£ 24.50

owed in this Dictionary

mien	nan	san	tan
min			
ming			
miu			
mo			
mou			
mu			

na
nai
nan
nang
nao
nei
nen
neng
ni
nian
niao
nieh
nien
ning
niu
no
nu
nü
nuan
nueh
nung

o
ou

pa	sa	ta	t'o	ts'uan
pai	sai	tai	t'ou	ts'ui
			t'u	ts'un

Chinese-English Dictionary of Contemporary Usage

Chinese-English Dictionary of Contemporary Usage

Compiled by

WEN-SHUN CHI

with the assistance of

JOHN S. SERVICE
MEI-HSIA HUANG
CHI-PING CHEN

University of California Press

Berkeley, Los Angeles, London

WE 01736

University of California Press
Berkeley and Los Angeles, California

University of California Press, Ltd.
London, England

Copyright © 1977 by
The Regents of the University of California

ISBN 0-520-02655-1
Library of Congress Catalog Card Number: 73-90663
Composition by Asco Trade Typesetting Ltd., Hong Kong
Printed in the United States of America
Designed by Jim Mennick

3 4 5 6 7 8 9 0

To the people of the Center for Chinese Studies

Contents

Foreword

UNINTENDED or unimagined consequences of organizational activity are the subject matter of the historical and social sciences. Interestingly enough, however, American historians and social scientists often carry on their research in organizations that themselves produce significant unintended consequences. I am thinking of the typical "organized research unit" attached to a large American university. Usually funded on "soft money" (i.e., by a piper, such as the Ford Foundation, who can call the tune or stop the music if he wants to), housed in temporary quarters, and having trouble knowing precisely what it ought to be doing or is doing at any given moment, such organized research units are likely to make their most important contributions in areas that the units' founders and leaders did not fully recognize.

The Center for Chinese Studies, an organized research unit attached to the Berkeley campus of the University of California, came into being in 1957. Undoubtedly reflecting the area studies approach that was developed during World War II and responding to national needs during the Cold War, the Center commissioned itself to undertake and promote scholarship on the People's Republic of China. Instrumental to this more-or-less explicitly articulated goal were the traditional requirements of all university life: books, and scholars who could read them. Thus the Center undertook as secondary goals the building of a first-rate research library on contemporary China and the training of students and faculty in the skills required to read and interpret the writings of the Chinese communists. Rather like the activities of the nineteenth century American missionaries in China or of the twentieth century American Peace Corps volunteers in other parts of the world, these instrumental activities—compiling dictionaries, translating important documents, teaching people to read Chinese—may turn out to be of more lasting importance than the primary goal of the organization itself.

Chi Wen-shun was the Center's first and only "senior tutor" in the language of the People's Republic during the Center's first twenty years of existence. He taught hundreds of graduate students how to read *Jen-min jih-pao* and *Hung-ch'i*, and he compiled three widely used texts for the guidance of those who did not necessarily

need to know how to read all forms of Chinese but who had to be able to translate accurately the statements of Mao Tse-tung and other leaders of the Chinese People's Republic. As a former student of Mr. Chi's in the Center (1958–1961) and as one who commonly complained to him of the difficulties of using "standard" dictionaries to read contemporary Chinese materials, it was my pleasure in 1971, as chairman of the Center (1967–1972), to make Mr. Chi's dictionary project one of the main programs in the Center's collective activities. My successor as chairman, Professor Frederic Wakeman, continued and reinforced the Center's support for Mr. Chi's endeavors, and he did so in a period when the Center's financial capabilities were drastically reduced.

This dictionary was a joint effort. It built on the glossaries contained in Chi Wen-shun's original texts of communist documents, but it was actually compiled by a committee of four devoted workers—Chi Wen-shun, John Service, Huang Mei-hsia, and Chen Chi-ping—who in thousands of hours selected each additional entry and verified all of the translations. Susan Alitto and Karl Slinkard provided invaluable editorial and typing service. The University of California Press also contributed financial assistance and expert guidance when it came time to publish the work of these scholars.

From the late 1950s through the 1970s the United States made a massive effort on many levels and through many different organizations to investigate and understand contemporary Chinese affairs. This dictionary is one product of one of the organizations engaged in that endeavor. I believe that its excellence is testimony to the seriousness which American scholars brought to the study of contemporary China and to the validity of the organized research unit approach in opening up a new area of research.

CHALMERS JOHNSON

February 1976

Preface

ONE NATIVE-BORN Chinese and long-time language teacher in the United States recently commented: "I have become an illiterate; I cannot read the *Jen-min jih-pao* (People's Daily)." Although made in jest, the comment serves to dramatize the enormous changes in the Chinese language in recent decades. Chinese, as all living languages, reflects a people's way of life, and has evolved accordingly in response to the demands of a rapidly changing world. In China, moreover, profound institutional and ideological transformations have accelerated the pace of linguistic change, producing a proliferation of newly coined terms and even new written forms in the now-standardized and officially promulgated simplified characters.

The purpose in compiling the present dictionary is to record as many of these changes as possible in one convenient volume for the benefit of the growing number of English-speaking people who use modern Chinese-language publications. By being selective rather than exhaustive in the choice of entries, the people who have worked on the dictionary have tried to provide a concise but comprehensive reference to terms and phrases not readily found translated and explained elsewhere. We assume that the user will already have some familiarity with the Chinese language and, therefore, that this volume will supplement other standard Chinese-English dictionaries.

Work on the compilation and translation of these linguistic changes began at the Center for Chinese Studies in the early 1960s. The three resulting volumes, prepared by me—*Readings in Chinese Communist Documents* (1963); *Readings in Chinese Communist Ideology* (1968); and *Readings in the Chinese Communist Cultural Revolution* (1971)*—contain a total of fifty-five carefully selected articles and extensive vocabulary lists of the important or unfamiliar terms and expressions appearing in each article. Since the documents themselves are drawn from a forty-year period of the Chinese Communist movement and deal with a wide range of issues, the language in which they are written, and thus the appended collection of 12,000 glossary terms, encompass an important part of the most useful and frequently occurring vocabulary items for the study of contemporary Chinese materials.

*All published by the University of California Press, Berkeley, California.

Within the limits set by our desire to produce a handy reference volume, we have endeavored to be as comprehensive and current as possible both in the terminology we have included and in the range of topics we have covered. We have therefore supplemented the basic core of entries taken from the Reader glossaries with terms gathered from a systematic examination of recent Chinese publications, including books, dictionaries, and journals on specialized subjects, and general periodicals, particularly the *Jen-min jih-pao* and *Hung-ch'i* (Red Flag). Consequently, the dictionary contains the basic vocabulary and specialized terminology essential to understanding Chinese discussions in economics, educational and cultural affairs, sociology, military affairs, law, agriculture, international affairs, science, and technology. Given the pervasiveness of politics in nearly every aspect of modern Chinese life, we have paid particular attention to political terms and expressions, the language of Marxism and Maoism, and the common slogans and catchwords associated with the wide variety of campaigns and movements, such as the 1973–1975 campaign to criticize Lin Piao and Confucius. There are also entries for important names, including Chinese transliterations of foreign names and frequently appearing contractions.

Although the dictionary concentrates on contemporary terms and phrases, it contains some traditional expressions that either function as key words to the sense of a sentence or that have had new and extended meanings attached to them. Within this category we have made a special effort to include both traditional and contemporary idiomatic expressions (*ch'eng-yü*). *Ch'eng-yü* constitute some of the colorful and expressive aspects of the Chinese language, but they can also present some of the greatest translation difficulties, even to advanced students of Chinese. Where possible, we have based our explanations on the *Hanyu chengyu xiao-cidian* (Pocket dictionary of Chinese idiomatic expressions), 3rd rev. ed. (Peking: Commercial Press, 1973), which reflects the impact of the new ideology on some of the traditional or more familiar meanings associated with these expressions. Also not easily found in other dictionaries, but included here, are some of the earthy colloquial and vernacular expressions which have gained currency and respectability in present-day China.

As far as possible, we have endeavored to keep the definitions succinct, but still indicative of the range of meaning in the Chinese context. Therefore, we have tried to let translations reinforce and support each other by intentionally varying the form of the English definition provided for similar Chinese terms and by supplying appropriate synonyms and alternate meanings. When more than one definition is given for a term, the most literal always appears first, and

marked differences in usage or grammatical function are separated with semicolons. We have not, however, tried to show parts of speech, because the grammatical function of so many Chinese terms depends on word order or context. Thus, a definition in noun or verbal form does not necessarily mean that usage of the term is restricted to that part of speech. We have provided explanations and important supplementary information in parentheses after the definitions and used brackets to supply words and meanings only implied by the original Chinese or necessary for idiomatic English. If a definition mentions a Chinese term that also appears as a separate entry, the romanization of the term is printed in boldface type with tone marks. Otherwise, the term is italicized and, if it is not commonly known, characters are supplied.

In addition to the references already mentioned, we have drawn on the following Chinese and Chinese-English dictionaries, both to verify our own translations and to broaden our coverage of specialized terminology: Dennis J. Doolin and Charles P. Ridley, eds., *A Chinese-English Dictionary of Communist Chinese Terminology* (Stanford: Hoover Institution Press, 1973); *Han-Ying k'o chi ch'ang-yung tz'u-hui* (Chinese-English dictionary of terms and phrases in science and technology) (Peking: Commercial Press, 1962); *Han-Ying shih-shih yung-yü tz'u-hui* (Chinese-English dictionary of common terms and phrases) (Peking: Commercial Press, 1964); *Han-yü tz'u-tien* (Chinese dictionary), ed. Li Chin-hsi (Shanghai: Commercial Press, 1957); C. Huang, *Hsien-tai Han-Ying hsueh-sheng tz'u-tien* (A modern Chinese-English dictionary for students) (Lawrence, Kansas: Center for East Asian Studies, University of Kansas, 1968); Liang Shih-ch'iu, ed., *Tsui-hsin shih-yung Han-Ying tz'u-tien* (A new practical Chinese-English dictionary) (Taipei: Far Eastern Publications, 1971); Lin Yutang, *Tang-tai Han-Ying tz'u-tien* (Chinese-English dictionary of modern usage) (Hong Kong: The Chinese University of Hong Kong, 1972); *Mathews' Chinese-English Dictionary*, comp. Robert Henry Mathews (Cambridge, Mass.: Harvard University Press, 1954); U. S. Joint Publications Research Service, *Chinese English Dictionary of Modern Chinese Usage*, 2nd ed. (Washington, D. C. 1965); *Standard Translations of Chinese Terms*, rev. ed. (Arlington, Virginia, 1972); Sybil Wong, comp., *Dictionary of Chinese Communist Agricultural Terminology* (Kowloon: Union Research Institute, 1968).

Our single most important source in compiling this dictionary has been the *Xinhua zidian* (New China dictionary) Peking: Commercial Press, 1971, 1973). As the best available representation of the current language standards in the People's Republic of China, it has been our main reference throughout, especially for deter-

mining correct pronunciations, tones, and character formations. Thus, entries in this dictionary that may differ from what is familiar to some Chinese speakers or what is indicated in other Chinese dictionaries, actually reflect the linguistic changes recorded in the *Xinhua zidian*.

W. S. C.

Acknowledgments

MY DEEP thanks are due to Professor Chalmers A. Johnson, former Chairman of the Center for Chinese Studies, who first suggested the idea of compiling this dictionary and whose support at all stages has made its completion possible. I am grateful also to the Center for financial support, to the present Chairman, Professor Frederic E. Wakeman, Jr., and to Professors Joyce K. Kallgren and John B. Starr for their kind provision of administrative assistance. My sincere thanks go to Mei-hsia Huang, who assisted in compiling the work from its very beginning, as well as to John S. Service and C. P. Chen, who joined it at a later stage. These colleagues worked with me on the final selection of terms to be included; Mr. Service was especially helpful in checking the English translations. My thanks also to Ms. Susan Alitto for her meticulous editorial work and to Karl Slinkard, who typed the whole manuscript. Needless to say, I am solely responsible for any mistakes or other shortcomings.

W. S. C.

Guide to Using the Dictionary

Romanization: The dictionary committee adopted the Wade-Giles romanization system to indicate the pronunciation of Chinese characters because we believe it is still generally more familiar to English-speaking students of Chinese than the *pinyin* system currently used in China. For readers who do know the *pinyin* system, however, we have supplied parenthetical *pinyin* equivalents with the Wade-Giles romanization headings throughout the dictionary. Conversion Table A at the back of the dictionary also lists the corresponding *pinyin*—Wade-Giles spellings.

In the interest of clarity and simplicity, we have eliminated most of the "luxury umlauts" that appear in standard Wade-Giles: *hsu*, *hsuan*, *hsueh*, *hsun*, *lueh*, *nueh*, *yuan*, *yueh*, *yun*. Exceptions are the umlauts in *chüeh* and *ch'üeh*, which we have retained so that these romanizations could be arranged together with the other syllables that start with the *chü* and *ch'ü* sounds. We have, of course, retained the umlauts where they indicate pronunciation differences in otherwise identical romanizations. Characters such as 私, which have been variously romanized as *ssu*, *szu*, and *sze*, are consistently spelled *szu* in this dictionary.

Tones and Hyphens: As a further guide to pronunciation, we have used the following system of tone marks over the romanization for ·each character: 1st tone, high level, ¯; 2nd tone, rising, ´; 3rd tone, low, ˇ; 4th tone, falling, `. Absence of a tone mark indicates that, in that particular context, the character is ordinarily pronounced in a neutral tone. We have, however, indicated only the most common neutral tones because we assume that most readers will want to know the tone in which the characters are normally pronounced, even though they might have a neutral tone in the given expression. Tone-sandhi changes have not been indicated. The character *i* 一, *ch'i* 七, and *pa* 八 are invariably marked as tone one, and *pu* 不 is always marked as tone four.

Hyphens are used to connect two or more romanized syllables into meaningful units.

Arrangement: The basic arrangement of the dictionary also depends on Wade-Giles romanization; the entries appear in alphabetical

order according to their character-by-character transcription in Wade-Giles. Terms having initial characters with identical romanizations are further arranged, first, according to tone, and second, according to stroke count. Thus, to locate an entry when its pronunciation is known: (1) turn to the section for the appropriate romanization and tone of the first character in the term; (2) count the number of strokes in the first character and locate it at the appropriate point among the other characters in that section; (3) if necessary, repeat the procedure for each succeeding character in the phrase.

We have treated aspirated and non-aspirated initials as different letters. Therefore, the aspirates in this dictionary are not integrated with the non-aspirates, but follow the entire sequence of their non-aspirated counterparts. Similarly, the initials "hs," "ts," "ts'," "tz," "tz'," "chü," and "ch'ü" are all treated as functional equivalents of initial letters and thus have their own sequences. We decided, however, that certain umlauted romanizations (lü, nü, and yü) are such minor variations that we have placed them immediately after their unumaluted counterparts. A chart on the inside front cover lists the romanization order followed in this dictionary, and romanization headings throughout the dictionary introduce each change in transcription and tone. Each new character entry has been assigned an entry number, which corresponds to the number given in the radical index.

Simplified Characters and Conversion Tables: Given our goal to record as completely as possible the current language changes in the People's Republic of China, we have naturally tried to adopt the officially promulgated simplified character forms. Again our standard has been the *Xinhua zidian*, but due to the difficulty printers have had in keeping their type fonts current with the changes, a few minor variations from the official character forms have been unavoidable. Where such deviations occur—such as 商 for the now official 商 —they are one of the previously accepted printed variations of a character element that has now been standardized. They do not affect the stroke count of the character. For the convenience of readers who are not familiar with the simplified characters or who are using materials written in the traditional, complex character forms, we have supplied two conversion tables. Table B contains the official list, arranged according to stroke order, of the simplified characters and their corresponding complex forms. Table C shows the conversion in reverse order, from complex character to simplified form.

Radical Index: Since this dictionary uses the simplified character forms, we have also adopted the new simplified radical system used in the *Xinhua Zidian*. The new radical system uses 189 radicals and

differs from the traditional 214-radical system in several respects:

1. Some of the traditional radicals are no longer used as radicals either because that element does not appear in the simplified character forms or because the radical itself and the characters formerly listed under it are now listed under simpler radicals— e.g., 非, formerly radical 175, is now listed under radical 3 " 丨 "; 靠, is now under radical 4 " 丿 ".
2. The form itself of several traditional radicals has been simplified or changed—e.g. ⺍ — ⺾.
3. Some variant forms of former single radicals are now treated as two separate radicals—e.g. 人, radical 9, and 亻, radical 10.
4. Characters that contain more than one apparent radical are now listed under all possible radical forms, rather than under a single unique radical—e.g. 共, under radical 2 "一"; radical 17 "八"; and radical 43 "廾".
5. Some characters with difficult-to-identify radicals are simply listed under the radical that corresponds to the first stroke in the character—e.g. 东, under radical 2 "一."

We have followed exactly the order of radicals as it appears in the *Xinhua zidian*, but for the readers' convenience we have assigned a number to each radical and arranged them in a chart, which appears on the inside back cover of this volume. The characters listed under each radical are arranged in ascending order of complexity according to their stroke count.

We have indexed only the first characters of the dictionary entries. Numbers refer to character entry numbers, not page numbers. More than one number indicates that the character will be found in more than one location because its pronunciation varies in different contexts.

To locate a term or expression by means of the radical index:

1. determine the initial character in the expression;
2. identify the radical element in the character and locate it in the radical index;
3. count the number of strokes in the character, *excluding* the number of strokes contained in the radical, and locate the character in the numerical stroke count order of characters listed under that radical;
4. turn to the entry number that is given opposite the character and locate the expression in the alphabetically arranged list under that entry.

At the end of the radical index is a short list of characters with difficult-to-identify radicals. These have been arranged by total stroke count in the character.

Chinese-English Dictionary
of Contemporary Usage

ā (ā)

1 阿昌族 **ā-ch'āng-tsú** the Achang people (a minority in Yunnan province: population 17,000 in 1957)
阿尔及尔 **ā-ěrh-chí-ěrh** Algiers
阿尔及尔会议 **ā-ěrh-chí-ěrh huì-ì** the Algiers Conference (of Asian-African countries, scheduled to meet in 1965 but postponed and never held)
阿尔及利亚 **ā-ěrh-chí-lì-yà** Algeria
阿尔巴尼亚 **ā-ěrh-pā-ní-yà** Albania
阿飞 **ā-fēi** a hooligan, rowdy, juvenile delinquent
阿富汗 **ā-fù-hàn** Afghanistan
阿訇 **ā-hūng** Mohammedan priest, a mullah
阿根廷 **ā-kēn-t'íng** Argentina, the Argentine
阿克拉 **ā-k'ò-lā** Accra [Ghana]
阿拉伯叙利亚共和国 **ā-lā-pó hsù-lì-yà kùng-hó-kuó** Arab Republic of Syria
阿拉伯联合共和国 **ā-lā-pó lién-hó kùng-hó-kuó** United Arab Republic
阿拉伯联盟 **ā-lā-pó lién-méng** the Arab League
阿曼伊斯兰教长国 **ā-màn ī-szū-lán chiào-chǎng-kuó** the Sultanate of Oman
阿姆斯特丹 **ā-mǔ-szū-t'è-tān** Amsterdam
阿批亚 **ā-p'ī-yà** Apia [Western Samoa]
阿Q思想 **ā Q szū-hsiǎng** Ah Q thinking (from Lu Hsun's famous story of Ah Q, satirizing the Chinese nation's rationalized acceptance of humiliation without effective resistance against the oppressor)
阿 **ā**: *also see* **ō**

āi (āi)

2 哀求 **āi-ch'iú** to beseech, entreat
哀愁 **āi-ch'óu** sadness and sorrow (usually as bourgeois feelings)
哀鸣 **āi-míng** a death wail, sigh of despair (of the bourgeoisie)
哀悼 **āi-taò** to mourn, grieve a death
3 挨家挨户 **āi-chīa āi-hù** from house to house
挨近 **āi-chìn** to approach, come near to
挨次 **āi-tz'ù** in order, by turns
挨 **āi**: *see also* **ái**
4 埃及 **āi-chí** Egypt
埃塞俄比亚 **āi-sāi-ò-pǐ-yà** Ethiopia

ái (ái)

5 挨饿 **ái-ò** to suffer hunger
挨打受饿 **ái-tǎ shòu-ò** to suffer beating and hunger
挨 **ái**: *see also* **āi**
6 癌症 **ái-chèng** cancer (the disease)

ǎi (ǎi)

7 矮稻 **ǎi-tào** short paddy rice (a newly developed rice with a short, heavy stalk and high yield, much used in areas—such as Hainan Island—subject to typhoons and strong winds)

ài (ài)

8 艾灸 **ài-chiǔ** sticks of dried moxa used in moxibustion
艾森豪威尔 **ài-sēn-háo-wēi-ěrh** Eisenhower
艾森豪威尔主义 **ài-sēn-háo-wēi-ěrh chǔ-ì** the Eisenhower Doctrine
9 爱情至上 **ài-ch'íng-chìh-shàng** love is supreme (a bourgeois trait)
爱尔兰 **ài-ěrh-lán** Ireland
爱好 **ài-hào** to love, be fond of; fondness
爱好正义的人民 **ài-hào chèng-ì te jén-mín** justice-loving peoples
爱护 **ài-hù** to protect, take loving care of, cherish

爱护公共财物　**ài-hù kūng-kùng ts'ái-wù** to have concern for public property

爱护备至　**ài-hù pèi-chìh** to cherish to the utmost

爱人　**ài-jén** loved one, fiancé, fiancée (now the equivalent of 'spouse" in mainland usage); to love people

爱国教育运动　**ài-kuó chiào-yǜ yùn-tùng** Patriotic Education Movement

爱国主义　**ài-kuó-chǔ-ì** patriotism

爱国主义还是卖国主义　**ài-kuó-chǔ-ì hái-shìh mài-kuó-chǔ-ì** "Patriotism or Betrayal" (the Ch'i Pen-yü article, in the *Jen-min jih-pao* of April 1, 1967, attacking Liu Shao-ch'i for his praise of the film "Ch'ing-kung mi-shih")

爱国献款　**ài-kuó hsièn-k'uǎn** patriotic donations (a movement in 1951–52 to help pay for the Korean War)

爱国一家　**ài-kuó-i-chiā** all patriots are of one family (a call for Chinese unity)

爱国公约　**ài-kuó kūng-yuēh** a patriotic covenant, patriotic pledge

爱国粮运动　**ài-kuó-líang yùn-tùng** Patriotic Grain Movement (an occasional drive in rural brigades for maximum contractual promises to sell grain to the state beyond their tax and compulsory procurement obligations)

爱国不分先后　**ài-kuó pù-fēn-hsīen-hòu** patriotism is never too late (a call for Chinese unity)

爱国增产运动　**ài-kuó tsēng-ch'ǎn yùn-tùng** patriotic production campaign

爱国卫生运动　**ài-kuó wèi-shēng yùn-tùng** patriotic public health campaign, the Patriotic Hygienic Movement

爱克斯光　**ài-k'ò-szū kuāng** X-rays

爱民模范　**ài-mín mó-fàn** Love-the-People Model (a title awarded by the Ministry of National Defense to soldiers)

爱莫能助　**ài-mò-néng-chù** sympathetic but unable to help

爱兵观念　**ài-pīng kuān-nièn** the attitude of cherishing the soldiers (usually refers to the attitude which officers should have of caring for their men)

爱不释手　**ài-pù-shìh-shǒu** so fond of it that one will not let it out of one's hand

爱社如家　**ài-shè-jú-chiā** to love the commune as one's family (the proper attitude for commune members)

爱戴　**ài-tài** to love and support, cherish and honor

爱憎　**ài-tsēng** love and hatred

爱憎分明　**ài-tsēng-fēn-míng** to make a clear distinction between [who should be] loved and [who should be] hated; a clear line between love and hate

10　碍手碍脚　**ài-shǒu-ài-chǐao** to hinder hand and foot (in the way)

11　暧昧　**ài-mèi** ambiguous, vague, obscure, indefinite

ān (ān)

12　安家插队　**ān-chiā ch'ā-tuì** to settle down and join a production team (used in connection with persons going from the city to the country)

安家费　**ān-chiā-fèi** settle-the-family fee (expense money given to workers' families when the breadwinner is sent to a new location)

安家落户　**ān-chiā-lò-hù** to set up a permanent home (refers to persons moving from urban to rural areas)

安之若素　**ān-chīh-jò-sù** to feel at ease as if things were normal (calm, uninvolved)

安置办公室　**ān-chìh pàn-kūng-shìh** an arranging office (an office set up in communes to help settle people coming from cities to the country-side)

安居乐业　**ān-chǔ-lè-yèh** to live in peace and enjoy one's work

安装　**ān-chuāng** to install [equipment or machinery], emplace

安插　**ān-ch'ā** to place [in employment]

安全　**ān-ch'uán** security, safety; safely

安全正点　**ān-ch'uán chèng-tǐen** safe and punctual (generally used on railways)

安全和卫生设备　**ān-ch'uán hó wèi-shēng shè-pèi** equipment for safety and sanitation

安全人员　**ān-ch'uán jén-yuán** personnel responsible for safety and security

安全理事会　**ān-ch'uán lǐ-shìh-huì** the Security Council [of the UN]

安全设施　**ān-ch'uán shè-shīh** safety device, safety installation

安全生产　**ān-ch'uán shēng-ch'ǎn** safety in production

安全措施　**ān-ch'uán ts'ò-shīh** security and safety measures

安分守己　**ān-fèn-shǒu-chǐ** to keep one's duty and have self-control (to mind one's own business)

安富根　**ān-fù-kēn** to plant roots of riches (to lay the foundations of future prosperity)

安心工作　**ān-hsīn kūng-tsò** to work contentedly, work calmly

安哥拉 **ān-kō-lā** Angola

安卡拉 **ān-k'ǎ-lā** Ankara

安理会 **ān-lǐ-huì** UN Security Council (contraction of **ān-ch'üán lǐ-shìh-huì**)

安曼 **ān-màn** Amman

安排 **ān-p'ái** to arrange, put in order, plan

安排河山 **ān-p'ái hó-shān** to plan [the utilization of] rivers and mountains

安排生活 **ān-p'ái shēng-huó** to arrange one's livelihood (to make a proper assignment of priorities, e.g., between ideological and practical, public and private, etc.)

安培 **ān-p'éi** ampere

安莎通讯社 **ān-shā t'ūng-hsùn-shè** ANSA News Agency [Italy]

安身之所 **ān-shēn-chīh-sǒ** a place to settle (a niche)

安道耳 **ān-tào-ěrh** Andorra

安定社会秩序 **ān-tìng shè-huì-chìh-hsù** to maintain social order, establish social order

安东尼奥尼 **ān-tūng-ní-ào-ní** Antonioni (an Italian film director)

安塔拉通讯社 **ān-t'ǎ-lā t'ūng-hsùn-shè** ANTARA [Indonesian National News Agency]

安营扎寨 **ān-yíng-chā-chài** to set up camp and erect a barricade (to settle down, establish a base)

安于现状 **ān-yú-hsièn-chuàng** satisfied with the status quo, content with existing conditions

13 鞍钢宪法 **ān-kāng hsièn-fǎ** the Anshan Steel Works Charter (in summary: (1) politics in command; (2) party leadership; (3) mass movement; (4) two participations, one reform, and three combinations; (5) technical innovation)

àn (àn)

14 按照革命利益的需要 **àn-chào kó-mìng lì-ì te hsū-yào** in accordance with the needs of revolutionary interests

按件计酬 **àn-chièn chì-ch'óu** to pay on a piece-work basis

按件计工 **àn-chièn chì-kūng** payment computed on a piece-work basis

按件包工 **àn-chièn pāo-kūng** contract by piece-work

按需分配 **àn-hsū fēn-p'èi** to each according to his needs

按人口平均计算 **àn-jén-k'oǔ p'íng-chūn-chì-suàn** to calculate on a per capita basis

按人口平均计算的产量 **àn-jén-k'ǒu p'íng-chūn chì-sūan te ch'ǎn-liàng** output calculated on a per capita basis (per capita output)

按人口平均计算的生产水平 **àn-jén-k'ǒu p'ing-chūn chì-sūan te shēng-ch'ǎn shuǐ-p'íng** per capita production level

按工分分配 **àn-kūng-fēn fēn-p'èi** distribution according to work-points

按劳计酬 **àn-láo chì-ch'óu** to compute pay according to work

按劳取酬 **àn-láo ch'ǔ-ch'óu** to receive compensation according to work

按劳分配 **àn-láo fēn-p'èi** to each according to his work

按摩治疗 **àn-mó chìh-liáo** to treat illness by massage; chiropractic

按捺不住 **àn-nà-pù-chù** unable to restrain [one's anger]

按比例发展 **àn-pǐ-lì fā-chǎn** to develop in proportion (to maintain a properly balanced development)

按兵不动 **àn-pīng-pù-tùng** to place troops and not move (to hold up and await the appropriate time)

按部就班 **àn-pù chìu-pān** to go step by step, follow the prescribed steps, carry out in proper sequence

按时计工 **àn-shíh chì-kūng** to compute work on a time basis

按语 **àn-yǔ** a commentary, note

15 案件 **àn-chièn** a legal case, political incident

案卷 **àn-chüàn** files, archives

16 暗礁 **àn-chiāo** rocks hidden under water (a hidden hazard)

暗箭 **àn-chièn** an invisible arrow (a stealthy blow)

暗箭伤人 **àn-chièn-shāng-jén** a secret arrow injures a man (slander, to defame another's reputation in secret)

暗中 **àn-chūng** underhandedly; clandestine

暗中支持 **àn-chūng-chīh-ch'íh** covert support

暗中反对 **àn-chūng-fǎn-tuì** veiled resistance

暗害 **àn-hài** to injure underhandedly

暗号 **àn-hào** a secret sign, password

暗河 **àn-hó** an underground river, sub-surface flow of water

暗流 **àn-liú** undercurrent (any clandestine trend against the orthodox doctrine)

暗杀 **àn-shā** to assassinate; assassination

暗算 **àn-suàn** to plot in secret

暗送秋波 **àn-sùng-ch'iū-pō** secretly to send an autumn ripple (to give a secret signal of assent, establish secret contact with an opposing

faction, etc.)

暗地里 **àn-tì-li** secretly, undercover, hidden

暗探 **àn-t'àn** a detective, plainclothesman

暗藏的反革命分子 **àn-ts'áng-te fǎn-kó-mìng fèn-tzǔ** hidden counter-revolutionaries

暗无天日 **àn-wú-t'iēn-jìh** darkness without sky and sun (a reference to the old society)

17 黯然失色 **àn-ján-shīh-sè** to appear very dull in comparison, to be eclipsed

āng (āng)

18 肮脏交易 **āng-tsāng chiāo-ì** dirty deals, shady transactions

áng (áng)

19 昂然挺立 **áng-ján-t'ǐng-lì** to stand straight with dignity

昂首阔步 **áng-shǒu-k'uò-pù** to raise the head and walk with big strides (complacent, self-satisfied)

昂首望天 **áng-shǒu-wàng-t'iēn** to raise one's head and look at the sky (to disregard the masses)

昂扬 **áng-yáng** elation; enthusiastic, exhilarated

áo (áo)

20 熬夜 **áo-yèh** to work until the small hours of the night

ào (ào)

21 傲然屹立 **ào-ján-ì-lì** proudly erect; to stand firmly

傲骨 **ào-kǔ** proud backbone (self-esteem, pride)

傲慢 **ào-màn** arrogant, haughty, overbearing

傲视旁人 **ào-shìh p'áng-jén** to look down upon others (arrogant, haughty)

22 奥林匹克运动会 **ào-lín-p'ǐ-k'ò yùn-tùng-hùi** the Olympics, the Olympic Games

奥斯陆 **ào-szū-lù** Oslo

奥地利 **ào-tì-lì** Austria

23 澳门 **ào-mén** Macao

澳大利亚 **ào-tà-lì-yà** Australia

24 懊丧 **ào-sàng** melancholy over a loss (dismayed, disappointed)

chā (zhā)

25 扎扎实实 **chā-chā shíh-shíh** plant solidly (careful and thorough, down to earth)

扎针 **chā-chēn** acupuncture; to insert a needle

扎正扎深 **chā-chèng chā-shēn** to take root correctly and deeply (refers to the attitude one should have in his assigned place of work)

扎下了根 **chā-hsià-le-kēn** to strike root in, to take root (usually figurative, referring to work)

扎伊尔 **chā-ī-ěrh** Zaïre (formerly, the Democratic Republic of the Congo, and still earlier, Belgian Congo; the capital is Kinshasa, formerly, Leopoldville)

扎根 **chā-kēn** to strike roots (usually refers to **hsià-fàng** cadres and youth)

扎根精神 **chā-kēn chīng-shén** a determination to strike roots (willingness to settle down in the countryside)

扎根群众中 **chā-kēn ch'ún-chùng-chūng** to take root amongst the masses

扎根农村 **chā-kēn núng-ts'ūn** to strike roots in the villages

扎深扎牢 **chā-shēn chā-láo** to become deeply and firmly rooted

扎实 **chā-shíh** solid, well-founded

扎实苦干 **chā-shíh k'ǔ-kàn** to work hard and earnestly

26 咋咋呼呼 **chā-chā hū-hū** blustery, noisy [of a person]

咋 **chā**: *see also* **tsǎ**

27 渣滓 **chā-tzu** dregs, sediment

渣油路面 **chā-yú lù-mièn** an oiled road, tarred road paving, asphalt road

chá (zhá)

28 轧钢厂 **chá-kāng-ch'ǎng** a steel-rolling mill

轧钢设备 **chá-kāng shè-pèi** steel-rolling equipment

轧 **chá**: *see also* **yà**

29 闸门 **chá-mén** a floodgate, sluice

chà (zhà)

30 乍得 **chà-té** Chad [Republic of]

31 诈骗犯 **chà-p'ièn-fàn** swindlers

32 炸开 **chà-k'āi** to blast open

33 榨取 **chà-ch'ǔ** to squeeze out, extract (to exploit, obtain by political pressure)

chāi (zhāi)

³⁴ 斋期 **chāi-ch'ī** religious fast days
斋戒节 **chāi-chièh-chiéh** Ramadan, the fast of Ramadan
³⁵ 摘下 **chāi-hsià** to take off, peel off, drop
摘下假面具 **chāi-hsià chiǎ-mièn-chù** to tear off the mask (to expose—usually political)
摘下伪善的面具 **chāi-hsià wěi-shán-te mièn-chù** to peel off a hypocritical mask
摘录 **chāi-lù** to excerpt; an excerpt
摘帽子 **chāi mào-tzu** to take off the hat (the hat refers figuratively to the high hat that symbolizes political disgrace—hence, to have the hat removed is to be rehabilitated)
摘棉机 **chāi-mién-chī** cotton picking machine, cotton harvester
摘掉右派帽子 **chāi-tiào yù-p'ài-mào-tzu** to take off the rightist hat
摘要 **chāi-yào** an abridgement, brief summary, epitome

chái (zhái)

³⁶ 宅邸 **chái-tǐ** a residence, dwelling, domicile

chǎi (zhǎi)

³⁷ 窄行播种法 **chǎi-háng pō-chùng-fǎ** close-row sowing method
窄轨铁路 **chǎi-kueǐ t'iěh-lù** narrow-gauge railway

chài (zhài)

³⁸ 债权人 **chài-ch'üán-jén** creditor
债台高筑 **chài-t'ái-kāo-chù** to build a high tower of debts (heavily in debt)
债务人 **chài-wù-jén** a debtor

chān (zhān)

³⁹ 沾沾自喜 **chān-chān-tzù-hsǐ** self-satisfied, complacent
沾染 **chān-jǎn** to taint, contaminate, pollute
沾边 **chān-piēn** to touch the edge (to be somewhat involved, to have some knowledge—generally with the connotation of incomplete commitment or participation)
⁴⁰ 瞻前顾后 **chān-ch'ién-kù-hòu** to look ahead and to look back (to be overly cautious and hesitant in reaching a decision)

瞻仰 **chān-yǎng** to pay respects to

chǎn (zhǎn)

⁴¹ 斩尽杀绝 **chǎn-chìn-shā-chüéh** total extermination
斩钉截铁 **chǎn-tīng-chiéh-t'iěh** to sever a nail and cut iron (to take decisive action)
斩断魔爪 **chǎn-tuàn mó-chǎo** to cut off the Devil's claws, to trim the claws of (usually in a political sense)
斩草除根 **chǎn-ts'ǎo-ch'ú-kēn** to cut weeds and dig out the roots (to eliminate the cause of the trouble completely)
⁴² 展期 **chǎn-ch'ī** to extend a time limit, postpone, delay, defer
展开 **chǎn-k'āi** to open, unfold, develop, start, inaugurate, extend
展览馆 **chǎn-lǎn-kuǎn** an exhibition hall
展望 **chǎn-wàng** to look toward; a prospect, outlook, expectation
展望未来 **chǎn-wàng wèi-lái** to look toward the future
⁴³ 崭新 **chǎn-hsīn** wholly new, brand new
⁴⁴ 辗转反侧 **chǎn-chuǎn-fǎn-ts'è** to toss about sleeplessly in bed

chàn (zhàn)

⁴⁵ 占着茅房不拉屎 **chàn-che máo-fáng pù lā-shǐh** to occupy the latrine without moving the bowels (to hold a position without doing the job)
占据 **chàn-chù** to occupy (usually by force or otherwise illegally)
占先 **chàn-hsiēn** to assume precedence, assume leadership
占领 **chàn-lǐng** to occupy (usually in the military sense)
占领军 **chàn-lǐng-chūn** occupation army
占领地 **chàn-lǐng-tì** occupied area
占上风 **chàn shàng-fēng** to steal the wind (to have the advantage over, gain the upper hand, prevail)
占有制 **chàn-yǔ-chìh** form of ownership, system of ownership
占优势 **chàn yū-shìh** to enjoy superiority, be superior to, get the advantage of; dominance
⁴⁶ 战战兢兢 **chàn-chàn-chīng-chīng** shivering and fearful (fearful of making mistakes, careful of one's steps, extremely cautious)
战争景气 **chàn-chēng chǐng-ch'ì** a war boom
战争状态 **chàn-chēng chuàng-t'ài** a

state of war

战争贩子 **chàn-chēng fàn-tzu** a warmonger

战争边缘政策 **chàn-chēng piēn-yuán chèng-ts'è** brink-of-war policy (brinksmanship)

战争万能论 **chàn-chēng wàn-néng lùn** the idea that all problems can be solved by war

战绩 **chàn-chī** war gains, war achievements

战场 **chàn-ch'ǎng** the battle-front, battlefield

战车 **chàn-ch'ē** a tank [military]

战区 **chàn-ch'ū** war zone

战犯 **chàn-fàn** war criminal

战俘 **chàn-fú** a prisoner of war

战壕 **chàn-háo** a trench [military]

战祸 **chàn-huò** the disaster of war, war calamities

战线 **chàn-hsièn** a front [military], battle line (figurative: the scene of any intensive political, social, or economic activity)

战役 **chàn-ì** a military campaign (a major series of military actions toward a particular goal)

战役学 **chàn-ì-hsuéh** the study of military campaigns

战役部署 **chàn-ì pù-shǔ** disposition of troops for a campaign

战鼓 **chàn-kǔ** a battle drum (a call to action)

战功 **chàn-kūng** merit achieved in war, distinguished military service

战果 **chàn-kuǒ** the fruits of battle, spoils of war

战利品 **chàn-lì-p'ǐn** spoils, booty, prizes of war

战例 **chàn-lì** a military precedent (battles having importance as examples)

战略 **chàn-luèh** military strategy (now often used in an extended sense)

战略学 **chàn-luèh-hsuéh** the science of military strategy (the systematic study of strategy)

战略任务 **chàn-luèh jèn-wù** a strategic task

战略上藐视敌人, 战术上重视敌人 **chàn-luèh-shang miǎo-shì tí-jén, chàn-shù-shang chùng-shìh tí-jén** slight the enemy strategically while taking full account of him tactically (a maxim also applied to the overcoming of difficulties in daily work or assigned tasks)

战略的持久战 **chàn-luèh-te ch'íh-chǐu-chàn** strategic protracted war

战略速决战 **chàn-luèh-te sù-chüéh-chàn** strategic war of quick solution

战略物资 **chàn-luèh wù-tzū** strategic materials

战略要地 **chàn-luèh yào-tì** strategic positions

战备 **chàn-pèi** military preparedness; military preparations

战备观念 **chàn-pèi kuān-nièn** the attitude of military preparedness

战胜灾害 **chàn-shèng tsāi-hài** to conquer natural calamities

战士 **chàn-shìh** a fighter, a soldier below the commissioned ranks (often figurative: e.g., a production worker, participant in a campaign)

战术 **chàn-shù** military tactics (often figurative)

战术学 **chàn-shù-hsuéh** the science of tactics, tactical studies

战斗 **chàn-tòu** to fight a battle (usually figurative: e.g., to struggle for production)

战斗号令 **chàn-tòu hào-lìng** combat orders (can be used in any intensive activity, as during a production campaign)

战斗化 **chàn-tòu-huà** martialization, making everything a struggle (the intensification of production activity —urged in the commune movement —*see* **szǔ-huà**）

战斗洗礼 **chàn-tòu hsǐ-lǐ** baptised by struggle

战斗意志 **chàn-tòu ì-chìh** the will to struggle

战斗任务 **chàn-tòu jèn-wù** combat duty, combat mission, a militant task (work to be done in a hurry)

战斗口号 **chàn-tòu k'ǒu-hào** battle cry, battle slogan

战斗力 **chàn-tòu-lì** fighting capacity

战斗力量 **chàn-tòu lì-liang** fighting strength

战斗历程 **chàn-tòu lì-ch'éng** the process of struggle, the course of struggle

战斗步伐 **chàn-tòu pù-fá** combat steps, combat stages (often figuratively)

战斗队 **chàn-tòu-tuì** a combat unit

战斗武器 **chàn-tòu wǔ-ch'ì** combat weapons (often figurative: e.g., Marxism, or the Thought of Mao Tse-tung)

战斗英雄 **chàn-tòu yīng-hsíung** a combat hero

战斗员 **chàn-tòu-yuán** fighter (enlisted men, as contrasted to officers)

战天斗地 **chàn-t'ien-tòu-tì** fight heaven and struggle against earth (to work with might and main against nature's obstacles)

战无不胜 **chàn wú-pù-shèng** no war not won (invincible)

战友 **chàn-yǔ** comrade-in-arms

47 站不住脚 **chàn-pù-chù-chiǎo** cannot stand (untenable, to be in a shaky position)

站在一旁说风凉话 **chàn-tsài ī-p'áng shuō fēng-liáng-huà** to make irresponsible and carping comments from the sidelines

站在一条战线上 **chàn-tsài ì-t'iáo chàn-hsièn-shang** to stand together on the same battleline

站稳立场 **chàn-wěn lì-ch'ǎng** to maintain a firm stand (generally in a political sense)

48 暂行 **chàn-hsíng** temporary, for the time being, provisional

暂行海关法 **chàn-hsíng hǎi-kuān-fǎ** the Provisional Customs Law

暂行条例 **chàn-hsíng t'iáo-lì** a provisional regulation, provisional measures

暂时利益服从长远利益 **chàn-shìh lì-ì fú-ts'úng ch'áng-yuǎn lì-ì** to subordinate temporary interests to long-range interests

暂定议程 **chàn-tìng ì-ch'éng** a tentative agenda

chāng (zhāng)

49 张惶失措 **chāng-huáng shīh-ts'ò** to be scared out of one's wits, to be frightened and at a loss as to what to do

张口结舌 **chāng-k'ǒu-chiéh-shé** to open the mouth and hold the tongue (astonished, dumbfounded; worsted in argument)

张冠李戴 **chāng-kuān-lǐ-tài** Li wears Chang's hat (a mistaken identification or inaccurate reference)

张国焘 **chāng kuó-t'āo** Chang Kuo-t'ao (1898—, one of the founders of the Communist party, became an apostate in 1936)

张牙舞爪 **chāng-yá-wǔ-chǎo** to display the teeth and brandish the claws (to challenge to fight; to act the bully)

50 章程 **chāng-ch'éng** regulations, rules, bylaws

章罗联盟 **chāng-ló lién-méng** the Chang-Lo alliance (an accusation against Chang Po-chün and Lo Lung-chi in the 1957 anti-Rightist campaign)

51 彰彰在目 **chāng-chāng-tsài-mù** manifest and before the eyes (obvious, public knowledge)

chǎng (zhǎng)

52 长成 **chǎng-ch'éng** to grow up, become an adult, grow into

长入 **chǎng-jù** to grow into, develop into

长大要当工农兵 **chǎng-tà yào-tāng kūng-núng-pīng** [when I] grow up [I] want to be a workman, farmer, or soldier

长自己的志气 **chǎng tzǔ-chǐ te chìh-ch'ì** to heighten one's will [to fight]

长 **chǎng**: see also ch'áng

53 涨潮 **chǎng-ch'áo** a rising tide

54 掌权 **chǎng-ch'üán** to hold [political] power, to rule

掌好权，用好权 **chǎng-hǎo-ch'üán, yùng-hǎo-ch'üán** to hold power and use it well

掌故 **chǎng-kù** historical anecdotes, national legends

掌柜 **chǎng-kuèi** a shop manager (a denunciatory epithet during the Cultural Revolution)

掌声雷动 **chǎng-shēng-léi-tùng** thunderous applause

掌握 **chǎng-wò** to grasp, control, take charge of, assume, handle, take into one's hands

掌握基本环节 **chǎng-wò chī-pěn huán-chiéh** to grasp the key link, grasp the key to a situation

掌握重点，照顾其他 **chǎng-wò chùng-tiěn, chào-kù ch'í-t'ā** to give priority to the most important aspects and due consideration to the rest

掌握分寸 **chǎng-wò fēn-ts'ùn** to handle down to the smallest detail (to control with great precision)

掌握规律 **chǎng-wò kuēi-lù** to master the law [of development of matters or things, etc.]

掌握敌情 **chǎng-wò tí-ch'íng** to grasp intelligence on the enemy (to understand through study the difficulties to be solved in an endeavor)

chàng (zhàng)

55 仗义执言 **chàng-ì chíh-yén** to speak boldly in defense of justice

仗义而起 **chàng-ì-érh-ch'ǐ** to act from righteousness

56 帐篷 **chàng-p'éng** a tent, awning, mat shed

57 障碍 **chàng-ài** obstacle, obstruction, hindrance, barrier

chāo (zhāo)

⁵⁸ 招致 **chāo-chìh** to cause, give rise to, incur; to expose oneself to, liable to, to run the chance of

招魂 **chāo-hún** to call back the soul (to revive)

招降纳叛 **chāo-hsiáng-nà-p'àn** to recruit deserters and traitors (usually in reference to reactionary forces)

招兵买马 **chāo-pīng-mǎi-mǎ** to raise troops and buy horses (to recruit—usually in the sense of reactionaries mobilizing their forces)

招牌 **chāo-p'ái** a signboard (usually pejorative and political)

招生制度 **chāo-shēng chìh-tù** student admission system

招生考试制度 **chāo-shēng k'ǎo-shìh chìh-tù** system for the admission of new students by examination

招待所 **chāo-tài-sǒ** guest house, hostel

招财进宝 **chāo-ts'ái-chìn-pǎo** to bring in wealth and treasure (Lin Piao was accused of saying that this was the main motive of the working people)

招摇撞骗 **chāo-yáo-chuàng-p'ièn** to bluff and deceive, swindle, hoax

招摇过市 **chāo-yáo-kuò-shìh** swaggering through the streets (to show off, unseemly self-advertising)

⁵⁹ 昭然若揭 **chāo-ján-jò-chiēh** as obvious as if [it had been] announced

⁶⁰ 朝气蓬勃 **chāo-ch'ì-p'éng-pó** the morning air is full of exuberance (alert and full of youthful vigor)

朝夕 **chāo-hsì** day and night, morning and evening; always, constantly

朝日新闻 **chāo-jìh hsīn-wén** *Asahi Shimbun* (Japanese daily newspaper)

朝令夕改 **chāo-lìng hsì-kǎi** an order given in the morning and changed in the evening (frequent changes, vacillation)

朝不保夕 **chāo-pù-pǎo-hsì** morning cannot ensure the evening (living from hand to mouth)

朝 **chāo**: *see also* **ch'áo**

chǎo (zhǎo)

⁶¹ 爪牙 **chǎo-yá** claws and teeth (a henchman, lackey—in a bad sense)

⁶² 找差距 **chǎo ch'ā-chù** to find disparities (the realization of disparities in ideology, knowledge, skills, or achievements so that ǒne can increase his efforts to learn from and emulate the advanced)

找窍门 **chǎo ch'iào-mén** to find the keyhole (to find better techniques, to get the knack of)

找煤报矿 **chǎo-méi pào-k'uàng** to search for coal and locate mines

找平补齐 **chǎo-p'íng pǔ-ch'í** equalization and compensation (an excessive concern of some members in the formation of communes)

找水探矿 **chǎo-shuǐ t'àn-k'uàng** to prospect for water and mines

⁶³ 沼气 **chǎo-ch'ì** marsh gas, methane

chào (zhào)

⁶⁴ 召唤 **chào-huàn** to summon, call

召回 **chào-húi** to recall (as the recall of a diplomat)

⁶⁵ 兆周 **chào-chōu** megacycle

⁶⁶ 照抄照搬 **chào-ch'āo-chào-pān** uncritical duplication and appropriation (usually of old or foreign things)

照葫芦画瓢 **chào-hú-lu huà-p'íao** to draw a ladle by copying a gourd (imitative, uncreative)

照会 **chào-huì** a diplomatic note

照顾 **chào-kù** to take care of; to take into consideration

照顾大局 **chào-kù tà-chú** to be mindful of the whole situation

照例 **chào-lì** according to rule, according to precedent

照亮 **chào-liàng** to light up, illuminate

照面 **chào-mièn** to show one's face; to meet face to face

照明 **chào-míng** lighting, illumination

照明弹 **chào-míng-tàn** illuminating shell, flare

照搬 **chào-pān** to move over without change (uncritical use or copying—usually of foreign models)

照本宣科 **chào-pěn-hsuān-k'ō** to explain from the book (uncreative, unimaginative)

照妖镜 **chào-yáo-chìng** a magic mirror which reflects the hidden ugliness of a monster (used in a political sense)

chē (zhē)

⁶⁷ 遮丑 **chē-ch'ǒu** to cover up ugliness

遮羞布 **chē-hsiū-pù** a loincloth, veil (figurative)

ché (zhé)

⁶⁸ 折旧 **ché-chìu** depreciation [of machinery or equipment in use]

折中 **ché-chūng** to compromise, mediate and intervene, conciliate,

take the middle way

折中主义 **ché-chūng-chǔ-ì** eclecticism (since Maoists hold that there can be no compromise between the proletarian and bourgeois lines, eclectism is usually tantamount to taking the side of the enemy)

折磨 **ché-mó** to torture; ordeal

69 哲学家 **ché-hsuéh-chiā** philosophers

哲学神秘论 **ché-hsuéh shén-mì lùn** the idea that philosophy is mysterious; making a fetish of philosophy

哲学研究 **ché-hsuéh yén-chiū** *Philosophical Studies* (Peking monthly journal, 1955—)

chè (zhè)

70 浙赣铁路 **chè-kàn t'iěh-lù** Hangchow [Chekiang] to Chuchow [Hunan] Railway

chēn (zhēn)

71 针织品 **chēn-chīh-p'ǐn** knit goods

针灸 **chēn-chiǔ** acupuncture and moxibustion

针插不进 **chēn-ch'ā-pù-chìn** a needle cannot be pushed in (impenetrable, airtight)

针锋相对 **chēn-fēng-hsiāng-tuì** points of needles facing each other (diametrically opposed, tit-for-tat)

针对 **chēn-tuì** pointing toward, to aim to, in the light of

针刺麻醉 **chēn-tz'ù má-tsuì** anesthesia by acupuncture

针无两头利 **chēn wú liǎng-t'óu lì** a needle cannot have two points (you can not have it both ways)

72 侦察 **chēn-ch'á** to investigate, examine, inquire into, survey, reconnoiter; an investigation, inquiry

侦察兵 **chēn-ch'á-pīng** a military scout

侦探 **chēn-t'àn** a detective, a spy; to spy upon, detect

73 珍珠港事件 **chēn-chū-kǎng shìh-chièn** the Pearl Harbor incident (December 7, 1941)

珍宝岛 **chēn-pǎo-tǎo** Damansky Island (in the Ussuri River on the Sino-Soviet border—scene of an incident in 1969)

74 真知 **chēn-chīh** true knowledge, insight

真金不怕火炼 **chēn-chīn pù-p'à huǒ-lièn** true gold does not fear smelting by fire

真枪实弹 **chēn-ch'iāng shíh-tàn** real guns and live bullets (serious, not to be played with)

真象 **chēn-hsiàng** the true appearance, phenomenon, real image

真相 **chēn-hsiàng** the real facts, truth

真相大白 **chēn-hsiàng tà-pái** the truth is completely clear

真心诚意 **chēn-hsīn-ch'éng-ì** the heart is true and the intention sincere (sincerely)

真空管 **chēn-k'ūng-kuǎn** vacuum tube

真理 **chēn-lǐ** truth, righteousness

真理报 **chēn-lǐ-pào** *Pravda* (Russian newspaper)

真灵 **chēn-líng** truly wonderful, miraculous; miraculously

真面目 **chēn-mièn-mù** true appearance, true shape or form (one's true self)

真凭实据 **chēn-p'íng-shíh-chù** positive proof and tangible evidence

真实性 **chēn-shíh-hsìng** truthfulness, factualness

真释 **chēn-shìh** the true interpretation

真刀真枪 **chēn-tāo chēn-ch'iāng** real sword and spear (from the theater: instead of using sham weapons, the actors use real weapons—a mark of outstanding skill and ability)

真才实学 **chēn-ts'ái shíh-hsuéh** very talented and learned

75 斟酌 **chēn-chó** to deliberate, consider carefully

chěn (zhěn)

76 诊疗所 **chěn-liáo-sǒ** a clinic, polyclinic, doctor's consulting room

诊断 **chěn-tuàn** to diagnose; diagnosis

77 枕木 **chěn-mù** railway sleeper; railroad tie

chèn (zhèn)

78 阵脚 **chèn-chiǎo** the keypoint in a battle formation

阵线 **chèn-hsièn** battle front (usually figurative)

阵地 **chèn-tì** battlefield, position, front (used broadly to refer to the scene of activity in any kind of intensive production or political work)

阵地战 **chèn-tì-chàn** positional warfare

阵地攻击战术 **chèn-tì kūng-chī chàn-shù** the tactic of attacking fixed positions

阵亡 **chèn-wáng** to be killed in action

阵营 **chèn-yíng** camp [military] (often political, e.g., the capitalist camp)

79 振振有词 **chèn-chèn-yǔ-tz'ú** to argue loudly [as if one had reason on one's side]

振奋人心 **chèn-fèn-jén-hsīn** to inspire, galvanize the morale of the people

振作精神 **chèn-tsò chīng-shén** to stimulate one's spirit

80 朕即世界 **chèn-chí-shìh-chièh** "I am the world" (a criticism of Soviet pretensions)

81 赈济 **chèn-chì** disaster relief

82 震耳欲聋 **chèn-ěrh-yù-lúng** it deafens the ear (a loud sound, deafening)

震撼全球 **chèn-hàn ch'üán-ch'íu** to shake the whole earth (earthshaking)

震撼人心 **chèn-hàn jén-hsīn** to shake people's hearts (to shock)

震天动地 **chèn-t'iēn-tùng-tì** earthshaking (a great accomplishment)

83 镇长 **chèn-chǎng** the head man of a town, mayor

镇反 **chèn-fǎn** to suppress counter-revolutionaries

镇压 **chèn-yā** to suppress, stamp out, subdue; suppression, repression

镇压反革命 **chèn-yā fǎn-kó-mìng** to suppress counterrevolutionaries

镇压反革命运动 **chèn-yā fǎn-kó-mìng yùn-tùng** the repression of counter-revolutionaries movement (1951)

镇压与宽大相结合 **chèn-yā yǔ k'uān-tà hsiāng-chiéh-hó** to combine suppression with leniency

chēng (zhēng)

84 争执 **chēng-chíh** controversy, dispute, contention; to argue

争执点 **chēng-chíh-tiěn** point of dispute, bone of contention

争气 **chēng-ch'ì** to be competitive, strive to excel, emulate

争求 **chēng-ch'íu** to fight for, strive toward

争取 **chēng-ch'ǔ** to fight for, strive for, to win over

争取主动 **chēng-ch'ǔ chǔ-tùng** to fight for the initiative

争取胜利 **chēng-ch'ǔ shèng-lì** to strive for victory (to fight resolutely for victory)

争权夺利 **chēng-ch'üán tó-lì** to struggle for power and advantage

争权夺势 **chēng-ch'üán tó-shìh** to fight for power

争分夺秒 **chēng-fēn tó-miǎo** to fight for minutes and seconds (to waste no time)

争相逃命 **chēng-hsiāng-t'áo-mìng** to flee for one's life; mass panic and flight

争先 **chēng-hsiēn** to contend for first place

争先进 **chēng-hsiēn-chìn** to strive to be the advanced

争先恐后 **chēng-hsiēn-k'ǔng-hòu** to fight for the lead and fear being left behind

争光 **chēng-kuāng** to win glory

争论 **chēng-lùn** a controversy, argument, debate; to argue, debate, engage in controversy

争论中心 **chēng-lùn chūng-hsīn** the main point of a controversy or dispute

争名夺利 **chēng-míng tó-lì** to struggle for fame and wealth

争霸世界 **chēng-pà shìh-chièh** to seek world hegemony

争辩 **chēng-pièn** to argue, dispute; a controversy, debate

争夺领导权 **chēng-tó lǐng-tǎo-ch'üán** to contend for the leadership

争端 **chēng-tuān** the point of dispute, cause of argument, bone of contention

争挑重担 **chēng-t'iāo chùng-tàn** to fight for taking a heavy load (eagerly to assume heavy responsibility)

85 征集 **chēng-chí** to collect, convene, gather together; a collection

征发 **chēng-fā** to levy, raise troops

征服 **chēng-fú** to conquer, vanquish, subjugate, compel submission by force

征腐恶 **chēng-fǔ-ò** to attack the corrupt and villainous

征购 **chēng-kòu** to requisition with compensation

征购粮 **chēng-kòu-liáng** tax and state-purchase grain

征粮 **chēng-liáng** tax levied in terms of food grains; tax grain; to levy a tax in grain

征收 **chēng-shōu** to levy and collect [taxes]

征途 **chēng-t'ú** a journey; the road traveled

征用 **chēng-yùng** to requisition; a requisition

86 挣扎 **chēng-chā** to struggle, fight desperately, free oneself

87 狰狞面貌 **chēng-níng mièn-mào** a grim visage, forbidding countenance; grisly

88 睁眼瞎子 **chēng-yěn hsiā-tzu** an open-eyed blind man (illiterate person)

89 蒸蒸日上 **chēng-chēng-jìh-shàng** like steam rising day by day (steady increase, daily improvement)

蒸汽透平 **chēng-ch'ì t'òu-p'íng** a steam turbine

chěng (zhěng)

⁹⁰ 拯救 **chěng-chìu** to rescue, relieve, save; relief

⁹¹ 整治 **chěng-chìh** to put in order, regulate, control

整装出发 **chěng-chuāng ch'ū-fā** all packed up and ready to start out (originally said of an army, now broadly used)

整装待命 **chěng-chuāng tài-mìng** waiting for orders in full battle array (ready to move at short notice)

整齐 **chěng-ch'í** neat, trim, tidy; in good order, well-arranged, forming a complete set

整军运动 **chěng-chūn yùn-tùng** ideological education movement (in the PLA)

整风 **chěng-fēng** rectification of work style

整风整社 **chěng-fēng chěng-shè** rectify [our] work style and tidy up the cooperatives

整风运动 **chěng-fēng yùn-tùng** rectification campaign, rectification of the work style movement (first carried out in 1942 by the Party)

整训 **chěng-hsùn** training and consolidation, reorganization and training

整垮 **chěng-k'uǎ** to topple, cause to collapse

整理 **chěng-lǐ** to put right, put in order, arrange; to revise, edit; to sort out, regulate, organize

整编 **chěng-piēn** to reorganize troops (to regroup, reshuffle, reorganize)

整编师 **chěng-piēn-shīh** a reorganized division [army]

整批交易 **chěng-p'ī chiāo-ì** a package deal

整社 **chěng-shè** rectification of the communes, to check up on the communes

整肃 **chěng-sù** to rectify, purge

整党 **chěng-tǎng** Party consolidation, Party reform

整党建党 **chěng-tǎng chièn-tǎng** Party consolidation and building

整掉 **chěng-tiào** to eliminate, discard [of persons]

整顿 **chěng-tùn** to rectify, reorganize, readjust; readjustment, check-up

整顿学风 **chěng-tùn hsuéh-fēng** rectify [the Party's] approach to study

整顿、巩固、充实、提高 **chěng-tùn, kǔng-kù, ch'ūng-shíh, t'í-kāo** readjustment, consolidation, filling up, elevation (a policy of the post-Great Leap period)

整顿三风 **chěng-tùn sān-fēng** rectify the three styles (an early name for the Cheng-feng Movement, coined by Mao in his speech of Feb. 1, 1942, inaugurating the campaign. The styles referred to: study, Party work, and literary work.)

《整顿党的作风》 **chěng-tùn tǎng te tsò-fēng** "To Rectify the Party's Working Style" (by Mao Tse-tung, Feb. 1, 1942)

整套 **chěng-t'ào** a whole set (can refer to a system of thought)

整体 **chěng-t'ǐ** the whole, an entirety, total

整体化 **chěng-t'ǐ-huà** integration; to integrate

整体观念 **chěng-t'ǐ kuān-nièn** the concept of the whole, viewing a situation as a whole (planning should take into account the interests of the whole industry, organization, or country)

整团建团 **chěng-t'úan chièn-t'úan** consolidation and expansion of the [Youth] League

chèng (zhèng)

⁹² 正常化 **chèng-ch'áng-huà** to normalize, to make sound; normalization

正气 **chèng-ch'ì** righteousness, spiritual strength for the right and just

正确 **chèng-ch'üèh** correct, accurate, proper, appropriate (usually in a political sense)

正确处理人民内部矛盾 **chèng-ch'üèh ch'ǔ-lǐ jén-mín nèi-pù máo-tùn** the correct handling of contradictions among the people (the theme of an essay by Mao Tse-tung on June 19, 1957)

正反两方面 **chèng-fǎn liǎng fāng-mièn** the positive and negative sides

正义战争 **chèng-ì chàn-chēng** a just war

正告 **chèng kào** to warn seriously

正规教育 **chèng-kuēi chiào-yù** regular education, school education

正规军 **chèng-kuēi-chūn** regular army, units of the regular army

正规化 **chèng-kuēi-huà** to regularize, standardize

正面 **chèng-mièn** the positive side, top, right side

正面教育 **chèng-mièn chiào-yù** positive education (teaching with an emphasis on activism and the good qualities of life and behavior in socialist society)

正面经验 **chèng-mièn chīng-yèn**

positive experiences

正面人物 **chèng-mièn jén-wù** positive personality, positive character (in a good sense)

正名 **chèng-míng** rectification of names (to conform one's actions to what is expected by one's title)

正比例 **chèng-pǐ-lì** direct ratio; in proportion to; directly proportional

正派人物 **chèng-p'ài jén-wù** people who are upright, honest, straightforward, positive, good

正式访问 **chèng-shìh fǎng-wèn** a formal visit

正式声明 **chèng-shìh shēng-míng** to declare formally; official statement

正式党员 **chèng-shìh tǎng-yuán** a full Party member

正视 **chèng-shìh** to face squarely, confront, look at things without flinching

正当 **chèng-tàng** legitimate, proper, valid, rightful, justified

正点率 **chèng-tiěn-lù** rate of punctuality

正统 **chèng-t'ǔng** orthodox

正统马克思主义 **chèng-t'ǔng mǎ-k'ò-szū-chǔ-ì** orthodox Marxism

正统思想 **chèng-t'ǔng szū-hsiǎng** orthodox ideology (such as Confucianism)

93 证据 **chèng-chù** evidence, proof

证人 **chèng-jén** a witness

证明 **chèng-míng** to attest to, bear witness to, identify, prove, substantiate; proof, evidence

证实 **chèng-shíh** to verify; verification

证书 **chèng-shū** a certificate, diploma, credentials

94 郑重其事 **chèng-chùng-ch'í-shìh** to do seriously, act with due care and respect

95 政界 **chèng-chièh** political circles, political personages

政治 **chèng-chìh** political; politics

政治集团 **chèng-chìh chí-t'úan** a political group, faction or clique

政治家长 **chèng-chìh chiā-chǎng** a political family head (an individual advanced in the study of the Thought of Mao Tse-tung and therefore regarded as the political head of his family)

政治僵尸 **chèng-chìh chiāng-shìh** a political corpse (such as Khrushchev before his actual demise)

政治界线 **chèng-chìh chièh-hsièn** political demarcation line

政治建厂 **chèng-chìh-chièn-ch'ǎng** politics builds factories

政治建军 **chèng-chìh chièn-chūn** politics builds the army

政治指导员 **chèng-chìh chǐh-tǎo-yuán** political director (political officer at company level [army])

政治经济学 **chèng-chìh chīng-chì-hsuéh** political economy

政治经历 **chèng-chìh chīng-lì** personal records of political activities

政治掮客 **chèng-chìh ch'ién-k'ò** a political broker (pejorative)

政治局 **chèng-chìh-chú** the Political Bureau, Politburo [of the Central Committee]

政治局面 **chèng-chìh chú-mièn** the political situation

政治觉悟 **chèng-chìh chüéh-wù** political awareness, political consciousness, political understanding, political awakening

政治权利 **chèng-chìh ch'üán-lì** political rights

政治犯 **chèng-chìh-fàn** a political offender, political prisoner

政治方向 **chèng-chìh fāng-hsiàng** political direction, political orientation

政治风向 **chèng-chìh fēng-hsiàng** direction of the political wind (political trend)

政治风浪 **chèng-chìh fēng-làng** political waves (political upheaval)

政治花招 **chèng-chìh huā-chāo** a political maneuver, political trick

政治活动 **chèng-chìh huó-tùng** political activity

政治协商会议 **chèng-chìh hsiéh-shāng hùi-ì** the Political Consultative Conference

政治行动 **chèng-chìh hsíng-tùng** political action, political activity

政治嗅觉 **chèn-chìh hsìu-chüéh** political sense of smell (political acumen)

政治学习 **chèng-chìh hsuéh-hsí** (1) political study; (2) *Political Studies* (Peking bi-monthly journal, 1955—)

政治热情 **chèng-chìh jè-ch'íng** political enthusiasm

政治任务 **chèng-chìh jèn-wù** a political task

政治纲要 **chèng-chìh kāng-yào** a political program

政治挂帅 **chèng-chìh-kuà-shuài** politics takes command (the main slogan of the Great Leap Forward)

政治观点 **chèng-chìh kuān-tiěn** political point of view

政治工作 **chèng-chìh kūng-tsò** political work

政治空气 **chèng-chìh k'ūng-ch'ì** the political atmosphere

政治理论课 **chèng-chìh lǐ-lùn k'ò** a class in political theory, political theory courses

政治力量 **chèng-chìh lì-liang** political strength

政治立场 **chèng-chìh lì-ch'ǎng** political stand, political standpoint

政治路线 **chèng-chìh lù-hsièn** political line

政治敏感 **chèng-chìh mǐn-kǎn** political sensitivity

政治目的 **chèng-chìh mù-tì** political aims or purposes

政治内容 **chèng-chìh nèi-júng** political content

政治讹诈 **chèng-chìh ó-chà** political blackmail

政治报告 **chèng-chìh pào-kào** political report (usually the principal report at a Party or national congress summarizing the achievements of the past period)

政治标准 **chèng-chìh piāo-chǔn** political criterion

政治部 **chèng-chìh-pù** political department (branch-type Party agencies, originally only in the army, but later also in finance, trade, communications, and industry)

政治骗子 **chèng-chìh p'ièn-tzu** a political swindler

政治上动摇 **chèng-chìh-shang tùng-yáo** to waver politically, to be unsteady politically

政治事故 **chèng-chìh-shìh-kù** a political accident (purposeful sabotage)

政治是灵魂 **chèng-chìh shìh líng-hún** politics is the soul

政治是统帅 **chèng-chìh shìh t'ǔng-shuài** politics is the commander

政治素质 **chèng-chìh sù-chíh** political qualities (good unless otherwise stated)

政治思想教育 **chèng-chìh szū-hsiǎng chiào-yù** political-ideological education

政治思想战线 **chèng-chìh szū-hsiǎng chàn-hsièn** the political-ideological front

政治特权 **chèng-chìh t'è-ch'üán** political prerogatives

政治责任感 **chèng-chìh tsé-jèn-kǎn** a sense of political responsibility

政治资本 **chèng-chìh tzū-pěn** political capital

政治危机 **chèng-chìh wéi-chī** a political crisis

政治委员 **chèng-chìh-wěi-yuán** political commissar, political commissioner

政治委员制度 **chèng-chìh-wěi-yuán chìh-tù** the political commissar system

政治问题 **chèng-chìh wèn-t'ì** (1) a political question; (2) a problem in one's political attitude which is regarded as serious

政治夜校 **chèng-chìh yèh-hsiào** political night school (usually for adult political study)

政治影响 **chèng-chìh yǐng-hsiǎng** political influence; political repercussions

政局 **chèng-chú** the political situation

政权 **chèng-ch'üán** political power, regime; government

政权机构 **chèng-ch'üán chī-kòu** political mechanism, structure of political power

政权机关 **chèng-ch'üán chī-kuān** organs of political power

政权建设 **chèng-ch'üán chièn-shè** the building of political power

政权性质 **chèng-ch'üán hsìng-chíh** the nature of a regime

政权到手，革命到头 **chèng-ch'üán tào-shǒu, kó-mìng tào-t'óu** [as soon as] political power is in hand, the revolution is ended (a doctrine contrary to Mao's theory of continuing revolution)

政权问题 **chèng-ch'üán wèn-t'í** the problem of [who is to hold] political power

政法 **chèng-fǎ** political and legal [affairs]; political-legal

政法干部 **chèng-fǎ kàn-pù** political-legal cadre

政法工作部 **chèng-fǎ kūng-tsò-pù** Political and Judicial Work Department [of the CCP Central Committee]

政法办公室 **chèng-fǎ pàn-kūng-shìh** Staff Office for Political and Legal Affairs [of the State Council]

政法研究 **chèng-fǎ yén-chiū** *Studies in Government and Law* (a Peking quarterly journal, 1954—)

政府机关 **chèng-fǔ chī-kuān** government organ, government administration

政府人士 **chèng-fǔ jén-shìh** government circles, members of the government

政协 **chèng-hsiéh** Chinese People's Political Consultative Conference (contraction of **Chūng-kuó jén-mín chèng-chìh hsiéh-shāng huì-ì**)

政协全国委员会 **chèng-hsiéh ch'üán-kuó wěi-yuǎn-huì** National Committee of the Chinese People's Political Consultative Conference

政纲 **chèng-kāng** political program, political platform, government program

政客 **chèng-k'ò** politician

政变 **chèng-pièn** a coup d'état, political uprising

政社合一 **chèng-shè-hó-ī** integration of governmental administration and commune management into one; to merge government and commune administration

政党 **chèng-tǎng** political party

政敌 **chèng-tí** political enemy

政体 **chèng-t'ǐ** form of government, political system, system of government

政策 **chèng-ts'è** a policy (usually political: more short-term than **chèng-kāng**, and more specific than **fāng-chēn**)

政策水平 **chèng-ts'è shuǐ-p'íng** the level of policy (the general understanding of government or party policies)

政策思想水平 **chèng-ts'è szū-hsiǎng shuǐ-p'íng** level of policy thinking (the general comprehension of political thought)

政委 **chèng-wěi** political commissar (abbreviation of **chèng-chìh wěi-yuán**)

政务院 **chèng-wù-yuàn** Government Administrative Council (renamed the **kuó-wù-yuàn** in 1954)

chī (jī)

96 几内亚 **chī-nèi-yà** Guinea [Republic of]

97 讥笑 **chī-hsiào** to ridicule, make fun of, laugh at

98 击中要害 **chī-chùng-yào-hài** to hit in the vitals (to strike at the root of, to strike home)

击溃 **chī-k'uèi** to defeat utterly, smash, disperse

击溃战 **chī-k'uèi-chàn** a military rout

击落 **chī-lò** to shoot down [aircraft]

击败 **chī-pài** to defeat, vanquish

击破 **chī-p'ò** to smash, foil, overcome

击退 **chī-t'uì** to repel, repulse, beat back

99 饥寒交迫 **chī-hán-chiāo-pò** to suffer from cold and hunger

饥荒 **chī-huāng** famine, destitution

饥饿 **chī-ò** hunger, starvation

100 机制纸 **chī-chìh-chǐh** machine-made paper

机警 **chī-chǐng** alert, sharp, quick-witted

机井 **chī-chǐng** a pump well, deep well [water]

机车 **chī-ch'ē** a railway locomotive; motorcycle; motorized vehicle

机车载重量 **chī-ch'ē tsài-chùng-liàng** hauling capacity of a locomotive

机器制造业 **chī-ch'ì chìh-tsào-yèh** machine building industry, machine tools industry

机器翻译 **chī-ch'ì-fān-ì** machine translation

机枪 **chī-ch'iāng** a machine-gun

机枪手 **chī-ch'iāng-shǒu** machine-gunner

机床 **chī-ch'uáng** machine tools

机床厂 **chī-ch'uáng-ch'ǎng** a machine tool factory

机具 **chī-chù** machine tools

机帆船 **chī-fán-ch'uán** motorized junk, motor boat

机帆化 **chī-fán-huà** to motorize junks

机会主义 **chī-huì-chǔ-ì** opportunism; opportunistic

机会主义路线 **chī-huì-chǔ-ì lù-hsièn** the line of opportunism

机会均等 **chī-huì-chūn-těng** principle of equal opportunity, equal opportunity

机械 **chī-hsièh** machinery; mechanical; mechanically

机械照搬 **chī-hsièh chào-pān** to imitate in a mechanical way

机械化 **chī-hsièh-huà** mechanization; to mechanize; mechanized

机械化耕作 **chī-hsièh-huà kēng-tsò** mechanized farming, mechanized cultivation

机械工业 **chī-hsièh kūng-yèh** engineering industry, machine industry

机械工业部 **chī-hsièh kūng-yèh-pù** Ministry of Machine Building (there are, or have been, several ministries of this name, numbered from one to seven)

机械论 **chī-hsièh lùn** mechanicalism, theory of mechanism, mechanistic theory

机械唯物论 **chī-hsièh wéi-wù lùn** mechanistic materialism, mechanical materialism

机耕 **chī-kēng** machine cultivated; mechanized farming

机耕农场 **chī-kēng núng-ch'ǎng** a mechanized farm

机构 **chī-kòu** institutional structure, organizational machinery, apparatus [of government]

机构臃肿，层次重叠 **chī-kòu yūng-chǔng, ts'éng-tz'ù ch'úng-tiéh** unwieldly and overlapping organizations, overstaffed and divided into many overlapping levels

机关 **chī-kuān** (1) a government agency, public organ, institution;

(2) a machine, mechanical contrivance; (3) a ruse, artifice, trick

机关报 **chī-kuān-pào** a serial publication of a government agency or political party

机率论 **chī-lù lùn** the theory of probability

机密 **chī-mì** secret, confidential, classified [information]

机不可失, 时不再来 **chī-pù-k'ŏ-shīh, shíh-pù-tsài-lái** an opportunity should not be lost [because] the time will never return

机动性 **chī-tùng-hsìng** flexibility, mobility

机动粮 **chī-tùng-liáng** flexible grain (grain reserves kept by local authorities at various levels)

机动灵活 **chī-tùng líng-huó** adaptable and flexible

机动兵力 **chī-tùng pīng-lì** mobile forces, mobile units [military]

机动队 **chī-tùng-tuì** a mobile unit (may be nonmilitary, as in the sparrow extermination campaign)

机动脱粒机 **chī-tùng t'ŏ-lì-chī** a power-driven shelling machine, husker

机动作战 **chī-tùng tsò-chàn** mobile operations, mobile warfare

机动物资 **chī-tùng wù-tzū** flexible materials (which planning or economic committees may assign to factories whose planned supply of raw materials proved to be insufficient)

机要秘书 **chī-yào mì-shū** confidential secretary

101 鸡犬不留 **chī-ch'ŭăn-pù-líu** not a fowl nor dog left (utter extermination, total destruction)

鸡犬不宁 **chī-ch'ŭăn-pù-níng** no peace even for chickens and dogs (a time of great trouble)

鸡毛还能上天 **chī-máo hái néng shàng-t'ién** can even a chicken feather go up to heaven? (how could the common people gain power?)

鸡毛蒜皮 **chī-máo suàn-p'í** chicken feathers and garlic skins (minor details, unimportant trifles; hangers-on, lackeys)

鸡毛当令箭 **chī-máo tàng lìng-chièn** to use a chicken feather as a badge of authority (overzealous in exercising command; to take too seriously a casual word dropped by a superior)

鸡瘟 **chī-wēn** chicken plague

102 迹象 **chī-hsiàng** outward appearances, evidences of, footprints, traces

103 积极 **chī-chí** active, positive, energetic, enthusiastic; actively

积极支持 **chī-chí chīh-ch'íh** to support actively

积极发挥 **chī-chí fā-huī** to give full play to, give full rein to

积极分子 **chī-chí fèn-tzŭ** positive elements, activists (the term implies positive commitment, optimistic activeness, and constructive effort)

积极性 **chī-chí-hsìng** initiative, enthusiasm, fervor, positiveness, zeal

积极人物 **chī-chí jén-wù** persons of an active, positive outlook (as contrasted to those with a passive, negative attitude)

积极因素 **chī-chí yīn-sù** positive factors, active factors

积聚 **chī-chù** to collect, gather, amass; accumulation

积肥 **chī-féi** to store manure, to lay in manure

积肥运动 **chī-féi yùn-tùng** fertilizer accumulation movement

积习 **chī-hsí** an old habit

积蓄 **chī-hsù** to accumulate, save, stock; savings, stock, accumulation

积谷防荒 **chī-kŭ fáng-huāng** to store grain against famine

积累 **chī-lěi** to accumulate, store up

积累经验 **chī-lěi chīng-yèn** to gather experience; accumulated experience

积累资金 **chī-lěi tzū-chīn** accumulated capital

积弊 **chī-pì** a long-standing abuse, an old irregularity

积德堂 **chī-té-t'áng** Hall of Accumulated Virtue (now used sarcastically to refer to the outwardly charitable, but actually selfish, pretensions of the leaders of the old society)

积压 **chī-yā** to neglect [one's work], hold up, postpone, allow [matters] to accumulate

积压物资交易会 **chī-yā-wù-tzū chiāo-ì-huì** accumulated goods exchange meeting

104 基加利 **chī-chiā-lì** Kigali [Rwanda]

基建 **chī-chièn** capital construction (contraction of **chī-pĕn chièn-shè**)

基建单位 **chī-chièn tān-wèi** capital construction units

基期 **chī-ch'í** base period; base

基础 **chī-ch'ŭ** a foundation, base, groundwork, basis

基础工业 **chī-ch'ŭ kūng-yèh** basic industry

基干 **chī-kàn** backbone (core element, basic cadre)

基干民兵 **chī-kàn-mín-pīng** basic unit of the militia (usually better trained

than the ordinary militia)

基年 **chī-nién** base year

基本建设 **chī-pěn chièn-shè** basic construction, capital construction

基本群众 **chī-pěn ch'ún-chùng** basic sections of the masses

基本好转 **chī-pěn hǎo-chuǎn** a fundamental turn for the better

基本核算单位 **chī-pěn hó-suàn-tān-wèi** basic accounting unit

基本功 **chī-pěn-kūng** basic skills

基本口粮 **chī-pěn k'ǒu-liáng** basic grain ration

基本劳动日 **chī-pěn láo-tùng-jìh** basic workday

基本粒子 **chī-pěn lì-tzǔ** fundamental particle

基本路线教育 **chī-pěn lù-hsièn chiào-yǜ** basic-line education (political indoctrination, including education and other forms, concerning fundamental issues such as mass line, socialist line, class struggle, etc.)

基本矛盾 **chī-pěn máo-tùn** a basic contradiction

基本生产关系 **chī-pěn shēng-ch'ǎn kuān-hsɪ** the basic relationships of production (i.e., primitive communalism, slavery, feudalism, capitalism, and socialism)

基本单位 **chī-pěn tān-wèi** basic unit

基本点 **chī-pěn-tiěn** a base point, a control plot [as in an agricultural experiment]

基本投资 **chī-pěn t'óu-tzū** capital investment

基本财政计划 **chī-pěn ts'ái-chèng chì-huà** a basic financial plan

基本原理 **chī-pěn yuán-lǐ** a fundamental principle, basic principle

基石 **chī-shíh** a foundation stone (often figurative)

基数 **chī-shù** base, base quantity, base number

基地网 **chī-tì-wǎng** a network of bases

基调 **chī-tiào** basic tune (theme, motif)

基多 **chī-tō** Quito [Ecuador]

基层 **chī-ts'éng** basic level, foundation, basic unit, basic level unit, primary unit, grass roots, grass roots level

基层政权 **chī-ts'éng chèng-ch'üán** basic unit of state power

基层选举 **chī-ts'éng hsuǎn-chǔ** elections at the lowest level, basic level elections

基层干部 **chī-ts'éng kàn-pù** basic level cadres

机层供销合作社 **chī-ts'éng kūng-hsiāo hó-tsò-shè** basic level supply and marketing cooperatives

基层单位 **chī-ts'éng tān-wèi** primary units, basic level units

基层党组织 **chī-ts'éng tǎng tsǔ-chīh** primary Party organization

基层组织 **chī-ts'éng tsǔ-chīh** basic level organization; [Party] organizations at the primary level

基层委员会 **chī-ts'éng wěi-yuán-huì** basic level [Party] committee

[105] 畸形发展 **chī-hsíng fā-chǎn** abnormal development

畸形现象 **chī-hsíng hsièn-hsiàng** an abnormal state of affairs

[106] 激战 **chī-chàn** a fierce battle, pitched battle

激战方酣 **chī-chàn-fāng-hān** at the climax of a bloody battle (usually figurative)

激进主义 **chī-chìn-chǔ-ì** radicalism, maximalism

激进派民主人士 **chī-chìn-p'ài mín-chǔ jén-shìh** a democrat of the radical type

激起公愤 **chī-ch'ǐ kūng-fèn** to provoke public indignation

激情 **chī-ch'íng** aroused emotions, excitement

激发 **chī-fā** to arouse, incite, stir up, spur on

激化 **chī-huà** intensification; to intensify

激光 **chī-kuāng** a laser beam

激烈 **chī-lièh** violent, fierce, sharp, keen, drastic, intemperate

激流 **chī-liú** a strong current, a torrent

激素 **chī-sù** a hormone

激荡 **chī-tàng** to surge wildly, be moved to renewed determination, be aroused to a new surge of spirit

激动 **chī-tùng** to excite; [emotionally] moving

激于义愤 **chī-yǘ-ì-fèn** aroused by righteous indignation

chí (jí)

[107] 及格 **chí-kó** to pass an examination; up to the mark, up to standard, qualified

及时 **chí-shíh** in good time; timely

[108] 吉隆坡 **chí-lúng-p'ō** Kuala Lumpur [Malaysia]

吉布提 **chí-pù-t'í** Djibouti [French Somaliland]

吉普车 **chí-p'ǔ-ch'ē** jeep (i.e., a small, all-purpose military vehicle)

吉田书简 **chí-t'ién shū-chiěn** the Yoshida Letter (written at the instance of John Foster Dulles stating that the Japanese govern-

ment would not finance trade with mainland China)

109 笈笈可危 **chí-chí-k'ǒ-wéi** in imminent danger, a precarious situation, extremely hazardous

110 级别 **chí-piéh** rank level

111 极权主义 **chí-ch'üán-chǔ-ì** totalitarianism

极力 **chí-lì** with the utmost effort

极点 **chí-tiěn** the farthest point, ultimate, extreme, absolute

极度关怀 **chí-tù kuān-huái** the utmost concern; to be extremely concerned about

极端仇视 **chí-tuān ch'óu-shìh** extremely hostile, violently hostile

极左思潮 **chí-tsǒ szū-ch'áo** ultra-left trend of thought

极右实质 **chí-yù shíh-chìh** ultra-rightist in essence

112 即将到来 **chí-chiāng-tào-lái** forthcoming, approaching, impending, imminent

即以其人之道还治其人之身 **chí ǐ ch'í-jén-chīh-tào huán chìh ch'í-jén-chīh-shēn** to pay back to a person his own principles (to deal with a man as he deals with you)

113 急起直追 **chí-ch'ǐ-chíh-chuī** to rise and pursue vigorously (to make amends as quickly as possible; to lose no time in emulating the leader)

急转直下 **chí-chuǎn-chíh-hsià** to take a sudden downward turn (a headlong fall, rapid deterioration)

急剧变化 **chí-chù pièn-huà** sudden change, precipitate change, sharp change

急风暴雨 **chí-fēng-pào-yǔ** strong wind and heavy rains (violent, sudden political events)

急先锋 **chí-hsiēn-fēng** a forerunner, vanguard, shock troops

急行军 **chí-hsíng-chǖn** a forced march

急性病 **chí-hsìng-pìng** (1) acute disease; (2) rashness, impatience

急如星火 **chí-jú-hsīng-huǒ** as urgent as sparks that may start a fire (extremely urgent)

急功近利 **chí-kūng-chìn-lì** quick success and early benefits (to seek position and wealth)

急,难,重症 **chí, nán, chùng-chèng** urgent, difficult, [and] serious diseases

急农业之所急 **chí-núng-yèh-chīh-sǒ-chí** [industry should] produce urgently whatever agriculture urgently needs

急不可待 **chì-pù-k'ǒ-tài** too urgent to wait (pressing)

急迫的问题 **chí-p'ò te wèn-t'í** an urgent problem

急刹车 **chí-shā-ch'ē** to apply the brakes sharply (often figurative)

急躁冒进 **chí-tsào-mào-chìn** to advance impatiently and impetuously; rash and adventuresome

急于求成 **chí-yǘ-chíu-ch'éng** over-anxiety to make achievements (impatient for success)

急用先学 **chí-yùng-hsiēn-hsuéh** to study first what is urgently needed

114 疾风知劲草 **chí-fēng-chīh-chìng-ts'ǎo** when the hard wind blows one can know the strong grass (fortitude is shown under difficult conditions)

疾恶如仇 **chí-ò-jú-ch'óu** to hate evil as an irreconcilable enemy

115 集结 **chí-chiéh** buildup, concentration, gathering; to concentrate

集结待命 **chí-chiéh tài-mìng** to assemble and await orders (originally, military, now may refer to any large project)

集装箱运输 **chí-chuāng-hsiāng yùn-shū** container transportation, container shipment

集中制 **chí-chūng-chìh** system of centralism, centralized control

集中指导 **chí-chūng-chǐh-tǎo** centralized guidance

集中经营 **chí-chūng-chīng-yíng** centralized management, centralized operation

集中反映 **chí-chūng-fǎn-yìng** to embody a concentrated reflection of

集中火力 **chí-chūng-huǒ-lì** to concentrate one's fire on; a concentrated attack (now often figurative)

集中领导,分散经营 **chí-chūng-lǐng-tǎo, fēn-sàn-chīng-yíng** centralized leadership and decentralized management

集中领导和群众运动相结合 **chí-chūng-lǐng-tǎo hó ch'ǘn-chùng-yùn-tùng hsiāng chiéh-hó** the combining of centralized leadership with mass movements

集中统一 **chí-chūng-t'ǔng-ī** centralized unity

集中营 **chí-chūng-yíng** a concentration camp

集中优势兵力 **chí-chūng yū-shìh pīng-lì** to muster superior forces

集权 **chí-ch'üán** centralization of power, to concentrate power

集二铁路 **chí-èrh t'iěh-lù** Inner Mongolia railway from Chining to Erhlien, connecting to Outer Mongolia and Siberia

集会自由 **chí-huì tzù-yú** freedom of

assembly

集日 **chí-jìh** market day, fair day

集市 **chí-shìh** a periodic rural market

集市贸易 **chí-shìh mào-ì** trading carried on at rural markets

集思广益 **chí-szū-kuǎng-ì** to canvas varying opinions and broaden the benefit

集体 **chí-t'ǐ** collective; a collective

集体安全 **chí-t'ǐ ān-ch'üán** collective security

集体智慧 **chí-t'ǐ chìh-huì** collective wisdom

集体经济 **chí-t'ǐ chīng-chì** collective economy

集体经营 **chí-t'ǐ chīng-yíng** collective management

集体主义 **chí-t'ǐ-chǔ-ì** collectivism

集体储备粮 **chí-t'ǐ ch'ú-pèi-liáng** collective reserve grain

集体福利 **chí-t'ǐ fú-lì** collective welfare

集体合同 **chí-t'ǐ hó-t'ung** a collective agreement, collective contract

集体化 **chí-t'ǐ-huà** collectivization (for application in the commune movement, *see* **szù-huà**)

集体领导 **chí-t'ǐ lǐng-tǎo** collective leadership; leading collective

集体领导和个人负责相结合 **chí-t'ǐ-lǐng-tǎo hó kò-jén-fù-tsé hsiāng-chiéh-hó** combining collective leadership with individual responsibility

集体农场 **chí-t'ǐ núng-ch'ǎng** collective farm [in the USSR]

集体生产 **chí-t'ǐ-shēng-ch'ǎn** collective production

集体生产劳动 **chí-t'ǐ-shēng-ch'ǎn-láo-tùng** collective labor for production

集体所有制 **chí-t'ǐ sǒ-yǔ-chìh** collective ownership system

集体饲养 **chí-t'ǐ-szù-yǎng** collective breeding of livestock

集体养猪 **chí-t'ǐ-yǎng-chū** collective pig breeding

集团 **chí-t'uán** a clique, faction, bloc

集团军 **chí-t'uán-chūn** a group army, army group

116 棘手 **chí-shǒu** thorny, prickly, baffling

117 瘠土 **chí-t'ǔ** poor land

118 籍贯 **chí-kuàn** place of origin (noted on official documents concerning persons—designates traditional family home, which need not be either birthplace or residence)

chǐ (jǐ)

119 几年辛苦, 万年幸福 **chǐ-nién hsīn-k'ǔ, wàn-nién hsìng-fú** hard work for a few years [and] happiness for ten

thousand

120 己所不欲, 勿施于人 **chǐ-sǒ-pù-yù, wù-shīh-yú-jén** do not inflict on others what you do not wish done to yourself

121 济南部队 **chǐ-nán pù-tuì** the Tsinan Forces [of the PLA]

122 挤垮 **chǐ-k'uǎ** to cause to collapse, push over, jostle

挤时间 **chǐ-shíh-chiēn** to make time [for something]

123 给养 **chǐ-yǎng** supplies [logistics]

给 **chǐ**, *see also* **kěi**

chì (jì)

124 计较个人名利 **chì-chiào kò-jén míng-lì** to be concerned for personal position and gain

计件工资 **chì-chièn kūng-tzū** piecework wages

计酬 **chì-ch'óu** to compute reward, compute compensation

计划 **chì-huà** to plan, arrange, map out, sketch, devise; a plan, program, project, intention

计划家庭 **chì-huà-chiā-t'íng** family planning

计划指标 **chì-huà-chǐh-piāo** a planned target

计划经济 **chì-huà-chīng-chì** (1) planned economy; (2) a monthly journal, Peking, Jan. 1955–Dec. 1958

计划管理 **chì-huà-kuǎn-lǐ** planned management

计划供应 **chì-huà-kūng-yìng** planned supply

计划生产 **chì-huà-shēng-ch'ǎn** planned production, planned output

计划生育 **chì-huà-shēng-yù** planned childbirth

计划收购 **chì-huà-shōu-kòu** planned purchasing

计划数字 **chì-huà-shù-tzù** a plan target, plan quota, plan figure

计划与统计 **chì-huà yǔ t'ǔng-chì** *Planning and Statistics* (a Peking monthly, 1959—)

计划用粮 **chì-huà-yùng-liáng** planned use of grain (to eat sparingly)

计量局 **chì-liáng-chú** Bureau of Standards and Measures [of the State Council]

计量科学 **chì-liáng k'ō-hsuéh** measurement science, metrology

计量单位 **chì-liáng tān-wèi** unit of measure

计时奖励工资 **chì-shíh chiǎng-lì kūng-tzū** reward system on a time-rate basis

计时工资 **chì-shíh kūng-tzū** time wages, time-rate wages

计算机 **chì-suàn-chī** calculating machine, computer

125 记账员 **chì-chàng-yuán** bookkeeper, accountant

记者招待会 **chì-chě chāo-tài-huì** press conference, news conference

记取 **chì-ch'ǔ** to remember, recollect, recall

记取教训 **chì-ch'ǔ chiào-hsùn** to learn a lesson

记分员 **chì-fēn-yuán** registrar of work-points

记忆犹新 **chì-ì-yú-hsīn** the memory is still fresh; to be fresh in mind

记工记账 **chì-kūng chì-chàng** to record work-points and keep accounts (usually in a commune)

记工员 **chì-kūng-yuán** work recorder, work-point recorder (a member of a production team)

记过 **chì-kuò** to impose demerits, to record mistakes (a nonlegal sanction)

记录片 **chì-lù-p'ièn** a documentary film, documentary, newsreel

记载 **chì-tsài** to record; on record, written records

126 纪律 **chì-lù** discipline, morale

纪律教育 **chì-lù-chiào-yù** education for discipline

纪律处分 **chì-lù-ch'ǔ-fèn** disciplinary action, disciplinary measures

纪律性 **chì-lù-hsìng** sense of discipline, disciplined character

纪念日 **chì-nièn-jìh** memorial day, commemoration day, anniversary

纪念白求恩 **chì-nièn pái-ch'íu-ēn** "In Memory of Bethune" (by Mao Tse-tung, 1939; one of the **lǎo-sān-p'iēn**)

纪念碑 **chì-nièn-pēi** monument, column, memorial tablet

纪要 **chì-yào** notes, a summary, minutes [of a meeting]

127 技巧 **chì-ch'iǎo** professional skill, artistic ability; skillful

技艺 **chì-ì** a feat, skillful act, acrobatics

技俩 **chì-liǎng** maneuver, trick, artifice, crafty practice

技能 **chì-néng** skill, technical proficiency, craftsmanship

技师 **chì-shīh** a skilled machine operater, technician

技术 **chì-shù** technical; technology; technique

技术经验交流会 **chì-shù chīng-yèn chiāo-líu-huì** skill and experience exchange meetings (held to improve work quality)

技术装备 **chì-shù chuāng-pèi** technical installation

技术辅导小组 **chì-shù fǔ-tǎo hsiǎo-tsǔ** technical assistance small groups (e.g., medical doctors in the early 1960s who toured rural hospitals to teach new techniques)

技术人员 **chì-shù jén-yuán** technician, technical expert

技术改革 **chì-shù kǎi-kó** technical transformation, technical improvement, technical innovation

技术革新 **chì-shù kó-hsīn** technical innovation

技术革新闯将 **chì-shù-kó-hsīn ch'uǎng-chiàng** a technical breakthrough general (a worker who wins special notice)

技术革命 **chì-shù kó-mìng** technical revolution, technological revolution

技术工人 **chì-shù kūng-jén** skilled workers, workers with technical skill

技术力量 **chì-shù lì-liang** technical strength (technological capacity)

技术兵种 **chì-shù pīng-chǔng** technical arms branches of the armed forces (i.e., chemical warfare, etc.)

技术神秘化 **chì-shù shén-mì-huà** to make a fetish of technology, making a mystery of technology

技术大军 **chì-shù tà-chūn** technical army (in a figurative sense)

技术第一 **chì-shù-tì-ī** technique first

技术队伍 **chì-shù tuì-wǔ** technical team, technical forces

技术推广站 **chì-shù t'uī-kuǎng-chàn** technical extension station (usually agricultural)

技术推广队 **chì-shù t'uī-kuǎng-tuì** technical extension teams (which went to factories to help solve problems—early 1960s)

技术作物 **chì-shù tsò-wù** industrial crops

技术资料 **chì-shù tzū-liào** technical data

技术操作规程 **chì-shù ts'āo-tsò kuēi-ch'éng** technical operating rules

技术无用论 **chì-shù wú-yùng lùn** the ·idea that technology is useless (an erroneous tendency to take too literally the idea that politics must be in command)

技术员 **chì-shù-yuán** a technician, technical expert

128 忌讳 **chì-huì** a taboo; to avoid things taboo

129 剂型 **chì-hsíng** forms of traditional medicine [pills, powders, etc.]

130 季节风 **chì-chiéh-fēng** monsoon, seasonal storm

季节性的 **chì-chiéh-hsìng-te** seasonal

季节工 **chì-chiéh-kūng** seasonal labor, seasonal laborer

季诺维也夫 **chì-nò-wéi-yěh-fū** Zinoviev, Grigori (1883–1936)

季度 **chì-tù** a quarter of a year

季度审订 **chì-tù-shěn-tìng** quarterly checks (of output and cultivated area in production teams)

131 既成事实 **chì-ch'éng-shìh-shíh** an established fact, a *fait accompli*

既得利益 **chì-té-lì-ì** vested interests

既定方针 **chì-tìng-fāng-chēn** the fixed policy

既往不咎 **chì-wǎng-pù-chiù** no punishment for past deeds (let bygones be bygones)

132 继承 **chì-ch'éng** to inherit, carry on; inheritance, succession

继续革命 **chì-hsù-kó-mìng** continuous revolution

继续大跃进 **chì-hsù tà-yuèh-chìn** to continue a great leap forward; a continuous great leap forward

继续当政 **chì-hsù tāng-chèng** to continue in power

继任 **chì-jèn** to succeed [to a post]

133 寄以希望 **chì-ǐ-hsī-wàng** to put one's hopes on

寄人篱下 **chì-jén-lí-hsià** to live under another's fence (to rely on another, to be under someone's thumb, to sponge)

寄生者 **chì-shēng-chě** a parasitic person

寄生虫 **chì-shēng-ch'úng** a parasitic worm (a common Cultural Revolution epithet)

寄生生活 **chì-shēng-shēng-huó** parasitism; parasitical life

寄宿学校 **chì-sù hsuéh-hsiào** boarding school

寄予期望 **chì-yú-ch'ī-wàng** to lodge hope in, to put hope in

134 觊觎 **chì-yú** to have aggressive designs against, to be ambitious to lay hands on

135 冀 **chì** Hopei province

chiā (jiā)

136 加紧 **chiā-chǐn** to hurry, speed up, tighten up; to intensify, aggravate, give a boost to

加强战备 **chiā-ch'iáng chàn-pèi** to strengthen military preparedness, increase war readiness

加剧 **chiā-chù** to intensify [in degree], deteriorate [of a situation]

加热炉 **chiā-jè-lú** heating furnace

加工 **chiā-kūng** to process; processing, finishing, refining

加工合同 **chiā-kūng hó-t'ung** a processing contract

加工生产组 **chiā-kūng shēng-ch'ǎn-tsǔ** processing production groups (set up by lane committees, 1959–1960)

加工订货 **chiā-kūng tìng-huò** orders placed by the state with small enterprises for manufacturing and processing; to process and manufacture goods

加拉加斯 **chiā-lā-chiā-szū** Caracas [Venezuela]

加纳 **chiā-nà** Ghana

加拿大 **chiā-ná-tà** Canada

加班 **chiā-pān** overtime work, extra shift, extra schedule

加蓬 **chiā-p'éng** [Republic of] Gabon

加深 **chiā-shēn** to intensify, deepen, aggravate, worsen

加速 **chiā-sù** to accelerate, quicken, expedite

加速器 **chiā-sù-ch'ì** [nuclear] accelerator

加德满都 **chiā-té-mǎn-tū** Kathmandu [Nepal]

加油 **chiā-yú** to add oil (to put out greater effort, pep up, buck up)

137 夹着尾巴 **chiā-che-wěi-pa** to put one's tail [between one's legs] (to flee in a cowardly manner)

夹杂 **chiā-tsá** to mix up, blend; mixed up, confused, impure

夹 **chiā**: see also **chiá**

138 枷锁 **chiā-sǒ** chains and shackles (bondage)

139 家长制 **chiā-chǎng-chìh** paternalism, patriarchy; patriarchal

家长会 **chiā-chǎng-huì** a meeting of [school pupils'] parents

家长式统治 **chiā-chǎng-shìh t'ǔng-chìh** to rule like patriarchs (to rule arbitrarily)

家长作风 **chiā-chǎng tsò-fēng** the paternal style

家给人足 **chiā-chǐ-jén-tsú** every family supplied and each person having enough (adequate supplies so that none suffer)

家产 **chiā-ch'ǎn** family property, patrimony

家丑外扬 **chiā-ch'ǒu-wài-yáng** to drag the family skeleton out into the light of day (to wash one's dirty linen in public)

家畜 **chiā-ch'ù** domestic animals or fowls

家传 **chiā-ch'uán** (1) family heritage; (2) handed down from generation to generation

家肥 **chiā-féi** natural fertilizer, night soil

家伙 **chiā-huo** (1) a tool; (2) a fellow, a guy (familiar or derisive)

家破人亡 **chiā-p'ò-jén-wáng** the family broken and people dead

家谱 **chiā-p'ǔ** family genealogy, family records

家史 **chiā-shǐh** family history (one of the **szù-shǐh**)

家属 **chiā-shǔ** family dependents

家属委员会 **chiā-shǔ wěi-yuán-huì** dependents' committee (in a residential building or factory)

家大业大浪费点没啥 **chiā-tà yèh-tà làng-feì-tiěn méi-shà** when the family is large or the business is big, it does not matter if there is a little waste (an attitude to be criticized)

家当 **chiā-tang** family property, family estate

家底 **chiā-tǐ** (1) family property (often figurative, as one's political capital); (2) family background and status

家庭教育 **chiā-t'íng-chiào-yù** family training, education in the home

家庭出身 **chiā-t'íng-ch'ū-shēn** family background and origin (the officially registered class history of any person—depends on the type of main income source of his family when he was a child)

家庭妇女 **chiā-t'íng-fù-nǚ** housewife (women who do not work outside the family)

家庭副业 **chiā-t'íng-fù-yèh** domestic sideline occupations

家庭副业生产 **chiā-t'íng-fù-yèh shēng-ch'ǎn** production by organized domestic side occupations

家庭开支 **chiā-t'íng k'āi-chīh** family budget, family expenditures

家庭补助 **chiā-t'íng pǔ-chù** family grants, family subsidy (supplemental to the family's regular income to meet special needs or conditions)

家庭手工业 **chiā-t'íng shǒu-kūng-yèh** domestic handicrafts industry

家族主义 **chiā-tsú-chǔ-ì** the clan system; clannishness

家务劳动 **chiā-wù-láo-tùng** housework, household chores

家务劳动社会化 **chiā-wù-láo-tùng shè-huì-huà** socialization of household work

家鱼 **chiā-yú** raised fish (fish farming in an organized way)

家喻戶晓 **chiā-yù-hù-hsiǎo** to make known to every family

140 嘉奖 **chiā-chǐang** a commendation, citation

chiá (jiá)

141 夹缝 **chiá-fèng** a narrow opening, a crack; in an interstice

夹攻 **chiá-kūng** to attack from two sides, hem in; a converging attack, pincer attack

夹道欢迎 **chiá-tào-huān-yíng** welcoming crowds lining the streets

夹 **chiá**: see also **chiā**

chiǎ (jiǎ)

142 贾桂思想 **chiǎ-kuèi szū-hsiǎng** Chia Kuei thinking (toadyism—usually connected with foreignism)

143 钾肥 **chiǎ-féi** potash or potassium fertilizer

144 假借名义 **chiǎ-chièh-míng-ì** to invoke the name of [usually in an improper or unauthorized way]

假话 **chiǎ-huà** falsehoods, lies

假红旗 **chiǎ-húng-ch'í** false red banner (refers to anti-Mao elements during the Cultural Revolution)

假象 **chiǎ-hsiàng** a false image, semblance

假想敌 **chiǎ-hsiǎng-tí** a hypothetical enemy

假惺惺 **chiǎ-hsīng-hsīng** spuriously; hypocritical

假公济私 **chiǎ-kūng-chì-szū** to promote one's private interests under the guise of serving the public, satisfy private ends by utilizing public means

假面具 **chiǎ-mièn-chù** a mask, false front (often used abstractly)

假释 **chiǎ-shìh** to parole, release on parole; parole, conditional release

假手于人 **chiǎ-shǒu-yǘ-jén** to put into the hands of others, let someone else do it (usually with the sense of shirking responsibility)

假定 **chiǎ-tìng** (1) a hypothesis, supposition; (2) supposing that, granting that

假裁军 **chiǎ-ts'ái-chūn** false disarmament, empty disarmament

chià (jià)

145 价值规律 **chià-chíh kuēi-lù** the law of value

价格 **chià-kó** price, value

146 架势 **chià-shih** a move in Chinese boxing (an affected style, an assumed manner)

架子 **chià-tzu** an affected manner,

airs, snobbishness

147 驾轻就熟 **chià-ch'īng-chìu-shú** to drive a light carriage over a familiar road (to perform a task easily because one has experience)

驾驶员 **chià-shǐh-yuán** a driver (can be used for either chauffeur or airplane pilot)

chiāng (jiāng)

148 江河日下 **chiāng-hó-jìh-hsià** the rivers are falling steadily (the situation is deteriorating, going from bad to worse)

江南 **chiāng-nán** south of the Yangtze river (loosely, Chekiang and south Kiangsu: usually suggests a lush and fertile area)

江南无煤论 **chiāng-nán wú-méi lùn** the doctrine that the Chiangnan [region] has no coal (economic defeatism)

江山 **chiāng-shān** rivers and mountains (territory, state, homeland)

江湾套里 **chiāng-wān t'ào-lǐ** slack water on the inside of the river bend

149 将计就计 **chiāng-chì-chìu-chì** to take advantage of an adversary's scheme, meet an adversary with his own strategy

将信将疑 **chiāng-hsìn-chiāng-í** wavering between belief and doubt

将一军 **chiāng-í-chūn** to checkmate, challenge; a checkmate

将功赎罪 **chiāng-kūng-shú-tsuì** to use meritorious service to atone for [past] mistakes

将错就错 **chiāng-ts'ò-chìu-ts'ò** to make the best of a mistake

将 **chiāng**: *see also* **chiàng**

150 僵持形势 **chiāng-chíh-hsing-shìh** a stalemated situation, a condition of stalemate

僵局 **chiāng-chú** a deadlock, stalemate

僵化 **chiāng-huà** to become rigid, stiff

151 疆界 **chiāng-chièh** frontier, border, boundary, limits

疆域 **chiāng-yù** territory [of a country]

chiǎng (jiǎng)

152 讲解 **chiǎng-chièh** to explain, expound [as a teacher to students]

讲究 **chiǎng-chiū** to analyze, make a careful study of

讲究 **chiǎng-chiu** meticulous; to be particular about

讲情面 **chiǎng-ch'íng-mien** to care for another person's face (to spare another's sensitivities)

讲习班 **chiǎng-hsí-pān** a lecture and study group, study group, class

讲稿 **chiǎng-kǎo** lecture notes

讲排场 **chiǎng-p'ái-ch'ang** to put on a grand or showy display (ostentatious)

讲评 **chiǎng-p'íng** to review and evaluate

讲师 **chiǎng-shīh** an instructor or lecturer [in a college or university]

讲授 **chiǎng-shòu** to lecture, instruct, teach [academic courses]

讲道理 **chiǎng-tào-lǐ** to appeal to reason, talk sense; to be reasonable

讲卫生 **chiǎng-wèi-shēng** to pay attention to hygiene

讲用会 **chiǎng-yùng-huì** meetings for discussion and application (such as were organized during the Cultural Revolution for the study of Mao's works and thought)

153 奖金 **chiǎng-chīn** a monetary reward, prize, bonus

奖励 **chiǎng-lì** to praise, commend, encourage by rewards; praise and encouragement

奖励制度 **chiǎng-lì chìh-tù** system of rewards

154 蒋政权 **chiǎng-chèng-ch'üán** the Chiang [Kai-shek] regime

蒋家王朝 **chiǎng-chiā wáng-ch'áo** the Chiang [Kai-shek] dynasty

蒋军 **chiǎng-chūn** the Chiang [Kai-shek] army

蒋管区 **chiǎng-kuǎn-ch'ǖ** the territory controlled by Chiang [during the Liberation War]

蒋帮 **chiǎng-pāng** the Chiang [Kai-shek] gang

chiàng (jiàng)

155 降级 **chiàng-chí** to demote, reduce to a lower grade; demotion

降职 **chiàng-chíh** a demotion [in position]

降落 **chiàng-lò** to land [an aircraft], to descend

降水量 **chiàng-shuǐ-liàng** amount of precipitation

降低成本 **chiàng-tī ch'éng-pěn** to reduce costs, cut down the cost of production

降低定额 **chiàng-tī tìng-ó** to cut down the norm, reduce the target goal

降低物价 **chiàng-tī wù-chià** to reduce prices; price reduction

降雨量 **chiàng-yǔ-liàng** amount of rainfall

156 将相 **chiàng-hsiàng** generals and ministers of state

将 **chiàng:** *see also* **chiāng**

chiāo (jiāo)

[157] 交战状态 **chiāo-chàn chuàng-t'ài** a state of war

交战权 **chiāo-chàn-ch'üán** belligerent rights

交战国 **chiāo-chàn-kuó** belligerent powers, belligerents

交战火网 **chiāo-ch'ā huǒ-wǎng** a cross-fire net

交叉射击 **chiāo-ch'á shè-chī** cross fire

交枪 **chiāo-ch'iāng** to hand over guns, lay down arms (to surrender)

交锋 **chiāo-fēng** to cross lances, meet in battle (often figurative)

交换价值 **chiāo-huàn chià-chíh** exchange value

交换意见 **chiāo-huàn ì-chièn** to exchange views, compare notes

交货 **chiāo-huò** to deliver goods; a consignment

交响乐团 **chiāo-hsiǎng-yuèh-t'uán** a symphony orchestra

交心 **chiāo-hsīn** to make a clean breast of

交心运动 **chiāo-hsīn-yùn-tùng** redeem-your-heart movement (to encourage declarations of loyalty)

交椅 **chiāo-ǐ** an armchair (a position, e.g., the first chair)

交易会 **chiāo-ì-huì** a trade fair

交口称誉 **chiāo-k'ǒu-ch'ēng-yù** to praise unanimously

交流 **chiāo-líu** exchange, interflow, crosscurrents; to exchange

交流经验 **chiāo-líu chīng-yèn** to exchange experiences

交流会议 **chiāo-líu huì-ì** an exchange-of-experience meeting (usually to demonstrate, on location, how a particular policy or project has been successfully carried out)

交流心得 **chiāo-líu hsīn-té** to exchange the mind's gain (to exchange personal knowledge derived after intense study)

交流电 **chiāo-líu-tièn** alternating current [electricity]

交纳 **chiāo-nà** to pay [tax]

交售余粮 **chiāo-shòu yǘ-liáng** to sell surplus grain [to the government]

交大 **chiāo-tà** Chiaotung [Communications] University (formerly at Shanghai, now at Sian)

交代 **chiāo-tài** (1) to hand over; (2) to review one's own history or actions for scrutiny by the group

交底 **chiāo-tǐ** to give all the facts

交头接耳 **chiāo-t'óu-chiēh-ěrh** to bend heads and whisper in the ear

交通工具 **chiāo-t'ūng kūng-chù** vehicles, means of transportation

交通部 **chiāo-t'ūng-pù** Ministry of Communications [of the State Council] (after 1969, absorbed the Ministry of Railways)

交通员 **chiāo-t'ūng-yuán** a message carrier, courier (during the Anti-Japanese and Liberation War periods)

交租 **chiāo-tsū** to pay rent

[158] 郊区 **chiāo-ch'ǖ** a suburb, suburban districts

郊外 **chiāo-wài** suburbs, outskirts, environs

[159] 娇气 **chiāo-ch'ì** frail, delicate, finicky

娇生惯养 **chiāo-shēng-kuàn-yǎng** to grow up in a soft environment (to live a sheltered life)

[160] 浇铸 **chiāo-chù** to cast metal; a metal mold

浇灌 **chiāo-kuàn** to water, irrigate

[161] 骄傲情绪 **chiāo-ào-ch'íng-hsù** arrogant sentiments, inner arrogance

骄傲自满 **chiāo-ào-tzù-mǎn** conceit and complacency; to be conceited and self-satisfied

骄傲自大 **chiāo-ào-tzù-tà** arrogant, overbearing; arrogance and conceit; to give oneself airs

骄气 **chiāo-ch'ì** arrogance, conceit

骄横 **chiāo-hèng** arrogant, overbearing

骄兵必败 **chiāo-pīng-pì-pài** an arrogant army is certain to meet defeat

骄奢淫逸 **chiāo-shē-yín-ì** lordly, luxurious, loose and idle

骄字顽症 **chiāo-tzù wán-chèng** haughtiness [like a] stubborn disease, the stubborn disease of the word "proud"

[162] 胶着状态 **chiāo-chó chuàng-t'ài** to be stuck, immobilized; condition of being stuck, or immobilized

胶合板 **chiāo-hó-pǎn** plywood

胶鞋 **chiāo-hsiéh** rubber-soled shoes, sneakers

[163] 教书不教人 **chiāo-shū pù chiāo-jén** teaching books [and] not teaching people (Cultural Revolution accusation of poor teaching methods employed by bookish intellectuals)

教书倒霉论 **chiāo-shū-tǎo-méi lùn** the idea that teaching is doomed

教 **chiāo:** *see also* **chiào**

[164] 焦急 **chiāo-chí** extremely anxious and restless, vexed, worried

焦煤 **chiāo-méi** coke, coking coal

焦点 **chiāo-tiěn** focus, focal point

焦头烂额 **chiāo-t'óu-làn-ó** with scorched head and smashed brow (working under conditions of great hardship)

焦土政策 **chiāo-t'ǔ-chèng-ts'è** scorched earth policy

焦裕禄 **chiāo yǜ-lù** Chiao Yü-lu (a *hsien* Party secretary, who was originally a peasant and then a forced laborer in the Manchurian mines. He joined the Resistance War and despite poor health, devoted himself to improving the soil and life of the peasants in a poor district of Honan until his death and subsequent glorification in 1964)

chiǎo (jiǎo)

165 角钢 **chiǎo-kāng** angle steel, angle steel bar

角落 **chiǎo-lò** an angle, a corner of a room

角度 **chiǎo-tù** (1) an angle [math.]; (2) point of view

角 **chiǎo**: *see also* **chuéh**

166 侥幸 **chiǎo-hsìng** a gambling attitude; to obtain by sheer luck; a lucky escape [from danger]

侥幸成功 **chiǎo-hsìng-ch'éng-kūng** success through good luck

167 绞杀 **chiǎo-shā** to strangle, throttle, stifle

168 狡猾 **chiǎo-huá** cunning, sly, untrustworthy, slippery

狡辩 **chiǎo-pièn** to argue deviously; artful self-defense, sophisticated argument

狡兔三窟 **chiǎo-t'ù-sān-k'ù** a sly rabbit has three exits to its burrow (crafty foresight; to take precautionary measures against danger)

169 脚镣 **chiǎo-liào** fetters, shackles

脚踏两只船 **chiǎo-t'à liǎng-chīh-ch'uán** to straddle two boats (to sit on the fence, be undecided)

脚踏实地 **chiǎo-t'à-shíh-tì** to plant one's feet on solid ground (to do a job honestly and practically)

170 矫揉造作 **chiǎo-jóu-tsào-tsò** to behave in an affected manner

矫枉过正 **chiǎo-wǎng-kuò-chèng** to over-correct something crooked (excessive measures, overstrictness)

171 搅浑 **chiǎo-hǔn** to muddy (to stir up, agitate, confuse matters)

172 缴获 **chiǎo-huò** to capture, take as booty

缴械 **chiǎo-hsièh** to disarm, hand over arms

缴纳 **chiǎo-nà** to pay to the authorities [taxes, fees, grain, etc.]

chiào (jiào)

173 叫好 **chiào-hǎo** applause; to applaud

叫器 **chiào-hsiāo** to clamor, raise a hue and cry; clamorous

叫苦连天 **chiào-k'ǔ-lién-t'iēn** to complain to high heaven (an endless recital of grievances)

174 较量 **chiào-lìang** to compare strength, match, contest

175 轿车 **chiào-ch'ē** an automobile sedan, limousine

176 教程 **chiào-ch'éng** a teaching manual

教具 **chiào-chù** teaching aids

教学基地网 **chiào-hsuéh chī-tì-wǎng** network of teaching bases (usually centers, away from the parent institution and often in the countryside, which serve a multiple purpose of providing practical experience, an opportunity for research [as in medicine], and improving the local educational level)

教学计划 **chiào-hsúeh chì-huà** teaching plan [for a particular field]

教学、劳动生产、科学研究三结合的学制 **chiào-hsuéh, láo-tùng-shēng-ch'ǎn, k'ō-hsuéh-yén-chiū sān-chiéh-hó te hsuéh-chìh** the three-combined educational system of teaching, productive labor, and scientific research

教学相长 **chiào-hsuéh-hsiāng-chǎng** teachers and students grow reciprocally, teachers and students benefit from each other

教学内容 **chiào-hsuéh nèi-júng** content of instruction

教学大纲 **chiào-hsuéh tà-kāng** teaching outline, lecture outline, teaching syllabus [for a particular course]

教学研究组 **chiào-hsuéh yén-chiū-tsǔ** teaching and research section (abbreviated as **chiào-yén-tsǔ**)

教学与研究 **chiào-hsuéh yǔ yén-chiū** *Teaching and Research* (Peking monthly, 1953—)

教训 **chiào-hsùn** to teach, instruct, rebuke, reproach; teaching, instruction, lesson

教义 **chiào-ì** religious doctrine, dogma

教改 **chiào-kǎi** educational reform (abbreviation of **chiào-yù kǎi-kó**)

教科书 **chiào-k'ō-shū** textbooks

教门 **chiào-mén** a church, sect; Mohammedans

教师节 **chiào-shīh-chiéh** Teachers' Day

教师中心论 **chiào-shīh-chūng-hsīn lùn** the view that teachers are the center of a school

教师报 **chiào-shīh-pào** *Teacher's Journal* (a semi-weekly newspaper)

教师倒霉论 **chiào-shīh tǎo-méi lùn** theory that teachers are doomed (exaggerated view attributed to reactionaries during the Cultural Revolution)

教师队伍建设 **chiào-shīh tuì-wǔ chièn-shè** to build up the ranks of the teachers

教师爷 **chiào-shīh-yéh** a drillmaster (usually sarcastic and critical of poor teaching methods)

教授治校 **chiào-shòu chìh-hsiào** professors [should] govern the university (a proposal made by intellectuals during the Hundred Flowers period, later heavily criticized)

教唆 **chiào-sō** to instigate, abet, incite, goad, stir up

教导 **chiào-tǎo** teaching, instruction; to teach, lead, conduct, educate

教导员 **chiào-tǎo-yuán** instructor, instruction officer (political officer of a PLA battalion)

教条 **chiào-t'iáo** dogma; doctrinaire, dogmatic

教条主义 **chiào-t'iáo-chǔ-ì** dogmatism, doctrinairism

教材 **chiào-ts'ái** teaching material

教养 **chiào-yǎng** to educate and bring up; culture, education and rearing

教研室 **chiào-yén-shìh** a [departmental] teaching and research group

教研组 **chiào-yén-tsǔ** a teaching and research section [subordinate to a *shih*]

教育战线 **chiào-yǔ-chàn-hsièn** the education front

教育机构 **chiào-yǔ-chī-kòu** educational institutions, educational organs

教育制度 **chiào-yǔ-chìh-tù** educational system

教育重点 **chiào-yǔ-chùng-tiěn** (1) important points in education, educational center; (2) a person singled out for concentrated educational attention as an example to others during the course of a political campaign

教育改革 **chiào-yǔ kǎi-kó** educational reform

教育革命 **chiào-yǔ-kó-mìng** revolution in education, the educational revolution

教育领域 **chiào-yǔ-lǐng-yǔ** the educational realm

教育部 **chiào-yǔ-pù** Ministry of Education

教育为政治服务 **chiào-yǔ wèi chèng-chìh fú-wù** education is to serve politics

教育与生产劳动相结合 **chiào-yù yǔ shēng-ch'ǎn-láo-tùng hsiāng-chiéh-hó** to combine education with productive labor

教 **chiào**: see also **chiāo**

chiēh (jiē)

阶级 **chiēh-chí** (1) steps, rank; (2) social class

阶级爱憎 **chiēh-chí-ài-tsēng** class love and hatred

阶级教育 **chiēh-chí-chiào-yǔ** class education (indoctrination in class struggle and class analysis)

阶级解放 **chiēh-chí-chiěh-fàng** class liberation [of the proletariat]

阶级界限 **chiēh-chí-chièh-hsièn** class boundaries [between the proletariat and the bourgeoisie]

阶级制度 **chiēh-chí-chìh-tù** the class system

阶级粥 **chiēh-chí-chōu** class congee (a coarse gruel sometimes served to sent-down personnel to remind them of pre-Liberation proletarian fare)

阶级差别 **chiēh-chí-ch'ā-piéh** class distinctions, class differentiation

阶级成分 **chiēh-chí-ch'éng-fèn** class status

阶级情谊 **chiēh-chí-ch'íng-í** class affection

阶级仇恨 **chiēh-chí-ch'óu-hèn** class hatred

阶级仇敌 **chiēh-chí-ch'óu-tí** class enemy

阶级出身 **chiēh-chí-ch'ū-shēn** class origin, class background

阶级觉悟 **chiēh-chí-chüéh-wù** class consciousness

阶级区分 **chiēh-chí-ch'ǖ-fēn** class distinctions, class differentiation

阶级分化 **chiēh-chí-fēn-huà** [internal] class differentiation (the process of sub-class stratification)

阶级分析 **chiēh-chí-fēn-hsī** class analysis

阶级合作 **chiēh-chí-hó-tsò** class cooperation (a tendency charged against revisionism)

阶级性 **chiēh-chí-hsìng** class character, class nature

阶级异己分子 **chiēh-chí ì-chǐ fèn-tzǔ** alien class element, individuals from alien classes, people of classes

different from one's own

阶级意识 **chiēh-chí-ì-shìh** class consciousness

阶级感情 **chiēh-chí-kǎn-ch'íng** class feelings

阶级关系 **chiēh-chí-kuān-hsi** relations among classes

阶级观念 **chiēh-chí-kuān-nièn** class concept, class view

阶级观点 **chiēh-chí-kuān-tiěn** class viewpoint (one of the **szù-tà-kuān-tiěn**)

阶级苦、民族恨 **chiēh-chí-k'ǔ, mín-tsú-hèn** class bitterness and national hatred

阶级烙印 **chiēh-chí-lào-yìn** class brand (an indelible mark of one's class)

阶级利己主义 **chiēh-chí-lì-chǐ-chǔ-ì** the theory of class self-interest

价级立场 **chiēh-chí-lì-ch'ǎng** class standpoint

阶级利害 **chiēh-chí-lì-hài** class gain or loss, class interest or disadvantage, class interests

阶级利益 **chiēh-chí-lì-ì** class interests, class benefits

阶级路线 **chiēh-chí-lù-hsièn** the class line

阶级矛盾 **chiēh-chí-máo-tùn** class contradictions

阶级内容 **chiēh-chí-nèi-júng** class content

阶级报复 **chiēh-chí-pào-fù** class revenge

阶级本质 **chiēh-chí-pěn-chìh** class essence, class character

阶级本性 **chiēh-chí-pěn-hsìng** class character

阶级本能 **chiēh-chí-pěn-néng** class instinct

阶级偏见 **chiēh-chí-p'iēn-chièn** class prejudice

阶级品质 **chiēh-chí-p'ǐn-chìh** class quality, class qualities

阶级社会 **chiēh-chí-shè-huì** a class society

阶级深情 **chiēh-chí-shēn-ch'íng** deep class feelings

阶级敌人 **chiēh-chí-tí-jén** class enemy

阶级地位 **chiēh-chí-tì-wèi** class position

阶级斗争 **chiēh-chí-tòu-chēng** class struggle

阶级斗争熄灭论 **chiēh-chí-tòu-chēng hsī-mièh lùn** the theory of the dying out of the class struggle (one of the accusations against Liu Shao-ch'i)

阶级斗争形式 **chiēh-chí-tòu-chēng hsíng-shìh** forms of class struggle

阶级斗争一抓就灵 **chiēh-chí-tòu-chēng ī-chuā-chìu-líng** once class struggle is grasped, miracles are possible

阶级队伍 **chiēh-chí-tuì-wǔ** class members, class corps, class ranks

阶级调和论 **chiēh-chí-t'iáo-hó lùn** the theory of class harmony (a view attributed to Liu Shao-ch'i)

阶级投降主义 **chiēh-chí-t'óu-hsiáng-chǔ-ì** class capitulationism

阶段 **chiēh-tuàn** a stage, a phase [in history or time]

阶梯 **chiēh-t'ī** a ladder, staircase (steps leading to success)

阶层 **chiēh-ts'éng** a stratum, sub-division of a single class

¹⁷⁸ 皆大欢喜 **chiēh-tà-huān-hsǐ** to the satisfaction of all concerned

¹⁷⁹ 接见 **chiēh-chièn** to receive, talk with [a visitor]

接近末日 **chiēh-chìn-mò-jìh** to approach the end; one's days are numbered

接踵而来 **chiēh-chǔng-érh-lái** to come on the heels of, follow in quick succession

接触 **chiēh-ch'ù** to contact, get in touch with; a contact

接任 **chiēh-jèn** to take over an office, assume a post

接连不断 **chiēh-lién-pù-tuàn** continuous, continuously

接班 **chiēh-pān** to relieve another in work, to take over a shift

接班人 **chiēh-pān-jén** a relief, successor (usually refers to "revolutionary successors")

接上关系 **chiēh-shang-kuān-hsi** to establish relations (usually with the Party)

接受教训 **chiēh-shòu-chiào-hsùn** to learn the lessons [of history]

接受教育 **chiēh-shòu-chiào-yù** to receive education [from the workers, peasants, and soldiers]

接受工农兵的再教育 **chiēh-shòu kūng-núng-pīng te tsài-chiào-yù** to be re-educated by the workers, peasants, and soldiers (one of the campaigns after the Cultural Revolution)

接受贫下中农再教育 **chiēh-shòu p'ín-hsià-chūng-núng tsài-chiào-yù** to be re-educated by the poor and lower-middle peasants (said of city workers, students, and cadres going to the countryside after the Cultural Revolution)

接待人员 **chiēh-tài jén-yuán** reception personnel

接头 **chiēh-t'óu** to make contact with; to have a firm grasp of a situation, have a clear view, know

¹⁸⁰ 街坊 **chiēh-fang** neighbor, neighbor-

hood

街道居民委员会 **chiēh-tào-chū-mín wěi-yuán-huì** neighborhood committee, administrative station in the neighborhood

街道妇女 **chiēh-tào-fù-nǚ** neighborhood women (usually unemployed housewives who are organized for various activities)

街道服务站 **chiēh-tào fú-wù-chàn** street service station (stations for repairing and patching work in urban communes)

街道小厂 **chiēh-tào-hsiǎo-ch'ǎng** small neighborhood factory

街道医生 **chiēh-tào-ī-shēng** street doctor (urban equivalent of barefoot doctors)

街道故事员 **chiēh-tào kù-shìh-yuán** street storyteller

街道工业 **chiēh-tào-kūng-yèh** street industry (small industrial units organized in the neighborhoods, often utilizing the part-time labor of housewives)

街道图书馆 **chiēh-tào t'ú-shū-kuǎn** a small library organized by a neighborhood

街谈巷议 **chiēh-t'án-hsiàng-ì** talked on the streets and discussed in the alleys (the talk of the town, on everyone's lips)

街头巷尾 **chiēh-t'óu-hsiàng-wěi** at street head and alley end (in every nook and cranny of the city)

181 揭穿 **chiēh-ch'uān** to expose, disclose, unmask; disclosure

揭穿骗局 **chiēh-ch'uān pièn-chú** to uncover a deception

揭发 **chiēh-fā** to denounce, unmask, reveal; denunciation, revelation

揭盖子 **chiēh-kài-tzu** to lift the lid, expose (Cultural Revolution phrase implying free criticism of power-holders and capitalist roaders)

揭竿而起 **chiēh-kān-érh-ch'ǐ** to raise a stick [as a banner] and revolt

揭老底 **chiēh-lǎo-tǐ** to expose the old bottom (to reveal old hidden facts)

揭露无余 **chiēh-lù-wú-yú** to thoroughly expose, completely unmask

揭矛盾,促转化 **chiēh-máo-tùn, ts'ù-chuǎn-huà** to reveal the contradiction and then to urge its transformation

揭幕 **chiēh-mù** to raise the curtain, inaugurate (to come into being, get under way)

揭示 **chiēh-shìh** to post a notice (to announce, proclaim, enunciate)

揭短 **chiēh-tuǎn** to reveal the failings [of another], expose blemishes

chiéh (jié)

182 孑孑小民 **chiéh-chiéh-hsiǎo-mín** insignificant common people

183 节节败退 **chiéh-chiéh-pài-t'uì** one defeat after another

节节胜利 **chiéh-chiéh-shèng-lì** to gain victory after victory; to push forward from victory to victory

节节抵御 **chiéh-chiéh-tǐ-yù** to resist in successive stages

节俭 **chiéh-chiěn** frugal, thrifty; thrift

节制 **chiéh-chìh** to control, regulate, limit, restrain; control, regulation; temperate, moderate

节制闸 **chiéh-chìh-chá** a flood regulator, regulating sluice gate

节制生育 **chiéh-chìh-shēng-yù** birth control

节气 **chiéh-ch'ì** the 24 periods into which a year is divided; seasonal changes

节气不饶人 **chiéh-ch'ì pù-jáo-jén** the seasons are unforgiving (farm work can not wait)

节衣缩食 **chiéh-ī-sō-shíh** to save on food and clothing

节日 **chiéh-jìh** festival, holiday

节骨眼 **chiéh-kǔ-yěn** the opening of a joint between bones (a particular moment, juncture)

节粮 **chiéh-liáng** to save grain

节煤 **chiéh-méi** to conserve coal

节省 **chiéh-shěng** to save, practice thrift, be economical; economy, conservation

节外生枝 **chiéh-wài-shēng-chīh** branches growing out from the joints (added complications apart from the main issue)

节育 **chiéh-yù** birth control (abbreviation of **chiéh-chìh-shēng-yù**)

节约 **chiéh-yuēh** to economize, be frugal; economy, austerity; thrifty, frugal

节约闹革命 **chiéh-yuēh nào-kó-mìng** be thrifty [in order to] make revolution

节约代用 **chiéh-yuēh-tài-yùng** economy through use of substitute [materials]

184 劫持 **chiéh-ch'íh** to hold under duress, abduct, seize

劫夺 **chiéh-tó** to loot, pillage, plunder, rob

185 杰出 **chiéh-ch'ū** eminent, outstanding [of thought, accomplishment, etc.]

杰作 **chiéh-tsò** a masterpiece, masterstroke

186 结案 **chiéh-àn** to close a case, wind up a lawsuit

结账 **chiěh-chàng** to settle balances, settle accounts

结成联盟 **chiéh-ch'éng lién-méng** to enter into an alliance, form a coalition; affiiliation

结局 **chiéh-chú** the final outcome, conclusion, ending

结合 **chiéh-hó** to combine, join together, coordinate, unite, merge; a combination, alliance, association

结合合同 **chiéh-hó-hó-t'ung** a combined contract

结构 **chiéh-kòu** a structure, arrangement, construction, composition

结构和构件 **chiéh-kòu hó kòu-chièn** structure and part (a structure as a whole and its component elements)

结论 **chiéh-lùn** to sum up, conclude; a summary, conclusion

结社、集会和人身自由 **chiéh-shè, chí-huì hó jén-shēn tzù-yú** freedom of association, assembly, and person

结党营私 **chiéh-tǎng-yíng-szū** to form cliques for selfish advantage

结余 **chiéh-yú** surplus, excess, remainder, balance

187 捷径 **chiéh-chìng** a short cut, the shortest way

捷克斯洛伐克 **chiéh-k'ò-szū-lò-fá-k'ò** Czechoslovakia

捷报频传 **chiéh-pào p'ín-ch'uán** victory reports keep pouring in (often used in reports of production)

捷足先登 **chiéh-tsú-hsiēn-tēng** the swift foot first reaches [the top] (the man who moves fast will be first to reach his goal)

188 截击机 **chiéh-chi-chī** fighter plane; interceptor

截长补短 **chiéh-ch'áng-pǔ-tuǎn** to trim the long to make up the short (to plead one's merits to overcome deficiencies; may also have the sense of one person's strong points making up for another's weaknesses—thus promoting effective teamwork)

截然不同 **chiéh-ján-pù-t'úng** entirely different

189 竭尽心力 **chiéh-chìn-hsīn-lì** with all one's heart

竭力鼓吹 **chiéh-lì-kǔ-ch'uī** to drum and blow with all one's strength (to promote with maximum effort)

chiěh (jiě)

190 解救 **chiéh-chiù** to rescue, save, relieve, succor, deliver

解除禁运 **chiéh-ch'ú chìn-yùn** to lift an embargo

解除武装 **chiéh-ch'ú wǔ-chuāng** to disarm

解决 **chiéh-chüéh** to solve [problems], settle [disputes]; settlement, solution

解放 **chiéh-fàng** (1) to liberate; (2) the Liberation; (3) a magazine published in Yenan during the Resistance War

解放战争 **chiéh-fàng-chàn-chēng** the War of Liberation [1946–49, against the Nationalists]

解放前 **chiéh-fàng-ch'ién** before Liberation (pre-1949)

解放初期 **chiéh-fàng-ch'ū-ch'ī** the early post-Liberation period

解放军 **chiéh-fàng-chūn** Liberation Army (the PLA)

解放军画报 **chiéh-fàng-chūn huà-pào** *Liberation Army Pictorial* (a Peking monthly, 1951—)

解放军学全国人民 **chiéh-fàng-chūn hsuéh ch'üán-kuó jén-mín** the People's Liberation Army [must] learn from all the people (slogan introduced after the purge of Lin Piao)

解放军报 **chiéh-fàng-chūn pào** *Liberation Army News* (a Peking daily newspaper, 1958—)

解放区 **chiéh-fàng-ch'ū** liberated area

解放妇女生产力 **chiéh-fàng fù-nǚ shēng-ch'ǎn-lì** liberate women's productive force

解放日报 **chiéh-fàng jìh-pào** *Liberation Daily* (published in Yenan during the Resistance War; since 1949, in Shanghai)

解放干部 **chiéh-fàng-kàn-pù** (1) liberated cadres; (2) to rehabilitate cadres [after they have gone through reform]

解放思想 **chiéh-fàng szū-hsiǎng** emancipation of thought; to emancipate someone ideologically, emancipate people's minds

解囊相助 **chiéh-náng-hsiāng-chù** to loosen the purse strings to give help (to assist generously)

解剖麻雀 **chiéh-p'ōu-má-ch'üèh** to dissect a sparrow (a small-scale, detailed experiment, usually before general application)

解散 **chiéh-sàn** to disperse, scatter, break up, dissolve; dismissal, dissolution

解释 **chiéh-shìh** to explain, clarify, expound; explanation, clarification, statement

解答 **chiéh-tá** to solve [problems], to

answer [questions]; solution, answer, explanation

解冻 **chièh-tùng** to thaw

解体 **chièh-t'ǐ** to disintegrate, fall apart, be dismembered; dissolution, collapse

解围 **chièh-wéi** to lift an encirclement (to save others from embarrassment or difficulties)

chièh(jiè)

191 介入 **chièh-jù** to interfere, enter, intervene

介绍信 **chièh-shào-hsìn** letter of introduction, credentials

192 戒骄戒躁 **chièh-chiāo-chièh-tsào** to shun pride and impatience

戒心 **chièh-hsīn** to be alert, on guard; alertness, vigilance

戒备 **chièh-pèi** to be on the alert, take precautionary measures; an alert

戒严 **chièh-yén** curfew; martial law

193 届满 **chièh-mǎn** to expire; a completed term (*chieh* means an item in a series. It thus serves the function of "th" or "rd." Hence, the common usage to indicate a session or term: *ti szu-chieh jen-min tai-piao ta-hui* = the Fourth People's Congress)

194 界桩 **chièh-chuāng** boundary marker, boundary stone

界限 **chièh-hsièn** an outer limit, border; limitation, restriction

界线 **chièh-hsièn** a boundary line, demarcation

195 借镜 **chièh-chìng** to borrow a mirror (to learn from the experience of others)

借古讽今 **chièh-kǔ-fěng-chīn** using ancient things to satirize the present (such as Wu Han's *Hai Jui pa-kuan*)

借口 **chièh-k'ǒu** a pretext, excuse, subterfuge

借尸还魂 **chièh-shīh-huán-hún** to come back to life through the possession of another person's body (e.g., capitalism reviving in the guise of revisionism)

借刀杀人 **chièh-tāo-shā-jén** to kill by using another's knife (to instigate a crime by others for one's own purposes)

借题发挥 **chièh-t'í-fā-huī** to make use of a topic to air one's own opinions

chiēn (jiān)

196 奸商 **chiēn-shāng** traitorous merchant

(a phrase used in several economic campaigns, especially in 1952 and 1955)

奸淫掳掠 **chiēn-yín-lǔ-luèh** to rape and plunder

197 尖锐 **chiēn-juì** sharp, pointed, barbed, acute, critical

尖锐冲突 **chiēn-juì ch'ūng-t'ū** acute conflict

尖锐化 **chiēn-juì-huà** to sharpen, become acute

尖兵 **chiēn-pīng** the point man (the lead man in a military patrol)

尖刀战术 **chiēn-tāo-chàn-shù** sharp knife tactics (a concentrated attack on a limited front)

尖端 **chiēn-tuān** apex, acme, pinnacle, the extreme point

尖端科学 **chiēn-tuān-k'ō-hsuéh** a pinnacle science (refers to any highly specialized, highly sophisticated science—such as nuclear physics)

198 歼灭战 **chiēn-mièh-chàn** a battle of annihilation (may be other activity such as a production effort which is assured of success by careful planning and ample manpower mobilization)

歼灭性打击 **chiēn-mièh-hsìng tǎ-chī** a crushing blow, annihilative attack

199 坚贞不屈 **chiēn-chēn-pù-ch'ū** to stand firm and unyielding [on moral principles]

坚强堡垒 **chiēn-ch'iáng pǎo-lěi** a stout bulwark, strong bastion (figurative)

坚强不屈 **chiēn-ch'iáng-pù-ch'ū** strong and unbending

坚持战斗 **chiēn-ch'íh-chàn-tòu** to persist in struggle; persistent struggle

坚持真理, 改正错误 **chiēn-ch'íh-chēn-lǐ, kǎi-chèng-ts'ò-wù** to hold fast to the truth [and] to correct mistakes

坚持不懈 **chiēn-ch'íh-pù-hsièh** consistent and untiring

坚持不渝 **chiēn-ch'íh-pù-yú** persistent, persevering, unremitting

坚持实践 **chiēn-ch'íh shíh-chièn** to insist on practice

坚持原则 **chiēn-ch'íh yuán-tsé** to stand firm on principles

坚决支持 **chiēn-chüéh chīh-ch'íh** to support resolutely, to give firm support

坚决、彻底、全面地消灭敌人 **chiēn-chüéh, ch'è-tǐ, kān-chìng, ch'üán-pù-te hsiāo-mièh tí-jén** to annihilate the enemy resolutely, thoroughly, wholly, and completely

坚决反对 **chiēn-chüéh fǎn-tuì** to oppose resolutely, to be firmly against; steadfast opposition

坚决手段 **chiēn-chüéh-shǒu-tuàn** a resolute method of handling, a firm hand

坚决地放、大胆地放、彻底地放 **chiēn-chüéh-te-fàng, tà-tǎn-te-fàng, ch'è-tǐ-te-fàng** [let the masses] resolutely, boldly, and thoroughly express [their views]

坚信 **chiēn-hsìn** to believe firmly

坚韧 **chiēn-jèn** resilience, endurance; resilient

坚忍不拔 **chiēn-jěn-pù-pá** determined, unwavering, unmovable

坚如磐石 **chiēn-jú-p'án-shíh** as firm as a rock

坚固 **chiēn-kù** strong, firm, unshakable; to make secure

坚壁清野 **chiēn-pì-ch'īng-yěh** to strengthen the bulwarks and leave no provisions outside (tactic of people's war)

坚守岗位 **chiēn-shǒu kǎng-wèi** to hold one's sentry post (to faithfully discharge one's duty)

坚定不移 **chiēn-tìng-pù-í** firm and unmoving, unswerving, unflinching, unshakable

200 艰巨 **chiēn-chù** arduous, formidable, difficult

艰巨任务 **chiēn-chù-jèn-wù** a formidable task, arduous task

艰险 **chiēn-hsiěn** difficulty and danger, perilous

艰苦 **chiēn-k'ǔ** hard and bitter, hardship, arduous

艰苦战斗 **chiēn-k'ǔ-chàn-tòu** a hard-fought battle, bitter fight

艰苦卓绝 **chiēn-k'ǔ-chō-chüéh** to endure hardship with fortitude (to surmount great difficulties)

艰苦创业 **chiēn-k'ǔ-ch'uàng-yèh** painstakingly to establish an enterprise

艰苦奋斗 **chiēn-k'ǔ-fèn-tòu** a hard and bitter struggle, to work hard and overcome difficulties

艰苦朴素 **chiēn-k'ǔ-p'ǔ-sù** hard-working and plain-living, hardship and austerity

艰难曲折 **chiēn-nán-ch'ǔ-ché** arduous and tortuous; difficulties and setbacks

艰难险阻 **chiēn-nán-hsiěn-tsǔ** difficulties and dangerous obstacles

艰难困苦 **chiēn-nán-k'ùn-k'ǔ** hardships and privations

201 肩并肩 **chiēn-pìng-chiēn** to stand shoulder to shoulder with, side by side

肩不能挑，手不能提 **chiēn-pù-néng-t'iāo, shǒu-pù-néng-t'í** shoulders unable to carry [and] hands unable to lift (incapable of physical labor—a caustic remark addressed to former intellectuals)

202 兼职 **chiēn-chíh** [holding] concurrent positions

兼职兼薪 **chiēn-chíh-chiēn-hsīn** having two jobs and collecting two salaries (a practice usually criticized)

兼学别样 **chiēn-hsuéh-piéh-yàng** to learn other things concurrently

兼任 **chiēn-jèn** double responsibility (one man in two jobs, e.g., in Party and State functional organs)

兼顾 **chiēn-kù** to attend to two or more matters at the same time

兼并 **chiēn-pìng** annexation; to annex

兼收并蓄 **chiēn-shōu-pìng-hsù** to take and store up (to include everything in one's study; to be broadminded)

兼听则明，偏信则暗 **chiēn-t'īng-tsé-míng, p'iēn-hsìn-tsé-àn** to hear both sides makes you enlightened [while] to trust only one side makes you benighted

203 监察 **chiēn-ch'á** to control, supervise, inspect (often in the sense of after-the-fact investigation)

监察委员会 **chiēn-ch'á wěi-yuán-huì** control committee [in the Party]

监视 **chiēn-shìh** to keep close watch over; surveillance

监督 **chiēn-tū** to supervise; supervision (differing from **chiēn-ch'á** in usually being before-the-fact)

监督留用 **chiēn-tū-liú-yùng** kept on the job but placed under supervision

监狱 **chiēn-yù** jail, prison

204 煎服 **chiēn-fú** to simmer and use [a decoction of Chinese medicine]

chiĕn (jiǎn)

205 拣取 **chiěn-ch'ǔ** to select, gather, pick up

拣破烂 **chiěn-p'ò-làn** to gather rags and other waste materials (applied figuratively to such persons as Liu Shao-ch'i and the old society for collecting rags and junk from the USSR)

206 柬埔寨 **chiěn-p'ǔ-chài** Cambodia

柬埔寨民族统一阵线 **chiěn-p'ǔ-chài mín-tsú t'ǔng-ī-chèn-hsièn** the National United Front of Cambodia (the united front organization headed

by Norodom Sihanouk)

柬埔寨王国民族团结政府 **chiĕn-pʼŭ-chài-wáng-kuó mín-tsú-tʼuán-chiéh chèng-fŭ** the Royal Government of the National Union of Cambodia

207 捡煤渣 **chiĕn-méi-chā** to pick up coal cinders (a reference to the hardships of the old society)

208 减产 **chiĕn-chʼăn** to decrease production or output; a drop in production

减轻 **chiĕn-chʼīng** to become lighter, make lighter; to extenuate, mitigate, lighten, reduce

减缓 **chiĕn-huăn** to retard, slacken, slow down, delay

减刑 **chiĕn-hsíng** to commute a sentence, to reduce punishment

减弱 **chiĕn-jò** to weaken, decrease [in degree], reduce

减料 **chiĕn-liào** cheating on materials, reduction in material

减色 **chiĕn-sè** to lose brilliance, fade, become less attractive

减租减息 **chiĕn-tsū chiĕn-hsī** reduction of rent and interest (1942–1944)

减租退押 **chiĕn-tsū tʼuì-yā** to reduce rents and refund land-rent deposits

减押 **chiĕn-yā** reduction of [land-rent] deposit money

209 检查 **chiĕn-chʼá** to inspect, check, examine; inspection, examination

检查站 **chiĕn-chʼá-chàn** a checkpoint, inspection station

检查质量 **chiĕn-chʼá chìh-liàng** to check for quality, to inspect the quality of

检查和保卫制度 **chiĕn-chʼá hó păo-wèi chìh-tù** examination and protection system (a fixed procedure in granaries, 1960)

检察 **chiĕn-chʼá** to examine or inspect [as by a public procurator]; the activities of the Procuratorate, which includes inspection, investigation, control, prosecution, and administration of law

检察长 **chiĕn-chʼá-chăng** chief procurator

检察机关 **chiĕn-chʼá-chī-kuān** procuratory organs, prosecution organs

检察权 **chiĕn-chʼá-chʼüán** procuratorial authority

检察委员会 **chiĕn-chʼá wĕi-yuán-huì** procuratorial committee, inspection committee

检察员 **chiĕn-chʼá-yuán** a procurator

检举 **chiĕn-chŭ** to prosecute; to report an accusation to the authorities

检举箱 **chiĕn-chŭ-hsiāng** accusation boxes (in campaigns such as that in 1952)

检举小组 **chiĕn-chŭ-hsiăo-tsŭ** informant small groups (in residents' committees to report any signs of discontent to public security organs and to assist in preparing accusations)

检修 **chiĕn-hsiū** to overhaul, repair

检疫 **chiĕn-ì** quarantine; to quarantine

检讨 **chiĕn-tʼăo** to discuss thoroughly, review [problems or failings]

检验制度 **chiĕn-yèn-chìh-tù** testing system

检阅 **chiĕn-yuèh** to review, inspect (originally, in the military sense, now more broadly used—as to review a parade)

210 剪纸 **chiĕn-chĭh** paper-cutting (one of the Chinese folk arts)

剪报 **chiĕn-pào** newspaper clippings

剪刀差 **chiĕn-tāo-chʼā** the scissors discrepancy (the disparity in prices of industrial goods and those of agricultural produce)

211 简洁 **chiĕn-chíeh** simple and clear, concise, terse

简称 **chiĕn-chʼēng** abbreviated as, in short; to abbreviate

简化 **chiĕn-huà** to simplify, reduce; simplification

简化汉字 **chiĕn-huà-hàn-tzù** to simplify Chinese characters; simplified characters

简化字 **chiĕn-huà-tzù** simplified characters

简易公路 **chiĕn-ì-kūng-lù** a simple road, an unpaved road

简易托儿所 **chiĕn-ì tʼŏ-érh-sŏ** simple nurseries (ordinary homes where infants were placed in daytime so that their mothers could work during the Great Leap period)

简明扼要 **chiĕn-míng-ò-yào** terse and concise

简报 **chiĕn-pào** a brief report, a bulletin

简便 **chiĕn-pièn** simple and convenient, handy

简便易行 **chiĕn-pièn-ì-hsíng** simple and convenient to do

简单化 **chiĕn-tān-huà** to simplify; simplification (often used in the sense of superficial over-simplication)

简单再生产 **chiĕn-tān tsài-shēng-chʼăn** simple reproduction (repetition of production on the same scale: Marx, *Capital*)

简单粗暴的方法 **chiĕn-tān tsʼŭ-pào te fāng-fă** simplified and crude methods (usually refers to criticism that is overly violent and not based on rational analysis)

简体字 **chiĕn-tʼĭ-tzù** simplified

characters
简要 **chiĕn-yào** simple and concise, brief and to the point
212 碱地 **chiĕn-tì** alkaline soil

chièn (jiàn)

213 见证 **chièn-chèng** evidence, clear proof; a witness

见解 **chièn-chiĕh** understanding, personal opinion, views, judgment

见重担就挑 **chièn chùng-tàn chiù t'iāo** to see a heavy load and immediately lift it to one's shoulders (eager to assume responsibility)

见风使舵 **chièn-fēng-shíh-tò** to observe the wind and use the helm (to temper one's action to the wind—unprincipled opportunism)

见缝插针 **chièn-fèng-ch'ā-chēn** to insert the needle wherever you see a tiny hole (turning every spare moment to advantage)

见效 **chièn-hsiào** to show results, clearly effective

见义勇为 **chièn-ì-yŭng-wéi** to see the righteousness and act boldly (to do the right thing bravely without caring about the risk)

见异思迁 **chièn-ì-szū-ch'iēn** seeing a difference and wishing to change (without fixed principles, inconstancy)

见困难就上 **chièn-k'ùn-nán chìu-shàng** to see a difficulty and immediately confront it

见利忘义 **chièn-lì-wàng-ì** to see profit and forget integrity

见面礼 **chièn-mièn-lǐ** a gift given at one's first meeting

见报第一 **chièn-pào-tì-ī** to want to see [one's name in] the newspaper (over-anxiety for public fame)

见不得人 **chièn-pù-te-jén** cannot face people (cannot stand the light of day)

见世面 **chièn-shìh-mièn** to see the world (to experience, gain sophistication)

见势不妙 **chièn-shìh-pù-miào** to view the prospects as unfavorable

见死不救 **chièn-szú-pù-chìu** to see death and still not try to save (without compassion, heartless)

见物不见人 **chièn-wù pù chièn-jén** to see [only] things but not men (to consider only material factors and to ignore the human element)

见物又见人 **chièn-wù yù chièn-jén** to see both things and human beings
214 间接经验 **chièn-chiēh-chīng-yèn** indirect experience

间隙 **chièn-hsì** a cleft, a crack, an interval [of time or space]; discord, misunderstanding

间歇 **chièn-hsiēh** intermittent; an interval, intermission, recess

间谍 **chièn-tiéh** a spy, secret agent (a traitor)

间断 **chièn-tuàn** to disconnect, interrupt, detach

间作密植 **chièn-tsò-mì-chíh** interplanting and close cropping

间作套种 **chièn-tsò-t'ào-chùng** interplanting between rows of a standing crop

215 建交 **chièn-chiāo** to establish [diplomatic] relations

建筑 **chièn-chù** to build, construct; a structure, an edifice

建筑工厂化 **chièn-chù kūng-ch'ǎng-huà** assembly-line method in construction; construction of prefabricated buildings

建筑工程部 **chièn-chù kūng-ch'éng-pù** Ministry of Construction [of the State Council]

建筑工地 **chièn-chù-kūng-tì** construction site

建筑材料 **chièn-chù-ts'ái-liào** building materials

建筑用手脚架 **chièn-chù-yùng shǒu-chiǎo-chià** construction scaffolding

建成 **chièn-ch'éng** to build up, complete construction

建军节 **chièn-chūn-chiéh** Army Day (August 1, the anniversary of the Nanchang Uprising in 1927, now regarded as the birth of the PLA)

建军路线 **chièn-chūn-lù-hsièn** the line for building up the army

建议 **chièn-ì** to suggest, make a proposal, give advice; a proposal, resolution, suggestion

建立 **chièn-lì** to establish, erect, create [an agency or institution]

建班子 **chièn-pān-tzu** to set up a leading team

建设 **chièn-shè** to construct, build, erect, establish; construction, building

建设边疆 **chièn-shè-piēn-chiāng** build up the border areas

建党 **chièn-tǎng** to build up the Party, to strengthen the Party; organizational development of the Party

建团 **chièn-t'uán** to build up the [Communist Youth] League, to strengthen the League
216 剑拔弩张 **chièn-pá-nǔ-chāng** swords drawn and bows stretched (belligerent behavior, saber-rattling)

217 贱买贵卖 **chièn-mǎi-kuèi-mài** to buy cheap and to sell dear
218 舰队 **chièn-tuì** naval fleet, naval unit
舰艇 **chièn-t'ǐng** warship, naval vessel
219 健全管理制度 **chièn-ch'üán kuǎn-lǐ-chìh-tù** to perfect the management system
健康水平 **chièn-k'āng-shuǐ-p'íng** general health level
健忘症 **chièn-wàng-chèng** amnesia
220 渐进 **chièn-chìn** to inch forward, to advance gradually
221 践踏 **chièn-t'à** to trample underfoot
222 鉴戒 **chièn-chièh** to take warning from past failure
鉴别 **chièn-piéh** to appraise, evaluate, pass judgment on; to differentiate
鉴定成分 **chièn-tìng-ch'éng-fèn** to determine class status
鉴往知来 **chièn-wǎng-chīh-lái** by reviewing the past one will know the future
223 箭在弦上 **chièn-tsài-hsíen-shang** the arrow is already fitted to the bow (action is imminent; the situation is tense)
箭靶子 **chièn-pǎ-tzu** an archery target (target)

chīh (zhī)

224 之流 **chīh-líu** the like of, ilk
225 支柱 **chīh-chù** a pillar, main support (may be figurative)
支撑点 **chīh-ch'ēng-tiěn** point of support
支前 **chīh-ch'íen** to support the front (contraction of **chīh-yuán ch'íen-hsièn** 支援前线)
支持 **chīh-ch'íh** to support, sustain, uphold; support, backing
支行 **chíh-háng** branches [of a firm or bank, etc.]
支线 **chīh-hsièn** branch line (usually of railway)
支离破碎 **chīh-lí-p'ò-suì** dismembered and fragmented, completely disintegrated
支流 **chīh-líu** a tributary stream, branch of a river
支农 **chīh-núng** to support agriculture
支农吃亏论 **chīh-núng-ch'īh-k'uēi lùn** the idea that supporting agriculture is a losing proposition
支部 **chīh-pù** a branch [of the Party or Youth League]
支部生活 **chīh-pù-shēng-huó** *Party Branch Life* (a Tientsin semi-monthly, 1950—)
支部书记 **chīh-pù-shū-chì** branch secretary [of the Party or Youth League]
支部大会 **chīh-pù-tà-huì** general membership meeting [of the Party or League branch]
支部委员会 **chīh-pù wěi-yuán-huì** branch committee [of the Party or League]
支配 **chīh-p'èi** to direct, dispose, administer, hold authority over
支书 **chīh-shū** branch secretary [of the Party or League] (contraction of **chīh-pù-shū-chì**)
支队 **chīh-tuì** detachment, a unit detached from the main force (usually military)
支左 **chīh-tsǒ** support the Left (Cultural Revolution instruction to the PLA)
支左、支农、支工 **chīh-tsǒ, chīh-núng, chīh-kūng** aid leftists, aid agriculture, aid industry (instruction to the PLA during the Cultural Revolution)
支左模范 **chī-tsǒ-mó-fàn** models in assisting the Left (commendations to picked PLA units)
支左办公室 **chīh-tsǒ pàn-kūng-shìh** Aid Left Bureau (agency set up to aid the Left)
支左不支派 **chīh-tsǒ pù-chīh-p'ài** support the Left but not factions (Cultural Revolution slogan urging PLA support for mass organizations)
支左委员会 **chīh-tsǒ wěi-yuán-huì** committee for assisting the Left
支援 **chīh-yuán** to support and aid
支援农业 **chīh-yuán núng-yèh** supporting agriculture (a justification for heavy industry investment)
支援巴拿马运动 **chīh-yuán pān-ná-mǎ yùn-tùng** Support Panama Campaign (1964)
226 只字不提 **chīh-tzù-pù-t'í** not a single word is mentioned
只 **chīh**: see also **chǐh**
227 织锦厂 **chīh-chǐn-ch'ǎng** silk brocade factory
织染 **chīh-jǎn** weaving and dyeing
228 枝节 **chīh-chiéh** branch and section (minor details, complications)
229 肢解 **chīh-chiěh** to dismember; dismemberment
230 知己知彼，百战不殆 **chīh-chǐ chīh-pǐ, pǎi-chàn-pù-tài** know the enemy and know yourself: a hundred battles without disaster
知和行 **chīh hó hsíng** knowing and doing; knowledge and action
知心人 **chīh-hsīn-jén** the person who understands [my] heart (the ideal for

cadre-people relations)

知行统一论 **chīh-hsíng-t'ǔng-ī lùn** the theory of the unity of knowledge and action

知名人士 **chīh-míng-jén-shìh** well-known people, outstanding personalities, celebrities

知难而进 **chīh-nán-érh-chìn** to know the difficulties yet press ahead

知难而退 **chīh-nán-érh-t'uì** realizing the difficulty one retreats

知识 **chīh-shíh** knowledge, learning

知识青年 **chīh-shíh-ch'īng-nién** educated youths, young intellectuals

知识青年上山下乡 **chīh-shíh ch'īng-nién shàng-shān hsià-hsiāng** educated youth go up to the mountains and down to the villages

知识青年到农村去 **chīh-shíh ch'īng-nién tào núng-ts'ūn-ch'ǜ** educated young people [should] go to the villages

知识分子 **chīh-shíh-fèn-tzǔ** educated elements, intellectuals

知识分子劳动化 **chīh-shíh-fèn-tzǔ láo-tùng-huà** to "labor-ize" the intellectuals (to cause the intellectuals to identify with the workers)

知识分子倒霉论 **chīh-shíh-fèn-tzǔ tǎo-méi lùn** the doctrine that intellectuals are doomed

知识里手 **chīh-shíh-lǐ-shǒu** an intellectual expert (a wiseacre)

知识私有 **chīh-shíh-szū-yǔ** knowledge is private (attacked as a bourgeois, individualist, unsocialist concept)

知识的新贵族 **chīh-shíh te hsīn-kuèi-tsú** the new aristocracy of knowledge, the new intellectual elite (critical)

知无不言，言无不尽 **chīh-wú-pù-yén, yén-wú-pù-chìn** say all you know and say it without reserve

chíh (zhí)

231 执政党 **chíh-chèng-tǎng** the party in power

执行机关 **chíh-hsíng-chī-kuān** executive organ, executive agency

执行任务 **chíh-hsíng-jèn-wù** to carry out a task, to perform one's duty, to discharge an obligation

执行委员会 **chíh-hsíng wěi-yuán-huì** executive council, executive committee

执迷不悟 **chíh-mí-pù-wù** to refuse to come to one's senses (to persist in error)

232 直接 **chíh-chiēh** direct, at first hand; directly

直接调拨 **chíh-chiēh-tiào-pō** direct allocation and delivery, direct assignment

直截了当 **chíh-chiéh-liǎo-tàng** simple and direct

直觉 **chíh-chüéh** intuition, intuitive perception, inspiration

直系亲属 **chíh-hsì-ch'īn-shǔ** immediate family members (direct line as opposed to branch lines)

直辖市 **chíh-hsiá-shìh** a municipality directly under central authority

直译 **chíh-ì** literal translation, literal interpretation

直流输电线 **chíh-líu shū-tièn-hsièn** direct-current transmission line

直升飞机 **chíh-shēng-fēi-chī** a helicopter

直属 **chíh-shǔ** directly controlled by, subordinate to

直率 **chíh-shuài** straightforward, outspoken, forthright, candid

直达火车 **chíh-tá-huǒ-ch'ē** a through train

直言不讳 **chíh-yén-pù-huì** to speak without concealment, frankly

233 值勤 **chíh-ch'ín** to be on duty (usually military, as to stand a watch)

值班 **chíh-pān** to be on duty (usually in a factory or office)

234 职权 **chíh-ch'üán** authority, jurisdiction, official powers

职权范围 **chíh-ch'üán-fàn-wéi** sphere of one's functions and powers, scope of authority, area of jurisdiction

职衔 **chíh-hsién** position and title, rank

职工 **chíh-kūng** staff and workers

职工代表大会 **chíh-kūng tài-piǎo-tà-huì** workers' congress

职工业余学校 **chíh-kūng yèh-yú-hsuéh-hsiào** workers' spare-time schools

职工运动 **chíh-kūng-yùn-tùng** labor movement

职能 **chíh-néng** function [of a position or organization]

职别 **chíh-piéh** job-rank (position and salary classification)

职责 **chíh-tsé** office and duty (duty)

职位 **chíh-wèi** title of a position

职务 **chíh-wù** duty or responsibility of a position

职业 **chíh-yèh** occupation, profession

职业病 **chíh-yèh-pìng** occupational disease

职员 **chíh-yuán** a functionary, office worker, clerical personnel

235 植保 **chíh-pǎo** plant protection, crop protection

植保植检站 **chíh-pǎo chíh-chiěn-chàn** plant protection and examination stations

植树造林 **chíh-shù-tsào-lín** afforestation

植物间种 **chíh-wù-chièn-chùng** hybridization

植物保护 **chíh-wù-pǎo-hù** plant protection

植物生长激素 **chíh-wù shēng-chǎng chī-sù** a plant growth hormone

植物油 **chíh-wù-yú** vegetable oils

236 殖民枷锁 **chíh-mín-chiā-sǒ** the colonial yoke, colonial shackles

殖民主义 **chíh-mín-chǔ-ì** colonialism

殖民主义恶棍 **chíh-mín-chǔ-ì ò-kùn** colonialist villain

殖民主义大国 **chíh-mín-chǔ-ì tà-kuó** colonialist great power

殖民地 **chíh-mín-tì** a colony

殖民特权 **chíh-mín-t'è-ch'üán** colonial prerogatives, special rights of the colonialist power

殖民体系 **chíh-mín-t'ǐ-hsì** colonial system, colonial control

殖民统治 **chíh-mín-t'ǔng-chìh** colonial control, colonial rule

chǐh (zhǐ)

237 止步不前 **chǐh-pù-pù-ch'ién** to stop and not go forward, to make no progress

238 只争朝夕 **chǐh-chēng-chāo-hsì** seize the day, seize the hour

只见树木不见森林 **chǐh-chièn-shù-mù, pù-chièn-sēn-lín** to see only the trees and not the forest

只专不红 **chǐh-chuān-pù-húng** merely expert [but] not red (technically proficient but not ideologically correct)

只能打天下，不能坐天下 **chǐh-néng tǎ-t'iēn-hsià, pù-néng tsò-t'iēn-hsià** only able to conquer the country, but not able to govern it (Rightist criticism of the Communist Party during the Hundred Flowers Campaign)

只打雷，不下雨 **chǐh-tǎ-léi, pù-hsià-yǔ** it only thunders [but] does not rain (talk without action)

只此一家 **chǐh-tz'ǔ-ì-chiā** there is only this single shop [we have no branches] (intellectuals' sarcasm directed at the Party during the Hundred Flowers Campaign)

只 **chǐh**: see also **chīh**

239 纸黄金 **chǐh-huáng-chīn** "paper gold" (Special Drawing Rights, established by international agreement in 1968 as an official fiscal reserve unit)

纸老虎 **chǐh-lǎo-hǔ** a paper tiger (not as dangerous as it looks)

纸包不住火 **chǐh pāo-pù-chù huǒ** fire cannot be wrapped in paper (the real issue cannot be concealed)

纸上谈兵 **chǐh-shàng-t'án-pīng** paper discussion of military matters (impractical and empty talk)

240 指战员 **chǐh-chàn-yuán** commanders and fighters, officers and men (contraction of **chǐh-huī yuán** and **chàn-tòu yuán**)

指针 **chǐh-chēn** a guiding needle (a guiding principle)

指出 **chǐh-ch'ū** to point out

指挥 **chǐh-huī** to command, direct, order (usually military)

指挥小组 **chǐh-huī-hsiǎo-tsǔ** command group (set up to solve bottlenecks in transportation during the Great Leap)

指挥棒 **chǐh-huī-pàng** conductor's baton (usually a satirical reference to the pretensions of the USSR)

指挥田 **chǐh-huī-t'ién** commanding farm plot (synonym for **shìh-yèn-t'ién**)

指挥员 **chǐh-huī-yuán** commander (synonymous with officer in Communist usage)

指向 **chǐh-hsiàng** to point toward

指路明灯 **chǐh-lù-míng-tēng** a bright lantern lighting the road (Mao Tse-tung's thought)

指名 **chǐh-míng** to mention by name, to name [as in an accusation]

指名道姓 **chǐh-míng tào-hsìng** to single out by surname and given name (usually implies explicit criticism)

指明 **chǐh-míng** to indicate clearly, demonstrate, point out

指南 **chǐh-nán** a guide book

指南针 **chǐh-nán-chēn** a compass (now a simile for the Thought of Mao Tse-tung)

指标 **chǐh-piāo** index, quota, target, indicator

指标落实 **chǐh-piāo-lò-shíh** (1) to fix targets realistically; (2) to realize a target

指桑骂槐 **chǐh-sāng-mà-huái** reviling the locust tree while pointing at the mulberry (to abuse indirectly)

指使 **chǐh-shǐh** to direct, instigate, abet

指示 **chǐh-shìh** a directive, instruction (usually not in legal form and carrying weight according to its source); to instruct, advise

指手划脚 **chǐh-shǒu-huà-chiǎo** to point with fingers and draw with the feet (to gesticulate or act dramatically often with the suggestion that the person is assuming unwarranted

authority)

指数 **chǐh-shù** index number

指导思想 **chǐh-tǎo-szū-hsiǎng** guiding thought, guiding theory

指导员 **chǐh-tǎo-yuán** a guide (company political officer in the PLA)

指定 **chǐh-tìng** to assign, prescribe, appoint, authorize

指责 **chǐh-tsé** to blame, censure

指望 **chǐh-wàng** to have hope

指压疗法 **chǐh-yā-liáo-fǎ** a method of treatment somewhat similar to acupuncture, but using pressure applied to certain points on the body by the thumbs

指引 **chǐh-yǐn** to lead, guide, conduct

241 趾高气扬 **chǐh-kāo-ch'ì-yáng** high-stepping [with] lofty airs (arrogant)

chìh (zhì)

242 至高无上 **chìh-kāo-wú-shàng** supreme, highest, ultimate

至理名言 **chìh-lǐ-míng-yén** self-evident truths and famous sayings, high principles and noble words, fine axioms

至宝 **chìh-pǎo** a treasure; most precious

243 志气 **chìh-ch'ì** determination, personal ambition, morale

志同道合 **chìh-t'úng-tào-hó** common goals and principles (to share the same ideals)

志愿 **chìh-yuàn** will, choice, preference, a wish, desire

志愿军 **chìh-yuàn-chūn** a volunteer force, volunteers, volunteer army

244 质询 **chìh-hsún** to question, inquire into, cross-examine; inquiry, cross-examination

质量 **chìh-liàng** (1) quality; qualitative (2) mass [physics]

质变 **chìh-pièn** qualitative change

质的飞跃 **chìh tè fēi-yuèh** a qualitative leap, a leap in the quality [of social development, etc.]

质子 **chìh-tzǔ** proton

质子同步加速器 **chìh-tzǔ t'úng-pù chiā-sù-ch'ì** proton synchrotron

质问 **chìh-wèn** to question, interpellate, interrogate; an inquiry, interrogation

245 制止 **chìh-chǐh** to forbid, prohibit, restrain, check; restraint, interdiction, an order to stop

制成 **chìh-ch'éng** to make into, manufacture, produce, enact [into law]

制服 **chìh-fú** uniform (attire)

制空权 **chìh-k'ūng-ch'üan** air supremacy, control of the air

制炼厂 **chìh-lièn-ch'ǎng** a refinery

制片厂 **chìh-p'ièn-ch'ǎng** a motion picture studio

制订 **chìh-tìng** to draw up, map out, formulate

制定 **chìh-tìng** to enact [into law], formulate, define

制度 **chìh-tù** institutional system, institutionalized methods; regime, rule, polity

制造事故 **chìh-tsào shìh-kù** to manufacture an accident, fabricate an incident

制裁 **chìh-ts'ái** punishment, sanction

制约 **chìh-yuēh** to restrict, set conditions, limit; restriction, limitation

246 治安 **chìh-ān** public order, security

治安保卫委员会 **chìh-ān-pǎo-wèi wěi-yuán-huì** security and protection committees

治洪 **chìh-húng** flood control

治理河流 **chìh-lǐ hó-líu** to bring a river under control, harness a river, tame a river

治疗 **chìh-liáo** treatment of disease

治本 **chìh-pěn** to treat the root (a long-term solution)

治本工程 **chìh-pěn-kūng-ch'éng** basic engineering projects

治标 **chìh-piāo** to treat the superficial (a temporary solution)

治病救人 **chìh-pìng-chìu-jén** cure the sickness to save the patient (an instruction by Mao Tse-tung in the first Cheng-feng Movement, 1942)

治丧委员会 **chìh-sāng wěi-yuán-huì** a funeral committee

治沙 **chìh-shā** desert regulation (measures to stop the advance of the sand, restrict the growth of deserts, and reclaim deserts)

治山治水 **chìh-shān-chìh-shuǐ** improve mountains and regulate water (measures, such as afforestation, to make the mountains productive and reduce flooding)

治山、治水、治碱 **chìh-shān, chìh-shuǐ, chìh-chiěn** regulate the mountains, water, and alkaline land

治田 **chìh-t'ién** field improvement (includes many types of measures such as soil improvement, desalinization, drainage, etc.)

治罪 **chìh-tsuì** to punish by law, to control crime

治外法权 **chìh-wài-fǎ-ch'üan** extra-territoriality

247 桎梏 **chìh-kù** fetters, bondage

248 致敬 **chìh-chìng** to pay respects, salute,

greet

致意 **chìh-ì** to send regards to, extend greetings, give one's best wishes

致力 **chìh-lì** to devote energy, exert one's strength, concentrate on

致命打击 **chìh-mìng-tǎ-chì** a fatal blow

致词 **chìh-tz'ú** to make a speech, deliver an address

249 秩序 **chìh-hsù** order, orderly procedure, arrangements

250 窒息 **chìh-hsī** to stifle, smother, suffocate, asphyxiate

251 滞而不进 **chìh-érh-pù-chìn** stagnant, without progress

滞留 **chìh-líu** (1) to detain, hold up, hinder; (2) to loiter, not move forward

滞纳金 **chìh-nà-chīn** a fine for being late in paying [taxes]

252 智取威虎山 **chìh-ch'ǔ-wēi-hǔ-shān** (1) "Taking Tiger Mountain by Strategy" (one of the **yáng-pǎn-hsì**). Adapted from Ch'ü Po's novel, *Lin-hai hsueh-yuan*); (2) a symphony version of the same play

智慧 **chìh-huì** wisdom, intelligence

智力 **chìh-lì** intelligence, mental power

智利 **chìh-lì** [Republic of] Chile

智谋 **chìh-móu** clever strategy, sagacity

智育 **chìh-yù** intellectual education, intellectual training (parallel with moral and physical)

253 置之不理 **chìh-chīh-pù-lǐ** to pay no regard to

置之死地 **chìh-chīh-szǔ-tì** to place [a person] in mortal danger

置之度外 **chìh-chīh-tù-wài** to put it out of mind (philosophical calm)

chìn (jīn)

254 斤斤计较 **chīn-chīn-chì-chiào** to weigh and calculate minutely (to be calculating and unwilling to make the smallest sacrifice, especially monetary)

斤两 **chīn-liǎng** catties and ounces (weight, significance)

255 今非昔比 **chīn-fēi-hsī-pǐ** the present cannot be compared with the past (the current usage is to suggest that the present is better than the past)

今不如昔 **chīn-pù-jú-hsī** things of the present are not equal to those of the past (worse off than before)

今是昨非 **chīn-shìh-tsó-fēi** the present is right and the past was wrong

今天说来 **chīn-t'iēn-shuō-lái** in terms of today

256 金鸡纳 **chīn-chī-nà** quinine

金钱挂帅 **chīn-ch'ién-kuà-shuà** money takes command (a criticism of economism)

金风送爽 **chīn-fēng-sùng-shuǎng** the "goldwind" [autumn breezes] brings salubrity (the sense of invigoration associated with brisk autumn weather)

金日成 **chīn jìh-ch'éng** Kim Il-sung [North Korean leader]

金融紧缩政策 **chīn-júng-chǐn-sō chèng-ts'è** tight money policy, deflationary policy

金融寡头 **chīn-júng-kuǎ-t'óu** financial oligarchs

金融共同体法郎 **chīn-júng kùng-t'úng-t'ǐ fǎ-láng** [African] Financial Community Franc

金融投机 **chīn-júng t'óu-chī** monetary speculation, financial speculation

金光大道 **chīn-kuāng-tà-tào** *The Golden Road* (title of a novel by Hao Jan)

金科玉律 **chīn-k'ō-yù-lǜ** an infallible rule (usually critical)

金陵 **chīn-líng** a literary name for Nanking

金缕玉衣 **chīn-lǚ-yù-ī** jade burial clothes (recently excavated from a Han dynasty tomb)

金碧辉煌 **chīn-pì-huī-huáng** glittering in gold and blue, elegant and beautiful [of a building]

金边 **chīn-piēn** Phnom Penh [Cambodia]

金属 **chīn-shǔ** metals, metallic

金属加工业 **chīn-shǔ chiā-kūng-yèh** metal-working industry

金属切削机床 **chīn-shǔ-ch'ièh-hsiāo chǐ-ch'uáng** metal-cutting machine tools

金属型铸范 **chīn-shǔ-hsíng chù-fàn** a metallic mold

金字标签 **chīn-tzù-piāo-ch'iēn** a label in golden characters (the label is good but the implication is that the contents may not be)

金字塔 **chīn-tzù-t'ǎ** pyramid, pyramidical

金银财宝 **chīn-yín-ts'ái-pǎo** bullion and valuables

金元主义 **chīn-yuán-chǔ-ì** dollar imperialism

257 津津乐道 **chīn-chīn-lè-tào** to speak of something happily with mouth watering

津津有味 **chīn-chīn-yǔ-wèi** mouth-watering (savory, very interesting)

津浦铁路 **chīn-p'ǔ t'ièh-lù** the Tientsin-Pukow railway

津贴 **chīn-t'ièh** a subsidy, subvention,

special allowance or assistance; subsidization

258 筋疲力尽 chǐn-p'í-lì-chìn the muscles are weary and the strength is used up (utterly exhausted)

筋斗 chǐn-tǒu a somersault

259 襟怀坦白 chǐn-huái-t'ǎn-pái a white bosom beneath the coat (open and magnanimous, frank, sincere)

chǐn (jǐn)

260 仅见 chǐn-chièn barely seen, rare

仅次于 chǐn-tz'ù-yú second best, second to, next only to

261 尽管 chǐn-kuǎn in spite of, notwithstanding, even though, nevertheless

尽量 chǐn-liàng to the best of one's ability

尽 chǐn: see also chìn

262 紧张 chǐn-chāng (1) tense, urgent, critical; (2) earnestness (part of the sān-pā tsò-fēng)

紧张局势 chǐn-chāng-chú-shìh a tense, critical or strained situation

紧急 chǐn-chí dangerously critical, pressing, imperative

紧急状态 chǐn-chí-chuàng-t'ài a state of emergency

紧急倡议 chǐn-chí-ch'àng-ì an urgent proposal or proposition

紧急呼吁 chǐn-chí-hū-yù an urgent appeal

紧急会议 chǐn-chí-huì-ì an emergency conference or meeting

紧急关头 chǐn-chí-kūan-t'óu critical moment, critical situation, crucial juncture

紧急时期 chǐn-chí-shíh-ch'ī urgent period, crucial stage

紧急通告 chǐn-chí-t'ūng-kào an urgent circular, urgent notification

紧紧跟上 chǐn-chǐn-kēn-shàng to follow up closely

紧抓 chǐn-chuā to grasp tightly, seize firmly (usually figurative)

紧相毗连 chǐn-hsiāng-p'í-lién with common borders

紧跟 chǐn-kēn to follow closely

紧固 chǐn-kù tight and strong

紧锣密鼓 chǐn-ló-mì-kǔ a rapid tattoo of drums and gongs (a fanfare; ostentatious preparations)

紧密 chǐn-mì tightly and closely, close

紧密联系 chǐn-mì-lién-hsì closely related, close integration

紧密的友谊关系 chǐn-mì-te yǔ-ì-kuān-hsi close ties of friendship

紧密团结 chǐn-mì-t'uán-chiéh to rally together closely; strong unity

紧迫 chǐn-p'ò pressing, urgent, imperative

紧缩编制 chǐn-sō-piēn-chìh to reduce staff, tighten up administration

紧握 chǐn-wò to grip firmly, hold tightly; a strong grasp

263 谨防 chǐh-fáng to beware of, guard against

谨小慎微 chǐn-hsiǎo-shèn-wēi timorous, overcautious, punctilious

谨慎的乐观 chǐn-shèn-te lè-kuān cautious optimism, restrained optimism

264 锦绣河山 chǐn-hsiù-hó-shān embroidered rivers and mountains (a splendid, beautiful country—China)

锦标主义 chǐn-piāo-chǔ-ì "trophy-ism" [winning of championships] (an attitude now discouraged: e.g., in international sport meetings friendship is more important than winning)

锦上添花 chǐn-shàng-t'iēn-huā to add flowers to embroidery (to gild the lily)

chìn (jìn)

265 尽其本分 chìn-ch'í-pěn-fèn to do one's full share

尽全力 chìn-ch'üán-lì to do one's best, exert one's utmost, spare no effort

尽心竭力 chìn-hsīn-chiéh-lì to exhaust one's mental and physical energy (to do one's utmost)

尽一切办法 chìn ī-ch'ièh pàn-fǎ by every means, to seek in every way to

尽人皆知 chìn-jén-chiēh-chīh everybody knows it, known to all

尽力 chǐn-lì to do one's best, exhaust one's strength; wholeheartedly

尽善尽美 chìn-shàn-chìn-měi perfectly good, perfectly beautiful (perfect)

尽做坏事 chìn-tsò huài-shìh to do all sorts of evil things; actively malevolent

尽 chìn: see also chǐn

266 劲头 chìn-t'óu vigor, zip, energy

劲头足足 chìn-t'óu-tsú-tsú extremely vigorous, energetic

劲足 chìn-tsú vigorously; energetic

劲 chìn: see also chìng

267 近郊 chìn-chiāo close suburbs, near environs [of a city]

近距离 chìn-chù-lí close quarters, at close range

近距离战斗 chìn-chù-lí chàn-tòu close quarters fighting, close combat

近现代史 chìn-hsièn-tài-shǐh modern and contemporary history (modern, from 1640 AD; contemporary, since

1917)

近路不走走远路 **chìn-lù pù-tsŏu tsŏu-yuǎn-lù** to take the long road instead of the short one

近视 **chìn-shìh** short-sighted, near-sighted

近视症 **chìn-shìh-chèng** myopia (often figurative)

近代社会诸矛盾 **chìn-tài-shè-huì chū-máo-tùn** the contradictions of modern society

近代史 **chìn-tài-shǐh** modern history

268 进展 **chìn-chǎn** development, progress; to advance, improve

进程 **chìn-ch'éng** progress [in a course of action]

进出口平衡 **chìn-ch'ū-k'ŏu p'íng-héng** balance between imports and exports

进军 **chìn-chūn** to stage a march, to advance troops (to advance toward a specific goal)

进军号 **chìn-chūn-hào** the signal [bugle call] for "advance"

进取 **chìn-ch'ǔ** to forge ahead aggressively, endeavor to improve one's lot; energetic, enterprising

进化论 **chìn-huà lùn** the theory of evolution

进洪闸 **chìn-húng-chá** flood-inlet gate, sluice gate

进校革委会 **chìn-hsiào kó-wěi-huì** revolutionary committees [formed by workers and PLA] after entering the schools [during the Cultural Revolution]

进行 **chìn-hsíng** to advance, carry out, engage in, initiate; progress, advancement

进行曲 **chìn-hsíng-ch'ǔ** a musical march, marching song

进行到底 **chìn-hsíng-tào-tǐ** to carry through to the end, carry out to a conclusion, press resolutely

进修 **chìn-hsīu** to study for one's improvement; carrying out further study

进修班 **chìn-hsīu-pān** a refresher class

进一步 **chìn-ī-pù** to go a step further

进入 **chìn-jù** to enter into, penetrate, make way into

进攻 **chìn-kūng** an attack; to attack, launch an attack (used broadly)

进攻战 **chìn-kūng-chàn** the offense [military]; an offensive

进攻的信号 **chìn-kūng-te hsìn-hào** the signal to attack

进攻的矛头 **chìn-kūng-te máo-t'óu** the spearhead of an attack

进口 **chìn-k'ŏu** importation; to import

进步人士 **chìn-pù-jén-shìh** progressive personage, progressives

进度 **chìn-tù** rate of progress, degree of progress [of work]

进退维谷 **chìn-t'uì-wéi-kǔ** advance or retreat [leaves one] still in a ravine (to be in a dilemma)

269 浸种 **chìn-chǔng** to soak seeds [to hasten germination]

浸染 **chìn-jǎn** to influence gradually; to contaminate

浸透 **chìn-t'òu** to soak through

270 晋 **chìn** Shansi province

晋冀鲁豫[边区] **chìn-chì-lǔ-yù [piēn-ch'ū]** Shansi-Hopei-Shantung-Honan [Border Region] (a CCP base area in the Resistance War)

晋冀豫[区] **chìn-chì-yù [ch'ū]** Shansi-Hopei-Honan [Region] (a CCP base area during the Resistance War)

晋察冀[边区] **chìn-ch'á-chì [piēn-ch'ū]** Shansi-Hopei-Chahar [Border Region] (a CCP base area during the Resistance War)

晋绥[边区] **chìn-suí [piēn-ch'ū]** Shansi-Suiyuan [Border Region] (a CCP base area in the Resistance War)

271 禁止 **chìn-chǐh** prohibition; to prohibit, forbid, suppress, outlaw

禁止流通 **chìn-chǐh-líu-t'ūng** to demonetize, ban circulation

禁止试验和使用原子武器 **chìn-chǐh shìh-yèn hó shǐh-yùng yuán-tzǔ-wǔ-ch'ì** the prohibition of testing and use of nuclear weapons

禁止原子弹氢弹世界大会 **chìn-chǐh yuán-tzǔ-tàn ch'īng-tàn shìh-chièh-tà-huì** World Conference Against Atomic and Hydrogen Bombs

禁区 **chìn-ch'ū** a forbidden area, closed area

禁锢 **chìn-kù** to confine, imprison (also in the abstract sense)

禁令 **chìn-lìng** a legal restriction or ban, injunction; to enjoin, interdict, proscribe

禁运 **chìn-yùn** to prohibit transport, embargo

禁 **chìn**: see also **chín**

chìng (jīng)

272 京剧 **chīng-chù** Peking opera

京剧革命 **chīng-chù-kó-mìng** the revolution in Peking opera

京剧团 **chīng-chù-t'uán** a Peking opera troupe

京剧院 **chīng-chù-yuàn** the Academy of Peking Opera

京戏 **chīng-hsì** Peking opera

京广线铁路 **chīng-kuǎng-hsièn t'iěh-lù**

the Peking-Canton railway

京包铁路 **chīng-pāo-t'iěh-lù** the Peking-Paotow railway

京沈铁路 **chīng-shěn-t'iěh-lù** the Peking-Shenyang [Mukden] railway

京族 **chīng-tsú** the Ching people (a minority in Kwangsi Chuang Autonomous Region: population 4,000 as of 1957)

[273] 泾渭分明 **chīng-wèi-fēn-míng** to clearly distinguish the Ching and the Wei (to make a clear differentiation between the clear and the muddy; to distinguish good and bad)

泾渭不分 **chīng-wèi-pù-fēn** unable to distinguish the Ching and Wei [rivers](unable to distinguish true from false)

[274] 经济 **chīng-chì** economy; economic, economical; economics

经济战线 **chīng-chì-chàn-hsièn** the economic front

经济基础 **chīng-chì-chī-ch'ǔ** the economic basis, economic foundation

经济建设 **chīng-chì-chièn-shè** economic construction, economic development

经济指数 **chīng-chì-chǐh-shù** economic index

经济主义 **chīng-chì-chǔ-ì** economism (the use of material incentives instead of political consciousness to induce workers and peasants to produce more)

经济主义黑风 **chīng-chì-chǔ-ì hēi-fēng** the black wind of economism

经济发展不平衡状态 **chīng-chì-fā-chǎn pù-p'íng-héng chuàng-t'ài** the condition of uneven economic development

经济发展速度 **chīng-chì-fā-chǎn sù-tù** the rate of economic development

经济封锁 **chīng-chì-fēng-sǒ** economic blockade

经济核算制度 **chīng-chì-hó-suàn chìh-tù** business accountability system, economic accounting system (broader than cost accounting as it covers almost the whole field of management)

经济恢复时期 **chīng-chì-huī-fù shíh-ch'ī** period of economic recovery (the period between Liberation and the beginning of the First Five-Year Plan)

经济形态 **chīng-chì-hsíng-t'ài** the economic form, economic structure

经济宣言 **chīng-chì-hsūan-yén** the economic manifesto (by the Algiers Conference in 1973 of leaders of the non-aligned countries)

经济改革 **chīng-chì-kǎi-kó** economic reform

经济林 **chīng-chì-lín** an economic forest (such as fruit orchards, wood-oil, lacquer trees, etc.)

经济掠夺 **chīng-chì-luèh-tó** economic plundering

经济命脉 **chīng-chì-mìng-mài** the economic pulse (economic arteries, economic lifeline, key points of the economy)

经济破产 **chīng-chì-p'ò-ch'ǎn** economic bankruptcy

经济渗透 **chīng-chì-shèn-t'òu** economic infiltration, economic penetration

经济水域 **chīng-chì shuǐ-yù** economic waters (coastal waters reserved for economic utilization by the bordering country)

经济作物 **chīng-chì-tsò-wù** economic crop, industrial crop, cash crop

经济危机 **chīng-chì-wéi-chī** economic crisis

经济研究 **chīng-chì-yén-chīu** (1) economic research; (2) *Economic Studies* (Peking monthly, 1955—)

经济援助 **chīng-chì-yuán-chù** economic aid

经久不息 **chīng-chiǔ-pù-hsī** prolonged, lasting, enduring, continuous

经常 **chīng-ch'áng** regular, current, frequent, continuous; currently

经常讲，反复讲 **chīng-ch'áng-chiǎng, fǎn-fù-chiǎng** to expound constantly [and] explain repeatedly (often refers to political study)

经常反复的实践 **chīng-ch'áng fǎn-fù-te shíh-chièn** recurrent practice, frequently repeated practice

经常费 **chīng-ch'áng-fèi** current expenditures, normal costs, operating expenses

经常化 **chīng-ch'áng-huà** routinization; to make regular

经常开支 **chīng-ch'áng-k'āi-chīh** ordinary expenditure, current expenditure

经常稳定 **chīng-ch'áng-wěn-tìng** long-term stabilization

经费 **chīng-fèi** expenditure, outlay, cost, funds

经风雨、见世面 **chīng-fēng-yǔ chièn-shìh-mièn** to pass the storm and know the world (to temper and broaden oneself)

经销 **chīng-hsiāo** to handle distribution; sale on commission [for the state]

经线 **chīng-hsièn** lines of longitude

经过改造的游民 **chīng-kuò-kǎi-tsào-te**

yú-mín remoulded loafers

经理 chīng-lǐ manager, director, administrator; to administer, manage

经历 chīng-lì to go through, experience, traverse

经不起考验 chīng-pu-ch'ǐ k'ǎo-yèn to fail to pass the test, unable to withstand the test of experience

经受 chīng-shòu to experience, undergo

经得住考验 chīng-te-chù k'ǎo-yèn able to pass [severe] testing, to withstand great stress (to prove one's strength and determination under severe requirements)

经得起风险 chīng-te-ch'ǐ fēng-hsiěn capable of weathering storms (staunch, steadfast)

经典著作 chīng-tiěn-chù-tsò classical works, great books (usually the Marxist classics)

经典文献 chīng-tiěn-wén-hsièn classical works

经度 chīng-tù longitude

经纬度测定 chīng-wěi-tù ts'è-tìng determination of latitude and longitude

经验 chīng-yèn to have experience of; practical experience; empirical, experimental

经验积累 chīng-yèn-chī-lěi the accumulation of experience, weight of experience

经验教训 chīng-yèn-chiào-hsùn lessons derived from experience; experience and lessons

经验主义 chīng-yèn-chǔ-ì empiricism

经验论 chīng-yèn lùn empiricism

经验批判论 chīng-yèn-p'ī-p'àn lùn empirical criticism

经营 chīng-yíng to operate, manage, administer, carry on, engage in [business]; business, enterprise, management

经营范围 chīng-yíng-fàn-wéi scope of operations

经营管理 chīng-yíng-kuǎn-lǐ management; to manage

经由 chīng-yú by way of, through, via

经院哲学 chīng-yuàn-ché-hsuéh scholasticism

275 荆棘丛中 chīng-chí-ts'úng-chūng surrounded by thorns (beset by difficulties)

276 惊奇 chīng-ch'í to be surprised, show astonishment; startling, shocking

惊慌 chīng-huāng panic; startled and confused

惊惶失措 chīng-huáng-shīh-ts'ò to be thrown into panic and dismay, paralyzed by fear

惊悉 chīng-hsī shocked to learn

惊险小说 chīng-hsiěn-hsiǎo-shuō novels of suspense and adventure

惊心动魄 chīng-hsīn-tùng-p'ò to startle the heart and shake the soul (hair-raising, deeply shocked)

惊异 chīng-ì to be amazed, be startled

惊人事件 chīng-jén-shìh-chièn a devastating surprise, a bombshell

惊弓之鸟 chīng-kūng-chīh-niǎo birds startled by the bow (to be alert, fearful, frightened)

惊动 chīng-tùng to alarm, rouse to vigilance

惊涛骇浪 chīng-t'āo-hài-làng frightful billows and fearful waves (a dangerous situation, a heavy blow)

惊天动地 chīng-t'iēn-tùng-tì to startle heaven and shake the earth (a great deed; earth-shaking)

惊讶 chīng-yà to be surprised or alarmed; astonishment, surprise

277 兢兢业业 chīng-chīng-yèh-yèh with fear and caution, wary, constantly on guard

278 精简 chīng-chiěn to simplify; simplified

精简机构 chīng-chiěn-chī-kòu to simplify the organizational structure; organizational streamlining

精简机关 chīng-chiěn-chī-kuān to simplify and reduce government organizations (equivalent to "reduction in force")

精简会议 chīng-chiěn huì-ì to simplify and reduce meetings

精简领导小组 chīng-chiěn lǐng-tǎo-hsiǎo-tsǔ a team for simplying leadership (usually involves reduction in personnel of an organization)

精巧技术 chīng-ch'iǎo chì-shù delicate workmanship, exquisite technique

精确 chīng-ch'üèh exact, accurate, precise

精华 chīng-huá essence, the best part

精细 chīng-hsì fine, delicate, meticulous, precise; thorough, careful

精细严密 chīng-hsì-yén-mì painstaking and thorough

精心 chīng-hsīn painstaking, done with meticulous care

精心设计 chīng-hsīn shè-chì painstakingly designed, thoroughly planned

精益求精 chīng-ì-ch'íu-chīng excellent but seek still greater excellence (never be content with what has been achieved)

精锐部队 chīng-juì-pù-tuì crack troops, an elite force

精干 chīng-kàn shrewd and capable,

rational and efficient

精耕细作 **chīng-kēng-hsì-tsò** careful and intensive cultivation [of crops]

精力充沛 **chīng-lì-ch'ūng-pèi** brimming with vigor and energy

精良 **chīng-liáng** excellent, of the highest quality, finest, first-class

精炼厂 **chīng-lièn-ch'ǎng** a refinery

精密机床 **chīng-mì chī-ch'uáng** a precision machine tool

精密仪器 **chīng-mì-í-ch'ì** precision tools, precision instruments

精明强干 **chīng-míng-ch'iáng-kàn** shrewd and capable

精明干练 **chīng-míng-kàn-lièn** sagacious, astute, wise; sagacity

精兵简政 **chīng-pīng-chiěn-chèng** fewer and better troops and simpler administration, picked troops and efficient government

精兵简政运动 **chīng-pīng-chiěn-chèng-yùn-tùng** the campaign for crack troops and simpler administration (Yenan, December 1941; in Peking, March 1968)

精疲力尽 **chīng-p'í-lì-chìn** completely tired out, exhausted

精辟分析 **chīng-p'ì-fēn-hsī** incisive analysis

精神 **chīng-shén** the spiritual part of a human [as opposed to the material being]; spirit, morale, elan; vigor, energy; mental and nervous [illness, etc.]

精神枷锁 **chīng-shén-chiā-sǒ** spiritual shackles

精神奖励 **chīng-shén-chiǎng-lì** spiritual incentive, moral incentive

精神支柱 **chīng-shén-chīh-chù** a spiritual pillar (chief moral support)

精神桎梏 **chīng-shén-chìh-kù** spiritual shackles

精神状态 **chīng-shén-chuàng-t'ài** the state of mind

精神准备 **chīng-shén-chǔn-pèi** psychological preparation; mentally prepared

精神反常 **chīng-shén-fǎn-ch'áng** mentally abnormal, to lose one's mental balance

精神和实质 **chīng-shén hó shíh-chìh** spirit and substance

精神焕发 **chīng-shén-huàn-fā** radiant spirit

精神贵族 **chīng-shén-kuèi-tsú** intellectual aristocrats (usually those trained in bourgeois schools)

精神面貌 **chīng-shén-mièn-mào** the outward manifestations of spirit, psychological and mental features

精神堡垒 **chīng-shén-pǎo-lěi** spiritual stronghold (in a good sense)

精神变物质 **chīng-shén pièn wù-chìh** spirit transforms matter (moral power changes material conditions)

精神实质 **chīng-shén-shíh-chìh** spiritual essence

精神堕落 **chīng-shén-tò-lò** spiritual decadence

精神抖擞 **chīng-shén-tǒu-sǒu** energies mustered [as for an important task], animated

精神财富 **chīng-shén-ts'ái-fù** spiritual wealth

精神武器 **chīng-shén-wǔ-ch'ì** a spiritual weapon (such as the Thought of Mao Tse-tung)

精神武库 **chīng-shén-wǔ-kù** spiritual armory

精神鸦片 **chīng-shén-yā-p'ièn** a spiritual opiate (usually religion)

精髓 **chīng-suǐ** marrow (essence)

精打细算 **chīng-tǎ hsì-suàn** to make a careful and detailed calculation

精度 **chīng-tù** degree of precision

精通 **chīng-t'ūng** well versed in, expert at

279 鲸吞 **chīng-t'ūn** to annex, swallow up

chǐng (jǐng)

280 井冈山 **chǐng-kāng-shān** Chingkang-shan (the mountain in Kiangsi where Mao took refuge in 1927)

井喷 **chǐng-p'ēn** an [oil] gusher

281 景气 **chǐng-ch'ì** economic prosperity, a boom

景象 **chǐng-hsiàng** prospects, condition, outlook, indication

景颇族 **chǐng-p'ǒ-tsú** the Ching-p'o people (a minority in Yunnan province: population 101,000 as of 1957)

景泰蓝 **chǐng-t'ài-lán** cloisonne, enamel

282 警戒 **chǐng-chièh** to keep watch, stand guard, hold oneself ready; to warn, caution; an alert, vigilance

警戒状态 **chǐng-chièh-chuàng-t'ài** a state of alert

警戒线 **chǐng-chièh-hsièn** a cordon, warning line

警钟 **chǐng-ch'ūng** an alarm bell, warning

警察 **chǐng-ch'á** the police, a policeman

警察暴力 **chǐng-ch'á-pào-lì** police brutality

警觉 **chǐng-chüéh** vigilance, alertness

警告 **chǐng-kào** a warning; to warn, caution

警备区 **chǐng-pèi-ch'ū** a garrison area,

a garrison command
警惕 **chǐng-t'ì** vigilant, alert, especially cautious; alertness
警卫 **chǐng-wèi** to stand guard, escort, protect
警卫员 **chǐng-wèi-yuán** a bodyguard

chìng (jìng)

283 劲敌 **chìng-tí** a strong enemy, worthy rival
劲 **chìng**: see also **chìn**
284 净重 **chìng-chùng** net weight
净收净打 **chìng-shōu-chìng-tǎ** all reaped [and] all thrashed
净载重 **chìng-tsài-chùng** the net weight of the load
285 竞争 **chìng-chēng** competition, contest; to compete with, vie with
竞放毒草 **chìng-fàng-tú-ts'ǎo** to compete in putting forth poisonous weeds
竞选 **chìng-hsǔan** to run for office, be a candidate for election; an election campaign
竞赛 **chìng-sài** to compete with; competition, contest, emulation
286 敬爱 **chìng-ài** to respect and love; respected
敬而远之 **chìng-érh-yuǎn-chíh** to respect but keep a distance
敬意 **chìng-ì** veneration, esteem, respect
敬老院 **chìng-lǎo-yuàn** homes for the aged
敬礼 **chìng-lǐ** to salute; a salute
敬仰 **chìng-yǎng** respectful; to look up to
287 境界 **chìng-chièh** (1) boundaries; position, location; (2) situation, condition; (3) state of mind
境况 **chìng-k'uàng** circumstances, situation (usually of a person)
境地 **chìng-tì** state, situation, position; territory under jurisdiction
境域 **chìng-yù** realm, territory
288 静止 **chìng-chǐh** static, stationary, without movement
静观态度 **chìng-kuān-t'ài-tù** a wait-and-see attitude; passive
289 镜子 **chìng-tzu** a mirror (a lesson)

chiū (jiū)

290 纠正 **chiū-chèng** to correct [an error or misconduct]
纠察队 **chiū-ch'á-tuì** discipline teams (to provide factory watchmen or to monitor crowds)
纠缠不清 **chiū-ch'án-pù-ch'īng** to be hopelessly entangled (deeply involved)
纠纷 **chiū-fēn** a dispute, conflict, differences
291 揪住不放 **chiū-chù pù-fàng** to hold in a tight grip (unrelenting pressure—on rightists or counterrevolutionaries)
揪出来 **chiū-ch'ū-lái** plucked out [of a person], to pluck out [a person]
揪出来示众 **chiū-ch'ū-lái shìh-chùng** to pluck out and show to the masses

chiǔ (jiǔ)

292 九·一八事变 **chiǔ-i-pā shìh-pièn** the September 18 Incident (the Japanese takeover of Manchuria in 1931)
九评 **chiǔ-p'íng** nine criticisms (the nine letters of the CCP Central Committee to the Central Committee of the USSR in 1963–64)
九三学社 **chiǔ-sān-hsuéh-shè** the September 3 Association (one of the democratic parties joining in the People's Political Consultative Conference)
九大 **chiǔ-tà** the Ninth Great (9th Party Congress, April, 1969)
九大路线 **chiǔ-tà-lù-hsièn** the line of the Ninth Party Congress (1969)
九月暗流 **chiǔ-yuèh-àn-líu** the September undercurrent (a trend in September 1967 to ultra-radical excesses in the Cultural Revolution)
293 久经锻炼 **chiǔ-chīng-tuàn-lièn** well-steeled, long-tested
久已向往 **chiǔ-ì-hsiàng-wǎng** long looked forward to
294 酒类 **chiǔ-lèi** alcoholic drinks, liquor

chiù (jiù)

295 旧知识分子 **chiù-chīh-shíh-fèn-tzǔ** old-type intellectuals (educated before 1949)
旧制度 **chiù-chìh-tù** the old [institutional] system, ancien régime
「旧翻新」服装加工商店 **"chiù-fān-hsīn" fú-chuāng chiā-kūng shāng-tièn** "old-into-new" clothing renovation shops
旧风俗 **chiù-fēng-sú** old customs (one of the **szù-chiù**)
旧习惯 **chiù-hsí-kuàn** old practices, old habits (one of the **szù-chiù**)
旧性 **chiù-hsìng** original [class] nature
旧学 **chiù-hsuéh** old learning (traditional Chinese learning)
旧框框 **chiù-k'uāng-k'uāng** old frames (traditional patterns or restrictions)
旧俄帝国 **chiù-ó tì-kuó** the tsarist

Russian empire

旧社会 **chiù-shè-huì** the old society (pre-communist society)

旧式 **chiù-shìh** old styled, old fashioned; the old pattern

旧事重提 **chiù-shìh-ch'úng-t'í** to repeat the old tale, to reopen an old case, to go over ground previously covered

旧思想 **chiù-szū-hsiǎng** old thought, old ideology (one of the **szù-chiù**)

旧调重弹 **chiù-tiào-ch'úng-t'án** to replay old tunes (usually derogatory)

旧文化 **chiù-wén-huà** old culture (one of the **szù-chiù**)

296　救急 **chiù-chí** to relieve an urgent need; first aid, fast relief

救济 **chiù-chì** to relieve, help, rescue, save; relief

救济粮 **chiù-chì-liáng** relief grain

救护飞机 **chiù-hù-fēi-chī** a mercy plane, air ambulance

救荒 **chiù-huāng** to [give] for natural disasters (such as famine relief)

救星 **chiù-hsīng** a savior (often applied to Mao Tse-tung)

救国 **chiù-kuó** to save the country

救苦救难 **chiù-k'ǔ-chiù-nàn** to relieve distress and difficulty

救命 **chiù-mìng** to save life; "Help!"

救生圈 **chiù-shēng-ch'üān** life preserver, life belt

救世主 **chiù-shìh-chǔ** the savior

救死扶伤 **chiù-szǔ-fú-shāng** to rescue the dying and heal the wounded

救灾 **chiù-tsāi** to provide relief in natural calamities

救亡文学 **chiù-wáng-wén-hsuéh** national salvation literature (important during the 1930s and early 1940s)

救药 **chiù-yào** [a disease] susceptible to medication, curable

297　就诊 **chiù-chěn** to go to receive treatment [at a doctor's office, hospital, clinic, etc.]

就职 **chiù-chíh** to take office, assume a post, commence duty

就事论事 **chiù-shìh-lùn-shìh** to confine the discussion to the matter at issue

就地取材 **chiù-tì-ch'ǔ-ts'ái** to obtain raw materials locally, use local materials

就地全歼 **chiù-tì-ch'üán-chiēn** to annihilate the enemy on the spot (to solve a problem on the spot)

就地改造 **chiù-tì-kǎi-tsào** on-the-spot reform

就地闹革命 **chiù-tì nào-kó-mìng** to make revolution on the spot

就地停火 **chiù-tì-t'íng-huǒ** a cease-fire

in place

就座 **chiù-tsò** to take [assigned] seats [at an assembly or formal gathering]

就业 **chiù-yèh** to get employment; employment

就业面 **chiù-yèh-miàn** total employment, range or scope of employment

就业委员会 **chiù-yèh wěi-yuán-huì** employment committee

chiǔng (jiǒng)

298　窘境 **chiǔng-chìng** an embarrassing situation, predicament, dilemma, quandary

chō (zhuō)

299　卓越成就 **chō-yuèh-ch'éng-chiù** outstanding achievement, superior accomplishment

300　拙劣 **chō-lièh** clumsy, awkward, stupid, inferior

301　捉襟见肘 **chō-chīn-chièn-chǒu** when tightening the lapel the elbow is exposed (in dire straits)

捉拿 **chō-ná** to arrest, to seize [a person]

chó (zhúo)

302　茁壮成长 **chó-chuàng-ch'éng-chǎng** to grow vigorously; vigorous growth, flourishing

303　酌情办理 **chó-ch'íng-pàn-lǐ** to handle according to the circumstances

酌处 **chó-ch'ǔ** to administer [a sanction] at the discretion of the authority

酌判 **chó-p'àn** to sentence at the discretion of the authority

酌退 **chó-t'uì** to make restitution at the discretion of the authority

304　着重 **chó-chùng** emphatically; emphatic; emphasis, stress

着手 **chó-shǒu** to put one's hand to, start, begin

着眼 **chó-yěn** to fix attention on, with a view to

chōu (zhōu)

305　周转 **chōu-chuǎn** turnover, circulation, turnaround

周转不开 **chōu-chuǎn-pù-k'āi** circulation constricted (clogged, financial tightness)

周转资金 **chōu-chuǎn-tzū-chīn** a revolving fund, circulating funds, fluid capital

周期 **chōu-ch'ī** a time period

周刊 **chōu-k'ān** a weekly publication

周率 **chōu-lǜ** [radio] frequency

周密 **chōu-mì** close-knit, thorough, comprehensive

周年 **chōu-nién** annual anniversary

週年纪念日 **chōu-nién chì-nièn-jìh** an anniversary

周报 **chōu-pào** a weekly journal

周围 **chōu-wéi** surroundings, periphery; around, circumference

周扬文艺路线 **chōu-yáng wén-ì-lù-hsièn** Chou Yang's literary line (attacked in the Cultural Revolution)

306　洲际导弹 **chōu-chì-tǎo-tàn** intercontinental ballistic missile

chóu (zhóu)

307　轴承厂 **chóu-ch'éng-ch'ǎng** a shaft bearing factory

轴心国 **chóu-hsīn-kuó** the Axis powers

chòu (zhòu)

308　咒骂 **chòu-mà** to curse, revile

309　昼夜 **chòu-yèh** day and night

chū (zhū)

310　朱毛 **chū-máo** Chu Teh and Mao Tse-tung (a common reference in the Kiangsi and Yenan periods)

311　诛杀 **chū-shā** to kill as punishment for crime

312　诸侯 **chū-hóu** a duke, feudal lord

诸葛亮会 **chū-kó-liàng-huì** a meeting of clever strategists (a "brain-storming" conference; a cadre seeks the opinion of experienced workers and peasants)

313　珠穆朗玛峯 **chū-mù-lǎng-mǎ-fēng** Mount Jolmo Lungma (Mt. Everest)

314　猪圈 **chū-chüàn** a pigsty, pigpen

猪肺疫 **chū-fèi-ì** swine plague (hemorrhagic septicemia)

猪舍 **chū-shè** hog pen (for large scale hog raising)

猪鬃 **chū-tsūng** hog bristles

猪瘟 **chū-wēn** hog plague

猪眼睛看不到天 **chū-yěn-chīng k'àn-pù-tào-t'iēn** the eyes of the pig cannot see the sky (ignorant, short-sighted)

chú (zhú)

315　竹简 **chú-chiěn** bamboo strips (used for writing before paper was invented)

竹制品 **chú-chìh-p'ǐn** articles made of bamboo

316　逐级下放 **chú-chí-hsià-fàng** downward transfer by gradual steps (an early form of *hsia-fang* where cadres merely moved down one step, e.g., from provincial to *hsien* offices)

逐出 **chú-ch'ū** to drive out, expel, evict

逐行逐业 **chú-háng chú-yèh** trade by trade, every trade

逐戶摸底 **chú-hù-mō-tǐ** to understand the true conditions of each household

逐步 **chú-pù** gradually, step by step; to proceed in an orderly way

逐步升级 **chú-pù-shēng-chí** step by step promotion, orderly ascent (escalation)

逐条 **chú-t'iáo** each article [of a treaty or document], article by article

逐字逐句 **chú-tzù chú-chù** word for word, literally

317　烛照 **chú-chào** to enlighten, illuminate

chǔ (zhǔ)

318　主将 **chǔ-chiàng** chief general (a derisive epithet in the Cultural Revolution)

主角 **chǔ-chiǎo** the principal actor, leading role

主持 **chǔ-ch'íh** (1) to take charge, preside over, direct, manage; (2) to uphold

主持正义 **chǔ-ch'íh chèng-ì** to uphold justice

主权 **chǔ-ch'üán** sovereignty; sovereign

主和派 **chǔ-hó-p'ài** the peace-advocating group

主席 **chǔ-hsí** chairman, president

主席团 **chǔ-hsí-t'uán** presidium, executive committee

主义 **chǔ-ì** [fundamental] doctrine, principle, -ism, theory (a principle guiding a set of ideas)

主意 **chǔ-ì** an opinion, proposal, suggestion; a decision

主人公 **chǔ-jén-kūng** master of the house [or country] (the proletariat)

主人翁 **chǔ-jén-wēng** master of the house (refers to the proletariat)

主人翁思想 **chǔ-jén-wēng szū-hsiǎng** master-of-the-house thinking (a member of the proletariat should be conscious that he is responsible)

主人翁态度 **chǔ-jén-wēng t'ài-tù** the attitude of a master (*see next above*)

主任 **chǔ-jèn** director, head [of a department]

主任委员 **chǔ-jèn-wěi-yuán** chief of a committee

主观 **chǔ-kuān** subjectivist, subjective

主观主义 **chǔ-kuān-chǔ-ì** subjectivism

主观忆造 **chǔ-kuān-ì-tsào** subjective fabrication

主观认识 **chǔ-kuān-jèn-shíh** subjective concepts, subjective views

主观观念论 **chǔ-kuān-kuān-nièn lùn** subjective idealism

主观能动性 **chǔ-kuān néng-tùng-hsìng** subjective initiative

主观能动作用 **chǔ-kuān néng-tùng tsò-yùng** subjective initiating function

主观世界 **chǔ-kuān-shìh-chièh** the subjective world

主观动机 **chǔ-kuān tùng-chī** subjective motive

主观唯心主义 **chǔ-kuān wéi-hsīn-chǔ-ì** subjective idealism

主观唯心论 **chǔ-kuān wéi-hsīn-lùn** the theory of subjective idealism

主观愿望 **chǔ-kuān-yuàn-wàng** subjective wishes, wishful thinking

主管 **chǔ-kuǎn** [person] in charge, the competent person; to manage, administer

主管机关 **chǔ-kuǎn-chī-kuān** the competent authorities, the authorities concerned

主攻 **chǔ-kūng** main direction for attack, the principal attack

主课 **chǔ-k'ò** the chief lesson

主力战 **chǔ-lì-chàn** the main action [military]

主力军 **chǔ-lì-chūn** the main military force; elite units

主力兵团 **chǔ-lì-pīng-t'uán** the main force [military]

主粮 **chǔ-liáng** the chief grains (rice and wheat)

主流 **chǔ-liú** main current, chief trend, mainstream

主流和支流 **chǔ-liú hó chīh-liú** mainstream and tributaries (main trend and side issues)

主办 **chǔ-pàn** to direct, undertake, be responsible for, sponsor

主送 **chǔ-sùng** main transmission (the direct transmission of action documents from superior to subordinate units)

主导思想 **chǔ-tǎo-szū-hsiǎng** dominant ideas, dominant ideology

主导原则 **chǔ-tǎo-yuán-tsé** leading principle, guiding principle

主动 **chǔ-tùng** to take action, take the initiative; initiative

主动权 **chǔ-tùng-ch'uán** power of initiative, the authority to initiate [an action or policy]

主动性 **chǔ-tùng-hsìng** the quality of being able to take initiative

主动地位 **chǔ-tùng-tì-wèi** a position of initiative

主题 **chǔ-t'í** main theme, thesis, subject

主题歌 **chǔ-t'í-kō** a theme song

主体 **chǔ-t'ǐ** main body, essential part, mainstay, main subject

主宰一切 **chǔ-tsǎi-í-ch'ièh** to have absolute supremacy

主子 **chǔ-tzu** boss, master, ruler, lord (pejorative)

主委 **chǔ-wěi** chief committee member (contraction of **chǔ-jèn wěi-yuán**)

主要环节 **chǔ-yào-huán-chiéh** key link

主要劳动 **chǔ-yào-láo-tùng** principal labor (the main agricultural work of each season: e.g., plowing)

主要矛盾 **chǔ-yào-máo-tùn** principal contradiction

主要矛盾转移论 **chǔ-yào-máo-tùn chuǎn-í lún** the concept that the principal contradiction changes

主要矛盾线 **chǔ-yào-máo-tùn-hsièn** the critical path (a term used in operations research)

319 贮藏 **chǔ-ts'áng** to hoard, store up; hoarding

chù (zhù)

320 住屋交换所 **chù-fáng chiāo-huàn-sǒ** residence exchange centers (offices to arrange the exchange of living quarters)

321 助教 **chù-chiào** a teaching assistant [college level]

助纣为虐 **chù-chòu-wéi-nuèh** to help [King] Chou to maltreat people (an accusation against followers of campaign targets)

助产士 **chù-ch'ǎn-shìh** a midwife

助理 **chù-lǐ** to assist, help, aid; an assistant, a helping hand

助手 **chù-shǒu** an assistant, helper, adjutant, adviser

助威 **chù-wēi** to give oral or moral support, root for

322 注脚 **chù-chiǎo** a footnote

注重 **chù-chùng** to stress, emphasize; emphasis

注入 **chù-jù** to introduce into, instil, inject

注明 **chù-míng** to state explicitly in a footnote

注射 **chù-shè** to inoculate, inject; inoculation

注射预防针 **chù-shè yù-fáng-chēn** to inoculate with a preventive injection

注音 **chù-yīn** phonetic, sound notation; to transcribe into phonetic notation

注音字母 **chù-yīn-tzǔ-mǔ** the National Phonetic Alphabet (introduced in 1918)

³²³ 驻扎 **chù-chā** to station [troops], to garrison

驻军 **chù-chūn** garrison forces

驻校工人毛泽东思想宣传队 **chù-hsiào kūng-jén máo-tsé-tūng-szū-hsiǎng hsūan-ch'úan-tuì** Workers' Mao Tse-tung Thought Propaganda Teams to Stay in the Schools

驻美联络处 **chù-měi lién-lò-ch'ù** [the Chinese] Liaison Office Resident in the United States [at Washington]

驻外人员 **chù-wài-jén-yuán** representatives to foreign states

³²⁴ 祝酒 **chù-chǐu** to drink a toast, to toast

祝贺 **chù-hò** congratulations, felicitations; to congratulate

祝词 **chù-tz'ú** a message of greetings, speech of congratulation

祝愿 **chù-yuàn** to felicitate, congratulate, send best wishes

³²⁵ 柱石 **chù-shíh** a pillar stone (main support—as the PLA)

³²⁶ 著作 **chù-tsò** writings, works, literary creation

³²⁷ 蛀虫 **chù-ch'úng** insects which eat clothes or books (often used figuratively)

³²⁸ 铸件 **chù-chièn** metal casting

铸件厂 **chù-chièn-ch'ǎng** a foundry

铸工 **chù-kūng** foundry works

chuā (zhuā)

³²⁹ 抓 **chuā** to grasp, seize, grab, clutch, pay close attention to (connotes complete, exclusive, and unrelenting control)

抓政治保险,抓业务危险 **chuā-chèng-chìh pǎo-hsiěn, chuā-yèh-wù wēi-hsiěn** concentrating on politics is safe [but] concentrating on professional work is dangerous

抓政治思想工作 **chuā-chèng-chìh-szū-hsiǎng kūng-tsò** grasp political-ideological work

抓紧 **chuā-chǐn** to grasp firmly, grasp tightly

抓紧革命大批判 **chuā-chǐn kó-mìng tà-p'ī-p'àn** grasp firmly revolutionary mass criticism

抓住重点 **chuā-chù-chùng-tiěn** to grasp the main points

抓抓放放 **chuā-chuā-fàng-fàng** to grasp and to let go intermittently (inconsistent)

抓创作的同志 **chuā-ch'uàng-tsò-te t'úng-chìh** Party worker guiding such work as the creation of a **yàng-pǎn-hsì**: not the actual writer or professional staff)

抓好 **chuā-hǎo** to grasp well

抓好两头 **chuā-hǎo-liǎng-t'óu** to grasp both ends well (to come to a thorough understanding of Party policy on the upper level and of the actual conditions on the lower level; or, to understand both advanced and backward elements)

抓好典型 **chuā-hǎo-tiěn-hsíng** to thoroughly master [the use of] models

抓人头 **chuā-jén-t'óu** to grasp heads (to merely count heads; to overemphasize numbers)

抓纲,抓线 **chuā-kāng-chuā-hsièn** to grasp the principle and [policy] line

抓革命保险,抓生产危险 **chuā-kó-mìng pǎo-hsiěn, chuā-shēng-ch'ǎn wēi-hsiěn** to grasp revolution is safe [but] to emphasize production is dangerous

抓革命,促生产,促工作,促战备 **chuā kó-mìng, ts'ù shēng-ch'ǎn, ts'ù kūng-tsò, ts'ù chàn-pèi** grasp revolution, push production, push work, and push war preparedness

抓两头,带中间 **chuā-liǎng-t'óu, tài-chūng-chiēn** grasp [keep watch over] the two ends [the most advanced and the most backward] to bring along [the majority] in between

抓路线 **chuā-lù-hsièn** grasp the [correct] line

抓生产 **chuā-shēng-ch'ǎn** to grasp production (to pay attention to production)

抓生活 **chuā-shēng-huó** to grasp livelihood (to take care of the livelihood of one's subordinates)

抓思想 **chuā-szū-hsiǎng** seize hold of thought (emphasize ideology)

抓大事 **chuā-tà-shìh** emphasize the important affairs [of the political line] (do not waste time on minor affairs)

抓得早,抓得紧 **chuā-té-tsǎo, chuā-té-chǐn** grasp [affairs] early and tightly

抓点 **chuā-tiěn** to take hold of points [selected basic units]

抓点带面 **chuā-tiěn-tài-mièn** to grasp the points and to bring along the plane [the whole area]

chuān (zhuān)

³³⁰ 专案 **chuān-àn** a particular case, a separate file

专案审查小组 **chuān-àn shěn-ch'á-hsiǎo-tsǔ** special case investigation groups

专政 **chuān-chèng** dictatorship

专政机关 **chuān-chèng-chī-kuān** organs of the [people's] dictatorship (any power-holding agency of the government)

专辑 **chuān-chí** a special publication on a particular subject

专家 **chuān-chiā** an expert, a specialist

专家治厂 **chuān-chiā-chìh-ch'ǎng** [to let] experts run the factories (criticized as a Rightist policy)

专家治校 **chuān-chiā-chìh-hsiào** experts [should] manage schools (attacked as a bourgeois revisionist concept)

专家路线 **chuān-chiā lù-hsièn** the expert line (the tendency of experts in a field to over-emphasize technical factors)

专职 **chuān-chíh** specific work (the person involved spends full time and holds no concurrent job)

专制 **chuān-chìh** despotic, autocratic; tyranny, absolutism

专制制度 **chuān-chìh-chìh-tù** autocratic system, despotic system

专治 **chuān-chìh** a specific cure, [a drug which] cures a specific illness [or trouble]

专长 **chuān-ch'áng** to be adept in, excel in, be a specialist in; proficient, expert

专区 **chuān-ch'ū** special region, administrative region; a government subdivision between *hsien* and *sheng*

专横跋扈 **chuān-hèng-pá-hù** arbitrary and overweening

专修科 **chuān-hsiū-k'ō** a concentrated course [of study]

专人分工负责 **chuān-jén fēn-kūng-fù-tsé** division of labor with fixed responsibilities

专刊 **chuān-k'ān** a special supplement [of a publication]

专科学校 **chuān-k'ò-hsuéh-hsiào** a specialized school (usually a technical school at upper-middle-school level)

专栏 **chuān-lán** a by-lined column [in a magazine or newspaper]

专利费 **chuān-lì-fèi** patent fee

专论 **chuān-lùn** a treatise or article on a specific subject

专卖 **chuān-mài** a monopoly; to monopolize

专门 **chuān-mén** specialized, professional, technical; a speciality

专门技能 **chuān-mén-chì-néng** specialized technical ability, technical know-how

专擅 **chuān-shàn** to act without proper authorization, take matters into one's own hands

专署 **chuān-shǔ** prefectural commissioner's office, office of a **chuān-ch'ū**

专断 **chuān-tuàn** arbitrary [in making decisions]

专题讨论 **chuān-t'í-t'ǎo-lùn** discussion on a special topic or subject; to discuss a specific topic

专文 **chuān-wén** a special article, feature article

专业 **chuān-yèh** a vocation, occupation, specialized field or profession; specialized, professional

专业教育 **chuān-yèh-chiào-yù** vocational or professional education

专业知识 **chuān-yèh-chìh-shíh** professional knowledge

专业厂矿 **chuān-yèh-ch'ǎng-k'uàng** specialized factories and mines

专业分工 **chuān-yèh-fēn-kūng** division of labor based on specialization

专业人员 **chuān-yèh-jén-yuán** professional workers, professional personnel

专业美术工作者 **chuān-yèh měi-shù-kūng-tsò-chě** professional practitioner of the fine arts, worker in fine arts

专业部门会议 **chuān-yèh-pù-mén huì-ì** specialist meeting (usually more narrow and more technical in scope than a **kūng-tsò huì-ì**)

专业生产会议 **chuān-yèh shēng-ch'ǎn huì-ì** a production meeting of specialized trades

专业队 **chuān-yèh-tuì** specialized task brigades

专业队伍 **chuān-yèh-tuì-wǔ** specialized personnel

专业文艺工作者 **chuān-yèh wén-ì-kūng-tsò-chě** a specialized worker in literature and the arts

专有 **chuān-yǔ** to possess exclusively, monopolize

专用 **chuān-yùng** exclusive use, for a particular purpose

331   砖瓦厂 **chuān-wǎ-ch'ǎng** brick and tile factory

chuǎn (zhuǎn)

332   转折关头 **chuǎn-ché-kuān-t'óu** a critical turning point

转折点 **chuǎn-ché-tiěn** a turning point

转诊 **chuǎn-chěn** to transfer for treatment [medical]

转嫁 **chuǎn-chià** to shift or transfer to someone else (usually implies

shifting the blame or responsibility)

转化 **chuǎn-huà** to transform, change; interconversion [chemical]; to transpose

转移 **chuǎn-í** to change place; to move, shift [direction]

转移目标 **chuǎn-í-mù-piāo** to shift targets

转入低潮 **chuǎn-jù-tî-ch'áo** to ebb, subside

转入地下 **chuǎn-jù-tì-hsià** to go underground (figurative)

转卖 **chuǎn-mài** to re-sell, to sell to a third party

转败为胜 **chuǎn-pài-wéi-shèng** to turn defeat into victory

转变 **chuǎn-pièn** to convert; change, transformation, conversion, remolding (often refers to the remolding of one's political thought)

转变关头 **chuǎn-pièn-kuān-t'óu** a turning point, juncture

转播 **chuǎn-pō** to rebroadcast, to relay

转瞬 **chuǎn-shùn** [in a] blink of the eye (a very short time)

转载 **chuǎn-tsài** to reprint

转弯抹角 **chuǎn-wān-mò-chiǎo** to turn a corner (to speak in an indirect and purposely obscure way)

转危为安 **chuǎn-wēi-wéi-ān** to turn peril into peace (to surmount a crisis)

转业 **chuǎn-yèh** to change occupation

转业军人 **chuǎn-yèh-chûn-jén** demobilized soldiers who have changed occupation (ex-soldiers who have transferred back to civilian duties other than their original occupations)

转业和复员 **chuǎn-yèh hó fù-yuán** to change occupation and be demobilized (soldiers transferred from active service to civilian work)

转业训练 **chuǎn-yèh-hsùn-lièn** training for changing jobs

转运站 **chuǎn-yùn-chàn** transshipment station, transfer post

转 **chuǎn**: *see also* **chuàn**

chuàn (zhuàn)

³³³ 转炉 **chuàn-lú** a Bessemer converter

转 **chuàn**: *see also* **chuǎn**

chuāng (zhuāng)

³³⁴ 庄稼 **chuāng-chia** agriculture; farm crops

庄户学 **chuāng-hù-hsuéh** farm schools in literacy and simple accounting

庄严 **chuāng-yén** solemn, dignified, noble, sublime

庄园 **chuāng-yuán** farm (refers to landlord holdings)

³³⁵ 装机总容量 **chuāng-chī tsǔng-júng-liàng** total installed [generating] capacity

装甲兵 **chuāng-chiǎ-pīng** Armored Corps (one of the service arms of the PLA)

装置 **chuāng-chìh** to install, to equip with; an installation

装腔作势 **chuāng-ch'iāng-tsò-shìh** to sing in falsetto and strike postures (affectation, pretense)

装潢门面 **chuāng-huáng-mén-mièn** to decorate the front of a building (superficial work)

装卸区 **chuāng-hsièh-ch'ǚ** loading districts, loading zones (a section of a port)

装卸工人 **chuāng-hsièh-kūng-jén** a docker, longshoreman

装模作样 **chuāng-mó-tsò-yàng** to indulge in histrionics, assume airs

装备 **chuāng-pèi** to equip, furnish with, fit out; equipment, installation

装配车间 **chuāng-p'èi-ch'ē-chiēn** an assembly shop

装饰品 **chuāng-shìh-p'ǐn** decorations, decorative articles

装点江山 **chuāng-tiěn-chiāng-shān** to decorate the rivers and mountains (to remake the face of the country)

装懂 **chuāng-tǔng** to pretend to understand

装药点炮 **chuāng-yào-tiěn-p'ào** to place and set off explosive charges [in construction work]

chuàng (zhuàng)

³³⁶ 壮举 **chuàng-chǔ** a magnificent act, great feat, impressive undertaking

壮丽 **chuàng-lì** grand and beautiful, impressive

壮大 **chuàng-tà** powerful, robust, stalwart; grown-up

壮胆 **chuàng-tǎn** to whip up courage, help to encourage, stimulate courage

壮族 **chuàng-tsú** the Chuang people (a minority in Kwangsi, Yunnan, and Kwangtung provinces: population 7,785,000 as of 1957—name changed from 僮族 **chuàng-tsú** in 1965)

³³⁷ 状况 **chuàng-k'uàng** conditions, circumstances, general aspects, situation

状态 **chuàng-t'ài** condition [of things], manner or appearance

338 僮 **chuàng** the Chuang people (a minority nationality: *see* 壮 **chuàng**)

chuì (zhuì)

339 追加支出 **chuī-chiā-chĭh-ch'ū** to appropriate additional expenditure; added expenditure

追剿 **chuī-chiǎo** to pursue and destroy

追缴 **chuī-chiǎo** to demand payment

追究 **chuī-chiū** to investigate thoroughly, inquire into, pursue [a matter] closely

追逐 **chuī-chú** to pursue, chase after, hunt

追查 **chuī-ch'á** to investigate, pursue an investigation

追求 **chuī-ch'iú** to seek for, seek after

追肥 **chuī-féi** topdressing, fertilizer added to maturing crop [in contrast to base fertilizer applied before seeding]

追认 **chuī-jèn** to confirm retroactively (may be posthumous confirmation of status such as Party membership or official confirmation after a temporary promotion)

追念古人 **chuī-nièn-kŭ-jén** to cherish the memory of the ancients

追述 **chuī-shù** to relate, recount

追索 **chuī-sŏ** search for, to recover [what is due from the past]

追算期限 **chuī-suàn-ch'ī-hsièn** a time limit for calculating back (the limitation set for computing past obligations, as by capitalists during the Five-Anti Movement)

追悼会 **chuī-tào-huì** a memorial ceremony, memorial service

340 锥子会 **chuī-tzu-huì** an "awl meeting" (a meeting at which workers criticize other's faults and expose their own faults)

chūn (zhūn)

341 谆谆告诫 **chūn-chūn-kào-chièh** to earnestly warn, emphatically enjoin

chŭn (zhŭn)

342 准确 **chŭn-ch'üèh** accurate, definite, correct; accuracy

准备 **chŭn-pèi** to prepare, make preparations

准备金 **chŭn-pèi-chīn** a reserve fund

准绳 **chŭn-shéng** a plumb line, marking line (a criterion, standard, rule of conduct)

准则 **chŭn-tsé** a criterion, standard, guideline

chūng (zhōng)

343 中级干部 **chūng-chí-kàn-pù** middle-level cadres

中间阶段 **chūng-chiēn-chiēh-tuàn** middle stage, intermediate stage

中间阶层 **chūng-chiēn-chiēh-ts'éng** the middle strata, middle stratum

中间分子 **chūng-chiēn-fèn-tzǔ** middle elements, middle-of-the-roaders (those who neither oppose nor actively support Communist policy)

中间人物 **chūng-chiēn-jén-wù** people in the middle (those who find it difficult in action or ideology to take a definite stand)

中间人物论 **chūng-chiēn-jén-wù lùn** the doctrine of middle characters (the idea that many people, even among such groups as poor peasants, have in fact vacillated between socialism and capitalism—one of the **hēi-pā-lùn**)

中间路线 **chūng-chiēn-lù-hsièn** middle-of-the-road line (an unwillingness to choose between socialism and capitalism)

中间派 **chūng-chiēn-p'ài** middle-of-the-roaders, compromisers

中间势力 **chūng-chiēn-shìh-lì** the third force

中间道路 **chūng-chiēn-tào-lù** the middle road

中间地带 **chūng-chiēn-tì-tài** the intermediate zone (1. Asia-Africa-Latin America; 2. the Common Market)

中坚分子 **chūng-chiēn-fèn-tzǔ** backbone elements, those who are the mainstay of

中坚力量 **chūng-chiēn-lì-liàng** the core strength, hard-core strength, nucleus of power

中近东 **chūng-chìn-tūng** Middle and Near East

中专生 **chūng-chuān-shēng** students of secondary technical schools

中产阶级 **chūng-ch'ǎn-chiēh-chí** the middle class, the bourgeoisie

中程飞弹 **chūng-ch'éng-fēi-tàn** intermediate-range ballistic missile

中曲发酵饲料 **chūng-ch'ū-fā-hsiào szù-liào** yeast fermentation of [animal] feed, silage

中非共和国 **chūng-fēi kùng-hó-kuó** the Central African Republic

中华全国青年联合国 **chūng-huá ch'üán-kuó ch'īng-nién lién-hó-huì**

All-China Federation of Youth

中华全国妇女联合会 **chūng-huá ch'üán-kuó fù-nǚ lién-hó-huì** All-China Women's Federation

中华全国新闻工作者协会 **chūng-huá ch'üán-kuó hsīn-wén kūng-tsò-chě hsiéh-huì** All-China Journalists' Association

中华全国学生联合会 **chūng-huá ch'üán-kuó hsuéh-shēng lién-hó-huì** All-China Students' Federation

中华全国科学技术普及协会 **chūng-huá ch'üán-kuó k'ō-hsuéh-chì-shù p'ǔ-chí hsiéh-huì** All-China Association for the Dissemination of Scientific and Technical Knowledge

中华全国体育总会 **chūng-huá ch'üán-kuó t'ǐ-yù tsǔng-huì** All-China Athletic Federation

中华全国总工会 **chūng-huá ch'üán-kuó tsǔng-kūng-huì** All-China Federation of Trade Unions

中华人民共和国 **chūng-huá jén-mín kùng-hó-kuó** People's Republic of China

中华人民共和国全国人民代表大会 **chūng-huá jén-mín kùng-hó-kuó ch'üán-kuó jén-mín tài-piǎo-tà-huì** National People's Congress of the People's Republic of China

中华人民共和国宪法 **chūng-huá jén-mìn kùng-hó-kuó hsièn-fǎ** Constitution of the People's Republic of China (promulgated January, 1975)

中华民国 **chūng-huá-mín-kuó** the Republic of China

中华民族 **chūng-huá-mín-tsú** the Chinese people of various nationalities (note: in previous usage, this referred only to the Chinese people)

中华苏维埃共和国 **chūng-huá sū-wéi-āi kùng-hó-kuó** The Chinese Soviet Republic (established at Juichin, Kiangsi, on November 7, 1931)

中西医结合 **chūng-hsī-ī chiéh-hó** the combination of traditional and Western medicine (now strongly urged)

中小型 **chūng-hsiǎo-hsíng** medium and small types

中小型企业 **chūng-hsiǎo-hsíng ch'ǐ-yèh** medium and small-sized enterprises

中心 **chūng-hsīn** center, core, heart, hub, nucleus; central

中心城市 **chūng-hsīn-ch'éng-shìh** metropolis, major city, metropolitan city

中心环节 **chūng-hsīn-huán-chiéh** central link, main point, keystone

中心任务 **chūng-hsīn-jèn-wù** central task, core work

中心工作 **chūng-hsīn-kūng-tsò** major work, important work, central task

中型 **chūng-hsíng** middle-sized, medium

中医 **chūng-ī** Chinese traditional medicine

中医师 **chūng-ī-shīh** doctors of traditional Chinese medicine

中日邦交正常化 **chūng-jìh pāng-chiāo chèng-ch'áng-huà** normalization of China-Japan [diplomatic] relations

中共 **chūng-kùng** Chinese Communist Party (contraction of **Chūng-kuó kùng-ch'ǎn-tǎng**)

中共中央 **chūng-kùng-chūng-yāng** Central Committee of the Chinese Communist Party (contraction of **Chūng-kuó kùng-ch'ǎn-tǎng chūng-yāng wěi-yuán-huì**; also contracted to **Chūng-yāng**)

中共中央政治局 **chūng-kùng-chūng-yāng chèng-chìh-chú** the Political Bureau of the CCP Central Committee (Politburo)

中共中央监察委员会 **chūng-kùng-chūng-yāng chiēn-ch'á wěi-yuán-huì** Control Committee of the CCP Central Committee

中共中央中南局 **chūng-kùng-chūng-yāng chūng-nán-chú** South-central Bureau of the CCP Central Committee (Hupeh, Hunan, and Kwangtung)

中共中央军事委员会 **chūng-kùng-chūng-yāng chūn-shìh wěi-yuán-huì** Military Commission of the CCP Central Committee

中共中央妇女工作委员会 **chūng-kùng-chūng-yāng fù-nǚ-kūng-tsò wěi-yuán-huì** Women's Work Committee of the CCP Central Committee

中共中央华北局 **chūng-kùng-chūng-yāng huá-pěi-chú** North China Bureau of the CCP Central Committee

中共中央华东局 **chūng-kùng-chūng-yāng huá-tūng-chú** East China Bureau of the CCP Central Committee

中共中央西南局 **chūng-kùng-chūng-yāng hsī-nán-chú** Southwest Bureau of the CCP Central Committee

中共中央西北局 **chūng-kùng-chūng-yāng hsī-pěi-chú** Northwest Bureau of the CCP Central Committee

中共中央宣传部 **chūng-kùng-chūng-yāng hsūan-ch'uán-pù** Propaganda Department of the CCP Central Committee

中共中央高级党校 **chūng-kùng-chūng-yāng kāo-chí tăng-hsiào** Higher Party School of the CCP Central Committee

中共中央工业交通政治部 **chūng-kùng-chūng-yāng kūng-yèh chiāo-t'ūng chèng-chìh-pù** Political Department for Industry and Communications of the CCP Central Committee

中共中央农林政治部 **chūng-kùng-chūng-yāng núng-lín chèng-chìh-pù** Political Department for Agriculture and Forestry of the CCP Central Committee

中共中央农村工作部 **chūng-kùng-chūng-yāng núng-ts'ūn kūng-tsò-pù** Rural Work Department of the CCP Central Committee

中共中央书记处 **chūng-kùng-chūng-yāng shū-chì-ch'ù** the Secretariat of the CCP Central Committee

中共中央对外联络部 **chūng-kùng-chūng-yāng tuì-wài lién-lò-pù** International Liaison Department of the CCP Central Committee

中共中央东北局 **chūng-kùng-chūng-yāng tūng-pěi-chú** Northeast Bureau of the CCP Central Committee

中共中央统一战线工作部 **chūng-kùng-chūng-yāng t'ǔng-ī-chàn-hsièn kūng-tsò-pù** United Front Work Department of the CCP Central Committee

中共中央组织部 **chūng-kùng-chūng-yāng tsǔ-chīh-pù** Organization Department of the CCP Central Committee

中共中央财贸政治部 **chūng-kùng-chūng-yāng ts'ái-mào chèng-chìh-pù** Political Department for Finance and Trade of the CCP Central Committee

中共中央委员会 **chūng-kùng-chūng-yāng wěi-yuán-huì** Central Committee of the CCP

中国致公党 **chūng-kuó chìh-kūng-tăng** the China Chih Kung Tang (one of the democratic parties)

中国旧民主主义革命时期 **chūng-kuó chìu mín-chǔ-chǔ-ì kó-mìng shíh-ch'ī** the period of the old Chinese democratic revolution (from 1840 to the May Fourth Movement in 1919)

中国青年 **chūng-kuó-ch'īng-nién** *Chinese Youth* (official organ of the Chinese Communist Youth League, founded in Shanghai in 1923 and published, with breaks, in Kiangsi, Yenan, and Peking until suspended in August, 1966)

中国青年报 **chūng-kuó-ch'īng-nién-pào** *Chinese Youth Journal* (newspaper published by the Communist Youth League until suspended in August, 1966)

中国轻工业 **chūng-kuó-ch'īng-kūng-yèh** *Light Industry of China* (Peking, semi-monthly, 1950—)

中国出口商品交易会 **chūng-kuó ch'ū-k'ǒu-shāng-p'ǐn chiāo-ì-huì** China Export Commodities Trade Fair (the Canton Fair)

中国纺织 **chūng-kuó-fǎng-chīh** *Chinese Textiles* (published at Peking, three times a month, 1950—)

中国封建社会 **chūng-kuó fēng-chièn-shè-huì** Chinese feudal society (475 B.C. to 1840 A.D.)

中国妇女 **chūng-kuó-fù-nǚ** *Women of China* (published in Peking, monthly, 1950—)

中国画院 **chūng-kuó-huà-yuàn** Academy of Chinese Painting

中国红军 **chūng-kuó-húng-chūn** the Chinese Red Army (1927–1937)

中国红十字会 **chūng-kuó húng-shíh-tzù-huì** Red Cross Society of China

中国新民主主义青年团 **chūng-kuó hsīn-mín-chǔ-chǔ-ì ch'īng-nién-t'uán** China New Democratic Youth League (before 1957)

中国新闻 **chūng-kuó-hsīn-wén** *China News* (published at Canton by the Chung-kuo-hsin-wen-she, 1954—)

中国新闻社 **chūng-kuó hsīn-wén-shè** China News Service (the foreign news counterpart of the Hsin-hua-she)

中国医学科学院 **chūng-kuó ī-hsuéh-k'ō-hsuéh-yuán** Chinese Academy of Medical Sciences

中国人民政治协商会议 **chūng-kuó-jén-mín chèng-chìh hsiéh-shāng-huì-ì** Chinese People's Political Consultative Conference

中国人民解放军 **chūng-kuó-jén-mín chiěh-fàng-chūn** The Chinese People's Liberation Army (the PLA, the official title of the armed forces since March, 1947)

中国人民志愿军 **chūng-kuó-jén-mín chìh-yuàn-chūn** Chinese People's Volunteers (the Chinese forces participating in the Korean War)

中国人民保卫世界和平委员会 **chūng-kuó-jén-mín pǎo-wèi shìh-chièh-hó-p'íng wěi-yuán-huì** Chinese People's Committee For World Peace

中国人民对外文化协会 **chūng-kuó-jén-mín tuì-wài wén-huà hsiéh-huì** Chinese People's Association for

Cultural Relations with Foreign Countries

中国人民外交学会 **chūng-kuó-jén-mín wài-chiāo hsuéh-huì** Chinese People's Institute of Foreign Affairs

中国人民银行 **chūng-kuó-jén-mín yín-háng** People's Bank of China

中国工人 **chūng-kuó-kūng-jén** *The Chinese Worker* (a journal first published at Yenan in 1940; since 1956, a semi-monthly published at Peking)

中国工商行政管理局 **chūng-kuó kūng-shāng hsíng-chèng kuǎn-lǐ-chú** Central Administrative Bureau of Industry and Commerce

中国工业 **chūng-kuó-kūng-yèh** *Chinese Industry* (a Shanghai monthly, 1949—)

中国共产主义青年团 **chūng-kuó-kùng-ch'ǎn-chǔ-ì ch'īng-nién-t'uán** Communist Youth League of China (before 1957 known as the China New Democratic Youth League)

中国共产党 **chūng-kuó-kùng-ch'ǎn-tǎng** Communist Party of China [the CCP]

中国共产党章程 **chūng-kuó-kùng-ch'ǎn-tǎng chāng-ch'éng** Party Constitution of the CCP (the latest version was adopted by the 10th Congress in August, 1973)

中国共产党中央委员会 **chūng-kuó-kùng-ch'ǎn-tǎng chūng-yāng-wěi-yuán-huì** Central Committee of the Chinese Communist Party

中国国际贸易促进委员会 **chūng-kuó kuó-chì-mào-ì ts'ù-chìn wěi-yuán-huì** Chinese Committee for the Promotion of International Trade

中国国民党革命委员会 **chūng-kuó-kuó-mín-tǎng kó-mìng wěi-yuán-huì** Revolutionary Committee of the Kuomintang (one of the democratic parties in the People's Republic)

中国科学院 **chūng-kuó k'ō-hsuéh-yuàn** Chinese Academy of Sciences (established November, 1949; also known as Academia Sinica)

中国旅行游览事业管理局 **chūng-kuó lǔ-hsíng-yú-lǎn-shìh-yèh kuǎn-lǐ-chú** China Travel and Tourism Bureau

中国民主建国会 **chūng-kuó mín-chǔ-chièn-kuó-huì** China Democratic National Construction Association (one of the democratic parties)

中国民主同盟 **chūng-kuó mín-chǔ-t'úng-méng** China Democratic League (one of the democratic parties, comprising many of the

non-Communist intellectuals)

中国民主促进会 **chūng-kuó mín-chǔ-ts'ù-chìn-huì** China Association for Promoting Democracy (one of the minor democratic parties)

中国民用航空总局 **chūng-kuó mín-yùng-háng-k'ūng tsǔng-chú** Civil Aviation Administration of China

中国奴隶社会 **chūng-kuó nú-lì-shè-huì** the Chinese slave society (now considered to have been from about 2100 B.C. to about 450 B.C.)

中国农工民主党 **chūng-kuó núng-kūng-mín-chǔ-tǎng** Chinese Peasants' and Workers' Democratic Party (one of the democratic parties)

中国农民 **chūng-kuó-núng-mín** *The Chinese Peasant* (a journal published at Canton under joint Kuomintang-Communist auspices in 1926 and edited by Mao Tse-tung)

中国农报 **chūng-kuó-núng-pào** *Chinese Agricultural Bulletin* (Peking semi-monthly, 1950—)

中国农业科学院 **chūng-kuó núng-yèh-k'ō-hsuéh-yuàn** Chinese Academy of Agricultural Sciences

中国贫油论 **chūng-kuó-p'ín-yú lùn** the theory that China is poor in oil (an old defeatist idea)

中国少年先锋队 **chūng-kuó shào-nién-hsiēn-fēng-tuì** Chinese Young Pioneers (from 7–14 years of age)

中国社会主义青年团 **chūng-kuó shè-huì-chǔ-ì ch'īng-nién-t'uán** Chinese Socialist Youth League (the CCP's first youth auxiliary, founded in 1922; in 1925, its name was changed to Communist Youth League)

中国是个大安排 **chūng-kuó shìh ko tà-ān-p'ái** China is a big arrangement (to rebuild China is a tremendous job)

中国的赫鲁晓夫 **chūng-kuó-te hò-lǔ-hsiǎo-fū** China's Khrushchev (Liu Shao-ch'i)

中国对外援助八项原则 **chūng-kuó tuì-wài-yuán-chù pā-hsìang yuán-tsé** Eight Principles of Foreign Aid (set forth by Chou En-lai during his Africa trip in 1964. Briefly summarized: (1) equality and mutual benefit, (2) respect for sovereignty, (3) long-term interest-free or low-interest loans, (4) help toward self-reliance, (5) low investment and quick results, (6) best quality equipment at international market prices, (7) training of recipient country personnel, (8) no special amenities for Chinese

personnel)

中国通 **chūng-kuó-t'ūng** China hand, China expert

中国作家协会 **chūng-kuó tsò-chiā hsiéh-huì** China Writers' Association

中国左翼作家联盟 **chūng-kuó tsǒ-ì-tsò-chiā lién-méng** League of Chinese Leftist Writers (in the 1930s)

中国文化 **chūng-kuó-wén-huà** *Chinese Culture* (a journal first published in Yenan in February, 1940)

中国文学艺术界联合会 **chūng-kuó wén-hsuéh-ì-shù-chièh lién-hó-huì** China Federation of Literary and Art Circles

中国文字改革委员会 **chūng-kuó wén-tzù-kǎi-kó wěi-yuán-huì** Committee for Reforming the Chinese Written Language [of the State Council]

中国亚非团结委员会 **chūng-kuó yà-fēi-t'uán-chiéh wěi-yuán-huì** Chinese Committee for Afro-Asian Solidarity

中国语文 **chūng-kuó-yǔ-wén** *The Chinese Language* (a Peking monthly, 1952—)

中国原始社会 **chūng-kuó yuán-shǐh-shè-huì** Chinese primitive society (from Lan-t'ien man to 2100 B.C.)

中看不中用 **chūng-k'àn pù-chūng-yùng** pleasing to the eye but not useful

中立主义 **chūng-lì-chǔ-ì** neutralism

中联部 **chūng-lién-pù** International Liaison Department (contraction of **Chūng-kùng-chūng-yāng tuì-waì-lién-lò-pù**)

中流砥柱 **chūng-liú-tǐ-chù** a stone pillar in mid-stream (an indomitable person)

中美大使会谈 **chūng-měi tà-shǐh-huì-t'án** Chinese-American ambassadorial talks (commenced in 1955, first in Switzerland, and later, in Warsaw)

中农 **chūng-núng** middle peasant (peasants who do not exploit others although they have a fair amount of producer goods)

中沙群岛 **chūng-shā-ch'ǘn-tǎo** Macclesfield Islands (eastern part of the Paracel Islands)

中枢 **chūng-shū** center, axis; central

中苏友好 **chūng-sū-yǔ-hǎo** *Chinese-Soviet Friendship* (a Peking monthly, 1949–1952)

中等专业教育 **chūng-těng chuān-yèh-chiào-yù** secondary vocational education

中等农业学校 **chūng-těng núng-yèh hsuéh-hsiào** secondary agricultural schools

中东 **chūng-tūng** the Middle East

中东通讯社 **chūng-tūng t'ūng-hsùn-shè** Middle East News Agency [MENA]

中途 **chūng-t'ú** midway, on the way, in course

中草药 **chūng-ts'ǎo-yào** Chinese medicinal herbs

中央 **chūng-yāng** center, central (usually refers to the Central Committee of the CCP, but may also include state agencies in Peking)

中央政治局 **chūng-yāng chèng-chìh-chú** Political Bureau of the Central Committee (Politburo)

中央集权 **chūng-yāng chí-ch'üán** centralization, centralization of authority

中央机关 **chūng-yāng-chī-kuān** central organs [of either Party or government]

中央气象局 **chūng-yāng ch'ì-hsiàng-chú** Central Meteorological Bureau

中央局 **chūng-yāng-chú** Central Bureau (usually refers to regional bureaus of the Central Committee)

中央军委 **chūng-yāng-chūn-wěi** Military Commission of the Central [Committee of the CCP]

中央妇女工作委员会 **chūng-yāng fù-nǔ-kūng-tsò wěi-yuán-huì** Women's Work Committee of the Central [Committee of the CCP]

中央宣传部 **chūng-yāng hsuān-ch'uán-pù** Propaganda Department of the Central [Committee of the CCP]

中央人民政府 **chūng-yāng jén-mín chèng-fǔ** the central people's government (the national government)

中央高级党校 **chūng-yāng kāo-chí-tǎng-hsiào** Higher Party School of the Central [Committee of the CCP]

中央工作会议 **chūng-yāng kūng-tsò-huì-ì** a central work conference [of the Party]

中央工业 **chūng-yāng-kūng-yèh** enterprise operated by the central [national] government

中央部委 **chūng-yāng-pù-wěi** central ministries and commissions

中央书记处 **chūng-yāng shū-chì-ch'ù** Secretariat of the CCP Central Committee

中央统战部 **chūng-yāng t'ǔng-chàn-pù** United Front Work Department of the Central [Committee of the CCP]

中央组织部 **chūng-yāng tsǔ-chíh-pù** Organization Department of the Central [Committee of the CCP]

中央为主, 地方为辅 **chūng-yāng wéi-chǔ, tì-fāng wéi-fǔ** the central authorities play the main role while the local authorities play a subsidiary role

中央委员 **chūng-yāng-wěi-yuán** Central Committee member

中央委员会 **chūng-yāng wěi-yuán-huì** The Central Committee [of the CCP]

中央慰问团 **chūng-yāng wèi-wèn-t'uán** a governmental delegation of sympathetic inquiry (a mission intended to show concern after a disaster or to show approbation for hard work in accomplishing a major task)

中央文化革命小组 **chūng-yāng wén-huà-kó-mìng hsiǎo-tsǔ** Central Cultural Revolution Small Group (established May 16, 1966, to replace an earlier group)

中叶 **chūng-yèh** middle period of a dynasty or century

中游 **chūng-yú** middle reach [of a river], midstream

中游保险论 **chūng-yú-pǎo-hsiěn lùn** the idea of midstream being safe (avoiding complete commitment)

中游思想 **chūng-yú-szū-hsiǎng** middle-of-the-stream thinking (being content with mediocrity and thus avoiding the risks of being either backward or too advanced)

中原 **chūng-yuán** (1) originally: the lower Yellow River basin; (2) the central plain of China; (3) loosely: China

中庸之道 **chūng-yūng-chīh-tào** the doctrine of the mean [of Confucius]

中 **chūng**: *see also* **chùng**

344　终结 **chūng-chiéh** to complete, to end; the end

终久 **chūng-chǐu** (1) sooner or later, in the end, eventually; (2) to last long

终年 **chūng-nién** all the year, the whole year round

终身服膺 **chūng-shēn-fú-yīng** to follow [a teaching or a principle] for one's whole life (steadfast faith)

终点 **chūng-tiěn** the end, terminal point

345　忠爱 **chūng-ài** loyalty and love, loyal love; to be loyal and to love

忠诚 **chūng-ch'éng** loyal and honest, reliable

忠君 **chūng-chūn** loyal to the sovereign (a criticized Confucian virtue)

忠孝节义 **chūng hsiào chiéh ì** loyalty, filial piety, purity, and righteousness (the conventional Confucianist virtues)

忠心耿耿 **chūng-hsīn-kěng-kěng** unswerving loyalty

忠信 **chūng-hsìn** honorable and sincere (Confucian virtue)

忠实 **chūng-shíh** loyal and honest (faithful)

忠字牌 **chūng-tzù-p'ái** a loyalty tablet (a tablet bearing the character "loyalty" intended to take the place of the traditional ancestral tablet, common since 1968)

忠言逆耳 **chūng-yén-nì-ěrh** good advice hurts the ears

忠于人民 **chūng-yú-jén-mín** loyal to the people

346　衷心拥护 **chūng-hsīn-yūng-hù** to support wholeheartedly

chǔng (zhǒng)

347　肿瘤 **chǔng-líu** a tumor

348　种间杂交 **chǔng-chiēn-tsá-chiāo** hybridization; an interspecies cross

种族 **chǔng-tsú** a race [human]

种族主义 **chǔng-tsú-chǔ-ì** racism, racialism

种族歧视 **chǔng-tsú-ch'í-shìh** racial discrimination

种族隔离 **chǔng-tsú-kó-lí** racial segregation, apartheid

种族奴隶制 **chǔng-tsú nú-lì-chìh** system of racial slavery

种族上 **chǔng-tsú-shang** ethnically, racially

种子 **chǔng-tzu** a seed

种子选手 **chǔng-tzu-hsuǎn-shǒu** seeded players (sport tournament participants who, on the record of their ability, are scheduled so that they will not eliminate each other in the earlier rounds)

种子田 **chǔng-tzu-t'ién** a field for growing seeds, seed plot

种 **chǔng**: *see also* **chùng**

chùng (zhòng)

349　中计 **chùng-chì** to play into someone's hands

中肯 **chùng-k'ěn** apposite, to the point

中伤 **chùng-shāng** to defame, vilify, harm a person's reputation

chùng: *see also* **chūng**

350　众志成城 **chùng-chìh-ch'éng-ch'èng** the will of the masses [is as firm as] a city wall

众人之事 **chùng-jén-chīh-shìh** the business of all the people (Sun Yat-sen's definition of politics)

众叛亲离 **chùng-p'àn-ch'īn-lí** opposed by the masses and deserted by one's

followers

众矢之的 **chùng-shǐh-chǐh-tì** a target of public attack

众所周知 **chùng sǒ chōu-chǐh** as everyone knows; common knowledge

351 仲家 **chùng-chiā** one of the minority nationalities in Kweichow and Yunnan; now known officially as the **pù-ī** 布依

仲裁 **chùng-ts'ái** arbitration; to arbitrate

352 种植地 **chùng-chíh-tì** a plantation, cultivated area

种试验田 **chùng shìh-yèn-t'ién** to cultivate the experimental field (often a special responsibility of the rural cadres to improve farm techniques; may also be any production work using bold steps to achieve ambitious goals)

种地的 **chùng-tì-te** a tiller of the soil, farmer

种痘 **chùng-tòu** smallpox vaccination; to vaccinate

种在人、收在天 **chùng-tsài-jén, shōu-tsài-t'iēn** man sows [but] the reaping depends on heaven (wrong thinking: man must depend on his own efforts and struggle against nature)

种 **chùng**: *see also* **chǔng**

353 重制造、轻修配 **chùng-chìh-tsào, ch'īng-hsiū-p'èi** emphasis on manufacture and neglect of maintenance (a tendency to be criticized)

重钱轻粮 **chùng-ch'ién-ch'īng-liáng** to emphasize money and neglect foodgrain (over-emphasis on cash crops)

重副轻农 **chùng-fù-ch'īng-núng** to emphasize subsidiary occupations and to neglect agriculture

重心 **chùng-hsīn** center of gravity; crucial point

重型轧钢厂 **chùng-hsíng chá-kāng-ch'ǎng** a heavy steel rolling mill

重型机床 **chùng-hsíng chī-ch'uáng** heavy machine tool

重轨铁路 **chùng-kuěi-t'iěh-lù** heavy-rail railway

重工业 **chùng-kūng-yèh** heavy industry

重工业通讯 **chùng-kūng-yèh t'ūng-hsùn** *Bulletin of Heavy Industry* (journal published at Peking three times a month, 1953—)

重量 **chùng-liàng** weight, substance

重男轻女 **chùng-nán-ch'īng-nǚ** to favor males and slight females (now heavily criticized)

重视 **chùng-shìh** to pay serious attention to, stress

重视敌人 **chùng-shìh-tí-jén** to take the enemy seriously

重大 **chùng-tà** weighty, important, serious

重点 **chùng-tiěn** key point, main point, point of emphasis

重点建设 **chùng-tiěn-chièn-shè** priority construction, major construction, key point construction

重点进攻 **chùng-tiěn-chìn-kūng** attacks against key sectors

重点防御 **chùng-tiěn-fáng-yù** defense of key points

重点任务 **chùng-tiěn-jèn-wù** major task

重点观察 **chùng-tiěn-kuān-ch'á** go to the key points for observation; key point inspection

重点工程 **chùng-tiěn-kūng-ch'éng** key point project, major project, priority project

重点工业 **chùng-tiěn-kūng-yèh** key industries, major industries, priority industries

重点批判 **chùng-tiěn-p'ī-p'àn** to criticise a representative example

重点突出、全面安排的方针 **chùng-tiěn-t'ū-ch'ū, ch'üán-mièn-ān-p'ái te fāng-chēn** the policy of giving priority to key sectors and making all round arrangements for the whole

重点文物保护单位 **chùng-tiěn-wén-wù pǎo-hù-tān-wèi** units for the protection of key cultural treasures

重点物资 **chùng-tiěn-wù-tzū** primary materials, basic supplies

重要任务 **chùng-yào-jèn-wù** an important task, important mission

重友谊、重团结 **chùng yǔ-ì, chùng t'uán-chiéh** emphasize solidarity and emphasize unity

重于泰山 **chùng-yú-t'ài-shān** heavier than Mount T'ai (very weighty, of great significance)

重用 **chùng-yùng** to assign [a person] to an important position

重 **chùng**: *see also* **ch'úng**

ch'ā (chā)

354 差距 **ch'ā-chù** gap, range of difference

差别 **ch'ā-piéh** difference, distinction, differentiation

差错 **ch'ā-ts'ò** an accident, mistake, error

差错事故难免论 **ch'ā-ts'ò shìh-kù nán-miěn lùn** the idea that mistakes and accidents are unavoidable (an idea to be criticized)

差 **ch'ā**: *see also* **ch'āi, ch'à**

355 插进 **ch'ā-chìn** to insert, intervene in

插话 **ch'ā-huà** to interrupt in speech,

interject; an irrelevant episode

插红旗 **ch'ā húng-ch'í** to plant the red flag (the signal of Communist control or of the accomplishment of a task)

插红旗, 拔白旗 **ch'ā húng-ch'í, pá pái-ch'í** plant the red flag and take out the white flag

插标布点 **ch'ā-piāo-pù-tiěn** to set up targets and designate units (to set up targets on the basis of the experience of an advanced production brigade)

插手 **ch'ā-shǒu** to put one's hand in, meddle in, interpose

插刀 **ch'ā-tāo** to stab; a murderous attack

插队 **ch'ā-tuì** to insert [cadres or urban youth] into the [rural] brigades

插队落戶 **ch'ā-tuì-lò-hù** to join a production team and settle down in the village

插足 **ch'ā-tsú** to insert a foot (to interfere)

插秧 **ch'ā-yāng** to transplant rice seedlings

ch'á (chá)

356 茬 **ch'á** (1) stubble left after harvesting a crop; (2) a crop designated by time of seeding (as, early sown crop); (3) a crop designated by place in crop rotation (as, crop following field pea)

茬口 **ch'á-k'ǒu** opening in a crop rotation—usually denoted by the crop in the previous season

茬口搭配 **ch'á-k'ǒu-tā-p'èi** rational crop rotation in order to guarantee a high yearly yield

茬轮 **ch'á-lún** crop rotation

茬地 **ch'á-tì** stubble field, stub land

357 查找 **ch'á-chǎo** to search, look for, prospect for

查究 **ch'á-chiu** to investigate, hold an inquest, examine

查抄 **ch'á-ch'āo** to take inventory and confiscate property

查清 **ch'á-ch'īng** to investigate thoroughly, ascertain [the facts]

查明 **ch'á-míng** to investigate thoroughly, clarify

查对 **ch'á-tuì** to verify, prove, check, test for accuracy

查田定产 **ch'á-t'ién-tìng-ch'ǎn** fixing output by land survey

查田运动 **ch'á-t'ién-yùn-tùng** Land Classification Campaign (launched by Mao Tse-tung in Kiangsi on June 1, 1933)

查阅 **ch'á-yuèh** to look up [usually a file], check, investigate

358 察 **ch'á** Chahar province

察觉 **ch'á-chüéh** to become conscious of, to have found out

察言观色 **ch'á-yén-kuān-sè** to examine words and look at countenances (to base one's own actions by watching others)

ch'à (chà)

359 差不多的思想 **ch'à-pù-tō te szū-hsiǎng** being content with "almost"

差 **ch'à**: *see also* ch'ā, ch'āi

360 岔子 **ch'à-tzu** an accident, mistake, error

ch'āi (chāi)

361 拆墙 **ch'āi-ch'iáng** to tear down walls, remove barriers (often political, as to remove the barriers between the Party and the people)

拆墙脚 **ch'āi-ch'iáng-chiǎo** to dig out the foot of the wall, undermine

拆穿 **ch'āi-ch'uān** to expose, uncover, reveal

拆卸 **ch'āi-hsièh** to dismantle

拆烂污 **ch'āi-làn-wū** to cause harm through slipshod work; to fail to meet a commitment or promise

拆被子 **ch'āi pèi-tzu** to remove the padding in a Chinese quilt [for cleaning and airing] (a service often performed to show support for soldiers or others whose arduous duties give them no time for this)

拆散 **ch'āi-sàn** to break up, split apart, scatter

拆台 **ch'āi-t'ái** to take down the stage (to wreck)

362 差徭 **ch'āi-yáo** government service (in pre-Republican period)

差 **ch'āi**: *see also* ch'ā, ch'à

ch'ái (chái)

363 柴、米、油、盐 **ch'ái, mǐ, yú, yén** fuel, rice, cooking oil [and] salt (the things necessary for livelihood)

柴油机 **ch'ái-yú-chī** a diesel motor, diesel engine

柴油机厂 **ch'ái-yú-chī-ch'ǎng** a diesel engine manufacturing plant

364 豺狼当道 **ch'ái-láng tāng-tào** a wolf bars the road (tyrannical government, wolves in power)

豺狼成性 **ch'ái-láng-ch'éng-hsìng** wolfish nature, cruel

豺狼野心 **ch'ái-láng-yěh-hsīn** rapacious ambition

ch'ān (chān)

365　掺砂子　**ch'ān-shā-tzu** to blend sand [in order to loosen heavy soil]; to adulterate [rice] with sand

掺杂　**ch'ān-tsá** to mix up; adulterate

ch'án (chán)

366　缠绕　**ch'án-jǎo** to wind up, reel, entangle

ch'ǎn (chǎn)

367　产假　**ch'ǎn-chià** maternity leave (normally 56 days)

产值　**ch'ǎn-chíh** output value, value of production

产销合同　**ch'ǎn-hsiāo-hó-t'ung** production-and-selling contract (e.g., during the Great Leap, between communes and county commercial departments)

产销平衡　**ch'ǎn-hsiāo-p'íng-héng** coordination of production and marketing, balance between production and marketing

产量　**ch'ǎn-liàng** capacity or volume of production, output, yield

产额　**ch'ǎn-ó** quantity of production, output

产品　**ch'ǎn-p'ǐn** product (usually manufactured)

产品交换　**ch'ǎn-p'ǐn-chiāo-huàn** exchange of products

产品设计革命　**ch'ǎn-p'ǐn shè-chì kó-mìng** products designing revolution (the meaning is that China should not be content with merely copying foreign models)

产生　**ch'ǎn-shēng** (1) to give birth, produce, bring forth; (2) to cause, give rise to, engender

产生办法　**ch'ǎn-shēng-pàn-fǎ** procedure for nominating or election [of candidates]

产物　**ch'ǎn-wù** product, result, outcome

产业军　**ch'ǎn-yèh-chūn** industrial army, production army (any group organized for production)

产业革命　**ch'ǎn-yèh-kó-mìng** the Industrial Revolution

产业工会　**ch'ǎn-yèh-kūng-huì** trade union (i.e., a mid-level union that organizes smaller unions in all of a region's enterprises that produce similar goods; a member of a municipal union federation)

产业工人　**ch'ǎn-yèh-kūng-jén** industrial worker

368　谄媚　**ch'ǎn-mèi** to flatter, toady; sycophancy

谄谀　**ch'ǎn-yú** to flatter, flattery

369　阐发　**ch'ǎn-fā** to expound, propagate

阐明　**ch'ǎn-míng** to explain, expound, elucidate, define; an explanation

阐述　**ch'ǎn-shù** to expound, explain [doctrine, etc.]

370　铲除　**ch'ǎn-ch'ú** to dig out, uproot, eradicate, abolish

铲式挖泥机　**ch'ǎn-shìh wā-ní-chī** a dipper dredge

铲土机　**ch'ǎn-t'ǔ-chī** a soil scraper, power shovel

ch'āng (chāng)

371　猖獗　**ch'āng-chüéh** to run wild; unbridled, on the rampage

猖狂　**ch'āng-k'uáng** unrestrained, defiant, ferocious; rash, reckless

猖狂进攻　**ch'āng-k'uáng-chìn-kūng** a savage onslaught, ferocious attack

ch'áng (cháng)

372　长征　**ch'áng-chēng** (1) a long march (any feat of endurance and courage in serving the revolution; (2) The Long March [from Kiangsi to Shensi in 1934–35]

长征干部　**ch'áng-chēng-kàn-pù** Long March cadres (i.e., Party members who were on the Long March of 1934–35)

长江大桥　**ch'áng-chiāng tà-ch'iáo** a Yangtze River bridge (one at Wuhan, the other at Nanking)

长江天堑　**ch'áng-chiāng-t'iēn-ch'ièn** the Yangtze River is Heaven's moat (a natural strategic barrier)

长治久安　**ch'áng-chìh-chiǔ-ān** lasting peace and order, a long period of prosperity

长期性　**ch'áng-ch'ī-hsìng** long-term, lasting nature

长期共存, 互相监督　**ch'áng-ch'ī-kùng-ts'ún, hù-hsiāng-chiēn-tū** long-term coexistence and mutual supervision (a promise first made to democratic parties in 1949 at the People's Political Consultative Conference)

长处　**ch'áng-ch'ù** a strong point, forte

长驱直入　**ch'áng-ch'ǔ-chíh-jù** to push deeply into (originally military)

长工　**ch'áng-kūng** hired hand, permanent [as opposed to seasonal] worker (pre-1949, usually rural)

长工屋　**ch'áng-kūng-wù** a shed for the

hired hands

长年互助组 **ch'áng-nién hù-chù-tsǔ** a long-term mutual-aid team

长篇大论 **ch'áng-p'iēn-tà-lùn** a long and ponderous article, tedious talk

长大铁路 **ch'áng-tà t'iĕh-lù** the Changchun-Dairen railroad

长吨 **ch'áng-tūn** a long ton (2240 pounds or 1016 kilograms)

长藤结瓜 **ch'áng-t'éng-chiéh-kuā** a long vine produces [many] melons

长足进展 **ch'áng-tsú-chìn-chǎn** to advance by long strides, great or rapid progress

长远打算 **ch'áng-yuǎn-tǎ-suàn** a long-range plan or project

长 **ch'áng**: *see also* **chǎng**

374 肠衣 **ch'áng-ī** casings (hog or sheep intestines)

375 尝试 **ch'áng-shìh** an attempt; to try something

376 偿还 **ch'áng-huán** to repay, compensate, refund, make reparation

377 常见病 **ch'áng-chièn-pìng** a common disease

常住性 **ch'áng-chù-hsìng** constancy, invariability

常会 **ch'áng-huì** a regular meeting

常任理事 **ch'áng-jèn-lǐ-shìh** a permanent [council or committee] member

常规 **ch'áng-kuēi** regular practice, normal, conventional

常规战争 **ch'áng-kuēi-chàn-chēng** conventional war

常备军 **ch'áng-pèi-chǔn** standing army, a ready force

常备不懈 **ch'áng-pèi-pù-hsièh** ever vigilant

常批常新 **ch'áng-p'ī-ch'áng-hsīn** constant criticism [and] constant renewal

常设机关 **ch'áng-shè-chī-kuān** a permanent agency, standing organization

常识 **ch'áng-shíh** common sense; common knowledge, elementary knowledge

常数 **ch'áng-shù** a constant number, a constant [mathematics]

常态 **ch'áng-t'ài** normal pace, usual condition

常委 **ch'áng-wěi** a member of a standing committee (contraction of **ch'áng-wù-wěi-yúan**)

常委会 **ch'áng-wěi-huì** a standing committee (contraction of **ch'áng-wù wěi-yuán-hùi**)

常务委员 **ch'áng-wù-wěi-yuán** member of a standing committee

常务委员会 **ch'áng-wù wěi-yuán-huì** a standing committee

ch'ǎng (chǎng)

378 厂长 **ch'ǎng-chǎng** a factory head

厂际竞赛 **ch'ǎng-chì-chìng-sài** interfactory competition (usually in production)

厂际协作 **ch'ǎng-chì-hsiéh-tsò** interfactory coordination

厂前区 **ch'ǎng-ch'ién-ch'ü** factory frontage (the area in front of a factory, including gate, watchman's shed, administration building, and other structures—where wasteful arrangement is likely to draw criticism)

厂房 **ch'ǎng-fáng** factory building

厂校挂钩 **ch'ǎng-hsiào-kuà-kōu** to link the schools with the factories

厂矿 **ch'ǎng-k'uàng** factories and mines (basic industry)

厂龄 **ch'ǎng-líng** years of service in a factory, seniority in a plant

厂社挂钩 **ch'ǎng-shè-kuà-kōu** to link factories and communes; factory-commune linkage

厂史 **ch'ǎng-shǐh** factory history (one of the **szǔ-shǐh**)

厂带专业 **ch'ǎng-tài-chuān-yèh** the factory guides specialization (in developing its fields of vocational instruction, the school should be guided by the needs of the factory)

厂地 **ch'ǎng-tì** factory site

379 场合 **ch'ǎng-hó** circumstances; a situation, occasion

ch'àng (chàng)

380 畅销 **ch'àng-hsiāo** to sell like wildfire; brisk sales

畅行无阻 **ch'àng-hsíng-wú-tsǔ** to go on smoothly without obstruction

畅观楼事件 **ch'àng-kuān-lóu shìh-chièn** the Changkuanlou incident (an alleged plot by P'eng Chen in 1961 to overthrow Mao Tse-tung; so called because the plotters met at the Changkuanlou in the Peking Zoo)

畅所欲言 **ch'àng-sŏ-yù-yén** to speak freely

畅谈 **ch'àng-t'án** to have delightful talk together, talk without restraint

畅通 **ch'àng-t'ūng** unimpeded and through [travel or communications]

381 倡议 **ch'àng-ì** to advocate, propose, initiate

倡导 **ch'àng-tǎo** initiative and gui-

dance; to initiate, lead

382 唱腔 **ch'àng-ch'iāng** singing style (in Peking opera)

唱反派 **ch'àng-fǎn-p'ài** to play a contrary role (from Peking opera and indicates a character playing a foil to the hero. Present use is: to express opinions contrary to the official line)

唱反调 **ch'àng-fǎn-tiào** to sing a different tune (to express opposite opinions—similar to above)

唱和 **ch'àng-hò** to respond in singing, to exchange poems (to echo)

唱先进 **ch'àng-hsiēn-chìn** to sing of advanced people (in contrast to the old Peking opera which celebrated kings and characters of the feudal past, the new Peking opera is to sing of new heroes)

唱高调 **ch'àng-kāo-tiào** to sing in a high pitch (high-flown but impractical talk)

唱对台戏 **ch'àng-tuì-t'ái-hsì** to put on a rival show

唱词 **ch'àng-tz'ú** words of a song or opera

ch'āo (chāo)

383 抄袭 **ch'āo-hsí** (1) to plagiarize; (2) to outflank [the enemy]

抄送 **ch'āo-sùng** to transmit copies (to send information or duplicate copies)

384 钞票 **ch'āo-p'iào** paper money, money

385 超级警察国家 **ch'āo-chí-chǐng-ch'á kuó-chiā** an ultra police state (usually refers to the USSR)

超级核大国 **ch'āo-chí hó-tà-kuó** a nuclear superpower

超级大国 **ch'āo-chí-tà-kuó** a superpower (usually either the USSR or USA)

超阶级 **ch'āo chiēh-chí** to stand above classes; supraclass

超阶级的道德观 **ch'āo chiēh-chí te tào-té-kuān** supraclass moral view (a revisionist, bourgeois point of view)

超阶级文学 **ch'āo-chiēh-chí wén-hsuéh** supraclass literature (to be criticized)

超支 **ch'āo-chīh** excess expenditure

超支戶 **ch'āo-chīh-hù** deficit household (a household in which expenditures are above income)

超产粮 **ch'āo-ch'ǎn-liáng** surplus production of grain

超现实主义 **ch'āo-hsièn-shíh-chǔ-ì** surrealism

超然 **ch'āo-ján** aloof, detached, not involved, independent in point of view

超人一等 **ch'āo-jén-ī-těng** one grade higher than other people (thinking oneself better than others)

超「纲要」 **ch'āo kāng-yào** to surpass [the per *mu* output set by] the National Agricultural Development Program

超高温 **ch'āo-kāo-wēn** super-high temperature

超高压输电线 **ch'āo-kāo-yā shū-tièn-hsièn** ultra high-tension transmission line

超过 **ch'āo-kuò** to exceed, surpass, overtake

超龄团员 **ch'āo-líng-t'uán-yuán** over-aged [Youth] League members

超额 **ch'āo-ó** to exceed a quota, overfulfill a norm; above norm, above quota

超额积累 **ch'āo-ó-chī-lěi** accumulation above the norm (of a factory's sales, a relatively large percentage of which may be retained as profits)

超额利润 **ch'āo-ó-lì-jùn** profit in excess of the plan

超额完成 **ch'āo-ó-wán-ch'éng** to overfulfill a quota, surpass a commitment

超包产 **ch'āo-pāo-ch'ǎn** to overfulfill a production target

超短波 **ch'āo-tuǎn-pō** ultra shortwave

超天才 **ch'āo-t'iēn-ts'ái** an outstanding genius

超音波 **ch'āo-yīn-pō** supersonic waves

超音速 **ch'āo-yīn-sù** supersonic speed

超音速飞机 **ch'āo-yīn-sù fēi-chī** supersonic aircraft

超英赶美 **ch'āo-yīng kǎn-měi** surpass England [and] catch up with America (a slogan of the Great Leap Forward)

超越 **ch'āo-yuèh** to exceed, surpass, surpassing

ch'áo (cháo)

386 巢穴 **cháo-hsuèh** a lair, den, hiding place

387 朝鲜 **ch'áo-hsiēn** Korea

朝鲜劳动党 **ch'áo-hsiēn láo-tùng-tǎng** Korean Workers' Party [North Korea]

朝鲜停战协定 **ch'áo-hsiēn t'íng-chàn hsiéh-tìng** Korean Military Armistice Agreement (July 27, 1953)

朝鲜族 **ch'áo-hsiēn-tsú** the Korean people (a minority in Liaoning, Kirin, and Heilungkiang provinces: population 1,255,000 as of 1957)

朝野 **ch'áo-yěh** those in power and out

of power (now may refer to the government and the people)

朝 **ch'áo:** *see also* **chāo**

388 潮流 **ch'áo-líu** tide, current, trend, (now often has political connotations)

潮头 **ch'áo-t'óu** the crest of a wave (the crucial moment)

389 嘲笑 **ch'áo-hsiào** to ridicule; ridicule

ch'ē (chē)

390 车技 **ch'ē-chì** trick-cycling, stunting on a bicycle

车间 **ch'ē-chiēn** an operational unit in a factory, workshop, shop, machine shop

车间主任 **ch'ē-chiēn-chǔ-jèn** workshop director, the head of a factory sub-unit, shop head

车床 **ch'ē-ch'uáng** a lathe, a machine tool

车厢 **ch'ē-hsiāng** the interior of a railway coach or freight car

车工 **ch'ē-kūng** a lathe operator

车马店 **ch'ē-mǎ-tièn** a country inn (in North China)

ch'ě (chě)

391 扯后腿 **ch'ě-hòu-t'uǐ** to pull the hind leg (to obstruct, to hinder)

扯不上 **ch'ě-pū-shàng** cannot reach to, unconnected, irrelevant

ch'è (chè)

392 彻底 **ch'è-tǐ** thorough, complete, exhaustive; fully

彻底解放社会生产力 **ch'è-tǐ-chiěh-fàng shè-huì-shēng-ch'ǎn-lì** to release fully the productive force of society

彻底决裂 **ch'è-tǐ chuéh-lièh** a complete severance, thorough separation

彻底消灭 **ch'è-tǐ hsiāo-mièh** to uproot, utterly destroy

彻底革命精神 **ch'è-tǐ kó-mìng-chīng-shén** a spirit of thorough revolution

彻底变化 **ch'è-tǐ-pièn-huà** radical change, fundamental transformation

彻底破产 **ch'ù-tǐ-p'ò-ch'ǎn** complete bankruptcy

彻底扫盲 **ch'è-tǐ sǎo-máng** to thoroughly wipe out illiteracy

彻头彻尾 **ch'è-t'óu ch'è-wěi** from head to tail, from beginning to end (thoroughly, to the core)

彻夜不眠 **ch'è-yèh-pù-mién** to stay up all night, keep vigil

393 撤职 **ch'è-chíh** dismissal from job (a non-legal sanction)

撤军 **ch'è-chūn** to withdraw troops

撤换 **ch'è-huàn** to replace, call back and replace

撤回 **ch'è-huí** to withdraw, take back

撤销 **ch'è-hsiāo** to nullify, revoke, abrogate, cancel, repeal, remove, eliminate

撤退 **ch'è-t'uì** to withdraw, evacuate, retreat, remove; evacuation

ch'én (chén)

394 陈旧 **ch'én-chìu** stale, old-fashioned, out-dated, obsolete

陈腔滥调 **ch'én-ch'iāng-làn-tiào** hackneyed tunes and stale melodies (cliches and stock arguments, worn-out allegations)

陈腐 **ch'én-fǔ** old and worthless (antiquated, stale, outworn)

陈货 **ch'én-huò** stale goods (often figurative)

陈规陋俗 **ch'én-kuēi-lòu-sú** out-dated regulations and bad customs

陈列 **ch'én-lièh** to arrange, exhibit, display

陈年账簿 **ch'én-nién chàng-pù** account books of past years (old and useless data; a lack of creative thinking)

陈年老规矩 **ch'én-nién lǎo-kuēi-chü** out-dated regulations

陈述 **ch'én-shù** to explain, recount, give an account of

陈粟大军 **ch'én-sù tà-chün** the PLA Third Field Army (led by Ch'en Yi and Su Yü during the civil war)

陈独秀 **ch'én tú-hsìu** Ch'en Tu-hsiu (1879–1942: a founder and the first General Secretary of the CCP)

陈永贵 **ch'én yǔng-kuèi** Ch'en Yung-kuei (the peasant leader of the famous Tachai Production Brigade in Shansi)

395 沉着应战 **ch'én-chó-yìng-chàn** cool in meeting battle (often figurative)

沉重打击 **ch'én-chùng-tǎ-chī** a heavy blow

沉船 **ch'én-ch'uan** a sunken ship, shipwreck; to scuttle a ship

沉默 **ch'én-mò** silent, quiet, reticent; silence

沉思 **ch'én-szū** to contemplate, ponder, reflect deeply

沉得住气 **ch'én-te-chù-ch'ì** able to remain calm under pressure, self-composed

沉痛 **ch'én-t'ùng** extremely painful, sad, tragic

ch'èn (chèn)

396 衬托 **ch'èn-t'ō** to show indirectly, set off, enhance, serve for contrast

397 称职 **ch'èn-chíh** up to the requirements of the post

称心如愿 **ch'èn-hsīn-jú-yuàn** just as one wishes

称 **ch'èn**: *see also* **ch'ēng**

398 趁机会 **ch'èn chī-huì** to seize the opportunity

趁火打劫 **ch'èn-huǒ tǎ-chiéh** to use [the occasion of] a fire in order to plunder (taking advantage of another's trouble)

趁热打铁 **ch'èn-jè-tǎ-tiěh** strike while the iron is hot

ch'ēng (chēng)

399 称号 **ch'ēng-hào** title, style, designation

称孤道寡 **ch'ēng-kū-tào-kǔa** to call oneself king (to claim the prerogatives of greatness)

称霸世界 **ch'ēng-pà-shìh-chìeh** to claim world hegemony

称颂 **ch'ēng-sùng** to pay tribute to, laud, praise

称赞 **ch'ēng-tsàn** to praise, commend, extol

称王称霸 **ch'ēng-wáng-ch'ēng-pà** to declare oneself king or despot (to lord it over others)

称 **ch'ēng**: *see also* **ch'èn**

400 撑腰打气 **ch'ēng-yāo-tǎ-ch'ì** to prop up the waist and inflate (to boost someone—generally with an unfavorable connotation)

ch'éng (chéng)

401 成长 **ch'éng-chǎng** growth, development

成绩 **ch'éng-chī** accomplishment, achievement, results; scholastic record

成见 **ch'éng-chièn** prejudice, bias, preconceived ideas

成就 **ch'éng-chiù** accomplishment, attainment, results, progress made

成器 **ch'éng-ch'ì** to amount to something [of a person], to accomplish something worthwhile

成千上万 **ch'éng-ch'iēn-shàng-wàn** thousands upon thousands, myriads

成群结队 **ch'éng-ch'ún-chiéh-tuì** [as if] in hordes and armies (large numbers)

成分 **ch'éng-fèn** (1) status, personal background, class characteristics; (2) element, constituent, component part, factor

成分论 **ch'éng-fèn-lùn** the doctrine of family background (emphasis on class background)

成分不纯 **ch'éng-fèn-pù-ch'ún** impurity in class composition

成效 **ch'éng-hsiào** positive result, success

成性 **ch'éng-hsìng** having the characteristics of; to become second nature

成人教育 **ch'éng-jén-chiào-yù** adult education

成规旧习 **ch'éng-kuēi-chiù-hsí** conventional criteria and old habits

成果 **ch'éng-kuǒ** fruits (results, achievement)

成昆铁路 **ch'éng-k'ūn t'iěh-lù** the railway from Chengtu [Szechwan] to Kunming [Yunnan]

成立 **ch'éng-lì** to found, establish, set up, erect

成龙配套 **ch'éng-lúng-p'ei-t'ào** to complete a dragon and match up a set (fit together [a machine, etc.], to make a whole)

成名成家 **ch'éng-míng-ch'éng-chiā** to become famous and an authority

成名成家，升官发财的阶梯 **ch'éng-míng-ch'éng-chiā shēng-kuān fā-ts'ái te chiēh-t'ī** becoming famous and an expert is the ladder to official position and riches (criticism of selfish ambition)

成败 **ch'éng-pài** success or failure (outcome)

成本 **ch'éng-pěn** cost, production costs

成批制造 **ch'éng-p'ī-chìh-tsào** to manufacture in large quantities

成片造林 **ch'éng-p'ièn tsào-lín** afforestation in a big area

成品 **ch'éng-p'ǐn** product, finished product

成熟 **ch'éng-shú** to mature, ripen, become fully developed

成都部队 **ch'éng-tū pù-tuì** Chengtu Military Forces [of the PLA] (formerly the Chengtu Military Region)

成套 **ch'éng-t'ào** a complete set; to form a whole; systematic

成套设备 **ch'éng-t'ào-shè-pèi** a complete set of equipment

成为泡影 **ch'éng-wéi-p'ào-yǐng** to become a bubble and shadow (complete failure, all comes to naught)

成文法 **ch'éng-wén-fǎ** written law, a statute

成药 **ch'éng-yào** patent medicine
成语 **ch'éng-yǔ** a phrase, idiom, set expression
成渝铁路 **ch'éng-yù t'iěh-lù** Chengtu-Chungking railroad
成员 **ch'éng-yuán** a member, constituent member [of a team or party, etc.]
成员国 **ch'éng-yuán-kuó** a member state

402 呈现 **ch'éng-hsièn** to manifest, reveal, show
呈递国书 **ch'éng-tì kuó-shū** to present [diplomatic] credentials

403 诚心诚意 **ch'éng-hsīn-ch'éng-ì** sincere in heart and intention, sincerely; sincerity
诚恳 **ch'éng-k'ěn** sincere, cordial
诚实 **ch'éng-shíh** honest; honesty

404 承袭 **ch'éng-hsí** to inherit
承认 **ch'éng-jèn** to recognize, admit, concede, confess to
承上启下 **ch'éng-shàng-ch'ǐ-hsià** to inherit from the past and open up the future; to receive [orders] from above and inform those below (to function at an intermediate level)
承担义务 **ch'éng-tān-ì-wù** to assume an obligation, commit oneself, accept responsibility

405 城镇 **ch'éng-chèn** cities and towns
城郊 **ch'éng-chiāo** suburbs
城乡 **ch'éng-hsīang** city and countryside, urban and rural
城乡交流 **ch'éng-hsīang-chiāo-líu** exchange [of goods] between city and village, urban-rural circulation
城乡结合 **ch'éng-hsīang-chiéh-hó** the integration of cities and countryside, urban and rural coordination
城乡兼顾 **ch'éng-hsīang-chiēn-kù** attention [must be given] to both city and countryside
城乡差异 **ch'éng-hsīang-ch'ā-ì** the differences between city and village, urban-rural differences
城乡互助 **ch'éng-hsīang-hù-chù** mutual aid between the cities and the countryside
城乡对立 **ch'éng-hsīang-tuì-lì** contrasts between town and country
城乡物资交流 **ch'éng-hsīang wù-tzū-chiāo-líu** exchange of goods between the city and the countryside
城市建设 **ch'éng-shìh-chièn-shè** municipal construction, urban development
城市小资产阶级 **ch'éng-shìh hsiǎo-tzū-ch'ǎn-chiēh-chí** urban petty bourgeoisie

城市人民公社 **ch'éng-shìh jén-mín-kūng-shè** urban commune
城市规划 **ch'éng-shìh-kuēi-huà** city planning
城市老爷卫生部 **ch'éng-shìh lǎo-yéh wèi-shēng-pù** the ministry of public health for urban lords (a criticism of public health neglect of the countryside)
城市民兵 **ch'éng-shìh-mín-pīng** urban militia
城市贫民 **ch'éng-shìh-p'ín-mín** the city poor, urban poor
城市卫生 **ch'éng-shìh-wèi-shēng** urban public health

406 乘机 **ch'éng-chī** to take advantage of an opportunity, take the chance
乘其不备 **ch'éng-ch'í-pù-pèi** to take advantage of a person's lack of preparation
乘风破浪 **ch'éng-fēng-p'ò-làng** to ride the wind and break the waves (to advance bravely)
乘虚而入 **ch'éng-hsū-érh-jù** to penetrate when [the enemy] is unguarded (to take advantage of another's lack of preparation)
乘人之危 **ch'éng-jén-chīh-wēi** to take advantage of another's critical situation
乘凉阅览处 **ch'éng-liáng yuèh-lǎn-ch'ù** enjoy-the-cool reading places (organized by lane committees)
乘胜前进 **ch'éng-shèng-ch'ién-chìn** to use victory for a continued advance (one success is a foundation for further successes)
乘势 **ch'éng-shìh** to exploit circumstances, make use of a situation (strike while the iron is hot)
乘务员 **ch'éng-wù-yuán** a train attendant
乘 **ch'éng**: *see also* **shèng**

407 惩治 **ch'éng-chìh** punishment; to punish, correct, suppress
惩治反革命条例 **ch'éng-chìh fǎn-kó-mìng t'iáo-lì** The Act for the Suppression of Counter-revolutionaires (February 21, 1951)
惩治贪污条例 **ch'éng-chìh t'ān-wū t'iáo-lì** Act for the Suppression of Corruption (April 21, 1952)
惩前毖后 **ch'éng-ch'ién-pì-hòu** to take warning from the past to be more careful for the future (learn from past mistakes)
惩罚 **ch'éng-fá** punishment, correction; to punish
惩办 **ch'éng pàn** to punish, deal severely with; punishment

惩办主义 **ch'éng-pàn-chǔ-ì** punitivism (contrary to the correct method of persuasion and education)

惩办和宽大相结合 **ch'éng-pàn hó k'uān-tà hsiāng-chiéh-hó** to combine punishment with leniency

408 程序 **ch'éng-hsù** order, sequence, procedure, channels, process

程式 **ch'éng-shìh** formula, form (used in the theater to refer to stage conventions); equation

程度 **ch'éng-tù** degree, level, extent

409 澄清 **ch'éng-ch'īng** to clarify, cleanse, purify

ch'ĕng (chěng)

410 逞强 **ch'ĕng-ch'iáng** to demonstrate power (to bully, rely on brute force)

ch'ī (qī)

411 七·七事变 **ch'ī-ch'ī-shìh-pièn** the Double Seven incident (the Marco Polo Bridge incident of July 7, 1937 —the start of the Sino-Japanese War)

七·二一指示 **ch'ī-èrh-ī chǐh-shìh** the July 21 directive (Mao Tse-tung's 1968 directive on the revolution of of education)

七沟八梁 **ch'ī-kōu-pā-liáng** seven gulleys and eight ridges (the heavily eroded loess country)

七类分子 **ch'ī-lèi fèn-tzǔ** the seven categories [of bad] elements (landlords, rich peasants, counter-revolutionaries, rightists, bad elements, bourgeoisie, and black gangsters [the last two were added during the Cultural Revolution])

七零八落 **ch'ī-líng-pā-lò** seven scatters and eight falls (in a state of utter confusion)

七拼八凑 **ch'ī-p'īn-pā-ts'òu** to scrape together, rig up, assemble together by hook or by crook

七十年代 **ch'ī-shíh-nién-tài** the seventh decade of any century (the 70s)

七手八脚 **ch'ī-shǒu-pā-chiǎo** seven hands and eight feet (in great haste, helter-skelter)

七嘴八舌 **ch'ī-tsǔi-pā-shé** seven mouths [and] eight tongues (many diverse opinions)

412 妻离子散 **ch'ī-lí-tzǔ-sàn** wife gone and children scattered (to break up families)

413 欺诈取胜 **ch'ī-chà-ch'ǔ-shèng** to achieve victory by fraud

欺负 **ch'ī-fu** to bully, browbeat, humiliate, take advantage of

欺人之谈 **ch'ī-jén-chīh-t'án** cheating, insincere talk, double-talk

欺软怕硬 **ch'ī-juǎn-p'à-yìng** to browbeat the weak but fear the strong (to be a bully)

欺骗 **ch'ī-p'ièn** deception, fraud; to cheat, swindle, impose on someone

欺压 **ch'ī-yā** to bully, browbeat; overbearing, high-handed behavior

414 期终考试 **chī-chūng-k'ǎo-shìh** a term-end [final] examination

期汇交易 **ch'ī-huì chiāo-ì** trade conducted on the basis of deferred payment

期限 **ch'ī-hsièn** a fixed period, time limit, term, deadline

期刊 **ch'ī-k'ān** a periodical, journal, serial publication

期满 **ch'ī-mǎn** expiration of a time or term; the deadline has passed

期待 **ch'ī-tài** to expect, anticipate, hope for

415 漆黑一团 **ch'ī-hēi-ī-t'uán** all is pitch dark (usually metaphorical)

ch'í (qí)

416 齐心协力 **ch'í-hsīn-hsiéh-lì** united in heart and strength (to work together wholeheartedly)

齐步前进 **ch'í-pù-ch'ién-chìn** to march forward in step, keep pace with

齐声高唱 **ch'í-shēng-kāo-ch'àng** to sing loudly in unison

齐动手 **ch'í-tùng-shǒu** everyone moves [his] hand (to work together)

齐头并进 **ch'í-t'óu-pìng-chìn** to advance side-by-side (to do many things simultaneously)

417 奇计 **ch'í-chì** a surprising stratagem, an ingenious plan

奇迹 **ch'í-chī** a miracle, a wonder

奇缺 **ch'í-ch'üēh** an acute shortage

奇袭白虎团 **ch'í-hsí pái-hǔ-t'uán** "Raid on the White-Tiger Regiment" (one of the **yàng-pǎn-hsì**)

奇功 **ch'í-kūng** distinguished service, meritorious achievement

奇谈怪论 **ch'í-t'án-kuài-lùn** strange talk (preposterous arguments)

418 歧视 **ch'í-shìh** to discriminate against; discriminating

歧途 **ch'í-t'ú** a fork in the road, a wrong road (usually figurative)

419 其势汹汹 **ch'í-shìh-hsiūng-hsiūng** bluster, blusterous

420 崎岖 **ch'í-ch'ū** uneven, rough, rugged [terrain]; to have difficulties on the way

421 骑墙派 **ch'í-ch'iáng-p'ài** those riding on
the wall (fence straddlers)
骑虎难下 **ch'í-hǔ-nán-hsià** when riding
the tiger it is difficult to dismount (a
situation which one is powerless to
leave)
骑兵 **ch'í-pīng** cavalry
骑在头上 **ch'í tsài t'óu-shang** riding on
the backs of (to oppress)

422 旗舰 **ch'í-chièn** a flagship [naval]
旗帜 **ch'í-chìh** banner, flag, standard
旗鼓相当 **ch'í-kǔ-hsiāng-tāng** flags and
drums standing opposite (evenly
matched in strength or influence)
旗开得胜 **ch'í-k'āi-té-shèng** to win
victory as soon as one's banner is
displayed (quick success)
旗手 **ch'í-shǒu** a flag carrier, standard
bearer
旗委 **ch'í-wěi** the Party committee of a
Mongol banner (equivalent to a
hsien committee)

ch'ǐ (qǐ)

423 乞求 **ch'ǐ-ch'iú** to beg, plead, implore
乞灵于 **ch'ǐ-líng-yú** to seek help from
(usually implying that one is helpless)
乞讨度日 **ch'ǐ-t'ǎo-tù-jìh** to depend on
alms for a living

424 企图 **ch'ǐ-t'ú** to attempt, try; an
attempt
企图复辟 **ch'ǐ-t'ú-fù-p'ì** to seek a
restoration (originally, restoration of
a dynasty or monarchy; now, may
refer to anything old or considered
bad)
企业 **ch'ǐ-yèh** an undertaking, enterprise (usually industrial or manufacturing)
企业家 **ch'ǐ-yèh-chiā** an entrepreneur,
industrialist
企业奖励基金 **ch'ǐ-yèh-chiǎng-lì chī-
chīn** funds allocated by the government to enterprises for meritorious
work
企业化 **ch'ǐ-yèh-huà** "enterprization"
(transforming simple, basic units into
larger, more modern operations)
企业下放 **ch'ǐ-yèh-hsià-fàng** the
transfer of enterprises to lower levels
(part of the process of decentralization: e.g., enterprises administered by
the central government being transferred to provincial or municipal
control)
企业会计 **ch'ǐ-yèh-k'uài-chì** (1) enterprise accounting; (2) a Peking semi-
monthly journal, 1952—
企业定型论 **ch'ǐ-yèh-tìng-hsíng lùn** the
theory that enterprises have a fixed
pattern (a line to be criticized)
企业自治 **ch'ǐ-yèh-tzù-chìh** enterprise
autonomy

425 启发 **ch'ǐ-fā** to enlighten, inspire,
arouse, give an impulse to; inspiration
启蒙时期 **ch'ǐ-méng-shíh-ch'ī** period of
enlightenment [in Europe]
启蒙运动 **ch'ǐ-méng-yùn-tùng** a movement of enlightenment (may refer to
periods such as the May 4th
Movement)
启示 **ch'ǐ-shìh** to enlighten, reveal;
revelation

426 起家 **ch'ǐ-chiā** to build up a fortune,
become prominent
起劲 **ch'ǐ-chìn** high-spirited, elated,
energetic
起重机 **ch'ǐ-chùng-chī** a crane, hoist,
derrick
起飞 **ch'ǐ-fēi** aircraft takeoff, departure; a flying start, a leap
起伏 **ch'ǐ-fú** undulating, wavy, up and
down
起哄 **ch'ǐ-hùng** to raise a hubbub,
create a disturbance, make a noise
起义 **ch'ǐ-ì** to rebel, rise in arms;
uprising, insurrection, revolt, armed
resistance (the term implies that the
rising was a righteous one)
起义部队 **ch'ǐ-ì-pù-tuì** (1) troops
involved in a righteous rebellion;
(2) troops who turn over from the
unjust to the just side in a war (e.g.,
Nationalist troops who joined the
Communists)
起码 **ch'ǐ-mǎ** at a minimum, at the
least, lowest limit
起码资格 **ch'ǐ-mǎ-tzū-kó** minimum
qualification
起色 **ch'ǐ-sè** signs of improvement; to
get better; indications of recovery
起死回生 **ch'ǐ-szǔ-huí-shēng** to bring
back to life
起点 **ch'ǐ-tiěn** starting point, point of
departure
起早贪黑 **ch'ǐ-tsǎo-t'ān-hēi** [to work]
from dawn to dark
起作用 **ch'ǐ-tsò-yùng** to have the
function of, to have the effect of, play
a role in
起草 **ch'ǐ-ts'ǎo** to prepare a draft [in
writing]
起源 **ch'ǐ-yuán** origin, source, genesis

ch'ì (qì)

427 气急败坏 **ch'ì-chí-pài-huài** desperate
and low-spirited

气节 **ch'ì-chiéh** moral integrity

气质 **ch'ì-chìh** disposition, temperament, character, aptitude

气井 **ch'ì-chǐng** a natural gas well

气壮如牛 **ch'ì-chuàng-jú-níu** as tough as an ox

气壮山河 **ch'ì-chuàng-shān-hó** spirit as strong as mountains and rivers (the people's spirit can improve nature)

气氛 **ch'ì-fēn** atmosphere, ambience [such as of a meeting or event]

气愤 **ch'ì-fèn** angry, irate; anger

气候预报 **ch'ì-hòu-yù-pào** weather forecasts, meteorological forecasts

气息奄奄 **ch'ì-hsī-yěn-yěn** with one's life ebbing fast away

气象 **ch'ì-hsiàng** weather, climatic phenomena (often used figuratively)

气象站 **ch'ì-hsiàng-chàn** weather station (usually rural)

气象记载 **ch'ì-hsiàng-chì-tsǎi** meteorological data

气象学 **ch'ì-hsiàng-hsuéh** meteorology

气象台 **ch'ì-hsiàng-t'ái** weather station, weather observatory, climatological station (usually the main stations, in cities)

气象测报网 **ch'ì-hsiàng ts'è-pào-wǎng** weather reporting network

气象万千 **ch'ì-hsiàng-wàn-ch'iēn** outward appearances change in countless [auspicious ways]

气象预报 **ch'ì-hsiàng-yù-pào** weather forecast

气概 **ch'ì-kài** bearing, manner, spirit (generally with the sense being impressive—a "heroic" bearing)

气功疗法 **ch'ì-kūng-liáo-fǎ** treatment through breath control and the use of one's inner strength

气量狭小 **ch'ì-liàng-hsiá-hsiǎo** narrow-minded, intolerant

气魄 **ch'ì-p'ò** spirit, soul, moral force

气势汹汹 **ch'ì-shìh-hsīung-hsīung** overbearing in attitude; truculently, savagely

气势磅礴 **ch'ì-shìh-p'áng-pò** great vitality

气体 **ch'ì-t'ǐ** gaseous state

气田 **ch'ì-t'ién** a natural gas field

气味 **ch'ì-wèi** flavor, taste, savor; odor, smell

气焰嚣张 **ch'ì-yèn-hsiāo-chāng** blazing unrestrainedly (overweening pride)

428 汽车制造业 **ch'ì-ch'ē chìh-tsào-yèh** motor-car industry

汽车队 **ch'ì-ch'ē-tuì** a convoy of trucks, motorcade

汽车外胎 **ch'ì-ch'ē-wài-t'āi** motor vehicle tires

汽船 **ch'ì-ch'úan** a motor boat, motor vessel

汽缸 **ch'ì-kāng** a cylinder

汽轮机 **ch'ì-lún-chī** steam turbine

汽笛 **ch'ì-tí** steam whistle, siren

汽艇 **ch'ì-t'ǐng** a power launch

汽压计 **ch'ì-yā-chì** a steam pressure gauge

汽油 **ch'ì-yú** gasoline

汽油弹 **ch'ì-yú-tàn** gasoline bomb, napalm bomb

429 奔暗投明 **ch'ì-àn-t'óu-míng** forsaking darkness [and] crossing over to the brightness (usually in a political sense—"joining the correct side")

弃旧图新 **ch'ì-chìu-t'ú-hsīn** to abandon the old for the new (to start afresh)

弃权 **ch'ì-ch'úan** to waive rights, abstain, relinquish

弃农经商 **ch'ì-núng-chīng-shāng** abandoning agriculture to take up commerce

430 契约 **ch'ì-yuēh** a contract (an old term)

431 砌墙 **ch'ì-ch'iáng** to build a wall (to isolate oneself)

砌石工程 **ch'ì-shíh-kūng-ch'éng** stone masonry work

432 器质性疾病 **ch'ì-chìh-hsìng chí-pìng** organic diseases

器械 **ch'ì-hsièh** apparatus, tools, equipment

器官 **ch'ì-kuān** sensory organs

器材 **ch'ì-ts'ái** equipment, materials and equipment

器材储备 **ch'ì-ts'ái-ch'ǔ-pèi** stock of equipment; stockpiling of equipment and materials

器乐 **ch'ì-yuèh** instrumental music

ch'iă (qiǎ)

433 卡介苗注射 **ch'iǎ-chièh-miáo chù-shè** anti-tuberculosis inoculation

卡路里 **ch'iǎ-lù-lǐ** a calory

卡宾枪 **ch'iǎ-pīn-ch'iāng** a carbine [rifle]

卡脖子 **ch'iǎ-pó-tzu** to seize by the neck, choke, throttle

卡达尔 **ch'iǎ-tá-ěrh** Kadar (the Hungarian Communist leader)

ch'ià (qià)

434 恰恰相反 **ch'ià-ch'ià-hsiāng-fǎn** just the opposite, on the contrary

恰如其分 **ch'ià-jú-ch'í-fèn** well-measured, just right, appropriate

恰当 **ch'ià-tàng** appropriately, precisely; pertinent, right [in degree or extent]

ch'iāng (qiāng)

435 羌族 **ch'iāng-tsú** the Ch'iang people (a minority in Szechwan: population 42,000 as of 1957)

436 枪杆诗 **ch'iāng-kǎn-shīh** gun-stock poetry (poetry composed by soldiers)
枪杆子里面出政权 **ch'iāng-kǎn-tzu lǐ-mièn ch'ū chèng-ch'üán** "political power grows out of gun barrels" (Mao Tse-tung, 1938)
枪口对外 **ch'iāng-k'ǒu-tuì-wài** turn the gun muzzles outward (do not fight a civil war)
枪林弹雨 **ch'iāng-lín-tàn-yǔ** a forest of rifles [and] a rain of bullets (a fierce battle)
枪毙 **ch'iāng-pì** to execute by shooting
枪托 **ch'iāng-t'ō** rifle butt, gun-stock
枪眼 **ch'iāng-yěn** firing slit, loophole through which a weapon can be discharged; a gun muzzle

437 腔调 **ch'iāng-tiào** (1) tune, melody; (2) tone of voice, accent

ch'iáng (qiáng)

438 强奸 **ch'iáng-chiēn** to rape, violate (often used abstractly)
强中有弱、弱中有强 **ch'iáng-chūng-yǔ-jò, jò-chūng-yǔ-ch'iáng** in strength there is also weakness: in weakness there is also strength (for example: every nation has its shortcomings, but even the weakest is not without hope)
强权政治 **ch'iáng-ch'üán-chèng-chìh** power politics
强化 **ch'iáng-huà** to strengthen
强项 **ch'iáng-hsiàng** strong and unbending (resolute, inflexible)
强弱搭配 **ch'iáng-jò-tā-p'eì** to pair the strong with the weak (to balance the strong and weak members—as in administrative reorganizations)
强攻硬上 **ch'iáng-kūng-yìng-shàng** to make a strong frontal attack and press resolutely forward (to push ahead despite difficulties)
强烈 **ch'iáng-lièh** strong, ardent, lively, keen
强烈对照 **ch'iáng-lièh-tuì-chào** to contrast sharply with
强烈愿望 **ch'iáng-lièh-yuàn-wàng** strong desire, fervent hope
强暴 **ch'iáng-pào** brutal, overbearing, ruthless; brute force
强盛 **ch'iáng-shèng** powerful and rich, strong and prosperous
强大 **ch'iáng-tà** strong and large (powerful)

强盗行为 **ch'iáng-tào-hsíng-wéi** a piratical act
强盗逻辑 **ch'iáng-tào-ló-chì** gangster logic, gun law, law of the jungle
强敌 **ch'iáng-tí** a formidable enemy
强调 **ch'iáng-tiào** to indicate accent [in music], stress, emphasize
强度 **ch'iáng-tù** degree of intensity
强有力 **ch'iáng-yǔ-lì** strong, vigorous, robust
强 **ch'iáng:** see also ch'iǎng

439 墙报 **ch'iáng-pào** a wall newspaper
墙上画饼好看不好吃 **ch'iáng-shang huà-pǐng hǎo-k'àn pù-hǎo-ch'īh** a cake painted on the wall is good to look at but not to eat (things without substance are useless)

ch'iǎng (qiǎng)

440 抢劫 **ch'iǎng-chiéh** to rob, plunder, loot
抢救 **ch'iǎng-chiù** to rush to the rescue
抢种 **ch'iǎng-chùng** to seize the right time for planting crops
抢险队 **ch'iǎng-hsiěn-tuì** a team for the most dangerous work, a rescue team
抢修险工 **ch'iǎng-hsiū-hsiěn-kūng** rush repair work on danger points
抢购 **ch'iǎng-kòu** "snatch buying" (rushing to buy wholesale supplies before state authorities can; panic buying in fear of shortages)
抢墒 **ch'iǎng-shāng** to seize moisture (to rush planting while the soil moisture content is adequate)
抢时间 **ch'iǎng-shíh-chiēn** fighting [against] time (to strive for the early completion of a task)
抢收 **ch'iǎng-shōu** to rush a harvest
抢收抢种 **ch'iǎng-shōu-ch'iǎng-chùng** to rush a harvest so the next crop can be planted in time
抢点 **ch'iǎng-tiěn** to make up time [in order to keep on schedule]
抢吨位超负荷 **ch'iǎng-tūn-wèi ch'āo-fù-hò** competing for tonnage to exceed the quota (the implication is that by competing for heavy goods in order to fulfill the quota, the longshoremen slight other types of cargo and neglect aspects such as safety)
抢在先 **ch'iǎng-tsài-hsiēn** to struggle to be first

441 强占 **ch'iǎng-chàn** to occupy or appropriate by force
强加于人 **ch'iǎng-chiā-yú-jén** to impose on others
强制劳动 **ch'iǎng-chìh-láo-tùng** forced

labor

强制保险 **ch'iǎng-chìh-pǎo-hsiěn** mandatory insurance (for many kinds of transactions; may also be a minor kind of turnover tax)

强制兵役 **ch'iǎng-chìh-pīng-ì** military conscription

强制手段 **ch'iǎng-chìh-shǒu-tuàn** compulsory administrative methods

强求 **ch'iǎng-ch'íu** to seek strenuously, insist on getting

强取豪夺 **ch'iǎng-ch'ǔ-háo-tó** rapacious, voracious

强不知以为知 **ch'iǎng-pù-chīh ǐ-wéi-chīh** to insist that one knows what one does not know (to pretend to know)

强迫 **ch'iǎng-p'ò** coercion; compulsory; to force, coerce

强迫命令 **ch'iǎng-p'ò-mìng-lìng** arbitrary orders, coercion and commandism

强渡 **ch'iǎng-tù** to cross a river by force (a river crossing opposed by the enemy)

强词夺理 **ch'iǎng-tz'ú-tó-lǐ** strained and specious argument (captious, artificial arguments)

强 **ch'iǎng**: *see also* **ch'iáng**

ch'iāo (qiāo)

442 敲诈 **ch'iāo-chà** to blackmail, extort, defraud; blackmail

敲诈勒索 **ch'iāo-chà-lè-sǒ** to blackmail and impose exactions on, extort and racketeer

敲起警钟 **ch'iāo-ch'ǐ-chǐng-chūng** to strike the alarm bell (to raise a warning)

敲响丧钟 **ch'iāo-hsiǎng-sǎng-chūng** to toll the death knell

敲骨吸髓 **ch'iāo-kǔ hsī-suǐ** break the bones and suck the marrow (to extract one's lifeblood)

敲锣打鼓 **ch'iāo-ló-tǎ-kǔ** to sound gongs and beat drums (a fanfare)

敲掠 **ch'iāo-lueh** to blackmail and plunder

敲门砖 **ch'iāo-mén-chuān** a stone for knocking at the gate (an open sesame, a means to success)

ch'iáo (qiáo)

443 乔治敦 **ch'iáo-chìh-tūn** Georgetown [British Guiana]

444 侨汇证 **ch'iáo-hui-chèng** overseas remittance card (a permit for residents of China to receive remittances from overseas Chinese

and to expend the proceeds in special shops)

侨乡 **ch'iáo-hsiāng** the native place [in China] of overseas Chinese

侨民 **ch'iáo-mín** fellow countrymen overseas; an alien resident, foreigners

侨胞 **ch'iáo-pāo** overseas [Chinese] compatriots

侨务报 **ch'iáo-wù-pào** *Bulletin of Overseas Chinese Affairs* (Peking bimonthly, 1956—)

445 荞麦 **ch'iáo-mài** buckwheat

446 桥梁作用 **ch'iáo-liáng-tsò-yùng** to function as a bridge (to serve as a link)

桥墩 **ch'iáo-tūn** bridge pier

桥头堡 **ch'iáo-t'óu-pǎo** bridge-head

447 翘首遥望 **ch'iáo-shǒu-yáo-wàng** to raise the head and look afar (to hope for eagerly, to look forward to)

翘 **ch'iáo**: *see also* **ch'iào**

ch'iǎo (qiǎo)

448 巧取豪夺 **ch'iǎo-ch'ǔ-háo-tó** to take by trick and plunder by force

巧干 **ch'iǎo-kàn** to work resourcefully

巧妙 **ch'iǎo-miào** ingenious, cunning, subtle

ch'iào (qiào)

449 俏皮话 **ch'iào-p'í-huà** a jibe, retort, witticism, clever remark; sarcasm

450 窍门 **ch'iào-mén** knack, gist, a clever [and usually easiest] way of doing something

451 翘尾巴 **ch'iào-wěi-pā** to raise the tail (to be cocky and self-satisfied)

翘 **ch'iào**: *see also* **ch'iáo**

452 撬开 **ch'iào-k'āi** to pry open

ch'iēh (qiē)

453 切削法 **ch'iēh-hsiāo-fǎ** cutting method

切煤机 **ch'iēh-méi-chī** mechanical coal cutter, cutting machine

切断 **ch'iēh-tuàn** to cut off, sever, amputate, disconnect, break apart

切 **ch'iēh**: *see also* **ch'ièh**

ch'ièh (qiě)

454 且战且退 **ch'ièh-chàn-ch'ièh-t'uì** to fight and retreat at the same time (a holding action)

ch'ièh (qiè)

455 切中要害 **ch'ièh-chùng-yào-hài** to

reach the vitals (to hit the nail on the head; pertinent, relevant)

切切实实 **ch'iĕh-ch'iĕh-shíh-shíh** practical, effective, feasible, thoroughly practical

切齿咒骂 **ch'iĕh-ch'ĭh-chòu-mà** to gnash the teeth and curse

切合时宜 **ch'iĕh-hó-shíh-í** fitting to the time (opportune, timely)

切身 **ch'iĕh-shēn** close, personal, intimate, vital to oneself

切身体会 **ch'iĕh-shēn-t'ĭ-huì** understanding or realization through personal experience

切实 **ch'iĕh-shíh** practical, actual, feasible, effective

切实可行 **ch'iĕh-shíh-k'ŏ-hsíng** practical and workable, thoroughly feasible

切题 **ch'iĕh-t'í** to be on the subject; pertinent, appropriate

切磋球艺 **ch'iĕh-ts'ō-ch'iu-ì** to cut and polish ball [playing] technique (mutual help in improving game skills)

切 **ch'iĕh**: *see also* **ch'iēh**

456 怯懦 **ch'iĕh-nò** timid, faint-hearted, cowardly

457 窃据 **ch'iĕh-chù** to usurp [office or position]

窃取 **ch'iĕh-ch'ŭ** to steal, take by stealth

窃国大盗袁世凯 **ch'iĕh-kuó tà-tào yuán shìh-k'ǎi** *Yuan Shih-k'ai, The Great Country-Stealing Robber* (title of a book by Ch'en Po-ta)

窃为私有 **ch'iĕh-wéi-szū-yŭ** to steal by treating as a personal possession (the implication is that public property or position is being converted to private gain)

ch'iēn (qiān)

458 千安培 **ch'iēn-ān-p'éi** kiloampere

千真万确 **ch'iēn-chēn-wàn-ch'üèh** a thousand [times] true and ten thousand [times] accurate (absolutely true)

千家万户 **ch'iēn-chiā-wàn-hù** thousands and tens of thousands of housholds (the people)

千斤县 **ch'iēn-chīn-hsièn** a *hsien* reaching the average output of 1,000 *chin* [500 kilograms] per *mu*

千周 **ch'iēn-chōu** kilocycle

千差万别 **ch'iēn-ch'ā-wàn-piéh** one thousand and ten thousand differences (great differences)

千秋万世 **ch'iēn-ch'iu-wàn-shìh** a thousand autumns and a myriad generations (very old, eternal)

千疮百孔 **ch'iēn-ch'uāng-pǎi-k'ŭng** one thousand boils and one hundred holes (all rotten; full of shortcomings and mistakes)

千锤百炼 **ch'iēn-ch'uí-pǎi-lièn** a thousand forgings and a hundred smeltings (well tested, to pass through a severe testing)

千钧重负 **ch'iēn-chūn-chùng-fù** a heavy load of 30,000 catties (a crushing burden)

千军万马 **ch'iēn-chūn-wàn-mǎ** a thousand soldiers and ten thousand horses (a vast number of people mobilized for a task)

千方百计 **ch'iēn-fāng-pǎi-chì** a thousand methods and a hundred plans (full of plans; to take every means possible)

千夫所指 **ch'iēn-fū-sǒ-chǐh** pointed at by a thousand men (condemned by the masses)

千伏特 **ch'iēn-fú-t'è** kilovolt

千辛万苦 **ch'iēn-hsīn-wàn-k'ŭ** a thousand hardships and ten thousand bitternesses (difficulties met and overcome in a good cause)

千难万险 **ch'iēn-nán-wàn-hsiĕn** a thousand difficulties and ten thousand dangers

千欧姆 **ch'iēn-ōu-mŭ** kiloohm

千变万化 **ch'iēn-pièn-wàn-huà** a thousand changes and myriad variations (kaleidoscopic, protean)

千篇一律 **ch'iēn-p'iēn-í-lù** a thousand volumes the same (stereotyped, monotonous, to apply a set rule to everything)

千山万崒 **ch'iēn-shān-wàn-lùng** a thousand mountains and ten thousand meadows (a vast mountainous area)

千丝万缕 **ch'iēn-szū-wàn-lŭ** thousands and tens of thousands of threads (many ramifications, very complicated relationships)

千刀万剐 **ch'iēn-tāo-wàn-kuǎ** death by a thousand slices (now only figurative)

千头万绪 **ch'iēn-t'óu-wàn-hsù** a thousand heads and ten thousand ends (very complicated, complex and difficult—usually said of a problem)

千瓦 **ch'iēn-wǎ** kilowatt

459 迁就 **ch'iēn-chiù** to appease, meet the demands of; appeasement, accomodation, compromise

迁徙 **ch'iēn-hsĭ** to change one's

residence, migrate, move away

迁移 **ch'iēn-í** to move [location]; to remove, shift

迁延 **ch'iēn-yén** to delay, procrastinate, dillydally

460　牵着鼻子走 **ch'iēn-che-pí-tzu-tsǒu** to lead [or be led] by the nose (a person of no initiative, a blind follower)

牵制 **ch'iēn-chìh** to impede, tie down, curb, check, restrain; to divert [enemy attention]

牵扯 **ch'iēn-ch'ě** to involve, drag others in

牵强附会 **ch'iēn-ch'iǎng-fù-huì** to reach a farfetched conclusion, make a forced interpretation, distort the meaning

牵线人 **ch'iēn-hsièn-jén** a string puller [the person who controls the puppet]

牵连 **ch'iēn-lién** to link, involve, implicate; involvement

牵涉 **ch'iēn-shè** to involve, be linked to, to implicate or be implicated

牵引机 **ch'iēn-yǐn-chī** haulage machine, traction machinery

461　铅字 **ch'iēn-tzù** lead type of Chinese characters

462　谦虚谨慎 **ch'iēn-hsū-chǐn-shèn** modest and cautious

谦逊谨慎 **ch'iēn-hsùn-chǐn-shèn** humble and cautious

谦让 **ch'iēn-jàng** modest and unobtrusive, self-effacing

463　签证 **ch'iēn-chèng** a passport visa, to visé [a passport]

签名运动 **ch'iēn-míng-yùn-tùng** a signature collection drive

签订 **ch'iēn-tìng** to sign [a formal instrument], to conclude [as a treaty]

签字国 **ch'iēn-tzù-kuó** signatory states

ch'ién (qián)

464　前者 **ch'ién-chě** the former

前进分子 **ch'ién-chìn-fèn-tzǔ** progressive elements (usually used to refer to the more liberal groups in other parties, such as the "progressive elements" in the Kuomintang during the Anti-Japanese War)

前景 **ch'ién-chǐng** the foreground of a painting (vista, prospect, outlook, future)

前车之鉴 **ch'ién-ch'ē-chīh-chièn** the warning of the front cart's [upset] (learn from other's mistakes)

前锋 **ch'ién-fēng** (1) vanguard, forerunner, precursor; (2) a Party journal, 1923–24

前赴后继 **ch'ién-fù-hòu-chì** [those in]

front advance [and those] behind press on

前夕 **ch'ién-hsī** the night before, on the eve

前线 **ch'ién-hsièn** (1) front line, battle line; (2) a journal of the CCP Peking branch: disgraced and closed during the Cultural Revolution

前已报导 **ch'ién-í-pào-tǎo** as already reported

前功尽弃 **ch'ién-kūng-chìn-ch'ì** to forfeit all previous achievements

前列 **ch'ién-lièh** (1) what is listed above; (2) the front row

前辈 **ch'ién-pèi** earlier generations, elders

前怕龙后怕虎 **ch'ién-p'à-lúng hòu-p'à-hǔ** to fear the dragon in front and the tiger behind (timid, overcautious)

前仆后继 **ch'ién-p'ū-hòu-chì** as those in front fall, those behind take their place (to advance wave upon wave)

前哨 **ch'ién-shào** outpost, sentry, forward patrol (originally military but now often figurative)

前哨阵地 **ch'ién-shào-chèn-tì** outpost position [military]

前身 **ch'ién-shēn** (1) a previous incarnation; (2) the precursor of an organization

前十条 **ch'ién-shíh-t'iáo** the First Ten Points (issued by the Central Committee in May, 1963, as a guide for the **szǔ-ch'īng** movement; superceded in September, 1963, by the **hòu-shíh-t'iáo**)

前述 **ch'ién-shù** the above-mentioned

前所未有 **ch'ién-sǒ-wèi-yǔ** previously nonexistent (unprecedented, unparalleled)

前敌指挥部 **ch'ién-tí chǐh-huī-pù** field command headquarters

前堵后追 **ch'ién-tǔ-hòu-chuī** to block the route of advance and pursue from the rear

前提 **ch'ién-t'í** the first and basic concern; a premise, precondition

前途暗淡 **ch'ién-t'ú-àn-tàn** the road ahead is dark and dull (gloomy prospects)

前途光明 **ch'ién-t'ú-kuāng-míng** the future is brilliant

前奏曲 **ch'ién-tsòu-ch'ǔ** an overture, prelude

前委 **ch'ién-wěi** front-line Party committees

前无古人 **ch'ién-wú-kǔ-jén** no ancient people before [such as this] (unprecedented, unparalleled)

前言 **ch'ién-yén** foreword [of a book]

465 钱财 **ch'ién-ts'ái** money, wealth

466 钳制 **ch'ién-chìh** to suppress [movement or action], to muzzle

钳工 **ch'ién-kūng** a fitter [factory laborer]

467 捐客 **ch'ién-k'ò** a broker

468 潜伏 **ch'ién-fú** to be in hiding, lie hidden (latent, concealed)

潜移默化 **ch'ién-í-mò-huà** to change and influence silently (imperceptible and gradual change—usually from education or the environment)

潜意识 **ch'ién-i-shíh** the subconscious

潜入 **ch'ién-jù** to infiltrate, creep in, move furtively

潜力 **ch'ién-lì** latent energy, potential strength; potentiality

潜力挖尽论 **ch'ién-lì wā-chìn lùn** the theory that all potentiality has been exhausted (usually to be criticized)

潜在力量 **ch'ién-tsài-lì-liang** potential strength, inherent strength, unutilized energy

469 黔 **ch'ién** Kweichow province

ch'iěn (qiǎn)

470 浅海养殖 **ch'iěn-hǎi yǎng-chíh** fish-farming in shallow marine water

浅耕粗作 **ch'iěn-kēng-ts'ū-tsò** shallow plowing and extensive cultivation

浅薄 **ch'iěn-pó** shallow and thin (superficial, cursory)

471 遣返战俘 **ch'iěn-fǎn chàn-fú** repatriation of prisoners of war

遣俘 **ch'iěn-fú** repatriation of prisoners of war

遣送 **ch'iěn-sùng** official action sending a person to a place

472 谴责 **ch'iěn-tsé** to rebuke; condemnation

ch'ièn (qiàn)

473 欠缺 **ch'ièn-ch'üēh** to need, lack, be short of; needs, shortcomings

474 歉收 **ch'ièn-shōu** a poor harvest, crop failure

ch'īh (chī)

475 吃脚行饭 **ch'īh-chiǎo-háng-fàn** to eat by the work of one's legs (to earn a living as a porter, carrier, etc.)

吃尽苦水 **ch'īh-chìn-k'ǔ-shuǐ** to drink all the bitter water (the most down-trodden people)

吃尽苦头 **ch'īh-chìn-k'ǔ-t'óu** one who has suffered all hardships

吃惊 **ch'īh-chīng** to be shocked, startled, astonished

吃二遍苦 **ch'īh-èrh-piēn-k'ǔ** to suffer a second time

吃饭不要钱 **ch'īh-fàn pù-yào-ch'ién** eating without need of money (free food—an early policy in some communes, soon abandoned)

吃、喝、玩、乐 **ch'īh, hō, wán, lò** eating, drinking, and sensual pleasures (the decadent bourgeois life style)

吃小灶 **ch'īh-hsiǎo-tsào** to eat from the small kitchen (better food for certain higher ranks)

吃现成饭 **ch'īh-hsièn-ch'éng-fàn** to eat ready-made food (to enjoy the fruits of others' labor)

吃一堑长一智 **ch'īh-í-ch'ién ch'ǎng-í-chìh** a drink of [to fall into] a moat [gives one] a gain in wisdom (learn from mistakes)

吃人礼教 **ch'īh-jén-lǐ-chiào** man-devouring moral teachings (the Confucian doctrines, now alleged to have a feudal class basis)

吃人的制度 **ch'īh-jén-te chìh-tù** a man-devouring system (usually refers to pre-socialist society)

吃光分光 **ch'īh-kuāng-fēn-kuāng** to eat bare and distribute all [profits] (lack of foresight)

吃过小米扛过枪, 住过窑洞开过荒 **ch'īh-kuò hsiǎo-mǐ k'áng-kuò-ch'iāng, chù-kuò yǎo-tùng k'āi-kuò-huāng** [we've] eaten millet and shouldered a gun, lived in caves and reclaimed the wild (said in ridicule of old cadres who are content to live on their guerrilla glory)

吃苦耐劳 **ch'īh-k'ǔ-nài-láo** to suffer bitterness and hard toil (the sense is usually to indicate praise for a willingness to work hard and diligently)

吃亏 **ch'īh-k'uēi** to suffer a loss, be taken in, cheated; disadvantaged

吃老本 **ch'īh-lǎo-pěn** (1) to eat up one's capital (to run a business at a loss); (2) to live on one's old achievements

吃力 **ch'īh-lì** to take a lot of doing, exhausting, strenuous

吃力不讨好 **ch'īh-lì pù t'ǎo-hǎo** to work hard without receiving thanks, a thankless task

吃大戶 **ch'īh-tà-hù** to eat the rich (to plunder the landlords in time of distress)

吃掉 **ch'īh-tiào** to swallow, to eat up (usually metaphorical, as to over-

71

come the enemy)

吃透两头 **ch'īh-t'òu-liǎng-t'óu** to digest thoroughly both ends (such as, to link theory with practice)

吃透用活 **ch'īh-t'òu-yùng-huó** thorough understanding and flexible application

吃统销粮 **ch'īh t'ǔng-hsiāo-liáng** to consume the unified marketing grains (insufficient production subsidized by grain from the state)

476 痴心妄想 **ch'īh-hsīn-wàng-hsiǎng** to engage in absurd thoughts, to daydream; foolish hopes

痴人说梦 **ch'īh-jén-shuō-mèng** an idiot's daydream

477 魑魅魍魉 **ch'īh-mèi-wǎng-liǎng** hobgoblins of the hills and rivers (bad elements)

ch'íh (chí)

478 驰名 **ch'íh-míng** celebrated, well known, famous

479 迟结婚 **ch'íh-chiéh-hūn** delayed marriage

迟滞 **ch'íh-chìh** a crawling pace, slow in progress [of production]

迟迟 **ch'íh-ch'íh** dilatory, slow, leisurely

迟疑不决 **ch'íh-í-pù-chüéh** to hesitate without being able to make a decision

迟早 **ch'íh-tsǎo** sooner or later

480 持家 **ch'íh-chiā** to manage family [affairs]

持久战 **ch'íh-chǐu-chàn** protracted war

持久和平 **ch'íh-chǐu-hó-p'íng** durable peace, enduring peace

持重 **ch'íh-chùng** to maintain caution, act with gravity

持续 **ch'íh-hsù** continuous, uninterrupted; to carry on

持续期间 **ch'íh-hsù-ch'ī-chiēn** a continuous period, duration

持续上升 **ch'íh-hsù shàng-shēng** continuous increase, steady growth

ch'ǐh (chǐ)

481 尺度 **ch'ǐh-tù** measurement, measuring stick, criterion

482 侈谈 **ch'ǐh-t'án** extravagant talk (to boast, brag)

483 齿轮 **ch'ǐh-lún** gear, cogwheel

484 耻辱 **ch'ǐh-jù** disgrace, humiliation; to humiliate

485 褫夺公权 **ch'ǐh-tó kūng-ch'üán** to deprive one of his civil rights,

ch'ìh (chì)

486 叱咤风云 **ch'ìh-chà-fēng-yún** to order about the wind and the clouds (to have great power)

487 斥骂 **ch'ìh-mà** to revile, curse, bawl out

斥责 **ch'ìh-tsé** to rebuke severely, condemn

488 赤脚教师 **ch'ìh-chiǎo-chiào-shīh** barefoot teachers

赤脚医生 **ch'ìh-chiǎo-ī-shēng** barefoot doctors (para-medical personnel working in the countryside)

赤脚兽医 **ch'ìh-chiǎo-shòu-ī** barefoot veterinarians

赤脚电工 **ch'ìh-chiǎo-tièn-kūng** barefoot electrical worker (semi-professional electrical workers who install electrical facilities in rural areas)

赤区 **ch'ìh-ch'ṻ** Red areas (Communist controlled areas, usually in the Kiangsi period)

赤裸裸 **ch'ìh-lǒ-lǒ** naked, bare, stark, undisguised; nakedly

赤膊上阵 **ch'ìh-pó-shàng-chèn** to go into battle without armor (to fight without aid or supporters)

赤贫化 **ch'ìh-p'ín-huà** pauperization

赤手空拳 **ch'ìh-shǒu-k'ūng-ch'üán** bare-handed (unarmed)

赤道 **ch'ìh-tào** the equator

赤字 **ch'ìh-tzù** red figures (a deficit)

赤卫队 **ch'ìh-wèi-tuì** red guards or scarlet guards (local militia defense forces during the Kiangsi and Yenan periods—not to be confused with the Red Guards of the Cultural Revolution)

ch'īn (qīn)

489 侵埃战争 **ch'īn-āi-chàn-chēng** the War of Aggression against Egypt (the 1956 attack on the Suez Canal)

侵占 **ch'īn-chàn** to occupy by force or aggression

侵朝战争 **ch'īn-ch'áo-chàn-chēng** War of Aggression Against Korea (the Korean War of 1950–1953)

侵犯 **ch'īn-fàn** to infringe upon [rights], to encroach upon [territory]; infringement, violation

侵害 **ch'īn-hài** to violate [territory or rights]

侵袭 **ch'īn-hsí** to encroach, make an attack on, steal [territory]

侵扰 **ch'īn-jǎo** invasion and harassment, aggressive disturbance

侵略战争 **ch'īn-luèh-chàn-chēng** aggressive war, war of aggression

侵略者 **ch'īn-luèh-chě** aggressor, invader

侵略主义 **ch'īn-luèh-chǔ-ì** jingoism

侵略成性 **ch'īn-luèh ch'éng-hsìng** aggression has become its nature

侵略魔爪 **ch'īn-luèh-mó-chǎo** the aggressor's evil claw

侵略本性 **ch'īn-luèh-pěn-hsìng** inherent aggression

侵略势力 **ch'īn-luèh-shìh-li** aggressive forces [political or military]

侵蚀 **ch'īn-shíh** to eat into gradually, deteriorate; to misappropriate [public funds]; to erode; corrosion

侵吞 **ch'īn-t'ūn** (1) to embezzle, peculate; peculation; (2) to annex, gobble up [territory], absorb

490 亲近 **ch'īn-chìn** close, intimate, to be close to; close friends or relatives

亲切 **ch'īn-ch'ièh** intimate, from the heart, sincere, warm and friendly, cordial, sympathetic

亲切关怀 **ch'īn-ch'ièh-kuān-huái** to be intimately and sincerely concerned

亲赴 **ch'īn-fù** to go in person

亲信 **ch'īn-hsìn** a confidant, right-hand man

亲人 **ch'īn-jén** blood relatives (now used figuratively to include compatriots and comrades)

亲如一家 **ch'īn-jú-ì-chiā** as close as members of the same family

亲临 **ch'īn-lín** to attend in person

亲美、恐美、崇美 **ch'īn-měi, k'ǔng-měi, ch'úng-měi** pro-America, fear America, and worship America (criticism of attitudes supposedly held by intellectuals during the early years after Liberation)

亲密战友 **ch'īn-mì-chàn-yǔ** close comrade-in-arms (a trusted supporter or follower)

亲密团结群众 **ch'īn-mì t'uán-chiéh ch'ún-chùng** to unite intimately with the masses

亲笔信 **ch'īn-pǐ-hsìn** a letter written in one's own hand, autograph letter

亲善 **ch'īn-shàn** friendship, goodwill, amity; rapprochement

亲身感受 **ch'īn-shēn-kǎn-shòu** deeply and intimately touched

亲手 **ch'īn-shǒu** by one's own hand (in person, personally)

亲自出马 **ch'īn-tzù-ch'ū-mǎ** to mount the horse personally (in person, to come forward, to take the field)

亲王 **ch'īn-wáng** prince [of the royal house]

亲友 **ch'īn-yǔ** relatives and friends

亲 **ch'īn:** *see also* **ch'ìng**

491 钦佩 **ch'ēn-p'èi** to admire, think highly of, respect; admiration, esteem

ch'ín (qín)

492 秦始皇[帝] **ch'ín-shǐh-huáng [tì]** the first emperor of the Ch'in Dynasty (whose reputation is being revived through the discussion of the Confucianist-Legalist controversy)

493 禽畜 **ch'ín-ch'ù** poultry and farm animals

禽兽 **ch'ín-shòu** (1) beasts; (2) subhuman, beastly

494 勤俭 **ch'ín-chiěn** hard work and thrift; industrious and frugal

勤俭建国 **ch'ín-chiěn-chièn-kuó** to build up the country by industry and frugality

勤俭持家 **ch'ín-chiěn-ch'íh-chiā** to manage the family with diligence and thrift (may also refer to the management of one's unit)

勤俭办学 **ch'ín-chiěn-pàn-hsuéh** to run schools with industry and frugality

勤俭办医 **ch'ín-chiěn-pàn-ī** to administer medical affairs with diligence and frugality

勤俭办工厂 **ch'ín-chiěn-pàn-kūng-ch'ǎng** to run the factories with hard work and thrift

勤俭办社 **ch'ín-chiěn-pàn-shè** to run the communes industriously and economically

勤巧结合 **ch'ín-ch'iǎo-chiéh-hó** to combine diligence and skillfulness

勤工俭学 **ch'ín-kūng-chiěn-hsuéh** to study while one works; a work-study program

勤劳朴素 **ch'ín-láo-p'ǔ-sù** industrious and plain

勤劳勇敢 **ch'ín-láo-yǔng-kǎn** industrious and courageous

勤勉 **ch'ín-miěn** earnest, diligent, assiduous, devoted

勤杂人员 **ch'ín-tsá-jén-yuán** personnel performing menial and miscellaneous duties

勤务 **ch'ín-wù** fatigue duty [military], service work

勤务员 **ch'ín-wù-yuán** an orderly, service person

ch'īng (qīng)

495 青 **ch'īng** Chinghai province

青出于蓝 **ch'īng-ch'ū-yú-lán** blue

comes from the indigo [plant] (the student excels the teacher; those who follow may surpass those who went before)

青储饲料 **ch'īng-ch'ú-szù-liào** silage crops, ensilage

青春 **ch'īng-ch'ūn** the spring (youth, vitality)

青黄不接 **ch'īng-huáng-pù-chiēh** when the grain of the previous crop is exhausted and the current crop is not yet ready (a temporary shortage)

青稞 **ch'īng-k'ō** barley

青霉素 **ch'īng-méi-sù** penicillin

青苗 **ch'īng-miáo** green shoots, a young crop

青年节 **ch'īng-nién-chiéh** Youth Day

青年农业建设队 **ch'īng-nién núng-yèh chièn-shè-tuì** Youths' Agricultural Construction Team (a prestige organization for **hsià-hsiāng** volunteers, 1964)

青年团 **ch'īng-nién-t'uán** the Youth League

青帮 **ch'īng-pāng** the Green Gang (most important of the Shanghai pre-1949 secret societies)

青少年 **ch'īng-shào nién** boys and young men

青松 **ch'īng-sūng** a green pine (a person with strength, endurance, and constancy—like an evergreen pine standing through winter and storm)

496 轻机关枪 **ch'īng-chī-kuān-ch'iāng** sub-machine gun

轻装前进 **ch'īng-chuāng-ch'ién-chìn** to advance lightly armed (to discard useless baggage: now usually figurative)

轻重缓急 **ch'īng-chùng-huǎn-chí** in order of importance and emergency, relative urgency

轻重倒置 **ch'īng-chùng-tào-chìh** to reverse light and heavy (to reverse the relative importance)

轻车熟道 **ch'īng-ch'ē-shú-tào** [to have] a light cart and familiar road (an easy task)

轻骑手 **ch'īng-ch'í-shǒu** light cavalry (mobile teams of doctors, artists, or technical workers)

轻举妄动 **ch'īng-chǔ-wàng-tùng** to behave recklessly; rash, impetuous

轻而易举 **ch'īng-érh-ì-chǔ** light and easy to do (any easy matter)

轻信谣言 **ch'īng-hsìn-yáo-yén** to give easy credence to rumors

轻型登陆艇 **ch'īng-hsíng- tēng-lù-t'īng** light landing craft

轻易 **ch'īng-ì** lightly, easily; easy [to do]

轻工业 **ch'īng-kūng-yèh** light industry

轻工业部 **ch'īng-kūng-yèh-pù** Ministry of Light Industry [of the State Council]

轻快 **ch'īng-k'uài** quick, agile, easy to handle, light

轻描淡写 **ch'īng-miáo-tàn-hsiěh** a light sketch and simple writing (to describe vaguely, to adumbrate)

轻便铁道 **ch'īng-pièn-t'iěh-tào** a light railway, a branch or spur railroad

轻炮 **ch'īng-p'ào** light artillery

轻视 **ch'īng-shìh** to look down upon, minimize, underestimate, disdain

轻视敌人 **ch'īng-shìh-tí-jén** to take the enemy lightly

轻率 **ch'īng-shuài** frivolously, light-minded

轻松 **ch'īng-sūng** relaxed, with a light touch, light

轻敌 **ch'īng-tí** to belittle the enemy, underestimate the enemy

轻微 **ch'īng-wēi** minor, petty, piddling, slight, light

497 氢弹 **ch'īng-tàn** hydrogen bomb

氢武器 **ch'īng-wǔ-ch'ì** hydrogen weapons

498 倾注 **ch'īng-chù** to pour from one receptacle to another, to overflow

倾巢出动 **ch'īng-ch'áo-ch'ū-tùng** to empty the nest and go out (a derogatory phrase that indicates a whole group has gone into action)

倾向 **ch'īng-hsiàng** tendency, trend, inclination; to be inclined toward

倾销 **ch'īng-hsiāo** to dump goods

倾盆大雨 **ch'īng-p'én-tà-yǔ** a torrential downpour

倾听意见 **ch'īng-t'īng-ì-chièn** to listen attentively

倾吐 **ch'īng-t'ǔ** to pour out [one's feelings] (to talk freely)

倾轧 **ch'īng-yà** to squeeze out (strife, discord, internecine dissension, intra-party struggle)

499 清账 **ch'īng-chàng** to clean up accounts, settle accounts

清真寺 **ch'īng-chēn-szù** a mosque

清洁工 **ch'īng-chiéh-kūng** cleaning work

清洁队 **ch'īng-chiéh-tuì** a cleaning squad

清查 **ch'īng-ch'á** to detect, investigate, ferret out

清产定股 **ch'īng-ch'ǎn-tìng-kǔ** clearing property and fixing shares (in the transition to socialism, 1956 and before)

清偿 **ch'īng-ch'áng** to pay up, settle [an

account], pay debts in full

清清白白 **ch'ing-ch'ing-pái-pái** pure, unsullied [reputation]

清除 **ch'ing-ch'ú** to remove, eradicate, clear out, clean up, purge, liquidate

清除出党 **ch'ing-ch'ú-ch'ū-tǎng** to purge [someone] from the Party

清除废料 **ch'ing-ch'ú-fèi-liào** to clean out rubbish (often figurative)

清华大学 **ch'ing-huá-tà-hsuéh** Tsinghua University (Peking)

清洗 **ch'ing-hsǐ** to cleanse, purge

清醒 **ch'ing-hsǐng** wide-awake, sober, clear-headed

清一色 **ch'ing-ǐ-sè** monochromatic (completely dominated by one group or party)

清高 **ch'ing-kāo** simple [living] and high [thinking] (highminded, of great prestige)

清官 **ch'ing-kuān** upright officials

清规戒律 **ch'ing-kuēi-chièh-lü** commandments and taboos, interdictions

清规律例 **ch'ing-kuēi-lü-lì** (same as next above)

清工分, 清思想 **ch'ing-kūng-fēn ch'ing-szū-hsiǎng** to straighten out work-points and clarify thinking

清宫秘史 **ch'ing-kūng mì-shǐh** "The Inside Story of the Ch'ing Court" (a film made in 1949 in which the Ch'ing court was portrayed favorably and the Boxers unfavorably, criticized during the Cultural Revolution)

清理 **ch'ing-lǐ** to liquidate, clear up, put in order, settle

清理阶级队伍 **ch'ing-lǐ chiēh-chí-tuì-wǔ** to cleanse the class ranks

清凉饮料 **ch'ing-liáng-yǐn-liào** cooling drinks

清末立宪党人 **ch'ing-mò lì-hsièn-tǎng-jén** the constitutionalists at the end of the Ch'ing period

清算 **ch'ing-suàn** to clear an account, settle old debts (to settle scores, eliminate or purge)

清算斗争 **ch'ing-suàn-tòu-chēng** an account-settling struggle (usually refers to a struggle against class enemies, as in the Land Reform when the debts between landlords and peasants were liquidated)

清算运动 **ch'ing-suàn-yùn-tùng** account-settling movement (as in the Land Reform)

清单 **ch'ing-tān** a detailed list of items, statement of account, inventory

清党 **ch'ing-tǎng** a Party purge

清党运动 **ch'ing-tǎng-yùn-tùng** a campaign to purge the Party

清点物资 **ch'ing-tiěn-wù-tzū** to make an inventory, make a list

清仓查库 **ch'ing-ts'āng-ch'á-k'ù** to make an inventory of granaries and warehouses

清仓运动 **ch'ing-ts'āng-yùn-tùng** warehouse clearance movement (mid-1959)

清样 **ch'ing-yàng** galley proof [of a manuscript]

ch'íng (qíng)

500 情节 **ch'íng-chiéh** (1) circumstances of a case; (2) a dramatic plot, incident

情景 **ch'íng-chǐng** a general aspect, general situation, how it looks

情场 **ch'íng-ch'ǎng** the [battle] field of love, amorous competition (a theme of old literature now criticized)

情绪 **ch'íng-hsù** personal feeling, state of mind, mood, spirit

情感 **ch'íng-kǎn** sentiment, emotion, feelings, friendship between two persons

情况 **ch'íng-k'uàng** circumstances, condition, state of affairs

情理 **ch'íng-lǐ** humanity and reason, reason, reasonableness

情面 **ch'íng-mièn** social consideration, "face"

情报 **ch'íng-pào** intelligence, information; an intelligence report

情报局 **ch'íng-pào-chú** (1) intelligence office or department; (2) an abbreviation for the Cominform

情不自禁 **ch'íng-pù-tzù-chìn** unable to control one's emotions (strongly tempted, cannot help but)

情势 **ch'íng-shìh** a situation, circumstances

情愿 **ch'íng-yuàn** to wish, want to; willing

501 晴天霹雳 **ch'íng-t'iēn-p'ī-lì** a thunderbolt out of the blue sky (sudden bad news)

晴雨表 **ch'íng-yǔ-piǎo** barometer

ch'ïng (qǐng)

502 请进来 **ch'ïng-chin-lai** to invite in (workers, peasants, and soldiers should be invited in to teach in the schools)

请求 **ch'ïng-ch'íu** to request, ask, petition for

请客送礼 **ch'ïng-k'ò-sùng-lǐ** to entertain guests and send presents (a

75

tradition now deplored, because
lavish entertaining is associated with
seeking favors)

请示 **ch'ìng-shìh** to ask for instructions'

请示报告 **ch'ìng-shìh pào-kào** to make
a report asking for clarification or
instructions

ch'ìng (qìng)

503 庆祝 **ch'ìng-chù** to celebrate,
commemorate, honor, observe;
celebration, commemoration

庆功会 **ch'ìng-kūng-huì** commendation
meeting, success celebration meeting

ch'iū (qiū)

504 邱吉尔 **ch'iū-chí-ěrh** Churchill [Sir
Wintson]

505 秋分工作 **ch'iū-fēn-kūng-tsò** the work
of dividing the autumn [harvest]

秋毫无犯 **ch'iū-háo-wú-fàn** without
violating the finest [autumn] hair
(troops so well disciplined that they
cause not the slightest injury to the
people's interests)

秋后算账 **ch'iū-hòu-suàn-chàng**
accounts will be reckoned after the
autumn harvest (revenge will come
after the harvest)

秋风扫落叶 **ch'iū-fēng săo lò-yèh** [as]
the autumn wind sweeps up the fallen
leaves

秋高气爽 **ch'iū-kāo-ch'ì-shuăng** brisk
late autumn weather

秋收起义 **ch'iū-shōu ch'ǐ-ì** Autumn
Harvest Uprising (the uprising led by
Mao Tse-tung in September 1927
near the Hunan-Kiangsi border)

秋收暴动 **ch'iū-shōu-pào-tùng** Autumn
Harvest Insurrections (a series of
rural uprisings in the central Yangtse
provinces from August through
September 1927: see also above)

ch'iú (qiú)

506 囚笼 **ch'iú-lúng** a convict's cage
(bondage)

507 求和 **ch'iú-hó** to sue for peace, offer
to surrender

求降 **ch'iú-hsiáng** to surrender,
capitulate

求神供鬼 **ch'iú-shén-kùng-kuěi** to seek
help from the gods and to make
offerings to the spirits (vainly to seek
help from improper sources)

求神拜佛 **ch'iú-shén-pài-fó** to seek help
from the gods and to worship

Buddha (vain hopes of aid)

求大同、存小异 **ch'iú-tà-t'úng, ts'ún-
hsiăo-ì** to seek agreement on major
issues while reserving differences on
minor points

求同存异 **ch'iú-t'úng-ts'ún-ì** to seek
unity and retain differences (see
above)

求稳怕乱 **ch'iú-wěn-p'à-luàn** seek
stability and fear disorder (applied
to cadres who hold back in applying
the mass line)

508 球艺 **ch'iú-ì** ball-playing skill

球类比赛 **ch'iú-lèi-pǐ-sài** a ball game
competition

球迷 **ch'iú-mí** a ball fan (an enthusiast
for basketball, ping-pong, etc.)

ch'iúng (qióng)

509 穷追 **chiúng-chuī** in hot pursuit; to
pursue relentlessly

穷富拉平 **ch'iúng-fù-lā-p'íng** to level
rich and poor

穷凶极恶 **ch'iúng-hsiūng-chí-ò**
extremely violent and evil (atrocious,
unbridled violence)

穷根究底 **ch'iúng-kēn-chiū-tǐ** to follow
the root to the limit (to get to the
bottom of a matter)

穷寇 **ch'iúng-k'òu** a tottering foe

穷苦 **ch'iúng-k'ǔ** poor, poverty-
stricken, destitute

穷困 **ch'iúng-k'ùn** needy, poverty-
stricken, in straitened circumstances

穷棒子 **ch'iúng-pàng-tzu** a bare stick
(an abject poor person, a penniless
person)

穷棒子精神 **ch'iúng-pàng-tzu chīng-shén**
pauper's spirit (to be willing to work
hard with very little)

穷兵黩武 **ch'iúng-pīng-tú-wǔ** ultra
militaristic

穷山恶水 **ch'iúng-shān-ò-shuǐ** barren
mountains and violent waters (a
barren landscape; unfavorable
natural conditions)

穷则思变 **ch'iúng-tsé-szū-pièn** at a dead
end one must think of change (the
more desperate the circumstances,
the more pecessary it is to find new
ways to alter one's condition and
carry on the revolution)

510 琼州海峡 **ch'iúng-chōu-hǎi-hsiá** the
Hainan Strait

ch'ō (chuō)

511 戳穿 **ch'ō-ch'uān** to expose by breaking
the cover, lay bare, poke a hole in

戳穿骗局 **ch'ō-ch'uān-p'ièn-chú** to expose a deception, to uncover a plot

ch'ōu (chōu)

512 抽出 **ch'ōu-ch'ū** to take away; pull out; select out of a group or number

抽取 **ch'ōu-ch'ǔ** to extract, draw out of

抽象 **ch'ōu-hsiàng** abstract, an abstraction

抽补 **ch'ōu-pǔ** to take from or to add (adjustment, repair, compensation)

抽水机 **ch'ōu-shuǐ-chī** water pump

抽调 **ch'ōu-tiào** to detach and transfer (may refer to the assignment of cadres in connection with any movement or undertaking)

抽样法 **ch'ōu-yàng-fǎ** sampling method

抽样调查 **ch'ōu-yàng tiào-ch'á** sampling investigation; to select a sample for investigation

ch'óu (chóu)

513 仇恨 **ch'óu-hèn** hatred, animosity; a feud

仇神 **ch'óu-shén** the Furies

仇视 **ch'óu-shìh** to be hostile to, regard as an enemy; hostility, hatred

仇敌 **ch'óu-tí** a hated enemy, bitter rival, foe, adversary

514 愁眉不展 **ch'óu-méi-pù-chǎn** with brows knit (to wear a troubled expression)

515 稠密 **ch'óu-mì** congested, crowded, dense

516 筹建 **ch'óu-chièn** to plan for constructing

筹划 **ch'óu-huà** to design, make plans for

筹款 **ch'óu-k'uǎn** to accumulate funds, collect funds

筹备 **ch'óu-pèi** to prepare, make preparations, arrange for; preparatory

筹备委员会 **ch'óu-pèi wěi-yuán-huì** a preparatory committee

517 酬答 **ch'óu-tá** to express appreciation, reciprocate, in return for

ch'ǒu (chǒu)

518 丑角 **ch'ǒu-chiǎo** a clown, comedian in a Chinese opera

丑剧 **ch'ǒu-chù** an ugly drama (a scandal, an unseemly affair)

丑化 **ch'ǒu-huà** to defame, besmirch, discredit, disgrace

丑类 **ch'ǒu-lèi** a gang of scoundrels, riffraff

丑恶面目 **ch'ǒu-ò-mièn-mù** a loathsome face (despicable, ugly)

丑事 **ch'ǒu-shìh** a scandal

丑态百出 **ch'ǒu-t'ài-pǎi-ch'ū** a hundred unseemly sights appear (all sorts of ugly behavior)

ch'òu (chòu)

519 臭架子 **ch'òu-chià-tzu** a stinking framework (disgusting airs of importance, offensive haughtiness)

臭知识分子 **ch'òu chīh-shíh-fèn-tzǔ** stinking intellectuals

臭气熏天 **ch'òu-ch'ì-hsūn-t'iēn** the stench reaches the sky

臭名昭彰 **ch'òu-míng-chāo-chāng** a notorious reputation luminously displayed (infamous)

臭名昭著 **ch'òu-míng-chāo-chù** extremely notorious (*see above*)

臭名远扬 **ch'òu-míng-yuǎn-yáng** a bad name known afar (notorious, of bad repute)

臭味相投 **ch'òu-wèi-hsiāng-t'óu** of the same foul odor (birds of a feather)

ch'ū (chū)

520 出诊 **ch'ū-chěn** going out to treat (a doctor's house call)

出击 **ch'ǔ-chī** an assault; to assault, sortie

出境 **ch'ū-chìng** to leave the country; to export

出主意 **ch'ū-chǔ-i** to make a suggestion, offer an idea, give a decision

出岔子 **ch'ū-ch'à-tzu** the untoward has happened, to meet with an accident

出差错 **ch'ū-ch'ā-ts'ò** an unforeseen error has happened

出产 **ch'ū-ch'ǎn** to produce; production; produce, products

出厂价 **ch'ū-ch'ǎng-chià** F.O.B. price

出场 **ch'ū-ch'ǎng** to make an entrance [on stage or field], to appear

出超 **ch'ū-ch'āo** export surplus (a favorable trade balance)

出奇 **ch'ū-ch'í** phenomenal, prodigious, wonderful, rare

出奇制胜 **ch'ū-ch'í chìh-shèng** victory by unusual tactics; to win by surprise

出其不意 **ch'ū-ch'í-pù-ì** to catch one off guard, to take by surprise

出勤 **ch'ū-ch'ín** to report for work, work attendance

出勤率 **ch'ū-ch'ín-lù** rate of attendance

出尔反尔 **ch'ū-ěrh-fǎn-ěrh** what has come from you [now] returns to you

(to have been contradicted by oneself in words or actions)

出发点 **ch'ū-fā-tiĕn** starting point, point of departure; basic viewpoint, premise, motive

出风头 **ch'ū-fēng-t'óu** to show off, seek the limelight, attract wide attention

出息 **ch'ū-hsī** interest, profit, to bear interest

出息 **ch'ū-hsi** a chance to better one's circumstances, a promising future

出席 **ch'ū-hsí** to be present at a meeting, attend a banquet or reception

出现 **ch'ū-hsièn** to emerge, appear, arise, become manifest; appearance, occurrence

出以公心 **ch'ū-ĭ-kūng-hsīn** with the public interest as the starting point

出人意外 **ch'ū-jén-ì-wài** beyond one's expectation, unexpectedly

出人头地 **ch'ū-jén-t'óu-tì** higher than others by a head (to stand out among the crowd, to excel)

出轨 **ch'ū-kuĕi** to derail, be derailed, an abnormal action

出口 **ch'ū-k'ŏu** to export; exports, exportation; an exit; to speak

出口商品交易会 **ch'ū-k'ŏu-shāng-p'ĭn chiāo-ì-huì** export trade fair [at Canton]

出路 **ch'ū-lù** an outlet, way out, exit; a profession, a future

出乱子 **ch'ū-luàn-tzu** a disturbance has arisen (to run into trouble)

出笼 **ch'ū-lúng** out of the basket (to set loose, put into circulation)

出马 **ch'ū-mǎ** to enter the lists, start, commence; to come out and assume a post

出卖 **ch'ū-mài** to sell out, betray; to offer for sale

出卖原则 **ch'ū-mài-yuán-tsé** to sell out one's principles

出满勤 **ch'ū-mǎn-ch'ín** full attendance [by workers or staff]

出面 **ch'ū-mièn** to appear publicly; to act publicly on the behalf of others or a group

出谋划策 **ch'ū-móu-huà-ts'è** to make plans and give advice

出版 **ch'ū-pǎn** to print, publish; a publication

出版消息 **ch'ū-pǎn hsiāo-hsī** *Publishing News* (a Peking weekly, 1958—)

出版人 **ch'ū-pǎn-jén** a publisher

出版社 **ch'ū-pǎn-shè** publishing firm

出版自由 **ch'ū-pǎn-tzù-yú** freedom of the press, freedom of publication

出版物 **ch'ū-pǎn-wù** a publication

出兵 **ch'ū-pīng** to dispatch troops

出色 **ch'ū-sè** outstanding, remarkable, splendid, noteworthy

出身 **ch'ū-shēn** social origin, to be born of

出身好 **ch'ū-shēn-hǎo** of good family origin (children of the proletariat)

出生入死 **ch'ū-shēng-jù-szǔ** to risk one's life, to defy all kinds of perils

出师不义 **ch'ū-shīh-pù-ì** unjustified military measures

出售 **ch'ū-shòu** to sell, offer for sale

出售余粮 **ch'ū-shòu-yǘ-liáng** to sell surplus grain

出敌不意 **ch'ū-tí-pù-ì** beyond the enemy's expectation

出点子 **ch'ū-tiĕn-tzu** to play a card (to use a tactic, offer a solution)

出动 **ch'ū-tùng** to start out [of groups or military units] (to commence an activity)

出题目 **ch'ū-t'í-mu** to set a topic, select the theme

出头 **ch'ū-t'óu** (1) to be successful [in one's career]; (2) to overcome oppression

出土文物 **ch'ū-t'ǔ-wén-wù** unearthed relics

出租汽车 **ch'ū-tsū-ch'ì-ch'ē** a taxi, rental car

出洋相 **ch'ū-yáng-hsiàng** to stand out with a foreign image (to make a fool of oneself in public)

出于自愿 **ch'ū-yǘ-tzù-yuàn** acting on one's own accord (on a voluntary basis)

[521] 初级社 **ch'ū-chí-shè** basic-level cooperative (agricultural producers cooperative of the elementary [team]-type)

初见成效 **ch'ū-chièn-ch'éng-hsiào** the first sight of results

初期 **ch'ū-ch'ī** the early period

初出茅庐 **ch'ū-ch'ū-máo-lú** just out of the straw hut (starting a career, inexperienced, green; a debut)

初年 **ch'ū-nién** early years

初步加工 **ch'ū-pù-chiā-kūng** initial processing, preliminary work

初步分析 **ch'ū-pù-fēn-hsī** preliminary analysis

初步协议 **ch'ū-pù-hsiéh-ì** a preliminary agreement

ch'ú (chú)

[522] 除旧布新 **ch'ú-chiù-pù-hsīn** to eliminate the old [and] unfold the new

除名 **ch'ú-míng** to strike off one's name (to expel, dismiss)

除霸 **ch'ú-pà** to get rid of local despots
除四害 **ch'ú-szù-hài** eliminate the four pests (flies, mosquitoes, rats, and sparrows)
523 锄奸反霸 **ch'ú-chiēn-fǎn-pà** to dig out traitors and local despots
锄头 **ch'ú-t'óu** a hoe
524 雏型 **ch'ú-hsíng** a miniature model, prototype

ch'ǔ (chǔ)

525 处置 **ch'ǔ-chìh** to handle, deal with, dispose of, take up, settle; disposition, settlement
处境 **ch'ǔ-chìng** circumstances, conditions, situation, state
处决 **ch'ǔ-chüéh** (1) to execute [a criminal]; (2) to decide [a matter]
处罚 **ch'ǔ-fá** to penalize, punish; a penalty, punishment, sanction
处方 **ch'ǔ-fāng** to prescribe for; a prescription
处分 **ch'ǔ-fèn** (1) to punish, censure, reprimand; a punishment, penalty, sanction; (2) to deal with; a settlement, disposition
处心积虑 **ch'ǔ-hsīn-chī-lǜ** to have in mind for a long time (deliberately, designedly; to work hard and deliberately at)
处刑 **ch'ǔ-hsíng** to impose criminal punishment
处理 **ch'ǔ-lǐ** to handle, deal with, treat, dispose of, manage, look after, take charge of
处于被动 **ch'ǔ-yú-pèi-tùng** to be in a passive situation
处 **ch'ǔ**: *see also* **ch'ù**
526 储蓄 **ch'ǔ-hsù** savings, stock, a deposit; to save, put aside
储蓄代办所 **ch'ǔ-hsù tài-pàn-sǒ** a savings agency (established in many rural basic units to accept deposits for the People's Bank)
储粮基金 **ch'ǔ-liáng chī-chīn** reserve foodgrain fund
储量定型论 **ch'ú-liàng tìng-hsíng lùn** the idea that natural resources have a fixed pattern (before the Communist period, mineral surveys—generally conducted by foreigners—had concluded that China's resources were very limited: this phrase attacks such defeatist thinking)
储备 **ch'ǔ-pèi** a reserve [of money], stockpile [of goods]
储备粮 **ch'ǔ-pèi-liáng** reserve grain
储藏量 **ch'ǔ-ts'áng-liàng** natural resource reserves

储存 **ch'ǔ-ts'ún** to store up, accumulate, save; accumulation
储运公司 **ch'ǔ-yùn-kūng-szū** a storage and transport corporation

ch'ù (chù)

527 处处设防 **ch'ù-ch'ù shè-fáng** to set up defenses everywhere
处处事事 **ch'ù-ch'ù shìh-shìh** in every place and every affair
处 **ch'ù**: *see also* **ch'ǔ**
528 畜产品 **ch'ù-ch'ǎn-p'ǐn** animal products
畜肥 **ch'ù-féi** animal manure
畜疫 **ch'ù-ì** animal disease
畜力 **ch'ù-lì** animal power, animal traction
畜力牵引工具 **ch'ù-lì-ch'iēn-yǐn kūng-chù** animal drawn implements
畜舍 **ch'ù-shè** livestock shed
畜 **ch'ù**: *see also* **hsù**
529 触及 **ch'ù-chí** to touch on, come in contact with
触及灵魂 **ch'ù-chí-líng-hún** to touch the soul
触角 **ch'ù-chiǎo** antennae, an insect's feeler, tentacle
触犯 **ch'ù-fàn** to offend, violate, outrage
触目惊心 **ch'ù-mù-chīng-hsīn** the sight brings horror (a ghastly sight)
触怒 **ch'ù-nù** to offend, affront, irritate, arouse wrath
触动 **ch'ù-tùng** to touch emotionally, arouse, excite
530 黜职 **ch'ù-chíh** to demote, depose, dismiss

ch'uān (chuān)

531 川 **ch'uān** Szechwan province
川流不息 **ch'uān-liú-pù-hsī** a continuously flowing stream (a steady flow)
532 穿插分割 **ch'uān-ch'ā-fēn-kō** to break through and cut off [military]
穿小鞋 **ch'uān-hsiǎo-hsiéh** [to force one] to wear small shoes (to inflict great discomfort, to assign one to an unnecessarily onerous task)
穿新鞋，走老路 **ch'uān-hsīn-hsiéh, tsǒu-lǎo-lù** wearing new shoes [but] traveling the old road (no real change in the situation)
穿孔卡 **ch'uān-k'ǔng-k'ǎ** a punch card

ch'uán (chuán)

533 传真电报机 **ch'uán-chēn tièn-pào-chī**

phototelegraph, telephoto

传家宝 **ch'uán-chiā-pǎo** a family heirloom, family treasure

传经送宝 **ch'uán-chīng-sùng-pǎo** passing on the classics and offering the treasures (to pass on one's experience or knowledge to some less advantaged unit or person)

传呼电话 **ch'uán-hū-tièn-huà** a public attended neighborhood telephone (the attendant calls the party wanted)

传下 **ch'uán-hsià** to hand down

传讯 **ch'uán-hsùn** to summon for trial

传染病 **ch'uán-jǎn-pìng** an infectious disease

传、帮、带 **ch'uán pāng tài** to teach, help, and lead

传播 **ch'uán-pō** to disseminate, spread, broadcast, bruit about

传布 **ch'uán-pù** to spread, disseminate, make widely known

传授 **ch'uán-shòu** to pass on, impart to, instruct

传说 **ch'uán-shuō** a story that goes around (rumor, gossip, legend, tradition)

传送带 **ch'uán-sùng-tài** conveyor belt

传达 **ch'uán-tá** (1) to transmit an order from above; (2) to communicate [thoughts, ideas]

传达会议 **ch'uán-tá-huì-ì** a transmission meeting (a conference at which higher level decisions are transmitted to the lower levels)

传达报告 **ch'uán-tá-pào-kào** to relay a report, transmit a report

传单 **ch'uán-tān** a leaflet, broadside, propaganda sheet

传导带 **ch'uán-tǎo-tài** transmission belt

传统 **ch'uán-t'ǔng** tradition, heritage; traditional

传统偏见 **ch'uán-t'ǔng-p'iēn-chièn** the bias of tradition

传统势力 **ch'uán-t'ǔng-shìh-lì** the forces of tradition

传宗接代 **ch'uán-tsūng-chiēh-tài** the tradition of continuing the family line (the desire for a son)

534 船厂 **ch'uán-ch'ǎng** a shipyard

船民 **ch'uán-mín** boat people (people making their living by transport or fishing and often, though less generally now, residing on their boats: formerly referred to by the derogatory term, **tàn-mín** 蜑民)

船舶 **ch'uán-pò** ships, vessels

船舱 **ch'uán-ts'āng** a ship's hold

船坞 **ch'uán-wù** a dockyard, ship repair yard

船员 **ch'uán-yuán** a member of a ship's crew, sailor, seaman

ch'uǎn (chuǎn)

535 喘息 **ch'uǎn-hsī** to pause for breath; a breathing spell

ch'uàn (chuàn)

536 串连 **ch'uàn-lién** to string or link together (during the Cultural Revolution the Red Guards used this term to describe their moving about to contact other groups and to exchange revolutionary experiences)

串连证明 **ch'uàn-lién-chèng-míng** an authorization to exchange experience (required, for instance, in Shanghai by an order of January 7, 1967)

串楼 **ch'uàn-lóu** from building to building (the implication is of a cadre spending all his time going from office to office and writing his report without actually visiting the field or shop)

串门 **ch'uàn-mén** to visit friends at their houses (to carry gossip)

串通 **ch'uàn-t'ūng** to conspire with [someone], to join with and plot

ch'uāng (chuāng)

537 窗花 **ch'uāng-huā** window pictures (paper-cut pictures used as window decoration, particularly in north China)

ch'uǎng (chuǎng)

538 闯将 **ch'uǎng-chiàng** a dauntless fellow, a daredevil (a term applied to the Red Guards during the Cultural Revolution)

闯劲 **ch'uǎng-chìn** dauntless vigor (the spirit of breaking with tradition or overcoming any difficulty)

闯新路 **ch'uǎng-hsīn-lù** to break through a new road (to strike out on a new line)

闯过关 **ch'uǎng-kuò-kuān** to storm a pass (to come through a severe test)

闯龙潭入虎穴 **ch'uǎng-lúng-t'án, jù-hǔ-hsuèh** to brave a dragon's pool or enter a tiger's lair (courageously to overcome great danger)

闯难关 **ch'uǎng-nán-kuān** to break through a difficult pass (to overcome a great difficulty)

ch'uàng (chuàng)

539 创纪录 **ch'uàng-chì-lù** to set a record, to establish a new record
创建 **ch'uàng-chièn** to create, build from scratch
创举 **ch'uàng-chǔ** a new creation, major breakthrough, new undertaking
创新 **ch'uàng-hsīn** to create something new
创立 **ch'uàng-lì** to establish, found, set up, open
创办 **ch'uàng-pàn** to start, found, establish (usually an enterprise, school, or newspaper)
创伤 **ch'uàng-shāng** a wound, injury, damage
创造经验 **ch'uàng-tsào-chīng-yèn** to create experience (to do something that one has not done before and thus to "create" experience)
创造奇迹 **ch'uàng-tsào ch'í-chī** to create miracles
创造发明 **ch'uàng-tsào-fā-míng** to create and invent
创造力 **ch'uàng-tsào-lì** originality, creative ability, creative force
创作 **ch'uàng-tsò** literary creations, literary works; to write literary works
创作自由 **ch'uàng-tsò-tzù-yú** freedom of writing [especially of literary works, such as novels]
创业 **ch'uàng-yèh** to start an enterprise, undertake a new project

ch'uī (chuī)

540 吹吹拍拍, 拉拉扯扯 **ch'uī-ch'uī p'āi-p'āi, lā-lā ch'ě-ch'ě** to resort to boasting, flattery and touting [among co-workers]
吹灰之力 **ch'uī-huī-chīh-lì** the strength to blow away dust (minimum effort)
吹嘘 **ch'uī-hsū** to say a good word for, praise
吹鼓手 **ch'uī-kǔ-shǒu** a member of a fife and drum corps (may have the connotation of being a propagandist or drumbeater for a discredited leader or cause)
吹毛求疵 **ch'uī-máo-ch'íu-tz'ū** blowing apart the fur to find blemishes (to find fault unfairly, to cavil at)
吹牛 **ch'uī-níu** to blow the cow [skin] (to brag)
吹牛皮 **ch'uī-níu-p'í** to brag, to bluff
吹捧 **ch'uī-p'ěng** to puff, ballyhoo
541 炊事员 **ch'uī-shìh-yuán** a cook (in army or messhall—has replaced the old term **huǒ-fū** 伙夫）

ch'uí (chuí)

542 垂直 **ch'uí-chíh** to hang down straight, perpendicular to
垂涎三尺 **ch'uí-hsién sān-ch'īh** the mouth waters three feet [down] (consumed with envy; to covet)
垂死挣扎 **ch'uí-szǔ-chēng-chá** a struggle as death approaches (a dying kick, last ditch struggle)
垂头丧气 **ch'uí-t'óu-sàng-ch'ì** head low and spirits despondent (crestfallen, dejected)
垂危 **ch'uí-wēi** near death (approaching a crisis)
543 锤炼 **ch'uí-lièn** to forge and temper, to steel, to temper

ch'ūn (chūn)

544 春季灭鼠突击活动 **ch'ūn-chì mièh-shǔ t'ū-chī huó-tùng** a spring rat-extermination drive
春节 **ch'ūn-chiéh** spring festival (the lunar new year)
春茶 **ch'ūn-ch'á** spring tea (the early picking from the tea bushes, considered to be the highest quality)
春寒 **ch'ūn-hán** [unseasonably] cold weather in the spring (of great potential harm to agriculture)
春耕 **ch'ūn-kēng** spring cultivation, spring plowing
春耕生产 **ch'ūn-kēng-shēng-ch'ǎn** spring production
春雷 **ch'ūn-léi** spring thunder (thunder in the spring wakens nature, hence, a harbinger of new life)
春播 **ch'ūn-pò** spring sowing
春色满园 **ch'ūn-sè-mǎn-yuán** spring colors fill the garden (great prosperity)

ch'ún (chún)

545 纯正 **ch'ún-chèng** upright, honest; unadulterated, pure [of thought or ideology]
纯技术观点 **ch'ún chī-shù-kuān-tiěn** a purely technical viewpoint (considering only the professional or technical aspects of a matter without regard for the political)
纯洁 **ch'ún-chiéh** pure, innocent, honest, sincere, faithful
纯碱 **ch'ún-chièn** soda ash
纯艺术 **ch'ún-ì-shù** pure art (art for

art's sake)

纯朴 **ch'ún-p'ŭ** plain, simple, honest and austere; simplicity

纯熟 **ch'ún-shú** well-learned, fluent, skillful

纯度 **ch'ún-tù** fineness, degree of purity [of metals, etc.]

纯粹 **ch'ún-ts'ùi** pure, genuine, unadulterated; completely, wholly, entirely

纯氧 **ch'ún-yǎng** pure oxygen

546 唇齿相依 **ch'ún-ch'ĭh-hsiāng-ī** lips and teeth depend on each other (mutually dependent, a reciprocal alliance)

ch'ŭn (chŭn)

547 蠢蠢欲动 **ch'ŭn-ch'ŭn-yù-tùng** stirring and anxious to make a move (itching for action—usually derogatory, as an enemy getting ready to strike)

蠢人 **ch'ŭn-jén** a foolish person

蠢事 **ch'ŭn-shìh** a stupid action, folly

蠢材 **ch'ŭn-ts'ái** a dimwit, imbecile, nincompoop

ch'ūng (chōng)

548 充饥 **ch'ūng-chī** to stop hunger, eat

充其量 **ch'ūng-ch'í-liàng** at most, at the maximum, at the worst

充斥 **ch'ūng-ch'ìh** to abound (said of bad things), overfull

充耳不闻 **ch'ūng-ěrh-pù-wén** to stuff the ears and not hear (to ignore what is said)

充分发挥 **ch'ūng-fēn-fā-hūi** to bring into full play, to make full use of, develop fully

充分理由 **ch'ūng-fēn-lǐ-yú** every reason, to have good reason, ample basis

充分动员 **ch'ūng-fēn-tùng-yuán** to mobilize to the fullest extent

充分条件 **ch'ūng-fēn-t'iáo-chièn** sufficient conditions

充行家 **ch'ūng háng-chiā** to pretend to be expert, pose as an expert

充满信心 **ch'ūng-mǎn-hsìn-hsīn** full of confidence

充实 **ch'ūng-shíh** crammed full, abundant, overflowing; to strengthen, improve, fill out; reinforcement

充当 **ch'ūng-tāng** to serve as, act, fill a post

充足 **ch'ūng-tsú** sufficient, adequate, full

充裕 **ch'ūng-yù** ample, abundant; affluence

549 冲击 **ch'ūng-chī** to pound against, to buffet; impact

冲决 **ch'ūng-chüéh** to smash, break

冲锋陷阵 **ch'ūng-fēng-hsièn-chèn** to charge with bayonets and break the lines (a hard-fought victory)

冲昏头脑 **ch'ūng-hūn-t'óu-nǎo** to have one's head turned, to be giddy with

冲垮 **ch'ūng-k'uǎ** to overwhelm [as by flooding]

冲破 **ch'ūng-p'ò** to break through, break down

冲淡 **ch'ūng-tàn** to dilute, water down; mild [temperament]

冲天干劲 **ch'ūng-t'iēn-kàn-chìn** soaring enthusiasm, boundless energy

冲突 **ch'ūng-t'ū** a clash, conflict, encounter; to clash with, to run counter to

ch'úng (chóng)

550 虫害与病害 **ch'úng-hài yǔ pìng-hài** insect pests and plant diseases

虫灾 **ch'úng-tsāi** an insect plague

551 重整旗鼓 **ch'úng-chěng-ch'í-kǔ** to re-adjust banners and drums (to regroup after a defeat; to resume a work after a failure; to rebuild one's strength and start anew)

重庆谈判 **ch'úng-ch'ìng t'án-p'àn** the Chungking Conference (between Mao Tse-tung and Chiang Kai-shek following Mao's arrival in Chungking on August 28, 1945)

重重危机 **ch'úng-ch'úng-wēi-chī** crisis on top of crisis

重犯 **ch'úng-fàn** to repeat a crime or mistake

重复 **ch'úng-fù** to repeat, double, multiply, overlap; repetition, duplication, redundancy

重新安排河山 **ch'úng-hsīn ān-p'ái hó-shān** to re-arrange the rivers and mountains (to conquer nature)

重新分配 **ch'úng-hsīn fēn-p'èi** to redistribute; redistribution

重新学习 **ch'úng-hsīn hsuéh-hsí** to study all over again

重新改写 **ch'úng-hsīn kǎi-hsiěh** to rewrite; be rewritten

重新调整 **ch'úng-hsīn t'iáo-chěng** to adjust anew; readjustment

重新做人 **ch'úng-hsīn-tsò-jén** to become a new man, make a fresh start in life, turn over a new leaf

重钢 **ch'úng-kāng** the Chungking Steel Works

重申 **ch'úng-shēn** to repeat a report, reiterate, reaffirm

重述 **ch'úng-shù** to repeat, restate

重蹈复辙 **ch'úng-tǎo-fù-ch'é** to follow

the track of an overturned cart (to repeat a mistake, fail to learn a lesson)

重叠 **ch'úng-tiéh** to duplicate, repeat, overlap

重定 **ch'úng-tìng** to re-schedule, re-fix, re-set

重弹老调 **ch'úng-t'án-lǎo-tiào** to sing the same old tune

重操旧业 **ch'úng-ts'āo-chiù-yèh** to practice again the old profession (usually critical: to engage in the same old business)

重温旧梦 **ch'úng-wēn-chiù-mèng** to re-warm old dreams (draw comfort from old memories)

重演 **ch'úng-yěn** to repeat a stage performance (to repeat, reappear)

重印 **ch'úng-yìn** to reprint

重 **ch'úng**: *see also* **chùng**

552 崇高品质 **ch'úng-kāo p'ǐn-chìh** excellent qualities [of a person]

崇美 **ch'úng-měi** to glorify America, worship America (attitudes for which intellectuals were criticized in the early post-1949 period)

崇拜 **ch'úng-pài** to worship, adore, idolize

崇拜权威 **ch'úng-pài ch'üán-wēi** a cult of authority, excessive awe of position

崇拜洋、名、古作品 **ch'úng-pài yáng-míng-kǔ tsò-p'ǐn** to worship foreign, famous, and ancient works [of art and literature]

崇山峻岭 **ch'úng-shān-chùn-lǐng** lofty mountains and high ranges

崇洋复旧 **ch'úng-yáng-fù-chiù** worship foreign and resurrect ancient [things or ideas]

ch'ŭng (chŏng)

553 宠儿 **ch'ŭng-érh** favorite son (often figurative)

chü (jū)

554 拘禁 **chü-chìn** to detain, confine, take into custody

拘留 **chü-líu** to detain forcibly; detention, custody

拘泥成法 **chü-ní-ch'éng-fǎ** to adhere rigidly to the established rule (formalistic, unimaginative)

拘票 **chü-p'iào** a warrant of arrest

拘束 **chü-shù** (1) to restrain, restrict the freedom of; (2) timid, shy, not at ease

555 狙击射手 **chü-chì-shè-shǒu** a sniper, one who shoots from ambush

556 居间人 **chü-chiēn-jén** a middleman, intermediary; a person in the middle

居住期限 **chü-chù-ch'ī-hsièn** term of residence, length of residence

居住和迁徙的自由 **chü-chù hó ch'iēn-hsǐ te tzù-yú** freedom of residence and freedom to change residence

居住条件 **chü-chù t'iáo-chièn** housing situation, housing conditions

居心何在 **chü-hsīn-hó-tsài** what is [his] motive?

居功 **chü-kūng** to claim credit [for a success]

居功自傲 **chü-kūng-tzù-ào** to be arrogant over one's accomplishment

居功自恃 **chü-kūng-tzù-shìh** to depend on one's past achievements, to rest on one's laurels

居留 **chü-líu** to stay, reside, sojourn

居民 **chü-mín** inhabitants, residents

居民证 **chü-mín-chèng** residence card (issued to households—important before the introduction of rations)

居民储蓄服务所 **chü-mín ch'ǔ-hsù fú-wù-sǒ** residents' savings service centers (established in late 1958 at residents' committee level to elicit funds from people who were not connected with larger organizations)

居民点 **chü-mín-tiěn** housing site, residential spot (usually on minor scale, smaller than a village)

居民团结大会 **chü-mín t'uán-chiéh tà-huì** residents' unity assemblies (an experiment in consolidating neighborhoods, 1964)

居民委员会 **chü-mín wěi-yuán-huì** neighborhood committee, residents' committee

557 鞠躬尽瘁 **chü-kūng-chìn-ts'uì** to humbly exhaust one's energies (to devote one's whole strength for the public good, to devote one's life to)

chü (jú)

558 局限 **chü-hsièn** limitation, restriction, constraint

局限性 **chü-hsièn-hsìng** of a limited nature, limited

局面 **chü-mièn** situation, general conditions, state of affairs

局部 **chü-pù** parts of a whole, partial, local

局部战争 **chü-pù-chàn-chēng** limited war, partial war

局部观点 **chü-pù-kuān-tiěn** a partial viewpoint (seeing only a part of the whole)

局部利益 **chü-pù-lì-ì** local interests,

partial interests

局部偏差 **chú-pù-p'iēn-ch'ā** partial deviations

局部错误 **chú-pù-ts'ò-wù** partially in error, to be mistaken in part, a local error

局势 **chú-shìh** circumstances, conditions, state of affairs, situation

局外人 **chú-wài-jén** an outsider, person not involved, third party

chǔ (jǔ)

559 沮丧 **chǔ-sàng** to be dispirited, downcast, dejected, gloomy

560 举棋不定 **chǔ-ch'í-pù-tìng** holding a chesspiece without deciding [the move] (indecisive, hesitant)

举枪致敬 **chǔ-ch'iāng-chìh-chìng** to salute with a rifle, to present arms

举出 **ch'ǔ-ch'ū** to cite, enumerate, itemize

举火把 **chǔ-huǒ-pǎ** to carry a torch (to lead, show the way)

举行 **chǔ-hsíng** to convene, hold [a meeting], carry out, arrange, conduct

举一反三 **chǔ-ī-fǎn-sān** given one [corner] to infer the other three

举国欢腾 **chǔ-kúo-huān-t'éng** the whole country joyous

举例 **chǔ-lì** to give an example, cite an example

举办 **chǔ-pàn** to initiate, sponsor, undertake

举不胜举 **chǔ-pù-shēng-chǔ** too numerous to cite

举世注目 **chǔ-shìh-chù-mù** the whole world looks attentively, the focus of universal attention

举世闻名 **chǔ-shìh-wén-míng** known to all the world

举世无敌 **chǔ-shìh-wú-tí** the best in the world, peerless, unique

举手表决 **chǔ-shǒu-piǎo-chüéh** to vote by a show of hands

举足轻重 **chǔ-tsú-ch'īng-chùng** lifting the foot is enough to change the balance (to play a decisive role)

561 龃龉 **chǔ-yǔ** upper and lower jaw mismatched (discord, disagreement, quarrel)

chù (jù)

562 巨细 **chù-hsì** large or small, importance

巨型 **chù-hsíng** a large model, giant, colossal

巨人 **chù-jén** giant, a great man

巨量 **chù-liàng** a great quantity

巨额 **chù-ó** a big amount, a large number

巨变 **chù-pièn** a great change, transformation (usually a major change, such as the contrast between pre- and post-Liberation)

巨大 **chù-tà** vast, immense, huge, substantial

巨大潜力 **chù-tà-ch'ién-lì** great potentiality, vast latent possibilities; to have much to offer

巨大财富 **chù-tà-ts'ái-fù** vast treasure, great wealth

巨头 **chù-t'óu** a magnate, giant, national leader

563 拒之于门外 **chù-chīh yú mén-wài** to be kept out of the door (to exclude)

拒绝 **chù-chüéh** to refuse, reject

564 具备 **chù-pèi** all complete, fully supplied with, ready

具备一切条件 **chù-pèi ī-ch'ièh t'iáo-chièn** there is every requisite, all conditions have been met

具体 **chù-t'ǐ** concrete [as opposed to abstract], specific

具体执行合同 **chù-t'ǐ chíh-hsíng hó-t'ung** a concrete executing contract

具体现实 **chù-t'ǐ-hsièn-shíh** concrete reality

具体实践 **chù-t'ǐ-shíh-chièn** actual practice, specific practice

具有 **chù-yǔ** to be provided with, there is, to carry with, to acquire

565 剧种特色 **chù-chǔng t'è-sè** the characteristics of the different opera styles

剧场 **chù-ch'ǎng** a theater

剧情 **chù-ch'íng** the plot of a play, a dramatic plot

剧烈 **chù-lièh** violent, vigorous, strenuous, drastic

剧目 **chù-mù** dramatic repertoire, a list of dramatic works

剧本 **chù-pěn** a play in written form, a script

剧毒 **chù-tú** highly poisonous; a deadly poison

剧团 **chù-t'uán** theatrical group, theatrical troupe

剧作家 **chù-tsò-chiā** a playwright

剧院 **chù-yuàn** a theater

566 惧怕 **chù-p'à** to fear, dread

567 据信 **chù-hsìn** according to belief

据了解 **chù-liǎo-chièh** according to understanding

据点 **chù-tièn** a base, stronghold, foothold

据推测 **chù-t'uī-ts'è** according to speculation, according to belief

568 距离 **chù-lí** distance, interval

569 锯床 **chù-ch'uáng** a sawing machine

570 聚精会神 **chù-chīng-huì-shén** to

concentrate one's attention and energy

聚居 **chù-chū** to live together [in hamlets or compact community groups]

聚合 **chù-hó** to assemble, come together

聚餐 **chù-ts'ān** to eat together, join for a meal (generally with each participant paying his share of the bill)

chüān (juān)

571 捐税繁重 **chüān-shuì fán-chùng** taxes are innumerable and crushing

捐赠 **chüān-tsèng** a donation, contribution, offering

chǔan (juǎn)

572 卷入 **chüǎn-jù** to involve, draw into, suck into

卷入漩涡 **chüǎn-jù-hsuán-wō** to be drawn into the whirlpool

卷土重来 **chüǎn-t'ǔ-ch'úng-lái** to roll up the dust and come back [as in battle] (to counter attack, to stage a comeback)

卷扬机 **chüǎn-yáng-chī** a hoisting machine, winch, windlass

chüèh (juè)

573 决战 **chüéh-chàn** a decisive battle; to fight a duel

决战决胜 **chüéh-chàn-chüéh-shèng** determined to fight and determined to win (committed to fight until ultimate victory)

决计 **chüéh-chì** (1) to decide, make up one's mind; (2) certainly, definitely

决心 **chüéh-hsīn** determination, resolution; a decision; to make up one's mind, be resolved to

决心书 **chüéh-hsīn-shū** letters of determination (sometimes posted by students or others as a public volunteering to go to the countryside

决一雌雄 **chüéh-ī-tz'ú-hsíung** to decide [which is] the female and the male (to match strength, to fight it out)

决议 **chüéh-ì** to pass a resolution; a resolution [adopted at a meeting]; to decide

决议如山 **chüén-ì-jú-shān** resolutions [pilling up] like a mountain (the implication is usually critical)

决议草案 **chüéh-ì-ts'ǎo-àn** a draft resolution

决口 **chüéh-k'ǒu** a break in a dike; to overflow; a breach, gap, opening

决口而出 **chüéh-k'ǒu-érh-ch'ū** to make an opening [in a dike] and rush forth (to break out of control)

决裂 **chüéh-lièh** to break apart from, break apart, come to a breaking point, quarrel and break off friendly relations

决不仁慈 **chüéh-pù-jén-tz'ú** without the slightest mercy

决不罢休 **chüéh-pù-pà-hsīu** to never give up, never give in

决算 **chüéh-suàn** a final account, balance sheet, financial report

决死战 **chüéh-szǔ-chàn** a fight to the death, mortal combat

决死斗争 **chüéh-szǔ-tòu-chēng** a life-and-death struggle

决定 **chüéh-tìng** to decide, determine; a decision; firmly resolved

决定性胜利 **chüéh-tìng-hsìng shèng-lì** a decisive victory, crucial victory

决定论 **chüéh-tìng lùn** determinism

决定因素 **chüéh-tìng-yīn-sù** deciding factor, determining agent

决策 **chüéh-ts'è** to make a decision; an adopted policy

574 诀窍 **chüéh-ch'iào** the secret [of doing something], knack

575 抉择 **chüéh-tsé** to make a choice, make a decision

576 角逐 **chüéh-chú** to contend for, to compete for

角逐地位 **chüéh-chú-tì-wèi** to compete for place

角色 **chüéh-sè** an actor, actress; an important person in any field

角斗 **chüéh-tòu** to fight, compete for mastery, contend

角 **chüèh**: *see also* **chiǎo**

577 绝招 **chüéh-chāo** a unique skill, matchless art, the secret skill of a master (the old peasants and workers are now urged to teach these skills to the younger generation)

绝交 **chüéh-chiāo** to break relations, sever relations

绝境 **chüéh-chìng** a place of doom, a desperate situation

绝非偶然 **chüéh-fēi-ǒu-ján** by no means accidental, certainly not by chance

绝口不谈 **chüéh-k'ǒu-pù-t'án** to refrain from saying a word; never to mention it again

绝路 **chüéh-lù** dead end

绝密 **chüéh-mì** strictly confidential

绝大多数 **chüéh-tà-tō-shù** the overwhelming majority

绝对 **chüéh-tuì** absolute [as opposed to

relative]; absolutely, definitely

绝对真理 **chüéh-tuì-chēn-lǐ** absolute truth

绝对控制 **chüéh-tuì k'ùng-chìh** uncontested control, absolute control

绝对民主 **chüéh-tuì-mín-chǔ** pure democracy, absolute democracy

绝对命令 **chüéh-tuì-mìng-lìng** a categorical command

绝对平均主义 **chüéh-tuì p'íng-chūn-chǔ-ì** absolute equalitarianism

绝对的同一性 **chüéh-tuì-te t'úng-ī-hsìng** absolute identity

绝望 **chüéh-wàng** to lose all hope, despair of; hopelessness, despair

绝无仅有 **chüéh-wú-chǐn-yǔ** very unique, rare

绝育手术 **chüéh-yù-shǒu-shù** sterilization [of the male], vasectomy

绝缘 **chüéh-yüán** (1) to break off relations; (2) to insulate; insulated

578 觉察 **chüéh-ch'á** to discover, disclose, reveal

觉醒 **chüéh-hsǐng** to awaken (usually refers to wakening of political or social consciousness)

觉悟 **chüéh-wù** to comprehend and become aware, consciousness (with political and social connotations)

觉悟程度 **chüéh-wù-ch'éng-tù** level of consciousness, degree of awareness

579 掘进手 **chüéh-chìn-shǒu** diggers, excavaters, miners (usually refers to expert coal miners)

掘壕 **chüéh-háo** to entrench, dig a trench

掘煤采油 **chüéh-méi-ts'ǎi-yú** to dig coal and extract oil

掘墓鞭尸 **chüéh-mù-piēn-shīh** to open the grave and scourge thè corpse (to revile the dead—as in the Soviet attacks on Stalin)

580 厥词 **chüéh-tz'ú** big talk, nonsense

581 攫取 **chüéh-ch'ǚ** to grab, seize and carry off

chün (jūn)

582 军爱民, 民拥军 **chün-ài-mín, mín-yūng-chün** the army loves the people and the people support the army

军长 **chün-chǎng** corps commander, army commander

军政一致 **chün-chèng-ī-chìh** [with] army and government united, military and political in full accord

军政人员 **chün-chèng-jén-yuán** military and administrative personnel

军政委员会 **chün-chèng wěi-yuán-huì** military and administrative committee (before 1954)

军纪 **chün-chì** military discipline

军舰 **chün-chièn** a naval vessel, warship

军警 **chün-chǐng** troops and police

军种 **chün-chǔng** military services, branches of the armed forces

军区 **chün-ch'ǚ** military region, military district, military command

军区司令部 **chün-ch'ǚ-szū-lìng-pù** military area command headquarters

军权 **chün-ch'üán** military power, military might

军阀 **chün-fá** warlords, militarists

军阀主义 **chün-fá-chǔ-ì** warlordism

军阀作风 **chün-fá-tsò-fēng** warlord style (disregard of Party or central authority; bullying behavior)

军法 **chün-fǎ** military law, military code of justice

军分区 **chün-fēn-ch'ǚ** military sub-district (below the provincial level)

军火 **chün-huǒ** ammunition, munitions

军火商 **chün-huǒ-shāng** munitions manufacturer, arms dealer

军械 **chün-hsièh** ordnance, military supplies, armaments

军衔制度 **chün-hsién-chìh-tù** the system of military ranks (now abolished)

军需品 **chün-hsü-p'ǐn** quartermaster goods

军宣队 **chün-hsuān-tuì** army propaganda team (contraction of: PLA Mao Tse-tung Thought Propaganda Team)

军人家属 **chün-jén-chiā-shǔ** army dependents, dependents of military personnel

军容风纪 **chün-júng-fēng-chì** military appearance and discipline

军干群 **chün-kàn-ch'ún** [revolutionary committees which combined] military, cadres, and the masses

军干群三结合 **chün-kàn-ch'ún sān-chiéh-hó** a three-way alliance of the PLA, cadres, and the masses

军官证 **chün-kuān-chèng** military officers' identification cards

军管军训 **chün-kuǎn-chün-hsùn** [set up] military administration [and introduce] military training (part of the **sān-chīh liǎng-chün** during the Cultural Revolution)

军国主义 **chün-kuó-chǔ-ì** militarism

军垦农场 **chün-k'ěn-núng-ch'ǎng** an army land reclamation farm

军龄 **chün-líng** length of military service

军马场 **chün-mǎ-ch'ǎng** a ranch for raising military horses

军民兼顾 **chün-mín-chièn-kù** to care

for both army and the people

军民一致 **chǔn-mín-í-chìh** army [and] people united

军民联防 **chǔn-mín-lién-fáng** joint defense by the army and the people

军农生产 **chǔn-núng-shēng-ch'ǎn** military agricultural production

军备竞赛 **chǔn-pèi-chìng-sài** arms race, contest of military preparedness

军部 **chǔn-pù** a military headquarters

军事基地网 **chǔn-shìh chī-tì-wǎng** a network of military bases

军事集团 **chǔn-shìh-chí-t'uán** military bloc, a militarist group

军事家 **chǔn-shìh-chiā** a military strategist, military man

军事法庭 **chǔn-shìh-fǎ-t'íng** a military court

军事化 **chǔn-shìh-huà** militarization (one of the goals of the communes in expanding the militia—see **szǔ-huà**)

军事训练 **chǔn-shìh-hsùn-lièn** military training

军事医学科学院 **chǔn-shìh ī-hsuéh k'ō-hsuéh-yuàn** Academy of Military Medical Sciences

军事艺术 **chǔn-shìh-ì-shù** the military arts

军事干涉 **chǔn-shìh-kān-shè** military intervention

军事观点 **chǔn-shìh-kuān-tiěn** the military viewpoint (to use only crude military methods)

军事管制委员会 **chǔn-shìh kuǎn-chìh wěi-yuán-huì** Military Control Commission (the first organs of temporary control after Liberation)

军事管理 **chǔn-shìh-kuǎn-lǐ** military administration, military supervision

军事工业 **chǔn-shìh-kūng-yèh** war industries, armament production

军事工业体制 **chǔn-shìh-kūng-yèh t'ǐ-chìh** the system of military industry, the administrative framework of armaments production

军事科学院 **chǔn-shìh k'ō-hsuéh-yuàn** The Academy of Military Science

军事扩张 **chǔn-shìh k'uò-chāng** military expansion

军事冒险 **chǔn-shìh-mào-hsiěn** military adventure, military gamble

军事包围 **chǔn-shìh-pāo-wéi** military encirclement

军事编制 **chǔn-shìh-piēn-chìh** military table of organization

军事素质 **chǔn-shìh-sù-chìh** quality of the military

军事压力 **chǔn-shìh-yā-lì** military pressure

军事野营活动 **chǔn-shìh yěh-yíng-huó-tùng** army field training, army field exercises

军事演习 **chǔn-shìh yěn-hsí** war exercises, maneuvers

军事院校 **chǔn-shìh yuàn-hsiào** military academies and schools

军属 **chǔn-shǔ** army dependents, army families

军代会 **chǔn-tài-huì** an army representative assembly

军团 **chǔn-t'uán** army group, corps

军委 **chǔn-wěi** The Military Commission (contraction of: **Chūng-kùng chūng-yāng chǔn-shìh wěi-yuán-huì**)

军用卡车 **chǔn-yùng-k'ǎ-ch'ē** army truck

军用品 **chǔn-yùng-p'ǐn** military supplies

583 均衡 **chǔn-héng** well balanced; equilibrium

均匀 **chǔn-yún** equal and even

584 君主立宪 **chǔn-chǔ-lì-hsièn** constitutional monarchy

chǔn (jùn)

585 俊杰 **chǔn-chiéh** a talented and superior person, man of extraordinary talent

586 竣工 **chùn-kūng** completion of a project [usually a construction project]

ch'ǖ (qū)

587 区分 **ch'ǖ-fēn** to separate [into classes or categories], to distinguish

区人民委员会 **ch'ǖ jén-mín wěi-yuán-huì** ward people's council (the ward is a sub-division of a municipality)

区别 **ch'ǖ-piéh** to discriminate, distinguish; difference, disparity, dissimilarity

区党委 **ch'ǖ-tǎng-wěi** ward or municipal district Party committee

区委 **ch'ǖ-wěi** district Party committee (may refer to a ward or other regional subdivisions)

区域自治 **ch'ǖ-yù-tzù-chìh** regional autonomy (always refers to minority areas)

588 曲折 **ch'ǖ-ché** twists and turns, ups and downs; the complications of an affair

曲解 **ch'ǖ-chiěh** to distort, misinterpret, misconstrue

曲直 **ch'ǖ-chíh** the crooked and straight (the right and wrong)

曲线 **ch'ǖ-hsièn** a curved line, curve

曲线救国 **ch'ǖ-hsièn-chiù-kuó** "save the nation by a devious path" (excuse

used by those who opposed open
conflict with Japan in the 1930s)
曲度 **ch'ǖ-tù** curvature [degree of]
曲 **ch'ǖ**: see also **ch'ǔ**
589　驱逐 **ch'ǖ-chú** to drive out, expel, oust,
evict
驱逐出境 **ch'ǖ-chú-ch'ǖ-chìng** deporta-
tion, to deport
驱散 **ch'ǖ-sàn** to scatter, disperse,
drive off, break up
驱使 **ch'ǖ-shǐh** to dictate to, impel,
order about, drive to
590　屈服 **ch'ǖ-fú** to yield, submit, admit
defeat; submission, subservience
屈辱 **ch'ǖ-jù** to humiliate; humiliation,
mortification, disgrace
屈尊就教 **ch'ǖ-tsūn-chiu-chiào** to go
humbly seeking advice
屈从 **ch'ǖ-ts'úng** to submit, yield to
591　躯壳 **ch'ǖ-ch'iào** the human body
(figuratively: the external shell,
material aspect)
592　趋向 **ch'ǖ-hsiàng** tendency, inclination,
trend; to trend to, incline toward
趋势 **ch'ǖ-shìh** tendency, trend

ch'ǘ (qú)

593　渠灌区 **ch'ǘ-kuàn-ch'ǚ** irrigation
district
渠道 **ch'ǘ-tào** irrigation canal, canal,
ditch, drain
594　瞿秋白 **ch'ǘ ch'iu-pái** Ch'ü Ch'iu-pai
(a Communist Party leader, b. 1899,
general secretary 1927–28, captured
and executed by the KMT in 1935)

ch'ǔ (qǔ)

595　曲艺 **ch'ǔ-ì** operas and ballads, ballad
singing and story telling
曲调 **ch'ǔ-tiào** a tune, song, melody
曲 **ch'ǔ**: see also **ch'ǖ**
596　取之不尽，用之不竭 **ch'ǔ-chīh pù-chìn,
yùng-chīh pù-chiéh** to take without
depleting and use without exhausting
(overflowingly abundant, inexhaustible)
取经 **ch'ǔ-chīng** going to get the
classics (the original reference is to
the Buddhist monk Hsuan Tsang
bringing the sutras from India; the
present meaning is that the less
advanced units should go to learn
from the more advanced units)
取长补短 **ch'ǔ-ch'áng-pǔ-tuǎn** taking
the long to mend the short (to overcome one's weaknesses by acquiring
the strong points of others)
取巧 **ch'ǔ-ch'iǎo** to take a short cut,

manage with dexterity, manipulate
skillfully, take advantage of a situation
取决于 **ch'ǔ-chüéh-yú** to be determined
by, depend on, contingent on
取而代之 **ch'ǔ-érh-tài-chīh** to replace,
take someone's place
取消 **ch'ǔ-hsiāo** to cancel, abolish,
nullify, revoke, liquidate
取消主义 **ch'ǔ-hsiāo-chǔ-ì** liquida-
tionism
取消资格 **ch'¨ǔ-hsiāo-tzū-kó** to deprive
someone of his status
取捨 **ch'ǔ-shě** to accept or refuse, make
a selection; a choice
取代 **ch'ǔ-tài** to replace, substitute
取得教训 **ch'ǔ-té-chiào-hsùn** to draw
lessons from
取得胜利 **ch'ǔ-té-shèng-lì** to gain the
victory
取缔 **ch'ǔ-tì** to prohibit, ban, repress

ch'ǜ (qù)

597　去其糟粕，取其精华 **ch'ǜ-ch'í-tsāo-p'ò,
ch'ǔ-ch'í-chīng-huá** to discard the
dross and select the best
去掉 **ch'ǜ-tiào** to throw away, abandon, discard, get rid of, remove,
eliminate
去掉盲目性 **ch'ǜ-tiào máng-mù-hsìng**
get rid of blindness (distinguish
between true and false Marxism)
去粗取精 **ch'ǜ-ts'ū-ch'ǔ-chīng** discard
the crude and select the refined
去伪存真 **ch'ǜ-wěi-ts'ún-chēn** discard
the false and retain the true
598　趣味 **ch'ǜ-wèi** interest [in or of a
subject], taste

ch'üān (quān)

599　圈套 **ch'üān-t'ào** a trap, snare, pitfall,
entrapment, intrigue, plot

ch'üán (quán)

600　全集 **ch'üán-chí** complete works
[literary], collected works
全球战略 **ch'üán-ch'iú-chàn-luèh** global
strategy
全局 **ch'üán-chú** the whole situation,
overall situation
全局观念 **ch'üán-chú-kuān-nièn** a view
that sees the whole situation (as
opposed to a partial viewpoint)
全局观点 **ch'üán-chú-kuān-tiěn** an
overall point of view (though
working hard at one's assigned task,
the interests of the whole are kept in

mind) 全军复没 **ch'üán-chün fù-mò** the whole army has been annihilated (may be figurative)

全权证书 **ch'üán-ch'üán-chèng-shū** full powers [diplomatic], plenipotentiary credentials

全权公使 **ch'üán-ch'üán-kūng-shǐh** a minister plenipotentiary

全权大使 **ch'üán-ch'üán-tà-shǐh** ambassador plenipotentiary

全权代表 **ch'üán-ch'üán-tài-piǎo** a plenipotentiary representative

全非青年大会 **ch'üán-fēi ch'īng-nién tà-huì** All-African Youth Conference

全非人民大会常设机构 **ch'üán-fēi jén-mín-tà-huì ch'áng-shè-chī-kòu** Permanent Organization of the All-African People's Conference

全副武装 **ch'üán-fù-wǔ-chuāng** fully armed, with full field pack

全行业 **ch'üán-háng-yèh** by whole trades

全行业公私合营 **ch'üán-háng-yèh kūng-szū-hó-yíng** whole lines of trade [changed over to] joint state-private enterprises

全县广播大会 **ch'üán-hsièn kuǎng-pò-tà-huì** broadcast assembly of the whole county (large groups assemble to hear broadcast messages, as in the launching of campaigns)

全线进攻 **ch'üán-hsièn chìn-kūng** to attack all along the front; a general attack

全线出击 **ch'üán-hsièn-ch'ū-chī** to launch attacks on all fronts

全线通车 **ch'üán-hsièn-t'ūng-ch'ē** a whole line open to traffic

全心全意 **ch'üán-hsīn-ch'üán-ì** whole-heartedly, with heart and soul

全心全意为人民服务 **ch'üán-hsīn-ch'üán-ì wèi jén-mín fú-wù** to serve the people with heart and soul, to be wholehearted in the service of the people

全新 **ch'üán-hsīn** brand-new, altogether new

全人类解放 **ch'üán-jén-lèi chiěh-fàng** the emancipation of all mankind

全日制 **ch'üán-jìh-chìh** full-time system, all-day

全日制学校 **ch'üán-jìh-chìh hsuéh-hsiào** full-time school

全国妇联 **ch'üán-kuó-fù-lién** All-China Women's Federation (contraction of **chūng-huá ch'üan-kuo fu-nü lien-ho hui**)

全国宣传工作会议 **ch'üán-kuó hsuān-ch'uán kūng-tsò-huì-ì** National Propaganda Work Conference (March 6–13, 1957)

全国一盘棋 **ch'üán-kuó ī-p'án-ch'í** the whole nation [is] a chess game (a slogan to emphasize overall strategy in planning production, popularized in 1959)

全国人口调查 **ch'üán-kuó jén-k'ǒu-tiào-ch'á** the national census

全国人民代表大会 **ch'üán-kuó jén-mín tài-piǎo tà-huì** National People's Congress

全国人民代表大会常务委员会 **ch'üán-kuó jén-mín tài-piǎo-tà-huì ch'áng-wù wěi-yuán-huì** Standing Committee of the National People's Congress

全国供销合作总社 **ch'üán-kuó kūng-hsiāo hó-tsò-tsǔng-shè** All-China Federation of Supply and Marketing Cooperatives

全国粮票 **ch'üán-kuó liáng-p'iào** all-China food tickets (food ration tickets available for use by travelers in any part of the country)

全国代表大会 **ch'üán-kuó tài-piǎo-tà-huì** National Congress (contraction of Ch'üan-kuo jen-min tai-piao-ta-hui)

全国总工会 **ch'üán-kuó tsǔng-kūng-huì** All-China Federation of Trade Unions

全劳动力 **ch'üán láo-tùng-lì** the work capacity of an able-bodied, full-time worker

全力以赴 **ch'üán-lì-ǐ-fù** to go all out, to do one's utmost

全面 **ch'üán-mièn** comprehensive, total, full-scale, all-out, all embracing

全面战争 **ch'üán-mièn-chàn-chēng** full-scale war, all-out war, total war

全面计划 **ch'üán-mièn-chì-huà** overall planning, comprehensive planning

全面专政 **ch'üán-mièn-chuān-chèng** dictatorship in all aspects, complete dictatorship

全面发展 **ch'üán-mièn-fā-chǎn** all-round development, overall development

全面复辟 **ch'üán-mièn-fù-pì** all-round restoration (usually refers to attempts to restore capitalism or the old regime)

全面规划 **ch'üán-mièn-kuēi-huà** over all planning

全面看问题 **ch'üán-mièn k'àn wèn-t'í** all-round view of things, to see a problem from all sides

全面胜利 **ch'üán-mièn-shèng-lì** overall victory, complete victory

全面大跃进 **ch'üán-mièn tà-yuèh-chìn** all-round big leap forward, a great

leap forward on all fronts

全面总结 ch'üán-mièn-tsǔng-chiéh comprehensive summing up

全面完成 ch'üán-mièn wán-ch'éng overall completion (such as an economic plan, etc.)

全民战争 ch'üán-mín-chàn-chēng all-out people's war, war of all the people

全民皆兵 ch'üán-mín-chiēh-pīng all the people are soldiers, all citizens are soldiers

全民竞赛运动 ch'üán-mín chìng-sài-yùn-tùng a nationwide emulation movement [in production]

全民防御体系 ch'üán-mín fáng-yù-t'ǐ-hsì defense system of all the people

全民性运动 ch'üán-mín-hsìng yùn-tùng a campaign participated in by the people of the whole country, a nationwide movement

全民搞工业运动 ch'üán-mín kǎo kūng-yèh yùn-tùng the movement to get everybody involved in industry (a campaign during the Great Leap)

全民国家 ch'üán-mín-kuó-chiā a state of the whole people (a critical reference to the Soviet Union which has announced that it no longer has class struggle)

全民炼钢 ch'üán-mín lièn-kāng everybody makes steel (Great Leap period)

全民办工业 ch'üán-mín pàn kūng-yèh development of industry by the whole people

全民办电 ch'üán-mín pàn-tièn the whole nation sets up electricity [generating plants]

全民表决 ch'üán-mìn-piǎo-chüéh a plebiscite, referendum

全民所有制 ch'üán-mín sǒ-yǔ-chìh system of ownership by the entire people

全民党 ch'üán-mín-tǎng a party of the whole people (a criticism of the CPSU—i.e., by claiming to be the part of all, it has given up class character)

全民族的全面抗战 ch'üán mín-tsú te ch'üán-mièn-k'àng-chàn total resistance by the whole nation

全民文艺 ch'üán-mín-wén-ì literature of the whole people (criticized as the Chou Yang line)

全能 ch'üán-néng all-round, versatile; omnipotent

全能厂 ch'üán-néng-ch'ǎng an all-capable factory (a manufacturing plant showing great initiative, self-reliance, and ability to handle a diversity of tasks)

全部 ch'üán-pù the whole, all, complete; totally, entirely

全盘机械化 ch'üán-p'án chī-hsièh-huà overall mechanization

全盘否定 ch'üán-p'án-fǒu-tìng complete denial, negation

全盘西化 ch'üán-p'án-hsī-huà wholesale Westernization (excessive aping of the West—to be criticized)

全盘电气化 ch'üán-p'án tièn-ch'ì-huà overall electrification

全神贯注 ch'üán-shén-kuàn-chù to be absorbed in, to concentrate one's whole attention [on], wholly concerned with

全盛时代 ch'üán-shèng-shíh-tài a golden age, peak period, heyday

全世界无产者联合起来 ch'üán-shìh-chièh wú-ch'ǎn-chě lién-hó-ch'ǐ-lái Proletarians of the world, unite! Workers of the world, unite!

全代会 ch'üán-tài-huì National Congress (contraction of ch'üán-kuo jen-min tai-piao ta-hui)

全党 ch'üán-tǎng all-Party, the whole Party, all ranks and levels of the [Communist] Party

全体会议 ch'üán-t'ǐ-huì-ì plenary meeting or session

全体人员 ch'üán-t'ǐ-jén-yuán the whole personnel, all the members of

全体利益 ch'üán-t'ǐ-lì-ì the interests of the whole

全体辞职 ch'üán-t'ǐ-tz'ú-chíh to resign en bloc

全托 ch'üán-t'ō full care (nursery or child care center providing room and board)

全文 ch'üán-wén the full text

权衡轻重 ch'üán-héng ch'īng-chùng to measure the light and heavy (to weigh the pros and cons)

权宜之计 ch'üán-í-chīh-chì an expediency plan, stop-gap measure, temporary expedient

权益 ch'üán-ì rights and interests, rights of ownership

权力 ch'üán-lì power, actual power to do things, governmental power, administrative authority

权力机关 ch'üán-lì-chī-kuān an organ of state authority, power organs, authoritative agencies

权力下放 ch'üán-lì-hsià-fàng downward delegation of authority [to lower government organs]

权力再分配 ch'üán-lì tsài-fēn-p'èi redistribution of power

权力无上 ch'üán-lì-wú-shàng supreme

in authority
权利 **ch'üán-lì** a right, a privilege; interests
权威 **ch'üán-wēi** an authority, a person who has special knowledge or status (now often has the connotation of self-importance)

602 泉源 **ch'üán-yuán** a spring, source

ch'üǎn (quǎn)

603 犬儒学派 **ch'üǎn-jú-hsuéh-p'ài** the Cynic school (from the Greek derivation: dog-like)
犬牙交错 **ch'üǎn-yá chiāo-ts'ò** dog's teeth gnashed together (like a jigsaw design—said of national borders that are excessively complex)

ch'üàn (quàn)

604 劝告 **ch'üàn-kào** to advise, admonish, exhort, teach; advice
劝说 **ch'üàn-shuō** to attempt to persuade; persuasion
劝阻随地吐痰 **ch'üàn-tsǔ suí-tì t'ù-t'án** persuade [others] not to spit at random

ch'üēh (quē)

605 缺秤 **ch'üēh-ch'èng** short weight (to give customers less than what they have paid for)
缺欠 **ch'üēh-ch'ièn** a shortcoming; to be short of, to owe
缺乏 **ch'üēh-fá** to lack; lack of, shortage
缺乏根据 **ch'üēh-fá kēn-chù** lacking in basis, groundless
缺席 **ch'üēh-hsí** to be absent from a meeting or class
缺陷 **ch'üēh-hsièn** a defect, failing, shortcoming
缺口 **ch'üēh-k'ǒu** a breach, a gap [in a wall or dike, etc.]
缺粮户 **ch'üēh-liáng-hù** a grain-deficient household
缺粮队 **ch'üēh-liáng-tuì** a grain-deficient production team
缺点 **ch'üēh-tiěn** a shortcoming, defect, lack, deficiency, fault, flaw
缺材代用 **ch'üēh-ts'ái-tài-yùng** to find substitutes for materials in short supply

ch'üèh (què)

606 确切 **ch'üèh-ch'ièh** valid, accurate, sound, exact, precise

确信 **ch'üèh-hsìn** to be certain of, to be convinced, sure of; reliable information
确认 **ch'üèh-jèn** to certify, definitely believe, acknowledge
确立 **ch'üèh-lì** to establish, build; to consolidate
确保 **ch'üèh-pǎo** to make sure, ensure, make safe, secure, guarantee
确实 **ch'üèh-shíh** exact, true, actual, correct, reliable; really genuine, authentic; really
确定 **ch'üèh-tìng** to affirm, make certain, make sure, fix, set; definite, sure, positive
确凿 **ch'üèh-tsò** definite, true, well-established

ch'ún (qún)

607 群众 **ch'ún-chùng** (1) the masses, the "people"—especially the workers, peasants, and soldiers; (2) *The Masses* (a Party journal—usually weekly, but often irregular—published in succession at Hankow, Chungking, Shanghai, and Hong Kong from December 1937 to October 1949)
群众积极性 **ch'ún-chùng chī-chí-hsìng** the initiative of the masses (the energy or aptitude of the masses to initiate action)
群众基础 **ch'ún-chùng-chī-ch'ǔ** mass foundation, mass basis (mass support)
群众教育运动 **ch'ún-chùng chiào-yù yùn-tùng** Mass Education Movement (1944)
群众接待站 **ch'ún-chùng chiēh-tài-chàn** mass reception stations (offices set up to receive suggestions, complaints, etc., from the masses)
群众监督 **ch'ún-chùng-chièn-tū** supervision by the masses; supervision of the masses
群众创造力 **ch'ún-chùng ch'uàng-tsào-lì** the creativeness of the masses
群众呼声 **ch'ún-chùng hū-shēng** the voice [demand] of the masses
群众性组织 **ch'ún-chùng-hsìng tsǔ-chīh** mass organizations, organizations of a mass character
群众学校 **ch'ún-chùng hsuéh-hsiào** mass schools (now generally known as **mín-pàn hsuéh-hsiào**)
群众观点 **ch'ún-chùng-kuān-tiěn** the mass point of view (one of the **szǔ-tà kuān-tiěn**)
群众工厂 **ch'ún-chùng-kūng-ch'ǎng** a

factory operated by the masses (small-scale neighborhood enterprise)

群众工作 **ch'ún-chùng-kūng-tsò** mass work, work among the masses

群众落后论 **ch'ún-chùng lò-hòu lùn** the theory that the masses are backward (a doctrine attributed to Liu Shao-ch'i)

群众路线 **ch'ún-chùng-lù-hsièn** the mass line ("from the masses and to the masses")

群众办报 **ch'ún-chùng pàn-pào** the masses run the papers (the columns of the newspapers should not be monopolized by their staffs)

群众评议推荐 **ch'ún-chùng p'íng-ì t'uī-chièn** evaluation and recommendation of the masses (selection by unit members for advanced training)

群众大会 **ch'ún-chùng-tà-huì** a mass rally, mass meeting

群众代表 **ch'ún-chùng-tài-piǎo** a representative of the masses

群众的眼睛是雪亮的 **ch'ún-chùng-te yěn-chīng shìh hsuěh-liàng-te** the eyes of the masses are crystal clear

群众斗争 **chún-chùng-tòu-chēng** struggle by the masses, struggle of the masses

群众团体 **ch'ún-chùng-t'uán-t'ǐ** a mass group, the body of the masses

群众推荐 **ch'ún-chùng-t'uī-chièn** recommendation by the masses

群众组织 **ch'ún-chùng-tsǔ-chīh** mass organization, organization of the masses

群众业余美术创作活动 **ch'ún-chùng yèh-yú měi-shù-ch'uàng-tsò huó-tùng** spare-time fine arts creative activities of the masses

群众业余文艺 **ch'ún-chùng yèh-yú wén-ì** spare-time arts and literature of the masses

群众运动 **ch'ún-chùng-yùn-tùng** mass movement, mass campaign

群起而攻之 **ch'ún-ch'ǐ érh kūng-chīh** to rally together to attack [him or it]

群防群治活动 **ch'ún-fáng ch'ún-chìh huó-tùng** the prevention and treatment of diseases by the masses [in rural villages]

群氓 **ch'ún-máng** the common people, the common herd (in the old, derogatory sense)

群魔乱舞 **ch'ún-mó-luàn-wǔ** a coven of devils dance confusedly (in derogation of the activities of one's opponents)

群声反对 **ch'ún-shēng-fǎn-tuì** every voice opposes, opposed by the masses

群策群力 **ch'ún-ts'è-ch'ún-lì** collective wisdom and strength, the plans and efforts of the masses

群威群胆 **ch'ún-wēi-ch'ún-tǎn** the power and courage of the masses [is great]

群言堂 **ch'ún-yén-t'áng** a hall [place, meeting] where all may speak freely

群英会 **ch'ún-yīng-huì** heroes' meeting (a meeting held to encourage others to emulate model workers)

群英会诊 **ch'ún-yīng-huì-chěn** joint consultation by a group of "heroes" (consultation on a problem by a group of technicians or experienced workers)

ēn (ēn)

608 恩情 **ēn-ch'íng** love, sentiment of friendship, kindness

恩人 **ēn-jén** benefactor, savior

恩格斯 **ēn-kó-szū** Engels, Friedrich (1820–1895)

恩赐观点 **ēn-tz'ù-kuān-tiěn** favor-granting viewpoint (an attitude to be criticized: help from a higher level is given because of need, not as a favor; those receiving the help should use it responsibly, not as a gratuity to be spent as a gift)

ĕrh (ér)

609 儿歌 **érh-kō** a children's rhyme, jingle

儿童节 **érh-t'úng-chiéh** Children's Day (June 1)

儿童队 **érh-t'úng-tuì** Children's Corps (Kiangsi and Anti-Japanese periods)

儿童团 **érh-t'úng-t'uán** Young Pioneers (Kiangsi and Anti-Japanese War periods)

ĕrh (ĕr)

610 尔虞我诈 **ĕrh-yú wǒ-chà** you cheat and I deceive (mutual dishonesty)

611 耳针疗法 **ĕrh-chēn-liáo-fǎ** using the acupuncture points in the ear as basis for treatment [of various ailments]

耳光 **ĕrh-kuāng** a slap in the face (figurative)

耳目一新 **ĕrh-mù-ī-hsīn** everything is new to ears and eyes (conditions have changed for the better)

耳目灵通 **ĕrh-mù-líng-t'ūng** ears and eyes penetrate afar (extremely well informed)

耳聰目明 **ěrh-ts'ūng-mù-míng** sharp in hearing and clear in seeing (a highly intelligent person)

耳聞目睹 **ěrh-wén-mù-tǔ** the ears hear and the eyes see (first-hand knowledge)

耳聞不如目睹 **ěrh-wén pù-jú mù-tǔ** hearing with one's ears is not as good as seeing with one's eyes (seeing is believing)

èrh (èr)

612 二者必居其一 **èrh-chě pì-chū-ch'í-ī** one must be [or do] one of the two [things]

二臣 **èrh-ch'én** twice an official (one who served two dynasties—hence, a traitor)

二七运动 **èrh-ch'ī-yùn-tùng** The February 7 Movement (a strike by railway workers at Hankow which was bloodily suppressed by the troops of Wu P'ei-fu on February 7, 1923)

二重性 **èrh-ch'úng-hsìng** dual nature, dual character, duality

二二八事变 **èrh-èrh-pā shìh-pièn** the February 28 Incident (the riots in Taiwan in February 1947)

二分法 **èrh-fēn-fǎ** dichotomy

二一一制 **èrh-ī-ī-ī chìh** the Two-One-One System (two fourths of the cadres are sent down to work at lower levels, one fourth are sent on inspection tours, the other fourth carry on normal duties: all roles are rotated at regular intervals)

二流子 **èrh-líu-tzu** idler, vagabond, do-nothing, loafer

二律矛盾 **èrh-lù-máo-tùn** the contradiction between two principles, antinomy

二律背反 **èrh-lù-pèi-fǎn** the opposition of two principles, antinomy

二把手 **èrh-pǎ-shǒu** the second hand (second in command)

二遍苦 **èrh-pièn-k'ǔ** to suffer a second time (living in the old society was the first suffering—any return to capitalism would be the second)

二部制 **èrh-pù-chìh** double sessioning [in schools]

二十年代 **èrh-shíh-nién-tài** the twenties of any century (if not specified, can be taken as the 1920s)

二十三条 **èrh-shíh-sān t'iáo** The Twenty-three Articles (set forth by Mao Tse-tung at the end of 1964 to guide the Socialist Education Movement)

二十大 **èrh-shíh-tà** the Twentieth Party Congress (of the CPSU, at which Khrushchev denounced Stalin)

二四三一制 **èrh-szù sān-ī chìh** the Two-Four and Three-One System (the workday of a cadre is divided into two four-hour periods—*erh-szu*. One period is spent in production as a laborer, inspector, or director; the other is in meetings, study, and routine official business. E.g., Loyang Tractor Factory, 1960)

二参一改 **èrh-ts'ān ī-kǎi** the Two Participations and One Change (workers participate in leadership and management of the enterprise, and change unreasonable regulations)

二次革命论 **èrh-tz'ù kó-mìng lùn** the dual revolution theory

二万五千里长征 **èrh-wàn-wǔ-ch'iēn lǐ ch'áng-chēng** the Long March (of the CCP from Kiangsi to Shensi, 1934–36)

二五制 **èrh-wǔ-chìh** the Two-Five System (a plan, instituted in 1960, by which cadres spent two days a week on meetings, inspections, and political studies, and the other five days working in the fields)

二元论 **èrh-yuán-lùn** dualism, dualistic theory

二月政变 **èrh-yuèh-chèng-pièn** the February Revolt (a coup allegedly planned by P'eng Chen and his group in February 1966)

二月复辟逆流 **èrh-yuèh fù-pì nì-líú** the February Restoration Counter-current (a phrase used by the radicals who met reverses in February 1967)

二月逆流 **èrh-yuèh-nì-líú** the February Counter-current (*see above*)

二月提纲 **èrh-yuèh t'í-kāng** the February Outline Report (an outline report on how to conduct the Cultural Revolution issued by the "Five-Man Group" on February 12, 1966, later repudiated by the Maoists)

fā (fā)

613 发展集体副业 **fā-chǎn chí-t'ǐ-fù-yèh** developing collective sideline occupations

发展进步势力 **fā-chǎn chìn-pù-shìh-lì** to develop the progressive forces

发展经济保障供给 **fā-chǎn-chīng-chì pǎo-chàng-kūng-chǐ** develop the economy to ensure supplies [of

necessities]

发展壮大 **fā-chǎn chuàng-tà** to develop and grow stronger and bigger

发展中国家 **fā-chǎn-chūng kuó-chiā** the developing countries

发展规律 **fā-chǎn-kuēi-lǜ** the law of development

发展生产 **fā-chǎn shēng-ch'ǎn** to develop production

发迹史 **fā-chì-shǐh** the history of development, developmental history

发家致富 **fā-chiā chìh-fù** to cause one's family to prosper (now criticized)

发家史 **fā-chiā-shǐh** the history of one family's prosperity

发酵 **fā-chiào** to ferment, to become sour

发起 **fā-ch'ǐ** to initiate, start, sponsor

发觉 **fā-chüéh** to find, discover; to sense, ferret out

发掘 **fā-chüéh** to excavate, dig out

发掘潜力 **fā-chüéh ch'ién-lì** to bring out potential abilities, tap potentialities

发掘古物 **fā-chüéh kǔ-wù** to unearth relics, discover ancient remains

发放 **fā-fàng** to dole out, send away, distribute

发奋图强 **fā-fèn t'ú-ch'iáng** to strive for strength with great vigor

发疯 **fā-fēng** to go crazy, lose one's senses, become frantic, run amuck

发航港 **fā-háng-kǎng** the port from which a ship's voyage originates

发号施令 **fā-hào-shīh-lìng** to give commands and orders

发慌 **fā-huāng** to panic, be uneasy, nervous

发挥 **fā-huī** to develop, expand on, give play to, give free scope to, manifest

发挥监督作用 **fā-huī chiēn-tū-tsò-yùng** to develop the supervisory function

发挥潜在力量 **fā-huī ch'ién-tsài-lì-liang** to tap potentialities, bring potentialities into play, make fuller use of latent resources

发挥作用 **fā-huī tsò-yùng** to fulfill a function, play a role, do one's proper part

发昏 **fā-hūn** to faint, grow dizzy, lose one's senses, go crazy

发祥地 **fā-hsiáng-tì** a place of auspicious omen (a place where a good or great thing has its origin)

发泄 **fā-hsièh** to release [pent up feelings or emotions], pour out, give vent to, dissipate

发现 **fā-hsièn** to discover, detect, uncover, bring to light; to appear, arise

发行 **fā-hsíng** to issue, publish

发热发光 **fā-jè fā-kuāng** to radiate heat and emit light (a good Party member, for example, will shine forth)

发人深思 **fā-jén-shēn-szū** to arouse one's deepest thoughts

发刊词 **fā-k'ān-tz'ú** an introductory editorial of a journal

发狂 **fā-k'uáng** to become crazy, mad, insane

发牢骚 **fā-láo-sāo** to complain, grumble

发明 **fā-míng** to invent; an invention

发表宣言 **fā-piǎo-hsuān-yén** to issue a manifesto

发表意见 **fā-piǎo ì-chièn** to express an opinion, make a statement of views

发表声明 **fā-piǎo shēng-míng** to make a statement, issue a statement

发病率 **fā-pìng-lù** incidence of illness

发布命令 **fā-pù mìng-lìng** to issue a command, publish an order

发票 **fā-p'iào** an invoice, cash receipt

发射器 **fā-shè-ch'ì** launching mechanism

发射台 **fā-shè-t'ái** launching platform

发生 **fā-shēng** to take place, occur, happen, arise, come about

发生问题 **fā-shēng wèn-t'í** to give rise to trouble, produce problems

发生影响 **fā-shēng yǐng-hsiǎng** to produce effects, affect, influence

发誓 **fā-shìh** to take an oath, vow

发思古幽情 **fā szū-kǔ yū-ch'íng** to cherish the memory of the good ancient days

发达 **fā-tá** to prosper, flourish, develop; developed

发达国家 **fā-tá-kuó-chiā** the developed countries

发电站 **fā-tièn-chàn** electrical generating plant (usually small scale)

发电机 **fā-tièn-chī** electric generator, dynamo

发电量 **fā-tièn-liàng** electrical output

发电能力 **fā-tièn néng-lì** electrical generating capacity

发电设备 **fā-tièn-shè-pèi** electrical generating equipment, electrical power installation

发抖 **fā-tǒu** to tremble, shiver (the usual connotation is that of an enemy quaking with fear)

发动战争 **fā-tùng chàn-chēng** to launch a war, initiate hostilities

发动群众 **fā-tùng ch'ún-chùng** to mobilize the masses, arouse the masses

发作 **fā-tsò** to flare up [in anger], break

out [in illness], develop into something

发财致富 **fā-ts'ái-chìh-fù** to make one's fortune, become rich

发扬 **fā-yáng** to develop, foster, expand, spread, unfold

发扬革命传统 **fā-yáng kó-míng ch'uán-t'ŭng** to foster the revolutionary tradition

发扬光大 **fā-yáng kuāng-tà** to foster and broaden

发扬优良的工作作风 **fā-yáng yū-liáng-te kūng-tsò tsò-fēng** to foster a good style of work

发言 **fā-yén** to speak out (individual expression in discussion sessions)

发言权 **fā-yén-ch'üán** the right to speak, right of expressing opinions

发言人 **fā-yén-jén** a [government or official] spokesman, speaker [at a large meeting]

发言提纲 **fā-yén-t'í-kāng** an outline of a statement or speech

发言盈庭 **fā-yén yíng-t'íng** talk fills the hall (too much talk)

发源 **fā-yuán** an origin, source; to originate

fá (fá)

⁶¹⁴ 伐木工 **fá-mù-kūng** a logger, tree cutter

⁶¹⁵ 罚款 **fá-k'uǎn** a penalty charge, fine

fǎ (fǎ)

⁶¹⁶ 法案 **fǎ-àn** a legislative bill, a draft act or law

法纪 **fǎ-chì** law and discipline

法家思想 **fǎ-chiā-szū-hsiǎng** the thought of the Legalist School

法制 **fǎ-chìh** a legal system, legislation, law

法治 **fǎ-chìh** rule based on law, constitutional government

法权 **fǎ-ch'üán** legal right, jurisdiction

法西斯 **fǎ-hsī-szū** fascist, fascism

法西斯蒂 **fǎ-hsī-szū-tì** fascist

法西斯独裁统治 **fǎ-hsī-szū tú-ts'ái-t'ǔng-chìh** the fascist dictatorship

法新社 **fǎ-hsīn-shè** Agence Francaise de Presse [AFP]

法学 **fǎ-hsuéh** the study of law, jurisprudence, legal science

法人 **fǎ-jén** juristic person, a legal entity [such as a corporation]

法官 **fǎ-kuān** a judge

法规 **fǎ-kuēi** laws and regulations, statutes, legislation

法兰西 **fǎ-lán-hsī** France (usually

contracted to Fa-kuo)

法郎 **fǎ-láng** franc

法令规章 **fǎ-lìng kuēi-chāng** laws and regulations

法律 **fǎ-lǜ** the law, laws, statute, legislation; legal, legitimate, statutory

法律制裁 **fǎ-lǜ-chìh-ts'ái** legal sanction

法律顾问处 **fǎ-lǜ kù-wèn-ch'ù** legal advice division

法办 **fǎ-pàn** to be dealt with under the law, judicial handling

法宝 **fǎ-pǎo** magic weapon (during the Cultural Revolution, one of the similes for the Thought of Mao Tse-tung)

法属西印度群岛 **fǎ-shǔ hsī-yìn-tù ch'ún-tǎo** French West Indies

法属圭亚那 **fǎ-shǔ kuēi-yà-nà** French Guiana

法属索马里 **fǎ-shǔ sǒ-mǎ-lǐ** French Somaliland

法典 **fǎ-tiěn** a law code

法定人数 **fǎ-tìng-jén-shù** a quorum

法庭 **fǎ-t'íng** a law court, tribunal (may refer to the actual courtroom or a division of a **fǎ-yuàn**)

法庭庭长 **fǎ-t'íng t'íng-chǎng** a chief judge

法统 **fǎ-t'ǔng** legal system [in a broad sense], the tradition of state political power

法则 **fǎ-tsé** a principle; a law, statute; a rule, regulations, a decree; a standard, pattern

法院 **fǎ-yuàn** law court, tribunal (usually in a broader sense than **fǎ-t'íng**)

fān (fān)

⁶¹⁷ 翻案 **fān-àn** to reopen a case, reverse a sentence, reverse a decision

翻案风 **fān-àn-fēng** case-reversing wind (a frequent aftermath of major campaigns when persons attacked during the campaign seek rehabilitation)

翻案书 **fān-àn-shū** a petition for rehabilitation

翻新 **fān-hsīn** to rebuild, renovate, remodel [the old into something new]

翻修 **fān-hsīu** to repair, remodel, overhaul

翻一番 **fān-ì-fān** to double [production]

翻译 **fān-ì** to translate, interpret; a translation; a translator or interpreter

翻然悔改 **fān-ján-huǐ-kǎi** to repent completely

翻然悔悟 **fān-ján-huǐ-wù** to make a clean break with the past, have a complete repentance

翻过筋斗 **fān-kuò kēn-tou** to turn a somersault (to suffer a reverse)

翻供 **fān-kùng** to withdraw testimony, retract testimony

翻脸 **fān-liěn** to reverse one's face (to break friendship, pretend not to know an old friend)

翻版 **fān-pǎn** to reprint, reproduce; reprint, reproduction

翻砂 **fān-shā** to pour [metal for casting] into a sand mold

翻山越岭 **fān-shān-yuèh-lǐng** to travel over mountains and ranges (tireless in accomplishing one's tasks)

翻身 **fān-shēn** to turn oneself around, reverse one's position [from the peasant's old inferiority to the landlord to a position of superiority] (to emancipate oneself, to become a new person)

翻身账 **fān-shēn-chàng** turning-over account (the history of one's change in status since Liberation)

翻身戶 **fān-shēn-hù** a family that has turn the tables, a liberated family (a family that formerly was oppressed, but whose condition has changed completely as the result of the new order)

翻身奴隶 **fān-shēn-nú-lì** a liberated slave

翻身农民 **fān-shēn-núng-mín** turned-over peasants (peasants who have overthrown the landlord's rule)

翻身农奴 **fān-shēn-núng-nú** serfs who have turned-over, emancipated serfs (generally refers to Tibet)

翻身斗争 **fān-shēn-tòu-chēng** a turn-over struggle

翻书查资料 **fān-shū ch'á tzū-liào** scanning the books and checking the data (implies over-emphasis on bookishness)

翻腾开 **fān-t'éng-k'āi** boiling turbulence (usually applied to ideological struggle in an active stage)

翻天覆地 **fān-t'iēn-fù-tì** to overturn sky and upset earth (to turn everything upside down, world-shaking, tremendous)

fán (fán)

618 烦闷 **fán-mèn** worried, vexed, melancholy

烦恼 **fán-nǎo** worries, annoyance; confusing, vexing

烦琐 **fán-sǒ** trivial, trifling

烦琐哲学 **fán-sǒ-ché-hsuéh** trivial philosophy, scholasticism

619 繁殖耕畜 **fán-chíh kēng-ch'ù** to breed draft animals

繁重劳动 **fán-chùng-láo-tùng** toilsome work, strenuous labor

繁复多样 **fán-fù-tō-yàng** complicated and varied

繁花盛开 **fán-huā-shèng-k'āi** in full bloom

繁华 **fán-huá** bustling, thriving, affluent

繁荣 **fán-júng** prosperous, thriving, flourishing

繁荣富强 **fán-júng-fù-ch'iáng** prosperous, rich and strong

繁荣兴旺 **fán-júng hsīng-wàng** prosperous and flourishing

繁体字 **fán-t'ǐ-tzù** complicated-form characters (the pre-simplification form of those characters which have now been standardized in simplified form)

繁文缛节 **fán-wén-jù-chiéh** superfluous rules and usages (useless procedures, red tape)

fǎn (fǎn)

620 反证 **fǎn-chèng** counter-evidence; to rebut

反击 **fǎn-chī** to counterattack, retaliate, retort, repulse

反集体决定论 **fǎn chí-t'ǐ-chüéh-tìng lùn** the doctrine of non-collective decision-making (the suggestion that not all decisions are in fact collective and that free will and leadership play a role—one of the **hēi-pā-lùn**)

反骄破满 **fǎn-chiāo-p'ò-mǎn** oppose arrogance and smash complacency

反间 **fǎn-chièn** to create discord [among the enemy], sow discontent

反殖民主义 **fǎn-chíh-mín-chǔ-ì** anti-colonialism

反转 **fǎn-chuǎn** to turn over, turn around; conversely

反常现象 **fǎn-ch'áng-hsièn-hsiàng** abnormal phenomena, anomaly

反潮流 **fǎn ch'áo-liú** going against the tide (to wage resolute struggle against opportunism, revisionism, and all other incorrect currents)

反其道而行之 **fǎn-ch'í-tào érh-hsíng-chíh** to do the opposite (however others do, we will proceed in the exactly opposite manner)

反侵略战争 **fǎn-ch'īn-luèh chàn-chēng** anti-aggressive war, war to resist aggression

反封建 **fǎn-fēng-chièn** anti-feudalism

反富农斗争 **fǎn-fù-núng tòu-chēng** anti-rich peasant struggle (launched in mid-1932 in the Kiangsi Soviet)

反复 **fǎn-fù** to repeat, reiterate, reduplicate, go over and over; now this now that, wavering

反复琢磨 **fǎn-fù-chó-mó** to polish repeatedly (painstaking deliberation)

反复古 **fǎn-fù-kǔ** oppose restoration of the old

反复无常 **fǎn-fù-wú-ch'áng** always changing, not dependable, capricious, fickle

反海洋霸权斗争 **fǎn hǎi-yáng pà-ch'uán tòu-chēng** the struggle against hegemony of the seas

反胡风运动 **fǎn-hú-fēng yùn-tùng** anti-Hu Feng Movement (1955); *see* **hú-fēng**

反华恶棍 **fǎn-huá ò-kùn** anti-China villains

反华大合唱 **fǎn-huá tà-hó-ch'àng** an anti-China chorus

反华影片《中国》 **fǎn-huá yǐng-p'ièn chūng-kúo** the anti-Chinese film "China" (the film documentary on China produced by Antonioni in 1972)

反"火药味"论 **fǎn huó-yào-wèi lùn** the doctrine of opposition to the smell of gunpowder (a desire to get away from the concentration on war and armed struggle—one of the **hēi-pā-lùn**)

反响 **fǎn-hsiǎng** echo, reaction [to a speech, etc.]; to reverberate

反省 **fǎn-hsǐng** self-reflection, self-examination, repentance

反修防修 **fǎn-hsiū fáng-hsiū** combating and preventing revisionism

反修粮 **fǎn-hsiū-liáng** anti-revisionism grain (to increase grain output to meet the threat of Soviet attack)

反人民 **fǎn-jén-mín** anti-popular; to turn against the people

反弱为强 **fǎn-jò-wéi-ch'iáng** to convert weakness into strength

反感 **fǎn-kǎn** resentment, antipathy

反戈一击 **fǎn-kō-ī-chī** to turn their weapons to attack the enemy

反革命 **fǎn-kó-mìng** a counter-revolutionary; counter-revolution

反革命集团 **fǎn-kó-mìng chí-t'uán** a counter-revolutionary clique

反革命经济主义 **fǎn-kó-mìng chīng-chì-chǔ-ì** counter-revolutionary economism

反革命分子 **fǎn-kó-mìng fèn-tzǔ** counter-revolutionary elements,

anti-revolutionary persons

反革命活动 **fǎn-kó-mìng huó-tùng** counter-revolutionary activities

反革命修正主义文艺 **fǎn-kó-mìng hsiū-chèng-chǔ-ì wén-ì** counter-revolutionary revisionist literary works

反革命修正主义文艺黑线 **fǎn-kó-mìng hsiū-chèng-chǔ-ì wén-ì hēi-hsièn** the black line of counter-revolutionary revisionist art and literature

反革命两面派 **fǎn-kó-mìng liǎng-mièn-p'ài** anti-revolutionary double-dealing factions

反革命暴力 **fǎn-kó-mìng pào-lì** anti-revolutionary violent forces

反革命地主武装 **fǎn-kó-mìng tì-chǔ wǔ-chuāng** the armed forces of the counter-revolutionary landlords

反革命罪行 **fǎn-kó-mìng tsuì-hsíng** anti-revolutionary crimes

反革命武装暴乱 **fǎn-kó-mìng wǔ-chuāng pào-luàn** counter-revolutionary armed disruptions

反官僚主义 **fǎn kuān-liáo-chǔ-ì** oppose bureaucratism (one of the **sān-fǎn**)

反攻 **fǎn-kūng** a counter-offensive; to fight back

反攻倒算 **fǎn-kūng tào-suàn** a counter-attack to reverse accounts (originally referred to the civil war counter-offensive by landlords to recover lands seized by the peasants)

反躬自问 **fǎn-kūng tzǔ-wèn** to examine oneself

反共 **fǎn-kùng** anti-Communism, anti-Communist

《反共启事》 **fǎn-kùng ch'ǐ-shìh** public confession of anti-communism (confessions by Communists in KMT prisons during 1936–37—a Cultural Revolution charge against Liu Shao-ch'i)

反共分子 **fǎn-kùng fèn-tzǔ** anti-Communist elements

反共老调 **fǎn-kùng lǎo-tiào** the old anti-Communist song, the stale theme of anti-Communism

反抗 **fǎn-k'àng** to resist, oppose, rise up against

反浪费 **fǎn làng-fèi** oppose waste (one of the **sān-fǎn**)

反理性主义 **fǎn-lǐ-hsìng-chǔ-ì** anti-rationalism

反马克思主义 **fǎn-mǎ-k'ò-szū-chǔ-ì** anti-Marxism

反冒进 **fǎn-mào-chìn** anti-adventurism

反美斗争 **fǎn-měi-tòu-chēng** the struggle against the USA, the anti-American struggle

反面 **fǎn-mièn** the negative aspect,

negative; the back side, obverse, reverse

反面教材 **fǎn-mièn chiào-ts'ái** material for negative education (personal histories or other materials that provide negative examples of conduct)

反面教育 **fǎn-mièn-chiào-yǜ** negative education (teaching by negative example to show the harmful results [of incorrect ideology, etc.]

反面教员 **fǎn-mièn-chiào-yuán** a person who serves as a negative example

反面经验 **fǎn-mièn-chīng-yèn** negative experience

反面人物 **fǎn-mièn-jén-wù** a villainous character, negative personality

反比例 **fǎn-pǐ-lì** inverse proportion

反驳 **fǎn-pó** to refute, rebut, disprove, to reply to a charge

反叛 **fǎn-p'àn** to rebel, revolt; insurrection, insurgence

反叛 **fǎn-p'an** a rebel, bandit, evil-doer

反扑 **fǎn-p'ū** a counter-lunge [by the enemy], an enemy counterattack

反扑黑纲领 **fǎn-p'ū hēi-kāng-lǐng** the black program of the [enemy] counter-attack

反三右 **fǎn sān-yù** oppose the three rightisms (oppose rightist opportunism, capitulationism, and splittism)

反射炉 **fǎn-shè-lú** a reverberatory furnace

反苏修 **fǎn sū-hsiū** óppose Soviet revisionism

反党集团 **fǎn-tǎng-chí-t'uán** an anti-Party bloc

反党活动 **fǎn-tǎng-huó-tùng** anti-Party activity

反党老手 **fǎn-tǎng lǎo-shǒu** old anti-Party hands

反党逆流 **fǎn-tǎng nì-liú** anti-Party reverse currents

反帝 **fǎn-tì** anti-imperialism, anti-imperialist; oppose imperialism

反帝, 反殖, 反霸 **fǎn-tì, fǎn-chíh, fǎn-pà** oppose imperialism, colonialism, and hegemony

反帝、反封建统一战线 **fǎn-tì fǎn-fēng-chièn t'ǔng-ī-chàn-hsièn** the United Front against imperialism and feudalism (1924–27)

反帝斗争 **fǎn-tì-tòu-chēng** the struggle against imperialism

反调 **fǎn-tiào** the opposite tune, a contrary idea

反颠复斗争 **fǎn-tiēn-fù tòu-chēng** struggle against subversion

反夺权 **fǎn-tó-ch'üán** counter-seizure

of power

反对核武器国际会议 **fǎn-tuì hó-wǔ-ch'ì kuó-chì-huì-ì** International Convention Against Atomic Arms

反对浪费 **fǎn-tuì làng-fèi** to oppose waste (one of the **sān-fǎn**)

反对派 **fǎn-tuì-p'ài** opposition faction

反对党 **fǎn-tuì-tǎng** opposition party; to oppose the Party

《反对党八股》 **fǎn-tuì tǎng-pā-kǔ** "Oppose Party Formalism" (essay by Mao Tse-tung, 1942)

反动 **fǎn-tùng** reaction [physical or political]; reactionary, conservative

反动集团 **fǎn-tùng-chí-t'uán** reactionary clique or faction

反动气焰 **fǎn-tùng-ch'ì-yèn** reactionary flames (reactionary arrogance and fury)

反动行为 **fǎn-tùng-hsíng-wéi** reactionary behavior or activities

反动观点 **fǎn-tùng-kuān-tiěn** reactionary viewpoint

反动浪潮 **fǎn-tùng-làng-ch'áo** the waves and tides of reaction

反动没落阶级 **fǎn-tùng mò-lò-chiēh-chí** the reactionary decadent class

反动堡垒 **fǎn-tùng-pǎo-lěi** a reactionary fortress, a stronghold of the reactionaries

反动本性 **fǎn-tùng-pěn-hsìng** reactionary nature

反动标语 **fǎn-tùng piāo-yǚ** reactionary slogans

反动派 **fǎn-tùng-p'ài** a reactionary clique

反动实质 **fǎn-tùng-shíh-chìh** reactionary essence, reactionary by nature

反动势力 **fǎn-tùng shìh-lì** reactionary forces

反动思潮 **fǎn-tùng szū-ch'áo** a reactionary current of thought

反动地方武装 **fǎn-tùng tì-fāng-wǔ-chuāng** reactionary local armed forces

反动透顶 **fǎn-tùng-t'òu-tǐng** reactionary in the extreme, thoroughly reactionary

反动统治 **fǎn-tùng-t'ǔng-chìh** reactionary rule

反动舆论 **fǎn-tùng-yú-lùn** reactionary public opinion

反贪污浪费 **fǎn t'ān-wū làng-fèi** oppose corruption and waste (two of the **sān-fǎn**)

反坦克砲 **fǎn-t'ǎn-k'ò-p'ào** anti-tank gun

反题材决定论 **fǎn t'í-ts'ái-chüéh-tìng lùn** the doctrine of opposition to

subject-matter as decisive (that writers should not be restricted to strictly revolutionary themes and should be free to write of such non-revolutionary themes as human interest and minor events—one of the **hēi-pā-lùn**)

反作用 **fǎn-tsò-yùng** reaction, counter-effect, to affect reciprocally, negative effect

反围攻 **fǎn-wéi-kūng** counter-encirclement

反问 **fǎn-wèn** to examine oneself; to counter-question

反应 **fǎn-yìng** reaction, response, repercussion

反应不一 **fǎn-yìng-pù-ī** mixed reaction, diverse reactions

反映 **fǎn-yìng** to reflect; to report; reflection

反映情况 **fǎn-yìng ch'íng-k'uàng** to reflect the conditions (to report the situation)

反映生活 **fǎn-yíng shēng-huó** to reflect life (e.g., literature should reflect real life)

反犹太主义 **fǎn-yú-t'ài-chǔ-ì** anti-Semitism

反右倾，鼓干劲 **fǎn-yù-ch'īng, kǔ-kàn-chìn** to fight against right deviation go all out, to oppose right devia-tion and summon up all one's energies (slogan of 1958–59)

反右派斗争 **fǎn-yù-p'ài tòu-chēng** the anti-rightist struggle

反语 **fǎn-yǔ** to say one thing and mean the opposite, ironic or sarcastic statements

621 返还 **fǎn-huán** to return [property], go back [to a place]; to make restitution

返销粮 **fǎn-hsiāo-liáng** reverse-sale grain (part of compulsory-purchase grain sold back to units whose own food production is insufficient)

返工 **fǎn-kūng** to do over again [due to poor work], repeat work; to return to work

返工重修 **fǎn-kūng-ch'úng-hsīu** to rebuild, reconstruct [due to faulty original construction]

返工废料 **fǎn-kūng-fèi-liào** waste of materials [due to the need] for redoing the work

返工浪费 **fǎn-kūng-làng-fèi** redoing and waste (waste of materials due to work that has to be redone)

fàn (fàn)

622 犯法 **fàn-fǎ** to violate the law, break the law

犯上作乱 **fàn-shàng-tsò-luàn** offending superiors and making disturbances (insubordination)

犯罪 **fàn-tsuì** to commit a crime

犯错误 **fàn-ts'ò-wù** to make a mistake, commit an error (usually refers to political or ideological errors)

623 泛期 **fàn-ch'ī** high-water season

泛泛之交 **fàn-fàn-chīh-chiāo** a slight acquaintance, a superficial friendship

泛滥 **fàn-làn** a flood; to flood

泛滥成灾 **fàn-làn-ch'éng-tsāi** inunda-tion grown to disaster (excessive bureaucratic paperwork)

泛美主义 **fàn-měi-chǔ-ì** pan-Americanism

泛亚社 **fàn-yà-shè** Pan-Asia News Agency [PANA]

624 饭堂 **fàn-t'áng** mess hall, dining hall

625 范畴 **fàn-ch'óu** categories [of thought], basic concepts

范例 **fàn-lì** a model, typical example, sample

范围 **fàn-wéi** scope, range, confines, parameters

626 贩卖死亡商人 **fàn-mài-szǔ-wáng shāng-jén** merchants of death (arms manufacturers)

627 梵蒂岗 **fàn-tì-kāng** the Vatican

fāng (fāng)

628 方案 **fāng-àn** a proposal, program, plan, suggestion

方针 **fāng-chēn** goal, principle; policy, course of action (usually a general policy line)

方针政策 **fāng-chēn chèng-ts'è** general and specific policies

方法 **fāng-fǎ** methods, operational practices, procedures

方法论 **fāng-fǎ-lùn** methodology

方向 **fāng-hsiàng** a direction, trend, orientation

方向性 **fāng-hsiàng-hsìng** orientation direction, directional

方向盘 **fāng-hsiàng-p'án** steering wheel

方兴未艾 **fāng-hsīng-wèi-ài** just starting to grow (on the ascent, on the upswing)

方略 **fāng-luèh** a general plan, tactics, strategy

方面 **fāng-mièn** aspect, side, phase, sector, sphere

方式 **fāng-shìh** method, form, mode, means

方园 **fāng-yuán** surface area

fáng (fáng)

629 防骄破满 **fáng-chiāo-p'ò-mǎn** guard

against arrogance and smash complacency

防止核战争协定 **fáng-chǐh hó-chàn-chēng hsiéh-tìng** the agreement on the prevention of nuclear war

防治结合 **fáng-chìh chiéh-hó** to combine prevention and treatment [usually medical]

防治风沙 **fáng-chìh fēng-shā** preventive control of blowing sand (protective measures taken against drifting sand)

防治病虫害 **fáng-chìh pìng-ch'úng-hài** prevention of pests and plant diseases

防范 **fáng-fàn** to take preventive measures, be on guard against

防风林 **fáng-fēng-lín** a windbreak of trees

防风林带 **fáng-fēng-lín-tài** forest strips [to serve as] windbreaks, shelterbelts

防护林 **fáng-hù-lín** protective forest, shelterbelt

防患于未然 **fáng-huàn-yú-wèi-ján** prevent disaster before it occurs (to nip in the bud)

防洪 **fáng-húng** flood control, flood prevention

防洪防涝 **fáng-húng fáng-lào** flood and waterlogging prevention

防洪大军 **fáng-húng tà-chün** flood prevention army (a large body of labor mobilized for flood prevention)

防火保卫工作 **fáng-huǒ pǎo-wèi-kūng-tsò** fire control and security work

防汛 **fáng-hsùn** flood prevention, measures to guard against seasonal high water

防汛排涝 **fáng-hsùn p'ái-lào** prevention of floods and the drainage of water-logged [fields]

防疫 **fáng-ì** prevention of epidemics, quarantine

防疫站 **fáng-ì-chàn** epidemic prevention station

防空 **fáng-k'ūng** air defense

防空兵 **fáng-k'ūng-pīng** Air Defense Forces

防空部队 **fáng-k'ūng-pù-tuì** anti-aircraft forces, anti-aircraft formations

防空洞 **fáng-k'ūng-tùng** air-raid shelter

防涝 **fáng-lào** waterlogging [of fields] prevention, field drainage measures

防病治病工作, 层层有人抓 **fáng-pìng chìh-pìng kūng-tsò ts'éng-ts'éng yǔ-jén-chuā** at every level there are persons firmly grasping the work of preventive medicine and treatment

防波堤 **fáng-pō-tí** a breakwater

防沙林 **fáng-shā-lín** sand-break trees (a stand of trees to act as a wind-break against the blowing sand)

防微杜渐 **fáng-wēi-tù-chièn** to guard against [while still] small and to block [the] gradual [growth] (to stop trouble before it becomes important, nip trouble in the bud)

防卫 **fáng-wèi** to defend, protect, guard; defense

防温降暑 **fáng-wēn-chiàng-shǔ** rebuff the heat and lower the temperature (measures to provide relief to workers in especially hot work in hot weather)

防务 **fáng-wù** defense measures

防御 **fáng-yù** to guard against; defense, defensive

防御战 **fáng-yù-chàn** a defensive war

防御体系 **fáng-yù-t'ǐ-hsì** defense system, defensive system

妨碍 **fáng-ài** to obstruct, hinder, impede, deter; obstacle, impediment

妨害 **fáng-hài** to jeopardize, endanger; to offend against

房产税 **fáng-ch'ǎn-shuì** real estate tax, property tax

房管局 **fáng-kuǎn-chú** housing bureau

房屋建筑专业 **fáng-wū chièn-chù chuān-yèh** housing construction specialization (may be professionalized training at the college level)

房无一间, 地无一垄 **fáng-wú-ī-chiēn, tì-wú-ī-lǔng** of house, not a single room, and of land, not even one furrow (very poor)

fǎng (fǎng)

访苦问苦 **fáng-k'ǔ-wèn-k'ǔ** to interview those who have suffered (one method by which the new generation are expected to learn about the old society)

访贫问苦 **fǎng-p'ín-wèn-k'ǔ** to interview the poor and miserable (*see above*)

访问 **fáng-wèn** to pay a visit to, call on; an interview, visit

访问团 **fǎng-wèn-t'uán** a visiting mission, visiting delegation

访问演出 **fǎng-wèn-yěn-ch'ū** visiting performance, a performance tour

仿效 **fǎng-hsiào** to follow the example of, copy, model after

仿造 **fǎng-tsào** to reproduce, imitate in manufacture, counterfeit

纺织工业部 **fǎng-chīh kūng-yèh-pù** Ministry of Textiles (absorbed into the Ministry of Light Industry in 1969)

纺纱织布 **fǎng-shā chīh-pù** to spin yarn and weave cloth (textile manufacturing)

fàng (fàng)

635 放之四海而皆准 **fàng-chïh-szù-hǎi érh chiēh-chǔn** [if it were] put [anywhere] in the four seas [it would] still be accurate (universally applicable—said of Marxism)

放长线钓大鱼 **fàng-ch'áng-hsièn tiào-tà-yú** to put out a long line to catch a big fish (to use foresight in pursuing large objectives)

放弃 **fàng-ch'ì** to give up, abandon, drop, discard, lay aside, relinquish

放下架子 **fàng-hsia-chià-tzu** to discard one's haughty airs

放下臭架子 **fàng-hsia ch'òu-chià-tzu** to shed the ugly mantle of pretentiousness

放下官架子 **fàng-hsia kuān-chià-tzu** to discard bureaucratic airs

放下包袱 **fàng-hsia pāo-fu** to lay down the burden (the burden is usually one's historical past or one's ideology)

放下屠刀，立地成佛 **fàng-hsia t'ú-tāo, lì-tì ch'éng-fó** to put down the [butcher's] knife [and] on the spot become a Buddha (anyone who completely repents his past can become a new man)

放下武器 **fàng-hsia wǔ-ch'ì** to lay down arms

放心大胆 **fàng-hsïn-tà-tǎn** get rid of anxiety and become confident; calm and bold

放任 **fàng-jèn** to let things go, let things take their course, laissez-faire; indulgent, permissive

放任主义 **fàng-jèn-chǔ-ì** laissez-faire, the laissez-faire principle

放任自流 **fàng-jèn-tzù-líu** to let something take its own course

放光芒 **fàng-kuāng-máng** to glow, radiate

放过机会 **fàng-kuò chï-huì** to let a chance go by, to let pass an opportunity

放开 **fàng-k'āi** to relax, loosen, release, set free; to lay aside

放开手干革命 **fàng-k'āi-shǒu kàn-kó-mìng** to free [one's] hands to carry on revolution

放宽限制 **fàng-k'uān-hsièn-chìh** to relax restrictions

放冷箭 **fàng lěng-chièn** to shoot an arrow from ambush (to stab in the back, make sarcastic remarks, snipe at)

放牧 **fàng-mù** to graze, pasture [animals] (a stage between pure nomadism and settled animal raising: herds are moved from pasture to pasture but the people are settled in a fixed location)

放炮 **fàng-p'ào** to set off an explosive, detonate a charge (also figurative—to utter bombast)

放哨 **fàng-shào** a sentinel, guard, scout; to be on watch, to stand sentry duty

放射性 **fàng-shè-hsìng** radioactivity, radioactive

放射性同位素 **fàng-shè-hsìng t'úng-wèi-sù** radioactive isotope

放射性测量 **fàng-shè-hsìng ts'è-liáng** surveying by use of radioactivity

放射性物质 **fàng-shè-hsìng wù-chìh** radioactive substance

放射性元素 **fàng-shè-hsìng yuán-sù** radioactive element

放手 **fàng-shǒu** to let go, let loose, give a free rein, remove the restraints; hands off

放手发动群众 **fàng-shǒu fā-tùng ch'ún-chùng** to mobilize the masses without restraint, give free rein to the masses

放松警惕 **fàng-sūng chǐng-t'ì** to slacken vigilance, relax one's guard, be off guard

放肆 **fàng-szù** unchecked, wanton, unruly

放大炮 **fàng-tà-p'ào** to set off a big gun (a bluff; to bluster)

放毒 **fàng-tú** to exude poison, spread poison (usually figurative)

放在第一位 **fàng tsài tì-ī-wèi** to put in the lead position, give priority to

放纵 **fàng-tsùng** to condone, indulge, give someone full freedom; uninhibited

放野火 **fàng-yěh-huǒ** to set fires in the wild (irresponsible trouble-making)

放阎王账 **fàng yén-wáng-chàng** to charge a high rate of interest; usury, loan sharking

放眼世界 **fàng-yěn-shìh-chièh** to open the eyes to the world (to have a broad viewpoint)

放映 **fàng-yìng** to project [a motion picture]

fēi (fēi)

636 飞机库 **fēi-chï-k'ù** aircraft hangar

飞机失事 **fēi-chï-shīh-shìh** aircraft accident

飞行队形 **fēi-hsíng tuì-hsíng** flight formation

飞蛾扑火 **fēi-ó-p'ū-huǒ** like moths

flying toward the flame (to seek one's own doom)

飞速前进 **fēi-shù-ch'ién-chìn** a flying advance (swift progress)

飞速发展 **fēi-sù-fā-chǎn** extremely rapid development

飞弹 **fēi-tàn** a flying bomb, missile

飞腾 **fēi-t'éng** to soar, rise rapidly

飞艇 **fēi-t'ǐng** an airship, dirigible, blimp

飞跃 **fēi-yuèh** a flying leap; to leap

飞跃过程 **fēi-yuèh-kuò-ch'éng** a process [or period] characterized by a great leap (rapid quantitative or qualitative change)

⁶³⁷ 非战斗人员 **fēi-chàn-tòu jén-yuán** a non-combatant

非正义战争 **fēi-chèng-ì chàn-chēng** unjust war

非正式 **fēi-chèng-shìh** unofficial, informal

非洲解放委员会 **fēi-chōu-chiěh-fàn wěi-yuán-huì** African Liberation Committee

非洲国家联盟 **fēi-chōu-kuó-chiā lién-méng** Union of African States

非洲统一组织 **fēi-chōu t'ǔng-ī tsǔ-chīh** Organization of African Unity

非军事的 **fēi-chün-shìh-te** non-military, demilitarized, civilian

非法 **fēi-fǎ** illegal, unlawful, illicit

非法监禁 **fēi-fǎ-chiēn-chìn** to detain illegally; illegal detention, illegal confinement, illegal imprisonment

非法地位 **fēi-fǎ-tì-wèi** a status of illegality, unlawful status

非凡 **fēi-fán** out of the ordinary (extraordinary, remarkable)

非国家津贴免费学校 **fēi-kuó-chiā-chīn-t'iēh miěn-fèi hsuéh-hsiào** non-state-subsidized free schools (run by the factories)

非驴非马 **fēi-lú fēi-mǎ** neither ass nor horse (neither fish nor fowl, nondescript)

非密封仓 **fēi-mì-fēng ts'āng** non-hermetic cabin

非难 **fēi-nàn** to blame, censure, critize, dispute

非暴力的反抗 **fēi-pào-lì-te fǎn-k'àng** non-violent resistance

非生产性建设 **fēi-shēng-ch'ǎn-hsìng chièn-shè** non-productive construction

非生产人员 **fēi-shēng-ch'ǎn jén-yuán** non-productive personnel

非党群众 **fēi-tǎng-ch'ún-chùng** a non-Party member [of the masses], the masses outside the Party

非党干部 **fēi-tǎng-kàn-pù** non-Party

cadres

非对抗性的 **fēi-tuì-k'àng-hsìng-te** non-antagonistic

非无产阶级思想 **fēi-wú-ch'ǎn-chiēh-chí szū-hsiǎng** non-proletarian thinking

⁶³⁸ 菲律宾 **fēi-lù-pīn** the Philippines

féi (féi)

⁶³⁹ 肥梁胖柱 **féi-liáng p'àng-chù** fat beams and stout pillars (extravagant construction beyond one's needs)

肥料 **féi-liào** fertilizer

肥田粉 **féi-t'ién-fěn** powdered fertilizer (chemical fertilizer)

肥沃 **féi-wò** fertile [soil]

fěi (fěi)

⁶⁴⁰ 诽谤 **fěi-pàng** to vilify, slander

⁶⁴¹ 匪帮 **fěi-pāng** a gang of bandits, bandits, gang (often political)

匪特 **fěi-t'è** a bandit agent, spy

匪徒 **fěi-t'ú** a bandit, vagrant

fèi (fèi)

⁶⁴² 废渣 **fèi-chā** clinkers, slag, solid industrial waste, dregs

废机器 **fèi-chī-ch'ì** scrap machines, unusable machinery

废纸 **fèi-chǐh** scraps of paper, waste paper (used figuratively)

废旧料 **fèi-chìu-liào** scrap industrial materials

废旧物资 **fèi-chìu-wù-tzū** scrap materials, waste products

废汽 **fèi-ch'ì** waste gas

废气 **fèi-ch'ì** waste steam

废寝忘食 **fèi-ch'ǐn-wàng-shíh** to neglect sleep and forget to eat (very hard working)

废除 **fèi-ch'ú** to abolish, discard, abrogate, annul, cancel, rescind, revoke, repeal, eliminate

废话 **fèi-huà** nonsense, persiflage, a superfluous statement

废钢 **fèi-kāng** scrap steel

废料 **fèi-liào** waste material (sometimes refers to a person)

废品 **fèi-p'ǐn** rejected product, rejects

废铁 **fèi-t'iěh** scrap iron

废次材料 **fèi-tz'ù-ts'ái-liào** waste [materials] and inferior materials

废物 **fèi-wù** wastes, a useless thing (can be applied to a person)

废物利用 **fèi-wù-lì-yùng** productive use of scrap, recycling

废物不废 **fèi-wù-pù-fèi** scrap materials are not waste (everything is useful)

废液 **fèi-yèh** waste liquids

643 肺都气炸了 **fèi-tū-ch'ì-chà-le** [my]·
lungs have exploded (great anger or
exasperation)

644 费工夫 **fèi-kūng-fu** it takes time,
time-consuming

费力 **fèi-lì** taking a lot of exertion,
laborious, strenuous; to take pains

费料, 费工, 费力 **fèi-liào, fèi-kūng,
fèi-lì** too consuming of labor, time,
and power (as a result of poor
design)

费边主义 **fèi-piēn-chǔ-ì** Fabianism

费用 **fèi-yùng** expenditure, cost,
expense, fee, charge

fēn (fēn)

645 分级 **fēn-chí** by levels, by grade

分级管理 **fēn-chí-kuǎn-lǐ** level-to-level
administration, administration by
different levels

分家 **fēn-chiā** to divide [the property
of] a family (to split any organization)

分解 **fēn-chiěh** to break up into several
elements, decompose; to explain,
analyze

分界线 **fēn-chiěh-hsièn** a demarcation
line, dividing line

分期 **fēn-ch'ī** to divide into time
periods; periodization, periodic

分期分批 **fēn-ch'ī-fēn-p'ī** period by
period, group by group; by time and
batch

分期付款 **fēn-ch'ī-fù-k'uǎn** installment
payments

分歧 **fēn-ch'í** to grow apart, diverge,
be divided over; discord, divergence,
disparity, differences; a schism

分遣队 **fēn-ch'iěn-tuì** a detachment,
task force, group detached [for a
special assignment]

分青 **fēn-ch'īng** to divide the green (in
the Land Reform there were divisions
even of the crops growing in the
fields)

分清界线 **fēn-ch'īng chièh-hsièn**
differentiate boundaries clearly,
draw a sharp line of demarcation

分清是非 **fēn-ch'īng shìh-fēi** to draw a
clear demarcation between right and
wrong

分清大是大非 **fēn-ch'īng tà-shìh tà-fēi**
to distinguish clearly the great rights
and wrongs (usually refers to basic
issues such as the line, viewpoint,
political stand)

分清敌我 **fēn-ch'īng tí-wǒ** to distinguish clearly between the enemy and
ourselves

分权 **fēn-ch'üán** decentralization of
authority

分而治之 **fēn-érh-chìh-chīh** divide and
rule

分发 **fēn-fā** to distribute, send out,
allot, disseminate

分化 **fēn-huà** to differentiate, split up,
disintegrate, divide, polarize;
dissension, [political] ferment,
polarization, disintegration

分化瓦解 **fēn-huà-wǎ-chiěh** dividing
and disintegrating

分洪 **fēn-húng** to divide the flood,
channel off flood waters

分析 **fēn-hsī** to analyze (especially
through the use of ideology);
analysis; analytical

分析态度 **fēn-hsī-t'ài-tù** analytical
approach, analytical attitude

分割 **fēn-kō** separately; to cut off, cut
up, divide, dismember

分割包围 **fēn-kō-pāo-wéi** to cut off and
encircle

分隔 **fēn-kó** to divide up, cut apart;
segmentation

分管 **fēn-kuǎn** separate control,
separate administration

分光, 吃光, 用光 **fēn-kuāng, ch'īh-
kuāng, yùng-kuāng** divide up
everything, eat up everything, and
use up everything (a criticized
tendency in some early communes)

分工 **fēn-kūng** division of labor; to
divide labor

分工合作 **fēn-kūng-hó-tsò** to divide the
work and work together, division of
labor and sharing of responsibility,
division of labor with coordination

分类 **fēn-lèi** classification; to classify,
sort

分离 **fēn-lí** to separate, divide, sever,
segregate

分裂 **fēn-lièh** to break up, split,
disunite, splinter; a schism, rift,
cleavage

分裂主义 **fēn-lièh-chǔ-ì** splittism,
secessionism, separatism (usually
refers to disruption of the international communist movement)

分路突进 **fēn-lù-t'ū-chìn** to advance
along several roads, penetrate from
different directions

分门别类 **fēn-mén-piéh-lèi** to classify
systematically, arrange by
categories

分秒必争 **fēn-miǎo-pì-chēng** to fight
for minutes and seconds (to make
every moment count)

分崩离析 **fēn-pēng lí-hsī** to disintegrate

and decompose (to lose unity, fall apart)

分别 **fēn-piéh** to separate; separately; to distinguish, tell apart; to part [from a person]

分别对待 **fēn-piéh tuì-tài** to deal separately with (to deal with each case on its merits)

分辨 **fēn-pièn** to compare and note the difference, to distinguish, differentiate

分布 **fēn-pù** to distribute, scatter, spread, diffuse; distribution

分配 **fēn-p'èi** to distribute, apportion, share, allocate, assign; distribution, allocation

分配制度 **fēn-p'èi-chìh-tù** distribution system

分配工作 **fēn-p'èi-kūng-tsò** to assign work, assign to a job, allocate work assignments (especially refers to work assignment of school-leaving students)

分配名单 **fēn-p'èi-míng-tān** distribution lists (of students admitted to university and middle schools)

分配到户 **fēn-p'èi-tào-hù** to supply directly to each household

分批 **fēn-p'ī** by groups, by batch, in separate groups

分散经营 **fēn-sàn-chīng-yíng** decentralized management

分散主义 **fēn-sàn-chǔ-ì** decentralization, fragmentationism (usually implies excessive decentralization)

分散兵力 **fēn-sàn-pīng-lì** dispersal of forces [military]

分散使用建设资金 **fēn-sàn-shǐh-yùng chièn-shè-tzū-chīn** to decentralize the use of construction funds

分散作战 **fēn-sàn-tsò-chàn** dispersed military operations, unconcentrated warfare

分数挂帅 **fēn-shù kuà-shuài** examination scores take command (excessive reliance on grades, especially in entrance examinations)

分数面前人人平等 **fēn-shù mièn-ch'ién jén-jén p'íng-těng** facing [school entrance] examination grades, all men are equal (reliance on entrance examinations, with a disregard of factors such as class background)

分数第一 **fēn-shù tì-ī** [school] grades are number one (excessive concern with grades)

分水岭 **fēn-shuǐ-lǐng** a watershed ridge (often figurative)

分等论价 **fēn-těng-lùn-chià** to price commodities according to grade

分摊 **fēn-t'ān** to divide pro rata, share equally

分田单干 **fēn-t'ién-tān-kàn** to divide the fields and work alone (some peasants in the early cooperative stage hoped to do better by themselves than by joining the cooperatives)

分庭抗礼 **fēn-t'íng-k'àng-lǐ** different in court but entitled to equal rites (to meet with equal standing, equal but rival, to match oneself against)

分头进行 **fēn-t'óu-chìn-hsíng** to carry out separately [by several persons or groups]

分赃 **fēn-tsāng** to share the plunder, divide the spoils

分组讨论 **fēn-tsǔ t'ǎo-lùn** to divide into groups for discussion

分子 **fēn-tzǔ** (1) element, particle, molecule; (2) numerator of a fraction [math]

分子辐射 **fēn-tzǔ-fú-shè** molecular radiation

分子式 **fēn-tzǔ-shìh** an equation [math]; a formula [chemical]

分层负责 **fēn-ts'éng-fù-ts'é** division of responsibility according to [organizational] levels

分娩 **fēn-wǎn** childbirth; to lie in, give birth

分野 **fēn-yěh** a dividing line, a division

分 **fēn:** *see also* **fèn**

646 芬芳香花 **fēn-fāng-hsiāng-huā** fragrant flowers (used figuratively as of good literary works)

芬兰 **fēn-lán** Finland

647 吩咐 **fēn-fu** to direct, command, instruct; instruction, direction

648 纷繁复杂 **fēn-fán-fù-tsá** confusing, tangled, complex

fén (fén)

649 坟墓 **fén-mù** a grave, tomb

650 焚书坑儒 **fén-shū-k'ēng-jú** burning the books and burying Confucian scholars alive (Ch'ín Shǐh-huáng-tì's long deplored action, now claimed to have been justified because of the Confucianists' opposition to progress)

fěn (fěn)

651 粉墨登场 **fěn-mò-tēng-ch'ǎng** to mount the stage in full make-up (to play a role—in a derogatory sense)

粉身碎骨 **fěn-shēn-suì-kǔ** body pow-

dered and bones shattered (stern determination that disregards the consequences)

粉饰 **fěn-shìh** to present a pleasant appearance, cover up, gloss over

粉饰太平 **fěn-shìh-t'ài-p'íng** to present a false appearance of peace and prosperity (to whitewash a bad situation)

粉碎 **fěn-suì** to pulverize, shatter, crush to pieces

粉碎机 **fěn-suì-chī** a crusher, pulverizer

粉碎枷锁 **fěn-suì chiā-sǒ** to smash the shackles, break the chains

fèn (fèn)

652 分子 **fèn-tzǔ** a part, member, or element of society

653 奋战 **fèn-chàn** to fight courageously

奋起抵抗 **fèn-ch'ǐ-tǐ-k'àng** to rise heroically to resist [attack]

奋发图强 **fèn-fā t'ú-ch'iáng** to strive to make [the country] strong

奋不顾身 **fèn-pù-kù-shēn** to brave dangers in disregard of one's own life; death-defying

奋斗 **fèn-tòu** to struggle, strive, fight for; a struggle

奋斗到底 **fèn-tòu tào-tǐ** to struggle to the end (to make no compromise or concession until victory is won)

奋勇 **fèn-yǔng** courageously, bravely

奋勇前进 **fèn-yǔng-ch'ién-chìn** to advance bravely

奋勇作战 **fèn-yǔng-tsò-chàn** to be fearless in battle

654 愤愤不平 **fèn-fèn pù-p'íng** indignant at injustice

愤慨 **fèn-k'ǎi** anger, indignation [over injustice]

愤怒 **fèn-nù** indignation, wrath, rage

愤怒文学 **fèn-nù-wén-hsuéh** the literature of indignation (allegedly a slogan used by Chou Yang during the early 1960s in urging writers to concern themselves with Party imperfections)

fēng (fēng)

655 丰产 **fēng-ch'ǎn** rich harvest, abundant production, bumper crop

丰产片 **fēng-ch'ǎn-p'ièn** a high-yield tract

丰富多采 **fēng-fù-tō-ts'ǎi** rich and variegated, abundant and many-colored

丰衣足食 **fēng-ī-tsú-shíh** abundant clothing and plentiful food

丰功伟绩 **fēng-kūng-wěi-chī** grand achievements

丰收 **fēng-shōu** bumper harvest, bumper crop

丰硕成果 **fēng-shuò-chéng-kuǒ** plentiful and large fruits, a fine crop (a good result, a fine achievement)

丰硕果实 **fēng-shuò-kuǒ-shíh** rich fruits, abundant fruits

656 风景区 **fēng-chǐng-ch'ǖ** a scenic spot, a resort area

风景画 **fēng-chǐng-huà** landscape painting

风潮 **fēng-ch'áo** a storm (used very broadly to include any intense social or political upheaval)

风起云涌 **fēng-ch'ǐ-yún-yǔng** winds rising and clouds gathering (to surge forward, to spread like a storm)

风气 **fēng-ch'ì** mores, customs, current fashion; bearing, air, manner

风吹两边倒 **fēng-ch'uī liǎng-piēn-tǎo** leaning this way and that as the wind blows (such as wavering between capitalism and socialism)

风吹草动 **fēng-ch'uī-ts'ǎo-tùng** the grass moves as the winds blow (any slight movement or disturbance)

风化 **fēng-huà** (1) moral atmosphere, public morals, influence, example; (2) wind erosion, weathering

风向 **fēng-hsiàng** the wind direction, direction

风险 **fēng-hsiěn** risk, danger

风行一时 **fēng-hsíng-ī-shíh** a current fashion, fad, vogue

风镐 **fēng-kǎo** a pneumatic pick

风格 **fēng-kó** literary style, the mode of a generation, the style of a person

风浪 **fēng-làng** wind and waves (a commotion, storm, crisis)

风里来雨里去 **fēng-lǐ-lái, yǔ-lǐ-ch'ǜ** come in the wind and go in the rain (originally—to work hard despite the trials of weather; now—to be tempered by storm and tribulation)

风里浪里不转向 **fēng-lǐ làng-lǐ pù-chuàn-hsiàng** to hold steadfast to one's course despite wind and wave (steadfast)

风凉话 **fēng-liáng-huà** cool, sly criticism; irresponsible talk

风马牛不相及 **fēng-mǎ-niú pù-hsiāng-chí** when a horse and a cow are in heat they have nothing to do with each other (totally unconnected, nothing in common, no relationship whatever)

风靡一时 **fēng-mí-ī-shíh** faddish, popular for a time

风暴 **fēng-pào** a storm, tempest (often figurative)

风波 **fēng-pō** wind and waves (disputes, quarrels, disturbances, a storm—in the figurative sense)

风平浪静 **fēng-p'íng làng-chìng** the wind abates and the waves subside (all quiet, the situation improves)

风尚 **fēng-shàng** fashion of the times, vogue, fad

风霜 **fēng-shuāng** wind and frost (harsh times, hardships)

风度 **fēng-tù** personal style, mien, manner

风动工具 **fēng-tùng-kūng-chù** pneumatic tool

风头主义 **fēng-t'óu-chǔ-ì** "show-offism," craving for popularity

风土人情 **fēng-t'ǔ-jén-ch'íng** local customs, local practices

风钻 **fēng-tsuàn** compressed air drill

风餐露宿 **fēng-ts'ān-lù-sù** to eat in the wind and sleep in the dew (to travel or work under conditions of physical hardship)

风云人物 **fēng-yún-jén-wù** important men of the day, man in the news, headliner

657 封建枷锁 **fēng-chièn-chiā-sǒ** the feudal yoke, shackles of feudalism

封建家长制 **fēng-chièn chiā-chǎng-chìh** feudal patriarchalism

封建制 **fēng-chièn-chìh** feudalism (one of the five relationships of production)

封建制度 **fēng-chièn-chìh-tù** feudalism, the feudal system

封建秩序 **fēng-chièn chìh-hsù** the feudal [social] order

封建主 **fēng-chièn-chǔ** feudal lord

封建主义 **fēng-chièn-chǔ-ì** feudalism

封建法西斯王朝 **fēng-chièn fā-hsī-szū wáng-ch'áo** a feudalist and fascist dynasty (refers to Liu Shao-ch'i and Lin Piao)

封建割据 **fēng-chièn-kō-chù** feudal separatism

封建买办法西斯王朝 **fēng-chièn mǎi-pàn fǎ-hsī-szū wáng-ch'áo** a feudal, comprador, fascist dynasty (a reference to the objective of Lin Piao's attempted coup)

封建迷信活动 **fēng-chièn mí-hsìn huó-tùng** feudalistic superstitious activities

封建农业经济 **fēng-chièn núng-yèh-chīng-chì** feudalistic agricultural economy

封建把头 **fēng-chièn pǎ-t'óu** feudalistic boss (a labor contractor or broker in the old society)

封建包办买卖婚姻 **fēng-chièn pāo-pàn mǎi-mài hūn-yīn** feudalistic arranged marriages involving monetary considerations

封建社会 **fēng-chièn shè-huì** feudal society

封建思想 **fēng-chièn szū-hsiǎng** feudalistic thinking

封建帝国 **fēng-chièn tì-kuó** a feudal empire

封建统治 **fēng-chièn t'ǔng-chìh** feudal control, feudal rule

封建统治阶级 **fēng-chièn t'ǔng-chìh-chiēh-chí** feudal ruling class

封建宗法思想 **fēng-chièn tsūng-fǎ szū-hsiǎng** feudalistic patriarchal thinking

封建残余 **fēng-chièn ts'án-yú** feudal remnants, feudal holdovers

封建余孽 **fēng-chièn yú-nièh** feudal dregs

封面 **fēng-mièn** the cover [of a book or magazine]

封闭 **fēng-pì** to seal up, close down, close completely

封山育林 **fēng-shān yù-lín** to close the mountains to raise forests (to set up forest preserves where firewood cutting is prohibited)

封锁 **fēng-sǒ** to seal and lock up (to blockade)

封锁禁运 **fēng-sǒ chìn-yùn** blockade and embargo

封资修 **fēng-tzū-hsiū** feudalism, capitalism and revisionism

658 疯人 **fēng-jén** a madman, lunatic, insane person

疯狗 **fēng-kǒu** a mad dog (figurative)

疯狂 **fēng-k'uáng** insane, mad, crazy, raving

659 烽火 **fēng-huǒ** war signals, a war beacon

660 锋芒毕露 **fēng-máng-pì-lù** the lance point is completely revealed (to show too much of one's ability)

锋芒所向 **fēng-máng-sǒ-hsiàng** the direction of the lance point (to threaten

661 蜂拥而来 **fēng-yūng-érh-lái** like bees coming in a swarm (to crowd in, surge forward, flock)

féng (féng)

662 逢迎 **féng-yíng** to anticipate and meet [a person's every wish] (to curry favor, toady, fawn upon)

663 缝纫机 **féng-jèn-chī** sewing machine

缝纫组 **féng-jèn-tsǔ** a sewing group

fĕng (fĕng)

664 讽刺 **fĕng-tz'ù** to satirize, laugh at, make fun of, ridicule; satire, irony, sarcasm

讽刺画 **fĕng-tz'ù-huà** a caricature, cartoon

fèng (fèng)

665 奉承 **fèng-ch'éng** to serve with particular attention (to toady, court favor, fawn upon)

奉劝 **fèng-ch'üàn** may I venture to advise you

奉献 **fèng-hsièn** to beg to present (to offer something to a superior)

奉行 **fèng-hsíng** to act as ordered, carry out orders

奉陪到底 **fèng-p'éi tào-tĭ** to have the honor of keeping company to the end (often used sarcastically)

fŏu (fŏu)

666 否决 **fŏu-chüéh** to veto, vote against; to fail to adopt

否决权 **fŏu-chüéh-ch'üán** veto power

否认 **fŏu-jèn** to deny, disavow, disclaim, repudiate, renounce

否定 **fŏu-tìng** to negate, decide in the negative

否定成绩 **fŏu-tìng ch'éng-chī** to ignore [the] achievements [of] (often refers to the refusal of rightists to recognize the positive achievements of the Party)

fū (fū)

667 夫权 **fū-ch'üán** the rights of the husband

夫权思想 **fū-ch'üán-szū-hsiăng** the mentality of the husband's authority (male chauvinism)

668 肤浅 **fū-ch'iĕn** skin-deep (superficial, vague)

669 敷衍了事 **fū-yĕn-liăo-shìh** to work perfunctorily, get by with the barest minimum

敷衍态度 **fū-yĕn-t'ài-tù** a perfunctory attitude, insincerity

fú (fú)

670 弗里敦 **fú-lĭ-tūn** Freetown [Sierra Leone]

671 伏击 **fú-chī** to attack from ambush

伏笔 **fú-pĭ** to contain an implication; a hint to be amplified later

伏辩 **fú-pièn** a statement of guilt; to admit defeat in an argument

伏特 **fú-t'è** volt

伏罪 **fú-tsuì** to admit guilt, accept punishment

672 扶植新生力量 **fú-chíh hsīn-shēng-lì-liang** to give active help to the newly emerging forces (usually with reference to the international field)

扶助工农 **fú-chù kūng-núng** to give assistance to the peasants and workers (one of Sun Yat-sen's New Three Principles)

扶持新生事物 **fú-ch'íh hsīn-shēng-shìh-wù** support newly created things (get out of old ruts and attitudes)

扶犁掌耙 **fú-lì chăng-p'á** hold the hoe and wield the harrow (engage in farm work)

673 拂晓 **fú-hsiăo** at the break of day, at dawn

674 服装 **fú-chuāng** apparel, clothing

服气 **fú-ch'ì** to concede superiority, to accept the merit [of another's position]

服刑 **fú-hsíng** to serve one's term of punishment

服役 **fú-ì** to serve [in military or labor service]

服饰 **fú-shìh** attire, costume and accessories (such as the national dress of the minority peoples)

服输 **fú-shū** to admit defeat, concede

服从命令 **fú-ts'úng-mìng-lìng** to obey a command, adhere to orders

服从组织分配 **fú-ts'úng tsŭ-chīh fēn-p'èi** to accept the organization's assignment (to cheerfully take up the duties assigned one by the Party)

服务 **fú-wù** to serve, render service, work as an employee; service

服务站 **fú-wù-chàn** a service station (normally a repair station providing various services to the public such as clothing repair, etc.)

服务性行业 **fú-wù-hsìng háng-yèh** service trades

服务上门 **fú-wù-shàng-mén** services to the door (for persons whose health or duties prevent them from going to the shop)

服务员 **fú-wù-yuán** an attendant, waiter, steward (a general term for persons performing all kinds of services)

675 俘获 **fú-huò** to capture, be taken prisoner

俘虏 **fú-lŭ** a prisoner of war, a captive

676 浮夸 **fú-k'uā** pompous exaggeration, prolixity

浮收滥取 **fú-shōu-làn-ch'ǔ** irregular levies [and] excessive extortion

浮动汇率 **fú-tùng-huì-lǜ** floating exchange rate

浮躁急迫 **fú-tsào-chí-p'ò** violent-tempered, hasty

浮财 **fú-ts'ái** movable property

浮于上层 **fú-yǘ-shàng-ts'éng** to float in upper levels (a bad style of work that is not based on contact with and knowledge of work and life of the lower level units)

浮云蔽日 **fú-yún-pì-jìh** floating clouds obscure the sun (like floating clouds, wrong ideas cannot lastingly obscure the right)

677 符号 **fú-hào** a symbol, mark, sign

符合 **fú-hó** to correspond to, conform to, accord with, be in agreement with, coincide with

符合人民愿望 **fú-hó jén-mín te yuàn-wàng** to accord with the desires of the people

678 幅度 **fú-tù** rate or range of rise or fall [of prices, production, etc], width, spread

幅员辽阔 **fú-yuán liáo-k'uò** a large territoried [country]

679 福州部队 **fú-chōu pù-tuì** the Foochow Forces [of the PLA]

福克兰群岛 **fú-k'ò-lán ch'ǘn-tǎo** Falkland Islands

福利 **fú-lì** well-being, benefit, welfare, social care

福利金 **fú-lì-chīn** welfare fund

福利工会 **fú-lì-kūng-huì** "benefits" labor unions (a Cultural Revolution accusation that some labor unions were more interested in worker benefits than politics)

福利设施 **fú-lì-shè-shīh** welfare facilities

福利事业 **fú-lì-shìh-yèh** welfare services

福特·杰勒尔德 **fú-t'è. chiéh-lè-ěrh-té** Gerald Ford

680 辐射 **fú-shè** nuclear radiation

辐射化学 **fú-shè-huà-hsuéh** radiation chemistry

辐射危害 **fú-shè-wēi-hài** radiation hazards, dangers of radiation

fǔ (fǔ)

681 抚恤金 **fǔ-hsù-chīn** survivor's pension

抚慰 **fǔ-wèi** to console, comfort, soothe

682 斧头镰刀 **fǔ-t'óu lién tāo** the hammer and sickle

683 辅助 **fǔ-chù** auxiliary, subsidiary, supplemental; to assist, back up

辅助工 **fǔ-chù-kūng** helper, unskilled worker

辅助劳动 **fǔ-chù láo-tùng** auxiliary labor, part-time work

辅导 **fǔ-tǎo** assistance and guidance; to guide; a coach, tutor

辅导老师 **fǔ-tǎo-lǎo-shīh** counseling teacher (attached to each class of a middle school—usually on a volunteer basis)

辅导员 **fǔ-tǎo-yuán** (1) guide, counselor (usually an adult working with Young Pioneers); (2) title of a publication

684 腐化 **fǔ-huà** corrupted, decadent; to corrupt, demoralize

腐化分子 **fǔ-huà-fèn-tzǔ** corrupt element (one who tries to injure society)

腐朽 **fǔ-hsiǔ** rotten, decayed, putrid, moribund

腐朽不堪 **fǔ-hsiǔ-pù-k'ān** rotten to an unbearable extent, hopelessly decadent

腐烂 **fǔ-làn** decayed, spoiled, rotten, musty

腐烂的文化 **fǔ-làn te wén-huà** decadent culture

腐败 **fǔ-pài** corrupt, debased, depraved

腐蚀 **fǔ-shíh** to erode, corrode, debase; erosion, decay

腐蚀剂 **fǔ-shíh-chì** a corrosive agent

腐蚀革命灵魂 **fǔ-shíh kó-mìng-líng-hún** to debase the revolutionary spirit

fù (fù)

685 付之一笑 **fù-chīh-ī-hsiào** to dismiss with a laugh (not worth serious attention)

付诸实践 **fù-chū shíh-chièn** to put into practice

付诸实施 **fù-chū shíh-shīh** to put into practice, carry into effect

付出 **fù-ch'ū** to pay out

付印 **fù-yìn** to send to press, to print

686 妇女节 **fù-nǚ-chiéh** Women's Day (March 8)

妇女工作委员会 **fù-nǚ-kūng-tsò wěi-yuán-huì** Women's Work Committee [of the CCP Central Committee]

妇女联合会 **fù-nǚ lién-hó-huì** All-China Women's Federation (contraction of **Chung-hua ch'üan-kuo fu-nü lien-ho-hui**)

妇女落后论 **fù-nǚ-lò-hòu lùn** the doctrine that women are [naturally] backward, the theory of female inferiority (to be criticized)

妇女顶半边天 **fù-nǚ tǐng pàn-piēn-t'iēn** women hold up half the sky (the

world is half women—which implies that women are equal in rights and work and have a great contribution to make)

妇女无用论 **fù-nǚ wú-yùng lùn** the idea that women are useless (a concept that is now criticized)

妇委 **fù-wěi** Women's Work Committee [of the CCP] (contraction of **Fu-nü-kung-tso wei-yuan-hui**)

妇幼保健站 **fù-yù pǎo-chièn-chàn** maternity and infant welfare station

687 负债 **fù-chài** liability, debt, indebtedness

负荷 **fù-hò** load, capacity (often electrical)

负伤 **fù-shāng** to be wounded, suffer injuries

负担 **fù-tān** to burden [oneself], to take upon oneself, to bear one's share of; a burden, an obligation

负责 **fù-tsé** to be responsible for, accountable for, in charge of; to bear the blame, liable for

负责人 **fù-tsé-jén** the responsible person, leading member, person in charge

负责任 **fù tsé-jèn** to assume the responsibility, accept the liability

负隅顽抗 **fù-yǔ-wán-k'àng** to hold a corner and resist stubbornly (a last ditch fight)

688 附加 **fù-chiā** additional, supplemental, appended, inserted

附加税 **fù-chiā-shuì** surtax, an additional tax

附件 **fù-chièn** an appendix, supporting documents, addendum

附注 **fù-chù** a note attached to a text

附和 **fù-hò** to follow another's lead in voicing opinions, agree without conviction

附录 **fù-lù** appendix, supplement

附设 **fù-shè** attached to, affiliated with

附属机构 **fù-shǔ chī-kòu** subordinate organization, affiliated agencies

附属医院 **fù-shǔ-ī-yuàn** an affiliated hospital

附属国 **fù-shǔ-kuó** a dependent country, dependency

附属物 **fù-shǔ-wù** a accessory article, a supplement, an auxiliary

附带 **fù-tài** collateral, related, supplementary; to carry with, annex, append

附带劳动 **fù-tài-láo-tùng** supplemental labor (agricultural work other than **chǔ-yào láo-tùng**; also, the labor of a presant who does not devote at least four months a year to **chǔ-yào láo-**

tùng)

附则 **fù-tsé** supplementary provisions; by-laws

附庸 **fù-yūng** a satellite [country], vassal

689 复交三原则 **fù-chiāo sān-yuán-tsé** three principles for normalization of relations [with Japan] (enunciated in 1972)

复职 **fù-chíh** to reinstate in office; to resume a post

复旧 **fù-chiù** to restore the old

复种 **fù-chùng** double cropping (the growing of two or more crops consecutively on the same field in the same year)

复种指数 **fù-chùng-chǐh-shù** multiple crop index

复种面积 **fù-chùng-mièn-chī** multiple cropping area, area on which several crops a year are grown

复查 **fù-ch'á** to reinvestigate, recheck

复仇 **fù-ch'óu** to take revenge, avenge; a reprisal

复发 **fù-fā** to recur, relapse [of illness]

复活 **fù-huó** to revive, resuscitate; resurrection

复兴 **fù-hsīng** to renew, revive, restore; regeneration, revival, renaissance

复古 **fù-kǔ** to revive the ancient

复国主义 **fù-kuó-chǔ-ì** irredentism

复课闹革命 **fù-k'ò nào-kó-mìng** to return to [school] classes to make revolution (slogan of the late period of the Cultural Revolution)

复辟 **fù-pì** to restore monarchy (now usually refers to the restoration of the old society)

复辟和反复辟的斗争 **fù-pì hó fǎn-fù-pì te tòu-chēng** the struggle between restoration and anti-restoration

复旦 **fù-tàn** (1) the return of light [after darkness], the dawn; (2) Futan University in Shanghai; (3) the title of an academic journal

复杂 **fù-tsá** mixed, intricate, complex, complicated

复杂化 **fù-tsá-huà** to make things complicated, to complicate

复杂性 **fù-tsá-hsìng** complexity

复员 **fù-yuán** to demobilize, deactivate; demobilized

复员军人 **fù-yuán-chūn-jén** a demobilized soldier [who has returned to his original job]

复员还乡 **fù-yuán-huán-hsiāng** a demobilized soldier [who has] returned to his native place

690 赴汤蹈火 **fù-t'āng tǎo-huǒ** to go through hot water and tread on fire

(to brave great dangers and
difficulties)

691 副政委 **fù-chèng-wěi** deputy political
commissar

副产品 **fù-ch'ǎn-p'ǐn** by-product,
subsidiary products

副产物 **fù-ch'ǎn-wù** by-product,
subsidiary product

副本 **fù-pěn** a duplicate copy, facsimile
reproduction

副博士 **fù-pó-shìh** Ph.D. candidate

副部长 **fù-pù-chǎng** a vice minister,
deputy minister

副食品 **fù-shíh-p'ǐn** non-staple foods,
subsidiary foodstuffs

副书记 **fù-shū-chì** deputy secretary [of
a Party or Youth League Committee]

副作用 **fù-tsò-yùng** side effect,
secondary effect, undesirable effects

副总理 **fù-tsǔng-lǐ** deputy premier

副业 **fù-yèh** secondary occupation, side
occupation, sideline

副业包产 **fù-yèh pāo-ch'ǎn** to take
responsibility for side-occupation
production

副业包产到人 **fù-yèh pāo-ch'ǎn tào-jén**
individual assumption of responsibility for [a commune unit] side-
occupation production (to be
criticized)

副业生产 **fù-yèh-shēng-ch'ǎn** subsidiary
production, sideline products

副业单干 **fù-yèh tān-kàn** to do auxiliary work on a private basis

副业作物 **fù-yèh-tsò-wù** subsidiary
crop

副业运输队 **fù-yèh yùn-shū-tuì** part-
time transport team

692 富强 **fù-ch'iáng** affluence [and military]
strength (national wealth and power)

富强康乐 **fù-ch'iáng-k'āng-lè** rich,
strong, peaceful, and happy (said of a
country and its people)

富豪 **fù-háo** wealthy and powerful
[persons]

富饶 **fù-jáo** fertile, rich in resources

富矿 **fù-k'uàng** high-grade ore

富农 **fù-núng** rich peasant

富农经济 **fù-núng-chīng-chì** rich-
peasant economy

富商 **fù-shāng** a rich merchant

富裕 **fù-yù** well-to-do, wealthy

富裕中农 **fù-yù-chūng-núng** rich
middle peasants

693 赋税 **fù-shuì** to levy or pay tax (land
tax and other levies in pre-Communist period)

694 腹背受敌 **fù-pèi-shòu-tí** exposed to the
enemy at front and rear

695 覆灭 **fù-mièh** to be completely

defeated; annihilation, doom

覆没 **fù-mò** to capsize, overturn

hā (hā)

696 哈尼族 **hā-ní-tsú** the Hani people (a
minority in Yunnan: population
549,000 as of 1957)

哈萨克族 **hā-sā-k'ò-tsú** the Kazakh
people (a minority in the Sinkiang-
Uighur Autonomous Region:
population 533,000 as of 1957)

哈达 **hā-tá** a ceremonial gift scarf (in
Tibet)

哈瓦那 **hā-wǎ-nà** Havana

哈 **hā**: *see also* **hǎ**

hǎ (hǎ)

697 哈巴狗 **hǎ-pa-kǒu** a Pekinese dog,
shameless dog (a Cultural Revolution
epithet)

哈 **hǎ**: *see also* **hā**

hǎi (hǎi)

698 海岸线 **hǎi-àn-hsièn** coastline

海岸砲兵 **hǎi-àn p'ào-pīng** coast
artillery, coastal battery

海疆 **hǎi-chiāng** coastal borders, the
sea frontier

海潮 **hǎi-ch'áo** sea tides

海军 **hǎi-chūn** the navy

海军陆战队 **hǎi-chūn lù-chàn-tuì** the
marine corps, marines

海防前哨 **hǎi-fáng ch'ièn-shào** coastal
defense outposts

海防部队 **hǎi-fáng pù-tuì** coastguards,
coastal defense units

海峡 **hǎi-hsiá** straits, a narrow passage
between two seas

海瑞罢官 **hǎi juì pà-kuān** "Hai Jui
Dismissed from Office" (historical
drama by Wu Han, reputedly
supporting P'eng Te-huai)

海港 **hǎi-kǎng** (1) harbor, port;
(2) "On the Docks" (one of the
yàng-pǎn hsì)

海口 **hǎi-k'ǒu** a seaport

海枯石烂 **hǎi-k'ū-shíh-làn** [until the]
seas dry up [and the] rocks decay
(forever, unchanging)

海里 **hǎi-lǐ** a nautical mile, knot

海洛英 **hǎi-lò-yīng** heroin

海陆丰苏维埃 **hǎi-lù-fēng sū-wéi-āi** the
Hailufeng Soviet (established in
northern Kwangtung in 1927 under
the leadership of P'eng P'ai, regarded
as the first soviet in China)

海陆空联合作战 **hǎi-lù-k'ūng lièn-hó**

tsò-chàn aero-amphibious warfare, combined operations on sea, land, and air

海绵田 **hǎi-mién-t'ién** a spongy field (field in which the soil has been carefully pulverized to reduce evaporation)

海拔 **hǎi-pá** above sea level

海商法 **hǎi-shāng-fǎ** maritime law

海上霸权 **hǎi-shàng pà-ch'üán** control of the seas

海事 **hǎi-shìh** a maritime accident (contraction of **hǎi-shàng shìh-chièn**)

海岛 **hǎi-tǎo** a sea island

海盗 **hǎi-tào** a pirate

海盗式武装侵略 **hǎi-tào-shìh wǔ-chuāng-ch'īn-lüèh** a piratical armed attack

海地 **hǎi-tì** Haiti

海涂 **hǎi-t'ú** tidelands, tidal marsh

海外奇谈 **hǎi-wài-ch'í-t'án** a traveler's tale (a fantastic story)

海外侨胞 **hǎi-wài-ch'iáo-pāo** overseas brothers (overseas Chinese)

海牙 **hǎi-yá** The Hague [Netherlands]

海牙公约 **hǎi-yá kūng-yuēh** The Hague Convention

海洋权 **hǎi-yáng-ch'üán** maritime rights

海洋法 **hǎi-yáng-fǎ** law of the sea

海洋法会议 **hǎi-yáng-fǎ huì-ì** Law of the Sea Conference (held in Caracas, Venezuela, 1974)

海洋学 **hǎi-yáng-hsuéh** oceanography

海洋霸权 **hǎi-yáng pà-ch'üán** control of the seas, maritime hegemony

海洋资源 **hǎi-yáng tzū-yuán** the resources of the oceans

海邮 **hǎi-yú** seamail

海运 **hǎi-yùn** maritime transport

hài (hài)

699 骇人听闻 **hài-jén-t'īng-wén** it frightens one to hear (dreadful, shocking)

700 害己害人 **hài-chǐ-hài-jén** to harm oneself and others

害群之马 **hài-ch'ún-chīh-mǎ** a horse that spoils the whole herd (one bad person can infect his whole group)

害人虫 **hài-jén-ch'úng** man-harming vermin, a noxious insect (often figurative)

hán (hán)

701 邯郸学步 **hán-tān-hsuéh-pù** to learn walking at Hantan (to lose one's own knowledge and originality by slavishly imitating others)

702 含糊 **hán-hu** unclear, not explicit, vague, ambiguous, equivocal

含糊其词 **hán-hú-ch'í-tz'ú** to speak equivocably, talk in vague terms, be ambiguous, slur over

含蓄 **hán-hsù** reserved [in manner], restrained [in speech or writing]

含义 **hán-ì** unexpressed meaning, implied, implicit by connotation

含沙射影 **hán-shā-shè-yǐng** to hold sand in the mouth and spurt at shadows (an insinuation, malicious)

含水量 **hán-shuǐ-liàng** water content

703 函授学校 **hán-shòu-hsuéh-hsiào** a correspondence school

704 涵养 **hán-yǎng** moral cultivation, culture, polite restraint; to keep one's temper

705 寒潮 **hán-ch'áo** a cold wave, a cold front

寒心 **hán-hsīn** to tremble with fear; daunted, dismayed, appalled by

寒流 **hán-liú** a cold wave, cold current

hǎn (hǎn)

706 罕见 **hǎn-chièn** seldom seen, rare

707 喊出 **hǎn-ch'ū** to make an outcry, to cry out

hàn (hàn)

708 汉奸 **hàn-chiēn** a traitor to China

汉奸文学 **hàn-chiēn wén-hsuéh** "traitor" literature (literary works during 1930s and 1940s accused of advocating capitulation to Japan)

汉城 **hàn-ch'éng** Seoul [South Korea]

汉族 **hàn-tsú** the Han people (the people of China excluding minorities)

汉子 **hàn-tzu** a man, stout fellow

汉字 **hàn-tzù** Chinese characters

汉字简化方案 **hàn-tzù chiēn-huà fāng-àn** Program for the Simplification of the Chinese Language

汉语 **hàn-yǔ** the Han language, the language of the Han Chinese people (the spoken form is based on Peking pronunciation and is the same as **p'ǔ-t'ūng-huà**; the written form includes simplified character forms; in both spoken and written forms it has displaced the old terms **kuó-yǔ** and **kuó-wén**)

汉语规范化 **hàn-yǔ kuēi-fàn-huà** standardization of the Chinese language

汉语拼音方案 **hàn-yǔ p'īn-yīn fāng-àn** Program for the Phonetic Spelling of the Chinese Language

汉字拼音符号 **hàn-yǔ p'īn-yīn fú-hào** the Chinese phonetic alphabet, phonetic transcription of the Chinese language

709 汗流浃背 **hàn-liú-chiā-pèi** sweat soaks the back (covered with perspiration)

汗牛充栋 **hàn-niú-ch'ūng-tùng** [so many books that the] ox sweats [and] the house is filled to the roof (excessively voluminous, over-abundant)

710 旱涝保收 **hàn-lào-pǎo-shōu** stable yields despite drought or excessive rain

旱涝不收 **hàn-lào pù-shōu** a bad harvest as a result of drought or flood

旱粮 **hàn-liáng** food reserves set aside for drought

旱魔 **hàn-mó** the drought demon

旱能灌涝能排 **hàn-néng-kuàn lào-néng-p'ái** drought can be irrigated [and] flooding can be drained

旱稻 **hàn-tào** upland rice (grown in dry fields)

旱地 **hàn-tì** non-irrigated land

旱灾 **hàn-tsāi** drought

711 悍然不顾 **hàn-ján-pù-kù** to rudely brush aside (high-handed, brusque)

712 捍海堰 **hàn-hǎi-yèn** a sea-restraining barrier, seawall

捍卫 **hàn-wèi** defense; to defend, protect, fend off

捍卫毛泽东思想 **hàn-wèi máo tsé-tūng szū-hsiǎng** defend the Thought of Mao Tse-tung (a slogan of the early stages of the Cultural Revolution)

捍卫祖国 **hàn-wèi tsǔ-kuó** defend the fatherland

713 焊接 **hàn-chiēh** to weld, solder

焊工 **hàn-kūng** a welder

hāng (hāng)

714 夯实地基 **hāng-shíh tì-chī** tamping the foundation, to compact

háng (háng)

715 行家 **háng-chiā** a specialist, expert; a profession, trade

行情 **háng-ch'íng** market conditions (sometimes figurative)

行行出状元 **háng-háng ch'ū chuàng-yuán** any walk of life can produce a winner in the imperial examinations (any field can produce top people; every job offers opportunities)

行会 **háng-huì** a guild, trade association

行列 **hán-lièh** rows, lines, ranks; a column formation

行商税 **háng-shāng-shuì** merchandising tax (placed on any re-sale transaction in the early 1950s)

行业 **háng-yèh** a trade, profession, occupation

行业界限 **háng-yèh-chièh-hsièn** demarcations between trades (now something to be broken down)

行 **háng**: see also **hsíng**

716 航程 **háng-ch'éng** range of navigation or flight, navigational distance

航向 **háng-hsiàng** sailing direction, a course

航线 **háng-hsièn** [air] navigation route, air route

航行 **háng-hsíng** to sail, navigate; a voyage

航行标志 **háng-hsíng-piāo-chìh** channel markers, aids to navigation

航空勘查 **háng-k'ūng k'ān-ch'á** aerial survey, aerial reconnaissance

航空母舰 **háng-k'ūng-mǔ-chièn** aircraft carrier

航空兵 **háng-k'ūng-pīng** air-force personnel (an informal term for the air branch of the PLA or members thereof)

航空测量 **háng-k'ūng ts'è-liáng** aerial surveying, aerial photographic survey

航道 **háng-tào** [sea] navigation line, sea route

航运公司 **háng-yùn-kūng-szū** shipping company, shipping line

háo (háo)

717 毫毛 **háo-máo** a fine hair (an iota)

毫不知耻 **háo-pù-chīh-ch'ǐh** without the least shame, impudence

毫不含糊 **háo-pù-hán-hu** without ambiguity, unequivocal, clear-cut

毫不怀疑 **háo-pù-huái-í** without the slightest doubt

毫不悔改 **háo-pù-huǐ-kǎi** without the slightest repentance, incorrigible

毫不利己专门利人 **háo-pù-lì-chǐ chuān-mén-lì-jén** with no [thought of] personal interests and exclusively [devoted to] the interests of others

毫不调和 **háo-pù-t'iáo-hó** uncom-promising, completely incompatible, irreconcilable

毫不在乎 **háo-pù-tsài-hu** completely unconcerned, "don't give a damn," nonchalant

毫不足怪 **háo-pù-tsú-kuài** nothing to be surprised at

毫无权利 **háo-wú ch'üán-lì** to have no rights at all, utter lack of rights

毫无二致 **háo-wú-èrh-chìh** cannot be distinguished, without any difference

毫无希望 **háo-wú-hsī-wàng** completely hopeless, without any chance of success

毫无信义 **háo-wú-hsìn-ì** utterly faithless

毫无疑义 **háo-wú-í-ì** definitely and beyond all doubt, withoug any doubt

毫无疑问 **háo-wú-í-wèn** not the slightest doubt

毫无骨气 **hào-wú-kǔ-ch'ì** utterly spineless (without any moral integrity)

毫无共同之处 **háo-wú kùng-t'úng-chīh-ch'ù** to have nothing in common

毫无例外 **háo-wú-lì-wài** without exception

毫无保留 **háo-wú-pǎo-liú** without qualification, unreservedly

毫无道理 **háo-wǔ-tào-lǐ** completely without justification, wholly unreasonable

毫无怨言 **háo-wú-yuàn-yén** without a word of complaint

毫无用处 **háo-wú-yùng-ch'u** completely useless, having no useful purpose

718 豪杰 **háo-chiéh** a hero, champion, person of great talent and ability

豪强 **háo-ch'iáng** the strong and the powerful (in the old society)

豪情壮志 **háo-ch'íng-chuàng-chìh** unbounded fervor and determination, ardor

豪放 **háo-fàng** vigorous and unrestrained, expansive, of heroic manner

豪迈 **háo-mài** gallant, magnanimous, energetic

豪迈誓言 **háo-mài shìh-yén** a gallant pledge

豪门资本 **háo-mén-tzū-pěn** the capital of rich and powerful families (usually refers to the four great families of the KMT era: Chiang, K'ung, Soong, and Ch'en)

豪绅恶霸分子 **háo-shēn-ò-pà fèn-tzǔ** bad gentry and local tyrant elements

豪言壮语 **háo-yén-chuàng-yǔ** bold and heroic words

719 壕沟 **háo-kōu** a trench, ditch, gutter

hǎo (hǎo)

720 好景不长 **hǎo-chǐng-pù-ch'áng** a good situation does not last, good things cannot be counted on to continue

好转 **hǎo-chuǎn** a turn for the better, a favorable change [in the situation]

好处 **hǎo-ch'ù** good points, benefits, advantages

好儿女 **hǎo-érh-nǔ** good sons and daughters (usually of Mao Tse-tung or the Party)

好汉 **hǎo-hàn** a gallant, stout-hearted, plucky fellow

好好先生 **hǎo-hǎo hsiēn-shēng** Mr. Good-Good (a person who is so nice that he never expresses any conviction or opinion)

好好学习天天向上 **hǎo-hǎo hsuéh-hsí, t'iēn-t'iēn hsiàng-shàng** diligently study [and] daily advance (slogan of the Young Pioneers)

好人好事 **hǎo-jén hǎo-shìh** good people and good deeds

好感 **hǎo-kǎn** a favorable impression, a good reaction

好了伤疤忘了疼 **hǎo-le-shāng-pā wàng-le-t'éng** when the scar heals, the pain is forgotten (living in a new society, one forgets the misery of the old)

好榜样 **hǎo-pǎng-yàng** a good example, fine model

好评 **hǎo-p'íng** a favorable evaluation, appreciation, approbation, acclaim

好事 **hǎo-shìh** a good deed, a good thing, charitable act

好 **hǎo**: see also **hào**

hào (hào)

721 号召 **hào-chào** to call for, appeal, urge, call

号角 **hào-chiǎo** a bugle, horn

号称 **hào-ch'ēng** to be called as, reputedly

号令 **hào-lìng** an order; to issue an order

号外 **hào-wài** a newspaper extra edition

722 好战 **hào-chàn** bellicose, warlike, hawkish

好逸恶劳 **hào-ì-wù-láo** to love ease and hate work

好大喜功 **hào-tà-hsǐ-kūng** to crave greatness and success

好 **hào**: see also **hǎo**

723 浩劫 **hào-chiéh** a great crisis, catastrophe, calamity, suffering

浩瀚 **hào-hàn** limitless, a vast expanse

浩浩荡荡 **hào-hào-tàng-tàng** coming with great force, in formidable array, in multitudes, overwhelming

浩如烟海 **hào-jú-yēn-hǎi** as vast as the misty sea (voluminous, countless)

浩大 **hào-tà** great, vast, imposing, huge

724 耗尽 **hào-chìn** to exhaust, drain, wear out, waste away

耗费 **hào-fèi** to spend; expenditure

耗时间 **hào-shíh-chiēn** to waste time, mark time, stretch out

hēi (hēi)

725 黑 **hēi** Heilungkiang province

黑暗 **hēi-àn** dark, darkness (usually with political connotations: reactionary, counter-revolutionary)

黑暗统治 **hēi-àn-t'ŭng-chìh** a black regime (a reactionary government)

黑旗 **hēi-ch'í** the black flag (a figurative reference to anti-Maoists during the Cultural Revolution)

黑风邪气 **hēi-fēng-hsiéh-ch'ì** black winds and evil emanations (reactionary influences)

黑话 **hēi-huà** black language (mysterious and obscure talk: a Cultural Revolution term for allegedly anti-Maoist opinions; the argot of criminals)

黑会 **hēi-huì** a black meeting (during the Cultural Revolution any group thought to be conspiring against Mao or the Party)

黑活 **hēi-huó** black work (illicit work)

黑货 **hēi-huò** smuggled goods, stolen goods, contraband (often figurative to refer to ideas or publications of the anti-Maoists)

黑线 **hēi-hsièn** the black line (a common Cultural Revolution term for allegedly anti-Mao or revisionist thought)

黑修养 **hēi hsiū-yăng** black "cultivation" (Liu Shao-ch'i's book, *How to be a Good Communist*)

黑秀才 **hēi-hsiù-ts'ái** a black *hsiù ts'ái* [scholar] (an epithet of the Cultural Revolution applied to anti-Maoist intellectuals)

黑人黑戶 **hēi-jén hēi-hù** black people, black households (people not registered in household books in the area where they actually live)

黑纲领 **hēi-kāng-lǐng** black program (any program regarded as anti-Mao or anti-Party)

黑格尔 **hēi-kó-ěrh** Hegel (1770-1831)

黑六论 **hēi-liù-lùn** the black six doctrines (attributed to Liu Shao-ch'i: (1) internal Party peace; (2) fusion of public and private; (3) the Party member an obedient tool; (4) backwardness of the masses; (5) joining the Party makes one an official; (6) the extinguishing of class struggle)

黑名单 **hēi-míng-tān** a black name list, black list

黑幕 **hēi-mù** black screen, black curtain (a cover-up for evil deeds—usually political)

黑八论 **hēi-pā-lùn** the black eight doctrines (a set of literary principles ascribed to Chou Yang, Hsia Yen, T'ien Han and others, and severely criticized during the Cultural Revolution—officially translated as: (1) truthful writing; (2) the broad path of realism; (3) the deepening of realism; (4) against collective decision-making; (5) middle characters; (6) opposition to subject-matter as the decisive factor; (7) the confluence of various trends as the spirit of the age; (8) opposition to the smell of gunpowder)

黑板报 **hēi-pǎn-pào** blackboard bulletin, blackboard newspaper

黑帮 **hēi-pāng** a black gang (anti-Party or anti-Maoist elements, especially intellectuals)

黑榜 **hēi-pǎng** a posted blacklist

黑笔记 **hēi-pǐ-chì** black reading notes (in 1974, used to refer to Lin Piao's personal notes on his reading)

黑三论 **hēi-sān-lùn** the three black theories (studying to become an official; studying is useless; teachers are doomed)

黑色臭染缸 **hēi-sè ch'òu-jǎn-kāng** a black, stinking dye vat

黑色冶金业 **hēi-sè yěh-chīn-yèh** ferrous metals industry, iron and steel industry

黑市 **hēi-shìh** black market

黑手揪红人 **hēi-shǒu chiū húng-jén** black hands purge red men (attacks on true revolutionaries by counter-revolutionaries)

黑穗病 **hēi-suì-pìng** smut, a crop disease caused by smut fungi

黑店 **hēi-tièn** a black inn (Cultural Revolution term for the headquarters or meeting place of an allegedly subversive group)

黑文 **hēi-wén** a black article (any writing regarded as critical of Mao Tse-tung or the Party)

黑五类 **hēi-wǔ-lèi** the black five elements (landlords, rightists, counter-revolutionaries, rich peasants, and bad elements)

hén (hén)

726 痕迹 **hén-chī** a mark left, imprint, footprint, trace, vestige, track

hĕn (hĕn)

727 狠揭猛批 **hĕn-chiéh měng-p'ī** to

relentlessly expose and criticize

狠抓 **hěn-chuā** to grasp forcefully

狠抓革命 **hěn-chuā kó-mìng** to grasp revolution firmly (now used very broadly)

狠下功夫 **hěn-hsià kūng-fu** to spend time unsparingly, painstaking

狠批克己复礼 **hěn-p'ī kò-chǐ-fù-lǐ** bitterly criticize "restrain [the] self [and] restore [the] rites" (slogan of the movement for criticism of Lin Piao and Confucius)

狠批孔孟之道 **hěn-p'ī k'ǔng-mèng-chīh-tào** determinedly criticize the way of Confucius and Mencius

狠挖老祖坟 **hěn-wā lǎo-tsǔ-fén** without compunction dig up one's ancestors' graves (ruthlessly rid oneself of the ideology of Confucius and Mencius)

hèn (hèn)

728   恨之入骨 **hèn-chīh-jù-kǔ** to hate to the bone

恨得要死 **hèn-te-yào-szǔ** to hate with extreme malice

héng (héng)

729   横征暴敛 **héng-chēng-pào-lièn** to extort taxes and levies, to impose unbearable burdens [on the people]

横加梗阻 **héng-chiā-kěng-tsǔ** willfully to set up obstacles, obstruct

横加威吓辱骂 **héng-chiā wēi-hò jǔ-mà** unreasonably to threaten and curse

横冲直撞 **héng-ch'ūng-chíh-chuàng** to collide horizontally and hit straight ahead (to clash in every direction, run amuck)

横幅标语 **héng-fú-piāo-yǔ** a pennant, streamer, banner

横行霸道 **héng-hsíng-pà-tào** to act against law and reason (to bully, terrorize, ride roughshod over)

横行天下 **héng-hsíng-t'iēn-hsià** to walk sideways under heaven (outrageous behavior; to seize power)

横贯 **héng-kuàn** across, connecting, from one side to the other

横扫 **héng-sǎo** to sweep clean

横生枝节 **héng-shēng-chīh-chiéh** to sprout branches abnormally (unreasonable complications apart from the main issue)

横施压力 **héng-shīh-yā-lì** unscrupulous pressure

横越 **héng-yuèh** to cross over, spanning, trans-

横 **héng**: see also **hèng**

730   衡量 **héng-liáng** to measure, weigh; a measure

hèng (hèng)

731   横蛮 **hèng-mán** arrogant, barbarous, ruthless

横暴 **hèng-pào** cruel, tyrannical, savage, violent

横财 **hèng-ts'ái** an ill-gotten fortune, windfall, illegal gains

横 **hèng**: see also **héng**

hō (hē)

732   呵责 **hō-tsé** to abuse, censure, reprimand, berate

733   喝采 **hō-ts'ǎi** to applaud and cheer, to acclaim; an ovation, applause

hó (hé)

734   禾苗 **hó-miáo** rice seedling

735   合金 **hó-chīn** an alloy

合金钢 **hó-chīn-kāng** steel alloy

合众国际社 **hó-chùng kuó-chì-shè** United Press International News Service [UPI]

合唱 **hó-ch'àng** a chorus; to sing in unison

合成氨 **hó-ch'éng-ān** synthetic ammonia

合成橡胶 **hó-ch'éng hsiàng-chiāo** synthetic rubber

合成纤维 **hó-ch'éng hsiēn-wéi** synthetic fiber

合成油类 **hó-ch'éng yú-lèi** synthetic oils

合情合理 **hó-ch'íng-hó-lǐ** in accord with human relations and reason

合二而一 **hó-èrh-érh-ī** combine two into one (philosophic theory, particularly linked to Yang Hsien-chen, which contradicts Mao's theory that "one divides into two," and is interpreted as looking toward class harmony rather than class struggle)

合二为一 **hó-èrh-wéi-ī** combine two into one (see above)

合法 **hó-fǎ** lawful, legal, legitimate, rightfully

合法政府 **hó-fǎ-chèng-fǔ** legal government

合法马克思主义 **hó-fǎ mǎ-k'ò-szū-chǔ-ì** legal Marxism

合法地位 **hó-fǎ tì-wèi** legal status

合法斗争 **hó-fǎ tòu-chēng** lawful struggle (one of the forms of class struggle employing nonviolent methods)

合伙 **hó-huǒ** partnership; to form a partnership

合一 **hó-ī** to unite, become one, integrate

合格 **hó-kó** qualified, up to standard, competent, eligible

合格证书 **hó-kó chèng-shū** qualification certificate

合格率 **hó-kò-lǜ** the rate [proportion] meeting the standard

合股 **hó-kǔ** in partnership, to pool capital

合理 **hó-lǐ** reasonable, logical, rational

合理发挥 **hó-lǐ fā-huī** to give proper scope to

合理负担 **hó-lǐ fù-tān** a rational division of] responsibility

合理化建议 **hó-lǐ-huà chièn-ì** rationalization proposals

合理密植 **hó-lǐ mì-chíh** reasonably close planting (a modification of close planting which proved disastrous)

合理布局 **hó-lǐ pù-chǘ** rational placement (usually refers to geographic location of industries)

合理使用劳动力 **hó-lǐ shǐh-yùng láotùng-lì** rational utilization of labor power

合并 **hó-pìng** to merge, amalgamate, consolidate, annex, absorb, unite

合适 **hó-shìh** suitable, appropriate, proper, fitting

合算 **hó-suàn** profitable, reasonable in price

合体字 **hó-t'ǐ-tzù** a composite character, a character made up of two or more component elements

合同 **hó-t'ung** a contract, written agreement

合同制度 **hó-t'úng chìh-tù** a contract system

合同工人 **hó-t'úng-kūng-jén** contract workers (who have fixed enforceable employment contracts)

合则两利离则俱伤 **hó-tsé-liǎng-lì, lítsé-chù-shāng** cooperation benefits both [but] separateness harms all

合作 **hó-tsò** to work together, work with, cooperate, collaborate; cooperation

合作化 **hó-tsò-huà** cooperativization

合作化运动 **hó-tsò-huà yùn-tùng** the cooperativization movement

合作医疗 **hó-tsò-ī-liáo** cooperative medicine (medical facilities based on cooperation of commune, brigade, team and individuals)

合作医疗站 **hó-tsò ī-liáo-chàn** a cooperative clinic (normally in a production brigade)

合作医疗基金 **hó-tsò-ī-liáo chī-chīn** cooperative medical fund

合作医疗制度 **hó-tsò-ī-liáo chìh-tù** cooperative medical service system

合作社 **hó-tsò-shè** a cooperative society, a collective

合资 **hó-tzū** joint capital, a partnership

合营 **hó-yíng** joint operation, jointly operated, partnership

合用 **hó-yùng** suitable, usable, practical

736 河湖港汊 **hó-hú-kǎng-ch'à** rivers, lakes, bays, and inlets

河内 **hó-nèi** Hanoi

河水不犯井水 **hó-shuǐ pù-fàn chǐng-shuǐ** water in the river does not offend the water in the well (non-conflicting)

河堤 **hó-tī** river dikes

河滩地 **hó-t'ān-tì** river-bank land, polder land (fields reclaimed from riverbeds)

737 和蔼可亲 **hó-ǎi-k'ǒ-ch'īn** amiable and lovable, a sweet disposition

和解 **hó-chiěh** to reconcile, reach an amicable settlement, settle differences

和衷共事 **hó-chūng-kùng-shìh** to work together harmoniously

和气 **hó-ch'ì** polite, agreeable, affable, cordial, good-natured

和风细雨 **hó-fēng-hsì-yǔ** mild breeze and fine rain (as, a mild, temperate and helpful method in criticism)

和缓 **hó-huǎn** mild, decreasing, mitigating

和谐 **hó-hsiéh** harmonious, friendly; to agree

和毛主席一条心 **hó máo-chǔ-hsí ī-t'iáohsīn** of one heart with Chairman Mao

和睦相处 **hó-mù-hsiāng-ch'ǔ** to live together harmoniously

和平阵营 **hó-p'íng chèn-yíng** the peace camp

和平奖金 **hó-p'íng chiǎng-chīn** peace prize

和平建国方针 **hó-p'íng chièn-kuó fāngchēn** policy of peace and national reconstruction

和平支柱 **hó-p'íng chīh-chù** a mainstay of peace

和平竞赛 **hó-p'íng chìng-sài** peaceful competition

和平主义 **hó-p'íng-chǔ-ì** pacifism

和平中立政策 **hó-p'íng-chūng-lì chèngts'è** policy of peace and neutrality

和平签名运动 **hó-p'íng ch'iēn-míng yùntùng** a peace appeal signature campaign

和平协商 **hó-p'íng hsiéh-shāng** peaceful negotiations, peace negotiations

和平宣言 **hó-p'íng hsuān-yén** a peace manifesto

和平改编 **hó-p'íng kǎi-piēn** peaceful reorganization (as, for example, the amalgamation of Fu Tso-yi's [Kuomintang] troops into the PLA in 1949)

和平攻势 **hó-p'íng-kūng-shìh** a peace offensive

和平共处 **hó-p'íng-kùng-ch'ǔ** peaceful coexistence

和平共处五项原则 **hó-p'íng-kùng-ch'ǔ wǔ-hsiàng-yuán-tsé** the five principles of peaceful coexistence (set forth by Chou En-lai at the Bandung Conference, 1955: mutual respect for territory and sovereignty; nonaggression; noninterference; equality and mutual benefit; peaceful coexistence)

和平过渡 **hó-p'íng-kuò-tù** peaceful transition

和平利用原子能 **hó-p'íng-lì-yùng yuán-tzǔ-néng** peaceful uses of atomic energy

和平民主新阶段 **hó-p'íng mín-chǔ hsīn chiēh-t'uàn** the new stage of peaceful democracy (a policy attributed to Liu Shao-ch'i, 1946)

和平民主运动 **hó-p'íng mín-chǔ yùntùng** movement of peace and democracy

和平堡垒 **hó-p'íng pǎo-lěi** a bulwark of peace

和平抵抗 **hó-p'íng tǐ-k'àng** civil disobedience, nonviolent resistance

和平调子 **hó-p'íng tiào-tzu** a peace tune; to talk peace

和平谈判 **hó-píng t'án-p'àn** peace negotiations

和平土改 **hó-p'íng t'ǔ-kǎi** peaceful land reform, nonviolent land reform

和平演变 **hó-p'íng-yěn-pièn** peaceful evolution, peaceful transformation (condemned in the Cultural Revolution as a retrogression to capitalism)

和事佬 **hó-shìh-lǎo** a peace-maker

和约 **hó-yuēh** peace treaty

和 **hó**: *see also* **huó**

738 荷兰 **hó-lán** Holland, Netherlands

荷属西印度群岛 **hó-shǔ hsī-yìn-tù chún-tǎo** Dutch West Indies, Dutch Antilles

荷属圭亚那 **hó-shǔ kuēi-yà-nà** Dutch Guiana

739 核战争 **hó-chàn-chēng** nuclear war

核基地 **hó-chī-tì** nuclear bases

核竞争 **hó-chìng-chēng** nuclear competition

核竞赛 **hó-chìng-sài** nuclear [arms] race

核冲突 **hó-ch'ūng-t'ū** nuclear conflict

核反应 **hó-fǎn-yìng** nuclear reaction

核反应堆 **hó-fǎn-yìng-tuī** nuclear reactor, nuclear pile

核分裂 **hó-fēn-lièh** nuclear fission

核海军 **hó-hǎi-chūn** a nuclear navy

核心 **hó-hsīn** core, nucleus, center, heart, focus, kernel

核心小组 **hó-hsīn hsiǎo-tsǔ** a core group, nuclear group

核心力量 **hó-hsīn lì-liang** a core force

核国家 **hó-kuó-chiā** a nuclear power

核能 **hó-néng** nuclear energy, nuclear capability

核讹诈 **hó-ó-chà** nuclear blackmail

核霸权 **hó-pà-ch'üán** nuclear hegemony

核保护 **hó-pǎo-hù** nuclear protection, nuclear shield

核骗局 **hó-p'ièn-chú** nuclear deception, nuclear plot

核实 **hó-shíh** to verify [a report or account]

核算 **hó-suàn** to estimate, calculate, to render an account

核算制度 **hó-suàn-chìh-tù** accounting system, computation system, auditing system

核弹头 **hó-tàn-t'óu** nuclear warhead, nuclear charge

核导弹 **hó-tǎo-tàn** nuclear guided missile

核定生产力 **hó-tìng shēng-ch'ǎn-lì** to evaluate production forces

核对 **hó-tuì** to verify, check the facts, confirm

核资 **hó-tzū** to compute the value of capital

核子辐射 **hó-tzǔ-fú-shè** nuclear radiation

核子物理学 **hó-tzǔ wù-lǐ-hsuéh** nuclear physics

核裁军 **hó-ts'ái-chūn** nuclear disarmament

核裁军谈判 **hó-ts'ái-chūn t'án-p'àn** nuclear disarmament talks (SALT talks)

核威协 **hó-wēi-hsiéh** nuclear threats

核武器 **hó-wǔ-ch'ì** nuclear weapons

核武器运载系统 **hó-wǔ-ch'ì yùn-tsài-hsī-t'ǔng** delivery system for nuclear weapons

核优势 **hó-yū-shìh** nuclear superiority

hò (hè)

740 贺词 **hò-tz'ú** a congratulatory message, message of greeting

740A 荷枪实弹 **hò-ch'iāng-shíh-tàn** guns at the ready and fully loaded

荷载 **hò-tsài** to carry, to bear, loaded

in; cargo

荷 **hō**: *see also* **hò**

741 赫哲族 **hò-chè-tsú** the Ho-che people (a minority in Heilungkiang province: population 700 as of 1957)

赫尔辛基 **hò-ěrh-hsīn-chī** Helsinki

赫赫战果 **hò-hò-chàn-kuǒ** magnificent war gains, impressive war results

赫赫有名 **hò-hò-yǔ-míng** far-famed, illustrious

赫鲁晓夫 **hò-lǔ-hsiǎo-fū** Khrushchev

hóu (hóu)

742 喉舌 **hóu-shé** throat and tongue (a mouthpiece, a spokesman for someone else)

743 猴子也为王 **hóu-tzu yěh wéi-wáng** even a monkey can become king (the full text: "when there is no tiger in the mountain, even a monkey can be king")

hǒu (hǒu)

744 吼声 **hǒu-shēng** a roaring cry, howl, yell

hòu (hòu)

745 后者 **hòu-chě** the latter

后继 **hòu-chì** to succeed; subsequent, following, posterior; a successor

后继有人 **hòu-chì-yǔ-jén** there are successors

后进 **hòu-chìn** underdeveloped, newly developed, developing, backward [persons]

后期 **hòu-ch'ī** later period

后起新手 **hòu-ch'ǐ-hsīn-shǒu** recently emerging new hands

后勤 **hòu-ch'ín** rear-echelon services, logistical elements

后勤机关 **hòu-ch'ín chī-kuān** rear-area service organizations

后勤工作 **hòu-ch'ín kūng-tsò** rear-area service work

后勤部队 **hòu-ch'ín pù-tuì** rear-echelon units

后觉 **hòu-chüéh** [those who are] slower to apprehend [principles]

后发制人 **hòu-fā-chìh-jén** the tactic of winning by not taking the first move (letting the other side commit themselves first)

后方 **hòu-fāng** the rear area [military]

后方勤务 **hòu-fāng ch'ín-wù** rear-echelon services

后方军事机关 **hòu-fāng chün-shìh chī-kuān** rear-area military organizations

后悔莫及 **hòu-huǐ-mò-chí** remorse

cannot help, regrets [after the event] are too late

后续部队 **hòu-hsù-pù-tuì** the follow-up force, the succeeding waves [of an attack]

后遗症 **hòu-í-chèng** sequel to a disease, an aftereffect of disease

后果 **hòu-kuǒ** results, consequences

后备储量 **hòu-pèi-ch'ǔ-liàng** amount held as a reserve

后备军 **hòu-pèi-chün** reserve troops

后十条 **hòu-shíh-t'iáo** the Later Ten Points (the second major directive during the Socialist Education Movement, issued in September 1963)

后代 **hòu-tài** posterity, descendants, later generations

后盾 **hòu-tùn** a prop to lean back on (backing, support, a supporter)

后台 **hòu-t'ái** backstage (a backer—usually covert)

后台老板 **hòu-t'ái-lǎo-pǎn** a backstage boss (a strong supporter behind the scenes)

后退 **hòu-t'uì** to retreat, withdraw; a retreat

后院 **hòu-yuàn** rear garden, backyard (may be figurative)

746 厚茧 **hòu-chiěn** calluses (a symbol of physical work)

厚今薄古 **hòu-chīn-pó-kǔ** to emphasize the new and de-emphasize the old

厚古薄今 **hòu-kǔ-pó-chīn** to stress the old and slight the new (a criticized Confucian trait)

厚颜无耻 **hòu-yén wú-ch'ǐh** brazen-faced and shameless, cynical

747 候选人 **hòu-hsuǎn-jén** a candidate for election

候选资格 **hòu-hsuǎn-tzū-kó** qualifications for candidacy

候补委员 **hòu-pǔ wěi-yuán** alternate members of a committee

hū (hū)

748 呼风唤雨 **hū-fēng-huàn-yǔ** to summon the wind and the rain (the masses have great power to conquer nature)

呼号 **hū-háo** a call signal; to wail aloud

呼和浩特 **hū-hó-hào-t'è** Huhehot (a city of Inner Mongolia, formerly Kweisui)

呼声 **hū-shēng** the noise of shouting, a great popular demand, an outcry

呼应 **hū-yìng** to echo, respond as an echo, act in cooperation

呼吁 **hū-yù** to appeal, petition, plead

for, call upon

749 忽略 **hū-lüèh** to neglect, slight, ignore; an oversight

忽视 **hū-shìh** to disregard, neglect, treat with indifference, lose sight of, overlook

忽视成分 **hū-shìh ch'éng-fèn** to take no account of class origin; to neglect the proper proportions

忽左忽右 **hū-tsǒ-hū-yù** suddenly [turning] left [and] suddenly right (wavering, without any convictions)

hú (hú)

750 狐群狗党 **hú-ch'ún-kǒu-tǎng** a pack of foxes and gang of dogs (a set of rogues and scoundrels)

狐狸尾巴 **hú-li-wěi-pa** a fox's tail (something that cannot be hidden, a betraying mark)

751 胡志明 **hú chìh míng** Ho Chi Minh (North Vietnamese leader, 1890–1969)

胡琴 **hú-ch'in** the Chinese violin

胡吹一顿 **hú-ch'ūi-i-tùn** to brag wildly

胡风 **hú-fēng** Hu Feng (Communist writer, liquidated in 1955 because of his criticism of the government's literary policy)

胡风反革命集团 **hú-fēng fǎn-kó-mìng chí-t'uán** Hu Feng's counter-revolutionary clique

胡搞 **hú-kǎo** to act without proper plan, make a mess of things; imprudent

胡乱 **hú-luàn** carelessly, at random, recklessly; without giving proper thought

胡说 **hú-shuō** to talk nonsense; wild talk, lies

胡说八道 **hú-shuō-pā-tào** drivel, rubbish, to talk nonsense

胡思乱想 **hú-szū-luàn-hsiǎng** to think and wish foolishly (to let the mind wander, to entertain foolish ideas)

胡同 **hú-t'ùng** a lane or side street [usually in Peking or Tientsin]

胡作非为 **hú-tsò-fēi-wéi** to act foolishly and recklessly, make mischief

胡诌 **hú-tsōu** to fabricate [a story], to talk rubbish

752 糊住了眼 **hú-chù-le-yěn** to paste up the eyes (figurative)

糊里糊涂 **hú-li-hú-t'ú** muddle-headed, careless, stupid; in a mess

糊涂观点 **hú-t'ú-kuān-tiěn** muddled viewpoint

糊涂思想 **hú-t'ú-szū-hsiǎng** confused

thinking, confused ideas (ideas contrary to Party ideology)

hǔ (hǔ)

753 虎口拔牙 **hǔ-k'ǒu-pá-yá** to draw the tiger's teeth (a dangerous undertaking)

虎视眈眈 **hǔ-shìh-tān-tān** to glare like a tiger (avaricious, covetous, waiting for a chance to attack)

虎头蛇尾 **hǔ-t'óu-shé-wěi** tiger's head and snake's tail (to start with great energy but to peter out at the end)

754 唬人 **hǔ-jén** to scare someone [by a trick]

hù (hù)

755 互教互学 **hù-chiào hù-hsuéh** mutually teach and learn from one another

互助 **hù-chù** mutual aid, cooperation

互助储金会 **hù-chù ch'ǔ-chīn-huì** mutual-aid savings societies (at lane level during the 1960s)

互助组 **hù-chù-tsǔ** mutual aid group, mutual aid team

互换原则 **hù-huàn yuán-tsé** the principle of reciprocity

互惠条约 **hù-huì t'iáo-yuèh** a treaty of reciprocity, a treaty based on full reciprocity

互相支援 **hù-hsiāng-chīh-yuán** mutual support

互相唱和 **hù-hsiāng ch'àng-hò** to exchange poems, to sing a duet together (often has an unfavorable political connotation)

互相呼应 **hù-hsiāng hū-yìng** mutually responsive

互相衔接 **hù-hsiāng hsién-chiēn** mutually linked, reciprocally connected

互相学习取长补短 **hù-hsiāng hsuéh-hsí ch'ǔ-ch'áng pǔ-tuǎn** to learn from each other and use others' strong points to overcome one's deficiencies

互相依赖 **hù-hsiāng-ī-lài** interdependence

互相让步 **hù-hsiāng-jàng-pù** mutual accommodation, a give-and-take attitude

互相关心 **hù-hsiāng-kuān-hsīn** a mutual concern, to be mutually concerned

互相攻讦 **hù-hsiāng-kūng-chiéh** mutual recrimination

互相利用 **hù-hsiāng-lì-yùng** each making use of the other

互相谅解 **hù-hsiāng-liàng-chiěh** mutual tolerance and understanding

互相联系 **hù-hsiāng-lién-hsì** reciprocal

relations, interlocking, having mutual connections

互相配合 **hù-hsiāng-p'èi-hó** to co-ordinate with; in coordination

互相独立 **hù-hsiāng-tú-lì** mutual independence

互相通知 **hù-hsiāng-t'ūng-chīh** to keep each other informed

互相尊重主权和领土完整 **hù-hsiāng tsūn-chùng chǔ-ch'üán hó lǐng-t'ǔ-wán-chěng** mutual respect for each other's sovereignty and territorial integrity (one of the five principles for coexistence)

互相影响 **hù-hsiāng yǐng-hsiǎng** to affect each other, interaction

互信 **hù-hsìn** mutual trust

互让互助 **hù-jàng-hù-chù** mutual accommodation and mutual aid

互利 **hù-lì** mutual benefit, mutually profitable, mutually beneficial

互谅互让 **hù-liàng-hù-jàng** mutual understanding and accommodation

互帮互学 **hù-pāng-hù-hsuéh** to help each other and learn from each other

互不侵犯 **hù-pù-ch'īn-fàn** mutual nonaggression (one of the five principles for coexistence)

互不干涉内政 **hù-pù-kān-shè-nèi-chèng** noninterference in each other's internal affairs (one of the five principles for coexistence)

互不通气 **hù-pù-t'ūng-ch'ì** mutually without communication [of information]

互派大使 **hù-p'ài tà-shǐh** exchange of ambassadors

互通情报 **hù-t'ūng ch'íng-pào** to exchange intelligence information (now often extended to exchange of scientific or technical information)

互通有无 **hù-t'ūng-yǔ-wú** to exchange what one has for what one lacks (each making up what the other lacks)

互为因果 **hù-wéi-yīn-kuǒ** reciprocal causation

756 户籍 **hù-chí** household records, list of inhabitants

户籍警 **hù-chí-chǐng** a census police-man, a neighborhood policeman

户籍科 **hù-chí-k'ō** household registration section [in each **p'ài-ch'ū-sǒ**—branch police station]

户口 **hù-k'ǒu** family, household, domicile, population

户口保证书 **hù-k'ǒu pǎo-chèng-shū** household guarantee certificates (issued c. 1965, in Shanghai, to persons whom the government

wished to send to the countryside promising restitution of their legal urban-residence status)

户口本 **hù-k'ǒu-pěn** household registers (the basis for the issuance of ration tickets)

户口簿 **hù-k'ǒu-pù** household book (recording all family members, with which rations or food tickets are obtained)

757 沪 **hù** Shanghai

沪剧 **hù-chù** the native Shanghai style of opera

沪杭铁路 **hù-háng t'iěh-lù** the Shanghai-Hangchow railway

沪宁铁路 **hù-níng t'iěh-lù** the Shanghai-Nanking railway

758 护岸 **hù-àn** to protect a shore; an embankment, shore erosion control

护照 **hù-chào** a passport

护符 **hù-fú** a charm for protection against demons (a protector)

护理 **hù-lǐ** nursing; to give medical care, to nurse, treat, take care of

护理员 **hù-lǐ-yúan** a nurses' aide, a practical nurse

护林 **hù-lín** forest protection

护身法宝 **hù-shēn-fǎ-pǎo** a protective talisman (figurative)

护士 **hù-shìh** a nurse

护送 **hù-sùng** to escort, convoy, send under protection

护堤工程 **hù-tī-kūng-ch'éng** dike works, levee system, dike project

护渔护航 **hù-yú hù-háng** to protect fisheries and navigation

759 怙恶不悛 **hù-ò-pù-ch'üān** to persist in evil and not repent (incorrigible)

huā (huā)

760 花招 **huā-chāo** showy and deceptive movements [in stage fighting], deception, sleight of hand

花架子 **huā-chià-tzu** a flower stand (a metaphor for formalism)

花费 **huā-fèi** to spend, dissipate, waste, squander; expenditure, expense

花岗岩脑袋 **huā-kāng-yén nǎo-tai** a head of granite (ultra-stubborn, diehard)

花天酒地 **huā-t'iēn-chǐu-tì** flower heaven and wine earth (to abandon oneself to a gay life, debauchery, wine and women)

花样繁多 **huā-yàng-fán-tō** multifarious, in many forms or styles

花言巧语 **huā-yén-ch'iǎo-yǔ** flowery words and cunning phrases (honeyed words, sweet talk to deceive)

761 哗哗啦啦 **huā-huā-lā-lā** the sound of flowing water (a mild hubbub)

哗 **huā**: *see also* **huà**

huá (huá)

762 华侨 **huá-ch'iáo** a Chinese residing abroad, overseas Chinese

华侨汇款 **huá-ch'iáo-huì-k'uǎn** remittances [into China] by overseas Chinese

华侨新村 **huá-ch'iáo hsīn-ts'ūn** an overseas Chinese new village (built by allowing real estate purchases and special rent contracts for recipients of large foreign remittances, and for returned overseas Chinese)

华侨购买证 **huá-ch'iáo kòu-mǎi-chèng** overseas Chinese purchase cards (ration tickets obtained by people classed as overseas Chinese in exchange for remittances they receive from abroad)

华侨联合会 **huá-ch'iáo lién-hó-huì** Federation of Overseas Chinese (a non-government group, led by the Overseas Chinese Affairs Division and the Party United Front Work Department)

华侨农场 **huá-ch'iáo núng-ch'ǎng** a farm operated by overseas Chinese (many of these in south China were set up to provide for returnees from Indonesia)

华侨事务委员会 **huá-ch'iáo-shìh-wù wěi-yuán-huì** Commission of Overseas Chinese Affairs [of the State Council]

华而不实 **huá-érh-pù-shíh** flowery but bears no fruit (mere show with no substance)

华尔街 **huá-ěrh-chiēh** Wall Street [New York]

华南抗日纵队 **huá-nán k'àng-jìh tsùng-tuì** South China Anti-Japanese Column (Communist force in Kwangtung during the Resistance War, also known as the East River Column)

华沙 **huá-shā** Warsaw

华沙条约组织 **huá-shā-t'iáo-yuēh tsǔ-chīh** Warsaw Pact Organization

华盛顿 **huá-shèng-tùn** Washington [D.C.]

华灯齐放 **huá-tēng-ch'í-fàng** colorful lights all alit (at a gala occasion)

763 哗众取宠 **huá-chùng-ch'ǔ-ch'ǔng** to seek popularity by wild statements (to engage in demagoguery)

哗然 **huá-ján** uproarious, boisterous, clamorous, tumultuous

哗 **huá**: *see also* **huā**

764 滑稽 **huá-chì** humorous, facetious, farcical, comical

滑稽傀儡剧 **huá-chī k'uéi-lěi-chù** puppet farce

滑雪 **huá-hsuéh** to ski

滑到邪路上去 **huá-tào hsiéh-lù shang-ch'u** to go astray, to slide into the wrong road, (to take the capitalist road)

huà (huà)

765 化整为零 **huà-chěng-wéi-líng** to transform unity into fragmentation, to break the whole into parts

化装 **huà-chuāng** to dress in disguise; masked

化除 **huà-ch'ú** to abolish, remove, dissolve, dispel

化肥 **huà-féi** chemical fertilizer

化害为利 **huà-hài-wéi-lì** to change a harm into an advantage

化合 **huà-hó** to combine into a compound [chemical]; chemical combination

化学 **huà-hsuéh** chemical; chemistry

化学肥料 **huà-hsuéh féi-liào** chemical fertilizers

化学纤维 **huà-hsuéh hsiēn-wéi** chemical fiber, synthetic fiber

化学工业部 **huà-hsuéh kūng-yèh-pù** Ministry of Chemical Industry [of the State Council (merged into the Ministry of Fuel and Chemical Industry after 1969)

化学武器 **huà-hsuéh wǔ-ch'ì** chemical warfare weapons

化工 **huà-kūng** chemical industry, chemical engineering

化工系统 **huà-kūng-hsì-t'ǔng** the chemical industry system

化公为私 **huà-kūng-wéi-szū** to change public into private

化零为整 **huà-líng-wéi-chěng** to gather parts into a whole

化悲痛为力量 **huà pēi-t'ùng wéi lì-liang** to transform grief into strength

化身 **huà-shēn** a personification, an incarnation

化生放战争 **huà-shēng-fàng chàn-chēng** chemical, biological, and radiological warfare

化大为小 **huà-tà-wéi-hsiǎo** to turn large [issues] into small ones

化为乌有 **huà-wéi-wū-yǔ** to be reduced to nothingness (to reduce to naught, vanish, disappear)

766 划成分 **huà-ch'éng-fèn** to determine

[class] status

划清界线 **huà-ch'īng chièh-hsièn** to draw a clear line of demarcation

划区医疗服务制 **huà-ch'ǚ ī-liǎo fú-wù-chìh** district clinic service system

划分阶级成分 **huà-fēn chiēh-chí-ch'èng-fèn** to determine class status

划一 **huà-ī** to make uniform, standardize, unify

划时代 **huà-shíh-tài** epoch-making, epochal

划策 **huà-ts'è** to give advice

767　画虎画皮难画骨 **huà-hǔ huà-p'í nán huà-kǔ** you may sketch a tiger's skin but not its bones (you can know a man's exterior but not his heart)

画龙点睛 **huà-lúng-tiěn-chīng** to add eyeballs to the painting of a dragon (the finishing stroke; the key phrase that gives forceful meaning to a speech or essay)

画饼充饥 **huà-pǐng-ch'ūng-chī** drawing a cake to satisfy hunger (using imagination to comfort oneself; a vain hope)

画皮 **huà-p'í** painted skin (a counter-revolutionary masquerading as one of the people)

画蛇添足 **huà-shé-t'iēn-tsú** to paint a snake and add feet (to add superfluous and inappropriate detail)

768　话剧 **huà-chù** modern prose drama

话柄 **huà-pǐng** a target of ridicule, material for gossip or scandalous talk

话不投机 **huà-pù-t'óu-chī** remarks that are unappealing to the other side, a disagreeable conversation

huái (huái)

769　怀着鬼胎 **huái-che-kuěi-t'āi** to bear the embryo of a demon (to scheme evil)

怀恨在心 **huái-hèn-tsài-hsīn** to harbor resentment, rankle

怀疑 **huái-í** to doubt, suspect, question

怀念 **huái-nièn** to cherish the memory, remember always; nostalgia

怀抱 **huái-pào** to hug, embrace; one's bosom; one's ambition

怀孕 **huái-yùn** to conceive, become pregnant; pregnancy

770　淮海战役 **huái-hǎi-chàn-ì** the Huaihai campaign (November 1948–January 1949)

huài (huài)

771　坏家伙 **huài-chiā-huo** a bad guy, rascal

坏分子 **huài-fèn-tzǔ** a bad element, undesirable person, riffraff (one of the **wǔ-lèi fèn-tzǔ**)

坏心眼 **huài-hsīn-yěn** bad intention, malicious intention

坏人坏事 **huài-jén huài-shìh** bad men and bad deeds

坏事变成好事 **huài-shìh pièn-ch'éng hǎo-shìh** bad things [can be] changed to good things

坏蛋 **huài-tàn** a bad egg (a villain, scoundrel, crook)

坏東西 **huài-tūng-hsi** a bad thing (a bad fellow)

huān (huān)

772　欢聚一堂 **huān-chù-ī-t'áng** well met, a happy gathering

欢呼 **huān-hū** to cheer, shout for joy, hail; ovation

欢欣鼓舞 **huān-hsīn-kǔ-wǔ** glad and dancing for joy (jubilant, elated)

欢乐 **huān-lè** happy, delighted, joy, good cheer

欢声雷动 **huān-shēng-léi-tùng** joyous shouts like thunder, thunderous applause

欢送 **huān-sùng** to give a farewell party, see off, wish bon voyage

欢天喜地 **huān-t'iēn-hsǐ-tì** rejoicing [in] heaven [and] happiness [on] earth (extremely happy)

欢迎 **huān-yíng** to welcome, greet

huán (huán)

773　还清 **huán-ch'īng** to repay in full, to pay off

还乡 **huán-hsiāng** to return to one's native place

还乡团 **huán-hsiāng-t'uán** home returning bands (armed groups sponsored by landlords during the Civil War period)

还本 **huán-pěn** repayment of principal

还原 **huán-yuán** to be restored to the original condition; chemical reduction

774　环节 **huán-chiéh** a link, segment

环境 **huán-chìng** environment, surroundings, material background

环境污染 **huán-chìng-wū-jǎn** environmental pollution

环子 **huán-tzu** a ring, ringlet, hoop

775　寰球 **huán-ch'iú** the world, globe

huǎn (huǎn)

776　缓急轻重 **huǎn-chí-ch'īng-chùng** slow, fast, heavy, or light (degree of

122

priority and importance)

缓期执行 **huǎn-ch'ī chíh-hsíng** to postpone a sentence, suspend execution, reprieve

缓冲国 **huǎn-ch'ūng-kuó** a buffer state

缓冲地带 **huǎn-ch'ūng-tì-tài** a buffer zone

缓和 **huǎn-hó** to appease, pacify, alleviate, allay, moderate; relaxation, easing of tensions, détente

缓和舆论 **huǎn-hó yǔ-lùn** to mollify public opinion

缓刑 **huǎn-hsíng** to suspend a sentence, to reprieve; suspension of punishment, probation

缓慢 **huǎn-màn** sluggish, slow-moving

缓兵之计 **huǎn-pīng-chīh-chì** delaying tactics, measures to stave off an attack

huàn (huàn)

777 幻想 **huàn-hsiǎng** illusion, fantasy, imagination; to imagine, daydream

778 涣散 **huàn-sàn** disorganization, disunity, disruption, dispersal

779 换成 **huàn-ch'éng** to alter, change, transform, turn into

换货 **huàn-huò** to exchange goods, barter

换工 **huàn-kūng** mutual exchange of labor, labor exchange

换汤不换药 **huàn-t'āng pù huàn-yào** to change the water [in which the herbs are brewed] without changing the medicine (to change the form without changing the substance)

换文 **huàn-wén** to exchange [diplomatic] notes

780 唤起注意 **huàn-ch'ǐ-chù-ì** to draw attention to

唤起民众 **huàn-ch'ǐ-mín-chùng** to arouse the masses

唤醒 **huàn-hsǐng** to awake, arouse, excite

781 焕发 **huàn-fā** shining, radiant

焕然一新 **huàn-ján-ī-hsīn** done over like new (to take on an entirely new aspect; completely renovated)

782 患难 **huàn-nán** predicament, troubles, tribulation

患难之交 **huàn-nàn-chīh-chiāo** a friendship cemented in adversity

患难与共 **huàn-nàn-yǔ-kùng** to meet tribulations together

患得患失 **huàn-té-huàn-shīh** to be worried about gaining and worried about losing (to worry about personal gains and losses; a small-minded man)

783 豢养 **huàn-yǎng** to feed or raise [animals]

huāng (huāng)

784 荒废 **huāng-fèi** neglected [studies], deserted and abandoned [gardens or fields]

荒谬 **huāng-miù** absurd, preposterous

荒谬绝伦 **huāng-miù-chuéh-lún** absolutely preposterous, completely absurd

荒年 **huāng-nién** year of a bad harvest, famine year

荒山僻野 **huāng-shān-p'ì-yěh** barren mountains and remote wilderness (desolate areas)

荒山秃岭 **huāng-shān-t'ū-lǐng** desolate mountains and barren ranges

荒诞不经 **huāng-tàn-pù-chīng** absurd, unbelievable, fantastic

荒地 **huāng-tì** uncultivated land, wasteland, wilderness

荒滩 **huāng-t'ān** uncultivated areas [along river banks or the seacoast]

荒唐 **huāng-t'ang** grossly exaggerated, absurd, wild; licentious, on a spree

荒芜 **huāng-wú** deserted and overgrown with weeds

荒淫 **huāng-yín** dissolute, dissipated, profligate, licentious

785 慌张 **huāng-chāng** desperate, frantic, helter-skelter

慌里慌张 **huāng-li-huāng-chāng** nervous and excited, to lose one's self-possession, panic-stricken

慌乱 **huāng-luàn** nervous and confused, in turmoil, hurried

huáng (huáng)

786 黄金时代 **huáng-chīn-shíh-tài** a golden age

黄忠 **huáng-chūng** the name of an old warrior in the Three Kingdoms period (a hard-working old man—an example extolled during the Great Leap)

黄泛区 **huáng-fàn-ch'ū** flood zone of the Yellow River

黄梁一梦 **huáng-liáng-ī-mèng** an evanescent dream, a vanished dream, disillusionment

黄连苦 **huáng-lién-k'ǔ** as bitter as *Coptis japonica* (very bitter—usually a reference to the bitterness experienced in the old society)

黄牛 **huáng-niú** an ox; a scalper (a person who buys in quantity while supply lasts and sells at a high price

later)

黄埔系 **huáng-p'ǔ-hsì** the Whampoa Clique [in the KMT army]

黄色歌曲 **huáng-sè kō-ch'ǔ** yellow songs (decadent music, bourgeois songs)

黄色工会 **huáng-sè kūng-huì** yellow labor unions (KMT-sponsored unions before Liberation)

黄色报刊 **huáng-sè pào-k'ān** the yellow press

黄豆 **huáng-tòu** the soya bean

787 惶惶然 **huáng-huáng-ján** agitatedly, panicky

惶惶不可终日 **huáng-huáng pù-k'ǒ-chūng-jih** so agitated that one cannot last out the day (fearful that each day is the last, hopelessly disturbed)

惶惶无主 **huáng-huáng-wú-chǔ** panicky and indecisive

惶恐不安 **huáng-k'ǔng-pù-ān** confused and uneasy, in fear and trepidation

788 蝗虫 **huáng-ch'úng** the locust, grasshopper

huǎng (huǎng)

789 谎话 **huǎng-huà** a lie, falsehood

谎言 **huǎng-yén** a lie, fabrication, untruth

790 幌子 **huǎng-tzu** a shop sign (pretext, guise, cover, smoke screen)

huī (huī)

791 灰心 **huī-hsīn** to feel discouraged, be disappointed, lose interest

灰溜溜 **huī-liū-liū** discouraged, very gloomy

灰色人生观 **huī-sè jén-shēng-kuān** a gray outlook on life, a pessimistic attitude toward life

792 恢复 **huī-fù** to recover, restore

恢复旧观 **huī-fù chiù-kuān** to restore the old appearance

恢复名誉 **huī-fù-míng-yù** to recover one's reputation, be rehabilitated

793 挥霍 **huī-huò** to squander money, spend lavishly

挥舞 **huī-wǔ** to brandish, wave

挥舞指挥棒 **huī-wǔ chǐh-huī-pàng** to wave a conductor's baton

794 辉煌成绩 **huī-huáng-ch'éng-chī** glorious achievements

795 徽章 **huī-chāng** a badge, insignia, emblem, medal

huí (huí)

796 回击 **huí-chī** to counterattack, rebuff,

repel, chase out

回潮 **huí-ch'áo** the returning tide

回合 **huí-hó** a round [in a bout or contest]

回乡 **huí-hsiāng** return to one's native village (a campaign in the early 1960s to relieve unemployment in the cities: distinct from **hsià-fàng**)

回乡知识青年 **huí-hsiāng chīh-shíh-ch'īng-nién** young educated people returning to the villages

回旋加速器 **huí-hsuán chiā-sù-ch'ì** cyclotron

回旋余地 **huí-hsuán yǔ-tì** room for maneuvering

回忆 **huí-ì** to recollect, recall, think back

回忆录 **huí-ì-lù** memoirs, reminiscences

回忆对比 **huí-ì-tuì-pǐ** recall past [suffering] to contrast with [present happiness]

回顾过去 **huí-kù-kuò-ch'ù** to look back on the past

回扣 **huí-k'òu** a discount, an agent's commission (now often carries the connotation of a kickback)

回民 **huí-mín** the Moslem people

回避 **huí-pì** to avoid confrontation, make way for, shun, draw back from

回升 **huí-shēng** to rise again, recover

回生现象 **huí-shēng-hsièn-hsiàng** the condition of returning to rawness (such as graduates of literacy classes failing to follow up and hence backsliding to their original illiterate state)

回声 **huí-shēng** an echo, response

回收 **huí-shōu** to recover [industrial waste]

回收废铁 **huí-shōu fèi-t'iěh** to retrieve scrap iron

回收率 **huí-shōu-lù** rate of retrieval

回头路 **huí-t'óu-lù** to come back on the old road

回头是岸 **huí-t'óu-shìh-àn** turn the head and there lies the shore (only when one has the determination to repent is there hope)

回族 **huí-tsú** the Hui people (a Moslem minority in the Ningsia Hui Autonomous Region, Kansu, Chinghai, and other provinces in North China; population 3,934,000 as of 1957)

huǐ (huǐ)

797 悔之无及 **huǐ-chīh-wú-chí** too late for regrets, regrets cannot help [the situation]

悔恨 **huǐ-hèn** repent and regret, regret

deeply, be penitent

悔改 **huǐ-kǎi** to repent and reform

悔过书 **huǐ-kuò-shū** a written critique of one's errors, self-criticism

悔过自新 **huǐ-kuò-tzù-hsïn** to repent and make a new start

798 毁灭 **huǐ-mièh** to destroy, wipe out, annihilate, ruin, lay waste, crush

毁谤 **huǐ-pàng** to slander, libel, defame

毁约 **huǐ-yuēh** [unilaterally] to break a contract, scrap a treaty, cancel an agreement

huì (huì)

799 汇集 **huì-chí** to gather together, to compile; convergent

汇价 **huì-chià** exchange rate

汇合 **huì-hó** to converge, flow together, meet, assemble; confluence, meeting, coincidence, assembly

汇款 **huì-k'uǎn** to remit money, transfer funds

汇报 **huì-pào** report back, feedback [generally the reporting of lower-level reaction to higher-level directives or actions]

汇报思想 **huì-pào szū-hsiǎng** to report one's own thinking [to one's unit or the Party]

汇报提纲 **huì-pào t'í-kāng** an outline of a report

汇报材料 **huì-pào ts'ái-liào** materials [data] for a report

汇编 **huì-piēn** a collection [of essays, materials, etc.]

汇兑 **huì-tuì** remittance of funds, currency exchange

800 会战 **huì-chàn** a battle (now often figurative, as a drive to complete a major project)

会诊 **huì-chěn** to consult [medical], group consultation and diagnosis [of any problem]

会见 **huì-chièn** to meet, to see a visitor, a meeting [of host and guest]

会聚 **huì-chù** to assemble, gather together

会议 **huì-ì** a conference, meeting, session

会议汇报制度 **huì-ì huì-pào chìh-tù** system of reporting the minutes of meetings (one of the earliest controls required of organizations in which the Party had no members)

会意文字 **huì-ì-wén-tzù** an ideographic written language

会理家 **huì-lǐ-chiā** good at home management (having a sense of responsibility for planning and managing the affairs of one's unit)

会门 **huì-mén** a secret religious sect, secret society

会盘算 **huì-p'án-suàn** good at the management of one's funds (frugal and economical)

会师 **huì-shïh** a meeting of military forces of the same side (now figurative, as a joining of task forces)

会道门 **huì-tào-mén** secret societies with religious character

会谈 **huì-t'án** talks, negotiations

会 **huì**: see also **k'uài**

801 讳疾忌医 **huì-chí-chì-ī** to conceal illness and fear treatment (to cover up one's mistakes and fear criticism)

讳言 **huì-yén** to avoid mentioning, to cover up

802 诲人不倦 **huì-jén-pù-chüàn** never tired of teaching others, an indefatigable teacher

诲淫诲盗 **huì-yín-huì-tào** to teach adultery and burglary (to debauch, to incite lewdness and violence)

803 绘声绘色 **hui-shēng-huì-sè** to paint sound and colors (to describe vividly)

804 贿赂 **huì-lù** to bribe; bribery

805 彗星 **huì-hsïng** a comet

806 晦涩 **hui-sè** unclear in meaning [of literary style], obscure

807 惠灵顿 **huì-líng-tùn** Wellington [New Zealand]

hūn (hūn)

808 昏昏沉沉 **hūn-hūn ch'én-ch'én** semiconscious, confused, dizzy, muddled

昏天黑地 **hūn-t'iēn-hēi-tì** heaven is obscured [and the] earth dark (in total darkness)

809 婚丧嫁娶 **hūn-sāng-chià-ch'ǚ** marriages and funerals (the major family affairs that impoverished families in the old society and on which heavy spending is now discouraged)

婚事新办 **hūn-shìh hsïn-pàn** a marriage in the new way (without the wasteful expenditures and social customs of the past)

婚姻法 **hūn-yïn-fǎ** the Marriage Law

婚姻自主 **hūn-yïn-tzù-chǔ** marriage determined and controlled by the principals themselves

hún (hún)

810 浑浑噩噩 **hún-hún-ò-ò** (1) simple and honest; (2) ignorant, muddle-headed

浑然一体 **hún-ján-ï-t'ǐ** an integral part,

inseparable, completely one

浑身发抖 **hún-shēn-fā-tǒu** to tremble with fear, shiver from head to foot

浑身是胆 **hún-shēn-shìh-tǎn** fearless, very daring

浑天仪 **hún-t'iēn-í** armillary sphere, celestial globe

811 魂飞魄散 **hún-fēi-p'ò-sàn** the soul flies and the spirit scatters (panic stricken, frightened out of one's senses)

hùn (hùn)

812 混战不已 **hùn-chàn-pù-ǐ** endless confused warfare [by many parties]

混进 **hùn-chìn** to sneak into

混合 **hùn-hó** to mix together, mingle, blend, compound

混合面 **hùn-hó-mièn** mixed flour (wheat flour heavily adulterated with coarse and cheap material; now a remembrance of the Japanese occupation)

混淆阶级阵线 **hùn-hsiáo chiēh-chí-chèn-hsièn** to obscure the class battle lines

混淆黑白 **hùn-hsiáo hēi-pái** to confuse black and white (to confuse right and wrong)

混淆是非 **hùn-hsiáo-shìh-fēi** to confuse right and wrong

混淆视听 **hùn-hsiáo-shìh-t'īng** to confuse the vision and the hearing [of the public] (to mislead)

混淆敌我 **hùn-hsiáo-tí-wǒ** to confuse friend with foe

混日子 **hùn-jìh-tzu** muddle through the days (to hold a job without real work)

混革命 **hùn-kó-mìng** to join the revolution without actually participating

混乱 **hùn-luàn** confusion, disorder, chaos

混凝土 **hùn-níng-t'ǔ** concrete, cement

混水摸鱼 **hùn-shuǐ-mō-yú** to feel for fish in murky water (to seek one's own advantage in another's trouble)

混沌 **hùn-tùn** nebulous; confused, undeveloped; ignorant and dumb

混同 **hùn-t'úng** to merge, combine, mix with

混杂 **hùn-tsá** mixed, of mixed quality or materials, of different kinds, motley; disorderly, chaotic, confused

混为一谈 **hùn-wéi-ī-t'án** to speak of different things as if they were one (to confuse the issue)

hūng (hōng)

813 轰轰烈烈 **hūng-hūng-lièh-lièh** roaringly

and blazingly (with vigor and vitality, dynamic, resoundingly)

轰赶队 **hūng-kǎn-tuì** scattering and chasing unit (from the sparrow elimination campaign)

轰动 **hūng-tùng** to arouse attention, excite, incite

814 哄传 **hūng-ch'uán** widespread word-of-mouth circulation of news

哄然大笑 **hūng-ján-tà-hsiào** a volley of laughter

哄堂大笑 **hūng-t'áng-tà-hsiào** roars of laughter fill the hall, the audience roared with laughter

哄 **hūng**: see also **hǔng**

815 烘云托月 **hūng-yún-t'ō-yuèh** to darken the clouds to bring out the moon (to make something more noticeable by contrast)

húng (hóng)

816 红专 **húng-chuān** red and expert (actively socialist and professionally qualified)

红专学校 **húng-chuān-hsuéh-hsiào** red and expert school (a half-work half-study school combining study and physical labor)

红专大学 **húng-chuān-tà-hsuéh** red and expert universities (half-work half-study universities set up during the Great Leap period)

红旗 **húng-ch'í** (1) a red flag (symbol of communism, China, victory, etc.); (2) *Red Flag* (the official theoretical journal of the Central Committee, Peking, usually semi-monthly, 1958—)

红旗招展 **húng-ch'í-chāo-chǎn** the red flag waves

红旗渠 **húng-ch'í-ch'ǘ** the Red Flag Canal (in Linhsien, Honan)

红旗下长大 **húng-ch'í-hsià chǎng-tà** to have grown up under the Red Flag (the post-1949 generation)

红旗手 **húng-ch'í-shǒu** bearer of the red flag (a model worker)

红旗单位 **húng-ch'í-tān-wèi** a red-flag unit (a commune or factory team that has excelled in output)

红旗田 **húng-ch'í-t'ién** a red-flag field (a high-yield field)

红枪会 **húng-ch'iāng-huì** the Red Spear Society (a North China rural secret society, dissolved after 1949)

红军 **húng-chūn** the Red Army

红军时期 **húng-chūn-shíh-ch'í** the Red Army period (pre-1937)

红军第一方面军 **húng-chūn tì-ī fāng-**

mièn-chǔn the First Front Army of the Red Army (the force led by Chu Teh and Mao Tse-tung in Kiangsi and on the Long March)

红花 húng-huā a red flower (a symbol of honor)

红小兵 húng-hsiǎo-pīng Red Little Soldiers (an organization for elementary school pupils which replaced the Young Pioneers after the Cultural Revolution)

红小兵宣传队 húng-hsiǎo-pīng hsuān-ch'uán-tuì little red soldier [Mao Tse-tung Thought] propaganda team

红线 húng-hsièn the red line (the current policies of the Party leadership)

红心 húng-hsīn a red heart (one who adheres faithfully to the Thought of Mao Tse-tung)

红星报 húng-hsīng-pào *Red Star* (a newspaper of the General Political Department of the Chinese Workers' and Peasants' Red Army, 1933–34)

红钢城 húng-kāng-ch'éng red steel city (such as the large community built for workers surrounding the steel works at Wuhan)

红根红苗 húng-kēn-húng-miáo red roots [and] red sprouts (of good class background and training)

红管家 húng-kuǎn-chiā a red housekeeper (a good and politically activated leader in group activities)

红利 húng-lì a dividend, bonus

红领巾 húng-lǐng-chīn (1) a red scarf (insignia of the Young Pioneers); (2) *Red Scarf* (periodical of the Young Pioneers)

红领巾铁路问讯台 húng-lǐng-chīn t'iěh-lù wèn-hsùn-t'ái Red Scarf railway enquiry desks (an assistance to travelers undertaken by the Young Pioneers)

红楼梦研究 húng-lóu-mèng yén-chiū *Studies in the Dream of the Red Chamber* (a critique by Yu Ping-po of the famous novel, attacked in 1954 as reactionary and used for an attack on the influence of Hu Shih)

红榜 húng-pǎng roll of honor

红宝书 húng-pǎo-shū the red precious book (*Quotations from Chairman Mao*)

红色 húng-sè red (the color symbolic of communism, the Party, China, and political virtue)

红色政权 húng-sè-chèng-ch'üán a red regime, socialist government

红色江山 húng-sè-chiāng-shān the red rivers and mountains (the land of China)

红色接班人 húng-sè chiēh-pān-jén red successors (the younger generation who will take over the Party and the government from the aging leaders)

红色专家 húng-sè chuān-chiā a red expert (a person technically competent and politically reliable)

红色中华 húng-sè chūng-huá *Red China* (organ of the Chinese Soviet Republic, 1931–1934)

红色种子 húng-sè chǔng-tzu red seeds (the term may have two meanings: (1) core elements in the society—especially among the youth—on whom the future will depend; (2) experienced workers and peasants who have the responsibility of training and indoctrinating the youth)

红色区域 húng-sè ch'ǖ-yǜ red areas (usually refers to territory controlled by the Communists before 1937)

红色好管家 húng-sè hǎo-kuǎn-chiā a red good housekeeper (who manages the affairs of a unit with proper responsibility for the public and Party good)

红色根据地 húng-sè kēn-chǜ-tì Red base areas (pre-1937)

红色革命熔炉 húng-sè kó-mìng júng-lú a red revolutionary crucible (which tempers and purifies those who pass through it)

红色娘子军 húng-sè niáng-tzu-chǖn "Red Detachment of Women" (a ballet dance-drama, one of the **yàng-pǎn hsì**)

红色保险箱 húng-sè pǎo-hsiěn-hsiāng a red safe (the mistaken idea that joining the Party relieves one of risk or responsibility)

红哨兵 húng-shào-pīng red sentinels, red patrols (political workers recruited from the masses in some factories and schools)

红十字会 húng-shíh-tzù-huì the Red Cross Society

红十字国际委员会 hùng-shíh-tzù kuó-chì wěi-yuán-huì International Committee of the Red Cross

红书 húng-shū a red book (a book approved by and conforming to the policies of the Party leadership)

红代会 húng-tài-huì a Red Guard representative assembly

红灯 húng-tēng a red lantern (an infallible guide, i.e., Mao's works)

红灯记 húng-tēng-chì "The Red

Lantern" (one of the **yàng-pǎn hsì**)

红太阳 **húng-t'ài-yang** the red sun (a metaphor referring to Mao Tse-tung)

红透专深 **húng-t'òu-chuān-shēn** thoroughly red and highly qualified

红彤彤 **húng-t'úng-t'úng** quintessentially red (completely loyal)

红卫报 **húng-wèi-pào** *The Red Guard* (a Canton newspaper, formerly the **Yáng-ch'éng wǎn pào**)

红卫兵 **húng-wèi-pīng** the Red Guards (organizations of militant youths formed in 1966 at the start of the Cultural Revolution)

红卫兵理发站 **húng-wèi-pīng lǐ-fà-chàn** Red Guard haircut stations (a service without cost during late 1966)

红五类 **húng-wǔ-lèi** the five red categories (children of workers, peasants, cadres, armymen, and revolutionary martyrs)

红与专 **húng-yǔ-chuān** red and expert (actively socialist and professionally qualified)

817 宏大 **húng-tà** great, vast, grand

宏图 **húng-t'ú** a vast plan, a determination on great things

818 洪泛区 **húng-fàn-ch'ū** flood-stricken area

洪峰 **húng-fēng** flood crest, flood peak

洪流 **húng-liú** the flood tide (figurative)

洪炉 **húng-lú** a large furnace, smelting oven (figurative)

洪水季节 **húng-shuǐ chì-chiéh** the high-water season

洪水猛兽 **húng-shuǐ měng-shòu** a great flood and fierce animals (a great disaster; the incalculable harm of heretical doctrines)

洪都拉斯 **húng-tū-lā-szū** Honduras

819 虹吸管 **húng-hsī-kuǎn** a siphon

820 鸿沟 **húng-kōu** a gap, gulf, chasm; a demarcation line

hǔng (hǒng)

821 哄骗 **hǔng-p'ièn** to defraud, cheat, swindle, hoax, inveigle

哄 **hǔng:** *see also* **hūng**

huō (huō)

822 豁出去 **huō-ch'ū-ch'ù** to risk, put everything at stake

豁 **huō:** *see also* **huò**

huó (huó)

823 和稀泥 **huó-hsī-ní** mixing thin mud (to

avoid a clear-cut stand)

和 **huó:** *see also* **hó**

824 活教材 **huó-chiào-ts'ái** live teaching material (non-book teaching materials)

活捉 **huó-chō** to capture alive, take prisoner

活期存款 **huó-ch'ī-ts'ún-k'uǎn** a current deposit, freely withdrawable deposit

活情况 **huó-ch'íng-kuàng** changing aspects (as opposed to inflexible or static)

活剧 **huó-chù** a drama in real life

活而不乱管而不死 **huó-érh-pù-luàn kuǎn-érh-pù-szǔ** initiative without disorder [and] control without stultification (the tasks of proper leadership)

活象 **huó-hsiàng** remarkably resembling, looking alike, a living image of

活学活用 **huó-hsuéh-huó-yùng** to study and apply [Mao's Thought] in a living [creative] way

活力 **huó-lì** vitality, vigor, dynamic energy

活龙活现 **huó-lúng-huó-hsièn** a live dragon appears (very vivid)

活埋 **huó-mái** to bury alive

活命哲学 **huó-mìng-ché-hsuéh** the philosophy of survival (putting survival above all else)

活靶子 **huó-pǎ-tzu** (1) a moving target [military]; (2) a living target [for criticism and reform: as contrasted, for instance, with a dead target such as Confucius]

活报剧 **huó-pào-chù** a living newspaper (news events acted out in theatrical skit form)

活标本 **huó-piāo-pěn** a live specimen

活生生 **huó-shēng-shēng** lively, vital, dynamic

活水 **huó-shuǐ** flowing water, fresh current

活思想 **huó-szū-hsiǎng** living thought (the changing and comprehensive mental processes of a person or a group: the ability to understand and tap these is an important requirement of leadership)

活动范围 **huó-tùng fàn-wéi** range of activities

活动余地 **huó-tùng yú-tì** leeway, room to maneuver

活材料 **huó-ts'ái-liào** living material [for study]

活样板 **huó-yàng-pǎn** live models (persons from the masses, or actual

128

life, who are expected to guide and instruct actors in **yàng-pǎn hsì**)

活页　**huó-yèh** loose-leaf [books]

活愚公　**huó yú-kūng** a living Yü-kung (a model of faith and perseverance)

活跃　**huó-yuèh** very lively, active

huǒ (huǒ)

825 火箭　**huǒ-chièn** a rocket

火箭发射台　**huǒ-chièn fā-shè-t'ái** rocket launching pad, rocket firing ramp

火箭核武器部队　**huǒ-chièn hó-wǔ-ch'ì pù-tuì** nuclear missile forces

火箭砲　**huǒ-chièn-p'ào** rocket launcher, rocket gun, bazooka

火箭筒　**huǒ-chièn-t'ǔng** rocket launcher, bazooka

火中取栗　**huǒ-chūng-ch'ǔ-lì** to pull chestnuts out of the fire (to be used by someone without gaining anything oneself)

火种　**huǒ-chǔng** fire seeds, embers kept for starting a new fire (the smoldering embers of revolution which can rekindle anew)

火车头　**huǒ-ch'ē-t'óu** a locomotive (sometimes a metaphor for the Thought of Mao Tse-tung)

火气　**huǒ-ch'ì** fiery-tempered, emotional; anger, chagrin

火炬　**huǒ-chù** a torch

火花　**huǒ-huā** a spark

火线　**huǒ-hsièn** firing line, line of fire, battle front

火星报　**huǒ-hsīng-pào** *Iskra* (a Russian newspaper published by Lenin)

火红青春　**huǒ-húng-ch'īng-ch'ūn** fiery youth

火热的斗争　**huǒ-jè-te-tòu-chēng** a fiery struggle

火坑　**huǒ-k'ēng** a fire pit, place of misery (the old society)

火力　**huǒ-lì** firepower [military]

火力发电厂　**huǒ-lì fā-tièn-ch'ǎng** a thermal power plant, thermo-electric power plant

火山　**huǒ-shān** a volcano

火山口　**huǒ-shān-k'ǒu** the crater of a volcano (the brink of disaster)

火上加油　**huǒ-shàng-chiā-yú** to add oil to the fire (to stir things up, exacerbate the situation)

火葬　**huǒ-tsàng** cremation, to dispose of bodies by burning

火网　**huǒ-wǎng** a barrage, cross fire

火焰　**huǒ-yèn** flames, fire

826 伙伴　**huǒ-pàn** a partner (a colleague, co-worker)

伙食　**huǒ-shíh** food for a group, meals

伙食团　**huǒ-shíh-t'uán** eating groups (in which meals are provided communally)

伙同　**huǒ-t'úng** to collude with; together, in unison

huò (huò)

827 或轻或重　**huò-ch'īng-huò-chùng** whether light or heavy, either light or heavy [in degree]

或多或少　**huò-tō-huò-shǎo** somewhat, to a greater or less degree

828 货车　**huò-ch'ē** a freight car, box car; a freight train; a truck

货船　**huò-ch'uán** a cargo vessel, freighter

货款　**huò-k'uǎn** payment for goods

货郎担　**huò-láng-tàn** a peddler (usually one who serves the people in the countryside)

货币　**huò-pì** currency, money, coins

货币流通量　**huò-pì liú-t'ūng-liàng** amount of currency in circulation

货币单位　**huò-pì tān-wèi** monetary unit

货色　**huò-sè** kinds and qualities of goods, varieties of merchandise (usually pejorative if used figuratively)

货物税　**huò-wù-shuì** commodity tax, excise tax, goods tax

货源　**huò-yuán** source of goods, source of supply

货运周转量　**huò-yùn chōu-chuǎn-liàng** circulation volume of freight transport

货运量　**huò-yùn-liàng** volume of freight

829 获得　**huò-té** to gain, acquire, obtain, achieve, receive

830 祸害　**huò-hài** harm, injury, evil, misfortune, disaster; to injure

祸心　**huò-hsīn** evil intention, malice

祸根　**huò-kēn** root of evil, seeds of misfortune, source of trouble

祸国殃民　**huò-kuó-yāng-mín** to bring disaster to the country and its people (traitorous actions)

祸乱　**huò-luàn** disaster and upheaval, chaos, disturbance, disorder

祸不单行　**huò-pù-tān-hsíng** misfortunes do not come singly

祸首　**huò-shǒu** ringleader, chief criminal, troublemaker

祸从口出　**huò-ts'úng-k'ǒu-ch'ū** disasters come from [careless] mouths

831 豁免　**huò-miěn** to exempt from [taxes, military service, etc.]

豁　**huò**: *see also* **huō**

hsī (xī)

832 吸取　**hsī-ch'ǔ** to absorb, extract, draw

out, accept

吸取经验教训 **hsī-ch'ǔ chīng-yèn chiào-hsùn** to absorb the lessons of experience

吸取先进经验 **hsī-ch'ǔ hsiēn-chìn chīng-yèn** to absorb [to learn from] advanced experience

吸血鬼 **hsī-hsuěh-kuěi** a bloodsucking ghost (a leech, vampire, bloodsucker)

吸收 **hsī-shōu** to absorb, take in, assimilate, admit, recruit

吸引力 **hsī-yǐn-lì** power of attraction, appeal

833 西安事件 **hsī-ān shìh-pièn** the Sian Incident (December 12, 1936, in which Chiang Kai-shek was captured)

西方世界 **hsī-fāng shìh-chièh** the Western world

西哈努克 **hsī-hā-nǔ-k'ò** [Prince] Sihanouk

西贡政权 **hsī-kùng chèng-ch'üán** the Saigon regime

西历 **hsī-lì** the Western calendar, Gregorian calendar

西南非洲 **hsī-nán fēi-chōu** Southwest Africa

西班牙 **hsī-pān-yá** Spain

西半球 **hsī-pàn-ch'iú** the Western Hemisphere

西萨摩亚 **hsī-sà-mó-yà** Western Samoa

西沙群岛 **hsī-shā ch'ǔn-tǎo** the Paracel Islands

西属几内亚 **hsī-shǔ chī-nèi-yà** Spanish Guinea

西属撒哈拉 **hsī-shǔ sā-hā-lā** Spanish Sahara

西藏 **hsī-tsàng** Tibet

西藏军区 **hsī-tsàng chūn-ch'ǔ** the Tibet Military Area Command [of the PLA]

西印度联邦 **hsī-yìn-tù lién-pāng** the Federation of the West Indies

834 希腊 **hsī-là** Greece

希特勒 **hsī-t'è-lè** Hitler

835 矽钢 **hsī-kāng** silicon steel (now known as **kūei-kāng**)

836 息息相关 **hsī-hsī-hsiāng-kuān** related as closely as each breath is to the next (closely linked with; vitally interrelated)

息息相通 **hsī-hsī-hsiāng-t'ūng** completely and mutually in touch, closely in touch [with each other]

837 牺牲 **hsī-shēng** to sacrifice; a sacrifice

牺牲个人服从组织 **hsī-shēng kò-jén fú-ts'úng tsǔ-chīh** sacrifice personal [interests] and obey the [Party] organization

838 奚落 **hsī-lò** to say things obliquely, laugh at, deride, make a fool of

839 稀奇 **hsī-ch'í** unusual, rare, strange, curious

稀缺材料 **hsī-ch'üēh ts'ái-liào** scarce materials, materials of high value due to their scarcity

稀里糊涂 **hsī-li-hú-t'u** muddled, confused, mixed-up

稀薄 **hsī-pó** watery and diluted (weak, thin)

稀少 **hsī-shǎo** few, little, scarce, sparse, rare

稀有金属 **hsī-yǔ chīn-shǔ** rare metals

840 锡金 **hsī-chīn** Sikkim

锡兰 **hsī-lán** Ceylon [Sri Lanka]

锡伯族 **hsī-pó-tsú** the Sibo people (a minority in the Sinkiang Uighur Autonomous Region: population 22,000 as of 1957)

841 熄灭 **hsī-mièh** to extinguish, die out, put out [a light]

hsí (xí)

842 习气 **hsí-ch'ì** habitual temperament, habits (usually has an unfavorable implication)

习惯势力 **hsí-kuàn-shìh-lì** force of habit

843 席卷 **hsí-chüǎn** to roll up like a mat; to engulf

席位 **hsí-wèi** a seat [as in an assembly]

席位主义 **hsí-wèi-chǔ-ì** "seat-ism" (contesting among various Cultural Revolutionary factions for seats in the Three-Way Alliance, etc.)

844 袭击 **hsí-chī** a surprise attack, raid; to assault, fall upon

袭用 **hsí-yùng** to inherit and use

845 媳妇 **hsí-fu** a wife; the wife of one's son

hsǐ (xǐ)

846 洗心革面 **hsǐ-hsīn-kó-mièn** cleanse the heart and change one's outlook (to make a complete change from bad to good)

洗心涤虑 **hsǐ-hsīn-tí-lù** to wash [one's] heart and cleanse [one's] thoughts

洗礼 **hsǐ-lǐ** baptism

洗脸 **hsǐ-liěn** to wash the face (self-criticism)

洗手不干 **hsǐ-shǒu-pù-kàn** to wash one's hands of, to be through with

847 铣床 **hsǐ-ch'uáng** a milling machine

848 喜见乐闻 **hsǐ-chièn-lè-wén** happy to see and pleased to hear (enthusiastically received—may refer to news events or art and literary works)

喜气洋洋 **hsǐ-ch'ì-yáng-yáng** a joyful atmosphere, to jump for joy

喜出望外 **hsǐ-ch'ū-wàng-wài** happiness beyond one's hopes

喜剧 **hsǐ-chù** a comedy

喜形于色 **hsǐ-hsíng-yǔ-sè** pleasure showing in one's face

喜人 **hsǐ-jén** pleasing, something that gives pleasure

喜人现象 **hsǐ-jén hsièn-hsiàng** pleasing events, pleasing aspects

喜怒哀乐 **hsǐ-nù-āi-lè** happiness, anger, sorrow, and joy (human feelings)

喜怒无常 **hsǐ-nù-wú-ch'áng** inconstant in joy and anger (capricious)

喜闻乐见 **hsǐ-wén-lè-chièn** happy to hear and pleased to see (enthusiastically received—of news event or art and literary production)

hsì (xì)

849 戏剧 **hsì-chù** drama, dramatic arts

戏剧研究 **hsí-chù yén-chiū** *Studies in Drama* (Peking, bi-monthly, 1959—)

戏曲 **hsì-ch'ǔ** native opera and other performing arts

戏法 **hsì-fǎ** sleight of hand, magic, a trick

戏弄 **hsì-nùng** to mock, tease, make fun of, hoax, make a fool of

850 系列 **hsì-lièh** a series, line or lineage, row

系数 **hsì-shù** coefficient, factor [mathematical]

系统 **hsì-t'ǔng** a system (a broad functional division or related grouping in governmental administration—may be vertical or horizontal, formal or informal)

系统化 **hsì-t'ǔng-huà** to systematize; systematization

系统选育 **hsì-t'ǔng-hsuǎn-yù** systematic [seed] selection and cultivation

851 细账 **hsì-chàng** detailed accounts [fiscal]

细节 **hsì-chiéh** minor points, trifles, details

细致 **hsì-chìh** delicate, exquisite, finely detailed

细菌 **hsì-chùn** bacteria

细菌战 **hsì-chùn-chàn** germ warfare, bacteriological warfare

细菌肥料 **hsì-chǔn-féi-lìao** bacterial fertilizer

细菌武器 **hsì-chǔn-wǔ-ch'ì** bacteriological weapons

细心 **hsì-hsǐn** careful, cautious, painstaking, circumspect

细粮 **hsì-liáng** fine food [as contrasted with coarse food] (in North China—wheat flour; in South China—

polished rice)

细毛羊 **hsì-máo-yáng** fine-wool sheep (a breed of sheep in Sinkiang)

细密 **hsi-mì** fine and delicate [materials], close [stitches], delicate handling

细目 **hsi-mù** items, clauses, specific details

细胞 **hsì-pāo** cell [biology]

细纱锭 **hsì-shā-tìng** ring spindle

细水长流 **hsì-shuǐ-ch'áng-liú** a small stream runs a long way (a little effort each day gets the job done; frugal management will have its reward)

hsiā (xiā)

852 瞎胡闹 **hsiā-hú-nào** blind [unplanned] activity

瞎说一气 **hsiā-shuō-ī-ch'ì** to talk as much nonsense as they like

瞎说八道 **hsiā-shuō-pā-tào** to tell lies, talk nonsense, make reckless or irresponsible statements

瞎子摸鱼 **hsiā-tzu-mō-yú** [like] a blind man groping for fish

hsiá (xiá)

853 狭隘经验论 **hsiá-ài chīng-yèn lùn** narrow empiricism

狭隘观点 **hsiá-ài kuān-tiěn** a narrow view, narrow-minded attitude

狭小天地 **hsiá-hsiǎo t'iēn-tì** a small world (usually in an abstract sense for narrow-minded concentration on one's own interests)

hsià (xià)

854 下级 **hsià-chí** lower level, subordinate

下级服从上级 **hsià-chí fú-ts'úng shàng-chí** the lower level obeys the higher level

下降 **hsià-chiàng** to drop, fall, decline, descend, decrease

下轿运动 **hsià-chiào yùn-tùng** stepping down from the sedan-chair movement (bureaucrats and cadres must go to the masses)

下贱 **hsià-chièn** cheap, low class, undignified, lowly, mean

下贱人 **hsià-chièn-jén** low status people (groups such as barbers and actors who suffered from discrimination in the old society)

下中农 **hsià-chūng-núng** lower-middle peasants

下厂下井 **hsià-ch'ǎng hsià-chǐng** go down to the factories and mines

下场 **hsià-ch'ǎng** to leave the stage (to leave the field, end a career; the end, finale)

下放 **hsià-fàng** transfer downward (either to a less developed geographical place or to a lower administrative level—may be downward transfer of either people or of administrative responsibility)

下放青年 **hsià-fàng-ch'īng-nién** young people sent to the countryside

下放权力 **hsià-fàng ch'üán-lì** relegation of power (usually refers to the downward transfer of power within the communes—when powers originally vested in the commune were passed to the brigades and the teams)

下放干部 **hsià-fàng kàn-pù** cadres transferred downward; to transfer cadres downward

下放工厂 **hsià-fàng kūng-ch'ǎng** to send down to the factory (to send non-worker personnel to the factory as workers)

下放劳动 **hsià-fàng láo-tùng** to send down to do manual labor

下放农村 **hsià-fàng núng-ts'ūn** to send down to the villages

下放资产 **hsià-fàng tzū-ch'ǎn** downward transfer of capital (decentralization of finance and credit)

下伙房 **hsià-huǒ-fáng** down to the [public] kitchen (due to complaints concerning public mess halls during the early communes, some *hsià-fàng* cadres were assigned this special task)

下乡 **hsià-hsiāng** to go down to the countryside

下乡青年 **hsià-hsiāng ch'īng-nién** young people going to the countryside

下乡上山 **hsià-hsiāng-shàng-shān** going down to the countryside and up to the mountains

下乡镀金论 **hsià-hsiāng tù-chīn lùn** the idea that going to the country is to be gilded (critical of the belief that a short period in the countryside will give one great merit)

下乡运动 **hisà-hsiāng yùn-tùng** Down to the Villages Movement (the sending of intellectuals to the villages, Yenan period, 1942–43)

下意识 **hsià-i-shíh** the subconscious; subconsciousness

下苦工夫 **hsià k'ǔ-kūng-fu** to devote much arduous effort and time

下里巴人 **hsià-lǐ-pā-jén** simple folksongs of the common people (popular literature and art works)

下列 **hsià-lièh** the following, as listed below

下连当兵 **hsià-lién tāng-pīng** to go down to the companies and serve as common soldiers (the PLA equivalent of **hsià-fàng**: in September 1958, army cadres at all levels were ordered to serve one month each year as privates)

下落 **hsià-lò** whereabouts; stopping-off place

下马 **hsià-mǎ** to dismount from a horse (to resign, to discontinue a course or policy)

下马观花 **hsià-mǎ-kuān-huā** to get off one's horse and examine the flowers (to make a slow, careful inspection)

下半旗 **hsià-pàn-ch'í** to fly a flag at half-mast

下水 **hsià-shuǐ** to launch, enter the water, go downstream; to lower oneself [by a disgraceful act], join [another camp]; the lower reaches of a river

下水道 **hsià-shuǐ-tào** a sewer, drains, channel outlet

下刀子也要干 **hsià-tāo-tzu yěh yào-kàn** even if it rains knives [we] will still persevere

下定决心 **hsià-tìng chüéh-hsīn** to make a resolution

下毒手 **hsià-tú-shǒu** to lay violent hands on someone, to use murderous means

下台 **hsià-t'ái** to leave the stage (leave office; go out of power, be ruined)

下层 **hsià-ts'éng** lower stratum, subordinate level

下文 **hsià-wén** in the next passage, a continuation, next installment, a sequel

下野 **hsià-yěh** to leave [the court] for the country (to leave high office)

下游 **hsià-yú** the lower reaches [of a stream or river] (downstream, below average, not up to par)

下游危险 **hsià-yú-wēi-hsiěn** it is dangerous to be downstream (it is dangerous to fall behind others)

855 吓唬 **hsià-hu** to bluff, scare, frighten, intimidate

吓不倒，压不垮 **hsià-pù-tǎo, yā-pù-k'uǎ** cannot be frightened and cannot be pressured

吓破胆 **hsià-p'ò-tǎn** to frighten [so as to] burst the gallbladder

吓倒 **hsià-tǎo** to be frightened into collapse

856 夏历 **hsià-lì** calendar of the Hsia dynasty (the lunar calendar, formerly **yīn-lì**; now generally replaced by the

term **núng-lì**)

夏粮 **hsià-liáng** summer-harvested grains

夏令营 **hsià-lìng-yíng** summer camp, summer playgrounds

夏收 **hsià-shōu** summer crop

夏收分配 **hsià-shōu fēn-p'èi** distribution after the summer harvest

夏收夏种 **hsià-shōu hsià-chùng** summer harvesting and planting

夏收作物 **hsià-shōu tsò-wù** crops harvested in the summer

夏收预分 **hsià-shōu yù-fēn** distribution in anticipation of the summer harvest

hsiāng (xiāng)

857 乡长会议 **hsiāng-chǎng-huì-ì** conference of township heads (1957)

乡政府 **hsiāng-chèng-fǔ** a *hsiāng* government (before the commune system)

乡社合一 **hsiāng-shè-hó-ī** the township and the commune become one entity, integration of village and commune

乡土教材 **hsiāng-t'ǔ chiào-ts'ái** local data [on livelihood, etc.] used as educational materials

乡村 **hsiāng-ts'ūn** village, hamlet, rustic area, the countryside

乡邮站 **hsiāng-yú-chàn** a rural postal agency

858 相安无事 **hsiāng-ān-wú-shìh** to be at peace mutually, peaceful and without conflict

相争 **hsiāng-chēng** to contend with each other, compete with, struggle with each other

相机 **hsiāng-chī** to watch for the right time [for action], at the opportune time

相继 **hsiāng-chì** in close succession, one after another

相结合 **hsiāng-chiéh-hó** to combine with, coordinate with, go hand in hand with

相称 **hsiāng-ch'èn** to correspond to, match, fit together with, suit, be commensurate with, symmetrical with

相持阶段 **hsiāng-ch'íh chiéh-tuàn** a stage of stalemate, a condition of neither side giving way

相处 **hsiāng-ch'ǔ** to live and work together, get along with

相反相成 **hsiāng-fǎn-hsiāng-ch'éng** mutually opposed [yet] mutually complementary

相仿 **hsiāng-fǎng** to resemble, look alike, similar to each other

相辅相成 **hsiāng-fǔ-hsiāng-ch'éng** mutually supplementary and complementary

相互 **hsiāng-hù** mutually, reciprocally

相互支持 **hsiāng-hù chīh-ch'íh** to support each other

相互援助 **hsiāng-hù yuán-chù** to assist each other

相信群众 **hsiāng-hsìn ch'ún-chùng** to trust the masses

相形见绌 **hsiāng-hsíng-chièn-ch'ù** found inferior by comparison, to lose by comparison

相容 **hsiāng-júng** mutually compatible

相关 **hsiāng-kuān** to have to do with, related, connected; correlation, concern

相配 **hsiāng-p'èi** to match each other, fit together, mutually agreeable

相适应又相矛盾 **hsiāng-shìh-yìng yù hsiāng-máo-tùn** mutual conformity as well as mutual contradiction

相当 **hsiāng-tāng** (1) appropriate, proper; (2) corresponding, equivalent; (3) considerable, to a great extent, fairly [large]

相等 **hsiāng-těng** equal to, equivalent, identical, corresponding

相对 **hsiāng-tuì** opposite, facing each other; relative, relatively; proportional

相对和绝对 **hsiāng-tuì hó chüéh-tuì** relative and absolute

相对性 **hsiāng-tuì-hsìng** relativity

相对论 **hsiāng-tuì-lùn** theory of relativity

相提并论 **hsiāng-t'í-pìng-lùn** mentioned and discussed as related things, to mention in the same breath, to put on a par with

相通 **hsiāng-t'ūng** intercommunicating; interrelated; interchangeable, synonymous

相应 **hsiāng-yìng** to act in response to, support each other; mutually supportive; appropriate, suitable

相 **hsiāng**: see also **hsiàng**

859 香花 **hsiāng-huā** fragrant flowers (literary works favored by the Party)

香花毒草 **hsiāng-huà-tú-ts'ǎo** fragrant flowers and poisonous weeds (approved and disapproved writings)

香料 **hsiāng-liào** condiments, spices

860 湘 **hsiāng** Hunan province

湘江评论 **hsiāng-chiāng p'íng-lùn** *The Hsiang River Review* (a journal founded by Mao Tse-tung in 1919)

湘桂铁路 **hsiāng-kuèi t'iéh-lù** the Hunan-Kwangsi railway

湘鄂西苏区 **hsiāng-ò-hsī sū-ch'ǔ**

Hunan-West Hupeh Soviet District (a CCP base during the Kiangsi period, under the leadership of Ho Lung and Hsiao K'o)

湘鄂赣苏区 **hsiāng-ò-kàn sū-ch'ü** Hunan-Hupeh-Kiangsi Soviet District (part of the Central Soviet District during the Kiangsi period)

hsiáng (xiáng)

861 详尽 **hsiáng-chìn** detailed and complete, exhaustively detailed, precise

详查 **hsiáng-ch'á** a detailed investigation; to investigate minutely

详情 **hsiáng-ch'íng** the detailed situation, full details of an event

hsiǎng (xiǎng)

862 享乐主义 **hsiǎng-lè-chǔ-ì** hedonism, self-indulgence

享年 **hsiǎng-nién** to live until, to die at the age of

享受 **hsiǎng-shòu** to enjoy (usually refers to enjoyment of material things)

享有很高的荣誉 **hsiǎng-yǔ hěn-kāo-te júng-yù** to enjoy a very high reputation

享用 **hsiǎng-yùng** to enjoy the use of, have at one's disposal

863 响彻全球 **hsiǎng-ch'è-ch'üán-ch'iú** to resound around the world

响彻云霄 **hsiǎng-ch'è-yún-hsiāo** echoing to the skies

响亮 **hsiǎng-liàng** sharply and clearly, loud and clear, forthright

响尾蛇导弹 **hsiǎng-wěi-shé tǎo-tàn** sidewinder guided missile

响应 **hsiǎng-yìng** to respond, answer, echo, reply, react to; a response

864 想象 **hsiǎng-hsiàng** to imagine, conceive, fancy; imagination, mental vision

想入非非 **hsiǎng-jù-fēi-fēi** to let one's fancy run wild (to indulge in wishful thinking)

想大事, 顾大局 **hsiǎng-tà-shìh, kù-tà-chú** to keep one's mind on great affairs [the revolution] and consider the overall situation [the country]

想当然 **hsiǎng-tāng-ján** to take for granted, to assume [something is so] without basis

想点子 **hsiǎng-tiěn-tzu** to think up a solution, work out a method

想透 **hsiǎng-t'òu** to think through

hsiàng (xiàng)

865 向群众交代 **hsiàng ch'ún-chùng chiāo-tài** to make a clean breast to the masses

向群众负责 **hsiàng ch'ún-chùng fù-tsé** to be responsible to the masses

向群众学习 **hsiàng ch'ún-chùng hsuéh-hsí** to learn from the masses

向废物夺宝 **hsiàng fèi-wù tó-pǎo** to snatch treasures from waste (to salvage, reclaim, or extract by-products from industrial waste)

向后倒退 **hsiàng-hòu tào-t'uì** to move backwards, retreat

向日葵 **hsiàng-jìh-k'uéi** a sunflower (because it always faces the sun, now a symbol of loyalty to Mao Tse-tung; *see* **hsiàng-yáng-huā**)

向国家伸手 **hsiàng kuó-chiā shēn-shǒu** looking to the government for a handout (attacked as contrary to Mao's emphasis on self-reliance)

向科学进军 **hsiàng k'ō-hsuéh chìn-chūn** to march forward to science (a slogan of 1956–57)

向山区进军 **hsiàng shān-ch'ü chìn-chūn** to advance to the mountain areas

向上伸手 **hsiàng-shàng shēn-shǒu** looking to the higher [levels] for a handout

向大自然宣战 **hsiàng tà-tzù-ján hsuān-chàn** to declare war against nature

向导 **hsiàng-tǎo** a guide; to guide

向导周报 **hsiàng-tǎo chōu-pào** *The Guide Weekly* (a CCP journal first published at Shanghai in September, 1922)

向纵深发展 **hsiàng tsùng-shēn fā-chǎn** toward penetrating and comprehensive development

向纵深推进 **hsiàng tsùng-shēn t'uī-chìn** toward a penetrating and comprehensive advance

向往 **hsiàng-wǎng** to crave, be attracted to, admire

向阳花 **hsiàng-yáng-huā** the sunflower (a symbol of loyalty to Mao Tse-tung; *see* **hsiàng jìh-k'uéi**)

向隅而泣 **hsiàng-yú-érh-ch'ì** to turn into a corner and weep (to mope)

866 项目 **hsiàng-mù** an item, article, clause, sum

867 相声 **hsiàng-shēng** comic dialogue

相 **hsiàng**: *see also* **hsiāng**

868 象章 **hsiàng-chāng** a badge having a picture on it (a Mao button)

象征 **hsiàng-chēng** to symbolize, signify; a symbol, token, emblem

象征主义 **hsiàng-chēng-chǔ-ì** symbolism

象棋比赛 **hsiàng-ch'í-pǐ-sài** a chess tournament

象牙之塔 **hsiàng-yá-chīh-t'ǎ** an ivory tower (the world of the petty-bourgeoisie divorced from reality)

象牙海岸 **hsiàng-yá-hǎi-àn** Ivory Coast [Republic of]

象牙雕刻品 **hsiàng-yá tiāo-k'ò-p'ǐn** ivory sculpture, carved ivory objects

象样 **hsiàng-yàng** proper in appearance (to look or act in a fitting or appropriate manner; exemplary, good, proper)

869 橡胶厂 **hsiàng-chiāo-ch'ǎng** rubber-goods factory

橡胶园 **hsiàng-chiāo-yuán** rubber plantation

hsiāo (xiāo)

870 消长 **hsiāo-chǎng** growth and decay, increase and decrease, wax and wane

消极 **hsiāo-chí** negative, inactive, passive, inert, sluggish

消极挨整 **hsiāo-chí-ái-chěng** to receive correction passively (instead of positively)

消极求稳 **hsiāo-chí-ch'iú-wěn** the negative [behavior of] seeking for stability, a negative seeking for safety

消极分子 **hsiāo-chí fèn-tzǔ** passive elements (usually contrasted with persons having the desired quality of activism)

消极平衡论 **hsiāo-chí-p'íng-héng lùn** the doctrine of a passive balance (to allow the weakest factor to be determining, instead of working to improve the weak factor or element)

消极怠工 **hsiāo-chí-tài-kūng** a work slowdown (usually suggests passive sabotage)

消极等待 **hsiāo-chí těng-tài** to wait passively

消除 **hsiāo-ch'ú** to abolish, eliminate, do away with, remove

消除异己 **hsiāo-ch'ú-ì-chǐ** to liquidate all those differing from oneself

消防民警 **hsiāo-fáng-mín-chǐng** fire prevention police

消防队 **hsiāo-fáng-tuì** fire brigades

消费 **hsiāo-fèi** to spend, consume; expenditure, consumption

消费合作社 **hsiāo-fèi hó-tsò-shè** consumers' cooperative society

消费品 **hsiāo-fèi-p'ǐn** consumer goods

消费资料 **hsiāo-fèi-tzū-liào** the raw materials of consumer goods (wheat, cotton, etc.)

消耗 **hsiāo-hào** to diminish, consume, exhaust, drain; attrition, consumption, cost of maintenance

消耗战 **hsiāo-hào-chàn** war of attrition

消息灵通人士 **hsiāo-hsī líng-t'ūng jén-shìh** well-informed persons, informed sources

消息报 **hsiāo-hsī-pào** *Izvestia* (Russian daily newspaper)

消弭 **hsiāo-mǐ** to put an end to, terminate

消灭 **hsiāo-mièh** to exterminate, destroy, eradicate, wipe out, annihilate, do away with

消磨 **hsiāo-mó** to wear away (to while away time)

消散 **hsiāo-sàn** to disperse, scatter

消逝 **hsiāo-shìh** to pass away, wither, fade

消毒剂 **hsiāo-tú-chì** a disinfectant, antiseptic agent

消亡 **hsiāo-wáng** to perish, wither away

871 宵禁 **hsiāo-chìn** a [night] curfew

872 逍遥法外 **hsiāo-yáo-fǎ-wài** outside the reach of the law, to go free

逍遥派 **hsiāo-yáo-p'ài** leisure groups (unproductive elements in society)

逍遥自在 **hsiāo-yáo-tzù-tsài** in a state of ease (to be at peace with the world and oneself, blissful abstraction)

873 萧墙之祸 **hsiāo-ch'iáng-chīh-huò** calamity within the walls [of the home] (internal trouble, civil war, etc.)

萧条 **hsiāo-t'iáo** a depression, recession, slump; desolate, lonely, forsaken

萧条萎缩 **hsiāo-t'iáo-wěi-sō** depressed and shrunken (said of economic conditions)

874 硝化甘油 **hsiāo-huà-kān-yú** nitroglycerine

硝石 **hsiāo-shíh** niter, nitrate

硝烟弥漫 **hsiāo-yēn-mí-màn** the smoke of gunpowder fills the sky (a battlefield)

875 销案 **hsiāo-àn** to close a case, dispose of a file

销毁 **hsiāo-huǐ** to destroy, ravage, devastate

销路 **hsiāo-lù** circulation, market demand, sales volume

销声匿迹 **hsiāo-shēng-nì-chī** to silence one's voice and hide one's traces (to conceal oneself)

销售 **hsiāo-shòu** to sell [goods]

876 潇洒 **hsiāo-sǎ** casual and elegant [in manner], dashing and refined

877 嚣张 **hsiāo-chāng** clamorous, blatant

hsiǎo (xiǎo)

878 小整风 **hsiǎo-chěng-fēng** a minor recti-

135

fication

小集体 **hsiǎo-chí-t'ǐ** a small collective

小集团 **hsiǎo-chí-t'uán** a small clique (a pejorative term: cliques are usually assumed to be organized for an illicit or anti-Party purpose)

小将 **hsiǎo-chiàng** little generals, "Young Turk," an active youngster (a good term)

小株密植 **hsiǎo-chū-mì-chíh** close planting of small [rice] plants (a method of increasing yield)

小注 **hsiǎo-chù** a note in smaller print (may be footnote or incorporated in the text)

小巧玲珑 **hsiǎo-ch'iǎo-líng-lúng** small and delicate, exquisite, petite

小丑 **hsiǎo-ch'ǒu** clown, comedian

小圈子 **hsiǎo ch'üān-tzu** a small circle (a group or clique—usually with an unfavorable connotation)

小恩小惠 **hsiǎo-ēn-hsiǎo-huì** small kindnesses and favors

小而全 **hsiǎo-érh-ch'üán** small but complete, compact (usually applied to local small-scale industry)

小贩管理小组 **hsiǎo-fàn kuǎn-lǐ hsiǎo-tsǔ** hawker management small group (an administrative organ in Shanghai, under a market management committee, before 1956)

小话剧 **hsiǎo-huà-chù** short prose dramas

小伙子 **hsiǎo-huǒ-tzu** a husky young fellow

小戏 **hsiǎo-hsì** a stage skit

小先生 **hsiǎo-hsiēn-shēng** young teachers (usually children who assist in basic literacy work with adults)

小型轧钢厂 **hsiǎo-hsíng chá-kāng-ch'ǎng** a small-scale steel rolling mill

小型农具 **hsiǎo-hsíng núng-chù** simple farm tools, hand-use implements [hoe, rake, etc.]

小型文艺宣传队 **hsiǎo-hsíng wén-ì hsuān-ch'uán-tuì** small-scale art propaganda teams (1964)

小型运动战 **hsiǎo-hsíng yùn-tùng-chàn** small-scale mobile warfare (figuratively: subsidiary work which can be done in slack seasons and spare time and requiring fewer workers than a mass project)

小学教师 **hsiǎo-hsuéh chiào-shīh** a primary school teacher; the title of a Peking monthly journal, 1952–1956

小学戴帽 **hsiǎo-hsuéh-tài-mào** a primary school wearing a hat (a primary school with a junior middle school attached)

小人 **hsiǎo-jén** (1) originally: a man of the lower classes (as opposed to the **chǔn-tzu** 君子); (2) a small or petty person; (3) now construed to be the working population throughout history

小高炉 **hsiǎo-kāo-lú** a small blast furnace

小歌剧 **hsiǎo-kō-chù** a short musical drama

小广播 **hsiǎo-kuǎng-pō** little broadcasts (a slang term for the gossip network among cadres and officials)

小看 **hsiǎo-k'àn** to despise, belittle, look down upon

小口径 **hsiǎo-k'ǒu-chìng** small caliber [guns]

小矿点 **hsiǎo-k'uàng-tiěn** a small [developed] mine (useful and adequate for local needs)

小骂大帮忙 **hsiǎo-mà tà-pāng-máng** to scold on minor issues but support on the major ones

小麦灌浆 **hsiǎo-mài kuàn-chiāng** the filling out of the wheat (approaching maturity)

小米加步枪 **hsiǎo-mǐ chiā pù-ch'iāng** millet plus rifles (recalling the hardships of guerrilla warfare which, nonetheless, brought victory)

小年 **hsiǎo-nién** a small year (a year, generally, following a heavy yield, when fruit trees produce a lighter crop)

小农经济 **hsiǎo-núng chīng-chì** small peasant economy

小额 **hsiǎo-ó** a small amount

小八路 **hsiǎo-pā-lù** young 8th Route (the young boys who joined the 8th Route Army as messengers and orderlies—often known as *hsiǎo-kuěi* [little devils])

小宝塔 **hsiǎo-pǎo-t'ǎ** the small pyramid (a reference to pre-socialist society where most received little or no education and only a few elite [the apex of the pyramid] received higher education)

小辫子 **hsiǎo-pièn-tzu** a small pigtail (an easily seized weakness)

小冰河时期 **hsiǎo-pīng-hó shíh-ch'ī** a lesser glacial age

小兵无大节 **hsiǎo-pīng wú tà-chiéh** a common soldier has no high principles (the reference is to the past, when the common soldier was more a mercenary than a man staking his life for his country)

小商小贩 **hsiǎo-shāng hsiǎo-fàn** small vendors and hawkers

小生产 **hsiǎo-shēng-ch'ǎn** small production, small-scale production

小生产者 **hsiǎo-shēng-ch'ǎn-chě** small producers

小生产力量 **hsiǎo-shēng-ch'ǎn lì-liang** small[-scale] productive forces (the capitalist spontaneous forces of small producers in the city and the country-side)

小市民 **hsiǎo-shìh-mín** petty bourgeoisie, narrow-minded town dwellers, philistines

小说 **hsiǎo-shuō** a novel

小道消息 **hsiǎo-tào-hsiāo-hsī** side-street news (news transmitted by word of mouth instead of through official media; grapevine news, gossip, rumor)

小调 **hsiǎo-tiào** informal songs, ballads, ditties folksongs

小读者 **hsiǎo-tú-chě** small readers, young readers, child readers

小段包工 **hsiǎo-tuàn pāo-kūng** a short-term labor agreement [for field work]

小队 **hsiǎo-tuì** a squad (any small unit)

小动作 **hsiǎo-tùng-tsò** mean and petty actions

小题大做 **hsiǎo-t'í-tà-tsò** to make a small matter into a big issue

小天地 **hsiǎo-t'iēn-tì** a small world (concentration on personal interests, a limited viewpoint)

小土群 **hsiǎo-t'ǔ-ch'ún** small indigenous groups (during the Great Leap Forward, small mass-run enterprises using indigenous production methods)

小土炉 **hsiǎo-t'ǔ-lú** a small indigenous blast furnace

小土地出租者 **hsiǎo t'ǔ-tì ch'ū-tsū-chě** small land leaseholder

小灾夺丰收, 大灾不减产 **hsiǎo-tsāi tó fēng-shōu, tà-tsāi pù chiěn-ch'ǎn** to wrest a good harvest from small disasters and a normal harvest from serious disasters

小灶 **hsiǎo-tsào** the small stove (specially prepared and higher-grade food reserved for personnel of certain grades in mess halls)

小卒 **hsiǎo-tsú** a common soldier; a pawn (an unimportant person being used by someone else)

小组 **hsiǎo-tsǔ** a section, small group, team, circle, cell (the lowest-level Party or work group)

小组会 **hsiǎo-tsǔ-huì** small group meeting, a meeting of a cell or small group

小组委员会 **hsiǎo-tsǔ wěi-yuán-huì** a subcommittee; a committee in charge of small groups

小资产阶级 **hsiǎo-tzū-ch'ǎn-chiēh-chí** the petty bourgeoisie

小资产阶级知识分子 **hsiǎo-tzū-ch'ǎn-chiēh-chí chīh-shíh-fèn-tzǔ** petty bourgeois intellectuals

小资产阶级民主派 **hsiǎo-tzū-ch'ǎn-chiēh-chí mín-chǔ-p'ài** petty bourgeois democratic groups

小自由 **hsiǎo-tzù-yú** little freedoms (usually refers to the cultivation of private plots and selling their products on the free market)

小册子 **hsiǎo-ts'è-tzu** a booklet, pamphlet, manual, brochure

小洋群 **hsiǎo-yáng-ch'ún** small foreign [method] groups (small mass-run enterprises using foreign production methods, or a group of small, foreign-style blast furnaces—during the Great Leap Forward)

小洋炉 **hsiǎo-yáng-lú** a small modern-style blast furnace

小宇宙 **hsiǎo-yǔ-chòu** microcosm

hsiào (xiào)

879 肖象 **hsiào-hsiàng** a portrait, likeness
肖 **hsiào:** *see also* **hsiāo**

880 孝子贤孙 **hsiào-tzǔ hsién-sūn** filial sons and worthy grandsons (used sarcastically)

881 校办工厂 **hsiào-pàn-kūng-ch'ǎng** a school-operated workshop

校办农场 **hsiào-pàn-núng-ch'ǎng** a school-operated farm

校舍 **hsiào-shè** school premises, school buildings

校史 **hsiào-shǐh** the school's history

校外辅导员 **hsiào-wài fǔ-tǎo-yuán** tutors from outside the school (usually volunteers rrom the PLA or workers who counsel activities such as the Young Pioneers)

校务委员会 **hsiào-wù wěi-yuán-huì** school affairs committee (the academic governing body of a university—now replaced by the school revolutionary committee)

校园 **hsiào-yuán** a school or college campus

882 效忠 **hsiào-chūng** to be loyal to, render loyalty to, show fidelity

效犬马之劳 **hsiào ch'ǔan-mǎ-chīh-láo** to render service like a dog or horse (servile)

效益 **hsiào-ì** an effective benefit, beneficial result

效果 **hsiào-kuǒ** an effect, result,

consequence

效劳 **hsiào-láo** to render service, serve faithfully

效力 **hsiào-lì** to put forth strength, render service; a result, effect; efficacy

效率 **hsiào-lù** efficiency, work capacity

效能 **hsiào-néng** function, effectiveness, efficiency, capacity

883 笑逐颜开 **hsiào-chú-yén-k'āi** a countenance beaming with smiles

笑容满面 **hsiào-júng-mǎn-mièn** a face covered with smiles

笑里藏刀 **hsiào-lǐ-ts'áng-tāo** a smile with a hidden knife (treacherous)

笑骂由人 **hsiào-mà-yú-jén** to take no heed of ridicule and scolding (without shame)

笑面虎 **hsiào-mièn-hǔ** a tiger with a smiling face (a wicked person with a hypocritical smile, a friendly-looking villain)

笑柄 **hsiào-pǐng** a laughing-stock, butt of ridicule

笑掉大牙 **hsiào-tiào-tà-yá** laugh one's tooth off (extremely laughable)

hsiēh (xiē)

884 歇歇脚的思想 **hsiēh-hsiēh-chiǎo te szū-hsiǎng** rest-a-while thinking (satisfied with one's present achievement)

歇人不歇车 **hsiēh-jén pù-hsiēh-ch'ē** rest the man but not the machine (multi-shift operation)

885 楔入 **hsiēh-jù** to wedge in, drive a wedge between

hsiéh (xié)

886 协会 **hsiéh-huì** an association, federation, society, institute

协议 **hsiéh-ì** to discuss, negotiate; an agreement

协力 **hsiéh-lì** to work together, combine efforts

协商 **hsiéh-shāng** to negotiate, seek agreement, consult, confer; a conference, consultation, negotiation; an agreement, understanding, entente

协定 **hsiéh-tìng** an agreement, pact, convention, accord (usually between nations but less formal than a treaty); to negotiate, come to an agreement

协调 **hsiéh-t'iáo** to harmonize, coordinate, synchronize, readjust relations [with]; harmonious

协同一致 **hsiéh-t'úng-ī-chìh** to collaborate fully, coordinate, bring into line; concerted, fully joined with

协同作战 **hsiéh-t'úng-tsò-chàn** combined military action (also figurative)

协作 **hsiéh-tsò** to combine efforts, collaborate, cooperate

协作风格 **hsiéh-tsò-fēng-kó** the style of coordinating efforts

887 邪气歪风 **hsiéh-ch'ì-wāi-fēng** evil influences and bad customs

邪恶 **hsiéh-ò** heretical and wicked, depraved, vicious

邪路 **hsiéh-lù** a wrong road (usually figurative)

邪门歪道 **hsiéh-mén-wāi-tào** improper channels or disreputable actions

邪不胜正 **hsiéh-pù-shèng-chèng** heresy cannot overthrow the truth

邪说 **hsiéh-shuō** a heresy, perverted view, immoral doctrine

888 胁迫 **hsiéh-p'ò** to threaten, intimidate, coerce, compel

胁从不问 **hsiéh-ts'úng-pù-wèn** not to inquire into [the misdeeds of] those coerced to join (leniency toward the misled)

889 挟恨 **hsiéh-hèn** to harbor hatred, bear a grudge

挟嫌 **hsiéh-hsién** to carry a grudge

890 携手并进 **hsiéh-shǒu-pìng-chìn** to march forward hand in hand

hsiěh (xiě)

891 写照 **hsiěh-chào** a portrayal, description, representation

写真实论 **hsiěh-chēn-shíh lùn** the doctrine of truthful writing (realism which may acknowledge faults even in a socialist society—one of the **hēi-pā-lùn**)

写作 **hsiěh-tsò** to write; literary works

hsièh (xiè)

892 泄气 **hsièh-ch'ì** to lose power or compression; to be frustrated, humiliated, deflated, disappointed

泄洪量 **hsièh-húng-liàng** spillway capacity, diversion capacity

泄露 **hsièh-lù** to leak [a secret], to divulge, reveal, disclose

泄露天机 **hsièh-lù t'iēn-chī** to leak out Heaven's plan (to reveal important secrets)

泄水闸 **hsièh-shuǐ-chá** a sluice gate, a spillway

泄水孔 **hsièh-shuǐ-k'ǔng** a sluice

泄私愤 **hsièh szū-fèn** to vent personal spite

893 卸肩 **hsièh-chiēn** to unburden the

shoulders (to lay down responsibility)
卸下 **hsièh-hsià** to unload
卸任 **hsièh-jèn** to retire from office
894 谢幕 **hsièh-mù** a curtain call, to take
bows
谢罪 **hièh-tsuì** to acknowledge a fault,
apologize
895 邂逅 **hsièh-hòu** to meet by chance,
meet without prior engagement

hsiēn (xiān)

896 仙丹 **hsiēn-tān** the pill of immortality,
elixir of life, panacea
897 先见之明 **hsiēn-chièn-chīh-míng** foresight, prescience, the ability to see
what is coming
先知先觉 **hsiēn-chīh-hsiēn-chüéh**
prophetic and perceptive
先进 **hsiēn-chìn** advanced, progressive,
a forerunner
先进集体 **hsiēn-chìn-chí-t'ǐ** an advanced collective, outstanding unit
先进阶级 **hsiēn-chìn-chiēh-chí** the
advanced class (the proletariat)
先进经验 **hsiēn-chìn-chīng-yèn** advanced experience
先进区域 **hsiēn-chìn-ch'ǖ-yǜ** advanced
areas, progressive districts
先进分子 **hsiēn-chìn-fèn-tzǔ** advanced
elements, progressive persons
先进人物 **hsiēn-chìn-jén-wù** an
advanced person [of some impor-
tance]
先进个人 **hsiēn-chìn-kò-jén** advanced
individuals
先进工人 **hsiēn-chìn-kūng-jén** an
advanced [factory] worker, outstanding worker
先进工作者 **hsiēn-chìn kūng-tsò-chě**
advanced workers (refers to performance of non-physical tasks—
Party, cadre, office, or intellectual)
先进工作方法 **hsiēn-chìn kūng-tsò-fāng-
fǎ** advanced working method
先进公社 **hsiēn-chìn-kūng-shè** an
advanced [progressive] commune
先进连队 **hsiēn-chìn-lién-tuì** an advanced company [in the PLA]
先进苗子 **hsiēn-chìn-miáo-tzu** good
sprouts (something young which is
promising and should be carefully
nurtured; may be youth, such as the
Young Pioneers, or any new
development)
先进模范单位 **hsiēn-chìn mó-fàn-tān-
wèi** an advanced model unit
先进生产者 **hsiēn-chìn shēng-ch'ǎn-chě**
advanced producers, innovative
producers

先进事迹 **hsiēn-chìn-shìh-chī** progressive deeds
先进水平 **hsiēn-chìn-shuǐ-p'íng** advanced level
先进思想 **hsiēn-chìn-szū-hsiǎng**
advanced thought, progressive ideas
先进大队 **hsiēn-chìn-tà-tuì** an advanced
[production] brigade
先进典型 **hsiēn-chìn-tiěn-hsíng** an
advanced model
先进因素 **hsiēn-chìn-yīn-sù** progressive
factors
先决条件 **hsiēn-chüéh-t'iáo-chièn** a
precondition, prerequisite
先驱 **hsiēn-ch'ǖ** a vanguard, pioneer,
forerunner, harbinger
先发制人 **hsiēn-fā-chìh-jén** he who
moves first can control others
(initiative is vital)
先锋 **hsiēn-fēng** a vanguard, forerunner
先锋战士 **hsiēn-fēng-chàn-shìh** vanguard fighters (usually refers to
members of the Party)
先锋模范作用 **hsiēn-fēng mó-fàn-tsò-
yùng** the model-serving role of the
vanguard
先锋队 **hsiēn-fēng-tuì** a vanguard unit,
vanguards
先锋作用 **hsiēn-fēng-tsò-yùng** role of
the vanguard, vanguard role
先后 **hsiēn-hòu** successively, one after
the other; order of precedence; at
various times; before and after; at
about the time
先行官 **hsiēn-hsíng-kuān** a forerunner,
vanguard
先人后己 **hsiēn-jén-hòu-chǐ** first [think
of] others [and] then of oneself
(unselfish)
先入为主 **hsiēn-jù-wéi-chǔ** the first
[idea] that enters [the mind] becomes
dominant (beware of having fixed
ideas)
先例 **hsiēn-lì** a former example, a
precedent
先烈 **hsiēn-lièh** a martyr [for the
nation or Party]
先搬后化 **hsiēn-pān-hòu-huà** transplant
first [and] transform later (said to
have been Liu Shao-ch'i's policy
toward borrowing from Soviet
models, as in education)
先破后立 **hsiēn-p'ò-hòu-lì** first destroy
and then build (referring to ideology
—an old phrase much used in the
Cultural Revolution)
先声 **hsiēn-shēng** the first voice,
precursor, herald
先声夺人 **hsiēn-shēng-tó-jén** the first
sounds [of a brilliant performance]

inspire awe (to make an impressive start)

先导 **hsiēn-tǎo** a leader, guide, forerunner, precursor

先天 **hsiēn-t'iēn** instinctive, innate, inborn; congenital, hereditary; the prenatal period

先头部队 **hsiēn-t'óu-pù-tuì** attacking echelon, spearhead units, advanced detachments

先验论 **hsiēn-yèn lùn** apriorism, presupposed by experience, derived from self-evident propositions

⁸⁹⁸ 纤维 **hsiēn-wéi** fibers

⁸⁹⁹ 掀起高潮 **hsiēn-ch'ǐ kāo-ch'áo** to stir up a high tide

⁹⁰⁰ 鲜血 **hsiēn-hsuěh** living blood, fresh blood

鲜明 **hsiēn-míng** sharp, distinct, clear, fresh

鲜明对比 **hsiēn-míng-tuì-pǐ** a distinct and clear contrast

⁹⁰¹ 暹罗 **hsiēn-ló** Siam (now known as Thailand)

hsién (xián)

⁹⁰² 闲散 **hsién-sǎn** with free time, at leisure, idle

闲地 **hsién-tì** idle land, fallow lands

闲谈 **hsién-t'án** gossip, idle talk; to chat

⁹⁰³ 弦乐器 **hsién-yuèh-ch'ì** stringed instruments

⁹⁰⁴ 贤明 **hsién-míng** wise, enlightened, sagacious

⁹⁰⁵ 衔级 **hsién-chí** title and rank

衔接 **hsién-chiēh** to connect up, link up, dovetail

⁹⁰⁶ 嫌疑 **hsién-í** suspicion; suspected; to be suspicious

嫌疑犯 **hsién-í-fàn** a suspect, suspected criminal

嫌低 **hsién-tì** to disapprove as too low [price, amount, or target objective]

嫌脏怕累 **hsién-tsāng-p'à-lèi** to hate dirt and fear fatigue (a bourgeois dislike of physical work)

嫌恶 **hsién-wù** to loathe, hate, dislike, abhor

hsiěn (xiǎn)

⁹⁰⁷ 险峯 **hsiěn-fēng** a strategic peak (a great challenge)

险恶用心 **hsiěn-ò-yùng-hsīn** to have devious or evil intentions

⁹⁰⁸ 显著 **hsiěn-chù** evident, conspicuous, clear, notable, renowned

显而易见 **hsiěn-érh-ì-chièn** apparent

and easily seen (obvious)

显露 **hsiěn-lù** to reveal, show, unveil, manifest

显示 **hsiěn-shìh** to indicate, show, reveal

显微镜 **hsiěn-wēi-chìng** a microscope

显眼 **hsiěn-yěn** conspicuous, striking, eye-catching

hsièn (xiàn)

⁹⁰⁹ 县级 **hsièn-chí** the *hsien* [county] level

县志 **hsièn-chìh** a county gazetteer (local history and descriptive handbook)

县人民代表大会 **hsièn-jén-mín tài-piǎo-tà-huì** a *hsien* people's congress

县联社 **hsièn-lién-shè** a *hsien* federation of communes

县、社、队三级农机修造网 **hsièn-shè-tuì-sān-chí núng-chī hsiū-tsào-wǎng** the three-level network of county, commune, and brigade for the repair and manufacture of agricultural machinery

县委 **hsièn-wěi** a *hsien* Party committee

⁹¹⁰ 限制 **hsièn-chìh** to restrict, control, set limits on

限制战略核武器协议 **hsièn-chìh chàn-lüèh hó-wǔ-ch'ì hsiéh-ì** Agreement on the Limitation of Strategic Nuclear Weapons (SALT I, 1972)

限制军备 **hsièn-chìh chūn-pèi** arms restriction

限期 **hsièn-ch'ī** a time limit; to set a time limit

限额 **hsièn-ó** a norm, quota

限定 **hsièn-tìng** to set a limit, fix, specify

限度 **hsièn-tù** extent, limits, degree

⁹¹¹ 线索 **hsièn-sǒ** a clue, hint, indication

线图 **hsièn-t'ú** a clear diagram

⁹¹² 现金交易 **hsièn-chīn-chiāo-ì** cash payment

现状 **hsièn-chuàng** present conditions, as things are, status quo

现场 **hsièn-ch'ǎng** the present locality, here, on the spot, at the site

现场会议 **hsièn-ch'ǎng-huì-ì** on-the-spot conference [to solve a technical or production problem]

现成 **hsièn-ch'éng** immediately available, ready-made, at hand

现成饭 **hsièn-ch'éng-fàn** ready-made food (to enjoy the product of another's labor)

现成路 **hsièn-ch'éng-lù** a ready-made road (to follow others)

现出 **hsièn-ch'ū** to show, reveal, grow, manifest, make apparent

现汇交易 **hsièn-huì-chiāo-ì** trade conducted on a sight draft basis

现货交易 **hsièn-huò-chiāo-ì** over-the-counter trading

现象 **hsièn-hsiàng** a phenomenon; external appearances

现行 **hsièn-hsíng** existing, currently valid, in effect

现行反革命分子 **hsièn-hsíng fǎn-kó-mìng fèn-tzǔ** currently [active] counter-revolutionary elements

现役 **hsièn-ì** on active service [military]

现实主义 **hsièn-shíh-chǔ-ì** realism, pragmatism

现实主义广阔道路论 **hsièn-shíh-chǔ-ì kuǎng-k'uò-tào-lù lùn** the doctrine of the broad path of realism (the idea that writers should be free to go beyond the worker-peasant-soldier orientation so as to explore broader fields of creativity—one of the **hēi-pā-lùn**)

现实主义深化论 **hsièn-shíh-chǔ-ì shēn-huà lùn** the doctrine of the deepening of realism (the idea that writers should be able to develop their character's inner contradictions and painful transition from an individual to a collective society—one of the **hēi-pā-lùn**)

现实性 **hsièn-shíh-hsìng** actuality, reality, realistic

现实生活 **hsièn-shíh shēng-huó** actual life

现实条件 **hsièn-shíh t'iáo-chièn** actual conditions

现代剧 **hsièn-tài-chù** a modern play, contemporary drama

现代汉语 **hsièn-tài-hàn-yǔ** the contemporary [spoken and written] language of the Han people [of China]

现代化 **hsièn-tài-huà** to modernize, make up-to-date; modernization

现代戏 **hsièn-tài-hsì** contemporary dramas (dramas or operas with modern themes)

现代修正主义 **hsièn-tài hsiū-chèng-chǔ-ì** modern revisionism (the revisionism of Khrushchev and his successors)

现存 **hsièn-ts'ún** in stock, on hand, available, extant

现有 **hsièn-yǔ** existing, to have on hand, available

现原形 **hsièn-yuán-hsíng** to show one's original [ugly] form (to show one's true colors)

⁹¹³ 宪章 **hsièn-chāng** a charter, constitution, set of regulations

宪法 **hsièn-fǎ** a national constitution; constitutional law

宪兵 **hsièn-pīng** military police, gendarmerie

⁹¹⁴ 陷阱 **hsièn-chǐng** a trap, booby-trap, pitfall

陷害 **hsièn-hài** to entrap, harm by a false charge, slander

陷入窘境 **hsièn-jù-chiǔng-chìng** to be in a tight corner, get into an awkward position

陷入圈套 **hsièn-jù-ch'üān-t'ào** to fall into a trap

陷入危机 **hsièn-jù-wēi-chī** to fall into a crisis

陷于破产 **hsièn-yǔ-p'ò-ch'ǎn** to fall into bankruptcy

⁹¹⁵ 羡慕 **hsièn-mù** to envy, admire, cherish, crave, long for

⁹¹⁶ 献计 **hsièn-chì** to offer plans, present a scheme

献出生命 **hsièn-ch'ū shēng-mìng** to offer one's life (to sacrifice oneself)

献花 **hsièn-huā** to present flowers

献媚 **hsièn-mèi** to fawn upon, curry favor, cater to

献身 **hsièn-shēn** to devote oneself, dedicate one's life

hsīn (xīn)

⁹¹⁷ 心安理得 **hsīn-ān-lǐ-té** a mind at peace [because it is] in accord with reason (to have achieved perfect peace of mind)

心照不宣 **hsīn-chào-pù-hsuān** mutually understood but not expressed (tacit agreement)

心交给党 **hsīn chiāo-kěi tǎng** to give one's heart to the Party

心惊肉跳 **hsīn-chīng-jòu-t'iào** heart startled [and] flesh palpitating (apprehensive, terrified)

心惊胆战 **hsīn-chīng-tǎn-chàn** heart startled [and] gallbladder trembling (palpitating with anxiety, fearful)

心中最红最红的太阳 **hsīn-chūng tsuì-húng tsuì-húng te t'ài-yang** the reddest, most red sun in our heart (a reference to Mao Tse-tung)

心中无数 **hsīn-chūng-wú-shù** no numbers in one's mind (to lack a grasp of the situation)

心中有鬼 **hsīn-chūng-yǔ-kuěi** a demon in the heart (ulterior motives, a guilty conscience)

心中有数 **hsīn-chūng-yǔ-shù** the mind has the numbers (to have a realistic grasp of the situation)

心肠 **hsīn-ch'áng** the heart; emotions;

mood; intentions

心窍 **hsīn-ch'iào** the openings of the heart (intelligence, cunning, resourcefulness, etc.)

心情舒畅 **hsīn-ch'íng shū-ch'àng** one's mind at ease (in a good mood)

心服 **hsīn-fú** to have one's heart won, submit sincerely, be convinced

心花怒放 **hsīn-huā-nù-fàng** the mind's flower in full bloom (in a very happy mood, elated)

心怀鬼胎 **hsīn-huái-kuěi-t'āi** with an evil embryo in the heart (an evil scheme)

心红似火 **hsīn-húng-szù-huǒ** hearts as red as fire (enthusiastically loyal to the Party)

心红眼亮 **hsīn-húng-yěn-liàng** heart red and eyes bright (when the ideology [of the Party] has been mastered the eyes become clear)

心心相印 **hsīn-hsīn-hsiāng-yìn** to share the same feelings, with hearts completely in tune, complete rapport

心虚 **hsīn-hsū** nervous, fainthearted; to feel guilty

心血 **hsīn-hsuèh** brain-taxing labor, heartfelt labor, a labor of love, a sudden idea

心血来潮 **hsīn-hsuèh-lái-ch'áo** a thought suddenly fills the mind, to have a brain storm

心如油煎 **hsīn-jú-yú-chiēn** as if one's heart were being fried in oil (extremely anguishing)

心甘情愿 **hsīn-kān-ch'íng-yuàn** content and willing (cheerful compliance)

心隔心, 谈不拢 **hsīn-kó-hsīn, t'án-pù-lǔng** hearts are apart [and] talk cannot pull them together

心坎 **hsīn-k'ǎn** the bosom, heartstrings, innermost feelings; the chest

心劳日拙 **hsīn-láo-jíh-chō** to work hard [to achieve evil intentions but] be worse off day-by-day (to get nothing for one's pains)

心里亮堂 **hsīn-li-liàng-t'ang** the heart is clear, the mind is satisfied and at ease

心理 **hsīn-lǐ** mentality, thought and ideas, psychology

心理战争 **hsīn-lǐ-chàn-chēng** psychological warfare

心连心 **hsīn-lién-hsīn** heart linked to heart (affectionately)

心领神会 **hsīn-lǐng-shén-hùi** profound comprehension

心明眼亮 **hsīn-míng-yěn-liàng** heart bright and eyes clear (a clear ability to differentiate right and wrong)

心目中 **hsīn-mù-chūng** in one's mind or heart; to keep an eye on

心平气和 **hsīn-p'íng-ch'ì-hó** mind quiet and disposition peaceful (friendly feelings, an equable temperament)

心得 **hsīn-té** [what the] heart gains (a personal insight, an individual's understanding or discovery)

心地光明 **hsīn-tì-kuāng-míng** with conscience clear (pure-hearted, open-minded, innocent)

心贴心, 谈得亲 **hsīn-t'iēh-hsīn, t'án-té-ch'īn** heart close to heart and able to talk with intimacy

心脏地区 **hsīn-tsàng-tì-ch'ü** the heartland

心有余而力不足 **hsīn-yǔ-yú érh lì-pù-tsú** the heart has the wish but the strength is insufficient

心愿 **hsīn-yuàn** a wish; willing

心悦诚服 **hsīn-yuèh-ch'éng-fú** to accept sincerely, heartily concur

918 辛勤 **hsīn-ch'ín** arduous, laborious, hard-working, diligent

辛亥革命 **hsīn-hài kó-mìng** The Revolution in [the] Hsin-hai [year] (the 1911 revolution against the Manchu dynasty)

辛苦 **hsīn-k'ǔ** laborious, toilsome; hardship; a colloquial expression of appreciation for someone's work

辛迪加 **hsīn-tǐ-chiā** a syndicate (*phonetic rendition*)

919 欣喜鼓舞 **hsīn-hsǐ-kǔ-wǔ** to be happy and excited

欣喜欲狂 **hsīn-hsǐ-yù-k'uáng** to be beside oneself with joy

欣欣向荣 **hsīn-hsīn-hsiàng-júng** joyous reviving and coming into bloom [of trees after winter] (blossoming, prospering, flourishing)

欣赏 **hsīn-shǎng** to appreciate, admire, enjoy

920 锌矿 **hsīn-k'uàng** a zinc mine

921 新 **hsīn** the Sinkiang-Uighur Autonomous Region

新安江发电站 **hsīn-ān-chiāng fā-tièn-chàn** the hydroelectric generating plant on the Hsinan River [in Chekiang]

新账旧账一起算 **hsīn-chàng chiù-chàng ī-ch'ǐ suàn** to settle old accounts and new accounts at the same time (to evaluate the new, the old must also be taken into consideration)

新针疗法 **hsīn-chēn-liáo-fǎ** the new method of acupuncture

新纪元 **hsīn-chì-yuán** a new era, new age

142

新加坡 **hsīn-chiā-p'ō** Singapore

新疆军区 **hsīn-chiāng chūn-ch'ü** the Sinkiang Military Area [of the PLA]

新疆生产建设兵团 **hsīn-chiāng shēng-ch'ǎn chièn-shè pīng-t'uán** Sinkiang Production and Construction Army Group

新建设 **hsīn chièn-shè** (1) new construction; (2) *New Construction* (a Peking journal, monthly, 1949—)

新殖民主义 **hsīn-chíh-mín-chǔ-ì** the new colonialism, neo-colonialism (usually refers to the USSR and the USA)

新陈代谢 **hsīn-ch'én-tài-hsièh** (1) replacement of the old by the new; (2) metabolism

新奇 **hsīn-ch'í** new and strange, novel, interesting, peculiar

新青年 **hsīn-ch'īng-nién** *New Youth* (a prominent journal of the May Fourth period)

新飞跃 **hsīn-fēi-yuèh** a new flying leap (a renewed intensive production or ideological drive)

新风气 **hsīn-fēng-ch'ì** new atmosphere, new prevailing practice

新风俗 **hsīn-fēng-sú** new customs (one of the **szù-hsīn** in the Cultural Revolution)

新富农 **hsīn-fù-núng** new rich peasants

新合营公司 **hsīn hó-yíng-kūng-szū** new joint enterprises (established in 1965)

新华日报 **hsīn-huá-jìh-pào** *New China Daily* (Communist Party newspaper published in Chungking during the Sino-Japanese War)

新华半月刊 **hsīn-huá pàn-yuèh-k'ān** *New China Semi-Monthly* (Peking, 1949—)

新华社 **hsīn-huá-shè** the New China News Agency (the official news agency of the People's Republic of China—contraction of **Hsīn-hua t'ung-hsun-she**)

新华通讯社 **hsīn-huá t'ūng-hsùn-shè** the New China News Agency (the official Chinese news agency)

新习惯 **hsīn-hsí-kuàn** new habits (one of the **szù-hsīn** in the Cultural Revolution)

新西兰 **hsīn-hsī-lán** New Zealand

新鲜事物 **hsīn-hsiēn-shìh-wù** something new, new things (the connotation usually is that these are "good" things)

新现实主义 **hsīn-hsièn-shíh-chǔ-ì** neo-realism

新兴力量 **hsīn-hsīng-lì-liang** the newly emerging forces (the Third World)

新兴力量运动会 **hsīn-hsīng-lì-liang yùn-tùng-huì** the Games of the New Emerging Forces (GANEFO)

新兴事业 **hsīn-hsīng shìh-yèh** new undertakings, newly established enterprises

新兴地主阶级 **hsīn-hsīng tì-chǔ-chiēh-chí** newly emerging landlord class (referring to the Ch'in dynasty and the end of feudalism)

新型 **hsīn-hsíng** of a new pattern, type, mould, etc.

新型农民 **hsīn-hsíng-núng-mín** the new type of peasants

新型大学 **hsīn-hsíng-tà-hsuéh** the new type of university (with its curriculum designed to serve politics and production, including children of peasants and laborers, and having some teachers who are peasants, workers, or soldiers)

新型大学生 **hsīn-hsíng tà-hsuéh-shēng** the new type of university students (students who are also able to work with their hands and whose outlook enables them to unite with workers, peasants, and soldiers)

新修正主义 **hsīn hsiū-chèng-chǔ-ì** neo-revisionism (Soviet revisionism—as contrasted with Kautsky's)

新血液 **hsīn-hsuèh-yèh** new blood (figurative: the new generation)

新人新事 **hsīn-jén hsīn-shìh** new people and new things

新人辈出 **hsīn-jén-pèi-ch'ū** mass emergence of new people

新高潮 **hsīn-kāo-ch'áo** a new high tide

新官上任三把火 **hsīn-kuān shàng-jèn sān-pǎ-huǒ** when a new official takes his post three fires [are started] (a new incumbent gets things done, a new broom sweeps clean)

新观察 **hsīn kuān-ch'á** *New Observer* (a Peking journal, semi-monthly, 1950—)

新贵 **hsīn-kuèi** a newly appointed official; an upstart

新康德主义 **hsīn k'āng-té-chǔ-ì** neo-Kantism

新浪漫主义 **hsīn làng-màn-chǔ-ì** neo-romanticism (revolutionary romanticism)

新老干部结合 **hsīn-lǎo-kàn-pù chiéh-hó** the union of new and old cadres

新苗 **hsīn-miáo** new shoots, young sprouts

新民主义 **hsīn-mín-chǔ-chǔ-ì** new democracy; new democratic

新民主主义青年团 **hsīn-mín-chǔ chǔ-ì ch'īng-nién-t'uán** The [China] New

Democratic Youth League (name changed in 1957 to Communist Youth League)

新民主主义革命 **hsīn-mín-chǔ-chǔ-ì kó-mìng** the New Democratic Revolution (ending in 1949)

新民主主义论 **hsīn-mín-chǔ-chǔ-ì lùn** "On New Democracy" (a treatise by Mao, 1940)

新民学会 **hsīn-mín hsuéh-huì** The Society for Study [of How to Make a] New People (organized by Mao Tse-tung in Changsha in late 1917)

新三反 **hsīn-sān-fǎn** the New Three-Antis (a 1962 campaign with targets similar to the "old three-antis": corruption, waste, bureaucracy)

新三民主义 **hsīn-sān-mín-chǔ-ì** the new Sun Yat-sen-ism (Sun's Three Great Policies: alliance with the Soviet Union; acceptance of Communists into the Kuomintang; aid to the workers and peasants)

新沙皇 **hsīn-shā-huáng** the new tsars (the Soviet leaders)

新生 **hsīn-shēng** (1) rebirth, rejuvenation, resurrection; (2) new students; an entering class

新生儿 **hsīn-shēng-érh** something newly born (anything newly made, produced, or created)

新生一代 **hsīn-shēng-ī-tài** the new generation

新生力量 **hsīn-shēng-lì-liang** new forces, new rising forces, budding forces (usually refers to the younger members in any group or unit)

新生事物 **hsīn-shēng-shìh-wù** new born things (anything new, a new creation)

新时代 **hsīn shíh-tài** a new age, new era

新式农具 **hsīn-shìh núng-chù** improved farm implements, new-style farm implements

新式步犁 **hsīn-shìh pù-lí** new-style walking [animal drawn] plow

新事物 **hsīn-shìh-wù** new phenomena, new things

新手 **hsīn-shǒu** a new hand, newcomer, novice

新思潮 **hsīn-szū-ch'áo** new thought tide (new ideological trend, new current of thought)

新思想 **hsīn-szū-hsiǎng** new thought, new ideas

新四军 **hsīn-szù-chǖn** the New Fourth Army (Communist force operating in the Yangtze and Huai River valleys, 1938–45)

新德里 **hsīn-té-lǐ** New Delhi

新动向 **hsīn-tùng-hsiàng** a new trend

新文化 **hsīn-wén-huà** new culture (one of the **szù-hsīn** during the Cultural Revolution)

新文学 **hsīn-wén-hsuéh** new literature (literature of the May Fourth period)

新闻 **hsīn-wén** news (material reported in a newspaper, newscast, or periodical; news, information, reporting)

新闻记者 **hsīn-wén-chì-chě** news reporter, journalist, correspondent

新闻封锁 **hsīn-wén-fēng-sǒ** news blackout

新闻报导队伍 **hsīn-wén pào-tǎo tuì-wǔ** the news reporting ranks

新闻参赞 **hsīn-wén ts'ān-tsàn** press attaché, press counsellor

新五反 **hsīn-wǔ-fǎn** the New Five-Antis (a 1962 campaign against: speculation, corruption, smuggling, espionage, and cadres' impure work style)

新五篇 **hsīn-wǔ-p'iēn** the New Five Articles (five articles first listed as such by Mao Tse-tung in March 1967: (1) On the Rectification of Erroneous Thought in the Party [December 1929]; (2) To Oppose Liberalism [September 1937]; (3) Directives on the Reaffirmation of the "Three Main Rules of Discipline and Eight Points for Attention" [October 1947]; (4) On the Rectification of the Party Style [February 1942]; (5) The Work Methods of the Party Committee [March 1949])

新业 **hsīn-yèh** a new enterprise, new undertaking

新英雄主义 **hsīn-yīng-hsiúng-chǔ-ì** new heroism (the use in literature of revolutionary heroes)

新愚公 **hsīn yú-kūng** a new Yü-kung (Yü-kung was the "Foolish Old Man" in Mao's article—a reference here to the Chinese people)

922 薪给标准 **hsīn-chǐ piāo-chǔn** rates of salary payment, pay scales

薪金 **hsīn-chīn** firewood money (salary)

薪水 **hsīn-shui** [money for] firewood and water (salary)

薪炭林 **hsīn-t'àn-lín** a forest for firewood and charcoal

hsìn (xìn)

923 信奉 **hsìn-fèng** to believe in, reverence

信服 **hsìn-fú** to believe in, trust, admire, have confidence in

信号 **hsìn-hào** a signal [lamp, flag, etc.]
信号灯 **hsìn-hào-tēng** a signal lantern
信息论 **hsìn-hsī-lùn** cybernetics, information theory
信心百倍 **hsìn-hsìn-pǎi-pèi** full of confidence, overflowing with confidence, to have complete faith in
信义 **hsìn-ì** good faith, honesty
信任投票 **hsìn-jèn-t'óu-p'iào** a vote of confidence
信口开河 **hsìn-k'ǒu-k'āi-hó** to say whatever comes into one's mind (to talk irrelevantly and not to the point)
信口雌黄 **hsìn-k'ǒu-tz'ú-huáng** to talk recklessly and irresponsibly
信赖 **hsìn-lài** to trust, rely on
信念 **hsìn-nièn** faith, belief; a creed
信贷资金 **hsìn-tài tzū-chīn** credit funds, funds for extending credit
信条 **hsìn-t'iáo** a creed, code of beliefs, dogma
信托部 **hsìn-t'ō-pù** trust department [of a bank]
信徒 **hsìn-t'ú** a disciple, follower, believer
信仰自由 **hsìn-yǎng-tzù-yú** freedom of religious belief
信用 **hsìn-yùng** credit; trustworthiness, reputation
信用证 **hsìn-yùng-chèng** letter of credit
信用合作社 **hsìn-yùng hó-tsò-shè** a credit cooperative society

hsīng (xīng)

924 兴建 **hsīng-chièn** to build, raise, construct, establish
兴起 **hsīng-ch'ǐ** to spring up, rise in numbers, gain power; to establish, found, start
兴废 **hsīng-fèi** rise or fall, prosperity or decline, destiny
兴风作浪 **hsīng-fēng-tsò-làng** to raise a wind and make waves (to start trouble)
兴修水利 **hsīng-hsiū shuǐ-lì** to build irrigation works, construct water conservancy projects
兴利除弊 **hsīng-lì-ch'ú-pì** to promote the beneficial and eliminate the bad
兴灭国，继绝世，举逸民 **hsīng mièh-kuó, chì chüéh-shìh, chǔ ì-mín** to revive the vanquished states, restore broken lines of succession, and recall refugee people (a charge against Lin Piao that he was, in effect, trying to follow some of the policies of Confucian times)
兴盛 **hsīng-shèng** prosperous, thriving, vigorous, flourishing

兴旺 **hsīng-wàng** prosperous, thriving, flourishing
兴无灭资 **hsīng-wú-mièh-tzū** to foster proletarian [ideology] and liquidate bourgeois [ideology], to promote proletarian and eliminate bourgeois
兴妖作怪 **hsīng-yāo-tsò-kuài** to act in a malicious and disorderly way, to play the devil
兴 **hsīng**: see also **hsìng**
925 星际飞船 **hsīng-chì-fēi-ch'uán** interplanetary space ship
星际飞行 **hsīng-chì-fēi-hsíng** interplanetary flight
星际航行 **hsīng-chì-háng-hsíng** interplanetary navigation, space travel
星际空间 **hsīng-chì-k'ūng-chiēn** interplanetary space
星际旅行 **hsīng-chì-lǚ-hsíng** space travel, interplanetary travel
星洲 **hsīng-chōu** Singapore
星星之火，可以燎原 **hsīng-hsīng-chǐh-huǒ, k'ǒ-ǐ-liáo-yuán** a single spark can start a prairie fire (a small act can have great consequences)
星罗棋布 **hsīng-ló-ch'í-pù** scattered about like stars in the sky or pieces on a chessboard (many in number but widely spread)
星岛 **hsīng-tǎo** Singapore
星座 **hsīng-tsò** a constellation [of stars]
星云 **hsīng-yún** a nebula

hsíng (xíng)

926 刑罚 **hsíng-fá** penal, criminal; punishment, penalty
刑法 **hsíng-fǎ** criminal law, penal code
刑讯逼供 **hsíng-hsùn pī-kūng** to extort confession by torture
刑事 **hsíng-shìh** criminal, penal; a criminal case
刑事案 **hsíng-shìh-àn** a criminal case
927 行政 **hsíng-chèng** administration, government; administrative, executive; to administer, manage
行政机关 **hsíng-chèng-chī-kuān** an administrative agency or organ
行政区 **hsíng-chèng-ch'ǖ** administrative district
行政区划 **hsíng-chèng ch'ǖ-huà** administrative district demarcation
行政工作人员 **hsíng-chèng kūng-tsò-jén-yuán** administrative personnel
行政班子 **hsíng-chèng pān-tzu** an administrative staff or group
行政村 **hsíng-chèng-ts'ūn** an administrative village (may comprise several

small "natural" villages)

行之有效 **hsíng-chīh-yǔ-hsiào** carried out with positive result

行军 **hsíng-chūn** to march troops, lead an army, deploy forces

行军打仗 **hsíng-chūn-tǎ-chàng** marching and fighting

行贿 **hsíng-huì** bribery; to bribe

行凶 **hsíng-hsiūng** to commit a violent crime, murder, kill

行不顾言 **hsíng-pù-kù-yén** to act in disregard of one's words, say one thing and do another

行不通 **hsíng-pù-t'ūng** impractical, unfeasible, unworkable, blocked

行使 **hsíng-shǐh** to exercise [powers], use, employ, carry out

行署区 **hsíng-shǔ-ch'ü** administrative office district (a large unit between the province and county levels that replaced and expanded the "special districts" for a period in the early 1950s)

行动 **hsíng-tùng** to act, move; conduct, behavior, actions, movement

行动指南 **hsíng-tùng chǐh-nán** a guide to action

行动一致 **hsíng-tùng-ī-chìh** actions in accord, to act in unison

行动离线 **hsíng-tùng lí-hsièn** [one's] actions deviate from the [correct] line

行动自如 **hsíng-tùng-tzù-jú** to move freely; freedom of movement

行踪 **hsíng-tsūng** traces, footprints (a person's whereabouts)

行刺 **hsíng-tz'ù** to carry out assasination

行为 **hsíng-wéi** conduct, actions, behavior

行为主义 **hsíng-wéi-chǔ-ì** behaviorism

行 **hsíng**: see also **háng**

928 形成 **hsíng-ch'éng** to take shape, become, form, produce as a result

形而上学 **hsíng-érh-shàng-hsuéh** metaphysics; metaphysical

形而上学唯物主义 **hsíng-érh-shàng-hsuéh wéi-wù-chǔ-ì** metaphysical materialism

形象 **hsíng-hsiàng** form, appearance; a statue or portrait

形象的塑造 **hsíng-hsiàng te sù-tsào** the portrait of, an image

形形色色 **hsíng-hsíng-sè-sè** of all shapes and colors (great variety and diversity)

形式主义 **hsíng-shìh-chǔ-ì** formalism

形式逻辑 **hsíng-shìh ló-chí** formal logic

形式上开门, 思想上关门 **hsíng-shìh-shang k'āi-mén szū-hsiǎng-shang kuān-mén** in form an open door [but]

ideologically a closed door

形势 **hsíng-shìh** the situation, general trend, outlook; terrain, contours, geographical layout

形势教育 **hsíng-shìh-chiào-yǜ** current affairs education (usually does not refer to formal course work in schools, but rather to informational material used in study groups and units)

形势逼人 **hsíng-shìh-pī-jén** circumstances impel one [to make a decision, put forth effort, etc.]

形势大好 **hsíng-shìh tà-hǎo** the situation is excellent

形势倒转 **hsíng-shìh tào-chuǎn** the situation has turned around; a drastic change in conditions; the tide has turned

形态 **hsíng-t'ài** appearance, form, state, general condition; posture

形体 **hsíng-t'ǐ** a material body of a certain shape, corporeal [as contrasted to spiritual]

形左实右 **hsíng-tsǒ shíh-yù** left in form but right in essence, seemingly left but actually right

929 型钢 **hsíng-kāng** shaped steel

型类 **hsíng-lèi** types, patterns, models

hsǐng (xǐng)

930 醒目 **hsǐng-mù** refreshing to the eye, attractive-looking, eye-catching

醒悟 **hsǐng-wù** to awaken, come to realize, reform, come to one's sense

hsìng (xìng)

931 兴之所至 **hsìng-chīh-sǒ-chìh** to follow one's inclination

兴致冲冲 **hsìng-chìh-ch'ūng-ch'ūng** very much interested, full of enthusiasm; overflowing high spirits

兴趣 **hsìng-ch'ù** interest, eagerness, enthusiasm, willingness

兴高采烈 **hsìng-kāo-ts'ǎi-lièh** interest high and spirits vigorous (excited, full of enthusiasm)

兴 **hsìng**: see also **hsīng**

932 性急 **hsìng-chí** impetuous, impatient, impulsive, vehement

性质 **hsìng-chìh** property, characteristics, nature

性格 **hsìng-kó** disposition, personality, temperament, character

性能 **hsìng-néng** capabilities, fitness or capacity [for work]; potency [of drugs]

性别 **hsìng-piéh** sex, sexual differences

933 幸福账 **hsìng-fú-chàng** the account book of happiness (the blessings of the new society must not be taken for granted: they should be remembered and added up)

幸福院 **hsìng-fú-yuàn** a happiness courtyard (a residence for the aged)

幸亏 **hsìng-k'uēi** fortunately, happily, thanks to

幸免 **hsìng-miěn** a lucky escape

幸灾乐祸 **hsìng-tsāi-lè-huò** to rejoice in calamity and take pleasure in the misfortune [of others]

934 悻悻 **hsìng-hsìng** gruff, surly, angry

hsiū (xiū)

935 休战 **hsiū-chàn** a truce, armistice, cease-fire, cessation of hostilities

休整 **hsiū-chěng** to rest and regroup (originally military, now figurative)

休假 **hsiū-chià** to have a holiday, go on vacation; a holiday, furlough, leave

休戚相关 **hsiū-ch'ī-hsiāng-kuān** mutual concern in happiness and sorrow (a feeling of solidarity)

休戚与共 **hsiū-ch'ì-yǔ-kùng** sharing common good and bad fortune

休会 **hsiū-huì** to adjourn a meeting; adjournment, recess

休闲地 **hsiū-hsién-tì** fallow land

休克 **hsiū-k'ò** a shock (*phonetic transliteration*)

休养所 **hsiū-yǎng-sǒ** a rest home, sanitarium

936 修整 **hsiū-chěng** to repair, remodel, fix

修整一新 **hsiū-chěng-ī-hsīn** to repair like new

修整耕地 **hsiū-chěng kēng-tì** to level farmland

修正案 **hsiū-chèng-àn** an amendment, suggestion for revision

修正主义 **hsiū-chèng-chǔ-ì** revisionism [of Marx-Leninism] (now refers to the policies of the USSR)

修正主义路线 **hsiū-chèng-chǔ-ì lù-hsièn** the line of revisionism, the revisionist line

修正主义统治集团 **hsiū-chèng-chǔ-ì t'ǔng-chìh-chí-t'uán** the ruling clique of revisionism (the Soviet leaders)

修建 **hsiū-chièn** to repair and build, erect

修旧利废 **hsiū-chiù lì-fèi** to repair the old and make use of waste

修筑 **hsiū-chù** to build, construct, erect

修复 **hsiū-fù** to renovate, make as good as new, restore

修修补补 **hsiū-hsiū-pǔ-pǔ** to repair and patch (a patchwork job; reformism—

as opposed to revolution)

修改党章 **hsiū-kǎi tǎng-chāng** revision of the Party Cons;itution

修理性行业 **hsiū-lǐ-hsìng háng-yèh** repairing ;rades

修补服务单位 **hsiū-pǔ fú-wù tān-wèi** repair service units (often neighborhood, or in factories)

修配厂 **hsiū-p'èi-ch'ǎng** a repair shop

修大寨田 **hsiū tà-chài-t'ién** to build Ta-chai [type of terraced] fields

修订 **hsiū-tìng** to edit and revise, amend

修梯田 **hsiū t'ī-t'ién** to build terraced fields

修造结合原则 **hsiū-tsào-chiéh-hó yuán-tsé** the principle of coordinating repair and manufacturing (equal emphasis should be given to servicing and repair)

修养 **hsiū-yǎng** (1) to seek perfection through study; moral nature as a result of training; self-cultivation; self-discipline; (2) a contracted form of reference to Liu Shao-ch'i's book **Lùn kùng-ch'ǎn-tǎng te hsiū-yǎng**)

937 羞耻 **hsiū-ch'ǐh** a sense of shame

羞辱 **hsiū-jǔ** to shame, insult, disgrace

hsiǔ (xiǔ)

938 朽木粪土 **hsiǔ-mù-fèn-t'ǔ** rotten wood and filth (a person beyond redemption, a useless thing)

朽木不可雕 **hsiǔ-mù pù-k'ǒ-tiāo** ro;ten wood cannot be carved (something useless and unsalvageable)

hsiù (xiù)

939 绣花 **hsiù-huā** embroidery, embroidered

940 袖手旁观 **hsiù-shǒu p'áng-kuān** to look on with hands in one's sleeves (to be unconcerned with the task at hand, be unmindful of another's need)

941 嗅觉不灵 **hsiù-chüéh-pù-líng** one's sense of smell is not keen (usually has a political connotation)

hsiūng (xiōng)

942 凶悍不化 **hsiūng-hàn-pù-huà** incorrigibly evil and violent

凶相毕露 **hsiūng-hsiàng-pì-lù** to bare one's ferocious features

凶猛 **hsiūng-měng** fierce, brutish, violent

凶年 **hsiūng-nién** a year of bad crops

凶恶 **hsiūng-ò** ferocious, brutish, violent

凶暴 **hsiūng-pào** cruel, brutal, vindictive, ruthless

凶焰万丈 **hsiūng-yèn-wàn-chàng** the fierce flames leap high

943 兄弟 **hsiūng-tì** brother, brothers (now used figuratively in the broadest sense of fraternal)

兄弟关系 **hsiūng-tì-kuān-hsi** brotherhood, fraternal relations

兄弟国家 **hsiūng-tì-kuó-chiā** fraternal countries

兄弟民族 **hsiūng-tì-mín-tsú** fraternal peoples (refers to the ethnic minorities in China)

兄弟单位 **hsiūng-tì-tān-wèi** fraternal units (usually neighboring organizational units)

兄弟党 **hsiūng-tì-tǎng** fraternal parties (parties in the same political camp or supporting each other)

兄弟组织 **hsiūng-tì-tsǔ-chíh** fraternal organizations (parties or associations friendly to the CCP

944 匈牙利 **hsiūng-yá-lì** Hungary

945 汹涌 **hsiūng-yǔng** turbulent, dashing [waters or waves]

汹涌澎湃 **hsiūng-yǔng-p'ēng-p'ài** rushing of water and roaring of waves (tumultuous)

946 胸中无数 **hsiūng-chūng-wú-shù** to have no numbers in one's bosom (to be without any clear grasp of a situation)

胸中有数 **hsiūng-chūng-yǔ-shù** to have numbers in one's bosom (to have a good grasp of a situation)

胸怀全局 **hsiūng-huái-ch'üán-chú** to keep the whole situation in mind

胸怀大志 **hsiūng-huái tà-chìh** to cherish a great ambition

胸怀祖国 **hsiūng-huái tsǔ-kuó** to keep the fatherland close to one's heart

胸无成竹 **hsiūng-wú-ch'éng-chú** without a perfect bamboo in one's mind (to start something without thinking it through; without a careful plan)

胸有全局 **hsiūng-yǔ-ch'üán-chú** to have the overall interest in mind

胸有百万雄兵 **hsiūng-yǔ pǎi-wàn hsiúng-pīng** *A Million Valiant Soldiers in His Bosom* (the title of a book by Mao Tse-tung's old bodyguard—referring to Mao as a great strategist and leader)

hsiúng (xióng)

947 雄纠纠 **hsiúng-chiū-chiū** imposing,

looking brave and resolute, strong and handsome

雄厚 **hsiúng-hòu** strong and solid (ample, powerful)

雄心壮志 **hsiúng-hsīn-chuàng-chìh** heroic heart and high ambitions

雄心勃勃 **hsiúng-hsīn-pó-pó** an overwhelmingly manly spirit (zealous, very ambitious)

雄辩 **hsiúng-pièn** eloquence of speech; forceful debate

雄才大略 **hsiúng-ts'ái-tà-luèh** a brave talent and a great strategist

雄伟 **hsiúng-wěi** stately, magnificent, impressive, majestic, strong, able

雄文四卷 **hsiúng-wén-szù-chüàn** four great volumes (the four volumes of Mao Tse-tung's *Selected Works*)

948 熊熊烈火 **hsiúng-hsiúng-lièh-huǒ** fiercely blazing fire

熊猫 **hsiúng-māo** the panda

hsū (xū)

949 须知 **hsū-chīh** it should be understood, one should know [that]

950 虚假 **hsū-chiǎ** false, deceitful, hypocritical; void, empty

虚张声势 **hsū-chāng-shēng-shìh** to make a deceptive show of force

虚惊 **hsū-chīng** a false alarm

虚怀若谷 **hsū-huái-jò-kǔ** a modest heart as open as a valley (very modest; free of pride and prejudice)

虚心使人进步, 骄傲使人落后 **hsū-hsīn shìh-jén chìn-pù, chiāo-ào shìh-jén lò-hòu** modesty helps a person to progress [whereas] conceit makes a person lag behind

虚弱本质 **hsū-jò-pěn-chìh** inherent weakness

虚弱无力 **hsū-jò wú-lì** weak and powerless

虚荣 **hsū-júng** vanity, vainglory

虚构 **hsū-kòu** to fabricate, trump up

虚夸 **hsū-k'uā** empty boasting, bragging, puffery

虚名 **hsū-míng** an empty reputation

虚报 **hsū-pào** a false report; to report untruthfully

虚评妄说 **hsū-p'íng-wàng-shuō** false criticisms and reckless talk

虚设 **hsū-shè** a nominal [position or title]; to exist in name only

虚伪 **hsū-wěi** spurious, false, hypocritical, insincere; hypocrisy

虚无主义 **hsū-wú-chǔ-ì** nihilism

虚无飘渺 **hsū-wú-p'iāo-miǎo** shapeless and elusive, floating and intangible (utterly visionary, lacking in reality)

虚与委蛇 **hsū-yǔ-wēi-í** to feign civility, pretend sympathy

951 嘘寒问暖 **hsū-hán-wèn-nuǎn** breathing on the cold and asking about the hot (to show great concern for the well-being of others)

hsǔ (xǔ)

952 许可证 **hsǔ-k'ǒ-chèng** a permit, license

许诺 **hsǔ-nò** to promise, consent, pledge

hsù (xù)

953 旭日东升 **hsù-jìh-tūng-shēng** the morning sun rises in the east (the vigor of youth)

954 序曲 **hsù-ch'ǔ** a musical overture (may also be overture in a broad sense)

序幕 **hsù-mù** a prologue, curtain raiser (beginning)

序言 **hsù-yén** introduction, preface, foreword, preamble

955 叙利亚 **hsù-lì-yǎ** Syria

叙述 **hsù-shù** to narrate, recount, state; a narration, account

956 畜牧区 **hsù-mù-ch'ǔ** pastoral area

畜牧兽医站 **hsù-mù shòu-ī-chàn** animal husbandry and veterinary stations

畜牧业 **hsù-mù-yèh** animal husbandry

畜 **hsù**: see also **ch'ù**

957 绪言 **hsù-yén** a preamble, foreword, preface

958 续篇 **hsù-piēn** a sequel [to an essay or a book]

959 絮棉 **hsù-mién** cotton wadding, quilting

960 蓄洪区 **hsù-húng-ch'ǔ** water retention basin, flood diversion area

蓄洪工程 **hsù-húng-kūng-ch'éng** flood storage, water detention project

蓄洪量 **hsù-húng-liàng** flood storage capacity

蓄意已久 **hsù-ì-ǐ-chiǔ** to have cherished an intention for a long time; long hoped for

hsuān (xuān)

961 宣战 **hsuān-chàn** to declare war

宣称 **hsuān-ch'ēng** to declare, announce, affirm, state, claim

宣传 **hsuān-ch'uán** to publicize, promote, carry on propaganda; propaganda, publicity, promotion

宣传工具 **hsuān-ch'uán-kūng-chù** publicity instruments, propaganda tools

宣传队 **hsuān-ch'uán-tuì** propaganda team

宣告 **hsuān-kào** to announce, declare, pronounce; an announcement

宣布 **hsuān-pù** to announce, declare, proclaim, promulgate

宣判 **hsuān-p'àn** to pronounce judgment, pass sentence

宣誓 **hsuān-shìh** to take a public oath, pledge, declare solemnly

宣读 **hsuān-tú** to read out in public, lecture

宣扬 **hsuān-yáng** to publicize, circulate, disseminate, spread

宣言 **hsuān-yén** a proclamation, manifesto, declaration, public statement, communique

962 喧哗 **hsuān-huá** noise [of a crowd], clamor, tumult, uproar

喧嚣一时 **hsuān-hsiāo-ī-shíh** irritatingly noisy for a time

喧宾夺主 **hsuān-pīn-tó-chǔ** the noisy guest usurps the place of the host (secondary things take the place of the important)

hsuán (xuán)

963 玄虚 **hsuán-hsū** abstruse, mystical, spurious, without substance; cunning schemes, evil tricks

玄学 **hsuán-hsuéh** metaphysics, mysticism

964 旋转 **hsuán-chuǎn** to revolve, turn round and round; rotation

旋转乾坤 **hsuán-chuǎn-ch'ién-k'ūn** to revolve heaven and turn earth (to reform the world, conquer nature)

旋律 **hsuán-lù** rhythm, cadence, melodic form

旋 **hsuán**: see also **hsuàn**

965 悬案 **hsuán-àn** a pending case, unresolved question, unsettled issue

悬而未决 **hsuán-érh-wèi-chüéh** pending and not yet settled, outstanding, left over

悬念 **hsuán-nièn** to think of [in one's absence], concerned about, in suspense, worried for

悬赏 **hsuán-shǎng** to offer a reward [for the capture or return of]

悬殊 **hsuán-shū** to differ by a large margin, very different; disparity, unevenness

悬崖勒马 **hsuán-yá-lè-mǎ** to rein in one's horse on the brink of a precipice (to realize a great danger just in time)

966 漩涡 **hsuán-wō** a whirlpool, eddy (a dispute, quarrel; a dangerous situation)

hsuǎn (xuǎn)

967　选集　**hsuǎn-chí** selected works, anthology

选种　**hsuǎn-chǔng** to select seeds; seed improvement

选种机　**hsuǎn-chǔng-chī** seed sorter, seed grader

选种浸种　**hsuǎn-chǔng chìn-chǔng** to select and soak seeds

选举　**hsuǎn-chǔ** to elect, vote; elections

选举权　**hsuǎn-chǔ-ch'üán** the right to vote, franchise, suffrage

选举法　**hsuǎn-chǔ-fǎ** laws governing elections

选举委员会　**hsuǎn-chǔ wěi-yuán-huì** election committees

选译　**hsuǎn-ì** to select and translate

选购　**hsuǎn-kòu** selective purchasing

选矿厂　**hsuǎn-k'uàng-ch'ǎng** ore dressing plant

选民　**hsuǎn-mín** voters, citizens eligible to vote, electorate

选民区　**hsuǎn-mín-ch'ǚ** an electoral constituency

选民登记　**hsuǎn-mín-tēng-chì** registration of voters

选拔　**hsuǎn-pá** to select [men], to pick out from a group, choose

选拔干部　**hsuǎn-pá kàn-pù** to select cadres [for advancement]

选拔赛　**hsuǎn-pá-sài** preliminary [selective] competition, trial heats

选派　**hsuǎn-p'ài** to select and send, nominate

选票　**hsuǎn-p'iào** a ballot

选手　**hsuǎn-shǒu** a selected contestant, team member

选送　**hsuǎn-sùng** to select and send [to school or for training]

选调　**hsuǎn-tiào** to select and transfer [in connection with work or duties]

选读　**hsuǎn-tú** selected readings

选段　**hsuǎn-tuàn** a selected piece, a song or aria from a larger work

选择　**hsuǎn-tsé** to select, choose, elect; a choice

选样　**hsuǎn-yàng** to sample; sampling

选用　**hsuǎn-yùng** to select and appoint [to a post]

hsuàn (xuàn)

968　炫耀　**hsuàn-yào** dazzling, beaming, radiant; to show off, flaunt

炫耀武力　**hsuàn-yào-wǔ-lì** to make a show of force

969　旋风　**hsuàn-fēng** a whirlwind, cyclone

旋工　**hsuàn-kūng** a lathe operator

旋　**hsuàn**: see also **hsuán**

970　渲染　**hsuàn-jǎn** to add touches of color (to enhance or distort by adding [fanciful] details)

hsuēh (xuē)

971　削弱　**hsuēh-jò** to weaken, enfeeble, devitalize

削足适履　**hsuēh-tsú-shìh-lǔ** to cut the foot to fit the shoe (procrustean methods)

削　**hsuēh**: see also **hsiāo**

hsuéh (xué)

972　学者　**hsuéh-chě** scholar (sometimes pejorative for pedants or bourgeois intellectuals)

学着干　**hsuéh-che-kàn** learning and doing at the same time, do while learning

学制　**hsuéh-chìh** the educational system (as the number of years in elementary and middle school, etc.)

学制改革　**hsuéh-chìh-kǎi-kó** reform of the educational system

学究　**hsuéh-chiū** a pedant, a man of limited knowledge

学成文武艺, 货与帝王家　**hsuéh-ch'éng wén-wǔ-ì, huò-yǔ tì-wáng-chiā** to master the civil and military arts in order to sell them to the imperial family (a criticism of the old idea that one studied in order to become an official)

学而不厌　**hsuéh-érh-pù-yèn** to be insatiable in learning

学而优则仕　**hsuéh-érh-yū tsé-shìh** [when one has] achieved excellence in studies one becomes an official (an old idea now criticized)

学阀　**hsuéh-fá** scholar-lords (the academic establishment—the comparison is to the warlords)

学风　**hsuéh-fēng** style of study (one of the **sān-fēng**)

学好用好　**hsuéh-hǎo yùng-hǎo** study well [and] apply well

学会　**hsuéh-huì** (1) an academic association, learned society; (2) a study group; (3) to learn a skill, master a subject

学会数理化, 走遍天下都不怕　**hsuéh-huì shù-lǐ-huà, tsǒu-p'ièn-t'iēn-hsià tōu-pù-p'à** when [I] have mastered mathematics, physics, and chemistry, [I] will not have to worry about holding down a job anywhere in the world (the tendency of many people to concentrate on technical excellence

but to avoid politics)

学习 **hsuéh-hsí** (1) to learn and review, study persistently, study and practice (in addition to school study, the term now applies to study of Party ideology, the Thought of Mao Tse-tung, etc.); (2) *Study* (a Peking semimonthly journal, 1949–58)

学习经验 **hsuéh-hsí chǐng-yèn** experience in study, method of study

学习小组 **hsuéh-hsi-hsiǎo-tsǔ** small study groups [within a unit]

学习先进经验 **hsuéh-hsí hsiēn-chìn-chǐng-yèn** to study and review advanced experiences

学习劳动英雄运动 **hsuéh-hsí láo-tùng-yīng-hsiúng yùn-tùng** the Emulation of Labor Heroes Movement (1943)

学习雷锋 **hsuéh-hsí léi-fēng** to learn from Lei Feng (*see* **léi fēng**)

学习路子 **hsuéh-hsí lù-tzu** the learning road (the method of learning)

学习班 **hsuéh-hsí-pān** a study group (usually a short-term group)

学习十大文件 **hsuéh-hsí shíh-tà wén-chièn** study the [CCP] Tenth Congress documents

学习铁人王进喜 **hsuéh-hsí t'iěh-jén wáng chìn-hsǐ** learn from the ironman Wang Chin-hsi (Wang was an oil driller and labor-hero from the Tach'ing oil field)

学习与批判 **hsuéh-hsí yǔ p'ī-p'àn** *Study and Criticism* (a Shanghai monthly journal, October 1973—)

学校教育 **hsuéh-hsiào-chiào-yù** school education, formal education

学校课堂与社会课堂 **hsuéh-hsiào-k'ò-t'áng yǔ shè-huì-k'ò-t'áng** the classroom in the school and the classroom in society (learning must not be confined to the school)

学校办工厂, 工厂办学校 **hsuéh-hsiào pàn kūng-ch'ǎng, kūng-ch'ǎng pàn hsuéh-hsiào** schools operate factories [and] factories operate schools

学先进 **hsuéh-hsiēn-chin** to learn from the advanced

学衔 **hsuéh-hsién** an academic title

学以致用 **hsuéh-ǐ-chìh-yùng** to learn in order to practice

学工学农学军 **hsuéh-kūng hsuéh-núng hsuéh-chūn** learn to work, farm, and soldier (responsibilities for students in addition to studying books)

学科 **hsuéh-k'ō** a subject or field of learning, a branch of study

学理 **hsuéh-lǐ** a [scientific] theory, explanation of scientific truth

学龄 **hsuéh-líng** of school age

学龄前儿童教育 **hsuéh-líng-ch'ién érh-t'úng chiào-yù** [teacher training courses in] preschool education; preschool or kindergarten education

学农基地 **hsuéh-núng-chī-tì** a location for agricultural study (an urban organization will normally have a rural base or site for agricultural work and training)

学, 摆, 分, 批, 改 **hsuéh, pǎi, fēn, p'ī, kǎi** to study [the policy and line], display [the facts], analyze [problems], criticize [defects], and reform [one's work] (the whole process of "line education")

学派 **hsuéh-p'ài** a school of thought

学深学透 **hsuéh-shēn-hsuéh-t'òu** to study deeply and thoroughly

学生运动 **hsuéh-shēng yùn-tùng** a student movement

学术 **hsuéh-shù** scholarship, learning; academic

学术权威 **hsuéh-shù ch'üán-wēi** academic authorities

学说 **hsuéh-shuō** a theory, doctrine, school of thought

学大寨 **hsuéh tà-chài** learn from Tachai [a famous production brigade in Shansi]

学大寨赶昔阳 **hsuéh tà-chài kǎn hsī-yáng** learn from Tachai, catch up with Hsiyang (Hsiyang is the *hsien* in which Tachai Production Brigade is located)

学到手 **hsuéh-tào-shǒu** to learn to hand (to learn a skill thoroughly and practically)

学得活用得上 **hsuéh-te-huó yùng-te-shàng** when study has been in a living way it will be usable; one should study in a living way and apply it practically

学懂弄通 **hsuéh-tǔng nùng-t'ūng** learn to understand and to master completely

学徒 **hsuéh-t'ú** an apprentice; pupil, student

学通 **hsuéh-t'ūng** to master completely

学王杰 **hsuéh wáng chiéh** to learn from Wang Chieh (a PLA exemplary hero)

学位 **hsuéh-wèi** academic degree

学员 **hsuéh-yuán** a student (usually a student who has worked as a farmer, worker, or in the PLA and has been chosen by his unit to attend college or university)

学院 **hsuéh-yuàn** an academic institute, college [in a university]

学院派 **hsuéh-yuàn-p'ài** scholastic schools, academic factions

学用结合 **hsuéh-yùng-chiéh-hó** to combine study and use

学用一致 **hsuéh-yùng-ī-chìh** the unity of study and use

学用会 **hsuéh-yùng-huì** a learning and application meeting (a meeting devoted to learning and applying the works and thought of Mao)

hsuĕh (xuĕ)

973　雪中送炭 **hsuĕh-chūng-sùng-t'àn** to send charcoal during snow (timely assistance)

雪耻 **hsuĕh-ch'īh** to wipe out a shame, avenge an insult

雪恨 **hsuĕh-hèn** to avenge a wrong, work out a grudge, get even with an enemy

雪亮 **hsuéh-liàng** crystal clear

雪灾 **hsuĕh-tsāi** a snow disaster, blizzard

雪冤 **hsuĕh-yuān** to clear of a false charge, vindicate oneself

hsuèh (xuè)

974　血案 **hsuèh-àn** a case involving blood (a murder case, homicide)

血债 **hsuèh-chài** a blood debt (a heinous crime)

血债血来还 **hsuèh-chài hsuèh-lái-huán** to demand blood for blood, make someone pay in blood for blood

血债累累 **hsuèh-chài-lĕi-lĕi** bloody crimes

血迹 **hsuèh-chì** bloodstains

血防区 **hsuèh-fáng-ch'ü̆** schistosomiasis prevention area

血汗 **hsuèh-hàn** blood and sweat

血吸虫病 **hsuèh-hsī-ch'úng-pìng** schistosomiasis, "snail fever," "liver fluke"

血洗 **hsuèh-hsī** a blood baptism, slaughter, massacre

血腥镇压 **hsuèh-hsīng-chèn-yā** bloody suppression

血肉 **hsuèh-jòu** blood and flesh

血肉相关 **hsuèh-jòu-hsiāng-kuān** blood and flesh relationship; to be closely related

血肉相连 **hsuèh-jòu-hsiāng-lién** mutually linked like flesh and blood, bound by the ties of flesh and blood

血肉关系 **hsuèh-jòu-kuān-hsi** flesh and blood relationship (may be figurative, e.g., relationship between the Party and the masses)

血泪斑斑 **hsuèh-lèi pān-pān** the stains of blood and tears (the sufferings of the poorer classes in the old society)

血淋淋 **hsuèh-lín-lín** blood dripping, sanguinary

血泊 **hsuèh-p'ò** a pool of blood

血丝虫病 **hsuèh-szū-ch'úng-pìng** filariasis

血统 **hsuèh-t'ŭng** the blood line, blood relationship, consanguinity

血统论 **hsuèh-t'ŭng lùn** the theory of blood line [determining class] (a doctrine now criticized)

血压 **hsuèh-yā** blood pressure

血 **hsuèh**: see also **hsiĕh**

hsūn (xūn)

975　勋章 **hsūn-chāng** a medal of honor, decoration, order

hsún (xún)

976　巡回辅导队 **hsún-huí fŭ-tăo-tuì** a circulating team to provide assistance and guidance

巡回医疗队 **hsún-huí-ī-liáo-tuì** medical patrol teams (circulating experts who go to suburban hospitals for fixed-term duties)

巡逻 **hsún-ló** to patrol; a patrol

巡逻警戒 **hsún-ló chǐng-chièh** to patrol on an alert basis

巡视 **hsún-shìh** a tour of inspection; to go around and inspect

巡洋舰 **hsún-yáng-chièn** a cruiser [naval]

巡游 **hsún-yú** to patrol; make an inspection tour

977　寻章摘句 **hsún-chāng-chāi-chù** to look for quotes and pluck sentences (to write pedantically and without creativity)

寻求 **hsún-ch'iú** to seek, try to get

978　驯服 **hsún-fú** to tame, subdue; subdued, obedient

驯服工具 **hsún-fú-kūng-chù** a docile tool [of the Party]

驯服工具论 **hsún-fú-kūng-chù lùn** the doctrine of docile instruments (the accusation that Liu Shao-ch'i said that Party members should be no more than docile instruments)

979　询问 **hsún-wèn** to inquire about, ask for, query, interrogate

980　循环 **hsún-huán** to come around in order, move in a cycle; circulation, rotation; cyclical

循环不息 **hsún-huán-pù-hsī** in unending succession, cyclically recurrent

循环往复 **hsún-huán-wăng-fù** cyclical repetition

循序渐进 **hsún-hsù-chièn-chìn** to follow in proper sequence and make gradual progress

循规蹈矩 **hsún-kuēi tǎo-chǔ** to observe all rules and regulations (law-abiding, quiet and well-behaved)

循此继进 **hsún-tz'ǔ-chì-chìn** to follow this [line] and continue to advance

hsùn (xùn)

981 训练 **hsùn-lièn** to train, instruct, discipline; training, drill

训练总监部 **hsùn-lièn tsǔng-chiēn-pù** General Supervisory Department of Military Training

训令 **hsùn-lìng** to order, command; instruction, order, command

982 汛期 **hsùn-ch'ī** the flood period, yearly flood

983 迅速 **hsùn-sù** fast, rapid, quick

984 徇私 **hsùn-szū** to profit oneself; favoritism, nepotism

985 殉国 **hsùn-kuó** to die for one's country

殉葬 **hsùn-tsàng** to bury the living with the dead (may be people, animals, or objects)

殉葬品 **hsùn-tsàng-p'ǐn** funerary objects, burial objects

ī (yī)

986 一张一弛 **ī-chāng ī-ch'íh** alternating between tension and relaxation (a fluid, changing situation)

一张考卷定终身 **ī-chāng-k'ǎo-chüàn tìng-chūng-shēn** a single examination paper determines one's whole life (the folly of excessive reliance on formal examinations)

一长制 **ī-chǎng-chìh** single-director system, one-man management

一着不慎满盘皆输 **ī-chāo-pù-shèn mǎn-p'án-chiēh-shū** a single careless move and the entire game is lost

一朝一夕 **ī-chāo ī-hsī** one dawn and one evening, a day (a short time)

一针见血 **ī-chēn-chièn-hsuèh** one [prick of the] needle brings blood (to come right to the point of the matter)

一枕黄粱 **ī-chěn-huáng-liáng** a pillow [dream] of millet (empty dreams)

一整套 **ī-chěng-t'ào** a complete set [of equipment or ideas]

一级军区 **ī-chí-chǔn-ch'ǔ** first-level military command (the highest level —the Peking Military Command)

一级行政区 **ī-chí hsíng-chèng-ch'ǔ** first-level administrative areas (including 22 provinces, 4 autonomous regions, and 3 municipalities)

一记耳光 **ī-chì-ěrh-kuāng** a slap [on the ear or face]

一技之长 **ī-chì-chīh-ch'áng** useful in some kind of work, having some strong points, a master of one technique

一家观 **ī-chiā-kuān** a one-family viewpoint (a narrow and selfish, individualistic viewpoint)

一脚踢开 **ī-chiǎo t'ī-k'āi** to kick aside abruptly (to discard something after having derived the benefit from it)

一箭双雕 **ī-chièn-shuāng-tiāo** to kill two birds with one arrow

一知半解 **ī-chīh-pàn-chiěh** a bit of knowledge half understood (a smattering; half-baked)

一纸空文 **ī-chǐh-k'ūng-wén** an empty document, dead letter

一致 **ī-chìh** unanimous, unitedly, one and all, in agreement, as one

一致对外 **ī-chìh tuì-wài** united against foreign [aggression, threats, etc.]

一祝二唱三读 **ī-chù èrh-ch'àng sān-tú** first, wish; second, sing; third, read (a public meeting should open by wishing Chairman Mao a long life, singing "Sailing the Seas Depends on the Helmsman," and then reading some quotations)

一抓就灵 **ī-chuā-chiù-líng** once [the policy, etc.] is grasped, miracles will follow

一抓三促 **ī-chuā-sān-ts'ù** one grasp and three pushes (grasp revolution; push production, one's tasks, and [war] preparedness)

一专多能 **ī-chuān-tō-néng** one specialty and many skills (mastering many skills while specializing in one)

一茬 **ī-ch'á** one crop; single cropping

一刹那 **ī-ch'à-nà** an instant, moment, twinkling

一场战斗一堂课，一次总结一层楼 **ī-ch'ǎng-chàn-tòu ī-t'áng-k'ò, ī-tz'ù-tsǔng-chiéh ī-ts'éng-lóu** one field of combat, one period of a class, one summing-up, [move up] one story (the process of advancement in ideology or technique through struggle, criticism and analysis)

一唱一和 **ī-ch'àng ī-hò** one singing and the other echoing, a duet (usually with a bad connotation—the person echoing is responding to subversive or incorrect leadership)

一成不变 **ī-ch'éng-pù-pièn** once formed and never changed (rigidly inflexible)

一气呵成 **ī-ch'ì-hō-ch'éng** to complete

in one breath (to carry through without break or interruption)

一窍不通 ī-ch'iào-pù-t'ūng not a single one of the sensory orifices is open (completely ignorant)

一切归公 ī-ch'ièh-kuēi-kūng everything belongs to the public

一前一后 ī-ch'ién ī-hòu one before and one after

一钱不值 ī-ch'ién-pù-chíh not worth a [single] cash

一清二楚 ī-ch'īng-èrh-ch'ǔ perfectly clear

一丘之貉 ī-ch'iu-chīh-hó badgers of the same mound (of the same ilk—derogatory)

一穷二白 ī-ch'iúng èrh-pái first poor and second blank, economically poor and culturally blank (a phrase used by Mao in 1958 to indicate that China is not developed economically and is like blank paper on which the new can be written)

一戳就穿 ī-ch'ō-chiù-ch'uān can be punctured with a mere stroke (can easily be exposed)

一筹莫展 ī-ch'óu-mò-chǎn not a single plan can be unfolded (none of one's plans or intentions can be realized)

一触即发 ī-ch'ù-chí-fā a [single] touch will release [the arrow] (a tense situation in which any incident may touch off hostilities)

一举成名 ī-chǔ ch'éng-míng one action makes one's name (to become famous overnight)

一举消灭 ī-chǔ-hsiāo-mièh to wipe out at one stroke

一举数得 ī-chǔ-shù-té one action with many gains

一去不复返 ī-ch'ù pù-fù-fǎn once gone [it can] never come back (such as the old society)

一二九运动 ī-èrh-chiǔ yùn-tùng the December 9 Movement (the student movement which began in Peking on December 9, 1935, to end further concessions to Japan)

一二三制 ī-èrh-sān chìh the one-two-three system (cadres spend one day a week studying, two days at meetings, and three days in work)

一发千钧 ī-fà-ch'iēn-chūn 30,000 catties hanging by a single hair (an extremely critical situation)

一帆风顺 ī-fān-fēng-shùn sails filled with a following wind (proceeding smoothly without hindrance or obstruction)

一反了事 ī-fǎn-liǎo-shìh one opposition and no more (brief opposition without a follow-through is not enough)

一放到底 ī-fàng-tào-tǐ transferred all the way to the bottom

一飞冲天 ī-fēi-ch'ūng-t'iēn as soon as flight starts it soars to the sky (quick success)

一分为二 ī-fēn-wéi-èrh one divides into two (Mao's theory of contradiction: a method of analysis in dialectical materialism with special reference to the inevitability of class struggle)

一风吹 ī-fēng-ch'uī blown by the same wind (to deal with indiscriminately)

一夫一妻制 ī-fū ī-ch'ī chìh monogamy

一好带四好，四好为一好 ī-hǎo tài szŭ-hǎo, szŭ-hǎo wèi ī-hǎo one good carries with it the other four goods; the four goods are for the attainment of the first good (refers to the qualifications of the "five-good" worker: (1) political work; (2) three-eight work style; (3) enterprise management; (4) managing one's livelihood; (5) implementing plans)

一呼百应 ī-hū-pǎi-yìng one person shouts and a hundred respond (widespread favorable response)

一户一猪 ī-hù-ī-chū one household one pig (each household should raise a pig)

一哄而散 ī-hùng-èrh-sàn one clamor and they scatter (helter-skelter)

一伙 ī-huǒ a gang

一系列 ī-hsì-lièh a series of

一下子 ī-hsià-tzu all at once, in a trice

一项 ī-hsiàng one item

一小撮 ī-hsiǎo-ts'ō a small handful, a few

一笑置之 ī-hsiào-chìh-chīh to dismiss with a smile

一线希望 ī-hsièn hsī-wàng a thread of hope

一线生机 ī-hsièn shēng-chī a thread of life

一心一意 ī-hsīn-ī-ì wholeheartedly, of one heart and mind, heart and soul

一心为革命 ī-hsīn wèi kó-mìng wholeheartedly for the revolution

一心为公 ī-hsīn-wèi-kūng devoted to the public [good]

一星半点 ī-hsīng pàn-tiěn one spark and half a dot (anything very small, few in number)

一意孤行 ī-ì-kū-hsíng to act stubbornly in one's own way, to do something against the advice of others

一人独吞 ī-jén-tú-t'ūn to devour by oneself (selfish, to refuse to share)

一日千里 ī-jìh-ch'iēn-lǐ a thousand *li* in

a day (rapid progress)

一干二净 **ī-kān èrh-chìng** completely cleaned up, empty, finished, totally, completely

一杆子插到底 **ī kān-tzu ch'ā tào-tǐ** to reach the bottom by one thrust of the pole (to carry out a policy promptly from the top to the lowest units)

一根稻草压弯腰 **ī-kēn-tào-ts'ǎo yā-wān-yāo** a single rice straw bends the back (without a goal the slightest task is onerous)

一个劲儿 **ī-ko-chìng-erh** [doing something] consistently or continually, without interruption, full of zest

一个心眼干革命 **ī-ko-hsīn-yěn kàn-kó-mìng** singlemindedly making revolution

一个萝卜顶一个坑 **ī-ko ló-po tǐng-ī-ko k'ēng** one turnip takes one hole (each person has his own job)

一个不杀大部不抓 **ī-ko-pù-shā, tà-pù-pù-chuā** not one killed and the great majority not to be detained (a civil war policy to encourage Nationalist defections)

一股黑风 **ī-kǔ hēi-fēng** a gust of black wind (a surge of the incorrect line)

一股脑儿 **ī-kǔ-nǎo-erh** completely, thoroughly; everything together

一官半职 **ī-kuān-pàn-chíh** one official and half a job (a petty official post)

一贯 **ī-kuàn** from beginning to end (consistent, unswerving, habitual)

一贯方针 **ī-kuàn-fāng-chēn** a consistent policy

一贯道 **ī-kuàn-tào** The Way of Perfect Truth (a secret society, dissolved after 1949)

一棍子打死 **ī-kùn-tzu tǎ-szǔ** to kill with a single blow (to deal with problems or people in an excessively arbitrary manner without attempting to salvage what may be good)

一锅端 **ī-kuō-tuān** to carry off the pot (to refuse to share tasks or benefits, monopolize)

一颗红心两只手 **ī-k'ō-húng-hsīn, liǎng-chīh-shǒu** one red heart and two hands (determined to take on any task)

一颗红心两种准备 **ī-k'ō-húng-hsīn, liǎng-chǔng-chǔn-pèi** one red heart [and] two kinds of preparation (graduates should obey the Party's instructions either to pursue further study or to work in the countryside)

一口气 **ī-k'ǒu-ch'ì** in one breath

一口观 **ī-k'ǒu-kuān** one-man viewpoint (egocentrism, individualism)

一孔之见 **ī-k'ǔng-chīh-chièn** a peephole view, partial view, limited viewpoint

一览表 **ī-lǎn-piǎo** a summary chart, tabular summarization

一揽子 **ī-lǎn-tzu** to monopolize, control everything (to be grasping for responsibility)

一揽子计划 **ī-lǎn-tzu chì-huà** a package plan, a package deal

一劳永逸 **ī-láo-yǔng-ì** one effort and lasting comfort (to do a job well so that one can relax—an idea now criticized)

一厘钱精神 **ī-lí-ch'ién chīng-shén** the tenth-of-a-cent spirit (the production drive should be accompanied by economy in making use of even the smallest bits of useful material)

一连串 **ī-lién-ch'uàn** an interlocked series

一露头 **ī-lòu-t'óu** as soon as it appears

一路货 **ī-lù-huò** one line of goods (the same ilk—generally derogatory)

一路哭不如一家哭 **ī-lù k'ū pù-jú ī-chiā k'ū** better one family weeping than a whole district (the interests of a few may have to be sacrificed for the benefit of the majority)

一路顺风 **ī-lù-shùn-fēng** may your whole journey have favorable winds (bon voyage)

一律平等 **ī-lù-p'íng-těng** everybody equal, equality without exception

一马当先 **ī-mǎ-tāng-hsiēn** one horse [man] takes the lead (to take the lead in any serious task)

一脉相承 **ī-mài-hsiāng-ch'éng** to derive from a common vein (to come from a single lineage)

一毛不拔 **ī-máo-pù-pá** to refuse to sacrifice a single hair (to refuse to give the slightest help)

一面之词 **ī-mièn-chīh-tz'ú** one-sided statement [in argument]

一面倒 **ī-mièn-tǎo** to lean to one side, favor one side

一鸣惊人 **ī-míng-chīng-jén** to astonish people by one shout (to be suddenly successful)

一模一样 **ī-mó-ī-yàng** exactly in the same form, similar, the same

一亩一猪 **ī-mǔ ī-chū** one pig per *mu* [of farmland] (an official ideal)

一年之计在于春 **ī-nién-chīh-chì tsài-yú-ch'ūn** the planning [or calculations] for the year depends on the spring (the planning and work done during the early part of the year lays the foundation for the year's accomplishment)

一年三造 **ī-nién-sān-tsào** one year three crops (triple cropping)

一年土，二年洋，三年不认爹和娘 **ī-niēn-t'ǔ, èrh-nién-yáng, sān-nién-pù-jèn tiēh-hó-niáng** the first year a country hick, the second foreignized, and in the third year refusing to recognize one's father and mother (criticizing young people who get swept off their feet when they leave home to study)

一把火烧两头 **ī-pǎ-huǒ shāo-liǎng-t'óu** a torch that burns both ends (one to illuminate the wrongdoings of freaks and monsters; the other to test the correctness of the leadership)

一败涂地 **ī-pài-t'ú-tì** a crushing defeat, complete failure

一般化 **ī-pān-huà** to generalize, uniformalize (to lose sight of particularities in a job or situation: hence, indiscriminate lumping together); ordinary

一班 **ī-pān** a class [of students], a squad [of soldiers], group

一班人 **ī-pān-jén** a group of people; the members of a squad (often implies the leading group)

一帮 **ī-pāng** a gang, clique, a group devoted to a common cause [usually unworthy]

一帮一 **ī-pāng-ī** one to help one (an activist works with a learner)

一帮一，一对红 **ī-pāng-ī, ī-tuì-húng** with one helping another, the pair will become red (the advanced must help the backward so that both may achieve "redness")

一褒一贬 **ī-pāo ī-piěn** one praise and one blame (to undercut, damn with faint praise)

一倍 **ī-pèi** to double, increase by 100 percent

一辈子 **ī-pèi-tzu** one lifetime, lifelong

一本账 **ī-pěn-chàng** the whole account book (a complete history)

一本书主义 **ī-pěn-shū chǔ-ì** one-book doctrine (critical of academics who think that their future depends on having at least one book published)

一鼻孔出气 **ī-pí-k'ǔng ch'ū-ch'ì** to breathe through the same nose (pejorative—slavishly to toe the same line)

一笔勾销 **ī-pǐ-kōu-hsiāo** to strike out with one stroke of the pen

一笔抹煞 **ī-pǐ-mǒ-shā** to cross out with one stroke (arbitrarily to deny someone's good points or achievements)

一边反，一边犯 **ī-piēn-fǎn, ī-piēn-fàn** on one hand to oppose [mistakes] and on the other to commit [mistakes] (the mistakes here committed are often those of self-complacency and pride)

一边干，一边盼 **ī-piēn-kàn, ī-piēn-p'àn** on one side to labor and on the other to hope [to leave the countryside and return home]

一边倒 **ī-piēn-tǎo** to lean to one side (to take a stand, not remain passive or neutral)

一兵多用 **ī-pīng-tō-yùng** every soldier [should be capable of] many functions

一不怕丑二不怕痛 **ī pù-p'à-ch'ǒu èrh pù-p'à-t'ùng** first, fear not ridicule and second, fear not pain

一不怕苦二不怕死 **ī pù-p'à-k'ǔ, èrh pù-p'à-szǔ** first, fear not hardship and second, fear not death

一步一个脚印 **ī-pù ī-ko chiǎo-yìn** each step leaves a footprint (every task should be done with care)

一步一层天 **ī-pù ī-ts'éng-t'iēn** each step is an advance to a higher level (usually refers to ideological progress)

一派繁荣兴旺景象 **ī-p'ài fán-júng hsīng-wàng chǐng-hsiàng** a thoroughly flourishing and prosperous outlook

一派大好形势 **ī-p'ài tà-hǎo hsíng-shìh** a thoroughly excellent situation

一批 **ī-p'ī** a batch, shipment [of goods], group [of people]

一批二用 **ī-p'ī èrh-yùng** both criticize and use (criticism and proper utilization of the person criticized are both essential)

一片哀鸣 **ī-p'ièn āi-míng** full of lamentations

一片欢腾 **ī-p'ièn huān-t'éng** full of rejoicing

一扫而光 **ī-sǎo-érh-kuāng** to sweep clean with one stroke

一闪念 **ī-shǎn-nièn** a flash of thought, a sudden idea

一身轻 **ī-shēn-ch'īng** the whole body [feels] light (the sense of shedding a burden that one feels in accepting mass criticism)

一声不吭 **ī-shēng pù-k'ēng** without even a sound

一省二快 **ī-shěng-èrh-k'uài** first [accomplish a task] economically and second, rapidly

一时一刻 **ī-shíh-ī-k'ò** every hour and every minute (all the time)

一事一议 **ī-shìh-ī-ì** one affair, one

discussion (everything should be discussed)

一事无成 **ī-shìh-wú-ch'éng** not a thing achieved

一视同仁 **ī-shìh-t'úng-jén** to treat all equally well

一手抓生产, 一手抓生活 **ī-shǒu chuā shēng-ch'ǎn, ī-shǒu chuā shēng-huó** with one hand grasp production [and] with the other grasp life (concentration on production does not relieve one of the responsibility for proper ordering of his political and social life)

一手拿枪, 一手拿锄 **ī-shǒu ná ch'iāng, ī-shǒu ná ch'ú** hold a rifle in one hand and a hoe in the other (a slogan associated with the campaign for training militia in 1958)

一手拿镐, 一手拿枪 **ī-shǒu ná kǎo, ī-shǒu ná ch'iāng** with a pick in one hand and a rifle in the other

一手包办 **ī-shǒu-pāo-pàn** to carry out single-handedly (to exclude others from participation)

一手导演 **ī-shǒu-tǎo-yěn** stage-managed single-handedly

一瞬即逝 **ī-shùn-chí-shìh** to vanish in a blink of the eyes

一丝一毫 **ī-szū-ī-háo** an iota, small amount

一丝不苟 **ī-szū-pù-kǒu** not negligent in one iota (meticulously attentive, scrupulously conscientious)

一打一拉的政策 **ī-tǎ ī-lā te chèng-ts'è** a policy of alternately striking and wooing

一打三反运动 **ī-tǎ sān-fǎn yùn-tùng** the One-Smash and Three-Anti Movement (smash the destructive activities of counter-revolutionaries, and counter: (1) corruption and theft; (2) ostentation and waste; (3) speculation and profiteering)

一大二公 **ī-tà-èrh-kūng** first, large and second, public (the basic characteristics of the commune)

一代新风 **ī-tài-hsīn-fēng** a generation with a new atmosphere (the new spirit since 1949)

一带而过 **ī-tài-érh-kuò** to touch and pass on (in passing, to mention in passing)

一党当政 **ī-tǎng-tāng-chèng** single-party government; monopolization of government by one party

一得之功 **ī-té-chīh-kūng** the merit of a humble achievement (a courtesy reference to oneself)

一得之愚 **ī-té-chīh-yú** one's humble opinion

一点两面战术 **ī-tiěn liǎng-mièn chàn-shù** one-point [and] two-plane tactics (a concentrated attack at a weak point with strong flanking attacks to encircle and cut off the rear)

一点论 **ī-tiěn lùn** a single point theory (criticized as a negation of **ī-fēn-wéi-èrh**)

一定条件 **ī-tìng-t'iáo-chièn** certain conditions, specific circumstances

一斗, 二批, 三改 **ī-tòu, èrh-p'ī, sān-kǎi** one struggle, two criticisms, and three reformations (from point 1 of the **shíh-liù-t'iáo**. Struggle against powerholders; criticize academic authorities and bourgeois ideology; reform education, literature, and the superstructure inconsistent with the socialist economic foundation)

一度 **ī-tù** once, at one time, formerly

一对红 **ī-tuì-húng** one pair red (a pair in which one person is helping the other's political development)

一塌糊涂 **ī-t'ā hú-t'ú** utterly confused, a great mess

一潭死水 **ī-t'án-szǔ-shuǐ** a pool of dead water (a situation of no movement, stalemate)

一套 **ī-t'ào** an integral group, a set [of ideas or things]

一体 **ī-t'ǐ** one body, as one body

一体化 **ī-t'ǐ-huà** integration

一条龙 **ī-t'iáo-lúng** a dragon (a chain or connected series)

一条龙运输 **ī-t'iáo-lúng yùn-shū** dragon [-like] transportation (the use of varied forms of transportation over different stages of a route)

一条鞭经营方式 **ī-t'iáo-piēn chīng-yíng-fāng-shìh** the single-whip method of management (vertical or hierarchical control)

一拖, 二骗, 三减免 **ī-t'ō, èrh-p'ièn, sān-chiěn-miěn** delays, cheating, reduction or exemption (methods of tax evasion)

一头扎进业务堆里 **ī-t'óu-chā-chìn yèh-wù-tuī-li** to bury one's head in heaps of professional work (to slight political work)

一团和气 **ī-t'uán-hó-ch'ì** full of agreeableness (unwilling to criticize, excessively passive)

一团糟 **ī-t'uán-tsāo** a hopeless mess, completely mixed up

一通百通 **ī-t'ūng-pǎi-t'ūng** when one [thing] is mastered, a hundred [can be] mastered (when the most important element is mastered, the

rest comes easily)

一统天下 ĭ-t'ǔng t'iēn-hsià to rule all below Heaven [China]; the unified kingdom (now suggests ruling the world)

一字之差 ĭ-tzù-chǐh-ch'ā a difference of one character (usually implies a significant difference in meaning)

一蹴而就 ĭ-ts'ù-érh-chiù to accomplish in one stroke

一次革命论 ĭ-tz'ù-kó-mìng lùn the theory of a single revolution (an idea that is rejected)

一次被蛇咬三年怕草绳 ĭ-tz'ù pèi shé-yǎo sān-nién p'à ts'ǎo-shéng once bitten by a snake, three years afraid of a straw rope (once bitten, twice shy)

一次完成论 ĭ-tz'ù-wán-ch'éng lùn the idea that [the revolution] can be completed once [and for all]

一碗水端平 ĭ-wǎn-shuǐ tuān-p'íng holding a bowl of water steady (to be fair to all parties concerned)

一往无前 ĭ-wǎng-wú-ch'ién to relentlessly move ahead so that nothing can stop one (indomitable, fearless)

一望无际 ĭ-wàng-wú-chì a look cannot see the margins (wide stretches, boundless)

一味 ĭ-wèi persistently, doggedly, habitually, invariably

一文不值 ĭ-wén-pù-chíh not worth a cent

一无例外 ĭ-wú-lì-wài without a single exception

一无是处 ĭ-wú-shìh-ch'ù having not the least good point (utterly without merit)

一无所有 ĭ-wú-sǒ-yǔ having not the least thing (completely poverty-stricken)

一物多用 ĭ-wù-tō-yùng each article has many uses

一叶障目，不见泰山 ĭ-yèh chàng-mù, pù-chièn t'ài-shān with a single leaf blocking the eye, one cannot see Tai mountain (to be so confused by minor aspects as to lose sight of the whole)

一业为主，多种经营 ĭ-yèh wéi-chǔ, tō-chǔng chǐng-yíng one line of work can be the main concern but many other kinds of work should be carried on simultaneously

一言难尽 ĭ-yén-nán-chìn difficult to finish in a word (a long story)

一言堂 ĭ-yén-t'áng a one-voice [meeting] hall (giving the masses no chance to express themselves)

一应俱全 ĭ-yìng-chǜ-ch'üán everything is ready, all is complete

一语道破 ĭ-yǔ-tào-p'ò a single phrase reveals [the truth]

一元化 ĭ-yuán-huà to unify, consolidate, simplify

一元化集体领导 ĭ-yuán-huà chí-t'ǐ-lǐng-tǎo unified collective leadership

一元化领导 ĭ-yuán-huà lǐng-tǎo unified leadership (may refer to organizational leadership or leadership which is unified by acceptance of the thought of Mao Tse-tung)

一月革命 ĭ-yuèh-kó-mìng the January Revolution (the power seizure initiated in Shanghai by the Left in January, 1967)

伊拉克 ĭ-lā-k'ò Iraq

伊朗 ĭ-lǎng Iran

伊斯兰教 ĭ-szū-lán chiào Islam (Mohammedanism)

衣锦还乡 ĭ-chǐn-huán-hsiāng coming home in fine raiment (to have achieved success in the world)

衣钵 ĭ-pō mantle and alms bowl (since an old monk's robe and bowl were passed down to a young monk, this is a metaphor for heritage and ideological succession)

医治 ĭ-chìh to treat medically, cure

医护人员 ĭ-hù-jén-yuán medical and nursing personnel

医学院 ĭ-hsuéh-yuàn a medical college

医疗 ĭ-liáo to cure, heal, treat; medical treatment, therapy

医疗证 ĭ-liáo-chèng medical card

医疗机构 ĭ-liáo-chǐ-kòu medical institutions and organizations

医疗教学点 ĭ-liáo chiào-hsuéh-tiěn medical school [field extension] stations (usually in rural areas to give practical training to medical students and to train local paramedical personnel)

医疗设施 ĭ-liáo-shè-shīh medical services and facilities

医疗卫生机构 ĭ-liáo wèi-shēng chǐ-kòu medical and public health organizations

医疗卫生工作 ĭ-liáo wèi-shēng kūng-tsò medical and public health activities

医士 ĭ-shìh a graduate of a short-term medical school, medical aide

医务人员 ĭ-wù-jén-yuán medical staff

医药 ĭ-yào medical care and medicine

医药结合 ĭ-yào-chiéh-hó the integration of medical treatment and pharmacy

医药费 ĭ-yào-fèi charges for medicines

医药工业 ĭ-yào-kūng-yèh the pharmaceutical industry

990 依照 **í-chào** according to, in accordance with; to obey, follow, accept
依据 **í-chù** in accordance with, based on, on the strength of
依法 **í-fǎ** according to law, by law, legally
依附 **í-fù** to depend on, adhere to, submit to, hang on to
依依不舍 **í-í-pù-shě** unwilling to part with, to cling to
依然故我 **í-ján-kù-wǒ** still the same old me, I am still what I used to be
依人定量 **í-jén tìng-liàng** rations determined according to individual [work requirements]
依靠群众 **í-k'ào ch'ún-chùng** to rely on the masses
依赖关系 **í-lài-kuān-hsi** a relationship of dependence
依率计征 **í-lǜ chì-chēng** taxation in accordance with fixed rates
依托 **í-t'ō** to depend on, rely on, trust
依存 **í-ts'ún** to depend on
依次 **í-tz'ù** in regular order, in sequence, consecutive, successive
依违两可 **í-wéi-liǎng-k'ǒ** to have no convictions of one's own, shilly-shally

í (yí)

991 仪仗队 **í-chàng-tuì** a guard of honor
仪器 **í-ch'ì** [scientific] apparatus, instruments
仪表 **í-piǎo** (1) a man's personal appearance; (2) a measuring or indicating instrument or meter
仪式 **í-shìh** ceremony, ritual, rites
992 沂蒙颂 **í-méng-sùng** "Ode of Yi Meng" (a dance drama provisionally accepted as one of the **yàng-pǎn-hsì**)
993 宜耕荒地 **í-kēng-huāng-tì** cultivable wasteland
宜林地 **í-lín-tì** land capable of being afforested
994 贻害无穷 **í-hài-wú-ch'iúng** long-lasting harmful consequences
贻笑大方 **í-hsiào-tà-fāng** to become a laughingstock [by showing one's ignorance, etc.]
贻人口实 **í-jén-k'ǒu-shíh** to give an occasion for gossip, to give others an excuse for criticism
贻误 **í-wù** to spoil, cause failure, disrupt
995 胰岛素 **í-tǎo-sù** insulin
996 移交 **í-chiāo** to hand [a position to a successor], transfer, turn over, convey
移植 **í-chíh** to transplant, implant

移植革命样板板戏 **í-chíh kó-mìng yàng-pǎn-hsì** a transplanted revolutionary model play (the transplanting may be the modification of a work in another art form, or the adaptation of another local style)
移风易俗 **í-fēng-í-sú** to change [old] habits and customs
移花接木 **í-huā-chiēh-mù** transplanting flowers and grafting trees (schemes to fool people by subterfuge)
移戏先移立足点 **í-hsì hsiēn-í lì-tsú-tiēn** to transplant a [revolutionary model] play it is first necessary to move one's standpoint
移民 **í-mín** immigrants, emigrants; to settle people in a new region, colonize
移山倒海 **í-shān-tǎo-hǎi** to shift mountains and move seas (man is able to overcome nature)
移东补西 **í-tūng-pǔ-hsī** shifting from east to make up west (using a surplus from one place to make up a deficit in another)
移动 **í-tùng** to move, shift, change, displace
移山造田 **í-shān tsào-t'ién** to move the mountains [in order to] make fields
997 遗迹 **í-chī** vestige, relic, trace, remains
遗嘱 **í-chǔ** a last will, testament, instructions of a dying person
遗产 **í-ch'ǎn** property left by a deceased person, legacy
遗臭万年 **í-ch'òu-wàn-nién** to leave a stench for ten thousand years
遗传 **í-ch'uán** to pass on to offspring, transmit to future generations; heredity
遗憾 **í-hàn** regret; regrettable
遗老 **í-lǎo** a survivor from an earlier period (usually pejorative)
遗留 **í-liú** to leave behind [usually at death]
遗漏 **í-lòu** to omit by mistake; an omission, oversight
遗毒 **í-tú** handed-down poison (the evil influence of old customs, an evil legacy)
遗体 **í-t'ǐ** a corpse, remains, dead body
998 疑惑 **í-huò** to doubt, suspect; a suspicion, misgiving, doubt
疑心 **í-hsīn** to suspect, doubt, distrust; a doubt, suspicion
疑义 **í-ì** doubtful meaning, dubious interpretation, inadequately explained
疑虑 **í-lǜ** misgiving, apprehension, anxiety
疑难杂症 **í-nán-tsá-chèng** puzzling diseases, illnesses difficult to diagnose

疑兵 **í-pīng** deceptively deployed troops, a feint to mislead the enemy

疑神疑鬼 **í-shén í-kuěi** to imagine all sorts of mysterious things

疑狱 **í-yù** an unsettled case, mysterious case

999 彝族 **í-tsú** the Yi people (a minority in Yunnan, Szechwan, and Kweichow provinces: population 3,264,432 as of 1957—formerly called Lólo 猡猡)

彝村苗寨 **í-ts'ūn miáo-chài** villages of the Yi [people] and stockades of the Miao (the areas in southwest China inhabited by the minority peoples)

ǐ (yǐ)

1000 以战止战 **ǐ-chàn-chǐh-chàn** to use war to end war

以战迫降 **ǐ-chàn-p'ò-hsiáng** to force surrender by means of war

以战养战 **ǐ-chàn-yǎng-chàn** to sustain war by war

以政治带文化 **ǐ-chèng-chìh tài-wén-huà** to use politics to bring along culture

以正视听 **ǐ-chèng-shìh-t'īng** to clarify what is seen and heard

以假乱真 **ǐ-chiǎ-luàn-chēn** to use the false to confuse the true

以骄反骄 **ǐ-chiāo-fǎn-chiāo** to use arrogance to counter arrogance

以节约为荣, 以浪费为耻 **ǐ-chiéh-yuēh wéi-júng ǐ-làng-fèi wéi-ch'ǐh** to take thrift as honorable and waste as shameful

以近为主, 远近结合 **ǐ-chìn-wéi-chǔ, yuǎn-chìn-chiéh-hó** to give priority to the short-term and to coordinate the short- and long-term

以儆效尤 **ǐ-chǐng-hsiào-yú** to warn those who would learn evil ways

以产定工制 **ǐ-ch'ǎn-tìng-kūng chìh** the system of using output to determine compensation for the working [day]

以耳代目 **ǐ-ěrh-tài-mù** to use the ears instead of the eyes (to listen to others instead of making a proper on-the-spot investigation)

以丰补歉 **ǐ-fēng-pǔ-ch'ièn** to use good [years] to make up for poor [years]

以副伤农 **ǐ-fù-shāng-núng** using sidelines to harm agriculture (basic agricultural production can be undermined by excessive concentration on sideline productive activities)

以副促农 **ǐ-fù-ts'ù-núng** using sidelines to promote agriculture

以红带专 **ǐ-húng-tài-chuān** use redness to guide expertness (loyalty to the Party comes before professional specialization)

以下 **ǐ-hsià** (1) including and less than [a specified number, level, or amount]; (2) the following, as below

以虚带实 **ǐ-hsū-tài-shíh** to use the abstract to guide the concrete (the political should guide the functional)

以学为主, 兼学别样 **ǐ-hsuéh-wéi-chǔ, chiēn-hsuéh-piéh-yàng** to give priority to study but concurrently to study other things (formal study must be accompanied with other activities such as farm and shop work and military training)

以一当十, 以十当百 **ǐ-ī-tāng-shíh, ǐ-shíh-tāng-pǎi** to pit one against ten and ten against a hundred

以衣帽取人 **ǐ-ī-mào ch'ǔ-jén** to judge a man by his hat and clothes (judging by outward appearances)

以逸待劳 **ǐ-ì-tài-láo** to wait at one's ease for the fatigued [enemy] (to await the enemy's exhaustion)

以柔克刚 **ǐ-jóu-k'ò-kāng** to use the soft to overcome the hard

以干代学 **ǐ-kàn-tài-hsuéh** to take work as a substitute for study (an attitude to be criticized)

以钢为纲 **ǐ-kāng-wéi-kāng** to take steel as the key link

以古非今 **ǐ-kǔ-fēi-chīn** to use the ancient to negate the present

以观后效 **ǐ-kuān-hòu-hsiào** to use observation of results, to check on the efficacy

以工代赈 **ǐ-kūng-tài-chèn** to give work instead of direct relief, relief through production

以攻为守 **ǐ-kūng-wéi-shǒu** using attack for defense

以苦为荣 **ǐ-k'ǔ-wéi-júng** to take hard work as honorable

以老带新 **ǐ-lǎo-tài-hsīn** to use the old to bring along the new (the experienced should assist the new hands)

以理服人 **ǐ-lǐ-fú-jén** to use reason to win over people

以力服人 **ǐ-lì-fú-jén** to subdue people by force

以粮食为主导 **ǐ-liáng-shíh wéi chǔ-tǎo** to take grain [production] as the leading [factor]

以粮为纲 **ǐ-liáng-wéi-kāng** with food grain as the key (to place primary emphasis on the production of foodstuffs)

以粮为纲, 全面发展 **ǐ-liáng-wéi-kāng, ch'üán-mièn fā-chǎn** make grain the key [link] and ensure all-round development

以粮为纲, 多种经营 **ǐ-liáng-wéi-kāng, tō-chǔng chīng-yíng** a diversified economy with grain as the key

以粮为纲, 五业并举 **ǐ-liáng-wéi-kāng, wǔ-yèh pìng-chǔ** treat foodstuff as basic and develop the five occupations simultaneously

以邻为壑 **ǐ-lín-wéi-hò** to use the neighbor's [field] as drainage [for the overflow from one's own field] (to shift one's troubles to others)

以卵击石 **ǐ-luǎn-chī-shíh** to use an egg to strike a stone (a reckless attack against a much stronger force)

以论带史 **ǐ-lùn-tài-shǐh** the use of theory to guide [the writing of] history (a reference to the work of historians under criticism)

以农村包围城市 **ǐ-núng-ts'ūn pāo-wéi ch'éng-shìh** to use the countryside to encircle the cities

以农为主, 以副养农 **ǐ-núng-wéi-chǔ, ǐ-fù-yǎng-núng** to regard agriculture as the main factor and let subsidiary production nurture agriculture (production of food grains is the main task while subsidiary production of vegetables, pigs, etc., generates capital for the former)

以农为主, 以农养副 **ǐ-núng-wéi-chǔ,ǐ-núng-yǎng-fù** to take agriculture as the main factor and let agriculture nurture the sidelines

以农为主, 农副结合 **ǐ-núng-wéi-chǔ, núng-fù-chiéh-hó** to take agriculture as the main factor and coordinate agriculture and sidelines

以农为荣, 以农为乐 **ǐ-núng-wéi-júng, ǐ-núng-wéi-lè** look upon agriculture as glory and joy

以农业为基础以工业为主导 **ǐ-núng-yèh wéi chī-ch'ǔ, ǐ-kūng-yèh wéi chǔ-tǎo** make agriculture the foundation and industry the guide [of the economy]

以色列 **ǐ-sè-lièh** Israel

以上 **ǐ-shàng** (1) including and more, or higher, than [a specified number, level, or amount]; (2) the above [listed or mentioned]

以社会为工厂 **ǐ-shè-huì wéi kūng-ch'ǎng** to take society as a workshop (an admonition to the students of the humanities)

以身殉职 **ǐ-shēn-hsùn-chíh** to give one's life in one's [official] work

以身作则 **ǐ-shēn-tsò-tsé** to make oneself an example [for others]

以师带徒 **ǐ-shīh-tài-t'ú** use the master [workman] to guide the apprentice

以势压人 **ǐ-shìh-yā-jén** to use one's power to pressure others

以...思想武装起来 **ǐ ... szū-hsiang wǔ-chuāng ch'ǐ-lái** to be armed with the thought of ...

以大吃小 **ǐ-tà-ch'īh-hsiǎo** to use the large to eat the small

以德报怨 **ǐ-té-pào-yuàn** to repay evil with good

以点带面 **ǐ-tiěn-tài-mièn** to use a point to guide the plane (to use the experience gained in a selected point to guide the work of a whole area)

以斗争求团结 **ǐ-tòu-chēng ch'iú-t'uán-chiéh** to attain unity through struggle

以毒攻毒 **ǐ-tú-kūng-tú** to use poison to attack poison (to utilize evil men to deal with other evil men)

以太 **ǐ-t'ài** ether [the anesthetic]

以退为进 **ǐ-t'uì-wéi-chìn** to use retreat to make an advance (to make a feint of retreat in order to advance)

以采带用, 以用促采 **ǐ-ts'ǎi-tài-yùng, ǐ-yùng-ts'ù-ts'ǎi** use the mining [of coal] to develop its use and the use [of coal] to promote its mining

以牙还牙 **ǐ-yá-huán-yá** a tooth for a tooth

ì (yì)

义正辞严 **ì-chèng-tz'ú-yén** speaking sternly and forcefully for justice

义气 **ì-ch'ì** sense of honor, sense of justice; loyalty, righteousness

义愤 **ì-fèn** righteous indignation

义愤填膺 **ì-fèn-t'ién-yīng** righteous indignation fills the breast

义和团 **ì-hó-t'uán** the Society of Righteous Harmony (the Boxers, 1900)

义形于色 **ì-hsíng-yú-sè** righteous [indignation] shows in one's face

义不容辞 **ì-pù-júng-tz'ú** public duty will not permit refusal (to be duty-bound)

义士 **ì-shìh** a martyr, man of honor, patriot

义胆忠肝 **ì-tǎn-chūng-kān** righteous gallbladder and loyal liver (righteous and loyal)

义无反顾 **ì-wú-fǎn-kù** righteousness does not look backward

义务 **ì-wù** obligation, duty, volunteer duty

义务安全检修队 **ì-wù ān-ch'uán chiěn-hsiū-tuì** volunteer safety inspection and repair teams (organized by Shanghai policemen in their spare time to repair buildings)

义务缝补站 **ì-wù féng-pǔ-chàn** voluntary sewing and mending stations (for Red Guards in late 1966)

义务劳动 **ì-wù láo-tùng** voluntary labor (labor without compensation)

义务兵役制 **ì-wù pīng-ì-chìh** voluntary armed-service system

义演 **ì-yěn** a charity performance

义勇军 **ì-yǔng-chūn** volunteers [military], a volunteer army

1002 亿万 **ì-wàn** hundreds of millions and tens of thousands (a very large number)

亿万群众 **ì-wàn-ch'ún-chùng** countless masses

1003 忆苦教育 **ì-k'ǔ-chiào-yù** education in recalling hardships (education to raise political consciousness by stressing the hardships of the past)

忆苦饭 **ì-k'ǔ-fàn** remembering-bitterness food (poor food sometimes given to youth or intellectuals to give them a taste of the hardness of the old society)

忆苦诉苦 **ì-k'ǔ-sù-k'ǔ** to recall and recount hardships

忆苦思甜 **ì-k'ǔ-szū-t'ién** to remember bitterness [of the past and to] think of the sweetness [of the present] (to compare the old and new societies)

忆比查活动 **ì-pǐ-ch'á huó-tùng** activity to recall, compare, and investigate [the differences between the past and present]

忆比会 **ì-pǐ-huì** a meeting to remember [the old society] and compare [it with the present]

1004 艺人 **ì-jén** artist, artiste, performer

艺术 **ì-shù** arts, fine arts (includes drama, opera, music, fine arts, dance, film, poetry, and literature)

艺术至上主义 **ì-shù-chìh-shàng-chǔ-ì** art for art's sake

艺术形式 **ì-shù hsíng-shìh** art forms

艺术观 **ì-shù-kuān** art viewpoint

艺术魅力 **ì-shù mèi-lì** the appealing power of art

艺徒 **ì-t'ú** an apprentice [in handicrafts or artistic work]

1005 议案 **ì-àn** a draft bill; a motion, resolution; proposal

议案审查委员会 **ì-àn-shěn-ch'á wěi-yuán-huì** resolutions examination committee (to collect and sift proposals from the public, before presentation to a people's congress)

议价 **ì-chià** discussion of price

议程 **ì-ch'éng** agenda (contraction of **ì-shìh jíh-ch'éng**)

议处 **ì-ch'ǔ** to deliberate over a punish-ment (an old term referring to punishment of an official)

议会 **ì-huì** a parliament, deliberative assembly, council

议会迷 **ì-huì-mí** a parliament addict (a criticism of persons—such as Liu Shao-ch'i—alleged to advocate moving toward parliamentarianism)

议会道路 **ì-huì-tào-lù** the parliamentary road

议会斗争 **ì-huì-tòu-chēng** parliamentary struggle (a legal, nonviolent form of political activity as contrasted to armed struggle)

议购合同 **ì-kòu-hó-t'ung** negotiated purchase contract

议事日程 **ì-shìh jìh-ch'éng** an agenda

议定书 **ì-tìng-shū** a protocol, *procès-verbal*, document of ratification

议员 **ì-yuán** a member of an assembly, parliament, etc.

1006 亦工亦农 **ì-kūng ì-núng** both a worker and a peasant (workers in the rural industries participate in farm work in the busy seasons)

亦步亦趋 **ì-pù-ì-ch'ū** [if you take a step] I also take a step; [if you hasten] I also hasten (to imitate or follow others—in a derogatory sense)

1007 异己分子 **ì-chǐ-fèn-tzǔ** disagreeing elements, alien elements, outsiders

异常 **ì-ch'áng** unusual, abnormal, extraordinary

异军突起 **ì-chūn-t'ū-ch'ǐ** a new army suddenly appears (a new force emerges)

异曲同工 **ì-ch'ǔ-t'úng-kūng** different tunes are equally excellent (different approaches can contribute to the same end)

异化作用 **ì-huà-tsò-yùng** catabolism, destructive metabolism

异想天开 **ì-hsiǎng-t'iēn-k'āi** to fancy that heavens will open (fanciful illusions, thinking that is divorced from reality)

异形钢管 **ì-hsíng-kāng-kuǎn** multi-shaped steel tubing

异议 **ì-ì** dissent, disagreement, objections

异口同声 **ì-k'ǒu-t'úng-shēng** different mouths with one sound (a chorus of approval, with one voice)

异实同名 **ì-shíh-t'úng-míng** differing in substance but alike in name

异党 **ì-tǎng** a differing party, opposing party, "the other party"

异党分子 **ì-tǎng-fèn-tzǔ** other-party elements

异端邪说 **ì-tuān-hsiéh-shuō** dissident

and heterodox theories

异体字 **ì-t'ǐ-tzù** variant [but acceptable] forms of characters

异族 **ì-tsú** an alien people, a foreign race

1008 译本 **ì-pěn** a translation, translated version [of a book]

1009 抑制 **ì-chìh** to repress, restrain, stifle, curb

1010 易货协定 **ì-huò-hsiéh-tìng** a barter agreement

易货贸易 **ì-huò-mào-ì** barter trade

易如反掌 **ì-jú-fǎn-chǎng** as easy as turning the palm [of one's hand]

1011 疫苗 **ì-miáo** vaccine

1012 益处 **ì-ch'ù** benefit, advantage, profit, good, usefulness

1013 溢洪道 **ì-húng-tào** a flood diversion channel, spillway

溢洪堰 **ì-húng-yèn** a flood storage dam

1014 意见 **ì-chièn** an opinion, view, idea, comment, proposal

意见本 **ì-chièn-pěn** a suggestion book (for criticisms and comments)

意见书 **ì-chièn-shū** a statement of opinions, memorandum of views, written proposal

意志 **ì-chìh** will, determination, ambition

意志坚决 **ì-chìh-chiēn-chüéh** the determination is firm; a steadfast will

意气风发 **ì-ch'ì-fēng-fā** in high spirits; boundless enthusiasm

意想不到 **ì-hsiǎng-pù-tào** to have never thought of it, unexpected, beyond expectation

意义 **ì-ì** significance, meaning, effect

意识 **ì-shíh** consciousness; to appreciate, be conscious of

意识形态 **ì-shíh-hsíng-t'ài** ideology; ideological

意识形态领域中的阶级斗争 **ì-shíh-hsíng-t'ài lǐng-yù-chūng-te chiēh-chí-tòu-chēng** class struggle in the realm of ideology

意大利 **ì-tà-lì** ʹtaly

意图 **ì-t'ú** to intend to do, plan, attempt

意外 **ì-wài** unexpected, unforeseen, accidental, by surprise

意味着 **ì-wèi-che** to mean, signify, imply

意味深长 **ì-wèi-shēn-ch'áng** profound in meaning, significant, expressive, meaningful

意愿 **ì-yuàn** wish, desire, volition

1015 毅然决然 **ì-ján-chüéh-ján** resolutely and firmly, in a determined manner

毅力 **ì-lì** perseverance, fortitude, determination, resoluteness, firmness,

tenacity

1016 臆想 **ì-hsiǎng** imagination, subjective thinking

臆造 **ì-tsào** to trump up, concoct, fabricate [a story]

ján (rán)

1017 燃放 **ján-fàng** to set off [firecrackers], ignite

燃料 **ján-liào** fuel, firewood

燃料化学工业部 **ján-liào huà-hsuéh kūng-yèh-pù** Ministry of Fuel and Chemical Industries (since 1969 has incorporated the former ministries of Petroleum Industry, Chemical Industry, and Coal Industry)

燃眉之急 **ján-méi-chīh-chí** an eyebrow-singeing urgency (imminent danger, threatening)

燃烧 **ján-shāo** to burn, be in flames, set on fire; combustion

jǎn (rǎn)

1018 染指 **jǎn-chǐh** to stain the fingers (to share in illegal profits, have a finger in the pie)

染缸 **jǎn-kāng** a dyeing vat (often figurative)

染料 **jǎn-liào** dyestuffs

jàng (ràng)

1019 让高山低头叫河水让路 **jàng kāo-shān tì-t'óu chiào hó-shuǐ jàng-lù** to make the mountains bow their heads and the rivers give way (the conquering of nature)

让步 **jàng-pù** to make a concession, compromise, yield ground, concede, back down

让步政策 **jàng-pù-chèng-ts'é** a policy of yielding, policy of concession

让步政策论 **jàng-pù-chèng-ts'è lùn** the doctrine of a policy of concessions (the theory that each new dynasty was able to show initial progress by making concessions to the accumulated grievances of the peasants)

让位 **jàng-wèi** to yield one's position, abdicate

jáo (ráo)

1020 饶恕 **jáo-shù** to forgive, pardon

饶漱石 **jáo shù-shíh** Jao Shu-shih (a Communist leader, purged with Kao Kang in 1954)

饶有风趣 **jáo-yǔ-fēng-ch'ù** full of a

sense of humor, abundantly humorous

jǎo (rǎo)

1021 扰乱 **jǎo-luàn** to disturb, agitate, harass, throw into disorder

jào (rào)

1022 绕过 **jào-kuò** to detour around, bypass, avoid, evade

绕不开 **jào-pù-k'āi** cannot be unentwined, unable to free from entanglement

绕道而过 **jào-tào-érh-kuò** to detour and pass by

绕道走 **jào-tào-tsǒu** to take a detour (avoid the issue)

绕月球飞行 **jào-yuèh-ch'iú fēi-hsíng** flight around the moon

jě (rě)

1023 惹起 **jě-ch'ǐ** to incite, provoke, set off, give rise to

惹事分子 **jě-shìh-fèn-tzǔ** agent provocateur, trouble-maker

jè (rè)

1024 热爱 **jè-ài** to love earnestly (now used chiefly for feelings toward Mao Tsetung, the Party, one's work, etc.)

热爱和平 **jè-ài-hó-p'íng** peace-loving; to cherish peace

热中(于) **jè-chūng [yú]** avid, restless, impatient; to have a mania for, hanker after, absorbed in

热潮 **jè-ch'áo** an enthusiastic tide

热忱 **jè-ch'én** enthusiasm, sincerity, warmheartedness

热诚 **jè-ch'éng** earnest, sincere, cordial

热气腾腾 **jè-ch'ì-t'éng-t'éng** the steam is rising (bubbling with enthusiasm)

热情 **jè-ch'íng** passion, ardor, fervor, enthusiasm

热讽 **jè-fěng** sharp satire

热核 **jè-hó** thermonuclear

热核反应 **jè-hó-fǎn-yìng** thermonuclear reaction

热核灾难 **jè-hó-tsāi-nàn** thermonuclear holocaust, thermonuclear calamity

热乎劲儿 **jè-hu-chìng-erh** intimate, affectionate, genial

热火朝天 **jè-hǔo-ch'áo-t'iēn** the hot fire reaches the sky (mass enthusiasm)

热心 **jè-hsīn** enthusiastic, ardent, zealous, earnest, eager

热量单位 **jè-liàng-tān-wèi** a thermal unit, caloric unit, calorie

热烈 **jè-lièh** warm, passionate, fervent, ardent, vehement

热闹地区 **jè-nao tì-ch'ū** the busy section [of town], downtown

热带 **jè-tài** tropical zone, the tropics

热电站 **jè-tièn-chàn** a thermal electric generating plant (usually on a small scale)

热电厂 **jè-tièn-ch'ǎng** a thermal electric generating plant (usually large)

热望 **jè-wàng** to hope ardently; a fervent hope, aspiration

jén (rén)

1025 人证 **jén-chèng** a witness; testimony of a witness, personal testimony

人给家足 **jén-chǐ-chiā-tsú** each person supplied and every family [has] enough (adequate supplies so that none suffer)

人间奇迹 **jén-chiēn-ch'í-chī** a miracle in the world of men (a miracle wrought by the masses—or by the Thought of Mao Tse-tung)

人间世 **jén-chiēn-shìh** the world of men

人间地狱 **jén-chiēn-tì-yù** hell on earth

人间天堂 **jén-chiēn-t'iēn-t'áng** a paradise on earth

人之常情 **jén-chìh-ch'áng-ch'íng** ordinary human feelings

人质 **jén-chìh** a hostage

人治 **jén-chìh** rule by men (as contrasted to rule by law)

人吃人的社会 **jén-ch'īh-jén te shè-huì** a society in which men eat men (the old exploitive society)

人情味 **jén-ch'íng-wèi** flavor of human feelings, sense of humanity, genuine human warmth, hospitality

人穷志气大 **jén-ch'iúng chìh-ch'ì-tà** the person is poor but his determination is great

人穷志不穷 **jén-ch'iúng chìh-pù-ch'iúng** poor in wealth but not in will

人穷志短 **jén-ch'iúng-chìh-tuǎn** [when a] person is poor, [his] will is deficient

人权 **jén-ch'üán** human rights, rights of the individual

人群 **jén-ch'ún** a crowd, throng, multitude; mankind

人浮于事 **jén-fú-yú-shìh** (1) men floating above business (the staff of an office larger than its affairs need); (2) more people than jobs, unemployment

人换精神地换貌 **jén-huàn chīng-shén tì-huàn-mào** [if] people change their spirit, [they can] change the land's appearance

人换思想地换装 **jén-huàn-szū-hsiǎng, tì-huàn-chuāng** [if] people change their thinking, [they can] change the landscape

人祸 **jén-huò** a man-made disaster

人小, 理想远大 **jén-hsiǎo, lǐ-hsiǎng yuǎn-tà** young in age but great in ideals

人心齐泰山移 **jén-hsīn-ch'í t'ài-shān-í** [if] men's hearts are as one then Mount T'ai [can be] moved

人心向背 **jén-hsīn-hsiàng-pèi** people's feelings for or against [a government, etc.], popular sentiment

人心所向 **jén-hsīn-sǒ-hsiàng** the trend of popular sentiment, weight of popular support

人心所背 **jén-hsīn-sǒ-pèi** rejected by popular feeling

人心同愤 **jén-hsīn-t'úng-fèn** the hatred of the people

人性论 **jén-hsìng lùn** the human nature theory (criticized as being abstract rather than being based on class)

人选 **jén-hsuǎn** persons chosen or selected [for a post or office]

人以群分 **jén-í-ch'ún-fēn** people divide themselves by categories (people of the same kind or mind tend to form themselves into groups)

人人动手 **jén-jén-tùng-shǒu** everyone moves a hand, all join in

人人为我, 我为人人 **jén-jén-wèi-wǒ, wǒ-wèi-jén-jén** everyone for me and I for everyone (all for one and one for all)

人格 **jén-kó** personal character, personality, stature

人工 **jén-kūng** human effort, work; man-made, artificial; man-day

人工流产 **jén-kūng-liú-ch'ǎn** induced abortion, artificial abortion

人工授粉 **jén-kūng-shòu-fěn** artificial pollination

人口稠密 **jén-k'ǒu ch'óu-mì** densely populated, populous

人类 **jén-lèi** the human species, mankind, human beings, humanity

人类之爱 **jén-lèi-chīh-ài** love of humanity

人类中心说 **jén-lèi-chūng-hsīn shuō** anthropocentrism

人类大同 **jén-lèi-tà-t'úng** universal harmony, the brotherhood of man, the ideal of one world

人力 **jén-lì** man power, manual labor, human force

人力资源 **jén-lì-tzū-yuán** human resources

人民 **jén-mín** the people, people's (refers on to the favored classes

under the people's democratic dictatorship—hence will exclude such groups as unreformed bureaucratic capitalists, etc.)

人民战争 **jén-mín-chàn-chēng** people's war

人民阵线 **jén-mín-chèn-hsièn** the people's front, popular front

人民政治协商会议 **jén-mín chèng-chìh hsiéh-shāng huì-ì** People's Political Consultative Conference

人民交通 **jén-mín chiāo-t'ūng** *People's Communications* (a Peking semi-monthly journal, 1950—)

人民教育 **jén-mín chiào-yù** *People's Education* (a Peking journal, semi-monthly, 1950—)

人民解放战争 **jén-mín chiěh-fàng chàn-chēng** (1) a people's liberation war; (2) the Liberation War (the final civil war against the Kuomintang government, 1946-49)

人民解放军 **jén-mín chiěh-fàng-chūn** the People's Liberation Army [the PLA]

人民检察院 **jén-mín chiěn-ch'á-yuàn** the People's Procuracy

人民志愿军 **jén-mín chìh-yuàn-chūn** the People's Volunteer Army (the Chinese forces in the Korean War)

人民警察 **jén-mín chǐng-ch'á** the people's police (the ordinary term for police)

人民装 **jén-mín-chuāng** the people's garb (the ordinary semi-uniform costume worn by most people, with minor differences for men and women)

人民勤务员 **jén-mín ch'ín-wù-yuán** the servitor of the people, one who serves the people (the kind of commitment a Party member should have toward the masses)

人民军队 **jén-mín chūn-tuì** the people's army, the army of the people

人民群众 **jén-mín ch'ún-chùng** the masses

人民群众是历史发展的动力 **jén-mín ch'ún-chùng shìh lì-shǐh fā-chǎn te tùng-lì** the masses are the motive force of historical development

人民法官 **jén-mín-fǎ-kuān** people's judges

人民法庭 **jén-mín-fǎ-t'íng** a people's court or tribunal (generally more limited than **fǎ-yuàn** and refers to the actual chamber in which trials are held)

人民法院 **jén-mín-fǎ-yuàn** the people's court (may refer in a broader sense

to the court organization)

人民日报 **jén-mín jìh-pào** *People's Daily* (the official Party newspaper, published in Peking with various local editions, 1948—)

人民革命战争 **jén-mín kó-mìng chàn-chēng** people's revolutionary war

人民革命力量 **jén-mín kó-mìng lì-liang** people's revolutionary forces

人民公社 **jén-mín-kūng-shè** a people's commune, commune

人民公敌 **jén-mín-kūng-tí** a public enemy, common enemy of the people

人民功臣 **jén-mín-kūng-ch'én** People's Hero (a military decoration)

人民共和国 **jén-mín-kùng-hó-kuó** a people's republic

人民民主制度 **jén-mín mín-chǔ-chìh-tù** people's democratic system, a people's democracy

人民民主主义 **jén-mín mín-chǔ-chǔ-ì** people's democracy

人民民主专政 **jén-mín mín-chǔ-chuān-chèng** people's democratic dictatorship

人民民主统一战线 **jén-mín mín-chǔ t'ǔng-ì-chàn-hsièn** the People's Democratic United Front

人民民主自治 **jén-mín mín-chǔ-tzù-chìh** people's democratic self-government

人民内部矛盾 **jén-mín nèi-pù máo-tùn** contradictions among the people

人民保卫工作 **jén-mín pǎo-wèi kūng-tsò** people's security work

人民币 **jén-mín-pì** people's currency (the legal tender of the People's Republic)

人民陪审制 **jén-mín p'éi-shěn-chìh** people's jury system

人民陪审员 **jén-mín p'éi-shěn-yuán** people's juror

人民评弹团 **jén-mín p'íng-t'án-t'uán** people's troupes for folk drama and chanting stories

人民事业 **jén-mín-shìh-yèh** the people's enterprise (the revolution and the building of the country)

人民手册 **jén-mín shǒu-ts'è** *People's Handbook* (published annually in Peking, 1951–1967)

人民税务 **jén-mín shuì-wù** *People's Taxation* (a Peking journal, semi-monthly, 1951–1958)

人民大会堂 **jén-mín tà-huì-t'áng** The Great Hall of the People (in Peking)

人民大学 **jén-mín-tà-hsuéh** the People's University (a university in Peking devoted to the social sciences and humanities)

人民代表大会 **jén-mín tài-piǎo tà-huì**

the People's Congress (at national and local levels)

人民的眼睛是雪亮的 **jén-mín te yěn-chīng shìh hsuěh-liàng-te** the eyes of the people are crystal clear

人民敌人 **jén-mín-tí-jén** enemies of the people (usually includes: bureaucratic capitalists, feudal landlords, counter-revolutionaries, and criminals)

人民体 **jén-mín-t'ǐ** people's [character] forms (a new printing type designed to reduce the differences between the usual handwritten and printed characters)

人民团体 **jén-mín-t'uán-t'ǐ** people's organization, mass organization, civic body

人民子弟兵 **jén-mín tzǔ-tì-pīng** the people's sons-and-brothers soldiers (the PLA)

人民财产 **jén-mín-ts'ái-ch'ǎn** people's property (public property)

人民委员会 **jén-mín wěi-yuán-huì** people's committee, people's council (formerly the governing body at government levels below the national)

人民文学 **jén-mín-wén-hsuéh** (1) literature of the people; (2) *People's Literature* (a Peking journal, monthly, 1949—)

人民武装 **jén-mín-wǔ-chuāng** the people's armed forces (the PLA)

人民武装部 **jén-mín wǔ-chuāng-pù** Department of the People's Arms (the office supervising militia affairs)

人民英雄纪念碑 **jén-mín-yīng-hsiúng chi-nièn-pēi** the cenotaph to the martyrs of the people (in T'ien-an-men Square, Peking)

人莫予毒 **jén-mò-yǔ-tú** others cannot harm me

人背畜驮 **jén-pēi-ch'ù-t'ó** men pack and animals carry (non-mechanized transport)

人本主义 **jén-pěn-chǔ-ì** humanism

人变质，权变色 **jén-pièn-chìh, ch'üán-pièn-sè** [when] men change quality, power changes color (when the ideology changes, there will be a change in [political] power)

人剥削人 **jén-pō-hsuēh-jén** exploitation of man by man

人不为己天诛地灭 **jén-pù-wèi-chǐ, t'iēn-chū-tì-mièh** [if] one does not look out for himself, heaven will punish and earth will destroy [him] (a sarcastic reference to individualism)

人身攻击 **jén-shēn-kūng-chí** to attack personally, *ad hominem* criticism

人身自由 **jén-shēn-tzù-yú** personal freedom

人生观 **jén-shēng-kuān** one's outlook on life, philosophy of life, life view

人士 **jén-shìh** people; personages

人事科 **jén-shìh-k'ō** personnel office

人事档案 **jén-shìh-tàng-àn** personal dossier, a personnel file

人是决定性因素 **jén shìh chüéh-tìng-hsìng yīn-sù** man is the decisive factor

人手 **jén-shǒu** hands, workers, personnel, manpower

人大 **jén-tà** (1) the National People's Congress (contraction of **jén-mín tài-piǎo-tà-huì**; (2) the People's University (contraction of **jén-mín tà-hsuéh**)

人代会 **jén-taì-huì** the National People's Congress (contraction of **jén-mín tài-piǎo-tà-huì**)

人道主义 **jén-tào-chǔ-ì** humanitarianism

人的阶级性 **jén-tè chiēh-chí-hsìng** man's class nature

人的因素第一 **jén-te-yīn-sù tì-ī** the human factor is supreme

人定胜天 **jén-tìng-shèng-t'iēn** man will certainly conquer nature

人体 **jén-t'ǐ** the human body

人头落地 **jén-t'óu-lò-tì** people's heads will fall to the ground (a serious matter—if it is not handled well, lives may be lost)

人造纤维 **jén-tsào-hsiēn-wéi** synthetic fiber

人造棉 **jén-tsào-mién** artificial cotton

人造丝 **jén-tsào-szū** artificial silk, rayon

人造地球卫星 **jén-tsào tì-ch'iú-wèi-hsīng** man-made earth satellite

人造羊毛 **jén-tsào-yáng-máo** artificial wool

人才 **jén-ts'ái** capable people, talented person; personnel; good looks; genius

人才辈出 **jén-ts'ái-pèi-ch'ū** each generation produces men of ability (there are men of talent in all generations; men of talent appear successively)

人材 **jén-ts'ái** (same as **jén-ts'ái**, second above)

人财两旺 **jén-ts'ái liǎng-wàng** men and finance both prosper (a slogan of the land reform period)

人次 **jén-tz'ù** "people-time" (numeral used in counting, e.g., number of participants at meetings, etc.)

人为障碍 **jén-wéi-chàng-ài** man-made difficulties, artificial obstacles

人为困难 **jén-wéi-k'ùn-nán** man-made difficulties

人文主义 **jén-wén-chǔ-ì** humanism

人文地理 **jén-wén-tì-lǐ** human geography, political geography, cultural geography

人武部 **jén-wǔ-pù** Militia Control Department (contraction of **jén-mín-wǔ-chuāng-pù**)

人物 **jén-wù** an outstanding personage; a character [in a novel, play, etc.]

人误地一时, 地误人一季 **jén wù-tì ī-shíh, tì wù-jén ī-chì** if man delays the land for an hour, the land will delay man for a season

人烟断绝 **jén-yēn-tuàn-chüéh** the smoke of men's [habitations] have ceased (a desolate and deserted place)

人员 **jén-yuán** personnel, staff, members

1026 仁爱 **jén-ài** humanity, kindness, benevolence, love

仁者爱人 **jén-chě-ài-jén** those who are benevolent love people (a Confucian doctrine criticized as lacking a class viewpoint)

仁政 **jén-chèng** a benevolent government, humanitarian rule

仁至义尽 **jén-chìh-ì-chìn** humanity fulfilled and justice done (to do the utmost to help those who have made mistakes)

仁义道德 **jén-ì-tào-té** humanity, righteousness and morality (a reference to Confucian ethics—now criticized)

仁慈 **jén-tz'ú** benevolence, charity, kindness, love

jěn (rěn)

1027 忍气吞声 **jěn-ch'ì-t'ūn-shēng** to restrain one's temper and swallow the voice (to endure without protest)

忍耐 **jěn-nài** to be patient; patience

忍无可忍 **jěn-wú-k'ǒ-jěn** having borne the unbearable (to reach the end of one's forbearance)

jèn (rèn)

1028 刃具 **jèn-chù** cutting tools

1029 认真看书学习 **jèn-chēn k'àn-shū hsuéh-hsí** conscientiously to read and study [the works of Marx, Mao, etc.]

认真读书 **jèn-chēn-tú-shū** to read conscientiously (normally refers to the study of Mao's works or Marxist literature)

认真对待 **jèn-chēn-tuì-tài** to take

seriously

认清 **jèn-ch'īng** to recognize clearly, discern, identify

认识 **jèn-shíh** cognition, awareness, understanding, comprehension; to be familiar with, recognize

认识过程 **jèn-shíh-kuò-ch'éng** the process of knowledge, cognition

认识论 **jèn-shíh lùn** the theory of knowledge, epistemology

认识模糊 **jèn-shíh-mó-hu** a vague comprehension, lack of a clear understanding

认识水平 **jèn-shíh-shuǐ-p'íng** level of comprehension

认识问题 **jèn-shíh-wèn-t'í** the problem of knowledge, a problem of comprehension

认输 **jèn-shū** to admit defeat, concede failure

认敌为我 **jèn-tí-wéi-wǒ** to take the enemy as ourselves (to be unable to draw a clear line between friend and the enemy)

认敌为友 **jèn-tí-wéi-yǔ** to take the the enemy as a friend (to confuse friend and the enemy)

认定 **jèn-tìng** to conclude, decide, confirm

认贼作父 **jèn-tséi-tsò-fù** to regard a bandit as one's father (to surrender willingly and completely to the enemy)

认罪 **jèn-tsuì** to admit guilt, concede fault, plead guilty

1030 任重道远 **jèn-chùng tào-yuǎn** a heavy burden and a long road (to assume a serious task that will require long and arduous effort)

任期 **jèn-ch'ī** a term of office, tenure in a post, tour of duty

任其浮沉 **jèn-ch'í-fú-ch'én** to leave him to float or sink (to refuse to give help, remain aloof)

任其自流 **jèn-ch'í-tzù-liú** to let things run their own course

任性 **jèn-hsìng** intractable, refractory, uninhibited, arbitrary; to do as one pleases

任意 **jèn-ì** to do as one pleases; unrestrained, at will, arbitrary, unceremoniously

任人摆布 **jèn-jén-pǎi-pù** to let others do the managing, let oneself be ordered about

任人唯亲 **jèn-jén-wéi-ch'īn** to appoint people only on the basis of closeness (to create a faction)

任人唯贤 **jèn-jén-wéi-hsién** appointing people solely on their merit

任免 **jèn-miěn** hiring and firing [usually in government employment]

任命 **jèn-mìng** to appoint, commission, assign, nominate; nomination

任务 **jèn-wù** an assigned task, duty, responsibility, mission

任用 **jèn-yùng** to appoint to an office; to hire, employ, engage

jēng (rēng)

1031 扔石子 **jēng-shíh-tzǔ** to throw a stone (to give an alerting warning)

jìh (rì)

1032 日照 **jìh-chào** sunlight, daylight

日积月累 **jìh-chī-yuèh-lěi** accumulating daily and piling up monthly, steady accumulation (may refer to the accumulation of experience, funds, etc.)

日久见人心 **jìh-chiǔ chièn jén-hsīn** the passage of time reveals a man's heart

日中备忘录贸易 **jìh-chūng pèi-wàng-lù mào-ì** trade conducted on the basis of the Japan-China Memorandum

日产量 **jìh-ch'ǎn-liàng** daily production output

日程 **jìh-ch'éng** agenda, daily program, itinerary

日清月结 **jìh-ch'īng yuèh-chiéh** daily clearance and monthly summarization (refers to accounting practice of daily entry and monthly balancing)

日趋腐败 **jìh-ch'ǖ-fǔ-pài** deteriorating daily

日全食 **jìh-ch'üán-shíh** a total solar eclipse

日新月异 **jìh-hsīn-yuèh-ì** daily new and monthly different (constant change and improvement)

日益增进 **jìh-ì-tsēng-chìn** increasing day by day

日日红 **jìh-jìh-húng** every day a red day (e.g., setting daily records in production)

日光灯 **jìh-kuāng-tēng** flourescent lamp

日寇 **jìh-k'òu** Japanese bandits (term used during the War of Resistance, 1937–45)

日理万机 **jìh-lǐ-wàn-chī** to handle myriad affairs each day (very busy)

日历 **jìh-lì** a calendar

日暮途穷 **jìh-mù-t'ú-ch'iúng** the day darkens and the road runs out (in a desperate situation, at the end of the road)

日内瓦会议 **jìh-nèi-wǎ huì-ì** the Geneva Conference (1954)

日内瓦公约 **jìh-nèi-wǎ kūng-yuēh** the Geneva Convention (1954)

日本 **jìh-pěn** Japan

日本鬼子 **jìh-pěn kuěi-tzu** Japanese devils (common during the War of Resistance, 1937–45)

日薄西山 **jìh-pó-hsī-shān** the sun nears the western mountains (close to the end, dying)

日偏食 **jìh-p'iēn-shíh** a partial solar eclipse

日食 **jìh-shíh** a solar eclipse

日子富了便生娇 **jìh-tzǔ fù-le pièn shēng-chiāo** when one's days become rich, then one becomes spoiled

日子不好过 **jìh-tzǔ pù-hǎo-kuò** hard times (may refer to either: (1) the life of the peasants and workers in the old society; (2) the difficulties and worsening situation of the opposition or the enemy)

日伪军 **jìh-wěi-chǖn** Japanese puppet troops (Chinese armies who served Japanese sponsored governments in occupied territories during the War of Resistance)

日夜奔忙 **jìh-yèh-pēn-máng** bustling about day and night

日月如梭 **jìh-yuèh-jú-sō** the sun and moon are like shuttles (time goes fast)

日用品 **jìh-yùng-p'ǐn** goods for daily use, daily necessities

jò (ruò)

1033 若即若离 **jò-chí-jò-lí** seemingly close and seemingly apart (halfhearted, lukewarm, uncertain ties)

若明若暗 **jò-míng-jò-àn** seemingly clear and seemingly dark (hazy, unclear, obscure)

若无其事 **jò-wú-ch'í-shìh** as if nothing had happened (to remain calm, perfect composure)

1034 弱肉强食 **jò-jòu-ch'iáng-shíh** the flesh of the weak is eaten by the strong (the survival of the fittest)

弱点 **jó-tiěn** a weak point, shortcoming, deficiency, vulnerability

jóu (róu)

1035 蹂躏 **jóu-lìn** to trample, devastate, ravage

jòu (ròu)

1036 肉中刺 **jòu-chūng-tz'ù** a thorn in the flesh

肉麻 **jòu-má** numb, a creepy sensation of the skin (disgusting, revolting, vulgar, coarse)

肉体 **jòu-t'ǐ** the human body, flesh (usually paired with **líng-hún**— "soul")

jú (rú)

1037 如饥似渴 **jú-chī-szù-k'ǒ** as if [one were] hungry and thirsty (urgently anxious for)

如期 **jú-ch'í** on schedule, at the time set, in time, on the date set

如出一辙 **jú-ch'ū-ī-ch'è** as if out of the same rut (a similarity between actions or statements by different people)

如法炮制 **jú-fǎ-p'ào-chìh** to brew [Chinese medicine] according to rules (to do something by the same formula)

如火如荼 **jú-huǒ-jú-t'ú** like fire and weeds (roaring, blazing, luxuriantly flowering, growing vigorously)

如获至宝 **jú-huò-chìh-pǎo** as if one had obtained the greatest treasure (to cherish what one has)

如意算盘 **jú-ì-suàn-p'án** an abacus that works out as one wishes (wishful thinking)

如鸟兽散 **jú-niǎo-shòu-sàn** to scatter like beasts and birds (to flee helter-skelter—derogatory)

如丧考妣 **jú-sàng-k'ǎo-pǐ** as if one had lost father and mother (worried and anxious—derogatory)

如释重负 **jú-shìh-chùng-fù** as if relieved of a heavy load

如数家珍 **jú-shù-chiā-chēn** like counting one's family treasures (something that one knows very well)

如数归还 **jú-shù-kuēi-huán** to return exactly the same quantity

如坐针毡 **jú-tsò-chēn-chān** like sitting on a rug full of needles (fearful and uneasy)

如此这般 **jú-tz'ǔ-chè-pān** in this way; and so on

如鱼得水 **jú-yǘ-té-shuǐ** like fish take to water (to get on well together)

1038 儒家学说 **jú-chiā-hsuéh-shuō** the doctrines of Confucius, Confucianism

儒法论争 **jú-fǎ lùn-chēng** the polemic between the Confucianists and the Legalists

儒法斗争史 **jú-fǎ tòu-chēng-shǐh** the history of the struggle between the Confucianists and the Legalists

1039 孺子牛 **jú-tzǔ-niú** children's ox (a phrase from a poem by Lu Hsun,

interpreted by Mao as referring to Communists serving the proletarian masses as an obedient ox)

jǔ (rǔ)

1040 辱骂 **jǔ-mà** to abuse, curse, insult, revile

jù (rù)

1041 入境签证 **jù-chìng-ch'iēn-chèng** entry visa

入场 **jù-ch'ǎng** to make an entrance, join a meeting; take an examination

入超 **jù-ch'āo** an adverse trade balance, trade deficit, import excess

入侵 **jù-ch'īn** to invade

入伙分赃 **jù-huǒ-fēn-tsāng** to join a gang and share the loot (figurative)

入门 **jù-mén** to have a rudimentary knowledge, to be initiated into; a primer or beginner's book

入迷 **jù-mí** to be obsessed, bewitched, captivated

入手 **jù-shǒu** a start; to commence, start, begin, get under way; to receive, get one's hands on

入党手续 **jù-tǎng-shǒu-hsù** the formalities of joining the Party

入党做官论 **jù-tǎng-tsò-kuān lùn** the doctrine of entering the Party to become an official (one of Liu Shao-ch'i's **hēi-liù-lùn**)

入伍 **jù-wǔ** to enlist, join the ranks, become a cadet

juǎn (ruǎn)

1042 软肩膀 **juǎn-chiēn-pǎng** soft shoulders (unwilling to take any responsibility)

软指标 **juǎn-chǐh-piāo** a soft target (usually an intangible target, such as quality standards, which cannot be as rigidly applied as quantitative targets)

软禁 **juǎn-chìn** house arrest

软席 **juǎn-hsí** soft seats (the more comfortable railway accomodations)

软任务 **juǎn-jèn-wù** a flexible task (usually refers to work that is not fixed in terms of output or time for completion, such as repair work)

软弱无能 **juǎn-jò-wú-néng** weak [willed] and incompetent

软骗硬逼 **juǎn-p'ièn-yìng-pī** by soft tricks and hard pressure (by menaces and tricks)

软刀子 **juǎn-tāo-tzu** a soft knife (indirect but deadly means)

软卧 **juǎn-wò** soft berths (the more comfortable sleeping accomodations on the railways)

软硬兼施 **juǎn-yìng-chiēn-shīh** to use both persuasion and force

juì (ruì)

1043 锐减 **juì-chiěn** to reduce sharply, decline markedly

锐利 **juì-lì** sharp, pointed, sharp-edged, cutting

1044 瑞士 **juì-shìh** Switzerland

瑞士联邦 **juì-shìh lién-pāng** the Swiss Confederation

瑞典 **juì-tiěn** Sweden

jùn (rùn)

1045 闰年 **jùn-nién** a year in which the lunar calendar has a thirteenth month, an intercalary year

1046 润滑油 **jùn-huá-yú** lubricating oil, lubricating grease, lubricant

润色 **jùn-sè** to add color, embellish, polish [one's writing], to add the final touches

júng (róng)

1047 荣复转退革命军人 **júng-fù-chuǎn-t'uì kó-mìng-chūn-jén** revolutionary soliders who are disabled, demobilized, changed work, or retired

荣誉 **júng-yù** to honor, respect, esteem

荣誉称号 **júng-yù-ch'ēng-hào** a title of honor

荣誉军人 **júng-yù-chūn-jén** a serviceman wounded in action, disabled veteran

1048 容积 **júng-chī** volume, capacity, holding space

容忍 **júng-jěn** to tolerate, bear; tolerance, forbearance

容量 **júng-liàng** capacity [of a container, etc.]

1049 溶剂 **júng-chì** solvents [chemical]

溶解 **júng-chiěh** to dissolve, melt, thaw

溶化 **júng-huà** to dissolve [chemistry], dissolution, melting

1050 熔炉 **júng-lú** a smelting furnace

熔铁 **júng-t'iěh** to smelt iron

熔铁炉 **júng-t'iěh-lú** a blast furnace

1051 融洽 **júng-ch'ià** harmonious [especially, human relations]; amity, concord; to be in unison

融化 **júng-huà** to melt

jǔng (rǒng)

1052 冗长 **jǔng-ch'áng** unnecessarily long [speech or writing]

kǎi (gǎi)

1053 改正 **kǎi-chèng** to correct, rectify, reform, improve

改进 **kǎi-chìn** to improve, better, make progress

改装 **kǎi-chuāng** to re-equip, provide new equipment, change dress, reconvert

改朝换代 **kǎi-ch'áo-huàn-tài** to change the dynasty (a change in regime without altering the character of the government)

改行 **kǎi-háng** to change profession, change one's trade

改换 **kǎi-huàn** to replace, change, substitute for

改邪归正 **kǎi-hsiéh-kuēi-chèng** to alter the crooked back to the straight (to reform, give up evil ways)

改弦更张 **kǎi-hsién-kēng-chāng** to tune the strings (to change course, policies, or methods)

改信 **kǎi-hsìn** to change one's belief, be converted

改选 **kǎi-hsuǎn** to hold a new election, elect new people

改革 **kǎi-kó** to reform, institute reforms; reformation

改观 **kǎi-kuān** to assume a new look, present a new appearance

改良 **kǎi-liáng** to improve, change for the better

改良主义 **kǎi-liáng-chǔ-ì** reformism (as contrasted to revolution)

改良土壤 **kǎi-liáng t'ǔ-jǎng** to improve soil [from infertile to fertile]

改版 **kǎi-pǎn** to make revision [of a book], to change format [of a newspaper]

改编 **kǎi-piēn** to revise [a book], to adapt [as a book into a drama]; to reorganize military units

改变 **kǎi-pièn** to transform, change, alter, modify

改变颜色 **kǎi-pièn-yén-sè** to change color (usually refers to a change away from redness—thus a backsliding from socialism)

改善 **kǎi-shàn** to improve, remedy, reform; improvement

改天换地 **kǎi-t'iēn-huàn-tì** to transform the sky and change the earth (usually refers to the conquest of nature)

改头换面 **kǎi-t'óu-huàn-mièn** to alter the head and change the face (to change appearance without changing in essence, to dissemble)

改土 **kǎi-t'ǔ** to change soil (to improve poor soil into fertile soil—contrac-

tion of **kǎi-liáng t'ǔ-jǎng**)

改土治水 **kǎi-t'ǔ-chìh-shuǐ** improve soil and regulate water

改造 **kǎi-tsào** to remodel, improve; to remold [as ideology]

改造红 **kǎi-tsào-húng** remolded red (persons whose redness has been arrived at through the proper process of study and practice—to be contrasted with **tzù-lái-húng**)

改造沙漠 **kǎi-tsào-shā-mò** to transform [reclaim] the deserts

改造山河 **kǎi-tsào-shān-hó** to change the mountains and rivers (may have an extended application to mean a change in political or social conditions)

改造世界 **kǎi-tsào-shìh-chièh** to change the world (usually refers to the change from capitalism to socialism)

改造世界观 **kǎi-tsào shìh-chièh-kuān** to reform one's world view

改造自然 **kǎi-tsào-tzù-ján** to change nature (to alter physical conditions, conquer nature)

改组 **kǎi-tsǔ** to reorganize, rearrange, reshuffle [a governing body]; reorganization

kài (gài)

1054 概况 **kài-k'uàng** general situation, overall conditions, a description of a general situation

概括 **kài-k'uò** to summarize, sum up; to generalize

概论 **kài-lùn** a general outline, statement of general principles, introduction to a subject

概莫能外 **kài-mò-néng-wài** all included, all covered

概念 **kài-nièn** a concept, general idea

概念化 **kài-nièn-huà** to conceptualize; abstract generalization, conceptualization

kān (gān)

1055 干旱 **kān-hàn** drought, arid

干扰 **kān-jǎo** to interfere, harass, jam [radio broadcasts]

干粮 **kān-liáng** non-perishable food (such as beans or grain); prepared foods capable of being carried while traveling

干量 **kān-liáng** dry measure

干涉 **kān-shè** to interfere, intervene, intrude into; intervention, interference

干死蛤蟆饿死老鼠 **kān-szǔ hā-ma ò-szǔ**

lăo-shu the frogs have died from drought and the rats have starved to death (a desperately poor place)

干脆 **kān-ts'uì** (1) straightforward, unequivocal; frankly, without mincing words; (2) crisp [of food]

干预 **kān-yù** to interfere, intervene, meddle in

干 **kān**: see also **kàn**

1056 甘 **kān** Kansu province

甘蔗 **kān-chè** sugarcane

甘居中游 **kān-chū-chūng-yú** content to stay in the middle reaches (happy with mediocrity; cadres who lack the ambition to forge ahead and yet fear to be left behind)

甘居下游 **kān-chū-hsià-yú** content to remain in the lower reaches [of the stream] (content to lag behind)

甘居人后 **kān-chū-jén-hòu** willing to remain behind others

甘心情愿 **kān-hsīn-ch'íng-yuàn** happily and willingly

甘苦 **kān-k'ǔ** sweetness and bitterness (joys and hardships, prosperity and adversity)

甘酒迪 **kān-năi-tí** Kennedy

甘把天下苦吃遍 **kān-pǎ t'iēn-hsià-k'ǔ ch'īh-pièn** to endure willingly any hardship in the world

甘薯 **kān-shǔ** the sweet potato

甘当群众小学生 **kān-tāng ch'ún-chùng hsiǎo-hsuéh-shēng** happy to be an elementary pupil of the masses

甘托克 **kān-t'ō-k'ò** Gangtok [Sikkim]

甘草剂 **kān-ts'ǎo-chì** a dose of licorice (often added to Chinese herb prescriptions to disguise a bitter taste without altering the value or efficacy of the medicine. Hence used to describe a person without strong character or opinion)

甘愿 **kān-yuàn** willingly, of one's own accord

1057 肝胆相照 **kān-tǎn-hsiāng-chào** liver and gallbladder facing each other (openheartedness between intimate friends)

1058 泔脚 **kān-chiǎo** swill (an important hog feed)

kăn (găn)

1059 赶紧 **kăn-chǐn** quickly, expeditiously; to lose no time

赶超小组 **kăn-ch'āo-hsiǎo-tsǔ** a small group for overtaking and surpassing (a term of experienced workers and specialists who are set up to solve a problem or increase production so as to surpass other enterprises)

赶下台 **kăn-hsià-t'ái** to drive off the stage (to force out of office)

赶先进 **kăn-hsiēn-chìn** to catch up with the advanced

赶跑 **kăn-p'ǎo** to drive away, chase off

赶上形势发展 **kăn-shàng hsíng-shìh-fā-chăn** to keep up with the development of conditions

赶走 **kăn-tsǒu** to drive away, expel, push back, banish

1060 敢教日月换新天 **kăn-chiào jìh-yuèh huàn-hsīn-t'iēn** bold enough to make the sun and moon shine in new skies (with courage to create a new world)

敢唱乱道 **kăn-ch'àng-luán-tào** boldly to advocate heretical principles

敢闯 **kăn-ch'uǎng** to boldly break through, dare to rush into

敢闯万重关 **kăn-ch'uǎng wàn-ch'úng-kuān** to dare to break through ten thousand passes (dauntless, fearless)

敢想敢闯 **kăn-hsiǎng-kăn-ch'uǎng** to dare to think and dare to charge in

敢想敢干 **kăn-hsiǎng-kăn-kàn** dare to think and dare to do

敢想, 敢说. 敢干, 敢革命 **kăn-hsiǎng, kăn-shuō, kăn-kàn, kăn-kó-mìng** dare to think, dare to speak, dare to act, and dare to make revolution

敢怒而不敢言 **kăn-nù érh pù-kăn-yén** angry but not daring to speak

敢上火焰山 **kăn-shàng huǒ-yèn-shān** to dare to climb the mountain of fire (fearless)

敢说, 敢想, 敢做 **kăn-shuō, kăn-hsiǎng, kăn-tsò** to be bold in speech, though, and action; dare to speak, think, and act

敢打必胜 **kăn-tǎ-pì-shèng** to dare to fight and be certain of victory

敢打大仗 **kăn-tǎ-tà-chàng** to dare to enter great battles (figurative)

敢打硬仗 **kăn-tǎ-yìng-chàng** to dare to fight hard battles

敢于反潮流 **kăn-yú fǎn ch'áo-liú** to dare to go against the current (to stand against a political counter-current)

敢于破旧 **kăn-yú p'ò-chiù** to dare to destroy the old

敢于斗争, 敢于胜利 **kăn-yú tòu-chēng, kăn-yú shèng-lì** dare to struggle and dare to be victorious

1061 感激不尽 **kăn-chī-pù-chìn** boundless gratitude

感激涕零 **kăn-chī-t'ì-líng** so grateful that tears are shed (now usually sarcastic)

感情 **kăn-ch'íng** sentiment, feeling, emotion, mutual rapport, devotion

[between friends, etc.]

感觉 **kǎn-chüéh** sensation, feeling; to feel, sense

感恩戴德 **kǎn-ēn-tài-té** gratitude for kindness and favors (used sarcastically)

感性知识 **kǎn-hsìng-chīh-shíh** perceptual knowledge (as contrasted with rational knowledge)

感性形象 **kǎn-hsìng-hsing-hsiàng** affective image, perceived image

感染 **kǎn-jǎn** colored by [of ideas], influenced by, imbued with, tinged with; to be infected [disease]

感人事迹 **kǎn-jén-shìh-chī** moving events, inspiring deeds

感官 **kǎn-kuān** the sensory organs

感伤主义 **kǎn-shāng-chǔ-ì** sensationalism

感到 **kǎn-tào** to sense, perceive, be sensible of, feel that

感动 **kǎn-tùng** to move, touch the feelings, impress, stir the emotions

1062 擀面杖吹火,一窍不通 **kǎn-mièn-chàng ch'uī-huǒ, ī-ch'iào pù-t'ūng** [if one tries to use a] rolling pin to blow on a fire, there is no hole through [it] (a person totally without the understanding to accomplish a task, totally ignorant)

kàn (gàn)

1063 干将 **kàn-chiàng** a very capable person

干劲 **kàn-chìn** energy to work, full of energy; vigor

干劲十足 **kàn-chìn-shíh-tsú** full of energy, full of drive; to go all out

干群关系 **kàn-ch'ún-kuān-hsi** the relationship of cadre and masses, cadre-masses relations

干校 **kàn-hsiào** a cadre training school (contraction of **kàn-pù hsuéh-hsiào**)

干线 **kàn-hsièn** trunk line, through route [railway or highway]

干革命 **kàn-kó-mìng** to engage in revolution, make revolution

干练 **kàn-lièn** competent, capable, experienced

干部 **kàn-pù** a cadre, activist, functionary

干部决定一切 **kàn-pù chüéh-tìng-ī-ch'ièh** cadres decide everything (a criticized attitude—equivalent to commandism)

干部下放 **kàn-pù hsià-fàng** to send down cadres (to transfer cadres from higher to lower organs, on a permanent or temporary basis)

干部下乡 **kàn-pù hsià-hsiāng** cadres go down to the villages

干部学校 **kàn-pù hsúeh-hsiào** cadre training school (see **kàn-hsiào**)

干部路线 **kàn-pù lù-hsièn** the cadre line (the policy guiding the recruitment, training, development and use of cadres)

干部保健制度 **kàn-pù pǎo-chièn chìh-tù** special health service for officials

干部参加生产劳动 **kàn-pù ts'ān-chiā shēng-ch'ǎn láo-tùng** cadre participation in productive labor

干事 **kàn-shìh** to manage business, handle affairs, do a job; an executive member of a committee, clerk

干 **kàn**: see also **kān**

1064 赣 **kàn** Kiangsi province

赣闽皖苏区 **kàn-mǐn-wǎn sū-ch'ǔ** the Kiangsi-Fukien-Anhwei Soviet Region (part of the Soviet Republic during the Kiangsi era)

kāng (gāng)

1065 冈比亚 **kāng-pǐ-yà** Gambia

1066 刚直 **kāng-chíh** upright, tough and honest, firm in principle

刚果(布) **kāng-kuǒ (pù)** [People's Republic of the] Congo (formerly the French Congo; capital: Brazzaville)

1067 纲举目张 **kāng-chǔ-mù-chāng** when the warp [of the fishing net] is raised, all the meshes are stretched (when the key factor of a problem is grasped, the other factors fall into place)

纲领 **kāng-lǐng** a program, guiding principle, leading thought, outline

纲领性文件 **kāng-lǐng-hsìng wén-chièn** programmatic documents

纲目 **kāng-mù** the outline and detailed items, a general outline [main topic and subdivisions]

纲要 **kāng-yào** essential points, an outline, summary

1068 钢渣 **kāng-chā** slag

钢筋 **kāng-chìn** reinforcing steel, reinforcing rods, wire mesh

钢筋混凝土 **kāng-chīn hùn-níng-t'ǔ** reinforced concrete

钢厂 **kāng-ch'ǎng** a steel mill, steel plant

钢琴 **kāng-ch'ín** a piano

钢琴协奏曲 **kāng-ch'ín hsiéh-tsòu-ch'ǔ** a piano concerto

钢琴伴唱 **kāng-ch'ín-pàn-ch'àng** singing with piano accompaniment

钢骨水泥 **kāng-kǔ-shuǐ-ní** reinforced concrete

钢管 **kāng-kuǎn** steel tubing, steel pipe

钢轨 **kāng-kuěi** steel rails

钢块 **kāng-k'uài** a steel ingot, bloom

钢板 **kāng-pǎn** steel plates

钢笔 **kāng-pǐ** a pen, fountain pen

钢帅 **kāng-shuài** commander-in-chief steel (steel production is the controlling factor)

钢锭 **kāng-tìng** a steel ingot, steel slab

钢条 **kāng-t'iáo** a steel bar, steel girder

钢铁重点企业 **kāng-t'iěh chùng-tiěn-ch'ǐ-yèh** key iron and steel enterprises

钢铁联合企业 **kāng-t'iěh lién-hó-ch'ǐ-yèh** an iron and steel complex, integrated iron and steel works

钢材 **kāng-ts'ái** steel stock, steel products, rolled steel

钢印 **kāng-yìn** a steel seal, impression seal

kǎng (gǎng)

1069 岗哨 **kǎng-shào** a sentry, sentinel

岗位 **kǎng-wèi** a sentry post (a citizen's responsibility in society)

岗位责任制 **kǎng-wèi tsé-jèn-chìh** a system of [each person] being responsibile for his post

1070 港口 **kǎng-k'ǒu** a port, harbor

港务局 **kǎng-wù-chú** port-control office

港务管理局 **kǎng-wù kuǎn-lǐ-chú** port [harbor] administrative office

kàng (gàng)

1071 杠杆 **kàng-kǎn** a pole, lever

kāo (gāo)

1072 高昂 **kāo-áng** rising, becoming higher; ambitious

高傲 **kāo-ào** arrogant, haughty

高瞻远瞩 **kāo-chān-yuǎn-chǔ** to look high and gaze far (farsighted)

高涨 **kāo-chàng** to rise; an upsurge, upswing; mounting, gaining momentum

高枕无忧 **kāo-chěn-wú-yū** to pile up pillows and sleep without worry (insensitive and blindly optimistic)

高级知识分子 **kāo-chí chīh-shíh-fèn-tzǔ** highly qualified intellectuals

高级合作社 **kāo-chí hó-tsò-shè** higher-level cooperatives, cooperatives of the advanced type

高级小学 **kāo-chí-hsiǎo-hsuéh** senior primary school

高级干部 **kāo-chí-kàn-pù** high-ranking cadres

高级农业生产合作社 **kāo-chí núng-yèh shēng-ch'ǎn hó-tsò-shè** advanced agricultural producers cooperative

高级社 **kāo-chí-shè** high-level cooperative, higher cooperative, advanced-level cooperative

高价收买 **kāo-chià shōu-mǎi** to buy at a high price

高价作物 **kāo-chià-tsò-wù** high-value crops

高教部 **kāo-chiào-pù** Ministry of Higher Education (contraction of **kāo-těng chiào-yǜ-pù**)

高精尖产品 **kāo-chīng-chīen ch'ǎn-p'ǐn** advanced products of high precision and quality

高中心外园磨床 **kāo-chūng-hsīn wài-yuán mò-ch'uáng** high-centered cylindrical grinding machine

高产规律 **kāo-ch'ǎn-kuēi-lù** the rules [for producing] high yields

高产良田 **kāo-ch'ǎn-liáng-t'ién** a high-yield field

高产试验田 **kāo-ch'ǎn shìh-yèn-t'ién** high-yield experimental plot

高产到顶 **kāo-ch'ǎn-tào-tǐng** the high-yield has reached a ceiling (a criticized idea that no further improvements in yield are possible)

高产作物 **kāo-ch'ǎn-tsò-wù** high-yield crop

高产稳产 **kāo-ch'ǎn-wěn-ch'ǎn** constant high-yielding, stabilized high yield

高潮 **kāo-ch'áo** high tide, flood tide, climax, upswing

高出一头 **kāo-ch'ū-ī-t'óu** higher by a head (to stand head and shoulders above others)

高举毛泽东思想红旗 **kāo-chǔ máo tsé-tūng szū-hsiǎng húng-ch'i** hold high the red banner of the Thought of Mao Tse-tung

高踞于人民之上 **kāo-chǜ yǘ jén-mín-chíh-shàng** to stand on the shoulders of the masses, to remain above the masses

高峰会议 **kāo-fēng-huì-ì** a summit meeting

高寒区域 **kāo-hán-ch'ū-yǜ** a high and cold region

高寒山区 **kāo-hán-shān-ch'ū** a high and cold mountainous area

高效利润 **kāo-hsiào-lì-jùn** super-profit

高兴 **kāo-hsìng** happy, pleased, glad, jubilant, amused

高一阵, 低一阵 **kāo-ī-chèn, tī-ī-chèn** sometimes up and sometimes down (fluctuating, unsteady)

高人一等 **kāo-jén-ī-těng** one grade above the others, to tower over the rest, stand out

高干 **kāo-kàn** higher-level cadres (contraction of **kāo-chí-kàn-pù**)

高岗 **kāo kāng** Kao Kang (a Communist and post-Liberation administrator of Manchuria, purged along with Jao Shu-shih in 1954)

高岗, 饶漱石反党联盟 **kāo kāng, jáo shù-shíh fǎn-tǎng-lién-méng** the anti-Party alliance of Kao Kang and Jao Shu-shih (see above)

高高在上 **kāo-kāo-tsài-shàng** to hold oneself loftily aloof, consider oneself superior

高贵品质 **kāo-kuèi-p'ǐn-chìh** noble qualities [of a person]

高考制度 **kāo-k'ǎo-chìh-tù** the system of entrance examination for admission to colleges and universities

高空观测 **kāo-k'ūng-kuān-ts'è** aerial reconnaissance

高空带电作业 **kāo-k'ūng tài-tièn tsò-yèh** aerial power transmission line work

高空作业 **kāo-k'ūng-tsò-yèh** high elevation work (construction work such as on bridges or high buildings)

高利贷 **kāo-lì-tài** usury

高粱 **kāo-liáng** kaoliang, sorghum

高楼建筑物 **kāo-lóu chièn-chù-wù** multi-story building

高楼深院 **kāo-lóu-shēn-yuàn** a high building and deep courtyards (to be isolated from the masses)

高炉 **kāo-lú** a blast furnace, iron-smelting furnace

高炉操作工人 **kāo-lú ts'ào-tsò-kūng-jén** a blast-furnace operator

高明 **kāo-míng** brilliant, discerning, clever, wise, highly competent

高额 **kāo-ó** a high fixed amount, high quota

高不可攀 **kāo-pù-k'ǒ-p'ān** so high that it is hard to reach (difficult to attain)

高山反应 **kāo-shān-fǎn-yìng** altitude sickness, the effects of high altitude

高山族 **kāo-shān-tsú** the Kao-shan people (a minority in Taiwan: population 200,000)

高射机关枪 **kāo-shè chī-kuān-ch'iāng** anti-aircraft machine gun

高射炮 **kāo-shè-p'ào** anti-aircraft gun

高渗透层 **kāo-shèn-t'òu-ts'éng** highly water-retentive strata

高速 **kāo-sù** high speed

高速轧钢法 **kāo-sù chá-kāng-fǎ** high-speed rolling method [of steel, etc.]

高速切削 **kāo-sù ch'iēh-hsuēh** high-speed [metal] cutting

高速度按比例发展 **kāo-sù-tù àn-pǐ-lì fā-chǎn** to develop at high speed and proportionately

高等教育 **kāo-těng-chiào-yù** higher education

高等教育部 **kāo-těng chiào-yù-pù** Ministry of Higher Education (see **kāo-chiào-pù**)

高等学校 **kāo-těng-hsuéh-hsiào** college and university-level schools

高等学校招生委员会 **kāo-těng hsuéh-hsiào chāo-shēng wěi-yuán-huì** an admissions committee for higher education

高等院校 **kāo-těng yuàn-hsiào** higher-level educational institutions (college, university and institute level)

高度 **kāo-tù** a high degree [of], highly, great; altitude, height, elevation

高度集中统一 **kāo-tù-chí-chūng t'ǔng-ī** highly centralized unity

高度现代化 **kāo-tù hsièn-tài-huà** highly modernized

高度意志力 **kāo-tù ì-chìh-lì** concentrated willpower

高度劳动热情 **kāo-tù láo-tùng jè-ch'íng** high enthusiasm for work

高度原则性 **kāo-tù yuán-tsé-hsìng** highly principled

高抬物价 **kāo-t'ái wù-chià** to force up the price

高谈阔论 **kāo-t'án-k'uò-lùn** a loud harangue, a broad lecture (usually suggests empty talk)

高温 **kāo-wēn** high temperature

高温车间 **kāo-wēn-ch'ē-chiēn** a high-temperature workshop

高屋建瓴 **kāo-wū chièn-líng** to pour a bottle [of water] from the roof of a high building (since the water must flow downward: an irresistible tendency)

高压 **kāo-yā** high pressure, high-tension

高压手段 **kāo-yā-shǒu-tuàn** repressive measures, high-handed tactics

高压输电线 **kāo-yā shū-tièn-hsièn** high-tension power transmission line

高压电焊 **kāo-yā tièn-hàn** high-tension electric welding

高于一切 **kāo-yǘ-ī-ch'ièh** the highest, ultimate, supreme

高原 **kāo-yuán** high plain, plateau

1073 膏、丹、丸、散、酊 **kāo, tān, wán, sǎn, tǐng** ointment, pills, pellets, powder, tincture (the five forms of Chinese medicine)

kǎo (gǎo)

1074 搞 **kǎo** to do, carry out, be engaged in, stir up, busy oneself with

搞成 **kǎo-ch'éng** to accomplish, bring

about, realize

搞出个名堂来 **kǎo-ch'ū ko míng-t'áng lai** to achieve something noteworthy

搞复辟 **kǎo fù-p'ì** to engage in restoration [of capitalism, etc.]

搞好 **kǎo-hǎo** to do well, accomplish thoroughly

搞好学习 **kǎo-hǎo hsuéh-hsí** to do well in studying

搞好关系 **kǎo-hǎo kuān-hsi** to achieve good relations

搞好生产 **kǎo-hǎo shēng-ch'ǎn** to do a good job with production

搞小广播 **kǎo hsiǎo-kuǎng-pō** to be a gossip-monger, engage in gossip

搞小动作 **kǎo hsiǎo-tùng-tsò** to engage in petty actions

搞革新 **kǎo kó-hsīn** to engage actively in renovation, to busy oneself in reform

搞革命 **kǎo kó-mìng** to engage in revolution, make revolution

搞垮 **kǎo-k'uǎ** to smash, shatter, wreck, disrupt, destroy, cause the collapse of

搞乱 **kǎo-luàn** to create confusion, make mischief

搞不清 **kǎo-pù-ch'īng** unable to make clear, unable to understand, confused

搞深搞透 **kǎo-shēn-kǎo-t'òu** to carry on [a campaign] deeply and penetratingly

搞施工 **kǎo-shīh-kūng** to engage in construction work

搞对头 **kǎo-tuì-t'óu** to do something correctly

搞懂 **kǎo-tǔng** to achieve understanding, understand

搞通 **kǎo-t'ūng** to obtain a clear understanding and acceptance

搞通思想 **kǎo-t'ūng szū-hsiǎng** to obtain a complete acceptance of [Communist] ideology without mental reservation

搞在一起 **kǎo-tsài-ī-ch'ǐ** to put together, merge, amalgamate, join with

搞糟 **kǎo-tsāo** to botch, bungle, make a mess of

搞资产阶级复辟 **kǎo tzū-ch'ǎn-chiēh-chí fù-p'ì** to engage in a capitalist restoration

搞卫生 **kǎo-wèi-shēng** to engage in public health, to do cleaning [of house, office, street, etc.]

搞右倾翻案 **kǎo-yù-ch'īng fān-àn** to engage in the rehabilitation of rightists

1075 稿件 **kǎo-chièn** a manuscript [submitted for publication]

稿费 **kǎo-fèi** writer's fees

稿子 **kǎo-tzu** a written draft, manuscript

kào (gào)

1076 告诫 **kào-chièh** to admonish, warn, enjoin, caution, reprimand

告状 **kào-chuàng** to file a legal complaint, accuse, charge

告终 **kào-chūng** to come to an end; to end, close, conclude

告发 **kào-fā** to inform on someone, to report, accuse, denounce

告密 **kào-mì** to make a secret report, report to the authorities on secret matters, give a tip

告别 **kào-piéh** to bid farewell, take one's leave, say goodbye

告示 **kào-shih** to make, announce, proclaim an official notice; proclamation, bulletin

告辞 **kào-tz'ú** to take leave of, bid farewell

kěi (gěi)

1077 给出路 **kěi ch'ū-lù** to leave one a way out (to give a person committing a fault some chance to continue useful work)

给小鞋穿 **kěi hsiǎo-hsiéh ch'ūan** to give one shoes that are too small (to treat badly, harass)

给以致命打击 **kěi ǐ chìh-mìng-tǎ-chī** to deal a fatal blow

给 **kei**: see also **chǐ**

kēn (gēn)

1078 根治海河 **kēn-chìh hǎi-hó** permanent control of the Hai River

根治淮河 **kēn-chìh huái-hó** permanent control of the Huai River

根治水患 **kēn-chìh shuǐ-huàn** permanent control of floods

根除 **kēn-ch'ú** to root out, uproot, exterminate, eradicate, wipe out

根据地 **kēn-chù-tì** a base area

根绝 **kēn-chüéh** to root out, eradicate

根红苗壮 **kēn-húng miáo-chuàng** red roots and strong sprouts (good class background and good education)

根本性 **kēn-pěn-hsìng** fundamental nature, basic character

根本性质的变化 **kēn-pěn hsìng-chìh-te pièn-huà** a change of fundamental character

根本立场 **kēn-pěn lì-ch'ǎng** basic standpoint

根本利益 **kēn-pěn-lì-ì** basic interests, fundamental interests

根深蒂固 **kēn-shēn tì-kù** roots deep and branches strong (deeply ingrained, inveterate)

根本对立 **kēn-pěn-tuì-lì** fundamentally opposed, diametrically opposed

根本态度 **kēn-pěn t'ài-tù** basic attitude

根子正 **kēn-tzu-chèng** the root is true (of good class background and experienced in struggle)

根源 **kēn-yuán** source, roots, origin, cause

1079 跟班劳动 **kēn-pān láo-tùng** [cadres] working with the shifts [in factories]

kēng (gēng)

1080 更正 **kēng-chèng** to put right, correct; correction

更换 **kēng-huàn** to change, replace, alter, remove

更新 **kēng-hsīn** to renew, renovate, improve

更 **kēng**: *see also* **kèng**

1081 耕者有其田 **kēng-chě yǔ-ch'í-t'ién** the tillers [should] possess their fields, land to the tillers

耕种 **kēng-chùng** to cultivate, engage in agriculture; farming

耕畜 **kēng-ch'ù** a plow animal

耕牛保险 **kēng-níu-pǎo-hsiěn** draft ox insurance

耕地面积 **kēng-tì-mièn-chī** cultivated acreage, crop area

耕读小学 **kēng-tú-hsiǎo-hsuéh** plow-and-read primary schools (for poor and lower-middle peasants, adults as well as children)

耕田队 **kēng-t'ién-tuì** a field-tilling squad

耕作区 **kēng-tsò-ch'ü** a plowed zone, plowed area

耕作时间 **kēng-tsò-shíh-chiēn** tillage time

耕作园田化 **kēng-tsò yuán-t'ién-huà** to intensify [garden-style] cultivation

kěng (gěng)

1082 梗阻 **kěng-tsǔ** to obstruct, hinder

kèng (gèng)

1083 更加壮大 **kèng-chiā-chuàng-tà** to grow even stronger

更加混乱 **kèng-chiā-hùn-luàn** to make the confusion even worse, intensify disorder; chaos compounded

更加巩固 **kèng-chiā-kǔng-kù** to consolidate even more firmly

更进一步 **kèng-chìn-í-pù** to go one step further, even further

更大胜利 **kèng-tà shèng-lì** an even greater victory

更 **kèng**: *see also* **kēng**

kō (gē)

1084 戈壁 **kō-pì** a desolate area of sand covered by pebbles, a desert; the Gobi Desert

1085 仡佬族 **kō-lǎo-tsú** the Ko-lao people (a minority in Kweichow province: population 20,000 as of 1957—often misread as Ch'i-lao)

1086 疙瘩 **kō-ta** a pimple, boil, knot; any small, round object (a problem that is difficult to solve)

疙瘩解不开 **kō-ta chiěh-pù-k'āi** a complication that cannot be unraveled

1087 哥老会 **kō-lǎo-huì** the Elder Brothers Society (a secret society, dissolved after 1949)

哥伦比亚 **kō-lún-pǐ-yà** [Republic of] Colombia

哥本哈根 **kō-pěn-hā-kēn** Copenhagen

哥斯达黎加 **kō-szū-tá-lí-chiā** [Republic of] Costa Rica

哥达纲领批判 **kō-tá kāng-lǐng p'ī-p'àn** [Marx's] *Critique of the Gotha Programme*

1088 割据 **kō-chü** to cut off [a territory], occupy [a region in derogation of national sovereignty]; territorial fragmentation

割据者 **kō-chü-chě** one who divides [country or territory], an annexationist

割让 **kō-jàng** to cede [territory]

割裂 **kō-lièh** to split, slash, rip open

割煤机 **kō-méi-chī** mechanical coal cutter, coal-cutting machine

割断 **kō-tuàn** to cut off, sever, separate

割草机 **kō-ts'ǎo-chī** hay-mowing machine, grass cutter

1089 搁置 **kō-chìh** to set aside, discontinue, postpone, table [a bill]

搁浅 **kō-ch'iěn** to be stranded in shallows, run aground, founder

1090 歌曲 **kō-ch'ǔ** songs (does not include selections from operas)

歌功颂德 **kō-kūng-sùng-té** to sing merits and praise virtues

歌手 **kō-shǒu** a singer (usually of folk songs)

歌颂 **kō-sùng** to sing praises, extol

歌舞团 **kō-wǔ-t'uán** a singing and dancing troupe

kó (gé)

革职 **kó-chíh** to dismiss from office, remove from a post, dismiss

革除 **kó-ch'ú** to get rid of, dismiss, expel, eliminate, exclude

革新 **kó-hsīn** to reform, renovate, change for the better

革心洗面 **kó-hsīn-hsǐ-mièn** change the heart and wash the face (to confess error and reform)

革新能手 **kó-hsīn-néng-shǒu** a good hand at technical improvements

革新派 **kó-hsīn-p'ài** reformist groups

革命 **kó-mìng** a revolution; revolutionary

革命战争 **kó-mìng-chàn-chēng** revolutionary war

革命朝气 **kó-mìng-chāo-ch'ì** revolutionary vitality, revolutionary elan

革命阵营 **kó-mìng-chèn-yíng** the revolutionary camp

革命政权 **kó-mìng-chèng-ch'üán** revolutionary regime, revolutionary government

革命政党 **kó-mìng-chèng-tǎng** a revolutionary party

革命积极性 **kó-mìng chī-chí-hsìng** revolutionary initiative, revolutionary activism

革命激情 **kó-mìng-chī-ch'íng** revolutionary fervor, revolutionary enthusiasm, revolutionary excitement

革命纪律 **kó-mìng-chì-lù** revolutionary discipline

革命家 **kó-mìng-chiā** a revolutionary

革命交响音乐 **kó-mìng chiāo-hsiǎng yīn-yuèh** revolutionary symphonic music

革命接班人 **kó-mìng-chiēh-pān-jén** a revolutionary successor (the younger generation of activist Party members)

革命接班人五个条件 **kó-mìng-chiēh-pān-jén wǔ-ko t'iáo-chièn** the five requisites for revolutionary successors (truly Marxist-Leninist; determined to serve the people of China and the great majority of the world; able to unite with and lead the proletariat; able to listen to the masses; willing to criticize himself and to correct mistakes in his work)

革命知识分子 **kó-mìng chīh-shíh-fèn-tzǔ** revolutionary intellectuals

革命秩序 **kó-mìng-chìh-hsù** revolutionary order, revolutionary discipline

革命进取心 **kó-mìng chìn-ch'ǔ-hsīn** a revolutionary aggressive spirit

革命进行到底 **kó-mìng chìn-hsíng tào-tǐ** the revolution [must be] carried to the end

革命精神 **kó-mìng-chīng-shén** revolutionary spirit

革命景象 **kó-mìng-chǐng-hsiàng** revolutionary outlook, revolutionary prospects

革命警惕 **kó-mìng-chǐng-t'ì** revolutionary alertness

革命竞赛 **kó-mìng-chìng-sài** revolutionary emulation, revolutionary competition

革命敬礼 **kó-mìng-chìng-lǐ** the revolutionary salute (a phrase in closing a letter)

革命转化 **kó-mìng-chuǎn-huà** revolutionary transformation

革命成果 **kó-mìng-ch'éng-kuǒ** revolutionary fruits, the achievements of the revolution

革命气氛 **kó-mìng-ch'ì-fēn** revolutionary atmosphere

革命前辈 **kó-mìng-ch'ién-pèi** revolutionary elders, revolutionary forerunners (refers to persons no longer living)

革命传统 **kó-mìng-ch'uán-t'ǔng** revolutionary tradition, revolutionary heritage

革命闯将 **kó-mìng-ch'uǎng-chiàng** a revolutionary pathbreaker, a revolutionary bravo (a Cultural Revolution term for the Red Guards)

革命军人 **kó-mìng-chǔn-jén** revolutionary soldiers

革命全局 **kó-mìng-ch'üán-chú** the overall situation of the revolution

革命权威 **kó-mìng-ch'üán-wēi** revolutionary prestige, revolutionary authority

革命群众 **kó-mìng-ch'ǔn-chùng** revolutionary masses

革命群众组织 **kó-mìng ch'ǔn-chùng-tsǔ-chīh** revolutionary mass organizations

革命群众运动 **kó-mìng ch'ǔn-chùng yùn-tùng** revolutionary mass movements (campaigns)

革命发展阶段论 **kó-mìng-fā-chǎn chiēh-tuàn lùn** the theory of the development of revolution by stages

革命分工 **kó-mìng-fēn-kūng** the division of labor in revolutionary tasks

革命风格 **kó-mìng-fēng-kó** revolutionary style (usually refers to personal bearing and actions)

革命风暴 **kó-mìng-fēng-pào** revolutionary storm

革命豪情 **kó-mìng-háo-ch'íng** revolu-

tionary vigor, revolutionary spirits
革命化建设 **kó-mìng-huà chièn-shè** to revolutionize construction (used in a broad sense, e.g., to rebuild [develop] education, industry, or a Party organization so that it will better serve the revolution)

革命洪流 **kó-mìng-húng-liú** revolutionary mainstream

革命活动纪念地 **kó-mìng-huó-tùng chì-nièn-tì** places memorializing revolutionary activities (revolutionary historical landmarks)

革命火炬 **kó-mìng-huǒ-chù** the revolutionary torch

革命小将 **kó-mìng-hsiǎo-chiàng** the little revolutionary generals (young students active in voluntary political agitation)

革命现实主义 **kó-mìng hsièn-shíh-chǔ-ì** revolutionary realism

革命现代京剧 **kó-mìng hsièn-tài-chǐng-chù** revolutionary Peking operas on contemporary themes (an early term for some of the dramas that eventually were modified to become **yàng-pǎn-hsì**)

革命现代舞剧 **kó-mìng hsièn-tài-wǔ-chù** modern revolutionary ballets

革命新风 **kó-mìng-hsīn-fēng** revolutionary new customs and habits

革命行动 **kó-mìng-hsíng-tùng** revolutionary actions

革命形势 **kó-mìng-hsíng-shìh** the revolutionary situation

革命性 **kó-mìng-hsìng** revolutionary nature, revolutionary character

革命一松生产必空 **kó-mìng ī-sūng, shēng-ch'ǎn pì-k'ūng** when revolutionary [spirit] is relaxed, production is sure to show a gap

革命热情 **kó-mìng-jè-ch'íng** revolutionary enthusiasm

革命人道主义 **kó-mìng jén-tào-chǔ-ì** revolutionary humanitarianism

革命人才 **kó-mìng-jén-ts'ái** revolutionary gifted persons, revolutionary talents

革命熔炉 **kó-mìng-júng-lú** the revolutionary crucible, the crucible of revolution

革命干劲 **kó-mìng-kàn-chìn** revolutionary drive, revolutionary Party energy

革命干部 **kó-mìng-kàn-pù** revolutionary cadres

革命根据地 **kó-mìng kēn-chù-tì** a revolutionary base area

革命歌曲 **kó-mìng-kō-ch'ǔ** a revolutionary song

革命科学技术人员 **kó-mìng k'ō-hsuéh**

chì-shù jén-yuán revolutionary scientific and technical personnel

革命浪漫主义 **kó-mìng làng-màn-chǔ-ì** revolutionary romanticism

革命老根据地 **kó-mìng lǎo-kēn-chù-tì** the old revolutionary bases (the old Soviet areas—pre-1937)

革命乐观主义 **kó-mìng lè-kuān-chǔ-ì** revolutionary optimism

革命理论 **kó-mìng-lǐ-lùn** revolutionary theories, revolutionary doctrines

革命领袖 **kó-mìng-lǐng-hsiù** revolutionary leaders

革命领导小组 **kó-mìng lǐng-tǎo-hsiǎo-tsǔ** a revolutionary leading small group (may be in any organization)

革命路线 **kó-mìng-lù-hsièn** the revolutionary line

革命怒火 **kó-mìng-nù-huǒ** the fierce fire of revolution

革命暴力 **kó-mìng-pào-lì** revolutionary violence

革命本色 **kó-mìng-pěn-sè** basic revolutionary color (true revolutionary spirit)

革命变化 **kó-mìng-pièn-huà** revolutionary change, revolutionary transformation

革命步子迈不出去 **kó-mìng-pù-tzu mài-pu-ch'ū-ch'ù** to be unable to start walking on the revolutionary path (e.g., to be lacking in the proper ideological motivation)

革命派 **kó-mìng-p'ài** revolutionaries, the revolutionary group

革命生产两不误 **kó-mìng shēng-ch'ǎn liǎng-pù-wù** neither revolution nor production are impeded (both activities are vital and should be pursued simultaneously)

革命圣地 **kó-mìng-shèng-tì** a sacred place of the revolution (normally refers to Yenan)

革命实践 **kó-mìng-shíh-chièn** revolutionary practice

革命事业 **kó-mìng-shìh-yèh** the revolutionary cause, revolutionary work

革命首创精神 **kó-mìng shǒu-ch'uàng-chǐng-shén** revolutionary pioneering spirit

革命思想 **kó-mìng-szū-hsiǎng** revolutionary thought, revolutionary ideology

革命大串连 **kó-mìng tà-ch'uàn-lién** traveling for extensive exchange of experiences in the [Cultural] Revolution

革命大好形势 **kó-mìng tà-hǎo-hsíng-shìh** the revolutionary situation is most favorable

革命大联合 **kó-mìng tà-lién-hó** The Revolutionary Great Alliance (a Cultural Revolution attempt to unite competing factions)

革命大批判 **kó-mìng tà-p'ī-p'àn** revolutionary mass criticism [and repudiation] (a Cultural Revolution call for public action in expunging revisionism and reactionary thought)

革命党人 **kó-mìng-tǎng-jén** revolutionary party members, members of a revolutionary party

革命导师 **kó-mìng-tǎo-shīh** the teacher of the revolution (usually refers to Mao Tse-tung)

革命到顶 **kó-mìng-tào-tǐng** the revolution has reached its culmination (the opposite of the theory of continuous revolution)

革命到头 **kó-mìng-tào-t'óu** the revolution has already reached its end

革命斗争 **kó-mìng-tòu-chēng** revolutionary struggle

革命斗志 **kó-mìng-tòu-chìh** revolutionary morale, revolutionary fighting spirit

革命队伍 **kó-mìng-tuì-wǔ** the revolutionary ranks

革命对象 **kó-mìng-tuì-hsiàng** a target of the revolution

革命动力 **kó-mìng-tùng-lì** the motive force of the revolution

革命团结 **kó-mìng-t'uán-chiéh** revolutionary solidarity, revolutionary unity

革命造反派 **kó-mìng-tsào-fǎn-p'ài** revolutionary rebels

革命才干 **kó-mìng-ts'ái-kàn** revolutionary ability, revolutionary talents

革命促生产 **kó-mìng ts'ù shēng-ch'ǎn** revolution promotes production

革命委员会 **kó-mìng wěi-yuán-huì** revolutionary committees (set up at all levels as "provisional organs of power" during the Cultural Revolution)

革命委员会筹备小组 **kó-mìng wěi-yuán-huì ch'óu-pèi hsiǎo-tsǔ** revolutionary committee preparatory team (a small group to prepare for [organize] the revolutionary committee)

革命文艺节目 **kó-mìng-wén-ì chiéh-mù** a program of revolutionary literature and arts (usually refers to an evening of drama and music)

革命文艺典型化 **kó-mìng-wén-ì tiěn-hsíng-huà** to make revolutionary literature and art into exemplary models

革命文物 **kó-mìng-wén-wù** cultural objects of the revolution, revolucultural relics

革命武装 **kó-mìng-wǔ-chuāng** revolutionary armed forces

革命样板戏 **kó-mìng yàng-pǎn-hsì** revolutionary model dramas (see **yàng-pǎn-hsì**)

革命要争先 **kó-mìng yào chēng-hsiēn** in revolution one should strive to be in the forefront

革命英雄 **kó-mìng-yīng-hsiúng** a revolutionary hero

革命英雄主义 **kó-mìng-yīng-hsiúng-chǔ-ì** revolutionary heroism

革命舆论 **kó-mìng-yǔ-lùn** revolutionary public opinion

革命原则 **kó-mìng-yuán-tsé** the basic principles of revolution

革命勇气 **kó-mìng-yǔng-ch'ì** revolutionary courage

革掉 **kó-tiào** to cut off, eliminate, get rid of

革自己的命 **kó tzù-chǐ te mìng** to wage revolution against oneself

革委会 **kó-wěi-huì** revolutionary committee (contraction of **kó-mìng wěi-yuán-huì**)

1092

格格不入 **kó-kó-pù-jù** neither fits into the other, incompatible with, completely unsuitable

格陵兰 **kó-líng-lán** Greenland

格杀 **kó-shā** to capture and summarily execute; to kill

格式 **kó-shìh** a form, style, pattern, sample

格外 **kó-wài** out of the normal, exceptional, unusual, extraordinary

格言 **kó-yén** a proverb, maxim, aphorism, motto, saying

1093

隔岸观火 **kó-àn-kuān-huǒ** to watch a fire from the opposite bank (to fail to help in another's distress, to take a bystander attitude)

隔绝 **kó-chüéh** to cut off, isolate, be separated from; blocked, obstructed

隔阂 **kó-hó** losing contact, out of touch, misunderstanding, a mental barrier

隔靴搔痒 **kó-hsuēh-sāo-yǎng** to scratch an itch through the shoe (failing to get to the point, having no effect)

隔离 **kó-lí** to isolate, separate; isolation, quarantine

隔膜 **kó-mó** (1) a barrier, diaphragm, the septum; (2) to have no communication or contact with; misunderstanding, disagreement, enmity

隔断 **kó-tuàn** to sever, cut off, isolate; obstructed, blocked

kò (gè)

1094 个性 **kò-hsìng** personality, individuality, individual character

个性解放 **kò-hsìng-chǐeh-fàng** emancipation of man's individual personality

个人 **kò-jén** individual [as contrasted with group]; personally, personal; oneself

个人整改阶段 **kò-jén chěng-kǎi chǐeh-tuàn** the stage of individual reform (a stage of somewhat reduced criticism in the main anti-rightist campaign; mid-December 1957)

个人经历 **kò-jén-chīng-lì** personal history, personal experience

个人主义 **kò-jén-chǔ-ì** individualism [as opposed to collectivism]

个人主义思想 **kò-jén-chǔ-ì szū-hsiǎng** individualistic thinking

个人主义野心家 **kò-jén-chǔ-ì yěh-hsīn-chiā** an individualistic careerist

个人成长史 **kò-jén ch'éng-chǎng-shǐh** the history of an individual's development (implies having reached maturity and stature and may include political growth or the achievement of outstanding skills or accomplishments)

个人成份 **kò-jén-ch'éng-fèn** individual [class] background

个人崇拜 **kò-jén-ch'úng-pài** the cult of personality

个人迷信 **kò-jén-mí-hsìn** the cult of the individual, personality cult

个人包办 **kò-jén-pāo-pàn** individual control of management; to monopolize management

个人所有制 **kò-jén sǒ-yǔ-chìh** individual private ownership, personal ownership

个人第一 **kò-jén-tì-ī** the individual comes first

个人野心 **kò-jén-yěh-hsīn** individual ambition, self-seeking

个人英雄主义 **kò-jén yīng-hsiúng-chǔ-ì** individualistic heroism

个别 **kò-pǐeh** individually, one by one, separately, isolated

个别辅导 **kò-pǐeh-fǔ-tǎo** individual tutoring

个体 **kò-t'ǐ** an entity; individual [as opposed to collective]

个体经济 **kò-t'ǐ-chīng-chì** individual economy [as contrasted with collective economy]

个体经营 **kò-t'ǐ chīng-yíng** individual operation [of an enterprise]

个体小农业 **kò-t'ǐ hsiǎo-núng-yèh** individual small-scale agriculture

个体劳动者 **kò-t'ǐ láo-tùng-chě** individual laborer, laborer work on his own

个体农民 **kò-t'ǐ-núng-mín** individual peasant

个体手工业 **kò-t'ǐ shǒu-kūng-yèh** individual handicraft industry

个体所有制 **kò-t'ǐ sǒ-yǔ-chìh** private ownership, individual ownership system

1095 各级 **kò-chí** various levels, at all levels

各阶层 **kò-chǐeh-ts'éng** at all levels, all walks of life, of all social strata

各界 **kò-chìeh** the various walks of life

各执一词 **kò-chíh-ī-tz'ú** each [disputant] holds fast to his own story

各尽所能，按需分配 **kò-chìn-sǒ-néng, àn-hsū-fēn-p'èi** from each according to his ability and to each according to his needs

各尽所能，按劳分配 **kò-chìn-sǒ-néng, àn-láo-fēn-p'èi** from each according to his ability and to each according to his work

各尽所能，按劳付酬 **kò-chìn-sǒ-néng, àn-láo-fù-ch'óu** from each according to his ability and to each according to his work

各尽所能，各取所需 **kò-chìn-sǒ-néng, kò-ch'ǔ-sǒ-hsū** from each according to his ability and to each according to his needs

各种形式 **kò-chǔng-hsíng-shìh** various forms, multiple forms, all forms

各种各样 **kò-chǔng-kò-yàng** of every kind, every variety, various

各取其长，补其所短 **kò-ch'ǔ-ch'í-ch'áng, pǔ-ch'í-sǒ-tuǎn** everyone should use others' strong points to correct his own weak points

各取所需 **kò-ch'ǔ-sǒ-hsū** to each according to his needs, each draws what he needs

各怀鬼胎 **kò-huái-kuěi-t'āi** each one [of them] bears a monster embryo (each member [of an opposition group] harbors evil intentions)

各行其是 **kò-hsíng-ch'í-shìh** each acts according to his sense of right and wrong (if ideology differs, actions will vary)

各人自扫门前雪 **kò-jén tzù-sǎo mén-ch'ién-hsuěh** each person sweeps the snow only in front of his own door (to lack public-spirited concern for others)

各个击破 **kò-kò-chī-p'ò** to smash [the enemy] one by one

各国议会联盟 **kò-kuó-ì-huì lién-méng**

181

the Inter-Parliamentary Union

各别 **kò-piéh** separate; separately, individually; different, various

各不相关 **kò-pù-hsiāng-kuān** each without relation to the other, independently

各得其所 **kò-té-ch'í-sǒ** each gets his proper position, each affair receives proper handling

各族人民 **kò-tsú-jén-mín** people of all nationalities [within China]

各自 **kò-tzù** each one himself, each one

各自为政 **kò-tzù wéi-chèng** each [office] administers its own affairs (independent administration without overall consideration)

kōu (gōu)

1096　勾结 **kōu-chiéh** to collude, be in league with, have secret connivance with

勾销 **kōu-hsiāo** to delete, cancel, strike out, nullify, annul

勾勾搭搭 **kōu-kōu-tā-tā** to conspire with, seduce, cooperate for evil purpose

勾 **kōu**: see also **kòu**

1097　沟渠 **kōu-ch'ǘ** a ditch, drain, gutter, channel

沟渠交错 **kōu-ch'ǘ-chiāo-ts'ò** crisscrossed with irrigation ditches

1098　钩心斗角 **kōu-hsīn-tòu-chiǎo** interlocked at the center and competing at the corners (a reference to the complicated roof construction of Chinese palaces: now has the meaning of political or personal maneuvering and competing for position)

kǒu (gǒu)

1099　苟延残喘 **kǒu-yén-ts'án-ch'uǎn** to prolong a dying gasp (to eke out a miserable existence)

1100　狗急跳墙 **kǒu-chí-t'iào-ch'iáng** a desperate dog will jump over a wall (an evil person faced with defeat will stop at nothing)

狗血淋头 **kǒu-hsuèh-lín-t'óu** to pour dog's blood on the head [of the accused] (to heap indignities on one)

狗肉账 **kǒu-jòu-chàng** dog meat account book (confused and worthless accounts)

狗奴才 **kǒu-nú-ts'ái** a dog-slave (a term of strong abuse)

狗腿子 **kǒu-t'uǐ-tzu** a dog's leg (lackey, flunkey, toady)

kòu (gòu)

1101　勾当 **kòu-tang** an underhanded job, plot, conspiracy, intrigue

勾 **kòu**: see also **kōu**

1102　构成 **kòu-ch'éng** to constitute, form, formulate

1103　购置 **kòu-chìh** to purchase, buy

购销服务处 **kòu-hsiāo fú-wù-ch'ù** marketing service office

购粮 **kòu-liáng** to procure food grains

购买力 **kòu-mǎi-lì** purchasing power

1104　夠劲 **kòu-chìn** strong enough, good enough

kū (gū)

1105　估计 **kū-chì** to estimate, calculate, reckon, conjecture

估计不足 **kū-chì-pù-tsú** an inadequate calculation, underestimation

估计错误 **kū-chì-ts'ò-wù** to miscalculate

估价 **kū-chià** to estimate cost, estimate value, appraise, evaluate

估产 **kū-ch'ǎn** to estimate production; estimated production

估量 **kū-liàng** to evaluate, calculate, estimate

估摸 **kū-mo** (1) to make a rough estimate, estimate roughly; (2) be on guard against

估算 **kū-suàn** to assess, evaluate

1106　沽名钓誉 **kū-míng-tiào-yù** to buy a good name and fish for fame (to use improper means to strive for fame)

1107　孤掌难鸣 **kū-chǎng-nán-míng** a single hand cannot clap (a single person's strength has limits)

孤寂 **kū-chì** lonely, solitary, friendless

孤家寡人 **kū-chiā-kuǎ-jén** your humble and unworthy king (a royal form of self-address; now refers to a person so isolated from the masses that no one will help him)

孤注一掷 **kū-chù-ī-chīh** to stake everything on a single throw [of the dice]

孤军作战 **kū-chūn-tsò-chàn** a fight by an isolated [military] unit (to carry on a single-handed struggle)

孤立 **kū-lì** isolated, unaided

孤立主义 **kū-lì-chǔ-ì** isolationism

孤立事件 **kū-lì-shìh-chièn** an isolated incident

孤立顽固势力 **kū-lì wán-kù-shìh-lì** to isolate the conservative forces

孤零零 **kū-líng-líng** singly, alone, lonely

1108　姑息 **kū-hsī** to be over lenient, spoil [a child] (appeasement, to appease)

姑息养奸 **kū-hsī-yăng-chiēn** appeasement nourishes villainy

1109 轱辘 **kū-lu** a wheel, pulley; to turn, revolve

1110 辜负 **kū-fù** to be unworthy [of expectations], be ungrateful to, let others down

kŭ (gŭ)

1111 古迹 **kŭ-chī** ancient remains, relics

古今中外 **kŭ-chīn-chūng-wài** ancient and modern and at home and abroad (everywhere and every time)

古晋 **kŭ-chìn** Kuching [Sarawak]

古怪 **kŭ-kuài** grotesque, strange, queer, weird, eccentric

古老 **kŭ-lăo** old, ancient, antiquated

古巴 **kŭ-pā** Cuba

古代汉语 **kŭ-tài-hàn-yŭ** the classical Han [Chinese] language

古典政治经济学 **kŭ-tiĕn chèng-chìh-chīng-chì-hsuéh** the classical [Western] political economy

古典文学 **kŭ-tiĕn-wén-hsuéh** classical literature

古董 **kŭ-tŭng** a curio, antique, old art object

古田会议 **kŭ-t'iĕn-huì-ì** the Kutien Conference (held at Kutien, Fukien, in December 1929)

古为今用, 洋为中用 **kŭ-wéi-chīn-yùng, yáng-wéi-chūng-yùng** the ancient to serve the present [and] and the foreign to serve the Chinese

1112 谷价 **kŭ-chià** the price of food grains

谷米 **kŭ-mĭ** food grains, cereals

谷穗 **kŭ-suì** ears of grain

谷仓 **kŭ-ts'āng** a granary, barn for storing grain

谷物 **kŭ-wù** grain, cereal

谷物丰收 **kŭ-wù-fēng-shōu** a bumper grain harvest

1113 股份 **kŭ-fèn** a stock share, a share of capital

1114 骨气 **kŭ-ch'ì** moral courage, uncompromising integrity

骨肥 **kŭ-féi** bone fertilizer

骨肉情谊 **kŭ-jòu-ch'íng-ì** the affection of flesh and bone

骨肉相连 **kŭ-jòu-hsiāng-lién** linked together as flesh and bone (an inseparable relationship)

骨干 **kŭ-kàn** backbone, core, mainstay

骨干份子 **kŭ-kàn-fèn-tzŭ** backbone elements, key persons

骨干力量 **kŭ-kàn-lì-liang** the core strength

骨干民兵 **kŭ-kàn-mín-pīng** core militia

骨干与配套结合 **kŭ-kàn yú p'èi-t'ào**

chiéh-hó to combine key projects with auxiliary projects

骨鲠在喉 **kŭ-kĕng-tsài-hóu** a bone stuck in the throat (something that one has to say)

骨子里 **kŭ-tzu-lĭ** in the bones (intrinsically, at heart, beneath the surface, in substance)

1115 蛊惑 **kŭ-huò** to seduce to wrongdoing, enchant (to engage in demagogy)

蛊惑人心 **kŭ-huò-jén-hsīn** to mislead and confuse people's minds

1116 鼓起勇气 **kŭ-ch'ĭ-yŭng-chì** to pluck up courage, arouse one's courage

鼓吹 **kŭ-ch'uī** to advocate, promote, uphold, incite, propagate

鼓风炉 **kŭ-fēng-lú** a blast furnace

鼓励 **kŭ-lì** to encourage, hearten

鼓动 **kŭ-tùng** to rouse, incite, stir up, instigate

鼓足干劲 **kŭ-tsú-kàn-chìn** to go all out, exert the utmost effort, summon up one's energy

鼓足干劲, 力争上游, **kŭ-tsú-kàn-chìn, lì-chēng-shàng-yú,** to go all out and aim high, to put forth the utmost effort and press consistently ahead

鼓足干劲, 力争上游, 多快好省 **kŭ-tsú-kàn-chìn, lì-chēng-shàng-yú, tō-k'uài-hăo-shĕng** go all out, aim high, and do more, faster, better, and more economically

鼓足干劲, 力争上游, 多快好省地建设社会主义 **kŭ-tsú-kàn-chìn, lì-chēng-shàng-yú, tō-k'uài-hăo-shĕng te chièn-shè shè-huì-chŭ-ì** to go all out and aim high for more faster, better, and more economical building of socialism

鼓舞 **kŭ-wŭ** to animate, inspire, spur on, incite, stimulate, encourage; dance for joy

鼓舞人心 **kŭ-wŭ-jén-hsīn** stirring, inspiring, stimulating, impressive

kù (gù)

1117 固执 **kù-chíh** obstinate, stubborn, opinionated, persistent

固沙防风 **kù-shā-fáng-fēng** sand stabilization and wind protection

固沙林 **kù-shā-lín** forestation for sand stabilization

固守 **kù-shŏu** to defend firmly, stand one's ground, adhere to

固定 **kù-tìng** to fix, make immovable; fixed, stationary, immovable, firm

固定协作 **kù-tìng-hsiéh-tsò** cooperation on a permanent basis

固定工人 **kù-tìng-kūng-jén** fixed work-

ers (holding permanent jobs)

固定设备 **kù-tìng-shè-pèi** fixed equipment

固定摊贩 **kù-tìng-t'ān-fàn** fixed hawkers (as contrasted with circulating or mobile hawkers)

固定资产 **kù-tìng-tzū-ch'ǎn** fixed assets

固体燃料 **kù-t'ǐ-ján-liào** solid fuel

1118 故障 **kù-chàng** a breakdown, hitch [in operation], obstacle, hindrance, accident

故技 **kù-chì** an old trick

故居 **kù-chū** a former residence

故乡 **kù-hsiāng** one's native place, home town or village

故意 **kù-ì** on purpose; intentionally

故弄玄虚 **kù-nùng-hsuán-hsū** to make things intentionally mysterious (to use sleight of hand to confuse and mislead people)

故步自封 **kù-pù-tzù-fēng** to continue in old steps and seclude oneself (to make no attempt to progress)

故事片 **kù-shìh-p'ièn** a feature film

故事员 **kù-shìh-yuán** a [professional] storyteller

故作姿态 **kù-tsò-tzū-t'ài** to [conceal one's intention by] making a gesture

1119 顾全大局 **kù-ch'üán-tà-chú** to bear the whole situation in mind; mindful of the whole situation

顾客 **kù-k'ò** a customer, patron

顾虑 **kù-lù** anxiety, scruple, apprehension, concern, careful consideration

顾问委员会 **kù-wèn wěi-yuán-huì** advisory committee, committee of advisers

1120 雇农 **kù-núng** hired peasant, a hired farm worker

雇佣 **kù-yūng** to hire [with reference to wage earners]

雇佣军 **kù-yūng-chūn** mercenaries

雇佣观点 **kù-yūng-kuān-tiěn** the mercenary point of view (of those who work only when paid, and work harder the more they are paid)

雇佣劳动 **kù-yūng-láo-tùng** wage labor

雇佣思想 **kù-yūng-szū-hsiǎng** mercenary thought or mentality

1121 痼疾 **kù-chí** chronic disease (figuratively—a recurring and problem)

kuā (guā)

1122 瓜分 **kuā-fēn** to cut up a melon (to partition, dismember)

瓜分中国 **kuā-fēn-chūng-kuó** to partition China

瓜分世界 **kuā-fēn-shìh-chièh** the partition of the world [into spheres

of influence] (now generally refers to the domination of the superpowers: the USSR and the USA)

1123 刮起一股冷风 **kuā-ch'ǐ ī-kǔ-lěng-fēng** to blow up a cold wind (a dampening of enthusiasm)

刮地皮 **kuā tì-p'í** to scrape off the earth (to embezzle and exploit, to benefit oneself at the public interest)

kuǎ (guǎ)

1124 寡头 **kuǎ-t'óu** an oligarch, boss, magnate

寡头政治 **kuǎ-t'óu-chèng-chìh** oligarchy, oligarchic government

kuà (guà)

1125 挂账 **kuà-chàng** to charge to one's account

挂号费 **kuà-hào-fèi** registration fee (usually a visit charge for medical outpatients)

挂钩 **kuà-kōu** to couple [railway cars], to link up (commonly refers to linking of schools with particular factories)

挂名 **kuà-míng** in name only, nominally, titular

挂名会员 **kuà-míng-huì-yuán** members in name only

挂牌子 **kuà-p'ái-tzu** to put a signboard up (usually with the connotation of false pretensions)

挂帅 **kuà-shuài** to hang up the commander-in-chief's insignia (to take command; to enjoy priority, as in production)

挂羊头卖狗肉 **kuà-yáng-t'óu, mài-kǒu-jòu** to hang a sheep's head [over the stall] and sell dog meat [to the public]

kuāi (guāi)

1126 乖张 **kuāi-chāng** perverse, recalcitrant, stubborn in wrongdoing, intractable

乖巧 **kuāi-ch'iǎo** clever, ingenious, sly

乖戾 **kuāi-lì** cantankerous, perverse, unreasonable, disagreeable

kuǎi (guǎi)

1127 拐骗 **kuǎi-p'ièn** to swindle, cheat; to abduct

kuài (guài)

1128 怪话 **kuài-huà** absurd statements,

strange talk
怪题 **kuài-t'í** tricky questions [in
student examinations] (criticized
during the Cultural Revolution)
怪物 **kuài-wù** a monster, strange
creature (an eccentric person)

kuān (guān)

1129 关照 **kuān-chào** to notify, inform; to
take care of, look after, take into
consideration
关节 **kuān-chiéh** (1) the joints [anatom-
ical]; (2) a secret request for official
assistance
关键 **kuān-chièn** a key, hinge, pivotal
point (a key to a problem)
关键性 **kuān-chièn-hsìng** crucial,
decisive, vital
关键人物 **kuān-chièn-jén-wù** key
personnel
关键时期 **kuān-chièn-shíh-ch'ī** a
crucially important period
关汽运行 **kuān-ch'ì-yùn-hsíng** to turn
off the steam and coast
关卡 **kuān-ch'iǎ** a check point, customs
barrier
关切 **kuān-ch'ièh** to be concerned
about; intimately related, connected
关怀 **kuān-huái** to be concerned about,
to look after; solicitude, care,
consideration
关系 **kuān-hsì** relationship, connection,
ties, association with, reference to
关系弄不好 **kuān-hsì nùng-pù-hǎo** to
make a mess of relations, fail to
establish good personal relations
关心 **kuān-hsīn** to be concerned about,
care for, be interested in, pay attention to
关连 **kuān-lién** to be related with,
interconnected; relations, connections
关门整风 **kuān-mén-chěng-fēng** rectification behind closed doors (to
ignore the people's opinions or
criticisms)
关门教学 **kuān-mén-chiào-hsuéh** teaching behind closed doors (a Cultural
Revolution accusation that educators
were separating schools from society
and social tasks)
关门主义 **kuān-mén-chǔ-ì** exclusivism,
closed-door policy, closed-door
sectarianism
关门办校 **kuān-mén-pàn-hsiào** running
schools behind closed doors (to
divorce the school from practical
life and work, and to reject mass
participation and guidance)

关门打基础 **kuān-mén tǎ-chī-ch'ǔ** lay-
ing a foundation behind closed doors
(the excuse that students should
acquire a solid foundation of theory
before applying it in practical work)
关门态度 **kuān-mén-t'ài-tù** a closed-
door attitude
关门育人 **kuān-mén-yù-jén** to educate
people behind closed doors
关闭 **kuān-pì** to close, shut, close down
[a business, etc.]
关税同盟 **kuān-shuì-t'úng-méng** tariff
union
关头 **kuān-t'óu** a crucial period, key
moment, juncture, turning point
关押 **kuān-yā** to confine, put under
detention; confinement
1130 观众 **kuān-chùng** the audience,
spectators
观众台 **kuān-chùng-t'ái** a spectators'
stand
观察 **kuān-ch'á** to observe, view,
examine, survey; observation
观察家 **kuān-ch'á-chiā** an [informed or
qualified] observer
观察员 **kuān-ch'á-yuán** an observer
[usually at a meeting or conference]
观风测云 **kuān-fēng-ts'è-yún** meteorological observation (often figurative:
to gauge one's moves according to
the situation)
观感 **kuān-kǎn** observations and comments, emotional reactions, impression from seeing or reading something
观光 **kuān-kuāng** to travel, view, visit;
sight-seeing
观礼台 **kuān-lǐ-t'ái** a rostrum, reviewing stand
观摩 **kuān-mó** to compare notes,
emulate the good points of others;
an exhibit to stimulate comparison
and emulation
观念 **kuān-nièn** an idea, notion,
concept, view
观念形态 **kuān-nièn-hsíng-t'ài** the form
of concepts, ideology
观赏艺术 **kuān-shǎng-ì-shù** the visual
arts
观点 **kuān-tiěn** a point of view, standpoint, position
观测 **kuān-ts'è** to prognosticate after
study, observe and survey, predict
观测站 **kuān-ts'è-chàn** an observation
station
观望 **kuān-wàng** to wait and see,
hesitate; watchful waiting
观望态度 **kuān-wàng-t'ài-tù** a wait-and-
see attitude, hopeful expectancy
1131 官架子 **kuān-chià-tzu** official airs,

bureaucratic pretensions

官教兵, 兵教官, 兵教兵 **kuān-chiào-pīng, pīng-chiào-kuān, pīng-chiào-pīng** officers teach soldiers, soldiers teach officers, and soldiers teach soldiers

官阶 **kuān-chiēh** official rank

官气 **kuān-ch'ì** bureaucratic behavior, bureaucratic airs

官气抬头 **kuān-ch'ì-t'ái-t'óu** bureaucratism raises its head

官方 **kuān-fāng** official; the government

官方宣传 **kuān-fāng hsuān-ch'uán** official propaganda, government publicity

官僚 **kuān-liáo** bureaucrat; bureaucratic (usually pejorative)

官僚主义 **kuān-liáo-chǔ-ì** bureaucratism (one of the **sān-fǎn**)

官僚主义作风 **kuān-liáo-chǔ-ì tsò-fēng** bureaucratic practices, bureaucratic style

官僚垄断资产阶级 **kuān-liáo lǔng-tuàn tzū-ch'ǎn chiēh-chí** the bureaucratic, monopolistic bourgeoisie

官僚买办资产阶级 **kuān-liáo-mǎi-pàn tzū-ch'ǎn chiēh-chí** the bureaucrat-comprador bourgeoisie

官僚资产阶级 **kuān-liáo tzū-ch'ǎn chiēh-chí** the bureaucrat-capitalist class

官僚资本 **kuān-liáo-tzū-pěn** bureaucratic capital

官僚资本主义 **kuān-liáo tzū-pěn-chǔ-ì** bureaucratic capitalism (the use of government position to engage in and control private business for personal profit)

官能 **kuān-néng** organic functions [human], physical functions

官逼民反 **kuān-pī-mín-fǎn** popular rebellion [resulting from] official repression (in the old society)

官兵 **kuān-pīng** officers and men

官兵一致 **kuān-pīng-ì-chìh** officers and soldiers united

官司 **kuān-szu** a lawsuit

官达菜 **kuān-tá-ts'ài** a low-quality vegetable (ordinarily for porcine consumption)

官字当头 **kuān-tzù-tāng-t'óu** always putting the word "official" first (very bureaucratic)

官样文章 **kuān-yàng wén-chāng** official-type documents, bureaucratic red tape, stereotyped formality

官员 **kuān-yuán** an official

¹¹³² 冠冕堂皇 **kuān-miěn-t'áng-huáng** dignified and noble bearing (high sounding, pompous)

冠 **kuān**: see also **kuàn**

kuǎn (guǎn)

¹¹³³ 管家 **kuǎn-chiā** to manage a household (said of a unit manager, such as of a production team)

管教 **kuǎn-chiào** to take care of and supervise [students or children], to discipline and educate

管制 **kuǎn-chìh** to control, administer, govern; control (a mild, punitive form of surveillance and correction)

管制分子 **kuǎn-chìh-fèn-tzǔ** a controlled person, person under surveillance

管制劳动 **kuǎn-chìh-láo-tùng** to work under surveillance, labor under public surveillance (usually under the surveillance of other peasants or commune members)

管卡压 **kuǎn ch'iǎ yā** to control, check, and suppress [counter-revolutionaries]

管而不死, 活而不乱 **kuǎn-érh-pù-szǔ, huó-érh-pù-luàn** control without stifling [and] enliven without disordering

管辖 **kuǎn-hsiá** to exercise control over, have jurisdiction over, regulate

管弦乐队 **kuǎn-hsién-yuèh-tuì** a symphony orchestra

管一漏百 **kuǎn-ì-lòu-pǎi** to control one and lose a hundred (overly narrow concentration of attention or effort)

管理 **kuǎn-lǐ** to manage, administer, handle, take care of, govern, regulate, supervise

管理制度 **kuǎn-lǐ-chìh-tù** system of administration

管理局 **kuǎn-lǐ-chú** administrative bureau (administers other agencies and enterprises but does not manage them operationally)

管理区 **kuǎn-lǐ-ch'ū** an administrative district

管理人员 **kuǎn-lǐ-jén-yuán** managerial personnel

管理民主化 **kuǎn-lǐ mín-chǔ-huà** management democratized

管理办法 **kuǎn-lǐ pàn-fǎ** administrative regulations, regulatory procedures

管理委员会 **kuǎn-lǐ wěi-yuán-huì** management committee, administrative committee

管理员 **kuǎn-lǐ-yuán** administrator, supervisor, custodial officer

管道 **kuǎn-tào** a pipeline

管天兵 **kuǎn-t'iēn-pīng** a heaven-

controlling soldier (an informal term for rural weather observers)

管乐器 **kuǎn-yuèh-ch'ì** a wind [musical] instrument

kuàn (guàn)

1134 贯彻 **kuàn-ch'è** to carry through, put into effect, go through with, carry out thoroughly, execute, permeate, penetrate, implement

贯彻执行 **kuàn-ch'è-chíh-hsíng** to carry out consistently and thoroughly

贯彻十大精神 **kuàn-ch'è shíh-tà-chīng-shén** to act in the spirit of the [CCP] Tenth Congress

贯穿 **kuàn-ch'uān** to penetrate, pierce through; to comprehend completely, know thoroughly

贯串 **kuàn-ch'uàn** to string together, piece together, interconnect, interrelate

贯通 **kuàn-t'ūng** to penetrate, master completely, achieve a thorough understanding

1135 冠军 **kuàn-chūn** a champion, winner, outstanding person

冠 **kuàn:** *see also* **kuān**

1136 惯例 **kuàn-lì** usual practice, established custom, usage, precedent

惯用伎俩 **kuàn-yùng-chì-liǎng** an often-used trick

1137 灌区 **kuàn-ch'ū** irrigated area

灌溉 **kuàn-kài** to irrigate, water

灌溉渠 **kuàn-kài-ch'ú** an irrigation canal

灌溉面积 **kuàn-kài-mièn-chī** the area under irrigation

灌迷魂汤 **kuàn mí-hún-t'āng** to pour a mind-muddling broth (to woo by flattery)

灌输 **kuàn-shū** to instill, teach, inculcate, indoctrinate

kuāng (guāng)

1138 光景 **kuāng-chǐng** situation, circumstances, conditions; prospects

光复 **kuāng-fù** to recover [lost territory], restore [old glory, etc.]

光滑度 **kuāng-huá-tù** degree of smoothness (in precision grinding)

光辉 **kuāng-huī** splendid, brilliant, magnificent, glorious

光辉照耀下 **kuāng-huī chào-yào-hsià** to be enlightened by; under the enlightenment of

光辉著作 **kuāng-huī-chù-tsò** glorious writings (of Marx, Engels, Lenin, Stalin, and Mao)

光辉形象 **kuāng-huī-hsíng-hsiàng** a glorious image, magnificent form

光辉榜样 **kuāng-huī-pǎng-yàng** a shining example

光辉典范 **kuāng-huī-tiěn-fàn** a glorious model

光辉体现 **kuāng-huī-t'ǐ-hsièn** a splendid manifestation

光辉灿烂 **kuāng-huī-ts'àn-làn** glorious and magnificent, brilliant and dazzling

光线 **kuāng-hsièn** a ray of light

光学 **kuāng-hsuéh** optics

光荣 **kuāng-júng** glory, splendor, honor

光荣称号 **kuāng-júng-ch'ēng-hào** a title of honor

光荣豪迈的事业 **kuāng-júng háo-mài-te shìh-yèh** the glorious and gallant enterprise (the revolution)

光荣人家 **kuāng-júng-jén-chiā** an honorable family (the family of a PLA man on active service)

光荣岗位 **kuāng-júng-kǎng-wèi** a glorious sentry post (any job or position, since all work serves the revolution)

光荣榜 **kuāng-júng-pǎng** a roster of honor (a citation of merit for workers and commune members)

光临 **kuāng-lín** brightness approaches (the arrival of a visitor; please honor [us] with your presence)

光芒万丈 **kuāng-máng-wàn-chàng** a flash of light shining afar (blazing ahead, a glorious prospect)

光明正大 **kuāng-míng-chèng-tà** sincere and straight (open and straightforward; honest and aboveboard)

光明前途 **kuāng-míng-ch'ién-t'ú** a bright future

光明日报 **kuāng-míng jìh-pào** *Kuangming Daily* (a Peking newspaper, organ of the Democratic League, 1949—)

光年 **kuāng-nién** a light year

光天化日 **kuāng-t'iēn-huà-jìh** in broad daylight (plainly visible)

光泽 **kuāng-tsé** luster, sheen

光彩夺目 **kuāng-ts'ǎi-tó-mù** brilliance that dazzles the eye

光阴似箭 **kuāng-yīn-szù-chièn** time [flies] like an arrow

kuǎng (guǎng)

1139 广积粮 **kuāng-chī-liáng** to store grain on a large scale

广交会 **kuǎng-chiāo-huì** the Canton Trade Fair (contraction of **Kuǎng-**

chōu chiāo-ì-huì)

广州交易会 **kuǎng-chōu chiāo-ì-huì** the Canton Trade Fair

广州部队 **kuǎng-chōu pù-tuì** the Canton Military Forces [of the PLA]

广场 **kuǎng-ch'ǎng** an urban square (for public gatherings)

广泛 **kuǎng-fàn** extensive, broad, widespread, comprehensive

广义 **kuǎng-ì** in the broad sense; the broad meaning

广告画 **kuǎng-kào-huà** poster art

广开言路 **kuǎng-k'āi yén-lù** to open wide the avenue of speech (to encourage free discussion)

广阔天地 **kuǎng-k'uò-t'iēn-tì** the vast land (usually refers to rural or mountain areas with potential for development)

广播 **kuǎng-pō** to broadcast, telecast; radio or television broadcast

广播节目 **kuǎng-pō-chiéh-mù** a program of broadcasts [radio or television]

广播事业局 **kuǎng-pō-shìh-yèh-chú** Broadcast Affairs Administrative Bureau [of the State Council]

广播电台 **kuǎng-pō-tièn-t'ái** radio station, broadcast station

广播体操 **kuǎng-pō-t'ǐ-ts'āo** broadcasted physical exercises

广播网 **kuǎng-pō-wǎng** radio broadcast network

广播演说 **kuǎng-pō-yěn-shuō** a broadcast speech

广博 **kuǎng-pó** wide, extensive, broad [in knowledge or experience]

广大 **kuǎng-tà** vast, large, spacious, immense

广度 **kuǎng-tù** width, breadth

kuēi (guī)

1140　归案法办 **kuēi-àn fǎ-pàn** to bring to court for judicial handling

归结 **kuēi-chiéh** to come to a conclusion, to sum up; in the end

归侨青年 **kuēi-ch'iáo-ch'īng-nién** overseas Chinese youth who have returned [to China]

归根 **kuēi-kēn** in the end, at last, finally, basically

归根结蒂 **kuēi-kēn chiéh-tì** in the end, finally, basically, fundamentally, in the final analysis

归根到底 **kuēi-kēn-tào-tǐ** in the last analysis

归公 **kuēi-kūng** to return something to the rightful public authorities; to go to [belong to] the public [the state]

归功 **kuēi-kūng** to attribute merit, give credit to

归国华侨农场 **kuēi-kuó-huá-ch'iáo núng-ch'ǎng** a farm operated by returned overseas Chinese

归纳法 **kuēi-nà-fǎ** the inductive method, induction, *a posteriori* reasoning

归宿 **kuēi-sù** the end, conclusion; a final settling place, permanent home

归档 **kuēi-tàng** to return to the files, file away

归队 **kuēi-tuì** to return to one's unit

归队闹革命 **kuēi-tuì nào kó-mìng** to return to one's original unit to carry on the revolution

归罪 **kuēi-tsuì** to put the blame on, hold someone responsible for a mistake, attribute error

归因 **kuēi-yīn** to attribute the cause

1141　圭亚那 **kuēi-yà-nà** Guiana

1142　龟缩 **kuēi-sō** to pull in like a tortoise (timid, to pull into one's shell)

1143　规章 **kuēi-chāng** regulations [usually printed], administrative rules, procedures, code

规程 **kuēi-ch'éng** rules, regulations, by-laws, procedures, requirements, process

规程万能 **kuēi-ch'éng-wàn-néng** rules and regulations can accomplish everything (criticized because it ignores the human factor)

规矩 **kuēi-chǔ** the compass and T-square (customary rules of good behavior; mannerly, well behaved)

规劝 **kuēi-ch'üàn** to admonish, exhort, persuade

规范 **kuēi-fàn** a norm, criterion; to regulate, normalize

规范化 **kuēi-fàn-huà** to normalize, standardize, regularize

规划 **kuēi-huà** to plan, design, draw up plans

规格 **kuēi-kó** standards, specifications

规规矩矩 **kuēi-kuēi-chǔ-chǔ** very orderly and properly, prim, conventional

规律 **kuēi-lù** laws [as in "economic laws"]; statutory law; rules and regularions; discipline

规律性 **kuēi-lù-hsìng** having the character of law, lawful, conformable to laws

规模 **kuēi-mó** scale, scope, extent

规模空前 **kuēi-mó-k'ūng-ch'ién** on a scale without precedent, very large

规避 **kuēi-pì** to evade, avoid, elude, sidestep

规定 **kuēi-tìng** to regulate, prescribe,

establish, formulate, enact, fix, determine; rules, regulations

规则 **kuēi-tsé** rules [usually procedural]; regulations [administrative], laws, statutes

1144 闺女 **kuēi-nǚ** a virgin, maiden, unmarried girl; daughter

1145 硅钢 **kuēi-kāng** silicon steel

kuěi (guǐ)

1146 轨距 **kuěi-chù** gauge [of railway tracks]

轨范 **kuěi-fàn** a rule, pattern, sample

轨道 **kuěi-tào** steel rails, a railway track; a planetary orbit; the proper way of doing things, conventional behavior

1147 诡计 **kuěi-chì** a trick, artful device, trap

诡计多端 **kuěi-chì-tō-tuān** crafty, tricky, full of stratagems

诡称 **kuěi-ch'ēng** to state spuriously

诡密 **kuěi-mì** furtive, stealthy, clandestine, secretive

诡辩 **kuěi-pièn** sophistry, subtle but fallacious argument

诡辩学派 **kuěi-pièn-hsuéh-p'ài** sophists

1148 鬼花招 **kuěi huā-chāo** devil's tricks, ghostly hanky-panky (a Cultural Revolution phrase for the alleged plots of anti-Maoists)

鬼话 **kuěi-huà** devil's talk (false words, lies, nonsense)

鬼话连篇 **kuěi-huà-lién-p'iēn** to tell a whole series of lies; lies from start to finish

鬼混 **kuěi-hùn** to live an idle life, make a nuisance of oneself, waste time

鬼怪 **kuěi-kuài** ghosts and monsters, demons and goblins

鬼鬼祟祟 **kuěi-kuěi-suì-suì** clandestine, furtive, shifty, evasive, surreptitious

鬼迷心窍 **kuěi-mí-hsīn-ch'iào** one's heart orifices stopped up by a demon (to make a person act in a very stupid manner)

鬼把戏 **kuěi-pǎ-hsì** a vicious trick

鬼胎 **kuěi-t'āi** an embryo of a demon (an evil plot, dark scheme)

鬼蜮伎俩 **kuěi-yù-chì-liǎng** the cunning of a demon and toad (dirty underhanded tricks, malicious treachery)

kuèi (guì)

1149 刽子手 **kuèi-tzu-shǒu** an executioner (figurative)

1150 柜台 **kuèi-t'ái** a sales counter

1151 贵重 **kuèi-chùng** valuable, precious, expensive, rare

贵宾 **kuèi-pīn** an honored guest

贵族 **kuèi-tsú** an aristocrat, noble

贵族老爷态度 **kuèi-tsú-lǎo-yéh t'ài-tù** the attitude of an aristocratic lord

贵族奴隶主阶级 **kuèi-tsú núng-lì-chǔ chiēh-chí** the aristocratic slave-owning class

1152 桂 **kuèi** Kwangsi Chuang Autonomous Region (formerly Kwangsi province)

桂系 **kuèi-hsì** the Kwangsi group (a military and political faction in the Kuomintang period)

1153 跪倒…脚下 **kuèi-tǎo … chüéh-hsià** to kneel at the feet of …

kǔn (gǔn)

1154 滚珠轴承厂 **kǔn-chū chóu-ch'éng-ch'ǎng** a ball-bearing manufacturing plant

滚一身泥巴, 炼一颗红心 **kǔn ī-shēn-ní-pa, lièn ī-k'ō-húng-hsīn** rolling about all covered with mud forges a red heart (farm work makes one a good revolutionary)

滚瓜烂熟 **kǔn-kuā-làn-shú** a round and very ripe melon (to know a passage of a book very thoroughly, to commit firmly to memory)

滚滚向前 **kǔn-kǔn-hsiàng-ch'ién** to roll forward, rush on

kūng (gōng)

1155 工交战线 **kūng-chiāo-chàn-hsièn** the battlefront of industry and communications

工间操 **kūng-chiēn-ts'āo** calisthenics during working hours

工种 **kūng-chǔng** types of work

工厂 **kūng-ch'ǎng** a factory, manufacturing plant, mill, works

工厂林立 **kūng-ch'ǎng-lín-lì** factories standing like a forest

工厂总管理委员会 **kūng-ch'ǎng tsǔng-kuǎn-lǐ wěi-yuán-huì** factory general management committee (in joint factories, with both public and private representatives)

工场 **kūng-ch'ǎng** a place of work, work site, workshop

工程 **kūng-ch'éng** planned construction, engineering; an engineering or building project; a job, task

工程兵 **kūng-ch'éng-pīng** Engineer Corps (one of the service arms of the PLA)

工程师 **kūng-ch'eng-shīh** an engineer

工期长, 见效慢 **kūng-ch'ī ch'áng, chièn-hsiào màn** the construction time is long and the visible results are slow

工愁善虑 **kūng-ch'óu-shàn-lǜ** given to melancholy and anxiety (the attitude of bourgeois writers)

工具 **kūng-chǜ** an instrument, tool, implement, equipment

工具改革 **kūng-chǜ-kǎi-kó** improvement of tools or implements

工具书 **kūng-chǜ-shū** a tool book, reference book (such as dictionary, manual, handbook)

工军宣传队 **kūng-chūn hsuān-ch'uán-tuì** [Mao Tse-tung's Thought] workers and soldiers propaganda team

工分 **kūng-fēn** work points, credits for work done

工分值 **kūng-fēn-chíh** work-point value

工分挂帅 **kūng-fēn-kuà-shuài** work points take command (a form of economism)

工会 **kūng-huì** labor union, trade union

工会总联合会 **kūng-huì tsǔng-lién-hó-huì** General Federation of Trade Unions

工效 **kūng-hsiào** labor efficiency, work efficiency

工序 **kūng-hsù** work procedures, operational sequence, process

工宣队 **kūng-hsuān-tuì** workers propaganda team (contraction for: Mao Tse-tung Thought Workers Propaganda Team)

工医班 **kūng-ī-pān** workers medical training class (to train paramedical personnel for factories)

工艺 **kūng-ì** technology, technical skill; craftsmanship

工艺规程 **kūng-ì-kuēi-ch'éng** technological regulations

工艺流程 **kūng-ì-liú-ch'éng** technical process

工人 **kūng-jén** a worker, a working man (blue-collar personnel)

工人政治学校 **kūng-jén chèng-chìh-hsuéh-hsiào** workers' political school

工人技术学校 **kūng-jén chì-shù-hsuéh-hsiào** workers' technical school

工人讲师 **kūng-jén-chiǎng-shīh** worker-teachers (usually at higher than middle school level)

工人阶级 **kūng-jén-chiēh-chí** the working class, proletariat

工人阶级必须领导一切 **kūng-jén-chiēh-chí pì-hsū lǐng-tǎo ī-ch'ieh** the working class must lead in everything

工人宣传队 **kūng-jén hsuān-ch'uán-tuì** workers propaganda teams (during the Cultural Revolution)

工人学员 **kūng-jén-hsuéh-yuán** worker students (university students selected from among the workers)

工人医生 **kūng-jén-ī-shēng** worker doctors (factory equivalent of the "barefoot doctors")

工人日报 **kūng-jén jìh-pào** *Workers' Daily* (a Peking newspaper, 1949—)

工人贵族 **kūng-jén-kuèi-tsú** labor aristocrats (pejorative)

工人工程师 **kūng-jén kūng-ch'éng-shīh** worker-engineers (an engineer from among the workers who has practical knowledge but no degree or has actually received advanced training and a degree in engineering)

工人毛泽东思想宣传队 **kūng-jén maó tsé-tūng szū-hsiǎng hsuān-ch'uán-tuì** Workers' Mao Tse-tung Thought Propaganda Team

工人造反联络站 **kūng-jén tsào-fǎn lién-lò-chàn** workers' rebel liaison station (set up in both urban and rural areas by many kinds of groups during 1967)

工人文化宫 **kūng-jén-wén-huà-kūng** workers' palace of culture

工人业余教育 **kūng-jén yèh-yú-chiào-yù** workers' spare-time education

工人业余文化学校 **kūng-jén yèh-yú wén-huà hsuéh-hsiào** workers' spare-time [basic] culture school

工人运动 **kūng-jén-yùn-tùng** a labor movement, worker movement

工科大学 **kūng-k'ō-tà-hsuéh** an engineering university (e.g., Chiaotung University)

工矿 **kūng-k'uàng** factories and mines

工联主义 **kūng-lién-chǔ-ì** syndicalism

工龄 **kūng-líng** length of time employed [in a factory], seniority, working years

工农 **kūng-núng** workers and peasants

工农中学 **kūng-núng-chūng-hsuéh** worker and peasant secondary schools (special schools for those whose early education was insufficient to meet the standards of the general schools)

工农出身 **kūng-núng-ch'ū-shēn** of peasant and worker origin

工农红军 **kūng-núng húng-chūn** the Workers and Peasants Red Army (pre -1937)

工农革命政府 **kūng-núng kó-mìng-chèng-fǔ** a workers' and peasants' revolutionary government

工农联盟 **kūng-núng-lién-méng** the alliance of workers and peasants

工农暴动队 **kūng-núng pào-tùng-tuì** workers' and peasants' insurrection teams

工农兵 **kūng-núng-pīng** workers, peasants, and soldiers

工农兵群众 **kūng-núng-pīng ch'ún-chùng** the masses of the workers, peasants, and soldiers

工农兵学员 **kūng-núng-pīng hsuéh-yuán** university students from the workers, peasants, and soldiers

工农兵论坛 **kūng-núng-pīng lùn-t'án** worker-peasant-soldier forums (used during the Anti-Rightist Campaign)

工农兵文艺 **kūng-núng-pīng wén-ì** worker-peasant-soldier literature and art

工农兵文艺战士 **kūng-núng-pīng wén-ì-chàn-shih** worker-peasant-soldier art warriors [workers]

工农兵英雄形象 **kūng-núng-pīng yīng-hsiúng hsíng-hsiàng** the heroic image of the workers, peasants, and soldiers

工农商学兵相结合 **kūng-núng-shāng-hsuéh-pīng hsiāng-chiéh-hó** to combine industry, agriculture, trade, education, and military affairs

工农速成中学 **kūng-núng sù-ch'éng-chūng-hsuéh** workers' and peasants' accelerated middle schools (*see* **kūng-núng-chūng-hsuéh**)

工农通讯员 **kūng-núng t'ūng-hsùn-yuán** worker and peasant correspondents (non-professional news correspondents)

工农业结合 **kūng-núng-yèh chiéh-hó** integration of industry and agriculture

工农业并举的方针 **kūng-núng-yèh pìng-chǔ-te fāng-chēn** the general policy of simultaneously developing industry and agriculture

工农业总产值 **kūng-núng-yèh tsǔng-ch'ǎn-chíh** gross industrial and agriculture output value

工农业余教育 **kūng-núng yèh-yǔ-chiào-yù** spare-time education for workers and peasants

工本 **kūng-pěn** operating costs, working capital

工兵团 **kūng-pīng-t'uán** engineer regiment

工伤事故 **kūng-shāng-shìh-kù** a work accident

工商户 **kūng-shāng-hù** industrial and commercial establishments

工商联 **kūng-shāng-lién** Federation of Industry and Commerce (contraction of **kūng-shāng-yèh lién-hó-huì**)

工商奴隶主 **kūng-shāng nú-lì-chǔ** industrial and merchant slaveholders (referring to the Ch'in period)

工商业资本家 **kūng-shāng-yèh tzū-pěn-**

chiā industrial and mercantile capitalists

工时 **kūng-shíh** work time, hours of work

工事 **kūng-shìh** engineering work; fortifications

工代会 **kūng-tài-huì** workers' representative assemblies

工地 **kūng-tì** construction site, work site

工读 **kūng-tú** to work and study

工团主义 **kūng-t'uán-chǔ-ì** syndicalism

工贼 **kūng-tséi** a strikebreaker, labor scab

工作 **kūng-tsò** to work; a task, work, activities, services, employment, operations

工作战斗化 **kūng-tsò chàn-tòu-huà** martialization of activities (one of the **sān-huà**)

工作方法 **kūng-tsò-fāng-fǎ** methods of work (usually refers to political, managerial, or mass work)

工作会议 **kūng-tsò-huì-ì** work conference (usually a comprehensive meeting which reviews past policy and decides upon future tasks)

工作效率 **kūng-tsò-hsiào-lù** working efficiency

工作需要 **kūng-tsò-hsū-yào** the necessity of the task, exigency of the work

工作人员 **kūng-tsò-jén-yuán** working personnel, staff

工作日 **kūng-tsò-jìh** working day

工作量 **kūng-tsò-liàng** amount of work

工作母机 **kūng-tsò-mǔ-chī** a machine tool

工作队 **kūng-tsò-tuì** an operations squad, task force, work team (often a group organized for a special task, as in connection with a campaign)

工作通讯 **kūng-tsò t'ūng-hsùn** *Bulletin of Activities* (a PLA army-party bulletin for limited circulation, irregular, 1961—)

工作作风 **kūng-tsò tsò-fēng** work style (refers to political or mass work)

工作组 **kūng-tsò-tsǔ** a work team, work group

工作语言 **kūng-tsò-yǔ-yén** working language [in the UN]

工资 **kūng-tzū** wages, pay, salary

工资照付的假期 **kūng-tzū chào-fù-te chià-ch'ī** a holiday with pay, paid vacation

工资制度 **kūng-tzū-chìh-tù** the wage system

工资制与供给制相结合 **kūng-tzū-chìh yǔ kūng-chǐ-chìh hsiāng-chiéh-hó**

combination of the wage and free supply systems

工资分 **kūng-tzū-fēn** wage unit

工资改革 **kūng-tzū-kǎi-kó** wage reform

工资等级 **kūng-tzū-těng-chí** wage scales, wage grade

工务 **kūng-wù** construction affairs, public works, public utilities

工业战线 **kūng-yèh-chàn-hsièn** the industrial front, industrial battle line

工业基地 **kūng-yèh-chī-tì** an industrial base, industrial complex

工业化 **kūng-yèh-huà** industrialization; to industrialize

工业学大庆 **kūng-yèh hsuéh tà-ch'ìng** in industry learn from Taching [oilfield]

工业革命 **kūng-yèh-kó-mìng** the Industrial Revolution

工业抗旱 **kūng-yèh-k'àng-hàn** struggle against raw material shortage; industrial combat against drought

工业垄断 **kūng-yèh-lǔng-tuàn** industrial monopoly

工业布局 **kūng-yèh-pù-chú** industrial deployment, geographical distribution of industry

工业生产 **kūng-yèh-shēng-ch'ǎn** industrial production

工业的合理布局 **kūng-yèh-te hó-lǐ pù-chú** rational distribution of industry

工业总产值 **kūng-yèh tsǔng-ch'ǎn-chíh** gross value of industrial output

工业突破 **kūng-yèh-t'ū-p'ò** an industrial breakthrough

工友同志 **kūng-yǔ-t'úng-chìh** worker comrade (a form of address used with porters, attendants, etc.)

公安 **kūng-ān** public security, law enforcement

公安局 **kūng-ān-chú** public security bureau (the primary law enforcement authority at various levels)

公安军 **kūng-ān-chǔn** public security forces

公安部 **kūng-ān-pù** the Ministry of Public Security [of the State Council]

公安部队 **kūng-ān-pù-tui** Public Security Force (also called **kūng-ān-chǔn**)

公安委员会 **kūng-ān wěi-yuán-hui** public security committee

公案 **kūng-àn** a case at law; a public issue, much-discussed problem

公债 **kūng-chài** government bonds, a state loan, public debt

公债还本抽签大会 **kūng-chài huán-pěn ch'ōu-ch'iēn tà-hui** assembly to exchange bonds and draw lots (prizes were given for lucky bond registra-

tion numbers in the mid-1950s)

公正 **kūng-chèng** just, fair, impartial, equitable

公积金 **kūng-chī-chīn** public accumulation fund, general reserve fund

公祭 **kūng-chì** a public funeral

公教人员 **kūng-chiào-jén-yuán** governmental functionaries and teachers

公检法 **kūng-chiěn-fǎ** public security, procuration, and courts (acronym for **kūng-ān-chú, chiěn-ch'á-yuàn** and **fǎ-yuàn**)

公职 **kūng-chíh** official post, official rank, government employment

公制 **kūng-chìh** the metric system

公斤 **kūng-chīn** a kilogram (2.205 pounds or 2 **shìh-chīn**)

公众 **kūng-chùng** public; the public

公众舆论 **kūng-chùng-yú-lùn** public opinion

公尺 **kūng-ch'ǐh** a meter (39.37 inches)

公顷 **kūng-ch'ǐng** a hectare (2.47 acres or 15 **shìh-mǔ**)

公方 **kūng-fāng** (1) the government side (government representation in joint enterprises); (2) a square meter

公费医疗 **kūng-fèi-ī-liáo** free medical treatment, free medical service

公海 **kūng-hǎi** the open sea, international waters

公害 **kūng-hài** harm to the public

公议 **kūng-ì** public discussion

公益 **kūng-ì** public welfare, community benefit, the general good

公益金 **kūng-ì-chīn** welfare fund

公然 **kūng-ján** publicly, openly

公认 **kūng-jèn** publicly acknowledged, generally recognized, widely accepted

公股董事 **kūng-kǔ-tǔng-shìh** public-share directors (in companies in which the state had bought or confiscated substantial stocks, during the early 1950s)

公共 **kūng-kùng** public, owned and shared by all, communal, common, joint

公共积累 **kūng-kùng-chī-lěi** public accumulation, accumulated public funds

公共汽车 **kūng-kùng-ch'ì-ch'ē** a public bus

公共墓园 **kūng-kùng-mù-yuán** public cemeteries

公共食堂 **kūng-kùng-shíh-t'áng** community dining halls, public service canteens

公共财产 **kūng-kùng-ts'ái-ch'ǎn** public property

公共卫生 **kūng-kùng-wèi-shēng** public health

公开 **kūng-k'āi** open, public, open to the public; to open, exhibit; overt

公开信 **kūng-k'āi-hsìn** an open letter

公开宣佈 **kūng-k'āi hsuān-pù** to proclaim publicly

公歀 **kūng-k'uǎn** public funds

公里 **kūng-lǐ** a kilometer (0.62 miles or 2 **shìh-lǐ**)

公历 **kūng-lì** the public numbering of years (the same as the Christian era —A.D. or B.C.)

公粮 **kūng-liáng** agricultural tax collected in grain, public grain

公路网 **kūng-lù-wǎng** highway network

公民 **kūng-mín** a citizen, national

公民权 **kūng-mín-ch'üán** civil rights, citizenship rights

公民投票 **kūng-mín-t'óu-p'iào** a general election, referendum

公报 **kūng-pào** an official communique, government gazette

公布 **kūng-pù** to promulgate, proclaim, announce, make public, publish

公平合理 **kūng-p'íng-hó-lǐ** fair and reasonable

公婆 **kūng-p'ó** mother-in-law and father-in-law [of the wife]

公社 **kūng-shè** a commune

公社化 **kūng-shè-huà** to convert to communes, communalization

公社管理委员会 **kūng-shè kuǎn-lǐ wěi-yuán-huì** commune administrative committee

公社工业化 **kūng-shè kūng-yèh-huà** industrialization of the communes

公社农业技术员 **kūng-shè núng-yèh chì-shù-yuán** commune agricultural technical personnel, a commune agricultural technologist

公社史 **kūng-shè-shǐh** commune history, the history of a commune

公社党委会 **kūng-shè tǎng-wěi-huì** Commune Party Committee

公升 **kūng-shēng** a liter [1.057 liquid quarts]

公使 **kūng-shǐh** a minister [diplomatic]

公使馆 **kūng-shǐh-kuǎn** a legation

公式 **kūng-shìh** a formula, prescribed form

公式主义 **kūng-shìh-chǔ-ì** "formula-ism" (adhering to a fixed program without taking into account the current situation)

公式化 **kūng-shìh-huà** to reduce to a formula, formularize; formularization

公事 **kūng-shìh** official business, public affairs

公说公有理, 婆说婆有理 **kūng-shūo kūng-yǔ-lǐ, p'ó-shūo p'ó-yǔ-lǐ** the husband says he is right and the wife says she is right (everyone thinks he is right)

公司法 **kūng-szū-fǎ** company law, corporate law

公私兼顾 **kūng-szū-chiēn-kù** to give concurrent consideration to public and private interests

公私合营 **kūng-szū-hó-yíng** state and private joint operation

公私合营企业 **kūng-szū-hó-yíng ch'ǐ-yèh** state-private joint enterprise

公私溶化 **kūng-szū-júng-huà** the dissolving of public and private (a slogan, attributed to revisionists, by which private interests could remain in control—one of the **hēi-liù-lùn**)

公私观 **kūng-szū-kuān** the public and private views

公私两利 **kūng-szū-liǎng-lì** both public and individual interests are benefited

公担 **kūng-tàn** 100 kilograms

公道 **kūng-tào** just, fair, reasonable

公德 **kūng-té** public ethics, public morals; a regard for public welfare

公敌 **kūng-tí** a public enemy

公地 **kūng-tì** public land

公吨 **kūng-tùn** a metric ton (2205 pounds)

公文 **kūng-wén** an official document, official despatch or letter

公务人员 **kūng-wù-jén-yuán** public employees, civil servants, staff of governmental agencies

公务员 **kūng-wù-yuán** civil servant (*see next above*)

公养猪 **kūng-yǎng-chū** pigs raised collectively

公养私养并举 **kūng-yǎng szū-yǎng pìng-chǔ** simultaneous public and private rearing (usually refers to raising of pigs both by production teams and as a domestic sideline occupation)

公营企业 **kūng-yíng-ch'ǐ-yèh** a public enterprise (usually industrial)

公有制 **kūng-yǔ-chìh** the public ownership system

公有化 **kūng-yǔ-huà** socialization [of ownership]

公有私养 **kūng-yǔ-szū-yǎng** public ownership and private care [of animals, etc.]

公寓 **kūng-yù** an apartment house

公元 **kūng-yuán** the public beginning (the system for numbering years: corresponds to A.D.)

公约 **kūng-yuēh** a treaty, pact, convention, covenant

功迹 **kūng-chì** a meritorious record

功绩 **kūng-chì** merit, a meritorious achievement, exploit, feat, distinguished service

功臣 **kūng-ch'én** a meritorious official (now refers to peasants, workers, or soldiers being honored for merit: similar to **yīng-hsiúng** [hero] or **mó-fàn** [model])

功臣思想 **kūng-ch'én-szū-hsiǎng** meritorious-official thinking (the alleged tendency of old cadres to sit back and rest on their past merits)

功臣自居 **kūng-ch'én-tzù-chū** the airs of a self-styled hero

功夫 **kūng-fu** hard work, time and energy expended; accomplishment

功勋 **kūng-hsūn** services [to the public], eminent contributions, meritorious achievement

功过 **kūng-kuò** merits and faults

功劳 **kūng-láo** merit, credit for good work, meritorious services

功劳簿 **kūng-láo-pù** a book of merits (the implication is of the individual being conscious of his own merits)

功利主义 **kūng-lì-chǔ-ì** utilitarianism

功率 **kūng-lǜ** power, output capacity [of a machine], work capacity

功能 **kūng-néng** function, effect, effectiveness, capability, use

功能性疾病 **kūng-néng-hsìng chí-pìng** a functional disease

功德 **kūng-té** achievement and virtue, contribution to the public good, meritorious works

功业 **kūng-yèh** great achievements, important contribution [to the public or national good]

1158 攻占 **kūng-chàn** to attack and occupy, capture [a place]

攻击 **kūng-chī** attack, assault; to criticize, reproach, attack verbally

攻讦 **kūng-chiéh** to attack, criticize, bring a charge against, expose

攻坚战术 **kūng-chiēn-chàn-shù** the tactics for attacking heavy fortifications

攻城 **kūng-ch'éng** to attack cities

攻下 **kūng-hsià** to take by assault, capture, batter down

攻心战术 **kūng-hsīn-chàn-shù** psychological warfare

攻关 **kūng-kuān** to attack the pass (to concentrate one's attack on the keypoint)

攻克敌阵 **kūng-k'ò-tí-chèn** to attack and capture enemy positions

攻破 **kūng-p'ò** to destroy by assault, conquer

攻守同盟 **kūng-shǒu-t'úng-méng** an offensive and defensive alliance (an accusation in the **sān-fǎn** campaign, that suspected transgressors had mutual agreements not to testify against each other)

攻无不克 **kūng-wú-pù-k'ò** there is no attack that was not won; there is no [position] that cannot be attacked and captured (invincible force)

1159 供给 **kūng-chǐ** to supply, distribute, equip, provide

供给制 **kūng-chǐ-chìh** supply system (an early arrangement for partial support of cadres by the supply of some daily needs in kind)

供给量 **kūng-chǐ-liàng** a supply quota

供产销 **kūng-ch'ǎn-hsiāo** supply, production, and marketing

供求 **kūng-ch'iú** supply and demand

供销 **kūng-hsiāo** supply and distribution, supply and sales, marketing

供销合同 **kūng-hsiāo-hó-t'ung** a supply and marketing agreement

供销合作社 **kūng-hsiāo hó-tsò-shè** a supply and marketing cooperative

供不应求 **kūng-pù-yìng-ch'iú** supply failing to meet demand

供应 **kūng-yìng** to supply, furnish, provide

供应站 **kūng-yìng-chàn** a supply station

供应紧张 **kūng-yìng-chǐn-chāng** a supply crisis, supply stringency

供应不上 **kūng-yìng-pù-shàng** supply cannot meet demand

供 **kūng**: *see also* **kùng**

1160 宫庭政变 **kūng-t'íng-chèng-pièn** a palace revolt (during the Cultural Revolution, a reference to the P'eng Chen case)

1161 恭喜发财 **kūng-hsǐ-fā-ts'ái** [wishing you] congratulations and riches (a term no longer in favor but an accusation against Lin Piao—that in his view this represented the attitude of the masses)

恭恭敬敬 **kūng-kūng chìng-chìng** very respectful, deferential

kǔng (gǒng)

1162 巩固 **kǔng-kù** to strengthen, consolidate, make more solid; strong, secure, solid; consolidation

巩固新民主义秩序 **kǔng-kù hsīn-mín-chǔ-chǔ-ì chìh-hsù** to consolidate the new democratic order (early post-Liberation period)

1163 拱桥 **kǔng-ch'iáo** an arch bridge

拱门 **kǔng-mén** an arched door or gateway, an arch

拱手 **kǔng-shǒu** to fold one's hands in a bow (to yield passively)

kùng (gòng)

¹¹⁶⁴ 共产主义 **kùng-ch'ǎn-chǔ-ì** communism, communist

共产主义精神 **kùng-ch'ǎn-chǔ-ì chīng-shén** the communist spirit

共产主义青年团 **kùng-ch'ǎn-chǔ-ì ch'īng-nién-t'uán** the Communist Youth League

共产主义觉悟 **kùng-ch'ǎn-chǔ-ì chüéh-wù** communist consciousness

共产主义风格 **kùng-ch'ǎn-chǔ-ì fēng-kó** the communist style [of work, or dealing with problems]

共产主义人生观 **kùng-ch'ǎn-chǔ-ì jén-shēng-kuān** the communist philosophy of life

共产主义理想 **kùng-ch'ǎn-chǔ-ì lǐ-hsiǎng** the communist ideals, communist vision

共产主义萌芽 **kùng-ch'ǎn-chǔ-ì méng-yá** the sprouts of communism, early beginnings of [organized] communism

共产主义世界观 **kùng-ch'ǎn-chǔ-ì shìh-chièh-kuān** the communist world view, communist *weltanschauung*

共产主义道德 **kùng-ch'ǎn-chǔ-ì tào-té** communist ethics

共产国际 **kùng-ch'ǎn-kuó-chì** the Communist International, Comintern

共产党 **kùng-ch'ǎn-tǎng** (1) the Communist party; (2) *The Communist Party* (a Party journal, monthly, published at Shanghai in 1921)

共产党宣言 **kùng-ch'ǎn-tǎng hsuān-yén** *The Communist Manifesto*

共产党人 **kùng-ch'ǎn-tǎng-jén** (1) Communist party members, a Communist; (2) *The Communist* (a CCP internal publication, Yenan, 1939)

共称 **kùng-ch'ēng** together known as; in combination called

共青团 **kùng-ch'īng-t'uan** Communist Youth League (abbreviation of **kùng-ch'ǎn-chǔ-ì ch'īng-nién-t'uán**)

共处 **kùng-ch'ǔ** coexistence; to coexist

共和国 **kùng-hó-kuó** a republic

共患难 **kùng-huàn-nàn** to share adversity and hardship

共性 **kùng-hsìng** common traits, shared characteristics

共甘苦 **kùng-kān-k'ǔ** to share the sweet and the bitter, work together through thick and thin

共鸣 **kùng-míng** resonance, sympathetic vibrations [physics]; sympathy, sympathetic understanding, to inspire a response in others

共命运 **kùng-mìng-yùn** to share the same destiny, a common fate

共谋 **kùng-móu** to conspire with, intrigue with, be in collusion with

共事 **kùng-shìh** to work together (to work on the same project or in the same place)

共通 **kùng-t'ūng** common, universal, universally applicable

共同 **kùng-t'úng** common, joint, collective, shared by all; together; to cooperate; concurrently

共同防御公约 **kùng-t'úng fáng-yù kūng-yuēh** joint defense pact, mutual defense treaty

共同奋斗 **kùng-t'úng fèn-tòu** to unite in a common struggle

共同感情与语言 **kùng-t'úng kǎn-ch'íng yǔ yǔ-yén** common sentiments and language

共同纲领 **kùng-t'úng-kāng-lǐng** The Common Program (adopted by the Chinese People's Political Consultative Conference, September 1949)

共同社 **kùng-t'úng-shè** Kyodo News Agency (Japan)

共同市场 **kùng-t'úng-shìh-ch'ǎng** the Common Market

共同对敌 **kùng-t'úng tuì-tí** together to face the enemy

共同体 **kùng-t'úng-t'ǐ** a community, collective

共同语言 **kùng-t'úng-yǔ-yén** a common language, [speaking] the same language

共存 **kùng-ts'ún** coexistence; to coexist

共有 **kùng-yǔ** to possess in common, owned by all; to communize

¹¹⁶⁵ 贡献 **kùng-hsièn** to contribute, offer oneself [to a cause]; contribution

¹¹⁶⁶ 供状 **kùng-chuàng** an affidavit

供认 **kùng-jèn** to admit, confess

供养 **kùng-yǎng** to nourish, support, rear, care for

供 **kùng:** *see also* **kūng**

kuō (guō)

¹¹⁶⁷ 锅炉 **kuō-lú** a boiler

锅灶 **kuō-tsào** a country stove built to hold the **kuō** [the cooking pot used mainly in north China]

锅碗瓢勺 **kuō-wǎn-p'iáo-sháo** cooking pot, bowl, dipper, and spoon [the common cooking utensils]

kuó (guó)

¹¹⁶⁸ 国籍 **kuó-chí** nationality, citizenship

国计民生 **kuó-chì-mín-shēng** fiscal administration and people's livelihood (the national economy as a whole)

国际 **kuó-chì** international; The [Communist] International

国际主义 **kuó-chì-chǔ-ì** internationalism

国际主义的内容 **kuó-chì-chǔ-ì te nèi-júng** the content of internationalism

国际专政论 **kuó-chì-chuān-chèng lùn** the doctrine of international dictatorship (the alleged USSR theory justifying intervention in Eastern Europe, Mongolia, etc.)

国际儿童节 **kuó-chì érh-t'úng-chiéh** International Children's Day (June 1)

国际反美统一战线 **kuó-chì fǎn-měi t'ǔng-ì-chàn-hsièn** the international anti-American front

国际合作 **kuó-chì-hó-tsò** cooperation among nations, international cooperation

国际货币 **kuó-chì-huò-pì** international currencies (the principal currencies of foreign trade and balancing of international accounts)

国际货币基金 **kuó-chì huò-pì chī-chīn** the International Monetary Fund [IMF]

国际新闻工作者协会 **kuó-chì hsīn-wén kūng-tsò-chě hsiéh-huì** International Organization of Journalists

国际形势 **kuó-chì-hsíng-shìh** the international situation

国际学生联合会 **kuó-chì hsuéh-shēng lién-hó-huì** the International Union of Students [IUS]

国际人权公约 **kuó-chì jén-ch'üán kūng-yuēh** International Charter of Human Rights

国际歌 **kuó-chì-kō** "The Internationale" [song]

国际关系 **kuó-chì-kuān-hsi** international relations

国际惯例 **kuó-chì kuàn-lì** international practice, international customs

国际公认 **kuó-chì kūng-jèn** internationally recognized

国际共产主义 **kuó-chì kūng-ch'ǎn-chǔ-ì** international communism

国际共产主义运动 **kuó-chì kūng-ch'ǎn-chǔ-ì yùn-tùng** the international communist movement

国际劳工协会 **kuó-chì láo-kūng-hsiéh-huì** The International Workingmen's Association: the First International

国际劳工组织 **kuó-chì láo-kūng tsǔ-chīh** the International Labor Organization [ILO]

国际劳动节 **kuó-chì láo-tùng-chiéh** International Labor Day (May 1)

国际列车 **kuó-chì lièh-ch'ē** an international train, a train crossing national borders

国际贸易 **kuó-chì-mào-ì** international trade, world trade

国际贸易促进会 **kuó-chì-mào-ì ts'ù-chìn-huì** Committee for the Promotion of International Trade

国际民主妇女联合会 **kuó-chì mín-chǔ fù-nǚ lién-hó-huì** Women's International Democratic Federation [WIDF]

国际奥林匹克委员会 **kuó-chì òu-lín-p'ǐ-k'ò wěi-yuán-huì** the International Olympic Committee [IOC]

国际霸权 **kuó-chì-pà-ch'üán** international hegemony (of the superpowers)

国际市场 **kuó-chì-shìh-ch'ǎng** the international market

国际事务 **kuó-chì-shìh-wù** international affairs

国际收支 **kuó-chì-shōu-chīh** international balance of payments

国际书店 **kuó-chì shū-tièn** the International Bookstore (a Peking publishing house, specializing in translations and books in foreign languages—usually known as Guozi Shudian)

国际地球物理年 **kuó-chì tì-ch'iú-wù-lǐ nién** the international geophysical year

国际地位 **kuó-chì-tì-wèi** international position, international prestige

国际托管制度 **kuó-chì t'ō-kuǎn chìh-tù** international trusteeship system

国际责任 **kuó-chì-tsé-jèn** international responsibility

国际问题 **kuó-chì-wèn-t'í** an international problem, foreign relations issues

国际舞台 **kuó-chì-wǔ-t'ái** the international stage (international scene)

国家 **kuó-chiā** the state; the formal instruments of rule; national; a country, nation

国家机器 **kuó-chiā-chī-ch'ì** the machinery of the state, state apparatus (generally abstract)

国家机构 **kuó-chiā-chī-kòu** state institutions, institutional machinery of the state, state structure

国家机关 **kuó-chiā-chī-kuān** state agencies, administrative organs of the state, state authorities

国家机关工作人员 **kuó-chiā-chī-kuān kūng-tsò jén-yuán** personnel of state

organs, members of state administration, civil service personnel

国家基本建设委员会 **kuó-chiā chī-pěn-chièn-shè wěi-yuán-huì** Commission of State Capital Construction [of the State Council]

国家基本财政计划 **kuó-chiā chī-pěn-ts'ái-chèng chì-huà** the national financial plan

国家计划 **kuó-chiā-chì-huà** state planning, the state plan

国家计划委员会 **kuó-chiā chì-huà wěi-yuán-huì** State Planning Commission [of the State Council]

国家建设委员会 **kuó-chiā chièn-shè wěi-yuán-huì** State Construction Commission

国家至上 **kuó-chiā-chìh-shàng** the state above all, the state is supreme

国家津贴 **kuó-chiā chīn-t'iēh** state subsidies

国家经济建设公债 **kuó-chiā chīng-chì-chièn-shè kūng-chài** state economic construction bonds

国家经济委员会 **kuó-chiā chīng-chì wěi-yuán-huì** State Economic Commission [of the State Council]

国家主权 **kuó-chiā-chǔ-ch'üán** national sovereignty

国家主席 **kuó-chiā-chǔ-hsí** the state chairman

国家储备金 **kuó-chiā ch'ǔ-pèi-chīn** state reserve funds

国家决算 **kuó-chiā chüéh-suàn** final account of state revenue and expenditure, the final state budget

国家权力 **kuó-chiā-ch'üán-lì** the state power

国家海洋局 **kuó-chiā hǎi-yáng-chú** National Hydrographic Bureau

国家宪法 **kuó-chiā-hsièn-fǎ** a national constitution

国家改变颜色 **kuó-chiā kǎi-pièn yén-sè** the state changes its color (to change to or from socialism)

国家观 **kuó-chiā-kuān** concept of the state, theory of the state

国家供应粮 **kuó-chiā kūng-yìng-liáng** state-supplied grain

国家科学技术委员会 **kuó-chiā k'ō-hsuéh chì-shù wěi-yuán-huì** the State Science and Technology Commission [of the State Council]

国家篮球队 **kuó-chiā lán-ch'iú-tuì** a national basketball team

国家粮食征购 **kuó-chiā liáng-shíh-chēng-kòu** state grain procurement

国家领导人 **kuó-chiā lǐng-tǎo-jén** the state leaders

国家垄断资本主义 **kuó-chiā lǔng-tuàn** tzū-pěn-chǔ-ì state monopoly capitalism

国家收入 **kuó-chiā-shōu-jù** state revenue

国家收购站 **kuó-chiā shōu-kòu-chàn** state purchasing station

国家收购机关 **kuó-chiā shōu-kòu chī-kuān** state purchasing organs

国家档案局 **kuó-chiā tàng-àn-chú** State Archives Bureau

国家地震局 **kuó-chiā tì-chèn-chú** National Seismographic Bureau

国家体育委员会 **kuó-chiā t'ǐ-yù wěi-yuán-huì** National Athletic Committee (commonly abbreviated as *kuó-chiā-t'ǐ-wěi*)

国家投资 **kuó-chiā t'óu-tzū** state investment

国家统计局 **kuó-chiā t'ǔng-chì-chú** State Statistical Bureau

国家资本主义的低级形式 **kuó-chiā tzū-pěn-chǔ-ì te tì-chí-hsíng-shìh** lower form of state capitalism (the pre-1955 policy of permitting private enterprise to continue, but with raw materials supplied and all finished products bought by the state)

国家资本主义的高级形式 **kuó-chiā tzū-pěn-chǔ-ì te kāo-chí hsíng-shìh** higher form of state capitalism (the 1955–56 program of establishing joint state-private operation of enterprises by paying fixed dividends to the private shareholders)

国家测绘总局 **kuó-chiā ts'è-huì-tsǔng-chú** State Surveying and Cartography Bureau

国家危机 **kuó-chiā-wēi-chī** a national crisis

国家预算 **kuó-chiā yù-suàn** the state budget

国家预算收入 **kuǒ-chiā yù-suàn-shōu-jù** budgetary revenue

国家元首 **kuó-chiā-yuán-shǒu** head of state

国境 **kuó-chìng** national territory

国境线 **kuó-chìng-hsièn** national boundary

国产 **kuó-ch'ǎn** domestic products, local products

国旗 **kuó-ch'í** national flag

国情 **kuó-ch'íng** national tradition; the current national situation or conditions

国庆 **kuó-ch'ìng** the national anniversary day [of any country]

国庆节日 **kuó-ch'ìng-chiéh-jìh** the National Day (October 1)

国庆观礼 **kuó-ch'ìng kuān-lǐ** review of the National Day parade

国军 **kuó-chǖn** the national army [pre-Liberation]

国防 **kuó-fáng** national defense

国防前哨 **kuó-fáng-ch'ién-shào** national defense outposts

国防军 **kuó-fáng-chǖn** national defense army, defense forces

国防工事 **kuó-fáng-kūng-shìh** permanent national defense works, fortifications

国防科学委员会 **kuó-fáng-k'ō-hsuéh wěi-yuán-huì** National Defense Scientific and Technological Commission [under the Ministry of Defense]

国防部 **kuó-fáng-pù** Ministry of National Defense [under the State Council]

国防委员会 **kuó-fáng wěi-yuán-huì** National Defense Committee (an advisory committee)

国防文学 **kuó-fáng-wén-hsuéh** national defense literature (a term coined by Chou Yang and others for patriotic literary and dramatic works in the 1930s, later criticized during the Cultural Revolution)

国富民穷 **kuó-fù mín-ch'iúng** the country is rich but the people are impoverished (a statement charged against Lin Piao)

国画家 **kuó-huà-chiā** a painter in the traditional Chinese style

国徽 **kuó-huī** state emblem, national insignia

国会 **kuó-huì** a national legislative body (parliament, diet, congress, etc.)

国歌 **kuó-kō** the national anthem

国共合作 **kuó-kùng-hó-tsò** Kumintang-Communist cooperation (1923–27 and 1937–45)

国库 **kuó-k'ù** the state treasury, exchequer

国民 **kuó-mín** a citizen, a national; the people of a country; national

国民经济 **kuó-mín-chīng-chì** the national economy

国民经济计划 **kuó-mín-chīng-chì chì-huà** national economic planning

国民经济军事化 **kuó-mín-chīng-chì chǖn-shìh-huà** militarization of the national economy

国民经济恢复时期 **kuó-mín-chīng-chì huī-fù-shíh-ch'ī** the period of recovery of the national economy (1950–1952)

国民经济各部门 **kuó-mín-chīng-chì kò pù-mén** various branches of the national economy

国民收入 **kuó-mín-shōu-jù** national income (gross personal income)

国民党 **kuó-mín-tǎng** the Kuomintang [KMT] (the Nationalist Party of China)

国民总产值 **kuó-mín tsǔng-ch'ǎn-chíh** gross national output

国内战争 **kuó-nèi-chàn-chēng** civil war

国内形势 **kuó-nèi hsíng-shìh** domestic situation, internal conditions

国内革命战争 **kuó-nèi kó-míng-chàn-chēng** revolutionary civil war

国宾 **kuó-pīn** a state guest

国事访问 **kuó-shìh-fǎng-wèn** a state visit

国书 **kuó-shū** diplomatic credentials, letter of credence

国典 **kuó-tiěn** national law codes

国度 **kuó-tù** a state, country, nation

国体 **kuó-t'ǐ** form of the state; national prestige

国策 **kuó-ts'è** national policies, the policies of the state

国粹主义 **kuó-ts'uì-chǔ-ì** the doctrine of national and cultural uniqueness ("everything Chinese is best")

国外投资 **kuó-wài-t'óu-tzū** investment in foreign countries

国务卿 **kuó-wù-ch'īng** the [US] secretary of state

国务院 **kuó-wù-yuàn** the State Council [in China]; the Department of State [in the US]

国务院副总理 **kuó-wù-yuàn fù-tsǔng-lǐ** vice premier of the State Council

国务院工交办公室 **kuó-wù-yuàn kūng-chiāo pàn-kūng-shìh** Industry and Communications Office of the State Council

国务院国防工业办公室 **kuó-wù-yuàn kuó-fáng-kūng-yèh pàn-kūng-shìh** Defense Industry Office of the State Council

国务院科教组 **kuó-wù-yuàn k'ō-chiào-tsǔ** the Science and Education Section of the State Council (has replaced the Ministry of Education since 1969)

国务院内务办公室 **kuó-wù-yuàn nèi-wù pàn-kūng-shìh** Internal Affairs Office of the State Council (formerly, the Political and Legal Affairs Office)

国务院农林办公室 **kuó-wù-yuàn núng-lín pàn-kūng-shìh** Agriculture and Forestry Office of the State Council

国务院总理 **kuó-wù-yuàn tsǔng-lǐ** premier of the State Council

国务院财贸办公室 **kuó-wù-yuàn ts'ái-mào pàn-kūng-shìh** Finance and Trade Office of the State Council

国务院参事室 **kuó-wù-yuàn ts'ān-shìh-**

shìh Councillor's Office of the State Council

国务院外事办公室 **kuó-wù-yuàn wài-shìh pàn-kūng-shìh** Foreign Affairs Office of the State Council

国务院文教办公室 **kuó-wù-yuàn wén-chìào pàn-kūng-shìh** Culture and Education Office of the State Council

国务院文化组 **kuó-wù-yuàn wén-huà-tsǔ** the Culture Section of the State Council (it has replaced the Ministry of Culture)

国宴 **kuó-yèn** a state banquet, state dinner

国营 **kuó-yíng** state-operated, owned and operated by the state

国营企业 **kuó-yíng-ch'ǐ-yèh** a state enterprise

国营工业 **kuó-yíng-kūng-yèh** a state-operated industry

国营农场 **kuó-yíng-núng-ch'ǎng** state farms (often on poor or reclaimed land)

国营商业 **kuó-yíng-shāng-yèh** state-operated trade, a state-operated business or commercial enterprise

国营商业机构 **kuó-yíng-shāng-yèh chǐ-kòu** state commercial agencies

国营商业部门 **kuó-yíng-shāng-yèh pù-mén** state trading departments

国有化 **kuó-yǔ-huà** conversion to national ownership, nationalization; to nationalize

国有土地使用证 **kuó-yǔ-t'ǔ-tì shǐh-yùng-chèng** deed for the use of state-owned land (granted after land reform, for surface rights)

kuǒ (guǒ)

1169 果敢 **kuǒ-kǎn** resolute and daring, stout-hearted

果木 **kuǒ-mù** a fruit tree

果实 **kuǒ-shíh** fruit of trees; results, consequences, an achievement

果断 **kuǒ-tuàn** decision with courage, decisive, resolute, determined

果园 **kuǒ-yuán** an orchard

1170 裹足不前 **kuǒ-tsú-pù-ch'ién** to bind the feet and not advance (indecisive and at a standstill)

kuò (guò)

1171 过急 **kuò-chí** too hasty, precipitate

过境贸易 **kuò-chìng-mào-ì** transit trade

过程 **kuò-ch'éng** process; [in the] course [of]; a stage

过期 **kuò-ch'ī** overdue, after a set time limit

过分 **kuò-fèn** excessively, too, unduly, superfluous

过黄河 **kuò-huáng-hó** to surpass the Yellow River (to produce more than 500 kg. per *mu*, the standard set for the Yellow River valley by the agricultural plan)

过火 **kuò-huǒ** to go beyond the proper limit, overdo; intemperate, exaggerated, excessive

过细 **kuò-hsì** very careful, to give close attention to; cautious, painstaking, squeamish

过日子 **kuò-jìh-tzu** to practice economy; to pass the time, to live

过高估计 **kuò-kāo-kū-chì** to over-estimate

过关 **kuò-kuān** to go through the pass (to pass a severe test, survive an ordeal)

过虑 **kuò-lù** over-anxious, unduly concerned

过目 **kuò-mù** to pass one's eye over, look over, read

过三关 **kuò-sān-kuān** to surmount three passes [tests] (ideology, life style, physical labor)

过剩 **kuò-shèng** surplus; excessive, superfluous

过失 **kuò-shīh** a fault, error, mistake; negligence

过时 **kuò-shíh** outdated, old-fashioned, obsolete, anachronistic

过得去了 **kuò-te-ch'ǜ-le** we've passed! (to be satisfied with a minimally sufficient achievement)

过得硬 **kuò-te-yìng** capable of toughness [in spirit, work style, and learning techniques]

过低估计 **kuò-tī-kū-chì** to under-estimate

过度 **kuò-tù** excessive, too much; to go beyond the normal limit

过渡 **kuò-tù** to cross over; a ferry, transition; transitional

过渡阶段 **kuò-tù-chiēh-tuàn** a transitional stage

过渡状态 **kuò-tù-chuàng-t'ài** transitional state

过渡形式 **kuò-tù-hsíng-shìh** a transitional form

过渡时期 **kuò-tù-shíh-ch'ī** a transitional period

过渡时期总路线 **kuò-tù-shíh-ch'ī tsǔng-lù-hsièn** general line for the transitional period (set forth by Mao Tse-tung at the end of 1952)

过早 **kuò-tsǎo** too early, prematurely

过左倾向 **kuò-tsǒ-ch'īng-hsiàng** an excessively leftist tendency

过问 **kuò-wèn** to ask about, make inquiries about; to show concern; to interfere with

过硬 **kuò-yìng** toughness, resoluteness; to be resolute and uncompromising

过于强调 **kuò-yú-ch'iáng-tiào** to over-emphasize, lay too much stress on

k'ā (kā)

¹¹⁷² 咖啡文学 **k'ā-fēi-wén-hsuéh** coffee literature (literature serving the function of being merely entertainment)

¹¹⁷³ 喀麦隆 **k'ā-mài-lúng** [Republic of] Cameroon

喀布尔 **k'ā-pù-ěrh** Kabul [Afghanistan]

喀土穆 **k'ā-t'ǔ-mù** Khartoum [Sudan]

k'ǎ (kǎ)

¹¹⁷⁴ 卡路里 **k'ǎ-lù-lǐ** a calorie [thermal unit]

卡宾枪 **k'ǎ-pīn-ch'iāng** a carbine [rifle]

卡片 **k'ǎ-p'ièn** a card, index card, visiting card

卡萨布兰卡非洲宪章 **k'ǎ-sà-pù-lán-k'ǎ fēi-chōu hsièn-chāng** the African Charter of Casablanca

卡塔尔酋长国 **k'ǎ-t'ǎ-ěrh chíu-chǎng-kuó** Sheikdom of Qatar

卡宴 **k'ǎ-yèn** Cayenne [French Guiana]

k'āi (kāi)

¹¹⁷⁵ 开展 **k'āi-chǎn** to develop, unfold, evolve; to launch; to promote

开展城乡交流 **k'āi-chǎn ch'éng-hsiāng-chiāo-líu** to promote rural-urban intercourse

开展贸易 **k'āi-chǎn mào-ì** to develop trade

开张营业 **k'āi-chāng yíng-yèh** to open a business (may be figurative and pejorative)

开支 **k'āi-chīh** expenses, expenditure, disbursements; to pay, spend, disburse

开场 **k'āi-ch'ǎng** to open a theatrical play, commence a public activity; to begin

开诚布公 **k'āi-ch'éng-pù-kūng** to reveal sincerity and show justice (sincerely and openly, frank, honest)

开窍 **k'āi-ch'iào** to open the orifices (to begin to see more and understand more)

开除 **k'āi-ch'ú** to dismiss [from Party, official post, school, etc.], to expel,

discharge dishonorably

开除出党 **k'āi-ch'ú-ch'ū-tǎng** to be expelled from the Party

开除党籍 **k'āi-ch'ú-tǎng-chí** expulsion from the Party rolls

开创 **k'āi-ch'uàng** to start, found, create, initiate

开春 **k'āi-ch'ūn** in early spring; the beginning of spring

开卷作题 **k'āi-chüàn-tsò-t'í** open-book examinations

开发山区 **k'āi-fā-shān-ch'ū** to develop mountain areas, reclaim hilly land

开放 **k'āi-fàng** to open up, liberalize; to lift a ban

开后门 **k'āi-hòu-mén** to open a back door (when someone in authority gives another person a favor or benefit to which he or she is not entitled)

开花结果 **k'āi-huā-chiéh-kuǒ** to flower and bear fruit (usually figurative)

开化 **k'āi-huà** civilized, developed

开荒 **k'āi-huāng** to open up uncultivated land

开荒生产 **k'āi-huāng-shēng-ch'ǎn** to reclaim wasteland for production

开荒造田 **k'āi-huāng-tsào-t'ién** to reclaim wasteland and make fields

开火 **k'āi-huǒ** to open fire

开心 **k'āi-hsīn** happy, enjoying oneself; to make fun of, play a joke on; to open one's heart, talk sincerely

开关 **k'āi-kuān** an electric switch, mechanical control to open or close a valve

开工 **k'āi-kūng** to begin construction, commence work, in operation

开工不足 **k'āi-kūng-pù-tsú** under-capacity operation

开国 **k'āi-kuó** to found a state, establish a government

开垦荒地 **k'āi-k'ěn-huāng-tì** to bring new land under cultivation, reclaim wasteland, open up virgin land

开课 **k'āi-k'ò** to being the school term, offer courses

开阔眼界 **k'āi-k'uò yěn-chièh** to widen one's vision

开历史倒车 **k'āi lì-shǐh tào-ch'ē** to reverse the cart of history (historical retrogression)

开罗 **k'āi-ló** Cairo

开路 **k'āi-lù** to open a new road, pioneer, lead the way (often figurative)

开门整风 **k'āi-mén-chěng-fēng** open-door rectification (signifying the willingness of the Party to receive outside criticism)

开门见山 **k'āi-mén-chièn-shān** to open the door and directly see the mountain (to be straightforward, conceal nothing, talk right to the point)

开门红 **k'āi-mén-húng** to open the door to red (to start the year [or season] with achievement—so that the whole season will be successful)

开门揖盗 **k'āi-mén-ī-tào** to open the door and greet robbers (to invite trouble)

开门办学 **k'āi-mén-pàn-hsuéh** open-door school management (schools run with public participation, with teachers coming from the community, and with links established with farms and factories)

开门排戏 **k'āi-mén-p'ái-hsì** open-door rehearsal (a means of inviting mass criticism of **yàng-pǎn-hsì** in development)

开明 **k'āi-míng** enlightened, progressive, liberal, open-minded

开明人士 **k'āi-míng-jén-shìh** enlightened persons

开明绅士 **k'āi-míng-shēn-shìh** enlightened gentry

开明地主 **k'āi-míng-tì-chǔ** enlightened landlords

开幕 **k'āi-mù** to raise the curtain, commence, inaugurate

开幕典礼 **k'āi-mù-tiěn-lǐ** inaugural ceremony

开办 **k'āi-pàn** to set up, start, operate, establish

开辟道路 **k'āi-p'ì-tào-lù** to open up a road (to make something possible)

开辟财政来源 **k'āi-p'ì ts'ái-chèng-lái-yuán** to develop financial resources

开普敦 **k'āi-p'ǔ-tūn** Cape Town

开山造田 **k'āi-shān-tsào-t'ién** digging out the mountains to make fields

开设 **k'āi-shè** to found, start, open

开刀 **k'āi-tāo** surgery (may be figurative)

开导 **k'āi-tǎo** to enlighten, explain and convince, guide

开倒车 **k'āi-tào-ch'ē** (1) to reverse the cart, back a train or car; (2) to be old-fashioned, retrograde

开端 **k'āi-tuān** the beginning; to make a start

开动 **k'āi-tùng** to start [a machine], set in motion

开动脑筋 **k'āi-tùng-nǎo-chīn** to use the brain

开天辟地 **k'āi-t'iēn-p'ì-tì** to open the heavens and spread the earth (epochal, a great achievement)

开脱 **k'āi-t'ō** to pardon, acquit, vindicate, extricate from difficulties

开脱责任 **k'āi-t'ō-tsé-jèn** to relieve of responsibility

开拓 **k'āi-t'ò** to expand, open up, enlarge

开头 **k'āi-t'óu** in the beginning, from the start

开凿 **k'āi-tsáo** to excavate, dig, drill

开足马力 **k'āi-tsú-mǎ-lì** to open up full horsepower (under full steam, going full blast)

开宗明义 **k'āi-tsūng-míng-ì** to cite clearly at the beginning [of a speech or article its] central theme, an introductory outline

开采 **k'āi-ts'ǎi** to mine, extract, exploit

开玩笑 **k'āi-wán-hsiào** to joke, play a joke, make fun of

开夜车 **k'āi-yèh-ch'ē** to drive a carriage at night (to travel by double stages; to burn the midnight oil)

开源节流 **k'āi-yuán-chiéh-liú** to broaden the sources of income and economize on expenditures

1176 揩油 **k'āi-yú** to wipe off the oil (to sponge off someone, take improper advantage of, squeeze a small profit)

k'ǎi (kǎi)

1177 凯旋 **k'ǎi-hsuán** a triumphant return [of an army]

凯歌 **k'ǎi-kō** a victory song, paean of triumph

k'ǎn (kǎn)

1178 刊登 **k'ǎn-tēng** to publish [in a periodical], to carry an article

刊载 **k'ǎn-tsǎi** to publish [an article in a newspaper or periodical], to carry, print, feature

刊物 **k'ǎn-wù** periodicals, serials, magazines

1179 勘察 **k'ǎn-ch'á** to investigate, review, examine (usually a field investigation)

勘探 **k'ǎn-t'àn** to survey [mines and resources], prospect; geological investigation

勘测 **k'ǎn-ts'è** to survey [land], prospect

1180 堪培拉 **k'ǎn-p'éi-lā** Canberra [Australia]

1181 戡乱时期 **k'ǎn-luàn-shíh-ch'ī** the period of suppression [of Communist activities, 1945–49]

k'ǎn (kǎn)

1182 坎儿井 **k'ǎn-érh-chǐng** pit wells (a

system of irrigation used in Sinkiang)

坎帕拉 **k'ǎn-p'à-lā** Kampala [Uganda]

1183 砍伐 **k'ǎn-fá** to fell [trees, etc.], chop
down

砍两头卡中间 **k'ǎn-liǎng-t'óu ch'iǎ-chūng-chiēn** to cut off the two ends
[the advanced and the backward] and
to strangle those in between (to allow
the masses no initiative)

砍掉 **k'ǎn-tiào** to chop off, eliminate,
get rid of

k'àn (kàn)

1184 看中 **k'àn-chùng** to prefer, choose,
favor, take a liking to, take a fancy to

看重 **k'àn-chùng** to think highly of,
esteem, regard as important, value,
stress

看齐 **k'àn-ch'í** "eyes right" (to keep in
line, keep abreast of)

看清局势 **k'àn-ch'īng-chú-shìh** to see
the situation clearly, have a correct
appraisal of the situation

看法 **k'àn-fǎ** way of looking [at a
problem, etc.], viewpoint, opinion

看惯 **k'àn-kuàn** accustomed to seeing,
used to the sight of

看守 **k'àn-shǒu** to guard, watch, keep a
lookout; to keep [a person] under
detention

看待 **k'àn-tài** to treat, view, look at

看得准 **k'àn-te-chǔn** able to see things
precisely

看得高 **k'àn-te-kāo** able to see high,
set high goals

看得远 **k'àn-te-yuǎn** able to see far,
having a broad view, farseeing

看台 **k'àn-t'ái** a reviewing stand

看透 **k'àn-t'òu** to see through [a trick];
understand fully, recognize the
inevitable

看菜吃饭, 量体裁衣 **k'àn-ts'ài-ch'īh-fàn,
liáng-t'ǐ-ts'ái-ī** to regulate the
appetite according to the dishes and
cut the dress according to the figure
(to fit one's actions to the circumstances)

k'āng (kāng)

1185 康庄大道 **k'āng-chuāng-tà-tào** a level
and easy thoroughfare, the broad
path (usually figurative)

康拜因收割机 **k'āng-pài-yīn shōu-kō-chī**
a combine harvester, harvesting
machine

1186 慷慨 **k'āng-k'ǎi** generous, unselfish,
liberal, hospitable; heroic, ardent

慷慨解囊 **k'āng-k'ǎi-chiěh-náng** gener-

ously to open the purse (to contribute
funds generously)

慷慨陈词 **k'āng-k'ǎi-ch'én-tz'ú** to speak
up bravely for justice

1187 糠秕 **k'āng-pǐ** rice bran (very poor
foodstuff)

k'áng (káng)

1188 扛长活打短工 **k'áng-ch'áng-huó tǎ-tuǎn-kūng** to do steady work or do
odd jobs (usually refers to farm
work)

扛起 **k'áng-ch'ǐ** to carry on the
shoulder (to lift a burden)

扛活 **k'áng-huó** a farm laborer (on a
regular basis)

扛大活 **k'áng-tà-huó** to do heavy work

k'àng (kàng)

1189 抗战 **k'àng-chàn** (1) war of resistance
[against aggression]; (2) The War of
Resistance [against Japan, 1937-
1945] (contraction of **k'àng-jìh-chàn-chēng**)

抗战戏剧 **k'àng-chàn-hsì-chù** dramas
for the Resistance War (plays with a
patriotic theme popularized during
the war against Japan)

抗战人员 **k'àng-chàn-jén-yuán** resistance fighters, resistance personnel

抗击 **k'àng-chī** to resist an attack,
defend against aggression

抗拒 **k'àng-chù** to resist, oppose,
withstand, defy

抗拒从严 **k'àng-chù-ts'úng-yén** stern
punishment for those who resist [as
by refusing to confess guilt or repent
errors]

抗旱 **k'àng-hàn** drought-resistant; to
guard against drought

抗旱保墒 **k'àng-hàn pǎo-shāng** to
protect against drought and conserve
moisture

抗旱排涝 **k'àng-hàn-p'ái-lào** to fight
against drought and drain off waterlogging

抗旱作物 **k'àng-hàn-tsò-wù** drought-
resistant crops

抗旱运动 **k'àng-hàn-yùn-tùng** anti-
drought campaign

抗衡 **k'àng-héng** to contend against,
compete, match, be equal to

抗议 **k'àng-ì** to protest; a protest

抗日 **k'àng-jìh** The War of Resistance
Against Japan [1937-1945] (contraction of **k'àng-jìh-chàn-chēng**)

抗日战争 **k'àng-jìh-chàn-chēng** The
War of Resistance Against Japan

[1937–1945]
抗日战争时期 **k'àng-jìh-chàn-chēng shíh-ch'ī** the period of The War of Resistance Against Japan (1937–1945)

抗日救国十大纲领 **k'àng-jìh chiù-kuó shíh-tà kāng-lǐng** The Ten Great Principles for Resisting Japan and for National Salvation (set forth by the CCP in July 1937)

抗日军政大学 **k'àng-jìh chŭn-chèng tà-hsuéh** the Resist-Japan Military and Political University (operated by the CCP at Yenan and in the main base areas, 1937–1945)

抗日根据地 **k'àng-jìh kēn-chù-tì** anti-Japanese base areas

抗日民族统一战线 **k'àng-jìh mín-tsú t'ŭng-ī-chàn-hsièn** the national anti-Japanese united front

抗日大学 **k'àng-jìh tà-hsuéh** Resist-Japan [Military and Political] University (operated in Yenan by the CCP during the Sino-Japanese War, 1937–1945—contraction of **k'àng-jìh chŭn-chèng tà-hsuéh**)

抗粮 **k'àng-liáng** to resist the grain levy

抗美救国战争 **k'àng-měi chiù-kuó-chàn-chēng** the anti-American national salvation war (referring to the war in Vietnam)

抗美援朝 **k'àng-měi yuán-ch'áo** Resist America [and] Aid Korea (a slogan during the Korean War)

抗暴 **k'àng-pào** to resist tyranny

抗生素 **k'àng-shēng-sù** antibiotics

抗大 **k'àng-tà** The Resist-Japan Military and Political University (contraction of **k'àng-jìh chŭn-chèng tà-hsuéh**)

抗大精神 **k'àng-tà-chīng-shén** the K'ang-ta spirit (unity, alertness, austerity, liveliness)

抗毒素 **k'àng-tú-sù** antitoxin

抗灾 **k'àng-tsāi** to contend against natural disasters

抗灾保畜 **k'àng-tsāi-pǎo-ch'ù** guard against natural disasters and protect the herd

抗灾斗争 **k'àng-tsāi-tòu-chēng** the struggle against natural disasters

k'ǎo (kǎo)

1190 考状元 **k'ǎo-chuàng-yuán** to win first place in the imperial examinations (now used to criticize the idea that one enters a university to gain an official career)

考查 **k'ǎo-ch'á** to investigate, study

[conditions, facts], inquire into, check

考察 **k'ǎo-ch'á** to investigate, examine, study

考察团 **k'ǎo-ch'á-t'uán** an observation group, study team

考据 **k'ǎo-chù** textual research

考核 **k'ǎo-hó** officially to examine and pass on, audit, check, review

考古 **k'ǎo-kǔ** (1) to study the ancient past, archaeology; (2) *Archaeology* (a Peking monthly journal)

考古学 **k'ǎo-kǔ-hsuéh** the science of archaeology

考古学报 **k'ǎo-kǔ hsuéh-pào** *Journal of Archaeology* (Peking journal, quarterly, 1949—)

考虑 **k'ǎo-lù** to consider, weigh, deliberate, take into account

考生 **k'ǎo-shēng** students taking an examination (usually refers to the college entrance examination)

考试制度 **k'ǎo-shìh-chìh-tù** the examination system

考茨基 **k'ǎo-tz'ú-chī** Kautsky [Karl] (1854–1938)

考验 **k'ǎo-yèn** to test, try; a test, trial

1191 拷打 **k'ǎo-tǎ** to flog, whip, torture

1192 烤烟 **k'ǎo-yēn** cured tobacco

k'ào (kào)

1193 靠吃老本过日子 **k'ào ch'īh-lǎo-pěn kuò-jìh-tzu** to live off accumulated capital (old cadres getting by on their old accomplishments)

靠吓人吃饭 **k'ào hsià-jén ch'īh-fàn** to live by frightening people (to depend on intimidation—as the threat of nuclear war, etc.)

靠老本吃饭 **k'ào lǎo-pěn ch'īh-fàn** to depend on old capital to eat (relying on one's former achievements)

靠拢 **k'ào-lǔng** to come close to, approach, draw up (generally in a political sense: to become sympathetic, come over [to the position of the Party—but without joining it])

靠边站 **k'ào-piēn-chàn** stand aside (an imperative phrase applied to cadres or officials under attack during the Cultural Revolution)

靠剥削起家 **k'ào-pō-hsuéh ch'ǐ-chiā** to build the family fortune on exploitation

靠山 **k'ào-shān** a mountain that one leans against (a supporter in high places, protector, patron, mainstay)

靠山吃山 **k'ào-shān-ch'īh-shàn** to live close to the mountain and make a living off the mountain (to make a

living in one's given circumstances;
to make do with what one has)
靠天靠国家 **k'ào-t'iēn k'ào-kuó-chiā** to
depend on heaven and the nation (a
passive attitude)
靠自己 **k'ào tzù-chǐ** to rely on oneself
靠文凭吃饭 **k'ào wén-p'íng ch'īh-fàn**
to make a living by depending on
one's diploma

k'ĕn (kĕn)

1194 肯尼迪 **k'ĕn-ní-tí** Kennedy
肯尼亚 **k'ĕn-ní-yà** Kenya
肯定 **k'ĕn-tìng** to affirm, confirm;
affirmative, positive, determined
1195 垦荒 **k'ĕn-huāng** to reclaim wasteland,
open up virgin soil
垦荒志愿队 **k'ĕn-huāng chìh-yuàn-tuì**
wilderness volunteer team (volunteer
land reclamation teams
1196 恳切 **k'ĕn-ch'ièh** very sincere, earnest
恳求 **k'ĕn-ch'íú** to entreat, beseech,
implore, plead
1197 啃咸菜 **k'ĕn-hsién-ts'ài** to gnaw on
pickled vegetables (to depend on
poor food)
啃老本 **k'ĕn-lǎo-pěn** to chew old capital
(to rest on one's laurels)
啃洋本本 **k'ĕn-yáng-pěn-pěn** to gnaw
on foreign books (ridiculing some
intellectuals)
啃硬骨头 **k'ĕn-yìng-kǔ-t'ou** chewing on
a hard bone (to work on a hard task)

k'ēng (kēng)

1198 坑道 **k'ēng-tào** a tunnel, underground
passage, trench
坑道战 **k'ēng-tào-chàn** tunnel warfare
坑道工事 **k'ēng-tào-kūng-shìh** tunnel
fortifications, underground forts

k'ō (kē)

1199 苛求 **k'ō-ch'íú** to be very exacting,
expect too much, apply a harsh
standard
苛捐杂税 **k'ō-chüān-tsá-shuì** exorbitant
taxes and miscellaneous levies
苛刻 **k'ō-k'ò** harsh, pitiless, relentless,
unfeeling, unkind
苛责 **k'ō-tsé** to castigate, denounce,
criticize harshly
1200 柯尔克孜族 **k'ō-ĕrh-k'ò-tzū-tsú** the
Kirghiz people (a minority in the
Sinkiang Uighur Antonomous
Region: population 68,000 as of
1957)
柯西金 **k'ō-hsī-chìn** Kosygin [Alexei

Nikolaevich]
1201 科技 **k'ō-chì** scientific and technical;
science and technology
科技大学 **k'ō-chì-tà-hsuéh** the University of Science and Technology [in
Peking]
科学技术委员会 **k'ō-hsuéh chì-shù wěi-yuán-huì** the Scientific and Technological Commission
科学种田 **k'ō-hsuéh-chùng-t'ién** scientific farming
科学分析 **k'ō-hsuéh-fēn-hsī** scientific
analysis
科学性 **k'ō-hsuéh-hsìng** imbued with a
scientific character, having a scientific
nature
科学规划委员会 **k'ō-hsuéh-kuēi-huà
wěi-yuán-huì** the Planning Committee
for Development of Science [of the
State Council]
科学考察 **k'ō-hsuéh-k'ǎo-ch'á** scientific
investigation
科学考察仪器 **k'ō-hsuéh-k'ǎo-ch'á í-ch'ì**
apparatus for scientific investigation
科学来自实践 **k'ō-hsuéh lái-tzù shíh-chièn** science derives from practice
科学论断 **k'ō-hsuéh lùn-tuàn** a scientific
assertion, scientific conclusion, thesis
科学普及读物 **k'ō-hsuéh-p'ǔ-chí tú-wù**
popular scientific reading materials
科学社会主义 **k'ō-hsuéh shè-huì-chǔ-ì**
scientific socialism
科学实验 **k'ō-hsuéh-shíh-yèn** (1) scientific experiment (one of the **sān-tà-kó mìng-tòu-chēng**); (2) *Scientific
Experiment* (a Peking journal,
monthly)
科学通报 **k'ō-hsuéh t'ūng-pào** *Scientia*
(a Peking journal, monthly, 1950—)
科学测量仪器 **k'ō-hsuéh ts'è-liáng-í-ch'ì**
scientific measuring apparatus
科学研究机关 **k'ō-hsuéh yén-chiū chī-kuān** scientific research institutions
科学园地 **k'ō-hsuéh-yuán-tì** the field of
science, the scientific field
科学院 **k'ō-hsuéh-yuàn** The Academy
of Sciences, Academia Sinica
科伦坡 **k'ō-lún-p'ō** Colombo [Sri
Lanka]
科伦坡计划 **k'ō-lún-p'ō chì-huà** the
Colombo Plan
科纳克里 **k'ō-nà-k'ò-lǐ** Conakry
[Guinea]
科室人员 **k'ō-shìh-jén-yuán** lower-level
technical and administrative
personnel
科威特 **k'ō-wēi-t'è** Kuwait
科威特城 **k'ō-wēi-t'è-ch'éng** Al Kuwait
[the capital of Kuwait]
科研 **k'ō-yén** scientific research (con-

traction of *k'ō-hsuéh yén-chīu*)

1202 颗粒状肥料 **k'ō-lì-chuàng féi-liào** pelletized fertilizer

颗粒归仓 **k'ō-lì-kuēi-ts'āng** [every] kernel to the granary

k'ŏ (kě)

1203 可敬 **k'ŏ-chìng** respectable, admirable

可乘之机 **k'ŏ-ch'éng-chīh-chī** an opportunity that one can utilize, advantage

可耻 **k'ŏ-ch'ǐh** shameful, disgraceful, ignominious

可取 **k'ŏ-ch'ǔ** worth selecting, merits, advantages, worthiness

可喜 **k'ŏ-hsǐ** pleasing, pleasurable

可喜成果 **k'ŏ-hsǐ-ch'éng-kuǒ** delightful fruit, pleasant results

可笑 **k'ŏ-hsiào** ridiculous, laughable

可疑 **k'ŏ-í** suspect, suspicious, questionable, doubtful, unreliable

可以休矣 **k'ŏ-í-hsiū-ǐ** it would be best to stop [what you are doing]

可以理解 **k'ŏ-í-lǐ-chiěh** understandable, lucid, clear, intelligible

可耕地 **k'ŏ-kēng-tì** arable land

可歌可泣 **k'ŏ-kō-k'ŏ-ch'ì** praiseworthy and moving, inspiring

可贵 **k'ŏ-kuèi** to be honored, to be prized

可考 **k'ŏ-k'ǎo** verifiable

可靠 **k'ŏ-k'ào** reliable, dependable, accurate, trustworthy

可怜虫 **k'ŏ-lién-ch'úng** a pitiable worm, poor creature, miserable wretch

可鄙 **k'ŏ-pǐ** contemptible

可兑换 **k'ŏ-tuì-huàn** convertible, exchangeable

可动产 **k'ŏ-tùng-ch'ǎn** liquid assets, transferable property

1204 渴望 **k'ŏ-wàng** to thirst for, long for, crave; earnestly hope, aspire to

k'ò (kè)

1205 克己奉公 **k'ò-chǐ-fèng-kūng** to be strict with oneself in serving the people, wholehearted devotion to the public good

克己复礼 **k'ò-chǐ-fù-lǐ** to restrain the self and restore the rites (a Confucian saying which Lin Piao is accused of using as an attempt to restore the old order)

克制 **k'ò-chìh** to control, exercise restraint, overcome, rule over, curb, subdue

克服 **k'ò-fú** to overcome, master, subjugate

克服官僚主义 **k'ò-fú kuān-liáo-chǔ-ì** to overcome bureaucratism

克服浪费 **k'ò-fú-làng-fèi** to eliminate waste

克扣 **k'ò-k'òu** to deduct, discount, withhold a part of a subordinate's wages

克里姆林宫 **k'ò-lǐ-mǔ-lín kūng** the Kremlin

克敌制胜 **k'ò-tí-chìh-shèng** to defeat the enemy and win a victory

1206 刻划 **k'ò-huà** to carve, inscribe, engrave (to describe vividly)

刻骨仇恨 **k'ò-kǔ ch'óu-hèn** hatred that is engraved in the bone (deep-seated hatred)

刻苦 **k'ò-k'ǔ** hard-working, painstaking, self-sacrificing, strenuous

刻苦学习 **k'ò-k'ǔ-hsuéh-hsí** to study with might and main

刻苦钻研 **k'ò-k'ǔ-tsuān-yén** to study arduously

刻板 **k'ò-pǎn** to engrave [for printing] (stereotyped, dull, monotonous; adhering strictly to the rules)

刻薄 **k'ò-pó** sharp, cutting, harsh, sarcastic, unfeeling, unkind

刻不容缓 **k'ò-pù-júng-huǎn** even a moment cannot be lost, no time to lose, most urgent, immediate

刻毒 **k'ò-tú** wicked, fiendish, cruel, devilish

1207 客机 **k'ò-chī** passenger aircraft

客车 **k'ò-ch'ē** a passenger car [railway], passenger train

客观 **k'ò-kuān** objective [as opposed to subjective], not biased

客观真理 **k'ò-kuān-chēn-lǐ** objective truth

客观效果 **k'ò-kuān-hsiào-kuǒ** an objective result, actual outcome

客观现实 **k'ò-kuān-hsièn-shíh** objective reality

客观形势 **k'ò-kuān-hsíng-shìh** the objective situation, true conditions

客观需要 **k'ò-kuān-hsū-yào** objective needs, objective requirements

客观规律 **k'ò-kuān-kuēi-lǜ** objective laws

客观过程 **k'ò-kuān-kuò-ch'éng** the objective process

客观过程的反映 **k'ò-kuān-kuò-ch'éng te fǎn-yìng** reflection of the objective process

客观可能性 **k'ò-kuān k'ŏ-néng-hsìng** objective probability

客观必然性 **k'ò-kuān pì-ján-hsìng** objective necessity, objective inevitability

客观实际 **k'ò-kuān-shíh-chì** objective

reality
客观世界 **k'ò-kuān-shìh-chìeh** the objective world
客观事实 **k'ò-kuān-shìh-shíh** objective facts
客观事物 **k'ò-kuān-shìh-wù** objective matter, objective things
客观存在 **k'ò-kuān-ts'ún-tsài** objective existence
客观外界 **k'ò-kuān-wài-chìeh** the objective external world
客满 **k'ò-mǎn** a full audience, a capacity house
客队 **k'ò-tuì** a visiting team, guest team
客运 **k'ò-yùn** passenger service
1208 课程 **k'ò-ch'éng** a course of study [in school]
课程下放 **k'ò-ch'éng-hsià-fàng** downward shift of studies (transferring basic courses from higher to lower-level schools)
课本 **k'ò-pěn** textbooks
课堂教学 **k'ò-t'áng-chìao-hsuéh** classroom teaching
课堂讨论 **k'ò-t'áng-t'ǎo-lùn** classroom discussion, seminar
课题 **k'ò-t'í** a problem or task [for students], subject of a test, assigned theme
课外活动 **k'ò-wài-huó-tùng** extra-curricular activities

k'ŏu (kŏu)

1209 口径 **k'ŏu-chìng** calibre [of gun or artillery]
口诛笔伐 **k'ŏu-chū-pǐ-fá** verbal and written exposure and criticism of wrongdoings
口气 **k'ŏu-ch'ì** tone of voice, way of speaking
口气强硬 **k'ŏu-ch'ì-ch'iáng-yìng** a strong tone [of speech or statement]
口琴 **k'ŏu-ch'ín** a harmonica, mouth organ
口出大言 **k'ŏu-ch'ū-tà-yén** the mouth utters big words (to talk big, brag)
口服 **k'ŏu-fú** (1) to express submission verbally; (2) to take [medicine] by mouth
口服心服 **k'ŏu-fú-hsīn-fú** to submit by word and in heart (total submission)
口号 **k'ŏu-hào** a slogan [usually political or patriotic]; a watchword, military oral command
口译 **k'ŏu-ì** oral interpretation
口若悬河 **k'ŏu-jò-hsuán-hó** to talk like a cataract (glib, voluble, loquacious, skilled in debate)

口供 **k'ŏu-kùng** testimony, a deposition, a verbal report by a suspect
口口声声 **k'ŏu-k'ŏu-shēng-shēng** every mouth and every voice (to say repeatedly and emphatically, reiterate)
口粮 **k'ŏu-liáng** rations [of food]
口令 **k'ŏu-lìng** a password; an oral order
口蜜腹剑 **k'ŏu-mì-fù-chièn** a mouth of honey but a dagger [concealed] in the bosom (dastardly intent)
口实 **k'ŏu-shíh** an excuse, pretext, gossip
口是心非 **k'ŏu-shìh-hsīn-fēi** the mouth is right but the heart is wrong (hypocritical)
口试 **k'ŏu-shìh** an oral examination
口头 **k'ŏu-t'óu** verbally, orally; oral communication
口头禅 **k'ŏu-t'óu-ch'án** a cliche, platitude, empty slogan
口头协议 **k'ŏu-t'óu-hsiéh-ì** a verbal agreement
口头革命派 **k'ŏu-t'óu kó-mìng-p'ài** revolutionaries in words, lip-service revolutionaries
口味 **k'ŏu-wèi** taste, flavor [of food]; a person's inclinations or tastes
口语化 **k'ŏu-yǔ-huà** to vernacularize [one's writing style]

k'òu (kòu)

1210 叩头 **k'òu-t'óu** to kneel and touch the ground with the forehead, kowtow (abject submission)
1211 扣人心弦 **k'òu-jén-hsīn-hsién** to pluck the strings of the heart (very moving)
扣留 **k'òu-líu** to detain, hold, intern; to confiscate, attach, withhold
扣帽子 **k'òu-mào-tzu** to put a hat on, to label (to accuse someone of being a reactionary)
扣压 **k'òu-yā** to suppress; to prevent [publication]
扣押 **k'òu-yā** to confine, detain, take into custody [persons]; to seize, attach, confiscate [property]

k'ū (kū)

1212 枯竭 **k'ū-chiéh** dried up, exhausted, used up
枯黄 **k'ū-huáng** dry and brown, withered
枯木逢春 **k'ū-mù féng-ch'ūn** a dried tree meets the spring (to come to life again, to revive)
1213 哭哭啼啼 **k'ū-k'ū-t'í-t'í** to whimper, blubber; tearful

哭丧着脸 **k'ū-sāng-che-liěn** a mournful countenance, dejected look

k'ŭ (kǔ)

1214　苦战 **k'ŭ-chàn** to fight against heavy odds; a bitter struggle

苦尽甘来 **k'ŭ-chìn-kān-lái** the bitter is over and the sweet has come (the hard times of the old society are past and good times are here)

苦境 **k'ŭ-chìng** a plight, distress, trouble, difficult circumstances

苦情账 **k'ŭ-ch'íng-chàng** an accounting for afflictions suffered

苦心 **k'ŭ-hsīn** with great patience and resolve; to go to great pains, persistent

苦心经营 **k'ŭ-hsīn-chīng-yíng** to manage painstakingly; with painstaking effort

苦心孤诣 **k'ŭ-hsīn-kū-ì** great pains [leading to] solitary achievement (notable achievement after persistent work)

苦役 **k'ŭ-ì** hard work, drudgery

苦干精神 **k'ŭ-kàn chīng-shén** the spirit of being willing to make strenuous efforts against great odds

苦干, 实干, 巧干 **k'ŭ-kàn, shíh-kàn, ch'iǎo-kàn** to work strenuously, preseveringly, and resourcefully

苦工 **k'ŭ-kūng** toil, heavy work, hard physical labor

苦功 **k'ŭ-kūng** strenuous effort [at study etc.]

苦口婆心 **k'ŭ-k'ŏu-p'ó-hsīn** bitter words but a motherly heart (to remonstrate with kindly intent)

苦劳 **k'ŭ-láo** credit for hard work, merit for strenuous efforts

苦练 **k'ŭ-lièn** arduous training, strenuous practice

苦练技术 **k'ŭ-lièn-chì-shù** to master a technique by hard practice; a hard-won skill

苦闷 **k'ŭ-mèn** boredom, melancholy; bored, low-spirited

苦难 **k'ŭ-nàn** privation, suffering, adversity, hardship, calamity

苦难史 **k'ŭ-nàn-shǐh** the history of bitterness and suffering

苦恼 **k'ŭ-nǎo** anxiety, misery, worry; irksome, miserable, vexing

苦大仇深 **k'ŭ-tà-ch'óu-shēn** the bitterness is great and the hatred deep (the old society)

苦读 **k'ŭ-tú** to study extremely hard

苦头 **k'ŭ-t'óu** hardship, a bitter experience

苦痛 **k'ŭ-t'ùng** suffering, pain, discomfort, misery

k'ù (kù)

1215　库存物资 **k'ù-ts'ún-wù-tzū** stockpiled materials

1216　酷刑 **k'ù-hsíng** torture, cruel punishment

k'uā (kuā)

1217　夸张 **k'uā-chāng** to exaggerate, brag

夸口 **k'uā-k'ǒu** to boast, brag; a braggart

夸夸其谈 **k'uā-k'uā-ch'í-t'án** bragging, bombast

夸大 **k'uā-tà** to exaggerate; arrogant, grandiloquent

夸耀 **k'uā-yào** to show off, flaunt oneself

k'uǎ (kuǎ)

1218　垮台 **k'uǎ-t'ái** to be overthrown, lose office, go out of power, collapse, fall

k'uà (kuà)

1219　挎包 **k'uà-pāo** a haversack (hanging from one shoulder across the chest)

1220　跨江过海 **k'uà-chiāng-kuò-hǎi** to stride over rivers and cross the seas

跨长江 **k'uà-ch'áng-chiāng** to cross the Yangtze River (to exceed the grain production level for the Yangtze valley set by the agricultural plan at 800 kg. per *mu*)

跨区供应 **k'uà-ch'ū-kūng-yìng** inter-area supply

跨行业 **k'uà-háng-yèh** spanning [several] trades

跨行业组织 **k'uà-háng-yèh tsǔ-chīh** inter-trade organizations

跨黄河 **k'uà-huáng-hó** crossing the Yellow River [grain] (exceeding the production standard for grain of 500 kg. per *mu* set for Yellow River farm areas by the agricultural plan)

跨入 **k'uà-jù** to stride into

跨国公司 **k'uà-kuó-kūng-szū** supranational corporation, multinational company

跨单位, 跨部门 **k'uà-tān-wèi, k'uà-pù-mén** spanning [several] units and departments

跨越 **k'uà-yuèh** to stride over

k'uài (kuài)

1221　会计 **k'uài-chì** accounting; account-

ancy; an accountant

会计制度 **k'uài-chì-chìh-tù** accounting system

会计年度 **k'uài-chì-nién-tù** fiscal year, accounting year

会计员 **k'uài-chì-yuán** an accountant

会 **k'uai**: *see also* **huì**

1222 快马加鞭 **k'uài-mǎ-chiā-piēn** to lay the whip on a speeding horse (extremely fast, to speed up)

快马还要加鞭 **k'uài-mǎ hái-yào chiā-piēn** [even though] the horse is fast, one should still apply the whip (even though progress is good, one should still try harder)

快板书 **k'uài-pǎn-shū** a storyteller using bamboo clappers

快速轧钢法 **k'uài-sù chá-kāng-fǎ** high speed method of rolling steel

快速舰 **k'uài-sù-chièn** a frigate [naval]

快速切削 **k'uài-sù-ch'iēh-hsiāo** fast-cutting [machine work]

快速电子计算机 **k'uài-sù tièn-tzǔ-chì-suàn-chī** high-speed electronic computer, automatic digital calculator

1223 块规 **k'uài-kuēi** Johannson [standard measurement] blocks

块块领导 **k'uài-k'uài lǐng-tǎo** piece-by-piece leadership (dispersed control lacking strong vertical or hierarchical leadership)

k'uān (kuān)

1224 宽敞明亮 **k'uān-ch'ǎng-míng-liàng** spacious and well-lit

宽宏大量 **k'uān-húng-tà-liàng** generous, magnanimous, open-hearted, broad-minded

宽以待人 **k'uān-ǐ-tài-jén** lenient in dealing with people, generous in personal relations

宽容 **k'uān-júng** to forgive, pardon, excuse, tolerate, forbear

宽广 **k'uān-kuǎng** vast, broad, extensive, spacious

宽阔 **k'uān-k'uò** spacious, wide, roomy

宽阔胸怀 **k'uān-k'uò-hsiūng-huái** broad-minded, having a large view, rising above trivialities

宽猛相济 **k'uān-měng-hsiāng-chì** to use a proper mixture of leniency and severity

宽恕 **k'uān-shù** to forgive, pardon

宽打窄用 **k'uān-tǎ-chǎi-yùng** to budget liberally and spend sparingly

宽大 **k'uān-tà** generous, lenient, magnanimous, forgiving, merciful

宽大政策 **k'uān-tà-chèng-ts'è** a policy

of leniency

宽大处理 **k'uān-tà-ch'ǔ-lǐ** to dispose of [a case] in a lenient way, to settle magnanimously

宽大为怀 **k'uān-tà-wéi-huái** magnanimous, liberal, tolerant, forgiving

宽贷 **k'uān-tài** to allow delay in payment of a debt; to forgive, pardon, show mercy

宽待 **k'uān-tài** to treat generously

宽银幕电影 **k'uān-yín-mù tièn-yǐng** wide-screen film, cinemascope

k'uǎn (kuǎn)

1225 款项 **k'uǎn-hsiàng** a sum of money, funds, money; an item of expenditure

k'uāng (kuāng)

1226 框框 **k'uāng-k'uang** a restricting framework, limiting standards

k'uáng (kuáng)

1227 狂潮 **k'uáng-ch'áo** violent waves (figurative)

狂犬吠日 **k'uáng-ch'ǔǎn-fèi-jìh** a mad dog barking at the sun (usually refers to reactionaries)

狂吠 **k'uáng-fèi** to bark madly (to yell nonsense, utter wild words, rant)

狂欢 **k'uáng-huān** to rejoice wildly; a revel, orgy, carnival

狂想曲 **k'uáng-hsiǎng-ch'ǔ** a musical fantasy, rhapsody

狂热 **k'uáng-jè** scorching heat (wild fervor, blind zeal, mad enthusiasm, obsession)

狂热性 **k'uáng-jè-hsíng** fanaticism

狂人 **k'uáng-jén** a lunatic, madman, fanatic; a person of unsound mind

狂澜 **k'uáng-lán** violent waves, violent disturbances

狂流 **k'uáng-líu** a deluge, outpouring

狂诵 **k'uáng-sùng** to recite feverishly

狂妄企图 **k'uáng-wàng-ch'ǐ-t'ú** an irrational scheme, frenzied ambition

狂妄自大 **k'uáng-wàng-tzù-tà** mad with [a sense of] self-greatness, vainglorious

狂妄野心 **k'uáng-wàng-yěh-hsīn** unbridled ambition

k'uàng (kuàng)

1228 旷日持久 **k'uàng-jìh-ch'íh-chiǔ** to extend over many days, be time-consuming; to procrastinate

旷古空前 **k'uàng-kǔ-k'ūng-ch'ién**

unprecedented in history
¹²²⁹ 矿井 **k'uàng-chǐng** a mine shaft, a mine
矿产资源 **k'uàng-ch'ǎn-tzū-yuán**
mineral resources
矿场 **k'uàng-ch'ǎng** a mine site
矿工 **k'uàng-kūng** a miner, mine
workers
矿坑 **k'uàng-k'ēng** a mine pit
矿砂 **k'uàng-shā** mineral ore in sand
form
矿山 **k'uàng-shān** an ore-bearing
mountain, a mine
矿石 **k'uàng-shíh** a mineral, ore
矿藏 **k'uàng-ts'áng** mineral reserves,
mineral deposits
矿务局 **k'uàng-wù-chú** mining bureau
矿物肥料 **k'uàng-wù-féi-liào** mineral
fertilizer
矿物资源 **k'uàng-wù-tzū-yuán** mineral
resources
矿冶设备 **k'uàng-yěh-shè-pèi** equipment
for mining and metallurgy
矿业 **k'uàng-yèh** mining industry

k'uēi (kuī)

¹²³⁰ 亏本 **k'uēi-pěn** to lose capital, lose
money
¹²³¹ 窥探 **k'uēi-t'àn** to spy on, peep into,
detect

k'uéi (kuí)

¹²³² 魁伟 **k'uéi-wěi** tall and large in stature,
stalwart, impressive, majestic

k'uěi (kuǐ)

¹²³³ 傀儡 **k'uěi-lěi** a puppet
傀儡政权 **k'uěi-lěi-chèng-ch'üán** a
puppet regime

k'uèi (kuì)

¹²³⁴ 匮竭 **k'uèi-chiéh** exhausted, used up
¹²³⁵ 溃烂 **k'uèi-làn** ulceration, inflamma-
tion, bursting of an abscess
溃不成军 **k'uèi-pù-ch'éng-chūn** defeated
to the point of no longer being an
army, utterly routed
溃散 **k'uèi-sàn** defeated and dispersed

k'ūn (kūn)

¹²³⁶ 昆明部队 **k'ūn-míng-pù-tuì** the Kun-
ming Military Forces [of the PLA]

k'ùn (kùn)

¹²³⁷ 困惑 **k'ùn-huò** at a loss, perplexed,

bewildered
困苦 **k'ùn-k'ǔ** poverty, want, hardship,
tribulation, suffering
困难 **k'ùn-nán** difficulty, distress,
trouble, hardship
困难时期 **k'ùn-nán shíh-ch'ī** the difficult
(the years 1960–1962)
困守 **k'ùn-shǒu** hemmed in, cornered
困兽犹斗 **k'ùn-shòu-yú-tòu** cornered
beasts will still fight

k'ūng (kōng)

¹²³⁸ 空战 **k'ūng-chàn** an air battle, air
combat
空讲 **k'ūng-chiǎng** to talk in an empty
way; a harangue without substance
空降 **k'ūng-chiàng** air-borne, air-
dropped, parachuted
空降部队 **k'ūng-chiàng-pù-tuì** para-
chute troops, airborne forces
空间 **k'ūng-chiēn** space; a limited
extent in one, two or three dimen-
sions
空间技术 **k'ūng-chiēn-chì-shù** space
technology
空中侦察 **k'ūng-chūng-chēn-ch'á** air
reconnaissance
空中观察 **k'ūng-chūng-kuān-ch'á** aerial
observation
空中楼阁 **k'ūng-chūng-lóu-kó** castles in
the air (unrealistic theories or plans)
空中堡垒 **k'ūng-chūng-pǎo-lěi** a Flying
Fortress [B-29 bomber]
空气调节设备 **k'ūng-ch'ì t'iáo-chiéh shè-
pèi** air-conditioning installations
空气污染 **k'ūng-ch'ì-wū-jǎn** air pollution
空前 **k'ūng-ch'ién** unprecedented
空前纪录 **k'ūng-ch'ién-chì-lù** all-time
record
空前绝后 **k'ūng-ch'ién-chüéh-hòu**
nothing [like it] before or since (a
unique occurrence)
空前高涨 **k'ūng-ch'ién-kāo-chàng** an
unprecedented upsurge
空前广泛 **k'ūng-ch'ién-kuǎng-fàn** [on a
scale] unprecedented in scope
空前未有 **k'ūng-ch'ién-wèi-yǔ** unprecedented, never before existing
空军 **k'ūng-chūn** an air force
空军陆战队 **k'ūng-chūn lù-chàn-tuì**
paratroops
空喊 **k'ūng-hǎn** to shout emptily (loud
shouts without action or result)
空话 **k'ūng-huà** empty talk, talk without content, verbiage
空话连篇 **k'ūng-huà-lién-p'iēn** to fill
endless pages with empty talk
空袭 **k'ūng-hsí** an air attack, an air raid

空想 **k'ūng-hsiǎng** an impractical hope, wishful thinking; to daydream, think of utopia

空想家 **k'ūng-hsiǎng-chiā** a dreamer, mere theorist

空想主义 **k'ūng-hsiǎng-chǔ-ì** utopianism

空想社会主义 **k'ūng-hsiǎng shè-huì-chǔ-ì** utopian socialism

空虚 **k'ūng-hsū** vacuous, empty, depleted

空名 **k'ūng-míng** in name only

空说不做 **k'ūng-shuō-pù-tsò** to say but not to act (empty promises, lip service)

空对空飞弹 **k'ūng-tuì-k'ūng fēi-tàn** air-to-air missiles

空洞 **k'ūng-tùng** without real substance, void, empty

空洞无物 **k'ūng-tùng-wú-wù** without substance, empty of content

空谈 **k'ūng-t'án** empty talk, aimless discussion, academic theorizing divorced from reality

空头 **k'ūng-t'óu** to sell short, buy or sell stocks on margin; [a check issued] without funds

空头政治家 **k'ūng-t'óu chèng-chìh-chiā** a political charlatan

空头支票 **k'ūng-t'óu-chìh-p'iào** a check written without sufficient funds (an empty promise)

空投接济 **k'ūng-t'óu-chiēh-chì** air-dropped supplies

空投物资 **k'ūng-t'óu-wù-tzū** to air-drop supplies, air-dropped supply

空邮 **k'ūng-yú** airmail

空 **k'ūng** see also k'ùng

k'ŭng (kŏng)

1239 孔家店 **k'ŭng-chiā-tièn** the Confucianist shop (a derogatory term for Confucianists)

孔老二 **k'ŭng-lǎo-èrh** the second son of the K'ung family (Confucius was the second son in his family; hence this is a disrespectful way of referring to him)

孔子 **k'ŭng-tzǔ** Confucius

1240 恐惧 **k'ŭng-chù** fear, awe, dread, fright

恐吓 **k'ŭng-hò** to intimidate, frighten, scare, threaten, menace

恐吓信 **k'ŭng-hò-hsìn** a threatening letter, blackmail letter

恐慌 **k'ŭng-huāng** a panic, fear; consternation, horror; [economic] depression

恐美崇美 **k'ŭng-měi-ch'úng-měi** fearing America and worshipping America

(errors targeted in the **ài-kuó chiào-yù yùn-tùng**)

恐怖 **k'ŭng-pù** terror, horror, fear

恐怖主义 **k'ŭng-pù-chǔ-ì** terrorism

k'ùng (kòng)

1241 空隙 **k'ùng-hsì** a vacant space, crevice, gap, loophole

空闲 **k'ùng-hsién** idle, at leisure, unoccupied

空白 **k'ùng-pái** a blank [in a paper form], blank

空白点 **k'ùng-pái-tiĕn** a blank spot, blank; blankness

空子 **k'ùng-tzu** a vacancy, an empty space; a weak point

空位 **k'ùng-wèi** an unoccupied seat, empty space, vacancy

空 **k'ùng**: see also k'ūng

1242 控制 **k'ùng-chìh** to control, dominate, master; control, domination, mastery

控制论 **k'ùng-chìh-lùn** theory of control

控制数字 **k'ùng-chìh-shù-tzù** control numbers (set by high authorities in the planning process to guide actions at lower levels)

控告 **k'ùng-kào** to accuse, lay charges, file a legal complaint

控诉 **k'ùng-sù** to accuse, complain against; to proceed against [in a court]

k'uò (kuò)

1243 扩展 **k'uò-chǎn** to stretch, expand, spread, extend, advance

扩张 **k'uò-chāng** to expand, spread, stretch, extend

扩张政策 **k'uò-chāng-chèng-ts'è** an expansionist policy

扩张主义 **k'uò-chāng-chǔ-ì** expansionism

扩张军备 **k'uò-chāng-chūn-pèi** to extend military preparations; an arms drive

扩张势力 **k'uò-chāng-shìh-lì** to expand influence, increase power

扩张武力 **k'uò-chāng-wǔ-lì** to expand military power

扩建 **k'uò-chièn** to build an addition; to enlarge, expand

扩充 **k'uò-ch'ūng** to expand, enlarge, increase, augment, amplify

扩充军备 **k'uò-ch'ūng chūn-pèi** to increase military preparedness; arms expansion

扩军竞赛 **k'uò-chūn-chìng-sài** an arms race

扩军备战 **k'uò-chūn-pèi-chàn** military

expansion and war preparations

扩大 **k'uò-tà** to enlarge, expand, broaden, widen; to magnify, amplify, exaggerate

扩大战果 **k'uò-tà-chàn-kuǒ** to exploit a victory

扩大接触 **k'uò-tà-chiēh-ch'ù** to broaden contacts, increase contacts

扩大会议 **k'uò-tà-huì-ì** an enlarged session

扩大地方权限 **k'uò-tà tì-fāng-ch'üán-hsièn** to expand the jurisdictional limits of local [authorities]

扩大再生产 **k'uò-tà tsài-shēng-ch'ǎn** extended reproduction (reproduction on an extended scale)

扩大眼界 **k'uò-tà-yěn-chièh** to take a wider view, broaden one's experience

扩音器 **k'uò-yīn-ch'ì** an amplifier, loud speaker

1244 阔气 **k'uò-ch'i** extravagant in spending habits; an extravagant manner

阔人 **k'uò-jén** an extravagant person, free spender, the rich

阔步前进 **k'uò-pù-ch'ién-chìn** to advance with great strides

阔少 **k'uò-shào** son of the rich (spoiled sons of the bourgeoisie)

lā (lā)

1245 拉紧 **lā-chǐn** to pull tight, fasten tighter, hang on firmly

拉长战线 **lā-ch'áng chàn-hsièn** to extend the battleline (often figurative)

拉出去, 打进来 **lā ch'ū-ch'ü, tǎ chìn-lai** to pull out and force a way in (the class enemy seeks to subvert [pull out] Party members and to infiltrate their own agents)

拉后腿 **lā-hòu-t'ǔi** to pull a hind leg (to hinder, obstruct someone)

拉祜族 **lā-hù-tsú** the Lahu people (a minority in Yunnan province: population 183,000 as of 1957)

拉话 **lā-huà** to make conversation, chat

拉回老路 **lā-huí-lǎo-lù** to pull back to the old road, revert to the old line

拉下马 **lā-hsià-mǎ** to pull [someone] off the horse (to force a cadre or official out of his position)

拉下水 **lā-hsià-shuǐ** to pull into the water (to get someone else involved in one's scheme or trouble)

拉一批, 打一批 **lā ī-p'ī, tǎ ī-p'ī** to win over one group and attack another group, to woo some and attack others

拉各斯 **lā-kò-szū** Lagos [Nigeria]

拉拉扯扯 **lā-lā-ch'ě-ch'ě** to pull and drag this way and that (to implicate

or involve; to indulge in aimless talk)

拉练 **lā-lièn** to take out and march (to go out camping and marching, to go on a long march to temper oneself)

拉拢 **lā-lǔng** to draw [someone] over to one's side (to win over, recruit, draw together; to ingratiate oneself with)

拉美 **lā-měi** Latin America (contraction of lā-tīng měi-chōu)

拉密堡 **lā-mì-pǎo** Fort Lamy [Chad]

拉巴斯 **lā-pā-szū** La Paz [Bolivia]

拉巴特 **lā-pā-t'è** Rabat [Morocco]

拉不开弓, 挑不起担, 压不住台 **lā-pù-k'āi-kūng, t'iao-pù-ch'ǐ-tàn, yā-pù-chù-t'ái** unable to pull the bow, unable to lift the load [and] unable to hold the audience

拉山头, 结死党, 耍阴谋, 搞分裂 **lā-shān-t'óu, chiéh-szǔ-tǎng, shuǎ-yīn-móu, kǎo-fēn-lièh** to seize the mountain-tops [commanding positions], to consolidate a party [of adherents loyal] to the death, to play with conspiracies, to engage in disunity (the alleged crimes of Lin Piao)

拉上马 **lā-shàng-mǎ** to boost [someone] onto the horse (to put someone into an official position)

拉丁美洲 **lā-tīng-měi-chōu** Latin America, Central and South America

拉丁美洲通讯社 **lā-tīng-měi-chōu t'ūng-hsùn-shè** Agencia Latina de Noticias

拉瓦尔品第 **lā-wǎ-ěrh-p'ǐn-tì** Rawalpindi [Pakistan]

1246 垃圾 **lā-chī** garbage, trash, waste, debris, rubbish

垃圾堆 **lā-chī-tuī** garbage heap, trash heap

lǎ (lǎ)

1247 喇嘛庙 **lǎ-ma-miào** a lamasery

lái (lái)

1248 来之不易 **lái-chīh-pù-ì** not easily available, not easy to obtain, hard to come by

来来去去 **lái-lái-ch'ù-ch'ù** to come and go in great numbers, to and fro, back and forth

来临 **lái-lín** to come, arrive; advent, arrival

来龙去脉 **lái-lúng-ch'ù-mài** [the source of] a dragon's coming and the flow of his pulse (the beginning and subsequent development of an event; cause and effect)

来宾 **lái-pīn** guests, visitors

来势汹汹 **lái-shìh-hsiūng-hsiūng** to come in a threatening manner; an ominous entrance; to come looking for trouble

来自五湖四海 **lái-tzù wǔ-hú-szù-hǎi** coming from the five lakes and the four seas (from all corners of the country)

来往 **lái-wǎng** to come and go; coming and going (friendly intercourse, social relations)

来由 **lái-yú** cause, reason; background, origin

来源 **lái-yuán** the source, origin

lài (lài)

1249 赖债 **lài-chài** to repudiate a debt

赖着不走 **lài-che-pù-tsǒu** to procrastinate and not move (to refuse to move, overstay one's time)

1250 癞皮狗 **lài-p'í-kǒu** a mangy dog, a dog with scabies (a repulsive or disgusting person)

lán (lán)

1251 兰州部队 **lán-chōu pù-tuì** the Lanchow Forces [of the PLA] (formerly, the Lanchow Military Region)

兰新铁路 **lán-hsīn t'iěh-lù** the Lanchow-Sinkiang railway

兰田人 **lán-t'ién-jén** the Lantien man (a fossil skull about 600,000 years old found at Lantien, Shensi)

1252 拦住 **lán-chu** to obstruct, hinder, check, block, hold back, stay, stop

拦住泥沙 **lán-chu-ní-shā** to check silting, hold back silt formation, curb silt formation

拦海造田 **lán-hǎi-tsào-t'ién** to make fields by holding back the sea, to reclaim marshlands

拦河闸 **lán-hó-chá** a dam to regulate the flow of a river, a river control sluice gate

拦蓄洪水 **lán-hsù-húng-shuǐ** to impound flood water

拦路虎 **lán-lù-hǔ** a road-blocking tiger (a highwayman—now usually figurative)

拦腰 **lán-yāo** to hold by the waist, cut across in the middle

1253 蓝本 **lán-pěn** an original manuscript from which copies are made, a model for copying; a blueprint

蓝图 **lán-t'ú** a blueprint

1254 谰言 **lán-yén** abusive words, slander, calumny, defamation

1255 篮球 **lán-ch'iú** basketball

篮球赛 **lán-ch'iú-sài** basketball competition

lǎn (lǎn)

1256 懒汉 **lǎn-hàn** a lazy fellow, indolent loafer

懒汉哲学 **lǎn-hàn-ché-hsuéh** lazybones philosophy

懒惰 **lǎn-tò** lazy, idle, indolent, slothful

làn (làn)

1257 烂种 **làn-chǔng** seeds rotted by excess moisture

烂下去 **làn-hsia-ch'ü** to become more and more dilapidated, become more rotten, continue to decay

烂泥 **làn-ní** soft mud, mire, quagmire

烂掉 **làn-tiào** rotted away (in a political sense)

烂摊子 **làn-t'ān-tzu** a broken-down stall, an awful mess (an affair or legacy that has been completely ruined)

1258 滥调 **làn-tiào** a platitude, cliche

滥用 **làn-yùng** to spend lavishly, misuse, abuse, waste

滥用职权 **làn-yùng chíh-ch'üán** to abuse one's official power, misuse the powers of one's position

láng (láng)

1259 狼藉 **láng-chí** in total disarray, in pandemonium; disorderly, messy, untidy; dishonorable, notorious

狼心狗肺 **láng-hsīn-kǒu-fèi** wolf's heart and dog's lung (extremely vicious)

狼狈处境 **láng-pèi-ch'ǔ-chìng** a helpless situation, predicament, quandary, dilemma

狼狈不堪 **láng-pèi-pù-k'ān** in utter disorder, in great distress

狼狈逃窜 **láng-pèi-t'áo-ts'uàn** to flee in panic

狼狈为奸 **láng-pèi-wéi-chiēn** to band together for evil; in collusion for an evil purpose

狼子野心 **láng-tzǔ-yěh-hsīn** wolfish ambitions (greedy, cruel, brutal, ferocious)

lǎng (lǎng)

1260 朗诺 **lǎng-nò** Lon Nol (Cambodian leader after Sihanouk)

朗诺叛国集团 **lǎng-nò p'àn-kuó-chí-**

t'uán the traitorous Lon Nol clique
朗诵 lǎng-sùng to recite, read aloud

làng (làng)

1261 浪潮 làng-ch'áo waves, tide, current
浪费 làng-fèi to waste, lavish; extravagant, wasteful
浪漫主义 làng-màn-chǔ-ì romanticism
浪涛滚滚 làng-t'āo-kǔn-kǔn rolling waves
浪头 làng-t'ou the crest of a wave; big waves, breakers
浪子回头 làng-tzǔ-huí-t'óu the return of a prodigal son, a profligate repents

lāo (lāo)

1262 捞一把 lāo-ĭ-pǎ to dredge up a handful (to make a profit by quick means)
捞业务资本 lāo yèh-wù-tzū-pěn to develop one's occupational capital (usually with the sense of concentrating on one's personal expertise at the expense of ideological education)

láo (láo)

1263 牢记 láo-chì to keep firmly in mind
牢记血泪仇 láo-chì hsuèh-lèi-ch'óu always remember the enmity of blood and tears
牢固 láo-kù secure, firm
牢靠 láo-k'ào solid, reliable, strong, sure
牢牢生根 láo-láo-shēng-kēn to root firmly
牢不可破 láo-pù-k'ǒ-p'ò invulnerable, impregnable, unshakable, indestructible
牢骚 láo-sāo discontent, grumbling, complaint
牢狱 láo-yù a jail, prison
1264 劳心者治人, 劳力者治于人 láo-hsīn-chě chìh-jén, láo-lì-chě chìh-yú-jén those who labor with their minds govern others [and] those who labor with their strength are governed by others (a saying by Mencius—now criticized)
劳役 láo-ì hard labor, conscripted labor (usually implies a penal sanction)
劳逸结合 láo-ì-chiéh-hó integrating labor and rest (a Great Leap slogan —when there was a tendency to reduce efficiency by overwork)
劳改 láo-kǎi reform through labor (contraction of láo-tùng kǎi-tsào)

劳改犯 láo-kǎi-fàn labor-reform convicts (generally somewhat less restricted than other criminals)
劳苦 láo-k'ǔ to work hard, toil; laborious, strenuous
劳苦功高 láo-k'ǔ-kūng-kāo to work hard and make great contributions
劳民伤财 láo-mín-shāng-ts'ái to work the people and waste money (to waste manpower and resources)
劳模 láo-mó a model of labor [i.e., model worker] (contraction of láo-tùng mó-fàn)
劳保 láo-pǎo labor insurance (contraction of láo-tùng pǎo-hsiěn)
劳保条例 láo-pǎo-t'iáo-lì labor insurance regulations
劳动 láo-tùng (1) to labor, do physical work; (2) Labor (a Peking journal, monthly, 1954—)
劳动纪律 láo-tùng-chì-lù labor discipline, work discipline
劳动教养 láo-tùng-chiào-yǎng re-education through labor (less onerous than reform through labor)
劳动教育 láo-tùng-chiào-yù (1) labor education (classroom instruction from kindergarten upward to familiarize children with the various kinds of productive work and to teach the honor of labor); (2) education through labor (a mild form of reform through labor)
劳动节 láo-tùng-chiéh Labor Day (May 1)
劳动介绍所 láo-tùng chièh-shào-sǒ labor introduction centers (mobile units to register unemployed workers)
劳动津贴 láo-tùng-chīn-t'iēh work allowances (small payments given by street committees to residents— almost all women—who participated in Great Leap street projects in Shanghai)
劳动竞赛 láo-tùng-chìng-sài labor competition (usually implies labor emulation rather than a formal competition)
劳动惩罚论 láo-tùng-ch'éng-fá lùn the doctrine of making a punishment out of labor (an accusation against Liu Shao-ch'i)
劳动强度 láo-tùng-ch'iáng-tù labor intensity, the amount of physical strength required in a job
劳动创造世界 láo-tùng ch'uàng-tsào shìh-chièh labor creates the world
劳动群众 láo-tùng-ch'ún-chùng the laboring masses, working masses
劳动分工 láo-tùng-fēn-kūng division of

labor

劳动服务站 **láo-tùng fú-wù-chàn** labor service station

劳动合作 **láo-tùng-hó-tsò** labor cooperation

劳动效率 **láo-tùng-hsiào-lù** labor efficiency

劳动人民 **láo-tùng-jén-mín** the working people

劳动人民知识化, 知识分子劳动化 **láo-tùng-jén-mín chīh-shíh-huà, chīh-shíh-fèn-tzŭ láo-tùng-huà** to cause laboring people to become educated and to make intellectuals competent in manual labor (to narrow the difference between manual and mental work)

劳动日 **láo-tùng-jìh** working days (can refer to either the number or length of working days)

劳动改造 **láo-tùng-kăi-tsào** reform through labor, labor reform, correction through labor (a penal sanction)

劳动观点 **láo-tùng-kuān-tiĕn** the laboring viewpoint (an attitude of respect for manual work: one of the **szŭ-tà-kuān-tiĕn**)

劳动力 **láo-tùng-lì** manpower, labor force; a laborer

劳动力的分配 **láo-tùng-lì-te fēn-p'èi** allocation of labor power

劳动模范 **láo-tùng-mó-fàn** a model worker, labor hero (a title of merit)

劳动能手 **láo-tùng-néng-shŏu** a skillful worker (a title of merit—lower than model worker)

劳动报酬 **láo-tùng-pào-ch'óu** payment for labor, remuneration of labor

劳动保险 **láo-tùng-păo-hsiĕn** labor insurance

劳动保险金 **láo-tùng-păo-hsiĕn-chīn** labor insurance funds

劳动保险条例 **láo-tùng-păo-hsiĕn t'iáo-lì** labor insurance laws and regulations

劳动部 **láo-tùng-pù** Ministry of Labor [of the State Council]

劳动生产率 **láo-tùng shēng-ch'ăn-lù** labor productivity

劳动生产定额 **láo-tùng shēng-ch'ăn tìng-ó** labor production quota

劳动手段 **láo-tùng-shŏu-tuàn** means of labor, work methods

劳动手册 **láo-tùng-shŏu-ts'è** labor handbook, working manual

劳动思想教育 **láo-tùng-szū-hsiăng chiào-yù** education in the ideology of work (*see* **láo-tùng-chiào-yù** [1])

劳动大军 **láo-tùng tà-chūn** a labor army (a large body of labor mobilized for any major or urgent task)

劳动底分 **láo-tùng-tĭ-fēn** basic labor-points

劳动镀金论 **láo-tùng-tù-chīn lùn** the doctrine that labor gilds one (a criticism of those who perform labor in a pro forma way)

劳动锻炼 **láo-tùng-tuàn-lièn** tempering through labor (usually means direct **hsià-fàng** of cadres to productive [farm] labor)

劳动条件 **láo-tùng-t'iáo-chièn** working conditions

劳资协商 **láo-tzū-hsiéh-shāng** labor-capital consultation (established in progressive factories during input shortage of the 1950s)

劳资关系 **láo-tzū-kuān-hsi** labor-capital relationship (during joint-operation)

劳资两利 **láo-tzū-liăng-lì** of benefit to both labor and capital

劳卫制 **láo-wèi-chìh** labor and defense training system (a program of physical training for labor and defense preparation)

劳武结合 **láo-wŭ-chiéh-hó** the integration of labor and military

劳武合一 **láo-wŭ-hó-ī** the combination of the labor and military forces

lăo (lăo)

1265 老将 **lăo-chiàng** an old general, veteran (an older man who spurns retirement and keeps on doing good work)

老解放地区 **lăo chiĕh-fàng-tì-ch'ŭ** old liberated areas (of the Resistance War period)

老奸巨猾 **lăo-chiēn-chù-huá** one experienced in trickery and deception; shrewd and crafty

老茧 **lăo-chiĕn** thick calluses (a mark of honorable labor)

老中青三结合 **lăo-chūng-ch'īng sān-chiéh-hó** a triple combination of the old, middle-aged, and young (a formula for leading groups in any kind of organization)

老成持重 **lăo-ch'éng-ch'íh-chùng** experienced and restrained (praising the maturity of a young man)

老好人 **lăo-hăo-jén** an agreeable person, soft-hearted person (having no strong viewpoint and not offering criticism of others)

老虎 **lăo-hŭ** a tiger (in the Five-Anti campaign: a capitalist who is being attacked)

老虎口 **lăo-hŭ-k'ŏu** the tiger's mouth

(a dangerous place; in the face of danger)

老虎屁股 **lǎo-hǔ-p'ì-ku** the tiger's rump (something too dangerous to touch)

老虎窝 **lǎo-hǔ-wō** the tiger's lair (in the Five-Anti campaign: the office of a capitalist under attack)

老话 **lǎo-huà** an old saying, often repeated remark, cliche

老黄历 **lǎo-huáng-li** an old almanac (obsolete standards and guidance)

老黄牛 **lǎo-huáng-níu** an old ox (a faithful servant of the people)

老红军 **lǎo-húng-chǖn** an old Red Army soldier (a veteran of the pre-1937 period)

老乡 **lǎo-hsiāng** fellow townsman, a person from the same province or place

老兄 **lǎo-hsiūng** elder brother (an affectionate salutation addressing a [male] friend)

老学究 **lǎo-hsuéh-chiū** an old pedant

老一辈 **lǎo-ī-pèi** the older generation; older by one generation

老一套 **lǎo-ī-t'ào** same old thing, in a rut, conventional

老人家 **lǎo-jén-chiā** an old person (a term of respect)

老干部 **lǎo-kàn-pù** an old cadre

老框框 **lǎo-k'uāng-k'uang** an old framework (old restrictions, constrictions, restraints)

老来青 **lǎo-lái-ch'īng** green in old age (a high-yield strain of rice)

老老实实 **lǎo-lǎo-shíh-shíh** honest, trustworthy, unpretentious, unassuming, plain

老路 **lǎo-lù** an old road, beaten track (now often figurative)

老农参谋处 **lǎo-núng ts'ān-móu-ch'ù** old peasants' counseling office (to seek advice from experienced peasants)

老百姓 **lǎo-pǎi-hsìng** the old hundred names, common people

老板 **lǎo-pǎn** a proprietor, manager, boss

老保 **lǎo-pǎo** old conservatives, old fogies

老标兵 **lǎo-piāo-pīng** a verteran who has consistently been a model soldier (may also refer to workers, etc.)

老部下 **lǎo-pù-hsià** a long-time subordinate

老牌 **lǎo-pái** an old brand; well known, old; old-fashioned

老牌殖民帝国 **lǎo-p'ái chíh-mín-tì-kuó** the old colonial imperial powers

老牌卖国贼 **lǎo-p'ái mài-kuó-tséi** a long standing traitor

老三篇 **lǎo-sān-p'iēn** the three venerable articles, three constantly read articles (three articles written by Mao in the Yenan days which were widely popularized during the Cultural Revolution: "In Memory of Norman Bethune," "Serve the People," and "The Foolish Old Man Who Removed the Mountain")

老沙皇 **lǎo-shā-huáng** the old czars (in contrast to the new czars—the present Soviet leaders)

老少互助组 **lǎo-shào hù-chù-tsǔ** mutual aid team of old and young (the old with experience and the young with education and ideology can benefit from each other)

老生常谈 **lǎo-shēng-ch'áng-t'án** the stale talk of an aged scholar (a threadbare argument, cliche)

老师 **lǎo-shīh** a teacher (a polite form of address)

老实 **lǎo-shih** honest, truthful, guileless, prudent, blunt

老鼠过街人人喊打 **lǎo-shǔ-kuò-chiēh jén-jén-hǎn-tǎ** a rat crossing the street is chased by all passers-by (everybody hates harmful people)

老鼠跌落天秤，自称自 **lǎo-shǔ tiēh-lò t'iēn-p'íng, tzù-ch'ēng-tzù** (the character "ch'ēng" means both "to weigh" and "to praise"—hence sarcasm at those who brag about themselves)

老大哥 **lǎo-tà-kō** old big brother (a term formerly used to designate the USSR)

老大难 **lǎo-tà-nán** old and very difficult

老大难单位 **lǎo-tà-nán tān-wèi** an old and extremely difficult unit (a long established unit that is resisting reform)

老大难问题 **lǎo-tà-nán wèn-t'í** old and very difficult problems (important problems that have remained unsolved for a long time)

老大娘 **lǎo-tà-niáng** elder aunt (a polite form of addressing any woman beyond youth—especially in the countryside)

老大自居 **lǎo-tà-tzù-chū** self-claimed to be important and great

老大错 **lǎo-tà-ts'ò** long–standing major errors

老大爷 **lǎo-tà-yéh** elder uncle (a polite form of addressing an elder man—especially in the countryside)

老当益壮 **lǎo-tāng-ì-chuàng** the old

should be even more sturdy (to gain vigor with age; still hale and hearty)

老底 **lǎo-tǐ** original capital (ancestry, pedigree; past background, experience; the seamy side of one's private life)

老调 **lǎo-tiào** the same old song, hackneyed tune (platitudes)

老调重弹 **lǎo-tiào-ch'úng-t'án** to replay the same old tune (to harp on a shopworn theme)

老调高弹 **lǎo-tiào-kāo-t'án** loudly to strike up the same old tune (unimagiative and inappropriate)

老套 **lǎo-t'ào** old ways, old methods

老天爷 **lǎo-t'iēn-yéh** the old man in Heaven, Heaven

老同志 **lǎo-t'úng-chìh** (1) an old comrade [in the Party]; (2) a polite way of addressing a mature [male] stranger

老造反 **lǎo-tsào-fǎn** old rebels, experienced rebels; undisciplined

老资格 **lǎo-tzū-kó** a senior, veteran, old hand

老子反动儿混蛋 **lǎo-tzu-fǎn-tùng érh-hún-tàn** the father reactionary [and the] son a bad egg (like father like son)

老子党 **lǎo-tzu-tǎng** the "father party" (a criticism of the Soviet Communist Party's pretensions)

老子天下第一 **lǎo-tzu t'iēn-hsià-tì-ī** this old man is number one (I will take no orders from anyone)

老子英雄儿好汉 **lǎo-tzu-yīng-hsiúng érh-hǎo-hàn** the father a hero, the son a brave man (like father like son)

老财 **lǎo-ts'ái** local [people of] wealth

老挝 **lǎo-wō** Laos

老五篇 **lǎo-wǔ-p'iēn** the venerable five articles (the **lǎo-sān-p'iēn** together with two additional articles by Mao: "On the Rectification of Erroneous Thought in the Party," and "To Oppose Liberalism")

老有所依 **lǎo-yǔ-sǒ-ī** to have someone to depend on in one's old age

lào (lào)

1266 涝灾 **lào-tsāi** waterlogging damage

涝洼地 **lào-wā-tì** waterlogged marsh land

1267 烙印 **lào-yìn** a mark made by a hot iron (an imprint, brand)

lè (lè)

1268 乐趣 **lè-ch'ù** delight, pleasure, joy, fun

乐意 **lè-ì** willing, agreeable to; to like

乐观 **lè-kuān** optimistic

乐观主义 **lè-kuān-chǔ-ì** optimism

乐观自信 **lè-kuān-tzù-hsìn** optimistic and self-confident

乐园 **lè-yuán** a garden of happiness, paradise, Elysium, Eden

乐 **lè**: see also **yuèh**

1269 勒令 **lè-lìng** to order, to compel by an order or instruction

勒索 **lè-sǒ** to extort, blackmail, wring from

勒 **lè**: see also **lēi**

lēi (lēi)

1270 勒紧裤带 **lēi-chǐn k'ù-tài** to tighten one's belt (to economize)

勒 **lēi**: see also **lè**

léi (léi)

1271 雷锋 **léi fēng** Lei Feng (a soldier who died on duty and was hailed as a model for the youth of China)

雷锋运动 **léi-fēng-yùn-tùng** the Lei Feng Movement (commenced in 1963)

雷管 **léi-kuǎn** a percussion cap, detonator

雷克雅末克 **léi-k'ò-yǎ-wèi-k'ò** Reykjavik [Iceland]

雷厉风行 **léi-lì-fēng-hsíng** with the violence of thunder and the speed of wind (vigorous and prompt action; to carry out rigorously)

雷声大雨点小 **léi-shēng-tà yǔ-tiěn-hsiǎo** the thunderclaps are big but the raindrops are small (a big fuss with little result)

雷打不动 **léi-tǎ-pù-tùng** even thunder cannot move him

雷霆万钧之力 **léi-t'íng-wàn-chǔn-chīh-lì** the thunderbolt has the force of 300,000 *chin* (extremely powerful)

lěi (lěi)

1272 累积 **lěi-chī** to accumulate, pile up (usually refers to capital accumulation)

累进税 **lěi-chìn-shuì** progressive tax

累犯 **lěi-fàn** a repeat offender [legal], recidivist

累累 **lěi-lěi** repeatedly, successively; consecutively; piling up, heavy [casualties]

lèi (lèi)

1273 类型 **lèi-hsíng** type, category, class

类别 **lèi-piéh** classification, categorization; kind, class, division, variety

类似 **lèi-szù** to resemble; similar to, like

1274 擂台 **lèi-t'ái** a platform from which the champion issues challenges (a place where production accomplishments are posted to invite challenge and emulation)

lĕng (lĕng)

1275 冷战 **lĕng-chàn** cold war; the Cold War

冷静 **lĕng-chìng** calm, composed, clear-minded; secluded, quiet

冷静说理 **lĕng-chìng-shuō-lĭ** to reason dispassinately

冷嘲热讽 **lĕng-ch'áo-jè-fĕng** cold laughter and searing mockery (scorn and sarcasm)

冷气暖气调节 **lĕng-ch'ì nuăn-ch'ì t'iáo-chiéh** air conditioning for heating an and cooling

冷气设备 **lĕng-ch'ì-shè-pèi** air-conditioning installation; air-conditioned

冷却 **lĕng-ch'üèh** to cool off, cool, reduce temperature

冷笑 **lĕng-hsiào** a cold smile, cynical leer, sarcastic laugh

冷若冰霜 **lĕng-jò-pīng-shuāng** as cold as ice and frost (cold and unemotional)

冷酷 **lĕng-k'ù** merciless, heartless, cruel, callous, grim

冷酷无情 **lĕng-k'ù-wú-ch'íng** cruel and merciless

冷落 **lĕng-lè** cold and lonely, on the decline; to slight, ignore, cold shoulder, be apathetic toward

冷冷清清 **lĕng-lĕng-ch'īng-ch'īng** cold and quiet (deserted, dreary, lifeless)

冷淡 **léng-tàn** cold, indifferent, apathetic

冷藏库 **lĕng-ts'áng-k'ù** cold storage

冷眼旁观 **lĕng-yĕn-p'áng-kuān** to watch from the side with a cold eye (to stand aloof, coldly indifferent)

lí (lí)

1276 离间 **lí-chièn** to drive a wedge between (alienate, sow discord, estrange)

离职 **lí-chíh** to leave one's job, retire from office, resign

离经叛道 **lí-chīng-p'àn-tào** to deviate from the Classics and betray the Tao (to rebel against orthodox teachings)

离差 **lí-ch'ā** deviation, variance

离乡背井 **lí-hsiāng-pèi-chĭng** to leave one's village and turn one's back to the well (to leave home)

离心倾向 **lí-hsīn-ch'īng-hsiàng** a tendency to separate from the center, centrifugal tendency

离心离德 **lí-hsīn-lí-té** apart in hearts and virtue (each going his own way; lacking unity)

离心作用 **lí-hsīn-tsò-yùng** centrifugal effects

离谱 **lí-p'ŭ** off the standard (too far away from what is normal or acceptable)

离题万里 **lí-t'í-wàn-lĭ** ten thousand *li* off the theme

1277 犁头 **lí-t'óu** the plowshare

1278 黎湛铁路 **lí-chàn t'iĕh-lù** the railway from Litang [Kwangsi] to Chanchiang [Kwangtung]

黎明 **lí-míng** dawn, daybreak

黎巴嫩 **lí-pā-nèn** Lebanon

黎族 **lì-tsú** the Li people (a minority on Hainan Island: population 395,000 as of 1957)

1279 篱笆 **lí-pa** a bamboo fence; a fence, hedge

lĭ (lĭ)

1280 礼节 **lĭ-chiéh** etiquette, decorum, courtesy, civility

礼义 **lĭ-i** propriety and righteousness

礼宾司 **lĭ-pīn-szū** protocol office

礼炮 **lĭ-p'ào** a gun salute

礼尚往来 **lĭ-shàng-wăng-lái** courtesy requires reciprocity

礼堂 **lĭ-t'áng** an auditorium, hall; site of a ceremony

礼物 **lĭ-wù** a gift, present, donation

1281 李立三 **lĭ lì-sān** Li Li-san (c. 1899—, a founder of the CCP in France; Party leader and "deviationist" 1928-1930; blamed for the "Li Li-san line" stressing urban insurrections)

1282 里程碑 **lĭ-ch'éng-pēi** a milestone (often figurative)

里弄 **lĭ-nùng** an urban neighborhood, subdivision of a *ch'ü̆*; small urban side streets, lanes (usually in the Shanghai area)

里弄储蓄服务站 **lĭ-nùng ch'ŭ-hsù fú-wú-chàn** lane savings service stations

里弄公共食堂 **lĭ-nùng kūng-kùng shíh-t'àng** lane public mess halls

里手 **lĭ-shŏu** an expert, professional (a Hunan dialect term, equivalent to **nèi-háng**)

里斯本 **lĭ-szū-pĕn** Lisbon

里通外国 **lĭ-t'ūng-wài-kuó** to be in [conspiratorial] communication with a foreign country

里应外合 **lĭ-yìng-wài-hó** responding

within and joining without (to plot together; to attack internally and externally; fifth column activity)

[1283] 俚语 **lǐ-yǔ** slang, vulgar speech, rustic expressions

[1284] 理解 **lǐ-chiěh** to apprehend, comprehend, understand, perceive

理直气壮 **lǐ-chíh-ch'i-chuàng** bold in speech [because] based on right (fearless in the knowledge that justice is on one's side)

理智 **lǐ-chìh** reason, sense, intellect; rational [as opposed to emotional]

里屈辞穷 **lǐ-ch'ǚ-tz'ú-ch'iúng** principle bent and words exhausted (without logic or words to support an argument; to be on the wrong side and unable to say anything in self-defense)

理会 **lǐ-huì** to understand, comprehend, realize, appreciate; to take care of, deal with, mediate, pay attention to; to feel, be sensitive to

理货 **lǐ-huò** freight forwarding, customs brokerage

理想 **lǐ-hsiǎng** ideal; idea, thought, dream

理想境界 **lǐ-hsiǎng-chìng-chièh** ideal state, ideal condition

理想化 **lǐ-hsiǎng-huà** to idealize

理想国 **lǐ-hsiǎng-kuó** an ideal state, utopia

理性 **lǐ-hsìng** the rational faculty; reasonableness

理性知识 **lǐ-hsìng-chīh-shíh** rational knowledge

理性认识 **lǐ-hsìng-jèn-shíh** rational cognition, rational knowledge

理工 **lǐ-kūng** science and engineering

理科大学 **lǐ-k'ō-tà-hsuéh** a physical science university

理亏心虚 **lǐ-k'uēi-hsīn-hsū** principle deficient and heart empty (with the guilty conscience of an unjust cause)

理论 **lǐ-lùn** a theory; theoretical; to argue, debate (often has the sense of truth, a correct or proven theory)

理论至上 **lǐ-lùn-chìh-shàng** theory is above everything else (divorced from practice—hence bad)

理论和实践相结合 **lǐ-lùn hó shíh-chièn hsiāng-chiéh-hó** the integration of theory and practice

理论和实践统一 **lǐ-lùn hó shíh-chièn t'ǔng-ī** the unity of theory and practice

理论根据 **lǐ-lùn-kēn-chù** theoretical foundation

理论联系实际 **lǐ-lùn lién-hsì shíh-chì** to unite theory with practice

理论脱离实际 **lǐ-lùn t'ō-lí shíh-chì**

theory divorced from practice

理事 **lǐ-shìh** to direct, manage; a director, manager, member of a board of directors

理事会 **lǐ-shìh-huì** an executive council, board of directors

理事国 **lǐ-shìh-kuó** a member of the UN Security Council

理所当然 **lǐ-sǒ-tāng-ján** in accordance with what is naturally right (as a matter of course, naturally)

理财 **lǐ-ts'ái** fiscal management; to administer finances

理睬 **lǐ-ts'ǎi** to pay attention to, take notice of, heed the presence of

lì (lì)

[1285] 力争 **lì-chēng** to strive for, struggle hard, compete strenuously

力争上游 **lì-chēng-shàng-yú** to strive for the upper reaches of a stream (to aim high)

力戒骄傲 **lì-chièh-chiāo-ào** to guard against arrogance

力求 **lí-ch'iú** to strive toward, try hard, seek vigorously

力学 **lì-hsuéh** (1) dynamics; (2) to study or learn diligently

力量对比 **lì-liàng-tuì-pǐ** balance of force, relative strength, ratio of pow power

力能胜任 **lì-néng-shēng-jèn** strength equal to the task

力不胜任 **lì-pù-shēng-jèn** strength inadequate to the task

力不从心 **lì-pù-ts'úng-hsīn** the strength not equal to the will (abilities not commensurate with ambitions)

力所能及 **lì-sǒ-néng-chí** within the reach of one's power

力图 **lì-t'ú** to try hard, strive for

[1286] 历届 **lì-chièh** successive previous [meetings, sessions, games, elections, etc]

历程 **lì-ch'éng** process, course of

历来 **lì-lái** as in the past, in times gone by, hitherto, up to now

历史渣滓 **lì-shǐh-chā-tzu** the dregs of history

历史真实 **lì-shǐh-chēn-shíh** historical reality, historical facts

历史僵尸 **lì-shǐh-chiāng-shīh** a historical corpse (historical characters with no meaning or significance)

历史阶段 **lì-shǐh-chiēh-tuàn** a historical stage, historical period

历史经验 **lì-shǐh-chīng-yèn** historical experience

历史主动性 **lì-shǐh chǔ-tùng-hsìng**

historical initiative

历史转折 **lì-shǐh-chuǎn-ché** historical turns, the twists and turns of history

历史潮流 **lì-shǐh-ch'áo-liú** the tide of history, historical trend, trend of historical development

历史车轮 **lì-shǐh-ch'ē-lún** the wheel of history

历史剧 **lì-shǐh-chù** a drama on an historical theme

历史发展规律 **lì-shǐh fā-chǎn kuēi-lù** the laws of historical development

历史性 **lì-shǐh-hsìng** historic, having historical significance

历史意义 **lì-shǐh-ì-ì** historical significance, historic meaning

历史任务 **lì-shǐh-jèn-wù** historic task, historical mission

历史关头 **lì-shǐh-kuān-t'óu** a critical moment in history

历史规律 **lì-shǐh-kuēi-lù** historical laws (the laws of historical development in the Marxist sense)

历史必然性 **lì-shǐh pì-ján-hsìng** historical inevitability

历史博物馆 **lì-shǐh pó-wù-kuǎn** a history museum

历史使命 **lì-shǐh-shǐh-mìng** historical mission (a task imposed by history)

历史的火车头 **lì-shǐh-te huǒ-ch'ē-t'óu** the locomotive of history

历史唯心主义 **lì-shǐh wéi-hsīn-chǔ-ì** historical idealism

历史唯物主义 **lì-shǐh wéi-wù-chǔ-ì** historical materialism

历史文物 **lì-shǐh wén-wù** historical objects, historical relics

历史问题 **lì-shǐh-wèn-t'í** historical problems (questionable personal or class background factors in one's personal history)

历史舞台 **lì-shǐh wǔ-t'ái** the stage of history

历史研究 **lì-shǐh yén-chiū** (1) historical research; (2) *Historical Studies* (a Peking journal, bi-monthly, 1954—)

历次 **lì-tz'ù** at various times, successively

1287 厉行 **lì-hsíng** to enforce, carry out vigorously, make a sustained effort

厉行节约 **lì-hsíng-chiéh-yuēh** to make a serious effort at economy

1288 立脚点 **lì-chiǎo-tién** where one places one's foot (a standpoint)

立志 **lì-chìh** to set one's mind, determine to accomplish some specific goal, fix an objective

立传 **lì-chuàn** to write a biography

立场 **lì-ch'ǎng** a position [on a given question], stand, attitude, standpoint

立场, 观点, 方法 **lì-ch'ǎng, kuān-tién, fāng-fǎ** position, viewpoint, method (the three key points in approaching a problem)

立法 **lì-fǎ** to legislate, make laws, enact laws

立法权 **lì-fǎ-ch'üán** legislative power, law-making authority

立方 **lì-fāng** cube; cubic; three-dimensional

立方米 **lì-fāng-mǐ** cubic meter

立宪政体 **lì-hsièn-chèng-t'ǐ** a constitutional state, constitutional form of government, constitutional regime

立新功, 立新劳 **lì-hsīn-kūng, lì-hsīn-láo** to achieve new merit

立竿见影 **lì-kān-chièn-yǐng** the shadow appears [as soon as] the pole is raised (immediate results)

立功受奖 **lì-kūng-shòu-chiǎng** to establish merit and receive awards

立功赎罪 **lì-kūng-shú-tsuì** to atone for past errors by meritorious deeds

立式车床 **lì-shìh-ch'ē-chuáng** a vertical lathe

立四新 **lì-szù-hsīn** establish the four news (a Cultural Revolution slogan: new thought, culture, customs, and habits)

立党为公 **lì-tǎng-wèi-kūng** building a party for public interests

立党为私 **lì-tǎng-wèi-szū** building a party for selfish interests

立地成佛 **lì-tì-ch'éng-fó** to become a Buddha right on the spot (even a person with a bad past can be converted and become a revolutionary)

立体 **lì-t'ǐ** three-dimensional

立体电影 **lì-t'ǐ-tièn-yǐng** three-dimensional [3-D] motion picture

立足本职 **lì-tsú-pěn-chíh** to set one's feet on his own job (to master one's own job)

立足本地 **lì-tsú-pěn-tì** to stand on one's own locality (for example, to create a factory using local labor, materials, etc.)

立足点 **lì-tsú-tién** one's standpoint

立于不败之地 **lì-yú pù-pài-chǐh-tì** to place in an invincible position

1289 吏治 **lì-chìh** administration of officials, statecraft

1290 利奥波德维尔 **lì-ào-pō-té-wéi-ěrh** Leopoldville [now called Kinshasa]

利己 **lì-chǐ** to benefit oneself, be selfish; selfishness

利己主义 **lì-chǐ-chǔ-ì** egoism, egotism

利害 **lì-hài** gains and losses; good and harm; advantages and disadvantages

利害 **lì-hai** (1) sharp, shrewd, very

capable; (2) severe, harsh, terrible

利害冲突 **lì-hài-ch'ūng-t'ū** a clash of interests, conflict of interests

利害相关 **lì-hài-hsiāng-kuān** to involve both advantages and disadvantages, to involve one's vital interests

利害关系 **lì-hài-kuān-hsi** a relationship based on practical considerations of interest

利息 **lì-hsī** interest on deposits

利益 **lì-ì** gains, benefits, profit, good; to benefit [society, others]

利润 **lì-jùn** profit, gain

利润挂帅 **lì-jùn-kuà-shuài** profits take command

利令智昏 **lì-lìng-chìh-hūn** profit makes wisdom blind (misled by greed)

利率 **lì-lù** interest rate [banking]

利马 **lì-mǎ** Lima [Peru]

利比里亚 **lì-pǐ-lǐ-yà** Liberia

利比亚 **lì-pǐ-yà** Libya

利伯维尔 **lì-pó-wéi-ěrh** Libreville [Gabon]

利他主义 **lì-t'ā-chǔ-ì** altruism

利雅得 **lì-yǎ-té** Riyadh [Saudi Arabia]

利诱 **lì-yù** to tempt by gain [usually money or material]

利用 **lì-yùng** to utilize, make use of, take advantage of, avail oneself of

利用系数 **lì-yùng-hsì-shù** utilization coefficient, capacity factor

利用, 限制和改造方针 **lì-yùng, hsièn-chìh hó kǎi-tsào fāng-chēn** the policy of utilization, restriction and transformation (policy toward private industry and commerce during 1949–1956)

利用率 **lì-yùng-lù** utilization rate, operation rate

利用沙漠 **lì-yùng-shā-mò** utilization [reclamation] of desert lands

利欲熏心 **lì-yù-hsūn-hsīn** so greedy for profit that the orifices of the heart are blocked (avarice that blinds one to right and wrong; lured by profit)

1291 隶属 **lì-shǔ** subordinate to, under the command of, attached to, dependent on

1292 例证 **lì-chèng** evidence, proof; an example; to cite an example, exemplify

例行公事 **lì-hsíng-kūng-shìh** normal transacting of official business, regular procedure, routine

例外 **lì-wài** an exception

1293 粒子加速器 **lì-tzǔ chiā-sù-ch'ì** particle accelerator

1294 傈僳族 **lì-sù-tsú** the Lisu people (a minority in Yunnan province: population 317,000 as of 1957)

1295 痢疾 **lì-chí** diarrhea, dysentery

liáng (liáng)

1296 良种 **liáng-chǔng** superior seed, of good breed

良种试验 **liáng-chǔng-shìh-yèn** experimentation with improved seeds

良好开端 **liáng-hǎo-k'āi-tuān** a good start, a fine beginning

良心 **liáng-hsīn** conscience, moral goodness, fairness

良民证 **liáng-mín-chèng** good citizen card (identity cards issued by Japanese occupation forces during the Resistance War)

良田 **liáng-t'ién** a fertile field, good soil

良药苦口 **liáng-yào-k'ǔ-k'ǒu** good medicine is bitter in the mouth (good advice may be hard to take)

1297 梁山泊 **liáng-shān-p'ò** the robbers roost in the novel **Shui-hu-chuan** (The Water Margin) [considered to depict peasant revolution]

1298 量具 **liáng-chù** measuring instruments

量具刃具厂 **liáng-chù jèn-chù ch'ǎng** a factory producing measuring instruments and cutting tools

量: see also **liàng**

1299 粮荒 **liáng-huāng** a grain shortage, food scarcity, famine

粮林间作 **liáng-lín-chièn-tsò** grain and forests should be worked in combination

粮票 **liáng-p'iào** grain ration card (includes flour, etc.)

粮食 **liáng-shih** grains, cereals, rice and flour; staple foods

粮食储备 **liáng-shíh ch'ǔ-peì** stockpiling of grains, food reserves

粮食部 **liáng-shíh-pù** Ministry of Food [of the State Council] (merged into the Ministry of Commerce in 1959)

粮食代销店 **liáng-shíh tài-hsiāo-tièn** food-selling agent (authorized by state companies to sell rationed items)

粮食作物 **liáng-shíh-tsò-wù** grain crops

粮帅 **liáng-shuài** cereal [is the] commander-in-chief (everything depends on basic food production)

粮草 **liáng-ts'ǎo** food and fodder [for troops and their animals]

liǎng (liǎng)

1300 两者之中择其一 **liǎng-chě-chìh-chūng tsé-ch'í-ī** one of the two alternatives [must] be chosen

两极分化 **liǎng-chí-fēn-huà** polarization

两种教育制度, 两种劳动制度 **liǎng-chǔng chiào-yǜ chìh-tù, liǎng-chǔng láo-tùng chìh-tù** a system of two kinds of education and two kinds of labor (a Cultural Revolution accusation that Liu Shao-ch'i was creating an elitist system)

两种思想 **liǎng-chǔng-szū-hsiǎng** two kinds of ideology (capitalism and socialism)

两重性 **liǎng-ch'úng-hsìng** dual nature, duality

两重天 **liǎng-ch'úng-t'iēn** two different skies (the dark sky of the old society and the bright sky of the new)

两军对垒 **liǎng-chūn-tuì-lěi** two armies facing each other (often figurative)

两全其美 **liǎng-ch'üán-ch'í-měi** to profit both parties; to attain two objectives by a single act

两耳不闻窗外事, 一心只读科技书 **liǎng-ěrh pù-wén ch'uāng-wài-shìh, ī-hsīn chǐh-tú k'ō-chì-shū** the ears ignore everything outside the window and the heart is entirely devoted to reading technical books (indifferent to politics and society)

两放 **liǎng-fàng** two decentralizations (the downward transfer—as to the communes—of both the personnel and the capital for banking, investment, and purchasing)

两飞 **liǎng-fēi** a double leap (a leap forward in both agriculture and industry)

两分法 **liǎng-fēn-fǎ** dichotomy

两相情愿 **liǎng-hsiāng-ch'íng-yuàn** both parties are willing, mutual consent

两忆三查 **liǎng-ì-sān-ch'á** two rememberings and three examinings [investigations] (A. During civil war period: remember class suffering and national suffering; examine one's standpoint, will to fight, and will to work. B. Cultural Revolution: remember the bitterness of the old society and the sweetness of this day of Mao Tse-tung; examine anti-Mao and anti-Party elements, elements engaging in corruption, theft, extravagance and waste, and elements engaged in speculation or who wish to escape the country)

两个肩膀一双手 **liǎng-ko-chiēn-pǎng ī-shuāng-shǒu** two shoulders and a pair of hands (one must rely on one's own hard work)

两个拳头主义 **liǎng-ko-ch'üán-t'ou-chǔ-ì** two-fist-ism (a mistaken policy

of trying to fight on two fronts— from the Kiangsi period)

两个黑司令部 **liǎng-ko hēi szū-lìng-pù** the two black headquarters (of Liu Shao-ch'i and Lin Piao)

两股道上跑的车 **liǎng-kǔ-tào-shang p'ǎo-te-ch'ē** vehicles traveling on different roads (following different policies)

两管 **liǎng-kuǎn** two [things to be] managed (water and manure)

两利 **liǎng-lì** to the advantage of both sides

两利用 **liǎng-lì-yùng** the two utilizations (utilize spare time to settle disputes at the village level; utilize market days for the mediation committee to carry on work at the market town level)

两论 **liǎng-lùn** the two treatises (by Mao Tse-tung: "On Practice" and "On Contradiction")

两面性 **liǎng-mièn-hsìng** two-sidedness, dual character

两面派 **liǎng-mièn-p'ài** two-faced elements, double-dealers

两面三刀 **liǎng-mièn-sān-tāo** two-faces and three-swords (two-faced, treacherous)

两面手法 **liǎng-mièn-shǒu-fǎ** two-faced tactics, duplicity

两面外交 **liǎng-mièn-wài-chiāo** two-sided diplomacy

两难论法 **liǎng-nán-lùn-fǎ** a dilemma [in logic]

两败俱伤 **liǎng-pài-chù-shāng** both [sides] defeated and ruined (war in which there are no winners)

两报一刊 **liǎng-pào-ī-k'ān** the two newspapers and one journal (the three chief Party organs: **Jen-min jih-pao Chieh-fang-chün pao,** and **Hung-ch'i**)

两手政策 **liǎng-shǒu-chèng-ts'è** a two-handed policy (double-edged policy)

两手空空 **liǎng-shǒu-k'ūng-k'ūng** empty-handed, penniless

两手并用 **liǎng-shǒu-pìng-yùng** to use both hands at the same time (simultaneous pursuit of two tactics)

两党制 **liǎng-tǎng-chìh** the two-party system

两斗皆仇, 两和皆好 **liǎng-tòu chiēh-ch'óu, liǎng-hó chiēh-hǎo** if two fight, all will become enemies, but if two are peaceful, all will benefit (an aphorism charged against Lin Piao and said to mean that he opposed class struggle)

两条战线的斗争 **liǎng-t'iáo-chàn-hsièn**

te tòu-chēng a two-front struggle

两条道路 liǎng-t'iáo tào-lù the two
roads (i.e., socialism and capitalism)

两条道路的斗争 liǎng-t'iáo-tào-lù te
tòu-chēng the struggle between the
two roads [of socialism and capi-
talism]

两条腿走路 liǎng-t'iáo-t'uǐ tsǒu-lù to
walk on two legs (the two legs may
be: industry and agriculture; or,
modern and native methods)

两头冒尖 liǎng-t'óu-mào-chiēn to issue
forth at both ends (to be both red
and expert)

两参一改 liǎng-ts'ān-ǐ-kǎi two participations and one change (participations: of cadres in production and
workers in management; change: of
regulations and procedures)

两参，一改，三结合 liǎng-ts'ān, ǐ-kǎi,
sān-chiéh-hó two participations, one
change, and triple combination
(workers participate in management,
administrative personnel participate
in production; change outmoded
rules and regulations; workers,
cadres, and technicians form a triple
combination)

两院制 liǎng-yuàn-chìh the bicameral
system [in parliamentary government]

liàng (liàng)

1301 亮出 liàng-ch'ū to reveal, expose,
display

亮相 liàng-hsiàng a stage entrance
[holding a pose for the audience's
admiration], to display one's role (to
come forward and clarify one's
position)

亮私 liàng-szū to reveal what is
private or selfish

亮私斗私 liàng-szū-tòu-szū to expose
and struggle against selfishness

亮思想 liàng-szū-hsiǎng to reveal one's
thinking

1302 谅解 liàng-chièh to reconcile, be
understanding of, forgive

1303 量入为出 liàng-jù-wéi-ch'ū to base
expenditures on the amount of
income

量变 liàng-pièn quantitative change

量体裁衣 liàng-t'ǐ-ts'ái-ī to cut the
clothes by the size of the body (to act
in conformity with reality)

量才录用 liàng-ts'ái-lù-yùng to assign
tasks in accordance with people's
abilities

量 liàng: see also liáng

liáo (liáo)

1304 辽阔 liáo-k'uò vast, distant, broad

辽沈战役 liáo-shěn-chàn-ì the Liao-
Shen campaign (the campaign in
October 1948 in the West Liaoning-
Shenyang area in which the KMT
forces were defeated by the PLA
Fourth Field Army)

1305 疗程 liáo-ch'éng medical treatment
period, a treatment period

疗法 liáo-fǎ a cure, therapy, method of
medical treatment

疗效 liáo-hsiào effectiveness of
[medical] treatment

疗养地 liáo-yǎng-tì a health resort, spa

疗养院 liáo-yǎng-yuàn a sanatorium,
convalescent home, rest home

1306 聊以自慰 liáo-ǐ-tzù-wèi somehow to
find solace in

聊天 liáo-t'iēn to chat idly

1307 寥若晨星 liáo-jò-ch'én-hsīng as few as
morning stars (scanty, sparse)

寥寥数语 liáo-liáo-shù-yǔ only a few
words

1308 燎原烈火 liáo-yuán-lièh-huǒ a wild
prairie fire (the irresistible forces of
revolution)

liǎo (liǎo)

1309 了解 liǎo-chièh to comprehend, understand, grasp

了解情况 liǎo-chièh-ch'íng-k'uàng to
have a full grasp of the situation

了解下情 liǎo-chièh-hsià-ch'íng to
comprehend the circumstances at
lower levels

了如指掌 liǎo-jú-chǐh-chǎng as plain as
pointing to the palm (very clear)

了事 liǎo-shìh to settle a dispute,
dispose of a matter; to understand a
matter

了 liǎo: see also liào

liào (liào)

1310 了望 liào-wàng to observe; outlook;
overlooking

了 liào: see also liǎo

1311 料子服 liào-tzu-fú suits of woolen cloth
(sometimes criticized as a mark of
bourgeois thingking)

1312 撂挑子 liào-t'iāo-tzu to put down the
load (to give up one's responsibilities)

lièh (liè)

1313 列支敦士登 lièh-chīh-tūn-shìh-tēng
[Principality of] Liechtenstein

列强 **lièh-ch'iáng** the Powers (implies the imperialist countries)
列举 **lièh-chǔ** to enumerate, cite item by item
列席 **lièh-hsí** to be present at a meeting as an observer, attend without voting rights
列宁 **lièh-níng** Lenin (1870–1924)
列宁主义 **lièh-níng-chǔ-ì** Leninism
列为 **lièh-wéi** to classify as, listed as
1314 劣货贵卖 **lièh-huò-kuèi-mài** poor-quality commodities with high prices
劣根性 **lièh-kēn-hsìng** innate wickedness, depravity, meanness
劣绅 **lièh-shēn** bad gentry (the old rural ruling elite)
劣势 **lièh-shìh** an inferior position, unfavorable situation
劣等人种 **lièh-těng-jén-chǔng** an inferior race (indicating racial discrimination)
1315 烈火见真金 **lièh-huǒ chièn chēn-chīn** [only] fierce fire reveals true gold (it is crisis that proves a person's greatness)
烈士 **lièh-shìh** a martyr [to revolution or country]
烈士纪念碑 **lièh-shìh chì-nièn-pēi** a monument to revolutionary martyrs
烈士陵园 **lièh-shìh-líng-yuán** a cemetery for revolutionary martyrs
烈属 **lièh-shǔ** the family of a martyr, dependents of war dead
1316 猎取 **lièh-ch'ǔ** to obtain by cunning; to hunt for, chase after
猎夺 **lièh-tó** to hunt and seize
1317 裂痕 **lièh-hén** a fissure, split, chasm

lién (lián)

1318 连结 **lién-chiéh** to connect, link together, join, couple, connect, associate
连珠炮 **lién-chū-p'ào** an artillery barrage
连串 **lién-ch'uàn** a whole series; to link together, string together in a series
连环合同 **lién-huán-hó-t'ung** a linked contract (between several masters and apprentices together)
连环画 **lién-huán-huà** serialized stories in picture book form
连续发表 **lién-hsù-fā-piǎo** to publish in succession
连续作战 **lién-hsù-tsò-chàn** continuous battles, battles in close succession
连贯性 **lién-kuàn-hsìng** continuity, the quality of being consistent
连绵不绝 **lién-mién-pù-chüéh** continuous without a break, uninter-

rupted; ceaselessly, continuously
连绵不断 **lién-mién-pù-tuàn** continuous, unbroken, uninterrupted
连年 **lién-nién** year after year
连篇累牍 **lién-p'iēn-lěi-tú** successive articles and piled up tablets (voluminous writings, repetitious, redundant)
连声称好 **lién-shēng-ch'ēng-hǎo** to praise repeatedly
连锁反应 **lién-sǒ-fǎn-yìng** a chain reaction
连队 **lién-tuì** a company [military], armed unit
连队建设 **lién-tuì-chièn-shè** the building of [strong] company units
连队史 **lién-tuì-shǐh** company history [military]
连载 **lién-tsǎi** to serialize, publish in a number of installments
连夜 **lién-yèh** [to continue] into the night, the same night, all night
1319 联结 **lién-chiéh** to form an alliance, join together, unite
联成一起 **lién-ch'éng-ī-ch'ǐ** to fuse together; to form into a unit
联合 **lién-hó** to unite, join together, combine, federate, associate, consolidate
联合战线 **lién-hó-chàn-hsièn** an allied battle front
联合诊所 **lién-hó-chěn-sǒ** a joint clinic (a clinic covering several medical fields)
联合政府 **lién-hó-chèng-fǔ** coalition government
联合行动委员会 **lién-hó hsíng-tùng wěi-yuán-huì** united action committee (a form of organization during the Cultural Revolution)
联合国 **lién-hó-kuó** the United Nations [UN]
联合国安全理事会 **lién-hó-kuó ān-ch'üán lǐ-shìh-huì** the UN Security Council
联合国军 **lién-hó-kuó-chǔn** the United Nations military forces
联合国和平部队 **lién-hó-kuó hó-p'íng-pù-tuì** UN peace-keeping forces
联合国宪章 **lién-hó-kuó hsièn-chāng** the United Nations Charter
联合国工业发展理事会 **lién-hó-kuó kūng-yèh-fā-chǎn lǐ-shìh-huì** the UN International Development Association [IDA]
联合国大会 **lién-hó-kuó tà-huì** the UN General Assembly
联合邦 **lién-hó-pāng** a confederation
联合兵种 **lién-hó-pīng-chǔng** combined military arms

联合收割机 **lién-hó shōu-kō-chī** a combine harvester

联合押汇集团 **lién-hó yā-huì chí-t'uán** United Underwriting Group (formed by the Government with banks and shippers in mid-1951 to finance transport and to gather economic information)

联合运输 **lién-hó-yùn-shū** combined transport

联欢 **lién-huān** a social gathering, party

联欢节 **lién-huān-chiéh** a festival, carnival, fiesta

联席会议 **lién-hsí-huì-ì** a joint conference

联系 **lién-hsì** to connect, link, join together, ally, make contact with

联系群众 **lién-hsì-ch'ún-chùng** to establish close links with the masses, keep close to the masses, have rapport with the masses

联购联销 **lién-kòu-lién-hsiāo** buying together and selling together (a mid-1950s policy for hawkers, who were urged to form and supervise their own buying and selling groups)

联共 **lién-kùng** (1) the Communist Party of the Soviet Union; (2) a policy of cooperation with the Communists (as in the KMT-CCP cooperation during the 1923–1927 period)

联共(布) **lién-kùng (pù)** the Communist Party of the Soviet Union (Bolshevik) [CPSU(b)]

联共(布)党史 **lién-kùng (pù) tăng-shǐh** *The History of the CPSU (b)* [*Short Course*] (the 1938 history compiled under the auspices of Stalin)

联络 **lién-lò** to maintain liaison, get in touch with, keep in contact, communicate with; liaison, contact

联络站 **lién-lò-chàn** a liaison station (a subordinate or local liaison office)

联络员 **lién-lò-yuán** liaison officers

联盟 **lién-méng** an alliance, federation, league; to ally with

联邦 **lién-pāng** a federation

联邦制 **lién-pāng-chìh** the federal system

联邦议会 **lién-pāng-ì-huì** a federal parliament

联赛 **lién-sài** a league competition [sports]

联社 **lién-shè** a federation of communes

联大 **lién-tà** the UN General Assembly (contraction of **lién-hó-kuó tà-huì**)

联动 **lién-tùng** united action committee (contraction of **lién-hó hsíng-tùng wĕi-yuán-huì**)

联动机 **lién-tùng-chī** a transmission gear [motor car]

联运 **lién-yùn** through transportation using various modes

1320 廉洁 **lién-chiéh** incorruptible, honest, clean

廉洁政治 **lién-chiéh-chèng-chìh** clean government

廉洁奉公 **lién-chiéh-fèng-kūng** to serve the public honestly

1321 镰刀斧头 **lién-tāo fǔ-t'óu** the sickle and hammer

liĕn (liǎn)

1322 脸谱 **liĕn-p'ǔ** facial make-up [in Peking opera, indicating role and character] (figuratively, a person's image)

脸上光彩 **liĕn-shàng-kuāng-ts'ǎi** a face that is shining [with achievement]

脸上无光 **liĕn-shāng-wú-kuāng** a face without brightness (indicating failure)

1323 敛迹 **liĕn-chǐ** to stop leaving traces (to mend one's ways, to stop illegal maneuvers)

lièn (liàn)

1324 练兵 **lièn-pīng** to train troops, drill troops

练武 **lièn-wǔ** to train [oneself] in martial arts

练硬功 **lièn-yìng-kūng** to train [ourselves to master] the highest skills

1325 炼焦 **lièn-chiāo** to make coke

炼焦炉 **lièn-chiāo-lú** a coke oven

炼焦煤 **lièn-chiāo-méi** coking coal

炼钢 **lièn-kāng** to smelt steel

炼钢厂 **lièn-kāng-ch'ǎng** a steel plant

炼钢炉 **lièn-kāng-lú** a steel-smelting furnace

炼钢又炼人 **lièn-kāng yù lièn-jén** smelting steel also tempers men

炼铁 **lièn-t'iĕh** iron-smelting

炼油厂 **lièn-yú-ch'ǎng** an oil refinery

1326 恋爱 **lièn-ài** romantic love, passionate devotion; to be enamoured

恋恋不舍 **lièn-lièn-pù-shĕ** reluctant to part company with

1327 链式反应 **lièn-shìh-fǎn-yìng** a chain reaction

lín (lín)

1328 邻接 **lín-chiēh** contiguous, bordering, adjacent

邻居 **lín-chū** people living next door, neighbors

邻户 **lín-hù** next-door neighbor, next household

1329 林家铺子 **lín-chiā p'ù-tzu** *The Lin Family Shop* (a novel and film by Mao Tun, criticized during the Cultural Revolution)

林家王朝 **lín-chiā wáng-ch'áo** the Lin [Piao] family dynasty

林场 **lín-ch'ǎng** a forest plantation, tree farm

林彪路线 **lín piāo lù-hsièn** the [revisionist] line of Lin Piao

林贼 **lín-tséi** the traitor Lin [Piao]

林业 **lín-yèh** forest industry, forestry

林业部 **lín-yèh-pù** Ministry of Forestry [of the State Council] (now merged into the Ministry of Agriculture and Forestry)

1330 临阵磨枪 **lín-chèn-mó-ch'iāng** to wait for the battle to sharpen the lance (to fail to prepare in advance; to cram for an exam)

临阵脱逃 **lín-chèn-t'ō-t'áo** to desert in the face of the battle (to absent oneself when most needed)

临机处置 **lín-chī-ch'ǔ-chìh** to confront an emergency and dispose of it [well]

临机应变 **lín-chī yìng-pièn** to make changes as the situation demands, act according to the circumstances

临近 **lín-chìn** located nearby, close by; to approach

临终 **lìn-chūng** near the end, on the point of death

临床诊断 **lìn-ch'uáng-chěn-tuàn** bedside diagnosis, clinical diagnosis

临行 **lín-hsíng** on the eve of departure

临渴掘井 **lín-k'ǒ-chüéh-chǐng** to wait for thirst to dig a well (to do something too late and without preparation)

临别 **lín-piéh** while leaving, on the point of departure

临时起作用的因素 **lín-shíh ch'ǐ tsò-yùng te yīn-sù** a factor which only temporarily plays a role

临时权力机构 **lín-shíh ch'uán-lì-chī-kòu** a temporary organ of authority

临时费 **lín-shíh-fèi** interim expenses

临时行商 **lín-shíh-háng-shāng** temporary business (individual private businesses, authorized under special circumstances for a limited period in the late 1950s, apparently to solve input or information shortages)

临时户口 **lín-shíh hù-k'ǒu** temporary residence

临时人口办公室 **lín-shíh jén-k'ǒu pàn-kūng-shìh** Temporary Population Office (to assist and direct movement of people out of urban centers, 1957)

临时工人 **lín-shíh-kūng-jén** temporary worker, casual worker

临时代办 **lín-shíh-tài-pàn** chargé d'affaires ad interim

临时采购小组 **lín-shíh ts'ǎi-kòu hsiǎo-tsǔ** temporary purchasing groups (set up by government-favored private grocers to go to the countryside to buy supplies directly from peasants, 1955)

临时应付办法 **lín-shíh yìng-fù-pàn-fǎ** a temporary expedient, improvised method

临危不惧 **lín-wéi-pù-chù** dauntless before danger

1331 淋漓尽致 **lín-lí-chìn-chìh** to fall like dripping rain (to soak thoroughly, imbue completely; vivid [description])

1332 琳琅满目 **lín-láng-mǎn-mù** the glittering of gems fills the eye (a dazzling display of fine objects)

1333 磷肥 **lín-féi** phosphate fertilizer

lìn (lìn)

1334 吝惜 **lìn-hsī** stingy, niggardly

líng (líng)

1335 灵芝仙草 **líng-chīh-hsiēn-ts'ǎo** the magic *fomes japonica* (a nonexistent, imaginary cure-all for any kind of problem)

灵巧 **líng-ch'iǎo** clever, dextrous, nimble, agile

灵魂 **líng-hún** the soul, vital essence, psyche, spirit

灵魂深处 **líng-hún-shēn-ch'ù** deep in the soul

灵活 **líng-huó** flexible, nimble, quick-minded, alert, alive, energetic, elastic

灵活机动 **líng-huó-chī-tùng** flexibly mobile

灵活性 **líng-huó-hsìng** elasticity, mobility, flexibility

灵感论 **líng-kǎn lùn** the theory of inspiration

灵敏 **líng-mǐn** sensitive, quick to respond, intelligent, facile

灵丹圣药 **líng-tān-shèng-yào** an efficacious pill and divine medicine (an illusory panacea)

1336 凌乱 **líng-luàn** in total disarray, disheveled, untidy; confusion

1337 陵墓 **líng-mù** a tomb, grave, mausoleum

1338 菱角 **líng-chiǎo** the water caltrop, water chestnut (the leaves and stems

of which are valuable as fertilizer)

1339 零件 **lǐng-chièn** spare parts, components [of machinery and equipment], replacement parts, accessories

零星 **lǐng-hsīng** fragmented, piecemeal, fractional

零工 **lǐng-kūng** casual labor, short-term worker, odd-job employee

零零星星 **lǐng-lǐng-hsīng-hsīng** scattered petty amounts

零部件 **lǐng-pù-chièn** spare parts and component parts

零售 **lǐng-shòu** to sell at retail; retail sales

零碎不全 **lǐng-suì-pù-ch'üán** fragmentary and incomplete

lǐng (lǐng)

1340 领进 **lǐng-chìn** to lead into, introduce into

领主 **lǐng-chǔ** a large landowner [in Tibet]

领取 **lǐng-ch'ǚ** to receive as due, draw out, get, acquire, fetch

领海 **lǐng-hǎi** territorial waters

领海权 **lǐng-hǎi-ch'üán** territorial water rights, sovereignty over territorial waters

领航 **lǐng-háng** to pilot, navigate; navigation

领会 **lǐng-huì** to comprehend, understand, appreciate

领先 **lǐng-hsiēn** to walk ahead, lead

领袖 **lǐng-hsiù** a leader, the leading figure

领港员 **lǐng-kǎng-yuán** a harbor pilot

领空 **lǐng-k'ūng** territorial air space

领路人 **lǐng-lù-jén** a guide (often refers to Mao Tse-tung)

领略 **lǐng-luèh** to grasp, comprehend, experience, taste

领事馆 **lǐng-shìh-kuǎn** a consulate

领事裁判权 **lǐng-shìh ts'ái-p'àn-ch'üán** extraterritorial jurisdiction, consular jurisdiction

领受 **lǐng-shòu** to receive, to enjoy

领, 代, 反, 叛, 坏 **lǐng, tài, fǎn, p'àn, huài** great owners, army, counter-revolutionaries, traitors, and evil people (the five bad elements in Tibet)

领导 **lǐng-tǎo** to lead, guide; leadership (includes one's direct superior or the head of an organization)

领导集团 **lǐng-tǎo-chí-t'uán** a leading group

领导, 专家, 群众三结合 **lǐng-tǎo, chuān-chiā, ch'ún-chùng sān-chiéh-hó** the three-way combination of leader-

ship [cadres], specialists, and masses

领导权 **lǐng-tǎo-ch'üán** leadership authority

领导方针 **lǐng-tǎo-fāng-chēn** a guiding policy

领导方法 **lǐng-tǎo-fāng-fǎ** method of leadership

领导核心 **lǐng-tǎo-hó-hsīn** leadership nucleus, leading core

领导干部 **lǐng-tǎo kàn-pù** leadership cadre (any Party or state cadre who holds executive position at any level)

领导干部, 工人, 技术人员三结合 **lǐng-tǎo-kàn-pù, kūng-jén, chì-shù-jén-yuán sān-chiéh-hó** a three-way coordination of leading cadres, workers, and technical personnel

领导岗位 **lǐng-tǎo-kǎng-wèi** leading posts, leadership positions

领导高明论 **lǐng-tǎo-kāo-míng lùn** the doctrine that leaders are brilliant (to be criticized)

领导骨干 **lǐng-tǎo-kǔ-kàn** the leadership backbone (the reliable leading group)

领导力量 **lǐng-tǎo-lì-liàng** leadership strength, leadership forces

领导班子 **lǐng-tǎo-pān-tzu** leading groups

领导偏一偏, 影响一大片 **lǐng-tǎo p'iēn-ǐ-p'iēn, yǐng-hsiǎng ǐ-tà-p'ièn** [if] the leadership deviates only a little, the effect will be very broad

领导水平 **lǐng-tǎo-shuǐ-p'íng** the level of leadership (the quality of leadership)

领导地位 **lǐng-tǎo-tì-wèi** a position of leadership, status as a leader

领导同志 **lǐng-tǎo-t'úng-chìh** a leading comrade

领导作风 **lǐng-tǎo-tsò-fēng** style of work of the leadership, leadership style

领导作用 **lǐng-tǎo-tsò-yùng** a leading role; the leadership function

领地 **lǐng-tì** domain, realm

领土 **lǐng-t'ǔ** territory under jurisdiction

领土权 **lǐng-t'ǔ-ch'üán** sovereign rights over territory

领域 **lǐng-yǜ** national territory, domain, sphere, realm

lìng (lìng)

1341 令人震惊 **lìng-jén-chèn-chīng** shocking, frightening

令人兴奋 **lìng-jén-hsīng-fèn** to make people excited; rousing, exciting

令人失望 **lìng-jén-shīh-wàng** disap-

pointing, discouraging

令人厌倦 **lìng-jén-yèn-chüàn** tiresome, boring, tedious

1342   另起炉灶 **lìng-ch'ǐ-lú-tsào** to rebuild a stove (to start a new household, make a new start)

另当别论 **lìng-tāng-piéh-lùn** to single out for separate handling

另眼相看 **lìng-yěn-hsiāng-k'àn** to see in a new light (to re-evaluate in a better way)

另眼相待 **lìng-yěn-hsiāng-tài** to see and treat in a better way

liū (liū)

1343   溜之大吉 **liū-chīh-tà-chí** to leave stealthily, slip out

liú (liú)

1344   刘胡兰 **liú hú-lán** Liu Hu-lan (a girl martyr of the Liberation War)

刘少奇一类骗子 **liú shào-ch'í í-lèi p'ièn-tzu** swindlers like Liu Shao-ch'i

刘邓大军 **liú-tèng-tà-chǖn** the Liu [Po-ch'eng] and Teng [Hsiao-p'ing] army (the PLA Second Field Army during the Liberation War)

刘毒 **liú-tú** Liu poison (the evil theories and influence of Liu Shao-ch'i)

1345   浏览 **liú-lǎn** to glance over, thumb through [a book], take a casual look

1346   流产 **liú-ch'ǎn** an abortion, miscarriage; abortive

流程 **liú-ch'éng** flow, work flow

流传 **liú-ch'uán** to spread [in time or place], circulate, transmit from person to person, hapd down to following generations

流芳百世 **liú-fāng-pǎi-shìh** leaving a fragrance for a hundred generations (to hand down a good reputation)

流线型 **liú-hsièn-hsíng** streamlined, sleek

流星 **liú-hsīng** a meteor

流行 **liú-hsíng** fashionable, popular, in vogue, prevalent; to spread rapidly [of a disease]

流行性乙型脑炎 **liú-hsíng-hsìng í-hsíng-nǎo-yén** Japanese type-B encephalitis

流行病 **liú-hsíng-pìng** a contagious disease affecting many persons, epidemic

流血的斗争 **liú-hsuèh-te tòu-chēng** bloody combat, sanguinary struggle

流寇 **liú-k'òu** roving bandits

流寇主义 **liú-k'òu-chǔ-i** roving banditism (the doctrine that guerrilla

warfare can be successful without the mobilization of popular support and the establishment of bases)

流寇思想 **liú-k'òu-szū-hsiǎng** roving-bandit mentality

流浪 **liú-làng** to wander about, drift, roam

流离失所 **liú-lí-shīh-sǒ** wandering and homeless

流利 **liú-lì** fluent, flowing, smooth; glib, flippant

流量 **liú-liàng** volume of flow

流露 **liú-lù** to reveal unknowingly, betray, manifest, show

流氓 **liú-máng** a hooligan, loafer, rascal, gangster, ruffian, riff-raff

流氓阿飞 **liú-máng ā-fēi** vagabonds and rowdies

流氓无产阶级 **liú-máng wú-ch'ǎn-chīeh-chí** lumpenproletariat

流派 **liú-p'ài** branch, division, school [of thought], faction; tributary

流沙 **liú-shā** shifting sands, quicksand, sediment

流水作业 **liú-shuǐ-tsò-yèh** running-water method of work (streamlined production; assembly-line production where work goes on without interruption)

流速 **liú-sù** the speed of flow, current velocity

流弹 **liú-tàn** stray bullets

流毒 **liú-tú** to spread poison (having evil effects)

流动 **liú-tùng** to be in flowing motion, float, drift; mobile, itinerant, circulating

流动摊贩 **liú-tùng-t'ān-fàn** a mobile hawker

流动资金 **liú-tùng-tzū-chīn** working capital, revolving funds

流动资产 **liú-tùng-tzū-ch'ǎn** liquid assets, floating assets, current assets

流动资本 **liú-tùng-tzū-pěn** floating capital, working capital

流通 **liú-t'ūng** to circulate; circulation, exchange, flow [of trade], turnover

流亡 **liú-wáng** to flee, wander in a strange land; and exile, refugee

流亡政府 **liú-wáng-chèng-fǔ** a government in exile

流言蜚语 **liú-yén-fēi-yǔ** idle talk and flying words (gossip, rumor, hearsay)

流域 **liú-yù** drainage basin, river valley, catchment area

1347   留情 **liú-ch'íng** to show mercy, relent

留学生 **liú-hsuéh-shēng** a student studying abroad, person who has studied abroad

留恋 **liú-lièn** to be sorry to leave,

reluctant to part with, keep in memory

留神 **liú-shén** to pay attention, be wary, on the look out; alert, vigilant

留声机 **liú-shēng-chī** a phonograph

留党察看 **liú-tǎng-ch'á-k'àn** to place on probation within the Party

留得青山在, 不愁没柴烧 **liú-te ch'īng-shān tsài, pù-p'à méi ch'ái shāo** as long as the green mountains are there, one should not fear there will be no fuel to burn (as long as one lives there is no need to despair)

留有余地 **liú-yǔ-yú-tì** to make allowance, leave ground for, provide leeway

留用 **liú-yùng** to retain for use, give employment; to retain someone in his post while on probation or under surveillance

1348 琉球 **liú-ch'iú** the Ryukyu [Islands]

1349 硫酸 **liú-suān** sulphuric acid

1350 榴弹炮 **liú-tàn-p'ào** a howitzer

liù (liù)

1351 六亲不认 **liù-ch'īn-pù-jèn** to deny the six relationships [of father, mother, elder brother, younger brother, wife, and child] (to be free of nepotism)

六号门 **liù-hào-mén** "Gate No. 6" (a famous motion picture with the Tientsin railway station as its locale)

六六六 **liù-liù-liù** [formula] 666 (a popular insecticide)

六论 **liù-lùn** the six doctrines (see **hēi-liù-lùn**)

六边运动 **liù-piēn-yùn-tùng** the Six-Alongside Movement (the **wǔ-piēn** with the addition of **piēn hsuéh-hsí** : all expected of theatrical workers engaged in **yàng-pǎn-hsì**)

六三运动 **liù-sān-yùn-tùng** the June Third Movement (a later phase of the May Fourth Movement in 1919)

六十分主义 **liù-shíh-fēn-chǔ-ì** 60 percentism (content to get by with a barely passing grade)

lō (luō)

1352 罗唆 **lō-so** wordy, verbose, prolix, rambling

罗 **lō**: see also **ló**

ló (luó)

1352A 罗安达 **ló-ān-tá** Luanda [Angola]

罗致 **ló-chìh** to select and use [people of talent], to recruit

罗经指向 **ló-chīng-chǐh-hsiàng** the compass shows the direction; a guide

罗列 **ló-lièh** to arrange for display, spread out

罗马 **ló-mǎ** Rome

罗马教皇 **ló-mǎ-chiào-huáng** the Pope

罗马尼亚 **ló-mǎ-ní-yà** Romania

罗马尼亚通讯社 **ló-mǎ-ní-yà t'ūng-hsùn-shè** the Romanian Press Agency [Agerpres]

罗斯福 **ló-szū-fú** Roosevelt

罗网 **ló-wǎng** a trap, snare, net

1353 逻辑 **ló-chì** logic

1354 锣鼓喧天 **ló-kǔ-hsuān-t'iēn** the gongs and drums disturb Heaven (a great clamor)

1355 螺丝钉 **ló-szū-tīng** a screw (a small but important element in a large entity, a small cog in the revolution)

螺纹 **ló-wén** a screw thread, spiral

lò (luò)

1356 洛川会议 **ló-ch'uān-huì-ì** the Lochuan Conference (the August 25, 1937, meeting at Lochuan, Shensi, that called for a united front against Japan)

洛伦索马贵斯 **ló-lún-sǒ mǎ-kuèi-szū** Lourenco Marques [Mozambique]

洛美 **lò-měi** Lome [Tago]

1357 络绎不绝 **lò-ì-pù-chüéh** one after another, in uninterrupted succession, continuous

1358 珞巴族 **lò-pā-tsú** the Lo-pa people (a minority in Tibet—population unknown)

1359 落脚生根, 开花结果 **lò-chiǎo shēng-kēn, k'āi-huā chiéh-kuǒ** to get feet, grow roots, bloom, and bear fruit (the expectation that young people sent to the countryside will settle and remain there)

落井下石 **lò-chǐng-hsià-shíh** to stone [a man] in a well (to be without mercy; kick a man when he is down)

落差 **lò-ch'ā** the head drop [in hydro-electric power plants], difference in elevation

落成典礼 **lò-ch'éng-tiěn-lǐ** a dedication ceremony [of a new building or project]

落后 **lò-hòu** to fall behind, lag; backward, underdeveloped

落后状态 **lò-hòu-chuàng-t'ài** backward conditions, undeveloped

落后分子 **lò-hòu-fèn-tzǔ** backward elements

落后面貌 **lò-hòu-mièn-mào** the appearances of backwardness,

primitive aspects

落戶 **lò-hù** to enter one's name in a resident register, establish a home (implies settling down in a strange land or difficult circumstances: often used in connection with the **hsià-fàng** of cadres and students)

落戶边疆 **lò-hù-piēn-chiāng** to settle in the frontier regions

落花流水 **lò-huà-liú-shuǐ** like fallen flowers on running water (vanished, scattered; severely defeated)

落入陷阱 **lò-jù-hsièn-chǐng** to fall into a trap, be ensnared

落空 **lò-k'ūng** to fail in an attempt, end up with nothing, suffer loss; in vain

落实 **lò-shíh** to conform [to reality], adjust, conform; to put into effect, realize, carry out, implement

落实政策 **lò-shíh-chèng-ts'è** to carry out a policy, implement a policy

落水狗 **lò-shuǐ-kǒu** the dog in the water (a reference to Lu Hsun's remark that one should go on hitting a dog in the water; in other words, do not take pity on a dangerous enemy)

落泊 **lò-p'ó** dejected, downhearted; to be a failure

落拓 **lò-t'ò** unorganized and undisciplined, desultory

lóu (lóu)

1360 楼房 **lóu-fáng** a building of more than one storey

楼梯 **lóu-t'ī** a staircase

1361 喽啰 **lóu-lo** a bandit's lackey, gangster underling

lòu (lòu)

1362 漏气漏油 **lòu-ch'ì-lòu-yú** leaking steam and oil (faulty machinery)

漏掉 **lòu-tiào** to omit, overlook, miss, leave out; omission

漏洞 **lòu-tùng** a loophole, shortcoming

漏洞百出 **lòu-tùng-pǎi-ch'ū** a hundred holes appear (full of loopholes)

漏网 **lòu-wǎng** to escape from the net

1363 露出马脚 **lòu-ch'ū-mǎ-chiǎo** the horse's hoof is revealed (to reveal one's true character; the plot is revealed)

露出破绽 **lòu-ch'ū-p'ò-chàn** the open seam is revealed (the matter is divulged)

露一手 **lòu-ī-shǒu** to show one's hand (to demonstrate skill)

露面 **lòu-mièn** to appear in public, show up, appear

露原形 **lòu-yuán-hsíng** to reveal one's

true colors

露 **lòu**: *see also* **lù**

lú (lú)

1364 卢萨卡 **lú-sà-k'ǎ** Lusaka [Zambia]

卢森堡 **lú-sēn-pǎo** Luxemburg

卢旺达 **lú-wàng-tá** [Republic of] Rwanda

1365 庐山会议 **lú-shān huì-ì** Lushan meeting (the 8th plenum of the 8th Central Committee in the fall of 1959, resulting in the purge of P'eng Te-huai)

lǔ (lǔ)

1366 掳掠 **lǔ-luèh** to plunder, rob, pillage

1367 鲁 **lǔ** Shantung province

鲁迅 **lǔ hsùn** Lu Hsun (the pen name of Chou Shu-jen, 1881–1936, novelist, essayist, and critic)

鲁莽 **lǔ-mǎng** rude, ill-mannered, uncivil, discourteous; reckless, rash, careless

lù (lù)

1368 陆军 **lù-chǔn** the army, land forces

陆续 **lù-hsù** one after another, continuous, successive, from time to time

1369 录音 **lù-yīn** to record sound, record on tape

录音机 **lù-yīn-chī** a recording machine, tape recorder

录音广播 **lù-yīn-kuǎng-pò** to broadcast by electrical transcription; a recorded broadcast

1370 路见不平, 拔刀相助 **lù-chièn-pù-p'íng, pá-tāo-hsiāng-chù** seeing in the street and injustice, [one] draws sword to help the victim

路线 **lù-hsièn** a course, road, route, direction, line (generally refers to a broad political policy directed toward ultimate, long-range goals)

路线教育 **lù-hsièn-chiào-yù** line education (political indoctrination, which may include education and all forms of propaganda activity, to obtain general acceptance and understanding of basic policies)

路线觉悟 **lù-hsièn-chüéh-wù** consciousness of the line (the successful result of line education)

路线是个纲, 纲举目张 **lù-hsièn shìh ko kāng, kāng-chǔ-mù-chāng** the line is the key and, once it is grasped, everything falls into place.

路线斗争 **lù-hsièn-tòu-chēng** the struggle between [socialist and capitalist] lines

路线对了头，一步一层楼 **lù-hsièn tùi-le-t'óu, ī-pù ī-ts'éng-lóu** when one is matched up with the [right] line then each step is like rising one storey

路线错误 **lù-hsièn-ts'ò-wù** errors of line

路易斯港 **lù-ì-szū-kǎng** Port Louis [Mauritius]

路人皆知 **lù-jén-chiēh-chīh** known to every man in the street (common knowledge)

路不拾遗 **lù-pù-shíh-í** [articles left] on the road are not lost (efficient government administration; high degree of peace and order)

路条 **lù-t'iáo** an internal travel pass, a safe-conduct pass

路透社 **lù-t'òu-shè** Reuter's News Agency

路子广 **lù-tzu-kuǎng** the road is wide (many opportunities; varied chances of improvement, progress or development)

路遥知马力，日久见人心 **lù-yáo chīh mǎ-lì, jìh-chiǔ chièn jén-hsīn** [it takes] a long road to know a horse's strength [and] a long time to see a man's heart

¹³⁷¹ 露骨 **lù-kǔ** the bones exposed (obvious, undisguised, plain, transparent; candid, outspoken, without reserve)

露天 **lù-t'iēn** open-air, under the sky

露天开采 **lù-t'iēn-k'āi-ts'ǎi** open-cut mining, surface mining, strip mining

露天矿 **lù-t'iēn-k'uàng** an open-cut mine, strip mine

露天作业 **lù-t'iēn-tsò-yèh** outdoor operation; to carry on work in the open

露头 **lù-t'óu** an outcropping

露 **lù:** *see also* **lòu**

lǚ (lǚ)

¹³⁷² 旅进旅退 **lǚ-chìn-lǚ-t'uì** to advance together and retreat together

旅行 **lǚ-hsíng** to travel, tour, journey in a group

旅行社 **lǚ-hsíng-shè** travel service (in China normally refers to the China Travel Service—Luxingshe)

旅行遊览事业 **lǚ-hsíng yú-lǎn shìh-yèh** travel and tourism

旅客 **lǚ-k'ò** a traveler, passenger, tourist

旅大 **lǚ-tà** Lushun-Dairen (a new municipality comprising the former Port Arthur and Dairen)

旅委 **lǚ-wěi** brigade Party committee

旅游 **lǚ-yú** travel and tourism

旅游局 **lǚ-yú-chú** Bureau of Tourism (under the Ministry of Foreign Affairs)

¹³⁷³ 铝制品 **lǚ-chìh-p'ǐn** aluminum articles, aluminum products

铝礬土 **lǚ-fán-t'ǔ** bauxite

¹³⁷⁴ 屡教不改 **lǚ-chiào-pù-kǎi** repeated teaching without correcting [one's mistakes]

屡见不鲜 **lǚ-chièn-pù-hsiēn** commonly seen and not rare

屡试不爽 **lǚ-shìh-pù-shuǎng** to undergo many tests without failure

屡次 **lǚ-tz'ù** again and again, time after time, frequently, repeatedly

¹³⁷⁵ 履行 **lǚ-hsíng** to implement, fulfill, discharge, carry out, accomplish, perform, observe, abide by

履行诺言 **lǚ-hsíng-nò-yén** to keep one's word, live up to one's promise

履带 **lǚ-tài** track [of a vehicle], caterpillar treads

lù (lù)

¹³⁷⁶ 律师 **lù-shīh** a lawyer

¹³⁷⁷ 绿洲 **lù-chōu** an oasis

绿肥 **lù-féi** green fertilizer (a crop which is plowed under while green for its nutrient value to the soil)

绿肥作物 **lù-féi-tsò-wù** green fertilizer crops

绿化 **lù-huà** to "green," afforestation (to cover denuded wasteland and mountains with greenery)

绿化荒山 **lù-huà huāng-shān** to "green" the barren mountains, afforestation

绿化祖国 **lù-huà-tsǔ-kuó** to make the fatherland green

luǎn (luǎn)

¹³⁷⁸ 卵翼 **luǎn-ì** to hatch under the wing (to shelter, protect)

luàn (luàn)

¹³⁷⁹ 乱纪 **luàn-chì** to violate discipline, break rules; disorder

乱抓 **luàn-chuā** to grab wildly (disregarding proper channels of authority and responsibility)

乱七八糟 **luàn-ch'ī-pā-tsāo** seven in disorder and eight in a mess (in great confusion, an awful mess, topsy-turvy)

乱反对一气 **luàn-fǎn-tuì-ī-ch'ì** a reckless spirit of opposition, willful and

non-selective opposition

乱放一通 **luàn-fàng-ì-t'ūng** to shoot [arrows] in every direction (irresponsible accusations)

乱放炮 **luàn-fàng-p'ào** to fire at random (often figurative)

乱干 **luàn-kàn** to do haphazardly, act in a disordered way

乱搞 **luàn-kǎo** to make a mess

乱搞男女关系 **luàn-kǎo nán-nǚ kuān-hsi** to engage in improper sexual relationships

乱来一阵 **luàn-lái-ì-chèn** to act foolishly, go off half-cocked

乱了套 **luàn-le-t'ào** to disarrange, mix up the proper order

乱骂 **luàn-mà** to vilify, abuse foully, curse without justification

乱跑乱说 **luàn-p'ǎo-luàn-shuō** to dash about and talk in a scatterbrained way

乱跑乱窜 **luàn-p'ǎo-luàn-ts'uàn** running about and fleeing in every direction

乱杀 **luàn-shā** to kill without discrimination; reckless slaughter

乱说一顿 **luàn-shuō-ì-tùn** irresponsible talk; to talk without restraint

乱说乱动 **luàn-shuō-luàn-tùng** to talk and act in a wholly irresponsible way

乱子 **luàn-tzu** a disturbance, trouble

lùeh (lüè)

1380 掠过 **lùeh-kuò** to flash past, sideswipe, brush past, "buzz" [of airplanes]

掠夺 **lùeh-tó** to plunder, pillage, despoil, rob, seize

1381 略加点缀 **lùeh-chiā-tièn-chuì** to add a few things for show

略见一斑 **lùeh-chièn-ì-pān** from a glimpse the whole can be inferred

略前详后 **lùeh-ch'ién-hsiáng-hòu** brief in the early period and detailed in the later period

略去 **lùeh-ch'ǜ** to omit, leave out, delete; a hiatus

略而不谈 **lùeh-érh-pù-t'án** to omit and not mention, skip over

略胜一筹 **lùeh-shèng-ì-ch'óu** slightly better in comparison to, somewhat superior

略述 **lùeh-shù** to describe briefly, summarize; brief, outline

略为 **lùeh-wéi** slightly, a little, somewhat

lūn (lūn)

1382 抡起胳膊 **lūn-ch'ǐ-kō-po** to swing the arm [to go to work]

lún (lún)

1383 伦理学 **lún-lǐ-hsuéh** ethics

伦敦 **lún-tūn** London

1384 轮换 **lún-huàn** to go by turns, alternate, rotate

轮换制度 **lún-huàn-chìh-tù** a rotation system

轮换劳动 **lún-huàn-láo-tùng** to take turns in physical labor, rotational work

轮训 **lún-hsùn** to receive training on a rotation basis

轮训班 **lún-hsùn-pān** a training class operating on a rotating basis

轮廓 **lún-k'uò** an outline, silhouette, contour, sketch, general layout

轮流 **lún-liú** to take turns, rotate

轮流下放 **lún-liú-hsià-fàng** to take turns in in going down [to the countryside]

轮流作庄 **lún-liú-tsò-chuāng** to take turns in being the dealer (an allegedly rightist idea that political power should not be the monopoly of one group or party)

轮班 **lún-pān** to take turns, rotate, take shifts

轮驳船 **lún-pó-ch'uán** steamships and lighters

轮作 **lún-tsò** crop rotation

lùn (lùn)

1385 论战 **lùn-chàn** a war of theories, polemic

论证 **lùn-chèng** to argue, prove, demonstrate; proof

论持久战 **lùn ch'íh-chiǔ-chàn** "On Protracted War" (written by Mao Tse-tung in 1938)

论处 **lùn-ch'ǔ** to deal with, punish [according to the offense]

论据 **lùn-chù** grounds [of an argument], data, evidence, facts

论共产党员的修养 **lùn kùng-ch'ǎn-tǎng-yuán te hsiū-yǎng** On Self-Cultivation of a Communist (a booklet by Liu Shao-ch'i in 1939: also translated as How to Be a Good Communist)

论理 **lùn-lǐ** to reason, logic

论理认识 **lùn-lǐ-jèn-shíh** logical knowledge, deductive knowledge

论联合政府 **lùn lién-hó-chèng-fǔ** "On Coalition Government" (written by Mao Tse-tung in 1945)

论述 **lùn-shù** to discuss, discourse, deal with

论调 **lùn-tiào** the tone of a statement,

theme of an argument

论点 **lùn-tiĕn** the point at issue; a standpoint, viewpoint; opinion, assertion, contention

论断 **lùn-tuàn** to discuss and judge; judgment, opinion, conclusion

论坛 **lùn-t'án** a forum, tribune of opinion

论资排辈 **lùn-tzū-p'ái-pèi** to consider qualifications and arrange ranks according to seniority

论文 **lùn-wén** an essay, discourse, treatise, thesis, dissertation

lúng (lóng)

1386　龙江颂 **lúng-chiāng-sùng** "Song of the Dragon River" (a later addition to the original group of **yàng pǎn hsì**)

龙须沟 **lúng-hsū-kōu** Dragon Whiskers Ditch (a notorious slum in Peking, whose clearance in the early 1950s was dramatized by Lao She in a novel and film as a model)

龙潭虎穴 **lúng-t'án-hǔ-hsuèh** dragon's pool and tiger's den (a very dangerous place)

龙套 **lúng-t'ào** a dragon coat (a reference to the costume in classical opera worn by guards of nobles: hence, a supernumerary or unimportant role)

龙腾虎跃 **lúng-t'éng-hǔ-yuèh** the dragon soars and the tiger leaps (full of vigor and vitality)

龙头 **lúng-t'óu** (1) a water faucet, hydrant; (2) the leader of a secret society

龙舞 **lúng-wǔ** dragon dance

1387　隆重接待 **lúng-chùng-chiēh-tài** an impressive reception

隆重举行 **lúng-chùng chǔ-hsíng** to carry out in an impressive and solemn manner

隆重开幕 **lúng-chùng k'āi-mù** to open with impressive ceremony

1388　聋哑针灸治疗 **lúng-yǎ chēn-chiǔ-chìh-liáo** acupuncture treatment of deaf mutes

lǔng (lǒng)

1389　陇 **lǔng** Kansu province

陇海铁路 **lǔng-hǎi t'iĕh-lù** the railway from Lienyunkang (Kiangsu) to Lanchow (Kansu)

1390　垄断 **lǔng-tuàn** to monopolize; a monopoly

垄断价格 **lǔng-tuàn-chià-kó** to impose a monopoly price

垄断市场 **lǔng-tuàn-shìh-ch'ǎng** to monopolize the market

垄断资产阶级 **lǔng-tuàn tzū-ch'ǎn-chiēh-chí** the monopoly capitalist class

垄断资本 **lǔng-tuàn-tzū-pĕn** monopoly capital

垄断资本主义 **lǔng-tuàn tzū-pĕn-chǔ-ì** monopoly capitalism

垄断财团 **lǔng-tuàn-ts'ái-t'uán** a monopolistic financial group

1391　笼罩 **lǔng-chào** to cover completely; overshadow; coop up; permeate

笼统 **lǔng-t'ǔng** generalized, sweeping, indiscriminate, unspecified

笼统平均数 **lǔng-t'ǔng p'íng-chǔn-shù** a general average

má (má)

1392　麻疹 **má-chĕn** measles

麻织品 **má-chīh-p'ǐn** linen fabrics

麻雀 **má-ch'uèh** sparrows

麻雀虽小，五脏俱全 **má-ch'uèh suī hsiǎo, wǔ-tsàng chù-ch'uán** though a sparrow is small, it is complete with all the essential organs

麻纺厂 **má-fǎng-ch'ǎng** flax-spinning factory

麻疯 **má-fēng** leprosy

麻木不仁 **má-mù-pù-jén** numbed and without feeling (paralyzed; indifferent, unsympathetic, callous)

麻痹 **má-pì** paralysis, palsy; insensitive, numb

麻痹思想 **má-pì szū-hsiǎng** insensitive thinking, insensitivity

麻痹大意 **má-pì tà-ì** insensitive and negligent, lacking vigilance, careless

麻丝 **má-szū** hemp and silk

麻醉 **má-tsuì** to numb the feelings, anesthetize, drug, dope, render unconscious

麻醉剂 **má-tsuì-chì** an anesthetic, narcotic

麻醉品 **má-tsuì-p'ǐn** anesthetics, narcotics

mǎ (mǎ)

1393　马鞍形 **mǎ-ān-hsíng** shaped like a saddle, U-shaped

马尔加什 **mǎ-ĕrh-chiā-shíh** Malagasy

马尔代夫 **mǎ-ĕrh-tài-fū** Maldives

马耳他 **mǎ-ĕrh-t'ā** Malta

马放南山 **mǎ-fàng-nán-shān** the horses have been put to pasture in the southern mountains (an end to hostilities, peaceful conditions)

马后炮 **mǎ-hòu-p'ào** to fire a [cere-

monial] salute after the [man on the] horse has passed (belated effort, useless talk after the event)

马虎 **mǎ-hu** perfunctory, careless, sloppy, slovenly

马戏团 **mǎ-hsì-t'uán** a circus

马歇尔 **mǎ-hsiēh-ěrh** Marshall [George C., 1880–1959]

马歇尔计划 **mǎ-hsiēh-ěrh chì-huà** the Marshall Plan

马日事变 **mǎ-jìh shìh-pièn** the Ma-jih Incident (the suppression of revolutionary organizations in Changsha by General Hsu K'o-hsiang on May 21, 1927; *mǎ* is 21st in the telegraphic code)

马克思 **mǎ-k'ò-szū** Marx [Karl, 1818–1883]

马克思主义 **mǎ-k'ò-szū-chǔ-ì** Marxism

马克思列宁主义 **mǎ-k'ò-szū lièh-níng chǔ-ì** Marxism-Leninism

马克思列宁主义政党 **mǎ-k'ò-szū lièh-níng chǔ-ì chèng-tǎng** the political party of Marxism-Leninism

马克思列宁主义理论 **mǎ-k'ò-szū lièh-níng-chǔ-ì lǐ-lùn** the theory of Marxism-Leninism

马拉维 **mǎ-lā-wéi** Malawi [formerly Nyasaland]

马来西亚 **mǎ-lái-hsī-yà** Malaysia

马来亚 **mǎ-lái-yà** Malaya

马累 **mǎ-lèi** Male [Republic of Maldives]

马里 **mǎ-lǐ** [Republic of] Mali

马力 **mǎ-lì** horsepower

马列 **mǎ-lièh** Marx and Lenin, Marxist-Leninist

马列主义 **mǎ-lièh-chǔ-ì** Marxism-Leninism

马列主义理论 **mǎ-lièh-chǔ-ì lǐ-lùn** Marxist-Leninist theory

马铃薯 **mǎ-líng-shǔ** the white potato

马马虎虎 **mǎ-ma hū-hu** perfunctory, careless, sloppy, mediocre, so-so

马那瓜 **mǎ-nà-kuā** Managua [Nicaragua]

马尼拉 **mǎ-ní-lā** Manila

马不停蹄 **mǎ-pù-t'íng-t'í** without stopping the horse's hooves (to do without stopping; continuous, unceasing, untiring)

马塞卢 **mǎ-sài-lú** Maseru [Lesotho (formerly Basutoland)]

马首是瞻 **mǎ-shǒu-shìh-chān** to look up to the head of [another's] horse (to follow obediently; be guided by; dance to the leadership of)

马斯喀特 **mǎ-szū-k'ā-t'è** Muscat [Oman]

马达 **mǎ-tá** a motor

马大哈 **mǎ tà-hā** the name of a minor stage character who was so careless that he ordered actual monkeys instead of Monkey brand soap (used to typify a feckless minor bureaucrat)

马到成功 **mǎ-tào-ch'éng-kūng** as soon as the horse arrives, it will be accomplished (quickly and easily done)

马德里 **mǎ-té-lǐ** Madrid [Spain]

1394 吗啡 **mǎ-fēi** morphine

1395 码头 **mǎ-t'óu** a wharf, dock, pier

码头主人, 吨位奴隶 **mǎ-t'óu chǔ-jén, tūn-wèi nú-lì** [be] the master of the docks, [not] the slave of tonnage (dock workers should take more thar. mere tonnage as the criterion of excellence)

1396 蚂蚁啃骨头 **mǎ-ì k'ěn kú-t'óu** ants gnawing at a bone (making huge machines with small machine tools)

蚂蚁社 **mǎ-ì-shè** the Ant Society (a group of Communist intellectuals in Shanghai in the 1930s)

蚂 **mǎ**: *see also* **mà**

mà (mà)

1397 蚂蚱 **mà-cha** the locust, grasshopper

蚂 **mà**: *see also* **mǎ**

mái (mái)

1398 埋伏 **mái-fú** to ambush, lie in wait for

埋头 **mái-t'óu** to bury one's head, devote oneself to, be immersed in, engrossed with

埋头干和抬头看结合起来 **mái-t'óu-kàn hó t'ái-t'óu-k'àn chiéh-hó ch'ǐ-lái** to combine engrossing oneself in action with raising one's head to see

埋头苦干 **mái-t'óu k'ǔ-kàn** to be engrossed in hard work

埋头读书 **mái-t'óu tú-shū** over-concentration on study (ignoring practice)

埋葬 **mái-tsàng** to bury [a corpse]

埋葬帝修反 **mái-tsàng tì-hsiū-fǎn** to bury imperialists, revisionists, and counter-revolutionaries

埋藏 **mái-ts'áng** to bury [a treasure, etc.], to conceal, hide

埋 **mái**: *see also* **mán**

mǎi (mǎi)

1399 买卖婚姻 **mǎi-mài hūn-yīn** marriage on a mercenary basis (traditional marriage with gifts and monetary considerations)

买办 **mǎi-pàn** a compradore

买办阶级 **mǎi-pàn chiēh-chí** the compradore class

买办封建制度 **mǎi-pàn fēng-chièn chìh-tù** the compradore-feudal system

买办大资产阶级 **mǎi-pàn tà-tzū-ch'ǎn-chiēh-chí** the compradore bourgeoisie

买办洋奴哲学 **mǎi-pàn yáng-nú ché-hsuéh** the compradore foreign slave mentality

买办洋奴爬行哲学 **mǎi-pàn yáng-nú p'á-hsíng ché-hsuéh** the compradore foreign slave, crawling mentality (the attitude of those who look abroad for solutions to China's problems)

mài (mài)

1400　迈进一大步 **mài-chìn ī tà-pù** to take a big stride forward

迈开 **mài-k'āi** to step out, take a big step

1401　麦贤得 **mài hsién-té** Mai Hsien-te (a sailor who performed heroically after having been injured by shrapnel, becoming a national examplar)

麦克马洪线 **mài-k'ò-mǎ-húng hsièn** the MacMahon line [between Tibet and India]

麦什哈特阿曼 **mài-shíh-hǎ-t'è ā-màn** Muscat and Oman [now simply Oman]

1402　卖狗皮膏药 **mài kǒu-p'í kāo-yào** to sell dog skin ointment (to offer a fake panacea; make wild claims)

卖光 **mài-kuāng** to sell out

卖国 **mài-kuó** to sell out one's country, sedition, treason

卖国集团 **mài-kuó-chí-t'uán** a traitorous clique

卖国主义 **mài-kuó-chǔ-ì** "traitor-ism"

卖国求荣 **mài-kuó-ch'iú-júng** to seek glory by selling out one's country, betray one's country for high position

卖国条约 **mài-kuó-t'iáo-yuēh** treasonable treaties

卖国贼 **mài-kuó-tséi** a traitor, one who collaborates with an enemy country

卖空买空 **mài-k'ūng-mǎi-k'ūng** to buy and sell empty (to speculate in politics)

卖力 **mài-lì** to work as a laborer; work hard willingly

卖命 **mài-mìng** to work hard at the risk of one's life

卖弄 **mài-nùng** to flaunt, flourish, show off, make a display

卖身契 **mài-shēn-ch'ì** a contract for the sale of a person [as a servant]

卖身投靠 **mài-shēn-t'óu-k'ào** to sell oneself in exchange for a livelihood and protection

1403　脉管 **mài-kuǎn** the pulse [physiology]

脉搏 **mài-pó** a pulse, pulsation, pulsating movement

mán (mán)

1404　埋怨 **mán-yuàn** to complain, grumble, blame

埋 **mán:** see also **mǎi**

1405　蛮横 **mán-hèng** barbarous, savage, unreasonable, overbearing

蛮横无理 **mán-hèng-wú-lǐ** outrageous and unreasonable

蛮干 **mán-kàn** to go ahead without considering the consequences, reckless action

蛮不讲理 **mán-pù-chiǎng-lǐ** impervious to reason, high-handed, brutal, rude

1406　瞒过 **mán-kuò** to deceive, conceal from, cover up

瞒天过海 **mán-t'iēn-kuò-hǎi** sailing the seas under a false flag (clever and daring in deceiving others)

mǎn (mǎn)

1407　满招损，谦受益 **mǎn-chāo-sǔn, chiēn-shòu-ì** haughtiness invites loss while modesty receives benefit

满架葡萄一条根 **mǎn-chià-p'ú-t'ao ī-t'iáo-kēn** the arbor is full of grapes, but there is only one root (everything depends on the root—which can normally be understood to be the Party)

满城风雨 **mǎn-ch'éng fēng-yǔ** the whole city [is covered by] wind and rain (news that quickly spreads and causes general concern)

满期 **mǎn-ch'ī** the expiration of a given period; run out of time, expire

满腔热情 **mǎn-ch'iāng-jè-ch'ing** one's breast full of warm emotion (full of patriotic fervor)

满腔悲愤 **mǎn-ch'iāng-pēi-fèn** the breast is full of grief and anger

满腔同情 **mǎn-ch'iāng-t'úng-ch'íng** heart-felt sympathy

满负荷 **mǎn-fù-hò** a capacity load [of electricity]

满怀 **mǎn-huái** a heart full [of sorrow, etc.]

满怀喜悦 **mǎn-huái-hsǐ-yuèh** full of joy

满怀信心 **mǎn-huái-hsìn-hsīn** full of confidence

满怀革命豪情 **mǎn-huái kó-mìng-háo-ch'íng** full of revolutionary élan

满意 **mǎn-ì** to satisfy; be satisfied,

content; satisfactory

满面春风 **măn-mièn-ch'ūn-fēng** a face full of spring breezes (beaming with pleasure)

满盘皆输 **măn-p'án-chiēh-shū** the whole board [of a chess game] is lost (all is lost, total defeat)

满身伤疤 **măn-shēn-shāng-pā** the body is covered with scars (may be figurative)

满、松、停错误思想 **măn-sūng-t'íng ts'ò-wù-szū-hsiăng** the ideological errors of self-complacency, relaxation of effort, and cessation [of the revolution]

满堂红 **măn-t'áng-húng** to cover the hall in red (glorious success; to make the whole production area prosperous)

满堂灌 **măn-t'áng-kuàn** the whole [class] period of forced feeding (continuous cramming by the teacher —without practical work or development of student initiative)

满天阴霾 **măn-t'iēn yĭn-mái** a sky full of dense clouds (dark prospects)

满载超轴运动 **măn-tsài ch'āo-chóu yùn-tùng** the campaign for hauling capacity loads

满座 **măn-tsò** all seats taken, full house, all the people present

满足现状 **măn-tsú hsièn-chuàng** satisfied with the status quo

满族 **măn-tsú** the Manchu people (a minority in Peking, Hopei, Inner Mongolia, and Northeast China: population 2,430,000 as of 1957)

màn (màn)

1408   曼谷 **màn-kŭ** Bangkok

曼纳马 **màn-nà-mă** Manamah [Bahrein]

1409   漫长 **màn-ch'áng** endless, infinite

漫长曲折 **màn-ch'áng-ch'ŭ-ché** long and tortuous

漫画 **màn-huà** a cartoon, caricature; a monthly magazine published in Peking by the Union of Chinese Artists

漫不经心 **màn-pù-chīng-hsīn** carelessly without taking heed (heedless, unmindful, inattentive)

漫山遍野 **màn-shān-p'ièn-yěh** all over the hills and fields (everywhere, very numerous)

漫谈 **màn-t'án** casual comment, rambling talk

漫天要价 **màn-t'iēn-yào-chià** to demand sky-high prices

1410   慢性病 **màn-hsìng-pìng** a chronic disease, creeping illness

慢条斯理 **màn-t'iáo-szū-lĭ** unhurriedly, leisurely, without haste

1411   蔓延 **màn-yén** to spread, sweep over, grow widely

máng (máng)

1412   忙来忙去 **máng-lái-máng-ch'ù** busily coming and busily going (usually suggests busily engaged in petty affairs)

1413   芒刺在背 **máng-tz'ù-tsài-pèi** thorns in one's back (to feel uneasy)

1414   盲人瞎马 **máng-jén-hsiā-mă** a blind man [on] a blind horse (frightening and dangerous, a dangerous situation)

盲人摸象 **máng-jén-mō-hsiàng** a blind man feeling the elephant (to know only a part of the whole)

盲目 **máng-mù** blind; lacking insight, without understanding; reckless, aimless

盲目抄袭 **máng-mù-ch'āo-hsí** blind imitation (such as excessive copying from Soviet models)

盲目崇拜 **máng-mù-ch'úng-pài** blind worship, blind faith

盲目发展 **máng-mù-fā-chăn** blind expansion, unplanned development

盲目活动 **máng-mù-huó-tùng** haphazard activity

盲目性 **máng-mù-hsìng** thoughtlessness, blindness

盲目乐观 **máng-mù-lè-kuān** blindly optimistic, recklessly optimistic

盲目乱干一通 **máng-mù luàn-kān ī-t'ūng** to do something in a blindly haphazard way

盲目生产 **máng-mù-shēng-ch'ăn** blind production (production without planning)

盲动主义 **máng-tùng-chŭ-ì** blind activism, adventurism, putschism

盲从 **máng-ts'úng** to blindly follow

1415   茫然 **máng-ján** vague, uncertain, bewildered, confused, ignorant

茫然无知 **máng-ján-wú-chīh** completely unaware of, helplessly ignorant, at a loss

茫茫千里 **máng-máng ch'iēn-lĭ** a vast area

茫茫然浑沌沌 **máng-máng-ján hún-t'ùn-t'ùn** hazy and obscure (politically unaware and fuzzy)

máo (máo)

1416   毛织品 **máo-chīh-p'ĭn** woolen fabrics,

woolen goods

毛斤定价 **máo-chīn-tìng-chià** price determined by gross weight [of pigs]

毛斤定等 **máo-chīn-tìng-těng** quality [of the pigs] determined by gross weight

毛竹 **máo-chú** heavy bamboo (used in construction, etc.)

毛主席十大军事原则 **máo chǔ-hsí shíh-tà chǔn-shìh yuán-tsé** Chairman Mao's Ten Military Principles (December 1947)

毛主席语录 **máo-chǔ-hsí yǔ-lù** *Quotations from Chairman Mao* (the "Little Red Book")

毛重 **máo-chùng** gross weight

毛产 **máo-ch'ǎn** gross output

毛儿盖会议 **máo-érh-kài huì-ì** the Maoerhkai Conference (a meeting of Communist leaders, including Chang Kuo-t'ao, at the town of this name in northern Szechwan in July 1935)

毛纺织厂 **máo-fǎng-chīh-ch'ǎng** woolen textile factory

毛线 **máo-hsièn** knitting wool

毛选 **máo-hsuǎn** *The Selected Works of Mao Tse-tung* (contraction of **máo tsé-tūng hsuǎn-chí**)

毛骨悚然 **máo-kǔ-sǔng-ján** hair rising and flesh creeping (frightening, horrible)

毛孔 **máo-k'ǔng** pores [of the skin]

毛里求斯 **máo-lǐ-ch'iú-szū** Mauritius

毛利 **máo-lì** gross profit

毛料 **máo-liào** woolen materials, wool cloth

毛毛楞楞 **máo-máo léng-léng** awkward and uncultivated, rough and unpolished

毛难族 **máo-nán-tsú** the Mao-nan people (a minority in the Kwangsi Chuang Autonomous Region: population 24,000 as of 1957)

毛病 **máo-ping** illness, sickness, disability, weakness, shortcoming, fault, trouble

毛皮 **máo-p'í** furs, pelts

毛泽东主义 **máo tsé-tūng chǔ-ì** "Maoism," the doctrines espoused by Mao Tse-tung (not an officially recognized term)

毛泽东选集 **máo tsé-tūng hsuǎn-chí** *The Selected Works of Mao Tse-tung*

毛泽东时代 **máo tsé-tūng shíh-tài** the era of Mao Tse-tung

毛泽东思想 **máo tsé-tūng-szū-hsiǎng** the Thought of Mao Tse-tung

毛泽东思想宣传队 **máo tsé-tūng szū-hsiǎng hsuān-ch'uán-tuì** Mao Tse-tung Thought propaganda team

(selected teams of workers under PLA guidance who entered schools and other units controlled by intellectuals during the Cultural Revolution to settle factional strife and apply the proletarian line)

毛泽东思想学习班 **máo tsé-tūng szū-hsiǎng hsuéh-hsí-pān** Thought of Mao Tse-tung study groups

毛泽东思想挂帅 **Máo Tsé-tūng szū-hsiǎng kuà-shuài** the Thought of Mao Tse-tung takes command

毛泽东思想大学校 **máo tsé-tūng szū-hsiǎng tà-hsuéh-hsiào** [the whole country should be] a great school of the Thought of Mao Tse-tung

毛泽东思想伟大红旗 **máo tsé-tūng szū-hsiǎng wěi-tà húng-ch'í** the great red flag of Mao Tse-tung's Thought

1417 矛盾 **máo-tùn** a contradiction, antagonism

矛盾尖锐化 **máo-tùn chiēn-juì-huà** the sharpening of contradictions, intensification of contradictions

矛盾重重 **máo-tùn ch'úng-ch'úng** the multiplicity of contradictions

矛盾论 **máo-tùn lù** the law of contradiction

矛盾论 **máo-tùn lùn** "On Contradiction" (by Mao Tse-tung, August 1937)

矛盾普遍性 **máo-tùn p'ǔ-pièn-hsìng** the universality of contradictions

矛盾的对立 **máo-tùn-le tuì-lì** the opposites in a contradiction

矛盾的对立面 **máo-tùn-te tuì-lì-mièn** the opposing facets of a contradiction

矛盾的统一 **máo-tùn-te t'ǔng-ī** the unity of contradictions

矛盾特殊性 **máo-tùn t'è-shū-hsìng** the particularity of contradictions

矛头 **máo-t'óu** the point of a lance, spearhead

矛头指向 **máo-t'óu chǐh-hsiàng** to be spearheaded at, the spearhead points toward

1418 茅房 **máo-fáng** the reed shelter (a privy)

茅棚 **máo-p'éng** a mat awning, a straw shed

茅台酒 **máo-t'ái-chiǔ** Maotai liquor (a distilled liquor of very high proof of a kind made in the Kweichow town of Maotai)

1419 牦牛 **máo-niú** the yak [Tibetan ox]

1420 锚地 **máo-tì** an anchorage

mǎo (mǎo)

1421 铆工 **mǎo-kūng** a riveter; riveting

mào (mào)

1422 冒尖 **mào-chiēn** outstanding, prominent, extraordinary

冒进 **mào-chìn** to advance recklessly (to proceed in an adventurist manner)

冒出 **mào-ch'ū** to put forth incautiously (imprudent publication of articles, etc.)

冒充 **mào-ch'ūng** to pretend to be someone else, use a substitute instead of the genuine, pose as

冒犯 **mào-fàn** to violate openly, offend

冒风险 **mào-fēng-hsiěn** to brave danger, take chances

冒险 **mào-hsiěn** to take risks, brave danger; adventure

冒险政策 **mào-hsiěn-chèng-ts'è** an adventurist policy

冒险主义 **mào-hsiěn-chǔ-ì** adventurism

冒冒失失 **mào-mao-shīh-shih** rash, imprudent, hasty, reckless; absent-minded, disorderly

冒昧 **mào-mèi** presumptuous, rash; to take the liberty of, presume [used as a polite expression]

冒牌 **mào-p'ái** to forge a label, infringe a trademark (bogus, counterfeit, false, fake)

冒天下之大不韪 **mào t'iēn-hsià chìh tà-pù-wěi** to dare to do what the whole country considers to be the greatest mistake

冒头 **mào-t'óu** to emerge, begin to appear

1423 贸易 **mào-ì** to trade, barter, exchange; trade

贸易协定 **mào-ì hsiéh-tìng** a trade agreement [between nations]

贸易议定书 **mào-ì ì-tìng-shū** a trade protocol, trade agreement

贸易枢纽 **mào-ì shū-niǔ** a trade center, nexus of trade

1424 帽子 **mào-tzu** a hat (figuratively—a label)

1425 貌合神离 **mào-hó-shén-lí** in appearance harmonious but in spirit divided

貌不惊人 **mào-pù-chīng-jén** an appearance that does not attract others (ordinary in appearance)

貌似强大 **mào-szù-ch'iáng-tà** to appear to be powerful, outwardly strong

貌似公正 **mào-szù-kūng-chèng** to pretend an air of justice

méi (méi)

1426 没精打采 **méi-chīng-tǎ-ts'ǎi** dispirited and discouraged (listless, indifferent, dejected, disheartened)

没棱没角 **méi-léng-méi-chiǎo** no ridges and no corners (a person lacking in individuality or character)

没有瓜不连在藤上 **méi-yǔ kuā pù-lién-tsài t'éng-shang** there is no melon that is not connected to a vine (everything depends on the correct line)

没有功劳，也有苦劳 **méi-yǔ kūng-láo, yěh-yǔ k'ǔ-láo** [although] there is no record of achievement, there is a record of hard work

没有什么了不起 **méi-yǔ-shén-ma liǎo-pu-ch'ǐ** nothing to be impressed by, nothing wonderful

没有调查研究就没有发言权 **méi-yǔ tiào-ch'á yén-chiū chiù méi-yǔ fā-yén-ch'üán** without having done investigation and research one has no right to speak

没 **méi:** see also **mò**

1427 玫瑰滑稽剧团 **méi-kuèi huá-chì chù-t'uán** the Rose Burlesque Troupe (a comedy company, attacked during mid-1957 for satirizing the Party)

1428 眉开眼笑 **méi-k'āi yěn-hsiào** eyebrows raised and eyes laughing (a beaming countenance, delighted)

眉头一皱计上心来 **méi-t'óu-ī-chòu chì-shàng-hsīn-lái** knit your brows and a strategem will come to mind

1429 梅雨 **méi-yǔ** the plum rains (a rainy season, usually in June–July, in the lower Yangtze valley which constitutes a sort of monsoon; also called *huáng-méi-yǔ* 黄梅雨)

1430 湄公河 **méi-kūng-hó** the Mekong River

1431 煤焦油 **méi-chiāo-yú** coal tar

煤井 **méi-chǐng** a coal mine shaft, a deep coal mine

煤气 **méi-ch'ì** coal gas

煤耗 **méi-hào** coal consumption

煤坑 **méi-k'ēng** a coal pit

煤矿 **méi-k'uàng** a coal mine, colliery

煤矿藏 **méi-k'uàng-ts'áng** coal reserves, coal deposits

煤斗车 **méi-tǒu-ch'ē** a hopper car

煤炭工业 **méi-t'àn kūng-yèh** coal industry

煤炭工业部 **méi-t'àn kūng-yèh-pù** Ministry of Coal Industry [of the State Council] (merged into the Ministry of Fuel and Chemical Industry after 1969)

煤田 **méi-t'ién** coal field

煤层 **méi-ts'éng** coal seam, coal vein

煤油 **méi-yú** kerosene

煤油大王 **méi-yú-tà-wáng** the kerosene king (John D. Rockefeller)

1432 糜子 **méi-tzu** a cereal grain

糜 **méi**: *see also* **mí**

měi (měi)

1433 每日快报 **měi-jìh k'uài-pào** the *Daily Express* [London]

每况愈下 **měi-k'uàng-yù-hsià** progressively worse, from bad to worse; to deteriorate, worsen

每年一度 **měi-nién-ī-tù** once a year, yearly

1434 美蒋匪帮 **měi-chiǎng-fěi-pāng** the US Chiang [Kai-shek] bandit gang

美好 **měi-hǎo** fine, good, favorable, exquisite, beautiful

美化 **měi-huà** to "prettify;" beautification; to "Americanize"

美人计 **měi-jén-chì** a snare using a beautiful woman as a lure

美国 **měi-kuó** the United States of America, America

美国新闻处 **měi-kuó hsīn-wén-ch'ù** the United States Information Service [USIS]

美国生活方式 **měi-kuó shēng-huó-fāng-shìh** the American way of life

美国第一主义 **měi-kuó tì-ī-chǔ-ì** America first-ism

美利坚众国 **měi-lì-chiēn hó-chùng-kuó** the United States of America

美丽富饶 **měi-lì-fù-jǎo** beautiful and fertile [of a land]

美联社 **měi-lién-shè** the Associated Press [AP]

美满 **měi-mǎn** happy, content, sweet, excellent, harmonious

美满幸福 **měi-mǎn-hsìng-fú** content and happy

美妙 **měi-miào** excellent, wonderful, delicate

美名 **měi-míng** a good reputation

美属维尔京群岛 **měi-shǔ wéi-ěrh-chīng ch'ǘn-tǎo** the Virgin Islands [US]

美术 **měi-shù** the fine arts; *Fine Arts* (a magazine published in Peking by the Union of Chinese Artists)

美术创作 **měi-shù-ch'uàng-tsò** works of fine art; artistic creation

美术工作者 **měi-shù kūng-tsò-chě** an art worker

美德 **měi-té** good virtue, good character

美帝 **měi-tì** American imperialism, American imperialists

美援 **měi-yuán** American aid

美元集团 **měi-yuán-chí-t'uan** the dollar bloc

1435 镁铝砖 **měi-lǚ-chuān** magnesite brick (high temperature refractory brick for furnaces)

mèi (mèi)

1436 媚敌求荣 **mèi-tí-ch'iú-júng** to flatter an enemy to gain favor

mén (mén)

1437 门径 **mén-chìng** an approach to, access to, proper channels

门户之见 **mén-hù-chīh-chièn** sectarian views, parochial prejudices

门户开放 **mén-hù-k'āi-fàng** the open door [policy]

门户开放主义 **mén-hù-k'āi-fàng chǔ-ì** the Open Door Doctrine

门类 **mén-lèi** category, division, classification, field [academic]

门罗主义 **mén-ló-chǔ-ì** the Monroe Doctrine

门路 **mén-lù** the door and road (1. contacts, connections, or means of approach [for a job, etc.]; 2. tricks of the trade, key or tip to a beginner)

门巴族 **mén-pā-tsú** the Men-pa people (a minority in Tibet: population unknown)

门票 **mén-p'iào** a ticket of admission

门市部 **mén-shìh-pù** retail sales department

门徒 **mén-t'ú** disciple, pupil, student

门外汉 **mén-wài-hàn** an outsider, novice, layman, greenhorn

méng (méng)

1438 萌芽 **méng-yá** to sprout, bud; the initial stage, beginning

萌芽状态 **méng-yá-chuàng-t'ài** the embryonic state, formative stage

萌芽性质 **méng-yá-hsìng-chíh** embryonic characteristics

萌芽时期 **méng-yá-shíh-ch'ī** in embryo, in the rudimentary stage

1439 蒙混 **méng-hùn** to deceive by assuming a similar appearance, hoodwink, swindle

蒙混过关 **méng-hùn-kuò-kuān** to hoodwink one's way through a pass (to pass a test—as during a campaign—by deceiving the masses)

蒙罗维亚 **méng-ló-wéi-yà** Monrovia

蒙昧无知 **méng-mèi-wú-chīh** ignorant and without knowledge, stupid and unlettered

蒙蔽 **méng-pì** to delude, swindle, deceive; to conceal, keep secret

蒙得维的亚 **méng-té-wéi-tí-yà** Montevideo [Uruguay]

蒙特卡洛 **méng-t'è-k'ǎ-lò** Monte Carlo

蒙 **méng**: *see also* **měng**

1440 盟主 **méng-chǔ** the chief of an alliance (such as the USSR in the Warsaw Pact)
盟军最高司令部 **méng-chūn tsuì-kāo szū-lìng-pù** the Supreme Allied Headquarters [of the UN forces in Korea]
盟国 **méng-kuó** an allied country, allies
盟员 **méng-yuán** a member of the Democratic League

1441 朦胧 **méng-lúng** dim, vague, hazy, drowsy

měng (měng)

1442 猛涨 **měng-chǎng** to rise suddenly, soar, shoot upward, skyrocket (such as a water level or prices)
猛追穷寇 **měng-chuī ch'iúng-k'òu** hotly to pursue the defeated enemy
猛攻 **měng-kūng** to attack fiercely; a vigorous assault
猛烈 **měng-lièh** fierce, violent, ruthless
猛扑 **měng-p'ū** to rush on fiercely, pounce on, swoop upon
猛上 **měng-shàng** to leap upon [a horse] (to engage in vigorously; to make a sudden increase in production)
猛兽 **měng-shòu** fierce wild beasts, beasts of prey
猛增 **měng-tsēng** a drastic increase, sudden increase
猛促生产 **měng-ts'ù shēng-ch'ǎn** to promote a drastic increase in production

1443 蒙古 **měng-kǔ** Mongolia, Mongolian
蒙古包 **měng-kǔ-pāo** a Mongolian yurt
蒙古族 **měng-kǔ-tsú** the Mongol people (a minority in the Inner Mongolia Autonomous Region and Northeast and Northwest China: population 1,645,000 as of 1957)
蒙 **měng:** see also **méng**

1444 锰钢 **měng-kāng** manganese steel

1445 懵懵懂懂 **měng-měng tǔng-tǔng** uncomprehending, unaware, dull-witted

mèng (mèng)

1446 孟加拉 **mèng-chiā-lā** Bangladesh [formerly East Pakistan]
孟什维克 **mèng-shíh-wéi-k'ò** Menshevik

1447 梦幻泡影 **mèng-huàn-p'ào-yǐng** a dreamy illusion and an empty bubble (utterly visionary, empty illusions, a total failure)
梦想 **mèng-hsiǎng** to daydream; vain hopes
梦呓 **mèng-ì** dream talk, nonsense

梦寐以求 **mèng-mèi-ì-ch'iú** to seek even in one's dreams while asleep (earnestly to wish for)

mí (mí)

1448 弥补 **mí-pǔ** to fill up [a gap], make up [a loss], patch, supplement
弥补赤字 **mí-pǔ-ch'ìh-tzù** to make up the red letters (to cover a deficit)
弥天大谎 **mí-t'iēn tà-huǎng** a lie as big as the sky

1449 迷航 **mí-háng** off course [in sea or aerial navigation]
迷糊 **mí-hu** vague, dim, indistinct, blurred, unclear; half-conscious, in a daze
迷惑 **mí-huò** to confuse, misguide, delude; to tempt, bewitch; puzzled, confused
迷惑人心 **mí-huò-jén-hsīn** to confuse the minds of the people, delude the public
迷惑敌人 **mí-huò-tí-jén** to confuse the enemy
迷惑舆论 **mí-huò-yǔ-lùn** to confuse public opinion, befuddle the public
迷信 **mí-hsìn** to believe blindly; superstition
迷信教条 **mí-hsìn-chiào-t'iáo** to believe blindly in dogma
迷信武力 **mí-hsìn-wǔ-lì** to have blind faith in armed force
迷信用品 **mí-hsìn yùng-p'ǐn** objects used in superstitions (such as incense, paper money for burning at funerals, etc.)
迷人眼目 **mí-jén-yěn-mù** to blur the eyes (to confuse one so that he cannot tell true from false)
迷了心窍 **mí-le-hsīn-ch'iào** to befuddle the openings of the heart (to be bewitched; a person completely under another's power)
迷恋 **mí-lièn** to be infatuated, enamored of
迷路 **mí-lù** to lose the road, get lost, go astray
迷乱 **mí-luàn** bewildered, confused
迷茫 **mí-máng** hazy, vague, indistinct, obscure
迷梦 **mí-mèng** a delusive dream, illusion, delusion
迷失方向 **mí-shīh-fāng-hsiàng** to lose direction (usually in a political sense)
迷途知返 **mí-t'ú-chīh-fǎn** to know enough to turn back when one has lost the way (to be able to correct one's mistakes)
迷惘 **mí-wǎng** mentally confused,

bemused, stupified

迷雾 **mí-wù** clouds of obscurity [over the mind]

1450 糜烂 **mí-làn** mashed, rotten, corrupted, downtrodden

糜 **mí:** *see also* **méi**

1451 靡靡之音 **mí-mí-chīh-yīn** soft, seductive music

mǐ (mǐ)

1452 米制 **mǐ-chìh** the metric system

米面加工 **mǐ-mièn chiā-kūng** processing of rice and flour (rice polishing and flour milling)

米面复制品票 **mǐ-mièn fù-chìh-p'ǐn-p'iào** tickets for reprocessed products of rice and flour

mì (mì)

1453 秘方 **mì-fāng** a proprietary prescription, a handed-down secret prescription

秘密 **mì-mì** secret, private, confidential; a secret

秘密会议 **mì-mì-huì-ì** a secret meeting, closed meeting

秘密入党 **mì-mì-jù-tǎng** to join [the Communist] Party secretly

秘密投票 **mì-mì-t'óu-p'iào** secret ballot; to vote by secret ballot

秘史 **mì-shǐh** a secret history; the "inside" story

秘书 **mì-shū** a secretary [of an organization, committee, or party]

秘书长 **mì-shū-chǎng** secretary-general

秘书处 **mì-shū-ch'ù** a secretariat

1454 密集 **mì-chí** to cluster together, mass; dense, close-packed

密件 **mì-chièn** confidential papers, secret documents, classified papers; a secret article in a treaty or agreement

密植 **mì-chíh** serried-row planting, close planting

密切注意 **mì-ch'ièh chù-ì** to pay close attention

密切关注 **mì-ch'ièh kuān-chù** to have intimate concern for

密切联系 **mì-ch'ièh lién-hsì** to keep close ties with, be closely concerned with

密封 **mì-fēng** to seal off tightly; hermetic, airtight

密封仓 **mì-fēng-ts'āng** watertight compartment [ship], airtight cabin [aircraft]

密告者 **mì-kào-chě** an informer

密锣紧鼓 **mì-ló chǐn-kǔ** a rapid tattoo of gongs and drums (a fanfare)

密码电报 **mì-mǎ tièn-pào** a telegram in secret code or cipher

密谋 **mì-móu** to conspire, plot, plan secretly; a plot, secret scheme

密不通风 **mì-pù-t'ūng-fēng** so close that wind cannot blow through (tight-packed, airtight)

密商 **mì-shāng** to hold secret talks, negotiate in private

密约 **mì-yuēh** a secret treaty, secret agreement

miáo (miáo)

1455 苗头 **miáo-t'óu** the tip of a sprout (early beginning, clues, the first signs of success or failure)

苗族 **miáo-tsú** the Miao people (a minority in Kweichow, Hunan, Yunnan, Kwangsi, and Szechwan provinces: population 2,687,000 as of 1957)

1456 描写 **miáo-hsiěh** to describe, depict, portray [in writing]

描绘 **miáo-huì** to paint, sketch, depict

描述 **miáo-shù** to describe; description

1457 瞄准 **miáo-chǔn** to aim at, take aim, sight on

miǎo (miǎo)

1458 渺小 **miǎo-hsiǎo** very small, insignificant, tiny, infinitesimal

渺茫 **miǎo-máng** vast, boundless; hazy, vague, indistinct, uncertain

渺无人烟 **miǎo-wú-jén-yēn** for long distances no smoke of human [habitations] (lonely and deserted)

1459 藐视 **miǎo-shìh** to treat with contempt, disdain, slight, look down on

miào (miào)

1460 妙计 **miào-chì** an ingenious plan, subtle scheme, clever device

妙论 **miào-lùn** an ingenious argument, clever remark, wonderful idea (may be sarcastic)

妙不可言 **miào-pù-k'ǒ-yén** too subtle to be described, ingenious beyond belief

1461 庙宇 **miào-yǔ** a temple, shrine

mièh (miè)

1462 灭绝人性 **mièh-chuéh-jén-hsìng** completely devoid of humanity

灭茬 **mièh-ch'á** to remove stubble, plow under after harvest

灭虫 **mièh-ch'úng** to exterminate insects

灭敌人的威风 **mièh tí-jén te wēi-fēng** to crush the enemy's arrogance

灭顶之灾 **mièh-tǐng chīh-tsāi** to be drowned (in danger of destruction, a fatal disaster)

灭资兴无 **mièh-tzū-hsīng-wú** down with the bourgeoisie and up with the proletariat

灭此朝食 **mièh-tz'ǔ-chāo-shíh** to wipe out the enemy before breakfast

1463 蔑视 **mièh-shìh** to disdain, flout, slight, defy, disregard

mién (mián)

1464 绵羊 **mién-yáng** sheep

1465 棉织厂 **mién-chīh-ch'ǎng** a cotton textile mill

棉织品 **mién-chīh-p'ǐn** cotton fabrics, articles made of cotton

棉纺机 **mién-fǎng-chī** cotton-spinning machinery, spindles

棉麦套种 **mién-mài-t'ào-chùng** inter-cropping of cotton and wheat

棉纱 **mién-shā** cotton yarn

miěn (miǎn)

1466 免职 **miěn-chíh** to be dismissed from office, separated from service

免除 **miěn-ch'ú** to avoid, exempt, remit, absolve, acquit

免费 **miěn-fèi** free of charge, gratis

免费医疗 **miěn-fèi-ì-liáo** free health services, medical treatment without charge

免刑 **miěn-hsíng** to be exempt from criminal punishment

免疫 **miěn-ì** immunity from infection; to immunize

免役力 **miěn-ì-lì** immunity (from disease)

免掉 **miěn-tiào** to dismiss, bypass, eliminate

免退 **miěn-t'uì** to be exempt from returning, exempt from repayment

免罪 **miěn-tsuì** to remit a crime, absolve, acquit, exonerate

1467 勉强 **miěn-ch'iǎng** in a forced manner, involuntarily, reluctantly, barely

勉励 **miěn-lì** to urge, encourage, exhort, incite, rouse to action

1468 缅甸 **miěn-tièn** Burma

mièn (miàn)

1469 面积 **mièn-chī** square [surface] measure, area

面值 **mièn-chíh** face value

面黄肌瘦 **mièn-huáng-chī-shòu** sallow-faced and emaciated

面红耳赤 **mièn-húng-ěrh-ch'ìh** with face flushed and ears red (angry, bashful, embarrassed)

面向农村 **mièn-hsiàng-núng-ts'ūn** to be oriented toward the villages (industry, commerce, and cultural circles should work for the benefit of the rural areas and agricultural production)

面孔 **mièn-k'ǔng** a person's face; facial expression

面临 **mièn-lín** to encounter, meet, be faced with, be confronted by

面貌 **mièn-mào** facial looks, features, visage

面貌一新 **mièn-mào-ī-hsīn** to assume a new appearance

面面俱到 **mièn-mièn-chù-tào** to attend to all faces [of affairs] (sometimes a suggestion of non-specialized or superficial activity)

面目全非 **mièn-mù-ch'üán-fēi** the appearance is entirely changed [for the worse]

面目一新 **mièn-mù-ī-hsīn** the appearance is completely new (generally implies improvement)

面目可憎 **mièn-mù-k'ǒ-tsēng** repulsive appearance

面壁虚构 **mièn-pì-hsū-kòu** to face a wall [meditate] and produce an empty scheme (a false idea conceived in isolation from practicality)

面塑 **mièn-sù** figures modeled in dough

面对面 **mièn-tuì-mièn** face to face, opposite each other, vis-à-vis

面对面的领导 **mièn-tuì-mièn te lǐng-tǎo** face-to-face leadership, leadership exerted through intimate personal contact

mín (mín)

1470 民安物阜 **mín-ān-wù-fù** the people at peace and goods plentiful (peace and prosperity)

民家族 **mín-chiā-tsú** the Minchia people (a minority in Yunnan, now known as the **pái-tsú**)

民间 **mín-chièn** among the people; of the people; folk

民间传说 **mín-chièn ch'uán-shuō** folklore, folk tales

民间艺人 **mín-chièn-ì-jén** folk artists

民间艺术 **mín-chièn-ì-shù** folk art

民间故事 **mín-chièn-kù-shìh** folk tales

民间故事编辑室 **mín-chièn-kù-shìh piēn-chì-shìh** folk-tale editorial office (to gather stories and re-write them with

greater political significance)

民间单方 **mín-chiēn tān-fāng** private folk prescriptions [medical]

民间文学 **mín-chiēn wén-hsuéh** *Folk Literature* (a Peking journal, bimonthly, 1955—)

民间文艺形式 **mín-chiēn-wén-ì hsíng-shìh** forms of folk art and literature

民间舞蹈 **mín-chiēn-wǔ-tǎo** folk dances

民间验方 **mín-chiēn yèn-fāng** an effective folk medicine

民间音乐 **mín-chiēn-yīn-yuèh** folk music

民建 **mín-chièn** the China Democratic National Construction Association (one of the minor democratic parties)

民脂民膏 **mín-chíh-mín-kāo** the fat and oil of the people (usually a reference to the corruption of officials who squeeze the people)

民主集中制 **mín-chǔ-chí-chūng-chìh** the system of democratic centralism

民主专政 **mín-chǔ-chuān-chèng** democratic dictatorship

民主化 **mín-chǔ-huà** "democratization" (one of the szù-huà during the commune period)

民主协商 **mín-chǔ-hsiéh-shāng** democratic consultation

民主人士 **mín-chǔ-hsièn-chèng** democratic constitutionalism

民主宪政 **mín-chǔ-jén-shìh** democratic personages, democratic elements

民主改革 **mín-chǔ-kǎi-kó** democratic reform

民主个人主义 **mín-chǔ kò-jén-chǔ-ì** democratic individualism

民主革命 **mín-chǔ-kó-mìng** democratic revolution

民主管理 **mín-chǔ-kuǎn-lǐ** democratic management

民主评定 **mín-chǔ-p'íng-tìng** democratic assessment (of work points, pay, etc.)

民主生活 **mín-chǔ-shēng-huó** democratic life [within the Party]

民主势力 **mín-chǔ-shìh-lì** democratic forces

民主税收评定组 **mín-chǔ shuì-shōu p'íng-tìng-tsǔ** democratic tax appraisal groups (1952–1956)

民主党派 **mín-chǔ-tǎng-p'ài** democratic parties, democratic groups

民主讨论 **mín-chǔ-t'ǎo-lùn** democratic discussion

民主同盟 **mín-chǔ-t'úng-méng** the China Democratic League (one of the minor democratic parties)

民众 **mín-chùng** the public, masses, people, populace

民穷财尽 **mín-ch'iúng-ts'ái-chìn** the people are impoverished and their wealth exhausted

民船运输合作社 **mín-ch'uán yùn-shū hó-tsò-shè** people's boat transport cooperatives

民权 **mín-ch'uán** the people's rights, civil rights; democracy

民权主义 **mín-ch'uán-chǔ-ì** democracy

民法 **mín-fǎ** civil law; the Civil Code

民愤 **mín-fèn** the people's indignation, public wrath

民风 **mín-fēng** customs of the people, popular custom

民心 **mín-hsīn** popular sentiments, popular support; the confidence of the people

民刑法律 **mín-hsíng fǎ-lǜ** civil and criminal laws

民选 **mín-hsuǎn** popular election

民意 **mín-ì** the people's will, public sentiment, popular opinion

民意机关 **mín-ì-chī-kuān** organizations expressing public opinion; a people's representative body

民意调查 **mín-ì tiào-ch'á** public opinion survey

民意测验 **mín-ì ts'è-yèn** public opinion poll

民歌 **mín-kō** folk songs

民革 **mín-kó** the Revolutionary Committee of the Kuomintang (one of the minor parties)

民工 **mín-kūng** workers, civilian workers

民盟 **mín-méng** the China Democratic League (one of the minor democratic parties—*see* mín-chǔ-t'úng-měng)

民办 **mín-pàn** run by the people (operated by the commune)

民办小学 **mín-pàn hsiǎo-hsuéh** primary schools set up and operated by local units (such as neighborhood associations or commune brigades)

民办学校 **mín-pàn-hsuéh-hsiào** schools run by the people (*see above*)

民办公助 **mín-pàn kūng-chù** popular management and public assistance (decentralization of financial and administrative responsibility—emphasizing local option and initiative)

民兵 **mín-pīng** militia forces; a militiaman

民兵建设 **mín-pīng-chièn-shè** the building up of militia

民兵军事体育运动 **mín-pīng chūn-shìh-t'ǐ-yù yùn-tùng** militia military sports movement (Socialist Education period)

民兵工作 **mín-pīng-kūng-tsò** militia

work (generally refers to organizational, administrative or training activities related to the militia)

民兵连 **mín-pīng-lién** a militia company

民兵营 **mín-pīng-yíng** a militia battalion (usually the militia unit of a commune)

民不聊生 **mín-pù-liáo-shēng** the people had nothing to depend on [for life] (the old society)

民事法规 **mín-shìh-fǎ-kuēi** civil laws and regulations

民贼 **mín-tséi** a robber of the people (a public enemy)

民族 **mín-tsú** an ethnic group, people, nation, race, tribe

民族战争 **mín-tsú-chàn-chēng** a war of nationalities, national war

民族教育 **mín-tsú-chiào-yù** education for national minorities, ethnic education

民族解放战争 **mín-tsú-chiěh-fàng chàn-chēng** National Liberation War (usually refers to the Resistance War against Japan)

民族解放运动 **mín-tsú-chiěh-fàng yùn-tùng** a national liberation movement

民族至上 **mín-tsú-chìh-shàng** the nation above all

民族经济 **mín-tsú chīng-chì** a national economy

民族主义 **mín-tsú-chǔ-ì** nationalism; nationalist

民族主义国家 **mín-tsú-chǔ-ì kuó-chiā** a nationalistic state

民族气节 **mín-tsú-ch'ì-chiéh** the moral strength of the people, will power of the people, spirit of the nation

民族区域自治 **mín-tsú-ch'ǚ-yù tzù-chìh** regional autonomy for nationalities

民族分裂主义 **mín-tsú fēn-lièh-chǔ-ì** ethnic secessionism

民族风格 **mín-tsú-fēng-kó** national style (of different nationality groups)

民族恨 **mín-tsú-hèn** national hatred, ethnic animosity

民族习惯 **mín-tsú-hsí-kuàn** national customs, habits of ethnic groups

民族形式 **mín-tsú-hsíng-shìh** forms [of dress, literature, music, etc.] indigenous to national groups

民族虚无主义 **mín-tsú hsū-wú-chǔ-ì** national nihilism

民族遗产 **mín-tsú-í-ch'ǎn** national heritage, ethnic legacy

民族艺术 **mín-tsú-ì-shù** national arts, ethnic arts

民族融合 **mín-tsú-júng-hó** assimilation of nationalities (now contrary to official policy toward national minorities)

民族感情 **mín-tsú-kǎn-ch'íng** national sentiments

民族革命战争 **mín-tsú kó-mìng-chàn-chēng** national revolutionary war

民族观 **mín-tsú-kuān** the concept of nationality, view of nationalism, attitude toward nationality

民族观点 **mín-tsú kuān-tiěn** nationalistic point of view, ethnic standpoint

民族工商业 **mín-tsú kūng-shāng-yèh** nationalistic industry and commerce (refers to enterprises of the national bourgeoisie, as contrasted with bureaucratic or foreign capital, during the pre-socialist period)

民族利己主义 **mín-tsú lì-chǐ-chǔ-ì** the doctrine of narrow national self-interest

民族利益 **mín-tsú-lì-ì** national interests

民族贸易 **mín-tsú-mào-ì** national minorities trade

民族矛盾 **mín-tsú-máo-tùn** contradictions between nations

民族民主革命 **mín-tsú mín-chǔ kó-mìng** national democratic revolution

民族败类 **mín-tsú-pài-lèi** the dregs of the nation

民族平等 **mín-tsú-p'íng-těng** ethnic equality, national equality

民族色彩 **mín-tsú-sè-ts'ǎi** national color, ethnic characteristics

民族事务委员会 **mín-tsú-shìh-wù wěi-yuán-huì** Commission of Nationalities Affairs [of the State Council]

民族大家庭 **mín-tsú tà-chiā-t'íng** the great family of nationalities (refers to China)

民族大义 **mín-tsú-tà-ì** the noble national cause

民族独立 **mín-tsú-tú-lì** national independence

民族特点 **mín-tsú t'è-tiěn** national characteristics, ethnic particularities

民族投降主义 **mín-tsú t'óu-hsiáng-chǔ-ì** national capitulationism

民族团结 **mín-tsú t'uán-chiéh** (1) national unity; an alliance of nationalities; (2) *Solidarity of National Minorities* (a Peking monthly journal, 1957—)

民族统一战线 **mín-tsú t'ǔng-ī-chàn-hsièn** national united front, united front of all the people

民族资产阶级 **mín-tsú tzū-ch'ǎn-chiēh-chí** the national bourgeoisie (in contrast to the bureaucratic capitalists)

民族资源 **mín-tsú tzū-yuán** national resources, natural resources of a

particular people

民族自治 **mín-tsú-tzù-chìh** national autonomy (autonomy of national minorities)

民族自决 **mín-tsú-tzù-chuéh** national self-determination

民族自尊心 **mín-tsú tzù-tsūn-hsīn** national self-respect

民族文化 **mín-tsú wén-huà** national culture, ethnic culture

民族压迫 **mín-tsú-yā-p'ò** national oppression, oppression of one national group by another

民族研究 **mín-tsú yén-chiū** *Studies on National Minorities* (a Peking journal, monthly, 1956—)

民族英雄 **mín-tsú yīng-hsiúng** national hero

民怨 **mín-yuàn** people's grievances

民怨沸腾 **mín-yuàn-fèi-t'éng** the people are seething with discontent

民乐演奏 **mín-yuèh-yěn-tsòu** a performance on [Chinese] native [musical] instruments

民用 **mín-yùng** for civilian use; civil

民用航空 **mín-yùng-háng-k'ūng** civil aviation

mǐn (mǐn)

1471 闽 **mǐn** Fukien province

闽浙赣苏区 **mǐn-ché-kàn sū-ch'ǖ** the Fukien-Chekiang-Kiangsi Soviet District (part of the Soviet Republic during the Kiangsi period)

闽粤赣苏区 **mǐn-yuèh-kàn sū-ch'ǖ** the Fukien-Kwangtung-Kiangsi Soviet District (part of the Soviet Republic during the Kiangsi period)

1472 敏锐 **mǐn-juì** keen, sharp, sensitive, quick-witted

敏感 **mǐn-kǎn** sensitive, sympathetic; keen feeling, quick reaction; allergic [medical]

míng (míng)

1473 名正言顺 **míng-chèng-yén-shùn** valid in name and reasoning (sufficient and correct reasons for carrying out an action)

名称 **míng-ch'ēng** a name, designation [of a thing]

名副其实 **míng-fù-ch'í-shíh** the name agrees with actuality (to be worthy of the reputation)

名义上 **míng-ì-shang** nominally, as a matter of form, in the name of

名人 **míng-jén** celebrities, notables, important personages, VIP's

名利 **míng-lì** fame and profit, fame and wealth

名利思想 **míng-lì-szū-hsiǎng** fame and wealth thinking (an epithet aimed at the bourgeoisie)

名额 **míng-ó** a quota of persons (e.g., the number of openings for university admission)

名不虚传 **míng-pù-hsū-ch'uán** one's eminence is not falsely reputed (a reputation well deserved)

名牌人物 **míng-p'ái-jén-wù** famous-brand people (derisive description of people whom the democratic parties tried to recruit, 1956–1957)

名胜 **míng-shèng** scenic spot, historical site, famous place

名单 **míng-tān** a roster, name list, roll

名堂 **míng-t'áng** (1) a dignified name, title; (2) a result worth mentioning

名存实亡 **míng-ts'ún-shíh-wáng** the name remains but the reality has perished (to exist in name only)

名言 **míng-yén** a maxim, adage, famous saying

名誉 **míng-yù** honor, repute, reputation; honorary

名誉主席 **míng-yù-chǔ-hsí** honorary chairman

名誉恢复 **míng-yù huī-fù** to have one's good name restored (to be rehabilitated)

名誉会员 **míng-yù-huì-yuán** honorary member

名誉扫地 **míng-yù-sǎo-tì** [one's] reputation sweeps the ground (totally discredited)

1474 鸣放 **míng-fàng** "contending and blooming" (abbreviation for the slogan of the Hundred Flowers Campaign: **pǎi-huā ch'í fàng, pǎi-chiā chēng-míng**)

鸣放辩论 **míng-fàng-pièn-lùn** to air one's views and carry on debates

鸣锣开道 **míng-ló-k'āi-tào** beat the drums and clear a road (to create public opinion for an action)

鸣炮致敬 **míng-p'ào-chìh-chìng** to fire a salute

鸣笛 **míng-tí** to blow a whistle; sound a siren

1475 明哲保身 **míng-ché-pǎo-shēn** the wise man protects his person (a sarcastic reference to individualistic concern for one's own interests and cautious avoidance of taking any position on principle)

明争暗斗 **míng-chēng-àn-tòu** overt and covert struggle

明证 **míng-chèng** clear evidence,

irrefutable proof

明知故犯 **míng-chïh kù-fàn** deliberately to commit a crime

明知山有虎, 偏向虎山行 **míng-chïh shān-yǔ-hǔ, p'ïen hsìang hǔ-shān hsíng** [I] know full well that the mountains have tigers but am still determined to go there (to fear no dangers)

明智 **míng-chìh** wise, sagacious

明察秋毫 **míng-ch'á-ch'ïu-háo** able to examine the tip of an autumn hair (a capacity for clear and precise discernment)

明枪暗箭 **míng-ch'iāng-àn-chièn** in the open with a spear and in stealth with an arrow (to attack publicly and in secret)

明确 **míng-ch'üèh** clear and definite

明确规定 **míng-ch'üèh kuēi-tìng** to define clearly; an explicit stipulation

明确表示 **míng-ch'üèh piǎo-shìh** to make clear, express explicitly

明火执仗 **míng-huǒ chíh-chàng** with torches and cudgels (armed robbery committed openly)

明信片 **míng-hsìn-p'ièn** a postcard

明来暗往 **míng-lái-àn-wǎng** publicly to come and secretly to go (a relationship conducted on both public and private levels)

明朗 **míng-lǎng** clear; to become clear, clarify; open-minded, straightforward

明里暗里 **míng-lǐ-àn-lǐ** openly and covertly

明目张胆 **míng-mù-chāng-tǎn** unblinking and boldly (to do a bad thing openly, brazen)

明文 **míng-wén** clearly written, explicitly stipulated

明眼人 **míng-yěn-jén** a clear-eyed man (a shrewd man not easily deceived by appearances)

1476 冥思苦索 **míng-szū-k'ǔ-sǒ** to think deeply and search for earnestly

1477 铭记于心 **míng-chì-yú-hsīn** engraved on the heart (unforgettable)

mìng (mìng)

1478 命中 **mìng-chùng** to hit the target, score a hit

命根子 **mìng-kēn-tzu** stem [of a plant]; the root of one's life (something vital; that which is dearest)

命令 **mìng-lìng** an order, command, decree, edict, fiat; to command, order, direct

命令主义 **mìng-lìng-chǔ-ì** "commandism" (excessive reliance on administration through the issuance of arbitrary orders)

命脉 **mìng-mài** the life pulse, life vein (often figurative: a lifeline, something vital)

命名 **mìng-míng** to give a name to, christen, dub

命定 **mìng-tìng** predestined, fated

命题 **mìng-t'í** a proposition [in logic]; to prepare examination questions

命途多舛 **mìng-t'ú-tō-ch'uǎn** the road of life is full of frustrations

命运 **mìng-yùn** fate, destiny, one's lot, luck

mìu (mìu)

1479 谬论 **mìu-lùn** false reasoning, fallacious argument, nonsense, preposterous ideas

谬误 **mìu-wù** an error, inaccuracy, fallacy

mō (mō)

1480 摸 **mō** to feel, touch lightly, grope for, explore, research estimate

摸清情况 **mō-ch'īng ch'íng-k'uàng** to grope for a clarification of the situation, to feel out the situation

摸清底细 **mō-ch'īng tǐ-hsì** to grope through to the substance (to get to the bottom of something; to explore a person's intentions)

摸黑 **mō-hēi** to do something in the dark (to work or travel late)

摸规律 **mō-kuēi-lǜ** to explore the regularity [of events, an enemy's movements, etc.]

摸不透 **mō-pu-t'òu** unable to feel out, unable to get to the bottom of something (bewildered, puzzled, confused)

摸索 **mō-sǒ** (1) to grope for, feel about; (2) to dawdle, do things slowly

摸索出一条路子 **mō-sǒ-ch'ū ī-tiáo lù-tzu** to feel out a way [of doing something]

摸底 **mō-tǐ** to grope all the way to the bottom [of a problem]

摸早贪黑 **mō-tsǎo-t'ān-hēi** to grope in the early darkness and grudge the dark (to work from dawn to dark; devoted to one's work)

摸营 **mō-yíng** to feel one's way into the [enemy] camp

mó (mó)

1481 模范 **mó-fàn** an exemplary thing, pattern for emulation, model,

standard, ideal

模范行动 **mó-fàn-hsíng-tùng** exemplary activity, actions worthy of emulation

模范农场 **mó-fàn-núng-ch'ǎng** a model farm

模范事迹 **mó-fàn-shìh-chī** exemplary deeds

模仿 **mó-fǎng** to copy, model after, emulate, imitate

模糊 **mó-hu** blurred, unclear, hazy, indistinct; ambiguous, unintelligible

模型 **mó-hsíng** a pattern, model; a miniature

模棱两可 **mó-léng-liǎng-k'ǒ** equivocal, ambiguous, unclear, fence-sitting, straddling

模 **mó**: *see also* **mú**

1482 麼些 **mó-hsiēh** Moso (a minority nationality of Yunnan and Sikang; also known as the **nà-hsī-tsú**)

麼加迪沙 **mó-chiā-tí-shā** Mogadiscio [Somali Republic]

1483 摩拳擦掌 **mó-ch'üán ts'ā-chǎng** grinding the fist and rubbing the palm (ready for action; eager for the fray)

摩洛哥 **mó-lò-kō** Morocco

摩纳哥(侯国) **mó-nà-kō [hóu-kuó]** [Principality of] Monaco

摩天大楼 **mó-t'iēn-tà-lóu** a skyscraper

摩托 **mó-t'ō** an internal combustion engine, motor

摩托化部队 **mó-t'ō-huà pù-tuì** motorized units [military]

摩擦 **mó-ts'ā** to chafe, rub together; friction (conflict, disagreement)

1484 磨床 **mó-ch'uáng** a grinder, grinding machine

磨房 **mó-fáng** a mill house (a building housing an old-style stone mill)

磨削 **mó-hsiāo** to cut by grinding; to grind

磨炼 **mó-lièn** to temper, forge (to train, harden, discipline)

磨灭 **mó-mièh** to obliterate, wear out

磨损 **mó-sǔn** to wear away, fray; wear and tear, attrition

磨刀 **mó-tāo** to sharpen a sword, hone a knife (prepare for action)

磨刀霍霍 **mó-tāo-huò-huò** saber-rattling

磨头 **mó-t'óu** a grinding head

1485 蘑菇战术 **mó-kú-chàn-shù** mushroom tactics (to dilly-dally and waste time without effective action)

1486 魔爪 **mó-chǎo** a demon's claw (the lackey of an evil person)

魔怪 **mó-kuài** a monster, repulsive and evil creature

魔鬼 **mó-kuěi** a devil, monster, demon, evil spirit

魔鬼横行 **mó-kuěi-héng-hsíng** demons running rampant

魔术 **mó-shù** witchcraft, wizardry; magic; juggling

魔术演员 **mó-shù-yěn-yuán** a magician, conjurer

mǒ (mǒ)

1487 抹黑 **mǒ-hēi** to blacken, smear, stain, besmirch

抹灰 **mǒ-huī** to smear with ashes, besmirch, stain

抹煞 **mǒ-shā** to wipe out, sweep away, erase (ignore, disregard, negate)

mò (mò)

1488 末节 **mò-chiéh** the last joint (unimportant details, minor considerations)

末期 **mò-ch'ī** the final period

末日 **mò-jìh** the last day, doomsday

末日可数 **mò-jìh-k'ǒ-shǔ** the last days can be counted (imminent collapse)

末端 **mò-tuān** the tip, extremity, end

末尾 **mò-wěi** the end; ending

1489 没落 **mò-lò** to sink, decline, fall; declining; ruination

没收 **mò-shōu** to confiscate, seize; confiscation

没 **mò**: *see also* **méi**

1490 莫知所措 **mò-chīh-sǒ-ts'ò** to not know what to do (at a loss, in a dilemma)

莫衷一是 **mò-chūng-ī-shìh** no agreement at all (very diverse opinions; unable to arrive at a consensus)

莫须有 **mò-hsū-yǔ** [though not certain] it could have happened (a trumped up charge, spurious accusation)

莫须有罪名 **mò-hsū-yǔ tsuì-míng** a false charge, concocted accusation

莫洛托夫 **mò-lò-t'ō-fū** Molotov [Vyacheslav]

莫名其妙 **mò-míng-ch'í-miào** impossible to fathom, mysterious, incomprehensible, hard to figure out, inexplicable

莫三鼻给 **mò-sān-pí-chǐ** Mozambique

莫斯科 **mò-szū-k'ō** Moscow

莫斯科会议宣言 **mò-szū-k'ō huì-ì hsuān-yén** Declaration of the Moscow Meeting (the declaration of the 1957 Moscow conference of Communist parties supporting the principle of co-existence)

莫斯科会议声明 **mò-szū-k'ō huì-ì shēng-míng** Statement of the Moscow Meeting (issued by the 1960 Moscow conference of 81 "fraternal parties")

莫测高深 **mò-ts'è-kāo-shēn** there is no way to measure the height or depth [of something], unfathomable (usually a euphemism for obscurantist scholarship)

莫此为甚 **mò-tz'ǔ-wéi-shèn** there is nothing that exceeds this (the usual implication is of something bad or harmful)

1491 漠不关心 **mò-pù-kuān-hsīn** completely unconcerned, indifferent, apathetic

1492 墨迹战术 **mò-chì-chàn-shù** ink-spot tactics (starting with scattered spots of resistance which—like ink on absorbent paper—will spread and eventually coalesce)

墨汁未干 **mò-chīh-wèi-kān** the ink is not yet dry (usually refers to breaking of a fresh commitment or promise)

墨西哥 **mò-hsī-kō** Mexico

墨西哥城 **mò-hsī-kō ch'éng** Mexico City

墨守成规 **mò-shǒu-ch'éng-kuēi** to adhere to stereotyped routine (hidebound, without initiative or imagination)

1493 默契 **mò-ch'ì** tacit understanding, implicit agreement

默许 **mò-hsǔ** tacit permission, implied consent

默认 **mò-jèn** tacit acceptance; to acquiesce

默默承认 **mò-mò-ch'éng-jèn** silently to recognize

默默无闻 **mò-mò-wú-wén** silent and unheard (an obscure person, a minor figure)

默不作声 **mò-pù-tsò-shēng** to be silent and not utter a word (reticent, taciturn; to refuse to speak)

móu (móu)

1494 牟取暴利 **móu-ch'ǔ-pào-lì** grasping for excessive profits; to graspingly seek extortionate advantages (to profiteer)

牟利 **móu-lì** to profiteer

1495 谋臣策士 **móu-ch'én-ts'è-shìh** clever ministers and smart counselors (idea men, brain trust)

谋求和平解决 **móu-ch'iú hó-p'íng-chiěh-chüéh** to seek a peaceful solution

谋取私利 **móu-ch'ǔ szū-lì** to scheme to derive personal advantage

谋利 **móu-lì** to seek profit

谋生 **móu-shēng** to make a living

谋士 **móu-shìh** a strategist, resourceful man, idea man

mǒu (mǒu)

1496 某种程度 **mǒu-chǔng ch'éng-tù** to a certain extent, in some degree

某些 **mǒu-hsiēh** certain [persons or things], some, several, such and such

mǔ (mǔ)

1497 母法 **mǔ-fǎ** the "mother law" (the foreign law which has been borrowed or adapted from)

1498 亩产量 **mǔ-ch'ǎn-liàng** per *mu* yield

1499 姆巴巴纳 **mǔ-pā-pā-nà** Mbabane [Swaziland]

mù (mù)

1500 木屐 **mù-chī** wooden sandals, clogs, pattens

木厂 **mù-ch'ǎng** a lumber yard, timber mill

木刻 **mù-k'ò** wood carving, woodcut, wood engraving

木刻雕版书 **mù-k'ò tiāo-pǎn-shū** books printed from wood blocks

木棉 **mù-mién** tree cotton, kapok

木偶剧团 **mù-ǒu-chǔ-t'uán** a puppeteer troupe

木偶戏 **mù-ǒu-hsì** a puppet show

木雕 **mù-tiāo** wood carving, sculpture in wood

木炭 **mù-t'àn** wood charcoal

木材 **mù-ts'ái** lumber, timber, wood

木材加工工业 **mù-ts'ái chiā-kūng kūng-yèh** wood-working industry,

木材工业 **mù-ts'ài kūng-yèh** timber industry

1501 仫佬族 **mù-lǎo-tsú** the Mu-lao people (a minority in Kwangsi Chuang Autonomous Region: population 44,000 as of 1957)

1502 目击 **mù-chī** to see personally, witness

目击报告 **mù-chī pào-kào** an eyewitness report

目中无人 **mù-chūng-wú-jén** in his eyes there is no one [else] (extremely arrogant)

目前 **mù-ch'ién** presently, at the present time, now

目前形势和任务 **mù-ch'ién hsíng-shìh hó jèn-wù** the present situation and tasks

目前的首要任务 **mù-ch'ién te shǒu-yào jèn-wù** the primary present task, most important immediate task

目光如豆 **mù-kuāng-jú-tòu** one's circle of vision is as [small as] a bean (to lack insight, short-sighted)

目光短浅 **mù-kuāng tuǎn-ch'iěn** short-

sighted, shallow, superficial

目空一切 **mù-k'ūng-ī-ch'ièh** [his] eyes are empty of everything (to look down on everyone, supercilious, arrogant)

目标 **mù-piāo** a target, objective, goal, aim, purpose

目不识丁 **mù-pù-shíh-tīng** the eye cannot recognize [even a character as simple as] "ting" (illiterate)

目瞪口呆 **mù-tèng-k'ŏu-tāi** eyes staring and mouth dumb (dumbfounded)

目的 **mù-tì** purpose, goal, objective, aim, destination, intention, design

目的地 **mù-tì-tì** a destination, goal

目睹 **mù-tŭ** to see with one's own eyes, witness

目无组织 **mù-wú tsŭ-chīh** to despise the [Party] organization, to disregard organization

1503 牧主 **mù-chŭ** an owner of animal herds (the nomadic equivalent of a landlord in pre-Communist Mongolia or Tibet)

牧场 **mù-ch'ǎng** pasture land; a livestock farm, ranch

牧区 **mù-ch'ǖ** pastoral area, stock-raising region

牧区商业 **mù-ch'ǖ shāng-yèh** commerce in the nomad areas

牧畜 **mù-hsù** livestock breeding, animal husbandry

牧歌式 **mù-kō-shìh** idyllic, pastoral

牧民 **mù-mín** herdsmen, shepherds; nomads

牧师 **mù-shīh** a pastor, minister

牧童 **mù-t'úng** a boy or young man assigned to herd livestock or water buffalo

牧草 **mù-ts'ǎo** pasture grass, fodder, forage plants

1504 墓葬 **mù-tsàng** a tomb (especially the contents of the grave of an important person)

1505 幕后 **mù-hòu** behind the scenes, behind the curtain

幕后人物 **mù-hòu-jén-wù** behind-the-scenes personalities; wire-pullers (secret manipulators, influential but secret supporters)

幕后操纵 **mù-hòu-ts'āo-tsùng** to pull strings behind the scene, manipulate events from backstage

1506 暮气 **mù-ch'ì** a spirit of decline (despondent, gloomy, apathetic)

暮气沉沉 **mù-ch'ì-ch'én-ch'én** the atmosphere of the evening is heavy (despondent and dejected; a defeatist attitude)

1507 睦邻关系 **mù-lín kuān-hsi** good neighborly relations

1508 穆桂英 **mù kuèi-yīng** Mu Kuei-ying (a woman general who lived, according to legend, during the Sung dynasty: now an exemplar of a courageous, hard-working woman)

穆斯林 **mù-szū-lín** Moslem

ná (ná)

1509 拿手好戏 **ná-shǒu-hǎo-hsì** an operatic role which an actor is especially effective in portraying (one's speciality, strong point, forte)

拿得稳 **ná-te-wěn** to hold firmly; able to hold securely; capable of being held tightly (sure in handling a situation, competent)

nà (nà)

1510 呐喊 **nà-hǎn** (1) to shout in battle, utter a loud cry; (2) the title of a volume of essays by Lu Hsun

1511 纳西族 **nà-hsī-tsú** the Na-hsi people (a minority in Yunnan province: population 155,000. Also known as the Moso; see **mó-hsiēh**)

纳入 **nà-jù** to receive into, receive [a sum of money, etc.] and enter it [into a ledger, or account]

纳凉晚会 **nà-liáng wǎn-huì** enjoy-the-coolness evening parties (organized by street committees, 1964)

纳粮 **nà-liáng** to pay taxes in kind

纳沙贡 **nà-shā-kùng** Nationalist, religious, and Communist [parties] (a policy followed by Sukarno in Indonesia of uniting these groups: usually written as NASAKOM)

纳税 **nà-shuì** to pay taxes

纳税服役 **nà-tsū-fú-ì** to pay taxes and perform labor service

纳粹主义 **nà-ts'uì-chǔ-ì** Nazism

nǎi (nǎi)

1512 奶酪 **nǎi-lò** cheese

nài (nài)

1513 奈温 **nài wēn** Ne Win (a Burmese leader)

1514 耐碱作物 **nài-chiěn tsò-wù** alkali-resistant crops

耐烦 **nài-fán** to be patient, have patience

耐火材料 **nài-huǒ ts'ái-liào** heat-resistant materials, fireproof materials; refractories, firebrick

耐心 **nài-hsīn** patience, perseverance;
to be long-suffering

耐心说服教育 **nài-hsīn-shuō-fú chiào-yǜ**
education by patient persuasion
(usually refers, not to classroom
education, but to persuasive tactics
used with prisoners of war or in mild
phases of campaigns)

耐心听取相反的意见 **nài-hsīn t'īng-
ch'ǔ hsiāng-fǎn-te ì-chièn** to listen
patiently to opinions contrary to
one's own

耐人寻味 **nài-jén hsún-wèi** providing
food for thought (intriguing,
perplexing, puzzling)

耐水作物 **nài-shuǐ tsò-wù** a crop
tolerant to excessive water

耐用 **nài-yùng** durable, sturdy, able to
stand wear and tear

nán (nán)

1515　男主角 **nán-chǔ-chiǎo** the chief male
role, title role, hero

男主女从 **nán-chǔ nǚ-ts'úng** the man
leads and the woman follows (an old
idea—now heavily criticized)

男高音 **nán-kāo-yīn** tenor [voice]

男女关系 **nán-nǚ-kuān-hsi** the
relationship between men and women

男女平等 **nán-nǚ-p'íng-těng** equality
between men and women, equal
rights for both sexes

男女同工同酬 **nán-nǚ t'úng-kūng t'úng-
ch'óu** equal pay for equal work of
men and women

男低音 **nán-tī-yīn** bass (the lowest
male singing voice)

男尊女卑思想 **nán-tsūn nǚ-pēi szū-
hsiǎng** thinking that regards the
male as superior and the female as
inferior

1516　南征北战 **nán-chēng-pěi-chàn** to attack
in the north and fight in the south
(to go through many battles)

南极光 **nán-chí-kuāng** aurora australis,
southern lights

南京长江大桥 **nán-chīng ch'áng-chiāng
tà-ch'iáo** the Yangtze River bridge
at Nanking (a double-deck railway
and highway bridge, completed in
1968)

南京路上好八连 **nán-chīng-lù-shang
hǎo-pā-lién** the Good Eighth
Company on Nanking Road [in
Shanghai] (a PLA model company in
the post-Liberation period)

南京部队 **nán-chīng pù-tuì** the Nanking
Military Forces [of the PLA]
(formerly the Nanking Military

Region)

南茶北种 **nán-ch'á-pěi-chùng** to plant
southern tea in the north (tea is now
being produced in some northern
provinces such as Shantung)

南昌起义 **nán-ch'āng ch'ǐ-ì** the
Nanchang Uprising (August 1, 1927;
led by Chou En-lai and Chu Teh)

南腔北调 **nán-ch'iāng-pěi-tiào** southern
tones and northern notes (a
confusion of dialects)

南方日报 **nán-fāng jìh-pào** *Southern
Daily* (a Canton newspaper)

南非 **nán-fēi** [Union of] South Africa;
southern Africa

南浔铁路 **nán-hsún t'iěh-lù** the
Nanchang-Kiukiang railway

南共 **nán-kùng** the Yugoslavian
Communist Party

南粮北调 **nán-liáng-pěi-tiào** grain from
the south transported to the north
(the historical dependence of
northern provinces for grain from
the Yangtze provinces—a situation
now claimed to have basically ended
in 1973)

南罗得西亚 **nán ló-té-hsī-yà** Southern
Rhodesia (now Rhodesia)

南麻北种 **nán-má-pěi-chùng** to plant
southern hemp in the north (to
reduce northern dependence on the
south)

南泥湾精神 **nán-ní-wān chīng-shén** the
Nanniwan spirit (Nanniwan was the
site of the much praised reclamation
by the Eighth Route Army in Shensi
—hence, a dauntless spirit in
overcoming great difficulties)

南沙群岛 **nán-shā ch'ún-tǎo** the
Spratly Islands

南水北调 **nán-shuǐ-pěi-tiào** to send
southern water to the north (a
project to divert the upper waters of
the Han River)

南斯拉夫 **nán-szū-lā-fū** Yugoslavia

南斯拉夫通讯社 **nán-szū-lā-fū t'ūng-
hsùn-shè** the Yugoslavian News
Agency [TANJUG]

南亚次大陆 **nán-yà tz'ù-tà-lù** the South
Asia sub-continent

南也门 **nán-yěh-mén** South Yemen
[the People's Democratic Republic
of Yemen]

南辕北辙 **nán-yuán-pěi-ché** a south-
bound cart [and] a northbound
track (action contrary to one's goal)

1517　难熬 **nán-áo** difficult to endure, hard
to get through, arduous to bear

难产 **nán-ch'ǎn** (1) difficult labor [in
childbirth]; (2) hard to materialize,

difficult to bring about

难局 **nán-chǘ** a difficult situation, impasse, dead end

难以制服 **nán-ǐ-chìh-fú** difficult to control, unruly, intractable

难以置信 **nán-ǐ-chìh-hsìn** difficult to be believed, unbelievable

难以否认 **nán-ǐ-fǒu-jèn** difficult to deny, irrefutable

难以相信 **nán-ǐ-hsiāng-hsìn** difficult to believe, incredible

难以形容 **nán-ǐ-hsíng-júng** difficult to describe, inexpressible, beyond description

难以估计 **nán-ǐ-kū-chì** hard to estimate, difficult to evaluate

难以比拟 **nán-ǐ-pǐ-nǐ** hard to match, difficult to equal

难以为继 **nán-ǐ-wéi-chì** difficult to follow up, hard to continue

难搞 **nán-kǎo** hard to do, difficult to arrange

难怪 **nán-kuài** little wonder that, it is understandable that; cannot be held responsible for

难关 **nán-kuān** a difficult pass (a crucial test, crisis, obstacle to be overcome)

难过 **nán-kuò** uncomfortable, uneasy; to feel badly, distressed; to feel sorrow, regrets

难免 **nán-miěn** hard to avoid, inescapable, inevitable

难能可贵 **nán-néng-k'ǒ-kuèi** rare and commendable

难办 **nán-pàn** difficult to manage, hard to operate

难办之事 **nán-pàn-chīh-shìh** an affair that is difficult to manage, difficult business

难保 **nán-pǎo** hard to be certain, impossible to guarantee, difficult to judge; hard to hold, difficult to guard

难上加难 **nán-shàng-chiā-nán** difficulties piled on difficulties

难上难 **nán-shàng-nán** difficult in the extreme, difficulties on top of difficulties

难得 **nán-té** (1) hard to get, rarely met, seldom come by; (2) fortunate, lucky, exceptionally fine

难度 **nán-tù** degree of difficulty

难题 **nán-t'í** a difficult problem, baffling problem, tough question

难忘的印象 **nán-wàng-te yìn-hsiàng** an impression hard to forget, indelible impression

难为久计 **nán-wéi-chiǔ-chì** difficult to make any long-range plan

难 **nán**: see also **nàn**

nàn (nàn)

1518 难民 **nàn-mín** a refugee, fugitives from disaster

难 **nán**: see also **nán**

náng (náng)

1519 囊中物 **náng-chūng-wù** something in one's pocket (a sure thing)

囊括 **náng-k'uò** to encompass, include, embrace, comprise

nǎo (nǎo)

1520 恼火 **nǎo-huǒ** to become irritated; vexed

恼怒 **nǎo-nù** to be irritated and angry, indignant

1521 脑筋 **nǎo-chīn** brains, intelligence, mental capacity

脑力劳动 **nǎo-lì-láo-tùng** brain work, mental work [labor]

脑满肠肥 **nǎo-mǎn-ch'áng-féi** a swelled head and fat belly (fat capitalist, idle rich)

脑袋瓜 **nǎo-tài-kuā** the cranium, skull, head (in a general sense: brains, mental capacity)

nào (nào)

1522 闹 **nào** to start, do in a vigorous way, cause to happen; disturb, agitate, stir up

闹情绪 **nào ch'íng-hsù** to brood, be moody, become distracted [from one's work]

闹意见 **nào-ì-chièn** to have differences of opinion (implying abrasive relations between the parties)

闹意气 **nào-ì-ch'ì** to pick quarrels, look for trouble

闹革命 **nào kó-mìng** to engage actively in revolution

闹名誉地位 **nào míng-yù tì-wèi** to strive avidly for fame and position

闹不团结 **nào-pù-t'uán-chiéh** to behave in a manner contrary to unity, foment disunity

闹派别 **nào p'ài-piéh** to engage in cliquism, foment factionalism

闹生产 **nào shēng-ch'ǎn** to devote oneself vigorously to production

闹市 **nào-shìh** a bustling market, busy street

闹事 **nào-shìh** to create a disturbance,

make trouble, stir up a fuss

闹独立性 **nào tú-lì-hsíng** to stir up independence (to foment insubordination)

nèi (nèi)

1523 内债 **nèi-chài** domestic debt, internal debt

内战 **nèi-chàn** civil war

内政 **nèi-chèng** internal affairs [of a country], domestic administration

内奸 **nèi-chiēn** [Party] traitor, enemy agent operating in any organization

内查外调 **nèi-ch'á-wài-tiào** to investigate from inside and outside (to investigate thoroughly)

内行 **nèi-háng** a professional, expert; someone in the know, "insider"

内河运输 **nèi-hó-yùn-shū** inland waterway transportation

内核 **nèi-hó** essence, vital element

内讧 **nèi-hùng** internal strife, factional squabbles, intramural dissension

内线 **nèi-hsièn** interior lines; an inside connection

内线作战 **nèi-hsièn-tsò-chán** to conduct military operations on interior lines (to operate from a central position against enemy forces converging from different directions)

内燃机车 **nèi-ján-chī-ch'ē** a diesel locomotive

内容 **nèi-júng** content, contents; meaning, substance

内容健康 **nèi-júng chièn-k'āng** healthy in content (usually refers to the subject matter and substance of literary works as being wholesome)

内容贫乏 **nèi-júng p'ín-fá** skimpy in content, meager in substance, empty

内阁改组 **nèi-kó-kǎi-tsǔ** a cabinet reorganization

内科 **nèi-k'ó** internal medicine

内罗毕 **nèi-ló-pì** Nairobi [Kenya]

内螺纹 **nèi-ló-wén** internal screw thread

内乱 **nèi-luàn** internal disorder, civil strife

内蒙 **nèi-měng** [kǔ tzǔ-chìh-ch'ǖ] Inner Mongolia [an Autonomous Region]

内蒙古军区 **nèi-měng-kǔ chǖn-ch'ǖ** the Inner Mongolian Military Area Command [of the PLA]

内幕 **nèi-mù** behind the curtain (the inside story)

内部 **nèi-pù** the interior, internal parts, internal, domestic; inherent, intrinsic

内部整顿 **nèi-pù-chěng-tùn** internal

rectification, internal readjustment or reorganization

内部纷争 **nèi-pù-fēn-chēng** internal strife, internal wrangling

内部联系 **nèi-pù lién-hsì** internal relationships, internal connections (often refers to formal or informal linkages between sub-units within a larger organization)

内部矛盾 **nèi-pù-máo-tún** internal contradiction, inner contradiction

内部通报 **nèi-pù t'ūng-pào** internal communication (informational communications within organizational channels)

内部资金 **nèi-pù-tzū-chīn** internal capital (capital generated within an enterprise)

内部参攷 **nèi-pù-ts'ān-k'ǎo** material for internal reference use

内地 **nèi-tì** the hinterland, interior, inland (China proper)

内定 **nèi-tìng** internally decided (a decision, such as an appointment, which has been reached within the government or an organization but has not yet been made public)

内在联系 **nèi-tsài-lién-hsì** inherent relationships, inner relationships, intrinsic relationships

内在因素 **nèi-tsài yīn-sù** internal factors

内藏 **nèi-ts'áng** hidden within, latent

内外夹攻 **nèi-wài-chiā-kūng** a pincer attack from within and without

内外交困 **nèi-wài chiāo-k'ùn** beset internally and externally

内外结合 **nèi-wài chiéh-hó** to integrate internal and external [factors]; internal and external corrdination

内外勾结 **nèi-wài-kōu-chiéh** a conspiracy involving internal and external elements [in a unit, party, country, etc.]

内外物资交流 **nèi-wài wù-tzū chiāo-liú** interflow of commodities between home and abroad

内务部 **nèi-wù-pù** Ministry of Internal Affairs [of the State Council]

内因 **nèi-yīn** intrinsic factor, internal cause

1524 那一套 **nèi-ī-t'ào** that set (often implying contempt)

néng (néng)

1525 能者为师 **néng-chě-wéi-shīh** the capable should be teachers ("capable" is now generally intended to include any persons, such as old peasants, with special knowledge and abilities)

能蓄能灌能排 **néng-hsù néng-kuàn néng-p'ái** able to store [water], to irrigate, and to drain (the requirements for a complete irrigation system)

能干 **néng-kàn** capable, competent, able, efficient

能官能民 **néng-kuān-néng-mín** able to be an official and]yet remain] one of the people

能工巧匠 **néng-kūng-ch'iǎo-chiàng** skilled workers, artisans, craftsmen

能工能农 **néng-kūng-néng-núng** capable as a worker and [also] as a farmer

能力 **néng-lì** (1) ability, capability, faculty; (2) capacity, potentiality; (3) power, energy [physics]

能耐 **néng-nài** skill, ability, resourcefulness

能排能灌 **néng-p'ái néng-kuàn** able to drain and to irrigate

能上能下 **néng-shàng néng-hsià** able to ascend and to descend (willing to assume both the great and the small tasks)

能手 **néng-shǒu** an experienced worker, competent person, expert

能动性 **néng-tùng-hsìng** initiative, the capacity of being able to move

能动的飞跃 **néng-tùng-te fēi-yuèh** a great leap through active initiative

能武能文 **néng-wǔ-néng-wén** capable in both military and civil]fields]

能源危机 **néng-yuán-wēi-chī** the energy crisis

ní (ní)

1526   尼加拉瓜 **ní-chiā-lā-kuā** [Republic of] Nicaragua

尼日尔 **ní-jìh-ěrh** [Republic of] Niger

尼日利亚 **ní-jìh-lì-yà** Nigeria

尼科西亚 **ní-k'ō-hsī-yà** Nicosia [Cyprus]

尼克松主义 **ní-k'ò-sūng chǔ-ì** the Nixon Doctrine

尼龙 **ní-lúng** nylon

尼泊尔 **ní-pó-ěrh** Nepal

尼亚美 **ní-yà-měi** Niamey [Niger]

尼亚萨兰 **ní-yà-sà-lán** Nyasaland (now Malawi)

1527   泥脚深陷 **ní-chiǎo shēn-hsièn** to sink deep in the quagmire (to get into a desperate situation)

泥坑 **ní-k'ēng** swamp, mire, morass

泥菩萨过河，自身难保 **ní-p'ú-sà kuò-hó, tzù-shēn nán-pǎo** a clay idol crossing a river cannot even protect itself (even someone revered cannot be counted on for help when he, himself, is in trouble)

泥塑 **ní-sù** made of clay, modeled in clay, terracotta [figures] (figurative: motionless, without emotion)

泥塑木雕 **ní-sù-mù-tiāo** modeled in clay and carved in wood (a person whose expression and actions are lifeless and dull)

泥潭 **ní-t'án** a muddy pond, mire, bog

泥腿子 **ní-t'uǐ-tzu** muddy legs (a person who has been doing farm work)

泥足巨人 **ní-tsú-chù-jén** a colossus with feet of clay

1528   呢绒 **ní-júng** woolen piece goods

1529   霓红灯 **ní-húng-tēng** a neon lamp, neon sign

霓红灯下的哨兵 **ní-húng-tēng-hsià te shào-pīng** "On Guard beneath the Neon Lights" (a play based on the devotion and incorruptibility of the PLA Eighth Company on Nanking Road in Shanghai in the post-Liberation period)

nǐ (nǐ)

1530   你争我夺 **nǐ-chēng-wǒ-tó** you wrangle and I snatch (a free-for-all where everyone competes for a share of the spoils, etc.)

你追我赶 **nǐ-chuī-wǒ-kǎn** you press forward and I will hurry on (both striving for the same objective)

你不吃掉他，他就吃掉你 **nǐ pù ch'īh-tiào-t'ā, t'ā chiù ch'īh-tiào-nǐ** If you do not eat him, then he will eat you

你死我活 **nǐ-szǔ wǒ-huó** you die and I live (a fight to the bitter end)

你死我活的斗争 **nǐ-szǔ-wǒ-huó-te tòu-chēng** life-and-death struggle (a struggle which must end in the elimination of one of the parties)

1531   拟订 **nǐ-tìng** to draw up [a plan], propose, draft, lay out

nì (nì)

1532   逆差 **nì-ch'ā** a deficit, adverse balance [of trade]

逆风 **nì-fēng** a head wind, adverse wind (a trend or tendency contrary to the correct line)

逆来顺受 **nì-lái shùn-shòu** to accept adversity philosophically (the attitude that exploiters are alleged to have inculcated in the exploited groups of the old society)

逆历史潮流 **nì lì-shǐh-ch'áo-liú** to go against the current of history

逆流 **nì-liú** an adverse current, countercurrent; to go against the stream

逆水 **nì-shuǐ** to go against the current

逆天 **nì-t'iēn** defiant of Heaven (to act against the laws of nature)

1533 匿迹消声 **nì-chī-hsiāo-shēng** to hide one's trace and voice (to be in complete hiding)

匿名 **nì-míng** to hide one's name, anonymous, secret

匿影藏形 **nì-yǐng-ts'áng-hsíng** to hide both one's shadow and one's body (not to reveal one's true self)

niàng (niàng)

1534 醸酒业 **niàng-chiǔ-yèh** the production of alcoholic beverages (of all kinds—including brewing, distilling, and wine-making)

niǎo (niǎo)

1535 鸟瞰 **niǎo-k'àn** a bird's-eye view

nieh (nie)

1536 捏造 **nieh-tsào** to fabricate [evidence, etc.], trump up

niēn (niān)

1537 拈轻怕重 **niēn-ch'īng-p'à-chùng** to prefer the light to the heavy (to fear heavy tasks or responsibility)

nién (nián)

1538 年鉴 **nién-chièn** a yearbook, almanac, annual

年景 **nién-chǐng** harvest condition, conditions at the time of the New Year, harvest outlook for the year

年终 **nién-chūng** the year's end

年产量 **nién-ch'ǎn-liàng** annual production

年产能力 **nién-ch'ǎn-néng-lì** annual production capability

年成 **nién-ch'éng** the harvest [usually followed by good or bad], condition of the year's harvest

年份 **nién-fèn** a year period [calendar]

年画 **nién-huà** New Year's wall pictures, New Year posters

年会 **nién-huì** an annual conference, annual session, yearly meeting

年龄 **nién-líng** a person's age

年迈 **nién-mài** advanced in age; old age

年满 **nién-mǎn** to have reached the age of

年报 **nién-pào** an annual report; to report on an annual basis

年谱 **nién-p'ǔ** a chronology of a person's life

年代 **nién-tài** an epoch, era, period; the times

年度 **nién-tù** a period of twelve months devoted to a certain pursuit or activity (as in fiscal year or academic year)

1539 黏性 **nién-hsìng** adhesiveness, viscosity

niěn (niǎn)

1540 碾米厂 **niěn-mǐ-chǎng** rice-hulling mill, rice-husking mill

1541 撵走 **niěn-tsǒu** to drive [someone] away, expel, cast out

nièn (niàn)

1542 念念不忘 **nièn-nièn pù-wàng** to keep constantly in mind, never forget [a person or thing]

念头 **nièn-t'ou** an idea, thought, hunch (what one is thinking of at a given moment)

níng (níng)

1543 宁 **níng** Ningsia [Hui Autonomous Region]

宁芜铁路 **níng-wú t'iěh-lù** the Nanking-Wuhu railway

宁 **níng**: see also **níng**

1544 凝集力 **níng-chí-lì** cohesion

凝固 **níng-kù** to congeal, coagulate, solidify

凝固汽油弹 **níng-kù ch'ì-yú-tàn** napalm bomb

nìng (nìng)

1545 宁缺毋滥 **nìng-ch'üēh-wú-làn** better to have a shortage than an overflowing (to sacrifice completeness in favor of discrimination; quality is more important than quantity)

宁肯 **nìng-k'ěn** would rather, it is preferable

宁可少些，但要好些 **nìng-k'ǒ-shǎo-hsiěh, tàn-yào-hǎo-hsiěh** it is better to have fewer but of better quality

宁死不屈 **nìng-szǔ-pù-ch'ü** to prefer death to submission

宁愿 **nìng-yuàn** would rather, would sooner; to prefer

宁 **nìng**; see also **níng**

niú (niú)

1546 牛车 **niú-ch'ē** bullock cart, ox cart

牛粪水　**niú-fèn-huǒ** a cow dung fire
牛鬼蛇神　**niú-kuěi-shé-shén** cow-demons and snake-spirits (freaks and monsters, weird and evil supernatural creatures: epithets, much used in the Cultural Revolution, to impugn persons alleged to be anti-Mao)
牛栏　**niú-lán** a cow pen (alludes to the phrase **niú-kuěi-shé-shén** and generally means a place of temporary detention for persons attacked in the Cultural Revolution
牛痘　**niú-tòu** smallpox vaccination
牛头马面　**niú-t'óu-mǎ-mièn** ox-headed and horse-faced (denizens of Hades; freakish and evil monsters: similar to **niú-kuěi-shé-shén**)
牛头不对马嘴　**niú-t'óu pù-tuì mǎ-tsuǐ** a cow's head does not fit a horse's mouth (an answer that does not correspond to the question; two incompatible statements)
牛瘟　**niú-wēn** rinderpest

niŭ (niǔ)

1547　扭转　**niǔ-chuǎn** to turn around, wrench, twist, divert, turn away; turn the tide
纽约时报　**niǔ-yuēh shíh-pào** the *New York Times*

nó (nuó)

1548　挪威　**nó-wēi** Norway
挪用　**nó-yùng** to use [money] for a purpose not originally intended, embezzle, misappropriate

nò (nuò)

1549　诺罗敦·西哈努克　**nò-ló-tūn hsī-hā-nǔ-k'ò** [Samdech] Norodom Sihanouk
诺言　**nò-yén** a promise, pledge
1550　懦夫　**nò-fū** a coward
懦弱　**nò-jò** timid and weak, incompetent, easily swayed by others

nú (nú)

1551　奴化思想　**nú-huà-szū-hsiǎng** slave ideology, slavish thought
奴役　**nú-ì** to subjugate, enslave, reduce to slavery, slavery, enslavement
奴役性商约　**nú-ì-hsìng shāng-yuēh** a commercial treaty of enslavement
奴隶　**nú-lì** a slave, serf
奴隶制　**nú-lì-chìh** the slave system, slavery
奴隶主　**nú-lì-chǔ** a slave holder, slave owner

奴隶主贵族　**nú-lì-chǔ kuèi-tsú** slave-owning aristocracy
奴隶起义　**nú-lì-ch'ǐ-ì** a slave uprising
奴隶社会　**nú-lì-shè-huì** a slave society (a society based on slavery)
奴卑　**nú-pèi** a bond servant (usually maid servants in a condition of semi-slavery)
奴仆　**nú-p'ǔ** a household slave, bond servant, lackey (indentured or otherwise bound to a master)
奴才　**nú-ts'ái** a slavish person, man of weak and contemptible character, a "yes-man"; a slave, serf; an old courteous phase [always used by the speaker] equivalent to "your humble servant"
奴颜婢膝　**nú-yén-pì-hsī** the face of a slave and the knee of a bondmaid (adject and shameless servility)

nŭ (nŭ)

1552　努力　**nǔ-lì** to strive, make efforts, endeavor, work hard
努瓦克肖特　**nǔ-wǎ-k'ò-hsiāo-t'è** Nouakchott [Mauritania]

nù (nù)

1553　怒江　**nù-chiāng** the Salween River [Burma]
怒潮　**nù-ch'áo** a raging tide, angry waves (usually figurative: e.g., the overwhelming force of a mass movement)
怒气冲冲　**nù-ch'ì-ch'ūng-ch'ūng** in a great rage, furious, bursting with anger
怒吼　**nù-hǒu** a furious roar
怒不可遏　**nù-pù-k'ǒ-ò** anger that cannot be restrained
怒族　**nù-tsú** the Nu people (a minority in Yunnan: population 13,724 as of 1957)

nŭ (nŭ)

1554　女主角　**nǔ-chǔ-chiǎo** the heroine [in a drama], leading female role
女飞行员　**nǔ-fēi-hsíng-yuán** an aviatrix, woman airplane pilot
女高音　**nǔ-kāo-yīn** soprano
女工　**nǔ-kūng** female worker
女低音　**nǔ-tī-yīn** alto
女铁人　**nǔ-t'iěh-jén** an iron woman (a woman who has distinguished herself by emulating the work-hero, Wang T'ieh-jen, of the Taching oil fields)

女演员 **nǔ-yěn-yuán** an actress

nuǎn (nuǎn)

1555 暖温带 **nuǎn-wēn-tài** warm temperate zone

nueh (nüè)

1556 虐待 **nueh-tài** to maltreat, persecute, torment, ill-treat

núng (nóng)

1557 农机 **núng-chī** farm machines, agricultural machinery

农家活 **núng-chiā-huó** farm work

农产品 **núng-ch'ǎn-p'ǐn** agricultural products, farm produce

农产品加工 **núng-ch'ǎn-p'ǐn chiā-kūng** processing of agricultural products

农产品收购价格 **núng-ch'ǎn-p'ǐn shōu-kòu-chià-kó** procurement prices for agricultural products

农场 **núng-ch'ǎng** a farm, farm land, agricultural [experimental] station

农具 **núng-chù** farm tools, agricultural implements

农具修造厂 **núng-chù hsiū-tsào-ch'ǎng** a factory for the manufacture and repair of farm implements

农副农品加工 **núng fù-ch'ǎn-p'ǐn chiā-kūng** processing of farm subsidiary products

农副业 **núng-fù-yèh** subsidiary agricultural production, sideline rural occupations

农副业产品 **núng-fù-yèh ch'ǎn-p'ǐn** subsidiary agricultural products, rural sideline products

农户 **núng-hù** peasant household, agricultural household, farming family

农会 **núng-huì** peasant association (during the Soviet period: contraction of **núng-mín hsiéh-huì**)

农活 **núng-huó** farm jobs, farm tasks, farm work (e.g., plowing, sowing, etc.)

农闲 **núng-hsién** the farm slack season

农学家 **núng-hsuéh-chiā** an agronomist, agriculturist

农艺学 **núng-ì-hsuéh** agronomy, the science of agriculture

农艺师 **núng-ì-shīh** an agricultural technician

农工 **núng-kūng** agricultural workers, farm workers

农垦部 **núng-k'ěn-pù** Ministry of State Farms and Land Reclamation [of the State Council] (merged in 1959 into the Ministry of Agriculture and Forestry)

农垦地区 **núng-k'ěn tì-ch'ǖ** land-reclamation areas

农历 **núng-lì** the lunar calendar, agricultural calendar

农林口 **núng-lín-k'ǒu** the agriculture and forestry "mouth" (an informal term for the highest level determining policy on agricultural and forestry matters—not a formal organization, but at a level superior to the administrative government organs)

农林轮作 **núng-lín lún-tsò** alternation of forest and agricultural crops

农林木副渔全面发展 **núng-lín-mù-fù-yú, ch'üán-mièn fā-chǎn** comprehensive development of farming, forestry, animal husbandry, side-occupations, and fishing

农林牧副渔互相结合方针 **núng-lín-mù-fù-yú hù-hsiāng-chiéh-hó fāng-chēn** the principle of combining farming, forestry, animal husbandry, side-occupations and fishery

农林部 **núng-lín-pù** Ministry of Agriculture and Forestry [of the State Council]

农忙季节 **núng-máng chì-chiéh** the farming busy season

农民 **núng-mín** farmers, peasants, farming population

农民阶级 **núng-mín chiēh-chí** the farming class, peasant class

农民起义 **núng-mín-ch'ǐ-ì** a peasant uprising, peasant revolt

农民群众 **núng-mín-ch'ún-chùng** the peasant masses

农民画家 **núng-mín-huà-chiā** peasant artists

农民协会 **núng-mín hsiéh-huì** peasant association (during the Soviet period)

农民意识 **núng-mín-ì-shìh** peasant mentality

农民革命 **núng-mín kó-mìng** peasant revolution

农民革命战争 **núng-mín kó-mìng-chàn-chēng** peasant revolutionary war

农民革命政权 **núng-mín kó-mìng-chèng-ch'üán** a peasant revolutionary regime (e.g., the Taiping government)

农民个体所有制 **núng-mín kò-t'ǐ sǒ-yǔ-chìh** the system of peasant individual [land] ownership

农民大翻身 **núng-mín tà fān-shēn** the great turn around of the peasants (see **fān-shēn**)

农民自卫军 **núng-mín tzù-wèi-chǖn** the peasants' self-protection forces (during the Soviet and Civil War

periods)

农民运动 **núng-mín-yùn-tùng** the peasant movement

农奴 **núng-nú** a serf

农奴制度 **núng-nú-chìh-tù** the serf system

农时 **núng-shíh** the seasons of husbandry (the time for specific operations—such as plowing in the spring)

农贷 **núng-tài** agricultural loans (government credit for agriculture)

农田 **núng-t'ién** farmland, fields, agricultural land

农田基本建设 **núng-t'ién chī-pěn chièn-shè** fundamental reconstruction of farm fields

农田水利 **núng-t'ién shuǐ-lì** farmland water conservancy (includes irrigation, drainage, and all other water-use facilities for maximum utilization of the land)

农作物 **núng-tsò-wù** farm products, crops

农作曳引机 **núng-tsò yèh-yǐn-chī** a field tractor

农村 **núng-ts'ūn** a farm village, agricultural community; rural

农村集市 **núng-ts'ūn chí-shìh** a village market

农村分校 **núng-ts'ūn fēn-hsiào** a village branch school (rural branches of city schools to give city students some farm experience and to assist in educating rural youth)

农村副业 **núng-ts'ūn fù-yèh** rural subsidiary industry, village side-occupations

农村合作医疗 **núng-ts'ūn hó-tsò ī-liáo** rural cooperative medicine

农村医疗卫生网 **núng-ts'ūn ī-liáo wèi-shēng-wǎng** rural medical and public health network

农村人民公社 **núng-ts'ūn jén-mín-kūng-shè** rural people's communes

农村干部 **núng-ts'ūn kàn-pù** rural cadres, cadres working in the rural areas

农村根据地 **núng-ts'ūn kēn-chǜ-tì** village bases, rural base areas (during the pre-Liberation period)

农村革命根据地 **núng-ts'ūn kó-mìng-kēn-chǜ-tì** village bases of revolution, rural revolutionary base areas

农村广播网 **núng-ts'ūn kuǎng-pō-wǎng** rural broadcasting network, a network of village loudspeakers

农村版图书 **núng-ts'ūn-pǎn t'ú-shū** village books (a special series of books edited and prepared for rural use)

农村包围城市 **núng-ts'ūn pāo-wéi ch'éng-shìh** the villages surround the cities

农村商业 **núng-ts'ūn shāng-yèh** rural commerce, village trade

农村社会主义教育运动 **núng-ts'ūn shè-huì-chǔ-ì chiào-yǜ yùn-tùng** the Rural Socialist Education Movement (1962–66: also referred to as Socialist Education Movement and **szù-ch'īng yùn-tùng**)

农村读物 **núng-ts'ūn tú-wù** reading materials for rural areas (usually in very elementary language with pictorial aids to understanding)

农村文化阵地 **núng-ts'ūn wén-huà-chèn-tì** the cultural battleground in the villages

农村业余教育 **núng-ts'ūn yèh-yǘ-chiào-yǜ** rural spare-time education

农药 **núng-yào** agricultural pesticides, insecticides

农药保管员 **núng-yào pǎo-kuǎn-yuán** custodian of agricultural pesticides

农业 **núng-yèh** agriculture, farming; agricultural

农业机器制造工业 **núng-yèh-chī-ch'ì chìh-tsào-kūng-yèh** the farm machinery industry

农业机械技术 **núng-yèh chī-hsièh chì-shù** the technology of mechanized agriculture

农业机械化 **núng-yèh chī-hsièh-huà** the mechanization of agriculture, agricultural mechanization

农业机械部 **núng-yèh chī-hsièh-pù** the Ministry of Farm Machine Industry

农业技术 **núng-yèh-chì-shù** agricultural technology, farming techniques

农业技术试验站 **núng-yèh-chì-shù shìh-yèn-chàn** agricultural technical experiment station

农业技术推广站 **núng-yèh chì-shù t'uī-kuǎng-chàn** stations for the propagation of agricultural technology (farm extension stations)

农业技术员 **núng-yèh chì-shù-yuán** agro-technicians (i.e., graduates of the new schools established after 1968)

农业经济学 **núng-yèh chīng-chì-hsuéh** agricultural economics

农业中学 **núng-yèh chūng-hsuéh** agricultural middle school (vocational secondary schools in agriculture)

农业产业军 **núng-yèh ch'ǎn-yèh-chūn** an industrial army for agriculture (intended to mean that modern farmers, different from the small-

scale producers of the past, are an organized force for large-scale mechanized production)

农业气象 **núng-yèh ch'ì-hsiàng** agricultural meteorology

农业发展纲要 **núng-yèh fā-chǎn kāng-yào** the National Program of Agricultural Development (1956)

农业副产品 **núng-yèh fù-ch'ǎn-p'ǐn** subsidiary farm products

农业合作化 **núng-yèh hó-tsò-huà** the cooperativization of agriculture

农业合作社 **núng-yèh hó-tsò-shè** agricultural [producers'] cooperatives (often referred to as APC; *see* **núng-yèh shēng-ch'ǎn hó-tsò-shè**)

农业系统 **núng-yèh hsì-t'ǔng** the agriculture system (the network of government organizations and institutions concerned with agriculture and including policy formulation, technical assistance, quota determination, and distribution)

农业现代化 **núng-yèh hsièn-tài-huà** to modernize agriculture; agricultural modernization

农业信用合作社 **núng-yèh hsìn-yùng hó-tsò-shè** agricultural credit cooperatives

农业学大寨 **núng-yèh hsuéh tà-chài** in agriculture, learn from Tachai (Tachai is a model brigade in Shansi)

农业工厂化 **núng-yèh kūng-ch'ǎng-huà** to industrialize agriculture; the industrialization of agriculture

农业工人 **núng-yèh-kūng-jén** agricultural workers (in contrast to industrial workers)

农业科学技术 **núng-yèh k'ó-hsuéh chì-shù** agricultural science and technology

农业科学试验 **núng-yèh k'ó-hsuéh shìh-yèn** agricultural scientific experiments; scientific experimentation in agriculture

农业八字宪法 **núng-yèh pā-tzù hsièn-fǎ** the Eight-Point Charter of Agriculture (water, fertilizer, soil, seed, close [planting], prevention [of insect pests and plant diseases], technical [innovation], and management)

农业泵 **núng-yèh-pèng** agricultural water pump

农业部 **núng-yèh-pù** Ministry of Agriculture [of the State Council] (superseded in 1969 by the Ministry of Agriculture and Forestry)

农业社会主义 **núng-yèh shè-huì-chǔ-ì** agrarian socialism, agricultural socialism (i.e., absolute egalitarianism

based on a small farm economy)

农业社会主义改造 **núng-yèh shè-huì-chǔ-ì kǎi-tsào** the socialist transformation of agriculture

农业社会化 **núng-yèh shè-huì huà** the socialization of agriculture, to socialize agriculture

农业生产合作社 **núng-yèh shēng-ch'ǎn hó-tsò-shè** agricultural producers' cooperatives (often abbreviated as APC)

农业生产资料 **núng-yèh shēng-ch'ǎn tzū-liào** agricultural means of production

农业试验站 **núng-yèh shìh-yèn-chàn** agricultural experiment station

农业水利工会 **núng-yèh shuǐ-lì kūng-huì** Agricultural Water Conservancy Trade Union (for specialized workers on irrigation projects)

农业税 **núng-yèh-shuì** agricultural tax, farm tax

农业四化 **núng-yèh-szù-huà** the four transformations ["-izations"] of agriculture (mechanization, water utilization, electrification, and chemical fertilization)

农业突破 **núng-yèh-t'ū-p'ò** an agricultural breakthrough

农业增产竞赛 **núng-yèh tsēng-ch'ǎn chìng-sài** competitive emulation for increased farm production

农业为基础 **núng-yèh wéi chī-ch'ǔ** [with] agriculture as the foundation

农业稳收 **núng-yèh wěn-shōu** stable farm yield (farm output stabilized, by such measures as irrigation, against the normal vagaries of weather and rainfall)

农渔盐业 **núng-yǘ-yén-yèh** agriculture, fishing, and salt industries (all associated with coastal areas)

1558 浓厚 **núng-hòu** thick and dense [of material things]; serious, deep, and profound [of feelings, etc.]

浓缩 **núng-sō** to condense; condensed, concentrated

1559 脓疮 **núng-ch'uāng** an abscess, boil (also figurative)

nùng (nòng)

1560 弄假成真 **nùng-chiǎ-ch'éng-chēn** to turn simulation into reality (something playful has become serious)

弄巧成拙 **nùng-ch'iǎo ch'éng-chō** to try to be clever but turn out to be stupid (to bungle, outsmart oneself)

弄清 **nùng-ch'īng** to achieve a clarification, arrive at a clarification

弄出 **nùng-ch'ū** to commit [an error, etc.]

弄坏 **nùng-huài** to bungle, spoil, break something

弄虚作假 **nùng-hsū-tsò-chiǎ** to engage in pretense and falsehood (swindling)

弄死 **nùng-szǔ** to do to death, do away with, kill

弄懂弄通 **nùng-tǔng nùng-t'ūng** to succeed in understanding and mastering

弄通 **nùng-t'ūng** to achieve a mastery of [a subject, etc.]

弄通马克斯主义 **nùng-t'ūng mǎ-k'ò-szū-chǔ-ì** to achieve a full comprehension of Marxism

弄错 **nùng-ts'ò** to commit an error, make a mistake

ō (ē)

1561 阿谀 **ō-yú** to flatter, toady, fawn on

阿谀逢迎 **ō-yú féng-yíng** to curry favor with, fawn on, toady to

阿 **ō**: *see also* **ā**

ó (é)

1562 讹诈 **ó-chà** to blackmail, extort money by false pretenses, swindle

1563 俄国 **ó-kuó** Russia, Russian (the old name, no longer used)

俄罗斯族 **ó-ló-szū-tsú** the Russian people (a minority in the Sinkiang-Uighur Autonomous Region: population 9,700 as of 1957)

1564 额外 **ó-wài** beyond the set amount, extra, non-quota

额外负担 **ó-wài fù-tàn** an extra burden, obligation beyond the set quota

1565 鹅卵石 **ó-luǎn-shíh** goose egg pebbles (used in construction)

ò (è)

1566 厄瓜多尔 **ò-kuā-tō-ěrh** Ecuador

1567 扼杀 **ò-shā** to strangle, choke to death, suffocate

扼守 **ò-shǒu** to hold and defend [a strategic position]

扼要 **ò-yào** (1) the main points, in summary, briefly; (2) a strategic position

1568 饿死事小 **ò-szǔ-shìh-hsiǎo** to die of hunger is a small affair [to lose virtue is a major matter]

1569 恶狠狠 **ò-hěn-hěn** ferociously

恶化 **ò-huà** to get worse, deteriorate, degenerate

恶习 **ò-hsí** a bad habit

恶性 **ò-hsìng** malignant, virulent, hyper- [inflation, etc.]

恶性发展 **ò-hsìng-fā-chǎn** malignant development, excessive or unhealthy development

恶性通货膨胀 **ò-hsìng t'ūng-huò p'éng-chàng** hyper-inflation, runaway inflation

恶意 **ò-ì** malice, spite, evil intention, sinister motive

恶人先告状 **ò-jén hsiēn-kào-chuàng** a scoundrel is the first to sue

恶感 **ò-kǎn** ill will, enmity, dislike, bad feelings

恶棍 **ò-kùn** a villain, scoundrel, hooligan, ruffian

恶果 **ò-kuǒ** bad results, undesirable consequences

恶劣 **ò-lièh** evil, very inferior, of low character (especially in morals); rude, distasteful

恶名昭著 **ò-míng chāo-chù** an evil reputation that is conspicuous, notorious, infamous

恶霸 **ò-pà** local tyrant, village despot, bully

恶霸反革命分子 **ò-pà fǎn-kó-mìng fèn-tzǔ** counter-revolutionary local tyrants

恶霸地主 **ò-pà-tì-chǔ** a despotic landlord, tyrannical landlord

恶毒 **ò-tú** malicious, malevolent, vicious, pernicious

恶语中伤 **ò-yǔ-chùng-shāng** to harm others by malicious accusations

恶 **o**: *see also* **wù**

1570 鄂 **ò** Hupeh province

鄂伦春族 **ò-lún-ch'ūn-tsú** the Olunchun people (a minority in Heilungkiang province: population 2,400 as of 1957)

鄂温克族 **ò-wēn-k'ò-tsú** the Evenki people (a minority in the Inner Mongolia Autonomous Region and Heilungkiang province: population 7,000 as of 1957)

鄂豫皖边区 **ò-yù-wǎn piēn-ch'ǖ** the Hupeh-Honan-Anhwei Border Region (one of the CCP New Fourth Army bases during the Resistance War)

鄂豫皖苏区 **ò-yù-wǎn sū-ch'ǖ** the Hupeh-Honan-Anhwei Soviet District (one of the Soviet areas, 1928–1932; under the leadership of Chang Kuo-t'ao)

1571 遏制 **ò-chìh** to restrain, check, curb, suppress, stop

ōu (ōu)

1572 讴歌 **ōu-kō** to sing in praise, glorify, laud, eulogize

1573 欧安会 **ōu-ān-huì** European Security Conference (*see next below*)

欧洲安全会议 **ōu-chōu ān-ch'üán huì-ì** European Security Conference (proposed by the USSR in 1972)

欧洲经济共同体 **ōu-chōu chīng-chì kùng-t'úng-t'ǐ** European Economic Community

欧洲核裁军大会 **ōu-chōu hó-ts'ái-chǖn tà-huì** European Congress for Nuclear Disarmament

欧洲新秩序 **ōu-chōu hsīn-chìh-hsù** the European New Order (a reference to Hitler)

欧洲共同市场 **ōu-chōu kùng-t'úng-shìh-ch'ǎng** European Common Market

欧洲年 **ōu-chōu nién** the "year of Europe" (the Nixon-Kissinger statement that 1973 was to be the "year of Europe")

欧洲原子能联营组织 **ōu-chōu yuán-tzǔ-néng lién-yíng-tsǔ-chǐh** European Atomic Energy Community [EURATOM]

欧美 **ōu-měi** Europe and America

欧姆 **ōu-mǔ** ohm

欧阳海之歌 **ōu-yáng-hǎi chīh kō** *Song of Ouyang Hai* (a famous novel by Chin Ching-mai, 1966)

1574 殴打 **ōu-tǎ** to beat up, attack with fists or clubs

ǒu (ǒu)

1575 呕心沥血 **ǒu-hsīn lì-hsuèh** to drip one's heart-blood (descriptive of exhausting mental labor: the struggle of literary creation)

1576 偶尔 **ǒu-ěrh** occasionally, not habitually

偶象 **ǒu-hsiàng** an idol, image

偶象崇拜 **ǒu-hsiàng ch'úng-pài** idol worship, idolatry

偶然现象 **ǒu-ján hsièn-hsiàng** a random phenomenon, chance event

偶然事件 **ǒu-ján shìh-chièn** an accidental occurrence, unexpected happening, accident

1577 藕断丝连 **ǒu-tuàn-szū-lién** the lotus root is cut but still linked by filaments (undercover liaisons still persist after personal relations have seemingly been severed)

pā (bā)

1578 八届九中全会 **pā-chièh chiǔ-chūng ch'üán-huì** the Ninth Plenary Session of the Eighth Central Committee (January 1961, which shifted emphasis away from heavy industry to consumer goods)

八届十中全会 **pā-chièh shìh-chūng ch'üán-huì** the Tenth Plenary Session of the Eighth Central Committee (September 1962)

八九不离十 **pā-chiǔ pù-lí shíh** eight and nine are not far from ten (ten being a top score, eight and nine have the sense of "almost" or "good enough")

八七会议 **pā-ch'ī huì-ì** the August 7 Conference (a secret emergency conference of Party leaders on August 7, 1927, where Ch'en Tu-hsiu was ousted and Ch'ü Ch'iu-pai was installed as Party leader)

八二六〇派 **pā-èrh-liù-líng p'ài** the 8260 group, clock watchers (8260 means going work at 8 a.m., 2 hours break at noon, and at 6 p.m. sharp, off they go refusing to take part in political meetings and the like)

八方呼应 **pā-fāng hū-yìng** all eight points of the compass responding (all activities coordinated on a broad scale)

八项注意 **pā-hsiàng-chù-ì** The Eight Points for Attention (longstanding rules of conduct for the Red Army, Eighth Route Army, and the PLA: polite speech, fair payment for goods, return of articles borrowed, payment for damage, no maltreatment of the people, avoidance of crop damage, no liberties with women, and no ill-treatment of captives; *see also:* **sān-tà-chì-lǜ**)

八一建军节 **pā-ī chièn-chūn-chiéh** the August 1 Army Day (the anniversary of the Nanchang Uprising in 1927)

八·一宣言 **pā-ī-hsuān-yén** the August 1 Manifesto (issued by the CCP in 1935, calling for an end to the civil war and united action against Japan)

八一三事件 **pā-ī-sān shìh-chièn** the August 13 Incident (the outbreak of Sino-Japanese hostilities at Shanghai on August 13, 1937)

八股 **pā-kǔ** eight-legged (a reference to the essay form in the imperial civil service exams—hence, stereotyped writing, jargon)

八股调 **pā-kǔ-tiào** eight-legged style (stereotyped, formalistic, empty of

content)

八国联军 **pā-kuó lién-chün** the allied forces of the eight Powers (the army which defeated the Boxers in 1900 and raised the siege of the Legations in Peking)

八路军 **pā-lù-chün** the Eighth Route Army (the designation given the Chinese Workers and Peasants Red Army in 1937 when it was incorporated into the National government forces in the war against Japan)

八大 **pā-tà** the Eighth Party Congress (September 1956)

八字方针 **pā-tzù fāng-chēn** the Eight Character Policy (a post-Great Leap slogan for agriculture consisting of four phrases: **t'iáo-chěng** [adjustment]; **kǔng-kù** [consolidation]; **ch'üng-shíh** [reinforcement]; **t'í-kāo** [elevation]

八字宪法 **pā-tzù hsièn-fǎ** the Eight Character Charter (a code for agricultural development: water; fertilizer; soil [improvement]; close [planting]; protection [against pests]; technical [innovation]; [good] management)

1579
巴基斯坦 **pā-chī-szū-t'ǎn** Pakistan

巴结 **pā-chieh** to curry favor, flatter, toady to

巴西 **pā-hsī** Brazil

巴西利亚 **pā-hsī-lì-yà** Brazilia [Brazil]

巴格达 **pā-kó-tá** Baghdad [Iraq]

巴格达条约组织 **pā-kó-tá t'iáo-yuēh tsǔ-chīh** the Baghdad Pact Organization [CENTO]

巴拉圭 **pā-lā-kuēi** Paraguay

巴黎 **pā-lí** Paris

巴黎公社 **pā-lí-kūng-shè** the Paris Commune [1871]

巴黎公社式选举 **pā-lí kūng-shè-shìh hsuǎn-chǔ** Paris Commune type of elections (referred to in the Sixteen Point Decision of August 1966)

巴林(酋长国) **pā-lín [chiú-chǎng kuó]** [Sheikdom of] Bahrein

巴马科 **pā-mǎ-k'ō** Bamako [Mali]

巴拿马 **pā-ná-mǎ** [Republic of] Panama

巴拿马城 **pā-ná-mǎ ch'éng** Ciudad Panama [Panama]

巴瑟斯特 **pā-sè-szū-t'è** Bathurst [Gambia]

巴苏陀兰 **pā-sū-t'ó-lán** Basutoland

巴斯特尔 **pā-szū-t'è-ěrh** Basse-Terre [Guadaloupe, French West Indies]

1580
芭蕾舞 **pā-lěi-wǔ** the ballet

芭蕾舞剧 **pā-lěi-wǔ-chù** ballet dance-drama

pá (bá)

1581
拔海 **pá-hǎi** above the sea level

拔河 **pá-hó** a tug of war

拔火罐 **pá-huǒ-kuàn** the application of a heated container, from which the air has been exhausted, to relieve pain

拔高 **pá-kāo** to lift up, raise, elevate

拔腿 **pá-t'uǐ** to lift up the legs (run away, take flight, take to one's heels)

拔秧 **pá-yāng** to pull up [rice] seedlings [for transplanting]

1582
跋扈 **pá-hù** to defy authority, overstep one's bounds

跋山涉水 **pá-shān-shè-shuǐ** to climb mountains and ford streams (to travel afar under difficult conditions)

pǎ (bǎ)

1583
把着手教 **pǎ-che-shǒu chiāo** to teach [writing] by guiding the hand [of a student] (careful, patient and meticulous instruction by old peasants or workers)

把枕头垫高睡大觉 **pǎ chěn-t'ou tièn-kāo shuǐ-tà-chiào** to pile up the pillows and have a big sleep (to be unconcerned and heedless)

把政治关 **pǎ chèng-chìh-kuān** to guard the political pass (to make no concessions in political or ideological matters)

把家庭关 **pǎ chiā-t'íng-kuān** to guard the family pass (one must ensure the political rectitude of one's own family)

把持 **pǎ-ch'íh** to monopolize, dominate, control (usually in a derogatory sense)

把持包办 **pǎ-ch'íh-pāo-pàn** to monopolize everything

把方便让给人家 **pǎ fāng-pièn jàng-kěi jén-chia** to yield the convenience to others

把风 **pǎ-fēng** a person posted as a lookout; to watch out (usually implies participation in an illegal act)

把好路线关 **pǎ-hǎo lù-hsièn-kuān** to guard well the pass of the line (to defend the correct policy line)

把戏 **pǎ-hsì** jugglery, deceptive sleight-of-hand, cheap trickery

把一步当全程 **pǎ-ī-pù tàng-ch'üán-ch'éng** to consider one step as the whole journey (to lack persistence and follow-through)

把荣誉让给别人 **pǎ júng-yù jàng-kěi pièh-jén** to leave the honors to others

把关 **pǎ-kuān** to hold a pass, guard a frontier gate (now figurative: i.e., to hold the line against bourgeois ideology)

把关守口 **pǎ-kuān-shǒu-k'ǒu** to guard the passes (*see above*)

把困难留给自己 **pǎ k'ùn-nan liú-kěi tzù-chǐ** to leave the difficulties to oneself

把炮口对着自己 **pǎ p'ào-k'ǒu tuì-che tzù-chǐ** to turn the muzzle of the gun against oneself (to criticize oneself)

把头 **pǎ-t'óu** a minor labor boss (in the old society)

把文化关 **pǎ wén-huà-kuān** to hold the cultural pass

把握 **pǎ-wò** to take hold of, seize, grasp; [to be] confident, sure; have a firm grasp of a situation

1584 靶子 **pǎ-tzu** a target (literal and figurative)

pà (bà)

1585 坝子 **pà-tzu** a flat piece of land

坝堰 **pà-yèn** an embankment, dike, dam

1586 罢休 **pà-hsiū** to stop, cease, have done with

罢工 **pà-kūng** to stage a [labor] strike; a strike, walk-out

罢课 **pà-k'ò** a student strike; to refuse to attend classes

罢免 **pà-miěn** to recall [officials], remove from office, dismiss from one's post

罢市 **pà-shìh** to close shops, stop doing business (usually a form of protest by shopkeepers—a commercial strike)

罢手 **pà-shǒu** to stop the hands (to discontinue an action, pause, give up, stop)

1587 霸佔 **pà-chàn** to occupy by force, seize illegally, grab, monopolize

霸主 **pà-chǔ** a powerholder, person [or country] exercising hegemony, dominant power

霸权 **pà-ch'üán** hegemony, mastery, supremacy

霸权政治 **pà-ch'üán-chèng-chìh** power politics

霸权主义 **pà-ch'üán-chǔ-ì** the doctrine of hegemony, "hegemon-ism"

霸道 **pà-tào** the tyrant's way (rule by force; overbearing, violent, bullying)

pái (bái)

1588 白昼做梦 **pái-chòu-tsò-mèng** to dream in broad daylight, daydream, indulge in reveries

白旗 **pái-ch'í** the white flag (may signify either: truce, surrender; or anti-Communist forces)

白求恩 **pái ch'iú-ēn** Bethune [Dr. Norman] (a Canadian surgeon who died of septicemia while working with the Eighth Route Army in 1939)

白军 **pái-chūn** the white army (KMT or anti-Communist military forces)

白区 **pái-ch'ū** white areas (areas under KMT control, 1927–36)

白费气力 **pái-fèi-ch'ì-li** to waste effort, dissipate one's energy without result

白费时间 **pái-fèi-shíh-chiēn** to waste time, fritter away time

白话 **pái-huà** vernacular speech, colloquial language

白话文 **pái-huà-wén** writings in vernacular style

白衣战士 **pái-ī chàn-shìh** white-clothed fighters (medical corpsmen, battlefield medical workers)

白热 **pái-jè** white-hot, incandescent

白日作梦 **pái-jìh tsò-mèng** to dream in the daytime, daydream, indulge in reveries

白狗偷食, 黄狗当灾 **pái-kǒu t'ōu-shíh, huáng-kǒu tāng-tsāi** the white dog steals the food [but] the yellow suffers for it (to receive unmerited punishment)

白骨蔽野 **pái-kǔ pì-yěh** white bones covering the fields (the remains of bitter war)

白宫 **pái-kūng** The White House [in Washington, D.C.]

白毛女 **pái-máo nǚ** "The White-haired Girl" (ballet dance-drama, one of the **yàng-pǎn-hsì**)

白白断送 **pái-pái tuàn-sùng** to give up [something] in vain (suggests a useless sacrifice of life or territory)

白璧微瑕 **pái-pì wēi-hsiá** white jade only a minor flaw (a good person or thing with a slight imperfection)

白皮书 **pái-p'í-shū** white book, "white paper" (i.e., the US White Paper on Sino-American relations)

白色恐怖 **pái-sè-k'ǔng-pù** white terror

白手起家 **pái-shǒu-ch'ǐ-chiā** to establish a family with bare hands (to start from scratch, establish and prosper, flourish in an undertaking)

白族 **pái-tsú** the Pai people (a minority in Yunnan province: population 684,000 as of 1957; previously called **mín-chiā**)

白卫军 **pái wèi-chūn** White Guards (during the civil war in Russia)

păi (băi)

¹⁵⁸⁹ 百战百胜 **păi-chàn-păi-shèng** a hundred battles and a hundred victories (invincible, ever-victorious)

百折不回 **păi-ché-pù-huí** to push forward despite a hundred failures (unflinching, indomitable, unswerving)

百折不挠 **păi-ché pù-náo** unflinching despite a hundred setbacks (persistent, unshakable, indomitable, unremitting)

百家争鸣 **păi-chiā chēng-míng** [let] a hundred schools [of thought] contend

百周年纪念 **păi-chōu-nién chì-nièn** centenary celebration

百尺竿头更进一步 **păi-ch'ĭh kān t'óu, kèng chìn ī-pù** make another forward step on the hundred foot pole (to not be satisfied but continue to strive for greater achievement)

百发百中 **păi-fā-păi-chùng** a hundred shots and a hundred hits (to make every shot count)

百废俱兴 **păi-fèi-chù-hsīng** all neglected [matters] have been attended to

百废待举 **păi-fèi-tài-chŭ** a hundred tasks wait to be accomplished

百分 **păi-fēn** (1) one hundred points; (2) a popular variety of poker

百分比 **păi-fēn-pĭ** percentage

百害而无一利 **păi-hài érh wú-ī-lì** a hundred disadvantages without one advantage (totally bad)

百花齐放 **păi-huā ch'í-fàng** [let] a hundred flowers bloom

百花齐放百家争鸣 **păi-huā ch'í-fàng, păi-chiā chēng-míng** Let a hundred flowers blossom and a hundred schools of thought contend (the slogan of the Hundred Flowers Movement, 1957)

百花齐放推陈出新 **păi-huā ch'í-fàng t'uī-ch'én ch'ū-hsīn** let a hundred flowers bloom and weed out the old to let the new emerge

百花盛开 **păi-huā shèng-k'āi** the flowers are opening in profusion (prosperity, in full bloom)

百货公司 **păi-huò-kūng-szū** a department store, emporium

百货商店 **păi-huò shāng-tièn** a department store

百日武斗 **păi-jìh wŭ-tòu** the hundred days of militant struggle (the conflict at Tsing Hua University between Cultural Revolution factions, 1968)

百科全书 **păi-k'ō ch'üán-shū** the complete book of a hundred sciences (an encyclopedia)

百孔千疮 **păi-k'ŭng ch'iēn-ch'uāng** battered and scarred (full of ills and troubles, in a disastrous state)

百炼成钢 **păi-lièn-ch'éng-kāng** made into steel by a hundred temperings (tempered through repeated struggle)

百年大计 **păi-nién tà-chì** a grand design for a hundred years

百般歌颂 **păi-pān kō-sùng** to sing praises in a hundred ways

百般辩护 **păi-pān pièn-hù** to defend in a hundred ways

百般盼望 **păi-pān p'àn-wàng** to hope for in a hundred ways

百般刁难 **păi-pān tiāo-nàn** to be obstructive in a hundred ways

百倍 **păi-pèi** one hundred times, hundredfold

百团大战 **păi-t'uán tà-chàn** the Hundred Regiments Offensive (by Eighth Route Army in North China during 1940)

百足之虫死而不僵 **păi-tsú-chĭh-ch'úng, szŭ-érh-pù-chiāng** a centipede when dead is not rigid (a powerful person or country does not immediately lose all of its powers)

百万富翁 **păi-wàn fù-wēng** a millionaire

百万雄师 **păi-wàn hsiúng-shīh** the brave divisions of a million men (a powerful army)

百万吨 **păi-wàn-tùn** a megaton

百万瓦特 **păi-wàn-wă-t'è** a megawatt

百闻不如一见 **păi-wén pù-jú ī-chièn** a hundred hearings are not as good as one seeing (seeing is believing)

百药园 **păi-yào-yuán** an herb garden

百业萧条 **păi-yèh hsiāo-t'iáo** all business languishes (a business depression)

百 **păi**: see also **pó**

¹⁵⁹⁰ 摆正 **păi-chèng** to set things right, arrange properly

摆架子 **păi chìà-tzu** to spread a scaffolding (to put on airs; arrogant, snobbish)

摆出样子 **păi-ch'ū yàng-tzu** to put on the airs of

摆夷 **păi-í** an ethnic minority in Yunnan province (now officially the **t'ài-tsú** 泰族, Thai people)

摆阔气 **păi k'uò-ch'i** to show off one's wealth; ostentatious

摆老资格 **păi lăo-tzū-kó** to pride oneself on seniority

摆表现, 查危害, 挖根源 **păi piăo-hsièn, ch'á wēi-hài, wā kēn-yuán** set forth what each has shown [and] examine the harms [and] dig out the root

sources

摆布 **pǎi-pù** to manage or handle [a person], to control, arrange

摆事实 **pǎi shìh-shíh** to set forth the facts

摆事实, 讲道理 **pǎi-shìh-shíh chiáng-tào-lǐ** to present the facts and explain the reasons

摆脱 **pǎi-t'ō** to shake off, free oneself from, get away from, get rid of

摆在首位 **pǎi-tsài-shǒu-wèi** to put in the first place, place in the leading position

pài (bài)

1591 败仗 **pài-chàng** a losing war, defeat

败家子 **pài-chiā-tzǔ** a son who impoverishes the family, prodigal son

败局 **pài-chǘ** a situation of certain defeat, in a hopeless situation

败坏风纪 **pài-huài fēng-chì** to corrupt discipline (demoralized; demoralization)

败兴而归 **pài-hsìng érh-kuēi** to lose interest and go home (to return with a defeated spirit)

败光 **pài-kuāng** to deplete one's resources, spend everything

败类 **pài-lèi** corrupt people, bad elements, dregs of society

败北 **pài-pěi** to suffer defeat, be defeated

败诉 **pài-sù** to lose a lawsuit

1592 拜金主义 **pài-chīn-chǔ-ì** the worship of gold, mammonism

拜群众为师 **pài ch'ún-chùng wéi shīh** to kneel to the masses as teachers

拜访 **pài-fǎng** to visit, call on [a person]

拜会 **pài-huì** to pay a visit, call on (often suggests an official visit)

拜老农为师 **pài lǎo-núng wéi shīh** to kneel to the old peasants as teachers (to become disciples of the old peasants)

拜师 **pài-shīh** to take as a teacher

拜倒 **pài-tǎo** to prostrate oneself

拜物教 **pài-wù-chiào** fetishism

pān (bān)

1593 班长 **pān-chǎng** a squad leader, leader of a small group

班机 **pān-chī** a scheduled plane, regularly scheduled flight

班吉 **pān-chí** Bangui [Central African Republic]

班加西 **pān-chiā-hsī** Benghazi [Libya]

班禅喇嘛 **pān-ch'án lǎ-ma** the Panchen Lama

班房 **pān-fáng** a jail, confinement awaiting trial

班门弄斧 **pān-mén nùng-fǔ** to brandish an ax before Lu Pan's gate (to foolishly try to show one's skill before a true expert)

班组 **pān-tsǔ** squads and sub-squads, basic units (in army, factory, or productive work)

班子 **pān-tzu** a troupe, operatic company (any organized group)

1594 颁发 **pān-fā** to issue, make public; bestow, award, give out, distribute

颁布 **pān-pù** to promulgate, proclaim, publish officially

1595 斑斑血渍 **pān-pān-hsuèh-chì** mottled with blood stains

1596 搬场汽车 **pān-ch'ǎng ch'ì-ch'ē** cars for moving (to help move people and their possessions)

搬起石头打自己的脚 **pān-ch'ǐ shíh-t'ou, tǎ tzǔ-chǐ-te chiǎo** lifting a rock only to drop it on one's own feet (to inflict harm on oneself)

搬弄是非 **pān-nùng shìh-fēi** to carry and spread gossip, engage in malicious talk, stir up trouble between people

搬山填沟 **pān-shān t'ién-kōu** to move mountains and fill the gulleys (to build terraced fields)

搬运 **pān-yùn** to transport, move goods

pǎn (bǎn)

1597 板门店谈判 **pǎn-mén-tièn t'án-p'àn** the Panmunjon negotiations [for a truce in Korea]

板式 **pǎn-shìh** a pattern [worthy of emulation]

1598 版权 **pǎn-ch'üán** copyright

版画 **pǎn-huà** woodcut prints

版本 **pǎn-pěn** an edition, text

版税 **pǎn-shuì** royalties [on books]

pàn (bàn)

1599 办 **pàn** to manage, run, operate, carry out, do, handle, deal with, take care of

办法 **pàn-fǎ** means, schemes, methods, ways, measures, procedures for handling; procedural regulations

办好 **pàn-hǎo** to manage well, operate effectively

办学 **pàn-hsuéh** to run schools

办公室 **pàn-kūng-shìh** an administrative office [of a unit]

办理 **pàn-lǐ** to deal with, handle, take care of, undertake; to manage, run,

administer, regulate; to transact, execute, carry out

办报 **pàn-pào** to run a newspaper

办事 **pàn-shìh** to handle affairs, transact business; to manage, administer

办事公道 **pàn-shìh kūng-tào** to be equitable in managing affairs

办水利 **pàn shuǐ-lì** to engage in water conservancy, carry out irrigation or drainage projects, improve water utilization

1600 半安粮 **pàn-ān-liáng** half-safe grain (stored grain with water content requiring frequent examination for spoilage)

半遮半掩 **pàn-chē-pàn-yěn** half-screened and half-covered (partially concealed; semi-covertly)

半机械化 **pàn chī-hsièh-huà** semi-mechanized

半价 **pà-chià** half-price

半截子 **pàn chiéh-tzu** half a stick (unfinished, broken off, ended halfway)

半截子革命思想 **pàn-chiéh-tzu kó-mìng-szū-hsiǎng** halfway revolutionary thinking (generally sympathetic but unwilling to give full commitment to the Party policy)

半殖民地 **pàn-chíh-mín-tì** a semi-colony; semi-colonial

半斤八两 **pàn-chīn pā-liǎng** half a catty [or] eight ounces (six of one and half a dozen of the other; no difference)

半径 **pàn-chìng** half a diameter, the radius

半成品 **pàn-ch'éng-p'ǐn** semi-finished products

半球 **pàn-ch'iú** a hemisphere

半封建 **pàn-fēng-chièn** semi-feudal

半心半意 **pàn-hsīn-pàn-ì** half-heartedly

半信半疑 **pàn-hsìn-pàn-í** half belief and half suspicion, between belief and doubt

半热带 **pàn-jè-tài** semi-tropical zone, the subtropics

半耕半读 **pàn-kēng pàn-tú** half-time farming and half-time study

半官方 **pàn-kuān-fāng** semi-official

半工半读 **pàn-kūng pàn-tú** part-work and part-study

半工半读专业学校 **pàn-kūng pàn-tú chuān-yèh hsuéh-hsiào** half-work half-study vocational [specialized training] schools

半劳动力 **pàn-láo-tùng-lì** half working strength (people who can perform only part of the normal work quota)

半路出家 **pàn-lù-ch'ū-chiā** to make a new start in midcourse (to change to a new profession)

半农半医 **pàn-núng-pàn-ī** part-time farming and part-time medicine (barefoot doctors)

半农半读专业学校 **pàn-núng-pàn-tú chuān-yèh hsuéh-hsiào** half-farm and half-study vocational schools

半壁江山 **pàn-pì-chiāng-shān** half of the national territory

半边天 **pàn-piēn-t'iēn** the other half of the sky (usually a reference to women)

半社会主义性质 **pàn-shè-huì-chǔ-ì hsìng-chìh** semi-socialist nature, semi-socialist in character

半导体 **pàn-tǎo-t'ǐ** a semi-conductor, transistor (in common speech, may refer to a small [transistor] radio)

半导体收音机 **pàn-tǎo-t'ǐ shōu-yīn-chī** a transistor radio

半吊子 **pàn tiào-tzu** a shallow person, half-educated, rash; a jack of all trades

半托 **pà-t'ō** part-time nursery care

半脱产干部 **pàn-t'ō-ch'ǎn kàn-pù** a cadre semi-separated from production (a cadre whose assigned duties—e.g., administration or study—entail that only a part of his time be devoted to labor)

半脱离生产 **pàn-t'ō-lí shēng-ch'ǎn** partially removed from production

半途而废 **pàn-t'ú-érh-fèi** to abandon [a task] in mid-course

半自耕农 **pàn-tzù-kēng-núng** a farmer who makes part of his living by cultivating his own land [and partially by tenantry]

半自动化 **pàn tzù-tùng-huà** semi-automated; semi-automatic

半渔半读渔民小学 **pàn-yǘ pàn-tú yǘ-mín hsiǎo-hsuéh** half-fish half-study fisher people's primary schools

半月刊 **pàn-yuèh-k'ān** a fortnightly publication, semi-monthly publica-

1601 伴随 **pàn-suí** to accompany, follow

伴随而来 **pàn-suí-érh-lái** to come in company with

伴奏 **pàn-tsòu** to accompany [in musical performance]

1602 扮作 **pàn-tsò** to dress up as, disguised as, play the role of

扮演 **pàn-yěn** to play a role, act a part

扮演走卒角色 **pàn-yěn tsǒu-tsú chüèh-sè** to play the role of an errand boy

1603 拌嘴 **pàn-tsuǐ** to squabble, wrangle, bicker, quarrel; bickering, altercation

1604 绊脚石 **pàn-chiǎo-shíh** a stumbling block, obstacle

pāng (bāng)

1605 邦交 **pāng-chiāo** diplomatic relations, international ties

1606 帮倒忙 **pāng-tào-máng** to harm while trying to help, render an [unintentional] disservice

帮腔 **pāng-ch'iāng** to sing in unison, chorus, follow (to give verbal support to someone in a higher position)

帮后进 **pāng-hòu-chìn** to help those behind, help the backward to advance

帮会 **pāng-huì** a secret society, association, group, clique

帮闲 **pāng-hsién** to give advice from idleness (to be a parasite, meddlesome idler)

帮凶 **pāng-hsiūng** an accomplice, henchman, accessory

帮工 **pāng-kūng** an assistant to a skilled worker

帮办 **pāng-pàn** an assistant manager, deputy director, vice chief

帮手 **pāng-shǒu** a helper, assistant

1608 梆子 **pāng-tzu** a local folk opera style originating in Shensi

pǎng (bǎng)

1609 绑票 **pǎng-p'iào** to seize for ransom, kidnap

1610 榜样 **pǎng-yàng** a model, example, pattern (something worthy of emulation)

pāo (bāo)

1611 包扎 **pāo-chā** to wrap, bandage, pack

包教保学 **pāo-chiào-pǎo-hsuéh** to undertake teaching and ensure learning (the elders—old peasants and workers—should pass on their knowledge and experience to ensure the education of the young)

包产 **pāo-ch'ǎn** to contract for production; contracted production

包产计划 **pāo-ch'ǎn chì-huà** a plan for contracted production

包产合同 **pāo-ch'ǎn-hó-t'ung** a contract for guaranteed output (a contract by which a production unit undertakes to meet a specified output target)

包产到户 **pāo-ch'ǎn-tào-hù** production contracted down to the household (a practice ended by universalization of the cooperative and commune system)

包成本 **pāo-ch'éng-pěn** to guarantee cost (usually an agreement specifying

a cost of production that will not be exceeded)

包袱 **pāo-fu** a pack, bundle (an undesirable [spiritual or ideological] burden)

包含 **pāo-hán** to contain, comprise, include

包一头, 包到底 **pāo ī-t'óu pāo tào-tǐ** to contract from beginning to end (to contract on an inclusive basis)

包医百病 **pāo-ī-pǎi-pìng** to cure all diseases; a panacea (often figurative)

包容 **pāo-júng** to forgive, pardon, be lenient to; tolerant, patient with

包干制 **pāo-kān-chìh** total subsistence system (an early arrangement for public support in kind of army and government personnel)

包钢 **pāo-kāng** the Paotow Steel Works

包工制 **pāo-kūng-chìh** a system of labor contract (to set an inclusive figure for labor services)

包工包料 **pāo-kūng pāo-liào** to contract for labor and material (to set guaranteed maximums for labor and material costs)

包工头 **pāo-kūng-t'óu** labor contractors (a pre-Liberation term)

包裹运价 **pāo-kuǒ-yùn-chià** parcel transport rates

包括 **pāo-k'uò** to include, comprise

包兰铁路 **pāo-lán t'iěh-lù** the Paotow-Lanchow railway

包罗万象 **pāo-ló wàn-hsiàng** to include a myriad of phenomena (to have everything that should be there)

包办 **pāo-pàn** to do everything for, take over and manage, assume full responsibility; arbitrarily to assume charge

包办代替 **pāo-pàn tài-t'ì** to take everything into one's own hands; to monopolize a project

包庇 **pāo-pì** to shelter, shield, harbor (to defend someone who does not deserve it)

包身工 **pāo-shēn-kūng** a bond servant, slave worker

包租 **pāo-tsū** to rent as prime tenant, to charter

包藏 **pāo-ts'áng** to hide, conceal, secrete

包藏祸心 **pāo-ts'áng huò-hsīn** to conceal malicious intent [under a fair countenance]

包围 **pāo-wéi** to surround, encircle, besiege; encirclement

包围歼灭 **pāo-wéi chiēn-mièh** to encircle and annihilate

包围攻击 **pāo-wéi-kūng-chī** an en-

circling attack

1612 褒贬 **pāo-piěn** praise and blame; to criticize, disparage

pǎo (bǎo)

1613 宝成铁路 **pěo-ch'éng t'iěh-lù** the Paochi-Chengtu railway

宝贵经验 **pǎo-kuèi chīng-yèn** valuable experience

宝库 **pǎo-k'ù** treasury, treasure vault; a collection of articles of great value (often figurative)

宝书 **pǎo-shū** treasured books (Mao Tse-tung's *Selected Works*)

宝座 **pǎo-tsò** the precious seat (a throne; seat of honor)

1614 饱经风霜 **pǎo-chīng-fēng-shuāng** to have had one's fill of wind and frost (to have experienced many years of hardship)

饱经忧患 **pǎo-chīng-yū-huàn** to have borne grief and calamity

饱和 **pǎo-hó** saturation; saturated

饱食终日 **pǎo-shíh-chūng-jìh** to spend one's day in eating (a life of idleness)

饱受 **pǎo-shòu** to suffer [insult, etc.] to the fullest extent (to have had all one can take)

1615 保安 **pǎo-ān** public security, peace protection

保安部队 **pǎo-ān-pù-tuì** peace preservation corps, security forces

保安队 **pǎo-ān-tuì** local security force (an old, pre-Liberation term)

保安族 **pǎo-ān-tsú** the Pao-an people (a minority in Kansu province: population 5,500 as of 1957)

保安措施 **pǎo-ān ts'ò-shīh** security precautions, security measures

保障 **pǎo-chàng** to safeguard, ensure, protect, defend, guarantee

保障生活 **pǎo-chàng shēng-huó** to ensure a livelihood; a guaranteed living

保证 **pǎo-chèng** to guarantee, pledge, assure; a surety, warranty for another's financial undertaking

保证金 **pǎo-chèng-chīn** a security deposit, cash deposited as collateral

保证书 **pǎo-chèng-shū** a deed of security, letter of guarantee

保加利亚 **pǎo-chiā-lì-yà** Bulgaria

保加利亚通讯社 **pǎo-chiā-lì-yà t'ūng-hsùn-shè** Bulgarian Telegraph Agency [BTA]

保家卫国 **pǎo-chiā wèi-kuó** protect our homes and defend our country (a slogan during the Korean War)

保甲制度 **pǎo-chiǎ chìh-tù** the *paochia*

system (household groupings held mutually responsible for security—an old system revived by the KMT)

保教 **pǎo-chiào** to guarantee education [for children] (one of the **wǔ-pǎo**)

保健 **pǎo-chièn** protection of health, hygiene; public health

保健站 **pǎo-chièn-chàn** a public health station

保健机构 **pǎo-chièn-chī-kòu** public health agencies, the institutional network concerned with public health

保健工作 **pǎo-chièn-kūng-tsò** public health work

保健旅馆 **pǎo-chièn lǚ-kuǎn** small hotels with facilities to care for transients who are ill or convalescent

保健事业 **pǎo-chièn-shìh-yèh** health services

保健室 **pǎo-chièn-shìh** a health room (usually in a small unit, such as a school)

保健网 **pǎo-chièn-wǎng** network of health protection facilities

保健药箱 **pǎo-chièn yào-hsiāng** health medicine box (may be portable or placed at a fixed location, as in a factory)

保健员 **pǎo-chièn-yuán** paramedical personnel

保吃, 保穿, 保烧, 保教, 保葬 **pǎo-ch'īh, pǎo-ch'uān, pǎo-shāo, pǎo-chiào, pǎo-tsàng** to guarantee food, clothing, fuel, education [of children], and burial (the Five Guarantees, **wǔ-pǎo**)

保持 **pǎo-ch'íh** to maintain, keep, hold, preserve

保持接触 **pǎo-ch'íh chiēh-ch'ù** to maintain contact, keep in touch with

保持艰苦奋斗作风 **pǎo-ch'íh chiēn-k'ǔ fèn-tòu tsò-fēng** keep to the style of plain living and hard work

保持警惕 **pǎo-ch'íh chǐng-t'ì** to maintain vigilance, keep alert

保持革命干劲 **pǎ-ch'íh kó-mìng kàn-chìn** to keep up one's revolutionary enthusiasm, maintain revolutionary ardor

保持冷静头脑 **pǎo-ch'íh lěng-chìng t'óu-nǎo** to keep a cool head (to keep calm)

保持市容整洁 **pǎo-ch'íh shìh-júng chěng-chiéh** keep the city clean

保穿 **pǎo-ch'uān** to guarantee clothing (one of the **wǔ-pǎo**)

保权捍线 **pǎ-ch'üán hàn-hsièn** protect the power [of the people] and safeguard the [socialist] line

保护 **pǎo-hù** to protect, guard

保护环境 **pǎo-hù huán-chìng** to protect

the [natural] environment

保护人 **pǎo-hù-jén** a guardian, protector

保护各族人民利益 **pǎo-hù kò-tsú jén-mín lì-ì** to protect the interests of the people of all nationalities

保护关税 **pǎo-hù-kuān-shuì** a protective tariff

保护国 **pǎo-hù-kuó** a protectorate [country]

保护伞 **pǎo-hù-sǎn** a protective umbrella

保护胜利果实 **pǎo-hù shèng-lì kuǒ-shíh** protect the fruits of victory (a slogan during the land reform of the early 1950s)

保皇派 **pǎo-huáng-p'ài** emperor-protecting groups (a Cultural Revolution epithet)

保皇党 **pǎo-huáng-tǎng** monarchist party, royalist party (during the Cultural Revolution, an epithet for Liu Shao-ch'i and his alleged supporters)

保险 **pǎo-hsiěn** to insure, guarantee; insurance; a protective device—such as a safety catch on a firearm

保钢 **pǎo-kāng** defend the steel (ensuring steel production by such measures as improving transportation, and the supply of raw materials, fuel, and power—from the Great Leap)

保管员 **pǎo-kuǎn-yuán** a custodian

保留 **pǎo-liú** to retain, reserve, keep back, lay aside, defer [for future discussion]; maintain reservations; to suspend, deduct

保留工资 **pǎo-liú kūng-tzū** to maintain one's earnings [at the original level]; to receive one's regular salary while on another assignment such as schooling

保密 **pǎo-mì** to keep secret, preserve confidentiality

保苗 **pǎo-miáo** to protect the seedlings (to protect and maintain proper seedling growth)

保姆 **pǎo-mǔ** a nurse for small children

保镖 **pǎo-piāo** a bodyguard, armed escort; to serve as a guard

保不住 **pǎo-pu-chù** cannot be saved, cannot be defended; there is no guarantee that

保墒 **pǎo-shāng** to preserve moisture, [soil] moisture conservation

保墒防旱 **pǎo-shāng-fáng-hàn** [measures for soil] moisture conservation and drought protection

保烧 **pǎo-shāo** to guarantee fuel (one

of the **wǔ-pǎo**)

保释 **pǎo-shìh** on parole; to be set at liberty under a guarantee

保守主义 **pǎo-shǒu-chǔ-ì** conservatism

保守派 **pǎo-shǒu-p'ài** conservatives, conservative groups

保守思想 **pǎo-shǒu szū-hsiǎng** conservative ideology

保送 **pǎo-sùng** to recommend and send [for advanced training or education]

保葬 **pǎo-tsàng** to guarantee burial (one of the **wǔ-pǎo**)

保存 **pǎo-ts'ún** to preserve, maintain, safeguard, keep from harm, protect from loss

保存自己，消灭敌人 **pǎo-ts'ún tzù-chǐ hsiāo-mièh tí-jén** to preserve oneself and annihilate the enemy

保卫 **pǎo-wèi** to defend, guard against

保卫和平 **pǎo-wèi hó-p'ing** to protect peace, defend peace

保卫工作 **pǎo-wèi kūng-tsò** security work (normally, political security)

保卫国家主权 **pǎo-wèi kuó-chiā-chǔ-ch'üán** to defend national sovereignty

保卫科 **pǎo-wèi-k'ō** security section (in most all work organizations)

保卫民族利益 **pǎo-wèi mín-tsú-lì-ì** to defend the interests of the nation

保卫社会主义江山 **pǎo-wèi shè-huì-chǔ-ì chiāng-shān** to defend the rivers and mountains of socialism (defend the socialist political power)

保卫祖国 **pǎo-wèi tsǔ-kuó** to defend the fatherland

保温育秧 **pǎo-wēn-yù-yāng** a hot-bed nursery

保有 **pǎo-yǔ** to possess, preserve, own

保佑 **pǎo-yù** protect and bless

保育工作 **pǎo-yù kūng-tsò** child-care work, child welfare

保育事业 **pǎo-yù shìh-yèh** child-care (in a broad sense)

1616 堡垒 **pǎo-lěi** fortress, bastion, stronghold, bulwark

堡垒政策 **pǎo-lěi chèng-ts'è** the policy of blockhouse warfare (used by the KMT during the Kiangsi period)

堡垒户 **pǎo-lěi-hù** bulwark families (families who sheltered Communist soldiers and aided them during the Civil War)

pào (bào)

1617 刨床 **pào-ch'uáng** a planer, planing machine

刨 **pào:** see also **p'áo**

1618 报界 **pào-chièh** the world of the press, press circles, the press

报请批准 **pào-ch'ǐng-p'ǐ-chǔn** to submit with a request for approval

报仇 **pào-ch'óu** to avenge [a grievance], take revenge

报废 **pào-fèi** to report as useless or unserviceable

报复 **pào-fù** to retaliate, avenge, take reprisals; retaliation, revenge; to report back [after investigation, etc.]

报话机 **pào-huà-chī** a telephone transmitter

报喜 **pào-hsǐ** to report happy news (to report success in a large project or the overcoming of a major difficulty —often with a view to stimulating emulation by other units)

报喜不报忧 **pào-hsǐ pù-pāo-yū** to report only the good things but not the bad

报销 **pào-hsiāo** to submit accounts for approval

报告 **pào-kào** to report, inform, give an account of, announce; a report [to higher authorities]

报告制度 **pào-kào-chìh-tù** system of reports (a schedule of regular reporting at specified intervals by subordinate units to the next higher level in all Party and government organizations)

报告文学 **pào-kào-wén-hsuéh** reportorial literature, reportage

报刊 **pào-k'ān** newspapers and journals

报考对象 **pào-k'ǎo tuì-hsiang** applicants for an entrance examination

报社 **pào-shè** a newspaper publishing organization, newspaper office

报税 **pào-shuì** to declare goods for duty

报答 **pào-tá** to repay kindness, pay a debt of gratitude, reciprocate

报导 **pào-tǎo** to report [in writing]

报到 **pào-tào** to report one's arrival, report for duty

报应 **pào-yìng** retribution

1619 抱歉 **pào-ch'ièn** to regret, feel sorry about, apologize

抱负 **pào-fù** ambition, aspiration

抱不平 **pào-pù-p'íng** to be indignant at injustice, protest unfairness to another

抱头鼠窜 **pào-t'óu-shǔ-ts'uàn** to cover the head like a cornered rat (to flee ignominiously)

抱头痛哭 **pào-t'óu-t'ùng-k'ū** to bury one's head and weep bitterly

抱残守缺 **pào-ts'án-shǒu-ch'üēh** to cherish broken and worn-out [things] (extremely conservative; reluctant to accept new things)

抱粗腿 **pào-ts'ū-t'uǐ** to embrace a stout leg (to rely on someone else for protection)

抱有幻想 **pào-yǔ huàn-hsiǎng** to cherish illusions

1620 暴政 **pào-chèng** tyrannical rule; a tyrannical government

暴发户 **pào-fā-hù** suddenly wealthy families, newly rich

暴风 **pào-fēng** a storm, tempest, gale

暴风雪 **pào-fēng-hsuěh** a blizzard

暴风骤雨 **pào-fēng-tsòu-yǔ** violent wind and gusty rain (a political or social tempest; the title of a novel by Chou Li-po)

暴风雨 **pào-fēng-yǔ** fierce wind and rain, storm, tempest

暴力 **pào-lì** violence, brute force

暴力机器 **pào-lì chī-ch'ì** the machinery of violence (repressive measures used by reactionary regimes)

暴力革命 **pào-lì kó-mìng** violent revolution

暴力统治 **pào-lì t'ǔng-chìh** control by violence, violent rule

暴露 **pào-lù** to expose, uncover, lay bare, reveal, disclose (the implication is that what is being exposed is bad or harmful)

暴露文学 **pào-lù-wén-hsuéh** exposé literature, muckraking

暴露无遗 **pào-lù-wú-í** completely unmasked

暴乱 **pào-luàn** a violent rebellion, riot, disturbance of internal security

暴动 **pào-tùng** an insurrection, riot, uprising

1621 爆炸 **pào-chà** to explode, blow up; explosion, blast

爆发 **pào-fā** to explode, break out, erupt, flare up

爆破 **pào-p'ò** to demolish by explosives; demolition

爆破手 **pào-p'ò-shǒu** a demolition man, sapper

pēi (bēi)

1622 卑贱者 **pēi-chièn-chě** outcasts (groups of inferior social status in the old society)

卑躬屈节 **pēi-kūng ch'ǖ-chiéh** to bow low and humiliate oneself (obsequious, servile, fawning)

卑躬屈膝 **pēi-kūng ch'ǖ-hsī** to bow low and bend the knee (to humiliate oneself; servile)

卑劣 **pēi-lièh** depraved, mean

卑鄙 **pēi-pǐ** contemptible, mean, debased, crooked; low, inferior

卑鄙手段 **pēi-pǐ shǒu-tuàn** unscrupulous methods

卑视 **pēi-shìh** to look down on, treat as inferior

1623 杯满必溢 **pēi-mǎn-pì-ì** when the cup is filled it must overflow (excessive pride will lead to a fall)

杯水车薪 **pēi-shuǐ-ch'ē-hsīn** [to use] a cup of water [to put out] a cart-load of [burning] firewood (to use means that are hopelessly inadequate)

1624 背篓商店 **pēi-lǒu shāng-tièn** "basket-on-back stores" (sales personnel of rural cooperative stores who act as peddlers to take goods to people in remote areas)

背 **pēi**: *see also* **pèi**

1625 悲哀 **pēi-āi** sad, sorrowful, mournful

悲剧 **pēi-chù** a tragedy

悲愤填膺 **pēi-fèn-t'ién-yīng** the breast is full of grief and anger

悲欢离合 **pēi-huān-lí-hó** grief in separation and joy in reunion

悲喜交集 **pēi-hsǐ-chiāo-chí** grief and joy intermingled

悲观 **pēi-kuān** pessimism; pessimistic

悲观主义 **pēi-kuān-chǔ-ì** pessimism

悲观厌世 **pēi-kuān yèn-shìh** pessimistic and cynical, despondent, misanthropic

悲悼 **pēi-tào** to mourn, lament, grieve for

悲天悯人 **pēi-t'ién-mǐn-jén** to lament against Heaven and sympathize with mankind (to lament the difficulties of the world and sympathize with the miseries of mankind)

悲惨生活 **pēi-ts'án-shēng-huó** a miserable life, pathetic existence

pěi (běi)

1626 北极 **pěi-chí** the North Pole

北极圈 **pěi-chí-ch'üān** the Arctic Circle

工京六厂二校经验 **pěi-chīng liù-ch'ǎng èrh-hsiào chīng-yèn** the experience of the six factories and two universities of Peking (who supported Mao Tse-tung during the Cultural Revolution in consolidating the line of proletarian dictatorship)

北京部队 **pěi-chīng pù-tuì** the Peking Military Forces [of the PLA] (formerly the Peking Military Region)

北伐 **pěi-fá** the Northern Expedition (1926–1928)

北方局 **pěi-fāng-chú** the Northern Regional Bureau (of the CCP Central Committee before 1949)

北非 **pěi-fēi** North Africa

北国江南 **pěi-kuó chiāng-nán** (1) [the greenness of] Chiang-nan in the north of the country (the new appearance of lush vegetation in irrigated areas of the north); (2) the title of a motion picture criticized during the Cultural Revolution

北罗得西亚 **pěi ló-té-hsī-yà** Northern Rhodesia [now included in Zambia]

北煤南调 **pěi-méi nán-tiào** northern coal transported to the south (a reference to the old situation, now being changed, when the south lacked coal which had to be shipped from north China)

北婆罗洲 **pěi p'ó-ló-chòu** North Borneo

北上告状 **pěi-shàng kào-chuàng** to go north to make accusations (i.e., to Peking, during the Cultural Revolution, for criticism of opposing factions)

北大 **pěi-tà** National Peking University (contraction of Pěi-chīng Tà-hsuéh 北京大学)

北大荒 **pěi-tà-huāng** the great northern wilderness (the large undeveloped areas in Heilungkiang, now being opened up by large-scale state farms)

北大西洋公约 **pěi-tà-hsī-yáng kūng-yuēh** the North Atlantic Treaty

北大西洋公约组织 **pěi-tà-hsī-yáng kūng-yuēh-tsǔ-chīh** North Atlantic Treaty Organization [NATO]

北戴河 **pěi-tài-hó** Peitaiho (a beachside resort near Chingwangtao, site of several important Party conferences)

北洋军阀 **pěi-yáng chǔn-fá** northern warlords (during the Repulican period, especially 1912–1928)

pèi (bèi)

1627 贝专纳 **pèi-chuān-nà** Bechuanaland (now Botswana)

贝尔格莱德 **pèi-ěrh-kó-lái-té** Belgrade [Yugoslavia]

贝鲁特 **pèi-lǔ-t'è** Beirut [Lebanon]

贝雕 **pèi-tiāo** shell carving

1628 备案 **pèi-àn** to register, record, file, keep on record

备战 **pèi-chàn** to prepare for war; war preparations

备战, 备荒, 为人民 **pèi-chàn, pèi-huāng, wèi jén-mín** be prepared for war, avoid shortages [by having grain reserves], and [do everything] for the people

备件 **pèi-chièn** spare parts

备荒 **pèi-huāng** to be prepared for famine

备耕 **pèi-kēng** preparatory plowing (all preparations of the fields prior to seeding)

备课 **pèi-k'ò** class preparations (by the teacher)

备料 **pèi-liào** materials held in readiness [for production]

备忘录 **pèi-wàng-lù** a memorandum, aide memoire

备忘录贸易 **pèi-wàng-lù mào-ì** memorandum trade (refers to Sino-Japanese trade from 1963–1967 which was conducted on the basis of a "non-governmental" memorandum signed by Liao Ch'eng-chih and T. Takasaki)

1629 背井离乡 **pèi-chǐng lí-hsiāng** to turn one's back on the well and leave one's native place (to be forced to leave one's native place to seek a living)

背景 **pèi-chǐng** background, setting, backdrop, surrounding circumstances, social connections

背弃 **pèi-ch'ì** to turn one's back on, renounce, abandon, relinquish, forsake

背后 **pèi-hòu** back, behind, at the back of, behind one's back, in secret

背信弃义 **pèi-hsìn-ch'ì-ì** faithless and unscrupulous, perfidious, treacherous

背靠背 **pèi-k'ào-pèi** back against back (facing in opposite directions, incompatible, having no connection)

背离革命路线 **pèi-lí kó-mìng lù-hsièn** to divorce oneself from the revolutionary line

背包 **pèi-pāo** a knapsack

背叛 **pèi-p'àn** to betray, defect, rebel, become an apostate

背熟 **pèi-shú** to memorize completely, learn by heart, recite easily from memory

背诵 **pèi-sùng** to recite from memory

背道而驰 **pèi-tào-érh-ch'íh** to gallop off in the opposite direction

背 **pèi**: *see also* **pēi**

1630 倍增 **pèi-tsēng** to increase by one-fold, to double

1631 被专政 **pèi-chuān-chèng** subjected to [the people's] dictatorship (elements of society, such as former landlords, who do not enjoy full civil rights)

被侵略者 **pèi-ch'īn-luèh-chě** victims of aggression

被俘 **pèi-fú** to be taken prisoner [of war]

被选举权 **pèi-hsuǎn-chǔ-ch'üán** the right to stand for office, eligibility for election

被告 **pèi-kào** the accused, defendant

被管制分子 **pèi-kuǎn-chìh fèn-tzǔ** persons under surveillance (usually persons who have committed minor offenses and are required to report regularly to the police)

被逼 **pèi-pī** to be forced to, compelled to

剥削阶级 **pèi-pò-hsuèh chiēh-chí** the exploited classes

被动 **pèi-tùng** to be moved [only by outside forces], (passive—as contrasted with active, initiating)

被压迫阶级 **pèi-yā-p'ò chiēh-chí** the oppressed classes

被压迫人民 **pèi-yā-p'ò jén-mín** the oppressed people

被压迫民族 **pèi-yā-p'ò mín-tsú** the oppressed nations

被压迫民族解放运动 **pèi-yā-pò mín-tsú chiēh-fàng yùn-tùng** the liberation movement of the oppressed peoples

pēn (bēn)

1632 奔放 **pēn-fàng** running free, galloping, running riot; expressive and emotional [in writing or artistic work]

奔赴农村 **pēn-fù núng-ts'ūn** to rush to the rural villages

奔腾 **pēn-t'éng** to run and jump, leap about, rush forward

奔走 **pēn-tsǒu** to busy oneself intently, to be in a hurry, work actively [for a cause, etc.], strive for something

奔走相告 **pēn-tsǒu-hsiāng-kào** to run hither and thither with the news

pěn (běn)

1633 本届 **pěn-chièh** the current session, the present sitting

本质 **pěn-chìh** innate character, essential qualities, intrinsic nature, essence

本质差别 **pěn-chìh-ch'ā-piéh** essential distinction

本钱 **pěn-ch'íen** capital investment, capital, principal, asset

本分 **pěn-fèn** one's part, role, duty; the limit to one's rights

本行 **pěn-háng** one's own special field, this profession, this firm

本息 **pěn-hsī** principal and interest

本性 **pěn-hsìng** innate [human] nature, inborn, natural character

本国 **pěn-kuó** one's own country, homeland

本来面目 **pěn-lái-mièn-mù** the true look, original appearance, something's real [unmasked] character

本利 **pěn-lì** principal and interest

本领 **pěn-lǐng** ability, skill, talent

本末 **pěn-mò** the beginning and end, root and branch (the essential and peripherial)

本末倒置 **pěn-mò tǎo-chìh** to have the proper order reversed (to neglect the essentials and attend to the superficial)

本能 **pěn-néng** instinct, inborn ability, faculty

本本主义 **pěn-pěn-chǔ-ì** bookishness

本票 **pěn-p'iào** a cashier's check, promissory note

本色 **pěn-sè** original color, real look, true qualities

本身 **pěn-shēn** oneself, personally, itself, in itself

本事 **pěn-shìh** (1) skill, ability, talent; (2) resume of a story, synopsis of a plot

本单位 **pěn-tān-wèi** one's own unit

本地干部 **pěn-tì-kàn-pù** local cadres

本体 **pěn-t'ǐ** noumenon, a thing-in-itself, substance

本体论 **pěn-t'ǐ-lùn** ontology; ontological

本位主义 **pěn-wèi-chǔ-ì** departmentalism, parochialism, group egoism, "vested-interest-ism" (to be concerned only with one's own organizational unit)

本位主义思想 **pěn-wèi-chǔ-ì szū-hsiǎng** departmentalistic thinking

本文 **pěn-wén** the text, this article

pèn (bèn)

1634 笨拙 **pèn-chō** clumsy, awkward, unskilled

笨重劳动 **pèn-chùng láo-tùng** heavy manual labor

笨重体力活 **pèn-chùng t'ǐ-lì-huó** heavy physical work

笨脑袋 **pèn-nǎo-tài** stupid, muddle-headed, dull-witted

笨鸟先飞 **pèn-niǎo hsiēn-fēi** the slow bird has to fly first (self-deprecatory phrase of a person who has to take the first move)

pēng (bēng)

1635 崩溃 **pēng-k'uèi** to collapse, break down, cave in, disintegrate

崩龙族 **pēng-lúng-tsú** the Peng-lung people (a minority in Yunnan province: population 6,000 as of 1957)

1636 绷带 **pēng-tài** a bandage

pèng (bèng)

1637 迸发 **pèng-fā** to burst forth, erupt

1638 泵站 **pèng-chàn** a pump station

pī (bī)

1639 逼真 **pī-chēn** life-like, almost real [of a stage performance, etc.], true to life

逼近 **pī-chìn** to close in, draw near, gain on

逼供 **pī-kùng** to coerce testimony, extort a confession

逼, 供, 信 **pī, kùng, hsìn** compulsion, confession, credence (strictly prohibited methods of extorting confessions by "third degree" methods and then accepting those confessions as the basis for punishment)

逼令 **pī-lìng** to comple one to

逼迫 **pī-p'ò** to compel, force, impel one to, put pressure on one; urgent

逼上梁山 **pī-shàng-liáng-shān** to be compelled to ascend the Liang mountains (to be forced to become rebels and outlaws; the title of a Peking opera)

pí (bí)

1640 荸荠 **pí-ch'i** the water chestnut [*Seirpus Tuberosus*]

pǐ (bǐ)

1641 比重 **pǐ-chùng** relative weight, specific gravity

比附 **pǐ-fù** to liken, compare by putting things together, draw an analogy

比划 **pǐ-huà** to gesticulate, make motions, make combative gestures

比先进 **pǐ-hsiēn-chìn** to compare [oneself] with the advanced [leaders]

比, 学, 赶, 帮 **pǐ, hsuéh, kǎn, pāng** compare [oneself with the more advanced], learn [from the more advanced], catch up [with the more advanced], help [the less advanced] (a slogan popularized during the Great Leap)

比学赶帮超运动 **pǐ hsuéh kǎn pāng ch'āo yùn-tùng** the campaign to compare, learn, catch up, help and overtake

比垮 **pǐ-k'uǎ** to cause to topple by being compared [with others] (to fall short in emulation)

比勒陀利亚 **pǐ-lè-t'ó-lì-yà** Pretoria [South Africa]

比利时 **pǐ-lì-shíh** Belgium

271

比例 **pǐ-lì** proportion, ratio

比例代表制 **pǐ-lì tài-piǎo chìh** the system of proportional representation

比率 **pǐ-lù** ratio, proportion, rate

比拟 **pǐ-nǐ** to compare with, liken to; analagous

比比皆是 **pǐ-pǐ-chiēh-shìh** everywhere and in great numbers, widespread and numerous, very common

比赛 **pǐ-sài** a contest, match, tournament; to compete in a contest

比绍 **pǐ-shào** Guinea-Bissau (formerly Portuguese Guinea; also the name of the capital city)

比武 **pǐ-wǔ** a contest in martial arts (a production contest)

比喻 **pǐ-yù** a metaphor, simile, parable, allegory

1642 彼此呼应 **pǐ-tz'ǔ-hū-yìng** mutually responsive (giving mutual support)

1643 笔记 **pǐ-chì** to take notes; notes [of lectures, etc.]

笔下生花 **pǐ-hsià shēng-huā** flowers spring up under one's pen (an elegant writing style)

笔译 **pǐ-ì** a written translation

笔杆子 **pǐ kǎn-tzu** the handle of a pen, penholder (usually contrasted with **ch'īang kǎn-tzu,** the barrel of a gun)

笔名 **pǐ-míng** pen name, nom de plume

笔调 **pǐ-tiào** writing style

笔误 **pǐ-wù** a slip of the pen, mistake in writing, typographical error

1644 鄙视 **pǐ-shìh** to look with contempt on, despise

pì (bì)

1645 匕首 **pì-shǒu** a dagger, stiletto

1646 必修课 **pì-hsiū-k'ò** a required course [in college or school]

必然王国 **pì-ján-wáng-kuó** the realm of necessity (in which the people, because they are ignorant of the [Hegelian-Marxist] objective laws of society, have no free choice)

必恭必敬 **pì-kūng pì-chìng** showing great respect, very politely

必要条件 **pì-yào-t'iáo-chièn** a necessary condition, essential terms, requisite

必由之路 **pì-yú-chìh-lù** the road that must be followed

1647 闭会 **pì-huì** to adjourn a meeting, close a session; adjournment

闭会期间 **pì-huì-ch'ī-chiēn** a period of adjournment, not in session

闭关政策 **pì-kuān-chèng-ts'è** a closed door policy, an isolationist policy

闭关主义 **pì-kuān-chǔ-ì** isolationism

闭关自守 **pì-kuān tzù-shǒu** [a policy of] exclusion and self-defense

闭口不谈 **pì-k'ǒu-pù-t'án** to shut the mouth and say nothing

闭路电视 **pì-lù-tièn-shìh** closed-circuit television

闭门修养 **pì-mén hsiū-yǎng** to cultivate oneself behind closed doors (to divorce oneself from the masses and the Party)

闭门读书 **pì-mén tú-shū** to study behind closed doors (to divorce oneself from practice and reality)

闭门造车 **pì-mén-tsào-ch'ē** to make a cart behind closed doors (to ignore reality and to approach problems subjectively)

闭目塞听 **pì-mù sè-t'īng** to shut the eyes and plug the ears

闭幕 **pì-mù** to lower the curtain (to conclude, close, end)

闭幕词 **pì-mù-tz'ú** a curtain speech (at the end of a meeting)

闭塞 **pì-sè** (1) to block up, obstruct, stop up; (2) backward, remote

1648 毕生 **pì-shēng** throughout one's lifetime, lifelong, during one's whole life

毕业生 **pì-yèh-shēng** a graduate

毕业实践 **pì-yèh shíh-chièn** pre-graduation practice (a final term before graduation of university students in which they serve an internship in the field of their study)

毕业式 **pì-yèh-shìh** commencement, graduation ceremony

1649 庇护 **pì-hù** to harbor, protect, shield, shelter

1650 秘鲁 **pì-lǔ** Peru

1651 弊病 **pì-pìng** corrupt practices, shortcomings, deficiencies, disadvantages

1652 避重就轻 **pì-chùng-chiù-ch'īng** to avoid the heavy and take up the light (to avoid serious problems or responsibilities)

避而不谈 **pì-érh-pù-t'án** to avoid and refuse to discuss

避开 **pì-k'āi** to get out of the way, keep away from, shun

避免 **pì-miěn** to avoid; to forestall, prevent from happening, avert, save from

避难 **pì-nàn** to seek refuge, escape calamity

避难权 **pì-nàn-ch'üán** the right of asylum

避难所 **pì-nàn-sǒ** a place of refuge, asylum, sanctuary

避孕 **pì-yùn** to avoid pregnancy; contraception

避孕指导室 **pì-yùn chǐh-tǎo shìh** contraception guidance room

避孕手术 **pì-yùn shǒu-hsù** surgery to prevent conception (applies to both male and female)

避孕药 **pì-yùn-yào** birth control pills, contraceptive medicines

避孕用品 **pì-yùn-yùng-p'ǐn** contraceptive devices

1653 壁画 **pì-huà** a wall picture, fresco, mural

壁垒 **pì-lěi** a barricade, breastworks, barrier, fortification

壁垒森严 **pì-lěi-sēn-yén** the fortifications are thick and impressive, an unassailable stronghold

壁报 **pì-pào** a wall newspaper

壁上观 **pì-shàng-kuān** to watch from atop a wall (to watch a fight or struggle without aiding either party; to remain aloof)

piāo (biāo)

1654 标志 **piāo-chìh** a mark, sign, symbol

标帜 **piāo-chìh** a banner, sign, mark [of recognition or distinction]

标准 **piāo-chǔn** standard, criterion, model; typical

标准轨 **piāo-chǔn-kuēi** standard gauge [railway]

标签 **piāo-ch'iēn** a label, price tag

标尺 **piāo-ch'ǐh** a surveying measure, water depth gauge (also figurative)

标新立异 **piāo-hsīn-lì-ì** to manifest the new and establish the novel (to try to be original, to write or act in an attention-getting manner)

标杆 **piāo-kān** surveying rod, marking pole

标杆队 **piāo-kān-tuì** a standard-setting [production] team, model team

标榜 **piāo-pǎng** to give favorable publicity to, glorify, laud; to profess, declare

标本 **piāo-pěn** a specimen

标兵 **piāo-pīng** standard bearers (model workers, an honorary title in schools and factories)

标题 **piāo-t'í** heading, title, newspaper headline

标题音乐 **piāo-t'í-yīn-yuèh** program music (music intended to suggest a sequence of images or incidents)

标音文字 **piāo-yīn wén-tzù** a phonetic written language

标语 **piāo-yǔ** a written slogan, inscription, watchword, political slogan or motto

1655 膘肥体壮 **piāo-féi t'ǐ-chuàng** well fleshed and healthy [of animals]

piǎo (biǎo)

1656 表彰 **piǎo-chāng** to honor, cite, commend, publicize; a citation

表决 **piǎo-chüéh** to put to vote, decide by vote

表决权 **piǎo-chüéh-ch'üán** voting rights, the right to decide by vote

表现 **piǎo-hsièn** to give evidence of, show [results], appear, demonstrate [ability], distinguish oneself

表现手法 **piǎo-hsièn-shǒu-fǎ** means of expression [in literature and the arts]

表里 **piǎo-lǐ** outside and inside (form and content)

表露 **piǎo-lù** to make plain, express, expose, reveal

表面 **piǎo-mièn** on the surface, superficial, external, outward

表面价值 **piǎo-mièn-chià-chíh** face value

表面服从, 暗里破坏 **piǎo-mièn fú-ts'úng, àn-lǐ p'ò-huài** superficial compliance but secret obstruction

表面化 **piǎo-mièn-huà** to externalize; externalization

表示 **piǎo-shìh** to show, express, demonstrate, indicate

表示态度 **piǎo-shìh-t'ài-tù** to define one's attitude, make one's attitude known

表率 **piǎo-shuài** a model, example, leader, paragon

表达 **piǎo-tá** to express [meaning or feelings], to convey, transmit, make known

表态 **piǎo-t'ài** to make plain one's attitude (contraction of **piǎo-shìh t'ài-tù**)

表态式 **piǎo-t'ài-shìh** to make a gesture of showing one's attitude (with the implication of concealing one's true attitude; to make a pretense)

表扬 **piǎo-yáng** to praise in public, commend, compliment, praise, cite

表扬信 **piǎo-yáng-hsìn** a letter of commendation (usually to the superior of the person being commended)

piéh (bié)

1657 别开生面 **piéh-k'āi-shēng-mièn** to create a new face (to create a new style; introduce a novel feature)

别名 **piéh-míng** an alias, a given name other than the one by which a person is usually known

别墅 **piéh-shù** a villa, country house

别动队 **piéh-tùng-tuì** special activities forces (a branch of the KMT special services which can be compared in function to the German S.S.)

别无分店 **piéh-wú-fēn-tièn** there is no branch shop elsewhere (this is the only true brand [of goods or ideology])

别有用心 **piéh-yǔ-yùng-hsīn** to have a hidden purpose; with an ulterior motive

piēn (biān)

1658 边际 **piēn-chì** a boundary, limit, margin; marginal

边疆 **piēn-chiāng** frontier regions, borderlands

边疆区党委 **piēn-chiāng-ch'ü̆ tăng-wěi** a frontier region Party committee

边疆民兵建设 **piēn-chiāng mín-pīng chièn-shè** the build-up of militia in the frontier regions

边界问题 **piēn-chièh-wèn-t'í** boundary questions, border problems

边境 **piēn-chìng** national boundary, frontier zone

边境贸易 **piēn-chìng mào-ì** frontier trade, trans-border trade

边境兑换 **piēn-chìng-tuì-huàn** currency exchange at the border

边卡 **piēn-ch'iǎ** a frontier post

边沁主义 **piēn-ch'ìn-chǔ-ì** Benthamism (utilitarianism)

边区 **piēn-ch'ü̆** border area [between provinces] (usually a Communist base area established during the Anti-Japanese War)

边防 **piēn-fáng** frontier defense

边防军 **piēn-fáng-chǖn** frontier defense force, border guards

边防部队 **piēn-fáng pù-tuì** frontier defense units

边学习, 边运用 **piēn-hsuéh-hsí, piēn-yùn-yùng** to study on one hand and apply on the other (simultaneous study and practice)

边学边干 **piēn-hsuéh-piēn-kàn** simultaneously to study and to [apply the study in] action, to learn while doing

边改造, 边使用, 边提高 **piēn-kǎi-tsào, piēn-shǐh-yùng, piēn-t'í-kāo** simultaneously to reform, use, and raise [the level]

边干边学 **piēn-kàn piēn-hsuéh** doing while learning

边实践, 边教学 **piēn-shíh-chièn, piēn-chiào-hsuéh** simultaneously to practice and to teach (developing teaching materials through experiment)

边实践, 边设计 **piēn-shíh-chièn, piēn-shè-chì** simultaneously to practice and to design (to carry on industrial design on the basis of practical use)

边实验, 边教学 **piēn-shíh-yèn, piēn-chiào-hsuéh** simultaneously to experiment and to teach

边谈边打 **piēn-t'án piēn-tǎ** on one hand to talk and on the other to fight, to negotiate and fight at the same time

边缘 **piēn-yuán** the edge, margin, rim, brink

1659 编者按(语) **piēn-chě àn [-yǔ]** editor's note

编辑部 **piēn-chì-pù** editorial department

编制 **piēn-chìh** to draw up, organize, draft, compile, codify; organizational system, table of organization

编制和定员制度 **piēn-chìh hó tìng-yuán chìh-tù** the principle of established organizational forms and specified personnel

编著者 **piēn-chù-chě** a compiler, editor

编剧 **piēn-chù** to write a play; a playwright

编号 **piēn-hào** a designation number, assigned identifying number [for a person, document, or thing]

编写 **piēn-hsiěh** to compile and write

编译 **piēn-ì** editing and translating; a translator, interpreter

编目 **piēn-mù** to prepare a catalog, arrange a table of contents; a cataloguer

编排 **piēn-p'ái** (1) to arrange in order; (2) write and direct [a play, etc.]

编造 **piēn-tsào** to fabricate, form, put together

编演 **piēn-yěn** to write and stage [a play]

编印 **piēn-yìn** to edit and print, publish

1660 鞭炮 **piēn-p'ào** firecrackers

鞭子 **piēn-tzu** a whip, lash (a symbol of the old ruling class)

鞭策自己 **piēn-ts'è-tzù-chǐ** to flog oneself (to push oneself to great efforts)

piěn (biǎn)

1661 贬值 **piěn-chíh** to devaluate [especially currency]; devaluation

贬低 **piěn-tī** to derogate, disparage, downgrade, put a low value on

pièn (biàn)

1662 变节 **pièn-chiéh** to desert a cause, defect, become an apostate, switch

变节分子 **pièn-chiéh-fēn-tzǔ** a turncoat,

renegade, deserter

变质 **pièn-chìh** to change in quality, degenerate, deteriorioate

变种 **pièn-chǔng** a mutant [of plant or animals]

变迁 **pièn-ch'iēn** to change in trend; evolution, change

变法 **pièn-fǎ** a reform in the form of government, political reform, constitutional reform

变废为宝 **pièn-fèi-wéi-pǎo** to transform waste into something of value

变化 **pièn-huà** to transform, change, transmute, metamorphose; vicissitudes

变换 **pièn-huàn** to convert, change, switch

变相 **pièn-hsiàng** changed only in appearance, disguised

变相劳改 **pièn-hsiàng láo-kǎi** a disguised form of labor reform (Lin Piao is accused of saying this about the movement to send youth to the mountains and villages)

变相失业 **pièn-hsiàng shìh-yèh** disguised form of unemployment (a statement attributed to Lin Piao in reference to **hsià-fàng**)

变心 **pièn-hsīn** a change of heart; to change loyalty, turn traitor

变更 **pièn-kēng** to change, alter, modify

变革 **pièn-kó** to reform, revolutionize; change, reform, reformation

变革现实 **pièn-kó hsièn-shíh** to alter reality, change actual circumstances

变工 **pièn-kūng** to exchange labor; labor exchange

变工互助 **pièn-kūng hù-chù** to exchange labor and help each other, labor exchange and mutual aid

变工队 **pièn-kūng-tuì** labor exchange teams

变乱 **pièn-luàn** rebellion, revolt, upheaval, chaos

变劣势为优势 **pièn luèh-shìh wéi yū-shìh** to change an unfavorable situation into a favorable one

变本加厉 **pièn-pěn-chiā-lì** to change something and make it more serious (from bad to worse)

变色 **pièn-sè** to change color (usually implies a change away from being "red" or Communist)

变数 **pièn-shù** a variable [in mathematics]

变电站 **pièn-tièn-chàn** tranformer station

变动 **pièn-tùng** to change, reorganize, reshuffle [an organization]; change, fluctuation, alteration, modification

变态 **pièn-t'ài** abnormality; metamorphosis [zoology]

变天 **pièn t'iēn** a change of weather (usually from fine to bad); a change of regime (implies a change away from socialism)

变天账 **pièn-t'iēn-chàng** accounts allegedly kept by landlords and capitalists so that they will be able to collect their losses when the Communist government is replaced

变天思想 **pièn-t'iēn szū-hsiǎng** restorationist thinking, the hope for the return of the old regime

变通 **pièn-t'ūng** to change method, adapt to circumstances, be flexible; expedient

变压器 **pièn-yā-ch'ì** an [electric] transformer

1663 便服 **pièn-fú** everyday dress, civilian garb, ordinary clothing

便衣警察 **pièn-i-chǐng-ch'á** a plainclothes policeman

便衣公安人员 **pièn-ī kūng-ān jén-yuán** plainclothes public-security personnel

便宜行事 **pièn-í hsíng-shìh** to act as circumstances may require [without asking for approval from superiors]

便利 **pièn-lì** a convenience, facility, accommodation, advantage

1664 遍地开花 **pièn-tì-k'āi-huā** the ground is covered with blossoms (to flourish on a broad scale)

1665 辨清方向 **pièn-ch'īng fāng-hsiàng** to distinguish clearly [the correct] direction

辨清是非 **pièn-ch'īng shìh-fēi** to distinguish clearly between right and wrong

辨认 **pièn-jèn** to recognize, identify, distinguish, perceive, discern

辨别 **pièn-piéh** to distinguish between, see the difference between, discriminate, differentiate

辨别力 **pièn-piéh-lì** the power of discernment

1666 辩证 **pièn-chèng** dialectical, dialectically

辩证法 **pièn-chèng-fǎ** dialectical method, dialectics

辩证发展过程 **pièn-chèng fā-chǎn kuò-ch'éng** the dialectical process

辩证唯物主义 **pièn-chèng wéi-wù-chǔ-ì** dialectical materialism

辩证唯物主义观点 **pièn-chèng wéi-wù-chǔ-ì kuān-tiěn** the viewpoint of dialectical materialism (one of the **szù-tà-kuān-tiěn**)

辩证唯物论 **pièn-chèng wéi-wù-lùn** dialectical materialism

辩解 **pièn-chiěh** to make excuses for, try to justify, palliate, explain, vindicate

辩护 **pièn-hù** to defend verbally, defend in a legal action, plead a case

辩护士 **pièn-hù-shìh** a lawyer, barrister; apologist

辩论 **pièn-lùn** to debate, carry on an argument; a debate, controversy

辩驳 **pièn-pó** to rebut, refute, debate,

1667　辫子 **pièn-tzu** a pigtail, queue (something that can easily be grabbed: hence, a vulnerable point)

pǐn (bǐn)

1668　宾至如归 **pǐn-chìh-jú-kuēi** the guests feel at home

宾馆 **pǐn-kuǎn** a guest house (usually for distinguished visitors)

1669　滨州铁路 **pǐn-chōu t'iěh-lù** the Harbin-Manchouli railway

滨长铁路 **pǐn-ch'áng t'iěh-lù** the Harbin-Changchun railway

滨绥铁路 **pǐn-suí t'iěh-lù** the Harbin-Suifenho railway

1670　濒临 **pǐn-lín** near, close, on the brink of, on the verge of

濒临崩溃 **pǐn-lín-pēng-k'uèi** on the brink of collapse

濒于灭亡 **pǐn-yú-mièh-wáng** on the brink of extermination

pìn (bìn)

1671　摈弃 **pìn-ch'ì** to push away, get rid of, reject, cast away, discard

pǐng (bǐng)

1672　冰川 **pǐng-ch'uān** a glacier

冰消瓦解 **pǐng-hsiāo-wǎ-chiěh** the ice has melted and the tiles are scattered (dissolution and complete collapse)

冰岛 **pǐng-tǎo** Iceland

冰点 **pǐng-tiěn** freezing point

冰天雪地 **pǐng-t'iēn-hsuěh-tì** icy skies and snowy land (bitterly cold)

1673　兵舰 **pǐng-chièn** a warship, naval vessel

兵种 **pǐng-chǔng** specialized branches of the armed forces

兵强马壮 **pǐng-ch'iáng mǎ-chuàng** strong soldiers and sturdy horses (a powerful army)

兵权 **pǐng-ch'üán** military power, military forces

兵法 **pǐng-fǎ** military arts, military strategy and tactics

兵荒马乱 **pǐng-huāng-mǎ-luàn** the soldiers are wild and the horses are in disorder (the chaos brought by unjust war)

兵役 **pǐng-ì** military service, conscription

兵役证 **pǐng-ì-chèng** draft card

兵役制 **pǐng-ì-chìh** conscription system

兵役委员会 **pǐng-ì wěi-yuán-huì** military service committee (units at district and *hsien* levels to select and notify new PLA recruits), draft boards

兵工厂 **pǐng-kūng-ch'ǎng** an ordnance factory, arsenal

兵力 **pǐng-lì** military strength, military manpower

兵变 **pǐng-pièn** a [military] mutiny

兵痞 **pǐng-p'ǐ** a soldier ruffian (usually an old professional soldier whose motives are mercenary and who exists by avoiding combat and living off the people)

兵团 **pǐng-t'uán** an army group, corps (usually a grouping of at least two armies)

兵营 **pǐng-yíng** a military camp, barracks

兵油子 **pǐng-yú-tzu** an oily soldier (*see* **pǐng-p'ǐ**)

pìng (bìng)

1674　并肩战斗 **pìng-chiēn chàn-tòu** to fight shoulder to shoulder

并肩前进 **pìng-chiēn ch'ién-chìn** to advance shoulder to shoulder

并肩作战 **pìng-chiēn tsò-chàn** to fight shoulder to shoulder

并重 **pìng-chùng** equally heavy (of equal importance)

并称 **pìng-ch'ēng** to mention together

并成 **pìng-ch'éng** to fuse together, merge, combine, amalgamate, unify

并举 **pìng-chǔ** to do simultaneously, carry out at the same time, develop concurrently

并非 **pìng-fēi** by no means, in no sense, really (used to reinforce a negative)

并行 **pìng-hsíng** to walk abreast; in parallel

并行不悖 **pìng-hsíng-pù-pèi** parallel and unopposed (to be able to carry on two things at the same time without conflict)

并列 **pìng-lièh** to juxtapose; parallel, side by side, coordinate

并排 **pìng-p'ái** in a row, in the same row, side by side, alongside

并社 **pìng-shè** to combine cooperatives (to form large cooperatives by merging smaller cooperatives)

并社升级 **pìng-shè-shēng-chí** to merge

cooperatives and raise them to a high-level [organization]

并吞 **pìng-t'ùn** to annex, absorb, swallow up

并网发电 **pìng-wǎng-fā-tièn** power transmission net [connecting various sources]

1675 病症 **pìng-chèng** disease, illness

病假 **pìng-chià** sick leave

病状 **pìng-chuàng** symptoms of a disease

病情公报 **pìng-ch'íng-kūng-pào** a medical bulletin [on the condition of the patient]

病虫害 **pìng-ch'úng-hài** disease and insect pest damage [to crops]

病菌 **pìng-chùn** microbe, germ, bacteria

病房 **pìng-fáng** a hospital room (may refer to either a ward or private room)

病号 **pìng-hào** a sick person (originally a military person on the sick list)

病入膏肓 **pìng-jù-kāo-huāng** a disease that has entered the vital organs (an incurable illness, terminal illness)

病容 **pìng-júng** a sickly appearance, emaciated look

病历 **pìng-lì** medical history [of a patient]

病室 **pìng-shìh** a hospital room or ward; a sick room or small medical facility

病毒 **pìng-tú** a virus

1676 摒弃 **pìng-ch'ì** to discard, abandon, reject, renounce, exclude

pō (bō)

1677 波及 **pō-chí** to affect, involve, spread to

波长 **pō-ch'áng** wave length

波恩 **pō-ēn** Bonn [West Germany]

波哥大 **pō-kō-tà** Bogota [Colombia]

波兰 **pō-lán** Poland

波兰通讯社 **pō-lán t'ūng-hsùn-shè** Polish Press Agency [PAP]

波澜壮阔 **pō-lán chuàng k'ùo** the great waves are strong and broad

波浪式起伏 **pō-làng-shìh ch'ǐ-fú** rising and falling like waves (undulating movement)

波浪式前进 **pō-làng-shìh ch'ién-chìn** to move ahead with a wavelike motion

波斯湾 **pō-szū-wān** the Persian Gulf

波多黎各 **pō-tō-lí-kò** Puerto Rico

波多诺伏 **pō-tō-nò-fú** Porto Novo [Dahomey]

波动 **pō-tùng** wavelike movement; undulations, fluctuations, unrest

波涛 **pō-t'āo** waves and billows,

breakers, large waves

波茨坦协定 **pō-tz'ú-t'ǎn hsiéh-tìng** the Potsdam Agreement

1678 拨款 **pō-k'uǎn** to allocate funds, appropriate money; an appropriation

1679 剥削 **pō-hsuēh** to exploit, despoil; exploitation

剥削阶级 **pō-hsuēh-chiēh-chí** the exploiting class

剥削阶级统治 **pō-hsuēh-chiēh-chí t'ǔng-chìh** control by the exploiting class

剥削方式 **pō-hsuēh fāng-shìh** form of exploitation

剥削行为 **pō-hsuēh hsíng-wéi** exploitive practices

剥削思想 **pō-hsuēh-szū-hsiǎng** exploitive thinking

剥削有功论 **pō-hsuēh yǔ-kūng lùn** the doctrine that exploitation has merit (an accusation against Liu Shao-ch'i)

剥削越多功劳越大 **pō-hsuēh yuèh tō, kūng-láo yuèh-tà** the more [the capitalists] exploit, the greater their merit (a statement charged against Liu Shao-ch'i)

剥夺 **pō-tó** to deprive of, take away, divest of, dispossess, despoil

剥夺自由刑 **pō-tó tzù-yú hsíng** to punish by depriving of liberty (usually refers to surveillance rather than imprisonment)

1680 玻利维亚 **pō-lì-wéi-yà** Bolivia

1681 播种机 **pō-chǔng-chī** a seeding machine, planter, sower

播种面积 **pō-chùng-mièn-chī** sown area

播出 **pō-ch'ū** to broadcast, disseminate

播送 **pō-sùng** to transmit [by radio], broadcast

pó (bó)

1682 伯恩斯坦 **pó-ēn-szū-t'ǎn** Bernstein [Eduard] (1850–1932, a German revisionist in the Second International)

伯尔尼 **pó-ěrh-ní** Berne [Switzerland]

伯利兹 **pó-lì-tzū** Belize [British Honduras]

1683 驳斥 **pó-ch'ìh** to refute, disprove, expose error, rebut; to dismiss [a lawsuit], reject an appeal

驳船 **pó-ch'uán** a barge, lighter

驳不胜驳 **pó-pù-shèng-pó** too many [arguments] to rebut successfully, too many [lies, arguments, mistakes] to deal with

驳倒 **pó-tǎo** to defeat in debate; utterly refuted

1684 勃列日涅夫 **pó-lièh-jìh-nièh-fū** Brezhnev

1685 柏林 **pó-lín** Berlin
柏油路 **pó-yú-lù** a tarred road, asphalt road
1686 博爱 **pó-ài** fraternity, love for all
博古通今 **pó-kǔ-t'ūng-chīn** to know well both the ancient and the present
博览会 **pó-lǎn-huì** a trade fair, exposition, exhibition
博得信任 **pó-té-hsìn-jèn** to win confidence
博物馆 **pó-wù-kuǎn** a museum
1687 渤海海峡 **pó-hǎi hǎi-hsiá** the Pohai Strait (off the coast of Shantung)
1688 搏斗 **pó-tòu** to engage in hand-to-hand combat, fight at close quarters
1689 薄弱 **pó-jò** weak, feeble, fragile, inadequate
薄弱环节 **pó-jò-huán-chiéh** weak links
薄利多销 **pó-lì tō-hsiāo** to cut profit in order to increase sales

pǒ (bǒ)

1690 簸扬机 **pǒ-yáng-chī** a winnowing machine

pǔ (bǔ)

1691 卜卦 **pǔ-kuà** to divine [by the Eight Diagrams]
1692 补给 **pǔ-chǐ** to provision, supply, replenish, reinforce; [military] provisions
补救 **pǔ-chiù** to remedy, save the situation, rectify shortcomings
补助 **pǔ-chù** to subsidize, assist, support financially
补助金 **pǔ-chù-chīn** a subsidy, subvention, grant-in-aid, special allowance
补偿 **pǔ-ch'áng** to compensate, indemnify, make good, pay reparation for
补齐 **pǔ-ch'í** to make even, compensate for deficiencies
补充 **pǔ-ch'ūng** to supplement, add to, make up, fill out
补缺 **pǔ-ch'üēh** to fill a vacancy, fill a vacant post
补发工资 **pǔ-fā kūng-tzū** to pay up back wages
补习 **pǔ-hsí** supplemental study, make-up study, private tutoring
补选 **pǔ-hsuǎn** a by-election
补课 **pǔ-k'ò** to make up a lesson usually figurative)
补办 **pǔ-pàn** to complete [formalities] belatedly
补税 **pǔ-shuì** to pay up unpaid tax, make good a tax deficiency

补丁摞补丁 **pǔ-tīng lò-pǔ-tīng** patches on patches, impoverished (may be figurative: piecemeal revision instead of fundamental change or improvement)
补短 **pǔ-tuǎn** to make up deficiencies, meet a deficit, correct shortcomings
补贴 **pǔ-t'iēh** to subsidize, help financially
补贴工分 **pǔ-t'iēh kūng-fēn** to subsidize in work points
补退不罚 **pǔ-t'uì pù-fá** no punishment if reimbursement is made
补足 **pǔ-tsú** to supply what is lacking, make whole, cover a deficit
1693 捕风捉影 **pǔ-fēng-chō-yǐng** to seize the wind and grasp the shadows (to talk or act without basis in fact, grasping at straws, pursuing chimeras)
1694 哺乳室 **pǔ-jǔ-shìh** a nursing room (usually for mothers working in factories)
哺育 **pǔ-yù** to nurture; nourishment

pù (bù)

1695 不战不和 **pù-chàn-pù-hó** neither war nor peace
不折不扣 **pù-ché-pù-k'òu** without discount (in full, fully, a hundred percent, absolutely)
不正之风 **pù-chèng-chīh-fēng** an unhealthy tendency, bad work style
不及 **pù-chí** not up to, cannot compare with, not as [good] as
不即不离 **pù-chí-pù-lí** neither close nor remote, to keep a certain distance
不计成本 **pù-chì ch'éng-pěn** to disregard the cost
不计其数 **pù-chì-ch'í-shù** too numerous to count, numberless, numerous
不假思索 **pù-chiǎ-szū-sǒ** not to depend on consideration (quick reaction)
不骄不躁 **pù-chiāo pù-tsào** not conceited or rash
不结盟国家 **pù-chiéh-méng kuó-chiā** the non-aligned nations
不竭源泉 **pù-chiéh-yuán-ch'üán** an inexhaustible source
不解之谜 **pù-chiěh-chīh-mí** an unfathomable enigma
不坚定分子 **pù-chiēn-tìng fèn-tzǔ** wavering elements
不见棺材不流泪 **pù-chièn kuān-ts'ai pù-liú-lèi** one who does not shed tears until he sees the coffin
不知所措 **pù-chīh-sǒ-ts'ò** at a loss as to what to do, in a dilemma
不知所云 **pù-chīh-sǒ-yún** not to know what is being said

不值一笑 **pù-chíh-í-hsiào** not worth a laugh (beneath consideration)

不值一驳 **pù-chíh-í-pó** not worth refuting

不止不行 **pù-chǐh pù-hsíng** without stopping [the old] there can be no carrying out [the new]

不治之症 **pù-chìh-chīh-chèng** an incurable disease, fatal illness (often figurative)

不置可否 **pù-chìh-k'ǒ-fǒu** without saying yes or no, without expressing agreement or disagreement (to make no comment)

不咎既往 **pù-chiù-chì-wǎng** not to go into past misdeeds

不着边际 **pù-chó-piēn-chì** without even touching the margin [of the issue]

不抓不行 **pù-chuā-pù-hsíng** without grasping firmly it cannot be done

不抓不行, 抓而不紧 **pù-chuā pù-hsíng, chuā érh pù-chǐn** it will not do to have no grasp at all—nor will it do if the grasp is not firm

不成 **pù-ch'éng** will not do, not going to succeed

不成功便成仁 **pù-ch'éng-kūng piènch'éng-jén** if it does not succeed, I must preserve virtue [by killing myself] (words allegedly used by Lin Piao before his attempted coup against Mao Tse-tung)

不成文 **pù-ch'éng-wén** unwritten [law]

不承担义务 **pù-ch'éng-tān ì-wù** not to assume any obligation, not to commit oneself

不期而遇 **pù-ch'í-érh-yù** to meet unexpectedly, encounter someone by chance

不期然而然 **pù-ch'í-ján érh-ján** without being expected, it turned out this way

不切实际 **pù-ch'ièh shíh-chì** not in touch with reality; unrealistic, impractical

不浅 **pù-ch'iěn** not superficial, not shallow (serious; seriously)

不齿 **pù-ch'ǐh** to condemn, despise; despicable

不耻下问 **pù-ch'ǐh-hsià-wèn** not ashamed to ask, not ashamed to learn [from one's inferiors]

不啻 **pù-ch'ìh** not less than, equivalent to, the same as, as if

不求进步 **pù-ch'iú chìn-pù** not striving to progress

不求甚解 **pù-ch'iú shèn-chiěh** not striving for a deep understanding

不出所料 **pù-ch'ū-sǒ-liào** not beyond expectations (just as expected)

不绝 **pù-chüéh** without an end,

uneasing, at all times

不绝其自新之路 **pù-chüéh ch'í tzù-hsīnchīh-lù** not to close off another person's chance to reform himself

不绝如缕 **pù-chüéh-jú-lǔ** only a single strand remains unbroken (a desperate situation); to be almost extinct (as a declining skill)

不均 **pù-chǔn** unequal; inequality

不屈 **pù-ch'ǖ** unbending, unyielding, unswerving

不屈战士 **pù-ch'ǖ chàn-shìh** an unwavering fighter, one who fights to the bitter end

不屈不挠 **pù-ch'ǖ pù-náo** not to be bent or cowed, unyielding

不全面 **pù-ch'üán-mièn** not comprehensive (partial)

不乏其人 **pù-fá ch'í-jén** that kind of person is not few, not lacking that kind of person

不法 **pù-fǎ** unlawful, illegal, illicit, illegitimate

不凡 **pù-fán** not common (extraordinary, exceptional, outstanding)

不妨 **pù-fáng** might as well, no harm [in trying, etc.]

不放一枪 **pù-fàng-í-ch'iāng** without firing a single shot

不分正反 **pù-fēn chèng-fǎn** without distinguishing the right [side] and the wrong [side], regardless of the rights or wrongs

不分昼夜 **pù-fēn-chòu-yèh** not to separate day and night (to work around the clock)

不分上下, 不分老少 **pù-fēn shàng-hsià, pù-fēn lǎo-shào** making no distinction of rank or age

不分敌我 **pù-fēn-tí-wǒ** to fail to distinguish between the enemy and ourselves

不敷 **pù-fū** not enough, insufficient

不服 **pù-fú** not to submit, to resist, rebel, be recalcitrant

不服气 **pù-fú-ch'ì** recalcitrant, unwilling to submit, rebellious disobedient, resentful

不负众望 **pù-fù chùng-wàng** not to fail the people's hopes

不负任何条件 **pù-fù-chiā jèn-hó t'iáochièn** without attaching any conditions, with no strings attached

不符合客观实际 **pù-fù-hó k'ò-kuānshíh-chì** inconsistent with objective reality

不寒而慄 **pù-hán-érh-lì** trembling with fear, terrified

不好的下场 **pù-hǎo-te hsià-ch'ǎng** an inauspicious exit, unhappy end

不合逻辑 **pù-hó ló-chì** not in accord with logic, illogical

不合作主义 **pù-hó-tsò-chǔ-ì** the principle of non-cooperation, civil disobedience, passive resistence

不和 **pù-hó** disharmony, not on good terms, incompatible

不怀好意 **pù-huái-hǎo-ì** not cherishing good intentions (with evil intent, bearing ill will)

不欢而散 **pù-huān-érh-sàn** an unhappy end of a meeting; to disperse in discord

不惜牺牲 **pù-hsī hsī-shēng** to spare no sacrifice, be ready for any sacrifice

不惜工本 **pù-hsī kūng-pěn** to spare neither labor nor cost

不惜笔墨 **pù-hsī pǐ-mò** unsparing of pen and ink (to write voluminously)

不下火线 **pù-hsià-huǒ-hsièn** never to retreat from the firing line (to stick resolutely to one's task; never give in)

不相干 **pù-hsiāng-kān** to have nothing to do with, does not concern, irrelevant

不相上下 **pù-hsiāng-shàng-hsià** neither higher nor lower than each other (mutual equality, on a par, about the same)

不祥之兆 **pù-hsiáng-chīh-chào** an omen of trouble, unlucky omen

不向国家伸手 **pù-hsiàng kuó-chiā shēn-shǒu** do not hold out hands to the state (solve problems at the local level)

不象样子 **pù-hsiàng-yàng-tzu** disreputable, not up to snuff, not up to the norm

不肖子孙 **pù-hsiāo tzǔ-sūn** unworthy descendants, good-for-nothing heirs

不孝有三，无后为大 **pù-hsiào yǔ-sān, wú-hòu wéi-tà** of the three unfilial [acts], to lack an heir is the greatest

不屑一顾 **pù-hsièh-ī-kù** not to condescend to give [even] one look, despise

不懈 **pù-hsièh** untiring, unremitting [effort]

不信邪 **pù hsìn-hsiéh** not to believe in ghosts (to have no imaginary fears, to be courageous)

不信任案 **pù-hsìn-jèn àn** a motion of no confidence [parliamentary]

不行 **pù-hsíng** [this] will not do, not up to standard, to no avail, unacceptable; not allowed; unsuccessful

不省人事 **pù-hsǐng-jén-shìh** unable to understand human events (unconscious, insensible)

不幸 **pù-hsìng** bad luck, unfortunate; unfortunately

不朽 **pù-hsiǔ** immortal, eternal, undying

不锈钢 **pù-hsiù-kāng** stainless steel

不宣而战 **pù-hsuān-érh-chàn** to go to war without a declaration (to wage an undeclared war)

不学无术 **pù-hsuéh-wú-shù** wanting in learning and without skill (incompetent, ignorant, uneducated)

不一而足 **pù-ī-érh-tsú** many, a great variety, and so forth, et cetera

不移 **pù-í** unchanging, consistent

不遗余力 **pù-í-yǘ-lì** to spare no effort, do one's utmost

不以人们意志为转移 **pù ǐ jén-mén ì-chìh wéi chuǎn-í** not to be moved by the will of men (independent of human will)

不以为意 **pù-ǐ-wéi-ì** to think nothing of, pay no attention to, heedless

不以为然 **pù-ǐ-wéi-ján** to not regard it as right (to come to a different conclusion; to disagree)

不义之财 **pù-ì-chīh-ts'ái** dishonest wealth, wealth gained illicitly, loot, dirty money

不翼而飞 **pù-ì-érh-fēi** without wings and yet flown (inexplicably missing, stolen; to travel without wings: i.e., fast-spreading news)

不入虎穴，焉得虎子 **pù-jù hǔ-hsuèh, yēn-té hǔ-tzǔ** how can one obtain tiger cubs if one does not enter the tiger's lair (no great feat is accomplished without risk)

不容置疑 **pù-júng-chìh-í** without permitting any doubt, indisputable

不容置辩 **pù-júng-chìh-pièn** permitting no argument, beyond dispute, undeniable, indisputable

不容抵赖 **pù-júng-tǐ-lài** to brook no denial

不干涉政策 **pù-kān-shè chèng-ts'è** a policy of nonintervention

不甘后人 **pù-kān-hòu-jén** not willing to be behind others (not wishing to be backward)

不甘心灭亡 **pù-kān-hsīn mièh-wáng** no [person or class] willingly accepts extermination (no class is exterminated without a struggle)

不甘示弱 **pù-kān-shìh-jò** reluctant to show weakness, unwilling to be shown as inferior

不顾前后 **pù-kù-ch'ién-hòu** not regarding what is in the front or back (rash, reckless, heedless, imprudent)

不顾生死 **pù-kù-shēng-szǔ** without

regard for life or death

不顾死活 **pù-kù-szǔ-huó** not regarding death or life

不顾条件 **pù-kù t'iáo-chièn** to take no account of [actual] circumstances, heedless of conditions

不管用 **pù-kuǎn-yùng** not practical in use, not suited [to the application]

不光彩 **pù-kuāng-ts'ǎi** adding no luster to the face (to lose face)

不攻自破 **pù-kūng-tzù-p'ò** to fall of itself without being attacked (usually refers to a false thesis, slander, etc.)

不共戴天 **pù-kùng-tài-t'iēn** not to share the same sky (cannot co-exist; implacable hostility)

不堪一击 **pù-k'ān-ī-chī** unable to withstand a single attack

不堪设想 **pù-k'ān-shè-hsiǎng** unthinkable, unimaginable [consequences]

不可战胜 **pù-k'ǒ-chàn-shèng** invincible, unconquerable

不可争辩 **pù-k'ǒ chēng-pièn** indisputable, irrefutable

不可知论 **pù-k'ǒ-chīh lùn** agnosticism

不可救药 **pù-k'ǒ-chiù-yào** cannot be saved by medication, incurable (hopeless, incorrigible)

不可侵犯 **pù-k'ǒ-ch'īn-fàn** cannot be encroached upon, inviolable

不可分性 **pù-k'ǒ-fēn-hsìng** indivisibility

不可分离 **pù-k'ǒ fēn-lí** indivisible, integral, inseparable, inalienable

不可或缺 **pù-k'ǒ huò-ch'üēh** cannot be dispensed with (vital, essential)

不可想象 **pù-k'ǒ hsiǎng-hsiàng** cannot be imagined, inconceivable

不可一世 **pù-k'ǒ ī-shìh** unable [to see others] in a generation (arrogant in the extreme)

不可告人 **pù-k'ǒ-kào-jén** [something that] cannot be told to others (covert intentions, a shameful act)

不可告人的动机 **pù-k'ǒ-kào-jén te tùng-chī** ulterior motives

不可抗拒 **pù-k'ǒ k'àng-chù** irresistible, inevitable; *force majeure*

不可抗拒的法则 **pù-k'ǒ k'àng-chù te· fǎ-tsé** an irresistible law, immutable law

不可克服 **pù-k'ǒ-k'ò-fú** unconquerable, insurmountable, insuperable

不可理喻 **pù-k'ǒ-lǐ-yù** cannot be convinced by reason, not susceptible to rational persuasion, unreasonable

不可磨灭 **pù-k'ǒ-mó-mièh** indestructible

不可偏废 **pù-k'ǒ-p'iēn-fèi** not to favor [one side] and neglect [the other]

不可少 **pù-k'ǒ-shǎo** cannot get along without, cannot be reduced in number, indispensable

不可胜计 **pù-k'ǒ shēng-chì** too numerous to count

不可收拾 **pù-k'ǒ shōu-shíh** cannot be put to rights, cannot be mended [of a situation]

不可思议 **pù-k'ǒ-szū-ì** [it] cannot be thought and told (inconceivable, incomprehensible; mysterious; wonderful)

不可调和 **pù-k'ǒ-t'iáo-hó** irreconcilable, implacable

不可推诿的义务 **pù-k'ǒ t'uī-wěi te ì-wù** an unshirkable obligation

不可同日而语 **pù-k'ǒ t'úng-jìh érh yǔ** cannot be spoken of on the same day (not to be mentioned in the same breath)

不可逾越的鸿沟 **pù-k'ǒ yǘ-yuèh te húng-kōu** a chasm that cannot be leaped (a schism that cannot be bridged)

不愧 **pù-k'uèi** not undeserving (deserving, apt, fit, suitable)

不劳而获 **pù-láo érh-huò** to not work and yet to obtain (to receive unearned income)

不离口 **pù-lí-k'ǒu** [words or objects that are] not separate from [always on] the lips (to keep on saying, repeating, eating, smoking, etc.)

不离手 **pù-lí-shǒu** not to leave the hand (to hold on to, keep on practicing)

不理 **pù-lǐ** to ignore, disregard, fail to consider, take no cognizance of, not to reply to

不利因素 **pù-lì-yīn-sù** unfavorable factors, adverse factors

不良倾向 **pù-liáng ch'īng-hsiàng** an unwholesome trend, unfavorable tendency

不良分子 **pù-liáng fèn-tzǔ** undesirable elements, bad people

不了了之 **pù-liǎo-liǎo-chīh** to leave [a matter] unsolved, to end inconclusively

不留情 **pù-liú-ch'íng** to be very strict, disregard feelings; without mercy

不流血革命 **pù-liú-hsuèh kó-mìng** a bloodless revolution

不伦不类 **pù-lún pù-lèi** not this class nor that species (hard to categorize, not true to type)

不毛之地 **pù-máo-chīh-tì** land on which not a hair [will grow] (sterile land which cannot be cultivated)

不谋而合 **pù-móu-érh-hó** to agree without prior consultation

不拿枪的敌人 **pù ná-ch'iāng te tí-jén** enemies not carrying guns (especially intellectuals or ideological opponents)

不能自拔 **pù-néng-tzŭ-pá** unable to free oneself [from a situation]

不念旧恶 **pù-nièn chiù-ò** to not remember old wrongs (let bygones be bygones)

不宁唯是 **pù-nìng-wéi-shìh** not only this way, not only

不白之冤 **pù-pái-chīh-yüān** a wrong that has not been righted; a false accusation

不败之地 **pù-pài-chīh-tì** an invincible position, unassailable ground

不变价格 **pù-pièn chià-kó** unchanging prices, fixed prices

不变资本 **pù-pièn-tzū-pĕn** fixed capital

不辩菽麦 **pù-pièn shū-mài** to not know beans from wheat (to lack experience in production, be divorced from practical matters)

不怕一万，就怕万一 **pù-p'à ī-wàn, chiù p'à wàn-ī** one is not afraid of ten thousand [but] is afraid of the one in ten thousand [possibility] (fear not the expected but fear the unexpected)

不怕苦, 不怕死 **pù-p'à-k'ŭ, pù-p'à-szŭ** fear neither hardship nor death

不偏不倚 **pù-p'iēn pù-ĭ** neither prejudiced nor leaning to one side (impartial)

不平等条约 **pù-p'íng-tĕng t'iáo-yüēh** an unequal treaty

不破不立 **pù-p'ò pù-lì** without destruction there can be no construction

不三不四 **pù-sān pù-szù** neither three nor four (not up to standard; incongruous, neither one thing nor the other)

不塞不流 **pù-sè pù-liú** without damming there can be no flow

不杀不辱 **pù-shā pù-jŭ** do not kill and do not humiliate

不上纲, 不上线 **pù-shàng-kāng, pù-shàng-hsièn** to fail to grasp the principles and fail to grasp the line

不赦 **pù-shè** unpardonable [crimes]

不胜其烦 **pù-shēng-ch'í-fán** unable to put up with the bother, cannot stand the nuisance

不胜枚举 **pù-shēng-méi-chŭ** too numerous to recount, too many to be cited

不失时机 **pù-shīh-shíh-chī** do not lose the opportunity; do not miss the opportune time

不失寸土 **pù-shīh-ts'ùn-t'ŭ** do not give up an inch of territory

不识大体 **pù-shíh-tà-t'ĭ** to fail to see the large issues, not to recognize the important matters

不时 **pù-shíh** occasionally, unexpectedly, unseasonably

不时之需 **pù-shíh-chīh-hsü** an unpredicted need, occasional requirements

不是东风压倒西风, 就是西风压倒东风 **pù-shìh tūng-fēng yā-tăo hsī-fēng, chiù-shìh hsī-fēng yā-tăo tūng-fēng** either the east wind prevails over the west wind, or the west wind prevails over the east wind

不识抬举 **pù-shíh t'ái-chŭ** not to know how to appreciate favors (unappreciative, ungrateful)

不速之客 **pù-sù-chīh-k'ò** an uninvited guest

不打自招 **pù-tă-tzù-chāo** to confess [fault] without pressure

不丹 **pù-tān** Bhutan

不得 **pù-té** may not, shall not, must not, cannot, unable; to refrain from

不得已而求其次 **pù-té-ĭ érh-ch'iú-ch'í-tz'ù** cannot help but take the second [best]; having no alternative except the inferior one

不得人心 **pù-té-jén-hsīn** not winning peoples' hearts (unpopular, discredited)

不得力 **pù-té-lì** ineffectual, ineffective, awkward, unable to achieve the desired result

不得了 **pù-té-liăo** to be in a bad way, disastrous, terrible

不得要领 **pù-té-yào-lĭng** to fail to grasp the key points, miss the point; not to the point, irrelevant

不等待, 不伸手 **pù-tĕng-tài, pù-shēn-shŏu** not to wait and not hold out the hands (to get on with one's task, to be self-reliant)

不抵抗主义 **pù-tĭ-k'àng-chŭ-ì** nonresistance, the principle of nonresistance

不顶事 **pù-tĭng-shìh** to not be on top of affairs (ineffective)

不断革命论 **pù-tuàn-kó-mìng lùn** the theory of uninterrupted revolution, theory of continual revolution

不断革命的精神 **pù-tuàn-kó-mìng te chīng-shén** the uninterrupted revolution spirit, the spirit of uninterrupted revolution

不断深入 **pù-tuàn-shēn-jù** ceaseless penetration (to not slacken efforts in going deep among the masses)

不断再分配 **pù-tuàn tsài fēn-p'èi** continuous redistribution [of wealth]

不断调整 **pù-tuàn-t'iáo-chĕng** continual

readjustment

不断跃进 **pù-tuàn-yuèh-chìn** a continuous leap forward

不对头 **pù-tuì-t'óu** not matching, not fitting (not right)

不懂事 **pù-tǔng-shìh** not to understand how one should behave (immature, undeveloped, lacking in basic worldly comprehension, naive)

不动产 **pù-tùng-ch'ǎn** fixed assests, immovable properties, real estate

不动脑筋, 不费气力 **pù-tùng nǎo-chīn, pù-fèi ch'ì-lì** not to stir the brain nor expand any effort

不动声色 **pù-tùng-shēng-sè** without changing voice or color (complete self-control, calm, unmoved)

不动摇 **pù tùng-yáo** unwavering, steady, steadfast, firm, resolute

不冻港 **pù-tùng-kǎng** an ice-free port

不挑担子 **pù-t'iāo tàn-tzu** unwilling to carry the load (one who shirks responsibility)

不脱产干部 **pù-t'ō-ch'ǎn kàn-pù** a cadre [continuing to be] engaged in production [while at the same time having leadership or administrative duties]

不通 **pù-t'ūng** ungrammatical, unclear [writing]; illogical, inarticulate [ideas]; stupid, bigoted [persons]; closed to traffic [roads]

不同凡响 **pù-t'úng-fán-hsiǎng** not like the ordinary sound (excellent, outstanding—usually referring to artistic or literary work)

不痛不痒 **pù-t'ùng-pù-yǎng** not painful and not itching (irrelevant and unimportant, not reaching to the key issues, pointless)

不在乎 **pù-tsài-hu** immaterial, could not care less; nonchalant

不在话下 **pù-tsài-huà-hsià** no need to mention at this point, not under discussion at present

不择手段 **pù-tsé shǒu-tuàn** to make no choice between plans (to resort to all means; by fair means or foul; the end justifies the means)

不足 **pù-tsú** insufficient, not enough; not qualified; undeserving

不足为奇 **pù-tsú-wéi-ch'í** not enough to cause surprise (nothing strange, in no way remarkable)

不足为凭 **pù-tsú-wéi-p'íng** not sufficient for evidence

不自量 **pù-tzù-liàng** to overrate one's strength

不测之祸 **pù-ts'è-chīh-huò** an unforeseen calamity, unexpected disaster

不辞而别 **pù-tz'ú-érh-piéh** to leave

without bidding farewell

不外 **pù-wài** nothing more than, only, no other than, most likely; invariably

不忘阶级苦 **pù-wàng chiēh-chí-k'ǔ** do not forget the sufferings of the [proletarian] class

不忘本 **pù-wàng-pěn** do not forget origins (an exhortation addressed to the proletarian class)

不违农时 **pù-wéi núng-shíh** do not violate the farming times (farm work must be done at the appropriate times)

不为名, 不为利 **pù-wèi-míng, pù-wèi-lì** for neither fame nor gain

不畏 **pù-wèi** not to fear, not in awe of (to be defiant of)

不谓 **pù-wèi** not spoken of (unexpectedly)

不闻不问 **pù-wén pù-wèn** to neither hear nor ask (to care nothing about, oblivious to, indifferent to; to cut off intercouse)

不问政治 **pù-wèn chèng-chìh** to be indifferent to politics

不问青红皂白 **pù-wèn ch'īng-húng tsào-pái** unconcerned whether blue, red, black or white (without asking for the facts, without distinguishing right from wrong)

不务正业 **pù-wù chèng-yèh** not engaging in a proper occupation (having no legitimate occupation; a playboy, wastrel)

不误农时 **pù-wù núng-shíh** do not delay the agricultural times

不夜城 **pù-yèh-ch'éng** (1) the nightless city (revelry, dissipation); (2) the title of a play and film of the 1930s, subsequently criticized

不言而喻 **pù-yén-érh-yù** it is understood without needing to be stated (obvious, understood without explanation)

不厌其烦 **pù-yèn-ch'í-fán** not oppressed by the wearisomeness [of a task] (very patient)

不厌其详 **pù-yèn-ch'í-hsiáng** the more detailed the better

不由分说 **pù-yú-fēn-shuō** not permitted to make an explanation (unreasonable)

不由自主 **pù-yú-tzù-chǔ** without control of oneself

不远千里而来 **pù-yuǎn ch'iēn-lǐ érh-lái** to consider it not far to have come a thousand *li*

不约而同 **pù-yuēh-érh-t'úng** unanimous action without prior consultation

布加勒斯特 **pù-chiā-lè-szū-t'è** Bucharest

[Romania]

布置 **pù-chìh** to make arrangements, place in position, arrange; to decorate [a room]

布景 **pù-chǐng** [stage] scenery, background, setting

布局 **pù-chú** the layout of a book, etc.], arrangement

布尔什维克 **pù-ěrh-shíh-wéi-k'ò** Bolshevik

布哈林 **pù-hā-lín** Bukharin (1888–1938, Russian Communist leader, purged by Stalin)

布依族 **pù-ī-tsú** the Pu-yi people (a minority in Kweichow province: population 1,311,000 as of 1957)

布宜诺斯艾利斯 **pù-í-nò-szū ài-lì-szū** Buenos Aires [Argentina]

布告 **pù-kào** a proclamation, public notice, announcement, bulletin, notification

布拉柴维尔 **pù-lā-ch'ái-wéi-ěrh** Brazzaville [People's Republic of Congo]

布拉格 **pù-lā-kó** Prague

布朗族 **pù-lǎng-tsú** the Pu-lang people (a minority in Yunnan province: population 41,000 as of 1957)

布鲁塞尔 **pù-lǔ-sāi-ěrh** Brussels

布隆迪 **pù-lúng-tí** Burundi [Republic of]

布票 **pù-p'iào** cloth ration coupons

布达佩斯 **pù-tá-p'èi-szū** Budapest

布点 **pù-tiěn** to designate points [or units] (may refer to the planning of geographical distribution or to the accomplishment of any task)

布点下伸,分散办学 **pù-tiěn hsià-shēn, fēn-sàn pàn-hsuéh** to lower the designated level for locating and disperse the establishment of schools (so that they will be close to and accessible to the children of poor and lower-middle peasants)

1697 步其后尘 **pù-ch'í-hòu-ch'én** to walk in another's dust (to follow in another's footsteps)

步伐 **pù-fá** paces [in military review, etc.], steps, strides

步行 **pù-hsíng** to walk, march, travel on foot

步行串连 **pù-hsíng ch'uàn-lién** exchanging [revolutionary] experiences on foot (a popular Red Guard activity during the Cultural Revolution)

步兵 **pù-pīng** a foot soldier, infantry

步兵炮 **pù-pīng-p'ào** artillery weapons [smaller than 105 mm] used by infantry

步步紧跟 **pù-pù-chǐn-kēn** to follow closely step-by-step

步步为营 **pù-pù-wéi-yíng** to advance step-by-step by building fortified camps (to advance by cautious and thoroughly prepared steps)

步哨 **pù-shào** a sentry, sentinel, guard, watch

步调 **pù-tiào** marching gait (refers to both length and rapidity of the stride; often figurative)

步调一致 **pù-tiào-ī-chìh** to march in step, to keep step with (in complete coordination with)

步骤 **pù-tsòu** steps, measures; procedure, sequence of actions

1698 部长 **pù-chǎng** the head of a government ministry, cabinet officer

部长级 **pù-chǎng-chí** ministerial rank

部长助理 **pù-chǎng chù-lǐ** assistants to the minister

部件 **pù-chièn** components, parts

部分核禁试条约 **pù-fèn hó chìn-shìh t'iáo-yuēh** Partial Nuclear Test Ban Treaty

部分利益服从整体利益 **pù-fèn-lì-ì fú-ts'úng chěng-t'ǐ-lì-ì** partial interest [must be] subordinate to the interests of the whole

部下 **pù-hsià** subordinates

部落 **pù-lò** a tribe which has not formed a nation, primitive tribe or clan; tribal region

部门 **pù-mén** a class, section, department, branches, units

部首 **pù-shǒu** radicals of Chinese characters

部署 **pù-shǔ** to make military deployment, put in order, make preparations, arrange

部队 **pù-tuì** a military unit, troops

部队建设 **pù-tuì chièn-shè** a build-up of troop units (includes expansion, training, and improvement)

部队干部 **pù-tuì kàn-pù** a cadre who is [or was] a member of the armed forces

部族主义 **pù-tsú-chǔ-ì** tribalism

部委 **pù-wěi** the Party committee of a ministry

p'á (pá)

1699 扒手 **p'á-shǒu** pickpocket

1700 爬起来 **p'á-ch'i-lai** to get up, climb up (to climb the ladder of success)

爬行哲学 **p'á-hsíng ché-hsuéh** crawling philosophy (being content to move forward very slowly; slavishly following foreign models instead of practicing self-reliance)

爬山涉水 **p'á-shān shè-shuǐ** to climb

mountains and ford rivers
爬山队 **p'á-shān-tuì** a mountain-climbing team, mountaineering group
爬得愈高，跌得愈重 **p'á té yù-kāo, tiēh té yù-chùng** the higher one climbs, the harder one falls
爬山越岭 **p'á-shān yuèh-lǐng** climbing mountains and crossing ranges

p'à (pà)

1701 怕沾边 **p'à chān-piēn** to fear being [even] slightly involved
怕苦怕累 **p'à-k'ǔ p'à-lèi** to fear hardship and fatigue
怕得罪人 **p'à té-tsuì jén** afraid of offending people
怕字当头 **p'à tzù tāng-t'óu** to put "p'a" [fear] at the head [in the first place] (to be excessively cautious and timid)
1702 帕拉马里博 **p'à-lā-mǎ-lǐ-pó** Paramaribo [Surinam]
帕米尔高原 **p'à-mǐ-ěrh kāo-yuán** the Pamir plateau

p'āi (pāi)

1703 拍案而起 **p'āi-àn-érh-ch'ǐ** to pound the table and stand, to stand up pounding the table
拍制 **p'āi-chìh** to shoot and edit [a motion picture]
拍马屁 **p'āi-mǎ-p'ì** to stroke a horse's rump (to flatter, toady)
拍摄 **p'āi-shè** to take photographs
拍手喝采 **p'āi-shǒu hō-ts'ǎi** to clap one's hands and applaud

p'ái (pái)

1704 排挤 **p'ái-chǐ** to push [someone] aside, expel [someone] from a group, squeeze a person out, boycott, discriminate against
排碱沟 **p'ái-chiěn-kōu** a ditch for draining alkaline salts from farmland
排斥 **p'ái-ch'ìh** to expel, exclude, discriminate against, proscribe, drive away, condemn
排球 **p'ái-ch'iú** volleyball
排出 **p'ái-ch'ū** to exclude, expel, drive out, drain out
排除 **p'ái-ch'ú** to exclude, push aside, overcome
排除异己 **p'ái-ch'ú-ì-chǐ** to expel those differing from oneself (get rid of those holding different views, eliminate those not belonging to one's own clique)

排除万难 **p'ái-ch'ú wàn-nán** to overcome all difficulties
排泄 **p'ái-hsièh** to excrete, let off [anger, etc.]
排险 **p'ái-hsiěn** to get rid of dangers (especially in construction work, to eliminate dangerous aspects)
排灌 **p'ái-kuàn** drainage and irrigation
排灌设备 **p'ái-kuàn shè-pèi** drainage and irrigation equipment, facilities for drainage and irrigation
排涝 **p'ái-lào** to drain waterlogged fields; to divert flood water
排涝治碱 **p'ái-lào chìh-chiěn** to drain water [as a means of] controlling alkaline soil
排列 **p'ái-lièh** to arrange in series, arrange in order; to rank, place; permutation [mathematics]
排难解纷 **p'ái-nàn-chiěh-fēn** to settle difficulties and clear up misunderstandings (to mediate disputes, offer good offices)
排内性 **p'ái-nèi-hsìng** internal antipathy, mutual hostility, sectarianism
排山倒海 **p'ái-shān tǎo-hǎi** to overthrow a mountain and upset the sea (a powerful and irresistible force)
排水 **p'ái-shuǐ** drainage; to drain out water
排水量 **p'ái-shuǐ-liàng** water displacement [in measurement of ship tonnage]
排队 **p'ái-tuì** to queue up, form a line, get into formation
排外 **p'ái-wài** to reject outsiders (xenophobic, chauvinistic, anti-foreign, provincial, parochial)
排外主义 **p'ái-wài-chǔ-ì** xenophobia, anti-foreignism, exclusive-ism
排外性 **p'ái-wài-hsìng** exclusiveness, exclusivity
排演 **p'ái-yěn** to rehearse for a show; a rehearsal
排 **p'ái**: see also p'ǎi
1705 徘徊 **p'ái-huái** to linger, hover, walk to and fro, move without purpose; hesitating, irresolute
徘徊歧路 **p'ái-huái-ch'í-lù** to hesitate at the crossroads (to have trouble in choosing right from wrong)
徘徊观望 **p'ái-huái-kuān-wàng** to observe without making up one's mind, wait and see, avoid commitment
1706 牌价 **p'ái-chià** the marked price, list price, official price
牌号不同货色一样 **p'ái-hào pù-t'úng hùo-sè ī-yàng** the labels are different but the goods are the same (different

in form but the same in essence)
牌购 **p'ái-kòu** to purchase at list price
牌子 **p'ái-tzu** (1) a brand, trademark [of goods or manufactures]; (2) a card, tag, label; (3) reputation

p'ǎi (pǎi)

1707　迫击炮 **p'ǎi-chī-p'ào** a mortar, trench mortar
迫 **p'ǎi**: *see also* **p'ò**
1708　排子车 **p'ǎi-tzu-ch'ē** a handcart, pushcart (used for hauling cargo, with one man pushing and one or more pulling)
排 **p'ǎi**: *see also* **p'ái**

p'ài (pài)

1709　派遣 **p'ài-ch'iěn** to dispatch, send on a mission
派遣军 **p'ài-ch'iěn-chūn** an expeditionary force
派出 **p'ài-ch'ū** to send out, dispatch
派出机关 **p'ài-ch'ū-chī-kuān** an extended agency (such as an office of a central agency set up in a regional area but not under the latter's jurisdiction)
派出所 **p'ài-ch'ū-sǒ** branch police station (the lowest unit of the police)
派系 **p'ài-hsì** affiliations, clique connections; cliques, factions, blocs
派性 **p'ài-hsìng** factionalism, a tendency to form into cliques
派购任务 **p'ài-kòu jèn-wù** the purchasing task (of a commerce bureau—to buy the state's quota from producers)
派别 **p'ài-piéh** categories, schools of thought, factions
派别活动 **p'ài-piéh huó-tùng** factional activity
派生 **p'ài-shēng** derivative, deriving from; a derivative
派头 **p'ài-t'óu** style [of dress or behavior], manner, air (usually unfavorable in implication)

p'ān (pān)

1710　攀亲戚 **p'ān-ch'īn-ch'i** to exploit a relationship, utilize family [or marriage] relationships to one's advantage
攀亲道故 **p'ān-ch'īn-tào-kù** to exploit a relationship or old friendship
攀登高峰 **p'ān-tēng-kāo-fēng** to scale the heights (to master skills and techniques, especially in science and technology)

p'án (pán)

1711　盘踞 **p'án-chù** to squat with the legs crossed (to take a fixed position, entrench oneself, occupy)
盘根错节 **p'án-kēn-ts'ò-chiéh** twisted roots and intricate gnarls (great complexity; a confused and difficult affair)
盘剥 **p'án-pō** to exploit, practice usury, fleece, cheat
盘山过岭 **p'án-shān kuò-lǐng** winding around the mountains and crossing the ridges (a long road)
盘问 **p'án-wèn** to interrogate closely
1712　磐石 **p'án-shíh** a massive rock (stable, enduring)
1713　蹒跚不前 **p'án-shān-pù-ch'ién** to falter, hesitate, totter

p'àn (pàn)

1714　判处 **p'àn-ch'ǔ** to pass sentence on; a sentence
判决 **p'àn-chüéh** a judgment, verdict, sentence, court decision, judicial determination; to sentence
判决书 **p'àn-chüéh-shū** a written decision of a court, judgment, legal opinion, decree
判刑 **p'àn-hsíng** to impose a criminal sentence, convict, sentence
判明 **p'àn-míng** to ascertain, discern clearly, determine
判别是非 **p'àn-piéh-shìh-fēi** to distinguish right and wrong
判定 **p'àn-tìng** to consider and decide, determine, judge
判断 **p'àn-tuàn** to judge [after consideration], decide, conclude; a decision, conclusion
判罪 **p'àn-tsuì** to convict, find guilty, impose sentence
1715　叛匪 **p'àn-fěi** rebel bandits (usually troops who have mutinied and become bandits)
叛国 **p'àn-kuó** to betray one's country, treason
叛国分子 **p'àn-kuó fēn-tzǔ** traitorous elements
叛国罪行 **p'àn-kuó tsuì-hsíng** the crime of treason
叛乱 **p'àn-luàn** revolt, rebellion, sedition, insurrection, mutiny, treason, anarchy
叛卖 **p'àn-mài** to sell out [one's country], betray
叛逆 **p'àn-nì** to revolt; sedition; a rebel
叛变 **p'àn-pièn** to revolt and change over, mutiny, insurgency

叛党 **p'àn-tǎng** to betray the Party
叛徒 **p'àn-t'ú** traitor, turncoat, renegade, deserter
1716 盼望 **p'àn-wàng** to hope for, wish

p'āng (pāng)

1717 滂沱大雨 **p'āng-t'ó-tà-yǔ** a torrential rain
1718 磅礴 **p'āng-pó** extensive, vast, filling all space

p'áng (páng)

1719 庞然大物 **p'áng-ján-tà-wù** a huge object (now generally suggests that despite its impressive outward appearance, the object is fragile and weak)
庞大 **p'áng-tà** huge, immense, tall
庞杂 **p'áng-tsá** disorderly, confused, motley
1720 旁征博引 **p'áng-chēng-pó-yǐn** with copious references and quotations (elaborate documentation of evidence)
旁证 **p'áng-chèng** circumstantial evidence
旁敲侧击 **p'áng-ch'iāo ts'è-chí** to knock from one side and strike from the other (to convey a secret meaning by metaphors and allusions; seemingly irrelevant talk with a hidden purpose)
旁若无人 **p'áng-jò-wú-jén** [to act] as if there were no bystanders (overconfident, arrogant, contemptuous of others)
旁观者清 **p'áng-kuān-chě-ch'īng** bystanders can see clearly (one directly involved cannot see as well as well as one outside the events)
旁听席 **p'áng-t'īng-hsí** seats for observers or auditors
旁听生 **p'áng-t'īng-shēng** an auditing student

p'āo (pāo)

1721 抛砖引玉 **p'āo-chuān yǐn-yù** to throw a brick and elicit jade (a polite phrase in advancing one's proposal and asking others to do likewise)
抛弃 **p'āo-ch'ì** to abandon, throw away, give up, reject [responsibility, etc.]
抛出 **p'āo-ch'ū** to throw out, cast away
抛锚 **p'āo-máo** to drop anchor (now has the meaning of a mechanical breakdown—of a car, machine, etc.—which leaves one unable to make further headway)

抛射体 **p'āo-shè-t'ǐ** a projectile
抛射筒 **p'āo-shè-t'ǔng** a projectile launching tube
抛售 **p'āo-shòu** to dump [goods on the market], sell at low prices
抛在后面 **p'āo-tsài-hòu-mièn** to leave behind, throw something to the rear

p'áo (páo)

1722 刨去 **p'áo-ch'ù** to take out of, deduct
刨树要刨根 **p'áo-shù yào p'áo-kēn** to dig out the tree one must dig out the roots
刨 **p'áo**: see also **pào**
1723 咆哮 **p'áo-hsiāo** to roar, bluster, rage
1724 炮制 **p'áo-chìh** to treat by low fire, decoct, brew [medicinal herbs]
炮 **p'áo**: see also **pào**
1725 袍哥 **p'áo-kō** a gown brother (a member of a secret society)

p'ǎo (pǎo)

1726 跑龙套 **p'ǎo lúng-t'ào** to run the "dragon set" (a bit player in old-style Peking opera who carried a flag onto the stage: hence, to play an insignificant role; now has the sense of a minor post or general utility man)
跑腿 **p'ǎo-t'uǐ** to run about, do leg work, run errands for

p'ào (pào)

1727 泡影 **p'ào-yǐng** the shadow of a bubble (an illusion, unreality)
1728 炮击 **p'ào-chī** to bombard; an artillery attack, barrage
炮舰 **p'ào-chièn** a gunboat, warship
炮舰政策 **p'ào-chièn chèng-ts'è** a gunboat policy [in diplomacy]
炮灰 **p'ào-huī** cannon fodder
炮火连天 **p'ào-huǒ lién-t'iēn** cannon fire covers the sky
炮楼 **p'ào-lóu** a gun turret
炮兵 **p'ào-pīng** (1) the Artillery Force [one of the service arms of the PLA]; (2) an artilleryman
炮声沉寂 **p'ào-shēng ch'én-chì** the guns fall silent
炮手 **p'ào-shǒu** a gunner, artilleryman
炮打司令部 **p'ào-tǎ szū-lìng-pù** "bombard the headquarters" [of the power-holders] (Mao Tse-tung's first tà-tzù-pào in the Cultural Revolution)
炮队 **p'ào-tuì** an artillery battery
炮台 **p'ào-t'ái** a gun platform, fort, fortification
炮 **p'ào**: see also **p'áo**

p'éi (péi)

¹⁷²⁹ 陪衬 **p'éi-ch'èn** to serve as background [in order to bring out the subject with greater brilliance], to add for contrast; serve as a prop [as in photography]; to accompany as a subordinate

陪审 **p'éi-shěn** to join in a trial, assist in trying a case; act as a juror

陪审团 **p'éi-shěn-t'uán** a jury

陪葬品 **p'éi-tsàng-p'ǐn** objects buried with a person

陪同 **p'éi-t'úng** to accompany; be accompanied by

¹⁷³⁰ 培植 **p'éi-chíh** to plant, cultivate, grow [plants]; to educate, train, develop

培训 **p'éi-hsùn** to cultivate and instruct, train, educate

培训教材 **p'éi-hsùn chiào-ts'ái** training materials, teaching materials for training courses

培养 **p'éi-yǎng** to cultivate, grow, nurture [plants]; to train, raise, bring up, develop [people]

培养典型 **p'éi-yǎng tiěn-hsíng** to foster exemplary experience

培养优良植物品种 **p'éi-yǎng yū-liáng chíh-wù p'ǐn-chǔng** to breed improved plant varieties

培育 **p'éi-yù** to raise, breed, cultivate, grow, nourish

¹⁷³¹ 赔偿 **p'éi-ch'áng** to compensate, indemnify, reimburse, make restitution, make good a loss

赔偿协定 **p'éi-ch'áng hsiéh-tìng** a reparations agreement

赔偿名誉 **p'éi-ch'áng míng-yù** an indemnity for defamation

赔款 **p'éi-k'uǎn** a payment for damages, [war] indemnity

赔本 **p'éi-pěn** to lose one's investment, run a business at a loss, fail in business

赔罪 **p'éi-tsuì** to apologize

¹⁷³² 裴多菲俱乐部 **p'éi-tō-fēi chù-lò-pù** the Petofi Club (a literary group associated with the Hungarian uprising in 1956)

p'èi (pèi)

¹⁷³³ 佩服 **p'èi-fú** to admire, respect

¹⁷³⁴ 配给 **p'èi-chǐ** to allocate, furnish, supply; rationing and supply

配给制 **p'èi-chǐ-chìh** a ration system

配角 **p'èi-chiǎo** a supporting actor or actress

配件 **p'èi-chièn** spare parts [of machinery], accessories

配种 **p'èi-chǔng** selective [animal] breeding

配种站 **p'èi-chǔng-chàn** an [animal] breeding station

配合 **p'èi-hó** to be adapted to, in tune with; to combine, join, pair, unite, match together, coordinate, synchronize; appropriate, well-matched, suitable

配偶 **p'èi-ǒu** a couple, husband and wife; spouse

配不上 **p'èi-pu-shàng** to be no match for; does not fit, unsuitable, unworthy

配上 **p'èi-shàng** to match with, join to, attach

配电板 **p'èi-tièn-pǎn** an electrical switchboard

配套 **p'èi-t'ào** to make up a set (to fit together parts or units to form a complete set or project; to supply all needed components)

配套成龙 **p'èi-t'ào-ch'éng-lúng** to make up a set to become a dragon (to supply all needed elements so that equipment will become operable— just as a dragon must have head, body, and tail to be complete)

p'ēn (pēn)

¹⁷³⁵ 喷气发动机 **p'iēn-ch'ì fā-tùng-chi** a jet engine

喷气式飞机 **p'ēn-ch'ì-shìh fēi-chi** a jet airplane

喷薄而出 **p'ēn-pó-érh-ch'ū** to spurt forth

喷水池 **p'ēn-shuǐ-ch'íh** a fountain

喷雾器 **p'ēn-wù-ch'ì** a spray gun, atomizer, spraying machine

p'én (pén)

¹⁷³⁶ 盆地 **p'én-tì** a basin [geographical]

p'ēng (pēng)

¹⁷³⁷ 抨击 **p'ēng-chī** to attack by words, censure, make accusations

¹⁷³⁸ 澎湃 **p'ēng-p'ài** the roaring of large waves

p'éng (péng)

¹⁷³⁹ 朋友遍天下 **p'éng-yǔ p'ièn t'iēn-hsià** friends covering the world; our friends are everywhere

¹⁷⁴⁰ 彭真 **p'éng chēn** P'eng Chen (1902—, Communist leader and mayor of Peking, purged in the Cultural

Revolution)

彭德怀 **p'éng té-huái** P'eng Te-huai (1898—, military leader and minister of National Defense, purged in 1959)

彭德怀反党集团 **p'éng té-huái făn-tăng chí-t'uán** the P'eng Te-huai anti-Party clique

1741 棚戶区 **p'éng-hù-ch'ǖ** an area of shack dwellings, "shantytown"

1742 蓬勃 **p'éng-pó** flourishing, booming, prospering

蓬勃兴起 **p'éng-pó hsīng-ch'ǐ** to rise luxuriantly

蓬勃发展 **p'éng-pó-fā-chăn** flourishing development, vigorous growth

蓬蓬勃勃 **p'éng-p'éng pó-pó** flourishing and prospering; luxuriantly

蓬头垢面 **p'éng-t'óu-kòu-mièn** [with] disheveled hair and grimy face

1743 膨胀 **p'éng-chàng** to expand, swell, bloat; expansion, inflation, swelling

p'ĕng (pĕng)

1744 捧场 **p'ĕng-ch'ăng** to applaud an actor (to praise, endorse, support by one's presence)

捧场文章 **p'ĕng-ch'ăng-wén-chāng** promotional literature, a laudatory review

捧上天 **p'ĕng-shàng-t'iēn** to praise to high heavens, over-praise

p'èng (pèng)

1745 碰机会 **p'èng chī-hui** to come upon an opportunity by chance

碰壁 **p'èng-pì** to collide with a wall (to meet rejection, encounter difficulties)

碰得头破血流 **p'èng-te t'óu-p'ò hsuèh-liú** to collide so that one's scalp is broken and blood flows (a hopeless struggle; to beat one's head against the wall)

碰钉子 **p'èng-tīng-tzu** to hit a nail (meet rejection, run into a snag)

碰头 **p'èng-t'óu** to bump heads (to meet, have a rendezvous)

碰头会 **p'èng-t'óu-hui** a bump-heads meeting (informal decisional meetings, usually small, often impromptu, and generally to deal with a specific, limited problem)

碰运气 **p'èng-yùn-ch'i** to depend on luck, try one's luck; to meet with good luck; a fluke

p'ī (pī)

1746 批转 **p'ī-chuăn** to approve [a docu-

ment] for forwarding [or circulation]

批准 **p'ī-chŭn** to approve, sanction, confirm, validate, ratify; official approval, authorization, validation

批准权 **p'ī-chŭn-ch'üán** authority to approve or disapprove

批发 **p'ī-fā** wholesale; to sell at wholesale

批发价 **p'ī-fā-chià** the wholesale price

批发部 **p'ī-fā-pù** wholesale department [of a commercial corporation]

批复请示 **p'ī-fù ch'ǐng-shìh** to answer a request for guidance, give an official reply

批修整风 **p'ī-hsiū-chĕng-fēng** rectification through criticism of revisionism

批孔 **p'ī-k'ŭng** to criticize Confucius (normally refers to the 1974 campaign to criticize Confucius)

批林整风 **p'ī-lín chĕng-fēng** rectification through criticism of Lin [Piao]

批林批孔 **p'ī-lín p'ī-k'ŭng** criticism of Lin [Piao] and Confucius

批驳 **p'ī-pó** to reject with adverse comment [a communication from a lower organization], to reverse a lower decision

批判 **p'ī-p'àn** to criticize, censure, repudiate; to judge

批判主义 **p'ī-p'àn-chŭ-ì** critical philosophy, Kantianism

批判会 **p'ī-p'àn-hui** a criticism meeting

批判现实主义 **p'ī-p'àn hsièn-shíh-chŭ-ì** critical realism (attacked during the Cultural Revolution as being contrary to Mao's literary formula of "combining revolutionary realism with revolutionary romanticism")

批判掉 **p'ī-p'àn-tiào** to criticize away, repudiate

批评 **p'ī-p'íng** to criticize; criticism, comment

批评从严, 处理从宽 **p'ī-p'íng ts'úng yén, ch'ŭ-lĭ ts'úng k'uān** to criticize severely but to deal with leniently

批评与自我批评 **p'ī-p'íng yŭ tzù-wŏ-p'ī-p'íng** criticism and self-criticism

批深, 批透, 批倒, 批臭 **p'ī-shēn, p'ī-t'òu, p'ī-tăo, p'ī-ch'òu** to criticize profoundly and thoroughly until [the enemy] is overthrown and becomes [merely] a stench

批示 **p'ī-shìh** to instruct, give directions (usually by a note on the incoming message from a subordinate)

批斗 **p'ī-tòu** criticism and struggle

1747 纰漏 **p'ī-lòu** negligence and errors

1748 披着羊皮的豺狼 **p'ī-chè yáng-p'í te ch'ái-láng** a wolf in sheep's clothing

披荆斩棘 **p'ī-chīng chăn-chí** to spread

thorns and cut brambles (to cope with a difficult situation)

披星戴月 **p'ī-hsīng tài-yuèh** to cloak oneself with the stars and wear the moon (to go out early and return home late; extremely hard-working)

披肝沥胆 **p'ī-kān-lì-tăn** to open the liver and empty the gall bladder (to speak unreservedly and with great sincerity)

1749 砒霜 **p'ī-shuāng** arsenic

1750 劈山治水 **p'ī-shān chìh-shuĭ** to cleave the mountains and control the waters (to build irrigation canals through mountains)

劈山造田 **p'ī-shān tsào-t'ién** to cleave the mountains and build fields

劈头 **p'ī-t'óu** at the very beginning; open up with

1751 霹雳一声 **p'ī-lì-ī-shēng** a sudden clap of thunder

p'í (pí)

1752 皮之不存毛将焉附 **p'í-chīh-p'ù-ts'ún, máo-chiāng-yēn-fù?** when the skin is lost, where can you place the hair? (when what one depends on is lost, all is lost)

皮筏 **p'í-fá** a raft [constructed of] inflated skins

皮肤晒黑, 脚板磨硬 **p'í-fū shài-hēi, chiăo-păn mó-yìng** skin sunburned and feet hardened (to show the [honorable] marks of physical labor)

皮革 **p'í-kó** hides, leather

皮开肉绽 **p'í-k'āi-jòu-chàn** the skin broken and the flesh exposed·(to have suffered a cruel beating)

皮棉 **p'í-mién** ginned cotton

皮破血流 **p'í-p'ó-hsuèh-liú** skin broken and bleeding (usually implies self-imposed bumps and bruises by blundering or futile action)

皮带轮 **p'í-tài-lún** a pulley for leather belts in power transmission

皮影戏 **p'í-yĭng-hsì** shadow show [using puppets of varnished skin]

1753 疲倦 **p'í-chüàn** fatigued, tired, exhausted, weary

疲劳 **p'í-láo** fatigue, weariness, exhaustion

疲塌 **p'í-t'ā** weak and weary, slack in performance, lackadaisical, languid

疲于奔命 **p'í-yŭ-pēn-mìng** weary of running as if life depended on it (wearied from coping with too many problems; utterly exhausted)

1754 蚍蜉撼大树 **p'í-fú hàn tà-shù** the ant tries to shake a large tree (to try

something beyond one's power; not to know one's limitations)

1755 琵琶 **p'í-pa** the pipa (a guitar-like musical instrument)

1756 脾气 **p'í-ch'i** temperament, disposition, nature

p'ĭ (pĭ)

1757 匹敌 **p'ĭ-tí** an equally matched rival, peer, rival, worthy opponent

1758 痞子 **p'ĭ-tzu** "riffraff," scoundrels, rascals (in 1926–1927, the KMT opposition denigrated the CCP-dominated peasants associations as a "riffraff movement" [*p'i-tzu yun-tung*]. Mao Tse-tung countered that the so-called riffraff were actually revolutionary peasants)

p'ì (pì)

1759 辟谣 **p'ì-yáo** to squelch a rumor, rebut a slander

1760 譬喻 **p'ì-yù** a simile, metaphor, analogy

p'iāo (piāo)

1761 漂浮 **p'iāo-fú** to drift, float about

漂浮在会议上 **p'iāo-fú tsài huì-ì shang** drifting about on [a sea of] conferences

漂来漂去 **p'iāo-lái-p'iāo-ch'ù** to drift hither and thither

漂 **p'iāo:** see also **p'iào**

1762 飘渺 **p'iāo-miăo** elusive, difficult to discern, obscure, misty

飘飘然 **p'iāo-p'iāo-ján** as if floating on the breeze (slightly euphoric, complacent, elated)

飘扬 **p'iāo-yáng** to be blown about in the wind, to flutter

p'iào (piào)

1763 票据交换 **p'iào-chù chiāo-huàn** exchange of negotiable instruments (bank-clearing)

票面价值 **p'iào-mièn chià-chíh** face value

1764 漂亮话 **p'iào-liang huà** handsome talk, pretty words

漂 **p'iào:** see also **p'iāo**

p'iēh (piē)

1765 撇开 **p'iēh-k'āi** to set aside, cast off (to dismiss from discussion; exclude from consideration)

p'iēn (piān)

1766 偏爱 **p'iēn-ài** to have special fondness for [someone], be partial to

偏见 **p'iēn-chièn** prejudice, bias, pre-conceived ideas, one-sided views

偏重 **p'iēn-chùng** to over-emphasize; stress one element of; lean heavily toward; have extraordinary faith in

偏差 **p'iēn-ch'ā** error, deviation

偏废 **p'iēn-fèi** doing one thing to the neglect of another; crippled

偏向 **p'iēn-hsiàng** to lean toward, be inclined toward; angle, tilt, slant

偏斜 **p'iēn-hsiéh** slanted, oblique; not fair

偏心 **p'iēn-hsīn** bias, favoritism, partiality

偏信 **p'iēn-hsìn** to believe one side only

偏高 **p'iēn-kāo** to set too high, over-state, overestimate; unrealistically high

偏离 **p'iēn-lí** to deviate from, stray

偏旁 **p'iēn-p'áng** a radical on one side of a character

偏偏 **p'iēn-p'iēn** stubbornly, against expectations, unfortunately, contrary to intention

偏题 **p'iēn-t'í** unfair [examination] questions (questions that are irre-levent to the topic or excessively narrow)

偏听 **p'iēn-t'īng** to listen to one side only

偏听偏信 **p'iēn-t'īng p'iēn-hsìn** to listen to and believe only one side; thoroughly biased

1767 篇章 **p'iēn-chāng** literary compositions, writings [in general]; a chapter, an article, poem

篇幅 **p'iēn-fù** width or length of paper (the space of a periodical or news-paper; length of an article)

p'ièn (piàn)

1768 片面 **p'ièn-mièn** one-sided, incomplete, unilateral

片面真理 **p'ièn-mièn chēn-lǐ** a partial truth

片面节约 **p'ièn-mièn chiéh-yuēh** one-sided thrift (stressing economy to the point of adversely affecting efficiency; penny-wise but pound-foolish)

片面强调 **p'ièn-mièn ch'iáng-t'iào** one-sided stress, unbalanced stress; to lay undue emphasis on

片面性 **p'ièn-mièn-hsìng** one-sidedness

片面夸大 **p'ièn-mièn k'uā-tà** one-sided exaggeration; to exaggerate certain

aspects of

片断 **p'ièn-tuàn** an incomplete section, part, fragment (usually suggests something taken out of context)

片断经验 **p'ièn-tuàn-chīng-yèn** frag-mentary experience

1769 骗局 **p'ièn-chú** fraud, trickery, decep-tion, chicanery; a hoax, swindle

骗取 **p'ièn-ch'ǚ** to obtain by fraud

骗人鬼话 **p'ièn-jén kuěi-huà** devilish talk that cheats people (totally false words)

骗术 **p'ièn-shù** a trick, ruse, wile; trickery

骗子 **p'ièn-tzu** a swindler, cheat, imposter, liar, charlatan

p'īn (pīn)

1770 拼憨力 **p'īn hān-lì** by brute force, depending on physical strength alone

拼消耗 **p'īn hsiāo-hào** to rely only on [increased] consumption [of raw materials to increase production] (to neglect technical factors)

拼命 **p'īn-mìng** to stake one's life (to go all out, to devote oneself without reservation to accomplishing a task)

拼命精神 **p'īn-mìng-chīng-shén** the spirit of going all out

拼命主义 **p'īn-mìng-chǔ-ì** "desperado-ism" (advocacy of a policy of serious but unwarranted risks: usually refers to foolhardy military actions)

拼死命 **p'īn-szǔ-mìng** to stake one's very life, desperately

拼凑 **p'īn-ts'òu** to scrape together from bits and pieces, assemble together by hook or by crook, rig up, patch together; cannibalize [machinery]

拼音字母 **p'īn-yīn tzǔ-mǔ** the phonetic symbols, the phonetic alphabet

p'ín (pín)

1771 贫穷 **p'ín-ch'iúng** poverty, destitution, penury; poor, needy, impoverished

贫乏 **p'ín-fá** scanty, meager, destitute, needy; wanting, insufficient, deficient

贫下中农 **p'ín-hsià-chūng-núng** poor and lower-middle peasants (poor peasants are those who, prior to 1949, owned too little land to be self-supporting; lower-middle peasants were barely self-supporting and constantly in danger of becoming poor peasants)

贫下中农接待站 **p'ín-hsià-chūng-núng chiéh-tài-chàn** a reception station for poor and lower-middle peasants (set

up in some city hospitals to assist people from rural areas)

贫下中农协会 **p'ín-hsià-chūng-núng hsiéh-huì** poor and lower-middle peasant associations

贫下中农毛泽东思想宣传队 **p'ín-hsià-chūng-núng máo-tsé-tūng-szū-hsiăng hsuān-ch'uán-tuì** poor and lower-middle peasant Mao Tse-tung Thought propaganda teams

贫协 **p'ín-hsiéh** poor and lower-middle peasant association (contracted form)

贫宣队 **p'ín-hsuān-tuì** poor and lower-middle peasant Mao Tse-tung Thought propaganda teams (contracted form)

贫雇农 **p'ín-kù-núng** poor peasants and hired laborers

贫雇农路线 **p'ín-kù-núng lù-hsièn** the poor peasant-farm laborer line

贫苦 **p'ín-k'ŭ** poverty and hardship; poor, destitute

贫矿 **p'ín-k'uàng** a mine producing low-grade ore

贫困 **p'ín-k'ùn** impoverished, poor, hard up

贫民 **p'ín-mín** poor people, impoverished people

贫民窟 **p'ín-mín-k'ū** a slum

贫农 **p'ín-núng** poor peasants (usually defined as those who, in 1949, owned no land or too little to be self-supporting)

贫农核心小组 **p'ín-núng hó-hsīn hsiăo-tsŭ** poor peasant core group

贫农代表大会 **p'ín-núng tài-piăo-tà-huì** poor peasants representative assembly

贫病交迫 **p'ín-pìng-chiāo-p'ò** oppressed by both poverty and disease

贫代会 **p'ín tài-huì** poor peasants' representative assembly (*see above*)

贫无立锥之地 **p'ín-wú lì-chuī chīh tì** so poor that he does not have enough land to stick an awl into

贫油 **p'ín-yú** deficient in oil (to lack petroleum resources)

1772 频繁 **p'ín-fán** frequent, incessant, multifarious, excessive

频率 **p'ín-lù** frequency (radio wave length)

p'ín (pìn)

1773 品级 **p'ín-chí** grade [of an article or product], quality

品质 **p'ín-chìh** quality [of a commodity, etc.]

品种 **p'ín-chŭng** species [fauna or flora]; variety [of goods]

品德 **p'ín-té** virtue, moral character

p'ìn (pìn)

1774 聘请 **p'ìn-ch'ĭng** to invite for service, engage, appoint, employ

p'īng (pīng)

1775 乒乓球 **p'īng-p'āng-ch'iú** the game of ping-pong; a ping-pong ball

乒坛老将 **p'īng-t'án lăo-chiàng** a ping-pong general (a veteran ping-pong competitor)

p'íng (píng)

1776 平战结合 **p'íng-chàn chiéh-hó** to integrate [the requirements of] peace and war (in such matters as militia formation, industrial planning, etc.)

平整土地 **p'íng-chĕng t'ŭ-tì** to level ground (to grade the surface of fields for proper irrigation and drainage)

平价 **p'íng-chià** par value, price parity; to lower prices; a fair price

平起平坐 **p'íng-ch'ĭ p'íng-tsò** to stand and sit as equals (to be on a basis of equality)

平局 **p'íng-chŭ** a draw, tie [in a game or contest]

平均 **p'íng-chūn** equal, even, average

平均主义 **p'íng-chūn-chŭ-í** equalitarianism, egalitarianism

平均工资 **p'íng-chūn kūng-tzū** average wages

工均数 **p'íng-chūn-shù** an average, mean [math.]

平均地权 **p'íng-chūn tì-ch'üán** equalization of land ownership (one of the economic policies of Sun Yat-sen)

平凡 **p'íng-fán** ordinary, common, usual, mediocre, undistinguished

平反 **p'íng-făn** to reverse a [judicial] decision, redress [a miscarriage of justice], rehabilitate

平方公里 **p'íng-fāng-kūng-lĭ** a square kilometer

平方米 **p'íng-fāng-mĭ** a square meter

平房 **p'íng-fáng** a house having only one storey

平分 **p'íng-fēn** to divide equally

平分秋色 **p'íng-fēn-ch'iū-sè** to divide equally the autumn colors (to equal each other [in honors, achievement, etc.])

平衡 **p'íng-héng** balance, equilibrium; to balance, equalize, counterpoise

平衡状态 **p'íng-héng-chuàng-t'ài** a state of equilibrium

平衡发展 **p'íng-héng-fā-chǎn** balanced development, even growth

平衡预算 **p'íng-héng yü-suàn** a balanced budget; to balance a budget

平息 **p'íng-hsī** to come to an end, subside; to quell, subdue, cause to stop

平心静气 **p'íng-hsīn chìng-ch'ì** [with an] even mind and calm breath (cool-headed, calm, self-possessed)

平行 **p'íng-hsíng** going together, parallel, of equal rank

平易近人 **p'íng-ì-chìn-jén** approachable, attractive, gentle and humble, easy to get along with; [of writing style] lucid, unpretentious

平壤 **p'íng-jǎng** Pyongyang [North Korea]

平沟 **p'íng-kōu** to level the ditches (to remove dividing barriers between the Party and non-Party people)

平炉 **p'íng-lú** an open-hearth furnace

平面磨床 **p'íng-mièn-mó-ch'uáng** a surface grinding machine

平面图 **p'íng-mièn-t'ú** a floor plan, plane chart

平民 **p'íng-mín** common people, commoner [as opposed to lord], plebian [as opposed to patrician], civilian [as opposed to military]

平白无故 **p'íng-pái-wú-kù** for no reason, without reason or cause, without provocation

平平展展 **p'íng-p'íng-chǎn-chǎn** level and extensive, well graded

平射炮 **p'íng-shè-p'ào** a flat trajectory gun, cannon (as distinct from a howitzer)

平时 **p'íng-shíh** ordinarily, as a rule, normally; in a time of peace

平时国际公法 **p'íng-shíh kuó-chì kūng-fǎ** international law in peacetime

平时兵力 **p'íng-shíh pīng-lì** peace-time military strength

平时审查 **p'íng-shíh shěn-ch'á** regular examinations, periodic audits

平淡 **p'íng-tàn** mild, insipid, commonplace, uninteresting, flat

平等 **p'íng-těng** equality; equal, even; to be equal

平等互惠通商友好条约 **p'íng-těng hù-huì t'ūng-shāng yǔ-hǎo t'iáo-yuēh** a treaty of trade and friendship [on the basis] of equality and reciprocity

平等互利 **p'íng-těng hù-lì** reciprocity based on equality; equality and mutual benefit

平等关系 **p'íng-těng kuān-hsi** relations on an equal basis; a relationship of equality

平等待人 **p'íng-íng-těng tài-jén** equal treatment; to treat others on an equal footing

平等待遇 **p'íng-těng tài-yü** equal treatment; equal payment

平等地位 **p'íng-těng tì-wèi** equal standing

平地一声春雷 **p'íng-tì ī-shēng ch'ūn-léi** suddenly a clap of spring thunder (a harbinger of spring, a good omen)

平定 **p'íng-tìng** to pacify, quell, put down [a rebellion, etc.]; to settle, conquer, subdue; peaceful

平坦 **p'íng-t'ǎn** level and easy [of a road] (a smooth and even course—without ups and downs)

平田改土 **p'íng-t'ién kǎi-t'ǔ** to level fields and improve the soil

平原作战 **p'íng-yuán tsò-chàn** "Battle on the Plain" (a provisionally accepted **yàng-pǎn hsì**)

1777 评级 **p'íng-chí** to review grade levels (usually involves group consideration of individual rankings)

评价 **p'íng-chià** to estimate, appraise, assess, evaluate

评教评学会 **p'íng-chiào-p'íng-hsuéh-huì** a meeting for group review of individual accomplishment in teaching and study

评剧 **p'íng-chù** a school of folk-drama from North China

评分 **p'íng-fēn** to evaluate work points

评薪 **p'íng-hsīn** to review salary scales

评薪评级 **p'íng-hsīn p'íng-chí** re-evaluation of salary and grade

评议会 **p'íng-ì-huí** an appraisal meeting, arbitration board, advisory council

评工记分 **p'íng-kūng chì-fēn** evaluation of work and allotment of [work] points

评功摆好 **p'íng-kūng pǎi-hǎo** to appraise merits and display good [achievements]

评论 **p'íng-lùn** to comment on, discuss; a commentary, critique

评论员 **p'íng-lùn-yuán** a commentator, critic

评比 **p'íng-pǐ** to evaluate and compare

评述 **p'íng-shù** a critique, review

评头品足 **p'íng-t'óu p'ǐn-tsú** to criticize from head to foot, find fault with

评语 **p'íng-yǔ** critical comment, criticism, remarks

1778 凭借 **p'íng-chièh** to depend on, rely upon

凭据 **p'íng-chù** proof, evidence, basis, ground [for belief]

凭空 **p'íng-k'ūng** relying on emptiness

(without substantial support or
proof)

凭票付款 **p'íng-p'iào-fù-k'ǔan** a note
payable to bearer, sight draft

p'ō (pō)

1779 泼冷水 **p'ō lěng-shuǐ** to pour cold
water on

泼水节 **p'ō-shuǐ-chiéh** water splashing
festival [among the Thai people]

1780 坡田 **p'ō-t'ién** a sloping field, hilly field

p'ó (pó)

1781 婆婆妈妈 **p'ó-p'ó mā-mā** [to act] like
an old woman (nagging, sentimental,
indecisive)

p'ò (pò)

1782 迫近 **p'ò-chìn** to press near, close in,
approach; imminent

迫近灭亡 **p'ò-chìn-mièh-wáng** nearing
destruction, imminent collapse

迫切希望 **p'ò-ch'ièh-hsī-wàng** urgently
to hope for, eagerly look forward to,
impatiently await

迫切要求 **p'ò-ch'ièh-yāo-ch'íú** a pressing demand; to request urgently

迫害 **p'ò-hài** to persecute, oppress
cruelly, injure, ruin

迫不及待 **p'ò-pù-chí-tài** too pressing to
wait, so urgent that it cannot be put
off

迫使 **p'ò-shǐh** to force [someone] to do
[something]

迫在眉睫 **p'ò-tsài-méi-chiéh** to be
pressing against the eyebrow
(imminent)

迫 **p'ò:** *see also* **p'ǎi**

1783 破案 **p'ò-àn** to break a case (to solve a
case, clear up a case)

破绽百出 **p'ò-chàn-pǎi-ch'ū** a hundred
flaws appear

破旧立新 **p'ò-chiù lì-hsīn** destroy the
old and establish the new

破中有立 **p'ò-chūng yǔ-lì** within
destruction there is creation

破产 **p'ò-ch'ǎn** to go bankrupt, become
insolvent, fail

破旗 **p'ò-ch'í** a tattered banner

破除 **p'ò-ch'ú** to dispel, eradicate,
eliminate, destroy, get rid of, remove

破除架子 **p'ò-ch'ú chià-tzu** to get rid of
pretense

破除封建迷信 **p'ò-ch'ú fēng-chièn mí-
hsìn** to get rid of feudal superstition

破除迷信 **p'ò-ch'ú mí-hsìn** get rid of
superstition

破除迷信解放思想 **p'ò-ch'ú mí-hsìn
chièh-fàng szū-hsiǎng** get rid of
superstition and liberate thought

破釜沉舟 **p'ò-fǔ ch'én-chōu** to smash
the cooking vessels and sink the
boats (to cut off one's own retreat,
burn one's bridges; determined to
fight it out)

破坏 **p'ò-huài** to ruin, destroy, subvert,
sabotage, disrupt, violate, infringe,
obstruct, frustrate

破坏中立 **p'ò-huài chūng-lì** to violate
neutrality

破坏分子 **p'ò-huài fèn-tzǔ** saboteurs,
subversive elements

破坏活动 **p'ò-huài-huó-tùng** acts of
sabotage, subversive activities

破坏革命 **p'ò-huài kó-mìng** to subvert
the revolution

破坏名誉 **p'ò-huài míng-yù** to defame
one's reputation, slander, libel

破坏社会秩序 **p'ò-huài shè-hui-chìh-hsù**
to disrupt social order, violate public
order

破坏停战 **p'ò-huài t'íng-chàn** to break a
truce; a truce violation

破坏团结 **p'ò-huài t'uán-chiéh** to wreck
solidarity, undermine unity

破获 **p'ò-huò** to detect and arrest,
uncover [criminal acts], disclose

破罐子破摔 **p'ò-kuàn-tzu p'ò-shuāi** to
throw a broken jar recklessly (letting
go since the situation is ruined)

破口大骂 **p'ò-k'ǒu-tà-mà** to unseal the
mouth and shout abuse (to curse
without restraint)

破烂货 **p'ò-làn-huò** rags and rubbish,
trash (often figurative)

破裂 **p'ò-lièh** to disrupt, rupture,
break off, sever; broken, cracked

破落户 **p'ò-lò-hù** a fallen family,
impoverished household

破门而出 **p'ò-mén-érh-ch'ū** to break
through the door and dash out

破冰船 **p'ò-pīng-ch'uán** an ice-breaker
ship

破私立公 **p'ò-szū lì-kūng** eliminate the
selfish and foster the public [good]
(renounce self for the sake of society)

破四旧 **p'ò szù-chiù** to destroy the
four olds (*see* **szù-chiù**)

破四旧, 立四新 **p'ò-szù-chiù, lì szù-hsīn**
to destroy the four olds and establish
the four news (*see* **szù-hsīn**)

破天荒 **p'ò t'iēn-huāng** breaking the
state of nature (unprecedented, for
the first time, epoch-making)

破土开工 **p'ò-t'ǔ k'āi-kūng** to break
ground and start work

破字当头 **p'ò-tzù tāng-t'óu** the word

"destroy" comes first (a Cultural Revolution slogan)

1784 魄力 **p'ò-lì** determination and vigor, courage, guts

p'ōu (pōu)

1785 剖析 **p'ōu-hsī** to analyze, distinguish, explain, dissect; analysis

剖开 **p'ōu-k'āi** to rip open, cut apart

剖明 **p'ōu-míng** to dissect and clarify

剖视 **p'ōu-shìh** to view analytically

p'ū (pū)

1786 扑克牌 **p'ū-k'ò-p'ái** the game of poker; playing cards

扑灭 **p'ū-mièh** to quell, exterminate, extinguish

1787 铺张 **p'ū-chāng** to arrange, lay in order, make an ostentatious show; to exaggerate; pompous, extravagant

铺张浪费 **p'ū-chāng làng-fèi** extravagance and waste

铺张门面 **p'ū-chāng mén-mièn** to fix up the front [of the house] (to keep up appearances; superficial prettification)

铺平道路 **p'ū-p'íng tào-lù** to smooth the road (to help make possible, facilitate)

铺垫 **p'ū-tièn** to level out, even out the high and low spots; to cushion, spead a cushion

铺天盖地 **p'ū-t'iēn-kài-tì** filling the air and covering the ground (overflowing abundance)

p'ú (pú)

1788 仆从 **p'ú-ts'úng** servant, follower, retainer, lackey, flunkey

仆从军 **p'ú-ts'úng-chūn** a satellite army, lackey army, mercenary force

仆从国 **p'ú-ts'úng-kuó** a satellite, vassal country

1789 匍伏 **p'ú-fú** to crawl, creep on all fours

匍匐 **p'ú-fú** to crawl, creep on all fours

1790 菩萨心肠 **p'ú-sà hsīn-ch'áng** the kindness of a Buddha's heart (kindhearted, compassionate)

1791 葡属几內亚 **p'ú-shǔ chī-nèi-yà** Portuguese Guinea [now Bissau]

葡萄牙 **p'ú-t'áo-yá** Portugal

1792 蒲式耳 **p'ú-shìh-ěrh** a bushel

p'ǔ (pǔ)

1793 朴正熙 **p'ǔ chèng-hsī** Pak Chong Hee (President of South Korea, also

written as Chung Hee Park)

朴素 **p'ǔ-sù** simple, unadorned, plain

朴素感恩思想 **p'ǔ-sù kǎn-ēn szū-hsiǎng** a simplistic ideology of gratitude (thinking based on gratitude to the Communist Party rather than class consciousness)

朴素的无产阶级感情 **p'ǔ-sù te wù-ch'ǎn-chiēh-chí kǎn-ch'íng** plain proletarian feelings

1794 普照 **p'ǔ-chào** to shine upon all, illuminating everything

普及 **p'ǔ-chí** extending to all, universal; to make generally available, popularize

普及教育 **p'ǔ-chí-chiào-yù** universal education, education for all

普及和提高 **p'ǔ-chí hó t'í-kāo** popularization and raising [of standards]; to disseminate and improve

普查 **p'ǔ-ch'á** a general survey, census

普选 **p'ǔ-hsuǎn** a general election

普选制度 **p'ǔ-hsuǎn-chìh-tù** universal franchise, universal suffrage

普米族 **p'ǔ-mǐ-tsǔ** the P'u-mi people (a minority in Yunnan province: population 15,000 as of 1957)

普那卡 **p'ǔ-nà-k'ǎ** Punakha [Bhutan]

普遍 **p'ǔ-pièn** universal, general, common, widespread, everywhere

普遍真理 **p'ǔ-pièn-chēn-lǐ** universal truth

普遍性 **p'ǔ-pièn-hsìng** universality

普遍意义 **p'ǔ-pièn-i-ì** universal significance

普遍规律 **p'ǔ-pièn kuēi-lù** a universal law

普遍深入 **p'ǔ-pièn-shēn-jù** extensive and thorough

普遍裁军 **p'ǔ-pièn-ts'ái-chūn** universal disarmament

普遍存在 **p'ǔ-pièn-ts'ún-tsài** to exist everywhere

普天之下 **p'ǔ-t'iēn-chīh-hsià** all over the world

普通话 **p'ǔ-t'ūng-huà** the common language (based on Peking pronunciation and now used in preference to the older term: *kuó-yǔ* 国语)

普通一兵 **p'ǔ-t'ūng ī-pīng** just an ordinary soldier (whether one is a general or a private, he is still just a soldier; the title of a novel)

普通人 **p'ǔ-t'ūng-jén** the average man, man in the street

普通民兵 **p'ǔ-t'ūng mín-pīng** an ordinary militiaman

1795 谱写一曲 **p'ǔ-hsiěh ī-chǔ** to compose the music for a song

sā (sā)

1796 撒谎 **sā-huǎng** to scatter falsehoods, tell lies, fib

撒拉族 **sā-lā-tsú** the Salar people (a minority in Chinghai province: population 31,000 as of 1957)

撒手 **sā-shǒu** to relax the hand, loosen the grasp, let go of (to neglect a responsibility)

撒手不管 **sā-shǒu-pù-kuǎn** to relinquish one's concern in, give up, take no further interest in, wash one's hands of

撒 **sā**: *see also* **sǎ**

sǎ (sǎ)

1797 撒种 **sǎ-chǔng** to scatter seeds

撒 **sǎ**: *see also* **sā**

sà (sà)

1798 萨尔瓦多 **sà-ěrh-wǎ-tō** [Republic of] El Salvador

萨那 **sà-nà** San'a [Yemen Arab Republic]

sāi (sāi)

1799 塞进 **sāi-chìn** to stuff into, insert in, smuggle into (to add something surreptitiously [into a document])

塞住 **sāi-chù** to stop up, block, seal, cork

塞拉勒窝内 **sāi-lā-lè-wō-nèi** [Republic of] Sierra Leone

塞满 **sāi-mǎn** to stuff full, fill completely

塞内加尔 **sāi-nèi-chiā-ěrh** [Republic of] Senegal

塞饱肚皮 **sāi-pǎo-tù-p'í** to eat simply to fill the stomach

塞浦路斯 **sāi-p'ǔ-lù-szū** [Republic of] Cyprus

sān (sān)

1800 三整 **sān-chěng** the Three Rectifications [of organization, ideology, and work]

三极政府委员会 **sān-chí chèng-fǔ wěi-yuán-huì** the three levels of government councils (rural: village, *hsiang*, *hsien*; urban: neighborhood, district, municipality)

三级所有制 **sān-chí sǒ-yǔ-chìh** three-level ownership system (the system in force during the early stage of the commune movement with ownership divided between commune, brigade, and production teams)

三级所有, 队为基础 **sān-chí-sǒ-yǔ, tuì-wéi-chī-ch'ǔ** ownership at three levels with the production team as the base (*see above*)

三家四户 **sān-chia szù-hù** three families and four households (a small inhabited place; a small collection of people)

三家村 **sān-chiā-ts'ūn** three-family village (*see below*: **sān-chiā-ts'ūn chá-chì**)

三家村札记 **sān-chiā-ts'ūn chá-chì** "Notes from Three-Family Village" (an essay column by Teng T'o, Wu Han, and Liao Mo-sha which appeared in the Peking semi-monthly *Ch'ien-hsien* from 1961 to July 1964 and became an early target of the Cultural Revolution)

三角洲 **sān-chiǎo-chōu** a delta

三教九流 **sān-chiào chiǔ-liú** the Three Doctrines [religions] and the Nine Streams [schools of philosophy]

三结合 **sān-chiéh-hó** triple unification, triple alliance (a form of organization, largely ad hoc, often utilized during campaigns and varying in components according to setting. For instance, during the Great Leap: cadres, technicians, and peasants; managers, technicians, and workers; old, middle-aged, and young. During the Socialist Education Movement: poor and lower-middle peasants, cadres, and work-team members. During the Cultural Revolution: representatives of mass organizations, former Party cadres, and members of the PLA. In the creation of **yàng-pǎn-hsì**: the leadership [the Party], professional theater workers, and the masses)

三支 **sān-chīh** the Three Supports (a Cultural Revolution slogan; support: the left, industry, and agriculture)

三支两军 **sān-chīh-liǎng-chǔn** the Three Supports and Two Militarys (support leftists, workers, and peasants; military control and military training [of Red Guards]

三就 **sān-chiù** the Three On-the-Spot (to promote local purchase, butchering, and sale of pork)

三抓 **sān-chuā** Three Grasp-Firmlys [Three Grab-Hold-Ofs] (the elements may vary: ideology, production, living; attitude, systems, mass supervision)

三忠于运动 **sān-chūng-yú yùn-tùng** the Three Loyal-To Movement (launched in early 1968: loyal to Chairman Mao, his thought, and his revolutionary line)

三查 **sān-ch'á** the Three Check-ups (to check the registration of: production teams, households, and cultivated land)

三查三整 **sān-ch'á-sān-chěng** the Three Check-ups and Three Improvements (checking on the class origin, ideology and work style; improving organization, ideology and work style)

三查运动 **sān-ch'á yùn-tùng** the Three Check-ups Campaign (*against*: (a) those taking the capitalist road; (b) renegades and spies; and (c) the five bad elements—unreformed landlords, rich peasants, counter-revolutionaries, bad elements and rightists)

三岔路口 **sān-ch'à-lù-k'ǒu** where three roads meet, a crossroads (often figurative)

三七指示 **sān-ch'ī chǐh-shìh** the March 7 Directive (Mao Tse-tung's directive of March 7, 1967, that the PLA should give military and political training in schools and universities)

三七制 **sān-ch'ī-chìh** the Three-Seven System (a plan, commenced in some areas in 1960, for cadres to spend three days in meetings and study, and seven days in production work)

三气 **sān-ch'ì** the Three Ires (dissatisfaction [**yuàn-ch'ì**], disappointment [**hsièh-ch'ì**], recalcitrance or resentment [**pù-fú-ch'ì**])

三清一改 **sān-ch'īng ī-kǎi** Three Inventories and One Improvement [Campaign] (launched in the spring of 1961 to meet retail shortages of commodities; inventories were to be by factories, commercial outlets, and the city economic committee in order to improve the flow of available goods)

三清运动 **sān-ch'īng yùn-tùng** the Three Clear-ups Movement (to clear-up accounts, properties and work points)

三秋 **sān-ch'iū** the three autumn [tasks] (harvesting, plowing, and sowing)

三去三不回 **sān-ch'ù sān-pù-huí** the Three Go's and Three Do-Not-Returns (a **hsià-fàng** cadre slogan. *Go*: to the fields to set an example of good work; to the production teams

to create experience; to the most difficult places to solve problems. *Do not return until*: the problems are solved; experience is created; the "physiognomy of production" is transformed)

三番五次 **sān-fān wǔ-tz'ù** three turns and five times (time and time again, repeatedly, over and over)

三反 **sān-fǎn** the Three Antis (a movement for government and Party, begun in 1952, opposing: corruption, waste, and bureaucratism)

三反分子 **sān-fǎn fèn-tzǔ** the three-anti elements (persons, such as Liu Shao-ch'i and his followers, who were alleged to be: anti-Party, anti-Mao, and anti-socialist)

三反双减 **sān-fǎn shuāng-chiěn** the three anti and the double reduction (a policy in Tibet after the suppression of the 1960 rebellion. *Anti*: rebellion, corvée, and slavery; *reduction of*: land rent and interest)

三反运动 **sān-fǎn yùn-tùng** the Three-Anti Movement (a campaign, commenced in 1952, against corruption, waste, and bureaucratism)

三废 **sān-fèi** the Three Wastes (to counter wastage of liquids, gases, and solids [dregs, slag])

三风 **sān-fēng** the Three Trends (three bad trends or work styles to be corrected: bureaucratism, subjectivism, and sectarianism)

三伏天 **sān-fú-t'iēn** the hottest days of summer, the three ten-day periods after the summer solstice

三害 **sān-hài** the Three Calamities (tactics allegedly employed by Liu Shao-ch'i and his followers: factionalism, anarchism, and economism)

三好 **sān-hǎo** the Three Goods (the "goods" have varied according to time and circumstance—in the education policy set by Mao Tse-tung in 1957: good health, study, and work; in lauding the compensation of peasants in the communes during 1964: clear accounts, exchange for cash, and democratic distribution; for the PLA: good unification, discipline, and combat ability)

三好学生 **sān-hǎo-hsuéh-shēng** a Three-Good Student (good in health, learning, and work)

三合土 **sān-hó-t'ǔ** a native mortar (consisting of sand, lime, and soil)

三和一少 **sān-hó ī-shǎo** the Three

Reconciliations and One Reduction
(an accusation by Chou En-lai at the
Third National People's Congress in
December 1964, that in 1959–1962,
there were some who wanted to come
to a reconciliation with the imperialists, the reactionaries, and the
modern revisionists; and to reduce
aid to other peoples in revolt)

三化 **sān-huà** the Three Transformations (in communes, organization
should be militarized, action
martialized, and life collectivized)

三环外交 **sān-huán wài-chiāo** three-link
diplomacy

三红 **sān-húng** the Three Reds (from
the Cultural Revolution: the
Proletarian Headquarters [of the Red
Guards]; the PLA; and the
Revolutionary Committees)

三下生活 **sān-hsià shēng-huó** repeated
going down to [the masses to acquire
experience of] real life (a prerequisite
for writers and actors producing
yàng-pǎn hsì)

三夏 **sān-hsià** the three summer [tasks]
(threshing, storing, and transporting
wheat)

三降一灭 **sān-hsiáng-ī-mièh** the Three
Capitulations and One Cut-off (a
Cultural Revolution accusation
against Liu Shao-ch'i that he
advocated capitulation to the Soviet
revisionists, the imperialists, and the
reactionaries; and a cut-off of aid to
foreign revolutionaries)

三项实践 **sān-hsiàng shíh-ch'ièn** the
Three Kinds of [social] Practice (*see*
sān-tà kó-mìng yùn-tùng)

三心二意 **sān-hsīn èrh-ì** [of] three
minds and two intentions, three
thoughts and two ideas (undecided,
changeable, not wholehearted)

三忆三比 **sān-ì sān-pǐ** three recollec-
tions and three comparisons (a 1967
motto for study classes in Mao's
Thought: remember the bitterness of
the old society, and compare the
sweetness of the new; remember
what the Party has given them in
nurture and education, and compare
their own contribution; remember
the crimes of the power-holders, and
compare the great achievements of
the Cultural Revolution)

三纲五常 **sān-kāng wǔ-ch'áng** the three
bonds and five constant [virtues]
(moral obligation, the classical view
of the duties of man—now criticized)

三革命化 **sān kó-mìng-huà** the Three

Revolutionizations (revolutionization
of enterprises, personnel, and government organs)

三个差别 **sān-ko ch'ā-piéh** the Three
Differences (between urban and rural,
worker and peasant, mental and
physical labor)

三个臭皮匠, 合成一个诸葛亮 **sān-ko
ch'òu-p'í-chiàng, hó-ch'éng ī-ko chū-
kó-liàng** putting together three
stinking cobblers makes one Chuko
Liang (three ordinary men can equal
the master strategist Chuko Liang if
they put their heads together)

三关 **sān-kuān** the Three Tests
(ideology, life style, and physical
labor)

三管齐下 **sān-kuǎn ch'í-hsià** to use
three [pens] at the same time (to do
three things simultaneously)

三光政策 **sān-kuāng chèng-ts'è** the
Three-All Policy (retaliatory tactics
used by the Japanese in North China
after the Eighth Route Army's
success in the Hundred Regiments
Offensive: kill all, burn all, loot all)

三光四不留 **sān-kuāng szù-pù-liú** the
Three Bares and Four No-
Retentions (a Cultural Revolution
accusation that the policies of Liu
Shao-ch'i encouraged the peasants to
share out, eat up, and use up
everything [thus having nothing left,
or being bare]; and to retain nothing
for food grain reserves and for
commune, welfare, and prodution
funds)

三过思想 **sān-kuò szū-hsiǎng** Three-
Pass Thinking (an attitude charged
against intellectuals of doing no more
than a minimum [to pass] in regard
to politics, physical labor, and a
frugal life style)

三开门方法 **sān-k'āi-mén fāng-fǎ** the
Three-Open-Door Policy (public
discussion of applicants for Party
membership; public participation in
Party rectification; public consideration of recipients of the "Four-
Good" award)

三老 **sān-lǎo** the Three Olds (old
peasants, old Party members, and old
cadres—those who fought against the
KMT, landlords, and the old society)

三老干部 **sān-lǎo kàn-pù** Three-Old
Cadres (old cadres who are sick,
good, or over the age of 60: cadre
categories receiving lenient treatment
in the Cultural Revolution and
approved for membership in the **sān-**

chiéh-hó)

三老四严 **sān-lǎo szù-yén** Three-Honest and Four Strict (honest as a person and in speech and deeds; strict in demands on oneself, and in organization, attitude, and discipline)

三令五申 **sān-lìng wǔ-shēn** three orders and five instructions (repeated commands)

三落实 **sān-lò-shíh** the Three Carrying-Outs (to properly and realistically carry out the three aspects of struggle, criticism, and transformation)

三轮车 **sān-lún-ch'ē** a three-wheeled car, pedicab

三门干部 **sān-mén kàn-pù** three-door cadres (cadres who have gone from the door of their home to school and then directly into a government office: i.e., lacking in practical experience and labor)

三灭 **sān-mièh** the Three Exterminations (of mosquitoes, flies, and rats)

三面红旗 **sān-mièn húng-ch'í** the Three Red Flags (the General Line for Socialist Construction, People's Communes, and the Great Leap Forward)

三面红旗运动 **sān-mièn húng-ch'í yùn-tùng** the Three Red Flags Campaign (a campaign begun in 1958: *see above*)

三民主义 **sān-mín-chǔ-ì** the Three People's Principles (of Sun Yat-sen)

三八作风 **sān-pā-tsò-fēng** the Three-Eight Work Style (three phrases and eight characters summarizing maxims for the army developed by Mao Tse-tung in the Kiangsi period. The three phrases: correct political direction; simple and arduous work style; flexible strategy and tactics. The eight characters are the terms for: unity, alertness, earnestness, and activeness)

三包制度 **sān-pāo chìh-tù** the Three-Contract System (to operate under agreed targets for output, labor input, and cost)

三包一奖 **sān-pāo ī-chiǎng** Three Contracts and One Award (fixed targets for output, labor, and cost, with a reward for added output)

三保田 **sān-pǎo-t'ién** a three-hold field (it retains water, soil, and fertilizer: opposite of **sān-p'ǎo-t'ién**)

三不 **sān-pù** the Three-Nots (not to recognize, support, or join any anti-revolutionary organization)

三不放 **sān-pù-fàng** the Three No-Loosenings (do not let go of [loosen one's hold on]: the Thought of Mao Tse-tung; line education; and the struggle between the two lines)

三不怕精神 **sān-pù-p'à chīng-shén** the Three-Not-Fearing Spirit (not fearing hardship, fatigue, or difficulty)

三不停 **sān-pù-t'íng** the Three No-Stoppings (do not stop: changing one's world view; making continuous revolution; criticizing the capitalist class)

三不脱离 **sān-pù-t'ō-lí** the Three Not-To-Be-Separated-Froms (do not become separated [divorced] from: productive labor, the masses, and objective reality)

三不要 **sān-pù-yào** the Three Not-Wants (revisionism, "splittism," and conspiracy)

三跑田 **sān-p'ǎo-t'ién** a three-runaway field (it does not retain water, soil, or fertilizer)

三三制 **sān-sān-chìh** the Three-Thirds System (A. In the representative assemblies of Liberated Areas during the Resistance War: one-third of the seats for CCP members, one-third for other parties including the KMT, and one-third for non-party progressive elements. B. During the **hsià-fàng** campaign [as in Shensi in 1960]: one-third of the cadres transferred downward, one-third on inspection tours, and one-third carrying on regular duties)

三三四制 **sān-sān-szù-chìh** the Three-Three-Four System (applied in some sales organizations: out of ten employees, three are transferred downward to production brigades, three to take goods for sale to the brigades, and four to carry on normal sales work at the home store)

三上桃峯 **sān-shàng t'áo-fēng** "Three Ascents of Peach Peak" (the title of of a Shansi folk-drama accused of being in defense of Liu Shao-ch'i and his wife)

三十六计，走为上计 **sān-shíh-liù chì, tsǒu wéi shàng-chì** [of the] thirty-six stratagems, the best is to flee

三十年代 **sān-shíh-nién-tài** the Thirties (usually refers to 1927–37, a period of great literary activity with which Chou Yang and his group are identified)

三史 **sān-shǐh** the Three Histories (a

movement begun in 1959 to collect historical materials to keep alive the memory of conditions before Liberation. The content of the three histories varied among different groups—for peasants: the history of one's family, village, and commune; for workers: family, factory [or mine], and its revolutionary struggles; for PLA members: family, company, and the revolutionary achievements of the PLA; for Party members: family, village, and Party history)

三熟制 **sān-shú-chìh** the Three-Harvest System

三大政策 **sān-tà-chèng-ts'è** the Three Cardinal Policies (adopted by Sun Yat-sen and the KMT in 1924 and sometimes referred to as the New Three People's Principles: alliance with the USSR; acceptance of CCP members in the KMT; benefits to workers and peasants)

三大纪律 **sān-tà-chì-lù** the Three Main Rules of Discipline (rules of the Eighth Route Army: follow orders in every activity; take not a single needle or thread from the masses; turn in everything captured)

三大纪律，八项注意 **sān-tà-chì-lù, pā-hsiàng-chù-ì** the Three Main Rules of Discipline and the Eight Points for Attention (for Three Main Rules, *see above*. The Eight Points: speak politely, pay fairly for all purchases, return everything borrowed, pay for any damage, do not hit or swear at people, do not damage crops, take no liberties with women, do not ill-treat prisoners)

三大差别 **sān-tà-ch'ā-piéh** the Three Great Differences (between urban and rural, worker and peasant, mental and physical labor: similar to **sān-kò ch'ā-piéh**)

三大任务 **sān-tà-jèn-wù** the Three Great Tasks (to grasp revolution, promote production, and push war-readiness: a slogan appearing in 1968)

三大改造 **sān-tà-kǎi-tsào** the Three Great Transformations (of agriculture, handicrafts, and industry and commerce)

三大革命 **sān-tà-kó-mìng** the Three Great Revolutions (class struggle, the struggle for production, and scientific experiment)

三大革命斗争实践 **sān-tà-kó-mìng tòu-chēng shíh-chièn** the practice of the three great revolutionary struggles (*see above*)

三大革命运动 **sān-tà-kó-mìng yùn-tùng** the movement for the three great revolutionary [goals] (class struggle, the struggle for production, and scientific experiment)

三大观点 **sān-tà kuān-tiěn** the Three Great Viewpoints (political viewpoint, laboring viewpoint, and the mass viewpoint)

三大民主 **sān-tà mín-chǔ** the Three Great Democracies (applied in the PLA during the Liberation War: politically, officers and men help each other to understand goals; economically, soldiers take part in running their own mess; militarily, all share knowledge and express their views)

三大实践 **sān-tà-shíh-chièn** the Three Great Practices (struggle for production, class struggle, scientific experiment—the same as **sān-tà-kó-mìng**)

三大敌人 **sān-tà-tí-jén** the Three Great Enemies (imperialism, feudalism, and bureaucratic capitalism)

三大作风 **sān-tà-tsò-fēng** the Three Great Work Styles (firm and correct political direction; plain and arduous work style; and flexible strategy and tactics: *see also* **sān-pā-tsò-fēng**)

三代会 **sān-tài-huì** the Three Representative Assemblies (mass organizations for workers, peasants, and red guards)

三定 **sān-tìng** the Three Fixeds (abbreviation for regulations promulgated by the State Council in August, 1955, concerning production, state purchase, and consumer sales of grain)

三定一顶 **sān-tìng ī-tǐng** the Three Fixeds and One Substitution (cadres participating in labor: report to work at fixed hours; labor for a fixed length of time each day; assume fixed responsibilities toward production and they must also know the job of ordinary workers so that they can substitute for them)

三多会议 **sān-tō-huì-ì** a Three-"Many" Conference (a conference during which the participants see many shows, attend many banquets, and receive many gifts—a criticism of bureaucratism)

三对比 **sān-tuì-pǐ** the Three Comparisons (the present with the past; the good and the bad features of present-

day life; and the socialism of today with the promise of full communism in the future)

三天打鱼, 两天晒网 **sān-t'iēn-tǎ-yǘ, liǎng-t'iēn-shài-wǎng** to fish for three days and dry the nets for two (inconsistent and not persistent in one's work, to dilly-dally)

三脱离 **sān-t'ō-lí** the Three Separations (there are several versions, all abjured: from proletarian politics, the workers and peasants, production; from the masses, productive labor, workers and peasants; from politics, the masses, and labor. [*see also* **sān-pù-t'ō-lí**])

三突出创作原则 **sān-t'ū-ch'ū ch'uàng-tsò yuán-tsé** the creative writing principle of three saliencies (*in ascending order of importance*: positive personalities, heroic persons, the central heroic figure)

三土 **sān-t'ǔ** the Three Locals (the use of traditional Chinese medicine: local doctors, indigenous medicines, and simple methods)

三同作风 **sān-t'úng tsò-fēng** the Three-Togetherness Style [*of Leadership*] (cadres were to eat, live, and work together with the workers— commenced in 1958)

三座大山 **sān-tsò tà-shān** the Three Great Mountains (*before Liberation*: imperialism, feudalism, and bureaucratic capitalism; *during the Cultural Revolution*: imperialism, revisionism, and reactionaries)

三足鼎立 **sān-tsú-tǐng-lì** standing like a tripod (usually refers to China, the USSR and the US)

三自爱国运动 **sān-tzù ài-kuó yùn-tùng** the Three-Self Patriotic Movement (a campaign to sever Christian churches in China from outside guidance and support through: self-administration, self-support, and self-propagation)

三自一包 **sān-tzù ī-pāo** the Three Freedoms and One Contract (a policy initiated by Liu Shao-ch'i in 1962: private plots, free markets, freedom to engage in sideline occupations for private profit; and contracts by individual households to produce a specified amount of grain)

三参一改 **sān-ts'ān ī-kǎi** the Three Supervisions and One Improvement (a program implemented in some commercial enterprises: cadres participate in physical work, workers and staff participate in administration, and masses participate in supervision—these measures result in overall improvement)

三从一大 **sān-ts'úng ī-tà** the Three Froms and One Great (success in athletic competition comes from: doing the difficult, strict training, keeping a competitive spirit; and by developing one's physical capacity by great physical effort)

三湾改编 **sān-wān-kǎi-piēn** the reorganization at Sanwan (after the failure of the Autumn Harvest Uprising, Mao Tse-tung reorganized his defeated forces at Sanwan, Kiangsi, in October 1927, before leading them to the Chingkangshan)

三弯腰 **sān-wān-yāo** the Three Waist Bendings (in rice production: thinning the sprouts, transplanting the shoots, and scything the crop)

三位一体 **sān-wèi ī-t'ǐ** the Trinity (now refers to any combination of three elements or groups into an integral whole)

三要三不要 **sān-yào sān-pù-yào** the Three Do's and Three Do-Not's (*do*: practice Marxism, unite, and be open and aboveboard; *do not*: practice revisionism, split, or intrigue and conspire)

三有 **sān-yǔ** the Three Haves (in the PLA: each squad has [at least one] Party member; each platoon, a Party cell; and each company, a branch committee)

三右 **sān-yù** the Three Right [-isms] (right opportunism, right capitulationism and right "splittism")

sǎn (sǎn)

1801 伞兵 **sǎn-pīng** a paratrooper; airborne [military unit]

1802 散漫 **sǎn-màn** scattered, untidy, diffuse, loosely organized

散 **sǎn**: *see also* **sàn**

sàn (sàn)

1803 散发 **sàn-fā** to scatter, distribute, circulate, spread, disseminate

散开 **sàn-k'āi** to disperse, spread out

散播 **sàn-pò** to disseminate, spread

散布 **sàn-pù** to scatter, sprinkle, strew; to spread, disseminate

散 **sàn**: *see also* **sǎn**

sāng (sāng)

1804　丧钟 **sāng-chūng** a funeral bell, death knell, knell
　　丧 **sāng**: see also sàng

1805　桑给巴尔 **sāng-chǐ-pā-ěrh** Zanzibar

sàng (sàng)

1806　丧气 **sàng-ch'i** to lose heart; dejected, despondent; bad luck
　　丧魂失魄 **sàng-hún-shīh-p'ò** to be deprived of one's wits and lose one's nerve (to lose self-control through fright, to panic)
　　丧心病狂 **sàng-hsīn pìng-k'uáng** to be seized with crazy ideas, to lose one's powers of judgment
　　丧失 **sàng-shīh** to lose, be deprived of, be stripped of
　　丧胆 **sàng-tǎn** to lose one's gall (to panic)
　　丧地辱国 **sàng-tì-jǔ-kuó** to surrender territory and bring humiliation to the country
　　丧 **sàng**: see also sāng

sāo (sāo)

1807　骚扰 **sāo-jǎo** to disturb, harass, agitate
　　骚乱 **sāo-luàn** disturbance, unrest, upheaval, tumult
　　骚动 **sāo-tùng** disturbance, unrest, upheaval, commotion, tumult, riot; to become restless, ready for revolt

1808　缫丝 **sāo-szū** silk reeling

sǎo (sǎo)

1809　扫尽 **sǎo-chìn** to sweep away completely, clear out, eliminate
　　扫清 **sǎo-ch'īng** to sweep clean
　　扫除 **sǎo-ch'ú** to sweep away, eliminate eradicate
　　扫除文盲 **sǎo-ch'ú wén-máng** to eliminate illiteracy
　　扫雷艇 **sǎo-léi-t'ǐng** a mine-sweeper
　　扫盲 **sǎo-máng** to eliminate illiteracy (abbreviation of **sǎo-ch'ú wén-máng**)
　　扫盲运动 **sǎo-máng yùn-tùng** anti-illiteracy campaign
　　扫灭 **sǎo-mièh** to wipe out, exterminate, liquidate
　　扫射 **sǎo-shè** to fire upon, strafe
　　扫荡 **sǎo-tàng** to make a clean sweep [of the enemy], exterminate, mop up, annihilate
　　扫地出门 **sǎo-tì ch'ū-mén** to sweep up and drive out of the door (to confiscate all of a person's property)

　　扫地荡尽 **sǎo-tì-tàng-chìn** swept up and completely exhausted, completely destroyed
　　扫尾工作 **sǎo-wěi kūng-tsò** tail-sweeping work, tidying-up, clean-up work (the finishing touches, final stages of a movement)

sè (sè)

1810　色情 **sè-ch'íng** sexual passion, lust; obscene, pornographic
　　色盲 **sè-máng** color blind; to be color blind
　　色彩缤纷 **sè-ts'ǎi-pīn-fēn** of motley and variegated character

sēn (sēn)

1811　森林工业 **sēn-lín kūng-yèh** the forestry industry
　　森严 **sēn-yén** stern, severe, awe-inspiring

sēng (sēng)

1812　僧道 **sēng-tào** Buddhist monks and Taoist priests

shā (shā)

1813　杀豺狼讨血债 **shā-ch'ái-láng t'ǎo-hsuèh-chài** to kill the wolf to avenge a blood debt
　　杀价 **shā-chià** to reduce prices drastically, slash prices
　　杀尽 **shā-chìn** to kill all, exterminate, give no quarter
　　杀气腾腾 **shā-ch'ì-t'éng-t'éng** a thirst for blood engulfing all, a blood-thirsty atmosphere
　　杀虫设备 **shā-ch'úng shè-pèi** insecticide equipment
　　杀虫药剂 **shā-ch'úng-yào-chì** insecticide
　　杀菌剂 **shā-chūn-chì** fungicide, bacteriophage, germicide
　　杀一儆百 **shā-ī chǐng-pǎi** to kill one in order to warn a hundred
　　杀人放火 **shā-jén-fàng-huǒ** to murder and set fires
　　杀人如麻 **shā-jén-jú-má** to kill people like [cutting a bundle of] hemp
　　杀人不眨眼 **shā-jén pù-chǎ-yěn** to kill without blinking an eye
　　杀人不见血 **shā-jén pù-chièn-hsuèh** to kill a person bloodlessly (to kill without leaving a trace)
　　杀人武器 **shā-jén wǔ-ch'ì** lethal weapons
　　杀, 关, 管, 放 **shā, kuān, kuǎn, fàng** kill,

imprison, restrict, release (options in the trials of counter-revolutionaries)

杀伤弹 **shā-shāng-tàn** anti-personnel fragmentation bombs

杀身成仁 **shā-shēn-ch'éng-jén** to sacrifice one's life for benevolence (the principle *jen* was formerly the highest Confucian virtue; it is now given a class character and is associated with feudalism)

1814 沙家浜 **shā-chiā-pāng** one of the **yàng-pǎn-hsì** (adapted from the Shanghai opera "Lú-tàng huǒ-chǔng")

沙海 **shā-hǎi** a sea of sand, a large area of sand

沙皇 **shā-huáng** the tsars [of Russia]

沙皇制度 **shā-huáng-chìh-tù** the tsarist system

沙皇主义 **shā-huáng-chǔ-ì** tsarism (usually refers to the policies of the post-Stalin Soviet leaders)

沙捞越 **shā-lāo-yuèh** Sarawak (now part of Malaysia)

沙漠 **shā-mò** a desert

沙石硲 **shā-shíh-yù** a famous commune north of Peking

沙特阿拉伯 **shā-t'è ā-lā-pó** Saudi Arabia

沙文主义 **shā-wén-chǔ-ì** chauvinism

1815 纱厂 **shā-ch'ǎng** a cotton spinning factory

纱绽 **shā-tìng** a [cotton] spindle

1816 刹车 **shā-ch'ē** (1) to apply the brake, stop the car (often figurative); (2) to tie goods on a truck (also written as 煞车)

1817 砂丘 **shā-ch'iū** sand dunes

砂型 **shā-hsíng** a sand mold for casting metal

shǎ (shǎ)

1818 傻子 **shǎ-tzu** fool, imbecile, simpleton, idiot, blockhead

shà (shà)

1819 煞费苦心 **shà-fèi-k'ǔ-hsīn** to expend painstaking efforts, take a great deal of trouble

煞有介事 **shà-yǔ-chièh-shìh** as if there were such a thing (making a great deal out of a trifle)

shān (shān)

1820 山岙 **shān-ào** a level piece of ground between mountains

山珍海味 **shān-chēn hǎi-wèi** delicacies from the mountains and the seas (a sumptuous repast)

山脊 **shān-chǐ** a mountain ridge, spine-like ridge

山中无老虎，猴子也称王 **shān-chūng wú lǎo-hǔ, hóu-tzu yěh ch'ēng-wáng** when there is no tiger in the mountains, the monkey can claim to be king

山穷水尽 **shān-ch'iúng-shuǐ-chìn** at the end of the mountains and waters (at the end of the road, in a desperate situation)

山区 **shān-ch'ū** mountainous areas, upland regions

山沟 **shān-kōu** a gully, ravine, eroded terrain

山脉 **shān-mài** a mountain range, mountains

山崩 **shān-pēng** an avalanche, landslide

山炮 **shān-p'ào** a mountain gun, pack howitzer

山塘 **shān-t'áng** hill ponds (small man-made ponds to conserve water for farming)

山头主义 **shān-t'óu-chǔ-ì** "mountain-top-ism" (the tendency of individuals or organizations to expand, stress their own importance and special character, and to act independently of centralized [Party] discipline and control)

山村 **shān-ts'ūn** hill villages

山窝 **shān-wō** a mountain nest (a glen or small valley where a few people may live and farm)

山腰 **shān-yāo** the waist of the mountain, mountain mid-slopes

山药蛋 **shān-yào-tàn** the Irish potato

山雨欲来风满楼 **shān-yǔ-yù-lái fēng-mǎn-lóu** the wind sweeping through the tower heralds a rising storm in the mountains (strong winds foretell the coming storm)

山岳地带 **shān-yuèh-tì-tài** an area of mountain peaks, a wild mountain district

1821 删节 **shān-chiéh** to abridge, condense

删去 **shān-ch'ù** to delete, eliminate, strike out

删繁就简 **shān-fán ch'iù-chiěn** to delete the complicated and attain simplicity (to epitomize and condense)

删改 **shān-kǎi** to delete superfluities and correct errors [in a manuscript], revise, edit

1822 舢板 **shān-pǎn** a small boat, sampan

1823 煽起 **shān-ch'ǐ** to stir up, incite, fan, instigate

煽风点火 **shān-fēng-tiěn-huǒ** to fan the wind and light a fire (to instigate, incite)

煽惑 **shān-huò** to rouse with falsehoods, incite, arouse, agitate

煽动 **shān-tùng** to incite, stir up, foment, instigate, arouse to [violent] action

煽阴风, 点鬼火 **shān-yīn-fēng, tiĕn-kuĕi-huǒ** to fan up dark winds and light devilish flames

shǎn (shǎn)

1824 闪击战 **shǎn-chī-chàn** lightning stroke war, blitzkrieg

闪光 **shǎn-kuāng** flash, glitter, sparkle

闪过一个念头 **shǎn-kuò ī-ko nièn-t'óu** an idea flashes through [one's mind]

闪烁其词 **shǎn-shuò-ch'í-tz'ú** his words flicker like lightning (to talk with many evasions and ambiguities)

闪电战 **shǎn-tièn-chàn** a lightning war, blitzkrieg

闪电害 **shǎn-tièn-hài** lightning damage

1825 陕 **shǎn** Shensi province

陕甘宁 [边区] **shǎn-kān-níng [p'iēn-ch'ǚ]** Shensi-Kansu-Ningsia [Border Region] (the main CCP base area during the Anti-Japanese War)

shàn (shàn)

1826 讪笑 **shàn-hsiào** to ridicule, sneer at, laugh at, mock

1827 扇形地区 **shàn-hsíng-tì-ch'ǚ** a fan-shaped area, sector

扇形推进 **shàn-hsíng t'uī-chìn** to push forward in fan formation, fan out [military]

1828 善后 **shàn-hòu** to relieve after [the effects of a disaster, tragedy, etc.], rehabilitate; rehabilitation

善心 **shàn-hsīn** kindhearted, compassionate

善意 **shàn-ì** good intentions, kindly motives; well-meaning

善观风色 **shàn-kuān-fēng-sè** good at observing the weather (shrewd in sensing—and being able to take advantage of—changes in the political climate; an opportunist)

善良 **shàn-liáng** good, gentle, law-abiding, decent

善本 **shàn-pĕn** a rare book, valuable edition

善变 **shàn-pièn** skilled in changing (changeable, fickle, capricious)

善择时机 **shàn-tsé-shíh-chī** shrewd in selecting the [right] opportunity

善于斗争 **shàn-yǘ tòu-chēng** to be good in [carrying out] struggle (able to achieve success in struggle)

1829 擅长 **shàn-ch'áng** to excel in, be good at; one's forte, special field of competence

擅自处理 **shàn-tzù-ch'ǔ-lǐ** to act without authority, act on one's own

1830 赡家费 **shàn-chiā-fèi** an allowance for family maintenance

赡家汇款 **shàn-chiā huì-k'uǎn** remittances for family maintenance

shāng (shāng)

1831 伤心 **shāng-hsīn** deeply hurt, heartbroken, very sad

伤脑筋 **shāng-nǎo-chīn** to rack one's brain; vexatious, troublesome

伤疤 **shāng-pā** a wound scar (often figurative)

伤亡 **shāng-wáng** wounded and dead, casualties

伤亡事故 **shāng-wáng shìh-kù** an accident causing injury or death

伤员 **shāng-yuán** wounded soldiers

1832 商榷 **shāng-ch'üèh** to discuss together, give consideration to

商会 **shāng-huì** a chamber of commerce

商量 **shāng-liang** to consult, confer, deliberate, discuss, exchange views

商标 **shāng-piāo** a trademark, brand

商品 **shāng-p'ǐn** commodities, goods, wares, merchandise

商品价格 **shāng-p'ǐn-chià-kó** commodity prices

商品猪 **shāng-p'ǐn-chū** pigs raised for sale

商品肥料 **shāng-p'ǐn-féi-liào** commercial fertilizer

商品下放 **shāng-p'ǐn hsià-fàng** downward transfer of commodities (improving distribution to rural areas)

商品小组 **shāng-p'ǐn hsiǎo-tsǔ** commodity small groups (in buying departments of retail firms)

商品性生产 **shāng-p'ǐn-hsìng shēng-ch'ǎn** commercial production, production for market

商品粮 **shāng-p'ǐn-liáng** commercial foodgrain

商品流转额 **shāng-p'ǐn liú-chuǎn-ó** volume of commodity turnover, volume of commodity circulation

商品流通 **shāng-p'ǐn liú-t'ūng** circulation of commodities, exchange of goods

商品流通环节 **shāng-p'ǐn liú-t'ūng huán-chiéh** the process of commodity circulation (the process of the sale of goods from producer to consumer)

商品排队 **shāng-p'ǐn-p'ái-tuì** the

mustering of merchandise (to arrange goods so that certain ones will be the first to be sold, etc.)

商品饲料 **shāng-p'ǐn-szù-liào** commercial feed

商品作物 **shāng-p'ǐn-tsò-wù** a cash crop, commercial crop

商谈 **shāng-t'án** to discuss, negotiate, confer in regard to

商讨 **shāng-t'ǎo** to discuss, exchange views

商务参赞 **shāng-wù-ts'ān-tsàn** a commercial counselor [diplomatic]

商业 **shāng-yèh** trade and commerce, commercial enterprise, business

商业机构 **shāng-yèh chī-kòu** the commercial apparatus, the institutional structure of commerce

商业殖民地 **shāng-yèh chíh-mín-tì** commercial colonies (foreign areas held in subservience through economic rather than political domination)

商业主 **shāng-yèh-chǔ** a proprietor of a business

商业区 **shāng-yèh-ch'ǖ** the commercial district, business area, "downtown"

商业部 **shāng-yèh-pù** (1) Ministry of Commerce [of the State Council]; (2) a commercial department or section [within an organization]

商约 **shāng-yuēh** (1) to decide together, come to an agreement; (2) a commercial treaty

1833 墒情 **shāng-ch'íng** moisture content [of the soil]

shǎng (shǎng)

1834 赏识 **shǎng-shíh** to recognize the worth of, appreciate, enjoy

shàng (shàng)

1835 上级机关 **shàng-chí-chī-kuān** higher authorities

上缴 **shàng-chiǎo** to transfer, pay, or deliver to a higher agency

上智下愚 **shàng-chìh-hsià-yú** the high [classes] are wise and the low are stupid (an accusation against Confucianism)

上进 **shàng-chìn** to go forward, make progress, advance

上中农 **shàng-chūng-núng** upper-middle peasants

上坟祭祖 **shàng-fén chì-tsǔ** to visit the tomb and sacrifice to the ancestors

上海机床厂 **shàng-hǎi chī-ch'uáng-ch'ǎng** the Shanghai Machine Tool Plant (commended by Mao Tse-tung in 1968 for in-plant training of engineering and technical personnel)

上海警备区 **shàng-hǎi chǐng-pèi-ch'ǖ** the Shanghai Garrison Headquarters

上海公报 **shàng-hǎi kūng-pào** the Shanghai Communique (signed by Nixon and Chou En-lai in February 1972)

上海公社 **shàng-hǎi kūng-shè** the Shanghai Commune (established in January 1967 in emulation of the Paris Commune)

上海电视大学 **shàng-hǎi tièn-shìh tà-hsuéh** Shanghai Television University

上下结合 **shàng-hsià chiéh-hó** to integrate upper and lower [levels]

上下串连 **shàng-hsià ch'uàn-lién** high and low [all levels] linked together, thoroughly coordinated

上下呼应 **shàng-hsià hū-yìng** upper and lower mutually responding (acting in coordination with each other)

上下文 **shàng-hsià-wén** the preceding and following passages [of written material], context

上旬 **shàng-hsún** the first ten-day period [of each month]

上一级 **shàng ī-chí** the next higher level; to rise one grade

上任 **shàng-jèn** to assume office, take up an official appointment

上纲上线 **shàng-kāng shàng-hsièn** to act on principles and the [policy] line

上钩 **shàng-kōu** to take the hook (fall into a trap, be tricked into [something])

上、管、改大学 **shàng-kuǎn-kǎi tà-hsuéh** to go to the university and manage and reform it (a slogan for worker-peasant-soldier students after the Cultural Revolution)

上马 **shàng-mǎ** to mount a horse (assume office, commence a major undertaking)

上面骄一点，下面骄一片 **shàng-mièn chiāo-ī-tiěn, hsià-mièn chiāo-ī-p'ièn** a little arrogance at the top [results in] a great deal of arrogance below

上班 **shàng-pān** to go on duty, attend office, start a shift, go to work

上不沾天，下不着地 **shàng-pù-chān-t'iēn, hsià-pù-cháo-tì** not touching the sky above nor reaching the ground below (suspended in mid-air)

上山取宝 **shàng-shān-ch'ǚ-pǎo** to go into the mountains to extract treasures (a slogan to urge the development of mountain areas)

上山下乡 **shàng-shān-hsià-hsiāng** up to

the mountains and down to the countryside (usually means going as pioneers to open new land)

上山下乡知识青年 **shàng-shān-hsià-hsiāng chīh-shíh-ch'īng-nién** educated youth who have gone up to the mountains and down to the countryside

上升 **shàng-shēng** to climb up, ascend, rise, lift up, elevate

上述 **shàng-shù** as stated above; the above-mentioned

上诉 **shàng-sù** to appeal [to a higher court or authority]

上诉程序 **shàng-sù ch'éng-hsù** the appellate procedure

上当 **shàng-tàng** to be taken in, fall into a trap, be folded, cheated, swindled, imposed upon

上动下不动 **shàng-tùng hsià-pù-tùng** change at the top without changing the bottom (may refer to organizational reorganization; or to the uselessness of attempting reforms at the top levels of government or Party without change and support among the masses)

上台 **shàng-t'ái** to appear on stage (to take over, assume power, be appointed to high office)

上层 **shàng-ts'éng** higher level, upper stratum; top echelons; superior

上层阶级 **shàng-ts'éng-chiēh-chí** the upper class

上层建筑 **shàng-ts'éng-chièn-chù** the superstructure (Marxist terminology for the social, political, and legal institutions resting upon, and determined by, the "economic foundation" of productive relations)

上层建筑领域的革命 **shàng-ts'éng-chièn-chù lǐng-yù te kó-mìng** the revolution in the realm of the superstructure

上文 **shàng-wén** the previous passage [in written material]

上沃尔特 **shàng wò-ěrh-t'è** [Republic of] Upper Volta

上演 **shàng-yěn** to stage [a performance]

上瘾 **shàng-yǐn** to form a habit, become addicted to [drugs, etc.]

上映 **shàng-yìng** to exhibit, show [a film, etc.]; now showing

上游 **shàng-yú** the upper reaches of a stream, upstream (at the head of, in front, the leading segment)

上游冒险 **shàng-yú mào-hsiěn** the upper part of the stream is risky (there are dangers in being ahead)

shāo (shāo)

1836　烧结 **shāo-chiéh** sintering

烧碱 **shāo-chiěn** caustic soda

烧砖瓦 **shāo chuān-wǎ** to fire bricks and tile [in a kiln] (to make bricks and tiles)

烧毁 **shāo-huǐ** to destroy by burning

烧香 **shāo-hsiāng** to burn incense

烧伤 **shāo-shāng** to suffer burns

1837　稍安勿躁 **shāo-ān-wù-tsào** [be] a little calmer and do not [let yourself] be vexed

shǎo (shǎo)

1838　少安毋躁 **shǎo-ān-wú-tsào** [be] a little calmer and do not [let yourself] be vexed

少种多收 **shǎo-chùng tō-shōu** planting less and reaping more (high-yield farming methods)

少而精 **shǎo-érh-chīng** fewer but better (refers to Mao's educational directive to reduce the course load and to concentrate on essentials)

少费多得 **shǎo-fèi-tō-té** to spend a little and gain a great deal

少花钱多办事 **shǎo-huā-ch'ién tō-pàn-shìh** to spend little money but accomplish a great deal

少扣多分 **shǎo-k'òu tō-fēn** retain little and distribute much (usually refers to distribution of the collective income of a production team, when too much is paid out to the members and an inadequate amount reserved for the collective's funds)

少量 **shǎo-liàng** a small amount, small quantity

少慢差费 **shǎo-màn-ch'à-fèi** fewer, slower, inferior, and wasteful (the reverse of the slogan: **tō, k'uài, hǎo, shěng**)

少数 **shǎo-shù** a minority, small number

少数服从多数 **shǎo-shù fú-ts'úng tō-shù** the minority must obey the majority

少数民族 **shǎo-shù-mín-tsú** minority nationalities, ethnic minorities

少数民族地区 **shǎo-shù-mín-tsú tì-ch'ū** a minority nationality region (area where one or more national minorities are substantially represented in the population)

少说为佳 **shǎo-shūo wéi-chiā** it is best to say little

　　shǎo: *see also* **shào**

306

shào (shào)

1839 少先队 **shào-hsiēn-tuì** the Young
Pioneers (contraction of **shào-nién
hsiēn-fēng-tuì**)

少先队辅导员 **shào-hsiēn-tuì fǔ-tǎo-yuán**
a counselor of Young Pioneers

少年儿童活动站 **shào-nién érh-t'úng
huó-tùng-chàn** a youth and childrens'
activities center

少年先锋宫 **shào-nién hsiēn-fēng kūng**
Palace of Young Pioneers (a building
set aside for youth activities)

少年先锋队 **shào-nién hsiēn-fēng-tuì** the
Youth Vanguards, Young Pioneers

少年宫 **shào-nién-kūng** a youth palace
(a building for youth activities)

少年共产国际 **shào-nién kùng-ch'ǎn
kuó-chì** Young Communist International

少爷兵 **shào-yéh-pīng** young gentleman
soldiers (a derisive Korean War term
for American soldiers)

少 **shào**: *see also* **shǎo**

1840 哨卡 **shào-ch'iǎ** a barrier guarded by a
sentry

哨兵 **shào-pīng** a sentry, sentinel

shē (shē)

1841 奢侈品 **shē-ch'ǐh-p'ǐn** luxury goods

奢华 **shē-huá** extravagant, showy,
luxurious [in dress or habits]

shě (shě)

1842 舍得 **shě-té** to be willing to part with,
willing to give up

舍得一身剐，敢把皇帝拉下马 **shě-té
ī-shēn-kuǎ, kǎn-pǎ huáng-tì lā-hsià-mǎ**
only a person willing to suffer death
by slicing dares to drag the emperor
from his horse (in the fight against
seemingly powerful reactionary
forces, one must be courageous and
fear no sacrifice)

shè (shè)

1843 设计 **shè-chì** to plan, design, devise;
designing

设计革命 **shè-chì kó-mìng** a revolution
in design

设计规范 **shè-chì kuēi-fàn** design
criteria, design standards

设计能力 **shè-chì néng-lì** designed
capacity

设计师 **shè-chì-shīh** a designer

设计师动口，工人动手 **shè-chì-shīh
tùng-k'ǒu, kūng-jén tùng-shǒu** the
designer uses his mouth [and] the
worker uses his hands [gets it done]

设计，施工，投产 **shè-chì, shīh-kūng,
t'óu-ch'ǎn** to design, construct, and
throw into production

设计研究人员 **shè-chì yén-chiū jén-yuán**
design and research personnel

设计院 **shè-chì-yuàn** a planning
institute

设置 **shè-chìh** to establish, found, set
up, institute, arrange for; establishment, installations

设法 **shè-fǎ** to devise ways, contrive a
method

设防 **shè-fáng** to set up a defense,
fortify

设想 **shè-hsiǎng** to think, imagine,
conceive, assume, suppose; an idea,
rough plan, scheme

设立 **shè-lì** to establish, set up, found,
institute, install, inaugurate

设备 **shè-pèi** equipment, installations,
facilities, furnishings; to equip,
install, furnish

设备利用率 **shè-pèi lì-yùng-lǜ** equipment utilization rate

设施 **shè-shīh** to arrange, manage, plan
and execute; installations, facilities;
administrative measures, management

设定 **shè-tìng** to set up, enact [laws,
regulations]; to define [certain rights]

1844 社长 **shè-chǎng** director [of a news-
paper]; head of a society

社交 **shè-chiāo** social intercourse, life

社会 **shè-huì** society, community;
social; socialist

社会渣滓 **shè-huì chā-tzu** social dregs

社会基础 **shè-huì chi-ch'ǔ** social basis,
social foundations

社会教育 **shè-huì chiào-yù** social
education, education derived from
[living in] society (education is
considered to have three elements:
family, school, and social)

社会阶级剥削关系 **shè-huì-chiēh-chí pō-
hsuēh kuān-hsi** the exploitative
relationship of social classes

社会阶层 **shè-huì-chiēh-ts'éng** social
strata

社会殖民主义 **shè-huì chíh-mín-chǔ-ì**
socialist colonialism (a reference to
the USSR's intervention in Czechoslovakia)

社会治安 **shè-huì chìh-ān** social order,
public security, the security of society

社会制度 **shè-huì-chìh-tù** social institutions, social system

社会秩序 **shè-huì chìh-hsù** social law
and order, social order, public order

社会进化 shè-huì-chìn-huà social evolution

社会主义 shè-huì-chǔ-ì socialism, socialist

社会主义阵营 shè-huì-chǔ-ì chèn-yíng the socialist camp

社会主义积极性 shè-huì-chǔ-ì chī-chí-hsìng socialist activism, socialist enthusiasm, socialist initiative

社会主义集体经济 shè-huì-chǔ-ì chí-t'ǐ-chīng-chì the socialist collective economy

社会主义集体所有制 shè-huì-chǔ-ì chí-t'ǐ sǒ-yǔ-chìh the system of socialist collective ownership

社会主义教育 shè-huì-chǔ-ì chiào-yǜ socialist education

社会主义教育普及网 shè-huì-chǔ-ì chiào-yǜ p'ǔ-chí-wǎng the network to universalize socialist education

社会主义教育运动 shè-huì-chǔ-ì chiào-yǜ yùn-tùng the Socialist Education Movement (a 1962–66 campaign, in the rural areas—usually known as the szù-ch'īng yùn-tùng)

社会主义建设 shè-huì-chǔ-ì chièn-shè socialist construction

社会主义建设事业 shè-huì-chǔ-ì chièn-shè shìh-yèh the work of building socialism; socialist construction enterprises

社会主义建设总路线 shè-huì-chǔ-ì chièn-shè tsǔng lù-hsièn the General Line for Socialist Construction (one of the sān-mièn húng-ch'í, 1958)

社会主义经济基础 shè-huì-chǔ-ì chīng-chì-chī-ch'ú the socialist economic base

社会主义经济成分 shè-huì-chǔ-ì chīng-chì-chī-ch'ǔ the socialist economic the economy

社会主义经济有计划,按比例发展 shè-huì-chǔ-ì chīng-chì yǔ chì-huà, àn-pǐ-lì fā-chǎn planned and proportionate development of socialist economy

社会主义竞赛 shè-huì-chǔ-ì chìng-sài socialist competition, socialist emulation

社会主义竞赛运动 shè-huì-chǔ-ì chìng-sài yùn-tùng a socialist competition campaign

社会主义成分 shè-huì-chǔ-ì ch'éng-fèn the socialist sector

社会主义觉悟 shè-huì-chǔ-ì chüéh-wù socialist consciousness

社会主义全民所有制 shè-huì-chǔ-ì ch'üán-mín sǒ-yǔ-chìh socialist ownership by all the people

社会主义好商店 shè-huì-chǔ-ì hǎo-shāng-tièn a socialist good shop

(name of a political movement in 1964)

社会主义化 shè-huì-chǔ-ì-huà to socialize; socialization

社会主义协作 shè-huì-chǔ-ì hsiéh-tsò socialist coordination and cooperation

社会主义现实主义 shè-huì-chǔ-ì hsièn-shíh-chǔ-ì socialist realism (Mao's early—"Yenan Forum Talks"—approach to literary and artistic criticism: replaced during the Cultural Revolution by "the combination of revolutionary realism and revolutionary romanticism")

社会主义现实主义艺术 shè-huì-chǔ-ì hsièn-shíh-chǔ-ì ì-shù the art of socialist realism

社会主义兄弟国家的大家庭 shè-huì-chǔ-ì hsiūng-tì-kuó-chiā te tà-chiā-t'íng big family of fraternal socialist countries

社会主义改造 shè-huì-chǔ-ì kǎi-tsào socialist transformation (of industry and commerce into joint state-private enterprises; of agriculture into communes; and of handicrafts into handicraft cooperatives)

社会主义高潮 shè-huì-chǔ-ì kāo-ch'áo a socialist high tide

社会主义革命 shè-huì-chǔ-ì kó-mìng the socialist revolution

社会主义革命时期 shè-huì-chǔ-ì-kó-mìng shíh-ch'ī the period of the [Chinese] socialist revolution (1949 to the present)

社会主义关 shè-huì-chǔ-ì kuān the socialist test (to meet the needs and requirements of socialist thought and practice)

社会主义工人党 shè-huì-chǔ-ì kūng-jén-tǎng the Socialist Workers' Party [Hungary]

社会主义工业化 shè-huì-chǔ-ì kūng-yèh-huà socialist industrialization

社会主义历史阶段 shè-huì-chǔ-ì lì-shǐh-chiēh-tuàn the historical period of socialism

社会主义所有制 shè-huì-chǔ-ì sǒ-yǔ-chìh the socialist ownership system

社会主义大家庭 shè-huì-chǔ-ì tà-chiā-t'íng the great family of socialism

社会主义大协作 shè-huì-chǔ-ì tà hsiéh-tsò the socialist great coordination (a slogan following the Cultural Revolution calling for coordination of production measures and ideological construction)

社会主义大学 shè-huì-chǔ-ì tà-hsuéh socialist universities

社会主义大民主 **shè-huì-chǔ-ì tà-mín-chǔ** socialist broad democracy

社会主义道德 **shè-huì-chǔ-ì tào-té** socialist morality

社会主义祖国 **shè-huì-chǔ-ì tsǔ-kuó** [our] socialist fatherland (China)

社会主义文化 **shè-huì-chǔ-ì wén-huà** socialist culture

社会主义文化阵地 **shè-huì-chǔ-ì wén-huà-chèn-tì** the socialist cultural battlefield

社会主义文化课 **shè-huì-chǔ-ì wén-huà-k'ò** socialist culture course (basic education stressing the three Rs)

社会主义文化大革命 **shè-huì-chǔ-ì wén-huà tà kó-mìng** Great Socialist Cultural Revolution (an early term for the Great Proletarian Cultural Revolution)

社会主义文艺创作 **shè-huì-chǔ-ì wén-ì-ch'uàng-tsò** socialist literary creative works

社会主义业余教育 **shè-huì-chǔ-ì yèh-yú-chiào-yù** socialist spare-time education

社会青年 **shè-huì ch'īng-nién** social youth (often unemployed or disinclined to work)

社会发展规律 **shè-huì fā-chǎn kuēi-lù** the law of the development of society, law of social development

社会发展史 **shè-huì fā-chǎn-shǐh** the history of social development

社会法西斯主义 **shè-huì fǎ-hsī-szū-chǔ-ì** social fascism (a reference to such USSR policies as the Czechoslovakia intervention)

社会风气 **shè-huì fēng-ch'ì** social mores [customs] [conventions]

社会活动 **shè-huì huó-tùng** social activity

社会贤达 **shè-huì hsién-tá** social worthies, public personages (an old term)

社会现象 **shè-huì-hsièn-hsiàng** social phenomena

社会性 **shè-huì-hsìng** social character, the social quality (the human tendency to form social groups)

社会意识 **shè-huì ì-shíh** social consciousness

社会关系 **shè-huì kuān-hsi** social relationships

社会公仆 **shè-huì kūng-p'ú** a public servant of society (refers to all cadres and members of the government)

社会课堂 **shè-huì k'ò-t'áng** the classroom of society (the whole of society is a school)

社会名流 **shè-huì míng-liú** noted public figures

社会保险 **shè-huì-pǎo-hsiěn** social insurance

社会生产力 **shè-huì shēng-ch'ǎn-lì** social productive forces

社会实践 **shè-huì shíh-chièn** practice of a society, social practice

社会帝国主义 **shè-huì tì-kuó-chǔ-ì** social imperialism (a term for USSR revisionism, first used in 1968)

社会再生产 **shè-huì tsài-shēng-ch'ǎn** social reproduction (the uninterrupted process of production in society which includes simple reproduction and extended reproduction)

社会财富 **shè-huì ts'ái-fù** social wealth

社会存在 **shè-huì ts'ún-tsài** social existence

社会危机 **shè-huì wēi-chī** a social crisis

社来社去 **shè-lái shè-ch'ù** coming from the communes and returning to the communes (the program of giving advanced schooling to young commune members who then return to their units to apply their new skills)

社论 **shè-lùn** a [newspaper] editorial

社办 **shè-pàn** operated by a commune, commune-run

社办工业 **shè-pàn-kūng-yèh** commune-operated industry

社办事业 **shè-pàn-shìh-yèh** commune-run undertakings

社队联办 **shè-tuì lién-pàn** jointly operated by the commune and the brigade

社仓 **shè-ts'āng** a commune granary

社养猪 **shè-yǎng-chū** hogs raised by the commune

社员 **shè-yuán** a commune member; a member of a society or association

社员大会 **shè-yuán-tà-huì** a general meeting of commune members

社员代表大会 **shè-yuán tài-piǎo-tà-huì** a commune congress (a meeting of representatives chosen by the commune members)

1845 涉及 **shè-chí** to involve, touch on, relate to incidentally

1846 射击 **shè-chí** to shoot [with a gun], shoot at; marksmanship

射程 **shè-ch'éng** range [of a projectile or gun]

射出 **shè-ch'ū** to launch, emit, jet, radiate

射流 **shè-liú** a jet

1847 畲族 **shè-tsú** the She people (a minority in Fukien, Kwangtung, Chekiang, and Kiangsi provinces: population 226,000 as of 1957—often mispro-

nounced as *yü*)

1848　摄制 **shè-chìh** to produce [a film or documentary], to film

摄影记者 **shè-yǐng-chì-chě** a news cameraman

摄影场 **shè-yǐng-ch'ǎng** a motion picture studio

摄影师 **shè-yǐng-shīh** a photographer, cameraman

1349　麝香 **shè-hsiāng** musk

麝牛 **shè-niú** musk ox

shéi (shéi)

1850　谁 **shéi** colloquial pronunciation for **shúi**

shēn (shēn)

1851　申斥 **shēn-ch'ìh** to reprimand, reproach, rebuke, censure

申请报告 **shēn-ch'ǐng pào-kào** a written statement in support of a request

申明 **shēn-míng** to explain clearly, elucidate, set forth, expound

申述 **shēn-shù** to state in full, elaborate on, explain in detail

申诉 **shēn-sù** to petition, complain, file a complaint; to appeal

申言 **shēn-yén** to enunciate; an announcement

1852　伸向 **shēn-hsiàng** to stretch toward, reach toward

伸手 **shēn-shǒu** to reach out, hold out hands, stretch out one's hand; meddle into

伸手向上 **shēn-shǒu hsiàng-shàng** to hold out one's hands to higher [authorities] (to ask the government for everything)

伸手派 **shēn-shǒu-p'ài** the "hand-stretched-out" group (those who rely on government help)

伸缩性 **shēn-sō hsìng** flexibility, elasticity

伸冤 **shēn-yuān** to right a wrong, redress a grievance, clear up a false charge

1853　身价百倍 **shēn-chià-pǎi-pèi** one's price increased by a hundredfold (to increase one's social status and reputation—often with an implied criticism)

身教 **shēn-chiào** to teach by personal example

身经百战 **shēn-chīng-pǎi-chàn** to pass through a hundred battles (to survive many tests and struggles)

身分 **shēn-fèn** one's social status, class status, official rank, position, identity

身分证 **shēn-fèn-chèng** identity card (used mostly in the KMT period)

身心全面发展的共产主义新人 **shēn-hsīn ch'üán-mièn fā-chǎn te kùng-ch'ǎn-chǔ-ì hsīn-jén** the new Communist man who is well developed both physically and intellectually

身入与深入 **shēn-jù yǔ shēn-jù** to participate physically and penetrate mentally

身败名裂 **shēn-pài míng-lièh** with body ruined and reputation shattered (to lose position and reputation)

身世 **shēn-shìh** personal background, life experience, one's life

身受 **shēn-shòu** to accept personally, receive in person; to experience or endure personally

身段 **shēn-tuàn** body figure and movement, physique, stature

身体好, 学习好, 工作好 **shēn-t'ǐ hǎo, hsuéh-hsí hǎo, kūng-tsò hǎo** keep healthy, study well, and work well (a phrase coined by Mao Tse-tung in 1955 to exhort students: *see* **sān-hǎo-hsuéh-shēng**)

身体刑 **shēn-t'ǐ-hsíng** corporal punishment, physical punishment

身体力行 **shēn-t'ǐ lì-hsíng** to put oneself into what one is doing, practice what one preaches, to carry out through personal experience

身在福中不知福 **shēn-tsài-fǔ-chūng pù-chīh-fú** in the midst of good fortune not to know good fortune (to take the good life [of the new society] for granted)

身在宝山不识宝 **shēn-tsài-pǎo-shān pù-shíh-pǎo** while in the midst of mountains of treasures to fail to recognize them

身材 **shēn-ts'ái** bodily figure, stature, physique

身外之物 **shēn-wài-chīh-wù** things that are not part of one's body (money, property, material wealth)

身为工农画工农 **shēn-wéi-kūng-núng huà-kūng-núng** those who are workers and peasants [should] paint workers and peasants

1854　深奥莫测 **shēn-ào-mò-ts'è** depth and profundity that cannot be measured, unfathomable

深重 **shēn-chùng** grave, serious

深长 **shēn-ch'áng** profound, deep, significant

深切 **shēn-ch'ièh** sincere, deep, penetrating, thorough, intense

深浅 **shēn-ch'iěn** deep or shallow [depth]; light or dark [colors];

seriousness [of intent]; depth [of
meaning]
深情厚谊 shēn-ch'íng-hòu-ì deep
feelings and close friendship
深仇大恨 shēn-ch'óu tà-hèn inveterate
hatred
深厚 shēn-hòu deep and thick; long
and close [friendship]; profound
[learning, etc.]
深化 shēn-huà to deepen, intensify
深入 shēn-jù to enter deeply, penetrate
(the conscious effort required of
cadres and Party members to
establish links with the masses or to
reach the heart of any problem)
深入基层 shēn-jù chī-ts'éng to enter
deeply into the basic levels
深入浅出 shēn-jù-ch'iěn-ch'ū to
penetrate deeply but express it plainly
深入群众 shēn-jù ch'ún-chùng to
penetrate deeply into the masses
(keep in close touch with the masses)
深入细致 shēn-jù hsì-chìh penetrating
and intensive, in great detail,
thorough
深入下去 shēn-jù hsià-ch'ù to enter
deeply downward (conscientious,
instead of merely superficial,
participation)
深入下层 shēn-jù hsià-ts'éng to enter
deeply into the lower levels
深入现场 shēn-jù hsièn-ch'ǎng to enter
deeply into the actual site [of
production]
深入人心 shēn-jù jén-hsīn to penetrate
into people's hearts (to win popular
confidence and support)
深入生活 shēn-jù shēng-huó to
penetrate deeply into life
深入实际 shēn-jù shíh-chì to enter
deeply into practice
深感 shēn-kǎn to feel deeply
深耕细作 shēn-kēng hsì-tsò deep
plowing and intensive cultivation
深刻 shēn-k'ò profound significance,
deep meaning; penetrating, acute,
indelible
深谋远虑 shēn-móu-yuǎn-lù to plan
profoundly and consider distantly (to
think and plan far ahead)
深不可测 shēn-pù-k'ǒ-ts'è depth that
cannot be measured (unfathomable,
abstruse)
深批 shēn-p'ī deep criticism, penetrating criticism
深山老林 shēn-shān-lǎo-lín deep
mountains and old forests (forest
primeval, remote wilds)
深山密林 shēn-shān-mì-lín deep
mountains and dense forests (often

refers to areas populated by
minorities)
深深 shēn-shēn deeply, profoundly
深思熟虑 shēn-szū-shú-lù deep contem-
plation and ripe consideration
深到底 shēn-tào-tǐ deep unto the
bottom (thoroughgoing shēn-jù)
深度和广度 shēn-tù hó kuǎng-tù depth
and width
深造 shēn-tsào to attain profundity (to
pursue advanced study)
深挖 shēn-wā to dig deeply
深挖洞 shēn-wā-tùng deeply dig
tunnels (air raid shelters, etc.)
深恶痛绝 shēn-wù t'ùng-chüéh to hate
deeply and sever definitively (to
regard with extreme repugnance)
深渊 shēn-yuān an abyss, chasm
深远 shēn-yuǎn deep and far [in
meaning], showing great forethought,
profound, significant

shén (shén)

1855 神经质 shén-chīng chìh nervous
temperament, neurotic
神经过敏 shén-chīng kuò-mǐn over-
sensitive, morbidly sensitive;
hyperesthesia
神经衰弱 shén-chīng shuāi-jò neuras-
thenia, nervous debility
神气十足 shén-ch'ì-shíh-tsú dignified in
the utmost degree, assuming
pompous airs
神情 shén-ch'íng facial expression,
look, appearance, air
神乎其神 shén-hū-ch'í-shén how
wonderful is the spirit (miraculous,
marvelous)
神化 shén-huà to deify, deified
神话 shén-huà a myth
神仙 shén-hsiēn a fairy, immortal, god
神仙会 shén-hsiēn-huì an Elysian
gathering (a lofty, free exchange of
ideas among intelligent beings freed
of the usual tensions and restraints)
神仙妖怪 shén-hsiēn-yāo-kuài fairies
and weird monsters
神秘主义 shén-mì-chǔ-ì mysticism
神秘化 shén-mì-huà mystification; to
make a fetish out of
神秘论 shén-mì lùn mystical doctrines
神圣领土 shén-shèng lǐng-t'ǔ sacred
territory, inviolable territory
神通广大 shén-t'ūng kuǎng-tà infinitely
powerful, possessing marvelous
abilities, omnipotent
神采奕奕 shén-ts'ǎi-ì-ì high-spiritedly,
full of vigor

shěn (shěn)

1856 沈丹铁路 **shěn-tān t'iěh-lù** the Shen-yang-Tantung railway (connecting with North Korea)
沈阳部队 **shěn-yáng pù-tui** the Shen-yang Forces [of the PLA]

1857 审计 **shěn-chì** to audit; auditing
审计制度 **shěn-chì chìh-tù** auditing system
审查 **shěn-ch'á** to examine, review, investigate, scrutinize
审察 **shěn-ch'á** to study carefully, look into, investigate
审核 **shěn-hó** to review, re-examine, check over, examine and consider, pass on audit
审讯 **shén-hsùn** a hearing, [judicial] interrogation
审议 **shén-ì** to review and consider, examine and deliberate
审判 **shén-p'àn** to try [a case], adjudicate, judge; a trial
审判权 **shěn-p'àn-ch'üán** judicial authority, jurisdiction
审判员 **shén-p'àn-yuán** a judge, judicial personnel
审慎 **shén-shèn** cautious, careful
审订 **shěn-tìng** to examine and decide, decide [a legal case], examine and approve [a document]; approval; a decision

shèn (shèn)

1858 甚嚣尘上 **shèn-hsiāo-ch'én-shàng** much noise amid a cloud of dust (widespread speculation, much talked about)

1859 渗入 **shèn-jù** to permeate, percolate, infiltrate, penetrate, seep into
渗透 **shèn-t'òu** to permeate, percolate, seep through

1860 慎重 **shèn-chùng** careful, cautious, serious

shēng (shēng)

1861 升级 **shēng-chí** promotion in rank [or grade]; to be promoted
升降机 **shēng-chiàng-chī** an elevator, lift
升学 **shēng-hsuéh** to advance from a lower to a higher school
升官发财 **shēng-kuān-fā-ts'ái** to become an official and make a fortune (a charge that some youths seek university training as an avenue to government or Party posts and personal advancement)

升水 **shēng-shuǐ** a premium charged in currency exchange transactions
升调 **shēng-tiào** to promote and transfer, transfer to a higher post

1862 生计 **shēng-chì** means of livelihood, living, profession
生猪 **shēng-chū** a live pig [before butchering]
生产 **shēng-ch'ǎn** to produce, bring forth, yield, bear, manufacture; production; childbirth
生产战斗连 **shēng-ch'ǎn chàn-tòu-lién** a production combat company (a small task force organized for a special production project)
生产战斗营 **shēng-ch'ǎn chàn-tòu-yíng** a production combat battalion (a medium-sized production task force)
生产积极性 **shēng-ch'ǎn chī-chí-hsìng** production activism, enthusiasm for production
生产基金 **shēng-ch'ǎn chī-chīn** a production fund
生产计划 **shēng-ch'ǎn chì-huà** production plans
生产假期 **shēng-ch'ǎn-chià-ch'ī** maternity leave (usually 56 days with pay)
生产建设兵团 **shēng-ch'ǎn chièn-shè pīng-t'uán** production and construction military corps (PLA units, often used to open new areas in Heilungkiang and Sinkiang)
生产指标 **shēng-ch'ǎn chǐh-piáo** a production target, output quota
生产劲头 **shēng-ch'ǎn chìn-t'óu** productive vigor
生产竞赛 **shēng-ch'ǎn-chìng-sài** a production competition, production emulation [campaign], production drive
生产就是一切 **shēng-ch'ǎn chiù-shìh ī-ch'ièh** production is everything (a revisionist concept that ignores class struggle and social objectives)
生产车间 **shēng-ch'ǎn ch'ē-chiēn** a production workshop (a section of a factory engaged in actual production, rather than repair, etc.)
生产成本 **shēng-ch'ǎn ch'éng-pěn** production costs, costs of production
生产潜力 **shēng-ch'ǎn-ch'ién-lì** latent productive capacity, potential for production
生产发展速度 **shēng-ch'ǎn fā-chǎn sù-tù** rate of increase of production
生产方式 **shēng-ch'ǎn fāng-shìh** mode of production
生产合作社 **shēng-ch'ǎn hó-tsò-shè** a producer's cooperative
生产小队 **shēng-ch'ǎn hsiǎo-tuì** a

production team

生产高潮 **shēng-ch'ǎn kāo-ch'áo** a high tide of production

生产关系 **shēng-ch'ǎn-kuān-hsi** relations of production

生产管理 **shēng-ch'ǎn kuǎn-lǐ** production management, production control

生产工具 **shēng-ch'ǎn kūng-chǜ** tools of production, means of production

生产劳动 **shēng-ch'ǎn-láo-tùng** productive labor

生产劳动模范 **shēng-ch'ǎn láo-tùng mó-fàn** a model [worker] in productive labor

生产力 **shēng-ch'ǎn-lì** production forces

生产量 **shēng-ch'ǎn-liàng** the quantity produced, volume of production, output

生产率 **shēng-ch'ǎn-lǜ** rate of productivity, productivity

生产能力 **shēng-ch'ǎn néng-lì** productive power; productivity

生产社会化 **shēng-ch'ǎn shè-huì-huà** the socialization of production

生产实践 **shēng-ch'ǎn shíh-chièn** production practice

生产大队 **shēng-ch'ǎn tà-tuì** the production brigade (the next organizational level under the commune)

生产淡季 **shēng-ch'ǎn tàn-chì** the slack period of production

生产到顶论 **shēng-ch'ǎn-tào-tǐng lùn** the idea that production has reached its peak (a type of thinking to be criticized because it assumes that no further progress is possible)

生产第一 **shēng-ch'ǎn-tì-ī** production comes first (to be criticized because it puts production ahead of politics)

生产第一线 **shēng-ch'ǎn tì-ī-hsièn** the first line of production, the production front line

生产定额 **shēng-ch'ǎn tìng-ó** a fixed production quota

生产斗争 **shēng-ch'ǎn tòu-chēng** the struggle for production

生产队 **shēng-ch'ǎn-tuì** a production team (the lowest level of the commune organization)

生产停顿 **shēng-ch'ǎn t'íng-tùn** a halt in production

生产突击队 **shēng-ch'ǎn t'ū-chī-tuì** a special production task force, production shock troops

生产责任制 **shēng-ch'ǎn tsé-jèn-chìh** the system of fixed responsibility in production

生产资金 **shēng-ch'ǎn tzū-chīn** a special

production fund

生产资料 **shēng-ch'ǎn tzū-liào** the means of production (the raw materials, auxiliary materials, machinery, tools, and buildings; whatever is necessary to carry out production)

生产资料所有制 **shēng-ch'ǎn tzū-liào sǒ-yǔ-chìh** public ownership of the means of production

生产资料私人占有 **shēng-ch'ǎn-tzū-liào szū-jén-chàn-yǔ** private ownership of the means of production

生产自援单位 **shēng-ch'ǎn tzǔ-yuán tān-wèi** production self-help units (for the unemployed, 1951–1952)

生产促革命 **shēng-ch'ǎn ts'ù kó-mìng** production promotes [the] revolution

生气勃勃 **shēng-ch'ì-pó-pó** lively and vigorous, zestful, energetic, active, dynamic

生趣盎然 **shēng-ch'ù-áng-ján** full of the pleasures of life, lively, zestful

生儿育女 **shēng-érh-yù-nǚ** to bear sons and nourish daughters (to raise children)

生而知之 **shēng-érh-chīh-chīh** [people are] born with [the possession of] knowledge

生荒地 **shēng-huāng-tì** virgin soil, uncultivated land

生活 **shēng-huó** life, living, livelihood, existence (if not otherwise limited, it may be taken to refer to the life style or conditions of existence of the worker and peasant masses, and to include cultural, social, and political —as well as purely material— factors)

生活集体化 **shēng-huó chí-t'ǐ-huà** collectivization of living; to live collectively

生活指数 **shēng-huó chǐh-shù** [cost of] living index

生活指导 **shēng-huó chǐh-tǎo** life guidance (a program for elementary school pupils in the early 1950s with specific rules of training in hygenic ·habits, organizational discipline, courtesy, and politics and ideology)

生活津贴 **shēng-huó chīn-t'iēh** a living expense subsidy (payments in addition to basic wages to meet special needs or conditions)

生活气氛 **shēng-huó-ch'ì-fēn** the atmosphere of living, ambience

生活费 **shēng-huó-fèi** living expenses, cost of living

生活费用 **shēng-huó fèi-yùng** living expenses, cost of living

生活服务站 **shēng-huó fú-wù-chàn** a service station for [needs of daily] life (to provide household and housekeeping services for workers or other persons unable to perform them)

生活管理 **shēng-huó kuǎn-lǐ** management of living (usually refers to the arrangement and administration of group living)

生活办公室 **shēng-huó pàn-kūng-shìh** a livelihood administration office (*see* **shēng-huó fú-wù-chàn**)

生活必需品 **shēng-huó pì-hsū-p'ǐn** the necessities of life, essential goods, staples

生活是创作泉源 **shēng-huó shìh ch'uàng-tsò ch'üán-yuán** life is the spring [source] of artistic creation

生活水平 **shēng-huó shuǐ-p'íng** the level of livelihood, standard of living

生活资料 **shēng-huó tzū liào** the means of subsistence, necessities of life, means of livelihood

生息 **shēng-hsī** to bear interest [of money]; to reproduce and multiply [of animals]; to increase

生效 **shēng-hsiào** to be effective, take effect, become valid, come into operation

生效期 **shēng-hsiào-ch'ī** effective period, period of validity

生性 **shēng-hsìng** one's natural disposition, temperament, nature; aloof, solitary

生锈 **shēng-hsiù** rusting, corrosion

生根 **shēng-kēn** to grow roots, take root (e.g., cadres are expected to *sheng-ken* in rural villages)

生根开花 **shēng-kēn k'āi-huā** to grow roots and produce blooms (to achieve unity with the people)

生根, 开花, 结果 **shēng-kēn, k'āi-huā, chiéh-kuǒ** to grow roots, produce blooms, and bear fruit (success in achieving unity with the masses)

生离死别 **shēng-lí-szǔ-piéh** separation in life and parting at death (the bitterest of sorrows)

生力军 **shēng-lì-chǔn** fresh troops, reinforcements

生灵涂炭 **shēng-líng-t'ú-t'àn** living souls are in mud and charcoal (to plunge people into misery and suffering)

生龙活虎 **shēng-lúng huó-hǔ** [like] a lively dragon and active tiger (with a strong and lively spirit; very energetic)

生命 **shēng-mìng** life, vitality; vital

生命线 **shēng-mìng-hsièn** the thread of life, lifeblood, lifeline

生命刑 **shēng-mìng-hsíng** capital punishment

生命力 **shēng-mìng-lì** life force, vital energy, vitality

生搬硬套 **shēng-pān yìng-t'ào** to import and use in a forced way, borrow and apply mechanically

生怕 **shēng-p'à** to fear, be afraid; apprehensive, anxious

生平 **shēng-p'íng** one's life history; a brief biographical sketch

生事 **shēng-shìh** to cause trouble, create trouble, make a disturbance

生疏 **shēng-shū** unfamiliar with, unskilled in, estranged from, losing contact with, no longer intimate, getting rusty

生死相依 **shēng-szǔ hsiāng-ī** in life or death to depend on each other (to share the same fate)

生死利害 **shēng-szǔ lì-hài** a serious matter [that may determine] life or death

生死搏斗 **shēng-szǔ pó-tòu** a life-and-death struggle

生死不明 **shēng-szǔ-pù-míng** not known whether dead or alive, whereabouts unknown

生死斗争 **shēng-szǔ tòu-chēng** a life-and-death struggle

生死存亡 **shēng-szǔ ts'ún-wáng** life or death and survival or extinction (the decisive stage of development of a situation or struggle)

生死攸关 **shēng-szǔ-yū-kuān** a matter of life and death

生死与共 **shēng-szǔ-yǔ-kùng** to live or die together (to share in a life-and-death struggle)

生的伟大, 死的光荣 **shēng-te-wěi-tà, szǔ-te-kuāng-júng** "Great in life, glorious in death" (Mao Tse-tung's epitaph for Liu Hu-lan, *q.v.*)

生动 **shēng-tùng** lively, vivid, lifelike, moving, stimulating

生动教材 **shēng-tùng chiào-ts'ái** stimulating teaching materials

生动活泼 **shēng-tùng huó-p'ō** lively and vivacious

生动事实 **shēng-tùng shìh-shíh** vivid facts

生铁 **shēng-t'iěh** pig iron

生吞活剥 **shēng-t'ūn huó-pō** to flay and swallow alive (to take over someone else's ideas without discrimination or analysis)

生存 **shēng-ts'ún** existence, survival

生物 **shēng-wù** a living thing, organism, plant or animal life

生物制品 **shēng-wù chìh-p'ǐn** biological products

生物学 **shēng-wù-hsuéh** biology

生硬 **shēng-yìng** awkward, stiff, rigid, crude

生育 **shēng-yù** to give birth to; childbirth

1863 声称 **shēng-ch'ēng** to assert, declare, announce, claim

声情并茂 **shēng-ch'íng-pìng-mào** voice and feeling both [are] excellent (said of singers)

声息相通 **shēng-hsī hsiāng-t'ūng** in mutual close communication

声浪 **shēng-làng** sound waves

声明 **shēng-míng** to declare, announce, assert, clarify publicly, make known

声名狼藉 **shēng-mìng-láng-chí** one's reputation is ruined (notorious, disreputable)

声色俱厉 **shēng-sè-chù-lì** harsh in voice and severe in countenance

声势 **shēng-shìh** influence, power, prestige; a dominating position, threatening [military] force

声势浩大 **shēng-shìh-hào-tà** an impressive display of power and influence

声嘶力竭 **shēng-szū-lì-chiéh** voice hoarse and energy exhausted

声东击西 **shēng-tūng-chī-hsī** [to make] a noise in the east [while] attacking in the west

声讨 **shēng-t'ǎo** to denounce, condemn, attack publicly

声望 **shēng-wàng** fame, prestige, reputation

声言 **shēng-yén** to announce, proclaim

声援 **shēng-yuán** to give moral support, declare in support of

1864 牲畜圈 **shēng-ch'ù-chüan** a cattle pen, corral

牲畜配种 **shēng-ch'ù p'èi-chǔng** livestock breeding

1865 胜任愉快 **shēng-jèn-yú-k'uài** to master a task with comfort and ease

胜 **shēng**: *see also* **shèng**

shéng (shéng)

1866 绳索牵引机 **shéng-sǒ ch'iēn-yǐn-chī** an aerial cable conveyer

shěng (shěng)

1867 省长 **shěng-chǎng** provincial governor (pre-Cultural Revolution term)

省级 **shěng-chí** the provincial level

省劲 **shěng-chìn** to save [physical] energy, labor-saving

省吃俭用 **shěng-ch'īh chiěn-yùng** to eat sparingly and use frugally

省军区 **shěng-chūn-ch'ū** a provincial-level military district

省辖市 **shěng-hsiá-shìh** municipality directly controlled by the provincial government

省人民代表大会 **shěng jén-mín tài-piǎo tà-huì** a people's congress of a province

省港大罢工 **shěng-kǎng tà-pà-kūng** the Great Port Strike (the seaman's strike at Hong Kong and Canton in 1925)

省力 **shěng-lì** to save strength, save labor; labor-saving

省略 **shěng-lüèh** to omit, abridge, cut off, delete; very brief

省事 **shěng-shìh** to save trouble; convenient, easy

省委 **shěng-wěi** a provincial [Party] committee

省无联 **shěng-wú-lién** "Sheng-wu-lien" (an ultra-leftist youth group in the Cultural Revolution; an abbreviated and generally used form of "Hunan Provincial Proletarian Revolutionary Great Alliance Committee")

shèng (shèng)

1868 圣胡安 **shèng hú-ān** San Juan [Puerto Rico]

圣人 **shèng-jén** a sage, saint

圣马力诺 **shèng mǎ-lì-nò** San Marino

圣萨尔瓦多 **shèng sà-ěrh-wǎ-tō** San Salvador [capital of El Salvador]

圣地 **shèng-tì** hallowed ground, a sacred place, place of pilgrimage

圣地亚哥 **shèng-tì-yà-kō** Santiago [Chile]

圣多美 **shèng tō-měi** Sao Tome [Portuguese]

圣多明各 **shèng tō-míng-kò** Santo Domingo [Dominican Republic]

圣约瑟 **shèng yuēh-sè** San Jose [Costa Rica]

1869 胜仗 **shèng-chàng** a victorious war

胜负 **shèng-fù** victory or defeat (the outcome of a contest)

胜过 **shèng-kuò** to be superior to, excel, surpass, prevail over

胜利 **shèng-lì** a victory, triumph

胜利折实公债 **shèng-lì ché-shíh kūng-chài** reduce-to-true-value victory bonds (capital and interest were partial functions of a staples price-index at the time of repayment; sold in early 1950s to contrast with KMT bonds that had been wiped out by inflation)

胜利前进 **shèng-lì ch'ién-chìn** to

advance victoriously

胜利冲昏头脑 **shèng-lì ch'ūng-hūn t'óu-nǎo** victory turns one's head, success makes one dizzy

胜利果实 **shèng-lì-kuǒ-shíh** the fruits of victory

胜利完工 **shèng-lì wán-kūng** sucessful completion of a task

胜败 **shèng-pài** victory or defeat (the outcome of a war)

胜 **shèng**: *see also* **shēng**

1870 盛极一时 **shèng-chí-ī-shíh** extremely flourishing at one time (faddish, modish)

盛产 **shèng-ch'ǎn** abundant production, rich in

盛气凌人 **shèng-ch'ì líng-jén** to put on airs and bully others (rude arrogance)

盛情 **shèng-ch'íng** great kindness, warm hospitality, utmost sincerity

盛会 **shèng-huì** a large gathering, splendid social affair

盛行 **shèng-hsíng** to be prevalent, popular, in vogue

盛世 **shèng-shìh** a prosperous age, halcyon days, great era, golden age

盛衰荣辱 **shèng-shuāi júng-jǔ** rise or fall and honor or disgrace (vicissitudes; waxing and waning)

盛大 **shèng-tà** grand, magnificent, majestic

盛赞 **shèng-tsàn** to praise profusely, compliment highly

盛业 **shèng-yèh** a great achievement, great enterprise, noble cause

1871 剩余价值 **shèng-yǘ-chià-chíh** surplus value

剩余劳动 **shèng-yǘ-láo-tùng** surplus labor

剩余劳动力 **shèng-yǘ-láo-tùng-lì** surplus labor force

shīh (shī)

1872 尸臭 **shīh-ch'òu** the smell of a corpse (putrescence—often figurative)

1873 失职 **shīh-chíh** to be delinquent in duty; dereliction of duty, malpractice

失传 **shīh-ch'uán** to lose through the generations, lose the tradition of; a lost [skill, art, etc.]

失去平衡 **shīh-ch'ù p'íng-héng** to throw out of balance, tip the balance

失去时效 **shīh-ch'ù shíh-hsiào** to lose validity, expire, lapse, lose effect because of time

失去威信 **shīh-ch'ù wēi-hsìn** to lose authority, become discredited

失权 **shīh-ch'üán** to lose [political] power

失魂落魄 **shīh-hún-lò-p'ò** to lose the soul and drop the spirit (despondent, downhearted, listless; frightened out of one's senses)

失笑 **shīh-hsiào** to laugh involuntarily; cannot help laughing

失修 **shīh-hsiū** wanting in repair, lacking maintenance (run-down, dilapidated)

失学 **shīh-hsuéh** to lose [the opportunity of] schooling; to have one's education cut short

失灵 **shīh-líng** to lose effect; out of order, inoperative

失眠 **shīh-mién** to suffer from insomnia; insomnia

失败主义 **shīh-pài-chǔ-ì** defeatism

失败为成功之母 **shīh-pài wéi ch'éng-kūng chīh mǔ** failure is the mother of success

失实 **shīh-shíh** inaccurate, erroneous, not true, fallacious

失事 **shīh-shìh** to run into trouble, meet with an accident, make a mistake; an accident

失算 **shīh-suàn** a miscalculation (a mistaken move, bad decision)

失道寡助 **shīh-tào kuǎ-chù** [one who has] an unjust cause [finds] few supporters

失调 **shīh-t'iáo** to lose the harmony; be out of tune; upset, unbalanced; maladjustment, dislocation

失踪 **shīh-tsūng** to lose traces of, disappear; missing [of a person]

失望 **shīh-wàng** to lose one's hope, be disappointed, discouraged

失物招领处 **shīh-wù chāo-lǐng-ch'ù** the lost-and-found division (in each police station)

失业 **shīh-yèh** to lose employment; unemployed, out of work; unemployment

失业工人救济基金 **shīh-yèh-kūng-jén chiù-chì-chī-chīn** unemployed workers relief fund

失言 **shìh-yén** to lose [control of] the tongue (to say what should not be said, make an improper remark)

失约 **shīh-yuēh** to fail to meet a commitment, break a promise, miss an appointment

1874 师范教育 **shīh-fàn-chiào-yù** normal education, teacher training

师范大学 **shīh-fàn tà-hsuéh** the Normal University (in several locations)

师傅 **shīh-fu** a master (a skilled worker with practical knowledge to impart)

师傅带徒弟 **shīh-fu tài t'ú-tì** the master carrying along the apprentice (the

master-apprentice system)

师生 **shīh-shēng** teachers and students

师大 **shīh-tà** the Normal University (contraction of **shīh-fàn tà-hsuéh**)

师道尊严 **shīh-tào tsūn-yén** the dignity of the teacher

师徒集会 **shīh-t'ú chí-huì** masters' and apprentices' assemblies

师徒关系 **shīh t'ú kuān-hsi** master-apprentice relations

师资 **shīh-tzū** the supply of teachers; qualifications of a teacher

1875 诗歌 **shīh-kō** poems and songs

诗刊 **shīh-k'ān** *Poetry* (a Peking monthly journal, 1957—)

诗报告 **shīh-pào-kào** a poem report (treatment of a current newsworthy event in poetic form)

1876 施展 **shīh-chǎn** to display [one's talents, skill], put to good use, put to good effect

施加压力 **shīh-chiā yā-lì** to exert pressure, bring pressure to bear on

施放 **shīh-fàng** to spread, apply widely; to dole out

施肥 **shīh-féi** to apply fertilizer; fertilization

施行 **shīh-hsíng** to enforce, apply, put into effect, put into operation; enforcement, application

施工 **shīh-kūng** to start construction, commence building; to work on, process; production

施工计划 **shīh-kūng-chì-huà** a work plan, operating schedule

施工程序 **shīh-kūng-ch'éng-hsù** order of construction, operational sequence

施工现场 **shīh-kūng-hsièn-ch'ǎng** a work site, project site

1877 湿度 **shīh-tù** [degree of] humidity, moisture content

shíh (shí)

1878 十之八九 **shíh-chīh-pā-chǐu** eight or nine [times, chances, etc.] out of ten (highly likely, in all probability)

十进币制 **shíh-chìn-pì-chìh** the decimal currency system

十进位制 **shíh-chìn-wèi-chìh** the decimal system

十全十美 **shíh-ch'üán-shíh-měi** ten complete [and] ten beautiful (wholly perfect)

十二年科学技术发展计划 **shíh-èrh-nién k'ō-hsuéh-chì-shù fā-chǎn chì-huà** the Twelve Year Plan for Development of Science and Technology (formulated in 1956 to guide development in these fields—assuming the con-

tinuation of Soviet aid)

十分指标十二分措施 **shíh-fēn chǐh-piāo shíh-èrh-fēn ts'ò-shīh** [to fix] a ten-point target and [adopt] twelve-point measures

十项倡议 **shíh-hsiàng-ch'àng-ì** the Ten-Point Proposal (militia tasks and requirements as formulated by the National Conference on Militia Work in 1960)

十项要求 **shíh-hsiàng-yāo-ch'íú** the Ten Requests (a program for the militia promulgated by the Ministry of Defense in 1966)

十六条 **shíh-liù t'iáo** the Sixteen Points (adopted by the Eleventh Plenum of the Central Committee on August 8, 1966, in regard to the Cultural Revolution and Red Guard activities)

十六字诀 **shíh-liù-tzù chüéh** the sixteen-character key (from Mao's "Strategic Problems of China's Revolutionary War," 1936)

十目所视,十手所指 **shíh-mù sǒ shìh, shíh-shǒu sǒ chǐh** watched by ten eyes and pointed at by ten hands (to receive the supervision and accusations of the masses)

十拿九稳 **shíh-ná chiǔ-wěn** to grasp at ten and get a firm hold on nine (a very good chance of success)

十年九旱 **shíh-nién-chiǔ-hàn** nine years of drought out of ten

十年一贯制 **shíh-nién-í-kuàn-chìh** the Ten-Year Straight-Through System (the present organization of primary and secondary education into ten years)

十大 **shíh-tà** the Tenth Congress [of the Communist Party of China, 1973]

十大精神 **shíh-tà chīng-shén** the Tenth [Party] Congress spirit

十大军事原则 **shíh-tà chǖn-shìh-yuán-tsé** the Ten Chief Military Principles (a series of strategic and tactical operating principles set forth by Mao Tse-tung in "The Present Situation and Our Tasks," December 1947)

十大关系 **shíh-tà kuān-hsi** the Ten Great Relationships (set forth by Mao Tse-tung in April, 1956: industry and agriculture; coastal and inland industrial development; economic construction and national defense; the state cooperatives and individuals; central and local authorities; the Han people and national minorities; Party and non-Party people; revolution and counter-revolution; right and wrong; inside

and outside the Party; international relations)

十大路线 **shíh-tà lù-hsièn** the line of the Tenth Congress [1973]

十大文件 **shíh-tà-wén-chièn** the documents of the Tenth [Party] Congress

十冬腊月 **shíh-tūng-là-yuèh** from the tenth to the last month (the winter)

十条经验 **shíh-t'iáo-chīng-yèn** Ten Experiences (a program for basic indoctrination in the PLA—formulated by the General Political Department in 1966 and extended to Party and administrative units in 1967)

十条绳子 **shín-t'iáo-shéng-tzu** the Ten Ropes (a term used in 1962 by Yang Han-shen—later purged in the Cultural Revolution—to describe restrictions on freedom in writing; they consist of **wǔ-kò-ì-tìng** and **wǔ-kò-pù-kǎn**)

十足 **shíh-tsú** complete, perfect, one hundred percent

十月怀胎一朝分娩 **shíh-yuèh huái-t'āi ì-chāo fēn-mièn** ten months in the womb but born in a day (preparation takes a long time but the solution can be rapid)

十月革命 **shíh-yuèh kó-mìng** the October Revolution (the Russian Communist Revolution of 1917)

十月社会主义革命 **shíh-yuèh shè-huì-chǔ-ì kó-mìng** the October Socialist Revolution (*see above*)

1879　石沉大海 **shíh-ch'én tà-hǎi** a stone sunk into the sea (vanished without a trace)

石方 **shíh-fāng** a cubic measure for rock (used in excavation or construction)

石河子垦区 **shíh-hó-tzu k'ěn-ch'ü** the Shihhotzu Reclaimed District (a development area in Sinkiang largely populated by people from Shanghai)

石灰厂 **shíh-huī-ch'ǎng** a lime kiln

石膏 **shíh-kāo** gypsum, plaster of Paris

石刻 **shíh-k'ò** stone carving, sculpture

石煤 **shíh-méi** stone coal, hard coal, anthracite

石棉 **shíh-mién** asbestos

石版画 **shíh-pǎn-huà** a lithographed picture

石雕 **shíh-tiāo** stone carving

石太铁路 **shíh-t'ài t'iěh-lù** the Shih-chiachuang-Taiyuan railway

石炭 **shíh-t'àn** coal

石油 **shíh-yú** petroleum, crude oil

石油气 **shíh-yú-ch'ì** petroleum gas

石油工业 **shíh-yú kūng-yèh** the petroleum industry

石油工业部 **shíh-yú kūng-yèh-pù** the Ministry of Petroleum Industry [of the State Council] (merged in 1969 into the Ministry of Fuel and Chemical Industry)

石油输出国组织 **shíh-yú shū-ch'ü-kuó tsǔ-chīh** the Organization of Petroleum Exporting Countries [OPEC]

1880　识别 **shíh-piéh** to distinguish, differentiate, discriminate, discern, identify

识破 **shíh-p'ò** to see through

识大体，看大局 **shíh tà-t'ǐ, k'àn tà-chú** to discern the general interest and keep watch on the whole situation

识字组 **shíh-tzù-tsǔ** a class to teach basic reading

1881　时机 **shíh-chī** a favorable moment, opportunity

时节 **shíh-chiéh** a seasonable festival; occasion; time

时间 **shíh-chiēn** time, duration, hour

时紧时松 **shíh-chǐn shíh-sūng** sometimes tense and sometimes loose, alternating between alert and relaxed

时差 **shíh-ch'ā** time difference, difference in time between two different locales

时期 **shíh-ch'ī** a period, time, era, age; duration; a time limit

时起时伏 **shíh-ch'ǐ-shíh-fú** sometimes rising and sometimes declining (to vary in intensity from time to time)

时局 **shíh-chú** the current situation, circumstances of the time (the political situation—national or world)

时效 **shíh-hsiào** validity in terms of time, a time limitation

时光 **shíh-kuāng** the time [early, late, etc.]; the passage of time

时刻 **shíh-k'ò** time, hour; every moment, constantly, continually

时刻紧记 **shíh-k'ò-chǐn-chì** always keep in mind, never forget

时髦 **shíh-máo** fashionable, in vogue

时时 **shíh-shíh** often, frequent; continually, constantly; always, at every moment

时时刻刻 **shíh-shíh k'ò-k'ò** constantly, continuously, at every moment

时事 **shíh-shìh** happenings of the time, current events

时事通讯社 **shíh-shìh t'ūng-hsùn-shè** the Jiji News Agency

时势 **shíh-shìh** the time and circumstances, general situation, current trend of events

时代 **shíh-tài** an epoch, era, age,

period, time

时代精神 **shíh-tài chīng-shén** the spirit of the age (the modern spirit)

时代精神汇合论 **shíh-tài-chīng-shén huì-hó lùn** the doctrine of the merging of various trends as the spirit of the age (the idea that the ideologies of different classes and groups are blending toward a reduction of class struggle—one of the **hēi pā lùn**)

时代洪流 **shíh-tài húng-liú** the mighty currents of the age

时代感 **shíh-tài-kǎn** the feeling of the time

时代声音 **shíh-tài shēng-yīn** the voice of the age

时作时辍 **shín-tsò shíh-ch'ò** to work for a while and stop for a while (to do something by fits and starts)

时务 **shíh-wù** current [public] affairs, circumstances of the time

时有时无 **shíh-yǔ shíh-wú** sometimes present and sometimes absent (to occur spasmodically)

1882 实证主义 **shíh-chèng-chǔ-ì** pragmatism

实际 **shíh-chì** real, actual, practical; actually; in fact

实际产量 **shíh-chì-ch'ǎn-liàng** the actual output

实际行动 **shíh-chì-hsíng-tùng** concrete actions, practical actions

实际工资 **shíh-chì-kūng-tzū** real wages

实际生活锻炼 **shíh-chì-shēng-huó tuàn-lièn** tempered by practical life [experience]

实际收入 **shíh-chì-shōu-jù** real income

实际锻炼 **shíh-chì-tuàn-lièn** tempering by reality (tempering by experience)

实践 **shíh-chièn** practice; practical experience; practical; to put into practice, execute, carry out, perform

实践经验 **shíh-chièn-chīng-yèn** practical experience, experience gained through practice

实践出真知 **shíh-chièn ch'ū chēn-chīh** practice produces true knowledge

实践出科学 **shíh-chièn ch'ū k'ō-hsuéh** practice produces science

实践活动 **shíh-chièn-huó-tùng** concrete [as opposed to theoretical] activities

实践论 **shíh-chièn lùn** "On Practice" (an essay by Mao Tse-tung, 1937)

实践第一 **shíh-chièn-tì-ī** practice above all; practice is supreme

实质 **shíh-chìh** essence, substance, inner quality; in reality, essentially

实职 **shíh-chíh** a substantive position, an official position with decision-making authority

实话 **shíh-huà** Truth (an organ of the

CCP Central Bureau for the Soviet Areas, 1932)

实习 **shíh-hsí** to practice [what one has been taught] (field training, intern training, training through actual work)

实习生 **shíh-hsí-shēng** a trainee student

实现 **shíh-hsièn** to realize, materialize, become real; realization, fruition

实行 **shíh-hsíng** to put into effect, carry out, put into practice, execute, effectuate, accomplish

实干 **shíh-kàn** to act positively; positive action

实力 **shíh-lì** [real] strength, power, [military] might

实力派 **shíh-lì-p'ài** the "real power faction"

实力地位 **shíh-lì-tì-wèi** a position of strength

实力地位政策 **shíh-lì-tì-wèi chèng-ts'è** a policy of positions of strength, a policy based on positions of strength

实利主义 **shíh-lì-chǔ-ì** utilitarianism

实施 **shíh-shīh** to implement, carry out, give effect to, enforce, exercise, realize

实事求是 **shíh-shìh ch'iú-shìh** by verification of the facts to seek truth (to be objective, follow objective methods; factual, based on facts, realistic)

实弹射击 **shíh-tàn-shè-chī** to fire with live ammunition, live firing

实地 **shíh-tì** on the scene, on the spot, in the field; concretely, practically, on firm ground

实在论 **shíh-tsài lùn** realism

实物交换 **shíh-wù-chiāo-huàn** exchange of good, barter

实物经济 **shíh-wù-chīng-chì** a barter economy

实验 **shíh-yèn** to experiment, test; experimentation; an experiment

实验主义 **shíh-yèn-chǔ-ì** pragmatism

实验农场 **shíh-yèn núng-ch'ǎng** an experimental farm, agricultural testing station

实验室 **shíh-yèn-shìh** a laboratory

实用 **shíh-yùng** practical, useful; usage utility, practical use; utilization

实用主义 **shíh-yùng-chǔ-ì** pragmatism

1883 拾粪 **shíh-fèn** to pick up manure, collect droppings

1884 食粮 **shíh-liáng** foodstuffs, provisions, food grains

食品工业 **shíh-p'ǐn kūng-yèh** (1) food [processing] industries; (2) Food Industry (a Peking journal, semi-monthly, 1957—)

食堂 **shíh-t'áng** a mass hall, dining room

食物 **shíh-wù** eatables, food, provisions

食言 **shíh-yén** to eat one's words, break a promise

食油 **shíh-yú** edible oils, cooking oils

食用 **shíh-yùng** edible

食用植物油 **shíh-yùng chíh-wù-yú** edible vegetable oils

食用油 **shíh-yùng-yú** edible oils, cooking oils

shǐh (shǐ)

1885　史学 **shǐh-hsúeh** history [as a science], the study of history

史学史 **shǐh-hsuéh-shǐh** historiography

史料 **shǐh-liào** historical materials, historical data

史诗 **shǐh-shíh** a historical poem, epic

史实 **shǐh-shíh** historical facts

史太林 **shǐh-t'ài-lín** Stalin (now written as **szū-tà-lín**)

史无前例 **shǐh-wú-ch'ién-lì** no precedent in history, without historical precedent

1886　使节 **shǐh-chiéh** an envoy, delegate, diplomatic representative

使劲 **shǐh-chìn** to exert one's strength, apply force, make a great effort

使尽 **shǐh-chìn** to exhaust

使馆随员 **shǐh-kuǎn suí-yuán** a diplomatic attaché, counselor

使领馆 **shǐh-lǐng-kuǎn** embassies and consulates

使命 **shǐh-mìng** an official mission, job, task, obligation, duty

使用 **shǐh-yùng** to use, employ, utilize

1887　始终 **shǐh-chūng** beginning and end, from beginning to end; always, as usual

1888　驶向 **shǐh-hsiàng** to sail toward (destined to)

shìh (shì)

1889　士气 **shìh-ch'ì** morale of the troops, temperament and trend of the educated class

士气沮丧 **shìh-ch'ì-chǔ-sàng** morale is downcast; demoralized

士气低落 **shìh-ch'ì-tī-lò** low morale, morale at a low ebb

士气旺盛 **shìh-ch'ì-wàng-shèng** high morale

士兵 **shìh-pīng** soldiers, enlisted men

士绅 **shìh-shēn** the gentry, a member of the gentry class

1890　氏族 **shìh-tsú** a clan, tribe, family

氏族贵族 **shìh-tsú-kùei-tsú** a clan aristocracy, clan aristocrats

1891　世纪 **shìh-chì** a century, era

世界 **shìh-chièh** the world

世界知识 **shìh-chièh chìh-shíh** *World Knowledge* (a semi-monthly journal)

世界主义 **shìh-chièh-chǔ-ì** cosmopolitanism

世界和平理事会 **shìh-chièh-hó-p'íng lǐ-shìh-hùi** the World Council of Peace

世界革命 **shìh-chièh kó-mìng** world revolution

世界观 **shìh-chièh-kuān** world view, *Weltanschauung*, one's basic outlook

世界工会联合会 **shìh-chièh kūng-hùi lién-hó-hùi** World Federation of Trade Unions [WFTU]

世界民主青年联盟 **shìh-chièh mín-chǔ-ch'īng-nién lién-méng** World Federation of Democratic Youth [WFDY]

世界霸权 **shìh-chièh-pà-ch'üán** world domination, world hegemony

世界水平 **shìh-chièh-shuǐ-p'íng** [of] world level, world caliber (of the highest standard)

世界卫生组织 **shìh-chièh wèi-shēng tsǔ-chīh** World Health Organization [WHO]

世界舆论 **shìh-chièh yú-lùn** world opinion

世界语 **shìh-chièh-yǔ** Esperanto

世间 **shìh-chiēn** in the world, on the earth

世袭领地 **shìh-hsí lǐng-tì** hereditary domains

世上无难事, 只怕有心人 **shìh-shàng wú nán-shìh, chǐh p'à yǔ-hsīn jén** nothing in the world is difficult for one who sets his mind to it

世世相传 **shìh-shìh hsiāng-ch'uán** handed down from generation to generation

世世代代 **shìh-shìh tài-tài** from generation to generation and age to age

世俗 **shìh-sú** worldly, secular, mundane; common practice, customs and traditions, ordinary social conventions

世代相传 **shìh-tài hsiāng-ch'uán** inherited from generation to generation

世外桃源 **shìh-wài t'áo-yuán** a peach orchard beyond this world (arcadia, elysium, a Shangri-la)

1892　市长 **shìh-chǎng** a mayor, city head

市政 **shìh-chèng** a city government, municipal administration

市斤 **shìh-chīn** a market catty (half a kilogram; 1.102 pounds)

市场 **shìh-ch'ǎng** a market, marketplace, bazaar; the domestic or world

market

市场活跃 **shìh-ch'ǎng huó-yuèh** brisk trade, a lively market

市场管理委员会 **shìh-ch'ǎng kuǎn-lǐ wěi-yuán-huì** market control committee (in practice, the representative of the municipal commerce bureau in each market)

市尺 **shìh-ch'ǐh** a market foot (one-third of a meter; 13.12 inches)

市辖区 **shìh-hsiá-ch'ǖ** a district subordinate to a municipality, a ward of a city

市人民代表大会 **shìh-jén-mín tài-piǎo-tà-huì** municipal people's congress

市人民委员会 **shìh-jén-mín wěi-yuán-huì** a municipal people's committee (the governing body of a municipality)

市容 **shìh-júng** the appearance of a city (buildings, roads, environment, etc.)

市侩 **shìh-k'uài** a broker, crafty business man, slick merchant, shark

市里 **shìh-lǐ** a market *li* (half a kilometer; 0.31 miles)

市民 **shìh-mín** city people, city dwellers, urbanites

市民扫盲班 **shìh-mín sǎo-máng-pān** urban literacy classes (organized for adults by street and lane committees)

市亩 **shìh-mǔ** a market *mu* (one-fifteenth of a hectare; 0.164 acres)

市委 **shìh-wěi** a municipal [Party] committee

1893 示众 **shìh-chùng** to exhibit to the public, expose before the masses (usually by parading the person accused through the streets or before a mass meeting)

示范 **shìh-fàn** to demonstrate, exemplify; a demonstration

示意图 **shìh-ì-t'ú** a plan, sketch, design, layout

示弱 **shìh-jò** to show weakness, give an opening [to an opponent]

示踪原子 **shìh-tsūng yuán-tzǔ** a tracer atom

示威 **shìh-wēi** to demonstrate, stage a parade; make a show of force [military]; a demonstration

示威游行 **shìh-wēi yú-hsíng** a demonstration march, political parade

1894 式样 **shìh-yàng** a sample, model, example, pattern; a style, fashion

1895 事迹 **shìh-chì** the traces of past happenings, exploit, achievement, exemplary record, noteworthy deeds

事件 **shìh-chièn** an incident, affair, event, occurrence

事后 **shìh-hòu** after the event, afterward; after the fact, ex post facto

事项 **shìh-hsiàng** an item, matter, incident (one out of a number of items or matters)

事小意义大 **shìh hsiǎo ì-ì tà** a small matter but of great significance

事先 **shìh-hsiēn** in advance of the event, beforehand

事故 **shìh-kù** an accident, troublesome incident

事故难免论 **shìh-kù nán-miěn lùn** the idea that accidents are unavoidable

事例 **shìh-lì** an example, instance, precedent

事变 **shìh-pièn** a sudden turn of events; a rebellion, coup d'etat, incident involving violence

事不关己高高挂起 **shìh pù kuān-chǐ kāo-kāo kuà-ch'ǐ** if the affair does not concern oneself then hang it high [out of the way] (to lack public spirit)

事实 **shìh-shíh** facts, truth, reality; actual, real; *de facto*

事态 **shìh-t'ài** situation, circumstances, state of affairs

事在人为 **shìh-tsài jén-wéi** [success in] an affair depends on the human [will to do it] (man is the determining factor)

事务 **shìh-wù** business, affairs, work, administrative matters

事务主义 **shìh-wù-chǔ-ì** routinism, operationalism (excessive concern with routine business or operations)

事物 **shìh-wù** a thing, object; facts

事业 **shìh-yèh** an undertaking, enterprise; work, occupation, profession, career; a cause

事业用费 **shìh-yèh yùng-fèi** operating expenses

事与愿违 **shìh-yǔ-yuàn-wéi** the fact contravenes the wish (things do not always turn out as one hopes)

1896 试制 **shìh-chìh** trial manufacture, experimental production

试金石 **shìh-chīn-shíh** a touchstone, criterion, standard

试井 **shìh-chǐng** a test well

试掘 **shìh-chüéh** to test drill, prospect for

试飞 **shìh-fēi** a test flight; to test fly

试航 **shìh-háng** a test run, test voyage, shakedown cruise

试行 **shìh-hsíng** to put into operation on an experimental basis, try out; tentative, proposed

试行生产 **shìh-hsíng-shēng-ch'ǎn** trial production

试行条例 **shìh-hsíng-t'iáo-lì** tentative regulations

试论 **shìh-lùn** to discuss tentatively; a

tentative discussion

试算 **shìh-suàn** a trial audit

试点 **shìh-tiěn** a selected experiment, pilot plan (usually a focus of work in order to achieve a breakthrough)

试点班 **shìh-tiěn-pān** an experimental class (to test new methods, teaching materials, etc.)

试探 **shìh-t'àn** to test, sound out, explore, grope for

试图 **shìh-t'ú** to attempt, scheme

试验 **shìh-yèn** to experiment, test, prove; an experiment; experimental

试验性的 **shìh-yèn-hsìng-te** experimental, trial, test

试验室 **shìh-yèn-shìh** a laboratory

试验田 **shìh-yèn t'ién** an experimental field, test plot

试验演出 **shìh-yèn yěn-ch'ū** an experimental presentation (usually refers to the public presentation of a dramatic production before it has finally received the official seal of approval as a **yàng-pǎn-hsì**)

试映 **shìh-yìng** a [cinema] preview

1897　侍从 **shìh-ts'úng** attendants, followers, servants, aides

1898　势均力敌 **shìh-chǔn-lì-tí** equal in influence and matched in strength (a balance of forces; of equal power)

势如怒潮 **shìh-jú-nù-ch'áo** as powerful as the angry tides

势如破竹 **shìh-jú-p'ò-chú** to advance as easily as splitting bamboo (to advance with irresistible force; with momentum that cannot be stopped)

势力 **shìh-lì** power, influence, force, strength

势力范围 **shìh-lì-fàn-wéi** a sphere of influence, extent of power

势不可挡 **shìh-pù-k'ǒ-tǎng** irresistible power, an irresistible trend

势不两立 **shìh pù liǎng-lì** unable to coexist, incompatible

势头 **shìh-t'óu** momentum

1899　视察 **shìh-ch'á** to inspect, examine, investigate, observe; inspection, investigation

视觉形象 **shìh-chüéh hsíng-hsiàng** a visual image

视而不见 **shìh-érh-pù-chièn** to look without seeing (to be absent-minded)

视若无睹 **shìh-jò-wú-tǔ** to gaze at it as nothing (to be undisturbed by what one has seen)

视力保护运动 **shìh-lì pǎo-hù yùn-tùng** the Eyesight Protection Movement

视死如归 **shìh-szǔ-jú-kuēi** to look upon death as going home (very brave; to face death without faltering)

视导科 **shìh-tǎo-k'ō** a supervision and guidance section (in a district-level education bureau, sending inspectors to check on schools' curricula)

视为至宝 **shìh-wéi-chìh-pǎo** to regard as most valuable

视为畏途 **shìh wéi wèi-t'ú** to regard it as a dangerous road (often figurative)

1899a　恃德者昌,恃力者亡 **shìh-té chě ch'āng, shìh-lì chě wáng** those who rely on virtue will thrive and those who rely on force will perish (allegedly cited by Lin Piao to criticize the dictatorship of the proletariat)

1900　适合 **shìh-hó** suitable, fit, appropriate, congruent, corresponding

适宜 **shìh-í** suitable, fitting, proper

适龄 **shìh-líng** having reached a particular age, the required age [for military service, etc.]

适龄儿童 **shìh-líng érh-t'úng** school-age children, children of school age

适时 **shìh-shíh** at the right time, in the nick of time; opportune, timely

适当 **shìh-tàng** just right, fitting and proper, suitable, appropriate

适当安排 **shìh-tàng ān-p'ái** suitable arrangement [of one's life, work, etc.]

适当照顾 **shìh-tàng chào-kù** to give appropriate consideration to

适当比例 **shìh-tàng pǐ-lì** in appropriate proportion, a suitable ratio

适得其反 **shìh-té-ch'í-fǎn** to get exactly the opposite, just the reverse

适应 **shìh-yìng** to adapt to, correspond to, adjust to, accommodate to, conform to; adaptation

适应性 **shìh-yìng-hsìng** adaptability

适于 **shìh-yú** appropriate to, suitable for

适用 **shìh-yùng** applicable, usable, suitable, valid, what is needed; to apply

1901　是非 **shìh-fēi** yes or no, right or wrong; the sense of right and wrong, principles; a dispute, quarrel, discord

是非曲直 **shìh-fēi-ch'ǔ-chíh** rights and wrongs (merits and demerits)

是非不分 **shìh-fēi-pù-fēn** to make no distinction between right and wrong

是非问题 **shìh-fēi-wèn-t'í** a problem of right and wrong, a question of who is right and who is wrong

是可忍,孰不可忍 **shìh-k'ǒ-jěn, shú-pù-k'ǒ-jěn** if this can be tolerated, what cannot be tolerated? (there must be limits)

1902　逝世 **shìh-shìh** to pass away, die

1903　释放 **shìh-fàng** to release [from prison], set free, liberate

释免 **shìh-miěn** to be acquitted of
释罪 **shìh-tsuì** to exonerate, acquit
1904 誓师大会 **shìh-shīh tà-huì** an [army] oath-taking meeting, a pledge assembly (a rally of workers to pledge themselves to a public enterprise)
誓词 **shìh-tz'ú** an oath, pledge, vow
誓言 **shìh-yěn** a solemn pledge, vow, oath

shōu (shōu)

1905 收缴 **shōu-chiǎo** to collect [taxes, rent], confiscate, sequester
收件人 **shōu-chièn-jén** the recipient, addressee
收支 **shōu-chīh** revenue and expenditure, income and expenses
收支平衡 **shōu-chīh p'íng-héng** income and expenditure in balance
收支统计制度 **shōu-chīh t'ǔng-chì chìh-tù** transactions statistical system, income and expenditure reporting system
收猪卖肉购销点 **shōu-chū mài-jòu kòu-hsiāo-tiěn** purchase-and-supply points for collecting hogs and selling meat (markets run by production units to distribute non-collectively raised pork, 1965)
收场 **shōu-ch'ǎng** to dismantle the stage (the end of a story or affair; conclusion, ending)
收成 **shōu-ch'éng** the harvest [good or bad]
收发 **shōu-fā** to receive and send out, dispatch, relay; a person handling the receipt and dispatch of correspondence, telegrams, etc.
收发室 **shōu-fā-shìh** a message center
收复 **shōu-fù** to recapture, regain, recover [lost territory, etc.]
收回 **shōu-huí** to take back, retake, reclaim, retrieve; to retract, rescind; to withdraw from circulation, redeem
收获 **shōu-huò** a harvest (fruits, results)
收获量 **shōu-huò-liàng** harvest output, amount of the yield
收效 **shōu-hsiào** to get the desired result or effect, prove effective, succeed
收讯台 **shōu-hsùn-t'ái** a receiving station [radio, etc.]
收益 **shōu-ì** to receive benefits; income, gain, profit, yield
收益分配政策 **shōu-ì-fēn-p'èi chèng-ts'è** the policy of distributing profits, income-distribution policy
收入 **shōu-jù** receipts, income, earnings,

revenue
收容 **shōu-júng** to give shelter to, accommodate, take in; to take into custody, intern
收容站 **shōu-júng-chàn** shelter stations (usually in disaster relief)
收割 **shōu-kō** to reap, scythe, harvest
收割机 **shōu-kō-chī** a harvesting machine, harvester
收购站 **shōu-kòu-chàn** a purchasing station
收购价格 **shōu-kòu-chià-kó** procurement price, purchasing price
收管吃 **shōu-kuǎn-ch'īh** harvesting, conservation, and consumption [of agricultural products]
收归国有 **shōu-kuēi-kuó-yǔ** to nationalize [property], nationalization
收罗 **shōu-ló** to assemble, gather
收拢 **shōu-lǔng** to draw the net
收买 **shōu-mǎi** to buy, purchase, buy up; to bribe
收报机 **shōu-pào-chī** a telegraph receiving set, teletype machine
收编 **shōu-piēn** to incorporate and reorganize [troops of another side]; to amalgamate
收兵 **shōu-pīng** to recall the troops (to end hostilities, discontinue a campaign)
收兵回营 **shōu-pīng-huí-yíng** to call the troops back to the barracks
收兵休整 **shōu-pīng hsiū-chěng** to discontinue hostilities to rest and regroup [one's forces]
收拾 **shōu-shíh** to put in order, mend, arrange, tidy up
收拾残局 **shōu-shíh ts'án-chǘ** to settle a disturbed situation (to deal with the aftermath of a war or great upheaval)
收缩 **shōu-sō** to shrink up, contract, curtail; shrinkage, contraction
收租 **shōu-tsū** to collect rent
收租院 **shōu-tsū-yuàn** the Rent-Collecting Court (a famous group sculpture depicting rent collection by a harsh Szechwanese landlord)

shǒu (shǒu)

1906 手掌心 **shǒu-chǎng-hsīn** the middle of the palm of the hand
手枪 **shǒu-ch'iāng** a handgun, pistol, revolver
手法 **shǒu-fǎ** dexterity, skill, workmanship, artistry; sleight of hand
手法翻新 **shǒu-fǎ fān-hsīn** new sleight of hand tricks
手风琴 **shǒu-fēng-ch'in** an accordion

手扶拖拉机 **shǒu-fú t'ō-lā-chī** a hand-guided tractor

手写体 **shǒu-hsiěh-t'ǐ** the handwritten form

手续 **shǒu-hsù** procedures, formalities, routine

手续费 **shǒu-hsù-fèi** a service charge, procedural fee

手工艺 **shǒu-kūng-ì** handicraft skill, craftsmanship

手工业 **shǒu-kūng-yèh** handicrafts, manual trades

手工业主 **shǒu-kūng-yèh chǔ** a master handicraftsman

手工业合作化 **shǒu-kūng-yèh hó-tsò-huà** the cooperativization of handicrafts, organization of handicraft trades into cooperatives

手工业工人 **shǒu-kūng-yèh kūng-jén** workers in handicraft trades

手工业生产合作社 **shǒu-kūng-yèh shēng-ch'ǎn hó-tsò-shè** handicraft producers' cooperatives

手工业作坊 **shǒu-kūng-yèh tsō-fāng** a handicraft workshop

手铐 **shǒu-k'ào** handcuffs, manacles

手榴弹 **shǒu-liú-tàn** a hand grenade

手忙脚乱 **shǒu-máng chiǎo-luàn** the hands are busy and the feet confused (helter-skelter, flustered)

手把 **shǒu-pǎ** a handle, lever

手把手教 **shǒu-pǎ-shǒu-chiāo** to teach by guiding the hand [of the student] (very careful and patient instruction)

手边 **shǒu-piēn** at hand, handy

手电筒 **shǒu-tièn-t'ǔng** a flashlight

手段 **shǒu-tuàn** means, measures, steps, procedures; tactics, devices, skill in dealing with people

手提机关枪 **shǒu-t'í chī-kuān-ch'iāng** a hand machine gun, sub-machine gun

手推车 **shǒu-t'uī-ch'ē** a pushcart, handcart, wheelbarrow

手足之情 **shǒu-tsú chīh ch'íng** the affections of hand and foot (fraternal feelings, class intimacy)

手足无措 **shǒu-tsú-wú-ts'ò** not [knowing what] to do with the hands and feet (at a loss as to what to do, confused, bewildered)

手册 **shǒu-ts'è** a handbook, manual, guidebook

手腕 **shǒu-wàn** (1) the wrist; (2) skill, dexterity, finesse

手舞足蹈 **shǒu-wǔ-tsú-tǎo** to wave the hands and stamp the feet

手印 **shǒu-yìn** a handprint; a thumb impression used as a signature

¹⁹⁰⁷ 守着煤山没煤烧 **shǒu-che méi-shān méi-méi-shāo** to sit on a mountain of coal without any coal to burn (to fail to develop natural resources)

守纪律 **shǒu chì-lù** to maintain discipline, observe discipline

守旧摊摊, 不创新业 **shǒu-chiù-t'ān-t'an, pù-chuàng-hsīn-yèh** to stick to the old stall without starting any new business (to keep to the old rut without trying to do anything new)

守法 **shǒu-fǎ** to observe the law; law-abiding

守信 **shǒu-hsìn** to keep promises, keep faith, abide by one's word

守口如瓶 **shǒu-k'ǒu-jú-p'íng** to keep the mouth closed like a bottle (to keep a secret, highly discreet)

守备 **shǒu-pèi** to watch, protect, defend; garrison duty

守势 **shǒu-shìh** defense [military]

守卫 **shǒu-wèi** to guard, defend, protect, keep watch

¹⁹⁰⁸ 首长 **shǒu-chǎng** a head [of a department, etc.], a superior

首创 **shǒu-ch'uàng** to produce first, found, start, initiate, originate

首创精神 **shǒu-ch'uàng chīng-shén** the spirit of initiative, pioneering spirit

首犯 **shǒu-fàn** a ringleader, chief criminal

首席 **shǒu-hsí** the first place; senior, chief, head

首相 **shǒu-hsiàng** a prime minister, premier (usually the executive head of a government)

首领 **shǒu-lǐng** a leader, head

首脑 **shǒu-nǎo** leading mind, head man, chief, top person

首脑会议 **shǒu-nǎo-huì-ì** a meeting of heads [of governments], a summit conference

首脑人物 **shǒu-nǎo-jén-wù** leading figures, chief personalities

首恶 **shǒu-ò** the chief criminal, principal offender

首批 **shǒu-p'ī** the first batch, first group

首当其冲 **shǒu-tāng-ch'í-ch'ūng** the first one to come into conflict (to bear the main brunt)

首都 **shǒu-tū** the capital [of a country] (Peking)

首次演出 **shǒu-tz'ù-yěn-ch'ū** the first performance, premiere

首位 **shǒu-wèi** the first place, seat of honor

首要战犯 **shǒu-yào-chàn-fàn** a chief war criminal

首演 **shǒu-yěn** a first performance, premiere (contraction of **shǒu-tz'ù-yěn-ch'ū**)

shòu (shòu)

1909 受制 **shòu-chìh** to be subject to
受宠若惊 **shòu-ch'ǔng jò-chīng** to receive more favors than one expected (to be agreeably surprised)
受二茬罪 **shòu-èrh-ch'á-tsuì** to endure a second suffering
受害 **shòu-hài** to suffer, be harmed, incur injury, be victimized
受贿 **shòu-huì** to accept bribes
受益 **shòu-ì** to benefit from, benefit by, gain advantage
受命 **shòu-mìng** to accept an order, be charged with, be authorized
受审 **shòu-shěn** to stand trial

1910 寿命 **shòu-mìng** a person's life span, one's age at death

1911 兽医 **shòu-ī** a veterinarian
兽力车 **shòu-lì-ch'ē** an animal-drawn cart

1912 授奖大会 **shòu-chiǎng tà-huì** awards assembly (to honor high producers)
授职 **shòu-chíh** to confer a rank, bestow an official position, invest in office
授旗宣誓大会 **shòu-ch'í hsuān-shìh tà-huì** receiving-the-colors pledge assembly (for students being formed into **hsìa-hsiāng** groups, 1964)
授权 **shòu-ch'üán** to authorize, empower, delegate powers
授粉 **shòu-fěn** pollination
授意 **shòu-ì** to give [someone else] an idea [for an action] (to suggest or inspire action in others)

1913 售票处 **shòu-p'iào-ch'ù** a ticket office, box office

1914 瘦弱 **shòu-jò** thin and weak, emaciated and frail

shū (shū)

1915 书记 **shū-chì** a secretary, scribe, clerk
书记处 **shū-chì-ch'ù** secretariat
书记挂帅 **shū-chì kuà-shuài** the secretary takes command (the Party secretary assumes personal charge and responsibility for a task)
书记动手，全党办社 **shū-chì tùng-shǒu, ch'üán-tǎng pàn-shè** the [Party] secretary initiates and the whole Party sets up communes
书法 **shū-fǎ** calligraphy, the art of calligraphy
书画 **shū-huà** calligraphy and painting
书刊 **shū-k'ān** books and periodicals
书刻工作者 **shū-k'ò kūng-tsò-chě** workers who carve seals
书面 **shū-mièn** in written form, in writing
书报 **shū-pào** books and newspapers
书本知识 **shū-pěn-chīh-shíh** bookish knowledge
书生之见 **shū-shēng-chīh-chièn** the ideas of a pedant (bookish, impractical, unrealistic)
书呆子 **shū-tāi-tzu** a bookish fool, bookworm
书摊 **shū-t'ān** a bookstall
书体 **shū-t'ǐ** forms of Chinese writing (such as seal characters or *k'ǎi-shū* 楷书)

1916 抒情诗 **shū-ch'íng-shīh** lyric poetry
抒发 **shū-fā** to pour out; to express [feelings]

1917 叔叔 **shū-shū** uncle, father's younger brother (used by children in addressing soldiers and visitors)

1918 枢纽 **shū-niǔ** focal point, axis, focus, hinge, key; pivotal
枢纽工程 **shū-niǔ-kūng-ch'éng** pivotal project

1919 殊死战 **shū-szǔ-chàn** a life-and-death battle; to fight to the last man

1920 梳妆 **shū-chuāng** to comb [the hair] and make up [the face]

1921 舒畅 **shū-ch'àng** cheerful, happy, in good spirits
舒服 **shū-fu** comfortable, cozy, relaxed
舒适 **shū-shìh** comfortable, pleasant

1922 疏浚 **shū-chùn** to clear and dredge [waterways]
疏忽 **shū-hū** careless, negligent, inadvertent; to neglect; an oversight
疏通 **shū-t'ūng** (1) to clear out [a waterway] and restore traffic; (2) to improve relations, bridge a misunderstanding, settle a conflict
疏远 **shū-yuǎn** distant from, estranged, alienated

1923 输出 **shū-ch'ū** to ship out; export
输入 **shū-jù** to import; imports
输光 **shū-kuāng** to lose everything, to be cleaned out
输送 **shū-sùng** to transport, send out, supply
输电线 **shū-tièn-hsièn** an electric transmission line
输电网 **shū-tièn-wǎng** electrical transmission net
输油管线 **shū-yú-kuǎn-hsièn** an oil pipeline

1924 蔬菜 **shū-ts'ài** vegetable

shú (shú)

1925 赎买政策 **shú-mǎi chèng-ts'è** the buying-out policy (under which the government paid 5 percent annual

interest to private shareholders of joint state-private enterprises that were taken from them during the Socialist Transformation of 1955–1956)

赎买金 **shú-maǐ chīn** a redemption fund

赎买到底 **shú-maǐ tào-tǐ** to continue redemption payments to the end (when the joint state-private enterprises were set up, the original intention was to make the 5 percent payments to the original owners for seven years, i.e., to 1962; later there was some demand that these payments be continued for twenty years so that the equivalent of 100 percent would be received. Actual payments were apparently made for two more years)

赎罪 **shú-tsuì** to atone for sin, redemption

1926 熟荒地 **shú-huāng-tì** abandoned cultivated land, wasteland that was under cultivation

熟悉 **shú-hsī** very familiar with, conversant with; to know well

熟练 **shú-lièn** experienced, skilled, qualified, dexterous

熟练工人 **shú-lièn kūng-jén** a skilled worker, experienced worker, veteran

熟能生巧 **shú-néng-shēng-ch'iǎo** skill is derived from practice, practice makes perfect

熟视无睹 **shú-shìh wú-tǔ** to have seen so often that one no longer notices (indifference bred by familiarity)

shǔ (shǔ)

1927 属性 **shǔ-hsìng** an attribute, quality, character, trait, property

属国 **shǔ-kuó** a vassal state, dependency

1928 暑期进修活动 **shǔ-ch'ī chìn-hsiū huó-tùng** summer progress activities

1929 鼠目寸光 **shǔ-mù ts'ùn-kuāng** the eyes of a rat [see] only an inch of light (very short-sighted)

1930 薯类 **shǔ-lèi** tuber crops

1931 曙光 **shǔ-kuāng** the dawn light, aurora (the beginning of hope)

shù (shù)

1932 术语 **shù-yǔ** technical terms, professional jargon

1933 束之高阁 **shù-chīh-kāo-kó** to tie up and put in the attic (to shelve, lay aside)

束缚 **shù-fù** to bind, tie together, restrict, fetter; restraints, bondage

束手束脚 **shù-shǒu-shù-chiǎo** bound hand and foot (overcautious)

束手待毙 **shù-shǒu-tài-pì** to wait for death [as if one's] hands were tied

束手无策 **shù-shǒu-wú-ts'è** without a solution [as if one's] hands were tied (perplexed, helpless)

1934 述说 **shù-shuō** to narrate, give a full report, recount

1935 树雄心，立壮志 **shù hsiúng-hsīn, lì chuàng-chìh** to set up heroic aspirations and establish stout determination

树靠根生鱼靠水养 **shù-k'ào kēn-shēng yú-k'ào shuǐ-yǎng** trees depend on roots for growth and fish depend on water for nourishment (figurative: trees and fish are the Party; roots and water are the masses)

树立新风尚 **shù-lì hsīn-fēng-shàng** to establish new mores

树立榜样 **shù-lì pǎng-yàng** to set up an example, establish a model

树碑立传 **shù-pēi-lì-chuàn** to erect tablets and write biographies (now criticized as glorification of individuals)

树倒猢狲散 **shù-tǎo hú-sūn-sàn** when the tree falls the monkeys scatter ("rats leave a sinking ship")

树得牢 **shù-te-láo** to establish firmly (as thought and ideology)

树敌 **shù-tí** to make enemies, antagonize (often with the implication of making enemies by one's own actions)

树欲静而风不止 **shù-yù-chìng érh fēng-pù-chǐh** the tree wishes to be quiet but the wind will not stop (class struggle is independent of human will)

1936 竖井矿 **shù-chǐng-k'uàng** a shaft mine [as opposed to a quarry or strip mine]

1937 数值 **shù-chíh** numerical value

数九隆冬 **shù chiǔ-lúng-tūng** the several nine-day periods of deep winter (bitterly cold weather)

数据 **shù-chù** data, numerical data

数学式子 **shù-hsuéh shìh-tzu** mathematical formulae

数理化 **shù-lǐ-huà** mathematics, physics, and chemistry (the "hard" sciences)

数量 **shù-liàng** quantity, amount, number

数码 **shù-mǎ** figures, numbers, numerals

数字 **shù-tzù** a numeral, figure

数字计算机 **shù-tzù chì-suàn-chī** a

digital computer
数字控制机床 **shù-tzù k'ùng-chìh chī-ch'uáng** numerically controlled machinery

shuǎ (shuǎ)

1938 耍花招 **shuǎ-huā-chāo** to take action to confuse or deceive others; to play tricks

耍花腔 **shuǎ-huā-ch'iāng** to sing in a fancy way (to speak in alluring tones; guileful)

耍弄 **shuǎ-nùng** to make a fool of, deceive, delude

耍手腕 **shuǎ-shǒu-wàn** to play tricks, maneuver in a clever way, use guileful tactics

耍坛子 **shuǎ-t'án-tzu** to juggle with jars

耍威风 **shuǎ-wēi-fēng** to make a pretense of authority

耍无赖 **shuǎ-wú-lài** to be deliberately dishonest

shuāi (shuāi)

1939 衰朽 **shuāi-hsiǔ** old and useless, senile

衰弱 **shuāi-jò** weak, sickly, feeble; weakening

衰落 **shuāi-lò** decayed, withered; decline, oblivion

衰败 **shuāi-pài** to decline, deteriorate, disintegrate; be defeated

衰退 **shuāi-t'uì** to decrease, decline, retrogress, fall; a slump, recession [economic]

衰亡 **shuāi-wáng** to wither away, decline and fall, perish

1940 摔跟斗 **shuāi kēn-tou** to fall flat (to fail ignominiously in an endeavor)

shuǎi (shuǎi)

1941 甩石子 **shuǎi shíh-tzǔ** to throw a stone (to give a warning)

甩手操 **shuǎi-shǒu-ts'āo** a form of calisthenics (by swinging the arms up and down)

甩掉帽子 **shuǎi-tiào mào-tzu** to throw off the hat (by one's own efforts to overcome an unfavorable label)

shuài (shuài)

1942 帅旗 **shuài-ch'í** the commander-in-chief's flag (a banner, standard, rallying point)

1943 率直 **shuài-chíh** candid, frank, honest, straightforward

率领 **shuài-lǐng** to lead, guide, head up

shuāng (shuāng)

1944 双季稻 **shuāng-chì-tào** double-crop rice (the growing of two crops of rice in one year on the same field)

双职工 **shuāng-chíh-kūng** double working (husband and wife both employed)

双抢 **shuāng-ch'iǎng** the two rush [jobs] (harvesting and plowing)

双抢劳动 **shuāng-ch'iǎng láo-tùng** double-rush labor (summer agricultural work for students and urban residents to meet the two summer periods of heavy farm work)

双重国籍 **shuāng-ch'úng-kuó-chí** dual nationality

双重领导 **shuāng-ch'úng lǐng-tǎo** dual leadership

双方 **shuāng-fāng** both sides, the two sides; bilateral, mutual

双方同意 **shuāng-fāng t'úng-ì** agreement on both sides, mutual consent

双簧 **shuāng-huáng** a kind of variety show with one person gesticulating in front and another speaking in the back (often figurative)

双任制 **shuāng-jèn-chìh** the double-appointment system (e.g., cadres may hold concurrent posts in both brigades and production teams)

双管齐下 **shuāng-kuǎn ch'í-hsià** to draw with two pens at the same time (to do two things simultaneously)

双轨 **shuāng-kuěi** double tracks; double-tracked

双轮双铧犁 **shuāng-lún shuāng-huá-lí** a two-wheeled double-shared plow

双面绣 **shuāng-mièn-hsiù** double-sided embroidery

双百分针 **shuāng-pǎi-fāng-chēn** the double-hundred policy (i.e., let a hundred flowers blossom and a hundred schools contend)

双边关系 **shuāng-piēn-kuān-hsi** bilateral relations

双边条约 **shuāng-piēn t'iáo-yuēh** a bilateral treaty

双十协定 **shuāng-shíh hsiéh-tìng** the Double Ten Agreement (between the Communists and the National Government at Chungking on October 10, 1945)

双水内冷汽轮发电机 **shuāng-shuǐ nèi-lěng ch'ì-lún fā-tièn-chī** double-acting internally water-cooled steam turbine generator

双引擎 **shuāng yǐn-ch'íng** twin-engined [aircraft, etc.]

shuǎng (shuǎng)

1945 爽直 **shuǎng-chíh** frank, outspoken, straightforward, open-hearted

shuí (shuí)

1946 谁战谁胜 **shuí chàn-shèng shuí** who defeats whom (the struggle to decide whether socialism or capitalism will prevail)

谁主浮沉 **shuí-chǔ fú-ch'éng** who controls whether [we] float or sink (we, the masses, control our own destiny)

谁种桃子谁收桃 **shuí-chùng-t'áo-tzu shuí-shōu-t'áo** whoever plants peaches should harvest peaches (one should be able to enjoy the fruits of one's labors—a slogan of the civil war period to justify Communist attempts to retain control of the areas they had liberated)

谁胜谁负 **shuí shèng shuí fù** who wins [and] who loses

谁养活谁 **shuí yǎng-huó shuí** who gives a living to whom (refers to peasant and landlord, worker and capitalist, or colony and imperialist power, etc.)

谁也管不着论 **shuí-yěh-kuǎn-pù-cháo lùn** the doctrine that nobody can tell [me] what to do (extreme individualism)

谁 **shuí**: also pronounced colloquially as **shéi**

shuǐ (shuǐ)

1947 水闸 **shuǐ-chá** a sluice gate, lock [in a canal]

水准 **shuǐ-chǔn** a water level, standard, level [of education, political consciousness, etc.]

水中捞月 **shuǐ-chūng lāo-yuèh** [to try] to scoop the moon out of the water (wasted effort, something impossible)

水产 **shuǐ-ch'ǎn** aquatic production; marine products

水产系统 **shuǐ-ch'ǎn hsì-t'ǔng** the marine products system (all units and agencies involved in the handling and marketing of aquatic products)

水产部 **shuǐ-ch'ǎn-pù** Ministry of Aquatic Products [of the State Council] (merged into the Ministry of Agriculture and Forestry in 1969)

水产品 **shuǐ-ch'ǎn-p'ǐn** aquatic products, marine products

水产养殖事业 **shuǐ-ch'ǎn yǎng-chíh shìh-yèh** aquatic cultivation enterprises

水车 **shuǐ-ch'ē** a water wheel, water mill

水渠 **shuǐ-ch'ú** a canal, channel

水分 **shuǐ-fèn** water content, humidity, moisture

水害 **shuǐ-hài** water damage [agricultural] (injury to plants or crops from excessive water)

水旱 **shuǐ-hàn** flood and drought

水浒传 **shuǐ-hǔ-chuàn** The Water Margin or All Men Are Brothers (traditional novel drawn from folklore about the courageous exploits of a group of loyal and just bandit-heroes; criticized in 1975)

水火 **shuǐ-huǒ** water and fire (incompatible things; disaster and calamity)

水火不相容 **shuǐ-huǒ pù-hsiāng-júng** incompatible with each other like fire and water

水系 **shuǐ-hsì** river systems

水泄不通 **shuǐ-hsièh-pù-t'ūng** even water cannot flow out (very crowded, clogged)

水乳交融 **shuǐ-jǔ-chiāo-júng** to blend like water and milk (two different things that mix together readily—such as the PLA and the masses)

水贵如油 **shuǐ-kuèi-jú-yú** water as expensive as oil (a reference to former times in North China where some areas had a serious lack of water)

水库 **shuǐ-k'ù** a water reservoir

水涝 **shuǐ-lào** waterlogging [of fields]

水力发电 **shuǐ-lì fā-tièn** hydroelectric power generation

水力采煤 **shuǐ-lì ts'ǎi-méi** hydraulic mining of coal

水利 **shuǐ-lì** water conservancy, water utilization, irrigation

水利工程 **shuǐ-lì kūng-ch'éng** water conservancy projects, engineering works for water control

水利枢纽 **shuǐ-lì shū-niǔ** a water control pivotal point, hydro-junction

水利电力部 **shuǐ-lì tièn-lì pù** the Ministry of Water Conservancy and Electric Power [of the State Council]

水利资源 **shuǐ-lì tzū-yuán** water resources

水利网 **shuǐ-lì-wǎng** a water conservancy network

水落石出 **shuǐ-lò shíh-ch'ū** the water recedes and the stones are exposed (the facts will eventually become clear)

水陆两用飞机 **shuǐ-lù-liǎng-yùng fēi-chī** an amphibian airplane

水路 **shuǐ-lù** a waterway, watercourse
水轮机 **shuǐ-lún-chī** a water wheel, hydraulic turbine
水龙头 **shuǐ-lúng-t'óu** water faucet, water tap
水磨房 **shuǐ-mò-fáng** a water mill
水墨画 **shuǐ-mò-huà** [Chinese] monochrome paintings
水泥 **shuǐ-ní** cement, concrete
水坝 **shuǐ-pà** a dam, dike
水泵 **shuǐ-pèng** a water pump
水兵 **shuǐ-pīng** a navy man, seaman, sailor
水平 **shuǐ-p'íng** water level; a level, standard; horizontal
水平面 **shuǐ-p'íng-mièn** a level surface; sea level
水平条田 **shuǐ-p'íng t'iáo-t'ién** level-graded strip-fields
水泼不进 **shuǐ-p'ō-pù-chìn** watertight, impermeable
水上长城 **shuǐ-shàng-ch'áng-ch'éng** the great wall on the water (the massive dikes along the lower Yellow River; also figuratively, the navy and coast defense forces
水上居民 **shuǐ-shàng chǔ-mín** residents on the water (the new term for what used to be called "boat people"— *tàn-mín*蛋民)
水上飞机 **shuǐ-shàng-fēi-chī** seaplane, flying boat
水深火热 **shuǐ-shēn-huǒ-jè** the water is deep and the fire is hot (the sufferings of the people in the old society)
水生植物 **shuǐ-shēng-chíh-wù** aquatic plant, water plant, hydrophyte
水手 **shuǐ-shǒu** a seaman, sailor, deckhand
水到渠成 **shuǐ-tào-ch'ú-ch'éng** when the water arrives, a channel is formed (when conditions are ripe, affairs are instantly accomplished)
水稻 **shuǐ-tào** rice grown in wet fields, paddy rice
水滴石穿 **shuǐ-tī-shíh-ch'uān** water drops can make a hole in stone (persistent effort, even though small, can accomplish great tasks)
水田 **shuǐ-t'ién** wet rice fields, paddy fields; irrigated land
水土流失 **shuǐ-t'ǔ liú-shīh** water losses and soil erosion
水土保持 **shuǐ-t'ǔ-pǎo-ch'íh** water and soil conservation
水土不服 **shuǐ-t'ǔ-pù-fú** the climate is not agreeable, not adjusted to the climate [of a new place]
水灾 **shuǐ-tsāi** a flood disaster; inundation, flooding

水足草肥 **shuǐ-tsú-ts'ǎo-féi** water sufficient and grass luxurious
水族 **shuǐ-tsú** the Shui people (a minority in Kweichow province: population 160,000 as of 1957; also known as *shuǐ-chiā-tsú* 水家族)
水彩画 **shuǐ-ts'ǎi-huà** watercolor pictures
水位 **shuǐ-wèi** water stage, water level [in rivers, lakes, etc.]
水文 **shuǐ-wén** hydrology, hydraulics
水文站 **shuǐ-wén-chàn** hydrographic station
水压机 **shuǐ-yā-chī** a hydraulic press

shui̇̀ (shui̇̀)

1948 税制 **shui̇̀-chìh** the tax system, system of taxation
税种 **shui̇̀-chǔng** kinds of taxes
税款 **shui̇̀-k'uǎn** tax funds; a tax, duty
税率 **shui̇̀-lǜ** tax rate, tariff
税目 **shui̇̀-mù** tax items, tax categories, taxables
税收 **shui̇̀-shōu** tax revenue, tax collections; taxation
税收法 **shui̇̀-shōu-fǎ** tax collection methods

shùn (shùn)

1949 顺风船 **shùn-fēng-ch'uán** a ship sailing with the wind (an easy passage)
顺利 **shùn-lì** going smoothly, having no trouble, doing well, without a hitch
顺藤摸瓜 **shùn-t'éng-mō-kuā** follow the vine and find the melon (to use a clue)
顺从 **shùn-ts'úng** to obey, comply with, acquiesce

shuō (shuō)

1950 说教 **shuō-chiào** to preach
说中 **shuō-chùng** to predict correctly
说穿 **shuō-ch'uān** to expose in speech, reveal
说法 **shuō-fa** way of expression, idiom, argument, interpretation
说服 **shuō-fú** to convince, persuade, prevail upon, win over; persuasion [especially in discussion]
说服教育 **shuō-fú-chiào-yǜ** education by persuasion
说服工作 **shuō-fú-kūng-tsò** persuading work, the task of convincing people by persuasion
说服力 **shuō-fú-lì** the power to convince; persuasive power
说老实话, 干老实事, 当老实人 **shuō lǎo-**

shih-huà, kàn lǎo-shih-shìh, tāng lǎo-shih-jén speak honest words, do honest deeds, and act as an honest man

说理 **shuō-lǐ** to talk reason, explain one's reasons, be reasonable

说明 **shuō-míng** to explain, clarify, enlighten, expound; an explanation, exposition

说明书 **shuō-míng-shū** a written explanation, instructions for use; a synopsis

说书 **shuō-shū** storytelling (a literary form practiced by professionals, often accompanied by a small drum)

说顺话, 少说话 **shuō-shùn-huà, shǎo-shuō-huà** to say only compliant things and say little

说到痛处 **shuō-tào t'ùng-ch'ù** to speak of painful matters ("to sting to the quick")

说到做到 **shuō-tào tsò-tào** to do what one says [he will do], to do as one speaks

说英雄 **shuō-yīng-hsiúng** to tell of heroes

sō (suō)

1951　唆使 **sō-shǐh** to instigate, incite, goad; incitement

1952　缩小 **sō-hsiǎo** to diminish, reduce, shrink, minimize, retrench, cut back; diminution

缩写 **sō-hsiěh** to abbreviate; abbreviation

缩手缩脚 **sō-shǒu-sō-chiǎo** to keep hands and feet drawn back (reluctant to act, timid)

缩短 **sō-tuǎn** to shorten, abridge, contract, condense

sǒ (suǒ)

1953　所向披靡 **sǒ-hsiàng p'ī-mǐ** wherever they went [the enemy] was dispersed (ever-triumphant)

所向无前 **sǒ-hsiàng-wú-ch'ién** wherever [our army advances] there is no one in front [of it] (the enemy refuses to stand and face us; an unopposed advance)

所向无敌 **sǒ-hsiàng-wú-tí** wherever [the army] goes it meets no rivals (invincible, ever-victorious)

所得 **sǒ-té** what one gets or receives, income

所得税 **sǒ-té-shuì** income tax

所在单位 **sǒ-tsài-tān-wèi** the unit in which one is situated (one's unit)

所在地区 **sǒ-tsài-tì-ch'ū** the area in which one works (or lives)

所作所为 **sǒ-tsò sǒ-wéi** what one has done (action, behavior, conduct)

所谓 **sǒ-wèi** so-called (usually implies doubt or illegitimacy)

所有制 **sǒ-yǔ-chìh** the ownership system, system of ownership

所有权 **sǒ-yǔ-ch'üán** rights of ownership, ownership

所有人 **sǒ-yǔ-jén** the owner, possessor, proprietor

所有物 **sǒ-yǔ-wù** something owned, property, possession

1954　索取 **sǒ-ch'ǔ** to demand, lay claim to, extort, extract; a demand, exaction

索尔兹伯里 **sǒ-ěrh-tzū-pó-lǐ** Salisbury [Rhodesia]

索非亚 **sǒ-fēi-yà** Sofia [Bulgaria]

索性 **sǒ-hsìng** simply, might just as well, without further ado

索马里 **sǒ-mǎ-lǐ** Somalia

索引 **sǒ-yǐn** to bring together; an index, concordance

1955　琐事 **sǒ-shìh** trifles, trivial matters, minor chores

琐碎 **sǒ-suì** fragmentary, petty and varied, tedious, multitudinous, annoying

1956　锁链 **sǒ-liàn** chains, shackles, fetters

sōu (sōu)

1957　搜集情报 **sōu-chí ch'íng-pào** to gather information, collect intelligence

搜罗 **sōu-ló** to collect from various sources, hunt up, muster

搜捕 **sōu-pǔ** to search for and arrest

搜捕队 **sōu-pǔ-tuì** a searching and capturing unit (as in the sparrow extermination campaign)

搜索 **sōu-sǒ** to search, inquire, reconnoiter

sū (sū)

1958　苏 **sū** Kiangsu province

苏区 **sū-ch'ū** soviet district (areas held by Communist forces during the war of 1927–1936)

苏醒 **sū-hsǐng** to revive, come to, awaken

苏修 **sū-hsiū** Soviet revisionists, Soviet revisionism

苏修集团 **sū-hsiū-chí-t'uán** the Soviet revisionist bloc

苏修侵捷事件 **sū-hsiū ch'ǐn-chiéh shìh-chièn** the Soviet revisionist invasion of Czechoslovakia (1968)

苏彝士运河 **sū-í-shìh yùn-hó** the Suez

Canal

苏共 **sū-kùng** the Communist Party of the Soviet Union

苏卡诺 **sū-k'ǎ-nò** Sukarno (Indonesian political leader)

苏联 **sū-lién** the Soviet Union (contracted form)

苏丹 **sū-tān** Sudan

苏维埃 **sū-wéi-āi** a soviet; Soviet

苏维埃政权 **sū-wéi-āi chèng-ch'üán** the Soviet regime (the Kiangsi Soviet Republic)

苏维埃社会主义共和国联盟 **sū-wéi-āi shè-huì-chǔ-ì kùng-hó-kuó lién-méng** the Union of Soviet Socialist Republics [USSR]

1959 酥油茶 **sū-yú-ch'á** butter tea (a food of Tibet)

sù (sù)

1960 诉诸武力 **sù-chū wǔ-lì** to resort to armed force

诉苦 **sù-k'ǔ** to tell of bitterness (as in a poor peasant's complaint against the landlord)

诉苦运动 **sù-k'ǔ-yùn-tùng** a "tell-of-bitterness" campaign

诉讼 **sù-sùng** to go to law, file a lawsuit, proceed against; a court action; litigation

1961 肃清 **sù-ch'īng** to wipe out, liquidate, exterminate, clear out

肃清反革命运动 **sù-ch'īng fǎn-kó-mìng yùn-tùng** the Movement for the Suppression of Counter-Revolutionaries (1955)

肃清反动势力 **sù-ch'īng fǎn-tùng-shìh-lì** to clear out the reactionary forces

肃反 **sù-fǎn** to clear out counter-revolutionaries (contraction of **sù-ch'īng fǎn-kó-mìng yùn-tùng**)

肃然起敬 **sù-ján-ch'ǐ-chìng** great respect rising in one's heart (to show great respect toward a person)

肃特 **sù-t'è** to clear out [Nationalist] agents

1962 速记员 **sù-chì-yuán** a shorthand stenographer

速成教学法 **sù-ch'éng chiào-hsuéh-fǎ** a quick method of teaching, intensive instruction

速成中学 **sù-ch'éng chūng-hsuéh** an accelerated middle school

速成识字法 **sù-ch'éng shíh-tzù-fǎ** a quick method for learning [Chinese] characters

速决 **sù-chüéh** to make a decision rapidly; a quick solution

速决战 **sù-chüéh-chàn** a war of quick

decision

速率 **sù-lǜ** rate of speed, velocity

速生树种 **sù-shēng-shù-chǔng** fast growing species of trees

速胜论者 **sù-shèng-lùn-chě** one who advocates quick victory (implies impatience in strategy)

速度 **sù-tù** speed, velocity, [musical] tempo

1963 素质 **sù-chìh** innate quality, natural character

1964 宿命论 **sù-mìng lùn** determinism, fatalism

宿舍 **sù-shè** group living quarters, dormitory

1965 塑胶 **sù-chiāo** plastics, vinyl

塑料厂 **sù-liào-ch'ǎng** a plastics plant, a factory manufacturing plastics

塑造 **sù-tsào** to form, model, sculpture, depict, portray

塑造典型 **sù-tsào tiěn-hsíng** to create an image [in art or literature]

suān (suān)

1966 酸辛 **suān-hsīn** pain, misfortune, suffering, hardship, misery

suàn (suàn)

1967 算帐 **suàn-chàng** to settle accounts, render an accounting; to get even

算细帐 **suàn-hsì-chàng** to compute an account in minute detail (to demand every penny owed)

算老帐 **suàn-lǎo-chàng** to settle old accounts

算命 **suàn-mìng** to tell fortunes; fortunetelling

算三帐 **suàn-sān-chàng** to reckon the Three Accounts (through self-examination, people are to see what progress they have made in their political, economic, and cultural accounts)

算数 **suàn-shù** valid, can be counted, to be taken as final

suí (suí)

1968 绥靖主义 **suí-chìng-chǔ-ì** appeasement, "compromise-ism"

绥靖公署 **suí-chìng-kūng-shǔ** pacification headquarters, headquarters of a pacification force

1969 随机应变 **suí-chī-yìng-pièn** to adapt quickly to changing circumstances

随风就俗 **suí-fēng-chiù-sú** to conform to custom

随心所欲 **suí-hsīn-sǒ-yù** to follow one's

wishes

随行人员 **suí-hsíng jén-yuán** an entourage, members of a retinue

随意 **suí-ì** as one pleases, according to wish, as one likes

随人俯仰 **suí-jén fŭ-yăng** to submit to other's whim and fancy

随便 **suí-pièn** as you like, as one pleases; casual, careless, lackadaisical

随波逐流 **suí-pō-chú-liú** to drift with the current (to have no views of one's own, do as others do)

随声附和 **suí-shēng-fù-hò** to echo others, to parrot

随时准备 **suí-shíh chŭn-peì** to be ready at all times

随手 **suí-shŏu** at hand, readily, immediately, without hesitation

随大流 **suí tà-liú** to follow the big flow, go along with the mainstream (follow the crowd, "go along")

随员 **suí-yuán** an attaché, escort, member of a suite

suì (suì)

1970 岁出 **suì-ch'ū** annual expenditure, expenditures during a year

岁入 **suì-jù** annual revenue, income during the year

岁入枯竭 **suì-jù-k'ū-chiéh** the yearly receipts have dried up; exhaustion of revenue sources

岁月 **suì-yuèh** years and months, time

1971 碎石路 **suì-shíh-lù** a gravel road

1972 隧道工程 **suì-tào kūng-ch'éng** tunnel construction work; a tunnel

1973 穗 **suì** Canton (a literary monosyllabic name)

sūn (sūn)

1974 孙中山 **sūn chūng-shān** Sun Yat-sen (1866–1925)

孙中山主义 **sūn chūng-shān chŭ-ì** Sun Yat-sen-ism (usually refers to the **hsìn-sān-mín-chŭ-ì**)

sŭn (sŭn)

1975 损害 **sŭn-hài** to damage, harm, impair, injure; damage

损坏 **sŭn-huài** to damage, injure, spoil, destroy

损人利己 **sŭn-jén lì-chĭ** to injure others [in order to] benefit oneself

损失 **sŭn-shīh** loss, damage, injury; damages, casualties

sūng (sōng)

1976 松劲 **sūng-chìn** to slacken, lose strength, relax efforts

松劲情绪 **sūng-chìn-ch'íng-hsù** a slack and insensitive state of mind

松劲泄气 **sūng-chìn hsièh-ch'ì** slackness and despondency

松弛 **sūng-ch'íh** to relax, loosen, slacken

松懈 **sūng-hsièh** negligent and lazy; to slacken, relax efforts

松口气 **sūng-k'ŏu-ch'ì** to take a breathing spell, relax for a while

松松垮垮 **sūng-sūng-k'uă-k'uă** loose and leisurely

松松爽爽 **sūng-sūng-shuăng-shuăng** leisurely and agreeably, amiably

sŭng (sŏng)

1977 怂动 **sŭng-tùng** to incite, instigate, drive, egg on

怂恿 **sŭng-yŭng** to instigate, incite, aid and abet

1978 耸人听闻 **sŭng-jén-t'īng-wén** to attract attention; sensational, startling

sùng (sòng)

1979 送教上门 **sùng-chiào shàng-mén** to bring education to the door (a program in extremely remote and isolated areas to send teachers to isolated students)

送货上门 **sùng-huò shàng-mén** to deliver goods to the door (to serve people in remote and isolated areas)

送行 **sùng-hsíng** to see someone off, give a farewell send-off

送医上门 **sùng-ī shàng-mén** to bring medical care to the door

送别宴会 **sùng-piéh-yèn-huì** a farewell banquet

送书下乡 **sùng-shū hsià-hsiāng** to send books to the countryside (a form of mobile library activity)

1980 颂歌 **sùng-kō** a song of praise, hymn, ode

颂古非今 **sùng-kŭ-fēi-chīn** to praise the ancient and deny the modern

颂词 **sùng-tz'ú** a eulogy; a message of congratulations, praise, felicitations

颂扬 **sùng-yúng** to eulogize, praise, acclaim

szū (sī)

1981 丝织品 **szū-chīh-p'ĭn** woven silk goods

丝毫 **szū-háo** the slightest bit, just a

little, in the least

丝弦乐队 **szū-hsién-yuèh-tuì** a string orchestra

1982 司政机关 **szū-chèng chì-kuān** headquarters and political department agencies [of PLA units]

司法 **szū-fǎ** judicial, juridical; to administer the law

司法改革 **szū-fǎ-kǎi-kó** judicial reform

司法部 **szū-fǎ-pù** the Ministry of Justice (before 1956)

司令部 **szū-lìng-pù** a [military] headquarters (often figurative)

司令员 **szū-lìng-yuán** a commanding officer, commander

1983 私债 **szū-chài** private debt, personal loans

私产 **szū-ch'ǎn** private property

私方 **szū-fāng** the private side, private parties

私方人员 **szū-fāng jén-yuán** personnel representing the capitalist interest [in joint enterprise]

私下 **szū-hsià** in secret, privately, between individuals

私心 **szū-hsīn** selfishness, favoritism, egotism; having a selfish motive

私心杂念 **szū-hsīn-tsá-nièn** selfish ideas and motley calculations

私股 **szū-kǔ** private shares [in a corporation or joint enterprise]

私利 **szū-lì** private profit; self-interest; selfisness

私卖 **szū-mài** to sell for private gain, sell illicitly

私念 **szū-nièn** selfish ideas

私商 **szū-shāng** a private merchant; private business; a smuggler

私党 **szū-tǎng** a private clique, personal faction

私造 **szū-tsào** to manufacture illicitly

"私"字作怪 **szū-tzù tsò-kuài** the word "private" creates mischief

私自 **szū-tzù** privately, secretly, by stealth

私养猪 **szū-yǎng-chū** pigs raised privately

私营 **szū-yíng** to operate by private ownership; operated privately

私营经济 **szū-yíng-chīng-chì** the private economy

私营企业 **szū-yíng ch'ĭ-yèh** privately owned enterprises

私营工商业 **szū-yíng kūng-shāng-yèh** private industry and trade

私营财产重估评审委员会 **szū-yíng ts'ái-ch'ǎn ch'úng-kū p'íng-shěn wěi-yuán-huì** the Private Capital Assessment and Review Committee (in Shanghai, mid-1951)

私有制 **szū-yǔ-chǐh** the private ownership system, private ownership

私有观念 **szū-yǔ kuān-nièn** the concept of private ownership; the viewpoint of [favoring] private property

私有财产 **szū-yǔ ts'ái-ch'ǎn** privately owned property, private property

私欲 **szū-yù** individual desires, selfish wishes

1984 思潮 **szū-ch'áo** the prevailing trend of thought, an ideological tide

思想 **szū-hsiǎng** thought, thinking, ideas, ideology (usually refers specifically to ideological thought)

思想战线 **szū-hsiǎng-chàn-hsièn** the ideological front

思想障碍 **szū-hsiǎng chàng-ài** an ideological obstacle (an impediment to one's ideological development)

思想阵地 **szū-hsiǎng-chèn-tì** an ideological battlefield

思想基础 **szū-hsiǎng chī-ch'ǔ** ideological foundation

思想僵化 **szū-hsiǎng chiāng-huà** mental stagnation; to become rigid in one's thinking; ideological rigidification

思想交锋 **szū-hsiǎng chiāo-fēng** ideological combat

思想教育 **szū-hsiǎng chiào-yù** ideological education

思想解放 **szū-hsiǎng chiěh-fàng** ideological emancipation, ideological liberation

思想见面 **szū-hsiǎng chièn-mièn** an ideological discussion, an exchange of views

思想健康 **szū-hsiǎng chièn-k'āng** [one's] ideology is healthy; ideological soundness

思想建设 **szū-hsiǎng chièn-shè** ideological reconstruction (to propagate an ideology so that it becomes widely and thoroughly accepted)

思想转不过弯来 **szū-hsiǎng chuàn-pù-kuò-wān-lai** one's thinking cannot make the [correct] turn (one's ideology is still inadequate)

思想准备 **szū-hsiǎng chǔn-pèi** ideological preparation

思想翻腾开 **szū-hsiǎng fān-t'éng-k'āi** to think seriously and over and over again

思想方法 **szū-hsiǎng fāng-fǎ** way of thinking, manner of thought, ideological method

思想和业务双丰收 **szū-hsiǎng hó yèh-wù shuāng-fēng-shōu** a bumper harvest in both ideology and occupational work

思想回潮 **szū-hsiǎng huí-ch'áo** an

ideological resurgence

思想混乱 **szū-hsiǎng hùn-luàn** ideologically confused, confused thinking

思想红作风硬 **szū-hsiǎng-húng tsò-fēng-yìng** ideology red and style of work firm

思想修养 **szū-hsiǎng hsiū-yǎng** ideological cultivation, ideological nourishment

思想一致 **szū-hsiǎng ī-chìh** ideological unity, unified in ideology

思想认识 **szū-hsiǎng jèn-shíh** ideological awareness, ideological recognition

思想改造 **szū-hsiǎng-kǎi-tsào** thought reform, reform through ideology, ideological remolding (the ideological process and method of changing one's mental identity)

思想盖子 **szū-hsiǎng kài-tzu** an ideological lid, a lid on ideology (anything that hampers ideological growth)

思想感情 **szū-hsiǎng kǎn-ch'íng** thoughts and feelings

思想根源 **szū-hsiǎng kēn-yuán** ideological origins

思想革命化 **szū-hsiǎng kó-mìng-huà** to revolutionize ideology; the revolutionization of ideology

思想懒汉 **szū-hsiǎng lǎn-hàn** an ideological lazy fellow (one who refuses to think profoundly and go beyond superficiality)

思想领域 **szū-hsiǎng lǐng-yù** the ideological realm

思想落后於实际 **szū-hsiǎng lò-hòu yú shíh-chì** thinking lagging behind actual events

思想包袱 **szū-hsiǎng pāo-fu** an ideological burden, ideological restraint (such as old ideas that make it difficult to accept the new)

思想变红 **szū-hsiǎng pièn-húng** [one's] ideology turns red

思想不纯 **szū-hsiǎng pù-ch'ún** impurity in ideology, ideologically impure

思想不通 **szū-hsiǎng pù-t'ūng** not thought through; ideologically immature or wrong

思想, 生产双丰收 **szū-hsiǎng, shēng-ch'ǎn shuāng-fēng-shōu** a bumper harvest in both ideology and production

思想动向 **szū-hsiǎng tùng-hsiàng** an ideological trend

思想问题 **szū-hsiǎng-wèn-t'í** an ideological problem (an ideological deviation—not subject to punishment)

思想原则 **szū-hsiǎng yuán-tsé** an ideological principle, a basic tenet of thought

思想原则上的团结 **szū-hsiǎng yuán-tsé shàng-te t'uán-chiéh** unity on [the basis of] ideological principles

思考 **szū-k'ǎo** to think, meditate, deliberate; thinking; deliberation

思路 **szū-lù** a thought path, train of thought

思索 **szū-sǒ** to search one's mind, ponder, reflect

思维 **szū-wéi** to think, cogitate; thinking, thought

1985　斯里兰卡 **szū-lǐ-lán-k'ǎ** Sri Lanka [formerly called Ceylon]

斯诺 **szū-nò** [Edgar] Snow (1906–1972, American writer on China)

斯大林 **szū-tà-lín** Stalin (1879–1953)

斯德哥尔摩 **szū-té-kō-ěrh-mó** Stockholm

斯威士兰 **szū-wēi-shìh-lán** Swaziland

1986　厮杀 **szū-shā** to slaughter one another, hand-to-hand combat, a melee

1987　撕毁 **szū-huǐ** to tear and destroy, tear to shreds

szŭ (sĭ)

1988　死记硬背 **szŭ-chì yìng-pèi** to remember mechanically and recite rigidly (to learn without comprehension)

死角 **szŭ-chiǎo** a dead angle, a blind corner, a neglected area (a place that cannot easily be reached, e.g., out of the line of fire)

死气沉沉 **szŭ-ch'ì ch'én-ch'én** the dead atmosphere is murky (hopelessly gloomy; dull and despondent)

死情况 **szŭ-ch'íng-kuàng** dead circumstances (static conditions)

死去活来 **szŭ-ch'ù-huó-lái** to faint and revive (in extreme pain or distress, very painful)

死分活评 **szŭ-fēn huó-p'íng** fixed rates with flexible assessment (flexible application of fixed rates in work points according to individual circumstances)

死分死记 **szŭ-fēn szŭ-chì** fixed rates inflexibly recorded

死胡同 **szŭ-hú-t'ùng** blind alley (dead end)

死灰复燃 **szŭ-huī-fù-ján** dying ashes [can be] rekindled (take care that defeated forces do not make a comeback)

死心塌地 **szŭ-hsin t'ā-tì** to set the heart and tread on firm ground (wholeheartedly, unreservedly)

死信 **szŭ-hsìn** [postal] dead letters, undeliverable mail

死刑 **szŭ-hsíng** the death penalty,
capital punishment; to sentence to
death

死学死用 **szŭ-hsuéh szŭ-yùng** dead
study and dead use (to learn superficially and apply inflexibly)

死里逃生 **szŭ-lĭ-t'áo-shēng** to grasp life
out of death (a narrow escape from
death)

死路 **szŭ-lù** a dead road (blind alley;
dangerous way)

死灭 **szŭ-mièh** to perish, die; extinction, death

死难 **szŭ-nàn** to die for the country

死搬硬套 **szŭ-pān yìng-t'ào** a strait
jacket

死板 **szŭ-păn** rigid, fixed, unchangeable, monotonous

死板教条 **szŭ-păn chiào-t'iáo** rigid
dogma

死不改悔 **szŭ-pù-kăi-huĭ** to die rather
than reform or repent (incorrigible)

死伤累累 **szŭ-shāng lĕi-lĕi** the dead and
wounded in heaps (to suffer heavy
casualties)

死守 **szŭ-shŏu** to defend to the last man,
hold to the end, defend bitterly

死水 **szŭ-shuĭ** dead water, stagnant
water (often figurative)

死党 **szŭ-tăng** sworn followers, a gang
of confederates swearing to face
death together

死得其所 **szŭ-té-ch'í-sŏ** to die a worthy
death

死敌 **szŭ-tí** a mortal enemy

死读书, 读死书, 读书死 **szŭ-tú-shū, tú-
szŭ-shū, tú-shū-szŭ** to read books in a
dead way [without thought or relating
to practice], to read dead books, and
to do nothing but read until [one is]
dead

死对头 **szŭ-tuì-t'óu** an arch adversary,
deadly enemy

死套子 **szŭ-t'ào-tzu** rigid forms,
inflexible rules

死亡 **szŭ-wáng** to die, perish; death;
dead

死要面子 **szŭ-yào-mièn-tzu** to seek face
to the point of death (to preserve
one's face at all costs)

死硬 **szŭ-yìng** stubborn, unyielding,
intransigent, rigid, diehard, irrecon-
cilables

死硬派 **szŭ-yìng-p'ài** diehards, irrecon-
cilables

死有重于泰山, 有轻于鸿毛 **szŭ-yŭ chùng
yú t'ài-shān, yŭ ch'īng yú húng-máo**
some deaths are heavier than T'ai-
shan [and] some are lighter than
swan's down

szù (sì)

四旧 **szù-chiù** the Four Olds (thoughts,
culture, habits and customs)

四周 **szù-chōu** on all sides, all around,
in the vicinity

四专 **szù-chuān** the Four Specifics
(specific: responsibility; storage and
management; uses for each grain;
storage accounts)

四清 **szù ch'īng** the Four Clarifications
(generally associated with the
Socialist Education Movement,
1962–1966. There have been a
number of different formulations:
A. work points, accounts, properties,
granaries; B. politics, ideology,
economics, organization; C. accounts, revisionism, capitalism,
superstition; D. political stand, work
style, family background, financial
situation)

四清运动 **szù-ch'īng yùn-tùng** the Four
Clarifications [Clean-ups] Campaign
(also known as the Socialist Education Movement: *see* **szù-ch'īng**)

四权 **szù-ch'üán** the Four Powers (of
government, clan, gods, and
husband: referred to by Mao Tse-
tung in his report on peasant
conditions in Hunan)

四反 **szù-făn** the Four Antis (a movement in 1952, later expanded into the
wŭ-făn; the targets were: bribery,
cheating, exorbitant profits, tax
evasion)

四废 **szù-fèi** the Four Wastages (in
industry: materials, water, gas, and
heat)

四分五裂 **szù-fēn-wŭ-lièh** divided into
four and split into five (to fall apart
in discord, disintegrate)

四害 **szù-hài** the Four Pests (mosquitoes, flies, sparrows, and rats; in
1960, bedbugs replaced sparrows)

四好 **szù-hăo** the Four Goods (good
in: political and ideological work,
carrying out "three-good" activities,
perfecting organizational life, and
maintaining ties with the masses)

四好连队 **szù-hăo lién-tuì** a Four Good
[PLA] Company (good in: political
and ideological work; the three-
eight style of work, military training,
and arrangement of daily life)

四好标兵 **szù hăo piāo-pīng** a Four
Good Example (*see above*)

四合一运动场 **szù-hó-ī yùn-tùng-ch'ăng**
a Four-in-One Athletic Field (serving
for: athletic exercise, military drill,

public meetings, and the drying of grain)

四化 **szù-huà** the Four Transformations or "-izations" (A. in commune organization: organization militarized, work martialized, individual living collectivized, management democratized; B. in agriculture: mechanization, electrification, irrigation, and "chemicalization")

四红运动 **szù-húng yùn-tùng** the Four Red Movement (to make every day, every ten-day period, every month, and the whole production area prosperous)

四新 **szù-hsīn** the Four New [Things] (a Cultural Revolution slogan calling for new: thought, culture, customs, and habits—to replace the **szù-chiù**)

四·一二 **szù-ī-èrh** April 12 (the date in 1927 of the suppression by Chiang Kai-shek of the Communist-led labor unions in Shanghai)

四个反党集团 **szù-ko fǎn-tǎng chí-t'uán** the four anti-Party cliques (of: Kao Kang, P'eng Chen, Liu Shao-ch'i, and Lin Piao)

四个一样 **szù-ko ī-yàng** the Four Sames (a work style urged for factory workers and staff, with varying versions. A. To work the same: day or night; in good or bad weather; with or without supervision; and whether or not the product is to be inspected. B. To work the same: whether or not there is leadership; whether working alone or in a group; whether conditions are good or bad; and whether one has been in the majority or minority)

四个关系 **szù-ko kuān-hsi** the Four Relations (in the PLA, between: weapons and men; professional and political work; administrative and ideological work; bookish ideology and living ideology)

四个面向 **szù-ko mièn-hsiàng** the Four Face-Towards (face toward: the rural areas; factories and mines; national borders; and the basic levels)

四个第一 **szù-ko tì-ī** the Four Firsts (enunciated by Lin Piao in 1960: the human factor, political work, ideological work and living ideology)

四个存在 **szù-ko ts'ún-tsài** the Four Continued Existences (1. class, class contradictions, and class struggle; 2. struggle between the socialist and capitalist roads; 3. the danger of capitalist restoration; 4. the threat of imperialism and modern revisionism)

四固定 **szù kù-tìng** the Four Fixeds (manpower, land, farm tools, and draft animals: elements of production fixed in production teams)

四快 **szù-k'uài** the Four Quicks (harvesting, selecting, drying, and selling)

四快一慢 **szù-k'uài ī-màn** the Four Quicks and One Slow (quick: in preparation, advance, exploitation of advantages gained, and pursuit; slow [cautious] in ordering a general attack)

四快一慢战法 **szù-k'uài ī-màn chàn-fǎ** the Four-Quicks One-Slow Military Tactics (quick in: approach, pursuit, exploiting success, and preparing encirclement; slow in: undertaking a general attack—which must be deliberately and carefully planned)

四类分子 **szù-lèi fèn-tzǔ** the Four [Bad] Elements (landlords, rich peasants, counter-revolutionaries, and local bad elements—such as thieves and criminals)

四留 **szù-liú** the Four Reserves (the four kinds of grain reserves to be held by peasants: individual rations, seeds, fodder, and emergency grain. From 1955 regulations)

四面楚歌 **szù-mièn-ch'ǔ-kō** on four sides the songs of Ch'u (to be surrounded by the enemy, in desperate straits)

四面八方 **szù-mièn-pā-fāng** the four sides and eight directions (everywhere, in all directions)

四不清 **szù pù-ch'īng** the Four Uncleans (*see* **szù-ch'īng**)

四不清干部 **szù-pù-ch'īng kàn-pù** Four-Unclean Cadres (cadres criticized in the **szù-ch'īng** campaign)

四旁植树 **szù-p'áng chíh-shù** to plant trees on the Four Besides (beside villages, homes, roads, and waters [canals and ponds])

四平八稳 **szù-p'íng-pā-wěn** four level and eight stable (safe and secure in every respect)

四史 **szù-shǐh** the Four Histories (a movement commenced in 1959, also known as the **sān-shǐh,** to collect historical materials to keep alive memories of pre-Liberation. Contents of the four histories varied among different groups, e.g., for peasants: family, village, brigade, and commune)

四算 **szù-suàn** the Four Plannings

(rural production teams should draw up plans for: household grain requirements and income; strengthening production; administration of labor; and management of finances)

四大 **szù-tà** the Four Greats (great contending, blooming, big character posters, and debate—the four methods for carrying out "struggle by reasoning")

四大家族 **szù-tà-chiā-tsú** the four great clans (the four families associated with the leadership of the KMT: Chiang, Soong, K'ung, and Ch'en)

四大古典小说 **szù-tà kǔ-tiěn hsiǎo-shuō** the four great classical novels (*Hunglou meng*, *San-kuo yen-i*, *Shui-hu chuan*, and *Hsi-yu chi*)

四大观点 **szù tà-kuān-tiěn** the Four Great Viewpoints (of class, physical work, the masses, and dialectical materialism)

四大自由 **szù-tà-tzù-yú** the Four Great Freedoms (Liu Shao-ch'i is alleged, during the early 1950s, to have promised peasants the freedoms to: engage in usury, hire labor, sell land, and run private enterprises)

四大文件 **szù tà wén-chièn** the Four Great Documents (by Mao: 1. "Talks at the Yenan Forum on Literature and Art" [May 1942]; 2. "On the Correct Handling of Contradictions Among the People" [February 1957]; 3. his speech at the national CCP Propaganda Work Conference [March 1957]; 4. "On New Democracy" [January 1940])

四大洋 **szù-tà-yáng** the four oceans (Atlantic, Pacific, Indian, and Artic)

四斗精神 **szù-tòu-chīng-shén** the Four Struggles Spirit (against heaven, earth, class enemies, and incorrect ideology)

四堵墙 **szù-tǔ-ch'iáng** four walls (criticizing schools that within their four walls are isolated from society)

四体不勤, 五谷不分 **szù-t'ǐ-pù ch'ín, wǔ-kǔ-pù-fēn** the arms and legs unwilling to toil and unable to differentiate the five grains (useless intellectuals)

四条汉子 **szù-t'iáo hàn-tzu** the four fellows (a pejorative reference to Chou Yang, Hsia Yen, T'ien Han, and Yang Han-sheng who were attacked in the Cultural Revolution)

四同 **szù-t'úng** the Four Togethers (in the commune movement, the cadres were enjoined to eat, live, labor, and consult with the peasants)

四同干部 **szù-t'úng-kàn-pù** a Four-Together Cadre (one who eats, lives, works, and consults with the masses)

四同作风 **szù-t'úng-tsò-fēng** the Four-Together Work Style (*see* **szù-t'úng**)

四统 **szù-t'ǔng** the Four Centralizations (a grain policy adopted in 1960 for centralized administration of: granaries, allocation, preservation, and processing)

四早 **szù-tsǎo** the Four Earlys (a slogan in rice growing calling for early [prompt] action to: weed, fertilize, control pests, and transport sprouts)

四组一队战法 **szù-tsǔ-ī-tuì chàn-fǎ** the military tactic of four elements in one unit (the use of a special combat team consisting of a firepower element, demolition element, assault infantry, and supporting elements)

四自创业 **szù-tzù-ch'uàng-yèh** the Four Self-Undertaken Enterprises (in connection with the local development of medicine: to gather, plant, and raise medicinal herbs; and to manufacture them into medicinal preparations)

四参加 **szù-ts'ān-chiā** the Four Participations (an urban movement in 1965 calling for participation in: political study; labor training; neighborhood [lane] work; and cultural and physical activities)

四无 **szù-wú** the Four No-Mores (no more flies, mosquitoes, rats, and sparrows: *see* **szù-hài**)

1990 似是而非 **szù-shìh-érh-fēi** seemingly true but actually false

1991 伺机 **szù-chī** to watch for a favorable opportunity, to bide one's time

伺 **szù**: *see also* **tz'ù**

1992 饲料 **szù-liào** fodder, animal food

饲料厂 **szù-liào ch'ǎng** a factory for animal feed

饲料谷物 **szù-liào kǔ-wù** feed grain

饲料作物 **szù-liào tsò-wù** fodder crops

饲养场 **szù-yǎng-ch'ǎng** feeding and raising farms (livestock and poultry farms)

饲养牲畜 **szù-yǎng shēng-ch'ù** animal husbandry, livestock breeding

饲养员 **szù-yǎng-yuán** stockman, herdsman, keeper, feeder

1993 肆意挥霍 **szù-ì-huī-huò** to squander recklessly

肆意歪曲 **szù-ì-wāi-ch'ū** to wantonly distort

肆无忌惮 **szù-wú-chì-tàn** inconsiderate,

audacious, unprincipled; to fear
nothing, act outrageously

tā (dā)

1994　配搭 **tā-p'èi** to match, mate, join as a
partner

tá (dá)

1995　达成协议 **tá-ch'éng hsiéh-ì** to reach an
agreement, achieve accord
达尔文主义 **tá-ĕrh-wén-chŭ-ì**
Darwinism
达荷美 **tá-hó-mĕi** [Republic of]
Dahomey
达喀尔 **tá-k'ā-ĕrh** Dakar [Senegal]
达赖喇嘛 **tá-lài lǎ-ma** the Dalai Lama
(Tibetan leader in exile)
达累斯萨拉姆 **tá-lèi-szū sà-lā-mǔ** Dar
es Salaam [Tanzania]
达斡尔族 **tá-wò-ĕrh-tsú** the Tahur
people (a minority in Heilungkiang
province: population 50,000 as of
1957)
1996　答卷 **tá-chüàn** a completed examination
paper
答复 **tá-fù** to reply, answer, respond;
an answer
答谢宴会 **tá-hsièh-yèn-huì** a banquet to
thank (usually a formal dinner by
a state guest to return the courtesy of
entertainment)
答辩 **tá-pièn** to speak in self-defense,
answer an attack; a rejoinder
1997　鞑靼 **tá-tá** Tartars (a general term for
the nomads of north and central
Asia)

tǎ (dǎ)

1998　打招呼 **tǎ chāo-hu** to greet a person,
bid welcome
打折扣 **tǎ ché-k'òu** to offer a discount,
at a discount
打着红旗反红旗 **tǎ-che húng-ch'í fǎn
húng-ch'í** to raise red flags to oppose
the Red Flag (to "don the cloak of
Marxism-Leninism and the Thought
of Mao Tse-tung to oppose Marxism-
Leninism and the Thought of Mao
Tse-tung")
打针 **tǎ-chēn** to inject [medicine or
drugs], to give an injection
打正规仗 **tǎ chèng-kuēi-chàng** to wage
a conventional war
打击一大片，保护一小撮 **tǎ-chī ī tà-p'ièn,
pǎo-hù ī hsiǎo-ts'ō** to hit hard at the
many to protect the handful (slogan
of the Cultural Revolution devised

for reactionary cadres accusing them
of inviting the masses to attack
cadres indiscriminately in order to
protect their own interests)
打击面 **tǎ-chī-mièn** scope of attack,
area of attack
打击歪风 **tǎ-chī wāi-fēng** to attack
unhealthy tendencies, eliminate
improper social trends
打家劫舍 **tǎ-chiā-chiéh-shè** to break
into a family and plunder the house
打交道 **tǎ chiāo-tào** to associate with,
have intercourse with, deal with
打劫 **tǎ-chiéh** to commit robbery,
plunder, rob, hold up
打歼灭战 **tǎ chiēn-mièh chàn** to fight an
extermination battle, fight a war of
annihilation (to concentrate one's
efforts in order to complete a task
thoroughly and effectively)
打井 **tǎ-chǐng** to dig or drill a well [for
water]
打主意 **tǎ chǔ-ì** to evolve an idea,
devise a course of action, plan what
to do
打肿脸充胖子 **tǎ-chǔng-liěn ch'ǔng-
p'àng-tzu** to slap one's face until it
swells in order to pretend to be a
fat man (a hollow pretense at being
a "big shot")
打中要害 **tǎ-chùng yào-hài** to hit a
vulnerable spot (to hit home)
打成反革命分子 **tǎ ch'éng fǎn-kó-mìng
fèn-tzǔ** to make someone into a
counter-revolutionary [unsupported
by the facts] (the implication is that
the person accused may not have
been, nor be inclined to become,
actually counter-revolutionary)
打成一片 **tǎ-ch'éng ī-p'ièn** to knead
into one, unite into a single whole,
combine into a single whole
打气 **tǎ-ch'ì** to fill with air, pump up,
inflate (to encourage, stimulate)
打气壮胆 **tǎ-ch'ì-chuàng-tǎn** to
embolden
打强心针 **tǎ ch'iáng-hsīn-chēn** to make
an injection of heart stimulant (to
give a "shot in the arm")
打前站 **tǎ-ch'ién-chàn** to establish a
forward position, fight in the front
line (to serve as a forerunner, to be a
vanguard)
打翻 **tǎ-fān** to overthrow, tip over
打夯 **tǎ-hāng** to tamp earth [with a
large stone weight raised by ropes],
stamp, pound
打回老家去 **tǎ-huí lǎo-chiā ch'ù** Fight
Back to Our Old Home! (the slogan
of the Manchurian exiles after 1931;

now used broadly in the sense of "never give up")

打昏 **tǎ-hūn** to beat [a person] unconscious

打下基础 **tǎ-hsià chī-ch'ǔ** to lay down a foundation

打响 **tǎ-hsiǎng** to fire [a shot] (to produce an effect, have a result)

打小算盘 **tǎ hsiǎo-suàn-p'an** to work a small abacus (to concern oneself with personal advantage and superficial trivialities)

打忧 **tǎ-jǎo** to disturb, bother, trouble

打入冷宫 **tǎ-jù lěng-kūng** to put [a queen or concubine no longer in the emperor's favor] in the cold palace [confinement] (to put someone on the back shelf)

打入十八层地狱 **tǎ-jù shíh-pā-ts'éng tì-yù** to be put into the eighteenth level of hell (to be plunged into the depths)

打开局面 **tǎ-k'āi chú-mièn** to open up a [new] prospect (to break new ground, embark on a new course)

打开缺口 **tǎ-k'āi ch'üēh-k'ǒu** to make a breach, drive a wedge

打开心窍 **tǎ-k'āi hsīn-ch'iào** to open up the heart orifices (to open up one's mind)

打垮 **tǎ-k'uǎ** to break down, crush, smash

打雷不下雨 **tǎ-léi pù-hsià-yǔ** it thunders but does not rain (to go through the motions without any real accomplishment)

打落水狗 **tǎ lò-shuǐ-kǒu** hit the dog in the water (do not take any pity on dangerous enemies: see lò-shuǐ-kǒu)

打乱 **tǎ-luàn** to throw into confusion

打马虎眼 **tǎ mǎ-hu-yěn** to exploit the carelessness of others, deceive, trick

打埋伏 **tǎ mái-fú** to prepare an ambush, conceal oneself, keep something in reserve

打扮 **tǎ-pàn** to make up, dress up, "prettify"

打报告 **tǎ-pào-kào** to make a report, render a report [to higher authorities]

打抱不平 **tǎ-pào pù-p'íng** to take up cudgels against injustice, be the champion of the oppressed

打漂亮仗 **tǎ p'iào-liàng-chàng** to fight a smart battle (to complete a task efficiently and economically)

打破纪录 **tǎ-p'ò chì-lù** to break the record

打破框框 **tǎ-p'ò chiù-k'uāng-k'uang** to smash old frames (to free oneself from old standards and restraints)

打破常规 **tǎ-p'ò ch'áng-kuēi** to shatter normal standards (to break with precedent)

打破沉寂 **tǎ-p'ò ch'én-chì** to break a dead silence (a sudden change in a situation)

打上烙印 **tǎ-shàng lào-yìn** to stamp with a brand (to brand, label)

打手 **tǎ-shǒu** a thug, man employed for violence, "bouncer"

打死老虎 **tǎ szǔ-lǎo-hǔ** beating a dead tiger (a term deriding targets selected for criticism by the work teams in the early phase of the Cultural Revolution)

打倒孔家店 **tǎ-tǎo k'ǔng-chiā-tièn** down with the shop of Confucius! (i.e., the Confucianists)

打得准，开得动，联得上 **tǎ-te-chǔn, k'āi-te-tùng, lién-te-shàng** to shoot [artillery] accurately, maintain mobility, and keep communications (a PLA slogan)

打得火热 **tǎ-te-huǒ-jè** to be heated up to a fiery pitch (to flirt ardently, be intimate with)

打得落花流水 **tǎ-te lò-huā liú-shuǐ** to beat [until it is like] flower petals fallen into flowing water (to beat the enemy completely beyond any hope of recovery)

打掉官气 **tǎ-tiào kuān-ch'ì** to strike off bureacratic airs

打短 **tǎ-tuǎn** to work on a short-term basis, do temporary work, work for a daily wage

打断 **tǎ-tuàn** to interrupt, break off, discontinue, cut short

打铁趁热 **tǎ-t'iěh chèn-jè** to strike while the iron is hot (to grasp an opportunity)

打听 **tǎ-t'īng** to inquire, ask, question, investigate

打退堂鼓 **tǎ t'uì-t'áng-kǔ** to beat the drum for leaving [the magistrate's] hall (to give up a task before completion)

打通思想 **tǎ-t'ūng szū-hsiǎng** to make an ideological breakthrough, break through a mental block, bring someone to correct ideology

打砸抢抄抓 **tǎ tsá ch'iǎng ch'āo chuā** beating, smashing, looting, house-raiding, and kidnapping (acts of violence which the Red Guards were warned not to commit)

打自己嘴巴 **tǎ tzǔ-chǐ-tsuǐ-pa** to slap one's own face (to contradict oneself)

打草站 **tǎ-ts'ǎo-chàn** a haying station

打草惊蛇 **tǎ-ts'ǎo chīng-shé** to beat the

grass and frighten the snake (to cause undesired agitation)

打错算盘 **tǎ-ts'ò suàn-p'an** to make an error on the abacus (to miscalculate, misjudge a situation)

打网 **tǎ-wǎng** to cast a net

打掩护 **tǎ yěn-hù** to put up a protective screen, lay down protective fire, cover, screen

打赢 **tǎ-yíng** to win [a law suit, etc.]

打硬仗 **tǎ yìng-chàng** to fight a relentless war, to wage all-out war (also figurative)

打游击 **tǎ yú-chī** to fight as a guerrilla (may be applied humorously to the improvization of tactics or dependence on one's wits)

打游击战 **tǎ yú-chī-chàn** to wage guerrilla war

tà (dà)

大寨 **tà-chài** Tachai (a place in Shansi and a famous production brigade, now a model for agriculture)

大寨精神 **tà-chài chīng-shén** the Tachai spirit (a revolutionary spirit of hard work and self-reliance exhibited by the Tachai Production Brigade in wasteland reclamation and agricultural development in a poverty-stricken setting)

大战役 **tà chàn-ì** a major battle, large campaign (may refer to a production project mobilizing great numbers and requiring a considerable time for completion)

大战略部署 **tà chàn-luèh pù-shǔ** the Great Strategic Plan (Mao Tse-tung's plan during the Cultural Revolution for revolutionary committees throughout the country)

大张旗鼓 **tà-chāng-ch'í-kǔ** to make a big display of banners and drums (with great fanfare)

大集体, 小自由 **tà chí-t'ǐ, hsiǎo-tzù-yú** the large collective and small freedoms (within the commune the peasant enjoys his private plot; individual freedoms depend on the collective)

大计 **tà-chì** a great plan (policy of a state, national plans or programs)

大将 **tà-chiàng** senior general [Chinese Army and Air Force]; senior admiral [Chinese Navy]; the star of a team, a champion

大街小巷 **tà-chiēh hsiǎo-hsiàng** streets and alleys, main roads and small streets

大捷 **tà-chiéh** a great victory, triumph

大检修 **tà-chiěn-hsiū** a major overhaul, general repairs

大致 **tà-chìh** on the whole, roughly, generally, with only a few exceptions

大惊小怪 **tà-chīng hsiǎo-kuài** to be alarmed at a trifle (much to do about nothing)

大专院校 **tà-chuān yuàn-hsiào** universities and colleges

大中小结合 **tà-chūng-hsiǎo chiéh-hó** to coordinate large, medium, and small [scale enterprises]

大众 **tà-chùng** the people, masses, public; all, everyone

大众化 **tà-chùng-huà** to popularize; popularization

大众文学 **tà-chùng wén-hsuéh** Popular Literature (a slogan used by Lu Hsün in the 1930s and which by 1966 had come to be praised as opposed to **kuó-fáng-wén-hsuéh**)

大众语 **tà-chùng-yǔ** language of the masses (a term popularized by left-wing writers in the 1930s)

大车 **tà-ch'ē** a big cart (a two-wheeled cart pulled by animals or men)

大气污染 **tà-ch'ì wū-jǎn** air pollution

大吃大喝 **tà-ch'īh tà-hō** big eating and drinking (over-eating and drinking—extravagant feasting)

大庆 **tà-ch'ìng** Taching (a famous oil field in Heilungkiang, now a national model for industry)

大庆精神 **tà-ch'ìng chīng-shén** the Taching spirit (the pioneering, hard-working, "overcome-any-obstacle" spirit of the Taching oil field workers)

大庆油田 **tà-ch'ìng yú-t'ién** the Taching oil field

大秋作物 **tà-ch'iū-tsò-wù** late autumn crops

大处着眼, 小处着手 **tà-ch'ù chó-yěn, hsiǎo-ch'ù chó-shǒu** with big issues one must start from a viewpoint and with small problems one must start by putting a hand [to them]

大吹大擂 **tà-ch'uī-tà-lèi** big blowing [the horns] and beating the drums (boasting, bragging; to boast)

大局 **tà-chú** the overall situation, general situation, national interests

大举进攻 **tà-chǔ chìn-kūng** to mount a major attack, attack in force

大军 **tà-chūn** a large army (may be any large body of people drafted and organized to serve a specific function in the socialist revolution and reconstruction)

大权在握 **tà-ch'üán tsài-wò** great

power within one's grasp; to hold great power

大而无当 **tà-érh-wú-tàng** large but not practical, big but not suitable

大发战争横财 **tà-fā chàn-chēng hèng-ts'ái** to reap large windfall war profits

大发雷霆 **tà-fā léi-t'íng** to raise a burst of thunder (to fly into a rage)

大放 **tà-fàng** to issue forth, bloom luxuriantly; a great blooming (usually refers to the "great blooming" of the Hundred Flowers Movement)

大放厥词 **tà-fàng chüéh-tz'ú** to let forth a lot of big talk, talk wildly (usually satirical)

大费唇舌 **tà-fèi ch'ún-shé** a great expenditure of lip and tongue (a long harangue)

大分化 **tà-fēn-huà** a great breaking up, separation, polarization [of the world situation]

大风浪中的考验 **tà-fēng-làng chūng te k'ǎo-yèn** the test of stormy times, a testing by storm

大幅度增长 **tà fú-tù tsēng-chǎng** a very broad increase [or growth]

大海航行靠舵手 **tà-hǎi-háng-hsíng k'ào tò-shǒu** sailing the seas depends on the helmsman

大汉族主义 **tà-hàn-tsú-chǔ-ì** Han chauvinism

大好 **tà-hǎo** very good, excellent, extremely favorable

大好局面 **tà-hǎo-chǘ-mièn** an excellent situation, extremely favorable situation

大好形势 **tà-hǎo-hsíng-shìh** an exceedingly favorable situation, promising outlook

大好时机 **tà-hǎo-shíh-chī** a very favorable opportunity, the best time

大后方 **tà-hòu-fāng** the great rear area (the country supporting the fighting front)

大呼隆 **tà-hū-lúng** a great flourish (implies frenzied activity without a proper long-term plan)

大话 **tà-huà** big talk, boasting, exaggeration

大红匾 **tà-húng-piěn** a large red [congratulatory] tablet with an inscription

大西洋宪章 **tà-hsī-yáng hsièn-chāng** the Atlantic Charter (1941)

大西洋公约 **tà-hsī-yáng kūng-yuēh** the Atlantic Pact (setting up NATO, 1949)

大喜若狂 **tà-hsǐ jò-k'uáng** almost insane with joy

大小强弱 **tà-hsiǎo ch'iáng-jò** size and strength

大校 **tà-hsiào** senior colonel [Chinese Army and Air Force]; senior captain [Chinese Navy]

大显身手 **tà-hsiěn-shēn-shǒu** to capacity (to do something to one's utmost capacity)

大兴水利 **tà-hsīng shuǐ-lì** large-scale water conservancy work

大兴土木 **tà-hsīng t'ǔ-mù** much construction of buildings

大行政区 **tà hsíng-chèng-ch'ǖ** the Great Administrative Regions (the six major administrative areas into which China was divided from 1950–1954)

大型企业 **tà-hsíng-ch'ǐ-yèh** large [scale] enterprises

大型掩护艇 **tà-hsíng yěn-hù-t'ǐng** landing ship support craft

大选 **tà-hsuǎn** a general election

大学大比 **tà-hsuéh tà-pǐ** great learning and great emulation; to study and emulate vigorously [by comparing oneself with the more advanced]

大雪封山 **tà-hsuěh fēng-shān** heavy snows have closed [the roads in the] mountains

大雪封地 **tà-hsuěh fēng-tì** heavy snows have sealed the land, snows cover the fields

大义凛然 **tà-ì-lǐn-ján** unswervingly to maintain righteousness

大意 **tà-ì** the gist, general content, general idea; careless, heedless

大人民呼拉尔 **tà jén-mín hū-lā-ěrh** Great People's Hural (the governing assembly of the People's Republic of Mongolia)

大人物 **tà jén-wù** a great man, important personage, VIP

大改组 **tà kǎi-tsǔ** a great change, major realignment [of the world situation]

大干苦干 **tà-kàn k'ǔ-kàn** to work hard with added vigor

大纲 **tà-kāng** a general program; an outline, summary; synopsis

大港油田 **tà-kǎng yú-t'ién** the Takang oil field (discovered in 1974 in North China)

大搞 **tà-kǎo** to do things on a large scale, do something in a big way

大搞群众运动 **tà-kǎo ch'ún-chùng-yùn-tùng** to start a full-scale mass movement, organize extensive mass movements

大搞农田基本建设 **tà-kǎo núng-t'ién**

chǐ-pěn-chièn-shè to engage in large-scale basic construction of fields

大规模 **tà kuēi-mó** large-scale, massive, extensive

大公报 **tà-kūng-pào** the *Ta-kung pao* (a daily newspaper published in Tientsin with separate editions in Shanghai and Hong Kong)

大公无私 **tà-kūng wú-szū** honest and without self-interest, all for the public good without selfish considerations

大功告成 **tà-kūng kào-ch'éng** to have brought a major task to successful completion, the success is complete

大国主义 **tà-kuó-chǔ-ì** Great Power chauvinism (contraction of: **tà-kuó-shā-wén-chǔ-ì**)

大国主宰世界命运 **tà-kuó chǔ-tsǎi shìh-chièh mìng-yùn** the Great Powers control the world's destiny

大国霸权 **tà-kuó pà-ch'üán** Great Power hegemony

大国沙民主义 **tà-kuó shā-wén-chǔ-ì** Great Power chauvinism

大砍 **tà-k'ǎn** to reduce drastically; a sharp reduction

大快人心 **tà-k'uài jén-hsīn** to lift the hearts of all, greatly to please the people

大块文章 **tà-k'uài wén-chāng** a major treatise, a large piece of writing (may be figurative)

大老粗 **tà-lǎo-ts'ū** a cloddish fellow, a big hick

大老爷 **tà-lǎo-yéh** sire, lord (formerly a form of address of common people toward an official: now used sarcastically)

大理石 **tà-lǐ-shíh** stone from Tali [Yunnan] (any marble)

大力 **tà-lì** strenuous effort, great effort, great force

大力支持 **tà-lì chǐh-ch'íh** to support energetically

大力普及 **tà-lì p'ǔ-chí** to popularize with great vigor

大立 **tà-lì** to establish in a big way, set up on a broad scale

大利大干 **tà-lì tà-kàn** [to see a] great benefit [and] undertake in a big way

大量生产 **tà-liàng shēng-ch'ǎn** mass production

大联合 **tà-lién-hó** a great alliance (especially used during the Cultural Revolution)

大联合誓师大会 **tà-lién-hó shìh-shīh-tà-huì** great-alliance pledge assemblies (among students especially during the fall of 1967)

大陆 **tà-lù** continent, mainland (usually refers to mainland China)

大陆棚 **tà-lù-p'éng** the continental shelf

大论战 **tà-lùn-chàn** a great polemic, great debate

大马士革 **tà-mǎ-shìh-kó** Damascus [Syria]

大忙季节 **tà-máng chì-chiéh** the busiest season (in agriculture, usually means summer or autumn)

大帽子压下来 **tà mào-tzu yā-hsia lai** to press down by the big hat (to invoke principles or pressures greater than required by the task at hand)

大面积增产运动 **tà mièn-chī tsēng-ch'ǎn yùn-tùng** the movement for increasing yields on large areas (going from experimental tracts to large-scale yield improvement)

大民主 **tà-mín-chǔ** Great Democracy (freedoms mentioned by Lin Piao's speech to the Red Guards on November 3, 1966, including: free expression of views, use of big character posters, exchange of revolutionary experience, supervision and criticism of all levels of the Party and government)

大民族主义 **tà-mín-tsú-chǔ-ì** nationalism of the major people, nationalism of the ethnic majority

大名鼎鼎 **tà-míng-tǐng-tǐng** a name known far and wide, very famous, celebrated

大鸣大放 **tà-míng tà-fàng** very loudly and very openly, a great blooming and great contending (free expression of opinion, unlimited criticism)

大鸣, 大放, 大争, 大辩 **tà-míng, tà-fàng, tà-chēng, tà-pièn** to air one's views, contend and debate to the fullest extent

大难临头 **tà-nàn-lín-t'óu** a great calamity is close to one's head; trouble is imminent

大年 **tà-nién** a big year [for the harvest of fruit]

大把头 **tà-pǎ-t'óu** the big boss (a labor contractor or broker in the old society)

大办民兵师 **tà-pàn mín-pīng-shīh** energetically to organize militia into divisions

大办农业, 大办粮食 **tà-pàn núng-yèh, tà-pàn liáng-shíh** to tackle energetically agriculture and foodstuff production

大棒政策 **tà-pàng chèng-ts'è** a "big stick" policy

大本营 **tà-pěn-yíng** a headquarters, base camp

大变动 tà pièn-tùng a great change, upheaval, cataclysm

大辩论 tà pièn-lùn a great debate, momentous controversy, vigorous discussions on basic principles

大兵团作战 tà-pīng-t'uán tsò-chàn warfare by large army corps (now figurative—the mobilization of large numbers of people to perform a task)

大批 tà-p'ī a large group; heavy criticism (see below)

大批判 tà p'ī-p'àn great criticism, vigorous criticism on a broad scale

大批生产 tà-p'ī shēng-ch'ǎn mass production

大平板车 tà p'íng-pǎn-ch'ē a heavy-duty flat-bed truck

大破私字，大立公字 tà-p'ò szū-tzù, tà-lì kūng-tzù destroy the word "self" and set up the word "public"

大破大立 tà-p'ò tà-lì great destruction and great construction

大扫除 tà-sǎo-ch'ú a big sweeping-out, housecleaning

大杀风景 tà-shā-fēng-chǐng to ruin the view (to disrupt the pleasant mood of a group)

大厦 tà-shà a large building

大少爷作风 tà-shào-yéh tsò-fēng the airs of a young lord (the manners of a spoiled brat)

大赦 tà-shè a general amnesty

大生产运动 tà shēng-ch'ǎn yùn-tùng the Great Production Movement (1943)

大声疾呼 tà-shēng chí-hū to shout loudly in desperation (a clarion call to warn of danger)

大牲畜 tà shēng-ch'ù big livestock (i.e., cattle and horses)

大师 tà-shīh a great teacher, master

大施威风 tà-shīh wēi-fēng to make a show of strength

大使 tà-shǐh an ambassador, diplomatic envoy of the highest rank

大使外交关系 tà-shǐh-chí wài-chiāo-kuān-hsi diplomatic relations at the ambassadorial level

大使馆 tà-shǐh-kuǎn an embassy

大事记 tà-shìh-chì a chronicle of important events

大事宣扬 tà shìh hsuān-yáng to give very wide publicity, play up, ballyhoo

大事铺张 tà-shìh p'ū-chāng to put on a lavish show, make much of a little; an exaggerated fanfare

大事做不来，小事又不做 tà-shìh tsò-pù-lái, hsiǎo-shìh yù-pù-tsò incapable of of handling an important job and yet refusing to do a minor job

大势 tà-shìh a general trend of events, overall situation

大势已去 tà-shìh ǐ-ch'ù the situation has gone, the trend of events has passed by (the situation is hopeless)

大势已定 tà-shìh ǐ-tìng the trend has become fixed (the conclusion is already determined, a foregone conclusion)

大势所趋 tà-shìh-sǒ-ch'ǚ the [irreversible] tendency of the situation (the die is cast)

大是大非 tà-shìh tà-fēi a major right and major wrong (a major dispute on basic political principles)

大手大脚 tà-shǒu tà-chiǎo [with] big hands and big feet (to do things carelessly; clumsy)

大书特书 tà-shū t'è-shū to write voluminously and elaborately on (to emphasize, play up, make an issue of)

大树特树 tà-shù t'è-shù to plant in a large and particular way (usually refers to efforts at increasing one's image or the authority of one's ideas)

大水冲倒龙王庙 tà-shuǐ ch'ūng-tǎo lúng-wáng-miào the flood has destroyed the temple of the Dragon King (the first line of a proverb followed by ǐ-chiā pù jèn-shíh ǐ-chiā jén 一家不认识一家人—people of the same family do not recognize each other; the first part is used to convey the meaning of the second part)

大肆 tà-szù dissolute, extravagant, reckless, excessive; great; to make a great display of

大肆叫器 tà-szù-chiào-hsiāo to set up a great clamor, allege vociferously

大肆泛滥 'tà-szù-fàn-làn an overwhelming inundation, great flood

大肆宣扬 tà-szù hsuān-yáng to preach unscrupulously, propagandize without restraint, disseminate recklessly

大肆蹂躏 tà-szù jóu-lìn to overrun heedlessly, lay waste recklessly, trample on without restraint

大肆鼓吹 tà-szù kǔ-ch'uī to praise loudly, promote extravagantly

大肆攻击 tà-szù kūng-chī to make a serious attack

大肆污蔑 tà-szù wū-mièh to slander violently, slander indiscriminately

大肆游说 tà-szù yú-shuì to go about energetically as a spokesman of (to engage in extensive lobbying)

大打矿山之战 tà-tǎ k'uàng-shān-chīh-chàn to fight vigorously the war of the mines

大胆革新 tà-tǎn kó-hsīn to innovate boldly

大胆实践 **tà-tăn shíh-chièn** to practice boldly

大敌当前 **tà-tí tāng-ch'ién** the great enemy confronts us

大抵 **tà-tǐ** for the most part, generally speaking, in most cases

大地 **tà-tì** the good earth, great land; the territory of the nation; China

大多数 **tà-tō-shù** majority, great majority, overwhelming majority

大都 **tà-tōu** the most, for the most part, probably, almost

大豆 **tà-tòu** the soy bean (the same as the **huáng-tòu**)

大队 **tà-tuì** a large team; a production brigade [in a commune]

大东亚共荣圈 **tà-tūng-yà kùng-júng-ch'ǖan** the Great East Asia Co-Prosperity Sphere (a propaganda slogan of the Japanese in the 1930s and early 1940s)

大动荡 **tà-tùng-tàng** great instability [of the world situation]

大踏步 **tà t'à-pù** great strides; to make great strides

大谈特谈 **tà-t'án-t'è-t'án** to talk voluminously and specifically

大体 **tà-t'ǐ** in principle, in essence; in general, on the whole; generally

大田生产 **tà-t'ién shēng-ch'ǎn** large-field production, production utilizing large fields

大田栽培 **tà-t'ién tsāi-p'éi** large-field cultivation, field practice (any agricultural practice or method used in ordinary fields, in contrast with those used in laboratory or experimental plots)

大田作物 **tà-t'ién-tsò-wù** a field crop (any crop grown in ordinary fields under more or less extensive cultivation)

大同 **tà-t'úng** great unity (the ideal of world harmony, universalism)

大同小异 **tà-t'úng-hsiǎo-ì** large similarities and small differences (generally similar, with only slight differences)

大杂烩 **tà-tsá-huì** a hodgepodge, melange, potpourri

大灾难 **tà-tsāi-nàn** a calamity, disaster, catastrophe, holocaust

大赞大颂 **tà-tsàn tà-sùng** to praise and commend extravagantly

大灶 **tà-tsào** a big stove, community kitchen (food prepared for a large group, institutional feeding)

大造革命舆论 **tà-tsào kó-mìng yú-lùn** to actively generate public opinion [favorable to] revolution

大作文章 **tà-tsò wén-chāng** energetically to write articles (often has an implication of much ado about little, or confusing the issue with lavish attention to extraneous matters)

大罪状 **tà-tsuì-chuàng** a serious indictment

大资产阶级 **tà tzū-ch'ǎn-chiēh-chí** the big bourgeoisie

大资本家 **tà tzù-pěn-chiā** a big capitalist, monopoly capitalist

大字报 **tà-tzù-pào** a big-character poster, big-character bulletin (a wall newspaper written in large characters widely used in major campaigns such as the Cultural Revolution)

大字标题 **tà-tzù piāo-t'í** a large-character headline, banner headline

大自然 **tà-tzù-ján** nature, the natural world

大材小用 **tà-ts'ái hsiǎo-yùng** large material for small uses (a waste of talent, to use a talented man in an inferior position)

大操大办 **tà-ts'āo tà-pàn** to do in a big way (implies extravagance and waste)

大错 **tà-ts'ò** a big mistake, gross blunder, serious error

大王 **tà-wáng** a king, magnate, big boss, chief brigand

大尉 **tà-wèi** senior captain [Chinese Army and Air Force]; senior lieutenant [Chinese Navy]

大无畏精神 **tà wú-wèi chīng-shén** a spirit of fearing nothing, dauntless spirit

大洋全 **tà-yáng-ch'ǖan** big, foreign, and complete (critical of those who scorn native methods and wish to ape foreign industrial methods and complete plants on a large scale)

大摇大摆 **tà-yáo-tà-pǎi** to strut, swagger

大言壮语 **tà-yén-chuàng-yǔ** big talk and lusty phrases (blustering speech, vainglorious talk)

大言不惭 **tà-yén-pù-ts'án** to boast without shame

大有进步 **tà-yǔ chìn-pù** to show great progress, much improved

大有好处 **tà-yǔ-hǎo-ch'ù** to have many advantages, be of great benefit

大有人在 **tà-yǔ-jén-tsài** many [such] people exist

大有可为 **tà-yǔ-k'ǒ-wéi** there are many possibilities [to accomplish something]; very promising, very hopeful [situation, etc.]

大有作为 **tà-yǔ-tsò-wéi** there is much that can be done

大鱼吃小鱼 **tà-yǘ ch'ǐh hsiǎo-yǘ** the big fish eat the little fish

大宇宙 **tà-yǘ-chòu** a macrocosm

大跃进 **tà yuèh-chìn** a great leap; the Great Leap Forward (1958)

tāi (dāi)

2000 呆滞 **tāi-chìh** cessation, stagnation; dull, inert; a stoppage

tǎi (dǎi)

2001 歹徒 **tǎi-t'ú** a vicious fellow, hoodlum, hooligan

2002 傣族 **tǎi-tsú** the T'ai [Thai] people (a minority in Yunnan province: population 500,000 as of 1957) [*tǎi is the correct pronunciation, but it is more generally pronounced* "t'ài"]

tài (dài)

2003 代价 **tài-chià** the price, cost, charge

代之而起 **tài-chīh-érh-ch'ǐ** to replace and then rise (political leaders who rise as others fall)

代主席 **tài-chǔ-hsí** an acting chairman

代销 **tài-hsiāo** to sell on behalf of, sell as an agent, sell on commission; a sales agent

代销人 **tài-hsiāo-jén** a sales agent, retail distributor

代谢 **tài-hsièh** (1) to express thanks on behalf of another; (2) metabolism

代议制 **tài-ì-chìh** the representative system of government, parliamentary government

代购代销 **tài-kòu tài-hsiāo** to buy and sell as an agent

代课 **tài-k'ò** to act as a substitute teacher

代理 **tài-lǐ** to act as agent of, be proxy for, act for, represent; acting; an agency, agent

代名词 **tài-míng-tz'ú** under another name; pronoun

代办 **tài-pàn** a charge d'affaires, deputy; to act for another

代本 **tài-pěn** the largest unit of native Tibetan military forces

代表 **tài-piǎo** a representative, delegate, deputy; to represent; be typical of

代表候选人 **tài-piǎo hòu-hsuǎn-jén** a candidate for election [to some representative body]

代表人物 **tài-piǎo jén-wù** representative persons, persons typical of a particular class or group

代表大会 **tài-piǎo-tà-huì** a representative assembly, congress, plenum, plenary session

代表团 **tài-piǎo-t'uán** a group of delegates, delegation, deputation

代表资格审查委员会 **tài-piǎo tzū-kó shěn-ch'á wěi-yuán-huì** a credential committee

代圣人立言 **tài shèng-jén lì-yén** to say worthy words in the name of the sage [Confucius]

代代相传 **tài-tài hsiāng-ch'uán** handed down from generation to generation

代替 **tài-t'ì** to replace, substitute for, stand proxy for; substitution, replacement

代言人 **tài-yén-jén** a spokesman, mouthpiece

代用器材 **tài-yùng ch'ì-ts'ái** substitute equipment, substitute materials

代用品 **tài-yùng-p'ǐn** a substitute, substitute goods

2004 带着问题学 **tài-che wèn-t'í hsuéh** when studying one should have [specific] problems [questions] in mind (the inference usually is that study is useless without having conscious awareness of ideological problems)

带劲 **tài-chìn** infused with vigor, energetic

带领 **tài-lǐng** to lead, conduct, guide

带路人 **tài-lù-jén** a guide, pathfinder (usually refers to the Party or Mao Tse-tung)

带电自由作业 **tài-tièn tzù-yú tsò-yèh** to work freely on charged electric [high tension] lines

带动 **tài-tùng** to drive, propel, set in motion, initiate, lead, activate

带动一大片 **tài-tùng ī-tà-p'ièn** to activate a large area

带头 **tài-t'óu** to take the lead, take the initiative, set an example (always in a laudatory sense)

带头作用 **tài-t'óu-tsò-yùng** an initiating function, leading role

带徒弟 **tài t'ú-ti** to train an apprentice (may be used in an extended sense: e.g., an experienced cadre is expected to help a junior cadre to perfect his leadership style)

带徒弟制度 **tài-t'ú-ti chìh-tù** the apprentice system

2005 待机破敌 **tài-chī p'ò-tí** to await the opportunity to smash the enemy (to bide one's time for action)

待遇 **tài-yù** to treat, benefit; the manner of treating people, treatment, pay, emoluments, compensation, wages, remuneration, benefits

²⁰⁰⁶ 怠工 **tài-kūng** to intentionally work slowly, loafing on the job, dragging out work; a work slowdown [a form of sabotage]

怠工者 **tài-kūng-chě** a person engaged in a work slowdown (a saboteur)

²⁰⁰⁷ 贷款 **tài-k'uǎn** a money loan; credit; to loan

²⁰⁰⁸ 逮捕 **tài-pǔ** to arrest, apprehend, nab

²⁰⁰⁹ 戴罪立功 **tài-tsuì lì-kūng** to atone for guilt by meritorious service

tān (dān)

²⁰¹⁰ 丹麦 **tān-mài** Denmark

²⁰¹¹ 担架 **tān-chià** a stretcher, litter

担惊受怕 **tān-chīng shòu-p'à** to carry alarms and suffer fears (for the well-being of someone else)

担风险 **tān-fēng-hsiěn** to assume a risk

担负 **tān-fù** to shoulder a burden, assume responsibility

担任 **tān-jèn** to assume a post, take over, take charge of, assume responsibility for

担保 **tān-pǎo** to guarantee, pledge, secure, endorse, vouch for; a guarantee, warranty, surety, collateral

担水 **tān-shuǐ** to carry water with a carrying pole

担当 **tān-tāng** to assume responsibility, take on oneself, undertake, accept the consequences

担 **tān**: *see also* **tàn**

²⁰¹² 单改双季 **tān-chì kǎi shuāng-chì** to change from single crop [rice] to double crop [rice]

单季稻 **tān-chì-tào** single crop rice

单价 **tān-chià** unit price, unit cost

单件修理 **tān-chièn hsiū-lǐ** piece-by-piece repair, single-unit repair

单产 **tān-ch'ǎn** unit yield

单枪匹马 **tān-ch'iāng-p'ǐ-mǎ** [entering battle with] single spear and single horse (to take on the enemy alone)

单纯 **tān-ch'ún** simple, plain, unembellished; pure, absolute; simply, solely, exclusively; simplicity, artlessness

单纯技术观点 **tān-ch'ún chì-shù kuān-tiěn** a purely technical viewpoint (one that does not take politics into consideration)

单纯军事观点 **tān-ch'ún chūn-shìh kuān-tiěn** a purely military viewpoint

单纯任务观点 **tān-ch'ún jèn-wù kuān-tiěn** a purely task-oriented viewpoint, a narrowly job-oriented viewpoint

单纯业务观点 **tān-ch'ún yèh-wù kuān-tiěn** a purely occupational viewpoint

单方 **tān-fāng** a prescription, recipe, formula [in Chinese medicine]

单行本 **tān-hsíng-pěn** a separate publication of an essay, play, or excerpt from a larger work or collection

单行条例 **tān-hsíng-t'iáo-lì** a special statute or regulation

单一 **tān-ī** single, unitary; simple, uncomplicated; singleness, unity

单一经营 **tān-ī-chīng-yíng** single operation (e.g., for a factory to concentrate on the manufacture of a single product)

单一全日制 **tān-ī ch'üán-jìh-chìh** single session all-day system (in contrast to schools operating on double sessions)

单一兵种 **tān-ī pīng-chǔng** a military force of a single arm

单干 **tān-kàn** to work on one's own, to do something single-handedly, independent operation (*see* **tān-kàn-hù**)

单干风 **tān-kàn-fēng** the do-it-alone trend, the spirit of individual enterprise (a target of the Socialist Education movement)

单干户 **tān-kàn-hù** do-it-alone households; individual farmers (who declined to join mutual-aid teams or the early cooperatives)

单练 **tān-lièn** a solo performance; to practice alone (usually refers to **wǔ-shù**)

单打一 **tān-tǎ-ī** a single shot [gun] (to take an overly narrow view of one's responsibilities, as a manufacturing plant that refuses to assume any responsibility for the repair or service of its products)

单调 **tān-tiào** a single tune (monotonous, dry, boring)

单层 **tān-ts'éng** single-storeyed

单位 **tān-wèi** a unit, standard of measurement, denominator; an organizational unit, one's place of work

单位面积产量 **tān-wèi mièn-chī ch'ǎn-liàng** yield per area unit

²⁰¹³ 耽心 **tān-hsīn** to have anxiety about; apprehensive, worried

耽误 **tān-wù** to delay, obstruct, hold up, interfere with

tǎn (dǎn)

²⁰¹⁴ 胆小如鼠 **tǎn-hsiǎo-jú-shǔ** as timid as a mouse

胆敢 **tǎn-kǎn** to dare; audacious

胆量 **tǎn-liàng** courage, bravery, daring, "guts"

胆略 **tǎn-lüèh** courage and resourcefulness

胆大心细 **tǎn-tà-hsīn-hsì** bold but prudent, daring but careful

tàn (dàn)

2015 但书 **tàn-shū** a proviso, reservation, a saving clause

2016 担 **tàn** a load (carried by one man); a hundredweight (100 **shìh-chīn** or market catties: 50 kilograms or 110.2 pounds)

担子 **tàn-tzu** a load, burden [carried on the shoulders]

担 **tàn**: *see also* **tān**

2017 诞生 **tàn-shēng** to be born, birth

2018 淡季 **tàn-chì** the off season, slack season (in business or agriculture)

淡而无味 **tàn-érh-wú-wèi** weak and without flavor (tasteless, insipid)

淡薄 **tàn-pó** thin, weak, deficient, mild, boring

淡水 **tàn-shuǐ** fresh water (as opposed to salty or brackish)

2019 弹尽粮绝 **tàn-chìn-liáng-chüéh** with ammunition expended and food exhausted

弹弓队 **tàn-kūng-tuì** a slingshot unit (in the sparrow extermination campaign)

弹道火箭 **tàn-tào-huǒ-chièn** ballistic rocket

弹道导弹 **tàn-tào-tǎo-tàn** a ballistic missile

弹药 **tàn-yào** ammunition

弹药筒 **tàn-yào-t'ǔng** a cartridge

2020 蛋白质 **tàn-pái-chìh** protein, albumin

蛋品 **tàn-p'ǐn** egg products

2021 氮肥 **tàn-féi** nitrogenous manure, nitrate fertilizer

tāng (dāng)

2022 当机立断 **tāng-chī-lì-tuàn** to make [correct] decisions quickly as the occasion requires (to act promptly and decisively)

当家作主 **tāng-chiā tsò-chǔ** to be the master in the house (to make the responsible decisions)

当之无愧 **tāng-chīh-wú-k'uèi** to accept without shame (to merit, deserve [an award, etc.])

当今 **tāng-chīn** the present time, now, today

当场 **tāng-ch'ǎng** on the spot, at the meeting

当前 **tāng-ch'ién** present, current, immediate, now facing [us]; now, presently

当局 **tāng-chú** constituted authority, official leadership; the authorities

当权 **tāng-ch'üán** to exercise power; in power, ruling

当权派 **tāng-ch'üán-p'ài** the clique in authority, faction in power

当群众的小学生 **tāng-ch'ǘn-chùng tè hsiǎo-hsuéh-shēng** to be an elementary pupil of the masses

当好参谋 **tāng-hǎo ts'ān-móu** to be a good counselor

当选 **tāng-hsuǎn** to be elected, be selected, be chosen

当一天和尚，撞一天钟 **tāng ī-t'iēn hó-shàng, chuàng ī-t'iēn chūng** to be a monk for a day and toll the bell for a day (to go through the motions; to live from day to day)

当仁不让 **tāng-jén-pù-jàng** to yield to no one when doing what is right (to be willing to take on any task that needs to be done)

当干部吃亏论 **tāng kàn-pù ch'īh-k'uēi lùn** the idea that to be a cadre brings misfortune

当面一套，背后一套 **tāng-mièn ī-t'ào, pèi-hòu ī-t'ào** to be one thing before one's face and another behind one's back ("two-faced," duplicitous)

当面不说，背后乱说 **tāng-mièn pù-shuō, pèi-hòu luàn-shuō** facing people to say nothing but behind their backs to talk irresponsibly

当牛做马 **tāng-niú tsò-mǎ** to be a cow and work like a horse (the life of the peasants in the old society)

当事人 **tāng-shìh-jén** the party concerned, participant, person involved; a party [to a legal action]

当代 **tāng-tài** in the present age, this generation, contemporary, today

当地 **tāng-tì** on the spot, local, a particular place (may have the sense of either "here" or "there")

当头一棒 **tāng-t'óu ī-pàng** a club [blow] to the head

当务之急 **tāng-wù-chīh-chí** the task of greatest present urgency, an affair of immediate importance

当 **tāng**: *see also* **tàng**

tǎng (dǎng)

2023 挡箭牌 **tǎng-chièn-p'ái** a shield [against arrows] (anything which can be used as a protective shield; an excuse)

挡住 **tǎng-chù** to block, impede, hinder, obstruct, halt

党章 **tǎng-chāng** the Party constitution; Party statutes, Party regulations

党政 **tǎng-chèng** the [Communist] Party and the government; the Party and politics

党籍 **tǎng-chí** Party membership, Party registration, Party affiliation

党纪 **tǎng-chì** Party discipline, Party rules

党支部 **tǎng-chīh-pù** a Party branch

党支部书记 **tǎng-chīh-pù shū-chì** a Party branch secretary

党支书 **tǎng-chīh-shū** a Party branch secretary (*contraction of above*)

党指向哪里, 就奔向哪里 **tǎng chíh-hsiàng nǎ-li, chiù pēn-hsiàng nǎ-li** wherever the Party points, there [I] will go

党中央 **tǎng-chūng-yāng** the Central Committee of the Chinese Communist Party (contraction of **chūng-kúo kùng-ch'ǎn-tǎng chūng-yāng wěi-yuán-huì**)

党群关系 **tǎng-ch'ún kuān-hsi** the relationship of the Party to the masses, Party-mass relationships

党阀 **tǎng-fá** a "Party lord," party establishment (any discredited Party leader accused of having an attitude similar to that of the warlords)

党费 **tǎng-fèi** Party membership fee, Party dues

党小组 **tǎng-hsiǎo-tsǔ** a Party small group, Party cell (the smallest Party unit)

党校 **tǎng-hsiào** a Party school

党性 **tǎng-hsìng** Party character, Party spirit, Party qualifications, "Party-ness"

党性不纯 **tǎng-hsìng pù-ch'ún** a deficiency in Party spirit, impure Party character, flawed in "Party-ness"

党性原则 **tǎng-hsìng yuán-tsé** principle based on Party spirit, the basic principles in "Party-ness"

党纲 **tǎng-kāng** a Party program (usually a broad statement of objectives)

党课 **tǎng-k'ò** Party training (usually classes for persons preparing for admission to the Party)

党老爷 **tǎng-lǎo-yéh** Party lords (satirical)

党龄 **tǎng-líng** the length of time one has been a Party member, period of Party membership

党内和平论 **tǎng-nèi hó-p'íng lùn** the doctrine of internal Party peace (one of the **hēi-liù-lùn**)

党内通讯 **tǎng-nèi t'ūng-hsùn** an intra-party bulletin, correspondence within the Party

党内外矛盾的交叉 **tǎng-nèi-wài máo-tùn te chiāo-ch'ā** the intertwining of the contradictions inside and outside the Party

党八股 **tǎng-pā-kǔ** the Party eight-legged essay, stereotyped Party writing, formalism (one of the targets in the Cheng Feng Movement of 1942)

党报 **tǎng-pào** a Party newspaper, Party journal; in Party press

党报委员会 **tǎng-pào wěi-yuán-huì** the Party Press Committee

党派 **tǎng-p'ài** political parties and factions

党史 **tǎng-shǐh** Party history

党代表 **tǎng-tài-piǎo** a Party representative (an early designation—pre-1937—for political commissars in the armed forces)

党的儿女 **tǎng-te-érh-nǔ** the Party's sons and daughters (distinguished Party members)

党的核心 **tǎng-te-hó-hsīn** Party nucleus (usually a small group of Party members within a non-Party unit or organization)

党的生活 **tǎng-te-shēng-huó** Party life (an individual's activities within the Party)

党天下 **tǎng-t'iēn-hsià** the Party kingdom (a 1957 criticism by Democratic League member Ch'u An-p'ing of Party monopolization of all important government posts)

党徒 **tǎng-t'ú** a party follower, party member

党团 **tǎng-t'uán** the [Communist] Party and [Youth] League

党团员 **tǎng-t'uán-yuán** [Communist] Party and [Youth] League members

党组 **tǎng-tsǔ** a Party fraction [within a non-Party organization], Party cell

党组织 **tǎng-tsǔ-chīh** the Party organization, Party apparatus

党外人士 **tǎng-wài jén-shìh** people outside the Party, non-Communist personages

党外民主人士 **tǎng-wài mín-chǔ-jén-shìh** democratic personages outside the [Communist] Party

党委 **tǎng-wěi** (1) a member of a Party committee; (2) Party Committee (abbreviation of **tǎng-wěi-huì**)

党委抓大事 **tǎng-wěi chuā tà-shìh** Party

committees [should] grasp the major issues

党委成员 **tǎng-wěi ch'éng-yuán** [regular] members of the Party committee

党委制 **tǎng-wěi-chìh** the Party committee system (collective leadership to prevent individuals from monopolizing the conduct of affairs)

党委会 **tǎng-wěi-huì** a Party committee

党委书记 **tǎng-wěi shū-chì** a secretary of a Party committee

党委第一书记 **tǎng-wěi tì-ī-shū-chì** the first secretary of a Party committee

党委委员 **tǎng-wěi wěi-yuán** a member of a Party committee

党务 **tǎng-wù** Party affairs, Party work

党羽 **tǎng-yǔ** a partisan adherent, follower of a political faction, member of a clique (pejorative)

党员 **tǎng-yuán** a Party member

党员大会 **tǎng-yuán tà-huì** a general meeting of Party members

tàng (dàng)

2025 当牛马使唤 **tàng-niú-mǎ shǐh-huàn** to be used like cows and horses (the life of peasants in the old society)

当牲畜倒卖 **tàng shēng-ch'ù tǎo-mài** to be sold like animals

当 **tàng**: *see also* **tāng**

2026 荡涤 **tàng-tí** to wash out, cleanse

2027 档案 **tàng-àn** files, records, archives; a file; a personal dossier

tāo (dāo)

2028 刀枪入库 **tāo-ch'iāng jù-k'ù** the swords and spears are returned to the storehouse (to abandon vigilance and preparedness)

刀耕火种 **tāo-kēng huǒ-chùng** the slash and burn [method of] agriculture

刀山火海 **tāo-shān-huǒ-hǎi** a mountain of knives and a sea of fire (a most dangerous situation)

2029 叨咕 **tāo-ku** to talk conspiratorially

叨唠 **tāo-lao** to nag, complain; garrulous, talkative

tǎo (dǎo)

2030 导致 **tǎo-chìh** to cause [something to happen], lead to, result in

导航 **tǎo-háng** to navigate; navigation

导火线 **tǎo-huǒ-hsièn** a fuse [for firecrackers or explosives] (a direct cause [of a development or event, such as war])

导师 **tǎo-shīh** a teacher, guide, mentor,

a homeroom teacher or teacher assigned to a particular group of students (now it often refers to Mao Tse-tung)

导弹 **tǎo-tàn** a guided missile

导言 **tǎo-yén** an introduction [to a book or article, normally by the author]

导演 **tǎo-yěn** a director [of a play or film); to direct

2031 倒霉 **tǎo-méi** to have bad luck; bad luck, ill fortune

倒把 **tǎo-pǎ** to speculate and profiteer

倒台 **tǎo-t'ái** the stage collapses (downfall, collapse—usually in a political sense)

倒 **tǎo**: *see also* **tào**

2032 捣毁 **tǎo-huǐ** to smash, willfully damage, demolish

捣鬼 **tǎo-kuěi** to play tricks, sow discord, cause trouble

捣乱 **tǎo-luàn** to cause a disturbance, create havoc, make trouble

捣乱, 失败, 再捣乱, 再失败 **tǎo-luàn, shǐh-pài, tsài tǎo-luàn, tsài shǐh-pài** to make trouble and fail, and again make trouble and again fail (Mao Tse-tung's description of the persistence of reactionaries)

捣蛋 **tǎo-tàn** to cause trouble, make a disburbance, commit sabotage, "raise hell"

2033 祷告 **tǎo-kào** to pray; a prayer

tào (dào)

2034 到处开花 **tào-ch'ù k'āi-huā** to blossom everywhere (figurative: plans coming to fruition)

到任 **tào-jèn** to assume [a high] office

到达港 **tào-tá-kǎng** the destination port, final port [of a ship's voyage]

到底 **tào-tǐ** to the very bottom, to the very end; to carry through, pursue relentlessly; after all, in the long run

2035 倒转 **tào-chuǎn** to turn backward, turn in another direction, change course

倒行逆施 **tào-hsíng nì-shīh** to act in opposition to right principles (to turn things upside down, take perverse action)

倒戈投敌 **tào-kō-t'óu-tí** to turn the lance downward and surrender to the enemy (to defect, capitulate, turn renegade)

倒流 **tào-liú** to flow backward; a countercurrent

倒退 **tào-t'uì** to go backward, withdraw, retreat

倒退复古 **tào-t'uì fù-kǔ** to go back and

revive the ancient (to retrogress, turn back the clock)

倒退复辟 **tào-t'uì fù-pì** to move backward and restore the sovereign (to go back to the old order)

倒 **tào**: *see also* **tǎo**

2036 悼念 **tào-nièn** to think of one who is gone, mourn, grieve for

悼词 **tào-tz'ú** a eulogy for someone who has died, memorial speech

2037 盗窃 **tào-ch'ièh** to rob, steal, plunder; theft, plundering

盗窃国家经济情报 **tào-ch'ièh kuó-chiā chīng-chì ch'íng-pào** to steal state economic intelligence; theft of state economic secrets (one of the **wǔ-fǎn**)

盗窃国家资财 **tào-ch'ièh kuó-chiā tzū-ts'ái** to steal state property; the theft of state assets (one of the **wǔ-fǎn**)

盗骗 **tào-p'ièn** to steal and cheat, embezzle

2038 道歉 **tào-ch'ièn** to excuse oneself, apologize

道会门 **tào-huì-mén** religious sects and secret societies

道义 **tào-ì** justice, a sense of righteousness, morality, ethics, honor; moral

道义之交 **tào-ì-chīh-chiāo** a relationship based on high principles

道理 **tào-lǐ** reason, rationality; principle, the right way

道路 **tào-lù** the way, path, road (often figurative)

道门 **tào-mén** religious sects, secret societies

道木 **tào-mù** railway ties

道德 **tào-té** morality, ethics, virtue, honor; moral, ethical

道德观 **tào-té-kuān** a moral view, moral concept

道德品质 **tào-té-p'ǐn-chìh** moral character, moral qualities

道听途说 **tào-t'īng-t'ú-shuō** to tell on the way what one heard by the road (to engage in gossip, rumor mongering)

té (dé)

2039 得逞 **té-ch'ěng** to achieve a presumptuous objective, succeed in an unworthy act, act in a presumptuous manner

得心应手 **té-hsīn-yìng-shǒu** the hand moves as the mind wishes (to do things easily and smoothly)

得意忘形 **té-ì-wàng-hsíng** so satisfied [that one] forgets appearances (so complacent that one forgets manners; to have one's head turned by success, dizzy with success)

得人心 **té jén-hsīn** to win the hearts of the people; popular, well liked

得过且过 **té-kuò-ch'iěh-kuò** if one can get by then get by (easygoing, without ambition; to work perfunctorily)

得力 **té-lì** capable, competent, able; very useful

得不偿失 **té-pù-ch'áng-shīh** the gain does not make up for the losses (not worth the effort)

得失 **té-shīh** gain or loss, success or failure, merits and demerits; expedience

得势 **té-shìh** to be in a powerful position, become influential, be in power

得当 **té-tàng** proper, fitting, appropriate

得道多助失道寡助 **té-tào tō-chù shīh-tào kuǎ-chù** the just is supported by many and the unjust by the few

得罪 **té-tsuì** to offend, give offense to, displease, annoy; to violate the law

得寸进尺 **té-ts'ùn-chìn-ch'ǐh** to receive an inch and take a foot (small concessions lead to greater demands)

得予 **té-yǔ** may [in the legal sense], to have permission to

2040 德黑兰 **té-hēi-lán** Teheran

德意志新闻社 **té-ì-chìh hsīn-wén-shè** Deutsche Presse Agentur [DPA]

德意志联邦共和国 **té-ì-chìh lién-pāng kùng-hó-kuó** Federal Republic of Germany [West Germany]

德意志民主共和国 **té-ì-chìh mín-chǔ kùng-hó-kuó** German Democratic Republic [East Germany]

德意志通讯社 **té-ì-chìh t'ūng-hsùn-shè** Allgemeiner Deutscher Nachrichtendienst [ADN]

德才兼备 **té-ts'ái-chiēn-pèi** to combine character and competence, having a full measure of both integrity and ability

德育 **té-yù** moral education, education in ethics

tēng (dēng)

2041 灯红酒绿 **tēng-húng-chiǔ-lù** red lanterns and green wines (the luxurious and decadent city life of the exploitative classes)

灯火管制 **tēng-huǒ kuǎn-chìh** restriction of illumination; a blackout

灯泡 **tēng-p'ào** an electric light bulb

灯丝 **tēng-szū** a lamp filament

灯塔 **tēng-t'ǎ** a lighthouse (a simile for the Thought of Mao Tse-tung)

2042　灯头 **tēng-t'óu** an electric light socket

登记 **tēng-chì** to register, enroll; note down, enter, record, list; registration

登峯造极 **tēng-fēng-tsào-chí** to scale the peak and achieve the ultimate (to obtain the highest level—in scholarship, literature, career, etc.)

登陆 **tēng-lù** to make a landing, disembark, go ashore

登陆艇 **tēng-lù-t'ǐng** a landing craft, landing vessel

登门求援 **tēng-mén-ch'iú-yuán** to go to someone's door and ask for help (to seek the benefit of another's experience: now usually refers to production units rather than persons)

登报 **tēng-pào** to appear in a newspaper, have printed in the press, make an announcement in the newspapers

登台 **tēng-t'ái** to mount the stage (to enter the political scene, commence playing an active role)

登载 **tēng-tsǎi** to publish, insert [in a book], record; publication

tĕng (dĕng)

2043　等级 **tĕng-chí** grade, class, rank; status, caste; rate, scale, gradation

等价交换 **tĕng-chià chiāo-huàn** to exchange at equivalent value; exchange of goods based on equivalent value

等距离 **tĕng-chù-lí** equidistant, separated by the same distance or interval

等闲视之 **tĕng-hsién-shìh-chīh** to treat casually, regard lightly, be négligent toward

等量齐观 **tĕng-liàng ch'í-kuān** to treat equally, put on the same footing, equate with, draw a parallel between

等待时机 **tĕng-tài shíh-chī** to await the opportune moment

等同 **tĕng-t'úng** to equate, put in the same position

tèng (dèng)

2044　鄧拓 **tèng-t'ō** Teng T'o (a writer and editor, one of the authors of "Notes from Three-Family Village," an early target of the Cultural Revolution)

tī (dī)

2045　低级 **tī-chí** lowest level [of schools, etc.], low rank, inferior grade, bottom echelon

低级趣味 **tī-chí ch'ù-wèi** in poor taste, vulgar

低级庸俗 **tī-chí yūng-sú** vulgar and mediocre

低贱 **tī-chièn** low and cheap, sordid

低产田 **tī-ch'ǎn-t'ién** a low-yield field, poor land

低产作物 **tī-ch'ǎn tsò-wù** a low-yield crop, short crop

低潮 **tī-ch'áo** a low tide, ebb tide (often figurative)

低人一头 **tī-jén-ī-t'óu** lower by a head than others (to be inferior)

低估 **tī-kū** to undervalue, underestimate, discount

低工资职工 **tī-kūng-tzū chíh-kūng** low-paid workers

低空飞行 **tī-k'ūng fēi-hsíng** low-altitude flying

低利贷款 **tī-lì tài-k'uǎn** a low-interest loan

低落 **tī-lò** to ebb, lower, recede, decline, depreciate; a fall, lowering, depreciation, depression

低能 **tī-néng** low efficiency; feeble-minded, incompetent; an imbecile

低三下四 **tī-sān-hsià-szù** to debase three and lower four (to lower one's dignity; mean, cheap, lowly, servile)

低声下气 **tī-shēng-hsià-ch'ì** to speak softly and lower the breath (to be meek and subservient, obsequious, cringing)

低头 **tī-t'óu** to lower the head (to acknowledge defeat, bow to the will of others)

低头认罪 **tī-t'óu-jèn-tsuì** to bow the head and admit guilt (accept guilt)

低头认错 **tī-t'óu jèn-ts'ò** to bow the head and confess error

低洼地区 **tī-wā tì-ch'ǚ** a low, swampy area, marshland

2046　提防 **tī-fáng** to guard against, be on the alert, be cautious

提 **tī**: see also **t'í**

2047　提坝 **tī-pà** a dam, dike, embankment

2048　滴水成冰 **tī-shuǐ-ch'éng-pīng** as water drops it immediately freezes (very cold weather)

滴滴弟 **tī-tī-t'ì** DDT [the insecticide]

tí (dí)

2049　迪拜 **tí-pài** Dibai [Trucial States]

2050　的确 **tí-ch'üèh** certainly, surely, truly, really

的确凉 **tí-ch'üèh-liáng** dacron cloth

的 **tí**: see also **tì**

2051　涤除 **tí-ch'ú** to wash out (figurative: to cleanse, purify [thought], get rid of

[old habits])

涤纶 **tí-lún** dacron yarn

2052 敌占区 **tí-chàn-ch'ǚ** zone of enemy occupation, enemy occupied zone

敌进我退, 敌驻我扰, 敌疲我打, 敌退我追 **tí-chìn wǒ-t'uì, tí-chù wǒ-jǎo, tí-p'í wǒ-tǎ, tí-t'uì wǒ-chuī** The enemy advances, we retreat; the enemy camps, we harass; the enemy tires, we attack; the enemy retreats, we pursue (military tactics set forth by Mao Tse-tung in 1928)

敌产 **tí-ch'ǎn** enemy property, enemy assets

敌情 **tí-ch'íng** the enemy's situation; intelligence concerning the enemy

敌军 **tí-chǖn** enemy forces, a hostile army

敌后 **tí-hòu** behind the enemy, the enemy's rear

敌后战场 **tí-hòu chàn-ch'ǎng** the war area behind the enemy

敌后抗日根据地 **tí-hòu k'àng-jìh kēn-chǚ-tì** anti-Japanese base areas in the enemy's rear

敌意 **tí-ì** a hostile attitude, animosity, enmity

敌人 **tí-jén** an enemy, foe, adversary, opponent (often used in a broad ideological or political sense)

敌国 **tí-kuó** an enemy country

敌视 **tí-shìh** to regard as an enemy, be hostile toward; hostility

敌得过 **tí-te-kuò** to be able to overcome; surmountable

敌对 **tí-tuì** opposing, hostile; hostility, antagonism, opposition

敌对分子 **tí-tuì fèn-tzǔ** hostile elements

敌对地带 **tí-tuì tì-tài** hostile territory

敌伪 **tí-wěi** the enemy and bogus [elements] (Japan and the Chinese military forces and governments created by the Japanese in China before 1945)

敌我关系 **tí-wǒ kuān-hsi** enemy-and-us relations (antagonistic relations, a relationship of hostility)

敌我矛盾 **tí-wǒ máo-tùn** contradictions between ourselves and the enemy (antagonistic contradictions)

敌我不分 **tí-wǒ-pù-fēn** to fail in differentiating [between] the enemy and ourselves

2053 嘀咕 **tí-ku** (1) to whisper privately; (2) restless and ill at ease

tǐ (dǐ)

2054 诋毁 **tí-huǐ** to slander, accuse falsely, malign, discredit

2055 底分 **tǐ-fēn** basic [work] points (work points based on a skill rating rather than piecework)

底子 **tǐ-tzu** (1) a foundation, basis, groundwork; (2) a manuscript, draft; (3) a shoe sole

2056 抵制 **tǐ-chìh** to resist, boycott; a boycott

抵触 **tǐ-ch'ù** to contradict, collide with, be in conflict with, contravene; conflicting, contradictory; contravention

抵消 **tǐ-hsiāo** to cancel, balance out, offset, compensate

抵抗 **tǐ-k'àng** to resist, oppose, fight against; resistance

抵赖 **tǐ-lài** to deny untruthfully, refuse to admit guilt

抵挡 **tǐ-tǎng** to resist, ward off, fend off, withstand

2057 砥柱 **tǐ-chù** a legendary rock in the Yellow River (an indomitable and upright person)

砥砺 **tǐ-lì** to discipline and polish (to polish one's character by close association)

tì (dì)

2058 地震区 **tì-chèn-ch'ǚ** an earthquake zone

地震观察站 **tì-chèn kuān-ts'è-chàn** a seismographic observatory

地基 **tì-chī** a foundation, groundwork

地质学 **tì-chìh-hsuéh** geological, geology

地质部 **tì-chìh-pù** Ministry of Geology [of the State Council]

地主 **tì-chǔ** a landlord, landholder

地主阶级 **tì-chǔ-chiēh-chí** the landlord class

地主阶级专政 **tì-chǔ-chiēh-chí chuān-chèng** the dictatorship of the landlord class

地主经济 **tì-chǔ-chīng-chì** a landlord economy

地主分子 **tì-chǔ-fèn-tzǔ** landlord elements (one of the szù-lèi-fèn-tzǔ)

地主老财 **tì-chǔ lǎo-ts'ái** landlords and rural rich

地主买办阶级 **tì-chǔ mǎi-pàn chiēh-chí** the landlord compradore class

地主资产阶级 **tì-chǔ tzū-ch'ǎn chiēh-chí** the landlord bourgeois class, the landowning class

地契 **tì-ch'ì** title deeds to land, land deeds

地球 **tì-ch'iú** the earth, globe

地球卫星 **tì-ch'iú wèi-hsīng** an earth satellite

地球物理探矿队 **tì-ch'iú-wù-lǐ t'àn-**

k'uàng-tuì a geophysical prospecting party

地区 **tì-ch'ü** area, district, region, zone, locality; local, regional (may refer to several territorial or administrative subdivisions: the jurisdiction of a street or neighborhood committee; an area of a province comprising several *hsièn*, formerly called **chuān-ch'ü**)

地权 **tì-ch'üán** land [ownership] rights

地方 **tì-fāng** local, regional, area (often contrasted with **chūng-yāng**, central)

地方政权 **tì-fāng chèng-ch'üán** local organs of [state] power, local government

地方主义 **tì-fāng-chǔ-ì** provincialism; localism, regionalism

地方戏 **tì-fāng-hsì** local plays, regional opera styles

地方性的事件 **tì-fāng-hsìng-te shìh-chièn** an incident of a local character

地方干部 **tì-fāng kàn-pù** local cadres (cadres working in local organs)

地方工业 **tì-fāng kūng-yèh** local industry

地方国营企业 **tì-fāng kuó-yíng ch'ǐ-yèh** state enterprises under local management

地方国营农场 **tì-fāng kuó-yíng núng-ch'ǎng** state farms under local management

地方兵团 **tì-fāng pīng-t'uán** local military forces

地方色彩 **tì-fāng sè-ts'ǎi** local characteristics, local traits, locally distinctive features [of handicrafts, etc.]

地方铁路 **tì-fāng-t'iěh-lù** local railways (railways built and operated by local authorities, such as provinces)

地方武装 **tì-fāng wǔ-chuāng** regional armed forces

地富反坏右 **tì-fù-fǎn-huài-yù** landlords, rich peasants, counter-revolutionaries, bad elements, and rightists (the **hēi-wǔ-lèi**)

地下核试验 **tì-hsià hó-shìh-yèn** underground nuclear tests

地下工厂 **tì-hsià kūng-ch'ǎng** an underground factory

地下工作 **tì-hsià kūng-tsò** underground work (secret and illegal political activity)

地下室 **tì-hsià-shìh** a basement, cellar

地下水 **tì-hsià shuǐ** subsurface water, ground water

地下党 **tì-hsià-tǎng** an underground party (the CCP while operating in KMT- or Japanese-controlled areas)

地下铁道 **tì-hsià-t'iěh-tào** an underground railroad, subway

地下资源 **tì-hsià-tzū-yuán** underground resources

地形 **tì-hsíng** topography, terrain; topographical

地热发电站 **tì-jè fā-tièn-chàn** a geothermal electric power generating plant

地瓜 **tì-kuā** the sweet potato

地广人稀 **tì-kuǎng-jén-hsī** the land broad and people sparse, thinly populated

地拉那 **tì-lā-nà** Tirana [Albania]

地雷 **tì-léi** land mines

地雷战 **tì-léi-chàn** land-mine warfare

地理知识 **tì-lǐ chīh-shíh** *Geographical Knowledge* (a monthly journal, Peking, 1950—)

地理学报 **tì-lǐ hsuéh-pào** *Acta Geographica Sinica* (a quarterly journal, Peking, 1934—)

地力 **tì-lì** productivity of the soil, soil fertility

地貌 **tì-mào** geomorphological

地薄人穷 **tì-páo jén-ch'iúng** the land is thin and the people poor (infertile land and impoverished people)

地步 **tì-pù** situation, position, condition; room for movement [for advance or retreat]

地盘 **tì-p'án** area of [a warlord's] control, sphere of power; a private kingdom

地痞流氓 **tì-p'ǐ liú-máng** riffraff, rabble, ruffians, hoodlums

地平线 **tì-p'íng-hsièn** the horizon

地上河 **tì-shàng-hó** the river above the land (the Yellow River)

地少人多 **tì-shǎo-jén-tō** little land but many people, densely populated

地瘦 **tì-shòu** the land is impoverished

地水面 **tì-shuǐ-mièn** water table

地大物博 **tì-tà wù-pó** the land is vast and its resources abundant

地带 **tì-tài** a zone of territory, a place and its vicinity, zone, area, district, region

地道战 **tì-tào-chàn** tunnel warfare

地地道道 **tì-tì-tào-tào** bona fide, very authentic

地点 **tì-tiěn** a site, locality, place, spot

地对空导弹 **ti-tuì-k'ūng tǎo-tàn** a ground-to-air missile

地对地导弹 **tì-tuì-tì tǎo-tàn** a ground-to-ground missile

地头蛇 **tì-t'òu-shé** a local snake (an influential local gangster who lives off the community)

地租 **tì-tsū** land rent, tenancy rent, ground rent

地层 **tì-ts'éng** a layer of earth, land stratum, a layer of sedimentary rock

地委 **tì-wěi** a district Party committee

地位 **tì-wèi** personal position, rank, status

地无立锥 **tì-wú-lì-chuī** [owning] no land even to stick an awl into (landless and very poor)

2059 弟兄单位 **tì-hsiūng tān-wèi** fraternal units

2060 的黎波里 **tì-lí-p'ō-lǐ** Tripoli [Libya]

的 **ti**: see also **tí**

2061 帝修反 **tì-hsiū-fǎn** imperialists, revisionists, and reactionaries

帝国主义 **tì-kuó-chǔ-ì** imperialism

帝国主义阵营 **tì-kuó-chǔ-ì chèn-yíng** the imperialist camp

帝国主义侵略集团 **tì-kuó-chǔ-ì ch'īn-lüèh chí-t'uán** the aggressive imperialist bloc

帝王将相 **tì-wáng-chiàng-hsiàng** emperors, kings, generals, and prime ministers (the feudal rulers, emblematic of the criticized great man theory of history and denounced as the common subjects of traditional opera and literature)

2062 递减 **tì-chiěn** to decrease or reduce progressively; progressive reduction

递补 **tì-pǔ** to fill vacancies in order of precedence

递增 **tì-tsēng** progressive increase; to increase gradually

2063 第二线 **tì-èrh-hsièn** the second line (a fall-back position)

第二线兵力 **tì-èrh-hsièn pīng-lì** second-line troops, reserves

第二共产国际 **tì-èrh kùng-ch'ǎn kuó-chì** the Second Communist International

第二国际 **tì-èrh kuó-chì** the Second International (see above)

第二国际修正主义 **tì-èrh-kuó-chì hsiū-chèng-chǔ-ì** the revisionism of the Second International

第二世界 **tì-èrh shìh-chièh** the Second World (Japan and the Common Market countries)

第二次国内革命战争时期 **tì-èrh-tz'ù kuó-nèi kó-mìng-chàn-chēng shíh-ch'ī** the Second Revolutionary Civil War Period (1928–1937)

第一政委 **tì-ī-chèng-wěi** the first political commissar, the leading political commissar

第一季度 **tì-ī-chì-tù** the first quarter (the first three months of the year)

第一线 **tì-ī-hsièn** the first line, front line (figurative: the masses, a factory, or a production site)

第一共产国际 **tì-ī kùng-ch'ǎn kuó-chì** the First Communist International

第一国际 **tì-ī kuó-chì** the First International (see above)

第一流 **tì-ī-liú** the first class, highest grade; first-rate

第一轮投票 **tì-ī-lún t'óu-p'iào** first round of voting, primary elections

第一把手 **tì-ī-pa-shǒu** the "number one man"

第一世界 **tì-ī-shìh-chièh** the First World (the US and USSR)

第一手材料 **tì-ī-shǒu ts'ái-liào** firsthand materials (data, sources, etc.], direct information

第一书记 **tì-ī-shū-chì** first secretary (the head of the Party committee)

第一次国内革命时期 **tì-ī-tz'ù kuó-nèi kó-mìng chàn-chēng shíh-ch'ī** the First Revolutionary Civil War Period (1926–1927)

第三共产国际 **tì-sān kùng-ch'ǎn kuó-chì** the Third Communist International, Comintern

第三国际 **tì-sān kuó-chì** the Third International (see above)

第三世界 **tì-sān shìh-chièh** the Third World (the developing countries of Asia, Africa, Latin America and other developing countries)

第三势力 **tì-sān shìh-lì** the Third Force (in the 1930s and 1940s, it usually meant the political groups in China that stood between the KMT and the CCP)

第三次国内革命战争时期 **tì-sān-tz'ù kuó-nèi kó-mìng-chàn-chēng shíh-ch'ī** the Third Revolutionary Civil War Period (1945–1949)

第五纵队 **tì-wǔ tsùng-tuì** the fifth column

2064 缔结 **tì-chiéh** to conclude [a treaty or contract]

缔结协定 **tì-chiéh hsiéh-tìng** to conclude an agreement

缔造 **tì-tsào** to found, establish, build up; to compose

缔约国 **tì-yüēh-kuó** a signatory state [to a treaty]

tiāo (diāo)

2065 刁难 **tiāo-nàn** to find fault, make difficulties, harass

刁徒 **tiǎo-t'ú** a cunning fellow, sly rascal

2066 凋谢 **tiāo-hsièh** to wither away, fade

凋敝 **tiāo-pì** emaciated, weakened, exhausted, chronically ill

2067 雕虫小技 **tiāo-ch'úng-hsiǎo-chì** one's petty craft of carving insects (a

derogatory phrase in reference to art or writing)

雕像 **tiāo-hsiàng** a sculptured portrayal of a person, statue, bust

雕刻 **tiāo-k'ò** to sculpt, carve, engrave; a sculpture

雕塑 **tiāo-sù** to carve [wood], mold [plastic], sculpt; sculpture

tiào (diào)

2068 吊车 **tiào-ch'ē** a crane, hoist, derrick; a car suspended from a cable, aerial transporter

吊桥 **tiào-ch'iáo** a suspension bridge

2069 钓鱼列岛 **tiào-yú lièh-tǎo** the Tiaoyü Islands (uninhabited islands about 190 nautical miles northeast of Taiwan and claimed by China, Taiwan, and Japan; the Japanese name is Senkaku Islands)

钓鱼台 **tiào-yú-t'ái** the Tiaoyü Islands (*see above*)

2070 调集 **tiào-chí** to concentrate [troops, forces], assemble

调查 **tiào-ch'á** to investigate (generally to learn facts, do research, and improve policies where needed— without the implications of deficiencies contained in **chiěn-ch'á**)

调查研究 **tiào-ch'á yén-chiū** investigation and research; to investigate and look into

调车 **tiào-ch'ē** to switch trains, change trains

调出 **tiào-ch'ū** to transfer [grain or other materials] from [one locality to another within the country]

调防 **tiào-fáng** to transfer [troops] for garrison duty

调换 **tiào-huàn** to transfer, replace, exchange, substitute, convert, transpose; substitution, replacement

调入 **tiào-jù** to bring in [grain, etc., from a source within the country]

调干 **tiào-kàn** a transferred cadre; to transfer cadres

调开 **tiào-k'āi** to transfer away, get rid of

调门 **tiào-mén** a tune, melody, pitch

调兵遣将 **tiào-pīng ch'iěn-chiàng** to move troops and dispatch generals (to transfer troops, deploy forces)

调拨 **tiào-pō** to assign, send, pass on, allocate; allocation

调配 **tiào-p'èi** to allocate, assign, distribute, allot; allocation, assignment (*see also* **t'iáo-p'èi**)

调配工作 **tiào-p'èi kūng-tsò** to assign work; allotment of tasks

调调 **tiào-tiao** [one's] tune (one's particular preference, fancy, hobby, etc.)

调度 **tiào-tù** to despatch, arrange, schedule, adjust according to need

调动 **tiào-tùng** to transfer, shift [troops, employees, cadres]

调动一切积极因素 **tiào-tùng ī-ch'ièh chī-chí-yīn-sù** to bring all positive factors into play

调研会 **tiào-yén-huì** an investigation and study meeting (a contraction of **tiào-ch'á yén-chiū-huì**)

调研提纲 **tiào-yén t'í-kāng** an outline for investigation and research

调 **tiào**: *see also* **t'iáo**

2071 掉以轻心 **tiào-ī-ch'īng-hsīn** to take a heedless attitude

掉队 **tiào-tuì** to straggle, fall out of formation, drop behind

tiēh (diē)

2072 爹亲娘亲不如毛主席亲 **tiēh-ch'īn niáng-ch'īn pù-jú máo chǔ-hsí ch'īn** Father is dear and Mother is dear, but not as dear as Chairman Mao

2073 跌交 **tiēh-chiāo** to trip and fall, fall over (to fail drastically, flop)

跌落 **tiēh-lò** to drop, fall, descend

tiéh (dié)

2074 谍报 **tiéh-pào** an espionage report, intelligence report

谍报员 **tiéh-pào-yuán** an espionage agent, spy

2075 喋喋不休 **tiéh-tiéh-pù-hsiū** to talk endlessly, chatter

tiēn (diān)

2076 滇 **tiēn** Yunnan province

2077 颠复活动 **tiēn-fù huó-tùng** subversive activities

颠复破坏 **tiēn-fù p'ò-huài** to subvert and wreck, sabotage

颠扑不破 **tiēn-p'ū-pù-p'ò** if it falls it will not break (unbreakable, immutable, irrefutable)

颠倒 **tiēn-tǎo** to reverse, turn upside down, invert

颠倒黑白 **tiēn-tǎo hēi-pái** to reverse black and white (to confuse right and wrong, call injustice, justice, etc.)

颠倒历史 **tiēn-tǎo lì-shǐh** to turn history upside down, distort history

颠倒是非 **tiēn-tǎo shìh-fēi** to confuse right and wrong, twist facts, distort the truth

tiěn (diǎn)

2078 典范 **tiěn-fàn** a model, example, sample, pattern

典型 **tiěn-hsíng** a model, exemplar, ideal [person, group, or unit] to be emulated; a prototype; typical, representative of

典型示范, 逐步推广 **tiěn-hsíng shìh-fàn, chú-pù t'uī-kuǎng** using a model [unit, etc.] for demonstration to gradually broaden [the experience gained from it]

典型事例 **tiěn-hsíng-shìh-lì** exemplary instances, sample cases

典故 **tiěn-kù** an allusion [from history or the Classics]

典礼 **tiěn-lǐ** a ceremony, rite, ritual; ceremonial

典当 **tiěn-tàng** to pawn, mortgage (involves transfer of possession)

2079 点缀 **tiěn-chuì** to provide decorative adornments, embellish

点火放毒 **tiěn-huǒ fàng-tú** to set fires and spread poison (to carry out covert subversion)

点线结合 **tiěn-hsièn-chiéh-hó** to integrate the points and lines (to spread the experience gained by concentrating on points)

点面结合 **tiěn-mièn chiéh-hó** to integrate the points and planes (*see above*)

点名批判 **tiěn-míng p'ī-p'àn** to criticize by name (direct criticism of individuals in public or unit meetings)

点事不点人 **tiěn-shìh pù tiěn-jén** to criticize the deed and not the person (a post-Cultural Revolution slogan)

点点滴滴 **tiěn-tiěn-tī-tī** drop by drop (may be said of the process of acquiring learning or gaining experience)

点头 **tiěn-t'óu** to nod the head (to approve, assent)

点子上 **tiěn-tzu-shang** to the point

tièn (diàn)

2080 电站 **tièn-chàn** a [small-scale] power generating plant

电唱机 **tièn-ch'àng-chī** a record player, electric phonograph

电气化 **tièn-ch'ì-huà** electrification; to electrify

电器 **tièn-ch'ì** electrical equipment (usually includes all materials, fixtures, appliances, machinery, etc., consuming or used in the generation and distribution of electricity)

电传打字机 **tièn-ch'uán tǎ-tzù-chī** a teletypewriter

电传影 **tièn-ch'uán-yǐng** an electrically transmitted picture, radiophoto

电焊 **tièn-hàn** electric welding

电话会议 **tièn-huà-huì-ì** a telephone conference

电热处理 **tièn-jè-ch'ǔ-lǐ** electrothermal treatment

电滚子 **tièn-kǔn-tzu** a dynamo, generator, rotor

电工 **tièn-kūng** an electrician, electrical technician

电力系统 **tièn-lì hsì-t'ǔng** the electrical power system

电力网 **tièn-lì-wǎng** the electric power net

电疗法 **tièn-liáo-fǎ** diathermy

电流 **tièn-liú** an electrical current

电码 **tièn-mǎ** a telegraphic code

电木 **tièn-mù** bakelite

电冰箱 **tièn-pīng-hsiāng** an electric refrigerator

电石 **tièn-shíh** calcium carbide

电视 **tièn-shìh** television

电视广播 **tièn-shìh kuǎng-pō** television transmission; a telecast

电动机车 **tièn-tùng chī-ch'ē** electric locomotives

电台 **tièn-t'ái** a radio broadcasting station; a radio sending or receiving station

电子 **tièn-tzǔ** an electron

电子计算机 **tièn-tzǔ chì-suàn-chī** electronic computer, electronic calculator

电子廻旋加速器 **tièn-tzǔ huí-hsuán chiā-sù-ch'ì** a betatron

电子显微镜 **tièn-tzǔ hsièn-wēi-chìng** an electron microscope

电子学 **tièn-tzǔ-hsuéh** electronics

电子管 **tièn-tzǔ-kuǎn** an electron tube

电子工业 **tièn-tzǔ kūng-yèh** the electronics industry

电子望远镜 **tièn-tzǔ wàng-yuǎn-chìng** a radio telescope

电子物理学 **tièn-tzǔ wù-lǐ-hsuéh** electronic physics

电影制片厂 **tièn-yǐng chìh-p'ièn-ch'ǎng** a cinema studio

电影剧本 **tièn-yǐng chù-pěn** a cinema script, scenario, screen play

电影放映机 **tièn-yǐng fàng-yìng-chī** a cinema projector, film projector

电影放映队 **tièn-yǐng fàng-yìng-tuì** a cinema projection team (usually circulating in a rural area)

电影配音译制 **tièn-yǐng p'èi-yīn ì-chìh** motion-picture-sound synchronization, dubbing

2081 佃富农 **tièn-fù-núng** a well-to-do tenant farmer (a well-to-do peasant who does not own his own land)
佃户 **tièn-hù** a tenant farmer
佃农 **tièn-núng** a tenant farmer
佃租 **tièn-tsū** tenancy rent, land rent, rent received from farmland; sharecropping
2082 店员 **tièn-yuán** a shop employee (an old term)
2083 奠定 **tièn-tìng** to found and consolidate, establish, found, settle

tīng (dīng)

2084 丁宁 **tīng-níng** to enjoin, exhort, impress on someone repeatedly
丁是丁，卯是卯 **tīng shìh tīng, mǎo shìh mǎo** a tenon is a tenon, and a mortise is a mortise (precise and conscientious, certain, without question)
丁点(儿) **tīng tiěn (-erh)** an iota; somewhat, a little, tiny
2085 钉螺蛳 **tīng-ló-shīh** spiral-shelled snail (the carrier of schistosomiasis)
钉梢 **tīng-shāo** to keep under secret surveillance

tǐng (dǐng)

2086 顶阵 **tǐng-chèn** to replace, substitute for, take the place of
顶住妖风 **tǐng-chù-yāo-fēng** to brace against an evil wind
顶峯 **tǐng-fēng** the highest peak, the apogee, apex
顶风冒雪 **tǐng-fēng-mào-hsuěh** to move against the wind and brave the snow
顶风破雾 **tǐng-fēng-p'ò-wù** to move against the wind and break through the fog
顶回去 **tǐng-hui-ch'ü** to push back, reject, repel
顶礼膜拜 **tǐng-lǐ mó-pài** to bow and kneel in worship (extremely obsequious)
顶牛 **tǐng-niú** (1) cows butting head against head (two people constantly contradicting one another); (2) a kind of domino game
顶班劳动 **tǐng-pān láo-tùng** substitute labor, [a cadre] taking over a shift as a laborer
顶, 驳, 揭, 整 **tǐng, pó, chiěh, chěng** to oppose, refute, expose, rectify (four methods to combat the rightist opportunist ideology)
顶点 **tǐng-tiěn** the pinnacle, apex;

topmost, utmost
顶替 **tǐng-t'ì** to substitute for [as an imposter], supplant falsely, pass oneself off as someone else
顶天立地 **tǐng-t'iēn-lì-tì** [with feet] on the ground and [head] supporting the sky (independent and indomitable, of the highest quality or caliber)
顶用 **tǐng-yùng** useful, serviceable
2087 鼎鼎大名 **tǐng-tǐng-tà-míng** [one's] illustrious name (now may be satirical)

tìng (dìng)

2088 订购 **tìng-kòu** to place an order, purchase
订立 **tìng-lì** to conclude, enter into [a treaty, contract, etc.]
2089 定案 **tìng-àn** to decide a case; a decision, judgment
定金 **tìng-chīn** a cash deposit, down payment, earnest money
定产 **tìng-ch'ǎn** fixed production [of grain for each peasant household] (one of the **sān-tìng**)
定厂办校 **tìng-ch'ǎng pàn-hsiào** specified factories to operate schools (refers to general rules for factory operation of schools, e.g., small and medium factories to operate elementary schools; large factories to operate middle schools)
定成分 **tìng ch'éng-fèn** to determine class status
定期 **tìng-ch'ī** periodic, regular, at fixed time intervals; to fix a time or date
定期轮换 **tìng-ch'ī lún-huàn** to rotate at fixed intervals
定期存款 **tìng-ch'ī-ts'ún-k'uǎn** a fixed deposit, a time deposit
定局论 **tìng-chú lùn** the idea that an unchangeable situation has been reached (a passive attitude that neglects the possibilities of improvement)
定息 **tìng-hsī** a fixed rate of interest
定息合营 **tìng-hsī hó-yíng** a fixed-interest joint enterprise (during the period of joint state-private enterprises)
定向系统 **tìng-hsiàng hsì-t'ǔng** orientation system (directional radio beams for aerial navigation)
定销 **tìng-hsiāo** the fixed amount of grain to be sold [by the state to grain-short peasant households] (one of the **sān-tìng**)
定型 **tìng-hsíng** a fixed pattern,

standard model, final form

定义 **tìng-ì** a definition, formulation

定稿 **tìng-kǎo** fixed documents, a final draft (as opposed to **ts'ǎo-kǎo**)

定购 **tìng-kòu** the fixed amount of grain for state purchase (one of the **sān-tìng**); to purchase, order

定理 **tìng-lǐ** law, principle; [mathematical] theorem

定量 **tìng-liàng** to determine the quantity; a fixed quantity, quota

定量供应 **tìng-liàng kūng-yìng** a fixed supply, set ration

定律 **tìng-lù** a [scientific] law

定论 **tìng-lùn** an accepted thesis, a conclusion, final judgment

定名 **tìng-míng** to give a name to, christen, dub

定牧 **tìng-mù** livestock raising on a fixed [locale] basis

定额 **tìng-ó** a fixed amount, norm, quota, target amount

定额储蓄存款 **tìng-ó ch'ǔ-hsù ts'ún-k'uǎn** fixed-amount savings deposits

定额管理 **tìng-ó-kuǎn-lǐ** norm control (control of production by a system of norms)

定评 **tìng-p'íng** definitive evaluation, final comment, ultimate judgment

定时炸弹 **tìng-shíh chà-tàn** a time bomb

定单 **tìng-tān** a purchase order, order form

定点 **tìng-tiěn** to fix a place, select a point or locality; a fixed place or point, a point of concentration

定点论 **tìng-tiěn lùn** "pinpointed" theories (as of art and literature)

定做 **tìng-tsò** to make to order, custom-made

定罪 **tìng-tsuì** to convict, find guilty; to fix the punishment, sentence

定员 **tìng-yuán** a fixed number of staff, the assigned personnel

tiū (diū)

丢盔卸甲 **tiū-k'uēi-hsièh-chiǎ** to throw away one's helmet and shed one's armor (to be defeated and give up)

丢面子 **tiū-mièn-tzu** to lose face (be humiliated, lose prestige)

丢在脑后 **tiū-tsài-nǎo-hòu** to throw into the back of the head (to forget)

丢卒保帅 **tiū-tsú pǎo-shuài** to sacrifice a pawn to save the king (often used in the sense of putting blame on subordinates to save the leading members)

tō (duō)

多级火箭 **tō-chí-huǒ-chièn** multistage rockets

多装快卸 **tō-chuāng-k'uài-hsièh** load heavily and unload quickly (a slogan for freight handlers)

多装快跑 **tō-chuāng-k'uài-p'ǎo** to load heavily and run [the train] rapidly

多中心即无中心 **tō-chūng-hsīn chí wú-chūng-hsīn** polycentrism means no center

多中心论 **tō-chūng-hsīn lùn** the theory of many centers, polycentrism

多种经营 **tō-chǔng-chīng-yíng** diversified operations (the implication is that narrow, over-specialization is to be avoided—especially in agriculture)

多种经营，全面发展 **tō-chǔng-chīng-yíng, ch'uán-mièn-fā-chǎn** diversified operations and all-round development

多种多样 **tō-chǔng tō-yàng** many types and many kinds, diversified and various, many kinds, varied

多哈 **tō-hǎ** Dohar [Qatar]

多如牛毛 **tō-jú-niú-máo** as numerous as the hairs on an ox

多哥 **tō-kō** [Republic of] Togo

多寡 **tō-kuǎ** many or few, much or little (number, quantity)

多，快，好，省 **tō-k'uài-hǎo-shěng** greater, faster, better, and more economical

多快好省地建设社会主义 **tō-k'uài-hǎo-shěng-te chièn-shè shè-huì-chǔ-ì** greater, faster, better and more economical building of socialism

多米尼加共和国 **tō-mǐ-ní-chiā kùng-hó-kuó** the Dominican Republic

多面手 **tō-mièn-shǒu** versatile person, a well-rounded person, having many skills

多民族的国家 **tō-mín-tsú te kuó-chiā** a multi-national state

多难兴邦 **tō-nàn-hsīng-pāng** [overcoming] difficulties helps a nation to grow strong

多边 **tō-piēn** many-sided, multilateral

多边协定 **tō-piēn hsiéh-tìng** a multilateral treaty, a multilateral agreement

多边形 **tō-piēn-hsíng** a polygon; polygonal

多边条约 **tō-piēn t'iáo-yuēh** a multilateral treaty

多兵种合成军队 **tō-pīng-chǔng hó-ch'éng chǔn-tuì** a combined force of different military branches

多数 **tō-shù** many, a large number; a majority; plural

多弹头导弹 **tō-tàn-t'óu tǎo-tàn** multi-warheaded ballistic missile

多党制度 **tō-tǎng chìh-tù** a multi-party system

多多益善 **tō-tō-ì-shàn** the more the better

多多少少 **tō-tō shǎo-shǎo** more or less, greater or lesser, to some extent

多头领导 **tō-t'óu-lǐng-tǎo** multi-headed leadership; multiple sources of command

多子多福 **tō-tzǔ-tō-fú** more children [and] more happiness (an old concept now criticized)

多才多艺 **tō-ts'ái-tō-ì** [possessing] much talent and many arts (gifted in many ways; versatile)

多采 **tō-ts'ǎi** multicolored, many-splendored, colorful

多样性 **tō-yàng-hsìng** diversity, variety

多余 **tō-yǘ** surplus, excess, superfluous, redundant; an excess, superfluity

多余人员 **tō-yǘ jén-yuán** excess personnel

多元论 **tō-yuán lùn** pluralism

多用少报 **tō-yùng shǎo-pào** to intentionally underestimate one's needs in submitting a budget

2092 咄咄怪事 **tō-tō-kuài-shìh** what a strange affair!

咄咄逼人 **tō-tō-pī-jén** to overawe alarmingly (to browbeat; overbearing)

tó (duó)

2093 夺取 **tó-ch'ǔ** to take by force, wrest from, grab, seize

夺取政权 **tó-ch'ǔ chèng-ch'üan** to seize governing power [of a country]

夺去 **tó-ch'ǜ** to take away, snatch from, remove, dispossess

夺权 **tó-ch'üan** to seize [political or administrative] power; a seizure of power

夺回 **tó-huí** to recapture, recover, reoccupy, take back

夺目 **tó-mù** to blind, dazzle; blinding, dazzling

tǒ (duǒ)

2094 躲避 **tǒ-pì** to dodge, shun, avoid, flee

躲躲闪闪 **tǒ-tǒ shǎn-shǎn** to move out of the way, dodge out of sight; evade, shirk

tò (duò)

2095 堕落 **tò-lò** to fall, go wrong, sink into oblivion, degenerate

堕落蜕化 **tò-lò t'uì-huà** degeneration and degradation

2096 舵手 **tò-shǒu** helmsman, pilot

2097 跺脚 **tò-chiǎo** to stamp one's foot [usually in anger]

tōu (dōu)

2098 兜圈子 **tōu-ch'üān-tzu** to take a stroll (to avoid a point, be circumlocutory, "beat about the bush")

兜售 **tōu-shòu** to peddle, sell merchandise from door to door

tǒu (dǒu)

2099 斗笠 **tǒu-lì** a broad-rimmed rain hat (usually worn by farmers)

斗 **tǒu:** see also **tòu**

2100 陡然 **tǒu-ján** suddenly, abruptly, unexpectedly

陡坡 **tǒu-p'ō** a steep slope, sharp incline

tòu (dòu)

2101 斗争 **tòu-chēng** to struggle, combat, fight; a struggle, combat, conflict; *Struggle* (a journal of the CCP Central Bureau in Kiangsi, 1933–1934)

斗争形式 **tòu-chēng-hsíng-shìh** the forms of struggle

斗争艺术 **tòu-chēng-ì-shù** the techniques of struggle

斗争纲领 **tòu-chēng-kāng-lǐng** a program of struggle, a guideline for struggle

斗争能手 **tòu-chēng-néng-shǒu** a person who is effective at struggle, a struggle expert

斗争实践 **tòu-chēng shíh-chièn** to practice struggle, the practice of struggle

斗争地主 **tòu-chēng tì-chǔ** to struggle against landlords

斗争对象 **tòu-chēng-tuì-hsiàng** struggle object, target of struggle (a person or persons being criticized in a campaign)

斗骄防变 **tòu-chiāo-fáng-pièn** to struggle against arrogance and to guard against reversion

斗志昂扬 **tòu-chìh áng-yáng** eager for the battle, full of fighting spirit

斗臭 **tòu-ch'òu** to struggle with until it stinks (to completely discredit)

斗绝了 **tòu-chüéh-le** to struggle to the extreme (to carry struggle beyond the

point of serving its useful purpose of bringing about unity)

斗垮 **tòu-k'uǎ** to struggle with until it collapses (to completely vanquish)

斗乱 **tòu-luàn** to struggle [so as to produce] confusion and disunity (since the purpose of struggle is to bring about unity, this implies excessive or an improper form of struggle)

斗批改 **tòu-p'ī-kǎi** struggle-criticism-transformation (became a widely used slogan during the Cultural Revolution meaning to struggle against those in authority taking the capitalist road; criticize and repudiate bourgeois ideas in oneself and others; transform education, literature and art, and other aspects of social life to make them correspond to the socialist economic base)

斗士 **tòu-shìh** a fighter

斗私批修 **tòu-szū-p'ì-hsiū** combat selfishness and repudiate revisionism (a Cultural Revolution slogan, 1967)

斗倒 **tòu-tǎo** to struggle with until it is overthrown; vanquish, defeat

斗倒我字 **tòu-tǎo wǒ-tzù** to vanquish the word "I"

斗掉 **tòu-tiào** to get rid of [by means of] struggle

斗错 **tòu-ts'ò** to struggle mistakenly [against someone]

斗 **tòu:** *see also* **tǒu**

2102 豆饼 **tòu-pǐng** soybean cake (the residue from pressing soybeans: an important animal feed)

tū (dū)

2103 都柏林 **tū-pó-lín** Dublin

都市 **tū-shìh** a large city, metropolis; metropolitan area

2104 督促 **tū-ts'ù** to admonish, spur on, inspire, drive forward; admonition, superintendence, enforcement

tú (dú)

2105 独占 **tú-chàn** to monopolize, a monoply

独占资本 **tú-chàn-tzū-pěn** monopoly capital

独唱 **tú-ch'àng** solo [in singing], a vocal recital

独出心裁 **tú-ch'ū-hsīn-ts'ái** to design out of one's mind alone (to have a plan that differs from those of others)

独创性 **tú-ch'uàng-hsìng** originality

独具匠心 **tú-chù-chiàng-hsīn** to have the heart of a good worker (to have originality in technique or arts)

独具慧眼 **tú-chù huì-yěn** to be possessed of a special eye (to be clairvoyant, able to see things clearly and truly)

独夫 **tú-fū** a man who is alone (a tyrant, cruel ruler, merciless autocrat)

独夫民贼 **tú-fū mín-tséi** a tyrant and plunderer of the people

独一无二 **tú-ī-wú-èrh** the only one, unique

独揽 **tú-lǎn** to be the sole holder [of power]

独立 **tú-lì** independent; independence

独立性 **tú-lì-hsìng** independence

独立思考 **tú-lì-szū-k'ǎo** independent thinking; to think independently

独立自主 **tú-lì tzù-chǔ** independent and self-governing

独立王国 **tú-lì wáng-kuó** an independent kingdom (an area or field of activity controlled by local leaders in a manner regarded as too independent of the central authority or Party)

独立运动 **tú-lì yùn-tùng** an independence movement

独龙族 **tú-lúng-tsú** the Tu-lung people (a minority in Yunnan province: population 2,700 as of 1957)

独木轮小车 **tú-mù-lún hsiǎo-ch'ē** a wheelbarrow

独木难支 **tú-mù-nán-chīh** it is difficult for a single pole to support (one person alone cannot accomplish much)

独木不成林 **tú-mù-pù-ch'éng-lín** one tree does not make a forest (it takes many)

独幕剧 **tú-mù-chù** a one-act play

独霸 **tú-pà** to exert hegemony, exercise absolute power, dominate

独树一帜 **tú-shù-ī-chìh** to set up a separate flag (to create a new style in art or a new situation in politics)

独胆沉着 **tú-tǎn-ch'én-chó** brave and composed when [fighting] alone

独当一面 **tú-tāng-ī-mièn** to take the whole responsibility in one sector

独到之处 **tú-tào-chīh-ch'ù** special merits, original aspects

独断专行 **tú-tuàn-chuān-hsíng** to take an arbitrary action

独断独行 **tú-tuàn-tú-hsíng** to decide and act on one's own, act arbitrarily

独体字 **tú-t'ǐ-tzù** a unitary character (a character which cannot be broken into elements that can stand alone)

独特 **tú-t'è** special, particular, distinguished, unique

独吞 **tú-t'ūn** to swallow by oneself (to pocket illicit profits without sharing)

独自 **tú-tzù** by oneself, alone, single-handedly; personally

独裁 **tú-ts'ái** dictatorial; dictatorship; to exercise [power] dictatorially, to act as a dictator

独有 **tú-yǔ** to possess solely

2106　毒剂 **tú-chì** a toxin, poison

毒气 **tú-ch'ì** poison gas

毒气弹 **tú-ch'ì-tàn** a poison gas shell, poison gas bomb

毒害 **tú-hài** to injure grievously, do great injustice to, poison [the mind]

毒化 **tú-huà** to empoison, envenom

毒辣 **tú-là** malicious, cruel, spiteful, ruthless

毒蛇 **tú-shé** poisonous snakes (an epithet often applied to intellectuals accused of being critical of Mao Tse-tung or the Party)

毒手 **tú-shǒu** malicious tactics, a venomous act

毒素 **tú-sù** poisonous matter, a toxin

毒草 **tú-ts'ǎo** poisonous weeds (literary or artistic works regarded as harmful to the Party or to the Thought of Mao Tse-tung)

毒雾迷尘 **tú-wù-mí-ch'én** poisonous fog and eye-smarting dust

2107　读卖新闻 **tú-mài hsìn-wén** the *Yomiuri Shimbun*

读报组 **tú-pào-tsǔ** newspaper-reading groups

读报员 **tú-pào-yuán** a newspaper reader (a person who reads news-papers aloud to illiterates in villages or factories)

读书 **tú-shū** to read books, study, *The Reader* (a Peking semi-monthly journal, 1955—)

读书做官 **tú-shū-tsò-kuān** to study [in order to] become an official (attacked as a reactionary concept recalling Confucian education)

读书无用论 **tú-shū wú-yùng lùn** theory that study is useless (condemned by Maoists as a leftist over-reaction in the Cultural Revolution)

读书务农 **tú-shū wù-núng** [those who] study should also engage in agriculture

2108　黩武主义 **tú-wǔ-chǔ-ì** crass militarism, saber rattling, jingoism

tǔ (dǔ)

2109　笃定 **tǔ-tìng** very sure of; to take

seriously

2110　堵江抗旱 **tǔ-chiāng k'àng-hàn** to dam rivers to guard against drought (raising the level of the water to reach the fields)

堵住 **tǔ-chù** to plug, close, block up, stop

堵塞 **tǔ-sāi** to stop up, block the way, close

堵死 **tǔ-szǔ** to block completely

2111　赌咒 **tǔ-chòu** to take an oath, pledge, vow, swear

赌博 **tǔ-pó** to gamble for money; gambling

tù (dù)

2112　杜撰 **tù-chuàn** to fabricate [a story, etc.], trump up

杜绝 **tù-chüéh** to stop completely, break off, terminate, eliminate, revoke

杜鹃山 **tù-chüān-shān** "Tu-chüan Mountain" (an addition to the original group of **yàng-pǎn-hsì**)

杜勒斯 **tù-lè-szū** Dulles (John Foster, 1888–1959)

杜林 **tù-lín** Dühring (Eugen, 1833–1921)

杜鲁门 **tù-lǔ-mén** Truman (President Harry S.)

杜鲁门主义 **tù-lǔ-mén-chǔ-ì** the Truman Doctrine (1946)

2113　度量 **tù-liàng** mass, capacity, measure; measuring instruments; degree of magnanimity, generosity

度量衡 **tù-liàng-héng** weights and measures

度数 **tù-shù** a reading in degrees, meter reading

2114　渡江作战 **tù-chiāng tsò-chàn** the river crossing campaign (the crossing of the Yangtze in April, 1949)

tuān (duān)

2115　端正 **tuān-chèng** correct, proper, decent, honest; well-formed, symmetric

端正思想 **tuān-chèng-szū-hsiǎng** correct ideology, proper thinking

端正态度 **tuān-chèng-t'ài-tù** a proper attitude

端倪已见 **tuān-ní-ǐ-chièn** the clue is already evident

tuǎn (duǎn)

2116　短暂 **tuǎn-chàn** short and temporary, transient, brief, temporarily

短期轮训 **tuǎn-ch'ī lún-hsùn** short-term training in rotation

短处 **tuǎn-ch'ù** shortcomings, faults, defects, weak points

短缺 **tuǎn-ch'üēh** to be deficient, fall short; a deficiency

短工 **tuǎn-kūng** a temporary employee, day laborer

短兵相接 **tuǎn-pīng-hsiāng-chiēh** to oppose with short weapons (hand-to-hand combat; fighting at close quarters)

短波 **tuǎn-pō** shortwave [radio, etc.]

短评 **tuǎn-p'íng** a short editorial, brief commentary (usually in a position of less prominence than the lead editorial)

短吨 **tuǎn-tūn** a short ton (907.2 kg.; 2000 lbs.)

短途运输 **tuǎn-t'ú yùn-shū** to transport over short distances; short distance transportation

tuàn (duàn)

2117 断章取义 **tuàn-chāng ch'ǔ-ì** to acquire the idea by broken sentences (to take a few sentences out of context; to take an excerpt for the whole)

断绝关系 **tuàn-chüéh kuān-hsi** to sever relations, break off relations

断线 **tuàn-hsièn** to break the thread (to lose contact)

断然 **tuàn-ján** certainly, absolutely, positively, categorically, emphatically, conclusively

断粮 **tuàn-liáng** short of food; to run out of food

断面 **tuàn-mièn** a cross section

断送 **tuàn-sùng** to throw away, lose for good; an irrevocable loss

断定 **tuàn-tìng** to decide, determine, conclude, fix; a judgment [in logic], conclusion

断言 **tuàn-yén** to say with certainty, assert confidently

2118 锻炼 **tuàn-lièn** to temper, steel, forge, harden, refine (to train or discipline oneself or others)

tuī (duī)

2119 堆积 **tuī-chī** to pile up, store up, accumulate, amass

堆场 **tuī-ch'ǎng** an open cargo storage area

堆砌 **tuī-ch'ì** to pile up; to lay [bricks]; to use superfluous words or phrases

tuì (duì)

2120 队界 **tuì-chièh** brigade boundaries [in the communes]

队校挂钩 **tuì-hsiào kuà-kōu** to set up linkages between [commune] brigades and schools

队队有储备，户户有余粮 **tuì-tuì yǔ ch'ǔ-pèi, hù-hù yǔ yú-liáng** every brigade has [grain] reserves and every household has leftover grain

队伍 **tuì-wǔ** troops, rank and file, an organized group

队养猪 **tuì-yǎng-chū** pigs raised by work teams or brigades

队员 **tuì-yuán** a member of a brigade or labor team [in the communes]; a member of the Young Pioneers

2121 对照 **tuì-chào** to check against, compare, contrast, place side by side

对峙 **tuì-chìh** to stand opposite, confront each other; confrontation (often implies a condition of stalemate)

对准 **tuì-chǔn** to aim at, set one's sights on; to adjust something to make it more accurate

对称 **tuì-ch'èn** symmetry; symmetrical

对方 **tuì-fāng** the other side, the other party [to a dispute]

对付 **tuì-fu** to deal with, cope with, respond to; a response

对象 **tuì-hsiàng** object [of an action], objective, target; subject [of consideration]; partner, opposite person

对人民负责的精神 **tuì jén-mín fù-tsé-te chīng-shén** the spirit of responsibility to the people

对抗 **tuì-k'àng** to face each other in opposition, encounter, confront, rival; to resist, oppose; antagonism; antagonistic

对抗阶级 **tuì-k'àng-chiēh-chí** antagonistic classes

对抗性 **tuì-k'àng-hsìng** antagonism

对口 **tuì-k'ǒu** the edges fit, fit exactly, correspond with (one's work corresponds with his training)

对口下厂 **tuì-k'ǒu hsià-ch'ǎng** to go and work in factories according to one's specialties

对立 **tuì-lì** to stand opposite each other; opposed

对立而又统一 **tuì-lì érh yù t'ǔng-ī** opposed and yet there is unity, both contradictory and in unity

对立关系 **tuì-lì-kuān-hsi** antagonistic relations

对立面 **tuì-lì-mièn** opposite sides,

opposites; confrontation

对立统一 **tuì-lì t'ǔng-ī** the unity of opposites

对立统一法则 **tuì-lì-t'ǔng-ī fǎ-tsé** the law of the unity of opposites

對流 **tuì-liú** convection currents [of heat or electrified particles], convection

对牛弹琴 **tuì-niú-t'án-ch'ín** to play a lute before an ox (to talk over people's heads; persuasion unsuited to the target)

对白 **tuì-pái** stage dialogue

对比 **tuì-pǐ** to contrast with, compare with; correlation, contrast; ratio, proportion

对不上号 **tuì-pù-shang-hào** cannot match the [correct] number (to make a mistake)

对待 **tuì-tài** to treat, deal with, behave toward; in regard to; treatment

对敌斗争 **tuì-tí tòu-chēng** the struggle against the enemy

对敌要狠, 对己要和 **tuì tí yào hěn, tuì chǐ yào hó** [struggle] against enemies must be ruthless [but struggle] among ourselves must be harmonious [i.e., non-antagonistic and constructive]

对台戏 **tuì-t'ái-hsì** a competitive dramatic performance on facing stages (may refer to political competition as between the USSR and US)

对天宣战 **tuì-t'iēn hsuān-chàn** to declare war against heaven (to overcome natural handicaps in production)

对外经济交流 **tuì-wài chīng-chì chiāo-liú** economic exchanges with foreign countries

对外经济联络部 **tuì-wài chīng-chì lién-lò-pù** Ministry of Economic Relations with Foreign Countries [of the State Council]

对外扩张政策 **tuì-wài k'uò-chāng chèng-ts'è** a policy of expansion abroad

对外贸易 **tuì-wài mào-ì** foreign trade

对外贸易逆差 **tuì-wài mào-ì nì-ch'ā** an unfavorable deficit in foreign trade

对外贸易部 **tuì-wài mào-ì-pù** Ministry of Foreign Trade [of the State Council]

对外文化联络委员会 **tuì-wài wén-huà lién-lò wěi-yuán-huì** Commission for Cultural Relations with Foreign Countries [of the State Council]

2122 兑换 **tuì-huàn** to exchange, convert [currencies]; exchange conversion; convertibility

兑换率 **tuì-huàn-lù** the rate of exchange [between currencies]

兑现 **tuì-hsièn** to exchange, convert, redeem, cash in; to fulfill a promise, keep one's word

tūn (dūn)

2123 吨 **tūn** a ton (now can be assumed to be 1000 kg.)

吨位 **tūn-wèi** tonnage

2124 敦促 **tūn-ts'ù** to urge sincerely, press for

2125 蹲试验室 **tūn shìh-yèn-shìh** to squat in the laboratory (spending too much time divorced from practical reality)

蹲点 **tūn-tiěn** to squat on a spot (to carry out concentrated field work to study conditions in a particular locality)

tùn (dùn)

2126 顿时 **tùn-shíh** immediately, promptly, at once

tūng (dōng)

2127 东张西望 **tūng-chāng-hsī-wàng** to stare east and look west (to look about furtively in every direction)

东江纵队 **tūng-chiāng tsūng-tuì** the East River Column (a Communist force near Canton during the Resistance War)

东京 **tūng-chīng** Tokyo

东抄西剪 **tūng-ch'āo hsī-chiěn** to copy from the east and clip from the west (no originality in writing, to copy shamelessly from others)

东翻西抄 **tūng-fān hsī-ch'āo** to turn [to reference books] in the east and copy from the west (*see above*)

东方红 **tūng-fāng-húng** the East is Red (1. the title of a song, written in 1942, to music based on a North Shensi folk song; 2. a musical pageant of the history of the CCP, first produced in 1964)

东风压倒西风 **tūng-fēng yā-tǎo hsī-fēng** the East wind prevails over the West wind (the forces of socialism prevail over the forces of imperialism; a quotation from the *Dream of the Red Chamber*, quoted by Mao in Moscow on November 17, 1957)

东海舰队 **tūng-hǎi chièn-tuì** the East Sea Fleet (of the PLA, based in Shanghai)

东方族 **tūng-hsiāng-tsú** the Tung-

hsiang people (a minority in Kansu province: population 159,000 as of 1957)

东南亚集体防务条约 **tūng-nán-yà chí-t'ǐ fáng-wù t'iáo-yuēh** the Southeast Asia Collective Defense Treaty (the basis of SEATO)

东欧 **tūng-ōu** Eastern Europe

东北 **tūng-pěi** the Northeast [provinces of China, commonly referred to in the West as Manchuria]

东奔西跑 **tūng-pēn-hsī-p'ǎo** to rush toward the east and run toward the west (to bustle about actively)

东拼西凑 **tūng-p'īn-hsī-ts'òu** to arrange in the east and collect in the west (to patch up from bits, to scrape together)

东沙群岛 **tūng-shā ch'ún-tǎo** the Paratus [Pratas] Islands (about 350 kilometers southeast of Hong Kong)

东山再起 **tūng-shān tsài-ch'ǐ** to rise again from the eastern mountain (to stage a comeback; a return to power)

东亚 **tūng-yà** East Asia

2128 冬小麦 **tūng-hsiǎo-mài** winter wheat

冬闲 **tūng-hsién** the winter slack season [in agriculture]

冬学 **tūng-hsuéh** winter school (part-time winter schools to teach peasant adults basic literacy and ideology)

冬令营 **tūng-lìng-yíng** winter camp (quasi-military training during winter vacation)

冬忙 **tūng-máng** the winter busy season (winter was formerly a slack season for farm work: major construction projects, study campaigns, etc., are now scheduled to change the old pattern and make winter a busy season)

冬有棉夏有单 **tūng-yǔ-mién hsià-yǔ-tān** in winter [we] have quilted [clothes] and in summer unlined [ones] (to have adequate and suitable clothing)

tǔng (dòng)

2129 董存瑞 **tǔng ts'ún-juì** Tung Ts'un-jui (a PLA hero in the 1946–1949 civil war who immolated himself in the process of blowing up a KMT blockhouse)

tùng (dòng)

2130 动辄得咎 **tùng-ché-té-chiù** to draw criticisms at every move, any action draws censure

动机 **tùng-chī** a motive, cause, inducement, occasion, intention

动静 **tùng-chìng** news of action, signs of movement; a noise, stir

动产 **tùng-ch'ǎn** liquid assets, movable property

动向 **tùng-hsiàng** direction of a movement, a trend, tendency

动人 **tùng-jén** very moving, touching, inspiring

动人情景 **tùng-jén ch'íng-chǐng** a touching scene, moving sight [involving people]

动工 **tùng-kūng** to commence work [on a project or construction]

动口 **tùng-k'ǒu** to move the mouth (to talk without doing; to argue without fighting)

动力 **tùng-lì** motive force, power, energy

动力车床 **tùng-lì ch'ē-ch'uáng** an engine lathe, power lathe

动力学 **tùng-lì-hsuéh** dynamics, kinetics

动力灌溉机械 **tùng-lì kuàn-kài chī-hsièh** power-driven irrigation machinery

动力来源 **tùng-lì lái-yuán** power resources

动脑筋 **tùng nǎo-chīn** to exercise the brain, think, consider, deliberate; to plan secretly

动手 **tùng-shǒu** to move the hands, start work, commence a project

动手派 **tùng-shǒu-p'ài** those who are real workers (people who work without wasting time on talk)

动荡 **tùng-tàng** uneasy, unstable, turbulent; to waver, shake; wavering

动荡不稳 **tùng-tàng-pù-wěn** shaky and unstable

动态 **tùng-t'ài** general trend [of affairs], development [of an event], overall situation, circumstances

动听 **tùng-t'īng** inspiring to listen to, persuasive, impressive

动作整齐 **tùng-tsò chěng-ch'í** [to make] movement in unison, march in step

动物学 **tùng-wù-hsuéh** zoology

动摇 **tùng-yáo** to waver, vacillate, wobble, shake; wavering

动摇不定的两面性 **tùng-yáo pù-tìng te liǎng-mièn-hsìng** the two-sidedness of wavering and uncertainty, vacillation

动员 **tùng-yuán** to mobilize, call up, rally; mobilization

动员一切积极因素 **tùng-yuán ī-ch'ièh chī-chí yīn-sù** to mobilize all positive factors

动用 **tùng-yùng** to use, employ, exercise, draw upon [funds]

2131 冻结 **tùng-chiéh** to freeze, congeal (also figurative)

364

冻结资金 **tùng-chiéh tzū-chīn** to freeze assets; frozen capital, blocked assets

冻疮 **tùng-ch'uāng** chilblains, frostbite

冻伤 **tùng-shāng** frostbite, injuries from exposure to cold

冻土 **tùng-t'ǔ** permafrost

2132　侗家 **tùng-chiā** the Tung-chia (a minority people now known as Tung —see below)

侗族 **tùng-tsú** the Tung people (a minority in Kweichow, Hunan, and Kwangsi provinces: population 825,000 as of 1957)

2133　洞察 **tùng-ch'á** to examine thoroughly, search carefully, see and understand clearly

2134　恫吓 **tùng-hsià** to menace, threaten, intimidate; a threat

t'ā (tā)

2135　塌台 **t'ā-t'ái** to break down, collapse, close shop, fail [in business, etc.]

2136　踏实 **t'ā-shíh** standing on firm ground (practical, realistic)

踏踏实实 **t'ā-t'ā shíh-shíh** practical, realistic (see above)

踏 **t'ā**: see also **t'à**

t'ǎ (tǎ)

2137　塔吉克族 **t'ǎ-chí-k'ò tsú** the Tajik people (a minority in the Sinkiang-Uighur Autonomous Region: population 15,000 as of 1957)

塔那那利佛 **t'ǎ-nà-nà-lì-fó** Tananarive [Malagasy]

塔斯社 **t'ǎ-szū-shè** the TASS News Agency

塔塔尔族 **t'ǎ-t'ǎ-ěrh-tsú** the Tatar people (a minority in the Sinkiang-Uighur Autonomous Region: population 4,000 as of 1957)

t'à (tà)

2138　踏脚石 **t'à-chiǎo-shíh** a stepping stone

踏步 **t'à-pù** to mark time [military], march in place

踏 **t'à**: see also **t'ā**

t'ái (tái)

2139　台 **t'ái** Taiwan province

台柱 **t'ái-chù** chief support, main pillar (the principal actor, central role)

台前 **t'ái-ch'ién** in front of the stage, the forestage

台风 **t'ái-fēng** a typhoon (a tropical cyclone in the China Sea)

台风联防 **t'ái-fēng-lién-fáng** coordinated defense against typhoons (a coordinated typhoon observation and warning network along the coast)

台湾海峡 **t'ái-wān hǎi-hsiá** the Taiwan Strait

台湾民主自治同盟 **t'ái-wān mín-chǔ tzù-chìh t'úng-méng** the Taiwan Democratic Self-Government League

台湾独立运动 **t'ái-wān tú-lì yùn-tùng** the Taiwan Independence Movement

2140　抬轿子的人 **t'ái chiào-tzu te jén** sedan-chair bearers (supporters of those in power)

抬出来 **t'ái-ch'u-lai** to raise and carry out (to elevate and make use of [a person, often dead])

抬高 **t'ái-kāo** to raise, elevate, enhance

抬高自己,贬低他人 **t'ái-kāo tzù-chǐ, piěn-tī t'ā-jén** to glorify oneself and belittle others

抬高物价 **t'ái-kāo wù-chià** to raise prices, force up prices

抬头 **t'ái-t'óu** to raise one's head (to gain self-respect and confidence)

抬头挺胸 **t'ái-t'óu t'ǐng-hsiūng** to raise the head and put out the chest

t'ài (tài)

2141　太极拳 **t'ài-chí-ch'uán** tai chi chuan, or more popularly, tai chi (an ancient form of boxing or gymnastics, with slow, circular movements combined with breath control)

太空 **t'ài-k'ūng** the great void, space

太空人 **t'ài-k'ūng-jén** a spaceman, astronaut

太平门 **t'ài-p'ing-mén** a safety door, emergency exit

太平盛世 **t'ài-p'íng shèng-shìh** a time of peace and prosperity

太平天国 **t'ài-p'íng t'iēn-kuó** the Taiping Heavenly Kingdom (1851–1864)

太平天国革命运动 **t'ài-p'íng t'iēn-kuó kó-mìng yùn-tùng** the revolutionary movement of the Taipings

太上皇 **t'ài-shàng-huáng** the father of the emperor (an eminence grise, kingmaker)

太子港 **t'ài-tzǔ kǎng** Port-au-Prince [Haiti]

太阳 **t'ài-yang** the sun (now a symbol representing the Party or Mao Tse-tung)

太阳系 **t'ài-yáng-hsì** the solar system

太阳能 **t'ài-yáng-néng** solar energy

太阳能电池 **t'ài-yáng-néng tièn-ch'íh** a solar battery

太阳灶 **t'ài-yáng-tsào** a solar stove

2142　态势 **t'ài-shìh** the [military] situation

态度 **t'ài-tù** attitude, behavior, manner

2143　泰然处之 **t'ài-ján-ch'ǔ-chīh** to handle in a calm manner, deal calmly [with a difficult situation]

泰然自若 **t'ài-ján-tzù-jò** as calm and easy as before, cool and collected, imperturbable

泰国 **t'ài-kuó** Thailand [Siam]

泰晤士报 **t'ài-wù-shìh pào** *The Times* [of London]

t'ān (tān)

2144　贪占 **t'ān-chàn** to take avariciously

贪官污吏 **t'ān-kuān wū-lì** avaricious officers and corrupt public servants (corrupt officials)

贪婪 **t'ān-lán** cupidity, avarice, greed

贪暴 **t'ān-pào** corrupt and brutal

贪大求洋 **t'ān-tà ch'iú-yáng** to love ostentation and seek foreign [ways]

贪得无厌 **t'ān-té-wú-yèn** insatiable covetousness

贪多求快 **t'ān-tō ch'iú-k'uài** to be greedy for quantity and to press for speed (to seek speed and quantity over considerations of quality and cost)

贪多反失 **t'ān-tō fǎn-shīh** to grasp for more but to lose [all]

贪图享乐 **t'ān-t'ú hsiǎng-lè** to be greedy for sensual pleasures

贪图享受 **t'ān-t'ú hsiǎng-shòu** to be greedy for a sybaritic life

贪污 **t'ān-wū** avaricious, corrupt; bribery (usually refers to official corruption or corruption of officials: one of the **wǔ-fǎn**)

贪污腐化 **t'ān-wū fǔ-huà** corrupt and degenerate; corruption and degeneration

贪污盗窃 **t'ān-wū-tào-ch'ièh** corruption and theft

贪慾 **t'ān-yǜ** avarice, greed

2145　摊贩 **t'ān-fàn** a vendor, stall keeper, peddler

摊开 **t'ān-k'āi** to spread out, open up, unfold, lay bare

摊牌 **t'ān-p'ái** to show one's cards, put one's cards on the table; a showdown

摊子 **t'ān-tzu** a peddler's stand, stall, booth

2146　瘫痪 **t'ān-huàn** paralyzed, paralytic

t'án (tán)

2147　昙花一现 **t'án-huā-ī-hsièn** like the blooming of a cereus (a fleeting phenomenon, to appear and then to be gone)

2148　谈家史 **t'án chiā-shǐh** to discuss family history (to relate the family histories of poor peasants and workers to arouse class consciousness especially among the youth)

谈虎色变 **t'án-hǔ-sè-pièn** mention of the tiger [causes] the countenance to change (unable to control one's emotions when something horrible is mentioned)

谈话记录 **t'án-huà chì-lù** minutes of talks, a record of a conversation

谈心 **t'án-hsīn** heart-to-heart talk, to pour out one's soul (often refers to political persuasion to aid the less advanced in raising their ideological understanding)

谈论 **t'án-lùn** to discuss, talk about; a detailed discussion

谈判 **t'án-p'àn** to negotiate, discuss, confer, deliberate; negotiations

谈问题 **t'án-wèn-t'í** to discuss problems (usually with the implication of seeking or offering help or clarification of thinking)

t'ǎn (tǎn)

2149　忐忑不安 **t'ǎn-t'è-pù-ān** indecisive and uneasy, apprehensive, nervous

2150　坦然 **t'ǎn-ján** calm, self-possessed, tranquil, composed, fully at ease

坦噶尼喀 **t'ǎn-ká-ní-k'ā** Tanganyika [now part of Tanzania]

坦克 **t'ǎn-k'ò** a [military] tank

坦白 **t'ǎn-pái** open, frank, honest; to tell the truth, speak frankly without reserve (politically, it refers to honesty and frankness in confessing one's own shortcomings)

坦白检查大会 **t'ǎn-pái chièn-ch'á tà-huì** confession and examination assemblies

坦白从宽，抗拒从严 **t'ǎn-pái ts'úng-k'uān, k'àng-chù ts'úng-yén** leniency toward those who acknowledge their crimes but severe punishment of those who stubbornly refuse

坦桑尼亚 **t'ǎn-sāng-ní-yà** Tanzania

坦率交换意见 **t'ǎn-shuài chiāo-huàn ì-chièn** to exchange views on a straightforward [candid] basis; a frank exchange of views

t'àn (tàn)

2151　叹气 **t'àn-ch'ì** to sigh; a sigh

叹为观止 **t'àn-wéi kuān-chǐh** to gasp in astonishment at the sight, to see something so great that there is no need to look further

2152 探照灯 **t'àn-chào-tēng** a searchlight, spotlight

探求 **t'àn-ch'iú** to seek, search for, pry out, look into

探出 **t'àn-ch'ū** to ferret out, search out, probe

探明 **t'àn-míng** to spy out, to find out by inquiry

探索 **t'àn-sǒ** to search for, look into, trace out, explore thoroughly

探讨 **t'àn-t'ǎo** to inquire into, ask about, examine, discuss [in an exploratory manner]

探头探脑 **t'àn-t'óu-t'àn-nǎo** to incline the head in a prying manner (to act stealthily, eavesdrop, be a secret listener)

t'āng (tāng)

2153 汤药 **t'āng-yào** a decoction of medicinal herbs

2154 蹚水 **t'āng-shuǐ** to walk through water, to ford [a stream, etc.]

t'áng (táng)

2155 堂而皇之 **t'áng-érh-huáng-chīh** with dignified bearing, in a grand manner

堂皇 **t'áng-huáng** imposing, impressive, stately

2156 塘肥 **t'áng-féi** pond-mud fertilizer

塘泥 **t'áng-ní** pond mud (used as a fertilizer—*see above*)

2157 镗床 **t'áng-ch'uáng** a boring machine

2158 糖衣炮弹 **t'áng-ī p'ào-tàn** sugar-coated bullets (deceitful propaganda; usually implies the use of economic inducements to subvert workers, etc., from a more austere revolutionary line)

2159 螳臂当车 **t'áng-pì-tāng-ch'ē** like a praying mantis using its feelers to stop the chariot (futile courage)

t'ǎng (tǎng)

2160 躺倒不干 **t'ǎng-tǎo-pù-kàn** to lie down and stop working (to refuse to work, lie down on the job)

t'āo (tāo)

2161 掏鸡窝 **t'āo chī-wō** to clean out chicken roosts

2162 滔滔不绝 **t'āo-t'āo-pù-chüéh** flowing endlessly, unceasing, inexhaustible (to talk fluently and endlessly)

滔天罪行 **t'āo-t'iēn-tsuì-hsíng** a crime that fills the sky, monstrous crime

t'áo (táo)

2163 逃荒要饭 **t'áo-huāng yào-fàn** to flee famine and beg for food

逃避 **t'áo-pì** to run away from, evade, dodge, escape, avoid

逃兵 **t'áo-pīng** a deserting soldier, deserter, fugitive, straggler

逃跑主义 **t'áo-p'ǎo-chǔ-ì** flightism

逃税 **t'áo-shuì** to avoid payment of taxes; tax evasion

逃脱 **t'áo-t'ō** to escape, evade, run away

逃窜 **t'áo-ts'uàn** to disperse and flee

逃亡 **t'áo-wáng** to flee, run away, escape, become fugitives

逃亡地主 **t'áo-wáng tì-chǔ** runaway landlords

2164 陶里亚蒂 **t'áo-lǐ-yà-tì** Togliatti (the Italian Communist leader)

2165 桃园经验 **t'áo-yuán chīng-yèn** "The Peach Garden Experience" (a report by the wife of Liu Shao-ch'i [Wang Kuang-mei] criticized during the Culture Revolution)

2166 淘汰 **t'áo-t'ài** to cull, eliminate inferior items, scour, wash thoroughly, [natural] selection; [athletic] elimination

t'ǎo (tǎo)

2167 讨债 **t'ǎo-chài** to call in a loan, demand payment of a debt, dun

讨伐 **t'ǎo-fá** to take punitive action, punish [militarily], subjugate

讨好 **t'ǎo-hǎo** to cater to, seek to make oneself liked, curry favor

讨还血债 **t'ǎo-huán hsuèh-chài** to pay back a blood debt, obtain revenge

讨论 **t'ǎo-lùn** to discuss, debate, argue; discussion (usually implies free and frank discussions where differences are revealed and resolved)

讨论会 **t'ǎo-lùn-huì** a discussion meeting (*see above*)

讨生活 **t'ǎo shēng-huó** to make a living, eke out a living

讨厌 **t'ǎo-yèn** disgusting, troublesome, annoying; to find [something] repulsive

t'ào (tào)

2168 套购 **t'ào-kòu** illicit buying; arbitrage

套上绞索 **t'ào-shang chiǎo-sǒ** to put a

noose around one's own neck

套用 **t'ào-yùng** to copy and use,
borrow

t'è (tè)

2169 特征 **t'è-chēng** defining qualities, distinctive features, unique marks,
characteristics

特制 **t'è-chìh** specially made, made to
order

特种戶口 **t'è-chǔng hù-k'ǒu** special
category families (families under
suspicion or surveillance)

特种钢 **t'è-chǔng-kāng** special [types
of] steel

特种部队 **t'è-chǔng pù-tuì** specialized
branches of the armed forces [such
as missile forces]

特产 **t'è-ch'ǎn** special products,
indigenous goods, articles
characteristic of a particular locality

特权 **t'è-ch'üán** special powers, special
privileges, unusual prerogatives;
especially empowered; immunity

特权阶级 **t'è-ch'üán-chiēh-chí** the
privileged classes

特惠关税制 **t'è-huì kuān-shuì-chìh** a
preferential tariff system

特写 **t'è-hsiěh** a feature article [in a
newspaper or magazine], a special
report; to write up one's impressions

特性 **t'è-hsìng** a special quality,
defining characteristic, distinctive
feature, peculiarity, individuality

特许 **t'è-hsǔ** special permission, special
grant; a concession, franchise

特意 **t'è-ì** purposely, intentionally

特古西加尔巴 **t'è-kǔ-hsī-chiā-ěrh-pā**
Tegucigalpa [Honduras]

特命全权公使 **t'è-mìng ch'üán-ch'üán
kūng-shǐh** envoy extraordinary and
minister plenipotentiary

特别刑法 **t'è-piéh hsíng-fǎ** special
criminal statutes, provisional
criminal laws

特别市 **t'è-piéh-shìh** special city (the
KMT designation for cities such as
Shanghai having special municipality
status)

特派代表 **t'è-p'ài tài-piǎo** a special
representative, special emissary

特色 **t'è-sè** unique features, special
characteristics, outstanding qualities

特赦 **t'è-shè** a special amnesty, pardon;
to pardon

特使 **t'è-shǐh** a special envoy

特殊 **t'è-shū** distinguished, special,
unusual, unique

特殊照顾 **t'è-shū chào-kù** special

treatment (treatment differing from
the usual, may be suggestive of
favoritism or impropriety)

特殊化 **t'è-shū-huà** to particularize
(treatment or status not enjoyed by
others)

特点 **t'è-tiěn** special features, characteristics, peculiarities, special traits,
specialties

特定 **t'è-tìng** designated specified;
particular, specific, limited

特务 **t'è-wu** special tasks (a special
agent, spy, undercover agent)

特务分子 **t'è-wù fèn-tzǔ** special elements (usually refers to KMT agents)

特务组织 **t'è-wù tsǔ-chīh** a special-
affairs organization (secret police,
espionage organization, secret
service)

特邀代表 **t'è-yāo tài-piǎo** a specially
invited delegate, representative by
invitation

特约演出 **t'è-yuēh yěn-ch'ū** a stage
presentation by special arrangement,
guest performance

t'éng (téng)

2170 腾出 **t'éng-ch'ū** to clear out, make
available, move aside, make space

t'í (tí)

2171 剔除 **t'í-ch'ú** to sort out and remove
[the bad], separate and discard

2172 梯田 **t'í-t'ién** terraced fields

2173 锑矿 **t'í-k'uàng** an antimony mine

2174 踢开 **t'í-k'āi** to kick [something] out of
the way; to kick open [a door]

踢皮球 **t'í p'í-ch'iú** to kick the ball
around (to pass the buck)

t'í (tí)

2175 提案 **t'í-àn** a proposal, proposition; a
resolution, bill, motion

提交 **t'í-chiāo** to deliver, forward, hand
over to the custody of, submit to

提倡 **t'í-ch'àng** to promote, advocate,
introduce, put forward, sponsor,
advance

提前 **t'í-ch'ién** ahead of schedule,
early; to move ahead, give priority to

提前释放 **t'í-ch'ién shìh-fàng** to move
up [the date of] release; release
before expiration of the sentence

提前完成 **t'í-ch'ién wán-ch'éng** to finish
[a task, etc.] ahead of schedule, pre-
schedule completion

提琴 **t'í-ch'ín** a violin

提请 **t'í-ch'ǐng** to submit a request,

make a proposal, appeal
提请注意 **t'í-ch'ǐng chù-ì** to request attention to
提出 **t'í-ch'ū** to bring forward, propose, raise, present, introduce
提纯复壮 **t'í-ch'ún-fù-chuàng** purification and rejuvenation
提心吊胆 **t'í-hsīn-tiào-tǎn** to lift the heart and hang the gall bladder (jittery, wary)
提议 **t'í-ì** to make a proposal, suggest, offer, move; a proposal, suggestion, motion
提意见 **t'í ì-chièn** to express an opinion, put forward views, advance criticism
提纲 **t'í-kāng** an outline, main points, principal thesis, summary
提纲挈领 **t'í-kāng-ch'iéh-lǐng** to select and bring forward the main points
提高 **t'í-kāo** to elevate, raise, lift, heighten, increase, improve, enhance, advance; elevation
提高纪律性 **t'í-kāo chì-lù-hsìng** to heighten one's sense of discipline
提高警惕 **t'í-kāo chǐng-t'ì** to heighten vigilance against
提高觉悟 **t'í-kāo chüéh-wù** to raise [one's level of political] consciousness
提高单位面积产量 **t'í-kāo tān-wèi mièn-chī ch'ǎn-liàng** to increase production per area unit
提高自觉性 **t'í-kāo tzù-chüéh-hsìng** raise one's self-awareness (to distinguish between true and false Marxism)
提供 **t'í-kùng** to provide, supply with, deliver, offer, place at the disposal of
提炼 **t'í-lièn** to refine, purify, extract, cleanse
提名 **t'í-míng** to nominate, recommend; nomination
提拔 **t'í-pá** to give [a person] a pull, promote, favor, help, act as a patron of
提审 **t'í-shěn** to bring up for trial, summon to appear in court; remove to a higher jurisdiction
提升 **t'í-shēng** to promote, elevate, advance, put into a higher position
提早 **t'í-tsǎo** ahead of time, in advance of schedule; to advance to an earlier date [or time]; to anticipate
提要 **t'í-yào** to bring forth the main points; an extract, synopsis, resume, summary
啼饥号寒 **t'í-chī-háo-hán** to wail with hunger and cold
啼笑皆非 **t'í-hsiào-chiēh-fēi** laughter and tears are both inappropriate (one does not know whether to laugh or cry; between tears and laughter)

题目 **t'í-mù** a subject, topic, heading, theme, title
题材 **t'í-ts'ái** subject matter, scope, content

t'ǐ (tǐ)

体积 **t'ǐ-chī** volume [of solids], cubic measure
体制 **t'ǐ-chìh** a system (normally of institutional form, rules, and hierarchical relationships)
体罚 **t'ǐ-fá** physical punishment (normally refers to school discipline)
体会 **t'ǐ-huì** to comprehend through intuition, realize, come to understand, appreciate through personal search
体系 **t'ǐ-hsì** a system (see **t'ǐ-chìh**); a system of concepts or ideas; orderliness
体现 **t'ǐ-hsièn** to embody, realize; an embodiment, materialization
体力 **t'ǐ-lì** physical strength, stamina; bodily, manual
体力劳动 **t'ǐ-lì láo-tùng** manual labor, physical work
体谅 **t'ǐ-liàng** to be understanding of, tolerant toward, sympathetic, considerate, forgiving
体体面面 **t'ǐ-t'ǐ mièn-mièn** extremely elegant, very fancy, most fashionable
体贴入微 **t'ǐ-t'iēh jù-wēi** to show solicitude even in minute [details] (extremely kind and thoughtful)
体总 **t'ǐ-tsǔng** the All-China Athletic Federation (contraction of **chūng-huá ch'üán-kuó t'ǐ-yù tsǔng-huì**)
体裁 **t'ǐ-ts'ái** form of writing, literary style
体操队 **t'ǐ-ts'āo-tuì** a gymnastic team
体温 **t'ǐ-wēn** body temperature
体无完肤 **t'ǐ-wù-wán-fū** no part of the bodily skin is still whole (often figurative and refers to violent verbal attacks)
体验 **t'ǐ-yèn** to experience firsthand, learn from personal experience
体育 **t'ǐ-yù** physical education, gymnastic instruction, athletics
体育新风尚 **t'ǐ-yù hsīn-fēng-shàng** the new style in athletics (the promotion of health should take precedence over winning competitive contests)
体育运动 **t'ǐ-yù yùn-tùng** physical culture and sports
体育运动委员会 **t'ǐ-yù yùn-tùng wěi-yuán-huì** the Physical Culture and Sports Commission [of the State Council]

t'ì (tì)

²¹⁷⁹ 替罪羔羊 **t'ì-tsuì-kāo-yáng** a scapegoat

t'iāo (tiāo)

²¹⁸⁰ 挑重担 **t'iāo-chùng-tàn** to shoulder a heavy load (to assume onerous responsibilities)

挑肥拣瘦 **t'iāo-féi chièn-shòu** to choose the fat and pick the lean (to think only of oneself; to be selfish)

挑粪 **t'iāo-fèn** to carry night soil

挑选 **t'iāo-hsuǎn** to select, choose, pick out

挑毛病 **t'iāo-máo-ping** to search out faults, find fault with

挑三拣四 **t'iāo-sān-chièn-szù** to choose three and pluck four (to pick and choose; hard to please)

挑剔 **t'iāo-t'i** to find fault with, pick faults; very fastidious, overly critical

挑剔和夸大缺点 **t'iāo-t'i hó k'uā-tà ch'üéh-tièn** to pick out faults and exaggerate shortcomings

挑子 **t'iāo-tzu** a load carried on the two ends of a pole, burden

挑 **t'iāo**: see also **t'iǎo**

t'iáo (tiáo)

²¹⁸¹ 条件 **t'iáo-chièn** (1) a condition; conditional (may include preconditions [a premise, requirement, conditions, strings attached]; or resulting conditions [circumstances, appearances, environment]) (2) terms, articles, clauses, proviso, provision

条件差 **t'iáo-chièh-ch'ā** the [natural] conditions are unfavorable

条件成熟 **t'iáo-chièn ch'éng-shú** the conditions are ripe

条件反射 **t'iáo-chièn fǎn-shè** a conditioned reflex

条分缕析 **t'iáo-fēn-lǚ-hsī** to analyze to the last detail; a detailed presentation

条幅 **t'iáo-fù** a vertical hanging scroll [of painting or calligraphy]

条款 **t'iáo-k'uǎn** a clause, proviso, term, article, section, paragraph [of a treaty or agreement]

条理 **t'iáo-lǐ** a line of reasoning, orderly presentation (reasonable, logical, orderly, sequential)

条例 **t'iáo-lì** a legislative act, statute, regulation, rule, by-law

条令 **t'iáo-lìng** regulations, prescriptions; a military instruction manual

条条框框 **t'iáo-t'iáo k'uāng-k'uāng** all kinds of restrictions, petty and multi-farious regulations

条条领导 **t'iáo-t'iáo lǐng-tǎo** vertical leadership (functional, hierarchical leadership)

条条是道 **t'iáo-t'iáo-shìh-tào** logical, reasonable, in good order

条田化 **t'iáo-t'ién-huà** to form strip fields (by combining small fields into large strip-shaped fields)

条文 **t'iáo-wén** the text [of a treaty, law, etc.]; clauses, terms, articles, stipulations

条文化 **t'iáo-wén-huà** codification; to codify

条约 **t'iáo-yuēh** a treaty, pact, agreement [between nations]

²¹⁸² 调整 **t'iáo-chěng** to adjust, regulate, put in order, alter, revise, reform, coordinate; adjustment, readjustment; regulatory

调整指标 **t'iáo-chěng chǐh-piāo** to adjust targets

调整房屋 **t'iáo-chěng fáng-wū** to readjust housing space (e.g., of offices, during administrative streamlining campaigns)

调整, 巩固, 充实, 提高 **t'iáo-chěng, kǔng-kù, ch'ūng-shíh, t'í-kāo** adjust, consolidate, fill-out, raise [standards] (a slogan during the hard years after the Great Leap Forward, about 1962)

调节 **t'iáo-chiéh** to set correctly, regulate, adjust, modulate; to tune [musical instruments]

调节水源 **t'iáo-chiéh shuǐ-yuán** to regulate water resources

调解 **t'iáo-chièh** to mediate, conciliate, settle [a quarrel]; mediation, intercession

调解人 **t'iáo-chièh-jén** a mediator, conciliator

调解委员 **t'iáo-chièh wěi-yuán** mediation members [of lane committees]

调和 **t'iáo-hó** to harmonize, reconcile, placate, bring about agreement; to mix, blend; to adjust, tune; reconciliation, accord, harmony

调和主义 **t'iáo-hó-chǔ-ì** "compromise-ism," "adjustism"

调和矛盾 **t'iáo-hó máo-tùn** to compromise contradictions, reconcile contradictions

调戏妇女 **t'iáo-hsì fù-nǚ** to take liberties with women, molest, dally with

调配 **t'iáo-p'èi** to arrange, coordinate; to blend, mix, prepare [a concoction] (see also **tiào-p'èi**)

调皮捣蛋 **t'iáo-p'í-tǎo-tàn** mischievous, trouble-making, ungovernable

调停 **t'iáo-t'íng** to mediate, reconcile, arbitrate, conciliate; mediation
调匀 **t'iáo-yún** to mix evenly, blend
调 **t'iáo**: *see also* **tiào**

t'iǎo (tiǎo)

2183 挑战 **t'iǎo-chàn** to provoke war (a challenge, as in a production campaign)
挑衅 **t'iǎo-hsìn** a provocation, challenge; to provoke; provocative
挑拨离间 **t'iǎo-pō lí-chièn** to foment dissension, sow discord, stir up ill will
挑灯夜战 **t'iǎo-tēng yèh-chàn** to carry lanterns and fight at night (to work at night, usually in the fields or on rush construction)
挑动 **t'iǎo-tùng** to instigate, incite, arouse
挑 **t'iǎo**: *see also* **t'iāo**

t'iào (tiào)

2184 跳板 **t'iào-pǎn** a diving board, springboard (often figurative)
跳跃欢呼 **t'iào-yuèh-hūan-hū** to leap and cheer [for joy]

t'iēh (tiē)

2185 贴切 **t'iēh-ch'ièh** proper, appropriate, fitting closely
贴心人 **t'iēh-hsīn-jén** a sympathetic person, a warmhearted person, a confidant
贴水 **t'iēh-shuǐ** a discount, exchange premium

t'iěh (tiě)

2186 铁案如山 **t'iěh-àn jú-shān** an ironclad case
铁证 **t'iěh-chèng** ironclad evidence, irrefutable proof
铁肩膀 **t'iěh-chiēn-pǎng** iron shoulders (able to carry heavy burdens or great responsibilities)
铁人精神 **t'iěh-jén chīng-shén** the iron man spirit (a reference to Wang Ching-hsi, a heroic worker in the Taching oilfields who earned the nickname of "Iron Man")
铁姑娘 **t'iěh-kū-niáng** an iron girl (a girl distinguishing herself by hard physical work, as the "iron girl team" which worked on the Red Flag Canal)
铁路运输 **t'iěh-lù-yùn-shū** railway transport, transport by rail
铁幕 **t'iěh-mù** the Iron Curtain
铁道兵 **t'iěh-tào-pīng** the Railway Corps (one of the service arms of the PLA)
铁道部 **t'iěh-tào-pù** the Ministry of Railways [of the State Council] (merged into the Ministry of Communications after 1969)
铁的事实 **t'iěh-te-shìh-shíh** ironclad facts, indisputable facts
铁托 **t'iěh-t'ō** Tito [Josip Brozovich, 1892—]

t'iēn (tiān)

2187 天安门广场 **t'iēn-ān-mén kuǎng-ch'ǎng** Tienanmen Square [Peking]
天堑变通途 **t'iēn-chàn pièn t'ūng-t'ú** a natural barrier becomes an open road (such as by the building of bridges across the Yangtze River)
天真烂漫 **t'iēn-chēn-làn-màn** innocent and carefree (honest and without affectation, naive)
天之骄子 **t'iēn-chīh-chiāo-tzǔ** heaven's favorite (to be extraordinarily blessed)
天经地义 **t'iēn-chīng-tì-ì** the principles of heaven and earth (absolutely correct, immutable, irrevocable)
天诛地灭 **t'iēn-chū tì-mièh** to be executed by heaven and destroyed by earth (universally condemned)
天气预报 **t'iēn-ch'ì yù-pào** a weather forecast, weather prediction
天翻地覆 **t'iēn-fān-tì-fù** the sky turns and the earth collapses (total disorder, chaos, pandemonium)
天赋 **t'iēn-fù** a natural aptitude, talent, innate endowment
天赋观念 **t'iēn-fù kuān-nièn** the concept of inherence [of intelligence, etc.]
天寒地冻 **t'iēn-hán tì-tùng** the sky is cold and earth frozen
天花 **t'iēn-huā** smallpox
天花乱坠 **t'iēn-huā luàn-chuì** flowers cascading from heaven (exaggerated description, overly optimistic eloquence)
天下大乱 **t'iēn-hsià-tà-luàn** the world in turmoil (widespread disorder)
天下太平 **t'iēn-hsià-t'ài-p'íng** the whole world is peaceful
天下无难事，只怕有心人 **t'iēn-hsià wú-nán-shìh, chǐh-p'à yǔ-hsīn-jén** there is no difficult task in the world that does not fear a stout-hearted man (the problem is not the difficulty of the task but one's determination)

天下乌鸦一般黑 **t'iēn-hsià wū-yā ī-pān-hēi** all the crows in the world are black (all bad people are the same)

天象仪 **t'iēn-hsiàng-í** a planetarium

天性 **t'iēn-hsìng** natural disposition, human nature, temperament, natural qualities; natural, by nature

天衣无缝 **t'iēn-i wú-fèng** a heavenly garment without seams (without a single flaw, unbroken, perfect)

天然 **t'iēn-ján** natural, inherent, native; naturally; [in a state of] nature

天然气 **t'iēn-ján-ch'ì** natural gas

天然资源 **t'iēn-ján tzū-yuán** natural resources

天然材料 **t'iēn-ján ts'ái-liào** natural materials, native materials

天壤之别 **t'iēn-jǎng-chǐh-piéh** the difference between heaven and earth (poles apart, vastly different)

天高皇帝远 **t'iēn kāo huáng-tì yuǎn** the heaven is high and the emperor far away (one may do as he pleases)

天罗地网 **t'iēn-ló tì-wǎng** nets in the sky and snares on the earth (no escape, surrounded on all sides)

天伦之乐 **t'iēn-lún-chǐh-lè** the happiness of natural bonds (the joys of family relationships)

天马行空 **t'iēn-mǎ hsíng-k'ūng** the heavenly horse flies through the skies (free, unrestrained and gifted with great power: Lin Piao is accused of having written this inscription on a scroll)

天命观 **t'iēn-mìng-kuān** predestination, a belief that fate is determined by heaven

天命论 **t'iēn-mìng lùn** the concept of the will of heaven (fatalism, predestination)

天兵天将 **t'iēn-pīng t'iēn-chiàng** heavenly soldiers and generals (supernatural agents)

天不怕地不怕 **t'iēn-pù-p'à tì-pù-p'à** to fear neither heaven nor earth (to fear no difficulties)

天生 **t'iēn-shēng** inborn, natural, innate

天大旱, 人大干 **t'iēn-tà-hàn, jén-tà-kàn** the greater the drought, the harder men must work

天地 **t'iēn-tì** heaven and earth (the world, universe, cosmos)

天堂 **t'iēn-t'áng** heaven, a paradise

天体 **t'iēn-t'ǐ** heavenly bodies; nude

天体力学 **t'iēn-t'ǐ lì-hsuéh** celestial mechanics

天天向上 **t'iēn-t'iēn-hsiàng-shàng** day-by-day to move upward (to improve oneself each day)

天灾 **t'iēn-tsāi** a natural disaster, natural calamity

天造地设 **t'iēn-tsào-tì-shè** created by heaven and put in place by earth (a natural match, perfect fit)

天才 **t'iēn-ts'ái** genius, inherent ability, natural aptitude; naturally gifted, a genius, brilliant person

天才教育 **t'iēn-ts'ái chiào-yù** education of talent (selective education for the more intelligent or gifted students: a policy charged against Liu Shao-ch'i)

天才论 **t'iēn-ts'ái lùn** the doctrine that talent [wisdom] is born in a person [and thus is independent of practice and experience]

天外还有天 **t'iēn-wài hái yǔ t'iēn** there is sky beyond the sky (never be satisfied; it is still possible to achieve greater things)

天文学 **t'iēn-wén-hsuéh** astronomy

天文仪 **t'iēn-wén-í** astronomical instruments

天文馆 **t'iēn-wén-kuǎn** a planetarium

天文台 **t'iēn-wén-t'ái** an astronomical observatory

天涯海角 **t'iēn-yá-hǎi-chiǎo** the horizon of heaven and the corners of the seas (very remote, the corners of the earth)

²¹⁸⁸ 添枝加叶 **t'iēn-chīh chiā-yèh** to add branches and leaves (to exaggerate, embellish)

添砖加瓦 **t'iēn-chuān chiā-wǎ** to add a brick or a tile (to make a contribution, however small, to the completion of a great task)

添油加醋 **t'iēn-yú chiā-ts'ù** to add oil and vinegar (to embellish a story, to misrepresent by overstating)

t'ién (tián)

²¹⁸⁹ 田间小路 **t'ién-chiēn hsiǎo-lù** small roads between the fields

田间管理 **t'ién-chiēn kuǎn-lǐ** tending to crops in the field, field care, field management

田间劳动 **t'ién-chiēn láo-tùng** field labor, farm work

田间地头学习组 **t'ién-chiēn tì-t'óu hsuéh-hsí-tsǔ** a field-end study group

田径 **t'ién-chìng** field and track athletics

田汉 **t'ién hàn** T'ien Han (a well-known playwright, 1898—, criticized in the Cultural Revolution and one of the **szù-t'iáo hàn-tzu**)

田里沒望头, 副业有奔头 **t'ién-lǐ méi wàng-t'ou, fù-yèh yǔ pèn-t'ou** farming

is not promising and sideline occupations seem attractive (an attitude now criticized)

田连阡陌 **t'ién-lién ch'iēn-mò** fields encompassing many paths (a wide expanse of farmland, rich landlord holdings)

田头会 **t'ién-t'óu-huì** a field-end conference (usually a study or discussion meeting during a meal or rest break in farm work)

田头民主会 **t'ién-t'óu mín-chǔ-huì** a field-end democratic conference (an informal field conference of cadres and peasants)

田园化 **t'ién-yuán-huà** to make fields into gardens, to intensify cultivation

2190 恬静安宁 **t'ién-chìng ān-níng** peaceful and quiet, tranquil

恬不知耻 **t'ién pù chīh-ch'ǐh** to be calm and not know shame, devoid of all sense of shame

2191 甜头 **t'ién-t'óu** a sweetness; a lure, bait

甜菜 **t'ién-ts'ài** the sugar beet

甜言蜜语 **t'ién-yén mì-yǔ** sweet words and honeyed phrases

2192 填写 **t'ién-hsiěh** to fill out [a form]

填沟 **t'ién-kōu** to fill up ditches (figurative: to wipe out barriers between the Party and the masses)

填补空白 **t'ién-pǔ k'ùng-pái** to fill in the blanks (to make up deficiencies)

填平鸿沟 **t'ién-p'íng húng-kōu** to fill in the gap, to close the gap

填平补齐 **t'ién-p'íng pǔ-ch'í** fill in and make even, level off and smooth out

填塞 **t'ién-sāi** to stuff, fill up, cram full

t'īng (tīng)

2193 听之任之 **t'īng-chīh jèn-chīh** leave it to his judgment; let it happen without taking action

听其言观其行 **t'īng-ch'í-yén kuān-ch'í-hsíng** to listen to one's words and watch his actions

听取 **t'īng-ch'ǔ** to listen attentively, to absorb by hearing

听喜不听忧 **t'īng-hsǐ pù t'īng-yū** to listen to good news but not to bad (the basis of unrealistically favorable reports)

听信 **t'īng-hsìn** to await news; to listen to others, believe in

听任 **t'īng-jèn** to allow one to do as he wishes, let something happen without taking action, leave to one's own judgment

听凭 **t'īng-p'íng** to let someone do as he likes (*synonymous with above*)

听天由命 **t'īng-t'iēn yú-mìng** to submit to heaven and accept fate

听从 **t'īng-ts'úng** to listen and follow, obey, take advice

t'íng (tíng)

2194 庭长 **t'íng-chǎng** a head of a court [of justice], chief judge

2195 停战 **t'íng-chàn** an armistice, truce, cease-fire

停职 **t'íng-chíh** to suspend from one's post, dismiss from service, remove from office

停滞不前 **t'íng-chìh-pù-ch'ién** to be stuck and not move forward; stagnation without progress

停火 **t'íng-huǒ** a cease-fire, to cease firing, suspend hostilities

停息 **t'íng-hsī** to stop, cease, a lull

停工 **t'íng-kūng** to suspend work, stop work, be out of [working] order; a work suspension, work stoppage

停课闹革命 **t'íng-k'ò nào-kó-mìng** to suspend classes [in order to] engage in revolution [as during the Cultural Revolution]

停留 **t'íng-liú** to tarry, linger, stay over

停步歇脚 **t'íng-pù hsiēh-chiǎo** to stop marching and rest the feet

停步不前 **t'íng-pù-pù-ch'ién** to halt marching, stop, mark time

停顿 **t'íng-tùn** to come to a standstill, halt, check, suspend action, remain still

t'ǐng (tǐng)

2196 挺起腰杆 **t'ǐng-ch'ǐ yāo-kǎn** to straighten up the backbone

挺身而出 **t'ǐng-shēn-érh-ch'ū** to come out with body erect (to thrust forward to meet a challenge)

2197 铤而走险 **t'ǐng-érh-tsǒu-hsiěn** to hurry forward toward danger (to become reckless in desperation)

t'ō (tuō)

2198 托儿所 **t'ō-érh-sǒ** a children's nursery

托管 **t'ō-kuǎn** a trusteeship, mandate

托管地 **t'ō-kuǎn-tì** a trust territory, mandated territory

托拉斯 **t'ō-lā-szū** a trust (a combination of firms or corporations)

托洛茨基 **t'ō-lò-tz'ū-chī** Trotsky, [Leon, 1877–1940]

托庇 **t'ō-pì** to harbor, shelter, screen, protect

托派 **t'ō-p'ài** the Trotskyite faction,

Trotskyites

托收承付 **t'ō-shōu ch'éng-fù** to entrust collections and disbursements to a bank or agent

托辞 **t'ō-tz'ú** to put forth a false reason, make excuses, give an alibi

托婴室 **t'ō-yīng-shìh** an infant care center

托运 **t'ō-yùn** to entrust for shipment; consigned shipment

2199 拖车 **t'ō-ch'ē** a trailer [vehicle]

拖船 **t'ō-ch'uán** a tugboat

拖后腿 **t'ō hòu-t'uǐ** to pull the hind leg (to check, hold back, hinder)

拖人下水 **t'ō-jén-hsià-shuǐ** to drag others into the water (to implicate others intentionally, to involve others in an inappropriate or improper activity)

拖拉机 **t'ō-lā-chī** a tractor

拖拉机站 **t'ō-lā-chī chàn** a tractor station

拖拉等待 **t'ō-lā těng-tài** to procrastinate and wait for, put off and wait

拖累 **t'ō-lěi** to involve, implicate [others in one's troubles]

拖泥带水 **t'ō-ní tài-shuǐ** to drag through mud and water (to be unable to make a decision; a sloppy and muddled style of writing or acting)

拖延 **t'ō-yén** to delay, stall, procrastinate, retard, postpone; delay, procrastination; to default [on a debt]

2200 脱节 **t'ō-chiéh** to become disconnected, out of joint, lose contact; incoherent, irrelevant, uncoordinated

脱产 **t'ō-ch'ǎn** to divorce [oneself] from production, withdraw from productive work, not participating in [actual] production

脱产干部 **t'ō-ch'ǎn kàn-pù** cadres divorced from production

脱销 **t'ō-hsiāo** to sell out, run out of stock; a shortage

脱鞋下田 **t'ō-hsiéh-hsià-t'ién** to take off one's shoes and go to the fields

脱离 **t'ō-lí** to break away, leave, break off, depart, separate, get rid of, become alienated from; separation, disengagement

脱离政治 **t'ō-lí chèng-chìh** to stand aloof from politics, discontinue involvement in politics

脱离群众 **t'ō-lí ch'ún-chùng** to separate oneself from the masses, lose touch with the masses

脱离人民 **t'ō-lí jén-mín** to cut oneself off from the people, lose touch with the people

脱离劳动 **t'ō-lí láo-tùng** to shun labor, separate oneself from physical work

脱离生产 **t'ō-lí shēng-ch'ǎn** to separate oneself from production [work], withdraw from production

脱离实际 **t'ō-lí shíh-chì** to separate oneself from practice, lose touch with reality

脱粒机 **t'ō-lì-chī** a threshing machine, husking machine, sheller

脱盲 **t'ō-máng** to escape from illiteracy (usually refers to adults who have undergone basic literacy education)

脱水蔬菜 **t'ō-shuǐ-shū-ts'ài** dehydrated vegetables

脱党 **t'ō-tǎng** to withdraw from a [political] party

脱胎换骨 **t'ō-t'āi-huàn-kǔ** to shed the womb and change one's bones (to change oneself completely, become a new person)

t'ó (tuó)

2201 驮畜 **t'ó-ch'ù** pack animals

2202 鸵鸟政策 **t'ó-niǎo chèng-ts'è** an ostrich policy ("head in the sand" policy)

t'ǒ (tuǒ)

2203 妥协 **t'ǒ-hsiéh** to compromise, reach a compromise; a compromise; appeasement

妥善 **t'ǒ-shàn** proper, appropriate, satisfactory, in order, well-arranged

妥善安排 **t'ǒ-shàn ān-p'ái** a satisfactory arrangement, thoroughly prepared

妥当 **t'ǒ-tàng** appropriate, adequate, satisfactory, sound, reliable, safe, well-arranged, secure; ready

妥妥贴贴 **t'ǒ-t'ǒ t'iēh-t'iēh** very properly, highly satisfactorily, firmly, securely

t'ò (tuò)

2204 唾弃 **t'ò-ch'ì** to spit on, spit at (reject, exclude, show contempt for)

唾余 **t'ò-yú** an excess of saliva, leftover saliva (platitudes)

t'ōu (tōu)

2205 偷窃 **t'ōu-ch'ièh** to steal; theft, thievery

偷袭 **t'ōu-hsí** a stealthy attack [military], surprise attack

偷入 **t'ōu-jù** to sneak into, enter covertly

偷工 **t'ōu-kūng** to cheat on work, cut corners on a job

偷工减料 **t'ōu-kūng chiěn-liào** to skimp on work and cheat on materials (to cheat on contracts for the state—one of the **wǔ-fǎn**)

偷梁换柱 **t'ōu-liáng huàn-chù** to steal a beam and substitute a post [of inferior size or quality] (deception, swindle, distortion of the facts)

偷税漏税 **t'ōu-shuì lòu-shuì** to evade and cheat on taxes (one of the **wǔ-fǎn**)

偷天换日 **t'ōu-t'iēn huàn-jìh** to steal the sky and replace the sun (to commit a great hoax, unscrupulously distort the facts)

t'óu (tuó)

2206 头重脚轻 **t'óu-chùng chiǎo-ch'īng** head heavy and foot light (upper-level offices over-staffed while lower-level offices are under-staffed; top-heavy administration or bureaucracy)

头号 **t'óu-hào** number one, the best, first class, greatest, chief

头号帝国主义 **t'óu-hào tì-kuó-chǔ-ì** the number one imperialist

头衔 **t'óu-hsién** a title of office, rank, grade

头人 **t'óu-jén** a headman, chief (a village chief of some minority peoples)

头面人物 **t'óu-mièn jén-wù** locally prominent persons, bigwigs, local notables

头目 **t'óu-mù** leader, chief, boss [in a derogatory sense]

头脑 **t'óu-nǎo** the leader, chief, boss, "brains"

头脑清醒 **t'óu-nǎo ch'īng-hsǐng** sober-minded, clearheaded, wide-awake, alert

头版 **t'óu-pǎn** the front page

头破血流 **t'óu-p'ò hsuèh-liú** [with] head cracked and blood flowing

头数 **t'óu-shù** a head count [of animals]

头等强国 **t'óu-těng ch'iáng-kuó** a first-class Power

头等大事 **t'óu-těng tà-shìh** a matter of the greatest importance

头头 **t'óu-t'óu** a chief (in a derogatory sense)

头头是道 **t'óu-t'óu-shìh-tào** on every side there is a [clear] road (a systematic and orderly [presentation], a logical and well-arranged [speech])

头痛医头，脚痛医脚 **t'óu-t'ùng-ī-t'óu, chiǎo-t'ùng-ī-chiǎo** to treat the head when the head aches and to treat the foot when the foot aches (to apply piecemeal remedies, to have no basic or overall plan, to fail to treat the root cause)

头子 **t'óu-tzu** headman, head, chief, boss (usually pejorative)

2207 投案自首 **t'óu-àn tzù-shǒu** to surrender voluntarily to a court

投机取巧 **t'óu-chī-ch'ǔ-ch'iǎo** to speculate and take advantage of opportunity; speculation, speculative manipulation, profiteering

投机分子 **t'óu-chī fèn-tzǔ** an opportunist, speculator, careerist

投机商人 **t'óu-chī shāng-jén** a speculating merchant

投机倒把 **t'óu-chī tǎo-pǎ** to speculate and manipulate [the market]

投产 **t'óu-ch'ǎn** to put into production, throw into [large scale] production

投降 **t'óu-hsiáng** to surrender, capitulate, submit

投降主义 **t'óu-hsiáng-chǔ-ì** capitulationism

投入怀抱 **t'óu-jù huái-pào** to throw oneself into the arms of, leap into the embrace of

投入生产 **t'óu-jù shēng-ch'ǎn** to put into operation, start production, plunge into production

投考 **t'óu-k'ǎo** to sign up for an examination

投靠 **t'óu-k'ào** to seek the patronage of, join and serve

投奔 **t'óu-pèn** to flee, seek protection

投票 **t'óu-p'iào** to cast a vote; a ballot, vote, plebiscite

投身 **t'óu-shēn** to plunge oneself into, to give oneself [to a cause], devote oneself to

投弹 **t'óu-tàn** to drop bombs, throw grenades

投敌 **t'óu-tí** to surrender to the enemy

投递 **t'óu-tì** to forward, dispatch, deliver [mail]

投资 **t'óu-tzū** to invest capital, make an investment; invested capital

投资额 **t'óu-tzū-ó** the amount of investment, the invested capital

投资比例 **t'óu-tzū pǐ-lì** ratio of investment

t'òu (tòu)

2208 透支 **t'òu-chīh** to overdraw; an overdraft

透彻 **t'òu-ch'è** thorough; thoroughly

透过 **t'òu-kuò** via, by way of, through the agency of; to pass through, penetrate

透露 **t'òu-lù** to seep through, disclose, reveal, divulge, let out

透视 **t'òu-shìh** perspective [in drawing]; to see through, examine by fluoroscope

透顶 **t'òu-tǐng** to the utmost, in the extreme, to the core

透雨 **t'òu-yǔ** a penetrating rain; rain leaking through

t'ū (tū)

2209 突击 **t'ū-chī** to attack by storm; a sudden attack (concentrated effort to meet a deadline)

突击花钱 **t'ū-chī huā-ch'ién** to squander money recklessly

突击任务 **t'ū-chī jèn-wù** an emergency task (an especially arduous task for volunteer "shock brigades")

突击工作队 **t'ū-chī kūng-tsò-tuì** sudden attack work teams (emergency task forces)

突击力量 **t'ū-chī lì-liàng** a shock force

突击队 **t'ū-chī-tuì** a shock brigade (usually a task force organized for the speedy accomplishment of a specific task)

突出 **t'ū-ch'ū** to protrude, stand out, be salient; give prominence to, give salience to; outstanding, salient, conspicuous, prominent

突出政治 **t'ū-ch'ū chèng-chìh** to give salience to politics, to give prominence to politics

突出无产阶级政治 **t'ū-ch'ū wú-ch'ǎn-chiēh-chí chèng-chìh** to give salience to proletarian politics

突飞猛进 **t'ū-fēi-měng-chìn** to advance by leaps and bounds; rapid development, swift advance, remarkable progress

突尼斯 **t'ū-ní-szū** Tunis [Tunisia]

突变 **t'ū-pièn** a sudden change, revolution, turn over; a mutation

突破 **t'ū-p'ò** to break through, to penetrate, smash, excel [by breaking old records]

突围 **t'ū-wéi** to break a siege, break through an encirclement

t'ú (tú)

2210 图案 **t'ú-àn** a design, pattern, sketch, plan

图章 **t'ú-chāng** a name seal [personal or business]

图解 **t'ú-chiěh** a presentation by means of graphs; diagrams or pictures for teaching, illustrations

图纸 **t'ú-chǐh** a diagram, layout paper, design sketch

图利 **t'ú-lì** to seek profit, be intent on making money

图名图利 **t'ú-míng t'ú-lì** to seek fame and gain, strive for glory and riches

图谋 **t'ú-móu** to scheme, plan, conspire, have evil intentions

图排场讲阔气 **t'ú p'ái-ch'ǎng chiǎng k'uò-ch'ì** ostentatious and pompous, putting on airs

图片 **t'ú-p'ièn** a picture, photograph, illustration

图书馆 **t'ú-shū-kuǎn** a library; *Libraries* (a Peking quarterly journal, 1961—)

图书馆工作 **t'ú-shū-kuǎn kūng-tsò** *Library Work* (a Peking monthly journal, 1955—)

图腾 **t'ú-t'éng** a totem

2211 涂脂抹粉 **t'ú-chīh mǒ-fěn** to smear on rouge and rub on powder (to gloss over, cover up)

涂掉 **t'ú-tiào** to strike out, erase, obliterate

2212 途径 **t'ú-chìng** a way, path, road; means

2213 徒费唇舌 **t'ú-fèi-ch'ún-shé** to use one's lips and tongue in vain (to waste one's breath; unsuccessful in persuading)

徒刑 **t'ú-hsíng** punishment by imprisonment; to imprison; a prison term

徒工 **t'ú-kūng** an apprentice worker, learner

徒劳无功 **t'ú-láo wú-kūng** to labor without effect, trouble oneself for nothing; futile

徒手 **t'ú-shǒu** bare-handed; empty-handed; unarmed

徒弟 **t'ú-tì** an apprentice, pupil, disciple

徒托空言 **t'ú-t'ō k'ūng-yén** depending only on empty words

徒有形式 **t'ú-yǔ-hsíng-shìh** merely having the appearance (empty; a mere formality)

2214 屠杀 **t'ú-shā** to massacre, slaughter on a large scale; a massacre

屠刀 **t'ú-tāo** a butcher's knife, massacre weapon

t'ǔ (tǔ)

2215 土家族 **t'ǔ-chiā-tsú** the Tu-chia people (a minority in Hunan and Hupeh provinces: population 603,000 as of 1957)

土教具 **t'ǔ-chiào-chù** locally made [simple] teaching aids

土质 **t'ŭ-chìh** soil quality, land fertility [or infertility]

土著 **t'ŭ-chù** natives, aborigines

土专家 **t'ŭ-chuān-chiā** an indigenous expert (a person competent at farming or a craft whose expertise depends on experience of handed-down skills rather than formal education)

土气 **t'ŭ-ch'ì** native flavor; rustic, unsophisticated

土产 **t'ŭ-ch'ǎn** native products, local products

土耳其 **t'ŭ-ěrh-ch'í** Turkey [Republic of]

土耳其斯坦 **t'ŭ-ěrh-ch'í-szū-t'ǎn** Turkestan [in the Soviet Union]

土法 **t'ŭ-fǎ** native methods, traditional ways, indigenous methods

土法上马 **t'ŭ-fǎ shàng-mǎ** to get going by using native methods

土方 **t'ŭ-fāng** (1) a unit of earthwork or excavation (formerly 100 cubic *ch'ih* [Chinese feet]; now one cubic meter); (2) a native or local medical prescription

土匪 **t'ŭ-féi** robber bands, bandits

土豪劣绅 **t'ŭ-háo lièh-shēn** local bullies and bad gentry, the local, oppressive, rich gentry and their minions of power (the despotic elements in the traditional rural society)

土豪恶霸 **t'ŭ-háo ò-pà** local despots, local ruffians

土话 **t'ŭ-huà** local dialects, language of the streets, idiom, patois

土化肥 **t'ŭ-huà-féi** indigenous chemical fertilizer, chemical fertilizer produced by native methods

土皇帝 **t'ŭ-huáng-tì** a local emperor (a local leader of reactionary feudal elements)

土壤 **t'ŭ-jǎng** soil, earth, dirt, land

土壤改良 **t'ŭ-jǎng kǎi-liáng** soil improvement

土壤流失 **t'ŭ-jǎng liú-shīh** soil erosion

土改 **t'ŭ-kǎi** land reform; the Land Reform (contraction of **t'ŭ-tì kǎi-kó**)

土钢 **t'ŭ-kāng** native steel (low-grade steel produced by indigenous methods)

土高炉 **t'ŭ-kāo-lú** an indigenous iron-smelting furnace (a "backyard" blast furnace)

土里土气 **t'ŭ-lǐ-t'ŭ-ch'ì** earthy manners; rustic, "countrified"

土木工程 **t'ŭ-mù kūng-ch'éng** civil engineering; construction and engineering

土办法 **t'ŭ-pàn-fǎ** indigenous and simple methods

土包子 **t'ŭ-pāo-tzu** a bumpkin, hick, rube

土崩瓦解 **t'ŭ-pēng-wǎ-chiěh** disturbance of the earth and collapse of the tiles (a great upheaval, total disorder, disintegration)

土布 **t'ŭ-pù** native cloth, homespun or handicraft material; unbleached cotton cloth

土设备 **t'ŭ-shè-pèi** crude installations, simple equipment

土生土长 **t'ŭ-shēng t'ŭ-chǎng** locally born and locally grown (a native, one who has not left his native place)

土地证 **t'ŭ-tì-chèng** a land [ownership] certificate, land title, land deed

土地法 **t'ŭ-tì-fǎ** the Land Law

土地小私有者 **t'ŭ-tì hsiǎo-szū-yǔ-chě** a small landowner

土地入股 **t'ŭ-tì jù-kǔ** to put land into shares, pool land on a share basis

土地改革 **t'ŭ-tì kǎi-kó** land reform, agrarian reform; the Land Reform (1947–1950)

土地改革法 **t'ŭ-tì kǎi-kó-fǎ** the Land Reform Law [1950]

土地革命 **t'ŭ-tì kó-mìng** agrarian revolution, the revolution on the land

土地关系 **t'ŭ-tì kuān-hsi** relations of land ownership

土地广阔 **t'ŭ-tì kuǎng-k'uò** the land is vast

土地公有 **t'ŭ-tì-kūng-yǔ** public ownership of land

土地买卖权 **t'ŭ-tì mǎi-mài-ch'üán** the right to buy and sell land

土地所有证 **t'ŭ-tì sǒ-yǔ-chèng** a land ownership deed (granted to all private holders after land reform)

土地所有制 **t'ŭ-tì sǒ-yǔ-chìh** the system of land ownership

土地私有制 **t'ŭ-tì szū-yǔ-chìh** system of private ownership of land, private land ownership

土单方 **t'ŭ-tān-fāng** a native [medical] prescription

土豆烧牛肉的共产主义 **t'ŭ-tòu shāo-niú-jòu te kùng-ch'ǎn-chǔ-ì** [Khrushchev's] "goulash" communism

土特产 **t'ŭ-t'è-ch'ǎn** local special products (well-known or special products of a particular locality)

土铁 **t'ŭ-t'iěh** native iron (pig iron produced by indigenous methods)

土族 **t'ŭ-tsú** the T'u people (a minority in Chinghai province: population 63,000 as of 1957)

土洋结合 **t'ŭ-yáng chiéh-hó** the integra-

tion of indigenous and foreign (usually refers to the integrated use of both native and Western [modern] methods and techniques in agriculture or industry)

土洋并举 **t'ǔ-yáng pìng-chǔ** using both indigenous and foreign [methods]

t'ù (tù)

2216 吐故纳新 **t'ù-kù nà-hsīn** to exhale the old and inhale the new (the constant process of renewal—in life, or to maintain the health and vigor of the Party)

吐苦水 **t'ù k'ǔ-shuǐ** to spit out the bitter water (to speak out of one's bitter life: a Land Reform slogan)

吐怨气 **t'ù-yuàn-ch'ì** to vent one's grievances

2217 兔子尾巴长不了 **t'ù-tzu wěi-pa ch'áng-pù-liǎo** the rabbit's tail cannot grow [any longer] (one's future is limited)

t'uán (tuán)

2218 团结 **t'uán-chiéh** to unify, rally together, form a group; unity, solidarity; union

团结, 紧张, 严肃, 活泼 **t'uán-chiéh, chǐn-chāng, yén-sù, huó-p'ō** unity, alertness, earnestness, activeness (the eight characters of the **sān-pā-tsò-fēng**)

团结一致 **t'uán-chiéh ī-chìh** to unite as one; unitary solidarity, complete unity

团结一切可能团结的力量 **t'uán-chiéh ī-ch'ièh k'ǒ-néng-t'uán-chiéh te lì-liang** to unite with all the forces that can be united

团结, 批评, 团结 **t'uán-chiéh p'ī-p'íng t'uán-chiéh** unity-criticism-unity (a form of ideological struggle in which criticism is a tool for the production of a new and heightened unity)

团结对敌 **t'uán-chiéh tuì-tí** to unite against the enemy

团结友谊 **t'uán-chiéh yǔ-ì** friendly solidarity, friendly unity

团支部 **t'uán-chīh-pù** a [Youth] League branch

团体 **t'uán-t'ǐ** a group, organization, corporate body

团团转 **t'uán-t'uán-chuàn** to pace about in an agitated manner, to act in a helter-skelter way

团组织 **t'uán-tsǔ-chīh** the [Youth] League organization

团委会 **t'uán-wěi-huì** a [Youth] League committee

t'uī (tuī)

2219 推荐 **t'uī-chièn** to recommend, endorse, nominate; a recommendation

推荐对象 **t'uī-chièn tuì-hsiàng** the applicants recommended, persons recommended

推进 **t'uī-chìn** to push forward, promote, advance, move ahead

推陈出新 **t'uī-ch'én chū-hsīn** to weed out the old and let the new emerge (a slogan first used by Mao Tse-tung in 1942)

推敲 **t'uī-ch'iāo** to push or knock [the door] (to choose words carefully, weigh words with care, consider precisely)

推崇 **t'uī-ch'úng** to esteem, respect

推翻 **t'uī-fān** to overthrow, upset, overturn; an overthrow

推销 **t'uī-hsiāo** to sell, push sales, seek to increase trade; sales promotion

推心置腹 **t'uī-hsīn-chìh-fù** to put one's heart in another's bowel (to treat others with utmost sincerity; complete trust)

推行 **t'uī-hsíng** to execute, put into application, carry out, implement, pursue, push through, carry on

推广 **t'uī-kuǎng** to propagate, popularize, broaden, extend, generalize; popularization, generalization

推广站 **t'uī-kuǎng-chàn** a promotion station, popularization center

推广经验 **t'uī-kuǎng chīng-yèn** to propagate experience (to extend and broaden the benefit of experience by sharing it with others)

推广典型 **t'uī-kuǎng tiěn-hsíng** to propagate exemplars

推理 **t'uī-lǐ** to reason out, infer, deduce; reasoning, inference

推理法 **t'uī-lǐ-fǎ** a method of reasoning; deductive method

推论 **t'uī-lùn** to infer; an inference, deduction, conclusion; a corollary [in mathematics]

推拿疗法 **t'uī-ná liáo-fǎ** massage therapy

推波助澜 **t'uī-pō chù-lán** to push the water to help the waves [become larger] (to instigate, egg on, incite, add fuel to the fire)

推动 **t'uī-tùng** to drive forward, motivate, further, foster, push, impel

推动力 **t'uī-tùng-lì** motive force, impetus, moving force, impelling force

推涛作浪 **t'uī-t'āo tsò-làng** to stir up

waves (to create trouble)

推脱 **t'uī-t'ō** to shirk, evade, avoid

推土机 **t'uī-t'ǔ-chī** a bulldozer, earth scraper

推测 **t'uī-ts'è** to calculate, conjecture, estimate, suppose, surmise; prognosis, predication

推诿 **t'uī-wěi** to make excuses, evade, shirk, avoid, equivocate, shift [the blame]; evasion, equivocation

t'uí (tuí)

2220   颓废 **t'uí-fèi** ruined, decadent, fallen to pieces; depressed, low-spirited

颓唐 **t'uí-t'áng** dispirited, dejected; decrepit, failing

t'uì (tuì)

2221   退职 **t'uì-chíh** to resign [from office], withdraw retire

退潮 **t'uì-ch'áo** an ebb tide; to ebb

退出 **t'uì-ch'ū** to step out, withdraw, retreat, evacuate, resign from, renounce; withdrawal

退却 **t'uì-ch'üèh** to retreat, withdraw, back down

退回 **t'uì-huí** to return [a gift, etc.], hand back, send back, reject; to retreat

退休 **t'uì-hsiū** to retire [from active life]

退休工人工作委员会 **t'uì-hsiū kūng-jén kūng-tsò wěi-yuán-huì** retired workers's activities committees (to recruit them to help in lane offices)

退学 **t'uì-hsuéh** to quit school, give up [one's] studies, drop out

退役 **t'uì-ì** to retire from [military] service

退让 **t'uì-jàng** to withdraw and yield, give precedence to yield, cede

退兵 **t'uì-pīng** to withdraw troops; defeated troops; to repel [enemy] troops

退步 **t'uì-pù** to move backward, retrogress, deteriorate; retrogression, deterioration

退色 **t'uì-sè** to shed color, fade (usually with the implication of losing "redness" or revolutionary ardor)

退党 **t'uì-tǎng** to withdraw from a [political] party, resign [one's] party membership

退佃 **t'uì-tièn** to revoke a land tenancy

退赃 **t'uì-tsāng** to return stolen goods, return the loot

退伍 **t'uì-wǔ** to retire from military service, be discharged from active

service, demobilize, deactivate

退伍军人 **t'uì-wǔ-chūn-jén** a veteran, retired armyman, ex-soldier

2222   蜕化 **t'uì-huà** to degenerate, deteriorate; degeneration

蜕化变质分子 **t'uì-huà pièn-chìh fèn-tzǔ** degenerate and backsliding elements

蜕变 **t'uì-pièn** to degenerate, change through exuviation

t'ūn (tūn)

2223   吞灭 **t'ūn-mièh** to engulf and destroy (to conquer and annex a country)

吞没 **t'ūn-mò** to take possession of [another's property], embezzle, misappropriate

吞并 **t'ūn-pìng** to swallow up; annex territory, take over and merge with

吞吐量 **t'ūn-t'ù-liàng** receiving and discharging capacity [of a port], volume of cargo handled

吞吞吐吐 **t'ūn-t'ūn t'ù-t'ù** swallowing and spitting (to hem and haw, speak in a manner not straightforward; equivocation)

t'ún (tún)

2224   屯田 **t'ún-t'ién** to station troops on the land and have them engage in agriculture

2225   囤积居奇 **t'ún-chī chǔ-ch'í** hoarding and speculation; to hoard for speculation

t'ūng (tōng)

2226   通缉 **t'ūng-chī** to order an arrest, issue an arrest warrant; search for a wanted person

通知 **t'ūng-chīh** to notify, make known, inform, announce, be in communication with; a notification, notice

通知书 **t'ūng-chīh-shū** a written notice, notification

通常 **t'ūng-ch'áng** usual, ordinary, common, general, normal

通车 **t'ūng-ch'ē** be open to traffic; a through train

通气 **t'ūng-ch'ì** (1) in touch with each other, in constant contact; sympathetic; (2) well ventilated; breathing freely

通情达理 **t'ūng-ch'íng-tá-lǐ** to understand the feeling and penetrate the principle (sound judgment; perceptive and judicious)

通风降温 **t'ūng-fēng chiàng-wēn** ventilation and cooling

通风报信 **t'ūng-fēng-pào-hsìn** to send a secret message

通风设备 **t'ūng-fēng shè-pèi** a ventilation system, ventilation facilities

通货 **t'ūng-huò** currency, money, medium of exchange

通货膨胀 **t'ūng-huò p'éng-chàng** currency inflation, inflation; inflationary

通货收缩 **t'ūng-huò shōu-sō** a reduction of the money in circulation, fiscal deflation, deflation; deflationary

通宵 **t'ūng-hsiāo** throughout the night, all night

通晓 **t'ūng-hsiǎo** to be familiar with, be acquainted with, know, understand

通信 **t'ūng-hsìn** to communicate by letter, be in correspondence with; correspondence, communications, signals

通信兵 **t'ūng-hsìn-pīng** the Signal Corps (one of the service arms of the PLA)

通讯 **t'ūng-hsùn** to communicate, correspond, report, give information; correspondence, communications

通讯线路 **t'ūng-hsùn hsièn-lù** postal and telecommunication lines

通讯工具 **t'ūng-hsùn kūng-chù** means of communication

通讯联络 **t'ūng-hsùn lién-lò** communications and liaison; to keep in touch

通讯报导 **t'ūng-hsùn pào-tǎo** reportage, reporting

通讯社 **t'ūng-hsùn-shè** a news agency, press service

通讯员 **t'ūng-hsùn-yuán** a news reporter, correspondent; a military courier, message carrier

通过 **t'ūng-kuò** (1) to pass, adopt, carry, confirm, approve [a bill or measure]; (2) to pass through, traverse, cross; (3) by way of, via, through

通令 **t'ūng-lìng** to issue a general order; a general order, decree

通报 **t'ūng-pào** to make known, inform, notify; a circular notice, announcement

通病 **t'ūng-pìng** a general illness, common deficiency, general fault

通盘 **t'ūng-p'án** overall, entire, as a whole, comprehensive

通盘构思 **t'ūng-p'án kòu-szū** overall considerations, comprehensive deliberations

通盘估计 **t'ūng-p'án kū-chì** an overall estimate

通商 **t'ūng-shāng** [foreign] trade, commerce; to carry on trade; open to trade

通商口岸 **t'ūng-shāng k'ǒu-àn** a treaty port, trading post, port

通史 **t'ūng-shǐh** a general history, history

通俗 **t'ūng-sú** popular, current, general; for mass tastes

通俗易懂 **t'ūng-sú-ì-tǔng** popular and easy to understand

通道 **t'ūng-tào** a through road, general thoroughfare, main road, passage

通电 **t'ūng-tièn** (1) to send a circular telegram, inform all concerned [by radio or telegram]; (2) to link up with a source of electricity, supply electricity to

通途 **t'ūng-t'ú** a through road, unobstructed road

通则 **t'ūng-tsé** general principles, basic rules, common regulations

通菜 **t'ūng-ts'ài** a low-quality vegetable (ordinarily for pig feed)

通用 **t'ūng-yùng** in general use, widely used, current; practical, usable; interchangeable

t'úng (tóng)

2227

同级 **t'úng-chí** at the same level, of equal rank; a coordinate level [of government, etc.], [organizationally] parallel

同济 **t'úng-chì** Tungchi University [Shanghai]

同志 **t'úng-chìh** to have the same goal (a comrade, fellow Party member, colleague; the customary and polite form of address within the Party or when addressing strangers)

同志态度 **t'úng-chìh t'ài-tù** a comradely attitude

同舟共济 **t'úng-chōu-kùng-chì** [those traveling] in the same boat help each other (to endure hardships and overcome difficulties by mutual help)

同住 **t'úng-chù** to live together (cadres to live with the people: one of the **szù-t'úng**)

同中之异 **t'úng-chūng-chīh-ì** differences among similarities

同期 **t'úng-ch'ī** at the same period, concurrently; the corresponding period

同吃 **t'úng-ch'īh** to eat together (cadres to eat with the people: one of the **szù-t'úng**)

同情 **t'úng-ch'íng** sympathy, compassion, pity; to sympathize with, feel comradely toward

同仇敌忾 **t'úng-ch'óu tí-k'ài** to share hatred of the same enemy (to fight a

common foe)

同床异梦 **t'úng-ch'uáng ì-mèng** to share a bed but have different dreams (to have hidden disagreements)

同群众打成一片 **t'úng ch'ún-chùng tǎ-ch'éng ī-p'ièn** to become one with the masses

同犯 **t'úng-fàn** fellow violator (the term of address required of prisoners)

同呼吸共命运 **t'úng-hū-hsī kùng-mìng-yùn** to breathe the same air and share the same fate

同化 **t'úng-huà** to assimilate; assimilation

同乡 **t'úng-hsiāng** a fellow native, a person from the same village, town, province, etc.

同心协力 **t'úng-hsīn-hsiéh-lì** with common heart and united strength (to work in cooperation, put forth united effort)

同心同德 **t'úng-hsīn t'úng-té** to be of the same heart and soul (of one mind)

同一性 **t'úng-ī-hsìng** identity, sameness, uniformity

同一律 **t'úng-ī-lù** the law of identity

同义语 **t'úng-ì-yǔ** a synonym

同意 **t'úng-ì** to agree, concur, assent, consent, be in agreement; agreement

同甘共苦 **t'úng-kān kùng-k'ǔ** to share the sweetness and bitterness together (to share weal and woe)

同归于尽 **t'úng-kuēi-yǘ-chìn** to end up in a common ruin [of both combatants]

同工农相结合 **t'úng-kūng-núng hsiāng-chiéh-hó** to integrate fully with the workers and peasants

同工同酬 **t'úng-kūng t'úng-ch'óu** equal pay for equal work

同劳动 **t'úng-láo-tùng** to labor together (cadres to work with the people: one of the *szù-t'úng*)

同流合污 **t'úng-liú hǒ-wū** to drift with the stream and combine with the filth (to collude with evil company)

同路人 **t'úng-lù-jén** a traveling companion (fellow-traveler, Communist sympathizer)

同盟 **t'úng-méng** an alliance, league, confederation; to ally with, confederate

同盟会 **t'úng-méng-huì** the Tung-meng Hui (the predecessor of the KMT, organized by Sun Yat-sen and Huang Hsing in Japan in 1905—full name Chung-kuo Tung-meng Hui)

同谋 **t'úng-móu** an accomplice, accessory, fellow plotter

同胞 **t'úng-pāo** children of the same parents (a fellow countryman, fellow citizen, compatriot)

同步加速器 **t'úng-pù chiā-sù-ch'ì** a synchrotron

同步回旋加速器 **t'úng-pù huí-hsuán chiā-sù-ch'ì** a synchrocyclotron

同步稳相加速器 **t'úng-pù wěn-hsiāng chiā-sù-ch'ì** synchrophasotron, proton synchrotron

同商量 **t'úng-shāng-liang** to consult together (the cadres to consult with the people: one of the *szù-t'úng*)

同上 **t'úng-shàng** as above, ditto

同时并举 **t'úng-shíh-pìng-chǔ** to do more than one thing at the same time, act at the same time, act simultaneously

同等 **t'úng-těng** of the same class or rank, equal in level, equal, coordinate, equivalent, of the same sort

同族 **t'úng-tsú** of the same race, nation, tribe, clan

同族三分亲 **t'úng-tsú sān-fēn-ch'īn** [members of the] same clan [start with at least] 30 percent affection

同位素 **t'úng-wèi-sù** an isotope

同业公会 **t'úng-yèh kūng-huì** a trade association, craft guild

2228 铜墙铁壁 **t'úng-ch'iáng t'iěh-pì** walls of copper and barriers of iron (an impregnable stronghold)

铜像 **t'úng-hsiàng** a bronze statue

铜管乐队 **t'úng-kuǎn yuèh-tuì** a brass band

2229 童话 **t'úng-huà** children's stories, nursery tales

童养媳 **t'úng-yǎng-hsí** a girl, who because of poverty is raised in and works for the family of her betrothed husband (a practice in the old society)

t'ŭng (tǒng)

2230 统战部 **t'ŭng-chàn-pù** the United Front Work Department [of the CCP Central and provincial committees] (contraction of *t'ŭng-ī-chàn-hsièn kūng-tsò-pù*)

统计 **t'ŭng-chì** statistics; to tabulate and total; statistical

统计工作 **t'ŭng-chì kūng-tsò** statistical work; *Statistical Work* (journal, Peking, semi-monthly, 1957–1958)

统计工作通讯 **t'ŭng-chì kūng-tsò t'úng-hsùn** *Statistical Work Bulletin* (a Peking, semi-monthly journal, 1954–1956)

统计研究 **t'ŭng-chì yén-chiū** *Statistical*

Studies (a Peking, monthly journal, 1958)

统治 **t'ŭng-chìh** to rule, govern, control, dominate, reign, hold the power of the state; rule, control

统治集团 **t'ŭng-chìh-chí-t'uán** a ruling group, power-holding faction

统治阶级 **t'ŭng-chìh-chiēh-chí** the ruling class

统筹 **t'ŭng-ch'óu** overall planning

统筹兼顾 **t'ŭng-ch'óu chiēn-kù** overall planning with due consideration for all proper arrangements (unified planning with attention to all components)

统筹方法 **t'ŭng-ch'óu fāng-fǎ** the overall planning method, operations research, linear programming

统筹学 **t'ŭng-ch'óu-hsuéh** operations research

统销 **t'ŭng-hsiāo** unified marketing, centrally controlled distribution

统一 **t'ŭng-ī** to unite, unify, consolidate, centralize, coordinate; unity; united, unified, consolidated; solely; uniform, consistent, standardized

统一安排 **t'ŭng-ī-ān-p'ái** overall arrangement, uniform arrangement, unified arrangement

统一战线 **t'ŭng-ī-chàn-hsièn** a united front

统一战线工作部 **t'ŭng-ī-chàn-hsièn kūng-tsò-pù** the United Front Work Department [of the CCP Central and provincial Committees]

统一帐册 **t'ŭng-ī-chàng-ts'è** standardized account books

统一计划 **t'ŭng-ī-chì-huà** unified planning; a unified plan

统一指挥 **t'ŭng-ī-chǐh-huī** unified command

统一经营 **t'ŭng-ī-chīng-yíng** centralized management

统一行动 **t'ŭng-ī hsíng-tùng** to act in unison; coordinated action

统一意志 **t'ŭng-ī ì-chìh** unified will; to consolidate determination; with one will

统一观 **t'ŭng-ī-kuān** the theory of unity [between knowing and doing]

统一规划 **t'ŭng-ī kuēi-huà** to map out a unified plan; unified planning

统一领导，全面安排 **t'ŭng-ī lǐng-tǎo, ch'üán-mièn ān-p'ái** centralized leadership and overall arrangement

统一领导，分级管理 **t'ŭng-ī lǐng-tǎo, fēn-chí kuǎn-lǐ** centralized leadership and management by levels

统一领导，分散经营 **t'ŭng-ī lǐng-tǎo, fēn-sàn chīng-yíng** the centralized leadership and decentralized operation

统一步伐 **t'ŭng-ī pù-fá** unified steps, uniform steps (to move forward together)

统一平均分配 **t'ŭng-ī p'íng-chūn fēn-p'èi** coordinated equal distribution, uniformly equal distribution

统一思想 **t'ŭng-ī szū-hsiǎng** to unify ideology; unified thinking

统一调度 **t'ŭng-ī tiào-tù** unified distribution

统一体 **t'ŭng-ī-t'ǐ** an entity, a unity

统购包销 **t'ŭng-kòu pāo-hsiāo** centralized [state] purchase and guaranteed distribution (applied to manufacturing firms before socialization)

统购统销 **t'ŭng-kòu t'ŭng-hsiāo** unified [state] purchase and distribution (through centralized monopoly wholesale agencies)

统帅 **t'ŭng-shuài** a supreme commander

²²³¹ 捅马蜂窝 **t'ŭng-mǎ-fēng-wō** to stir up a hornet's nest (to make trouble for oneself)

t'ùng (tòng)

²²³² 痛陈 **t'ùng-ch'én** to state earnestly, say with great feeling

痛切 **t'ùng-ch'ièh** deeply, earnestly, sincerely, trenchantly

痛斥 **t'ùng-ch'ìh** to scold severely, inveigh against, denounce

痛恨 **t'ùng-hèn** to hate bitterly; abhorrence, hatred

痛下决心 **t'ùng-hsià chüéh-hsīn** to make a solemn determination

痛心疾首 **t'ùng-hsīn-chí-shǒu** heartache and headache (to hate deeply; feel bitterly about)

痛改前非 **t'ùng-kǎi ch'ién-fēi** earnestly to correct past mistakes (to improve oneself and overcome faults)

痛哭流涕 **t'ùng-k'ū liú-t'ì** to shed tears in bitter sorrow

痛打落水狗 **t'ùng-tǎ lò-shuǐ-kǒu** "Beat hard the dog that has fallen into the water" (from a story by Lu Hsun: one should show no mercy to an enemy, even though he be in a desperate plight, because, if saved, he will again be dangerous)

痛定思痛 **t'ùng-tìng szū-t'ùng** when the hurt has eased one thinks [more rationally] about it (do not forget painful lessons learned in the past)

痛痒相关 **t'ùng-yǎng hsiāng-kuān** pain and itch are mutually related (to be

in close touch with each other, close sympathy)

tsá (zá)

2233 杂技团 **tsá-chì t'uán** an acrobatic troupe, jugglers

杂交 **tsá-chiāo** hybridization, cross-breeding

杂志 **tsá-chìh** a magazine, periodical, journal

杂七杂八 **tsá-ch'ī-tsá-pā** an assortment of sevens and eights (a jumble, motley of various things, hodge-podge)

杂居 **tsá-chū** mixed living (people of different races, nationalities, or customs living together)

杂货店 **tsá-huò-tièn** a variety store, shop selling sundries, retail grocery store

杂粮 **tsá-liáng** miscellaneous grains (food grains other than wheat and rice)

杂牌军 **tsá-p'ái-chūn** troops of mixed labels (usually refers to provincial or warlord armies in the KMT period not under direct Chiang Kai-shek or Central Government command)

杂色部队 **tsá-sè pù-tuì** troops of mixed colors (*see above*)

杂耍 **tsá-shuǎ** juggler's feats; a variety show

杂税 **tsá-shuì** a sundry tax, miscellaneous tax (usually an irregular or excessive tax levied locally by warlords or the KMT)

杂文 **tsá-wén** writings or essays on various subjects

杂务员 **tsá-wù-yuán** an "officer of miscellaneous tasks" (now used for persons performing menial functions such as orderly, messenger, janitor, office boy, etc.)

2234 砸锅 **tsá-kuō** to break the kettle (to ruin something for oneself, to fail in an attempted task)

砸烂 **tsá-làn** to smash to bits, crush completely

砸伤 **tsá-shāng** to be injured by a crashing object

砸碎 **tsá-suì** to smash to pieces, break into fragments

砸碎我字 **tsá-suì wǒ-tzù** to smash the word "I" (to look always beyond oneself)

tsǎ (zǎ)

2235 咋说咋办 **tsǎ-shuō-tsǎ-pàn** whatever

[you] say [I] will do it

咋 **tsǎ**: *see also* **chā**

tsāi (zāi)

2236 灾情 **tsāi-ch'íng** the extent of a disaster or calamity

灾区 **tsāi-ch'ū** a disaster area, the area affected by a calamity

灾害 **tsāi-hài** a disaster, calamity; the damages or effects caused by a natural disaster

灾荒 **tsāi-huāng** a famine caused by natural disaster

灾祸 **tsāi-huò** a disaster, calamity, catastrophe, trouble

灾民 **tsāi-mín** calamity-stricken people, refugees from a disaster

灾难 **tsāi-nàn** a disaster, catastrophe, suffering

2237 栽跟头 **tsāi-kēn-t'ou** to stumble, fall over (to meet a sudden or sharp reverse)

栽培 **tsāi-p'éi** to plant and cultivate; care for, nurture

tsǎi (zǎi)

2238 宰割 **tsǎi-kō** to cut up, dismember, partition, divide up; to slaughter, kill, destroy

宰杀 **tsǎi-shā** to butcher, slaughter, kill

2239 载入 **tsǎi-jù** to make an entry of, place on record, appear in [a book, etc.]

载文 **tsǎi-wén** to carry an article [in a publication]; published in

载 **tsǎi**: *see also* **tsài**

tsài (zài)

2240 再教育 **tsài-chiào-yù** to re-educate; re-education (commonly refers to Mao's May 7 [1968] directive ordering cadres and intellectuals to be re-educated by the workers, peasants, and soldiers)

再接再厉 **tsài-chiēh tsài-lì** to make unremitting efforts, forge ahead, be undismayed by failures

再版 **tsài-pǎn** to reprint; a second edition, new printing

再三 **tsài-sān** again and again, repeatedly

再生 **tsài-shēng** reborn; saved from death; a rebirth, revival

再生产 **tsài-shēng-ch'ǎn** reproduction ("the simple repetition of production," as in Marx, *Capital*)

2241　在案 **tsài-àn** on the record, in the file

在职 **tsài-chíh** to be in office, hold an office; incumbency; incumbent

在职干部 **tsài-chíh kàn-pù** cadres performing the functions of their post, incumbent cadres

在职工作 **tsài-chíh kūng-tsò** to carry on the duties of one's post (in contrast to cadres who may continue to hold their post or title while in a May 7th School or on **hsià-fàng**)

在场 **tsài-ch'ǎng** present, on the scene, at the spot; to be present at

在朝 **tsài-ch'áo** to be in power, hold [high] office, control the government

在一定程度上 **tsài ī-tìng ch'éng-tù shang** to a certain degree, to a specified extent

在意 **tsài-ì** to bear in mind, be careful, attentive to

在暴风雨中成长 **tsài pào-fēng-yǔ chūng ch'éng-chǎng** to grow to maturity amid stress and storm

在傍 **tsài-p'áng** beside, alongside, side by side

在世 **tsài-shìh** living, still alive

在所不惜 **tsài-sǒ-pù-hsī** regardless of the cost or sacrifice

在所不辞 **tsài-sǒ-pù-tz'ú** there is nothing that will make [me] shirk, to defy all kinds of perils

在党的总路线光辉照耀下 **tsài tǎng te tsǔng-lù-hsièn kuāng-huī-chào-yào-hsià** under the glorious illumination of the Party's general line (guided by the beacon light of the Party's general line)

在斗争中锻炼，在斗争中成长 **tsài toù-chēng chūng tuàn-lièn, tsài tòu-chēng chūng ch'éng-chǎng** in struggle tempered and in struggle matured

在途保险 **tsài-t'ú pǎo-hsiěn** transport insurance

在座 **tsài-tsò** to be present [at a meeting, etc.]

在望 **tsài-wàng** within sight

在野 **tsài-yěh** out of power, not in office; to be in the opposition

在延安文艺座谈会上的讲话 **tsài yén-ān-wén-ì tsò-t'án-huì shang te chiǎng-huà** "Talks at the Yenan Forum on Literature and Art," (by Mao Tse-tung, May 1942)

2242　载重量 **tsài-chùng-liàng** loading capacity, deadweight tonnage [of a ship]

载歌载舞 **tsài-kō-tsài-wǔ** to sing and dance at the same time (very joyful)

载波电路 **tsài-pō-tièn-lù** carrier wave electrical circuits

载 **tsài**: *see also* **tsǎi**

tsān (zān)

2243　糌粑 **tsān-pā** dried barley meal, tsamba

tsàn (zàn)

2244　赞助 **tsàn-chù** to support, patronize, favor, sponsor; auspices, support

赞成 **tsàn-ch'éng** to agree to, agree with, support, approve, vote for, endorse, favor; endorsement, approval, agreement

赞歌 **tsàn-kō** a song of praise

赞美 **tsàn-měi** to praise, extol, exalt, glorify

赞比亚 **tsàn-pǐ-yà** Zambia

赞不绝口 **tsàn-pù-chüéh-k'ǒu** to praise without ceasing, praise profusely

赞赏 **tsàn-shǎng** to commend, admire, praise

赞颂 **tsàn-sùng** to praise, eulogize, extol

赞同 **tsàn-t'úng** to approve of, consent to, agree with

赞扬 **tsàn-yáng** to exalt, glorify, extol

tsāng (zāng)

2245　赃物 **tsāng-wù** stolen goods, loot, plunder

2246　脏累活 **tsāng-lèi-huó** filthy and heavy work

tsàng (zàng)

2247　葬礼 **tsàng-lǐ** a funeral ceremony, burial service

葬身鱼腹 **tsàng-shēn yǔ-fù** to be buried in the maws of a fish (to be drowned)

葬送 **tsàng-sùng** to bury [one's talents, etc.], to waste or fritter away [one's future]

2248　藏 **tsàng** the Tibetan Autonomous Region

藏族 **tsàng-tsú** the Tibetan people (a minority in Tibet, Kansu, Chinghai and Yunnan: population 2,775,000 as of 1957)

藏 **tsàng**: *see also* **ts'áng**

tsāo (zāo)

2249　遭受 **tsāo-shòu** to suffer, undergo, bear, incur [loss]

遭殃 **tsāo-yāng** to meet with misfortune, suffer disaster, encounter bad luck

遭殃军 **tsāo-yāng-chūn** the meeting-with-calamity army (a reference to KMT troops in the Liberation War)

遭遇 **tsāo-yù** to encounter, meet with, suffer; vicissitudes [of life]; one's lot in life, fate

2250 糟糕透顶 **tsāo-kāo t'òu-tǐng** ruined to the utmost, hopelessly messed up, completely spoiled

糟粕 **tsāo-p'ò** dregs, refuse, sediment, worthless leftover

糟踏 **tsāo-t'a** to waste, misuse, debase, degrade; to scoff at, mock, libel, insult

tsáo (záo)

2251 凿井 **tsáo-chǐng** to drill a well, sink a shaft

tsǎo (zǎo)

2252 早茬 **tsǎo-ch'á** an early sown crop (usually refers to early wheat)

早请示, 晚汇报 **tsǎo ch'ǐng-shìh, wǎn huì-pào** in the morning seek directives and in the evening report [accomplishments]

早生贵子 **tsǎo-shēng-kuèi-tzǔ** [to hope for] early birth of a son (now criticized as an old concept)

早熟 **tsǎo-shú** premature; early maturing, precocious

早熟作物 **tsǎo-shú tsò-wù** early ripening crops (crop varieties requiring a shorter growing period)

早稻 **tsǎo-tào** early rice, early maturing rice (planted in early spring with a complete growth cycle of less than 120 days)

tsào (zào)

2253 灶王爷 **tsào-wáng-yéh** the kitchen god

2254 造价 **tsào-chià** the cost of building, construction, production, or manufacture

造纸厂 **tsào-chǐh-ch'ǎng** a paper mill

造就 **tsào-chiù** to make [something] complete (to educate, bring up; one's accomplishments, experiences)

造中有修, 修中有造, 修建结合 **tsào-chūng yǔ-hsiū, hsiū-chūng yǔ-tsào, hsiū-chièn chiéh-hó** manufacturing comprises repairing, repairing comprises manufacturing [and] the two [should be] integrated

造成 **tsào-ch'éng** to create, produce, form, bring about, result in, cause to happen

造船厂 **tsào-ch'uán-ch'ǎng** a shipyard, shipbuilding yard

造反 **tsào-fǎn** to rebel, revolt, rise up; rebellion, uprising, (had a bad connotation until 1949, but given a new and highly favorable meaning in the Cultural Revolution)

造反精神 **tsào-fǎn chīng-shén** rebellious spirit, the rebelling spirit (*see above*)

造反有功 **tsào-fǎn-yǔ-kūng** to rebel brings merit (usually suggests criticism of the youthful or immature assumption that the mere act of rebellion, whether correct or not, brings honor to its perpetrators)

造反有理 **tsào-fǎn-yǔ-lǐ** to rebel is justified (a statement made by Mao Tse-tung encouraging the Red Guards during the early phase of the Cultural Revolution)

造福 **tsào-fú** to create happiness, do good deeds

造型艺术 **tsào-hsíng-ì-shù** plastic arts, formative arts

造诣 **tsào-ì** degree of education, scholarly attainment; to call on, visit

造林 **tsào-lín** to afforest; afforestation

造林区 **tsào-lín-ch'ū** an afforestation area

造谣生事 **tsào-yáo shēng-shìh** to spread rumors and incite incidents

造谣污蔑 **tsào-yáo-wū-mièh** to spread rumors and slander

tsé (zé)

2255 择优录取 **tsé-yū lù-ch'ǔ** to select and admit the superior ones (usually refers to admission to university, etc.)

2256 责任 **tsé-jèn** responsibility, duty, obligation

责任制 **tsé-jèn-chìh** a responsibility system, system, system of [personal] responsibility

责任感 **tsé-jèn-kǎn** a sense of responsibility

责任事故 **tsé-jèn shìh-kù** an accident for which there is liability, an incident of culpable negligence

责任田 **tsé-jèn-t'ién** a plot assigned as a special responsibility

责令 **tsé-lìng** to order, place a responsibility on; an order

责难 **tsé-nán** to wish success in a difficult task

责难 **tsé-nàn** to upbraid, demand an explanation, reproach, scold

责备 **tsé-pèi** to criticize, blame, reproach, admonish, reprimand

责问 **tsé-wèn** to blame and demand an explanation, interrogate as a suspect

责无旁贷 **tsé-wú-p'áng-tài** a responsibility that cannot be shirked,

2257 啧啧赞赏 **tsé-tsé tsàn-shǎng** to make sounds showing admiration or praise

inescapable duty; duty-bound

tséi (zéi)

2258 贼巢 **tséi-ch'áo** bandits' lair, robbers' den, thieves' hideout

贼喊捉贼 **tséi hǎn chō-tséi** [it is the] thief [himself who] calls "stop thief" (to accuse someone else of one's own misdeeds)

贼心不死 **tséi-hsīn-pù-szǔ** a robber's heart never dies (evil ambition never rests)

贼过兴兵 **tséi-kuò hsīng-pīng** to mobilize the army after the bandits have gone (to lock the barn door after the horse has been stolen; too late for effective action)

贼眉鼠眼 **tséi-méi shǔ-yěn** having a bandit's brow and a rat's eyes (to look cunning and insincere)

贼头贼脑 **tséi-t'óu-tséi-nǎo** the head [i.e., appearance] of a thief (to act stealthily; thief-like, villainous)

贼赃 **tséi-tsāng** robber's loot, stolen goods, booty

tsēng (zēng)

2259 憎恶 **tsēng-wù** to hate, loathe, detest, abhor

2260 增长 **tsēng-chǎng** to grow, increase, enlarge; growth, increase, increment

增加 **tsēng-chiā** to add to, increase, enhance, augment, raise; an increase, enhancement

增进 **tsēng-chìn** to advance, increase, promote, make progress, develop, improve, strengthen

增产 **tsēng-ch'ǎn** to increase production; increased production

增产节约 **tsēng-ch'ǎn chiéh-yuēh** to increase production and practice economy

增产节约运动 **tsēng-ch'ǎn chiéh-yuēh yùn-tùng** the campaign [movement] to increase production and practice economy

增产不增税 **tsēng-ch'ǎn pù tsēng-shuì** an increase in production will not increase the tax [amount]

增产到顶 **tsēng-ch'ǎn tào-tǐng** [the idea that] production has reached the ultimate level

增强 **tsēng-ch'iáng** to strengthen, reinforce, fortify; reinforcement

增强人民体质 **tsēng-ch'iáng jén-mín t'ǐ-chìh** to strengthen the physique of the people

增光 **tsēng-kuāng** to add to the luster of (to glorify, honor)

增刊 **tsēng-k'ān** a supplement, special edition (usually a literary supplement, weekly or otherwise, to newspaper or journal)

增删 **tsēng-shān** to add and delete, to emend, to revise; emendation, revision

增设 **tsēng-shè** to add to

增多 **tsēng-tō** to grow in number, increase, augment; augmentation

增添 **tsēng-t'iēn** to increase, enlarge, add to, supplement

增援 **tsēng-yuán** to send reinforcements, reinforce; to build up troop strength

tsō (zuō)

2261 作坊 **tsō-fáng** a small workshop

作揖 **tsō-ī** an old-fashioned gesture in greeting (the greeter holds his own hands together in an up-and-down motion)

作 **tsō**: see also **tsò**

tsŏ (zuŏ)

2262 左倾 **tsŏ-ch'īng** an inclination toward the left, left-leaning, a leftist tendency, leftist (normally only has a political meaning: placing it within quotation marks suggests ultra-leftism or infantile leftism)

左倾机会主义 **tsŏ-ch'īng chī-huì-chǔ-ì** left opportunism

左倾分子 **tsŏ-ch'īng fèn-tzǔ** left deviationists, leftists, leftist elements

左倾空谈主义 **tsŏ-ch'īng k'ūng-t'án-chǔ-ì** leftist empty talk-ism, leftist phrase mongering

左倾路线 **tsŏ-ch'īng lù-hsièn** the leftist line, left deviationist line

左倾冒险主义 **tsŏ-ch'īng mào-hsiěn-chǔ-ì** left adventurism

左倾幼稚病 **tsŏ-ch'īng yù-chìh-pìng** leftist infantilism, the infantile disorder of the left wing

左翼 **tsŏ-ì** the left wing [in politics, literature, art, etc.]; the left flank [of an army formation]

左翼分子 **tsŏ-ì fèn-tzǔ** left-wing elements, a member of a left-wing group

左翼作家 **tsŏ-ì tsò-chiā** left-wing writers

左翼作家联盟 **tsŏ-ì tsò-chiā lién-méng** the League of Left-Wing Writers (established by Lu Hsun and others in 1930)

左顾右盼 **tsŏ-kù-yù-p'àn** looking to the left and beholding the right (to show lack of concentration on a task; inattentive; flirtatious; to act in a self-important manner)

左联 **tsŏ-lién** the League of Left-Wing Writers (contraction of **tsŏ-ì tsò-chiā lién-méng**)

左轮手枪 **tsŏ-lún shŏu-ch'iāng** a revolver, six- shooter

左派 **tsŏ-p'ài** the leftist faction, left wing, leftists, the left

左派幼稚病 **tsŏ-p'ài yù-chìh-pìng** "Left-Wing Communism, An Infantile Disorder" (by Lenin, 1920)

左道旁门 **tsŏ-tào p'áng-mén** the left path and the side door (heresy, heretical doctrines; improper and devious ways)

"左"得出奇 **"tsŏ" te ch'ū-ch'í** "leftist" to an unreasonable degree

左袒 **tsŏ-t'ǎn** to favor one side, be biased, give improper protection to

左右 **tsŏ-yù** left and right [of], approximately, near, about, in the neighborhood of, more or less, perhaps; to influence, sway

左右手 **tsŏ-yù-shŏu** the left and right hands (valuable assistants, top aides, entourage)

左右大局 **tsŏ-yù tà-chú** to right or left the trend (to be able to manipulate or control the trend of events)

左右摇摆 **tsŏ-yù yáo-pǎi** to stagger from left to right (to vacillate, be indecisive, without convictions)

tsò (zuò)

²²⁶³ 作战 **tsò-chàn** to fight, make war; a military operation, warfare

作战线 **tsò-chàn-hsièn** a military front, fighting line

作家 **tsò-chiā** a writer, author, playwright

作茧自缚 **tsò-chiĕn tzŭ-fù** to make a cocoon and bind oneself (to work hard and merely get oneself into trouble; to be one's own undoing)

作主 **tsò-chŭ** to be one's own master, exercise independent authority, take charge, decide

作曲 **tsò-ch'ŭ** to compose music; a musical composer

作法 **tsò-fǎ** (1) work method, way of doing things (implies an approach to a task as well as the actual methods used); (2) to exercise magic powers, engage in hocus-pocus

作法自毙 **tsò-fǎ-tzù-pì** to make a law that kills oneself (to get into trouble through one's own scheme; a plan that boomerangs)

作风 **tsò-fēng** style of work, work-style (generally refers to one's attitude, manner, and conduct in carrying out work, especially as it involves associates and the masses)

作风不纯 **tsò-fēng pù-ch'ún** an impurity in work-style (a work-style that is deficient, inadequate, or lacking in the proper attitude)

作怪 **tsò-kuài** to make mischief, behave badly, play malicious tricks

作客 **tsò-k'ò** to be a guest; sojourn in a strange land

作孽 **tsò-nièh** to do evil, cause misfortune to others

作恶多端 **tsò-ò-tō-tuān** to commit many kinds of evil, commit all sorts of crimes

作品 **tsò-p'ĭn** literary or artistic works, products of the arts of painting and calligraphy

作祟 **tsò-suì** to do mischief, play tricks, cause trouble

作对 **tsò-tuì** to oppose [one thing against another], contrast; to act against, choose to be a rival of, be hostile toward

作威作福 **tsò-wēi tsò-fú** to be severe and lenient by turns (to act in an oppressive manner; give oneself airs)

作为 **tsò-wéi** (1) behavior, conduct, way of acting, deeds, actions; (2) to serve as, to regard as; in the capacity of

作物 **tsò-wù** an agricultural crop

作物品种 **tsò-wù p'ĭn-chŭng** varieties of crops, the kinds of farm crops

作业 **tsò-yèh** work to be done; activity, task, operations, duty; a student's homework

作业计划 **tsò-yèh-chì-huà** a work plan, operations plan

作业区 **tsò-yèh-ch'ū** an area of operations, work district

作业队 **tsò-yèh-tuì** an operations team

作业组 **tsò-yèh-tsŭ** a job group (a small work unit—usually part of a work team)

作用 **tsò-yùng** a role, part played; a function, use, purpose; application, operation; usefulness, effect

作 **tsò**: see also **tsō**, and also "做" **tsò**)

²²⁶⁴ 坐井观天 **tsò-chĭng-kuān-t'iēn** to sit in a well and look at the sky (to have a narrow view, short-sighted, ignorant)

坐吃山空 **tsò-ch'ih-shān-k'ūng** sitting [idle] one can eat away a whole

387

mountain (ruin is certain if one does not work and produce)

坐庄 **tsò-chuāng** to sit as dealer [in a game of chance] (to take charge; be the ruling party in the government)

坐牢 **tsò-láo** to sit in jail, be imprisoned

坐牢不怕, 把牢底来坐穿 **tsò-láo pù-p'à, pǎ láo-tǐ lái tsò-ch'uān** [we are] not afraid of prison and will sit here until the prison floor wears out (a statement attributed to General Yeh T'ing after the South Anhwei Incident of 1941)

坐冷板凳 **tsò-lěng-pǎn-tèng** to sit on a cold bench (to hold a position with little authority; to be suspended from one's post and given no work to do; to be in limbo)

坐门等客 **tsò-mén těng-k'ò** to sit at the door to await customers (the traditional way of doing business: in contrast to new methods of taking goods to the customers, as in the countryside)

坐山观虎斗 **tsò-shān kuān-hǔ-tòu** to sit on a mountain and watch the tigers fight (to watch safely from the sidelines; to avoid involvement)

坐失时机 **tsò-shīh-shíh-chī** to sit and lose an opportunity, to miss a chance through idleness

坐视 **tsò-shìh** to sit and watch (to watch without helping)

坐等依赖 **tsò-těng ī-lài** to sit waiting and depend on others (the opposite of self-reliance)

坐等办法 **tsò-těng pàn-fǎ** the sitting and waiting method [of solving one's problems] (*see above*)

坐等病人叩门 **tsò-těng pìng-jén k'òu-mén** to sit and wait for the patients to knock at the door (the old attitude, instead of taking health services to the patients in the countryside etc.)

坐在火山口上 **tsò-tsài huǒ-shān k'ǒu-shang** sitting on the crater of a volcano

坐卧不宁 **tsò-wò-pù-níng** no peace in either sitting or lying (to be very uneasy in one's mind)

²²⁶⁵ 柞蚕丝 **tsò-ts'án-szū** tussah silk, wild silk (also known as Shantung silk)

²²⁶⁶ 座谈会 **tsò-t'án-huì** a sit and talk meeting (a symposium, forum, or consultative meeting, generally quite informal and intended more for an exchange of views than to reach decisions)

座位 **tsò-wèi** a seat, place

座无虚席 **tsò-wú-hsū-hsí** no seat is empty (a full house)

座右铭 **tsò-yù-míng** a motto at the right of one's chair (a favorite motto for one's guidance)

²²⁶⁷ 做出好样子 **tsò-ch'ū hǎo-yàng-tzu** to set a good example

做出榜样 **tsò-ch'ū pǎng-yàng** to set an example, be a model

做绝了 **tsò-chüéh-le** to carry to an extreme, overdo, run into the ground

做法 **tsò-fǎ** method, way of doing things, mode of action

做好人的工作 **tsò-hǎo jén-te kūng-tsò** to handle well the human factor, to do a good job of the work of dealing with men

做一天和尚, 撞一天钟 **tsò-ī-t'īen hó-shang, chùang-ī-t'iēn chūng** to be a monk for a day and toll the bell for a day (to go through the motions, do one's task in a perfunctory way)

做人 **tsò-jén** to conduct oneself [in a proper manner], to act as a man [in a moral society]

做官 **tsò-kuān** to be an official

做官享福 **tsò-kuān hsiǎng-fú** to be an official and enjoy a good life

做官当老爷 **tsò-kuān tāng lǎo-yeh** to be an official and [act as] a lord

做思想工作 **tsò szū-hsiǎng-kūng-tsò** to do ideological work (to carry on political indoctrination, to explain and motivate the masses to carry out the policy line or undertake a project)

做到老, 学到老 **tsò-tào-lǎo, hsuéh-tào-lǎo** work until one is old and learn until one is old

做天下的主人 **tsò t'iēn-hsià te chǔ-jén** to be the masters of the world (the role of the proletariat)

做贼心虚 **tsò-tséi hsīn-hsū** a thief has a guilty conscience (to act in a furtive or guilty manner)

做 **tsò**: see also "作" (**tsò**)

tsŏu (zǒu)

²²⁶⁸ 走集体富裕道路 **tsŏu chí-t'ǐ fù-yù tào-lù** to take the road of collective prosperity

走家串户 **tsŏu-chiā ch'uàn-hù** to visit every household from door to door

走街串户 **tsŏu-chiēh ch'uàn-hù** to walk the street from door to door (to canvas the neighborhood)

走出去, 请进来 **tsŏu-ch'u-ch'ù, ch'ǐng-chin-lai** to go out and invite [people] in (the students and school teachers should go out and invite the workers,

peasants, and soldiers in)

走风 **tsǒu-fēng** to leak wind (divulge information, leak out news, blab secrets)

走后门 **tsǒu hòu-mén** to use the back door (to gain something by improper means; to "pull strings")

走回头路 **tsǒu huí-t'óu-lù** to turn back on the road, take a reverse course, lose ground already gained

走下坡路 **tsǒu hsià-p'ō-lù** to go on a downward road (follow a dangerous and slippery course)

走向灭亡 **tsǒu-hsiàng mièh-wáng** to go toward ruin

走向胜利 **tsǒu-hsiàng shèng-lì** to march toward victory

走议会道路 **tsǒu ì-huì tào-lù** to take the parliamentary road

走狗 **tsǒu-kǒu** a running dog, lackey, stooge, henchman, hireling

走过场 **tsǒu-kuò-ch'ǎng** to cross the stage (a brief performance, transition scene)

走了一段弯路 **tsǒu-le ī-tuàn wān-lù** to have gone through a stretch of zig-zag road, followed a roundabout course

走马观花 **tsǒu-mǎ kuān-huā** to view flowers from a pacing horse (to take a cursory glance, gain only superficial knowledge, an overly hasty examination of conditions or a problem)

走马看花 **tsǒu-mǎ k'àn-huā** to look at flowers from a pacing horse (*see above*)

走马灯 **tsǒu-mǎ-tēng** a lantern with revolving silhouettes of horses (the succession of political leaders in office)

走不通 **tsǒu-pù-t'ūng** cannot go through, unfeasible, impossible to carry out

走私 **tsǒu-szū** to smuggle; smuggling, unsanctioned private business

走投无路 **tsǒu-t'óu wú-lù** to go down a blind alley, come to an impasse, no way out, with no one to depend on

走卒 **tsǒu-tsú** a henchman, lackey, stooge, errand boy

走资本主义道路 **tsǒu tzū-pěn-chǔ-ì tào-lù** to take the road of capitalism

走资派 **tsǒu-tzū-p'ài** capitalist roaders (those who, in Maoist terms, use or advocate capitalist methods: followers of Liu Shao-ch'i)

走村串帐 **tsǒu-ts'ūn ch'uàn-chàng** to go to the villages and visit each yurt (refers to grasslands or nomad areas)

走弯路 **tsǒu-wān-lù** to take a zig-zag

road, follow a roundabout path

走为上计 **tsǒu wéi shàng-chì** to leave is the best stratagem (retreat to fight another day)

走样子 **tsǒu-yàng-tzu** to deviate from the pattern, fail to conform to the norm

tsòu (zòu)

2269 奏鸣曲 **tsòu-míng-ch'ǔ** a sonata

奏乐 **tsòu-yuèh** to play music

tsū (zū)

2270 租界 **tsū-chièh** a foreign concession, leased territory

租借法案 **tsū-chièh fǎ-àn** the Lend-Lease Act

租赁 **tsū-lìn** to lease, rent; rental, leaseholding

租税 **tsū-shuì** a tax; taxation; to tax

租佃 **tsū-tièn** a farm lease; land tenancy

tsú (zú)

2271 足跡 **tsú-chī** footprints, tracks, traces; a person's whereabouts

足见 **tsú-chièn** it is evident that, suffice to show, from this it is clear

足智多谋 **tsú-chìh tō-móu** sufficient wisdom and many plans (wise and resourceful)

足球 **tsú-ch'iú** soccer football

足夠 **tsú-kòu** sufficient, enough, ample

2272 族主 **tsú-chǔ** a clan chief

族权 **tsú-ch'ǔan** clan authority

族谱 **tsú-p'ǔ** a clan book, clan genealogy

tsǔ (zǔ)

2273 诅咒 **tsǔ-chòu** to curse, revile, berate

2274 阻碍 **tsǔ-ài** to obstruct, block, hinder, prevent; an obstruction, hindrance

阻击战 **tsǔ-chī-chàn** a blocking [military] operation, preventive action, delaying action

阻击阵地 **tsǔ-chī chèn-tì** a defensive [military] position

阻止 **tsǔ-chǐh** to stop, prevent, hold up, retard, hinder

阻隔 **tsǔ-kó** to cut off, separate, interrupt, isolate; cut off, separated, isolated

阻拦 **tsǔ-lán** to stop, prevent, retard, obstruct

阻力 **tsǔ-lì** the force of resistance, resistance

阻挠 **tsǔ-náo** to obstruct, hinder, resist

阻挡 **tsǔ-tǎng** to block, hinder, place in the way, stop

阻援 **tsǔ-yuán** to block [enemy] reinforcement (to isolate and cut off from support)

2275 组织 **tsǔ-chīh** to organize, systematize, set up; an organization, body, structure, system; organized; organizational ("the organization" without further specification usually refers to the Party or Youth League)

组织照顾 **tsǔ-chīh chào-kù** to receive special care from the [Party] organization [of one's unit]

组织者 **tsǔ-chīh-chě** an organizer, ring leader

组织纪律性 **tsǔ-chīh chì-lù-hsìng** organizational discipline

组织建设 **tsǔ-chīh chièn-shè** to build [Party or League] organization

组织起来 **tsǔ-chīh-ch'ǐ-lái** "Get Organized!" (the title of an article by Mao Tse-tung)

组织处分 **tsǔ-chīh ch'ǔ-fèn** to be disciplined by the [Party or League] organization

组织军事化 **tsǔ-chīh chǔn-shìh-huà** militarization of organization (one of the **sān-huà**)

组织分配 **tsǔ-chīh fēn-p'èi** the assignment [of tasks] by the [Party or League] organization

组织学 **tsǔ-chīh-hsuéh** histology

组织工作队 **tsǔ-chīh kūng-tsò-tuì** organizing work teams (sent from higher levels to streamline lower bureaucracy, as in 1957)

组织疗法 **tsǔ-chīh-liáo-fǎ** tissue therapy, histotherapy

组织办公室 **tsǔ-chīh pàn-kūng-shìh** the office of a Party organization

组织上 **tsǔ-chīh-shang** organizationally

组织生活 **tsǔ-chīh shēng-huó** (1) life in the [Party] organization, organizational life; (2) *Party Life* (a Peking journal)

组成 **tsǔ-ch'éng** to form, constitute, compose, make up, organize; to consist of, comprise; formation, composition; component

组成人员 **tsǔ-ch'éng jén-yuán** component members

组成部分 **tsǔ-ch'éng pù-fèn** a component part, integral part

组曲 **tsǔ-ch'ǔ** a musical suite

组阁 **tsǔ-kó** to form a Cabinet [of a government]

组员 **tsǔ-yuán** a member of a party cell, a member of a small group

2276 祖传秘方 **tsǔ-ch'uán mì-fāng** a hereditary secret [medical] recipe

祖先 **tsǔ-hsiēn** ancestors, forebears, forefathers

祖国 **tsǔ-kuó** the fatherland, motherland, homeland

祖国神圣领土 **tsǔ-kuó shén-shèng lǐng-t'ǔ** the sacred territory of the fatherland

祖师爷 **tsǔ-shīh-yéh** venerable master

祖祖辈辈 **tsǔ-tsǔ pèi-pèi** ancestor upon ancestor and generation upon generation

祖宗 **tsǔ-tsūng** remote ancestors, forefathers

tsuān (zuān)

2277 钻劲 **tsuān-chìn** penetrative strength, delving energy

钻进 **tsuān-chìn** to worm into, penetrate, infiltrate

钻井机 **tsuān-chǐng-chī** a well-boring machine, well-drilling equipment

钻井队 **tsuān-chǐng-tuì** an [oil] well-drilling team

钻故纸堆 **tsuān-kù-chǐh-tuī** to bore into piles of old paper (to be absorbed in the study of old books; pedantry)

钻空子 **tsuān k'ùng-tzu** to sneak through a gap, take advantage of a loophole, exploit an opportunity

钻探 **tsuān-t'àn** to do exploratory drilling, prospect, investigate

钻探机 **tsuān-t'àn-chī** a drilling machine, boring machine, drilling rig

钻探队 **tsuān-t'àn-tuì** a team doing test drilling and prospecting

钻研 **tsuān-yén** to scrutinize thoroughly, research deeply, study assiduously

tsuǐ (zuǐ)

2278 嘴紧 **tsuǐ-chǐn** tight-lipped, close-mouthed (a person who can trusted with secrets)

嘴快心直 **tsuǐ-k'uài hsīn-chíh** the mouth is quick and the heart is straight (blunt and straightforward, frank and sincere)

嘴脸 **tsuǐ-liěn** the visage; face (in a derogatory sense)

tsuì (zuì)

2279 最近点 **tsuì-chìn tiěn** the nearest point [in an orbit, etc.], perigee

最前列 **tsuì-ch'ién-lièh** the very front row, the front rank

最亲密的战友 **tsuì ch'īn-mì te chàn-yǔ** the most intimate comrade-in-arms

最崇高的模范 **tsuì-ch'úng-kāo te mó-fàn** the most noble model

最后挣扎 **tsuì-hòu chēng-chá** the ultimate effort, final struggle

最后寄港 **tsuì-hòu-chì-kǎng** the last previous port of call [of a vessel]

最后决定权 **tsuì-hòu chüéh-tìng-ch'üán** the final decision-making authority

最后一息 **tsuì-hòu ī-hsī** the last breath, expiring breath

最后堡垒 **tsuì-hòu pǎo-lěi** the last fortress, innermost line of fortifications (the last stand of the opposition)

最后胜利 **tsuì-hòu shèng-lì** the final victory, ultimate victory

最后通牒 **tsuì-hòu t'ūng-tiéh** the final note, an ultimatum

最惠国待遇 **tsuì-huì-kuó tài-yǜ** most-favored-nation treatment

最惠国条款 **tsuì-huì-kuó t'iáo-k'uǎn** a most-favored-nation clause

最新指示 **tsuì-hsīn chǐh-shìh** the most recent instruction, latest directive

最凶恶的敌人 **tsuì-hsiūng-ò-te tí-jén** the most vicious enemy

最高级会议 **tsuì-kāo-chí huì-ì** a meeting at the highest level, summit conference

最高指示 **tsuì-kāo chǐh-shìh** the highest directive (usually understood to mean originating from Mao Tse-tung)

最高峰 **tsuì-kāo-fēng** the highest peak, summit, climax

最高人民检察院 **tsuì-kāo jén-mín chǐěn-ch'á-yuàn** the Supreme People's Procuratorate

最高人民法院 **tsuì-kāo jén-mín fǎ-yuàn** the Supreme People's Court

最高国家权力机关 **tsuì-kāo kuó-chiā ch'üán-lì chī-kuān** highest state authority, highest organ of the state power

最高国务会议 **tsuì-kāo kuó-wù huì-ì** a top-level state conference, the Supreme State Council

最高流量 **tsuì-kāo liú-liàng** maximum volume of flow, peak flow

最高年分 **tsuì-kāo nién-fèn** the highest year, peak year [in production, etc.]

最大限度 **tsuì-tà hsièn-tù** the greatest extent, maximum degree, utmost limit; the most; maximal

最远点 **tsuì-yuǎn-tiěn** the farthest point [in an orbit, etc.], apogee

2280　罪证确凿 **tsuì-chèng ch'üèh-tsò** criminal evidence beyond any doubt; criminal guilt reliably established

罪状 **tsuì-chuàng** a statement of crime, indictment, charge

罪犯 **tsuì-fàn** a criminal, offender, culprit

罪行 **tsuì-hsíng** a criminal act, crime; guilt

罪人 **tsuì-jén** a criminal, convict, sinner

罪该万死 **tsuì-kāi-wàn-szǔ** an offense deserving ten thousand deaths

罪魁祸首 **tsuì-k'uéi-huò-shǒu** the chief offender and ringleader

罪名 **tsuì-míng** a criminal charge, accusation, crime

罪恶昭彰 **tsuì-ò-chāo-chāng** one's sin is luminously displayed (said of a flagrant offender)

罪恶累累 **tsuì-ò-lěi-lěi** evil deeds piled upon each other, multiple offenses, crime-ridden

罪不容诛 **tsuì-pù-júng-chū** a crime beyond punishment

罪不容恕 **tsuì-pù-júng-shù** a crime which cannot be excused

罪大恶极 **tsuì-tà-ò-chí** the crime is great and the evil extreme, a heinous crime, capital offense

罪有应得 **tsuì-yǔ-yīng-té** the punishment is well deserved

2281　醉心 **tsuì-hsīn** infatuated with, charmed by, wholly absorbed in

醉生梦死 **tsuì-shēng mèng-szǔ** to live drunk and die dreaming (to live a befuddled life)

tsūn (zūn)

2282　尊重 **tsūn-chùng** to honor, respect, esteem, venerate, uphold

尊崇 **tsūn-ch'úng** to revere, venerate, idolize, worship

尊儒反法 **tsūn-jú fǎn-fǎ** to uphold the Confucianists and oppose the Legalists

尊干爱兵 **tsūn-kàn aì-pīng** [soldiers should] respect cadres and [cadres should] take care of soldiers

尊孔反法 **tsūn-k'ǔng fǎn-fǎ** to uphold Confucius and oppose the Legalist [school]

尊师爱生 **tsūn-shīh aì-shēng** [students should] respect teachers and [teachers should] cherish students

尊严 **tsūn-yén** dignity, honor, respectability; dignified, worthy

2283　遵照 **tsūn-chào** to follow, comply with, obey, accord with

遵循 **tsūn-hsún** to follow, accord with, act in accordance, comform to, obey; in conformance with

遵义会议 **tsūn-ì huì-ì** the Tsunyi Conference (the meeting of Communist

leaders during the Long March at Tsunyi, Kweichow, in January, 1935)

遵守 **tsŭn-shǒu** to comply with, abide by, observe, follow, adhere to, uphold; adherence, compliance

遵从 **tsŭn-ts'úng** to follow, comply with, obey, act in accord

tsŭn (zŭn)

2284　撙节 **tsŭn-chiéh** to economize, retrench, save

tsūng (zōng)

2285　宗教信仰自由 **tsūng-chiào hsìn-yǎng tzù-yú** freedom of religious belief, freedom of worship

宗教事务局 **tsūng-chiào shìh-wù-chú** Religious Affairs Office [of the State Council]

宗旨 **tsūng-chǐh** a principle, goal, aim, purpose; essential ideas, main points

宗主权 **tsūng-chǔ-ch'üán** suzerainty

宗主国 **tsūng-chǔ-kuó** a suzerain country (the country exercising suzerainty)

宗法制 **tsūng-fǎ-chìh** patriarchy, patriarchal system

宗派 **tsūng-p'ài** a sect, faction, clique

宗派纠纷 **tsūng-p'ài-chiū-fēn** factional strife

宗派主义 **tsūng-p'ài-chǔ-ì** sectarianism, cliquism, sectism, factionalism

宗派分裂活动 **tsūng-p'ài fēn-lièh huó-tùng** sectarian "splittist" activities, divisive clique activity

宗派观念 **tsūng-p'ài kuān-nièn** factional concepts, sectarian views

宗族主义 **tsūng-tsú-chǔ-ì** "clan-ism"

宗族关系 **tsūng-tsú kuān-hsi** clan relationships, clan ties

宗族观念 **tsūng-tsú kuān-nièn** clan concepts, a clan outlook

2286　综合 **tsūng-hó** to combine, synthesize, integrate, coordinate, recapitulate; synthesis, combination, coordination; synthetic, composite, integrated; multi-, poly-

综合技术 **tsūng-hó chì-shù** polytechnical

综合加工厂 **tsūng-hó chiā-kūng-ch'ǎng** a multi-product processing factory, an integrated processing plant

综合指标 **tsūng-hó chǐh-piāo** a general indicator, aggregate indicator

综合指数 **tsūng-hó chǐh-shù** an aggregate index, composite index

综合治疗 **tsūng-hó chìh-liáo** composite treatment

综合经济 **tsūng-hó chīng-chì** the integrated economy, aggregate economy

综合经营 **tsūng-hó chīng-yíng** integrated administration, coordinated operations, combined management

综合性红专学校 **tsūng-hó-hsìng húng-chuān hsuéh-hsiào** comprehensive red and expert schools

综合性企业 **tsūng-hó-hsìng ch'ǐ-yèh** an integrated enterprise (an enterprise producing a number of different but usually related products)

综合性工厂 **tsūng-hó-hsìng kūng-ch'ǎng** an integrated factory, a plant producing a number of products

综合医务所 **tsūng-hó ī-wù-sǒ** a comprehensive medical facility, polyclinic

综合利用 **tsūng-hó lì-yùng** comprehensive utilization, multipurpose use

综合报导 **tsūng-hó pào-tǎo** a comprehensive report, summing-up

综合平衡 **tsūng-hó p'íng-héng** integral equilibrium (a balance between various factors [of the economy])

综合大学 **tsūng-hó tà-hsuéh** a comprehensive university (a university covering several general fields)

综合研究 **tsūng-hó yén-chiū** coordinated research; to coordinate research

综括 **tsūng-k'uò** to sum up, recapitulate, generalize; comprehensive, all-embracing, all-inclusive

2287　踪迹 **tsūng-chī** a footprint, trace, track

tsŭng (zŏng)

2288　总政治部 **tsŭng chèng-chìh-pù** the General Political Department [of the PLA]

总计 **tsŭng-chì** a total sum, total amount, gross, aggregate; to add up, amount to, total to

总结 **tsŭng-chiéh** to summarize, recapitulate; a summing-up, synopsis, summary

总结经验 **tsŭng-chiéh chīng-yèn** to sum up experiences

总结报告 **tsŭng-chiéh pào-kào** a concluding report, summary report

总监 **tsŭng-chiēn** the Inspector-General [of the PLA]

总支部 **tsŭng-chīh-pù** a general Party branch (a main office with smaller branch offices subordinate to it)

总产值 **tsŭng-ch'ǎn-chíh** gross output value

总产量 **tsŭng-ch'ǎn-liàng** gross output, total production

总前委 **tsŭng-ch'ién-wěi** a general front

committee (a war-theater Party organization)

总和 **tsǔng-hó** a sum, total; to sum, total

总后勤部 **tsǔng hòu-ch'ín-pù** the General Logistics Department [of the PLA]

总纲 **tsǔng-kāng** the general principles [of a statement], an outline, preamble, introduction

总根子 **tsǔng-kēn-tzu** a main root, taproot

总管 **tsǔng-kuǎn** a supervisor, superintendent, director, boss (derogatory epithet during the Cultural Revolution)

总工会 **tsǔng-kūng-huì** a general trade union

总开关 **tsǔng-k'āi-kuān** a main switch, master switch

总理 **tsǔng-lǐ** a premier, prime minister

总理办公室 **tsǔng-lǐ pàn-kūng-shìh** the premier's secretariat

总领事 **tsǔng-lǐng-shìh** a consul-general

总路线 **tsǔng-lù-hsièn** the general line (Mao's formula for building socialism, announced in 1957)

总额 **tsǔng-ó** the total amount, gross amount, total volume, total value; total, gross

总罢工 **tsǔng-pà-kūng** a general strike

总编辑 **tsǔng-piēn-chí** an editor-in-chief, chief editor

总部 **tsǔng-pù** a general headquarters, base headquarters

总书记 **tsǔng-shū-chì** a general secretary, secretary-general

总数 **tsǔng-shù** the total number [amount, value, etc.], grand total

总司令 **tsǔng-szū-lìng** a commander-in-chief

总动员 **tsǔng-tùng-yuán** a general mobilization

总体规划 **tsǔng-t'ǐ kuēi-huà** overall planning, comprehensive planning, planning for the totality

总体设计 **tsǔng-t'ǐ shè-chì** overall design, comprehensive design, designing for the whole

总统 **tsǔng-t'ǔng** a president [of a republic]

总则 **tsǔng-tsé** general principles, general rules, general provisions [of a statute, etc.]

总参谋长 **tsǔng-ts'ān-móu-chǎng** the chief-of-staff (the head of the General Staff Department of the PLA)

总参谋部 **tsǔng-ts'ān-móu-pù** the General Staff Department [of the PLA]

总危机 **tsǔng-wēi-chī** a general crisis

tsùng (zòng)

2289 纵横交错 **tsùng-héng chiāo-ts'ò** the interlocking of vertical and horizontal, crosswise, crisscrossing

纵横驰骋 **tsùng-héng-ch'íh-ch'ěng** to gallop a horse lengthwise or crosswise (to move freely in any direction without challenge)

纵横捭阖 **tsùng-héng-pǎi-hó** [to move] vertically and horizontally and to open and close (to use skillfully diplomatic or political maneuvers)

纵火 **tsùng-huǒ** to set fire, commit arson; incendiarism, arson

纵容 **tsùng-júng** to tolerate, condone, be indulgent of, connive at; permissive, indulgent

纵深 **tsùng-shēn** extensive and deep; depth (for example, in a political movement, military operation, or one's work as a leader)

纵断面 **tsùng-tuàn-mièn** a vertical section

纵队 **tsùng-tuì** a column, detachment, brigade

tzū (zī)

2290 孜孜不倦 **tzū-tzū-pù-chüàn** to work diligently and without fatigue

2291 咨询 **tzū-hsún** to seek advice, inquire and consult; advisory

2292 姿态 **tzū-t'ài** carriage, deportment, bearing, poise; a gesture, pose, attitude

2293 资金 **tzū-chīn** a capital fund, capital, fund

资金积累 **tzū-chīn chī-lěi** capital accumulation, accumulation of funds

资金周转 **tzū-chīn chōu-chuǎn** capital turnover, turnover of capital

资助 **tzū-chù** to aid financially, contribute to, subsidize, support, aid

资产者 **tzū-ch'ǎn-chě** a person of means, property owner, an owner of the means of production

资产阶级 **tzū-ch'ǎn-chiēh-chí** the bourgeoisie, the capitalist class

资产阶级知识分子 **tzū-ch'ǎn-chiēh-chí chīh-shíh-fēn-tzǔ** bourgeois intellectuals (may refer to either persons born in bourgeois families, or having received a bourgeois education)

资产阶级专政 **tzū-ch'ǎn-chiēh-chí chuān-chèng** bourgeois dictatorship, the dictatorship of the bourgeoisie

资产阶级法权 **tzū-ch'ǎn-chiēh-chí fǎ-ch'üán** bourgeois legal rights (the

system of legal rights sponsored by the bourgeoisie)

资产阶级反动路线 **tzū-ch'ǎn-chiēh-chí fǎn-tùng lù-hsièn** bourgeois reactionary line

资产阶级人性论 **tzū-ch'ǎn-chiēh-chí jén-hsìng lùn** the bourgeois theory of human nature (assumes all people are basically the same, and contradicts the theory that human nature is shaped by social and material conditions based on class)

资产阶级个人主义 **tzū-ch'ǎn-chiēh-chí kò-jén-chǔ-ì** bourgeois individualism

资产阶级民主革命 **tzū-ch'ǎn-chiéh-chī mín-chǔ-kó-mìng** the bourgeois-democratic revolution

资产阶级民族主义 **tzū-ch'ǎn-chiēh-chí mín-tsú-chǔ-ì** bourgeois nationalism

资产阶级名利思想 **tzū-ch'ǎn-chiēh-chí míng-lì szū-hsiǎng** the bourgeois mentality of [seeking] fame and profit

资产阶级派性 **tzū-ch'ǎn-chiēh-chí p'ài-hsìng** bourgeois cliquishness, the factional nature of the bourgeoisie

资产阶级世界观 **tzū-ch'ǎn-chiēh-chí shìh-chièh-kuān** the bourgeois world view

资产阶级思想 **tzū-ch'ǎn-chiēh-chí szū-hsiǎng** bourgeois ideology

资产阶级代理人 **tzū-ch'ǎn-chiēh-chí tài-lǐ-jén** an agent of the bourgeoisie

资产阶级唯心主义 **tzū-ch'ǎn-chiēh-chí wéi-hsīn-chǔ-ì** bourgeois idealism

资产阶级文化专制主义 **tzū-ch'ǎn-chiēh-chí wén-huà chuān-chìh-chǔ-ì** bourgeois cultural absolutism

资产阶级文艺黑线 **tzū-ch'ǎn-chiēh-chí wén-ì hēi-hsièn** the black line of bourgeois literature and art

资产阶级野心家 **tzū-ch'ǎn-chiēh-chí yěh-hsīn-chiā** a bourgeois careerist

资产阶级右派 **tzū-ch'ǎn-chiēh-chí yù-p'ài** bourgeois rightists

资产阶级庸人 **tzū-ch'ǎn-chiēh-chí yūng-jén** bourgeois mediocrities, bourgeois philistines

资方人员 **tzū-fāng jén-yuán** persons of the capitalist sector, entrepreneurs

资格 **tzū-kó** qualifications, competence, capacity [of a person], requirements, seniority

资料 **tzū-liào** reference material, data, information

资本 **tzū-pěn** capital, assets, investment

资本积累 **tzū-pěn chī-lěi** capital accumulation

资本家 **tzū-pěn-chiā** a capitalist

资本家所有制 **tzū-pěn-chiā sǒ-yǔ-chìh** the capitalist ownership system

资本主义 **tzū-pěn-chǔ-ì** capitalism; capitalist, capitalistic

资本主义经济成分 **tzū-pěn-chǔ-ì chīng-chì ch'éng-fèn** the capitalist sector of the economy

资本主义企业 **tzū-pěn-chǔ-ì ch'ǐ-yèh** capitalist enterprise

资本主义倾向 **tzū-pěn-chǔ-ì ch'īng-hsiàng** a leaning toward capitalism, a capitalist trend

资本主义复辟 **tzū-pěn-chǔ-ì fù-pì** the restoration of capitalism

资本主义工商业的社会主义改造 **tzū-pěn-chǔ-ì kūng-shāng-yèh te shè-huì-chǔ-ì kǎi-tsào** the socialist transformation of capitalist industry and commerce

资本主义剥削制度 **tzū-pěn-chǔ-ì pō-hsuèh chìh-tù** the capitalist exploitative system

资本主义社会 **tzū-pěn-chǔ-ì shè-huì** a capitalist society

资本主义势力 **tzū-pěn-chǔ-ì shìh-lì** capitalist forces, the influence of capitalism

资本主义所有制 **tzū-pěn-chǔ-ì sǒ-yǔ-chìh** the capitalist ownership system

资本主义总危机 **tzū-pěn-chǔ-ì tsǔng-wēi-chī** the general crisis of capitalism

资本主义自发倾向 **tzū-pěn-chǔ-ì tzù-fā ch'īng-hsiàng** the spontaneous trend toward capitalism

资本主义自发势力 **tzū-pěn-chǔ-ì tzù-fā shìh-lì** the self-generating force of capitalism, the spontaneous strength of capitalism

资本主义尾巴 **tzū-pěn-chǔ-ì wěi-pa** the tail of capitalism (vestiges of capitalism, capitalist remnants)

资本论 **tzū-pěn lùn** *Das Kapital* [by Karl Marx]

资本额 **tzū-pěn-ó** the amount of capital, capital investment

资敌 **tzū-tí** to give supplies to the enemy, assist the enemy, treason

资财 **tzū-ts'ái** assets, property, capital, wealth

资源 **tzū-yuán** resources (usually refers to natural resources)

资源勘探 **tzū-yuán k'ān-t'àn** natural-resources prospecting

²²⁹⁴ 滋长 **tzū-chǎng** to grow, thrive, multiply

滋味 **tzū-wèi** taste, flavor

滋养 **tzū-yǎng** to nourish; nourishment; nutritious

²²⁹⁵ 孳生 **tzū-shēng** to grow and multiply, beget in large numbers

²²⁹⁶ 辎重 **tzū-chùng** military supplies, impedimenta

tzŭ (zǐ)

2297　子宫 **tzŭ-kūng** the womb, uterus
子孙后代 **tzŭ-sūn-hòu-tài** decendents, offspring, posterity
子弹 **tzŭ-tàn** bullets, small arms ammunition (often used in an extended sense to include: cartridge, shell and projectile)
子弟小学 **tzŭ-tì hsiǎo-hsuéh** a dependents' elementary school (a school for families of a factory's workers or an organization's employees)
子弟兵 **tzŭ-tì-pīng** sons and brothers soldiers (a common reference to the PLA)
子午线 **tzŭ-wǔ-hsièn** a meridian line [in geography]
2298　籽棉 **tzŭ-mién** seed cotton, raw cotton, unginned cotton
2299　紫外线 **tzŭ-wài-hsièn** ultra-violet rays
紫雲英 **tzŭ yún-yīng** *Astragalus sinicus* (a grassy plant with purple flowers which is plowed into the earth as fertilizer)

tzù (zì)

2300　自爱 **tzù-ài** self-respect, self-esteem
自己解放自己 **tzù-chǐ chiéh-fàng tzù-chǐ** each person liberates himself
自己人 **tzù-chǐ-jén** our own people; one of our own, within the same circle or group, having a close relationship
自己动手 **tzù-chǐ tùng-shǒu** to do it oneself, to take direct action
自给户 **tzù-chǐ-hù** self-supporting household, self-sufficient family
自给率 **tzù-chǐ-lù** rate of self-sufficiency
自给自足 **tzù-chǐ tzù-tsú** self-reliant, self-supporting, self-contained
自建公助 **tzù-chièn kūng-chù** construction by oneself with public [state] help (a plan for loans to employees for building homes, popular in 1957)
自知 **tzù-chīh** self-knowledge; to know oneself
自制 **tzù-chìh** self-restraint, self-control; made by oneself, locally made
自治 **tzù-chìh** self-government, autonomy; autonomous
自治州 **tzù-chìh-chōu** an autonomous district (a sub-provincial grouping of several *hsien*)
自治旗 **tzù-chìh-ch'í** an autonomous banner (the equivalent of a *hsien* in Inner Mongolia)
自治区 **tzù-chìh-ch'ü** an autonomous region (a governmental body at the provincial level where a relatively high concentration of one or more ethnic minorities makes a special status desirable)
自治县 **tzù-chìh-hsièn** autonomous county (usually a *hsien* with relatively high ethnic minority concentration)
自救 **tzù-chiù** self-help, self-salvation
自主 **tzù-chǔ** self-determination, independence; independent; independently
自产自销 **tzù-ch'ǎn tzù-hsiāo** to produce and market independently; independent production and marketing
自称 **tzù-ch'ēng** to call or declare oneself [to be], to claim or profess [to be]
自成系统 **tzù-ch'éng hsì-t'ǔng** to form one's own system [network] (to act in an independent manner)
自欺欺人 **tzù-ch'ī-ch'ī-jén** to delude oneself and others as well
自吹自擂 **tzù-ch'uī-tzù-lèi** oneself to blow the horn and beat the drum (to boast and brag)
自居 **tzù-chǖ** to consider oneself [to be a genius, etc.]
自决 **tzù-chüéh** to decide by oneself, self-determination; self-determined
自绝于人民 **tzù-chüéh yú jén-mín** to cause oneself to be rejected by the people, to isolate oneself from the people
自觉 **tzù-chüéh** self-awakening, self-realization; consciousness, awareness
自觉行动 **tzù-chüéh hsíng-tùng** conscious activity
自觉性 **tzù-chüéh-hsìng** consciousness, self-awareness, self-perception
自觉批修 **tzù-chüéh p'ī-hsiū** to spontaneously [with full self-awareness] criticize revisionism
自觉斗，同志帮，群众促 **tzù-chüéh-tòu, t'úng-chìh-pāng, ch'ún-chùng-ts'ù** to struggle spontaneously [against selfishness] with the help of comrades and the [vigilant] urging of the masses
自觉自愿 **tzù-chüéh tzù-yuàn** consciously and willingly, of one's own volition
自掘坟墓 **tzù-chüéh fén-mù** to dig one's own grave (to bring about one's own downfall)
自趋灭亡 **tzù-ch'ü mièh-wáng** to hasten towards one's own destruction, rush toward ruin
自取灭亡 **tzù-ch'ü mièh-wáng** to invite one's own destruction, court disaster
自发 **tzù-fā** self-initiated, spontaneous,

voluntary; automatic

自发倾向 **tzù-fā ch'īng-hsiàng** a spontaneous trend

自发趋向 **tzù-fā ch'ǚ-hsiàng** a spontaneous inclination toward

自发趋势 **tzù-fā ch'ǚ-shìh** a spontaneous tendency

自发工业户 **tzù-fā kūng-yèh hù** spontaneous [industrial] house (an extra-legal productive enterprise)

自发罢工 **tzù-fā pà-kūng** a spontaneous strike, wildcat strike

自发势力 **tzù-fā shìh-lì** spontaneous forces, an influence that arises spontaneously

自费 **tzù-fèi** at one's own expense, pay one's own way

自封 **tzù-fēng** to appoint oneself; self-styled; to isolate oneself

自负盈余 **tzù-fù yíng-yǘ** [firms that] assume responsibility for their own profits (usually small independently organized cooperative production units)

自豪 **tzù-háo** to pride oneself on, be proud of

自下而上 **tzù-hsià-érh-shàng** from lower [levels] to higher [levels], from bottom to top

自相矛盾 **tzù-hsiāng-máo-tùn** self-contradictory; to contradict oneself

自相残杀 **tzù-hsiāng-ts'án-shā** to engage in mutual slaughter; internecine strife

自新 **tzù-hsīn** to make a new person out of oneself, reform oneself; self-renewal

自新之路 **tzù-hsīn-chīh-lù** the road to self-renewal, the way for self-reform (self-education)

自信 **tzù-hsìn** self-confident

自信心 **tzù-hsìn-hsīn** self-confidence

自行 **tzù-hsíng** by oneself, on one's own, individually, independently, by itself

自行车 **tzù-hsíng-ch'ē** bicycle

自省 **tzù-hsīng** self-examination, reflection, introspection

自学 **tzù-hsuéh** private study, self-teaching

自学辅导广播讲座 **tzù-hsuéh fǔ-tǎo kuǎng-pō chiǎng-tsò** self-study broadcast lectures

自以为是 **tzù-ǐ-wéi-shìh** to consider oneself to always be in the right, regard oneself as infallible; cocksure

自然 **tzù-ján** natural, spontaneous, free, by itself; of course, doubtless, sure, self-evident; nature, pertaining to nature

自然界 **tzù-ján-chièh** the natural world (including plants, animals, and minerals)

自然主义 **tzù-ján-chǔ-ì** naturalism, naturalistic

自然区划 **tzù-ján ch'ǚ-huà** physiographical demarcation, natural regionalization

自然红 **tzù-ján-húng** naturally red, becoming red naturally (the incorrect idea that one is "naturally red" merely by coming from a proletarian family background or by being born into the new society)

自然现象 **tzù-ján hsièn-hsiàng** natural phenomena

自然科学 **tzù-ján k'ō-hsuéh** the natural sciences

自然力 **tzù-ján-lì** natural forces, the forces of nature

自然保护区 **tzù-ján pǎo-hù-ch'ǚ** a nature protection area

自然辩证法 **tzù-ján-pièn-chèng-fǎ** *Natural Dialectics* (a Shanghai quarterly journal, November 1973—)

自然地理 **tzù-ján tì-lǐ** physical geography

自然淘汰 **tzù-ján t'áo-t'ài** natural selection

自然灾害 **tzù-ján tsāi-hài** natural calamities

自然资源 **tzù-ján tzū-yuán** natural resources, natural wealth

自然村 **tzù-ján-ts'ūn** a natural village (usually a hamlet or small cluster of farm homes which is administered as a unit of an administrative village [hsíng-chèng-ts'ūn])

自高自大 **tzù-kāo-tzù-tà** conceited, high and mighty, proud and arrogant

自告奋勇 **tzù-kào-fèn-yǔng** to offer oneself undauntedly, volunteer one's services

自耕 **tzù-kēng** to farm on one's own

自耕农 **tzù-kēng-núng** an individual farmer, farmer working his land

自购自销 **tzù-kòu tzù-hsiāo** to buy and market on one's own

自顾不暇 **tzù-kù pù-hsiá** to have trouble even in taking care of oneself (so busy that one cannot help others)

自供状 **tzù-kūng-chuàng** a statement of confession

自夸 **tzù-k'uā** to boast, brag

自来红 **tzù-lái-húng** red by nature, naturally red (those who claim political merit by birth and social background rather than by study and personal action)

自来水 **tzù-lái-shuǐ** running water,

piped water

自力更生 **tzù-lì-kēng-shēng** [to achieve] self-renewal [through] one's own efforts; self-reliance (a slogan first popularized by Mao Tse-tung during the KMT blockade of Yenan)

自力更生为主，国家支援为辅 **tzù-lì kēng-shēng wéi chǔ, kuó-chiā chīh-yuán wéi fǔ** self-reliance as basic and government aid as supplemental

自力更生样样有 **tzù-lì kēng-shēng yàng-yàng-yǔ** with self-reliance all sorts of things will be had

自利 **tzù-lì** self-interest; selfishness

自流井 **tzù-liú-chǐng** an artesian well

自流观点 **tzù-liú kuān-tiěn** the laissez-faire point of view

自流灌溉 **tzù-liú kuàn-kài** gravity-flow irrigation, irrigation by natural flow

自留地 **tzù-liú-tì** land reserved for private use, private plots, household plots

自流组合 **tzù-liú tsǔ-hó** to organize on a purely voluntary basis, organize in a laissez-faire way

自满自足 **tzù-mǎn-tzù-tsú** conceited and self-satisfied, haughty, arrogant

自鸣得意 **tzù-míng-té-ì** to crow over one's own success (smug)

自命不凡 **tzù-mìng-pù-fán** to regard oneself as extraordinary (to consider oneself superior)

自谋出路 **tzù-moú ch'ū-lù** to find one's own way out (to find a means of self-support, to solve one's own problems)

自拔来归 **tzù-pá lái-kuēi** to lift oneself [out of bad habits or associations] and come back [to the correct road]

自白 **tzù-pái** a personal statement, confession, self-confession; to reveal oneself; a monologue

自办 **tzù-pàn** self-established, self-operated

自报公议 **tzù-pào kūng-ì** self-assessment [to determine the amount of food ration or salary due an individual, or the amount of grain tax a commune owes the government] and subsequent public discussion [on the matter]

自暴自弃 **tzù-pào-tzù-ch'ì** to abandon oneself [to dissipation, etc.], throw oneself away, have no ambition

自卑感 **tzù-pēi-kǎn** a feeling of inferiority, inferiority complex

自不量力 **tzù-pù-liàng-lì** to fail to measure one's own strength or resources (to try something beyond one's ability)

自喷油井 **tzù-p'ēn yú-chǐng** a self-flowing oil well, gusher

自杀 **tzù-shā** to commit suicide; suicide

自上而下，自下而上 **tzù-shàng-érh-hsià tzù-hsià-érh-shàng** from the top downward and from the bottom upward (the proper operation of the mass line, with action impulses coming from both top and bottom, and both interacting with the other)

自生自灭 **tzù-shēng-tzù-mièh** to grow and die without outside influences

自食其果 **tzù-shíh-ch'í-kuǒ** to eat one's own fruit (to suffer the consequences of one's own actions)

自食其力 **tzù-shíh-ch'í-lì** to live by one's own labor

自食其言 **tzù-shíh-ch'í-yén** to eat one's own words (to fail to keep one's promise)

自始至终 **tzù-shǐh-chìh-chūng** from beginning to end, from start to finish (throughout, in every part of, from A to Z)

自恃 **tzù-shìh** to presume on [one's talent, etc.], to overestimate oneself

自首 **tzù-shǒu** to submit voluntarily to the authorities, give oneself up

自私自利 **tzù-szū-tsù-lì** to selfishly pursue one's own interests; selfish, egotistical

自打耳光 **tsù-tǎ-ěrh-kuāng** to give oneself a slap in the face (to embarrass oneself, to do something that results in one's own humiliation)

自打嘴巴 **tsù-tǎ-tsuǐ-pà** to slap one's own cheek (*see above*)

自大 **tzù-tà** proud, arrogant, conceited

自大狂 **tzù-tà-k'uáng** megalomania

自动 **tzù-tùng** at one's own will, voluntarily; self-moving, self-propelled, automatic

自动化 **tzù-tùng-huà** automation; to automate

自动行星际站 **tzù-tùng hsíng-hsīng-chì chàn** an automatic interplanetary station

自动流水线 **tzù-tùng liú-shuǐ-hsièn** a self-propelled [production] line, automated [production] line

自动步枪 **tzù-tùng pù-ch'iāng** an automatic rifle

自动作业线 **tsù-tùng tsò-yèh-hsièn** an automated production line

自讨苦吃 **tzù-t'ǎo-k'ǔ-ch'īh** to go seeking trouble for oneself

自讨没趣 **tzù-t'ǎo-méi-ch'ǜ** to invite rejection, court humiliation

自投罗网 **tzù-t'óu-ló-wǎng** to snare oneself, fall into a trap through one's

own fault

自在 **tzù-tsài** at ease [with oneself and the world], free and unconstrained, contented, comfortable

自作聪明 **tzù-tsò-ts'ūng-míng** to pretend to be clever (to act in a subjective way, act pretentiously)

自走绝路 **tzù-tsŏu-chüéh-lù** to put oneself on a dead-end road (to adopt a disastrous policy)

自足小农经济 **tzù-tsú hsiăo-núng chīng-chì** a self-sufficient small peasant economy

自尊心 **tsù-tsūn-hsīn** a sense of self-respect, self-esteem

自卫战 **tzù-wèi-chàn** a war of self-defense

自卫反击战 **tzù-wèi făn-chī-chàn** self-defensive counterattack

自卫还击 **tzù-wèi huán-chī** to return fire in self-defense

自卫队 **tzù-wèi-tuì** a self-defense corps, militia

自我 **tzù-wŏ** the self, ego; I

自我教育 **tzù-wŏ chiào-yù** self-education

自我教育运动 **tzù-wŏ chiào-yù yùn-tùng** a self-education movement

自我解嘲 **tzù-wŏ chiěh-ch'áo** to flatter one's ego, console oneself

自我检查 **tzù-wŏ chiěn-ch'á** self-investigation, self-examination

自我检讨 **tzù-wŏ chiěn-t'ǎo** self-examination

自我出丑 **tzù-wŏ ch'ū-ch'ǒu** to disgrace oneself, expose oneself to ridicule

自我出发 **tzù-wŏ ch'ū-fā** to start from oneself, use oneself as the starting point

自我牺牲 **tzù-wŏ hsī-shēng** self-sacrifice

自我牺牲精神 **tzù-wŏ hsī-shēng chīng-shén** a spirit of self-sacrifice

自我改造 **tzù-wŏ kăi-tsào** self-remolding, self-reeducation

自我革命 **tzù-wŏ kó-mìng** self-revolution

自我辩解 **tzù-wŏ pièn-chiěh** self-apology, self-justification

自我批评 **tzù-wŏ p'ī-p'íng** self-criticism

自我陶醉 **tzù-wŏ-t'áo-tsuì** self-intoxicated (to lose one's objective grasp; self-delusion)

自由经营 **tzù-yú chīng-yíng** free management, free operation, free enterprise

自由竞争 **tzù-yú chìng-chēng** free competition

自由主义 **tzù-yú-chŭ-ì** liberalism

自由泛滥 **tzù-yú fàn-làn** to flood freely, spread unchecked

自由放任 **tzù-yú fàng-jèn** unrestrained self-indulgence, laissez faire

自由平等博爱 **tzù-yú p'íng-těng pó-ài** liberty, equality, and fraternity

自由散漫 **tzù-yú săn-màn** unrestrained and disorganized (an individualistic aversion to discipline)

自由市场 **tzù-yú shìh-ch'ăng** the free market

自由讨论 **tzù-yú t'ǎo-lùn** free discussion

自由天地 **tzù-yú-t'iēn-tì** a free world (a place or sphere in which one has a feeling of freedom)

自由王国 **tzù-yú-wáng-kuó** the realm of freedom (in which mankind, aware of the [Hegelian-Marxist] objective laws of society, have the free choice of serving the cause of socialism)

自有资金 **tzù-yŭ tzū-chīn** self-owned capital

自圆其说 **tzù-yuán-ch'í-shuō** to make round one's statement (to make one's story sound plausible, to justify one's argument)

自愿互利, 等价交换 **tzù-yuàn hù-lì, těng-chià chiāo-huàn** voluntary and mutually profitable exchange on a basis of equality of value

自愿互利原则 **tzù-yuàn hù-lì yuán-tsé** the principles of willingness and mutual benefit

自用棉 **tzù-yùng-mién** self-used cotton, cotton for private use

自用物品 **tzù-yùng wù-p'ín** articles for personal use, goods for private use, personal effects

2301 字里行间 **tzù-lĭ háng-chiēn** among the words and between the lines (the implicit [but not precisely stated] sense of a piece of writing)

2302 恣意 **tzù-ì** to act wilfully, do as one wishes, indulge one's tastes

ts'ā (cā)

2303 擦脂抹粉 **ts'ā-chīh-mŏ-fěn** to apply rouge and powder (to gloss over faults or defects)

擦亮眼睛 **ts'ā-liàng yěn-chīng** to wipe clear the eyes (to be on the watch for reactionary elements)

ts'ái (cái)

2304 才智 **ts'ái-chìh** talent and wisdom, intelligence, brilliance

才学 **ts'ái-hsuéh** talent and learning, intelligence and scholarship

才干 **ts'ài-kàn** ability to get things

done, competence, practical skill
才能 **ts'ái-néng** natural endowment, natural gifts, aptitude, talent
才子佳人 **ts'ái-tzǔ chiā-jén** a scholar and a beautiful woman (one of those themes of traditional literature which has come under criticism)
才子佳人部 **ts'ái-tzǔ-chiā-jén-pù** the ministry of scholars and beauties (a sarcastic reference to the Ministry of Culture during the Cultural Revolution)
2305 材料 **ts'ái-liào** (1) materials (a general term covering raw materials, construction materials, drygoods materials, supplies, etc.) (2) data, statistics, figures, information (all types of materials for writing, research, reporting, etc.)
2306 财政 **ts'ái-chèng** financial affairs [of the government], finances; financial, fiscal, monetary: *Finance* (a Peking semi-monthly journal, 1956—)
败政金融危机 **ts'ái-chèng chīn-júng wēi-chī** a financial and monetary crisis
财政部 **ts'ái-chèng-pù** the Ministry of Finance [of the State Council]
财经 **ts'ái-chīng** financial and economic (contraction of **ts'ái-chèng chǐng-chì**)
财经部门 **ts'ái-chīng pù-mén** the financial and economic departments and related units
财经体制 **ts'ái-chīng t'ǐ-chìh** the financial and economic systems
财产 **ts'ái-ch'ǎn** property, assets, possessions
财权 **ts'ái-ch'üán** property rights
财阀 **ts'ái-fá** a plutocrat, tycoon
财富 **ts'ái-fù** wealth, riches, resources
财力 **ts'ái-lì** financial power, financial resources
财贸系统 **ts'ái-mào hsì-t'ǔng** the finance and trade system
财团 **ts'ái-t'uán** a financial group, consortium, syndicate
财务 **ts'ái-wù** financial affairs, finance; financial
财务管理 **ts'ái-wù kuǎn-lǐ** financial administration, financial management
财物 **ts'ái-wù** property, valuables, belongings (usually refers to personal or movable property)
2307 裁决 **ts'ái-chüéh** to make a decision, render a judgment; a decision, verdict, sentence
裁军 **ts'ái-chūn** disarmament
裁军委员会 **ts'ái-chūn wěi-yuán-huì** the Disarmament Commission [United Nations]

裁判员 **ts'ái-p'àn-yuán** an umpire, referee, arbitrator

ts'ǎi (cǎi)

2308 采茶 **ts'ǎi-ch'á** to pick tea; tea picking
采掘工业 **ts'ǎi-chüéh kūng-yèh** extractive industries
采取 **ts'ǎi-ch'ǔ** to select and use, employ, adopt [a policy], take [an action], assume [an attitude]
采伐 **ts'ǎi-fá** to fell [timber, trees, etc.]; logging, timbering
采访新闻 **ts'ǎi-fǎng hsīn-wén** to report the news, cover the news
采割橡胶 **ts'ǎi-kó hsiàng-chiāo** to tap rubber [trees]
采购站 **ts'ǎi-kòu-chàn** a purchasing station, procurement station
采购人员 **ts'ǎi-kòu-jén-yuán** purchasing personnel
采矿 **ts'ǎi-k'uàng** to work a mine; mining
采矿设备 **ts'ǎi-k'uàng shè-pèi** mining equipment
采煤机 **ts'ǎi-méi-chī** a coal mining machine
采纳 **ts'ǎi-nà** to accept [a suggestion], receive, entertain, adopt
采挖 **ts'ǎi-wā** to excavate, dig out
采药 **ts'ǎi-yào** to gather medicinal [herbs]
采用 **ts'ǎi-yùng** to adopt and use, introduce [the use of], apply, utilize, embrace, have recourse to
采 **ts'ǎi**: see also **ts'ài**
2309 彩号 **ts'ǎi-hào** a wounded soldier
彩排 **ts'ǎi-p'ái** a dress rehearsal (in Chinese opera)
彩色影片 **ts'ǎi-sè yǐng-p'ièn** a color motion picture film
彩釉 **ts'ǎi-yù** pottery glaze, colored enamel
2310 踩到脚下 **ts'ǎi-tào-chiǎo-hsià** to trample underfoot

ts'ài (cài)

2311 菜圃 **ts'ài-p'ǔ** a vegetable plot, vegetable garden
菜籽 **ts'ài-tzǔ** vegetable seeds, rapeseed (usually seeds producing edible oils)

ts'ān (cān)

2312 参照 **ts'ān-chào** to refer to, compare with; in accordance with
参政 **ts'ān-chèng** to participate in government [affairs], be politically active

参加 **ts'ān-chiā** to participate in, take part in, join, attend, associate with; participation

参加比例 **ts'ān-chiā-pǐ-lì** ratio of participation

参军 **ts'ān-chǔn** to join the army, enter military service

参议会 **ts'ān-ì-huì** a representative assembly, legislature

参观 **ts'ān-kuān** to look over, observe, tour, visit; a visit

参观团 **ts'ān-kuān-t'uán** observation groups

参考 **ts'ān-k'ǎo** to refer to, collate, examine and compare, consult, confer; references, reference [data]; advisory

参考消息 **ts'ān-k'ǎo hsiāo-hsī** *Reference News* (a news digest for Party and governmental internal use containing broad summaries of news not appearing in the public media)

参考资料 **ts'ān-k'ǎo tzū-liào** (1) reference data, reference material (2) *Reference Materials* (a secret news bulletin for high-level Party and governmental officials)

参谋 **ts'ān-móu** a staff officer, counselor (now used more broadly than the original military/governmental sense: a **hsià-fàng** cadre is expected to be a *ts'ān-móu* to the basic-level cadre; an experienced old peasant is to be treated as a *ts'ān-móu* by the rural cadre)

参谋长 **ts'ān-móu-chǎng** a chief-of-staff

参事 **ts'ān-shìh** a counselor, consultant; a Counselor of Embassy

参数 **ts'ān-shù** a parameter

ts'án (cán)

2313 残渣余孽 **ts'án-chā-yú-nièh** leftover dregs and evil remnants (weakened but persisting evil remnants in society)

残废 **ts'án-fèi** crippled, maimed, disabled

残废军人 **ts'án-fèi chǔn-jén** a disabled ex-soldier, disabled veteran

残废军人证 **ts'án-fèi-chǔn-jén chèng** a disabled veteran's [identification] card

残害人民 **ts'án-hài jén-mín** to oppress the people cruelly

残忍 **ts'án-jěn** pitiless, cruel, brutal, barbarous

残羹余汤 **ts'án-kēng-yú-t'āng** leftover soup (anything leftover, scraps)

残酷 **ts'án-k'ù** cruel, brutal, ruthless

残酷斗争 **ts'án-k'ù tòu-chēng** a ruthless struggle, bitter fight

残暴 **ts'án-pào** cruel and heartless, pitiless, cold-blooded, ruthless

残兵败卒 **ts'án-pīng pài-tsú** defeated and disorganized troops, remnants of a defeated army

残杀 **ts'án-shā** to kill indiscriminately, massacre, slaughter; carnage

残次商品 **ts'án-tz'ù shāng-p'ǐn** defective merchandise, damaged goods, second-rate products (usually sold at special discounts)

残存 **ts'án-ts'ún** to remain as a residue, be left over

残余 **ts'án-yú** a remnant, residue, remainder

2314 蚕茧 **ts'án-chiěn** a silkworm cocoon

蚕桑业 **ts'án-sāng-yèh** the silk-raising industry

蚕食 **ts'án-shíh** to eat like a silkworm, to nibble away; encroachment

蚕食进攻 **ts'án-shíh-chìn-kūng** a nibbling attack, encroaching attack

蚕丝 **ts'án-szū** raw silk, silk yarn

ts'ǎn (cǎn)

2315 惨案 **ts'ǎn-àn** a tragic case, cruel murder case, cold-blooded massacre

惨重 **ts'ǎn-chùng** tragic, dire, calamitous

惨绝人寰 **ts'ǎn-chüéh-jén-huán** so tragic that it is rare in human life

惨痛 **ts'ǎn-t'ùng** greatly aggrieved; saddening, tragic

ts'àn (càn)

2316 灿烂夺目 **ts'àn-làn-tó-mù** the luster dazzles the eye (resplendent, dazzling, brilliant)

ts'āng (cāng)

2317 仓库 **ts'āng-k'ù** a warehouse, storehouse, treasury, depot

仓卒从事 **ts'āng-ts'ù-ts'úng-shìh** to attend to affairs in a hasty manner (to work in a slapdash way)

仓存保险 **ts'āng-ts'ún-pǎo-hsiěn** storage insurance

2318 沧海一粟 **ts'āng-hǎi ī-sù** a grain in the boundless sea (infinitely small)

沧海桑田 **ts'āng-hǎi sāng-t'ién** a vast ocean [may become] a field of mulberry trees (the great changes in the world; the vicissitudes in human affairs)

2319 苍蝇 **ts'āng-ying** the common housefly

ts'áng (cáng)

2320 藏垢纳污 **ts'áng-kòu-nà-wū** to store
filth and receive dirt (to harbor
criminals, shelter evil people; a
disreputable place)
藏身 **ts'áng-shēn** to hide oneself
藏头露尾 **ts'áng-t'óu-lù-wěi** to hide the
head and expose the tail (to reveal
only part of the truth)
藏 **ts'áng**: *see also* **tsàng**

ts'āo (cāo)

2321 操之过急 **ts'āo-chīh-kuò-chí** to handle
with excessive haste (to be overly
eager for success)
操心 **ts'āo-hsīn** to worry, be perturbed
about
操作 **ts'āo-tsò** to work on, care for,
operate [a machine, etc.], manipulate,
handle; operating; operations,
procedures, work
操作规程 **ts'āo-tsò-kuēi-ch'éng** working
regulations, operating procedures,
order of procedure
操纵 **ts'āo-tsùng** to control, manage,
manipulate, steer, maneuver, operate;
manipulation

ts'áo (cáo)

2322 草案 **ts'áo-àn** a draft [of a bill or
document], proposed resolution,
preliminary plan
草芥 **ts'áo-chièh** weeds and wild
mustard (things without meaning or
value, trash)
草菅人命 **ts'áo-chiēn-jén-mìng** to treat
people's lives like grass (to show an
utter disregard for the lives of people)
草场 **ts'áo-ch'áng** a field of grass, lawn,
pasture
草肥 **ts'áo-féi** seaweed fertilizer
草鞋医生 **ts'áo-hsiéh ī-shēng** a grass-
sandal doctor ("barefoot" doctor)
草木皆兵 **ts'áo-mù-chiēh-pīng** [to see]
every plant and tree as [enemy]
soldiers (the nervousness of a
defeated army, imaginary fears)
草率 **ts'áo-shuài** careless, perfunctory,
negligent; superficially
草甸 **ts'áo-tièn** a meadow, grassy field
草田轮作 **ts'áo-t'ién lún-tsò** grass and
field crop rotation
草草了事 **ts'áo-ts'áo-liǎo-shìh** to be in
too great a haste to finish, carelessly
dispose of an affair; perfunctory
草药 **ts'áo-yào** medicinal herbs
草鱼 **ts'áo-yǘ** the grass carp

草原儿女 **ts'áo-yuán-érh-nǚ** "Children
of the Grasslands" (a modern
revolutionary ballet)
草原造林 **ts'áo-yuán tsào-lín** steppe
silviculture

ts'è (cè)

2323 厕所 **ts'è-sǒ** latrine, lavatory, privy
2324 侧击 **ts'è-chī** to attack obliquely; a
flank attack
侧重 **ts'è-chùng** to attach special
importance to something; partial to,
one-sided
侧翼 **ts'è-ì** a flank [military]
侧面 **ts'è-mièn** a side, flank; profile,
side view
2325 测绘 **ts'è-huì** to survey [land] and draw
[maps]
测量 **ts'è-liáng** to measure, survey;
measurement
测深 **ts'è-shēn** depth measurement,
sounding
测定 **ts'è-tìng** to determine after
making a survey or analysis;
determination, titration
测验 **ts'è-yèn** to test, examine, try out;
testing
2326 策划 **ts'è-huà** to plot, plan, scheme,
conspire
策略 **ts'è-lüèh** a plan, scheme, tactic,
stratagem, device, maneuver
策谋 **ts'è-móu** a plot, intrigue;
scheming
策动 **ts'è-tùng** to set in motion,
instigate, incite, contrive, machinate,
maneuver; instigation, incitement
策应 **ts'è-yìng** to act in concert,
coordinate actions by plan, fight in
various places in accordance with a
single plan
策源地 **ts'è-yuán-tì** place of origin [of a
revolutionary movement], point of
departure, source, base

ts'éng (céng)

2327 层出不穷 **ts'éng-ch'ū-pù-ch'iúng** to
appear endlessly, happen again and
again, occur repeatedly
层峦叠嶂 **ts'éng-luán-tiéh-chàng** peaks
rising one upon another, range upon
range
层层负责 **ts'éng-ts'éng fù-tsé** each level
must be responsible for the affairs
[within its own sphere]
层层下放 **ts'éng-ts'éng hsià-fàng**
downward transfer from one level to
the next lower
层次 **ts'éng-tz'ù** sequence, order, rank,

priority

层次重叠 **ts'éng-tz'ù ch'úng-tiéh** a duplication of ranks (overlapping, organizational duplication)

层次分明 **ts'éng-tz'ù fēn-míng** the graduation is distinct, ranks are clear (clear arrangement according to order)

2328 曾几何时 **ts'éng-chǐ-hó-shíh** not many moments ago, how short a time! (suggesting drastic and rapid change)

曾 **ts'éng**: see also **tsēng**

ts'ō (cuō)

2329 磋商 **ts'ō-shāng** to consult, confer, negotiate, discuss; consultation, negotiation

ts'ò (cuò)

2330 挫折 **ts'ò-ché** a setback, defeat, reverse, rebuff, failure; to suffer a setback

挫败 **ts'ò-pài** a failure, defeat, setback

挫伤 **ts'ò-shāng** to bruise, fracture, blunt, break

2331 措施 **ts'ò-shīh** measures, steps, arrangements, preparations

措手不及 **ts'ò-shǒu-pù-chí** to be unable to place one's hand [on something] at the right time (to be caught unaware, taken by surprise)

措词 **ts'ò-tz'ú** phrasing, wording, diction

2332 锉刀 **ts'ò-tāo** a file (tool), rasp

2333 错觉 **ts'ò-chüéh** an hallucination, illusion, misconception

错乱 **ts'ò-luàn** mixed up, in disorder, confused, deranged; aberration, disorder

错杀 **ts'ò-shā** to kill by mistake

错综复杂 **ts'ò-tsūng fù-tsá** intermixed and complicated

错误估计 **ts'ò-wù kū-chì** to miscalculate, make a wrong estimate; a miscalculation

错误路线 **ts'ò-wù lù-hsièn** an incorrect line

ts'òu (còu)

2334 凑成 **ts'òu-ch'éng** to succeed in putting together, assemble into a whole

凑巧 **ts'òu-ch'iǎo** by chance, by luck; accidentally, fortuitously

凑合 **ts'òu-hó** (1) to improvise, scrape together, make do with what is available; (2) to assemble, collect, amass

ts'ū (cū)

2335 粗枝大叶 **ts'ū-chīh-tà-yèh** coarse branches and big leaves (sketchy, roughly finished, careless, superficial)

粗制滥造 **ts'ū-chìh-làn-tsào** coarsely made and overflowingly produced (mass production that stresses quantity rather than quality)

粗浅 **ts'ū-ch'iěn** coarse and shallow (crude, superficial; basic, elementary)

粗心大意 **ts'ū-hsīn tà-ì** rash and careless, thoughtless, negligent

粗粮 **ts'ū-liáng** coarse cereals (usually refers to food grains, excluding rice and wheat)

粗卤 **ts'ū-lǔ** boorish, rude, rough, coarse

粗略 **ts'ū-luèh** a general impression, sketchy, undetailed

粗暴 **ts'ū-pào** rude, rough, violent, brusque

粗手笨脚 **ts'ū-shǒu pèn-chiǎo** a rough hand and clumsy foot (awkward, clumsy, lacking grace or dexterity)

粗糙 **ts'ū-ts'āo** coarse, rough, unpolished, crude

ts'ù (cù)

2336 促战备 **ts'ù chàn-pèi** to urge war preparedness

促进 **ts'ù-chìn** to promote, expedite, press forward

促进派 **ts'ù-chìn-p'ài** progressive groups, an activist faction for progress

促转化 **ts'ù chuǎn-huà** to push transformation

促成 **ts'ù-ch'éng** to push to materialization, cause to happen, bring about, precipitate

促膝谈心 **ts'ù-hsī-t'án-hsīn** to sit with knees touching and talk heart to heart (to sit closely facing a person and talk intimately, converse as friends)

促工作 **ts'ù kūng-tsò** to promote work, push a task

促生产 **ts'ù shēng-ch'ǎn** to promote production, push production

促使 **ts'ù-shǐh** to compel, hasten, provoke, impel

促大干 **ts'ù tà-kàn** to push for a greater effort

促退派 **ts'ù-t'uì-p'ài** retrogressive elements, a faction opposing progress

ts'uàn (cuàn)

2337 篡改 **ts'uàn-kǎi** to alter [a writing,

entry] with evil intent

篡党夺权 **ts'uàn-tǎng tó-ch'üán** to usurp [the position of the] Party and seize power (an accusation against Lin Piao)

篡夺 **ts'uàn-tó** to seize by force and without right, usurp

ts'uī (cuī)

²³³⁸ 催化剂 **ts'uī-huà-chì** a catalyst [chemical]

催泪弹 **ts'uī-lèi-tàn** a tear gas bomb

催泪毒气 **ts'uī-lèi tú-ch'ì** tear gas

催芽播种 **ts'uī-yá-pò-chǔng** bud forcing and seeding

²³³⁹ 摧毁 **ts'uī-huǐ** to destroy, smash, wreck

摧枯拉朽 **ts'uī-k'ū-lā-hsiǔ** to break down the decayed and pull out the rotten [branches, etc.] (an easy victory: not requiring great strength)

摧垮 **ts'uī-k'uǎ** to destroy, shatter, overthrow

摧残 **ts'uī-ts'án** to destroy, demolish, disable, spoil; to humiliate

ts'uì (cuì)

²³⁴⁰ 脆弱 **ts'uì-jò** brittle and weak, fragile, frail; fragility, weakness

ts'ūn (cūn)

²³⁴¹ 村寨 **ts'ūn-chài** a village stockade, walled village

村长 **ts'ūn-chǎng** a village chief (a denunciatory epithet in the Cultural Revolution—referring to the **sān-chiā-ts'ūn** group)

村史 **ts'ūn-shǐh** a village history (the history of the past sufferings of a village—one of the **szù-shǐh**)

村屯 **ts'ūn-t'ún** a small village, hamlet

ts'ún (cún)

²³⁴² 存案 **ts'ún-àn** to put in the files, keep a record

存而不论 **ts'ún-érh-pù-lùn** to put aside without further discussion [for the time being] (to defer a decision or conclusion)

存货 **ts'ún-huò** stock, inventory, goods in stock; to stock goods, stockpile

存心为恶 **ts'ún-hsīn-wéi-ò** with intent to do evil (malice aforethought)

存款 **ts'ún-k'uǎn** a money deposit, funds on deposit; to deposit funds

存栏量 **ts'ún lán-liàng** the number [of animals] herded

存栏牲畜 **ts'ún-lán shēng-ch'ù** herded animals

存在 **ts'ún-tsài** to exist, survive, subsist; to be; existence, being; in existence

存在决定意识 **ts'ún-tsài chüéh-tìng ì-shíh** [Man's social] being determines [his] consciousness

存亡绝续 **ts'ún-wáng-chüéh-hsù** existence or extermination and termination or continuation (a critical stage for death or survival)

存养量 **ts'ún-yǎng-liàng** the number [of pigs, etc.] being raised

ts'ùn (cùn)

²³⁴³ 寸权必夺 **ts'ùn-ch'üán pì-tó** every inch of power must be seized [from the existing power holder]

寸利必得 **ts'ùn-lì pì-té** every inch of advantage must be obtained

寸步难行 **ts'ùn-pù nán-hsíng** it is difficult to move even an inch (a very difficult situation)

寸土必争 **ts'ùn-t'ǔ pì-chēng** even an inch of land has to be fought for

ts'ūng (cōng)

²³⁴⁴ 从容就义 **ts'ūng-júng-chiù-ì** to follow the path of virtue calmly (calmly to sacrifice one's life for principle)

从容考虑 **ts'ūng-júng k'ǎo-lǜ** to consider [a matter] in a leisurely manner

从容不迫 **ts'ūng-júng pù-p'ò** relaxed and unpressured

从 **ts'ūng**: see also **ts'úng**

²³⁴⁵ 匆忙 **ts'ūng-máng** hasty, hurried, in a great rush

匆促 **ts'ūng-ts'ù** hurried, hasty

匆匆忙忙 **ts'ūng-ts'ūng-máng-máng** in great haste, precipitately, suddenly

²³⁴⁶ 聪明能干 **ts'ūng-míng néng-kàn** intelligent and capable

ts'úng (cóng)

²³⁴⁷ 从今以后 **ts'úng-chīn-ì-hòu** from now on, from today forward, henceforth

从中取利 **ts'úng-chūng-ch'ǔ-lì** to obtain advantage from amidst [the trouble or disharmony of others] (to fish in troubled waters)

从长计议 **ts'úng-ch'áng-chì-ì** to take time to make careful deliberations

从群众中来，到群众中去 **ts'úng ch'ún-chùng chūng-lái, tào ch'ún-chùng chūng-ch'ù** to come from the masses and go to the masses (to gather and

sum up the views of the masses and take the resulting conclusions back to the masses)

从犯 **ts'úng-fàn** an accomplice, accessory [to a crime]

从下到上 **ts'úng-hsià-tào-shàng** from the bottom to the top

从公社来, 回公社去 **ts'úng kūng-shè lái, huí kūng-shè ch'ǜ** coming from the communes and returning to the communes (usually refers to commune members receiving outside training and then returning to the commune)

从宽处理 **ts'úng-k'uān ch'ǔ-lǐ** lenient treatment; to handle in a lenient manner

从理论到理论 **ts'úng lǐ-lùn tào lǐ-lùn** from theory to theory (education that ignores practice and deals only in theories)

从上到下 **ts'úng-shàng-tào-hsià** from top to bottom (usually suggests "commandism" and insufficient attention to the mass line)

从实际出发 **ts'úng shíh-chì ch'ū-fā** to start from reality, proceed from the actual situation

从事 **ts'úng-shìh** to engage in, work at, occupy oneself with, devote oneself to, pursue [a task], embark on

从属 **ts'úng-shǔ** to be subordinate to, dependent on; subordinate, secondary, collateral, incidental

从思想上找根源 **ts'úng szū-hsiǎng shang chǎo kēn-yuán** from [examining] ideology we can find the root [of a mistake, etc.]

从头到尾 **ts'úng-t'óu-tào-wěi** from head to tail, from beginning to end; throughout

从团结的愿望出发 **ts'úng t'uán-chiéh te yuàn-wàng ch'ū-fā** starting from the desire for unity

从无到有 **ts'úng-wú-tào-yǔ** from lacking to having (to develop from scratch)

从严 **ts'úng-yén** severe, stern, strict; to be severe

从 **ts'úng:** *see also* **ts'ūng**

2348 丛林 **ts'úng-lín** a dense forest, jungle

丛书 **ts'úng-shū** collectanea, literary items forming a collection

tz'ú (cí)

2349 词句 **tz'ú-chù** words and phrases, expressions, text of a writing, wording

2350 茨菇 **tz'ú-kū** the arrowhead [plant],

Sagittaria sagittifolia

2351 慈善 **tz'ú-shàn** charity, philanthropy, compassion, kindness

慈善事业 **tz'ú-shàn shìh-yèh** philanthropic undertakings

2352 辞职 **tz'ú-chíh** to resign from office; resignation

tz'ǔ (cǐ)

2353 此疆彼界 **tz'ǔ-chiāng pǐ-chièh** the boundary between [what is] mine [and what is] his

此起彼落 **tz'ǔ-ch'ǐ-pǐ-lò** rising here and falling there (endless, without a break, unceasing)

此呼彼应 **tz'ǔ-hū pǐ-yìng** one calls and the other responds (to act in concert)

此路不通 **tz'ǔ-lù pù-t'ūng** this road does not go through (a dead end)

此地无银三百两 **tz'ǔ-tì wú yín sān-pǎi-liǎng** no 300 taels of silver at this place (a man, having buried some treasure, put this sign at the place: hence, a denial that amounts to an admission)

tz'ù (cì)

2354 次货 **tz'ù-huò** inferior goods, low quality merchandise

次日 **tz'ù-jìh** the following day, next day, on the second day

次料顶好料 **tz'ù-liào tǐng hǎo-liào** inferior materials displace good materials

次生盐碱化 **tz'ù-shēng yén-chièn-huà** secondary alkalinization

次大陆 **tz'ù-tà-lù** a sub-continent

次等 **tz'ù-těng** second-rate, low grade, inferior

次要 **tz'ù-yào** secondary, subordinate, minor

次要矛盾 **tz'ù-yào máo-tùn** a secondary contradiction

2355 伺机反扑 **tz'ù-chī fǎn-p'ū** to wait for an opportunity to fight back

伺 **tz'ù:** *see also* **szù**

2356 刺激 **tz'ù-chī** to stimulate, provoke, incite; a stimulus; provocative

刺耳 **tz'ù-ěrh** to irritate the ears; harsh, screechy, grating

刺巴林 **tz'ù-pā-lín** a thicket of thorns, briar patch

刺杀 **tz'ù-shā** to stab to death, assassinate

刺伤 **tz'ù-shāng** a stab wound, bayonet wound

刺刀 **tz'ù-tāo** a bayonet, dagger

刺探 **tz'ù-t'àn** to search for, probe for,

spy, find out secretly

2357 赐与 **tz'ù-yǔ** to bestow, confer, grant

wā (wā)

2358 挖蒋根运动 **wā chiǎng-kēn yùn-tùng** a movement to dig out the roots of Chiang [Kai-shek] (a movement to eradicate KMT vestiges, ideological or organizational)

挖节找代 **wā chiéh chǎo tài** digging, saving, searching, and substituting (methods of getting the most out of raw materials)

挖进手 **wā-chìn-shǒu** diggers (usually refers to expert coal miners)

挖墙脚 **wā ch'iáng-chiǎo** to dig under the foot of a wall (to undermine)

挖穷根 **wā ch'iúng-kēn** to dig out the roots of poverty, uproot poverty

挖掘潜力 **wā-chüéh ch'ién-lì** to dig out hidden resources, bring out latent power, tap potential strength

挖黑线，清流毒 **wā hēi-hsièn, ch'īng liú-tú** to dig out the black line and purge the poison

挖心战术 **wā-hsīn chàn-shù** the tactic of removing the vital point (to weaken [the enemy] by eliminating the core strength, strike at the heel)

挖苦 **wā-k'u** to deride, be caustic about, ridicule with malice

挖空心思 **wā-k'ūng hsīn-szū** to exhaust one's mind, cudgel one's brains

挖宝思想 **wā-pǎo-szū-hsiǎng** treasure-digging thinking (the mistaken idea that the value of archaeological finds is in their monetary value)

挖山不止 **wā-shān pù-chǐh** to dig the mountain unceasingly (persistence can achieve great things—a reference to the spirit of "The Foolish Old Man Who Moved the Mountain"; *see* **yǔ-kūng í-shān**)

挖祖坟 **wā tsǔ-fén** to dig up one's ancestor's tomb (sometimes it has the sense of severing one's ideological or family ties)

wá (wá)

2359 娃娃 **wá-wa** a baby, young child; a doll; a pretty girl

wǎ (wǎ)

2360 瓦加杜古 **wǎ-chiā-tù-kǔ** Ouagadougou [Upper Volta]

瓦解 **wǎ-chiěh** (1) to disintegrate, collapse, fall apart, crumble, dissolve;

disintegration; (2) to destroy, subvert, undermine, disrupt, overthrow; destruction

瓦杜兹 **wǎ-tù-tzū** Vaduz [Liechtenstein]

瓦窑堡会议 **wǎ-yáo-pǎo huì-ì** the Wayaopao Conference (a meeting of the Politburo held at Wayaopao, North Shensi, on December 25, 1935, to decide on united-front policies for resistance against Japan)

2361 佤族 **wǎ-tsú** the Wa people (a minority people in Yunnan province: population 286,000 as of 1957 [formerly known as K'ǎ-wǎ 佧佤])

wāi (wāi)

2362 歪曲 **wāi-ch'ǖ** to twist, warp, distort; distortion

歪风 **wāi-fēng** an oblique wind (erroneous trend, perverted tendency)

歪风邪气 **wāi-fēng hsiéh-ch'ì** an evil wind and heterodox vapors (incorrect tendencies)

歪门邪路 **wāi-mén hsiéh-lù** a side door and oblique road (evil and heterodox ways)

wài (wài)

2363 外债 **wài-chài** foreign debts, foreign loans

外交 **wài-chiāo** foreign relations, relations between states; diplomacy; diplomatic

外交支持 **wài-chiāo chǐ-ch'íh** diplomatic support

外交关系 **wài-chiāo kuān-hsi** diplomatic relations

外交部 **wài-chiāo-pù** the Ministry of Foreign Affairs [of the State Council]

外交使团 **wài-chiāo-shǐh-t'uán** the diplomatic corps

外交事务 **wài-chiāo shìh-wù** foreign affairs, diplomatic matters

外交代办 **wài-chiāo tài-pàn** a chargé d'affaires

外界 **wài-chièh** the external world, one's environment; on the outside, those who are not "in the know"

外强中干 **wài-ch'iáng chūng-kān** outward strength but inner weakness, externally strong but internally weak

外侨汇款 **wài-ch'iáo huì-k'uǎn** foreign resident remittances, immigrant remittances

外行 **wài-háng** [someone] outside the profession, a layman, outsider;

unpracticed, unskilled

外户不闭 **wài-hù-pù-pì** the front door [need] not be closed (a condition of ideal peace and order)

外汇 **wài-huì** foreign exchange

外汇牌价 **wài-huì p'ái-chià** rates of foreign exchange

外协工作 **wài-hsiéh kūng-tsò** work done with outside help (subcontracted work)

外线 **wài-hsièn** the exterior line (in military operations: in contrast to interior lines)

外线作战 **wài-hsièn tsò-chàn** warfare on exterior lines; to fight on exterior lines

外国专家局 **wài-kuó chuān-chiā-chú** the Foreign Experts Bureau [of the State Council]

外国侨民 **wài-kuó ch'iáo-mín** foreign residents, resident aliens

外国侵略者 **wài-kuó ch'īn-luèh-chě** foreign aggressors

外国死人部 **wài-kuó szŭ-jén-pù** the ministry of dead foreigners (a sarcastic reference to the Ministry of Culture during the Cultural Revolution)

外国语学院 **wài-kuó-yŭ hsuéh-yuàn** the Foreign Languages Institute

外科 **wài-k'ō** surgery

外来干部 **wài-lái kàn-pù** cadres from other areas

外来干涉 **wài-lái kān-shè** outside interference

外来势力 **wài-lái shìh-lì** foreign forces, external forces

外流人口 **wài-liú jén-k'ŏu** population that drifts outside (usually refers to the drift from villages to towns, or people who seek to move during economic crises)

外贸 **wài-mào** foreign trade

外包工人 **wài-pāo kūng-jén** subcontracted workers (in a relatively small economic unit, which may be temporary, who do processing work for a major unit)

外表 **wài-piǎo** outer appearance, exterior, surface

外宾 **wài-pīn** foreign guests

外事系统 **wài-shìh hsì-t'ŭng** the foreign affairs system (the complex of organization having a relationship to foreign affairs)

外事口 **wài-shìh-k'ŏu** the foreign affairs "mouth" (an informal term for the highest level determining foreign policy—superior to administrative government organs but not

itself a formal body)

外事往来 **wài-shìh wǎng-lái** diplomatic comings and goings, diplomatic intercourse

外在 **wài-tsài** external, existing outside, extraneous, extrinsic

外族 **wài-tsú** foreign peoples, foreign nations, non-Han nationalities in China

外层空间 **wài-ts'éng k'ūng-chiēn** outer space

外为中用 **wài-wéi-chūng-yùng** to cause the foreign to serve China

外围 **wài-wéi** the outer surroundings; a perimeter (used to refer to "front" organizations)

外因 **wài-yīn** an external cause

外因论 **wài-yīn lùn** the theory of external causality

外语 **wài-yŭ** foreign languages

外园磨床 **wài-yuán mó-ch'uáng** a cylindrical grinding machine

外援 **wài-yuán** foreign aid

wān (wān)

2364　弯路 **wān-lù** a road with many curves, a roundabout way, detour

弯弯曲曲 **wān-wān-ch'ŭ-ch'ŭ** having many twists and turns, winding, tortuous

2365　剜肉补疮 **wān-jòu pǔ-chuāng** to cut off a piece of flesh to patch a boil (to disregard future misery in order to meet a current emergency)

2366　豌豆茬 **wān-tòu-ch'á** field pea stubble (refers to the crop planted in rotation immediately following the cutting of the field peas)

wán (wán)

2367　丸散膏丹针剂 **wán sǎn kāo tān chēn chì** pellets, powders, ointments, pills, injections, and potions (the six most common forms of Chinese medicine now in use; the old brews and decoctions, plus injections)

2368　完整 **wán-chěng** intact, complete, unbroken, undamaged

完结 **wán-chiéh** to conclude, terminate, culminate, fulfill, draw a conclusion

完成 **wán-ch'éng** to accomplish, complete, fulfill, perform; completion, fulfillment

完成任务 **wán-ch'éng jèn-wù** to complete a task

完成品 **wán-ch'éng-p'ĭn** finished products

完全 **wán-ch'üán** complete, whole,

total, entire, perfect; completely,
wholly

完小 **wán-hsiǎo** a full primary [school]
(offering the full number of years—a
contraction of *wán-ch'üán hsiǎo-
hsuéh*)

完粮 **wán-liáng** to pay taxes in kind

完美无缺 **wán-měi-wú-ch'üēh** perfect
and without defect

完备 **wán-pèi** well prepared, all ready;
completely equipped, complete with
everything

完毕 **wán-pì** to finish, complete, end;
completion

完善 **wán-shàn** perfect, immaculate,
untarnished, excellent

完蛋 **wán-tàn** ruined, done for, busted,
doomed

2369 玩具 **wán-chü** a toy, plaything

玩火自焚 **wán-huǒ tzù-fén** one who
plays with fire gets burned

玩笑 **wán-hsiào** to joke, tease, jest;
jokes

玩弄花招 **wán-nùng huā-chāo** to engage
in sleight of hand, play sly tricks

玩弄词句 **wán-nùng tz'ú-chü** to toy
with words, trifle with words (to use
deceptive phraseology)

2370 顽强 **wán-ch'iáng** stubborn, obstinate,
recalcitrant, unyielding

顽固 **wán-kù** headstrong, stubborn,
obstinate, inflexible, bigoted, thick-
skulled, conservative

顽固分子 **wán-kù fèn-tzǔ** diehard
elements, obstinate conservatives

顽固堡垒 **wán-kù pǎo-lěi** a diehard
fortress (may either be a group of
stubborn conservatives or an organization that shelters them)

顽固不化 **wán-kù-pù-huà** obstinate and
unchanging, inflexibly thick-headed,
incorrigibly conservative

顽固派 **wán-kù-p'ài** diehard groups,
bigoted elements, reactionaries

wǎn (wǎn)

2371 宛转 **wǎn-chuǎn** (1) in a roundabout
manner; (2) to explain or persuade in
a pleasant and tactful, but indirect
way

2372 挽救 **wǎn-chiù** to save, rescue, remedy
[a situation], help, extricate

挽回 **wǎn-huí** to win back, bring back,
restore [to an earlier state of affairs]

挽歌 **wǎn-kō** a song of mourning, dirge

2373 惋惜 **wǎn-hsī** to regret, feel sorry for,
deplore

2374 晚节有终 **wǎn-chiéh-yǔ-chūng** one's

integrity does not end in old age

晚会 **wǎn-huì** an evening meeting,
evening gathering

晚婚 **wǎn-hūn** late marriage (an official
part of the population control policy)

晚婚节育 **wǎn-hūn chiéh-yü** late
marriage and birth control

晚点 **wǎn-tiěn** later than the fixed
[time], behind schedule (usually
refers to trains or planes)

2375 皖 **wǎn** Anhwei province

皖南事变 **wǎn-nán shìh-pièn** The South
Anhwei Incident (the Kuomintang
attack on the headquarters of the
New Fourth Army during January
1941, in which Yeh T'ing was captured and Hsiang Ying killed—also
referred to as the New Fourth Army
Incident)

wàn (wàn)

2376 万金油干部 **wàn-chīn-yú kàn-pù** a
"tiger balm" cadre (a non-specialized
cadre who can fill-in at any kind of
job that needs to be done)

万众欢腾 **wàn-chùng huān-t'éng** the
applause of a multitude, thunderous
ovation

万众一心 **wàn-chùng ī-hsīn** united as
one man, complete unity

万象 **wàn-hsiàng** Vientiane [Laos]

万象更新 **wàn-hsiàng-kēng-hsīn** all
things are changed into new (a new
year, new epoch)

万古长青 **wàn-kǔ-ch'áng-ch'īng** eternally green, perennial freshness (a
spirit that never flags, or a friendship
that never fades)

万古长存 **wàn-kǔ-ch'áng-ts'ún** immortal, undying

万里长征 **wàn-lǐ-ch'áng-chēng** a long
march of ten thousand *li*; The Long
March (of the Communist forces
from Kiangsi to Shensi, 1934–1935)

万里长征第一步 **wàn-lǐ-ch'áng-chēng tì-
ī-pù** [to take] the first step of a long
march (to begin a long-term undertaking)

万里长城 **wàn-lǐ-ch'áng-ch'éng** the ten
thousand *li* long wall (i.e., the Great
Wall of China)

万里神州 **wàn-lǐ-shén-chōu** the divine
land of ten thousand *li* [China]

万里迢迢 **wàn-lǐ-t'iáo-t'iáo** thousands
of *li* and very remote

万隆会议 **wàn-lúng huì-ì** the Bandung
Conference (an Asian-African conference, April 18–24, 1955, at

Bandung, Indonesia in which Chou
En-lai stressed peaceful coexistence
and friendly cooperation among
nations)

万马奔腾 **wàn-mǎ-pēn-t'éng** ten
thousand stampeding horses (a
thunderous or roaring sound)

万能 **wàn-néng** versatile, all-purpose,
universal; all-powerful, omnipotent

万能机床 **wàn-néng chǐ-ch'uáng** a
universal machine tool

万能法宝 **wàn-néng fǎ-pǎo** an all-powerful magic weapon (a simile for the
Thought of Mao Tse-tung)

万能铣床 **wàn-néng hsǐ-ch'uáng** a
universal milling machine

万恶不赦 **wàn-ò-pù-shè** myriad evils
that cannot be pardoned (reprehen-
sible and inexcusable)

万般皆下品，唯有读书高 **wàn-pān chiēh
hsià-p'ǐn, wéi yǔ tú-shū kāo** all pro-
fessions are lowly things [and] only
studying is honorable (criticized as
exploitative and demeaning of work)

万变不离其宗 **wàn-pièn pù-lí ch'í-tsūng**
a myriad variations without separating from the ancestral root (methods
may vary but the principle remains
the same)

万炮齐鸣 **wàn-p'ào ch'í-míng** ten
thousand cannon sounding together

万世长存 **wàn-shìh ch'áng-ts'ún** to last
for countless generations (everlasting,
eternal)

万事不求人 **wàn-shìh pù ch'iú-jén** to
ask no help from others in anything
(to admit no personal fault or
inadequacy)

万事不帮人 **wàn-shìh pù pāng-jén** to
give no help to others in anything (to
be completely self-centered and
selfish)

万事大吉 **wàn-shìh tà-chí** everything is
fine

万寿无疆 **wàn-shòu wú-chiāng** [may you
attain] boundless longevity

万岁 **wàn-suì** ten-thousand years! long
live! hurrah!

万代 **wàn-tài** myriad generations,
eternity

万紫千红 **wàn-tzǔ-ch'iēn-húng** ten
thousand purples and a thousand
reds (a vast array of dazzling colors)

万无一失 **wàn wú ī-shīh** not one failure
in ten thousand (certain to succeed,
absolutely safe, sure)

万物 **wàn-wù** everything in creation,
all things, all living things

万应良药 **wàn-yìng liáng-yào** a medicine for a myriad needs, panacea

wáng (wáng)

²³⁷⁷ 亡国 **wáng-kuó** national extermination,
national subjugation; a country's
downfall, doom

亡国论者 **wáng-kuó-lùn-chě** one who is
pessimistic of the country's ability to
survive, a defeatist (especially during
the Resistance War period)

亡国奴 **wáng-kuó-nú** a slave in a sub-
jugated country, conquered people

亡命之徒 **wáng-mìng-chīh-t'ú** a fugitive,
desperado, lawless elements

²³⁷⁸ 王杰 **wáng chiéh** Wang Chieh (a PLA
soldier who became a national hero
and model in 1965 by throwing
himself on exploding dynamite to
save the lives of others)

王朝 **wáng-ch'áo** a royal house,
dynasty

王国 **wáng-kuó** a kingdom, monarchy
(has the meaning, in domestic affairs,
of aspiring to excessive independence
of the Party or central control)

王明 **wáng míng** Wang Ming (the
Party name of Ch'en Shao-yü, 1907–
1974, a leader of the Russian-trained
faction in the CCP and long-time
rival of Mao Tse-tung)

王明路线 **wáng míng lù-hsièn** the Wang
Ming line (regarded as capitulationist
toward the KMT by Mao Tse-tung
during the Resistance War, and
attacked as bourgeois during the
Cheng-feng Movement, 1942–1944)

王牌 **wáng-p'ái** a trump card

王实味思想 **wáng shíh-wèi szū-hsiǎng**
Wang Shih-wei thinking (Wang's
short novel, *Wild White Lilies*,
published in Yenan in 1942, was
heavily criticized as counter-revolutionary)

王道 **wáng-tào** the kingly way (the way
of an enlightened ruler, an enlightened reign of righteousness—as
contrasted with **pà-tào**)

wǎng (wǎng)

²³⁷⁹ 往返徒劳 **wǎng-fǎn-t'ú-láo** to waste
time going to and from (futile effort,
wasted effort)

往复 **wǎng-fù** to and fro, come and go,
there and back; repetitious, continuous

往昔 **wǎng-hsī** in the past, in ancient
times

往个人帐上挂 **wǎng kò-jén chàng-shang-
kuà** to charge to an individual's
account (to assign blame)

往事 **wǎng-shìh** past events, old stories

2380 枉费心机 **wǎng-fèi hsīn-chī** to have wasted one's mind (to scheme in vain)

2381 魍魉鬼魅 **wǎng-liǎng kuěi-mèi** apparitions and specters (epithet for anti-Mao elements during the Cultural Revolution)

wàng (wàng)

2382 妄想 **wàng-hsiǎng** absurd hopes, frivolous wishes, daydreams; to daydream, desire wildly

妄动 **wàng-tùng** to act recklessly; impulsive action

妄图 **wàng-t'ú** to attempt in vain; preposterous schemes

妄自菲薄 **wàng-tzù-fěi-pó** to underestimate oneself, to lack self-confidence, have a sense of inferiority

妄自尊大 **wàng-tzù tsūn-tà** to falsely overrate oneself; ignorantly conceited, egotistical, self-important

2383 忘其所以 **wàng-ch'í-sǒ-ǐ** to forget oneself, be carried away [by enthusiasm, etc.]

忘恩负义 **wàng-ēn-fù-ì** to forget kindness [and one's] obligations to right conduct (ungrateful, to turn against a friend or benefactor)

忘本 **wàng-pěn** to forget one's [proletarian class] origins

忘我战斗 **wàng-wǒ chàn-tòu** to struggle without regard for oneself; selfless struggle, self-sacrificing struggle

忘我劳动 **wàng-wǒ láo-tùng** selfless labor

2384 旺盛 **wàng-shèng** prosperous, flourishing, prolific, productive, blooming

2385 望尘莫及 **wàng-ch'én mò-chí** to look at the dust [raised by another] but be unable to catch up (to be hopelessly behind)

望风披靡 **wàng-fēng p'ǐ-mí** to watch the wind and scatter (to flee pell-mell)

望天田 **wàng-t'iēn-t'ién** heaven-depending fields (non-irrigated fields)

望子成龙 **wàng-tzǔ-ch'éng-lúng** to hope that their children will become dragons (to seek official careers for their children through becoming scholars—rather than by physical labor)

望远镜 **wàng-yuǎn-chìng** a telescope

望远镜和显微镜 **wàng-yuǎn-chìng hó hsiěn-wēi-chìng** a telescope and microscope (a reference to the Thought of Mao Tse-tung, which is said to perform both functions)

wēi (wēi)

2386 危机 **wēi-chī** a crisis, critical juncture

危机四伏 **wēi-chī szù-fú** a crisis of danger lurks in all four directions (beset by crises, danger wherever one turns)

危急 **wēi-chí** very dangerous, hazardous, urgent, pressing; an emergency

危局 **wēi-chú** a dangerous situation

危害 **wēi-hài** to endanger, harm, injure; dangerous, menacing

危险 **wēi-hsiěn** danger; dangerous, unsafe

危险粮 **wēi-hsiěn-liáng** dangerous grain (grain with high water content, requiring care in storage and frequent examination)

危如累卵 **wēi-jú-lěi-luǎn** as precarious as a pile of eggs

危地马拉 **wēi-tì-mǎ-lā** [Republic of] Guatemala

危在旦夕 **wēi-tsài-tàn-hsī** the danger lies between morning and evening (the crisis will come within a day; imminent danger)

危言耸听 **wēi-yén-sǔng-t'īng** to use exaggerated talk to shock the hearers (to resort to sensationalism)

2387 委蛇 **wēi-í** in a roundabout way, evasive, lacking in sincerity, carefree

委 **wēi**: *see also* **wěi**

2388 威震全国 **wēi-chèn-ch'üán-kuó** to awe the whole country (be universally acclaimed)

威风 **wēi-fēng** grandeur; imposing, awe-inspiring

威风凛凛 **wēi-fēng-lǐn-lǐn** awe-inspiring, imposing, demanding respect

威胁 **wēi-hsiéh** to threaten, menace, intimidate, coerce; a threat

威胁利诱 **wēi-hsiéh-lì-yù** threats and lures, coercion and bribery

威信 **wēi-hsìn** public confidence, prestige [based on good faith], authority

威信扫地 **wēi-hsìn-sǎo-tì** [to have one's] prestige dragged in the dust (to suffer a drastic loss of prestige)

威力 **wēi-lì** strength, power, force, might; military force; destructive force

威力无穷 **wēi-lì wú-ch'iúng** inexhaustible force, limitless power

威廉斯塔特 **wēi-lién-szū-t'ǎ-t'è** Willemstad [Netherlands West Indies]

威迫 **wēi-p'ò** to coerce, intimidate

威迫利诱 **wēi-p'ò-lì-yù** coercing and cajoling; to menace and offer bribes

威慑力量 **wēi-shè lì-liang** deterrent

power, deterrent capability, capacity
to deter

威德兼施 **wēi-té-chiēn-shīh** to use both
justice and mercy

威武雄壮 **wēi-wǔ hsiúng-chuàng**
majestic and powerful, impressively
martial, imposing and powerful

2389 微型汽车 **wēi-hsíng ch'ì-ch'ē** a miniature motorcar

微粒子 **wēi-lì-tzǔ** micro-particles

微妙 **wēi-miào** fine, subtle, minute,
delicate; mysterious, ethereal

微不足道 **wēi-pù-tsú-tào** so small [that
it is] not worth speaking of (trifling,
insignificant, negligible)

微生物 **wēi-shēng-wù** micro-organisms,
germs, bacteria, microbes

2390 巍然屹立 **wēi-ján-ch'ì-lì** to stand out
majestically

wéi (wéi)

2391 为政以德 **wéi-chèng-ǐ-té** to govern by
means of morality [virtue] (a Confucian doctrine now criticized as
counter to Legalism)

为之神往 **wéi-chīh-shén-wǎng** to be
completely absorbed in, to have one's
mind carried away

为止 **wéi-chǐh** until, till; no further

为仇 **wéi-ch'óu** to be hostile to, be an
enemy

为非作歹 **wéi-fēi-tsò-tǎi** to do mischief
and evil, do wrong and evil; sinful,
depraved

为富不仁 **wéi-fù pù-jén** to be rich but
not benevolent, rich and immoral

为虎作伥 **wéi-hǔ tsò-ch'āng** to act as
the ghost of one eaten by a tiger (the
ghost of the tiger's victim urges the
tiger to eat others, hence: to assist
or incite evil acts)

为人所不齿 **wéi-jén-sǒ-pù-ch'ǐh** to be
[so despicable, etc.] that people
regard [him] as not worth mentioning
(infamous, disreputable, beyond
contempt)

为妙 **wéi-miào** to be good, better, best

为难 **wéi-nán** to make things difficult
or embarrassing, create an obstruction; to cause or be in trouble, a
dilemma, a distressing position

为时过早 **wéi-shíh kuò-tsǎo** too early,
premature, inopportune

为首 **wéi-shǒu** as the head of, be the
leader, act as leader

为数不多 **wéi-shù pù-tō** not many in
number, limited in number

为所欲为 **wéi-sǒ-yù-wéi** to do as one
wishes, have one's own way; unscru-

pulous, self-willed, without restraint

为 **wéi**: *see also* **wèi**

2392 违法 **wéi-fǎ** unlawful, illegal

违法乱纪 **wéi-fǎ luàn-chì** to violate laws
and disrupt discipline; contrary to
law and precept

违反 **wéi-fǎn** to contradict, act against,
disregard, do the opposite, contravene

违犯 **wéi-fàn** to violate a law, disobey,
trespass, defy

违抗 **wéi-k'àng** to oppose, resist, defy,
disobey

违背 **wéi-pèi** to defy, place oneself in
opposition to, go against; give
offense to

2393 围剿 **wéi-chiǎo** to encircle and suppress, attack from all sides; encirclement, eradication (may be figurative)

围剿派性 **wéi-chiǎo p'ài-hsìng** to wipe
out factionalism

围海造田 **wéi-hǎi tsào-t'ién** to enclose
the sea and make fields (to reclaim
land from the sea)

围绕 **wéi-jǎo** to surround, encircle,
enclose

围攻 **wéi-kūng** to surround and attack,
besiege; encirclement

围点打援 **wéi-tiěn tǎ-yuán** [the tactic
of] encircling a point and striking at
[enemy attempts to send] support

围堰 **wéi-yèn** a cofferdam

2394 桅灯 **wéi-tēng** a masthead lantern,
boat's riding light

2395 唯成分论 **wéi-ch'éng-fèn lùn** the doctrine of [considering] only class
origin

唯心主义 **wéi-hsīn-chǔ-ì** idealism

唯心论 **wéi-hsīn lùn** idealism

唯心论的先验论 **wéi-hsīn lùn te hsiēn-
yèn lùn** idealist apriorism

唯理论 **wéi-lǐ lùn** rationalism

唯利是图 **wéi-lì-shìh-t'ú** to think only
of profit; unscrupulous profit-seeking

唯美主义 **wéi-měi-chǔ-ì** aestheticism
(the devotion to beauty, art for art's
sake)

唯名论 **wéi-míng lùn** nominalism

唯命是从 **wéi-mìng-shìh-ts'úng** any
command will be obeyed (to do
whatever one is told to do; unconditionally obedient)

唯派性论 **wéi-p'ài-hsìng lùn** the idea
that there is only factionalism, the
doctrine that factionalism in inevitable

唯生产力论 **wéi shēng-ch'ǎn-lì lùn** the
theory [that social development
results] only from productive forces

唯我论 **wéi-wǒ lùn** solipsism, the theory

that the self is the existent thing

唯我独革 **wéi-wǒ-tú-kó** [to regard] oneself as the only true revolutionary, "I, alone, am revolutionary"

唯我独左 **wéi-wǒ-tú-tsǒ** "I, alone, am a Leftist" (a form of factional pretension during the Cultural Revolution)

唯武器论 **wéi-wǔ-ch'ì lùn** the doctrine that only weapons [are important]

唯物主义 **wéi-wù-chǔ-ì** materialism

唯物主义认识论 **wéi-wù-chǔ-ì jèn-shíh lùn** the materialistic theory of knowledge, materialistic epistemology

唯物论 **wéi-wù lùn** materialism

唯物论的反映论 **wéi-wù-lùn te fǎn-yìng lùn** the materialist theory of reflection

唯物辩证法 **wéi-wù pièn-chèng-fǎ** materialist dialectics, dialectical materialism

唯 **wéi**: see also **wěi**

2396 维持 **wéi-ch'íh** to maintain, preserve, uphold, support, sustain; maintenance, support

维护 **wéi-hù** to defend, safeguard, protect, preserve, uphold, support

维护保养 **wéi-hù pǎo-yǎng** protection and maintenance

维新 **wéi-hsīn** to renew, reform, modernize; reform (usually refers to government or politics)

维修 **wéi-hsiū** maintenance, upkeep

维他命 **wéi-t'ā-mìng** vitamin

维吾尔族 **wéi-wǔ-ěrh-tsú** the Uighur people (a minority in Sinkiang: population 3,900,000 as of 1957)

维也纳 **wéi-yěh-nà** Vienna [Austria]

wěi (wěi)

2397 伪装 **wěi-chuāng** to disguise oneself, feign, simulate, camouflage; camouflage, disguise

伪军 **wěi-chǔn** troops of an illegal or bogus government, puppet forces

伪君子 **wěi-chǔn-tzǔ** a hypocrite

伪国大 **wěi-kuó-tà** the bogus National Assembly (convened by the Kuomintang in November 1946, and boycotted by the Chinese Communist Party and the Democratic League)

伪善面孔 **wěi-shàn mièn-k'ǔng** a hypocritical appearance, a face of hypocrisy

伪造 **wěi-tsào** to falsify, counterfeit, forge

2398 伟人 **wěi-jén** a great person (someone who has made a major historical contribution)

伟大 **wěi-tà** great, extraordinary, grand, noble; greatness

伟大业绩 **wěi-tà yèh-chī** a great career, monumental achievements

2399 尾巴主义 **wěi-pā-chǔ-ì** "tailism" (usually refers to followers of opposition figures)

尾巴翘上天 **wěi-pā ch'iào-shang-t'iēn** with the tail lifted toward the sky (arrogant and complacent)

尾随 **wěi-suí** to tail after, follow close after, go in the wake of

尾大不掉 **wěi-tà-pù-tiào** the tail is so large that it cannot be moved about (an organization so bloated that it cannot be effectively controlled from the top)

2400 纬线 **wěi-hsièn** parallels of latitude

2401 委曲求全 **wěi-ch'ǔ ch'iú-ch'üán** to twist and turn in order to accomplish something (to lower oneself in seeking a compromise)

委屈 **wěi-ch'ǔ** an injustice, grievance, wrong; to be wronged, frustrated

委任 **wěi-jèn** to appoint, delegate, commission, authorize; an appointment, commission

委靡不振 **wěi-mǐ-pù-chèn** dispirited and lethargic, downhearted and inactive

委内瑞拉 **wěi-nèi-juì-lā** Venezuela

委派 **wěi-p'ài** to appoint and dispatch, commission, delegate, accredit, assign

委托 **wěi-t'ō** to deputize, commission, entrust, authorize, delegate; a trust, commission

委员 **wěi-yuán** a member of a committee, board, commission, etc.

委员会 **wěi-yuán-huì** a committee, commission, council, board

委 **wěi**: see also **wéi**

2402 唯唯否否 **wěi-wěi fǒu-fǒu** [to answer] only yes or no (to have no independent opinion, to echo others)

唯唯诺诺 **wěi-wěi-nò-nò** to always say yes yes; to be a yes man

唯 **wěi**: see also **wéi**

wèi (wèi)

2403 卫星 **wèi-hsīng** a satellite

卫星工厂 **wèi-hsīng kūng-ch'ǎng** satellite factories

卫星田 **wèi-hsīng-t'ién** satellite fields (established around factories)

卫国战争 **wèi-kuó chàn-chēng** a defensive war, war of national defense

卫兵 **wèi-pīng** a guard, military escort, sentry

卫生 **wèi-shēng** sanitation, hygiene, health; hygienic

卫生局 **wèi-shēng-chú** a health bureau

卫生系统 **wèi-shēng hsì-t'ǔng** public health system

卫生工作 **wèi-shēng kūng-tsò** public health work

卫生部 **wèi-shēng-pù** the Ministry of Public Health [of the State Council]

卫生所 **wèi-shēng-sǒ** a health clinic

卫生大扫除 **wèi-shēng tà-sǎo-ch'ú** a big sanitation clean-up

卫生突击 **wèi-shēng t'ū-chī** a sanitation commando attack (a non-regular clean-up)

卫生员 **wèi-shēng-yuán** a sanitation worker, public health worker (usually with only basic training)

卫戍区 **wèi-shù-ch'ǖ** a garrison area

卫道者 **wèi-tào-chě** a defender of the faith (now refers to alleged supporters of Confucianism)

2404 为艺术而艺术 **wèi ì-shù érh ì-shù** art for art's sake

为人民服务 **wèi jén-mín fú-wù** "To Serve the People" (an article by Mao Tse-tung, September 1944, commemorating a military hero; later it became a PLA motto; and during the Cultural Revolution, it became one of the **lǎo-sān p'iēn** and a national slogan)

为人民立功 **wèi jén-mín lì-kūng** to achieve merit for the people

为革命种田 **wèi kó-mìng chùng-t'ién** to farm for the sake of the revolution

为革命而学 **wèi kó-mìng érh hsuéh** to study for the sake of the revolution

为革命甘当无名英雄 **wèi kó-mìng kān-tāng wú-míng yīng-hsiúng** willingly to be a nameless hero for the revolution

为革命当好配角 **wèi kó-mìng tāng-hǎo p'èi-chiǎo** to play a minor role for the sake of the revolution

为工人阶级政治服务 **wèi kūng-jén-chiēh-chí chèng-chìh fú-wù** to serve working-class politics

为工农兵服务 **wèi kūng-núng-pīng fú-wù** to serve the workers, peasants, and soldiers

为谁开门 **wèi-shéi k'āi-mén** for whom shall the doors [of the schools] be opened?

为无产阶级政治服务 **wèi wú-ch'ǎn-chiēh-chí chèng-chìh fú-wù** to serve proletarian politics

为 **wèi**: see also **wéi**

2405 未证实消息 **wèi-chèng-shíh hsiāo-hsi** an unconfirmed report, unverified news

未加工 **wèi chiā-kūng** to have not yet processed; unprocessed, crude, raw, in a rough state

未竟之业 **wèi-chìng-chīh-yèh** an unfinished cause, unfulfilled undertaking

未成熟 **wèi-ch'éng-shú** immature, unripe, premature, undeveloped

未可厚非 **wèi-k'ǒ-hòu-fēi** not meriting serious blame

未来 **wèi-lái** the future, in the future; not as yet, to come

未必 **wèi-pì** not necessarily, not sure, not always, improbable, uncertain

未卜先知 **wèi-pǔ-hsiēn-chīh** to foresee without divination (to foresee accurately)

未遂 **wèi-suí** attempted without success, not yet accomplished, unfulfilled, aborted

未雨绸缪 **wèi-yǔ ch'óu-móu** to thatch a roof before it rains (to take timely precautions, show forethought)

2406 位置 **wèi-chìh** a position, location, site, place; a post, rank, organizational position

2407 味道 **wèi-tào** a taste, flavor, smell

2408 畏惧 **wèi-chù** to fear, dread, be scared of, anxious about

畏难 **wèi-nán** to fear difficulty, be awed by a difficulty

畏首畏尾 **wèi-shǒu-wèi-wěi** to fear both the head and the tail (to be anxious about a whole affair; excessive fears)

畏缩 **wèi-sō** to fear and draw back (to recoil, cringe, flinch, shrink from; hesitant)

畏缩不前 **wèi-sō-pù-ch'ién** to flinch and stop progress

2409 胃口 **wèi-k'ǒu** appetite, desire to eat

2410 蔚然成风 **wèi-ján ch'éng-fēng** an overwhelming trend, sweeping vogue

2411 慰问 **wèi-wèn** to ask in solicitude, console, send condolences

慰问信 **wèi-wèn-hsìn** a letter of condolence, message of sympathy

慰问团 **wèi-wèn-t'uán** a sympathetic inquiry mission (a group sent to the scene of a disaster, to cheer up workers on a large project, to comfort the troops, etc.)

wēn (wēn)

2412 温情 **wēn-ch'íng** warmheartedness, kindness, affection, sentiment

温情主义 **wēn-ch'íng-chǔ-ì** sentimentalism (usually implies misguided softness or lack of revolutionary firmness)

温床 **wēn-ch'uáng** a hotbed, forcing frame (a garden frame which is heated, by fermenting manure or

otherwise, for early plant growth; may also be used metaphorically in a pejorative sense)

温和 **wēn-hó** gentle, mild, temperature, moderate, friendly

温和派 **wēn-hó-p'ài** moderates, moderate groups (normally political)

温和手段 **wēn-hó shǒu-tuàn** moderate means, mild methods

温故知新 **wēn-kù chīh-hsīn** to rediscover or learn new things by reviewing the old

温饱 **wēn-pǎo** a warm [back] and full [belly] (adequately clothed and fed)

温室 **wēn-shìh** a hothouse, greenhouse

温带 **wēn-tài** the temperate zone

温得和克 **wēn-té-hó-k'ò** Windhoek [Southwest Africa]

温度 **wēn-tù** temperature, heat, degree of temperature

温文典雅 **wēn-wén tiěn-yǎ** cultured and elegant (lacking any spirit of struggle)

2413 瘟疫 **wēn-ì** a plague, pestilence, epidemic

瘟神 **wēn-shén** the god of plague (someone who brings disaster on mankind)

wén (wén)

2414 文教战线 **wén-chiào chàn-hsièn** the cultural and educational battle line [front]

文教事业 **wén-chiào shìh-yèh** the cause of culture and education, cultural and educational undertakings

文教组织 **wén-chiào tsǔ-chīh** UNESCO

文件 **wén-chièn** documents, written materials, a writing, paper; documentary

文质彬彬 **wén-chìh pīn-pīn** fine both in accomplishments and in nature, elegant and refined (refers to the educational ideal of the Confucianists)

文权 **wén-ch'üán** the leadership power in the cultural realm, powerful figures in cultural matters

文风 **wén-fēng** literary style, literary tendency; a popular cultural interest

文化 **wén-huà** culture, civilization, education; cultural

文化战线 **wén-huà chàn-hsièn** the cultural battle line [front]

文化基础知识 **wén-huà chī-ch'ǔ chīh-shíh** basic cultural knowledge (elementary education)

文化交流 **wén-huà chiāo-liú** cultural exchange, cultural interchange

文化教育战线 **wén-huà chiào-yǜ chàn-hsièn** the battle front of culture and education

文化界 **wén-huà-chièh** cultural circles, the cultural sphere [realm]

文化程度 **wén-huà ch'éng-tù** cultural standard, educational achievement (the amount of schooling a person has had)

文化翻身 **wén-huà fān-shēn** the cultural turning over (the great change from culture for the elite few to culture being available to the masses)

文化遗产 **wén-huà í-ch'ǎn** a cultural heritage, cultural inheritance

文化革命 **wén-huà kó-mìng** a revolution in culture, a cultural revolution

文化革命小组 **wén-huà kó-mìng hsiǎo-tsǔ** the Cultural Revolutionary Small Group

文化馆 **wén-huà-kuǎn** a cultural center, museum of culture

文化宫 **wén-huà-kūng** a palace of culture

文化考查 **wén-huà k'ǎo-ch'á** a cultural examination (to review academic or educational qualifications)

文化课 **wén-huà-k'ò** a cultural course (usually classes in basic education and literacy)

文化领域 **wén-huà lǐng-yǜ** the sphere of culture, the cultural realm

文化补习学校 **wén-huà pǔ-hsí hsuéh-hsiào** cultural make-up schools (established in some factories in the 1960s for employees needing basic literacy education)

文化部 **wén-huà-pù** the Ministry of Culture [of the State Council]

文化水平 **wén-huà shuǐ-p'íng** the cultural level, educational standing

文化大军 **wén-huà tà-chǔn** a cultural army (the many people who are engaged in cultural work)

文化大革命 **wén-huà tà kó-mìng** the Great [Proletarian] Cultural Revolution

文化低 **wén-huà tī** of low cultural level

文化团体 **wén-huà t'uán-t'ǐ** cultural organizations, cultural bodies

文化摇篮 **wén-huà yáo-lán** the cradle of culture [civilization]

文汇报 **wén-huì-pào** the *Wen-hui Daily* (a daily newspaper published in Shanghai and Hong Kong)

文献 **wén-hsièn** records, documents, archives, literature

文献记录片 **wén-hsièn chì-lù-p'ièn** a documentary film

文选 **wén-hsuǎn** selected literary works,

an anthology

文学 **wén-hsuéh** literature

文学和艺术服从政治 **wén-hsuéh hó ì-shù fú-ts'úng chèng-chìh** literature and the arts [must] serve politics

文学遗产 **wén-hsuéh í-ch'ǎn** a literary legacy, literature heritage

文学艺术遗产 **wén-hsuéh ì-shù í-ch'ǎn** the literary and artistic heritage

文艺 **wén-ì** literature and art; literature as one of the fine arts, belles-lettres

文艺节目 **wén-ì chiéh-mù** a program of artistic performances

文艺界 **wén-ì-chièh** literary and artistic circles, the art and literature world

文艺创作神秘论 **wén-ì ch'uàng-tsò shén-mì lùn** the doctrine that literary creation is a mystery (a concept now derided, since the masses are now considered able to create their own literature)

文艺活动 **wén-ì huó-tùng** literary and artistic activities

文艺革命 **wén-ì kó-mìng** a revolution in literature and the arts

文艺理论 **wén-ì lǐ-lùn** theories of literature and the arts

文艺报 **wén-ì-pào** *Literature and Art* (a Peking semi-monthly journal, October 1949—)

文艺评论 **wén-ì p'íng-lùn** literary and artistic criticism

文艺沙龙 **wén-ì shā-lúng** literary salons (places where elite intellectuals congregate)

文艺调演 **wén-ì tiào-yěn** performances [in Peking] at which regional troupes present their adaptations of the various **yàng pǎn hsì**

文艺为工农兵服务 **wén-ì wèi kūng-núng-pīng fú-wù** literature and art is to serve the workers, peasants, and soldiers

文告 **wén-kào** an [official] statement, written bulletin

文革 **wén-kó** the Great Proletarian Cultural Revolution (abbreviation for: **wú-ch'ǎn-chiēh-chí wén-huà tà kó-mìng**)

文革十六条 **wén-kó shíh-liù-t'iáo** the Sixteen Points of the Cultural Revolution (the sixteen point resolution of the Central Committee on August 8, 1966)

文工队 **wén-kūng-tuì** cultural work groups (troupes for the performing arts [song, dance, drama, etc.] to provide recreation and education—originally in or attached to the army, but now also in factories, schools,

文工团 **wén-kūng-t'uán** cultural work troupes (*see above*)

文攻武卫 **wén-kūng wǔ-wèi** to attack with reason and to defend with force (a Red Guard slogan credited to Chiang Ch'ing in July 1967)

文过饰非 **wén-kuò shìh-fēi** [to use fine words] to conceal and gloss over fault

文科 **wén-k'ō** the humanities, liberal arts

文科大学 **wén-k'ō tà-hsuéh** a liberal arts college, humanities university

文莱 **wén-lái** Brunei [North Borneo]

文联 **wén-lién** the China Federation of Literary and Art Circles (contraction of **chūng-kuó wén-hsuéh-ì-shù-chièh lién-hó-huì**)

文盲 **wén-máng** illiteracy; illiterate; an illiterate

文明社会 **wén-míng shè-huì** a civilized society

文笔 **wén-pǐ** a writing style, literary skill

文斗 **wén-tòu** civil struggle, nonviolent struggle, persuasion

文牍主义 **wén-tú-chǔ-ì** "documentism" (the excessive reliance on writing and reading memos and reports instead of direct contacts and investigation)

文字改革 **wén-tzù kǎi-kó** (1) language reform of Chinese characters; (2) *Language Reform* (a Peking monthly journal, 1956—)

文物 **wén-wù** (1) cultural objects (relics and documents of cultural or historical significance); (2) *Cultural Relics* (a Peking monthly journal, 1950—)

文物古迹 **wén-wù-kǔ-chī** cultural objects and historical landmarks

文言文 **wén-yén-wén** writings in classical style

文娱活动 **wén-yǘ huó-tùng** cultural and recreational activities

2415 闻风丧胆 **wén-fēng-sàng-tǎn** on hearing the wind [of the enemy's coming] one becomes terrified (panicky, cowardly, nervous)

闻过则喜 **wén-kuò-tsé-hsǐ** to be pleased to hear of one's mistakes (to receive criticism gladly)

闻名 **wén-míng** famous, renowned, well-known

闻所未闻 **wén-sǒ-wèi-wén** to hear what has never been heard before (unheard of, most unusual, extraordinary)

2416 蚊子 **wén-tzu** the mosquito (one of the **szù-hài**)

wěn (wěn)

2417　吻合　**wěn-hó** to harmonize, match with, coordinate, correspond, tally

2418　稳扎稳打　**wěn-chā-wěn-tǎ** to take a firm position and deliver a sure blow (to advance methodically, slow and sure progress)

稳健　**wěn-chièn** firm and steady, stable (as contrasted with rash or whimsical)

稳住敌人　**wěn-chù tí-jén** to immobilize the enemy

稳产高产　**wěn-ch'ǎn kāo-ch'ǎn** steady production and high yield (the goal of conservancy measures to reduce dependence on rainfall)

稳产高产田　**wěn-ch'ǎn kāo-ch'ǎn t'ién** stable and high-yield fields (*see above*)

稳步　**wěn-pù** steady steps; steadily

稳步前进　**wěn-pù ch'ién-chìn** to proceed by steady steps; steady advance

稳步上升　**wěn-pù shàng-shēng** to move up by steady steps; steady promotion

稳定　**wěn-tìng** stable, steady, firm, fixed; to stabilize, steady

稳妥　**wěn-t'ǒ** safe and appropriate, secure and dependable, reliable, safe

wèn (wèn)

2419　问题　**wèn-t'í** a question, problem, matter [for concern], an affair, issue, dispute

问题不大　**wèn-t'í pù-tà** the problem is not great (it can be done)

问题的关键　**wèn-t'í te kuān-chièn** the key [to the solution] of a problem

问题的实质　**wèn-t'í te shíh-chìh** the substance of a problem (the actual point at issue)

wō (wō)

2420　涡轮机　**wō-lún-chī** a turbine

2421　窝工　**wō-kūng** to cause workers to be idle (to waste manpower, employ more workers than necessary)

窝工待料　**wō-kūng tài-liào** to have workers idle awaiting materials

窝窝囊囊　**wō-wō-nāng-nāng** stupid and cowardly, faint-hearted, good-for-nothing

窝窝头　**wō-wō-t'óu** a steamed muffin (usually of corn meal or other cheap cereals)

wò (wò)

2422　卧车　**wò-ch'ē** a sleeping car [on a train]

卧薪尝胆　**wò-hsīn-ch'áng-tǎn** to lie on faggots and taste gall (to nurse a vengeance; to goad oneself)

2423　渥太华　**wò-t'ài-huá** Ottawa [Canada]

2424　斡旋　**wò-hsúan** to mediate, conciliate, intercede, use one's good offices

wū (wū)

2425　乌七八糟　**wū-ch'ī-pā-tsāo** black seven and disordered eight (in total disorder, pandemonium; messy, untidy)

乌合之众　**wū-hó-chīh-chùng** a mass of people assembled like crows (an undisciplined mob, rabble)

乌干达　**wū-kān-tá** Uganda

乌拉圭　**wū-lā-kuēi** Uruguay

乌兰牧骑　**wū-lán mù-ch'í** red cultural team [Mongolian] (a traveling cultural group performing for herdsmen and villagers in Inner Mongolia)

乌兰巴托　**wū-lán-pā-t'ǒ** Ulan Bator [the capital of Outer Mongolia—formerly Urga]

乌鲁木齐　**wū-lǔ-mù-ch'í** Urumchi [the capital of Sinkiang—formerly Tihwa]

乌松布拉　**wū-sūng-pù-lā** Usumbura [Burundi]

乌托邦　**wū-t'ǒ-pāng** utopia; utopian

乌托邦社会主义　**wū-t'ǒ-pāng shè-huì-chǔ-ì** utopian socialism

乌孜别克族　**wū-tzū-piéh-k'ò-tsú** the Uzbek people (a minority in Sinkiang: population 11,000 as of 1957)

乌烟瘴气　**wū-yēn-chàng-ch'ì** black smoke and pestilential vapors (heavily polluted, noisome; corruption, confusion)

乌云乱翻　**wū-yún-luàn-fān** black clouds turbulently rolling (a threatening situation)

2426　污浊　**wū-chó** dirty, muddy, filthy, unclean

污染　**wū-jǎn** to pollute, contaminate, soil, taint; pollution

污蔑　**wū-mièh** to libel, slander, malign, vilify, defame, revile, desecrate

污泥浊水　**wū-ní-chó-shuǐ** mud and sewage (things which are backward, corrupt, or reactionary)

污水处理　**wū-shuǐ-ch'ǔ-lǐ** treatment of polluted water, sewage treatment

污毒　**wū-tú** filth and poison (often figurative)

2427　巫师　**wū-shīh** a sorcerer, wizard, witch

2428　诬告　**wū-kào** to accuse falsely, bring a false charge against; a false accusation

诬赖　**wū-lài** to accuse falsely, slander, shift the blame to

诬蔑 **wū-mièh** to calumniate, spread lies about, slander; calumny

2429 屋檐 **wū-yén** the eaves of a house

2430 钨砂 **wū-shā** wolframite [tungsten] ore

wú (wú)

2431 无碍大局 **wú-ài tà-chú** without hindrance of the broad [national] interest, without effect on the overall situation

无政府主义 **wú-chèng-fǔ-chǔ-ì** anarchism

无政府状态 **wú-chèng-fǔ chuàng-t'ài** a condition of anarchy, anarchy; anarchical

无稽之谈 **wú-chī-chīh-t'án** an unfounded statement, wild rumors, baseless gossip, foolish talk

无记名投票 **wú-chì-míng t'óu-p'iào** a secret ballot

无际 **wú-chì** limitless, boundless

无济于事 **wú-chì-yú-shìh** of no avail in the matter, of no help, useless, inadequate

无价宝 **wú-chià-pǎo** a priceless treasure, invaluable asset; very precious

无坚不摧 **wú-chiēn-pù-ts'uī** there is nothing so strong that [it] cannot be broken (very powerful)

无知 **wú-chīh** without knowledge, ignorant, stupid

无精打采 **wú-chīng-tǎ-ts'ǎi** to lack spirit [and] withdraw one's interest (listless, inert, discouraged, apathetic, exhausted)

无中生有 **wú-chūng-shēng-yǔ** to make something out of nothing (to fabricate, imagine, invent)

无产者 **wú-ch'ǎn-chě** the propertyless, the proletariat; a proletarian

无产阶级 **wú-ch'ǎn-chiēh-chí** the proletariat

无产阶级政治 **wú-ch'ǎn-chiēh-chí chèng-chìh** proletarian politics

无产阶级政治挂帅 **wú-ch'ǎn-chiēh-chí chèng-chìh kuà-shuài** proletarian politics takes command

无产阶级政治自觉 **wú-ch'ǎn-chiēh-chí chèng-chìh tzù-chuéh** the political consciousness of the proletariat, proletarian political consciousness

无产阶级政权 **wú-ch'ǎn-chiēh-chí chèng-ch'üán** proletarian political power, a proletarian regime

无产阶级政党 **wú-ch'ǎn-chiēh-chí chèng-tǎng** the political party of the proletariat (a Communist party)

无产阶级纪律 **wú-ch'ǎn-chiēh-chí chì-lù** proletarian discipline

无产阶级教育革命 **wú-ch'ǎn-chiēh-chí chiào-yù kó-mìng** the proletarian educational revolution

无产阶级教育路线 **wú-ch'ǎn-chiēh-chí chiào-yù lù-hsièn** the proletarian educational line, the line of proletarian education

无产阶级专政 **wú-ch'ǎn-chiēh-chí chuān-chèng** the dictatorship of the proletariat

无产阶级先锋队 **wú-ch'ǎn-chiēh-chí hsiēn-fēng-tuì** the vanguard of the proletariat (the Communist Party)

无产阶级学风 **wú-ch'ǎn-chiēh-chí hsuéh-fēng** the proletarian style of study

无产阶级感情 **wú-ch'ǎn-chiēh-chí kǎn-ch'íng** proletarian feelings, proletarian sympathies

无产阶级革命 **wú-ch'ǎn-chiēh-chí kó-mìng** proletarian revolution, the revolution of the proletariat

无产阶级革命接班人 **wú-ch'ǎn-chiēh-chí kó-mìng chiēh-pān-jén** proletarian revolutionary successors, successors to the revolution of the proletariat

无产阶级革命接班人的五个条件 **wú-ch'ǎn-chiēh-chí kó-mìng chiēh-pān-jén te wǔ-ko t'iáo-chièn** the five conditions for being a proletarian successor (*see* **wǔ-kò t'iáo-chièn**)

无产阶级革命路线 **wú-ch'ǎn-chiēh-chí kó-mìng-lù-hsièn** the line of the proletarian revolution, the proletarian revolutionary line

无产阶级革命派 **wú-ch'ǎn-chiēh-chí kó-mìng-p'ài** the revolutionary group of the proletariat, revolutionary elements of the proletariat

无产阶级革命事业 **wú-ch'ǎn-chiēh-chí kó-mìng shìh-yèh** the revolutionary cause of the proletariat; the cause of the proletarian revolution

无产阶级革命事业接班人 **wú-ch'ǎn-chiēh-chí kó-mìng shìh-yèh chiēh-pān-jén** the successors of the proletarian revolutionary cause [endeavor]

无产阶级革命党 **wú-ch'ǎn-chiēh-chí kó-mìng-tǎng** the revolutionary party of the proletariat

无产阶级革命队伍 **wú-ch'ǎn-chiēh-chí kó-mìng tuì-wǔ** the revolutionary ranks of the proletariat; the forces of the proletarian revolution

无产阶级革命文艺路线 **wú-ch'ǎn-chiēh-chí kó-mìng wén-ì lù-hsièn** the revolutionary literary line of the proletariat; the literary line of the proletarian revolution

无产阶级国际主义 **wú-ch'ǎn-chiēh-chí kuó-chí-chǔ-ì** proletarian inter-

nationalism

无产阶级国际主义原则 **wú-ch'ǎn-chiēh-chí kuó-chì-chǔ-ì yuán-tsè** the principle of proletarian internationalism

无产阶级暴力革命 **wú-ch'ǎn-chiēh-chí pào-lì kó-mìng** the catastrophic revolution of the proletariat

无产阶级世界革命 **wú-ch'ǎn-chiēh-chí shìh-chièh kó-mìng** the world revolution of the proletariat, the worldwide proletarian revolution

无产阶级世界观 **wú-ch'ǎn-chiēh-chí shìh-chièh-kuān** the proletarian world view

无产阶级党性 **wú-ch'ǎn-chiēh-chí tǎng-hsìng** the proletarian party spirit

无产阶级文化大革命 **wú-ch'ǎn-chiēh-chí wén-huà tà kó-mìng** the Great Proletarian Cultural Revolution (literally: the great revolution [to establish] a proletarian culture)

无产阶级文艺革命 **wú-ch'ǎn-chiēh-chí wén-ì kó-mìng** the proletarian literary revolution; the revolution in proletarian literature and art

无产阶级文艺路线 **wú-ch'ǎn-chiēh-chí wén-ì lù-hsièn** the line of proletarian literature and art

无产阶级英雄形象 **wú-ch'ǎn-chiēh-chí yīng-hsiúng hsíng-hsiàng** the image of the proletarian hero, the heroic image of the proletariat

无偿 **wú-ch'áng** without payment, uncompensated, free

无偿经援 **wú-ch'áng chīng-yuán** gratis economic aid, economic aid without compensation

无期徒刑 **wú-ch'ī t'ú-hsíng** life imprisonment (may be imprisonment for an indefinite period)

无耻之徒 **wú-ch'ǐ-chīh-t'ú** a shameless fellow

无耻谰言 **wú-ch'ǐh lán-yén** shameless and irresponsible talk

无情打击 **wú-ch'íng tǎ-chī** a merciless attack; to strike a merciless blow

无穷无尽 **wú-ch'iúng-wú-chìn** endless, boundless, limitless, interminable

无冲突论 **wú-ch'ūng-t'ū lùn** the doctrine that there are no longer conflicts (a tendency charged against some writers during the Cultural Revolution of reducing the emphasis on class struggle and other social conflicts)

无权过问 **wú-ch'üán kuò-wèn** without right to question, having no authority intervene (not within one's jurisdiction)

无法可依 **wú-fǎ k'ǒ-ī** [there is] no law

to be relied on

无法投递 **wú-fǎ t'óu-tì** an undeliverable [letter] (dead letter)

无法无天 **wú-fǎ wú-t'iēn** without law and without gods (devoid of conscience and respect for law; anarchy)

无非 **wú-fēi** nothing but, no other than, only this, merely

无风起浪 **wú-fēng-ch'ǐ-làng** to create waves without wind (to stir up trouble out of nothing)

无缝钢管 **wú-fèng kāng-kuǎn** seamless steel tubing, seamless steel pipe

无核区 **wú-hó-ch'ǖ** a nuclear-free zone

无核国家 **wú-hó kuó-chiā** non-nuclear countries

无后顾之忧 **wú hòu-kù chīh yū** without fear of an attack from the rear

无隙之乘 **wú-hsì-k'ǒ-ch'éng** there is no gap that can be utilized (to have no vulnerability that can be exploited)

无懈可击 **wú-hsièh-k'ǒ-chī** no negligence that can be attacked (invulnerable, impregnable, unassailable, unimpeachable)

无限忠心 **wú-hsièn chūng-hsīn** boundless loyalty, absolute loyalty

无限关怀 **wú-hsièn kuān-huái** limitless concern, unlimited sympathy

无限上纲 **wú-hsièn shàng-kāng** unlimited escalation [of accusations] (to inflate small matters into accusations of serious offenses so as to incriminate a person or group)

无线电 **wú-hsièn-tièn** a radio, wireless

无线电传真 **wú-hsièn-tièn ch'uán-chēn** a radio facsimile, radiophoto

无线电控制 **wú-hsièn-tièn k'ùng-chìh** radio control

无线电导航 **wú-hsièn-tièn tǎo-háng** radio navigation

无线电测向仪 **wú-hsièn-tièn ts'è-hsiàng-í** a radio direction finder, radio locator

无形 **wú-hsíng** without shape or form, invisible, intangible

无一漏网 **wú-ī lòu-wǎng** no one gets through the net (no escape)

无依无靠 **wú-ī wú-k'ào** [with] no one to turn to or rely on (alone and helpless, to have no family)

无疑 **wú-í** doubtless, undoubtedly, unquestionably

无以自解 **wú-ī-tzù-chièh** there is no way to explain oneself (unable to excuse [defend] oneself)

无意 **wú-ì** unintentionally, unexpectedly

无意识 **wú-ì-shíh** unconsciously; the subconscious

无人过问 **wú-jén kuò-wèn** nobody asks

about it (nobody cares; long neglected)

无辜 **wú-kū** innocent, guiltless; the innocent

无故 **wú-kù** without cause, without reason, groundless, uncalled for

无怪 **wú-kuài** no wonder that, not strange, nothing extraordinary; naturally

无关紧要 **wú-kuān chǐn-yào** of no importance, without significance, insignificant, inconsequential

无关大局 **wú-kuān tà-chú** not related to the overall situation

无关痛痒 **wú-kuān t'ùng-yǎng** it does not cause [one] any pain or itch (of no consequence, of no importance)

无轨电车 **wú-kuěi-tièn-ch'ē** a trackless tram, trolley bus

无攻不克 **wú-kūng-pù-k'ò** no assault without capturing [the objective] (no battle was lost; invincible)

无可争辩 **wú-k'ǒ-chēng-pièn** indisputable, irrefutable, incontestable

无可置疑 **wú-k'ǒ-chìh-í** there is nothing to be doubted (conclusive)

无可讳言 **wú-k'ǒ-huì-yén** no way to avoid mentioning (undeniable, beyond question, impossible to gloss over)

无可奈何 **wú-k'ǒ-nài-hó** having no alternative, it cannot be helped (hopeless, irremediable)

无可比拟 **wú-k'ǒ-pǐ-nǐ** there is nothing comparable [to this] (incomparable, without precedent)

无愧 **wú-k'uèi** nothing to be ashamed of (with clear conscience)

无孔不入 **wú-k'ǔng-pù-jù** nọ hole not entered (to exploit every loophole, to serve one's own interest by every device)

无赖 **wú-lài** a scoundrel, rascal; scandalous

无理取闹 **wú-lǐ-ch'ǔ-nào** to make trouble without a cause, quarrel without provocation

无立锥之地 **wú lì-chuī chǐh tì** without enough land to insert an awl [in] (landless, poverty-stricken)

无利可图 **wú-lì k'ǒ-t'ú** without any profit to be gained (profitless)

无聊 **wú-liáo** dejected, unhappy, listless, indifferent; boring, tasteless, uninteresting; boredom, ennui

无路可走 **wú-lù k'ǒ-tsǒu** no road that can be taken (no way out, in a hopeless situation, at a dead end)

无论如何 **wú-lùn-jú-hó** no matter what, in any case, come what may, anyway,

under all circumstances

无米之炊 **wú-mǐ-chǐh-ch'uī** to cook a meal without rice (to attempt the impossible; to lack the bare essentials)

无名小卒 **wú-míng hsiǎo-tsú** a nameless soldier (a nobody, person of little importance)

无能为力 **wú-néng-wéi-lì** unable to exert one's strength (unable to help, powerless to do anything)

无恶不作 **wú-ò-pù-tsò** [there is] no evil one would not do (capable of any possible crime; thoroughly evil)

无保留的 **wú-pǎo-liú-te** without reservation; unreservedly, unconditionally

无本之木 **wú-pěn-chǐh-mù** a tree without roots (something without foundation)

无比优越性 **wú-pǐ yū-yuèh-hsìng** incomparable superiority

无标题音乐 **wú piāo-t'í yīn-yuèh** nonprogrammatic music (music characterized by form or tempo, rather than theme or content)

无兵司令 **wú-pīng szū-lìng** a commander without an army

无病呻吟 **wú-pìng shēn-yín** to groan without being ill (to complain without cause; affected sentimentality)

无上 **wú-shàng** nothing higher, the highest (unsurpassed, matchless)

无神论 **wú-shén-lùn** atheism

无声无色 **wú-shēng wú-sè** no sound and no color (drab and unexciting, impassive)

无时无刻 **wú-shíh wú-k'ò** [there is] no time and no moment [that something is not done] (at all times, constantly, always)

无时无地 **wú-shíh wú-tì** [there is] no time and no place [where something is not being done] (every minute and everywhere, at all times and places)

无事生非 **wú-shìh-shēng-fēi** to make trouble out of nothing (intentionally to create trouble)

无视 **wú-shìh** not wishing to see (to consider unimportant, show contempt, undervalue, slight, ignore)

无数 **wú-shù** innumerable, countless, numberless

无双 **wú-shuāng** without equal, unmatched, peerless

无霜期 **wú-shuāng-ch'ī** the frost-free period

无所逞其技 **wú-sǒ ch'ěng ch'í-chì** unable to use one's tricks (to be frustrated)

无所顾忌 **wú-sǒ kù-chì** to have nothing

one fears (to have no scruples; unscrupulous)

无所不至 **wú-sǒ-pù-chìh** [there is] no place that has not been reached (1. ubiquitous, omnipresent; omnipresence; 2. very thorough, extremely attentive)

无所不在 **wú-sǒ pù-tsài** no place where it is not present (ubiquity, omnipresence)

无所不用其极 **wú-sǒ pù-yùng ch'í-chí** there is nothing in which extreme measures are not used (to go to any ends, to be relentless in every endeavor)

无所事事 **wú-sǒ shìh-shìh** to not do a thing (to loaf around, be idle)

无所适从 **wú-sǒ shìh-ts'úng** to not know whom to follow (to not know what to do; helpless, at a loss, bewildered)

无所作为 **wú-sǒ-tsò-wéi** to be without accomplishment, without achievement

无所措手足 **wú-sǒ ts'ò shǒu-tsú** to be unable to employ the hands and feet (at a loss as to what to do, bewildered, confused)

无所畏惧 **wú-sǒ wèi-chù** to fear nothing at all, have no worries; nothing to fear

无所用心 **wú-sǒ yùng-hsīn** to be completely inattentive, entirely unconcerned

无私援助 **wú-szū yuán-chù** selfless aid, altruistic support

无党派人物 **wú-tǎng-p'ài jén-wù** nonparty personages, public figures without party affiliation

无敌于天下 **wú-tí yǘ t'iēn-hsià** unmatched in the world, unrivaled, the strongest, peerless, invincible

无底洞 **wú-tǐ-tùng** a bottomless pit (desires or a need that can never be filled)

无的放矢 **wú-tì-fàng-shǐh** to shoot an arrow without a target (premature or foolish activity)

无独有偶 **wú-tú-yǔ-ǒu** not singly but a pair (most things, especially bad events or people, come in pairs)

无端 **wú-tuān** without cause, for no reason, groundless, unprovoked unjustified

无动于衷 **wú-tùng-yǘ-chūng** not moved in the heart (unconcerned, apathetic, callous; to be unmoved, stand pat)

无条件 **wú-t'iáo-chièn** without conditions, unconditional, unqualified, absolute

无足轻重 **wú-tsú-ch'īng-chùng** insufficient to carry any weight (of no appreciable importance, of no consequence)

无往不胜 **wú-wǎng-pù-shèng** to go nowhere without victory (to be successful in every endeavor)

无微不至 **wú-wēi-pù-chìh** not [even the] smallest [detail] unreached (with utmost care, very thoughtful, thorough, meticulous)

无谓 **wú-wèi** meaningless, senseless

无影无踪 **wú-yǐng-wú-tsūng** without shadow or clue (without a trace; to vanish, disappear)

无原则 **wú-yuán-tsé** without principles; unprincipled

无原子武器区 **wú-yuán-tzǔ wǔ-ch'ì ch'ǖ** a zone without atomic weapons, atom-free zone

无源之水 **wú-yuán-chīh-shuǐ** a river without a source (something having no foundation)

无用 **wú-yùng** useless, worthless

wǔ (wǔ)

五爱教育 **wǔ-ài-chiào-yù** Five-Loves Education (to inculcate love for: the motherland, the people, labor, science, and public property)

五角大楼 **wǔ-chiǎo-tà-lóu** the Pentagon [Washington, D.C.]

五节一储 **wǔ-chiéh ī-ch'ǔ** the Five Economies and One Saving (the economies: grain, coal, water, electricity, and birth control; the saving: savings accounts)

五节运动 **wǔ-chiéh yùn-tùng** the Five Austerities Movement (to save: water, electricity, rice, coal, and cloth; popularized in 1957)

五金 **wǔ-chīn** the five metals [gold, silver, copper, iron and tin]; metals in general; hardware

五七指示 **wǔ-ch'ī chǐh-shìh** The May 7 Instruction (a statement by Mao Tse-tung on May 7, 1966, calling for the PLA, workers, peasants, and students to learn some capability in the main fields outside their own)

五七一工程纪要 **wǔ-ch'ī-ī kūng-ch'éng chì-yào** the "Outline of Project 571" (the alleged plan for a coup by Lin Piao in 1971: "571" is presumed to be an allusion to "armed uprising"— **wǔ**-[chuāng] ch'ī-ì 武(装)起义)

五七干校 **wǔ-ch'ī kàn-hsiào** May 7 cadre schools (schools established in late 1968 where cadres were sent to

do manual work and study Mao's Thought [see **wǔ-ch'ǐ chíh-shìh** *above*])

五气 **wǔ-ch'ì** the Five Airs (attitudes to be avoided: bureaucratic, apathetic, extravagant, arrogant, and finicky)

五反 **wǔ-fǎn** the Five-Anti [Movement] (an important movement, begun in 1952 to oppose: bribery; tax evasion; theft of state property; skimping on work and cheating on materials; theft of state economic information)

五分制 **wǔ-fēn-chìh** the five-part grading system (a system of grading students from 1 to 5, now abandoned)

五风不正 **wǔ-fēng-pù-chèng** the Five [Work] Styles [which are] Incorrect (cadre tendencies criticized during the Socialist Education Campaign: absolute egalitarianism; commandism; maladministration; exaggeration of production figures; claiming special prerogatives)

五害 **wǔ-hài** the Five Pests (flies, mosquitoes, fleas, sparrows, and rats; bedbugs were subsequently included and sparrows deleted)

五好 **wǔ-hǎo** the Five Goods (usually refers to the **wǔ-hǎo yùn-tùng**, and may include differing five-goods for many different groups such as: army, communes, factories, students, collectives, etc.)

五好战士 **wǔ-hǎo chàn-shìh** a Five-Good Soldier (good in: ideology; military techniques; three-eight work style; carrying out assigned tasks; and physical training)

五好集体 **wǔ-hǎo-chí-t'ǐ** a Five-Good Collective

五好车间 **wǔ-hǎo ch'ē-chiēn** a Five-Good Workshop

五好妇女 **wǔ-hǎo fù-nǚ** a Five-Good Woman (good in: neighborly relations; family health care; cleanliness; economical management; self-improvement through study)

五好学生 **wǔ-hǎo hsuéh-shēng** a Five-Good Student

五好公社 **wǔ-hǎo kūng-shè** a Five-Good Commune

五好标准 **wǔ-hǎo piāo-chǔn** the Five-Good Standards (criteria established for cadres engaged in commune rectification in late 1958: (1) good results in commune rectification; (2) respect for local cadres; (3) good relations with commune members; (4) accurate in investigation and summing up experiences; (5) good in

thought reform)

五好运动 **wǔ-hǎo yùn-tùng** the Five-Good Movement (a general movement, commenced in late 1958, setting up criteria or standards for various groups such as the PLA, communes, schools, etc.)

五湖四海 **wǔ-hú szù-hǎi** the five lakes and four seas (usually China, but may also refer to the world)

五花八门 **wǔ-huā-pā-mén** five flowers and eight categories (full of tricks; many changes)

五项原则 **wǔ-hsiàng yuán-tsé** the Five Principles [of Peaceful Coexistence] (set forth by Chou En-lai at the Bandung Conference in April 1955)

五小工业 **wǔ-hsiǎo kūng-yèh** the Five Small Industries (industries which communes are encouraged to operate on a local, small-scale basis: iron, cement, coal mining, electrical generation; chemical fertilizer)

五星红旗 **wǔ-hsīng húng-ch'í** the five-starred red flag (the national flag)

五一国际劳动节 **wǔ-ī kuó-chì láo-tùng-chiéh** the May First International Labor Day

五一六指示 **wǔ-ī-liù chǐh-shìh** The May 16 Instruction (a Central Committee order, issued by Mao Tse-tung on May 16, 1966, dissolving P'eng Chen's group and establishing a new "Cultural Revolution Small Group," eventually headed by Ch'en Po-ta and Mao's wife, Chiang Ch'ing)

五一六分子 **wǔ-ī-liù fèn-tzǔ** May 16 elements (radicals, claiming to base themselves on Mao's directive of May 16, 1966, who came under attack in the later phase of the Cultural Revolution for anarchistic and nihilistic tendencies)

五一六兵团 **wǔ-ī-liù pīng-t'uán** the May 16 Corps (an alleged organization of ultra-leftist groups in the Cultural Revolution, later accused of active opposition to Chou En-lai and Mao Tse-tung)

五一六通知 **wǔ-ī-liù t'ūng-chīh** the May 16 Notification (also referred to as the May 16 Instruction: *see* **wǔ-ī-liù chǐh-shìh** *above*)

五人小组 **wǔ-jén hsiǎo-tsǔ** the Five-Man Group (set up under the leadership of P'eng Chen in late 1965 to conduct the Cultural Revolution; dissolved by Mao's instruction of May 16, 1966)

五改 **wǔ-kǎi** the Five Improvements

(to better living conditions in the countryside, peasants were urged to improve: wells supplying drinking water; privies; animal pens; stoves; and the surroundings)

五个一定 **wǔ-ko-ī-tìng** the Five Musts (part of Yang Han-shen's 1962 characterization of strictures on writers; they must: deal with significant themes, write about heroic characters, engage in collective writing; finish within a set time; receive the approval of the leadership)

五个一样运动 **wǔ-ko ī-yàng yùn-tùng** the Five-Sames Movement (rural cadres in 1960 were expected to be on the same basis as the peasants in: food and living conditions; physical labor; work points; pay; and treatment of their own families)

五个不敢 **wǔ-ko-pù-kǎn** the Five Dare-Nots (part of Yang Han-shen's characterization of strictures on writers; they dare not: deal with internal contradictions among the people, particularly between the leaders and the led; write satirical dramas; write tragedy; write about faults or defeats of heroes; mention the defects of Party members or leadership)

五个条件 **wǔ-ko t'iáo-chièn** the Five Requisites [for revolutionary successors] (they must be: true Marxist-Leninists; determined to serve the people of China and the great majority of the world; able to unite with and lead the proletariat; able to listen to the masses; and willing to criticize themselves and correct their mistakes)

五谷 **wǔ-kǔ** the five cereals (rice, wheat, kaoliang, millet, beans)

五光十色 **wǔ-kuāng shíh-sè** five lights and ten colors (gay with variegated colors; colorful)

五过硬 **wǔ-kuò-yìng** the Five Toughnesses (ideology; physical fitness; mastering skills; arduous training; and doing one's utmost; originally a PLA training slogan, later applied to other fields)

五老 **wǔ-lǎo** the Five Elders (five old, non-military, members of the Party who are highly respected: Hsu T'eh-li, Lin Pai-ch'ü, Hsieh Chüeh-tsai, Wu Yü-chang, and Tung Pi-wu)

五类分子 **wǔ-lèi fèn-tzǔ** the five-category elements (landlords, rich peasants, counter-revolutionaries, bad elements, and rightists; also known as **hēi-wǔ-lèi**)

五年计划 **wǔ-nién chì-huà** a Five-Year Plan (there have been several Five-Year Plans with dates believed to be: First, 1953–1957; Second, 1958–1962; Third, 1966–1970; and Fourth, 1971–1975)

五年试验，十年推广 **wǔ-nién shìh-yèn, shíh-nién t'uī-kuǎng** five years of trial and ten years of popularization (a 1965 phrase regarding the steady and cautious application of the half-work, half-study educational reforms)

五保 **wǔ-pǎo** the Five Guarantees (pledges to members of the advanced cooperatives and communes: food, clothing, fuel, education of children, and proper burial)

五保户 **wǔ-pǎo-hù** households enjoying the Five Guarantees (commune members—*see above*)

五边 **wǔ-piēn** the Five Alongsides (persons engaged in the **yàng-pǎn-hsì** are also urged, concurrently with their regular work, to: engage in labor, write, research, help and guide, engage in propaganda)

五卅惨案 **wǔ-sā ts'ǎn-àn** the May 30 Massacre (the incident in Shanghai on May 30, 1925, when the Municipal Council police shot into a crowd of strikers and students, killing twelve)

五卅运动 **wǔ-sā yùn-tùng** the May 30 Movement (a nationwide movement in 1925 to protest the May 30 Incident—*see above*)

五四运动 **wǔ-szù yùn-tùng** the May Fourth Movement (a general term for the broad political and intellectual currents arising from Peking student demonstrations on May 4, 1919, against the China provisions of the Versailles Treaty)

五大减少 **wǔ-tà-chiěn-shǎo** the Five Big Reductions (a rural campaign in the pre-commune period to reduce: purchase and sale of land; grain hoarding; hired labor; renting of land; speculation)

五大件 **wǔ-tà-chièn** the Five Big Articles (consumer goods indicative of a good standard of living: wristwatch, camera, bicycle, radio, and sewing machine)

五大洲 **wǔ-tà-chōu** the five continents (the world)

五大运动 **wǔ-tà-yùn-tùng** the five great

movements (Land Reform; Resist the U.S. and Aid Korea; Suppression of Counter-revolutionaries; Three-Anti and Five-Anti; Thought Reform)

五定 **wŭ-tìng** the Five Decisions (A. Before establishing new schools in rural areas, there should be decisions on: leadership, instructors, system, location, and activities. B. At the beginning of the farm year, commune units should decide: area to be sown, cost, output, quality, and total wages)

五多五少 **wŭ-tō wŭ-shǎo** the Five Too-Many and Five Too-Few (a radical slogan in 1967 criticizing the too many people who wished to: preside at meetings, ride in motorcars, sit in their office, attend operas, hold commemorative meetings; and the too few who were interested in: study, labor, struggle-criticism-transformation, contacting the masses, and having a rebel spirit)

五毒 **wŭ-tú** the Five Poisons (traditionally: snakes, scorpions, toads, lizards, and centipedes—now it refers to the **wŭ-fǎn**)

五体投地 **wŭ-t'ĭ-t'óu-tì** the five members [of the body: head, two hands, and two knees] fall to the earth (to recognize the superiority of another's position—especially in intellectual or technical matters)

五同 **wŭ-t'úng** the Five Togethers (as part of Mao Tse-tung's policy of revolution in education [1967], teachers should engage together with students in: study, struggle, military drill, physical labor, and recreation)

五灾 **wŭ-tsāi** the Five [Natural] Calamities (drought, water-logging, alkalinity, wind, and sand)

五脏俱全 **wŭ-tsàng-chù-ch'üán** [even though the sparrow is small] all its five organs are complete

五彩缤纷 **wŭ-ts'āi-pīn-fēn** many-colored and luxuriant (colorful and beautiful)

五次反围攻 **wŭ-tz'ù fǎn-wéi-kūng** the five counter-encirclements (the defense against the five KMT encirclement campaigns against the Kiangsi Republic, 1930–1934)

五位一体 **wŭ-wèi i-t'ĭ** five positions [in] one body (a reference to the commune, which combines the functions of agriculture, industry, commerce, education, and militia)

五业 **wŭ-yèh** the Five Occupations (the chief non-industrial occupations: agriculture, forestry, livestock, fisheries, and sideline occupations)

武装 **wŭ-chuāng** to arm, equip with weapons; armed; arms, armament; armed forces, militia (figurative: armed with [Marxism-Leninism and the Thought of Mao Tse-tung])

武装政变 **wŭ-chuāng chèng-pièn** a military coup d'etat, armed insurrection

武装基干民兵 **wŭ-chuāng chī-kàn mín-pīng** the armed backbone militia

武装较量 **wŭ-chuāng chiǎo-liàng** relative strength of armed forces, a test of military strength

武装进攻 **wŭ-chuāng chìn-kūng** an armed attack; to attack with military forces

武装起义 **wŭ-chuāng ch'ĭ-ì** an armed uprising (usually in a righteous cause)

武装侵略 **wŭ-chuāng ch'īn-luèh** armed aggression, military aggression

武装革命左派 **wŭ-chuāng kó-mìng tsŏ-p'ài** to arm the revolutionary leftists; armed revolutionary leftists

武装工作队 **wŭ-chuāng kūng-tsò-tuì** an armed work detachment (small, cadre-led armed units in the guerrilla areas during the Resistance War)

武装暴动 **wŭ-chuāng pào-tùng** an armed insurrection, armed rebellion

武装叛乱 **wŭ-chuāng p'àn-luàn** armed rebellion, armed revolt

武装到牙齿 **wŭ-chuāng tào yá-ch'ĭh** armed to the teeth

武装颠覆 **wŭ-chuāng tiēn-fù** armed subversion

武装夺取政权 **wŭ-chuāng tó-ch'ŭ chèng-ch'üán** to seize political power by armed force

武装斗争 **wŭ-chuāng tòu-chēng** armed struggle

武装挑衅 **wŭ-chuāng t'iǎo-hsìn** armed provocation

武装自卫 **wŭ-chuāng tzù-wèi** armed self-defense

武器 **wŭ-ch'ì** a weapon, arms, armament, ordnance (figuratively: the Thought of Mao Tse-tung)

武汉长江大桥 **wŭ-hàn ch'áng-chiāng tà-ch'iáo** the Yangtse River Bridge at Wuhan (completed in 1957)

武汉钢铁公司 **wŭ-hàn kāng-t'ĭěh kūng-szū** the Wuhan Iron and Steel Corporation

武汉部队 **wŭ-hàn pù-tuì** the Wuhan Military Forces [of the PLA] (formerly, the Wuhan Military Region)

武训传 **wǔ hsùn chuàn** "The Life of Wu Hsun" (a popular film criticized by Mao Tse-tung in 1951 as advocating bourgeois reformism)

武钢 **wǔ-kāng** the Wuhan Iron and Steel Corporation (contraction of **wǔ-hàn kāng-t'iěh kūng-szū**)

武关和文关 **wǔ-kuān hó wén-kuān** the military ordeal and cultural ordeal (the experience of armed revolutionary struggle and ideological testing during the Cultural Revolution)

武官 **wǔ-kuān** a military attaché [in an embassy]; a military officer

武工队 **wǔ-kūng-tuì** armed work detachments (small, cadre-led armed units in the guerrilla areas during the Resistance War—contraction of **wǔ-chuāng kūng-tsò-tuì**)

武功 **wǔ-kūng** military merits, fighting skills, martial arts

武库 **wǔ-k'ù** an armory, arsenal, weapon storehouse (often figurative)

武力解决 **wǔ-lì chiěh-chüéh** a settlement imposed by military force; to settle by force

武士道精神 **wǔ-shìh-tào chīng-shén** the Bushido spirit (the "way of the warrior," code of the Japanese samurai)

武术 **wǔ-shù** martial arts (a general term embracing various schools of stylized combat used in gymnastics, and for health and recreation)

武术表演 **wǔ-shù piǎo-yěn** a performance of martial arts, martial arts peformance

武斗 **wǔ-tòu** armed struggle, violent struggle (contrasted with **wén-tòu** during the Cultural Revolution)

武断 **wǔ-tuàn** to decide arbitrarily; an arbitrary decision; arbitrary, dogmatic, unreasonable

武卫 **wǔ-wèi** armed defense; to defend with force

2434 侮辱 **wǔ-jǔ** to insult, humiliate, dishonor, disgrace

侮谩 **wǔ-màn** to be rude to, insulting and rude

2435 舞剧 **wǔ-chù** a ballet, dance-drama (generally used in preference to **pā-léi-wǔ**)

舞弊 **wǔ-pì** to abuse one's official position, engage in malfeasance, accept bribes, act corruptly; corruption, bribery

舞蹈 **wǔ-tǎo** to dance; dancing

舞台 **wǔ-t'ái** a stage, theatre (often figurative)

舞台演出 **wǔ-t'ái yěn-ch'ū** to have performed on the stage (to stage, produce)

wù (wù)

2436 务虚 **wù-hsū** to give attention to the abstract [aspects] (to make political-ideological preparations for a task)

务农光荣 **wù-núng kuāng-júng** to engage in agriculture is honorable

务必 **wù-pì** must, should, by all means

务实 **wù-shíh** to attend to practical matters, strive for thoroughness

2437 物证 **wù-chèng** material evidence, physical evidence

物极必反 **wù-chí-pì-fǎn** when [something] reaches its limit, it reverses itself (when things are at their worst, they begin to mend)

物价 **wù-chià** commodity prices

物价指数 **wù-chià chǐh-shù** a commodity price index, price index

物价飞涨 **wù-chià fēi-chàng** skyrocketing prices, a sudden and sharp rise in prices

物价波动 **wù-chià pō-tùng** price fluctuations, instability of prices

物价稳定 **wù-chià wěn-tìng** stability of commodity prices, price stability

物质 **wù-chìh** matter, substance; material, physical; material goods, things

物质基础 **wù-chìh chī-ch'ǔ** material basis, physical base

物质力量 **wù-chìh lì-liàng** physical forces, material strength, tangible force

物质不灭定律 **wù-chìh pù-mièh tìng-lǜ** the law of conservation of matter

物质生活 **wù-chìh shēng-huó** material life, physical life, material well-being

物质第一性 **wù-chìh tì-ī-hsìng** the primacy of material things

物质财富 **wù-chìh ts'ái-fù** material wealth

物质刺激 **wù-chìh tz'ù-chī** material incentives

物质文明 **wù-chìh wén-míng** a material civilization, materialist culture, physical progress

物尽其用 **wù-chìn-ch'í-yùng** the utility of things should be exhausted, to use to the full

物权 **wù-ch'üán** property rights, rights over things

物候学 **wù-hòu-hsuéh** phenology (the science dealing with the relation between climate and periodic biological phenomena)

物以类聚 **wù-ǐ-lèi-chù** things group themselves by kind ("birds of a feather flock together")

物理学 **wù-lǐ-hsuéh** physics

物力 **wù-lì** material power, physical means, natural resources

物量 **wù-liàng** quantity of goods, physical volume, output

物品 **wù-p'ǐn** articles, goods, things, materials, substances

物色 **wù-sè** to select, choose, look for [talented men, etc.]; color, all kinds of goods

物体 **wù-t'ǐ** a body [in physics], object, substance

物资 **wà-tzū** materials, supplies, assets; goods, commodities

物资交流 **wù-tzū chiāo-liú** exchange of goods, interchange of commodities

物资交流会 **wù-tzū chiāo-liú-huì** a commodities exchange fair, materials exchange conference

物资储备 **wù-tzū ch'ǔ-pèi** commodity reserves, material stocks

物欲诱惑 **wù-yù yù-huò** to be led astray by the craving for material things; seduced by worldly desires

2438 误解 **wù-chiěh** to misunderstand, misconstrue, misinterpret, misinterpretation

误会 **wù-huì** a misunderstanding, misconception, misapprehension; to misapprehend

误人 **wù-jén** to mislead, misguide, lead [someone] astray

误认 **wù-jèn** to make a mistake in recognition, identify incorrectly; a mistaken recognition

误入歧途 **wù-jù-ch'í-t'ú** to take the wrong road in error, go mistakenly astray

误国 **wù-kuó** to harm the country, damage national interests (mismanage national affairs)

yā (yā)

2439 压榨 **yā-chà** (1) to oppress, exploit; oppression, exploitation; (2) to compress, squeeze, extract [liquids] by applying pressure

压制 **yā-chìh** to suppress, restrain, quash, oppress; suppression, constraint

压服 **yā-fú** to subjugate, subdue, force to submit

压抑 **yā-ì** to curb, repress, suppress

压钢厂 **yā-kāng-ch'ǎng** a steel rolling mill

压根儿 **yā-kēn-erh** totally, entirely, completely, fundamentally

压力 **yā-lì** pressure

压路机 **yā-lù-chī** a road-rolling machine, steamroller

压迫 **yā-p'ò** oppression; to oppress

压缩 **yā-sō** to compress, reduce, curtail, cut down; compression, reduction

压缩空气 **yā-sō-k'ūng-ch'ì** compressed air

压倒 **yā-tǎo** to overcome, prevail over, overpower, overwhelm, hold down, force under; win over, excel

压倒多数 **yā-tǎo-tō-shù** the overwhelming majority

压倒优势 **yā-tǎo-yū-shìh** overwhelming superiority, crushingly superior

压碗边 **yā wǎn-piēn** to put pressure on one side of the bowl (to intervene on behalf of one party in a dispute)

压延金属 **yā-yén chīn-shǔ** rolled metals

压延能力 **yā-yén néng-lì** rolling capacity

2440 鸦雀无声 **yā-ch'üèh wú-shēng** [even] the crows and sparrows [make] no sound (a dead silence, still as death)

鸦片战争 **yā-p'ièn chàn-chēng** the Opium War (1839–1842)

yá (yá)

2441 牙雕 **yá-tiāo** ivory carving

yǎ (yǎ)

2442 哑剧 **yǎ-chù** a pantomime play, mummery, mime

哑口无言 **yǎ-k'ǒu wú-yén** silent, dumbfounded, speechless

2443 雅加达 **yǎ-chiā-tá** Djakarta [Indonesia]

雅致 **yǎ-chìh** refined, genteel, delicate, elegant, tasteful

雅尔达协定 **yǎ-ěrh-tá hsiéh-tìng** the Yalta Agreement

雅谑 **yǎ-nuèh** an elegant joke

雅典 **yǎ-tiěn** Athens [Greece]

雅温得 **yǎ-wēn-té** Yaounde [Cameroon]

yà (yà)

2444 轧花 **yà-huā** to gin cotton

轧棉机 **yà-mién-chī** a cotton gin

轧棉厂 **yà-mién-ch'ǎng** a cotton ginning mill, cotton gin

轧 **yà**: *see also* chá

2445 亚洲 **yà-chōu** Asia

亚洲集体安全体系 **yà-chòu chí-t'ǐ ān-ch'üán t'ǐ-hsì** the Asia collective security system (proposed by the

USSR)

亚军 **yà-chün** the runner-up, winner of second place

亚非 **yà-fēi** Asia and Africa; Afro-Asian

亚非人民团结理事会 **yà-fēi jén-mín t'uán-chiéh lǐ-shìh-huì** Afro-Asian People's Solidarity Council

亚非拉国家 **yà-fēi-lā kuó-chiā** the countries of Asia, Africa, and Latin America

亚热带 **yà-jè-tài** the subtropics, subtropical

亚麻厂 **yà-má-ch'ǎng** a flax mill

亚庇 **yà-pì** Api [formerly known as Jesselton; the capital city of Sabah, formerly known as British North Borneo and now part of Malaysia]

亚松森 **yà-sūng-sēn** Asuncion [Paraguay]

亚的斯亚贝巴 **yà-tí-szū yà-pèi-pā** Addis Ababa [Ethiopia]

亚丁 **yà-tīng** Aden [People's Democratic Republic of Yemen]

亚运会 **yà-yùn-huì** the Asian Games

2446 揠苗助长 **yà-miáo-chù-chǎng** to pull the [rice] shoots to help them grow (to try to force growth or development by unnatural and violent means)

yāng (yāng)

2447 秧歌 **yāng-kō** the rice-sprout song (a folk-music genre, often accompanied by a simple dance, popularized by the Communists)

秧苗 **yāng-miáo** rice sprouts, rice seedlings

yáng (yáng)

2448 阳极 **yáng-chí** the anode, positive electrode

阳春白雪 **yáng-ch'ūn-pái-hsuěh** bright snow on a spring day (classical songs for an effete audience)

阳奉阴违 **yáng-fèng yīn-wéi** to overtly obey but covertly disobey (to feign compliance)

阳沟 **yáng-kōu** an open drain, exposed ditch, open sewer

阳历 **yáng-lì** the solar calendar, Gregorian calendar, Western chronology

阳谋 **yáng-móu** "an open conspiracy" (a plan openly arrived at—as contrasted with "secret conspiracy")

2449 扬场 **yáng-ch'áng** to winnow [grain]

扬眉吐气 **yáng-méi t'ǔ-ch'ì** to raise the eyebrows and blow out the breath (to be pleased with having risen from the oppressed conditions of the past)

扬水站 **yáng-shuǐ-chàn** a water pumping station

扬言 **yáng-yén** to spread the word, declare publicly, make a clamor

2450 羊城晚报 **yáng-ch'éng wǎn-pào** Canton Evening News (yang-ch'eng [City of Rams] is a legendary name for Canton)

羊圈 **yáng-chüàn** a sheepfold, sheep pen

羊绒 **yáng-júng** fine wool; angora wool

羊肚子毛巾 **yáng-tǔ-tzu máo-chīn** a terry-cloth towel (usually white and used by peasants in North China as a headcloth)

2451 杨献珍 **yáng hsièn-chēn** Yang Hsien-chen (c. 1899—, an important Party philosopher and head of the Higher Party School until 1964 when it was charged that his analysis of contradictions, stressing "two combining into one," was at variance with Mao Tse-tung's emphasis that "one divides into two," and was thus a form of revisionism)

2452 洋气 **yáng-ch'ì** foreign airs, smacking of foreign (usually suggests an uncritical preference for foreign things to things Chinese)

洋法 **yáng-fǎ** foreign methods (often used to mean modern, as contrasted with traditional or native, methods of manufacture, etc.)

洋灰 **yáng-huī** cement, portland cement

洋学堂 **yáng-hsuéh-t'áng** Western schools, modern institutions of learning (as contrasted with traditional schools: in current usage may be a criticism of the excessive reliance on foreign models)

洋镐 **yáng-kǎo** pickaxe, pick, mattock

洋框框 **yáng k'uāng-k'uāng** foreign frames (foreign ideas or models that are excessively relied on so that they restrict practical or native initiative)

洋奴哲学 **yáng-nú ché-hsuéh** a foreign slave philosophy (ideas derived from the West; an attitude of slavish imitation of the West)

洋奴爬行哲学 **yáng-nú p'á-hsíng ché-hsuéh** a foreign slave crawling philosophy (a cautious attitude of slavishly imitating foreign models instead of self-reliance and rapid progress)

洋布 **yáng-pù** foreign cloth (machine-made piece goods)

洋玩意儿 **yáng-wán-ì-erh** foreign toys (foreign things, ways, ideas, etc.—with a contemptuous connotation)

洋为中用 **yáng-wéi-chūng-yùng** to utilize foreign [things] to serve China

洋洋大观 **yáng-yáng tà-kuān** a grand sight (grand, magnificent, imposing)

洋洋得意 **yáng-yáng té-ì** copiously contented (self-contented, elated, puffed up with success)

洋油时代 **yáng-yú shíh-tài** the kerosene age (the period of Chinese dependence on foreign sources of petroleum)

yǎng (yǎng)

²⁴⁵³ 仰人鼻息 **yǎng-jén-pí-hsì** to watch another's breathing (to live at another's mercy, rely wholly on others, be entirely subservient)

仰光 **yǎng-kuāng** Rangoon [Burma]

²⁴⁵⁴ 氧气 **yǎng-ch'ì** oxygen

氧气炼钢法 **yǎng-ch'ì lièn-kāng-fǎ** the oxygen-blown steel process

²⁴⁵⁵ 养鸡场 **yǎng-chī-ch'ǎng** a chicken farm, poultry ranch

养精蓄锐 **yǎng-chīng-hsù-juì** to nourish the spirit and save vigor (to nurse one's strength, prepare for a challenging task)

养猪积肥 **yǎng-chū chī-féi** raise pigs [and] accumulate manure

养成习惯 **yǎng-ch'éng hsí-kuàn** to form into a habit, develop habits (implies the development of good habits)

养成工人 **yǎng-ch'éng kūng-jén** formative workers (who have learned simple machine skills—higher ranking than apprentices)

养儿防修 **yǎng-érh fáng-hsiū** to raise children to prevent revisionism (a turn of the old phrase that children are raised to provide support for the parent's old age: now the goal is to preserve Mao Tse-tung's revolutionary line)

养儿防老 **yǎng-érh-fáng-lǎo** to raise children to forestall [the troubles of] old age (the old philosophy of child rearing [*for the new, see above*])

养蜂场 **yǎng-fēng-ch'ǎng** a beekeeping establishment, apiary

养护维修 **yǎng-hù wéi-hsiū** upkeep and maintenance

养活 **yǎng-huó** to support life (to provide a living, bring up, support a family)

养人文艺 **yǎng-jén wén-ì** appetite-meeting literature (a view of literature—now criticized—that its function is to cater to peoples' desires rather than to serve an ideological or educational function)

养老金 **yǎng-lǎo-chīn** an old-age pension, old-age benefits

养路 **yǎng-lù** road maintenance; to keep the roads in repair

养女 **yǎng-nǚ** a foster daughter, adopted daughter (in the old society she sometimes suffered from an inferior, semi-servant status)

养蚕业 **yǎng-ts'án-yèh** the production of raw silk by raising silkworms, sericulture

养育 **yǎng-yù** to raise and educate, rear

yàng (yàng)

²⁴⁵⁶ 样板 **yàng-pǎn** a template, model, pattern, prototype, exemplar (may refer to advanced experience which is to serve as a model)

样板戏 **yàng-pǎn-hsì** the model dramas (the new-style Peking opera sponsored by Chiang Ch'ing and popularized during the Cultural Revolution)

样板田 **yàng-pǎn-t'ién** a model field (an experimental plot for demonstrating new agricultural techniques—may also be figurative)

样本 **yàng-pěn** a specimen copy, sample [of printing], test sample

样品 **yàng-p'ǐn** a sample of goods or merchandise, specimen

yāo (yāo)

²⁴⁵⁷ 夭折 **yāo-ché** to die young; premature death

²⁴⁵⁸ 妖氛 **yāo-fēn** ominous conditions, a sinister atmosphere

妖风 **yāo-fēng** a demonic wind, ill wind (heterodox ideas)

妖魔鬼怪 **yāo-mó-kuěi-kuài** monsters and ghosts, evil spirits of all kinds (a general term having political connotations referring to heterodox, evil, and monstrous people)

²⁴⁵⁹ 要挟 **yāo-hsiéh** to demand by threats, blackmail

要 **yāo**: *see also* **yào**

²⁴⁶⁰ 腰斩 **yāo-chǎn** to sever the body at the waist (to cut in two, to sever—usually figurative)

腰鼓 **yāo-kǔ** a waist drum, hip drum

²⁴⁶¹ 邀集 **yāo-chí** to invite to a gathering

邀请 **yāo-ch'ǐng** to invite; an invitation

邀请赛 **yāo-ch'ǐng-sài** an invitational
 tournament
邀功讨赏 **yāo-kūng t'ǎo-shǎng** to seek
 merit and ask for a reward (to seek
 to advance oneself)

yáo (yáo)

2462 窑洞 **yáo-tùng** homes excavated from
 loess cliffs (often called "caves")
2463 谣言 **yáo-yén** an unfounded report,
 rumors, gossip
2464 遥相呼应 **yáo-hsiāng hū-yìng** to
 respond to each other from a
 distance
遥控 **yáo-k'ùng** remote control
遥控测量 **yáo-k'ùng ts'è-liáng** tele-
 metric measurement
遥测讯号 **yáo-ts'è hsùn-hào** a tele-
 metric signal
遥远 **yáo-yuǎn** far and remote, distant
2465 摇旗纳喊 **yáo-ch'í nà-hǎn** to wave flags
 and shout (to cheer on, encourage,
 show support for)
摇篮 **yáo-lán** a cradle (usually figurative)
摇摆 **yáo-pǎi** to oscillate, swing to and
 fro, vacillate, waver
摇身一变 **yáo-shēn-ī-pièn** with one
 shake the body is transformed (a
 swift and drastic change in a person)
摇动 **yáo-tùng** to shake, vacillate, move
 back and forth, waver, totter, sway;
 wavering
摇头叹气 **yáo-t'óu-t'àn-ch'ì** to shake
 the head and give a sigh (may
 indicate disapproval or resignation)
摇尾乞怜 **yáo-wěi ch'ǐ-lién** to wag the
 tail and beg charity (to be fawning
 and obsequious)
摇摇欲坠 **yáo-yáo-yù-chuì** to sway as if
 to fall (tottering, shaky)
2466 瑶族 **yáo-tsú** the Yao people (a
 minority in Kwangsi, Kwangtung,
 Hunan, and Yunnan provinces:
 population 748,000 as of 1957)

yǎo (yǎo)

2467 咬文嚼字 **yǎo-wén chiáo-tzù** to chew
 words and gnaw on characters (to be
 highly pedantic, ostentatious of one's
 learning; semantic quibbling)
咬牙切齿 **yǎo-yá-ch'ièh-ch'ǐh** to gnash
 and grind the teeth

yào (yào)

2468 药厂 **yào-ch'ǎng** a pharmaceutical
 plant, drug factory

药方 **yào-fāng** a medicinal prescription, drug recipe
药房 **yào-fáng** a pharmacy, drugstore,
 dispensary
药理学 **yào-lǐ-hsuéh** pharmacology
药品 **yào-p'ǐn** medicines, medical drugs
药材 **yào-ts'ái** medical material,
 pharmaceutical substances, drugs
 (materials for native Chinese medicines)
药物制剂 **yào-wù chìh-chì** processed
 pharmaceutical preparations
药物学 **yào-wù-hsuéh** pharmacology
药物麻醉 **yào-wù-má-tsuì** anaesthesia
 by means of drugs
2469 要旨 **yào-chǐh** the essential idea, key
 point, theme, epitome, main principle
要饭 **yào-fàn** to beg food (be a beggar)
要害 **yào-hài** vital point, fatal spot,
 strategic location
要货计划 **yào-huò chì-huà** plan for
 demanded goods (an estimate of
 anticipated demand)
要写革命文，先做革命人 **yào hsiěh kó-
 mìng-wén, hsiēn tsò kó-mìng-jén** in
 order to write revolutionary literature, one must first become a revolutionary (applied to writers during the
 Cultural Revolution)
要领 **yào-lǐng** the vital point, essential
 element, important point
要塞 **yào-sài** a fortress, stronghold,
 bastion, strategic point
要点 **yào-tiěn** the essential point, main
 point, salient point
要言不烦 **yào-yén-pù-fán** essential
 words are not verbose (brief, concise, to the point, appropriately said)
要 **yào:** *see also* **yāo**
2470 钥匙 **yào-shih** a key
2471 耀武扬威 **yào-wǔ yáng-wēi** to dazzle
 with force and display power (to
 make a demonstration of force)

yēh (yē)

2472 耶路撒冷 **yēh-lù-sā-lěng** Jerusalem
 [Israel]
2473 椰子 **yēh-tzu** a coconut
椰菜 **yēh-ts'ài** savoy cabbage (usually
 used for feeding pigs)

yĕh (yĕ)

2474 也门 **yĕh-mén** Yemen
2475 冶金工业 **yĕh-chīn kūng-yèh** metallurgical industry
冶金工业部 **yĕh-chīn kūng-yèh-pù** the
 Ministry of Metallurgical Industry
 [of the State Council]

冶炼 **yěh-lièn** to smelt, refine

冶炼炉 **yěh-lièn-lú** a smelting furnace

2476 野战军 **yěh-chàn-chün** a field army

野战兵团 **yěh-chàn pīng-t'uán** an army corps

野心 **yěh-hsīn** wild ambition, greed for power

野心家 **yěh-hsīn-chiā** a careerist, person with a greed for power, one who schemes for power

野蛮 **yěh-mán** barbarous, savage, uncouth, rude, brutal, uncivilized

野板参三 **yěh-pǎn shēn-sān** Nozaka Sanzo (a leader of the Japanese Communist Party who spent most of the Resistance War period in Yenan under the name of Okana Susumu 冈野进)

野生植物 **yěh-shēng chíh-wù** wild plants, undomesticated plants

野生动物 **yěh-shēng tùng-wù** wild animals, undomesticated animals

野营 **yěh-yíng** outdoor camping; a field camp

野营训练 **yěh-yíng hsùn-lièn** field camp training

yèh (yè)

2477 叶群 **yèh ch'ún** Yeh Ch'ün (Lin Piao's wife, alleged to have been a co-conspirator and to have died with him)

叶公好龙 **yèh-kūng hào-lúng** Duke Yeh fancied dragons [when painted, but was frightened when a real one appeared] (to pretend to like something but actually to fear it [note: *yeh* in this usage was traditionally pronounced *shè*])

2478 业务 **yèh-wù** profession, work, business, occupation, task, function, job; functional, operational, occupational, professional, vocational

业务挂帅 **yèh-wù kuà-shuài** business takes command, professional needs should come first (an attitude criticized as denying the paramount role of ideology)

业务部门 **yèh-wù pù-mén** operational departments

业务第一 **yèh-wù-tì-ī** to put profession first

业余 **yèh-yú** spare-time, avocational, amateur

业余教育 **yèh-yú chiào-yù** spare-time education, after-hours education

业余中学 **yèh-yú chūng-hsuéh** a spare-time middle school

业余剧团 **yèh-yú chù-t'uán** an amateur dramatic troupe

业余函授教育 **yèh-yú hán-shòu chiào-yù** spare-time correspondence education

业余大学 **yèh-yú tà-hsuéh** an after-work university, spare-time college

2479 曳引机 **yèh-yǐn-chī** a vehicle for towing loads, tractor

2480 页岩 **yèh-yén** oil shale

页岩油 **yèh-yén-yú** shale oil

2481 夜战 **yèh-chàn** a night battle, night operations (to work at night, to continue a task into the night)

夜校 **yèh-hsiào** evening school, night school

夜以继日 **yèh-ī-chì-jìh** to use the night to continue the day (day and night, continuously, around the clock)

夜郎自大 **yèh-láng tzù-tà** the megalomania of [the king of] Yeh-lang [who asked the envoy of the Han empire which state was larger] (braggadocio; ignorant and boastful)

夜班 **yèh-pān** the night shift, a night class

2482 液量 **yèh-liàng** liquid measurement, liquid capacity

液体 **yèh-t'ǐ** the liquid state, a liquid substance, liquid

液体燃料 **yèh-t'ǐ ján-liào** liquid fuels

液体有机肥料 **yèh-t'ǐ yǔ-chī féi-liào** liquid organic fertilizer

yēn (yān)

2483 咽喉 **yēn-hóu** (1) the throat, larynx; (2) a narrow passage of strategic importance, a key point

2484 烟煤 **yēn-méi** smoky coal (bituminous coal, soft coal)

烟幕 **yēn-mù** a smoke screen (often figurative)

烟草 **yēn-ts'ǎo** the tobacco plant, tobacco

烟囱 **yēn-ts'ūng** a smokestack, chimney

2485 淹没 **yēn-mò** submerged, inundated, sunk

2486 阉鸡 **yēn-chī** to castrate a male chicken; a capon

阉割 **yēn-kō** to castrate, emasculate, geld (often figurative)

2487 腌肉 **yēn-jòu** salt-cured pork

2488 燕山夜话 **yēn-shān yèh-huà** "Evening Chats at Yenshan" (essays by Teng T'o in the *Pei-ching wan-pao* in 1961–1962 which became an early target of the Cultural Revolution)

燕 **yēn**: *see also* **yèn**

yén (yán)

2489 严阵以待 **yén-chèn-ī-tài** to await [the

enemy] in battle array (ready for any eventuality)

严正声明 **yén-chèng shēng-míng** a solemn declaration, serious declaration

严加谴责 **yén-chiā ch'iěn-tsé** to reprimand severely

严禁 **yén-chìn** a strict prohibition; to strictly forbid

严重 **yén-chùng** serious, grave, severe, critical; important, of great consequence

严重打击 **yén-chùng tǎ-chī** a severe blow, devastating attack, serious setback

严惩不贷 **yén-ch'éng-pù-tài** to punish severely without leniency

严峻 **yén-chùn** severe, harsh, exacting, stern

严防 **yén-fáng** to guard carefully, maintain strict vigilance, defend strongly

严寒 **yén-hán** bitter cold

严以责己 **yén-i-tsé-chǐ** to be strict in [one's] demands on oneself

严格 **yén-kó** strict, exacting, rigorous, austere, severe

严酷 **yén-k'ù** stern, severe, caustic, hard, cruel, pitiless, merciless, ruthless; cruelty, harshness

严厉 **yén-lì** stringent, stern, severe, ruthless

严密 **yén-mì** precise, exact; tight-knit; rigid, rigorous, strict, thorough; secretive, uncommunicative

严明 **yén-míng** strict but fair, disciplined

严肃 **yén-sù** solemn, serious, grave, austere; severity, gravity, seriousness

严辞 **yén-tz'ú** stern words, a solemn statement

2490 延安精神 **yén-ān chīng-shén** the Yenan spirit (a general invocation of the self-reliance, austerity, determination, and high morale associated with Yenan under Mao's leadership during the Resistance War)

延安文学艺术座谈会 **yén-ān wén-hsuéh i-shù tsò-t'án-huì** the Yenan Forum on Literature and Art (held in May 1942, and addressed by Mao Tsetung)

延长 **yén-ch'áng** to lengthen, extend, prolong

延期 **yén-ch'ī** to postpone, defer, delay; to extend a time limit, stay, hold over

延缓 **yén-huǎn** to postpone, put off, defer, delay; slow [in getting Something done], behindhand

延续 **yén-hsù** to continue, drag on, last

2491 言者无罪闻者足戒 **yén-chě-wú-tsuì, wén-chě-tsú-chièh** the [well-intentioned] speaker should not be punished [but] the hearer should take heed

言教 **yén-chiào** to teach by words; oral instruction

言之无物 **yén-chīh-wú-wù** words of no substance, empty talk

言近旨远 **yén-chìn-chǐh-yuǎn** the words are near but the meaning far (profound thoughts expressed in simple language)

言出法随 **yén-ch'ū-fǎ-suí** the order, once given, will be strictly enforced

言传身教 **yén-ch'uán shēn-chiào** to transmit by words and teach by example

言传身带 **yén-ch'uán shēn-tài** to teach by words and lead by deeds (to pass on experience)

言而无信 **yén-érh-wú-hsìn** to fail to live up to one's word

言行 **yén-hsíng** words and deeds

言行一致 **yén-hsíng-i-chìh** words and deeds in accord

言行不一 **yén-hsíng-pù-ī** words and deeds differing

言过其实 **yén-kuò-ch'í-shíh** the words exceed the reality (to exaggerate, boast, brag)

言论 **yén-lùn** open discussion, public speech; public opinion

言不尽意 **yén-pù-chìn-ì** the words do not fully express [my] meaning

言词 **yén-tz'ú** words and expressions, wording, speech

言外之意 **yén-wài-chīh-ì** the meaning beyond the words (implied meaning, between-the-lines meaning, overtones)

言为心声 **yén-wéi-hsīn-shēng** the words are the voice of the heart

言语 **yén-yǔ** the spoken language, words, speech

2492 沿海渔场 **yén-hǎi yú-ch'ǎng** coastal fishing grounds, offshore fisheries

沿袭 **yén-hsi** to follow old practices, continue according to tradition

沿革 **yén-kó** the process of inheritance and change, history, successive change

2493 岩层 **yén-ts'éng** a rock layer, stratum

2494 研究 **yén-chiū** to study, research, investigate thoroughly; research, investigation, study of

研究分析 **yén-chiū fēn-hsī** research and analysis; to study and analyze

研究生 **yén-chiū-shēng** research student, postgraduate student (as in the

U.S.)

研究员 **yén-chiū-yuán** a research fellow (the highest rank for members of a research institute, equivalent to full professor)

研究院 **yén-chiū-yuàn** a research institute, graduate school [outside China]

2495 盐碱化 **yén-chiěn-huà** alkalinization

盐碱地 **yén-chiěn-tì** alkaline land, alkaline soil

盐场 **yén-ch'ǎng** a salt field, salt production site

盐水选种 **yén-shuǐ hsuǎn-chǔng** salt water selection of rice

盐地 **yén-tì** saline soil

盐渍土 **yén-tzù-t'ǔ** saline soil, salinized soil

2496 阎王 **yén-wáng** the king of Hades; a tyrant

阎王债 **yén-wáng-chài** a loan from the king of Hell (extreme usury)

yěn (yǎn)

2497 掩耳盗铃 **yěn-ěrh-tào-líng** to cover one's ears while stealing a bell (to deceive oneself, cheat oneself)

掩护 **yěn-hù** to protect, cover [military]

掩护部队 **yěn-hù pù-tuì** covering forces

掩护艇 **yěn-hù-t'ǐng** support craft [naval], covering ships

掩人耳目 **yěn-jén-ěrh-mù** to cover people's ears and eyes (to deceive, swindle)

掩盖 **yěn-kài** to cover up, conceal, hide, shield

掩埋 **yěn-mái** to bury, inter

掩饰 **yěn-shìh** to cover up [an error], conceal [the truth], gloss over, disguise, dissemble; pretense, palliation

掩藏 **yěn-ts'áng** to hide, conceal

2498 眼界 **yěn-chièh** the field of one's vision, scope of sight, outlook, horizon

眼睛向下 **yěn-chīng hsiàng-hsià** the eyes should look downward [toward the masses]

眼中钉 **yěn-chūng-tīng** a thorn in the eye (an offense to the eye; the most hated person)

眼前 **yěn-ch'ién** before one's eyes (at this moment, now, at present)

眼高手低 **yěn-kāo-shǒu-tī** one's eyes are high but the hands are low (to be incapable of fulfilling one's own high expectations)

眼光 **yěn-kuāng** discerning ability, power of judgment, perception, outlook, vision

眼科 **yěn-k'ō** opthalmology, opthalmology department [of a university]

眼力 **yěn-lì** eyesight, vision; power of judgment, discernment, insight

2499 演唱工农兵 **yěn-ch'àng kūng-núng-pīng** to perform and sing of workers, peasants, and soldiers

演出节目 **yěn-ch'ū chiéh-mù** items or acts presented, the program of a performance

演化论 **yěn-huà-lùn** the theory of evolution

演习 **yěn-hsí** (1) a military exercise, maneuver, war games; (2) to practice, exercise

演绎法 **yěn-ì-fǎ** the deductive method, deduction

演变 **yěn-pièn** to develop and change, evolve, transform; evolution, evolutionary change

演算 **yěn-suàn** to do mathematical problems, calculate

演奏 **yěn-tsòu** to perform [music]

演员 **yěn-yuán** a performer, actor, actress

yèn (yàn)

2500 厌战情绪 **yèn-chàn ch'íng-hsù** war fatigue, war weariness

厌倦 **yèn-chüàn** to be tired of, weary, exhausted

厌恶 **yèn-wù** to detest, loathe, greatly dislike

2501 宴会 **yèn-huì** a banquet, feast, dinner party

2502 验方 **yèn-fāng** effective medical prescriptions

验墒 **yèn-shāng** to test [soil] moisture

验收 **yèn-shōu** to accept products after inspection, test and accept

2503 谚语 **yèn-yǔ** a proverb, aphorism, adage, saying

2504 堰堤 **yèn-tī** an earthen embankment, dam

2505 焰火 **yèn-huǒ** fireworks, pyrotechnics

2506 燕麦 **yèn-mài** oats

燕 **yèn**: *see also* **yēn**

yīn (yīn)

2507 阴暗 **yīn-àn** dark, dim, shady, gloomy, dusky, dreary, dismal

阴暗面 **yīn-àn-mièn** the dark side, seamy side

阴极 **yīn-chí** the negative electrode, negative pole, cathode

阴风 **yīn-fēng** a chilly wind (a wind that precedes the appearance of a ghost: hence, a foreboding wind)

阴魂不散 **yīn-hún-pù-sàn** the evil spirit has not left

阴险毒辣 **yīn-hsiěn-tú-là** insidious and ruthless

阴沟 **yīn-kōu** a covered drainage ditch, sewer

阴历 **yīn-lì** the lunar calendar

阴谋 **yīn-móu** a plot, conspiracy, intrigue, scheme, ruse; to plot, conspire

阴谋家 **yīn-móu-chiā** a person addicted to intrigue or conspiracy, conspirator

阴谋分子 **yīn-móu fèn-tzǔ** conspiratorial elements, plotters, intriguers, subversive elements

阴谋活动 **yīn-móu huó-tùng** conspiratorial activity, subversive activities

阴谋诡计 **yīn-móu kuěi-chì** dark plots and crafty schemes, intrigues, dark machinations

阴森森 **yīn-sēn-sēn** ominous, weird, dark and mysterious, obscure

阴阳怪气 **yīn-yáng-kuài-ch'ì** to talk in a strange and obscure way, act in an odd and weird manner

阴影 **yīn-yǐng** shades, shadows

阴雨 **yīn-yǔ** cloudy and rainy, rainy weather

2508　因循 **yīn-hsún** to follow along, take the course of least resistance procrastinate; negligent, perfunctory

因循守旧 **yīn-hsún shǒu-chiù** to stick to old ways, follow along in the same old rut

因公 **yīn-kūng** in the line of duty, because of official business

因果 **yīn-kuǒ** cause and effect, causality; karma

因果论 **yīn-kuǒ lùn** the theory of causation

因陋就简 **yīn-lòu-chiù-chiěn** to bring the mean to the simple (to make do with whatever is available; to take the easiest way)

因时制宜 **yīn-shíh-chìh-í** to do what is suitable to the occasion, do as the times demand

因势利导 **yīn-shìh-lì-tǎo** to give judicious guidance according to the situation, be guided by circumstances

因素 **yīn-sù** elements, factors, components

因地制宜 **yīn-tì-chìh-í** to adapt working methods to local conditions, do what local circumstances require, "get the best out of each area"

因噎废食 **yīn-yēh-fèi-shíh** to refuse to eat for fear of choking (to lose a great advantage because of fears of small difficulties)

2509　荫蔽 **yīn-pì** to conceal, cover up, shelter, protect

2510　殷鉴不远 **yīn-chièn pù-yuǎn** the mirror of Yin is not far away (the lessons of history are close at hand)

殷切 **yīn ch'ièh** fervent, courteous, polite

殷勤 **yīn-ch'ín** civil, courteous, polite, obliging, attentive

2511　音速 **yīn-sù** the speed of sound

音调 **yīn-tiào** pitch, tone; melody, tune

音乐研究 **yīn-yuèh yén-chiū** *Studies in Music* (A Peking bi-monthly journal, 1958—)

yín (yín)

2512　银行信贷 **yín-háng hsìn-tài** bank credit, bank loans

银幕 **yín-mù** the silver screen (a cinema screen, motion pictures)

银币 **yín-pì** silver money, silver coinage

银样蜡枪头 **yín-yàng là-ch'iāng-t'óu** the silver-like head of a pewter spear (impressive in appearance but without utility)

yǐn (yǐn)

2513　引者 **yǐn-chě** "the quoter" (an indication of changes, explanation, or emphasis added to cited material by the present writer or editor)

引证 **yǐn-chèng** to cite as proof, adduce, quote; a reference

引经据典 **yǐn-chīng-chù-tiěn** to cite the classics and rely on the canons (pedantic)

引种驯化 **yǐn-chǔng hsún-huà** to introduce and acclimatize [a new species, seed variety, etc.]

引擎 **yǐn-ch'íng** an engine, motor

引黄淤地 **yǐn-huáng-yǔ-tì** to bring in the Yellow [River water] to build land by siltation

引火烧身 **yǐn-huǒ shāo-shēn** to bring the fire to burn oneself (to take the initiative in exposing one's own errors in order to stimulate others; to get oneself in trouble)

引向深入 **yǐn-hsiàng shēn-jù** to lead toward a deep penetration (to go beyond superficialities)

引以为戒 **yǐn-ǐ-wéi-chièh** to take as a warning (to take the mistakes of others as an admonition)

引人注目 **yǐn-jén-chù-mù** to attract people's attention

引人入胜 **yǐn-jén-jù-shèng** to delight others very much, excite interest; fascinating, absorbing

引鬼入邦 **yǐn-kuěi-jù-pāng** to bring demons into [one's] country (to

engage in subversion; treason)

引狼入室 **yǐn-láng-jù-shìh** to invite the wolf into the house (to bring trouble on oneself)

引蛇出洞 **yǐn-shé-ch'ū-tùng** to induce the snake out of its hole (to lure the enemy out of hiding)

引伸 **yǐn-shēn** to deduce and elaborate, enlarge upon, extend in meaning, expound; to string out, prolong

引水发电 **yǐn-shuǐ fā-tièn** to divert water to generate electricity

引水坝 **yǐn-shuǐ-pà** a diversion dam

引水隧道 **yǐn-shuǐ suì-tào** a water diversion tunnel

引水渡槽 **yǐn-shuǐ tù-ts'áo** a water aqueduct

引水员 **yǐn-shuǐ-yuán** a harbor pilot

引导 **yǐn-tǎo** to guide, lead, show the way, conduct; to teach

引渡 **yǐn-tù** to extradite; extradition

引文 **yǐn-wén** a quotation

引言 **yǐn-yén** a preface, introduction, foreword [to a book or article]

引诱 **yǐn-yù** to entice, lure, seduce, tempt, inveigle

引玉之砖 **yǐn-yù-chīh-chuān** the jade-attracting brick (*see* p'āo-chuān yǐn-yù)

引用 **yǐn-yùng** to quote; to adopt for use

2514 饮鸩止渴 **yǐn-chèn-chǐh-k'ǒ** to drink poison to quench one's thirst (to take short-sighted and eventually disastrous action)

饮食服务部 **yǐn-shíh fú-wù-pù** a food service department (usually a canteen or cafeteria in a factory)

2515 隐患 **yǐn-huàn** a concealed evil, lurking peril, latent danger

隐晦 **yǐn-huì** obscure, hidden, secret

隐姓埋名 **yǐn-hsìng mái-míng** to hide one's surname and bury one's given name (to try to hide one's identity)

隐瞒 **yǐn-mán** to cover up, conceal; dupe, deceive; concealment, deception

隐匿 **yǐn-nì** to conceal, hide, give refuge to, shelter; concealment [of wrongdoing, etc.]

隐蔽 **yǐn-pì** to conceal, hide, cover up; concealed, covert; concealment

隐蔽活动 **yǐn-pì huó-tùng** covert activities, undercover action

隐身草 **yǐn-shēn-ts'ǎo** a grass that can make one invisible (cover, front, blind, disguise [as a police cover, etc.])

隐藏 **yǐn-ts'áng** to hide, conceal, secrete, cache; hidden, secreted,

camouflaged; latent, dormant, suppressed

隐喻 **yǐn-yù** a metaphor

yìn (yìn)

2516 印章 **yìn-chāng** a seal, stamp [usually official]

印发 **yìn-fā** to print and issue, reproduce and distribute

印花布 **yìn-huā-pù** printed cloth, calico

印花税 **yìn-huā-shuì** a stamp tax, revenue tax

印象 **yìn-hsiàng** a mental image, impression

印象派 **yìn-hsiàng-p'ài** the Impressionist school

印染厂 **yìn-jǎn-ch'ǎng** a printing and dyeing [textile] mill

印尼 **yìn-ní** Indonesia (contraction of yìn-tù-ní-hsī-yà)

印把子 **yìn-pǎ-tzu** an official seal (a symbol of authority)

印刷 **yìn-shuā** to print; printing

印第安人 **yìn-tì-ān jén** an American Indian

印度 **yìn-tù** India

印度新闻处 **yìn-tù hsīn-wén-ch'ù** the Indian Information Service [IIS]

印度卢比 **yìn-tù lú-pǐ** the Indian rupee

印度尼西亚 **yìn-tù-ní-hsī-yà** Indonesia

印度尼西亚新闻社 **yìn-tù-ní-hsī-yà hsīn-wén-shè** Persbiro Indonesia Agency [PIA]

印度报业托辣斯 **yìn-tù pào-yèh t'ō-là-szū** Press Trust of India [PTI]

yīng (yīng)

2517 应得 **yīng-té** that which one deserves to receive (deserved, due)

应有尽有 **yīng-yǔ-chìn-yǔ** to have everything that should be had (to have everything needed)

应 **yīng**: *see also* yìng

2518 英雄 **yīng-hsiúng** a hero, heroine

英雄主义 **yīng-hsiúng-chǔ-ì** heroism, heroics, valor (may be good or bad depending on the context, e.g., individual heroism or revolutionary heroism)

英雄气慨 **yīng-hsiúng ch'ì-kài** heroic airs, heroic behavior

英雄创造历史 **yīng-hsiúng ch'uàng-tsào lì-shǐh** heroes create history (the criticized theory that great men make history)

英雄形象 **yīng-hsiúng hsíng-hsiàng** the image of a hero, a heroic image

英雄人物 **yīng-hsiúng jén-wù** heroic

personages, heroes

英雄无用武之地 **yīng-hsiúng wú yùng-wǔ-chìh-tì** the hero has no chance to show his might (a capable person without an opportunity to use his skill)

英烈 **yīng-lièh** brave and ardent, heroic, valiant (usually implies martyrdom)

英明 **yīng-míng** intelligent, talented, wise, clever, sagacious

英镑集团 **yīng-pàng chí-t'uán** the pound sterling bloc

英属洪都拉斯 **yīng-shǔ húng-tū-lā-szū** British Honduras

英属圭亚那 **yīng-shǔ kuēi-yà-nà** British Guiana

英姿飒爽 **yīng-tzū sà-shuǎng** dashing and lively in appearance

英勇 **yīng-yǔng** brave, courageous, valiant, gallant, heroic, militant

英勇旗手 **yīng-yǔng ch'í-shǒu** the valiant standard-bearer

英勇奋战 **yīng-yǔng fèn-chàn** to fight bravely

英勇奋斗 **yīng-yǔng fèn-tòu** to battle valiantly, fight courageously

英勇善战 **yīng-yǔng shàn-chàn** valiant and skilled in combat

英勇斗争 **yīng-yǔng tòu-chēng** to struggle valiantly; a valiant combat

英勇顽强 **yīng-yǔng wán-ch'iáng** brave and unyielding

2519 鹦鹉学舌 **yīng-wǔ-hsuéh-shé** like a parrot imitating one's tongue (parrot-like imitation)

2520 鹰犬 **yīng-ch'üǎn** falcons and dogs [once used in hunting] (hired ruffians, brawlers, rowdies)

鹰厦铁路 **yīng-hsià t'iěh-lù** the Yintan [Kiangsi] to Amoy [Fukien] railway

yíng (yíng)

2521 迎接 **yíng-chiēh** to receive, greet, welcome

迎风踏雪 **yíng-fēng t'à-hsuěh** to breast the wind and tread the snow

迎合 **yíng-hó** to meet [another's] wishes (to yield, give in, cater to)

迎新晚会 **yíng-hsīn wǎn-huì** a party to welcome new students or new members of an organization; a New Year's Eve party

迎刃而解 **yíng-jèn-érh-chiěh** to meet the knife's edge and split (a problem that is neatly solved; neatly and quickly done)

迎头赶上 **yíng-t'óu kǎn-shàng** to catch up with and get ahead of, to surpass

迎头痛击 **yíng-t'óu-t'ùng-chī** to meet head-on, deal [the enemy] a stunning blow by a direct attack; to repulse a frontal attack

2522 盈余 **yíng-yú** a surplus, earnings, profit

盈余分配 **yíng-yú fēn-p'èi** the distribution of a surplus, division of earnings

2523 营建 **yíng-chièn** to manage construction; to build, construct

营林工作 **yíng-lín kūng-tsò** management and control of forests, forestry work

营私舞弊 **yíng-szū wǔ-pì** to seek personal advantage and illicit gain [from a public post], corruption and embezzlement

营造 **yíng-tsào** to build, construct, erect; construction

营养 **yíng-yǎng** nutrition, nourishment

营养状况 **yíng-yǎng chuàng-k'uàng** nutritional well-being [of the public]

营业 **yíng-yèh** to do business, engage in trade; a business, enterprise, industry; trade, commerce; commercial

营业日 **yíng-yèh-jìh** a business [work] day, operating hours

营业税 **yíng-yèh-shuì** a business tax

营业所 **yíng-yèh-sǒ** a business office (usually a small branch of a bank, etc.)

2524 赢利 **yíng-lì** profit, return [on investment], earnings

赢得 **yíng-té** to win, gain, earn, profit, get, obtain

yǐng (yǐng)

2525 影响 **yǐng-hsiǎng** shadow and echo (influence, impact, impression, effect, results; to influence, affect)

影象 **yǐng-hsiàng** an image, portrait, likeness

影片 **yǐng-p'ièn** a cinema film, motion picture, movie

影射 **yǐng-shè** to hint by suggestion, make false representations, talk behind one's back; to delude

影子 **yǐng-tzu** a shadow, trace, track

影子内阁 **yǐng-tzu nèi-kó** a "shadow cabinet"

影印 **yǐng-yìn** a photograph, photogravure, photo print

yìng (yìng)

2526 应战 **yìng-chàn** to accept battle (to take up a challenge)

应征入伍 **yìng-chēng jù-wǔ** to respond to conscription and enter the ranks [of the army], be conscripted, enter

military service

应届 **yìng-chièh** the present term [or year] (usually refers to the current graduating class of students)

应酬 **yìng-ch'ou** to extend hospitality, receive guests; social intercourse, entertainment

应付 **yìng-fù** to deal with, cope with, adjust to

应声虫 **yìng-shēng-ch'úng** an "echo worm" (a servile sycophant, "yes" men)

应邀 **yìng-yāo** to accept an invitation; at the invitation of

应用 **yìng-yùng** to utilize, make use of; application, use; applicable, useful

应用文 **yìng-yùng-wén** practical writing, business correspondence

应 **yìng**: *see also* **yīng**

2527   硬指标 **yìng-chǐh-piāo** a firm [quantitative] target

硬创 **yìng-ch'uàng** to accomplish [something] despite difficulties, to create in the face of obstacles

硬席 **yìng-hsí** hard seats (the ordinary class on railways)

硬性 **yìng-hsìng** obstinate, inflexible, stubborn [disposition]; hardness [of materials]

硬性规定 **yìng-hsìng kuēi-tìng** rigid regulations, inflexible rules

硬任务 **yìng-jèn-wù** a firm task (a job with fixed terms of quantity or time of completion)

硬骨头 **yìng-kǔ-t'ou** a hard bone (a steadfast, incorruptible person)

硬骨头六连 **yìng-kǔ-t'ou liù-lién** the hard-boned Sixth Company (a PLA unit praised for battle readiness, military technique, and military and political discipline; a model for emulation by all PLA units)

硬拉 **yìng-lā** to pull over firmly (to apply unrelenting pressure to persuade)

硬煤 **yìng-méi** hard coal, anthracite

硬搬和模仿 **yìng-pān ho mó-fǎng** uncritical borrowing and imitation [particularly of foreign models]

硬币 **yìng-pì** hard money coins, metallic currency (as opposed to paper currency)

硬手 **yìng-shǒu** a strong hand, good worker

硬说 **yìng-shuō** to assert arbitrarily, stand on one's opinion, insist on one's view

硬套 **yìng-t'ào** to arbitrarily apply

硬卧 **yìng-wò** hard berths (ordinary accommodations on overnight trains)

硬要 **yìng-yào** to demand insistently, insist on

yū (yōu)

2528   优质钢 **yū-chìh-kāng** high-quality steel

优种 **yū-chǔng** a superior strain [of seeds or livestock]

优抚工作委员会 **yū-fǔ kūng-tsò wěi-yuán-huì** special treatment work committees (to arrange relief or jobs for dependents of Korean War casualties)

优惠贷款 **yū-huì tài-k'uǎn** loans on favorable terms, preferential loans

优惠条件 **yū-huì t'iáo-chièn** favorable terms, favorable conditions

优先 **yū-hsiēn** priority, precedence; to have priority over; preferential

优先权 **yū-hsiēn-ch'üán** the right of prior consideration, priority, preferential privileges

优先发展 **yū-hsiēn fā-chǎn** priority development; to develop on a preferential basis

优先录取 **yū-hsiēn lù-ch'ǔ** priority of acceptance [for admission to schools, etc.]

优秀 **yū-hsiù** distinguished, excellent, outstanding, the best

优秀干部 **yū-hsiù kàn-pù** an outstanding cadre

优秀工作者 **yū-hsiù kūng-tsò-chě** an outstanding worker

优秀生免试直升 **yū-hsiù-shēng miěn-shìh chíh-shēng** excellent students promoted directly without examination (a 1957 policy to counter domination of college entrance examinations by students from bourgeois families)

优秀团员 **yū-hsiù t'uán-yuán** Excellent [Youth] League Member (a high honor given to youths, e.g., to enthusiastic Sinkiang volunteers)

优选法 **yū-hsuǎn-fǎ** optimization

优良 **yū-liáng** excellent, fine, good, choice, superior

优良传统 **yū-liáng ch'uán-t'ǔng** an excellent tradition, fine tradition

优良作风 **yū-liáng tsò-fēng** an excellent working style

优劣 **yū-lièh** good and bad, fit and unfit, bright and dull (quality)

优生学 **yū-shēng-hsuéh** eugenics

优胜 **yū-shèng** superior; pre-eminence, superiority

优势 **yū-shìh** superiority, dominance, supremacy, holding the advantage, in a favorable condition, the upper

hand

优待 **yū-tài** special benefits, favorable treatment, preferential care

优点 **yū-tiěn** good points, merits, advantages, good qualities

优越性 **yū-yuèh-hsìng** superiority, excellence

2529　忧心忡忡 **yū-hsīn-ch'ūng-ch'ūng** deeply worried, care-ridden

忧虑 **yū-lǜ** to worry; anxious, apprehensive; anxiety

忧伤 **yū-shāng** worried and grieved, sad, dejecteď, despondent

2530　幽灵 **yū-líng** the spirit of a deceased person, ghost, apparition

幽默 **yū-mò** humor; humorous

2531　悠久 **yū-chiǔ** long in time, for a long time, of long duration, enduring

悠悠万事, 唯此为大, 克己复礼 **yū-yū wàn-shìh, wéi-tz'ǔ wéi-tà, k'ò-chǐ fù-lǐ** "Of all things, this is the most important: to restrain the self and restore the rites" (a scroll alleged to have been written by Lin Piao reflecting his Confucian attitude)

yú (yóu)

2532　由衷之言 **yú-chūng-chīh-yén** words spoken from the heart

由浅入深 **yú-ch'iěn-jù-shēn** from the shallow to the deep (from the superficial to the serious, from the simple to the complex)

由弱变强 **yú-jò-pièn-ch'iáng** to change from weakness to strength

由来已久 **yú-lái-ǐ-chiǔ** it has been so for a long time (well established, longstanding)

由实践到认识, 由认识到实践 **yú shíh-chièn tào jèn-shíh, yú jèn-shíh tào shíh-chièn** from practice to knowledge and from knowledge to practice

由思想到存在 **yú szū-hsiǎng tào ts'úntsài** from ideology to existence

由低级到高级 **yú tì-chí tào kāo-chí** from a lower stage to a higher stage

由土到洋 **yú-t'ǔ tào-yáng** [to progress] from indigenous [methods] to modern [methods]

由存在到思想 **yú ts'ún-tsài tào szūhsiǎng** from existence to ideology

由此及彼, 由表及里 **yú-tz'ǔ chí-pǐ, yúpiǎo chí-lǐ** to proceed from here to there and from the surface to the interior

由物质到精神, 由精神到物质 **yú wù-chíh tào chīng-shén, yú chīng-shén tào wù-chìh** from matter to spirit and from spirit to matter

2533　邮政工人 **yú-chèng kūng-jén** postal workers

邮船 **yú-ch'uán** a mail steamer, passenger liner

邮电 **yú-tièn** posts and telecommunications

邮电局 **yú-tièn-chú** a post and telegraph office

邮电部 **yú-tièn-pù** the Ministry of Posts and Telecommunications [of the State Council]

邮电所 **yú-tièn-sǒ** a post and telegraph [branch] office

2534　犹太复国主义 **yú-t'ài fù-kuó-chǔ-ì** Zionism

犹太人 **yú-t'ài-jén** a Jew

犹豫不决 **yú-yù-pù-chüéh** hesitating and indecisive

2535　油脂 **yú-chīh** fats, oils, and greases, olein

油井 **yú-chǐng** an oil well

油茶树 **yú-ch'á-shù** the tea-oil tree

油气 **yú-ch'ì** petroleum gas, natural gas

油腔滑调 **yú-ch'iāng huá-tiào** oily tones and slippery tunes (suave and sly, utterly insincere)

油船 **yú-ch'uán** an oil tanker

油画 **yú-huà** an oil painting

油管 **yú-kuǎn** an oil pipeline

油粮供应站 **yú-liáng kūng-yìng-chàn** [cooking] oil and grain supply stations

油料 **yú-liào** petroleum products

油料作物 **yú-liào tsò-wù** vegetable oil crops

油轮 **yú-lún** an [oil] tanker

油苗 **yú-miáo** oil seepage, surface indications of petroleum

油母页岩 **yú-mǔ yèh-yén** oil [bearing] shale

油票 **yú-p'iào** oil tickets (ration coupons for cooking oil)

油水 **yú-shuǐ** (1) the cream or essence of something; (2) a side profit, outside gains, squeeze, kickbacks

油田 **yú-t'ién** an oil field

油田会战 **yú-t'ién huì-chàn** the oil field campaign

油桐 **yú-t'úng** the tung oil [tree]

油嘴滑舌 **yú-tsuǐ-huá-shé** an oily mouth and slippery tongue (insincere, slick and smooth in talk)

油菜籽 **yú-ts'ài-tzǔ** rapeseed

油层 **yú-ts'éng** an oil stratum, oil zone

油盐酱醋柴米茶 **yú yén chiàng ts'ù ch'ái mǐ ch'á** oil, salt, condiments, vinegar, fuel, rice, and tea (the basic necessities of daily life)

油印 **yú-yìn** to mimeograph, duplicate, reproduce

²⁵³⁶ 铀矿 **yú-k'uàng** a uranium mine

²⁵³⁷ 游击战 **yú-chī-chàn** guerrilla warfare, guerrilla operations

游击战争 **yú-chī-chàn-chēng** a guerrilla war

游击主义 **yú-chī-chǔ-ì** guerrilla-ism (excessive reliance on guerrilla tactics, such as neglecting the need for established bases)

游击军 **yú-chī-chūn** a guerrilla force, guerrilla army

游击区 **yú-chī-ch'ū** a guerrilla area, guerrilla zone

游击队 **yú-chī-tuì** guerrilla forces, a guerrilla unit, partisans, irregulars

游记 **yú-chì** an account of travels, travelogue, travel notes

游行 **yú-hsíng** a parade, demonstration, procession; to demonstrate (normally for a political purpose or protest)

游行示威 **yú-hsíng shìh-wēi** a demonstration march; to stage a demonstration

游刃有余 **yú-jèn-yǔ-yú** room for the blade and some to spare (more than capable of the task, highly proficient)

游客 **yú-k'ò** a traveler, tourist

游览 **yú-lǎn** to tour, see the sights; sightseeing

游离 **yú-lí** ionization

游历 **yú-lì** a sightseeing tour, pleasure trip; tourism

游民 **yú-mín** a vagrant, vagabond, homeless person, loafer

游民无产阶级 **yú-mín wú-ch'ǎn-chiēh-chí** the lumpen-proletariat

游牧制度 **yú-mù chìh-tù** the nomadic system, nomadism

游手好闲 **yú-shǒu hào-hsién** idle of hands and fond of leisure (dawdling, indolent, lazy)

游艇 **yú-t'ǐng** a yacht, motor cruiser

游资 **yú-tzū** idle funds, unemployed capital, hot money

游园会 **yú-yuán-huì** a celebration held in public parks (on May Day, October 1, etc.)

游园联欢会 **yú-yuán lién-huān-huì** a public parks get-together meeting (*see above*)

游泳场 **yú-yǔng-ch'ǎng** a swimming place (a natural, rather than artificial, setting)

游泳池 **yú-yǔng-ch'íh** a swimming pool

yǔ (yǒu)

²⁵³⁸ 友爱 **yǔ-ài** friendship, affection, fraternal love

友方 **yǔ-fāng** the friendly side, friendly party

友好 **yǔ-hǎo** friendly, amicable, cordial; friendship, amity, goodwill

友好交流 **yǔ-hǎo chiāo-liú** friendly intercourse, cordial exchange (usually refers to such activities as cultural exchange)

友好交往 **yǔ-hǎo chiāo-wǎng** friendly intercourse

友好接触 **yǔ-hǎo chiēh-ch'ù** friendly contacts

友好城 **yǔ-hǎo-ch'éng** a friend city (similar to but has replaced the term, "sister city")

友好访问 **yǔ-hǎo fǎng-wèn** a friendly visit (usually on an official basis)

友好协商 **yǔ-hǎo hsiéh-shāng** friendly negotiations, amicable discussions

友好关系 **yǔ-hǎo kuān-hsi** friendly relations, cordial connections, amicable bonds

友好款待 **yǔ-hǎo k'uǎn-tài** friendly treatment

友好代表团 **yǔ-hǎo tài-piǎo-t'uán** a friendship delegation

友好谈话 **yǔ-hǎo t'án-huà** friendly discussions, cordial talks

友好团结事业 **yǔ-hǎo t'uán-chiéh shìh-yèh** the cause of friendly unity

友好同盟互助条约 **yǔ-hǎo t'úng-méng hù-chù t'iáo-yuēh** a treaty of friendship, alliance, and mutual assistance

友好往来 **yǔ-hǎo wǎng-lái** friendly intercourse

友好邀请赛 **yǔ-hǎo yāo-ch'ǐng-sài** a friendly invitational competition

友谊重于胜负 **yǔ-ì chùng-yú shèng-fù** friendship is more important than winning or losing

友谊赛 **yǔ-ì-sài** friendly competition, a friendly game

友谊商店 **yǔ-ì shāng-tièn** a "Friendship Store" (established in the principal Chinese cities to cater to foreigners)

友谊第一，比赛第二 **yǔ-ì-tì-ī, pǐ-sài-tì-èrh** friendship first, competition second

²⁵³⁹ 有朝一日 **yǔ-chāo-ī-jìh** some day in the future, some day, there will be a day

有机结合 **yǔ-chī chiéh-hó** an organic combination, an integral combination

有机肥料 **yǔ-chī féi-liào** organic fertilizer, manure

有机合成化学 **yǔ-chī hó-ch'éng huà-hsuéh** organic synthetic chemistry

有机化学 **yǔ-chī-huà-hsuéh** organic chemistry

有机可乘 **yǔ-chī-k'ǒ-ch'éng** there is an opportunity to be taken advantage of, to have loopholes that can be

exploited; to show vulnerability

有机体 **yǔ-chī-t'ǐ** an organic body, organism

有机物 **yǔ-chī-wù** organic matter

有计划按比例发展的客观规律 **yǔ chì-huà àn pǐ-lì fā-chǎn te k'ò-kuān kuēi-lǜ** the objective law governing planned and proportionate development

有计划的 **yǔ-chì-huà-te** in a planned way, planned

有纪律的 **yǔ-chì-lǜ-te** disciplined, orderly

有加无已 **yǔ-chiā-wú-ǐ** incessant increase without cease

有奖储蓄 **yǔ-chiǎng ch'ǔ-hsù** lottery savings (under which bond numbers are drawn for prizes)

有主有从 **yǔ-chǔ yǔ-ts'úng** there is a main [point, element, or contra-diction] and subordinate [ones]

有产者 **yǔ-ch'ǎn-chě** one who has property (a member of the bourgeoisie)

有产阶级 **yǔ-ch'ǎn-chiēh-chí** the propertied class, bourgeoisie, capitalist class

有期徒刑 **yǔ-ch'ī-t'ú-hsíng** imprisonment for a fixed period

有情况 **yǔ-ch'íng-k'uàng** there are circumstances (an alteration in a situation usually under tense circumstances)

有求必应 **yǔ-ch'iú-pì-yìng** any request will be granted (unfailingly helpful)

有仇 **yǔ-ch'óu** to have bitter enmity, deep hostility

有据 **yǔ-chù** there is proof, having evidence, well substantiated

有法难依 **yǔ-fǎ nán-ī** there are laws but they are difficult [for the people] to follow

有法不依 **yǔ-fǎ pù-ī** there are laws but they are not followed [by the government]

有反必肃, 有错必纠 **yǔ-fǎn pì-sù, yǔ-ts'ò pì-chiū** counter-revolutionaries must be suppressed whenever they are found and mistakes must be corrected whenever they are discovered

有限主权论 **yǔ-hsièn chǔ-ch'üán lùn** the doctrine of limited sovereignty (the Brezhnev doctrine of the right to intervene in backsliding socialist countries)

有线广播 **yǔ-hsièn kuǎng-pō** broadcasting transmitted by wire or cable

有线电话 **yǔ-hsièn tièn-huà** the ordinary [wire transmitted] telephone

有线电报 **yǔ-hsièn tièn-pào** the telegraph, cable

有心人 **yǔ-hsīn-jén** a strong-willed person, a determined person, a thoughtful person

有血有肉 **yǔ-hsuèh-yǔ-jòu** having blood and flesh (lifelike, living)

有一套 **yǔ-ī-t'ào** to have one's own set of ideas, skills, or way of dealing with people or problems

有益 **yǔ-ì** advantageous, beneficial, profitable, useful, conducive, helpful

有意 **yǔ-ì** to intend; purposeful, intentional; intentionally, purposely; with intent

有意识 **yǔ-ì-shíh** conscious; consciously

有关方面 **yǔ-kuān-fāng-mièn** the concerned parties, interested parties, relevant groups

有关部门 **yǔ-kuān-pù-mén** the relevant departments, departments or offices concerned

有关当局 **yǔ-kuān-tāng-chú** the authorities concerned, proper authorities

有功 **yǔ-kūng** to have a meritorious record, have rendered distinguished service

有口皆碑 **yǔ-k'ǒu-chiēh-pēi** everyone who has a mouth becomes a [laudatory] tablet (to be praised by everyone)

有口难言 **yǔ-k'ǒu-nán-yén** to have a mouth but find it difficult to speak (unable to speak in self-defense)

有理 **yǔ-lǐ** reasonable, logical, right, rational; reasoned, in the right

有力 **yǔ-lì** strong, forceful, powerful, mighty

有力打击 **yǔ-lì tǎ-chī** a heavy blow

有利 **yǔ-lì** favorable, useful, advantageous, beneficial

有利因素 **yǔ-lì yīn-sù** a favorable factor

有例在先 **yǔ-lì-tsài-hsiēn** there are precedents

有门儿 **yǔ-mén-erh** there is a way, it can be done, likely to be realized

有名无实 **yǔ-míng-wú-shíh** there is a name but no substance (to exist in name only)

有目共赏 **yǔ-mù-kùng-shǎng** anybody who has eyes can share in the enjoyment (universally acclaimed)

有目共睹 **yǔ-mù-kùng-tǔ** anybody who has eyes can see [it] (known to everyone, obvious)

有奶便是娘 **yǔ-nǎi pièn-shìh-niáng** she who has milk is the mother (go to whoever has the resources)

有办法 **yǔ-pàn-fǎ** there is a way, it can

be done (resourceful, competent, efficient)

有备无患 **yǔ-pèi-wú-huàn** there is no danger when one is prepared; there will be no disaster when there is preparedness

有步骤 **yǔ-pù-tsòu** to have steps (to have a plan of procedure)

有色金属 **yǔ-sè-chīn-shǔ** nonferrous metals

有色金属工业 **yǔ-sè-chīn-shǔ kūng-yèh** nonferrous metals industry

有色冶金 **yǔ-sè-yěh-chīn** nonferrous metallurgy

有伤大雅 **yǔ-shāng-tà-yǎ** offensive against good taste, inelegant

有神论者 **yǔ-shén-lùn-chě** one who believes in the existence of a deity, theist

有生气 **yǔ-shēng-ch'ì** having vital force, vital

有生力量 **yǔ-shēng lì-liàng** effective strength, vital forces, active forces

有声有色 **yǔ-shēng-yǔ-sè** full of sound and color (vivacious, vivid, impressive)

有识之士 **yǔ-shíh-chīh-shìh** a far-sighted personage, knowledgeable person

有始有终 **yǔ-shǐh-yǔ-chūng** to have a start and an end (to do the whole job, completed, finished)

有事和群众商量 **yǔ-shìh hó ch'ǘn-chùng shāng-liang** to consult the masses whenever problems arise

有恃无恐 **yǔ-shìh wú-k'ǔng** having support one does not fear

有损无益 **yǔ-sǔn wú-ì** having loss and no profit (wholly disadvantageous, without redeeming benefit)

有代表性 **yǔ tài-piǎo-hsìng** having representative character, representative

有待于 **yǔ-tài-yǘ** to have dependence on, wait until

有的放矢 **yǔ-tì-fàng-shǐh** to shoot the arrow [only when] there is a target (purposive, sure of the goal)

有条件 **yǔ-t'iáo-chièn** the conditions are right, circumstances are favorable (since objective requirements are met, the outlook is promising)

有条件的 **yǔ-t'iáo-chièn-te** conditional, with conditions attached

有条不紊 **yǔ-t'iáo pù-wěn** well organized and without confusion (orderly, systematic, in regular sequence)

有头无尾 **yǔ-t'óu wú-wěi** to have a beginning but no end (to leave a job unfinished, quit halfway)

有团结有斗争, 以斗争求团结 **yǔ t'uán-chiéh yǔ tòu-chēng, ǐ tòu-chēng ch'iú t'uán-chiéh** there is unity and there is struggle and [we must] use struggle in order to achieve unity

有则改之, 无则加勉 **yǔ-tsé-kǎi-chīh, wú-tsé-chiā-miěn** [if I] have [mistakes] then [I will] correct them; [if I] have none then [I will] work harder

有闻必录 **yǔ-wén pì-lù** if it is heard it will be written down (if there is news it must be printed—an alleged fault of the capitalist press since there is no concern whether the news is correct or not)

yù (yòu)

2540 又红又专 **yù-húng yù-chuān** both red and expert (both politically and professionally qualified)

又联合, 又斗争 **yù lién-hó, yù tòu-chēng** both unity and struggle

又团结, 又斗争 **yù t'uán-chiéh, yù tòu-chēng** both unity and struggle (simultaneously to unite with and wage struggle against)

2541 右倾 **yù-ch'īng** tending to the right, rightist, right-wing, rightist deviation

右倾机会主义 **yù-ch'īng chī-huì-chǔ-ì** rightist opportunism

右倾机会主义路线 **yù-ch'īng chī-huì-chǔ-ì lù-hsièn** the line of rightist opportunism

右倾主义 **yù-ch'īng-chǔ-ì** rightist deviationism

右倾主义投机分子 **yù-ch'īng-chǔ-ì t'óu-chī-fèn-tzǔ** rightist opportunists

右倾情绪 **yù-ch'īng ch'íng-hsù** right-deviationist sentiments, right-wing sympathies

右倾翻案黑风 **yù-ch'īng fān-àn hēi-fēng** the black wind of rightist case reversing

右倾分裂主义 **yù-ch'īng fēn-lièh-chǔ-ì** rightist splittism

右倾分子 **yù-ch'īng fèn-tzǔ** rightist deviationists, rightist elements

右倾保守思想 **yù-ch'īng pǎo-shǒu szū-hsiǎng** rightist conservative thinking

右倾思想 **yù-ch'īng szū-hsiǎng** rightist thinking, rightist ideas

右倾投降主义路线 **yù-ch'īng t'óu-hsiáng-chǔ-ì lù-hsièn** the rightist capitulationist line

右舷 **yù-hsièn** the right side of a vessel, starboard

右翼 **yù-ì** (1) the [political] right wing, rightists, conservatives; (2) the right flank [of an army]

右翼分子 **yù-ì fèn-tzǔ** a right-winger, right-wing elements

右派分子 **yù-p'ài fèn-tzǔ** a rightist, member of the right wing or rightist groups

右得要命 **yù-té-yào-mìng** rightist to an extreme

2542 幼稚 **yù-chìh** childish, immature, juvenile, naive

幼稚可笑 **yù-chìh k'ǒ-hsiào** childish and laughable, ridiculously immature, puerile

幼儿教育 **yù-érh chìao-yù** preschool education

幼儿园 **yù-érh-yuán** a kindergarten (formerly called **yù-chìh-yuán** 幼稚园)

幼芽 **yù-yá** a young shoot, sprout, primary bud

2543 诱惑 **yù-huò** to entice, seduce, lead astray, deceive

诱导 **yù-tǎo** to lead, guide, induce; induction

诱敌深入 **yù-tí shēn-jù** to lure the enemy into deep penetration [so that he may be entrapped]

诱压兼施 **yù-yā-chiēn-shìh** to act both by coaxing and pressure

yǔ (yū)

2544 迂回 **yǔ-huí** winding, roundabout, circuitous, tortuous

迂回战术 **yǔ-huí-chàn-shù** flanking tactics

迂回曲折 **yǔ-huí-ch'ǔ-ché** twists and turns, tortuous and devious, circuitous, not straightforward

2545 淤积 **yǔ-chī** to silt up, clog up

淤地 **yǔ-tì** filled land, land built up by sedimentation

yú (yú)

2546 余粮 **yú-liáng** surplus grain (the grain remaining after meeting all requirements such as public grain, state purchase, and the producing unit's own subsistence)

余粮户 **yú-liáng-hù** households having surplus grain, households with grain reserves

余粮队 **yú-liáng-tuì** a production team or brigade producing surplus grain

余孽 **yú-nièh** remnant evils, [feudal] dregs, [outlaw] holdovers

余波 **yú-pō** the swell after a storm (aftermath, postlude, sequel)

余地 **yú-tì** spare space, leeway, elbow room, room to maneuver

余毒 **yú-tú** leftover poison (lingering pernicious influences, noxious remnants)

余痛 **yú-t'ùng** lingering pain

2547 鱼场 **yú-ch'ǎng** a fishing ground, fishery

鱼肝油 **yú-kān-yú** cod-liver oil

鱼雷艇 **yú-léi-t'ǐng** a torpedo boat

鱼龙混杂 **yú-lúng-hùn-tsá** to mix fish and dragons together (good and bad people intermingled)

鱼苗 **yú-miáo** fry, spawn, small fish

鱼目混珠 **yú-mù-hùn-chū** to mix fish eyes with pearls (to offer something bogus; masquerade, counterfeit)

2548 娱乐 **yú-lè** amusement, recreation, pleasure, fun

娱乐工具论 **yú-lè kūng-chù lùn** the doctrine that [literature] is an instrument for pleasure (to be criticized)

2549 渔船 **yú-ch'uán** a fishing boat, trawler

渔具 **yú-chù** fishing gear, fishing tackle

渔人之利 **yú-jén-chīh-lì** the fisherman's profit (when the bird and clam are engaged in fighting each other, the fisherman takes them both: hence, to make capital out of another's trouble)

渔民 **yú-mín** fishermen, fishing folk

渔村 **yú-ts'ūn** fishing village

渔业 **yú-yèh** the fishery industry

渔业大队 **yú-yèh tà-tuì** fishing brigade [of a commune]

渔运大队 **yú-yùn tà-tuì** a fishing and transport brigade [of a commune]

2550 舆论 **yú-lùn** public opinion

2551 愚忠愚孝 **yú-chūng yú-hsiào** simpleminded loyalty and filial piety

愚蠢 **yú-ch'ǔn** stupid, dull, thickwitted, foolish

愚惑 **yú-huò** to fool, deceive, cheat

愚公精神 **yú-kūng chīng-shén** the Yü Kung spirit (*see next below*)

愚公移山 **yú-kūng í-shān** "How Yü Kung Removed the Mountain" (also translated as "The Foolish Old Man Who Moved the Mountain," a classical story of humble perseverance, first used by Mao Tse-tung in 1945, now one of the **lǎo-sān-p'iēn**)

愚昧无知 **yú-mèi wú-chīh** foolish and ignorant, rude and unenlightened

愚民政策 **yú-mín chèng-ts'è** a policy of keeping the people ignorant; obscurantism, obfuscation

愚民主义 **yú-mín-chǔ-ì** obscurantism

愚弄 **yú-nùng** to make a fool of, mock, deride, ridicule, tease, deceive

愚弄人民 **yú-nùng jén-mín** to hoodwink the people

yǔ (yǔ)

2552　与己无关 **yǔ-chǐ-wú-kuān** of no concern to me (to look at all questions in a self-centered way)

与众不同 **yǔ-chùng-pù-t'úng** different from the multitude (standing out from the crowd, distinguished)

与其 **yǔ-ch'í** rather than

与其......宁可 **yǔ-ch'í...níng-k'ǒ...** rather than . . . it is better to . . .

与传统观念彻底决裂 **yǔ ch'uán-t'ǔng-kuān-nièn ch'è-tǐ chüéh-lièh** to make a complete break from traditional concepts

与虎谋皮 **yǔ-hǔ-móu-p'í** to ask a tiger to give up his pelt (to ask someone—e.g., a landlord—to give up something vital to his existence; a futile request; a doomed petition)

与人为善 **yǔ-jén wéi-shàn** to help others to practice virtue (to help someone for his own good)

与日俱增 **yǔ-jìh-chǔ-tsēng** to grow with each passing day (to grow with time)

与生俱来 **yǔ-shēng-chǔ-lái** something every person is born with (to come with birth, innate, inborn)

与世长辞 **yǔ-shìh-ch'áng-tz'ú** to depart from the world for good (to pass away, die)

与世隔绝 **yǔ-shìh-kó-chüéh** to be cut off from the world

与世无争 **yǔ-shìh-wú-chēng** to have no conflict with the world (to remain aloof, avoid conflicts that should be faced, take an escapist attitude)

与 **yǔ**: *see also* **yù**

2553　宇宙 **yǔ-chòu** the universe, cosmos, space

宇宙飞船 **yǔ-chòu fēi-ch'uán** a space ship

宇宙飞行 **yǔ-chòu fēi-hsíng** space flight

宇宙飞行站 **yǔ-chòu fēi-hsíng-chàn** a space station

宇宙飞行员 **yǔ-chòu fēi-hsíng-yuán** an astronaut, cosmonaut

宇宙火箭 **yǔ-chòu huǒ-chièn** a space rocket

宇宙线 **yǔ-chòu-hsièn** cosmic rays

宇宙观 **yǔ-chòu-kuān** cosmic view, world outlook

宇宙空间 **yǔ-chòu-k'ūng-chiēn** cosmic space, outer space

宇宙射线 **yǔ-chòu-shè-hsièn** cosmic radiation

宇称守恒定律 **yǔ-ch'èn shǒu-héng tìng-lù** the law of parity conservation

2554　羽毛球 **yǔ-máo-ch'iú** badminton

羽毛未丰 **yǔ-máo-wèi-fēng** the feather isn't yet fully grown (still fledgling, immature, inexperienced)

2555　雨后春笋 **yǔ-hòu-ch'ūn-sǔn** like bamboo shoots after a spring rain (springing up everywhere, very numerous, growing rapidly)

雨过天晴 **yǔ-kuò-t'iēn-ch'íng** the rain passes and the sky clears (*figurative*)

雨量 **yǔ-liàng** amount of rainfall, precipitation

雨量表 **yǔ-liàng-piǎo** a rain gauge

2556　语重心长 **yǔ-chùng-hsīn-ch'áng** weighty words and a thoughtful heart

语汇 **yǔ-huì** vocabulary

语录 **yǔ-lù** notes of discourses by a master, quotations, sayings; after 1966, also used to refer to the *Quotations from Chairman Mao*

语录牌 **yǔ-lù-p'ái** a quotation board (usually for quotations from Mao Tse-tung)

语体 **yǔ-t'ǐ** the vernacular style [of writing]

语无伦次 **yǔ-wú-lún-tz'ù** to talk incoherently; jumbled speech

语言 **yǔ-yén** language, speech

语言学 **yǔ-yén-hsuéh** linguistics

yù (yù)

2557　与会者 **yù-huì-chě** participants in a meeting

与会国 **yù-huì-kuó** countries attending a conference, participating nations

与 **yù**: *see also* **yǔ**

2558　玉米 **yù-mǐ** Indian corn, maise

玉米脱粒机 **yù-mǐ t'ō-lì-chī** a corn shelling machine, corn husker

玉石俱焚 **yù-shíh-chù-fén** jade and stone are all destroyed (to destroy indiscriminately)

玉蜀黍 **yù-shǔ-shǔ** Indian corn, maize

玉雕 **yù-tiāo** jade carving

2559　芋头 **yù-t'ou** the taro (an edible starchy tuber grown in the tropics)

2560　郁愤 **yù-fèn** suppressed indignation, exasperation

2561　育种 **yù-chǔng** selective breeding, seed cultivation

育秧 **yù-yāng** a rice seedling

2562　浴血奋战 **yù-hsuèh fèn-chàn** a bloody battle, sanguinary warfare

浴堂 **yù-t'áng** a public bathhouse

2563　预兆 **yù-chào** an omen, premonition, portent

预计 **yù-chì** to estimate, calculate in advance, project; an estimate

预计估产 **yù-chì kū-ch'ǎn** a preharvest estimate of production

预见 **yù-chièn** to foresee, anticipate, envision, see ahead; foresight, prudence

预期 **yù-ch'ī** to anticipate, expect; anticipation

预防 **yù-fáng** to take precautions, forestall, prevent beforehand

预防针 **yù-fáng-chēn** preventive inoculation

预防接种 **yù-fáng-chiēh-chùng** preventive inoculation, prophylactic inoculation, vaccination

预防为主, 治疗为辅 **yù-fáng wéi-chǔ, chìh-liáo wéi-fǔ** prevention is basic and treatment is secondary

预分 **yù-fēn** anticipatory distribution (a partial distribution before the completion of the harvest)

预想 **yù-hsiǎng** to anticipate, expect, envision

预先 **yù-hsiēn** in advance, beforehand, in anticipation; prior, preliminary

预先装配 **yù-hsiēn chuàng-p'èi** to prefabricate, preassemble; prefabrication

预购合同 **yù-kòu-hó-t'ung** an advance purchase contract (a contract made before the harvest)

预料 **yù-liào** to predict, expect, assume, anticipate, forecast; a prediction, forecast

预谋 **yù-móu** to scheme, plot in advance; premeditated [with malice]

预报 **yù-pào** a forecast, advance announcement; to forecast

预备役 **yù-pèi-ì** [military] reserve service

预备党员 **yù-pèi tǎng-yuán** a probationary Party member

预示 **yù-shìh** an advance warning, sign, omen

预算 **yù-suàn** a budget, estimate; to calculate in advance, budget

预算决算制度 **yù-suàn chüéh-suàn chìh-tù** a system [requiring] preliminary budgets and final accounting

预算审查委员会 **yù-suàn shěn-ch'á wěi-yuán-huì** a budget examination committee

预算收入 **yù-suàn shōu-jù** to budget one's income; a budget

预定 **yù-tìng** to decide beforehand, establish in advance, schedule, reserve, place an order for, subscribe to [a magazine, etc.]

预测预报 **yù-ts'è yù-pào** to predict and forecast [weather]

预言 **yù-yén** a prophesy, prediction, forecast; to predict

预应力混凝土 **yù-yìng-lì hùn-níng-t'ǔ** prestressed concrete

预约制度 **yù-yuēh chìh-tù** the appointment system (e.g., in medical clinics)

2564 欲盖弥彰 **yù-kài-mí-chāng** the more one tries to cover up [faults, etc.] the more apparent they become

欲罢不能 **yù-pà-pù-néng** wishing to stop [a course of action, etc.] but unable [to do so]

欲速不达 **yù-sù-pù-tá** desiring haste one fails to attain (haste makes waste)

2565 寓言 **yù-yén** a fable, allegory

2566 遇到 **yù-tào** to meet, encounter

2567 裕仁天皇 **yù-jén t'iēn-huáng** Emperor Hirohito [the emperor of Japan, b. 1901, reigning since 1926]

裕固族 **yù-kù-tsú** the Yü-ku people [a minority in Kansu province: population 4,600 as of 1957]

2568 豫 **yù** Honan province

yuān (yuān)

2569 冤家 **yuān-chiā** an enemy, adversary, opponent

冤屈 **yuān-ch'ǔ** a grievance, wrong, injustice, false accusation; to do an injustice

冤枉 **yuān-wǎng** to wrong, accuse falsely, do an injustice; an injustice, wrong, grievance

冤有头, 债有主 **yuān-yǔ-t'óu, chài-yǔ-chǔ** every grievance has a source, and every obligation is owed to someone

冤狱 **yuān-yù** an unjust verdict, miscarriage of justice

2570 鸳鸯蝴蝶派 **yuān-yāng-hú-tiéh-p'ài** the mandarin duck and butterfly school (a school of modern literature characterized by sentimental love stories)

2571 渊薮 **yuān-sǒu** the gathering ground of fish and beasts (a haunt, hotbed, haven)

渊源 **yuān-yuán** a source, origin, wellspring, fountainhead; cause

yuán (yuán)

2572 元件 **yuán-chièn** a basic part, primary element [of machinery, etc.]

元气 **yuán-ch'ì** vitality and constitution, stamina, strength

元老 **yuán-lǎo** an elder (usually a person of great prestige in political life who has held high position for long periods, or who has seniority as an old Party member)

元麦 **yuán-mài** naked barley

元首 **yuán-shǒu** the head of state, chief executive

元素 **yuán-sù** a [chemical] element

元旦 **yuán-tàn** New Year's Day

元旦献词 **yuán-tàn hsièn-tz'ú** a New Year's message

2573 园艺 **yuán-ì** gardening, horticulture

园陵 **yuán-líng** an imperial tomb, mausoleum

园田化 **yuán-t'ién-huà** intensive cultivation, garden farming; to intensify cultivation

2574 原籍 **yuán-chí** orginal domicile, home district, native place

原职 **yuán-chíh** a former post, original position

原封不动 **yuán-fēng pù-tùng** the original sealing has not been touched (intact, untouched, unopened)

原形毕露 **yuán-hsíng pì-lù** the true form is completely revealed (completely unmasked)

原型 **yuán-hsíng** a primitive form, prototype; standard, mold

原意 **yuán-ì** original meaning, original intention

原任 **yuán-jèn** [one's] original post, formerly held the post of; a late incumbent, predecessor

原稿 **yuán-kǎo** a manuscript, original copy

原告 **yuán-kào** a plaintiff, complainant, person bringing a suit

原耕 **yuán-kēng** original tillage (a term used during the Land Reform Campaign for the basis of land division)

原来如此 **yuán-lái-jú-tz'ǔ** it has always been thus, so that is how things are, now I understand

原理 **yuán-lǐ** a principle, [scientific] theory, doctrine

原料 **yuán-liào** raw materials, resources

原料输出国组织 **yuán-liào shū-ch'ū-kuó tsǔ-chīh** organizations of raw material exporting countries [such as OPEC]

原煤 **yuán-méi** unprocessed coal

原木 **yuán-mù** unprocessed wood, timber, logs

原始 **yuán-shǐh** primitive, original; a source, origin, beginning

原始公社制 **yuán-shǐh kūng-shè-chìh** the primitive communal system (one of the five basic relations of production)

原始森林 **yuán-shǐh sēn-lín** the primeval forest, virgin forest

原始社会 **yuán-shǐh shè-huì** primitive society

原始武器 **yuán-shǐh wǔ-ch'ì** primitive weapons

原地固守 **yuán-tì kù-shǒu** to stubbornly defend their original positions

原订 **yuán-tìng** originally planned, ordered, contracted

原定 **yuán-tìng** originally fixed, decided, planned, scheduled

原动力 **yuán-tùng-lì** natural forces, driving force, power, impetus

原载 **yuán-tsǎi** originally published in

原则 **yuán-tsé** a fundamental rule, general principle [usually political or ideological], doctrine; principled

原则问题 **yuán-tsé wèi-t'í** a problem of principle, fundamental question, question of principle

原子 **yuán-tzǔ** an atom

原子战争 **yuán-tzǔ chàn-chēng** atomic war

原子击破器 **yuán-tzǔ chī-p'ò-ch'ì** atomic accelerator, atom smasher

原子基地 **yuán-tzǔ chī-tì** an atomic [military] base

原子氢复合炸弹 **yuán-tzǔ ch'īng-fù-hó chà-tàn** a combined atomic-hydrogen bomb, hydrogen bomb

原子反应堆 **yuán-tzǔ fǎn-yìng-tuī** atomic reactor pile

原子核 **yuán-tzǔ-hó** the atomic nucleus; nuclear

原子学 **yuán-tzǔ-hsuéh** the science of atoms, nuclear physics

原子感应加速运动器 **yuán-tzǔ kǎn-yìng chiā-sù yùn-tùng-ch'ì** a betatron

原子论 **yuán-tzǔ-lùn** atomic theory, atomism

原子能 **yuán-tzǔ-néng** atomic energy

原子能发电站 **yuán-tzǔ-néng fā-tièn-chàn** an atomic power station, nuclear power station

原子讹诈政策 **yuán-tzǔ ó-chà chèng-ts'è** policy of atomic blackmail

原子时代 **yuán-tzǔ shíh-tài** the atomic age

原子弹 **yuán-tzǔ-tàn** an atomic bomb

原子弹头 **yuán-tzǔ tàn-t'óu** an atomic warhead

原子外交 **yuán-tzǔ wài-chiāo** atomic diplomacy

原子武器 **yuán-tzǔ wǔ-ch'ì** atomic weapons, atomic weaponry

原文 **yuán-wén** the original text

原样 **yuán-yàng** the original form

原盐 **yuán-yén** raw salt, unrefined salt, unprocessed salt

原油 **yuán-yú** crude oil, petroleum

原原本本 **yuán-yuán-pěn-pěn** from beginning to end, the whole story, in complete detail

2575 圆桌会议 **yuán-chō-huì-ì** a round-table conference

圆锥 **yuán-chuī** a cone

圆规 **yuán-kuēi** a pair of compasses, dividers

圆满结束 **yuán-mǎn chiéh-shù** to conclude satisfactorily, round off, wind up; a completely satisfactory conclusion

圆盘犁 **yuán-p'án-lí** a disc plow, harrow

圆筒 **yuán-t'ǔng** a cylinder

圆屋顶 **yuán-wū-tǐng** a dome, vault

圆舞曲 **yuán-wǔ-ch'ǔ** a waltz [dance]

2576 援救 **yuán-chiù** to come to the aid of, rescue, save, relieve

援助 **yuán-chù** aid, assistance, help, support; to assist, aid

援助协定 **yuán-chù hsiéh-tìng** an [international] aid agreement

援例 **yuán-lì** to follow a precedent, rely on a previous case

援兵 **yuán-pīng** reinforcing troops, reinforcements

援外 **yuán-wài** to give foreign aid; foreign aid

援引经典 **yuán-yǐn chīng-tiěn** to quote from the classics, cite the classics

援越抗美 **yuán-yuèh k'àng-měi** Aid Vietnam and Resist America

2577 缘故 **yuán-kù** a cause, reason, motive

缘木求鱼 **yuán-mù-ch'iú-yú** to climb a tree to seek fish (useless effort, misdirected activity)

缘由 **yuán-yú** the whys and wherefores, cause, reason

2578 源泉 **yuán-ch'üán** a wellspring, fountainhead, source

源远流长 **yuán-yuǎn-liú-ch'áng** the source is far and the course is long (to have a long history)

源源不绝 **yuán-yuán-pù-chüéh** to continue without end

2579 猿人 **yuán-jén** the anthropoids, apes

yuǎn (yuǎn)

2580 远征 **yuǎn-chēng** to do battle in a distant land (a military expedition)

远征军 **yuǎn-chēng-chǔn** an expeditionary force

远见 **yuǎn-chièn** foresight, perspective, vision, prescience; farsighted

远见卓识 **yuǎn-chièn chō-shíh** farsighted and outstandingly intelligent

远近闻名 **yuǎn-chìn wén-míng** renowned far and near, famous in every quarter

远景 **yuǎn-chǐng** the long view, outlook, perspective; a vista, distant view

远景计划 **yuǎn-chǐng-chì-huà** a long-term plan

远景规划 **yuǎn-chǐng-kuēi-huà** a long-range plan

远程火箭 **yuǎn-ch'éng-huǒ-chièn** a long-range rocket

远程导弹 **yuǎn-ch'éng-tǎo-tàn** a long-range guided missile

远距离自动操纵 **yuǎn-chǜ-lí tzǔ-tùng ts'āo-tsùng** automatic remote control

远离 **yuǎn-lí** to be far removed from, keep at a distance

远射 **yuǎn-shè** to fire over a long range, shoot from a distance; a long shot

远射程 **yuǎn-shè-ch'éng** long range [of a projectile, etc.]

远水不解近渴 **yuǎn-shuǐ pù-chiěh chìn-k'ǒ** distant waters cannot assuage present thirst

远大 **yuǎn-tà** large, immense, great; bold, ambitious; far-reaching, promising

远走高飞 **yuǎn-tsǒu-kāo-fēi** to travel far and fly high (to leave home and find a new, bright future)

远足 **yuǎn-tsú** an outing, an excursion

远洋巨轮 **yuǎn-yáng chǜ-lún** ocean-going large ships

远洋班船 **yuǎn-yáng-pān-ch'uán** ocean-going ships operating on a schedule or regular run

yuàn (yuàn)

2581 院长 **yuàn-chǎng** the chief officer of a *yuan*, head of a college, chief judge

院系 **yuàn-hsì** schools and departments in a university or institute

院系调整 **yuàn-hsì t'iáo-chěng** the reorganization of colleges and departments [in institutions of higher learning]

2582 怨气 **yuàn-ch'ì** strong dissatisfaction, ill-will, resentment, spite, grudge

怨恨 **yuàn-hèn** to hate, resent; hatred, animosity, enmity, ill-will

怨命 **yuàn-mìng** to blame fate, complain against one's lot

怨声载道 **yuàn-shēng-tsài-tào** complaints are heard everywhere (a reference to bad administration, etc.)

怨天尤人 **yuàn-t'iēn-yú-jén** to complain about heaven and blame others (to avoid blame by shifting it to others)

怨言 **yuàn-yén** spiteful words, dissatisfied talk, complaints, grumbling, recrimination

2583 愿望 **yuàn-wàng** a hope, wish, what one's heart desires

yuēh (yuē)

2584 约法八章 **yuēh-fǎ pā-chāng** the eight articles of provisional law (a statement of Communist policy toward the population of the cities issued during the Liberation War)

约翰逊 **yuēh-hàn-hsùn** Johnson [U.S. President Lyndon B.]

约会 **yuēh-huì** an appointment, engagement, scheduled meeting

约束 **yuēh-shù** to restrain, bind, commit, limit, repress, curb

约旦 **yuēh-tàn** Jordan

约定俗成 **yuēh-tìng-sú-ch'éng** agreed upon and become customary (one of the bases for the adoption of simplified characters)

yuèh (yuè)

2585 月计表 **yuèh-chì-piǎo** a monthly statement [of accounts, quantities, etc.]

月经 **yuèh-chīng** the menstrual period, menses

月清月结 **yuèh-ch'īng yuèh-chiéh** monthly clearing and settling [financial]

月球火箭 **yuèh-ch'iú-huǒ-chièn** a moon rocket, lunik

月刊 **yuèh-k'ān** a monthly magazine or journal

月台 **yuèh-t'ái** a railway station platform

2586 乐曲 **yuèh-ch'ǔ** a musical composition, piece of music

乐谱 **yuèh-p'ǔ** a musical score, sheet music

乐队 **yuèh-tuì** an orchestra, band

乐 **yuèh**: see also **lè**

2587 悦服 **yuèh-fú** to submit willingly, gladly comply, agree, be satisfied with

2588 阅览室 **yuèh-lǎn-shìh** a reading room

阅兵 **yuèh-pīng** to review troops, inspect troops

2589 粤 **yuèh** Kwangtung province

2590 跃进 **yuèh-chìn** to leap forward, proceed in jumps; a leap forward

跃跃欲试 **yuèh-yuèh-yǜ-shìh** impatient to have a try, eager to do something

2591 越轨 **yuèh-kuěi** to leave the track (exceed the bounds, violate the rules, deviate from the permissible)

越共 **yuèh-kùng** the Viet Cong

越南 **yuèh-nán** Vietnam

越南民主共和国 **yuèh-nán mín-chǔ kùng-hó-kuó** the Democratic Republic of Vietnam (the government of North Vietnam before the collapse of South Vietnam)

越南南方共和临时革命政府 **yuèh-nán nán-fāng kùng-hó lín-shíh kó-mìng chèng-fú** the Provisional Revolutionary Government of the Republic of South Vietnam

越南南方民族解放阵线 **yuèh-nán nán-fāng mín-tsú chiěh fàng chèn-hsièn** the South Vietnam National Liberation Front

越南通讯社 **yuèh-nán t'ūng-hsùn-shè** the Vietnam News Agency [VNA]

越俎代庖 **yuèh-tsǔ-tài-p'áo** the one in charge of sacrifices leaves his post to act for the cook (to go beyond one's duties to meddle in the affairs of others)

越狱 **yuèh-yù** to escape from prison, break out of jail; a jail break

yūn (yūn)

2592 晕头转向 **yūn-t'óu-chuàn-hsiàng** to feel dizzy and giddy (completely befuddled)

yǔn (yǔn)

2593 允许 **yǔn-hsǔ** to permit, allow, authorize, approve, promise; permission, approval

2594 陨石 **yǔn-shíh** a meteor

yùn (yùn)

2595 运转 **yùn-chuǎn** to turn around, revolve, rotate

运筹学 **yùn-ch'óu-hsuéh** operations research

运费 **yùn-fèi** freight charges, transportation costs, shipping fees

运河 **yùn-hó** a [barge] canal; the Grand Canal

运搬带 **yùn-pān-tài** a conveyer belt

运输 **yùn-shū** transport, transportation, shipping, hauling, carrying, transit, freight

运算 **yùn-suàn** to compute, calculate; operation [mathematics]

运动 **yùn-tùng** motion, physical exercise (exercise of influence, agitation, organized political or social pressure, "a movement," campaign)

运动战 **yùn-tùng-chàn** mobile warfare

运动学 **yùn-tùng-hsuéh** kinetics

运动员 **yùn-tùng-yuán** an athlete, sports participant

运用自如 **yùn-yùng tzù-jú** to apply as one wishes, use with ease, handle with great smoothness

²⁵⁹⁶ 酝酿 **yùn-niàng** to ferment, brew, distill, foment (in an extended sense, the preliminary exchange of views, preparation of mood and opinions, and laying the groundwork for settlement of an important issue or the introduction of a new policy)

²⁵⁹⁷ 蕴藏 **yùn-ts'áng** to have in store, collected, hidden

yūng (yōng)

²⁵⁹⁸ 佣工 **yūng-kūng** a hired laborer
佣佃 **yūng-tièn** a tenant
佣 **yūng**: *see also* **yùng**

²⁵⁹⁹ 拥政爱民 **yūng-chèng-ài-mín** support the government and cherish the people (a movement within the PLA)
拥挤 **yūng-chǐ** to crowd, throng; crowded, packed
拥军爱民 **yūng-chǔn-ài-mín** [the people should] support the army [and the army should] cherish the people
拥军优属 **yūng-chǔn yū-shǔ** to support the army and give preferential treatment to their dependents
拥护 **yūng-hù** to support, uphold, protect, assist, espouse; support, approval
拥干爱民 **yūng-kàn ài-mín** [the people should] support the cadres [and the cadres should] cherish the people
拥干爱兵 **yūng-kàn āi-pīng** [the soldiers should] support the cadres [and the cadres should] cherish the soldiers
拥有 **yūng-yǔ** to have, possess

²⁶⁰⁰ 庸人自扰 **yūng-jén tzù-jǎo** stupid people create trouble for themselves (upset by one's own folly)
庸俗 **yūng-sú** vulgar, unrefined, ordinary, mediocre
庸俗政治经济学 **yūng-sú chèng-chìh-chīng-chì-hsuéh** vulgar political economy (bourgeois economics)
庸俗进化论 **yūng-sú chìn-huà lùn** vulgar evolutionism, the unrefined theory of evolution (the concept that evolution can occur only in gradual stages without the possibility of major leaps; hence, something equivalent to reformism as opposed to revolution)
庸俗化 **yūng-sú-huà** to vulgarize; vulgarization, Philistinism
庸庸碌碌 **yūng-yūng-lù-lù** undistinguished and mediocre, very ordinary, of no consequence

²⁶⁰¹ 壅塞 **yūng-sè** to clog up, obstruct, block, impede the flow of

²⁶⁰² 臃肿 **yūng-chǔng** fat and clumsy, swollen, bloated, unwieldy (over-expanded, over-staffed)

yǔng (yǒng)

²⁶⁰³ 永垂不朽 **yǔng-ch'uí-pù-hsiǔ** to hand down forever without decay (to be remembered forever, immortal)
永恒不变 **yǔng-héng-pù-pièn** eternal and unchanging
永保人民的江山 **yǔng-pǎo jén-mín te chīang-shān** to preserve forever the people's rivers and mountains (to protect the country, uphold the regime)
永不卷刃的尖刀 **yǔng-pù chǔǎn-jèn te chiēn-tāo** a knife that never loses its edge (a company or team that goes on to greater and greater achievements)
永不变色 **yǔng-pù-pièn-sè** never to change color (i.e., never to lose redness)
永世长存 **yǔng-shìh-ch'áng-ts'ún** to exist eternally; everlasting, eternal
永无休止 **yǔng-wú-hsiū-chǐh** to be eternally without ceasing, never to come to an end, endless

²⁶⁰⁴ 勇气 **yǔng-ch'ì** courage, bravery, valor, prowess, gallantry, heroism
勇敢 **yǔng-kǎn** brave, bold, courageous, heroic, fearless; bravery, courage
勇敢牺牲 **yǔng-kǎn hsī-shēng** a heroic sacrifice; to bravely sacrifice oneself
勇往直前 **yǔng-wǎng chíh-ch'ién** to march fearlessly forward, advance courageously, go straight ahead
勇于创新 **yǔng-yǔ ch'uàng-hsīn** to be brave in creating new things, boldly innovative
勇于革新 **yǔng-yǔ kó-hsīn** to be brave in renovating

²⁶⁰⁵ 涌现 **yǔng-hsièn** to suddenly spring forth, emerge
涌上心头 **yǔng-shàng hsīn-t'óu** to come to mind, leap into one's mind

²⁶⁰⁶ 踊跃 **yǔng-yuèh** to jump with joy (joyful, happy, enthusiastic)

yùng (yòng)

²⁶⁰⁷ 用非所学 **yùng-fēi-sǒ-hsuéh** to use [a man] in ways other than his training (his job is unrelated to his training)
用户 **yùng-hù** a customer, user, consumer, patron
用心 **yùng-hsīn** to be attentive, diligent, careful, exercise caution, pay close

attention

用心摸索 **yùng-hsīn-mō-sǒ** to grope for carefully, feel out, to ponder with great care

用血汗换来 **yùng-hsuèh-hàn huàn-lái** to use one's blood and sweat in exchange [for something] (to gain something through strenuous effort)

用意 **yùng-ì** an intention, aim, purpose leading idea

用功 **yùng-kūng** to study hard, work diligently, apply oneself

用苦水洗过的眼睛最亮 **yùng-k'ǔ-shuǐ hsǐ-kuò-te yěn-chīng tsuì-liàng** eyes that have been washed with bitter water are the brightest (those who have suffered can see [right and wrong] the clearest)

用粮 **yùng-liáng** rations, grain for consumption

用粮计划 **yùng-liáng chì-huà** a grain consumption plan

用得上 **yùng-te-shàng** practical, usable, feasible, applicable

用材林 **yùng-ts'ái-lín** a timber forest (a forest producing usable timber and lumber in contrast to a forest maintained for natural beauty or firewood and charcoal)

用语 **yùng-yǔ** phraseology, terminology

佣金 **yùng-chīn** a commission, brokerage fee

佣 **yùng**: *see also* **yūng**

2608

Conversion Table A:
Pinyin to Wade-Giles

Pinyin	Wade-Giles	Pinyin	Wade-Giles	Pinyin	Wade-Giles	Pinyin	Wade-Giles
a	a	chun	ch'un	fu	fu	jie	chieh
ai	ai	chuo	ch'o			jin	chin
an	an	ci	tz'u	ga	ka	jing	ching
ang	ang	cong	ts'ung	gai	kai	jiong	chiung
ao	ao	cou	ts'ou	gan	kan	jiu	chiu
		cu	ts'u	gang	kang	ju	chü
ba	pa	cuan	ts'uan	gao	kao	juan	chüan
bai	pai	cui	ts'ui	ge	ke, ko	jue	chüeh
ban	pan	cun	ts'un	gei	kei	jun	chün
bang	pang	cuo	ts'o	gen	ken		
bao	pao			geng	keng	ka	k'a
bei	pei	da	ta	gong	kung	kai	k'ai
ben	pen	dai	tai	gou	kou	kan	k'an
beng	peng	dan	tan	gu	ku	kang	k'ang
bi	pi	dang	tang	gua	kua	kao	k'ao
bian	pien	dao	tao	guai	kuai	ke	k'o
biao	piao	de	te	guan	kuan	ken	k'en
bie	pieh	dei	tei	guang	kuang	keng	k'eng
bin	pin	deng	teng	gui	kuei	kong	k'ung
bing	ping	di	ti	gun	kun	kou	k'ou
bo	po	dian	tien	guo	kuo	ku	k'u
bu	pu	diao	tiao			kua	k'ua
		die	tieh	ha	ha	kuai	k'uai
ca	ts'a	ding	ting	hai	hai	kuan	k'uan
cai	ts'ai	diu	tiu	han	han	kuang	k'uang
can	ts'an	dong	tung	hang	hang	kui	k'uei
cang	ts'ang	dou	tou	hao	hao	kun	k'un
cao	ts'ao	du	tu	he	ho, he	kuo	k'uo
ce	ts'e	duan	tuan	hei	hei		
cen	ts'en	dui	tui	hen	hen	la	la
ceng	ts'eng	dun	tun	heng	heng	lai	lai
cha	ch'a	duo	to	hong	hung	lan	lan
chai	ch'ai			hou	hou	lang	lang
chan	ch'an	e	o	hu	hu	lao	lao
chang	ch'ang	ei	ei	hua	hua	le	le
chao	ch'ao	en	en	huai	huai	lei	lei
che	ch'e	eng	eng	huan	huan	leng	leng
chen	ch'en	er	erh	huang	huang	li	li
cheng	ch'eng			hui	hui	lia	lia
chi	ch'ih	fa	fa	hun	hun	lian	lien
chong	ch'ung	fan	fan	huo	huo	liang	liang
chou	ch'ou	fang	fang			liao	liao
chu	ch'u	fei	fei	ji	chi	lie	lieh
chuai	ch'uai	fen	fen	jia	chia	lin	lin
chuan	ch'uan	feng	feng	jian	chien	ling	ling
chuang	ch'uang	fo	fo	jiang	chiang	liu	liu
chui	ch'ui	fou	fou	jiao	chiao	lo	lo

Pinyin	Wade-Giles	Pinyin	Wade-Giles	Pinyin	Wade-Giles	Pinyin	Wade-Giles
long	lung	pang	p'ang	shen	shen	xiong	hsiung
lou	lou	pao	p'ao	sheng	sheng	xiu	hsiu
lu	lu	pei	p'ei	shi	shih	xu	hsu
luan	luan	pen	p'en	shou	shou	xuan	hsuan
lun	lun	peng	p'eng	shu	shu	xue	hsueh
luo	lo	pi	p'i	shua	shua	xun	hsun
lü	lü	pian	p'ien	shuai	shuai		
lüe	lueh	piao	p'iao	shuan	shuan	ya	ya
		pie	p'ieh	shuang	shuang	yan	yen
ma	ma	pin	p'in	shui	shui	yang	yang
mai	mai	ping	p'ing	shun	shun	yao	yao
man	man	po	p'o	shuo	shuo	ye	yeh
mang	mang	pou	p'ou	si	szu, ssu	yi	i
mao	mao	pu	p'u	song	sung	yin	yin
mei	mei			sou	sou	ying	ying
men	men	qi	ch'i	su	su	yong	yung
meng	meng	qia	ch'ia	suan	suan	you	yu
mi	mi	qian	ch'ien	sui	sui	yu	yü
mian	mien	qiang	ch'iang	sun	sun	yuan	yuan
miao	miao	qiao	ch'iao	suo	so	yue	yueh
mie	mieh	qie	ch'ieh			yun	yun
min	min	qin	ch'in	ta	t'a		
ming	ming	qing	ch'ing	tai	t'ai	za	tsa
miu	miu	qiong	ch'iung	tan	t'an	zai	tsai
mo	mo	qiu	ch'iu	tang	t'ang	zan	tsan
mou	mou	qu	ch'ü	tao	t'ao	zang	tsang
mu	mu	quan	ch'üan	te	t'e	zao	tsao
		que	ch'üeh	teng	t'eng	ze	tse
na	na	qun	ch'ün	ti	t'i	zei	tsei
nai	nai			tian	t'ien	zen	tsen
nan	nan	ran	jan	tiao	t'iao	zeng	tseng
nang	nang	rang	jang	tie	t'ieh	zha	cha
nao	nao	rao	jao	ting	t'ing	zhai	chai
ne	ne	re	je	tong	t'ung	zhan	chan
nei	nei	ren	jen	tou	t'ou	zhang	chang
nen	nen	reng	jeng	tu	t'u	zhao	chao
neng	neng	ri	jih	tuan	t'uan	zhe	che
ni	ni	rong	jung	tui	t'ui	zhei	chei
nian	nien	rou	jou	tun	t'un	zhen	chen
niang	niang	ru	ju	tuo	t'o	zheng	cheng
niao	niao	ruan	juan			zhi	chih
nie	nieh	rui	jui	wa	wa	zhong	chung
nin	nin	run	jun	wai	wai	zhou	chou
ning	ning	ruo	jo	wan	wan	zhu	chu
niu	niu			wang	wang	zhua	chua
nong	nung	sa	sa	wei	wei	zhuai	chuai
nou	nou	sai	sai	wen	wen	zhuan	chuan
nu	nu	san	san	weng	weng	zhuang	chuang
nü	nü	sang	sang	wo	wo	zhui	chui
nuan	nuan	sao	sao	wu	wu	zhun	chun
nüe	nueh	se	se			zhuo	cho
nuo	no	sen	sen	xi	hsi	zi	tzu
		seng	seng	xia	hsia	zong	tsung
o	o	sha	sha	xian	hsien	zou	tsou
ou	ou	shai	shai	xiang	hsiang	zu	tsu
		shan	shan	xiao	hsiao	zuan	tsuan
pa	p'a	shang	shang	xie	hsieh	zui	tsui
pai	p'ai	shao	shao	xin	hsin	zun	tsun
pan	p'an	she	she	xing	hsing	zuo	tso
		shei	shei				

Conversion Table B: Simplified to Complex Character Forms
(arranged by stroke order)

简化字总表检字

JIANHUAZI ZONGBIAO JIANZI

说　明

一、为了便利读者检查已经公布推行的简化字，我们根据《简化字总表》第二版编了这本检字。

二、本检字分三个表：A. 从拼音查汉字；B. 从简体查繁体；C. 从繁体查简体。

三、A 表是按汉语拼音字母的顺序排列的，一字异读的互见，一音异调的只列一调。†

四、B 表和 C 表是按汉字笔数排列的，同笔数的字以横、竖、撇、点、折为序。

五、凡《简化字总表》规定可作偏旁用的简化字，都用 ＊ 号标在字前，以便同不标 ＊ 号的，即不作偏旁用的简化字区别开来。

六、《简化字总表》第二表中的14个简化偏旁：讠〔言〕饣〔食〕、为〔昜〕、纟〔糸〕、収〔取〕、𮥼〔𤇾〕、収〔臨〕、只〔戠〕、钅〔金〕、兴〔𦥯〕、𡍼〔睪〕、圣〔坙〕、亦〔䜌〕、呙〔咼〕，一般不能独立成字，本检字没有收录。

七、凡《简化字总表》中附有注释的字，都用数码标在字后，注释统一排在 C 表的后面。‡

文字改革出版社　1964 年 8 月

---

2 笔
厂〔廠〕
卜〔蔔〕
儿〔兒〕
＊几〔幾〕
了〔瞭〕

3 笔
干〔乾〕⑧,
〔幹〕
亏〔虧〕
才〔纔〕
＊万〔萬〕
＊与〔與〕
千〔韆〕

亿〔億〕
个〔個〕
么〔麼〕⑳
＊广〔廣〕
＊门〔門〕
＊义〔義〕㉖
卫〔衛〕
飞〔飛〕
习〔習〕
＊马〔馬〕㉙
＊乡〔鄉〕

4 笔
【一】
＊丰〔豐〕⑥

开〔開〕
＊无〔無〕㊴
＊韦〔韋〕
＊专〔專〕
＊云〔雲〕
＊艺〔藝〕
厅〔廳〕㉔
＊历〔歷〕
〔曆〕
＊区〔區〕㉕
＊车〔車〕
【丨】
＊冈〔岡〕
＊贝〔貝〕

＊见〔見〕
【丿】
＊气〔氣〕
＊长〔長〕④
仆〔僕〕㉗
币〔幣〕
＊从〔從〕
＊仑〔侖〕
＊仓〔倉〕
＊风〔風〕
仅〔僅〕
凤〔鳳〕
＊乌〔烏〕㉓
【丶】

闩〔閂〕
＊为〔爲〕
斗〔鬥〕
忆〔憶〕
订〔訂〕
计〔計〕
讣〔訃〕
认〔認〕
讥〔譏〕
【一】
丑〔醜〕
队〔隊〕
办〔辦〕
邓〔鄧〕

劝〔勸〕
＊双〔雙〕
书〔書〕

5 笔
【一】
击〔擊〕
扑〔撲〕
＊节〔節〕
术〔術〕㉛
＊龙〔龍〕
厉〔厲〕
灭〔滅〕
＊东〔東〕

轧〔軋〕
【丨】
＊卢〔盧〕
＊业〔業〕
旧〔舊〕
帅〔帥〕
＊归〔歸〕
＊叶〔葉〕㊺
号〔號〕
电〔電〕
只〔隻〕
〔祗〕
叽〔嘰〕
叹〔嘆〕
【丿】
们〔們〕

仪〔儀〕
丛〔叢〕
＊尔〔爾〕
＊乐〔樂〕
处〔處〕
冬〔鼕〕
＊鸟〔鳥〕㉔
务〔務〕
＊刍〔芻〕
饥〔饑〕
【丶】
邝〔鄺〕
冯〔馮〕
闪〔閃〕
兰〔蘭〕

---

† Table A is a conversion table of characters arranged by Pinyin and is omitted in this dictionary.

‡ The notes referred to in item 7 are omitted in this dictionary.

*汇〔匯〕
〔彙〕
头〔頭〕
汉〔漢〕
*宁〔寧〕㉕
讦〔訐〕
讧〔訌〕
讨〔討〕
*写〔寫〕㊷
让〔讓〕
礼〔禮〕
讪〔訕〕
讫〔訖〕
训〔訓〕
议〔議〕
讯〔訊〕
记〔記〕

【乛】

辽〔遼〕
*边〔邊〕
出〔齣〕
*发〔發〕
〔髮〕
*圣〔聖〕
*对〔對〕
台〔臺〕
〔檯〕
〔颱〕
纠〔糾〕
驭〔馭〕
丝〔絲〕

6 笔

【一】

玑〔璣〕
*动〔動〕
*执〔執〕
巩〔鞏〕
圹〔壙〕
扩〔擴〕
扪〔捫〕
扫〔掃〕
扬〔揚〕
场〔場〕
*亚〔亞〕
芗〔薌〕
朴〔樸〕
机〔機〕
权〔權〕
*过〔過〕
协〔協〕
压〔壓〕㊸
*厌〔厭〕
厍〔厙〕
*页〔頁〕
夸〔誇〕
夺〔奪〕
*达〔達〕
*夹〔夾〕
轨〔軌〕
*尧〔堯〕㊹
划〔劃〕
迈〔邁〕
*毕〔畢〕

【丨】

贞〔貞〕
*师〔師〕
*当〔當〕
〔噹〕
尘〔塵〕
吁〔籲〕㊽
吓〔嚇〕㊳
*虫〔蟲〕
曲〔麯〕
团〔團〕
〔糰〕
吗〔嗎〕
屿〔嶼〕
*岁〔歲〕
回〔迴〕
*岂〔豈〕
则〔則〕
刚〔剛〕
网〔網〕

【丿】

钆〔釓〕
钇〔釔〕
朱〔硃〕
*迁〔遷〕
*乔〔喬〕
伟〔偉〕
传〔傳〕
伛〔傴〕
优〔優〕
伤〔傷〕
伥〔倀〕
价〔價〕
伦〔倫〕
伧〔傖〕
*华〔華〕
伙〔夥〕⑩
伪〔僞〕
向〔嚮〕
后〔後〕
*会〔會〕
*杀〔殺〕
合〔閤〕
众〔衆〕
爷〔爺〕
伞〔傘〕
创〔創〕
杂〔雜〕
负〔負〕
犷〔獷〕
犸〔獁〕
凫〔鳧〕
邬〔鄔〕
饦〔飥〕
饧〔餳〕

【丶】

壮〔壯〕
冲〔衝〕
妆〔妝〕
庄〔莊〕51
庆〔慶〕㉘
*刘〔劉〕
*齐〔齊〕
*产〔産〕
闭〔閉〕
问〔問〕
闯〔闖〕
关〔關〕
灯〔燈〕
汤〔湯〕
忏〔懺〕
兴〔興〕
讲〔講〕
讳〔諱〕
讴〔謳〕
军〔軍〕
讵〔詎〕
讶〔訝〕
讷〔訥〕
许〔許〕
讹〔訛〕
䜣〔訢〕
论〔論〕
讻〔訩〕
讼〔訟〕
讽〔諷〕
*农〔農〕
设〔設〕
访〔訪〕
诀〔訣〕

【乛】

*寻〔尋〕
*尽〔盡〕
〔儘〕
导〔導〕
*孙〔孫〕
阵〔陣〕
阳〔陽〕
阶〔階〕
*阴〔陰〕
妇〔婦〕
妈〔媽〕
戏〔戲〕
观〔觀〕
欢〔歡〕
*买〔買〕
纡〔紆〕
红〔紅〕
纣〔紂〕
驮〔馱〕
纤〔縴〕
〔纖〕㊴
纥〔紇〕
驯〔馴〕
纨〔紈〕
约〔約〕
级〔級〕
纩〔纊〕
纪〔紀〕
驰〔馳〕
纫〔紉〕

7 笔

【一】

*寿〔壽〕
*麦〔麥〕
玛〔瑪〕
*进〔進〕
远〔遠〕
违〔違〕
韧〔韌〕
刬〔剗〕
运〔運〕
抚〔撫〕
坛〔壇〕
〔罎〕
抟〔摶〕
坏〔壞〕⑨
抠〔摳〕
坜〔壢〕
扰〔擾〕
坝〔壩〕
贡〔貢〕
㧏〔掆〕
折〔摺〕㊾
抡〔掄〕
抢〔搶〕
坞〔塢〕
坟〔墳〕
护〔護〕
*壳〔殼〕⑮
块〔塊〕
声〔聲〕
报〔報〕
拟〔擬〕
㧐〔㩳〕
芜〔蕪〕
苇〔葦〕
芸〔蕓〕
苈〔藶〕
苋〔莧〕
苁〔蓯〕
苍〔蒼〕
*严〔嚴〕
芦〔蘆〕
劳〔勞〕
克〔剋〕
苏〔蘇〕
〔囌〕
极〔極〕
杨〔楊〕
*两〔兩〕
*丽〔麗〕⑰
医〔醫〕
励〔勵〕
还〔還〕
矶〔磯〕
奁〔奩〕
歼〔殲〕
*来〔來〕
欤〔歟〕
轩〔軒〕
连〔連〕
轫〔軔〕

【丨】

*卤〔鹵〕
〔滷〕
邺〔鄴〕
坚〔堅〕
*时〔時〕
呒〔嘸〕
县〔縣〕㊵
里〔裏〕
呓〔囈〕
呕〔嘔〕
园〔園〕
呖〔嚦〕
旷〔曠〕
围〔圍〕
吨〔噸〕
旸〔暘〕
邮〔郵〕
困〔睏〕
员〔員〕
呗〔唄〕
听〔聽〕
呛〔嗆〕
呜〔嗚〕
别〔彆〕
财〔財〕
囵〔圇〕
觃〔覎〕
帏〔幃〕
岖〔嶇〕
岗〔崗〕
岘〔峴〕
帐〔帳〕
岚〔嵐〕

【丿】

针〔針〕
钉〔釘〕
钊〔釗〕
钋〔釙〕
钌〔釕〕
乱〔亂〕
体〔體〕
佣〔傭〕
㑩〔儸〕
彻〔徹〕
余〔餘〕㊼
*佥〔僉〕
谷〔穀〕
邻〔鄰〕
肠〔腸〕
*龟〔龜〕
*犹〔猶〕
狈〔狽〕
鸠〔鳩〕
*条〔條〕㉝
岛〔島〕
邹〔鄒〕
饨〔飩〕
饩〔餼〕
饪〔飪〕
饫〔飫〕
饬〔飭〕
饭〔飯〕
饮〔飲〕
系〔係〕
〔繫〕⑪

【丶】

冻〔凍〕
状〔狀〕
亩〔畝〕
庑〔廡〕
库〔庫〕
疖〔癤〕
疗〔療〕
应〔應〕
这〔這〕
庐〔廬〕
闰〔閏〕
闱〔闈〕
闲〔閑〕
间〔間〕
闵〔閔〕
闷〔悶〕
灿〔燦〕
灶〔竈〕
炀〔煬〕
沣〔灃〕
沤〔漚〕
沥〔瀝〕
沦〔淪〕
沧〔滄〕
沨〔渢〕
沟〔溝〕
沩〔潙〕
沪〔滬〕
沈〔瀋〕
怃〔憮〕
怀〔懷〕
怄〔慪〕
忧〔憂〕
忾〔愾〕
怅〔悵〕
怆〔愴〕
*穷〔窮〕
证〔證〕
诂〔詁〕
诃〔訶〕
启〔啓〕
评〔評〕
补〔補〕
诅〔詛〕
识〔識〕
诇〔詗〕
诈〔詐〕
诉〔訴〕
诊〔診〕
诋〔詆〕
诌〔謅〕
词〔詞〕
诎〔詘〕
诏〔詔〕
译〔譯〕
诒〔詒〕

【乛】

*灵〔靈〕
层〔層〕
迟〔遲〕
张〔張〕
际〔際〕
陆〔陸〕
陇〔隴〕
陈〔陳〕
坠〔墜〕
陉〔陘〕
妪〔嫗〕
妩〔嫵〕
妫〔媯〕
刭〔剄〕
劲〔勁〕
鸡〔鷄〕
纬〔緯〕
纭〔紜〕
驱〔驅〕
纯〔純〕
纰〔紕〕
纱〔紗〕
纲〔綱〕
纳〔納〕
纴〔紝〕
驳〔駁〕
纵〔縱〕
纶〔綸〕
纷〔紛〕
纸〔紙〕
纹〔紋〕

纺〔紡〕 驴〔驢〕 纠〔糾〕 纽〔鈕〕 纾〔紓〕

8 笔

【一】

玮〔瑋〕 环〔環〕 责〔責〕 现〔現〕 表〔錶〕 玱〔瑲〕 规〔規〕 匦〔匭〕 拢〔攏〕 拣〔揀〕 垆〔壚〕 担〔擔〕 顶〔頂〕 拥〔擁〕 势〔勢〕 拦〔攔〕 扩〔擴〕 拧〔擰〕 拨〔撥〕 择〔擇〕 茏〔蘢〕 苹〔蘋〕 茑〔蔦〕 范〔範〕 茔〔塋〕 茕〔煢〕 茎〔莖〕 枢〔樞〕 枥〔櫪〕 柜〔櫃〕 枧〔梘〕 枨〔棖〕 板〔闆〕 枞〔樅〕 松〔鬆〕 枪〔槍〕 枫〔楓〕 构〔構〕 丧〔喪〕 *画〔畫〕 枣〔棗〕

*卖〔賣〕[21] 郁〔鬱〕 矾〔礬〕 矿〔礦〕 砀〔碭〕 码〔碼〕 厕〔廁〕 奋〔奮〕 态〔態〕 瓯〔甌〕 欧〔歐〕 殴〔毆〕 垄〔壟〕 郏〔郟〕 轰〔轟〕 顷〔頃〕 转〔轉〕 轭〔軛〕 斩〔斬〕 轮〔輪〕 软〔軟〕 鸢〔鳶〕

【丨】

*齿〔齒〕 *虏〔虜〕 肾〔腎〕 贤〔賢〕 县〔縣〕 *国〔國〕 昽〔曨〕 帆〔颿〕 *黾〔黽〕[23] 鸣〔鳴〕 咛〔嚀〕 咝〔噝〕 *罗〔羅〕 〔囉〕 岽〔崬〕 岿〔巋〕 帜〔幟〕 岭〔嶺〕[19] 剀〔剴〕 凯〔凱〕 峄〔嶧〕 败〔敗〕 账〔賬〕 贩〔販〕 贬〔貶〕

贮〔貯〕 图〔圖〕 购〔購〕

【丿】

钍〔釷〕 钎〔釺〕 钏〔釧〕 钐〔釤〕 钓〔釣〕 钒〔釩〕 钔〔鍆〕 钕〔釹〕 钖〔鍚〕 钗〔釵〕 制〔製〕 迭〔疊〕[5] 刮〔颳〕 侠〔俠〕 侥〔僥〕 侦〔偵〕 侧〔側〕 凭〔憑〕 侨〔僑〕 侩〔儈〕 货〔貨〕 侪〔儕〕 侬〔儂〕 *质〔質〕 征〔徵〕[50] 径〔徑〕 舍〔捨〕 剑〔劍〕 郐〔鄶〕 怂〔慫〕 籴〔糴〕 觅〔覓〕 贪〔貪〕 贫〔貧〕 饯〔餞〕 肤〔膚〕 胀〔脹〕 肮〔骯〕 胁〔脅〕 迩〔邇〕 *鱼〔魚〕 狞〔獰〕 *备〔備〕 枭〔梟〕

钱〔錢〕 饰〔飾〕 饱〔飽〕 饲〔飼〕 饴〔飴〕

【丶】

变〔變〕 庞〔龐〕 庙〔廟〕 疟〔瘧〕 疠〔癘〕 疡〔瘍〕 剂〔劑〕 废〔廢〕 闸〔閘〕 闹〔鬧〕[14] *郑〔鄭〕 卷〔捲〕 *单〔單〕 炜〔煒〕 炝〔熗〕 炉〔爐〕 浅〔淺〕 泷〔瀧〕 泸〔瀘〕 泺〔濼〕 泞〔濘〕 泻〔瀉〕 泼〔潑〕 泽〔澤〕 泾〔涇〕 怜〔憐〕 怅〔悵〕 怿〔懌〕 峃〔嶨〕 学〔學〕 宝〔寶〕 宠〔寵〕 *审〔審〕 帘〔簾〕 实〔實〕 诓〔誆〕 诔〔誄〕 试〔試〕 诖〔詿〕 诗〔詩〕 诘〔詰〕 诙〔詼〕 诚〔誠〕

衬〔襯〕 袆〔褘〕 视〔視〕 诛〔誅〕 话〔話〕 诞〔誕〕 诟〔詬〕 诠〔詮〕 诡〔詭〕 询〔詢〕 诣〔詣〕 诤〔諍〕 该〔該〕 详〔詳〕 诧〔詫〕 诨〔諢〕 诩〔詡〕

【乛】

*肃〔肅〕[22] 隶〔隸〕 *录〔録〕 弥〔彌〕 〔瀰〕 陕〔陝〕 驽〔駑〕 驾〔駕〕 *参〔參〕 艰〔艱〕 线〔線〕 绀〔紺〕 绁〔絏〕 绂〔紱〕 练〔練〕 组〔組〕 驵〔駔〕 绅〔紳〕 细〔細〕 驶〔駛〕 驸〔駙〕 驷〔駟〕 驹〔駒〕 终〔終〕 织〔織〕 驺〔騶〕 绉〔縐〕 驻〔駐〕 绊〔絆〕

驼〔駝〕 绋〔紼〕 绌〔絀〕 绍〔紹〕 驿〔驛〕 绎〔繹〕 经〔經〕 骀〔駘〕 给〔給〕

9 笔

【一】

贰〔貳〕 帮〔幫〕 珑〔瓏〕 顸〔頇〕 轪〔軑〕 垭〔埡〕 挜〔掗〕 挝〔撾〕 项〔項〕 挞〔撻〕 挟〔挾〕 挠〔撓〕 赵〔趙〕 贲〔賁〕 挡〔擋〕 垲〔塏〕 挢〔撟〕 垫〔墊〕 挤〔擠〕 挥〔揮〕 挦〔撏〕 *荙〔薘〕 荚〔莢〕 贳〔貰〕 荛〔蕘〕 荜〔蓽〕 *带〔帶〕 茧〔繭〕 荞〔蕎〕 荟〔薈〕 荠〔薺〕 荡〔蕩〕 垩〔堊〕 荣〔榮〕 荦〔犖〕 荧〔熒〕 荥〔滎〕 荨〔蕁〕

荩〔藎〕 荪〔蓀〕 荫〔蔭〕 荬〔蕒〕 荭〔葒〕 荮〔葤〕 药〔藥〕 标〔標〕 栈〔棧〕 栉〔櫛〕 栊〔櫳〕 栋〔棟〕 栌〔櫨〕 栎〔櫟〕 栏〔欄〕 柠〔檸〕 柽〔檉〕 树〔樹〕 䴓〔鳾〕 郦〔酈〕 咸〔鹹〕 砖〔磚〕 砗〔硨〕 砚〔硯〕 砜〔碸〕 面〔麵〕 牵〔牽〕 鸥〔鷗〕 奂〔奐〕 残〔殘〕 殇〔殤〕 轱〔軲〕 轲〔軻〕 轳〔轤〕 轴〔軸〕 轵〔軹〕 轷〔軤〕 轸〔軫〕 轹〔轢〕 轺〔軺〕 轻〔輕〕 鸦〔鴉〕

【丨】

战〔戰〕 觇〔覘〕 点〔點〕

临〔臨〕[18] 览〔覽〕 竖〔豎〕 *尝〔嘗〕[3] 眍〔瞘〕 哒〔噠〕 哓〔嘵〕 哔〔嗶〕 贵〔貴〕 虾〔蝦〕 蚁〔蟻〕 蚂〔螞〕 虽〔雖〕 骂〔罵〕 哕〔噦〕 剐〔剮〕 郧〔鄖〕 勋〔勛〕 哗〔嘩〕 响〔響〕 哙〔噲〕 哝〔噥〕 哟〔喲〕 峡〔峽〕 峣〔嶢〕 帧〔幀〕 罚〔罰〕 峤〔嶠〕 贱〔賤〕 贴〔貼〕 贶〔貺〕 贻〔貽〕

【丿】

钘〔鈃〕 钙〔鈣〕 钚〔鈈〕 钛〔鈦〕 钜〔鉅〕 钝〔鈍〕 钞〔鈔〕 钟〔鐘〕 〔鍾〕 钢〔鋼〕 钠〔鈉〕 钥〔鑰〕 钦〔欽〕

以下为简繁对照表，按列自上而下、自左而右阅读。

第 1 列

钧[鈞]
铃[鈴]
钨[鎢]
钩[鉤]
钪[鈧]
钫[鈁]
钬[鈥]
钭[鈄]
钮[鈕]
钯[鈀]
毡[氈]
氢[氫]
选[選]
适[適]⑧⓪
种[種]
秋[鞦]
复[復]
　[複]
　[覆]⑦
笃[篤]
传[傳]
俨[儼]
俩[倆]
俪[儷]
贷[貸]
顺[順]
俭[儉]
剑[劍]
鸽[鴿]
须[須]
　[鬚]
胧[朧]
胨[腖]
胪[臚]
胆[膽]
胜[勝]
胫[脛]
鸰[鴒]
狭[狹]
狮[獅]
独[獨]
狯[獪]
狱[獄]
狲[猻]
贸[貿]
饵[鉺]
饶[饒]
蚀[蝕]
饷[餉]
饸[餄]
饹[餎]

第 2 列

饺[餃]
侬[儂]
饼[餅]
【丶】
恸[慟]
怄[慪]
恺[愷]
恻[惻]
恼[惱]
恽[惲]
*将[將]⑫
奖[奬]⑫
疬[癧]
疮[瘡]
疯[瘋]
*亲[親]
飒[颯]
闺[閨]
闻[聞]
闼[闥]
闽[閩]
闾[閭]
阀[閥]
阁[閣]
阂[閡]
养[養]
姜[薑]
类[類]⑯
娄[婁]
总[總]
炼[煉]
炽[熾]
烁[爍]
烂[爛]
烃[烴]
洼[窪]
洁[潔]
洒[灑]
浇[澆]
浃[浹]
浈[湞]
浊[濁]
测[測]
浏[瀏]
浐[滻]
浑[渾]
浒[滸]

第 3 列

浓[濃]
浔[潯]
浕[濜]
勋[勳]
觉[覺]
宪[憲]
窃[竊]
诚[誠]
诬[誣]
语[語]
袄[襖]
诮[誚]
祢[禰]
误[誤]
诰[誥]
诱[誘]
诲[誨]
鸩[鴆]
说[說]
诵[誦]
诶[誒]
【→】
垦[墾]
昼[晝]
费[費]
逊[遜]
陨[隕]
险[險]
贺[賀]
怼[懟]
垒[壘]
娅[婭]
娆[嬈]
娇[嬌]
绑[綁]
绒[絨]
结[結]
绔[絝]
骁[驍]
绕[繞]
绖[絰]
骄[驕]
骅[驊]

第 4 列

绘[繪]
骆[駱]
骈[駢]
绞[絞]
骇[駭]
统[統]
绗[絎]
给[給]
绚[絢]
绛[絳]
络[絡]
绝[絕]

10 笔

【一】
艳[艷]
项[項]
珲[琿]
蚕[蠶]①
较[較]
盏[盞]
捞[撈]
载[載]
赶[趕]
盐[鹽]
埘[塒]
损[損]
埙[塤]
埚[堝]
捡[撿]
贽[贄]
挚[摯]
热[熱]
捣[搗]
壶[壺]
*聂[聶]
莱[萊]
莲[蓮]
莳[蒔]
莴[萵]
获[獲]
　[穫]
莸[蕕]
恶[惡]
　[噁]
劳[勞]
莹[瑩]
崂[嶗]
峥[崢]
鸪[鴣]
莼[蒓]

第 5 列

桡[橈]
桢[楨]
档[檔]
桤[榿]
桥[橋]
桦[樺]
桧[檜]
桩[樁]
样[樣]
贾[賈]
逦[邐]
砺[礪]
砾[礫]
础[礎]
砻[礱]
顾[顧]
轼[軾]
轾[輊]
轿[轎]
辂[輅]
【丨】
眦[眥]
鸬[鸕]
*虑[慮]
*监[監]
紧[緊]
*党[黨]
唛[嘜]
晒[曬]
晓[曉]
唝[嗊]
唠[嘮]
鸭[鴨]
哂[哂]
晔[曄]
晕[暈]
鸮[鴞]
积[積]
称[稱]
笕[筧]
*笔[筆]
债[債]
借[藉]⑬
倾[傾]
赁[賃]
颀[頎]
徕[徠]

第 6 列

觊[覬]
贼[賊]
贿[賄]
赂[賂]
赃[臟]
赅[賅]
【丿】
钰[鈺]
钲[鉦]
钳[鉗]
钴[鈷]
钵[缽]
钶[鈳]
钷[鉕]
钹[鈸]
钺[鉞]
钼[鉬]
钽[鉭]
钿[鈿]
铀[鈾]
铁[鐵]
铂[鉑]
铃[鈴]
铄[鑠]
铅[鉛]
铆[鉚]
铈[鈰]
铉[鉉]
铊[鉈]
铋[鉍]
铌[鈮]
铍[鈹]
铎[鐸]
氩[氬]
牺[犧]
敌[敵]
称[稱]
笕[筧]
*笔[筆]
债[債]
借[藉]⑬
倾[傾]
赁[賃]
顾[頎]
徙[徙]

第 7 列

舰[艦]
舱[艙]
耸[聳]
*爱[愛]⑫
颁[頒]
颂[頌]
【丿】
脏[臟]
脐[臍]
脑[腦]
胶[膠]
脓[膿]
鸱[鴟]
玺[璽]
鸲[鴝]
鸵[鴕]
袅[裊]
驾[駕]
皱[皺]
饽[餑]
饿[餓]
馁[餒]
请[請]
诸[諸]

第 8 列

烩[燴]
烬[燼]
递[遞]
涛[濤]
涝[澇]
涞[淶]
涟[漣]
涠[潿]
涢[溳]
涡[渦]
涂[塗]
涤[滌]
润[潤]
涧[澗]
涨[漲]
烫[燙]
涩[澀]
悭[慳]
悯[憫]
宽[寬]
家[傢]
*宾[賓]
窍[竅]
窎[窵]
诹[諏]
诺[諾]
诼[諑]
读[讀]
诽[誹]
袜[襪]㉟
祯[禎]
课[課]
诿[諉]
谀[諛]
谁[誰]
谂[諗]
调[調]
谄[諂]
谅[諒]
谆[諄]
谇[誶]
谈[談]
谊[誼]
谞[諝]
【→】
恳[懇]
剧[劇]
娲[媧]
娴[嫻]

*难[難]　屃[屓]　铟[銦]　猓[餜]　祸[禍]　级[緅]　睑[瞼]　鹄[鵠]
预[預]　硕[碩]　铠[鎧]　馄[餛]　谒[謁]　缁[緇]　喷[噴]　鹅[鵝]
缜[縝]　硖[硤]　铡[鍘]　馅[餡]　谓[謂]　　　　畴[疇]　颐[頤]
骊[驪]　硗[磽]　铢[銖]　馆[館]　谔[諤]　**12 笔**　践[踐]　筑[築]
绡[綃]　砲[礮]　铣[銑]　　　　谕[諭]　【一】　遗[遺]　筚[篳]
骋[騁]　硏[硏]　铤[鋌]　【丶】　谖[諼]　靓[靚]　蛱[蛺]　筛[篩]
绢[絹]　鸸[鴯]　铥[銩]　鸾[鸞]　谗[讒]　琼[瓊]　蛲[蟯]　牍[牘]
绣[綉]　聋[聾]　铧[鏵]　庼[廎]　谘[諮]　辇[輦]　蛳[螄]　傥[儻]
验[驗]　龚[龔]　铨[銓]　痒[癢]　谙[諳]　鼋[黿]　蛴[蠐]　傧[儐]
绥[綏]　袭[襲]　铩[鎩]　鸡[雞]　谚[諺]　趄[趄]　鹃[鵑]　储[儲]
绦[縧]　驾[駕]　铪[鉿]　旋[鏇]　谛[諦]　揽[攬]　喽[嘍]　傩[儺]
继[繼]　殒[殞]　铫[銚]　阉[閹]　谜[謎]　颉[頡]　嵘[嶸]　惩[懲]
绨[綈]　殓[殮]　铭[銘]　阊[閶]　谝[諞]　揿[撳]　嵚[嶔]　御[禦]
骏[駿]　赉[賚]　铬[鉻]　阋[鬩]　谞[諝]　搀[攙]　嵝[嶁]　颌[頜]
鸶[鷥]　辄[輒]　铮[錚]　阌[閿]⑭　　　　蛰[蟄]　赋[賦]　释[釋]
　　　　辅[輔]　铯[銫]　阍[閽]　【一】　絷[縶]　腈[腈]　鹆[鵒]
11 笔　辆[輛]　铰[鉸]　阎[閻]　弹[彈]　搁[擱]　赌[賭]　腊[臘]
【一】　堑[塹]　铱[銥]　阏[閼]　堕[墮]　搂[摟]　赎[贖]　腘[膕]
焘[燾]　　　　铲[鏟]　阐[闡]　随[隨]　搅[攪]　赐[賜]　鱿[魷]
逴[逴]　【丨】　铳[銃]　羟[羥]　粜[糶]　蒇[蕆]　赒[賙]　鲁[魯]
琏[璉]　颅[顱]　铵[銨]　盖[蓋]　*隐[隱]　蒉[蕢]　赔[賠]　鲂[魴]
琐[瑣]　啧[嘖]　银[銀]　粝[糲]　婍[嫿]　蒋[蔣]　赕[賧]　颍[潁]
狭[狹]　悬[懸]　铷[銣]　*断[斷]　婶[嬸]　蒌[蔞]　　　　飓[颶]
掳[擄]　唛[嘜]　矫[矯]　兽[獸]　颇[頗]　韩[韓]　【丿】　觞[觴]
掴[摑]　跃[躍]　鸹[鴰]　焖[燜]　颈[頸]　椟[櫝]　铸[鑄]　惫[憊]
鸷[鷙]　啮[嚙]　秽[穢]　渍[漬]　绩[績]　椤[欏]　铹[鐒]　馇[餷]
掷[擲]　跄[蹌]　笺[箋]　鸿[鴻]　绪[緒]　赍[齎]　铺[鋪]　馈[饋]
掸[撣]　蛎[蠣]　笼[籠]　渎[瀆]　绫[綾]　椭[橢]　铼[錸]　馉[餶]
壶[壺]　蛊[蠱]　笾[籩]　渐[漸]　骐[騏]　鹁[鵓]　铽[鋱]　馊[餿]
悫[愨]　蛏[蟶]　债[債]　淹[潯]　续[續]　鹂[鸝]　链[鏈]　馋[饞]
据[據]　累[纍]　偾[僨]　渊[淵]　绮[綺]　觌[覿]　铿[鏗]　
掺[摻]　啸[嘯]　偻[僂]　渔[漁]　骑[騎]　硷[鹼]　销[銷]　【丶】
掼[摜]　帻[幘]　躯[軀]　淀[澱]　绯[緋]　确[確]　锁[鎖]　亵[褻]
职[職]　崭[嶄]　皑[皚]　渗[滲]　绰[綽]　詟[讋]　锃[鋥]　装[裝]
聍[聹]　逻[邏]　衅[釁]　惬[愜]　骒[騍]　殚[殫]　锄[鋤]　蛮[蠻]
菥[蓁]　帼[幗]　鸺[鵂]　惭[慚]　绲[緄]　颊[頰]　锂[鋰]　脔[臠]
勖[勗]　赈[賑]　衔[銜]　惧[懼]　绳[繩]　雳[靂]　锅[鍋]　痨[癆]
萝[蘿]　婴[嬰]　舻[艫]　惊[驚]　骓[騅]　辊[輥]　锆[鋯]　痫[癇]
萤[螢]　赊[賒]　盘[盤]　惮[憚]　维[維]　辋[輞]　锇[鋨]　赓[賡]
营[營]　　　　鸼[鵃]　惨[慘]　绵[綿]　椠[槧]　锈[銹]　颏[頦]
萦[縈]　【丿】　龛[龕]　惯[慣]　绶[綬]　暂[暫]　锉[銼]　鹇[鷴]
萧[蕭]　铏[鉶]　鸽[鴿]　祷[禱]　绷[繃]　辍[輟]　锋[鋒]　阑[闌]
萨[薩]　铐[銬]　敛[斂]　谌[諶]　绸[綢]　辎[輜]　锌[鋅]　阒[闃]
梦[夢]　铑[銠]　领[領]　谋[謀]　绺[綹]　翘[翹]　锎[鐦]　阔[闊]
觋[覡]　铒[鉺]　脶[腡]　谍[諜]　绻[綣]　【丨】　锏[鐧]　阕[闋]
检[檢]　铓[鋩]　脸[臉]　谎[謊]　综[綜]　辈[輩]　锐[銳]　粪[糞]
梘[梘]　铕[銪]　象[像]④①　谏[諫]　绽[綻]　凿[鑿]　锑[銻]　*窜[竄]
*啬[嗇]　铝[鋁]　猎[獵]　皲[皸]　绾[綰]　辉[輝]　锒[鋃]　窝[窩]
匮[匱]　铜[銅]　猡[玀]　谐[諧]　绿[綠]　赏[賞]㉓　锓[鋟]　喾[嚳]
酝[醞]　铞[銱]　猕[獼]　裆[襠]　骖[驂]　睐[睞]　锔[鋦]　愤[憤]
　　　　　　　　　　　　谑[謔]　　　　　　　　　　　　愦[憒]

	13 笔	鉴〔鑒〕	稣〔穌〕	谬〔謬〕	【丨】	蛙〔蛙〕	**15 笔**
滞〔滯〕		魋〔魋〕	鲋〔鮒〕		觜〔觜〕	鲒〔鮚〕	
湿〔濕〕	**【一】**	嗫〔囁〕	卿〔卿〕	**【乛】**	龈〔齦〕	鲔〔鮪〕	**【一】**
溃〔潰〕		跷〔蹺〕	鲍〔鮑〕	辟〔闢〕	鹡〔鶺〕	鲖〔鮦〕	耧〔耬〕
溅〔濺〕	耢〔耮〕	跸〔蹕〕	鲅〔鮁〕	媛〔嬡〕	颡〔顙〕	鲗〔鰂〕	璎〔瓔〕
溇〔漊〕	鹉〔鵡〕	跻〔躋〕	鲐〔鮐〕	嫔〔嬪〕	暧〔曖〕	鲙〔鱠〕	赪〔赬〕
湾〔灣〕	鹋〔鶓〕	跹〔躚〕	颖〔穎〕	缙〔縉〕	暖〔曖〕	鲚〔鱭〕	撵〔攆〕
谟〔謨〕	辊〔輥〕	蜗〔蝸〕	鸽〔鴿〕	缜〔縝〕	鹘〔鶻〕	鲛〔鮫〕	撷〔擷〕
裢〔褳〕	骛〔騖〕	嗳〔噯〕	飔〔颸〕	缚〔縛〕	蹰〔躕〕	鲜〔鮮〕	撸〔擼〕
裣〔襝〕	摄〔攝〕	赗〔賵〕	飗〔飀〕	缛〔縟〕	蜡〔蠟〕	鲟〔鱘〕	聩〔聵〕
裤〔褲〕	摅〔攄〕		触〔觸〕	辔〔轡〕	蝈〔蟈〕	飖〔飖〕	聪〔聰〕
裥〔襇〕	摆〔擺〕	**【丿】**	雏〔雛〕	缝〔縫〕	蝇〔蠅〕	飕〔颼〕	觐〔覲〕
禅〔禪〕	〔襬〕	锗〔鍺〕	傅〔賻〕	骝〔騮〕	蝉〔蟬〕	廑〔廑〕	鞑〔韃〕
谠〔讜〕	赪〔赬〕	错〔錯〕	馍〔饃〕	缞〔縗〕	鹦〔鶊〕	馑〔饉〕	靳〔鞽〕
谡〔謖〕	摈〔擯〕	锘〔鍩〕	馏〔餾〕	缟〔縞〕	噎〔噫〕	馒〔饅〕	蕲〔蘄〕
谢〔謝〕	毂〔轂〕	锚〔錨〕	馐〔饈〕	缠〔纏〕②	罴〔羆〕		颐〔頤〕
谣〔謠〕	摊〔攤〕	锛〔錛〕		缡〔縭〕	赊〔賒〕	**【丶】**	蕴〔蘊〕
谤〔謗〕	鹊〔鵲〕	锝〔鍀〕	**【丶】**	缢〔縊〕	罂〔罌〕	銮〔鑾〕	樯〔檣〕
谥〔謚〕	蓝〔藍〕	锞〔錁〕	酱〔醬〕⑫	缣〔縑〕	赙〔賻〕	瘥〔瘥〕	樱〔櫻〕
谦〔謙〕	蓦〔驀〕	锟〔錕〕	鹑〔鶉〕	缤〔繽〕	罂〔罌〕	瘘〔瘻〕	飘〔飄〕
谧〔謐〕	鹌〔鵪〕	锡〔錫〕	瘄〔瘥〕	骟〔騸〕	赚〔賺〕	阈〔闃〕	履〔屧〕
【乛】	蓟〔薊〕	锢〔錮〕	瘆〔瘮〕		鹐〔鵮〕	鲞〔鯗〕	樾〔櫪〕
*属〔屬〕	蒙〔矇〕	锣〔鑼〕	鹧〔鷓〕	**14 笔**		鲎〔鱟〕	魇〔魘〕
屦〔屨〕	〔濛〕	锤〔錘〕	阉〔閹〕		**【丿】**	飧〔飱〕	履〔屨〕
骘〔騭〕	〔懞〕	锥〔錐〕	阊〔閶〕	**【一】**	锲〔鍥〕	鹚〔鷀〕	霉〔黴〕
毓〔鹼〕	颐〔頤〕	锦〔錦〕	阋〔鬩〕	瑷〔璦〕	锴〔鍇〕	潇〔瀟〕	辎〔輜〕
骜〔驁〕	献〔獻〕	锨〔鍁〕	誉〔譽〕	赘〔贅〕	锷〔鍔〕	潋〔瀲〕	
翠〔翬〕	颏〔頦〕	锫〔錇〕	粮〔糧〕	觏〔覯〕	锹〔鍬〕	潍〔濰〕	**【丨】**
骛〔鶩〕	榄〔欖〕	锭〔錠〕	数〔數〕	韬〔韜〕	锸〔鍤〕	赛〔賽〕	蝤〔齰〕
缂〔緙〕	榇〔櫬〕	键〔鍵〕	滗〔潷〕	叆〔靉〕	锻〔鍛〕	窭〔窶〕	龉〔齬〕
缃〔緗〕	桐〔櫚〕	锯〔鋸〕	溇〔漊〕	墙〔牆〕	锼〔鎪〕	谭〔譚〕	觑〔覷〕
缄〔緘〕	楼〔樓〕	锰〔錳〕	满〔滿〕	撄〔攖〕	锾〔鍰〕	谮〔譖〕	瞒〔瞞〕
缅〔緬〕	榉〔櫸〕	锱〔錙〕	滤〔濾〕	蔷〔薔〕	锵〔鏘〕	禤〔襬〕	题〔題〕
缆〔纜〕	赖〔賴〕	辞〔辭〕	滥〔濫〕	蔹〔蘞〕	镍〔鎳〕	褛〔褸〕	颙〔顒〕
缇〔緹〕	碛〔磧〕	颊〔頰〕	滗〔潷〕	蔟〔蔟〕	镀〔鍍〕	谯〔譙〕	颛〔顓〕
缈〔緲〕	碍〔礙〕	穇〔穇〕	漓〔灕〕	蔺〔藺〕	镁〔鎂〕	谰〔讕〕	踬〔躓〕
缉〔緝〕	磋〔磋〕	筹〔籌〕	滨〔濱〕	蔼〔藹〕	镂〔鏤〕	谱〔譜〕	踯〔躑〕
缊〔縕〕	鹕〔鶘〕	签〔簽〕	滩〔灘〕	鹕〔鶘〕	镃〔鎡〕	谲〔譎〕	蝾〔蠑〕
缌〔緦〕	尴〔尷〕	〔籤〕	预〔澦〕	槚〔檟〕	锁〔鐄〕		蝼〔螻〕
缎〔緞〕	殡〔殯〕	简〔簡〕	慑〔懾〕	槛〔檻〕	镅〔鎇〕	**【乛】**	噜〔嚕〕
缑〔緱〕	雾〔霧〕	觎〔覦〕	誊〔謄〕	槟〔檳〕	鸳〔鴛〕	鹛〔鶥〕	嘱〔囑〕
缓〔緩〕	辏〔輳〕	觐〔覲〕	鲨〔鯊〕	槠〔櫧〕	稳〔穩〕	嫱〔嬙〕	颟〔顢〕
缒〔縋〕	辐〔輻〕	频〔頻〕	鹫〔鶩〕	酽〔釅〕	箦〔簣〕	鹙〔鶖〕	
缔〔締〕	辑〔輯〕	腻〔膩〕	寝〔寢〕	酾〔釃〕	篑〔簀〕	缥〔縹〕	**【丿】**
缕〔縷〕	输〔輸〕	鹏〔鵬〕	窥〔窺〕	酿〔釀〕	箨〔籜〕	骠〔驃〕	镊〔鑷〕
骗〔騙〕		腾〔騰〕	窦〔竇〕	霁〔霽〕	箩〔籮〕	缦〔縵〕	镇〔鎮〕
编〔編〕	**【丨】**	鲅〔鮁〕	谨〔謹〕	愿〔願〕	箪〔簞〕	骡〔騾〕	镉〔鎘〕
缗〔緡〕	频〔頻〕	鲆〔鮃〕	谩〔謾〕	殡〔殯〕	箓〔籙〕	缧〔縲〕	镋〔钂〕
骚〔騷〕	龃〔齟〕	鲇〔鮎〕	谪〔謫〕	辕〔轅〕	箫〔簫〕	缨〔纓〕	镌〔鐫〕
缘〔緣〕	龄〔齡〕	鲈〔鱸〕	谫〔譾〕	辖〔轄〕	辕〔轅〕	骢〔驄〕	镍〔鎳〕
飧〔饗〕	鲍〔鮑〕	鲊〔鮓〕	谬〔謬〕	辗〔輾〕	膑〔臏〕	缩〔縮〕	镏〔鎦〕
	龆〔齠〕					缪〔繆〕	镐〔鎬〕
						缫〔繰〕	镑〔鎊〕

Column 1

镒[鎰]
镓[鎵]
镔[鑌]
锦[錦]
篑[簣]
篓[簍]
鸥[鷗]
鹇[鷳]
鹞[鷂]
鲠[鯁]
鲢[鰱]
鲣[鰹]
鲥[鰣]
鲤[鯉]
鲦[鰷]
鲧[鯀]
鲩[鯇]
卿[鄉]
馓[饊]
馔[饌]
【丶】
瘪[癟]
瘫[癱]
斋[齋]
颜[顏]
鹐[鵮]
鲨[鯊]
澜[瀾]
额[額]
谳[讞]
褴[襤]
遣[譴]

Column 2

鹤[鶴]
谵[譫]
【一】
屦[屨]
缥[縹]
缧[縲]
缟[縞]
缙[縉]
缛[縟]
毵[毿]
赞[贊]

16 笔

【一】
耦[耦]
撷[擷]
颞[顳]
颟[顢]
薮[藪]
颡[顙]
橹[櫓]
橼[櫞]
骘[騭]
赝[贗]
飙[飆]
飗[飈]
螯[螯]
辙[轍]
辚[轔]

【丨】

龉[齬]
螨[蟎]
鹦[鸚]
赠[贈]

【丿】

镨[錯]

Column 3

镖[鏢]
镗[鏜]
锼[鎪]
锁[鎖]
镛[鏞]
镜[鏡]
镝[鏑]
镞[鏃]
穑[穡]
赞[贊]
耧[耬]
篮[籃]
篱[籬]
魉[魎]
鲭[鯖]
鲮[鯪]
鲰[鯫]
鲱[鯡]
鲲[鯤]
鲳[鯧]
鲵[鯢]
鲷[鯛]
鲸[鯨]
獭[獺]

【丿】

鸰[鴒]
蟥[蟥]
瘘[瘻]
瘾[癮]
斓[斕]
辫[辮]
潋[瀲]

Column 4

濒[瀕]
懒[懶]
黉[黌]

【一】

鹨[鷚]
颣[纇]
缰[繮]
缱[繾]
缲[繰]
缳[繯]
缴[繳]

17 笔

【一】
薜[薜]
鹣[鶼]
鳓[鰳]

【丨】

龋[齲]
龌[齷]
瞩[矚]
蹒[蹣]
蹑[躡]
蟏[蠨]
啮[嚙]
羁[羈]
赡[贍]

【丿】

镨[鐯]
瘿[癭]
镁[鎂]
镂[鏤]
镄[鐨]
锏[鐧]

Column 5

镨[鐥]
镨[錯]
镨[鐺]
簖[籪]
鹕[鶘]
鳍[鰭]
鳎[鰨]
鳏[鰥]
鳒[鰜]
鳑[鰟]
鳋[鰠]
鳌[鰲]
鲾[鰏]
鳀[鯷]
鳅[鰍]
鳆[鰒]
鳇[鰉]
鳈[鰁]
鳉[鱂]

【丶】

鹫[鷲]
辩[辯]
赢[贏]
潍[濰]

【一】

鹬[鷸]
骤[驟]

18 笔

【一】

鳌[鰲]
鞯[韉]
魇[魘]

Column 6

【丨】
龇[齜]
颢[顥]
鹭[鷺]
翳[翳]
臁[臁]

【丿】

镳[鑣]
镭[鐳]
镮[鐶]
镯[鐲]
镰[鐮]
镱[鐿]
雠[讎]
臌[臌]
鳍[鯺]
鳎[鰳]
鳏[鯬]
鳐[鰩]
鳑[鰟]
鳒[鰜]

【丶】

鹳[鸛]
鹰[鷹]
癞[癩]
辗[輾]
谶[讖]

【一】

鹮[䴉]

19 笔

【一】

撄[攖]
蕲[蘄]

Column 7

【丨】

黉[黌]
颦[顰]
颟[顢]
髋[髖]
髌[髕]

【丿】

镲[鑔]
镳[鑣]
镴[鑞]

【丶】

禳[禳]
蟹[蠏]

【一】

鬓[鬢]
缵[纘]

20 笔

【一】

瓒[瓚]
鬓[鬢]
颥[顬]

【丨】

黩[黷]
颥[顬]

Column 8

镳[鑣]
镴[鑞]
膑[臏]
鳔[鰾]
鳕[鱈]
鳖[鱉]
鳗[鰻]

【一】

骦[驦]

21 笔

攥[攥]
蹒[躦]
鳘[鱈]
鳟[鱒]
癫[癲]
赣[贛]
灏[灝]

22 笔

鹳[鸛]
镶[鑲]

23 笔

趱[趲]
颥[顬]
躜[躦]

25 笔

镵[鑱]
馕[饢]
戆[戇]

Conversion Table C: Complex to Simplified Character Forms

(arranged by stroke order)

7 笔
*[車]车
*[夾]夹
*[貝]贝
*[見]见
[壯]壮
[妝]妆

8 笔
【一】
*[長]长④
*[亞]亚

[軋]轧
*[東]东
[協]协
*[來]来
[戔]戋
【丨】
*[門]门
*[岡]冈
【丿】
*[侖]仑

[兒]儿
【一】
[狀]状
[糾]纠

9 笔
【一】
[剋]克
[軌]轧
[庫]库
*[頁]页
[郟]郏

[剄]刭
[勁]劲
【丨】
[貞]贞
[則]则
[閂]闩
[迴]回
【丿】
[俠]侠
[係]系
[兔]兔

[帥]帅
[後]后
[釓]钆
[釔]钇
[負]负
*[風]风
【丶】
[訂]订
[計]计
[訃]讣
[軍]军

[祇]只
【一】
[陣]阵
*[韋]韦
[陝]陕
[陘]陉
[飛]飞
[紆]纡
[紅]红
[紂]纣
[納]纳

[級]级
[約]约
[紇]纥
[紀]纪
[紉]纫

10 笔
【一】
*[馬]马⑳
[挾]挟
[貢]贡
*[華]华

[英]英
[莖]茎
[莧]苋
[莊]庄㉛
[軒]轩
[連]连
[軔]轫
[剗]刬
【丨】
[鬥]斗
*[時]时

455

*[畢]毕　[財]财　[眍]眍　[閃]闪　[唄]呗　[員]员　*[豈]岂　[峽]峡　[蜆]蚬　[剛]刚　[剮]剐

【丿】
*[氣]气　[郵]邮　[倀]伥　[倆]俩　*[條]条[33]　[們]们　[個]个　[倫]伦　[隻]只　[島]岛　*[烏]乌[43]　*[師]师　[徑]径　[釘]钉　[針]针　[釗]钊　[釙]钋　[釕]钌　*[殺]杀　*[倉]仓　[脅]胁　[狹]狭　[狽]狈　*[芻]刍

【丶】
[訐]讦　[訌]讧　[討]讨　[訕]讪　[訖]讫　[訓]训　[這]这　[訊]讯　[記]记　[凍]冻　[畝]亩　[庫]库　[浹]浃　[涇]泾

【一】
[書]书　[陸]陆　[陳]陈　[孫]孙　[陰]阴　[務]务　[紜]纭　[純]纯　[紕]纰　[紗]纱　[納]纳　[紝]纴　[紛]纷　[紙]纸　[紋]纹　[紡]纺　[紐]纽　[紓]纾

11 笔

【一】
[責]责　[現]现　[匭]匦　[規]规　*[殼]壳[15]　[堊]垩　[掗]挜　[捨]舍　[捫]扪　[摑]掴　[堝]埚　[頂]顶　[掄]抡　*[執]执　[捲]卷　[掃]扫　[萊]莱　[萵]莴　[乾]干[8]　[梘]枧　[輒]辄　[斬]斩　[軟]软　*[專]专

*[區]区[28]　[堅]坚　*[帶]带　[厠]厕　[硃]朱　*[麥]麦　[頃]顷

【丨】
*[鹵]卤　[處]处　[敗]败　[販]贩　[眨]贬　[啞]哑　[閉]闭　[問]问　*[婁]娄　[喎]㖞　*[國]国　[帳]帐　[崬]岽　[崍]崃　[崗]岗　[圇]囵　*[過]过

【丿】
[氫]氢　*[動]动　[偵]侦　[側]侧　[貨]货　*[進]进　[梟]枭　*[鳥]鸟[24]　[偉]伟　[徠]徕　[術]术[31]　*[從]从　[釷]钍　[釺]钎　[釧]钏　[釤]钐　[釣]钓　[釩]钒　[釹]钕　[釵]钗　[貪]贪　[飥]饦

【丶】
[貧]贫　[脛]胫　*[魚]鱼
[詎]讵　[訝]讶　[訥]讷　[許]许　[訛]讹　[訩]讻　[訟]讼　[設]设　[訪]访　[訣]诀　[牽]牵　[烴]烃　[淶]涞　[淺]浅　[渦]涡　[淪]沦　[悵]怅　[郟]郏　[啟]启　[視]视

【一】
*[將]将[12]　[晝]昼　[張]张　[階]阶　[陽]阳　*[隊]队　[婭]娅　[媧]娲　[婦]妇　[習]习　*[參]参　[紺]绀　[紲]绁　[紱]绂　[組]组　[紳]绅　[紬]紬　[細]细　[終]终　[絆]绊　[紼]绋　[絀]绌　[紹]绍　[給]给　[貫]贯　*[鄉]乡

12 笔

【一】
[貳]贰　[頇]顸　*[堯]尧[44]　[揀]拣　[馭]驭　[項]项　[賁]贲　[場]场　[揚]扬　[塊]块　*[達]达　[報]报　[揮]挥　[壺]壶　[惡]恶　[葉]叶[46]　[貰]贳　*[萬]万　[葷]荤　[喪]丧　[葦]苇　[葒]荭　[椏]桠　[棟]栋　[棧]栈　[棡]㭎　[極]极　[軲]轱　[軻]轲　[軸]轴　[軼]轶　[軤]轷　[軫]轸　[軺]轺　*[畫]画　[腎]肾　[棗]枣　[硨]砗　[硤]硖　[硯]砚　[殘]残　*[雲]云

【丨】
[覘]觇　[睏]困　[貼]贴　[貺]贶　[貯]贮　[貽]贻　[閏]闰　[開]开　[閑]闲　[間]间　[閔]闵　[悶]闷　[貴]贵　[鄖]郧　[勛]勋　*[單]单　[喲]哟　*[買]买　[剴]剀　[凱]凯　[幀]帧　[嵐]岚　[幃]帏　[圍]围

【丿】
*[無]无[37]　[氬]氩　*[喬]乔　*[筆]笔　[備]备　[貸]贷　[順]顺　[傖]伧　[傯]傯　[傢]家　[鄔]邬　[眾]众　[復]复　[須]须　[鈃]钘　[鈣]钙　[鈈]钚　[鈦]钛　[鈍]钝　[鈔]钞　[鈉]钠　[鈐]钤　[欽]钦　[鈞]钧　[鈎]钩　[鈧]钪　[鈁]钫　[鈕]钮　[鈀]钯　[傘]伞　[爺]爷　[創]创　[飩]饨　[飪]饪　[飫]饫　[飭]饬　[飯]饭　[飲]饮　*[為]为　[脹]胀　[腖]胨　[腡]脶　[勝]胜　*[猶]犹　[貿]贸　[鄒]邹

【丶】
[詁]诂　[詞]词　[評]评　[詛]诅　[詐]诈　[訴]诉　[診]诊　[詆]诋　[詘]诎　[詔]诏　[詒]诒　[馮]冯　[痙]痉　[勞]劳　[渙]涣　[測]测　[湯]汤　[淵]渊　[渢]沨　[渾]浑　[愷]恺　[惻]恻　[惲]恽　[惱]恼

[運]运　[補]补　[禍]祸

【乛】
*[尋]寻　[費]费　[違]违　[軔]轫　[隕]陨　[賀]贺　*[發]发　[綁]绑　[絨]绒　[結]结　[絝]绔　[經]经　[絎]绗　[給]给　[絢]绚　[絳]绛　[絡]络　[絞]绞　[統]统　[絕]绝　[絲]丝　*[幾]几

13 笔

【一】
[頊]顼　[琿]珲　[瑋]玮　[頑]顽　[載]载　[馱]驮　[馴]驯　[馳]驰　[塒]埘　[塤]埙　[損]损　[遠]远　[塏]垲　[勢]势　[搶]抢　[搗]捣　[塢]坞　[壼]壸　*[聖]圣　[蓋]盖　[蓮]莲

[蒔]莳	[骯]肮	[頌]颂	[湞]浈	[蔞]蒌	[閬]阆	[銀]银	[滿]满
[華]华	【丿】	[腸]肠	[滌]涤	[蔦]茑	[嘔]呕	[鉚]铆	[漸]渐
[夢]梦	[筧]笕	[腫]肿	[溮]浉	[蓯]苁	[蝸]蜗	[餞]饯	[漚]沤
[蒼]苍	*[節]节	[剹]剹	[塗]涂	[蔔]卜	[團]团	[餌]饵	[滯]滞
[幹]干	*[與]与	[像]象④	[愷]恺	[蔣]蒋	[嘍]喽	[蝕]蚀	[滷]卤
[蓀]荪	[債]债	[猹]猹	[愾]忾	[薌]芗	[鄲]郸	[餉]饷	[漊]溇
[蔭]荫	[僅]仅	[獁]犸	[愴]怆	[構]构	[鳴]鸣	[餄]饸	[漁]渔
[蒓]莼	[傳]传	[鳩]鸠	[窩]窝	[樺]桦	[幘]帻	[餎]饹	[滸]浒
[楨]桢	[傴]伛	[獅]狮	[禎]祯	[榿]桤	[嶄]崭	[餃]饺	[滬]沪
[楊]杨	[傾]倾	[猻]狲	[褘]袆	[覡]觋	[嶇]岖	[餏]饻	[滻]浐
*[薔]蔷	[僂]偻	【丶】	【一】	[槍]枪	[罰]罚	[餅]饼	[漲]涨
[楓]枫	[賃]赁	[誆]诓	*[肅]肃㊵	[輒]辄	[嶗]崂	[領]领	[滲]渗
[軾]轼	[傷]伤	[誄]诔	[裝]装	[輔]辅	[圖]图	[鳳]凤	[慚]惭
[輕]轻	[傭]佣	[試]试	[遜]逊	[輕]轻	【丿】	[颱]台	[慪]怄
[輅]辂	[裊]袅	[註]注	[際]际	[塹]堑	[製]制	[獄]狱	[慳]悭
[較]较	[頎]颀	[詩]诗	[媽]妈	[匱]匮	[種]种	【丶】	[慟]恸
[竪]竖	[鉦]钲	[詰]诘	[預]预	*[監]监	[稱]称	[誠]诚	[慘]惨
[買]买	[鉗]钳	[誇]夸	[叠]迭⑤	[緊]紧	[箋]笺	[誣]诬	[慣]惯
*[匯]汇	[鈷]钴	[詼]诙	[綆]绠	[厲]厉	[僥]侥	[語]语	[寬]宽
[電]电	[缽]钵	[誠]诚	[經]经	*[厭]厌	[僨]偾	[誚]诮	*[賓]宾
[頓]顿	[鉅]钜	[誅]诛	[綃]绡	[碩]硕	[僕]仆㉗	[誤]误	[窪]洼
[盞]盏	[鈳]钶	[話]话	[絹]绢	[碭]砀	[僑]侨	[誥]诰	*[寧]宁㉕
【丨】	[鈸]钹	[誕]诞	[綉]绣	[碸]砜	[僞]伪	[誘]诱	[寢]寝
*[歲]岁	[鉞]钺	[詬]诟	[綏]绥	【丨】	[銜]衔	[誨]诲	[實]实
*[虜]虏	[鉬]钼	[詮]诠	[綈]绨	*[對]对	[鉶]铏	[誑]诳	[皸]皲
*[業]业	[鉭]钽	[詭]诡	[彙]汇	[幣]币	[銬]铐	[說]说	[複]复
*[當]当	[鉀]钾	[詢]询	**14 笔**【一】	[彆]别	[銠]铑	[認]认	【一】
[睞]睐	[鈾]铀	[詣]诣	[瑪]玛	*[嘗]尝③	[鉺]铒	[誦]诵	[劃]划
[賊]贼	[鈿]钿	[靜]静	[璡]琎	[嘖]啧	[銪]铕	[誒]诶	*[盡]尽
[賄]贿	[鉑]铂	[該]该	[瑣]琐	[曄]晔	[鋮]铖	*[廣]广	[屢]屡
[賂]赂	[鈴]铃	[詳]详	[瑲]玱	[夥]伙⑩	[銷]销	[麼]么㉙	[獎]奖⑫
[賅]赅	[鉛]铅	[詫]诧	[馭]驭	[賑]赈	[鋁]铝	[廎]庼	[墮]堕
[嗎]吗	[鉚]铆	[詡]诩	[摶]抟	[賒]赊	[銅]铜	[瘞]瘗	[隨]随
[嘩]哗	[鈰]铈	[裏]里	[摳]抠	[嘆]叹	[銦]铟	[瘺]瘘	[翬]翚
[嗊]唝	[鈮]铌	[準]准	[趙]赵	[暢]畅	[銖]铢	[瘋]疯	[墜]坠
[暘]旸	[鈹]铍	[頑]顽	[趕]赶	[嘜]唛	[銑]铣	[塵]尘	[嫗]妪
[閘]闸	*[僉]佥	[資]资	[摟]搂	[閨]闺	[鋌]铤	[颯]飒	[頗]颇
*[黽]黾	*[會]会	[羥]羟	[摑]掴	[聞]闻	[銓]铨	[適]适㉚	[態]态
[暈]晕	[亂]乱	*[義]义㊻	[臺]台	[閩]闽	[銚]铫	*[齊]齐	[鄧]邓
[號]号	*[愛]爱	[煉]炼	[撾]挝	[閭]闾	[銘]铭	[養]养	[緒]绪
[園]园	[飾]饰	[煩]烦	[墊]垫	[閥]阀	[鉻]铬	[鄰]邻	[綾]绫
[蛺]蛱	[飽]饱	[煬]炀	*[壽]寿	[閤]合	[錚]铮	*[鄭]郑	[綺]绮
[蜆]蚬	[飼]饲	[塋]茔	[摺]折㊾	[閣]阁	[鉸]铰	[燁]烨	[綫]线
*[農]农	[飿]饳	[熒]荧	[摻]掺	[閡]阂	[銥]铱	[熗]炝	[緋]绯
[嗩]唢	[頜]颔	[煒]炜	[摜]掼		[銃]铳	[榮]荣	[綽]绰
[嗶]哔		[遞]递	[勩]勩		[銨]铵	[滎]荥	[緄]绲
[嗚]呜		[溝]沟				[熒]荧	[綱]纲
[嗆]呛		[漣]涟				[漢]汉	[網]网
[圓]圆		[滅]灭					[維]维
							[綿]绵

457

〔綸〕纶
〔綬〕绶
〔綳〕绷
〔綢〕绸
〔綹〕绺
〔綣〕绻
〔綜〕综
〔綻〕绽
〔綰〕绾
〔綠〕绿
〔綴〕缀
〔緇〕缁

15 笔

【一】
〔鬧〕闹⑭
〔璡〕琎
〔靚〕靓
〔輦〕辇
〔髮〕发
〔撓〕挠
〔墳〕坟
〔撻〕挞
〔駔〕驵
〔駛〕驶
〔駟〕驷
〔駙〕驸
〔駒〕驹
〔駐〕驻
〔駝〕驼
〔駘〕骀
〔撲〕扑
〔頡〕颉
〔撣〕掸
*〔賣〕卖㉑
〔撫〕抚
〔撟〕挢
〔撳〕揿
〔熱〕热
〔鞏〕巩
〔摯〕挚
〔撈〕捞
〔穀〕谷
〔慤〕悫
〔撏〕挦
〔撥〕拨
〔蕘〕荛
〔蕆〕蒇
〔蕓〕芸
〔邁〕迈

〔黌〕黉
〔蕪〕芜
〔蕎〕荞
〔蕕〕莸
〔蕩〕荡
〔蕁〕荨
〔樁〕桩
〔樞〕枢
〔標〕标
〔樓〕楼
〔樅〕枞
〔麩〕麸
〔賚〕赉
〔樣〕样
〔橢〕椭
〔輛〕辆
〔輥〕辊
〔輞〕辋
〔槧〕椠
〔暫〕暂
〔輪〕轮
〔輟〕辍
〔輜〕辎
〔甌〕瓯
〔歐〕欧
〔毆〕殴
〔賢〕贤
*〔遷〕迁
〔鴉〕鸦
〔憂〕忧
〔碼〕码
〔磑〕硙
〔確〕确
〔賫〕赍
〔遼〕辽
〔殤〕殇

【丨】
〔輩〕辈
〔劌〕刿
*〔齒〕齿
〔劇〕剧
〔膚〕肤
*〔慮〕虑
〔鄴〕邺
〔輝〕辉
〔賞〕赏㉓
〔賦〕赋

〔賬〕账
〔賭〕赌
〔賤〕贱
〔賜〕赐
〔賙〕赒
〔賠〕赔
〔賧〕赕
〔曉〕哓
〔噴〕喷
〔嘩〕哗
〔噁〕恶
〔閫〕阃
〔閭〕闾
〔閱〕阅
〔閬〕阆
〔數〕数
〔踐〕践
〔遺〕遗
〔蝦〕虾
〔嘸〕呒
〔嘮〕唠
〔噝〕咝
〔嘰〕叽
〔嶢〕峣
*〔罷〕罢
〔嶠〕峤
〔嶔〕嵚
〔幟〕帜
〔嶗〕崂

【丿】
〔頲〕颋
〔篋〕箧
〔範〕范
〔價〕价
〔儂〕侬
〔儉〕俭
〔儈〕侩
〔億〕亿
〔儀〕仪
〔皚〕皑
*〔樂〕乐
*〔質〕质
〔徵〕征㉒
〔衝〕冲
〔慫〕怂
〔徹〕彻
〔衛〕卫
〔盤〕盘
〔鋪〕铺
〔鋏〕铗

〔鋱〕铽
〔銷〕销
〔鋥〕锃
〔鋰〕锂
〔鋇〕钡
〔鋤〕锄
〔鋯〕锆
〔鋨〕锇
〔銹〕锈
〔銼〕锉
〔鋒〕锋
〔鋅〕锌
〔銳〕锐
〔鋃〕锒
〔鋟〕锓
〔領〕领
〔劍〕剑
〔劊〕刽
〔鄶〕郐
〔餑〕饽
〔餓〕饿
〔餒〕馁
〔膞〕䏝
〔腡〕脶
〔膠〕胶
〔鵓〕鹁
〔魷〕鱿
〔魯〕鲁
〔魴〕鲂
〔穎〕颖
〔颳〕刮
*〔劉〕刘
〔皺〕皱

【丶】
〔請〕请
〔諸〕诸
〔諏〕诹
〔諾〕诺
〔諑〕诼
〔誹〕诽
〔課〕课
〔諉〕诿
〔諛〕谀
〔論〕论
〔諗〕谂

〔調〕调
〔諂〕谄
〔諒〕谅
〔諄〕谆
〔誶〕谇
〔談〕谈
〔誼〕谊
〔廟〕庙
〔廠〕厂
〔廡〕庑
〔瘞〕瘗
〔瘡〕疮
〔慶〕庆㉔
〔廢〕废
〔敵〕敌
〔頦〕颏
〔導〕导
〔瑩〕莹
〔潔〕洁
〔澆〕浇
〔潿〕涠
〔潤〕润
〔澗〕涧
〔潰〕溃
〔潷〕滗
〔潯〕浔
〔潑〕泼
〔憤〕愤
〔憫〕悯
〔憒〕愦
〔憚〕惮
〔憮〕怃
〔憐〕怜
*〔寫〕写㊹
*〔審〕审
*〔窮〕穷
〔褳〕裢
〔褲〕裤
〔鳩〕鸠

【乛】
〔遲〕迟
〔層〕层
〔彈〕弹
〔選〕选
〔槳〕桨⑫
〔漿〕浆⑫

〔險〕险
〔嬈〕娆
〔嫻〕娴
*〔駕〕驾
〔蕭〕萧
〔嫵〕妩
〔嬌〕娇
〔嬀〕妫
〔嫿〕婳
〔頤〕颐
〔鴰〕鸹
〔薩〕萨
〔橈〕桡
〔樹〕树
〔樸〕朴
〔橋〕桥
〔機〕机
〔輳〕辏
〔輻〕辐
〔輯〕辑
〔輸〕输
〔賴〕赖
〔頭〕头
〔醞〕酝
〔醜〕丑
〔勵〕励
〔磧〕碛
〔磚〕砖
〔磣〕碜
*〔歷〕历
〔曆〕历
〔奮〕奋
〔頰〕颊
〔殫〕殚
〔頸〕颈

〔緙〕缂
〔緗〕缃
〔緘〕缄
〔緬〕缅
〔緹〕缇
〔緝〕缉
〔緼〕缊
〔緦〕缌
〔緞〕缎
〔緱〕缑
〔緩〕缓
〔締〕缔
〔編〕编
〔緡〕缗
〔緯〕纬
〔緣〕缘

16 笔

【一】
〔璣〕玑
〔墻〕墙
〔駱〕骆
〔駭〕骇
〔駢〕骈
〔擓〕㧟
〔擄〕掳
〔擋〕挡
〔擇〕择
〔赬〕赪
〔撿〕捡
〔擔〕担
〔壇〕坛
〔擁〕拥
〔據〕据
〔薔〕蔷

〔疊〕叠

【丨】
〔噸〕吨
〔鴞〕鸮
〔噥〕哝
〔踴〕踊
〔螞〕蚂
〔獅〕狮
〔噹〕当
〔罵〕骂
〔噲〕哙
〔戰〕战
〔噯〕嗳
〔嘯〕啸
〔還〕还
〔嶧〕峄
〔嶼〕屿

【丿】
〔積〕积
〔頹〕颓
〔穆〕穆
〔篤〕笃
〔築〕筑
〔篳〕筚
〔篩〕筛
*〔舉〕举
〔興〕兴
〔學〕学
〔儔〕俦
〔憊〕惫
〔儕〕侪
〔儐〕傧
〔盡〕尽
〔鴕〕鸵
〔艙〕舱
〔錶〕表
〔錯〕错
〔鍺〕锗
〔錨〕锚
〔錛〕锛
〔錸〕铼
〔錢〕钱
〔鍀〕锝
〔錁〕锞
〔錕〕锟
〔釘〕钉
〔錫〕锡

〔縣〕县㊺

〔錮〕锢　〔謂〕谓　〔縉〕缙　〔檳〕槟　【丿】　〔鮮〕鲜　〔彌〕弥　〔櫚〕榈

〔鋼〕钢　〔諤〕谔　〔縝〕缜　〔檔〕档　〔矯〕矫　〔颶〕飓　〔嬪〕嫔　〔檳〕槟

〔鍋〕锅　〔諭〕谕　〔縛〕缚　〔櫛〕栉　〔鴰〕鸹　〔獷〕犷　〔績〕绩　〔檸〕柠

〔錘〕锤　〔諼〕谖　〔縟〕缛　〔檢〕检　〔簀〕箦　〔獰〕狞　〔縹〕缥　〔鵓〕鹁

〔錐〕锥　〔諷〕讽　〔緻〕致　〔檜〕桧　〔簍〕篓　　　　　〔縷〕缕　〔轉〕转

〔錦〕锦　〔諮〕谘　〔縲〕缧　〔麯〕曲　〔輿〕舆　【丶】　〔縵〕缦　〔轆〕辘

〔欽〕钦　〔諳〕谙　〔縫〕缝　〔轅〕辕　〔歟〕欤　〔講〕讲　〔縲〕缧　〔覆〕复⑦

〔鋯〕锆　〔諦〕谛　〔縐〕绉　〔轄〕辖　〔鵪〕鹌　〔謨〕谟　〔總〕总　〔醫〕医

〔錠〕锭　〔謎〕谜　〔縭〕缡　〔輾〕辗　*〔龜〕龟　〔謖〕谡　〔縱〕纵　〔礎〕础

〔鍵〕键　〔諢〕诨　〔縑〕缣　〔擊〕击　〔優〕优　〔謝〕谢　〔縴〕纤　〔殯〕殡

*〔錄〕录　〔諞〕谝　〔縊〕缢　〔臨〕临⑱　〔償〕偿　〔謠〕谣　〔縮〕缩　〔霧〕雾

〔鋸〕锯　〔諱〕讳　　　　　〔磽〕硗　〔儲〕储　〔謅〕诌　〔繆〕缪

〔錳〕锰　〔諝〕谞　**17 笔**　〔壓〕压㊸　〔魎〕魉　〔謗〕谤　〔繅〕缫　【丨】

〔錨〕锚　〔憑〕凭　【一】　〔礄〕硚　〔鴒〕鸰　〔謚〕谥　〔繈〕缰　*〔豐〕丰⑥

〔錛〕锛　〔鄺〕邝　〔檁〕檩　〔磯〕矶　〔禦〕御　〔謙〕谦　〔嚮〕向　〔覷〕觑

〔墾〕垦　〔瘐〕瘐　〔環〕环　〔鴯〕鸸　〔聳〕耸　〔謐〕谧　　　　　〔懟〕怼

〔餞〕饯　〔瘆〕瘆　〔贅〕赘　〔邁〕迈　〔鵃〕鸼　〔襃〕褒　**18 笔**　〔叢〕丛

〔餜〕馃　*〔親〕亲　〔璦〕瑷　〔尷〕尴　〔鍥〕锲　〔氈〕毡　【一】　〔矇〕蒙

〔錕〕锟　〔辦〕办　〔覯〕觏　〔鵂〕鸺　〔鍇〕锴　〔應〕应　〔耮〕耢　〔題〕题

〔餡〕馅　*〔龍〕龙　〔黿〕鼋　〔殮〕殓　〔鍘〕铡　〔癇〕痫　〔鬩〕阋⑭　〔韙〕韪

〔館〕馆　〔劑〕剂　〔幫〕帮　　　　　〔錫〕锡　〔療〕疗　〔瓊〕琼　〔瞼〕睑

〔頜〕颌　〔燒〕烧　〔騁〕骋　【丨】　〔鍶〕锶　〔癇〕痫　〔擷〕撷　〔闔〕阖

〔鴿〕鸽　〔燜〕焖　〔駸〕骎　〔齔〕龀　〔鍔〕锷　〔癉〕瘅　〔鬆〕松　〔闐〕阗

〔膩〕腻　〔熾〕炽　〔駿〕骏　〔戲〕戏　〔鍤〕锸　〔癆〕痨　〔翹〕翘　〔闒〕阘

〔鴟〕鸱　〔螢〕萤　〔趨〕趋　〔虧〕亏　〔鍛〕锻　〔鵁〕䴔　〔擼〕撸　〔闕〕阙

〔鮁〕鲅　〔營〕营　〔擱〕搁　〔斃〕毙　〔鎪〕锼　〔齋〕斋　〔擻〕擞　〔顒〕颙

〔鮃〕鲆　〔縈〕萦　〔擬〕拟　〔瞭〕了　〔鍬〕锹　〔鯗〕鲞　〔擾〕扰　〔曠〕旷

〔鮎〕鲇　〔燈〕灯　〔擴〕扩　〔顆〕颗　〔鍰〕锾　〔糞〕粪　〔騏〕骐　〔蹣〕蹒

〔鮓〕鲊　〔濛〕蒙　〔壙〕圹　〔購〕购　〔鍍〕镀　〔糝〕糁　〔騎〕骑　〔嚙〕啮

〔穌〕稣　〔燙〕烫　〔擠〕挤　〔賻〕赙　〔鎂〕镁　〔燦〕灿　〔騍〕骒　〔壘〕垒

〔鮒〕鲋　〔澠〕渑　〔蟄〕蛰　〔嬰〕婴　〔鎡〕镃　〔燭〕烛　〔騅〕骓　〔蟯〕蛲

〔鮑〕鲍　〔濃〕浓　〔縶〕絷　〔賺〕赚　〔鎇〕镅　〔燴〕烩　〔攄〕摅　*〔蟲〕虫

〔鮍〕鲏　〔澤〕泽　〔擲〕掷　〔嚇〕吓㊳　〔懇〕恳　〔鴻〕鸿　〔擻〕擞　〔蟬〕蝉

〔鮐〕鲐　〔濁〕浊　〔擯〕摈　〔闌〕阑　〔餷〕馇　〔濤〕涛　〔鼕〕冬　〔蟣〕虮

〔鮞〕鲕　〔澮〕浍　〔擰〕拧　〔闃〕阒　〔餳〕饧　〔濫〕滥　〔擺〕摆　〔鵑〕鹃

〔獲〕获　〔澱〕淀　〔轂〕毂　〔闊〕阔　〔餶〕馉　〔濕〕湿　〔贄〕贽　〔嚕〕噜

〔穎〕颖　〔澦〕滪　〔聲〕声　〔闆〕板　〔餿〕馊　〔濟〕济　〔燾〕焘　〔顓〕颛

〔獨〕独　〔懞〕蒙　〔藉〕借⑬　〔闈〕闱　〔斂〕敛　〔濱〕滨　*〔聶〕聂

〔獫〕猃　〔懌〕怿　〔聰〕聪　〔闋〕阕　〔鴿〕鸽　〔濘〕泞　〔聵〕聩　【丿】

〔獪〕狯　〔憶〕忆　〔聯〕联　〔曖〕暧　〔膿〕脓　〔濜〕浕　〔職〕职　〔鵠〕鹄

〔駕〕驾　〔憲〕宪　〔艱〕艰　〔蹕〕跸　〔臉〕脸　〔澀〕涩　*〔藝〕艺　〔鵝〕鹅

　　　　〔窺〕窥　〔藍〕蓝　〔蹌〕跄　〔膾〕脍　〔濰〕潍　〔覲〕觐　〔穫〕获

【丶】　〔窶〕窭　〔舊〕旧　〔蟎〕螨　〔膽〕胆　〔懨〕恹　〔鞦〕秋　〔穡〕穑

〔謀〕谋　〔寫〕写　〔薺〕荠　〔螻〕蝼　〔謄〕誊　〔襇〕裥　〔藪〕薮　〔穢〕秽

〔諶〕谌　〔褸〕褛　〔藎〕荩　〔蟈〕蝈　〔鮭〕鲑　〔襖〕袄　〔蠆〕虿　〔簡〕简

〔諜〕谍　〔禪〕禅　〔韓〕韩　〔雖〕虽　〔鮚〕鲒　〔禮〕礼　〔繭〕茧　〔簣〕篑

〔謊〕谎　　　　　〔隸〕隶　〔嚀〕咛　〔鮪〕鲔　　　　　〔藥〕药　〔簞〕箪

〔諫〕谏　【乛】　〔檉〕柽　〔覬〕觊　〔鮦〕鲖　【乛】　〔藭〕䓖　*〔雙〕双

〔諧〕谐　*〔隱〕隐　〔檣〕樯　〔嶺〕岭⑲　〔鮫〕鲛　〔屨〕屦　〔賾〕赜　*〔軀〕躯

〔謔〕谑　〔嬙〕嫱　　　　　〔嶸〕嵘　　　　　　　　　〔蘊〕蕴　*〔邊〕边

〔謁〕谒　〔嬡〕嫒　　　　　〔點〕点　　　　　　　　　〔檯〕台　*〔歸〕归

　　　　　　　　　　　　　　　　　　　　　　　　　　〔櫃〕柜　〔鏵〕铧

　　　　　　　　　　　　　　　　　　　　　　　　　　〔檻〕槛

〔鎮〕镇　〔濾〕滤　〔顛〕颠　〔鏜〕镗　〔瀝〕沥　【丨】　〔釋〕释　〔繼〕继
〔鏈〕链　〔鯊〕鲨　〔櫝〕椟　〔鏤〕镂　〔瀕〕濒　〔鹹〕咸　〔饒〕饶　〔饗〕飨
〔鎘〕镉　〔濺〕溅　〔櫟〕栎　〔鏝〕镘　〔瀘〕泸　〔鹺〕鹾　〔饊〕馓　〔響〕响
〔鎖〕锁　〔瀏〕浏　〔櫓〕橹　〔鏰〕镚　〔瀧〕泷　〔齟〕龃　〔饋〕馈

21 笔

〔鎧〕铠　〔濼〕泺　〔櫧〕槠　〔鏞〕镛　〔懶〕懒　〔齡〕龄　〔饌〕馔
【一】

〔鎝〕锝　〔瀉〕泻　〔櫞〕橼　〔鏡〕镜　〔懷〕怀　〔齣〕出　〔饑〕饥　〔耰〕耰
〔鎳〕镍　〔瀋〕沈　〔轎〕轿　〔鏟〕铲　〔寵〕宠　〔齙〕龅　〔臚〕胪　〔瓔〕璎
〔鍛〕锻　*〔竄〕窜　〔鏊〕鏊　〔鏑〕镝　〔襪〕袜㉟　〔齠〕龆　〔朧〕胧　〔鰲〕鳌
〔鎪〕锼　〔竅〕窍　〔轍〕辙　〔鏃〕镞　〔襤〕褴　*〔獻〕献　〔騰〕腾　〔攝〕摄
〔鎦〕镏　〔額〕额　〔轔〕辚　〔鏇〕旋　【﹁】　*〔黨〕党　〔鰆〕鲼　〔騾〕骡
〔鎬〕镐　〔禰〕祢　〔繫〕系⑪　〔鏘〕锵　〔韜〕韬　〔懸〕悬　〔鰈〕鲽　〔驅〕驱
〔鎊〕镑　〔襠〕裆　〔鶉〕鹑　〔辭〕辞　〔騭〕骘　〔鶪〕䴗　〔鰏〕鲾　〔驃〕骠
〔鎰〕镒　〔襝〕裣　*〔麗〕丽⑰　〔饉〕馑　〔鶩〕鹜　〔罌〕罂　〔鰐〕鳄　〔驄〕骢
〔鎵〕镓　〔襖〕袄　〔厴〕厣　〔饅〕馒　〔顙〕颡　〔闥〕闼　〔鰍〕鳅　〔驂〕骖
〔鎇〕镅　【﹁】　〔礪〕砺　〔鵬〕鹏　〔繮〕缰　〔闡〕阐　〔鰒〕鳆　〔攙〕搀
〔鵒〕鹆　〔醤〕酱⑫　〔礙〕碍　〔臘〕腊　〔繩〕绳　〔鶡〕鹖　〔鰉〕鳇　〔攛〕撺
〔鏌〕镆　〔韞〕韫　〔礦〕矿　〔鯖〕鲭　〔繾〕缱　〔蠣〕蛎　〔鰁〕鳈　〔鞽〕鞒
〔鵠〕鹄　〔隴〕陇　〔贋〕赝　〔鯪〕鲮　〔繰〕缲　〔蠐〕蛴　〔鰌〕鳅　〔韉〕鞯
〔饃〕馍　〔嬸〕婶　〔願〕愿　〔鯫〕鲰　〔繹〕绎　〔蠑〕蝾　〔編〕鳊　〔歡〕欢
〔餺〕馎　〔繞〕绕　〔鶇〕鸫　〔鯡〕鲱　〔繯〕缳　〔巏〕㠓　〔獼〕猕　〔權〕权
〔餼〕饩　〔繚〕缭　〔璽〕玺　〔鯤〕鲲　〔繽〕缤　〔嚶〕嘤　〔觸〕触　〔櫻〕樱
〔餾〕馏　〔織〕织　〔豶〕豮　〔鯧〕鲳　〔繡〕绣　〔鶚〕鹗　【丶】　〔欄〕栏
〔饉〕馑　〔繕〕缮　【丨】　〔鯢〕鲵　〔鶥〕鹛　〔髏〕髅　〔護〕护　〔轟〕轰
〔臍〕脐　〔繒〕缯　〔贈〕赠　〔鯰〕鲶　〔鶿〕鹚　〔鶻〕鹘　〔譴〕谴　〔覽〕览
〔鯁〕鲠　*〔斷〕断　〔闞〕阚　〔鯛〕鲷　　　　　　　　　　〔譯〕译　〔鄲〕郸
〔鯉〕鲤　　　　　〔關〕关　〔鯨〕鲸　**20 笔**　　　　　　　　　〔譫〕谵　〔飆〕飙
〔鯀〕鲧

19 笔　〔嚦〕呖　〔鯔〕鲻　　　　　　　　　　〔議〕议　〔殲〕歼
〔鯇〕鲩

　　　　〔疇〕畴　〔獺〕獭　【一】　　　　　　〔癥〕症
【一】

〔卿〕卿　〔鶘〕鹕　〔蹺〕跷　〔鶬〕鸧　〔瓏〕珑　　　　　〔辮〕辫　【丨】
〔颸〕飔　〔鶻〕鹘　〔蟶〕蛏　〔颼〕飕　〔鶯〕莺　【丿】　〔龑〕䶮　〔齜〕龇
〔颺〕飏　〔黠〕黠　〔蠅〕蝇　　　　　〔驊〕骅　〔犧〕牺　〔競〕竞　〔齦〕龈
〔觴〕觞　〔騙〕骗　〔蟻〕蚁　【丶】　〔騮〕骝　〔鶩〕鹜　〔贏〕赢　〔齬〕龉
〔獵〕猎　〔騷〕骚　*〔嚴〕严　〔譚〕谭　〔騶〕驺　〔籌〕筹　〔糲〕粝　〔齩〕咬
〔雛〕雏　〔壢〕坜　〔獸〕兽　〔譖〕谮　〔騸〕骟　〔籃〕篮　〔糰〕团　〔囁〕嗫
〔膪〕膪　〔壚〕垆　〔嚨〕咙　〔譙〕谯　〔攖〕撄　〔譽〕誉　〔鶃〕鹝　〔囂〕嚣
　　　　〔壞〕坏⑨　〔羆〕罴　〔識〕识　〔攔〕拦　〔覺〕觉　〔爐〕炉　〔闢〕辟
【丶】　〔攏〕拢　*〔羅〕罗　〔譜〕谱　〔攙〕搀　〔譽〕誊　〔瀾〕澜　〔囀〕啭
〔謹〕谨　〔擻〕擞　　　　　〔證〕证　〔聹〕聍　〔巇〕巇　〔瀲〕潋　〔顥〕颢
〔謳〕讴　*〔難〕难　【丿】　〔譎〕谲　〔顢〕颟　〔艦〕舰　〔瀰〕弥　〔躊〕踌
〔謾〕谩　〔鵲〕鹊　〔氌〕氇　〔譏〕讥　〔鶈〕蓍　〔鐃〕铙　〔鐠〕镨　〔躋〕跻
〔謫〕谪　〔麕〕麇　〔犢〕犊　〔鶊〕鹒　〔蘭〕兰　〔鐝〕镢　〔鐘〕钟　〔躑〕踯
〔謬〕谬　〔蘋〕苹　〔贊〕赞　〔廬〕庐　〔蘞〕蔹　〔�〕铜　〔鐋〕镗　〔躍〕跃
〔癧〕疬　〔蘆〕芦　〔穩〕稳　〔癟〕瘪　〔蘚〕藓　〔鐦〕锎　〔鐠〕镨　〔纍〕累
〔雜〕杂　〔鵓〕鹁　〔簽〕签　〔癢〕痒　〔鶓〕鹋　〔鐐〕镣　【﹁】　〔蠟〕蜡
*〔離〕离　〔藺〕蔺　〔簾〕帘　〔龐〕庞　〔飄〕飘　〔鐓〕镦　〔鶻〕鹘　〔矕〕矕
〔顔〕颜　〔躉〕趸　〔簫〕箫　〔壟〕垄　〔櫪〕枥　〔鏹〕镪　〔驀〕蓦　〔髒〕脏
〔糧〕粮　〔蘄〕蕲　〔牘〕牍　〔鶼〕鹣　〔櫨〕栌　　　　　〔纊〕纩　【丿】
〔燼〕烬　〔勸〕劝　〔懲〕惩　〔類〕类⑯　〔櫸〕榉　　　　　〔繽〕缤　〔儷〕俪
〔鵜〕鹈　〔蘇〕苏　〔鐯〕镨　〔爍〕烁　〔礬〕矾　　　　　　　　　　〔儸〕㑩
〔瀆〕渎　〔藹〕蔼　〔鏗〕铿　〔瀟〕潇　〔麵〕面　【一】　　　　　　　〔儼〕俨
〔懣〕懑　〔蘢〕茏　〔鏢〕镖　〔瀨〕濑　〔櫬〕榇　〔鶺〕鹡
　　　　　　　　　　　　　　　　　〔櫳〕栊　〔鐺〕铛
　　　　　　　　　　　　　　　　　〔礫〕砾　〔鐳〕镭
　　　　　　　　　　　　　　　　　〔礦〕砾　〔鐵〕铁

〔鷗〕鸥
〔鐵〕铁
〔鏷〕镤
〔鐳〕镭
〔鐺〕铛
〔鐸〕铎
〔鐶〕镮
〔鐲〕镯
〔鐮〕镰
〔鐿〕镱
〔鷸〕鹬
〔鷄〕鸡
〔鷂〕鹞
〔臟〕脏
〔騰〕腾
〔鰭〕鳍
〔鰱〕鲢
〔鰣〕鲥
〔鰨〕鳎
〔鰥〕鳏
〔鰷〕鲦
〔鰟〕鳑
〔鰜〕鳒
【丶】
〔癩〕癞
〔癧〕疬
〔癮〕瘾
〔斕〕斓
〔辯〕辩
〔礱〕砻
〔鷀〕鹚
〔爛〕烂
〔鷥〕鸶
〔灄〕滠
〔灃〕沣
〔灘〕滩
〔儷〕俪
〔懼〕惧
〔竈〕灶

〔顧〕顾
〔襯〕衬
〔鶴〕鹤
【一】
*〔屬〕属
〔纈〕缬
〔續〕续
〔纏〕缠②

22 笔

【一】
〔鬚〕须
〔驍〕骁
〔驕〕骄
〔攤〕摊
〔覿〕觌
〔攢〕攒
〔鷙〕鸷
〔聽〕听
〔蘿〕萝
〔驚〕惊
〔轢〕轹
〔鷗〕鸥
〔鑒〕鉴
〔邏〕逻
【丶】
〔讀〕读
〔讅〕谉
【丨】
〔巒〕峦
〔彎〕弯
〔孿〕孪
〔變〕变
〔顫〕颤
〔鷓〕鹧
〔癭〕瘿
〔癬〕癣
〔聾〕聋
〔龔〕龚
〔襲〕袭
〔灑〕洒
〔灕〕漓
〔懾〕慑
〔儺〕傩
〔巔〕巅

〔邏〕逻
〔體〕体
【丿】
〔罎〕坛
〔籜〕箨
〔籟〕籁
〔籙〕箓
〔籠〕笼
〔鑾〕銮
〔儻〕傥
〔艫〕舻
〔鑄〕铸
〔鑌〕镔
〔鑠〕铄
〔鱈〕鳕
〔鱔〕鳝
〔鰳〕鳓
〔鰹〕鲣
〔鰵〕鳘
【丶】
〔讀〕读
〔讅〕谉
【丨】
〔戀〕恋
〔彎〕弯
〔孿〕孪
〔變〕变
〔顫〕颤
〔癰〕痈
〔瘭〕瘭
〔癰〕癣
〔讋〕詟
〔羅〕罗

〔灑〕洒
〔竊〕窃
【一】
〔罎〕坛
〔鷥〕鸶

23 笔

【一】
〔瓚〕瓒
〔驛〕驿
〔驗〕验
〔攬〕揽
〔欏〕椤
〔轤〕轳
〔靨〕靥
〔魘〕魇
〔饜〕餍
〔鷦〕鹪
〔讎〕雠
〔顬〕颥
【丨】
〔曬〕晒
〔鷴〕鹇
〔顯〕显
〔蠱〕蛊
〔髖〕髋
〔髕〕髌
【丿】
〔籤〕签
〔讎〕雠
〔鷯〕鹩
〔黴〕霉
〔鑠〕铄
〔鑕〕锧
〔鱭〕鲚
〔鱧〕鳢
〔鱠〕鲙
〔鱣〕鳣
〔攣〕挛
〔鷸〕鹬
〔灝〕灏

〔鱗〕鳞
〔鱘〕鲟
〔鱏〕鲟
【丶】
〔讌〕䜩
〔欒〕栾
〔攣〕挛
〔孌〕娈
〔變〕变
〔戀〕恋
〔鷺〕鹭
〔癰〕痈
〔鱉〕鳖
【一】
〔鸛〕鹳
〔纓〕缨
〔纖〕纤⑤
〔纔〕才
〔鷥〕鸶

24 笔

【一】
〔鬢〕鬓
〔攬〕揽
〔驟〕骤
〔壩〕坝
〔韆〕千
〔觀〕观

25 笔

【一】
〔鹽〕盐
〔釀〕酿
〔靂〕雳
*〔靈〕灵
〔欞〕棂
〔鸞〕鸾
【丨】
〔顱〕颅
〔躡〕蹑
〔躥〕蹿
〔鼉〕鼍
〔鼊〕䴗
〔鼉〕鼍
〔鑷〕镊
〔鑽〕钻
〔鱨〕鲿
〔鱭〕鲚
〔鑭〕镧

〔鱗〕鳞
〔鱒〕鳟
〔鱘〕鲟
【丶】
〔讕〕谰
〔讖〕谶
〔讒〕谗
〔讓〕让
〔鸇〕鹯
〔鷹〕鹰
〔癱〕瘫
〔癲〕癫
〔贛〕赣
〔灝〕灏
【丶】
〔讞〕谳
〔讜〕谠
〔讛〕诶
〔鸝〕鹂
〔鸚〕鹦
〔顰〕颦
〔齷〕龌
〔齶〕腭
〔齲〕龋
【丨】
〔矚〕瞩
〔躪〕躏
〔躦〕躜
【丿】
〔纘〕缵
〔鑼〕锣
〔鑲〕镶
【丶】
〔灤〕滦

27 笔

【一】
〔鬮〕阄⑭
〔驤〕骧
〔顳〕颞

〔鑰〕钥
〔鑷〕镊
〔鱺〕鲡
〔鱨〕鲿
〔鰾〕鲼
〔鑌〕镔

26 笔

【一】
〔驥〕骥
〔驢〕驴
〔趲〕趱
〔顴〕颧
〔癱〕瘫
〔癲〕癫
〔贛〕赣
〔灥〕瀍
【丨】
〔矚〕瞩
〔躙〕躏
〔躦〕躜
【丿】
〔纜〕缆

【丨】
〔鸕〕鸬
〔顙〕颡
【丿】
〔钁〕镢
〔钂〕镗
【丶】
〔讕〕谰
〔讞〕谳
〔欒〕栾
〔灩〕滟
【一】
〔纜〕缆

28 笔

【一】
〔鸛〕鹳
〔欖〕榄
〔鑿〕凿
〔鸚〕鹦
〔钂〕镋
〔戀〕恋

29 笔

〔驪〕骊
〔鬱〕郁

30 笔

〔鸝〕鹂
〔饢〕馕
〔鱺〕鲡
〔鸞〕鸾

32 笔

〔籲〕吁⑭

SOURCE: *Jianhuazi Zongbiao Jianzi* (The complete list of simplified characters; Peking: Language Reform Press, 1964)

Index

Characters are arranged by new radicals (for table see inside of back cover) and stroke count (excluding the radical itself). References are to entry number (*not* page number) of the first character. Listing is by simplified character forms, with old forms in parentheses. Note that, in accordance with the practice followed in the *Xinhua Zidian*, a character may appear under more than one radical.

Characters with Difficult-to-Identify Radicals

2 strokes

刁 2065

3 strokes

亡 2377
义 1001
干 1055
  1063
才 2304
与 2552
  2557
  2367
丸 107
及 842
习 182
孑 2474
刃 268
乡 857

4 strokes

为 2391
  2404
丰 655
夫 667
开 1175
井 280
无 2431
专 330
支 225
牙 2441
屯 2224
中 343
  349
内 1523
升 1861
长 52
  372
丹 2010
氏 1890
月 2585
以 1000
尺 481
丑 518
巴 1579
书 1915

5 strokes

头 2206

玄 963
半 1600
平 1776
未 2405
末 1488
击 98
世 1891
本 1633
东 2127
卡 1174
北 1626
且 454
申 1851
电 2080
由 2532
史 1885
生 1862
乍 30
甩 1941
乐 1268
  2586
司 1982
民 1470
弗 670
出 520
发 613

6 strokes

农 1557
夹 137
考 1190
亚 2445
再 2240
更 1289
死 1988
成 401
至 242
师 1874
曳 2479
曲 588
  595
肉 1036
兆 65
年 1538
朱 310
乔 443
乒 1775
行 715
  927

7 strokes

来 1248

求 507
严 2489
巫 2427
束 1933
串 536
卯 1378

8 strokes

奉 665
表 1656
丧 1804
  1806
其 419
直 232
事 1895
非 637
果 1169
畅 380
垂 542
乖 1126
卑 1622
周 305
隶 1291
肃 1961
承 404

9 strokes

举 560
将 149
  156
叛 1715
奏 2269
甚 1858
柬 206
威 2388
歪 2362
临 1330
幽 2530
拜 1592
香 859
重 353
  551

10 strokes

高 1072
哥 1087
乘 406

---

11 strokes

爽 1945
夠 1104

12 strokes

就 297
棘 116
鼎 2087
舒 1921
释 1903
粤 2589

13 strokes

鼓 1116
赖 1249

14 strokes

聚 570
幹 2424
舞 2435
疑 998

15 strokes

靠 1193
豫 2568

16 strokes

整 91
翼 135

17 strokes

戴 2009

22 strokes

囊 1519

Table of Radicals 部

	10	20	30	40	50	60	70	80	90	100
1	[1] stroke 、	十	几	力	土	巾	己	斗	犬	水	斤
2	一	厂	儿	[3] strokes 氵	士	山	弓	文	歹	贝	爪
3	丨	匚	厶	忄	艹	彳	子	方	车	见	月
4	丿	卜	又	宀	大	彡	屮	火	戈	父	欠
5	乙	刂	廴	广	艹 (below)	夕	女	心	比	牛	风
6	[2] strokes 亠	冂	卩	门	尢	夂	幺	户	瓦	手	殳
7	冫	八	阝 (at left)	辶	弋	犭	纟	礻	止	毛	聿
8	冖	人	阝 (at right)	寸	小	饣	马	王	攴	气	爿
9	讠	亻	凵	扌	口	彐	巛	韦	日	攵	毌
10	二	勹	刀	工	囗	尸	[4] strokes 灬	木	曰	片	[5] strokes 穴